THE CHIEF EUROPEAN DRAMATISTS

THE CHIEF EUROPEAN DRAMATISTS

TWENTY-ONE PLAYS FROM THE DRAMA OF
GREECE, ROME, SPAIN, FRANCE, ITALY
GERMANY, DENMARK, AND NORWAY

FROM 500 B.C. TO 1879 A.D.

SELECTED AND EDITED
WITH NOTES, BIOGRAPHIES, AND
BIBLIOGRAPHIES

BY

BRANDER MATTHEWS

PROFESSOR OF DRAMATIC LITERATURE IN COLUMBIA UNIVERSITY
MEMBER OF THE AMERICAN ACADEMY OF ARTS AND LETTERS

BOSTON NEW YORK CHICAGO
HOUGHTON MIFFLIN COMPANY
The Riverside Press Cambridge

PN
6112
M4

The Riverside Press
CAMBRIDGE . MASSACHUSETTS
U . S . A

TO
H. C. CHATFIELD-TAYLOR
ACCOMPLISHED INTERPRETER OF TWO
CHIEF EUROPEAN DRAMATISTS
GOLDONI AND MOLIÈRE

CONTENTS

INTRODUCTION

IT is in response to a wider and more intelligent interest in dramatic literature, and in the drama as an art, that the playwrights of every modern language now publish their plays promptly in order that these may be read both by those who have already witnessed the performance and by those deprived of this pleasure by remoteness from the play-house. Preceding and accompanying this interest in the drama of the immediate present there is also a constantly increasing attention to the drama of the past, and more especially to the dramatic literature of the English language. Professor Neilson has made a selection of the most important tragedies and comedies of the dramatists who were Shakespeare's contemporaries under Queen Elizabeth and his successors under King James; and Professor Baker is preparing a corresponding collection chosen from out the works of the Restoration dramatists. In Professor Dickinson's volume, the *Chief Contemporary Dramatists*, there is ample representation of the foremost British and American playmakers at the beginning of the twentieth century.

Hitherto, however, no adequate attempt has been made to select, out of the drama of the remoter past and out of the drama of other tongues than English, a group of plays, tragic and comic, which might illustrate and illuminate the development of dramatic literature from the Greek of the fifth century B.C. to the Scandinavian of the end of the nineteenth century A.D. This is the difficult task which has been undertaken by the editor of this volume. It has been his duty to ascertain who, among the scores and the hundreds of play-wrights that have flourished in the different countries of Europe during the past twenty-four centuries, were entitled to be recognized as acknowledged masters of the art of the drama or as indisputable representatives of their race and of their era. This selection has proved to be a matter of unexpected delicacy; and the editor cannot hope that the scholars, into whose hands this volume may come, will all of them agree with his choice or accept the principles upon which it has been guided.

Yet, when every allowance has been made, it ought to be admitted that any selection like this must inevitably be affected by the personal equation of the editor, from which he cannot free himself, however much he may struggle. And this editor confesses frankly that if he could have had his own way, disregarding the necessary limitation of a single volume, he would have been glad to include the most amusing mediæval *Pierre Pathelin* of an unknown Frenchman and a corresponding German farce by Hans Sachs. He would have hesitated long before deciding upon the exclusion of Seneca, of Grillparzer and Freytag, of Alfred de Musset and the elder Dumas. It was to him a personal grief that his conscience compelled him to leave out Kotzebue and Scribe, playwrights rather than dramatists, master technicians who made the path straight for artists of a richer endow-ment and of a more significant message.

Even after the list of dramatists had been drawn up, there remained the almost equally difficult duty of deciding upon the single play which should best represent the total achievement of each of them. There is no doubt that Æschylus is satisfactorily repre-sented by *Agamemnon* and Sophocles by *Œdipus the King;* but is *Medea* necessarily the best

play to select from Euripides or *Phormio* from Terence? What should be the choice from
Goethe, from Schiller, and from Holberg? For Beaumarchais ought the *Barber of Seville*
to be taken or the *Marriage of Figaro?* And from Calderon ought *Life is a Dream* to be
picked out or the *Devotion to the Cross?* All that the editor can urge in justification of
the selection that he finally made is that he has been guided by a variety of reasons — by
the availability of a satisfactory translation, in some cases, and in others by the superior
fitness of the chosen play for the general reader.

A collection of masterpieces of the drama extending over a score of centuries serves to
make plain something which ought never to be overlooked. The principles of dramatic
art are unchanging through the ages, the same to-day in Paris or in New York that they
were in Athens twenty-four hundred years ago. They are to be deduced from the tragedies of Sophocles as clearly as from the tragedies of Shakespeare, from the comedies of
Molière as obviously as from the comedies of Lessing and Goldoni and Augier; and they
are all the result of the fact that a dramatist always composes his plays with the desire
and the intent that they shall be performed by actors in a theater and before an audience. He takes thought of the performers of his own time and city; and Sophocles and
Molière, while they were creating characters for the appreciation of posterity, were also
preparing parts for contemporary performers in whom they had confidence. He adjusts
the stories he tells on the stage to the physical conditions of the only playhouse with
which he is familiar. And he feels constrained always to choose the kind of story which
will arouse and retain the interests of his contemporaries in his own country, giving no
thought to the possible likings of any other audience either abroad or in the future.

A dramatist is a playwright who is also a poet — in the largest meaning of the word;
and he is a playwright before he is a poet. As a playwright he has an intuitive percep-
tion of the undeniable fact that spectators massed in a theater are always likely to be
most keenly interested in an action which deals with the deeds of strong-willed men;
and therefore he is prone to provide plots caused by the clash of contending desires.
As a playwright he is aware that the massed spectators insist on seeing for themselves
the culminating moments of the essential struggle, and therefore these necessary episodes are always shown in action and never tamely related. As a playwright he knows
that an audience will not be moved unless it understands fully what is happening before
its eyes; and therefore he takes infinite pains with the problem of exposition, making
clear so much of the past as may be essential for the understanding of the present. As
a playwright he is conscious that the playgoers need to have their attention kept alive
as the story is unrolled before them; and therefore he articulates his plot adroitly that
suspense thickens and that the stress of the contest is steadily intensified. And as a
playwright, finally, he never forgets that the audience has eyes as well as ears; and therefore he provides the utmost spectacle possible in his own theater so far as this is in accord with the quality of his work.

To the many friends who have aided him with encouragement and helped him with
counsel — especially to his colleague Professor Edward Delavan Perry — the editor
desires to express his abiding gratitude. And he takes pleasure in recording here his obligation to the kindly courtesy of the translators and of the owners of copyright who have
made possible the inclusion of translations especially desirable: to the President and
fellows of Harvard University for permission to use the late Professor Morris H. Morgan's
rendering of *Phormio* of Terence; to the American-Scandinavian Foundation for permission to use the version of *Rasmus Montanus* prepared by Professor Oscar James

Campbell and Mr. Frederic Schenck; to the Wisconsin Dramatic Society for permission to use Miss Merle Pierson's translation of Goldoni's *Mistress of the Inn;* to the Oxford University Press, American Branch, and Professor Gilbert Murray for permission to include his metrical rendering of the *Medea* of Euripides; to the Cambridge University Press for permission to reprint Jebb's prose version of *Œdipus;* to G. P. Putnam's Sons and Professor Curtis Hidden Page for permission to include his verse translation of *Tartuffe;* to Charles Scribner's Sons and Mr. William Archer for permission to use the latest version of his rendering of *A Doll's House;* to the Macmillan Company for permission to use Morshead's *Agamemnon;* to George Bell & Sons for permission to use the translations from Hugo, Lessing, and Racine; to J. M. Dent & Co. for permission to include the translation of the *Barber of Seville;* and to D. Appleton & Co. for permission to reprint the translation of the *Cid.*

AGAMEMNON

By ÆSCHYLUS

Translated into English verse by E. D. A. MORSHEAD

CHARACTERS

A WATCHMAN.

CHORUS.

CLYTEMNESTRA.

A HERALD.

AGAMEMNON.

CASSANDRA.

ÆGISTHUS.

---

*The Scene is the Palace of Atreus at Mycenæ. In front of the Palace stand
statues of the gods, and altars prepared for sacrifices.*

AGAMEMNON

A WATCHMAN. I pray the gods to quit
me of my toils,
To close the watch I keep, this livelong
year;
For as a watch-dog lying, not at rest,
Propped on one arm, upon the palace-roof
Of Atreus' race, too long, too well I know
The starry conclave of the midnight sky,
Too well, the splendors of the firmament,
The lords of light, whose kingly aspect
shows —
What time they set or climb the sky in
turn —
The year's divisions, bringing frost or fire.

And now, as ever, am I set to mark
When shall stream up the glow of signal-
flame,
The bale-fire bright, and tell its Trojan
tale —
Troy town is ta'en: such issue holds in hope
She in whose woman's breast beats heart
of man.

Thus upon mine unrestful couch I lie,
Bathed with the dews of night, unvisited
By dreams — ah me! — for in the place of
sleep
Stands Fear as my familiar, and repels
The soft repose that would mine eyelids seal.

And if at whiles, for the lost balm of sleep,
I medicine my soul with melody
Of trill or song — anon to tears I turn,
Wailing the woe that broods upon this
home,
Not now by honor guided as of old.

But now at last fair fall the welcome hour
That sets me free, whene'er the thick night
glow
With beacon-fire of hope deferred no more.
All hail!
　　　[*A beacon-light is seen reddening
　　　　the distant sky.*]

Fire of the night, that brings my spirit day,
Shedding on Argos light, and dance, and
song,
Greetings to fortune, hail!

Let my loud summons ring within the ears
Of Agamemnon's queen, that she anon
Start from her couch and with a shrill
voice cry
A joyous welcome to the beacon-blaze,
For Ilion's fall; such fiery message gleams
From yon high flame; and I, before the rest,
Will foot the lightsome measure of our joy;
For I can say, *My master's dice fell fair —
Behold! the triple sice, the lucky flame!*
Now be my lot to clasp, in loyal love,
The hand of him restored, who rules our
home:
Home — but I say no more: upon my
tongue
Treads hard the ox o' the adage.
　　　　　　　　　　　Had it voice,
The home itself might soothliest tell its
tale;
I, of set will, speak words the wise may
learn,
To others, nought remember nor discern.
　　　　[*Exit. The chorus of old men of
　　　　Mycenæ enter, each leaning on a
　　　　staff. During their song CLY-
　　　　TEMNESTRA appears in the back-
　　　　ground, kindling the altars.*]
CHORUS. Ten livelong years have rolled
away,
Since the twin lords of sceptered sway,
By Zeus endowed with pride of place,
The doughty chiefs of Atreus' race,
Went forth of yore,
To plead with Priam, face to face,
Before the judgment-seat of War!

A thousand ships from Argive land
Put forth to bear the martial band,
That with a spirit stern and strong
Went out to right the kingdom's wrong —

Pealed, as they went, the battle-song,
Wild as the vultures' cry;
When o'er the eyrie, soaring high,
In wild bereavèd agony,
Around, around, in airy rings,
They wheel with oarage of their wings,
But not the eyas-brood behold,
That called them to the nest of old;
But let Apollo from the sky,
Or Pan, or Zeus, but hear the cry,
The exile cry, the wail forlorn,
Of birds from whom their home is torn —
On those who wrought the rapine fell,
Heaven sends the vengeful fiends of hell.

Even so doth Zeus, the jealous lord
And guardian of the hearth and board,
Speed Atreus' sons, in vengeful ire,
'Gainst Paris— sends them forth on fire,
Her to buy back, in war and blood,
Whom one did wed but many woo'd!
And many, many, by his will,
The last embrace of foes shall feel,
And many a knee in dust be bowed,
And splintered spears on shields ring loud,
Of Trojan and of Greek, before
That iron bridal-feast be o'er!
But as he willed 't is ordered all,
And woes, by Heaven ordained, must fall—
Unsoothed by tears or spilth of wine
Poured forth too late, the wrath divine
Glares vengeance on the flameless shrine.

And we in gray dishonored eld,
Feeble of frame, unfit were held
To join the warrior array
That then went forth unto the fray:
And here at home we tarry, fain
Our feeble footsteps to sustain,
Each on his staff — so strength doth wane,
And turns to childishness again.
For while the sap of youth is green,
And, yet unripened, leaps within,
The young are weakly as the old,
And each alike unmeet to hold
The vantage post of war!
And ah! when flower and fruit are o'er,
And on life's tree the leaves are sere,
Age wendeth propped its journey drear,
As forceless as a child, as light
And fleeting as a dream of night
Lost in the garish day!

But thou, O child of Tyndareus,
Queen Clytemnestra, speak! and say
What messenger of joy to-day
Hath won thine ear? what welcome news,
That thus in sacrificial wise
E'en to the city's boundaries
Thou biddest altar-fires arise?
Each god who doth our city guard,
And keeps o'er Argos watch and ward
From heaven above, from earth below —
The mighty lords who rule the skies,
The market's lesser deities,
To each and all the altars glow,
Piled for the sacrifice!
And here and there, anear, afar,
Streams skyward many a beacon-star,
Conjur'd and charm'd and kindled well
By pure oil's soft and guileless spell,
Hid now no more
Within the palace' secret store.

O queen, we pray thee, whatsoe'er,
Known unto thee, were well revealed,
That thou wilt trust it to our ear,
And bid our anxious heart be healed!
That waneth now unto despair —
Now, waxing to a presage fair,
Dawns, from the altar, Hope — to scare
From our rent hearts the vulture Care.

List! for the power is mine, to chant on high
The chiefs' emprise, the strength that omens gave!
List! on my soul breathes yet a harmony,
From realms of ageless powers, and strong to save!

How brother kings, twin lords of one command,
Led forth the youth of Hellas in their flower,
Urged on their way, with vengeful spear and brand,
By warrior-birds, that watched the parting hour.

Go forth to Troy, the eagles seemed to cry —
And the sea-kings obeyed the sky-kings' word,
When on the right they soared across the sky,
And one was black, one bore a white tail barred.

High o'er the palace were they seen to soar,
Then lit in sight of all, and rent and tare,
Far from the fields that she should range
    no more,
Big with her unborn brood, a mother-hare.

And one beheld, the soldier-prophet true,
And the two chiefs, unlike of soul and will,
In the twy-colored eagles straight he knew,
And spake the omen forth, for good and ill.

(Ah, woe and well-a-day! but be the issue
    fair!)

Go forth, he cried, *and Priam's town shall*
    fall.
Yet long the time shall be; and flock and herd,
The people's wealth, that roam before the
    wall,
Shall force hew down, when Fate shall give
    the word.

But O beware! lest wrath in heaven abide,
To dim the glowing battle-forge once more,
And mar the mighty curb of Trojan pride,
The steel of vengeance, welded as for war!

For virgin Artemis bears jealous hate
Against the royal house, the eagle-pair,
Who rend the unborn brood, insatiate —
Yea, loathes their banquet on the quivering
    hare.

(Ah, woe and well-a-day! but be the issue
    fair!)

For well she loves — the goddess kind and
    mild —
The tender new-born cubs of lions bold,
Too weak to range — and well the sucking
    child
Of every beast that roams by wood and wold.

So to the Lord of Heaven she prayeth still,
"*Nay, if it must be, be the omen true!*
Yet do the visioned eagles presage ill;
The end be well, but crossed with evil too!"

Healer Apollo! be her wrath controll'd,
Nor weave the long delay of thwarting gales,
To war against the Danaans and withhold
From the free ocean-waves their eager sails!

She craves, alas! to see a second life
Shed forth, a curst unhallowed sacrifice —
'Twixt wedded souls, artificer of strife,
And hate that knows not fear, and fell device.

At home there tarries like a lurking snake,
Biding its time, a wrath unreconciled,
A wily watcher, passionate to slake,
In blood, resentment for a murdered child.

Such was the mighty warning, pealed of
    yore —
Amid good tidings, such the word of fear,
What time the fateful eagles hovered o'er
The kings, and Calchas read the omen clear.

(In strains like his, once more,
Sing woe and well-a-day! but be the issue
    fair!)

Zeus — if to The Unknown
That name of many names seem good —
Zeus, upon Thee I call.
Thro' the mind's every road
I passed, but vain are all,
Save that which names thee Zeus, the
    Highest One,
Were it but mine to cast away the load,
The weary load, that weighs my spirit
    down.

He that was Lord of old,
In full-blown pride of place and valor bold,
Hath fallen and is gone, even as an old tale
    told!
And he that next held sway,
By stronger grasp o'erthrown
Hath pass'd away!
And whoso now shall bid the triumph-chant
    arise
To Zeus, and Zeus alone,
He shall be found the truly wise.
'T is Zeus alone who shows the perfect way
Of knowledge: He hath ruled,
Men shall learn wisdom, by affliction
    schooled.

In visions of the night, like dropping rain,
Descend the many memories of pain
Before the spirit's sight: through tears and
    dole
Comes wisdom o'er the unwilling soul —

A boon, I wot, of all Divinity,
That holds its sacred throne in strength,
   above the sky!

And then the elder chief, at whose com-
   mand
The fleet of Greece was manned,
Cast on the seer no word of hate,
But veered before the sudden breath of
   Fate —

Ah, weary while! for, ere they put forth
   sail,
Did every store, each minish'd vessel, fail,
While all the Achæan host
At Aulis anchored lay,
Looking across to Chalcis and the coast
Where refluent waters welter, rock, and
   sway;
And rife with ill delay
From northern Strymon blew the thwart-
   ing blast —
Mother of famine fell,
That holds men wand'ring still
Far from the haven where they fain would
   be! —
And pitiless did waste
Each ship and cable, rotting on the sea,
And, doubling with delay each weary hour,
Withered with hope deferred th' Achæans'
   warlike flower.

But when, for bitter storm, a deadlier re-
   lief,
And heavier with ill to either chief,
Pleading the ire of Artemis, the seer
   avowed,
The two Atridæ smote their scepters on the
   plain,
And, striving hard, could not their tears
   restrain!
And then the elder monarch spake aloud —
Ill lot were mine, to disobey!
And ill, to smite my child, my household's
   love and pride!
To stain with virgin blood a father's hands,
   and slay
My daughter, by the altar's side!
'Twixt woe and woe I dwell —
I dare not like a recreant fly,
And leave the league of ships, and fail each
   true ally;

For rightfully they crave, with eager fiery
   mind,
The virgin's blood, shed forth to lull the ad-
   verse wind —
God send the deed be well!

Thus on his neck he took
Fate's hard compelling yoke;
Then, in the counter-gale of will abhorr'd,
   accursed,
To recklessness his shifting spirit veered —
Alas! that Frenzy, first of ills and worst,
With evil craft men's souls to sin hath ever
   stirred!

And so he steeled his heart — ah, well-a-
   day —
Aiding a war for one false woman's sake,
His child to slay,
And with her spilt blood make
An offering, to speed the ships upon their
   way!

Lusting for war, the bloody arbiters
Closed heart and ears, and would nor hear
   nor heed
The girl-voice plead,
Pity me, Father! nor her prayers,
Nor tender, virgin years.

So, when the chant of sacrifice was done,
Her father bade the youthful priestly train
Raise her, like some poor kid, above the
   altar-stone,
From where amid her robes she lay
Sunk all in swoon away —
Bade them, as with the bit that mutely
   tames the steed,
Her fair lips' speech refrain,
Lest she should speak a curse on Atreus'
   home and seed,

So, trailing on the earth her robe of saffron
   dye,
With one last piteous dart from her be-
   seeching eye
Those that should smite she smote —
Fair, silent, as a pictur'd form, but fain
To plead, *Is all forgot?*
How oft those halls of old,
Wherein my sire high feast did hold,
Rang to the virginal soft strain,

When I, a stainless child,
Sang from pure lips and undefiled,
Sang of my sire, and all
His honored life, and how on him should fall
Heaven's highest gift and gain!
And then — but I beheld not, nor can tell,
What further fate befell:
But this is sure, that Calchas' boding
strain
Can ne'er be void or vain.
This wage from Justice' hand do sufferers
earn,
The future to discern:
And yet — farewell, O secret of To-morrow!
Fore-knowledge is fore-sorrow.
Clear with the clear beams of the morrow's
sun,
The future presseth on.
Now, let the house's tale, how dark soe'er,
Find yet an issue fair! —
So prays the loyal, solitary band
That guards the Apian land.

> [*They turn to* CLYTEMNESTRA, *who
> leaves the altars and comes for-
> ward.*]

O queen, I come in reverence of thy sway—
For, while the ruler's kingly seat is void,
The loyal heart before his consort bends.
Now — be it sure and certain news of good,
Or the fair tidings of a flatt'ring hope,
That bids thee spread the light from shrine
to shrine,
I, fain to hear, yet grudge not if thou hide.
CLYTEMNESTRA. As saith the adage,
From the womb of Night
*Spring forth, with promise fair, the young
child Light.*
Aye — fairer even than all hope my news —
By Grecian hands is Priam's city ta'en!
CHORUS. What say'st thou? doubtful
heart makes treach'rous ear.
CLYTEMNESTRA. Hear then again, and
plainly — Troy is ours!
CHORUS. Thrills thro' my heart such joy
as wakens tears.
CLYTEMNESTRA. Aye, thro' those tears
thine eye looks loyalty.
CHORUS. But hast thou proof, to make
assurance sure?
CLYTEMNESTRA. Go to; I have — un-
less the god has lied.

CHORUS. Hath some night-vision won
thee to belief?
CLYTEMNESTRA. Out on all presage of a
slumb'rous soul!
CHORUS. But wert thou cheered by
Rumor's wingless word?
CLYTEMNESTRA. Peace — thou dost chide
me as a credulous girl.
CHORUS. Say then, how long ago the city
fell?
CLYTEMNESTRA. Even in this night that
now brings forth the dawn.
CHORUS. Yet who so swift could speed
the message here?
CLYTEMNESTRA. From Ida's top He-
phæstus, lord of fire,
Sent forth his sign; and on, and ever on,
Beacon to beacon sped the courier-flame.
From Ida to the crag, that Hermes loves,
Of Lemnos; thence unto the steep sublime
Of Athos, throne of Zeus, the broad blaze
flared.
Thence, raised aloft to shoot across the sea,
The moving light, rejoicing in its strength,
Sped from the pyre of pine, and urged its
way,
In golden glory, like some strange new sun,
Onward, and reached Macistus' watching
heights.
There, with no dull delay nor heedless
sleep,
The watcher sped the tidings on in turn,
Until the guard upon Messapius' peak
Saw the far flame gleam on Euripus' tide,
And from the high-piled heap of withered
furze
Lit the new sign and bade the message on.
Then the strong light, far-flown and yet
undimmed,
Shot thro' the sky above Asopus' plain,
Bright as the moon, and on Cithæron's
crag
Aroused another watch of flying fire.
And there the sentinels no whit disowned,
But sent redoubled on, the hest of flame —
Swift shot the light, above Gorgopis' bay,
To Ægiplanctus' mount, and bade the peak
Fail not the onward ordinance of fire.
And like a long beard streaming in the
wind,
Full-fed with fuel, roared and rose the
blaze,

And onward flaring, gleamed above the
cape,
Beneath which shimmers the Saronic bay,
And thence leapt light unto Arachne's peak,
The mountain watch that looks upon our
town.
Thence to th' Atrides' roof — in lineage
fair,
A bright posterity of Ida's fire.
So sped from stage to stage, fulfilled in
turn,
Flame after flame, along the course or-
dained,
And lo! the last to speed upon its way
Sights the end first, and glows unto the
goal.
And Troy is ta'en, and by this sign my lord
Tells me the tale, and ye have learned my
word.
CHORUS. To heaven, O queen, will I up-
raise new song:
But, wouldst thou speak once more, I fain
would hear
From first to last the marvel of the tale.
CLYTEMNESTRA. Think you — this very
morn — the Greeks in Troy,
And loud therein the voice of utter wail!
Within one cup pour vinegar and oil,
And look! unblent, unreconciled, they war.
So in the twofold issue of the strife
Mingle the victor's shout, the captives'
moan.
For all the conquered whom the sword has
spared
Cling weeping — some unto a brother
slain,
Some childlike to a nursing father's form,
And wail the loved and lost, the while their
neck
Bows down already 'neath the captive's
chain.
And lo! the victors, now the fight is done,
Goaded by restless hunger, far and wide
Range all disordered thro' the town, to
snatch
Such victual and such rest as chance may
give
Within the captive halls that once were
Troy —
Joyful to rid them of the frost and dew,
Wherein they couched upon the plain of
old —

Joyful to sleep the gracious night all
through,
Unsummoned of the watching sentinel.
Yet let them reverence well the city's gods,
The lords of Troy, tho' fallen, and her
shrines;
So shall the spoilers not in turn be spoiled.
Yea, let no craving for forbidden gain
Bid conquerors yield before the darts of
greed.
For we need yet, before the race be won,
Homewards, unharmed, to round the
course once more.
For should the host wax wanton ere it
come,
Then, tho' the sudden blow of fate be
spared,
Yet in the sight of gods shall rise once more
The great wrong of the slain, to claim re-
venge.
Now, hearing from this woman's mouth of
mine,
The tale and eke its warning, pray with me,
Luck sway the scale, with no uncertain poise,
For my fair hopes are changed to fairer joys.
CHORUS. A gracious word thy woman's
lips have told,
Worthy a wise man's utterance, O my
queen;
Now with clear trust in thy convincing tale
I set me to salute the gods with song,
Who bring us bliss to counterpoise our
pain.   [*Exit* CLYTEMNESTRA.]
Zeus, Lord of heaven! and welcome night
Of victory, that hast our might
With all the glories crowned!
On towers of Ilion, free no more,
Hast flung the mighty mesh of war,
And closely girt them round,
Till neither warrior may 'scape,
Nor stripling lightly overleap
The trammels as they close, and close,
Till with the grip of doom our foes
In slavery's coil are bound!

Zeus, Lord of hospitality,
In grateful awe I bend to thee —)
'T is thou hast struck the blow!
At Alexander, long ago,
We marked thee bend thy vengeful bow,
But long and warily withhold
The eager shaft, which, uncontrolled

And loosed too soon or launched too high,
Had wandered bloodless through the sky.

Zeus, the high God! — whate'er be dim in
doubt,
This can our thought track out —
The blow that fells the sinner is of God,
And as he wills, the rod
Of vengeance smiteth sore. One said of old,
The gods list not to hold
A reckoning with him whose feet oppress
The grace of holiness —
An impious word! for whensoe'er the sire
Breathed forth rebellious fire —
What time his household overflowed the
measure
Of bliss and health and treasure —
His children's children read the reckoning
plain,
At last, in tears and pain.

On me let weal that brings no woe be sent,
And therewithal, content!
Who spurns the shrine of Right, nor wealth
nor power
Shall be to him a tower,
To guard him from the gulf: there lies his
lot,
Where all things are forgot.
Lust drives him on — lust, desperate and
wild,
Fate's sin-contriving child —
And cure is none; beyond concealment clear,
Kindles sin's baleful glare.
As an ill coin beneath the wearing touch
Betrays by stain and smutch
Its metal false — such is the sinful wight.
Before, on pinions light,
Fair Pleasure flits, and lures him childlike
on,
While home and kin make moan
Beneath the grinding burden of his crime;
Till, in the end of time,
Cast down of heaven, he pours forth fruit-
less prayer
To powers that will not hear.

And such did Paris come
Unto Atrides' home,
And thence, with sin and shame his wel-
come to repay,
Ravished the wife away —

And she, unto her country and her kin
Leaving the clash of shields and spears and
arming ships,
And bearing unto Troy destruction for a
dower,
And overbold in sin,
Went fleetly thro' the gates, at midnight
hour.
Oft from the prophets' lips
Moaned out the warning and the wail —
Ah, woe!
Woe for the home, the home! and for the
chieftains, woe!
Woe for the bride-bed, warm
Yet from the lovely limbs, the impress of
the form
Of her who loved her lord, awhile ago!
And woe! for him who stands
Shamed, silent, unreproachful, stretching
hands
That find her not, and sees, yet will not
see,
That she is far away!
And his sad fancy, yearning o'er the sea,
Shall summon and recall
Her wraith, once more to queen it in his
hall.
And sad with many memories,
The fair cold beauty of each sculptured
face —
And all to hatefulness is turned their grace,
Seen blankly by forlorn and hungering
eyes!
And when the night is deep,
Come visions, sweet and sad, and bearing
pain
Of hopings vain —
Void, void and vain, for scarce the sleeping
sight
Has seen its old delight,
When thro' the grasps of love that bid it
stay
It vanishes away
On silent wings that roam adown the ways
of sleep.

Such are the sights, the sorrows fell,
About our hearth — and worse, whereof I
may not tell.
But, all the wide town o'er,
Each home that sent its master far away
From Hellas' shore,

Feels the keen thrill of heart, the pang of
    loss, to-day.
For, truth to say,
The touch of bitter death is manifold!
Familiar was each face, and dear as life,
    That went unto the war,
But thither, whence a warrior went of old,
Doth nought return —
Only a spear and sword, and ashes in an
    urn!
For Ares, lord of strife,
Who doth the swaying scales of battle hold,
War's money-changer, giving dust for gold,
Sends back, to hearts that held them dear,
Scant ash of warriors, wept with many a
    tear,
Light to the hand, but heavy to the soul;
Yea, fills the light urn full
With what survived the flame —
Death's dusty measure of a hero's frame!

Alas! one cries, *and yet alas again!*
Our chief is gone, the hero of the spear,
And hath not left his peer!
Ah, woe! another moans — *my spouse is*
    slain,
The death of honor, rolled in dust and blood,
Slain for a woman's sin, a false wife's shame!
Such muttered words of bitter mood
Rise against those who went forth to re-
    claim;
Yea, jealous wrath creeps on against th'
    Atrides' name.

And others, far beneath the Ilian wall,
Sleep their last sleep — the goodly chiefs
    and tall,
Couched in the foeman's land, whereon
    they gave
Their breath, and lords of Troy, each in his
    Trojan grave.

Therefore for each and all the city's breast
Is heavy with a wrath supprest,
As deep and deadly as a curse more loud
Flung by the common crowd:
And, brooding deeply, doth my soul await
Tidings of coming fate,
Buried as yet in darkness' womb.
For not forgetful is the high gods' doom
Against the sons of carnage: all too long
Seems the unjust to prosper and be strong,

Till the dark Furies come,
And smite with stern reversal all his home,
Down into dim obstruction — he is gone,
And help and hope, among the lost, is none!

O'er him who vaunteth an exceeding fame,
Impends a woe condign;
The vengeful bolt upon his eyes doth flame,
Sped from the hand divine.
This bliss be mine, ungrudged of God, to
    feel —
To tread no city to the dust,
Nor see my own life thrust
Down to a slave's estate beneath another's
    heel!

Behold, throughout the city wide
Have the swift feet of Rumor hied,
Roused by the joyful flame:
But is the news they scatter, sooth?
Or haply do they give for truth
Some cheat which heaven doth frame?
A child were he and all unwise,
Who let his heart with joy be stirred,
To see the beacon-fires arise,
And then, beneath some thwarting word,
Sicken anon with hope deferred.
The edge of woman's insight still
Good news from true divideth ill;
Light rumors leap within the bound
That fences female credence round,
But, lightly born, as lightly dies
The tale that springs of her surmise.

Soon shall we know whereof the bale-fires
    tell,
The beacons, kindled with transmitted
    flame;
Whether, as well I deem, their tale is true,
Or whether like some dream delusive came
The welcome blaze but to befool our soul.
For lo! I see a herald from the shore
Draw hither, shadowed with the olive-
    wreath —
And thirsty dust, twin-brother of the clay,
Speaks plain of travel far and truthful
    news —
No dumb surmise, nor tongue of flame in
    smoke,
Fitfully kindled from the mountain pyre;
But plainlier shall his voice say, *All is well,*
Or — but away, forebodings adverse, now,

And on fair promise fair fulfillment come!
And whoso for the state prays otherwise,
Himself reap harvest of his ill desire!

[*Enter* HERALD.]

HERALD. O land of Argos, fatherland of
mine!
To thee at last, beneath the tenth year's
sun,
My feet return; the bark of my emprise,
Tho' one by one hope's anchors broke
away,
Held by the last, and now rides safely here.
Long, long my soul despaired to win, in
death,
Its longed-for rest within our Argive land:
And now all hail, O earth, and hail to thee,
New-risen sun! and hail our country's God,
High-ruling Zeus, and thou, the Pythian
lord,
Whose arrows smote us once — smite thou
no more!
Was not thy wrath wreaked full upon our
heads,
O king Apollo, by Scamander's side?
Turn thou, be turned, be savior, healer,
now!
And hail, all gods who rule the street and
mart
And Hermes hail! my patron and my pride,
Herald of heaven, and lord of heralds here!
And Heroes, ye who sped us on our way —
To one and all I cry, *Receive again*
With grace such Argives as the spear has
spared.

Ah, home of royalty, belovèd halls,
And solemn shrines, and gods that front
the morn!
Benign as erst, with sun-flushed aspect
greet
The king returning after many days.
For as from night flash out the beams of
day,
So out of darkness dawns a light, a king,
On you, on Argos — Agamemnon comes.
Then hail and greet him well! such meed
befits
Him whose right hand hewed down the
towers of Troy
With the great axe of Zeus who righteth
wrong —

And smote the plain, smote down to noth-
ingness
Each altar, every shrine; and far and wide
Dies from the whole land's face its off-
spring fair.
Such mighty yoke of fate he set on Troy —
Our lord and monarch, Atreus' elder son,
And comes at last with blissful honor home;
Highest of all who walk on earth to-day —
Not Paris nor the city's self that paid
Sin's price with him, can boast, *Whate'er*
befall,
The guerdon we have won outweighs it all.
But at Fate's judgment-seat the robber
stands
Condemned of rapine, and his prey is torn
Forth from his hands, and by his deed is
reaped
A bloody harvest of his home and land
Gone down to death, and for his guilt and
lust
His father's race pays double in the dust.
CHORUS. Hail, herald of the Greeks,
new-come from war.
HERALD. All hail! not death itself can
fright me now.
CHORUS. Was thine heart wrung with
longing for thy land?
HERALD. So that this joy doth brim
mine eyes with tears.
CHORUS. On you, too, then, this sweet
distress did fall —
HERALD. How say'st thou? make me
master of thy word.
CHORUS. You longed for us who pined
for you again.
HERALD. Craved the land us who craved
it, love for love?
CHORUS. Yea, till my brooding heart
moaned out with pain.
HERALD. Whence thy despair, that
mars the army's joy?
CHORUS. *Sole cure of wrong is silence,*
saith the saw.
HERALD. Thy kings afar, couldst thou
fear other men?
CHORUS. Death had been sweet, as thou
didst say but now.
HERALD. 'T is true; Fate smiles at last.
Throughout our toil,
These many years, some chances issued
fair,

And some, I wot, were checkered with a
curse.
But who, on earth, hath won the bliss of
heaven,
Thro' time's whole tenor an unbroken
weal?
I could a tale unfold of toiling oars,
Ill rest, scant landings on a shore rock-
strewn,
All pains, all sorrows, for our daily doom.
And worse and hatefuller our woes on land;
For where we couched, close by the foeman's
wall,
The river-plain was ever dank with dews,
Dropped from the sky, exuded from the
earth,
A curse that clung unto our sodden garb,
And hair as horrent as a wild beast's fell.
Why tell the woes of winter, when the birds
Lay stark and stiff, so stern was Ida's
snow?
Or summer's scorch, what time the stirless
wave
Sank to its sleep beneath the noonday sun?
Why mourn old woes? their pain has passed
away;
And passed away, from those who fell, all
care,
Forevermore, to rise and live again.
Why sum the count of death, and render
thanks
For life by moaning over fate malign?
Farewell, a long farewell to all our woes!
To us, the remnant of the host of Greece,
Comes weal beyond all counterpoise of
woe;
Thus boast we rightfully to yonder sun,
Like him far-fleeted over sea and land.
The Argive host prevailed to conquer Troy,
And in the temples of the gods of Greece
Hung up these spoils, a shining sign to Time.
Let those who learn this legend bless aright
The city and its chieftains, and repay
The meed of gratitude to Zeus who willed
And wrought the deed. So stands the tale
fulfilled.
CHORUS. Thy words o'erbear my doubt:
for news of good,
The ear of age hath ever youth enow:
But those within and Clytemnestra's self
Would fain hear all; glad thou their ears
and mine.

[Re-enter CLYTEMNESTRA.]

CLYTEMNESTRA. Last night, when first
the fiery courier came,
In sign that Troy is ta'en and razed to
earth,
So wild a cry of joy my lips gave out,
That I was chidden — *Hath the beacon*
watch
Made sure unto thy soul the sack of Troy?
A very woman thou, whose heart leaps light
At wandering rumors! — and with words
like these
They showed me how I strayed, misled of
hope.
Yet on each shrine I set the sacrifice,
And, in the strain they held for feminine,
Went heralds thro' the city, to and fro,
With voice of loud proclaim, announcing
joy;
And in each fane they lit and quenched
with wine
The spicy perfumes fading in the flame.
All is fulfilled: I spare your longer tale —
The king himself anon shall tell me all.

Remains to think what honor best may
greet
My lord, the majesty of Argos, home.
What day beams fairer on a woman's eyes
Than this, whereon she flings the portal
wide,
To hail her lord, heaven-shielded, home
from war?
This to my husband, that he tarry not,
But turn the city's longing into joy!
Yea, let him come, and coming may he find
A wife no other than he left her, true
And faithful as a watch-dog to his home,
His foemen's foe, in all her duties leal,
Trusty to keep for ten long years unmarred
The store whereon he set his master-seal.
Be steel deep-dyed, before ye look to see
Ill joy, ill fame, from other wight, in me!
HERALD. 'T is fairly said: thus speaks a
noble dame,
Nor speaks amiss, when truth informs the
boast.   *[Exit* CLYTEMNESTRA.]
CHORUS. So has she spoken — be it
yours to learn
By clear interpreters her specious word.
Turn to me, herald, — tell me if anon

The second well-loved lord of Argos comes?
Hath Menelaus safely sped with you?
HERALD. Alas — brief boon unto my
friends it were,
To flatter them, for truth, with falsehoods
fair!
CHORUS. Speak joy, if truth be joy, but
truth, at worst —
Too plainly, truth and joy are here di-
vorced.
HERALD. The hero and his bark were
rapt away
Far from the Grecian fleet? 't is truth I say.
CHORUS. Whether in all men's sight
from Ilion borne,
Or from the fleet by stress of weather torn?
HERALD. Full on the mark thy shaft of
speech doth light,
And one short word hath told long woes
aright.
CHORUS. But say, what now of him each
comrade saith?
What their forebodings, of his life or death?
HERALD. Ask me no more: the truth is
known to none,
Save the earth-fostering, all-surveying
Sun,
CHORUS. Say, by what doom the fleet
of Greece was driven?
How rose, how sank the storm, the wrath
of Heaven?
HERALD. Nay, ill it were to mar with
sorrow's tale
The day of blissful news. The gods demand
Thanksgiving sundered from solicitude.
If one as herald came with rueful face
To say, *The curse has fallen, and the host*
Gone down to death; and one wide wound has
reached
The city's heart, and out of many homes
Many are cast and consecrate to death,
Beneath the double scourge, that Ares loves,
The bloody pair, the fire and sword of doom—
If such sore burden weighed upon my
tongue,
'T were fit to speak such words as gladden
fiends.
But — coming as he comes who bringeth
news
Of safe return from toil, and issues fair,
To men rejoicing in a weal restored —
Dare I to dash good words with ill, and say

How the gods' anger smote the Greeks in
storm?
For fire and sea, that erst held bitter feud,
Now swore conspiracy and pledged their
faith,
Wasting the Argives worn with toil and
war.
Night and great horror of the rising wave
Came o'er us, and the blasts that blow
from Thrace
Clashed ship with ship, and some with
plunging prow
Thro' scudding drifts of spray and raving
storm
Vanished, as strays by some ill shepherd
driven.
And when at length the sun rose bright, we
saw
Th' Ægean sea-field flecked with flowers
of death,
Corpses of Grecian men and shattered
hulls.
For us, indeed, some god, was well I deem,
No human power, laid hand upon our helm,
Snatched us or prayed us from the powers
of air,
And brought our bark thro' all, unharmed
in hull:
And saving Fortune sat and steered us fair,
So that no surge should gulf us deep in
brine,
Nor grind our keel upon a rocky shore.

So 'scaped we death that lurks beneath the
sea,
But, under day's white light, mistrustful all
Of Fortune's smile, we sat and brooded
deep,
Shepherds forlorn of thoughts that wan-
dered wild,
O'er this new woe; for smitten was our
host,
And lost as ashes scattered from the pyre.
Of whom if any draw his life-breath yet,
Be well assured, he deems of us as dead,
As we of him no other fate forebode.
But Heaven save all! If Menelaus live,
He will not tarry, but will surely come:
Therefore if anywhere the high sun's ray
Descries him upon earth, preserved by
Zeus,
Who wills not yet to wipe his race away,

Hope still there is that homeward he may
    wend.
Enough — thou hast the truth unto the
    end.   [*Exit* HERALD.]
   CHORUS. Say, from whose lips the pres-
    age fell?
Who read the future all too well,
And named her, in her natal hour,
Helen, the bride with war for dower?
'T was one of the Invisible,
Guiding his tongue with prescient power.
On fleet, and host, and citadel,
War, sprung from her, and death did lour,
When from the bride-bed's fine-spun veil
She to the Zephyr spread her sail.
Strong blew the breeze — the surge closed
    o'er
The cloven track of keel and oar,
But while she fled, there drove along,
Fast in her wake, a mighty throng —
Athirst for blood, athirst for war,
Forward in fell pursuit they sprung,
Then leapt on Simois' bank ashore,
The leafy coppices among —
No rangers, they, of wood and field,
But huntsmen of the sword and shield.

Heaven's jealousy, that works its will,
Sped thus on Troy its destined ill,
Well named, at once, the Bride and Bane;
And loud rang out the bridal strain;
But they to whom that song befell
Did turn anon to tears again;
Zeus tarries, but avenges still
The husband's wrong, the household's
    stain!
He, the hearth's lord, brooks not to see
Its outraged hospitality.

Even now, and in far other tone,
Troy chants her dirge of mighty moan,
Woe upon Paris, woe and hate!
Who wooed his country's doom for mate —
This is the burden of the groan,
Wherewith she wails disconsolate
The blood, so many of her own
Have poured in vain, to fend her fate;
Troy! thou hast fed and freed to roam
A lion-cub within thy home!

A suckling creature, newly ta'en
From mother's teat, still fully fain

Of nursing care; and oft caressed,
Within the arms, upon the breast,
Even as an infant, has it lain;
Or fawns and licks, by hunger pressed,
The hand that will assuage its pain;
In life's young dawn, a well-loved guest,
A fondling for the children's play,
A joy unto the old and gray.

But waxing time and growth betrays
The blood-thirst of the lion-race,
And, for the house's fostering care,
Unbidden all, it revels there,
And bloody recompense repays —
Rent flesh of kine, its talons tare:
A mighty beast, that slays, and slays,
And mars with blood the household fair,
A God-sent pest invincible,
A minister of fate and hell.

Even so to Ilion's city came by stealth
A spirit as of windless seas and skies,
A gentle phantom-form of joy and wealth,
With love's soft arrows speeding from its
    eyes —
Love's rose, whose thorn doth pierce the
    soul in subtle wise.

Ah, well-a-day! the bitter bridal-bed,
When the fair mischief lay by Paris' side!
What curse on palace and on people sped
With her, the Fury sent on Priam's pride,
By angered Zeus! what tears of many a
    widowed bride!

Long, long ago to mortals this was told,
How sweet security and blissful state
Have curses for their children — so men
    hold —
And for the man of all-too prosperous fate
Springs from a bitter seed some woe in-
    satiate.

Alone, alone, I deem far otherwise;
Not bliss nor wealth it is, but impious
    deed,
From which that after-growth of ill doth
    rise!
Woe springs from wrong, the plant is like
    the seed —
While Right, in Honor's house, doth its
    own likeness breed.

Some past impiety, some gray old crime,
Breeds the young curse, that wantons in
   our ill,
Early or late, when haps th' appointed
   time —
And out of light brings power of darkness
   still,
A master-fiend, a foe, unseen, invincible;

A pride accursed, that broods upon the race
And home in which dark Atè holds her
   sway —
Sin's child and Woe's, that wears its parents' face;
While Right in smoky cribs shines clear as
   day,
And decks with weal his life, who walks
   the righteous way.

From gilded halls, that hands polluted
   raise,
Right turns away with proud averted eyes,
And of the wealth, men stamp amiss with
   praise,
Heedless, to poorer, holier temples hies,
And to Fate's goal guides all, in its ap-
   pointed wise.

Hail to thee, chief of Atreus' race,
Returning proud from Troy subdued!
How shall I greet thy conquering face?
How nor a fulsome praise obtrude,
Nor stint the meed of gratitude?
For mortal men who fall to ill
Take little heed of open truth,
But seek unto its semblance still:
The show of weeping and of ruth
To the forlorn will all men pay,
But, of the grief their eyes display,
Nought to the heart doth pierce its way.
And, with the joyous, they beguile
Their lips unto a feignèd smile,
And force a joy, unfelt the while;
But he who as a shepherd wise
Doth know his flock, can ne'er misread
Truth in the falsehood of his eyes,
Who veils beneath a kindly guise
A lukewarm love in deed.
And thou, our leader — when of yore
Thou badest Greece go forth to war
For Helen's sake — I dare avow
That then I held thee not as now;

That to my vision thou didst seem
Dyed in the hues of disesteem.
I held thee for a pilot ill,
And reckless, of thy proper will,
Endowing others doomed to die
With vain and forced audacity!
Now from my heart, ungrudgingly,
To those that wrought, this word be said—
Well fall the labor ye have sped —
Let time and search, O king, declare
What men within thy city's bound
Were loyal to the kingdom's care,
And who were faithless found.

[*Enter* AGAMEMNON *in a chariot, accompanied by* CASSANDRA. *He speaks
   without descending.*]

   AGAMEMNON. First, as is meet, a king's
    All-hail be said
To Argos, and the gods that guard the
   land —
Gods who with me availed to speed us home,
With me availed to wring from Priam's
   town
The due of justice. In the court of heaven
The gods in conclave sat and judged the
   cause,
Not from a pleader's tongue, and at the
   close,
Unanimous into the urn of doom
This sentence gave, *On Ilion and her men,
Death:* and where hope drew nigh to par-
   don's urn
No hand there was to cast a vote therein.
And still the smoke of fallen Ilion
Rises in sight of all men, and the flame
Of Atè's hecatomb is living yet,
And where the towers in dusty ashes sink,
Rise the rich fumes of pomp and wealth
   consumed.
For this must all men pay unto the gods
The meed of mindful hearts and gratitude:
For by our hands the meshes of revenge
Closed on the prey, and for one woman's
   sake
Troy trodden by the Argive monster lies —
The foal, the shielded band that leapt the
   wall,
What time with autumn sank the Pleiades.
Yea, o'er the fencing wall a lion sprang
Ravening, and lapped his fill of blood of
   kings.

Such prelude spoken to the gods in full,
To you I turn, and to the hidden thing
Whereof ye spake but now: and in that
thought
I am as you, and what ye say, say I.
For few are they who have such inborn
grace,
As to look up with love, and envy not,
When stands another on the height of weal.
Deep in his heart, whom jealousy hath
seized,
Her poison lurking doth enhance his load;
For now beneath his proper woes he chafes,
And sighs withal to see another's weal.

I speak not idly, but from knowledge
sure —
There be who vaunt an utter loyalty,
That is but as the ghost of friendship dead,
A shadow in a glass, of faith gone by.
One only — he who went reluctant forth
Across the seas with me — Odysseus — he
Was loyal unto me with strength and will,
A trusty trace-horse bound unto my car.
Thus — be he yet beneath the light of day,
Or dead; as well I fear — I speak his praise.

Lastly, whate'er be due to men or gods,
With joint debate, in public council held,
We will decide, and warily contrive
That all which now is well may so abide:
For that which haply needs the healer's
art,
That will we medicine, discerning well
If cautery or knife befit the time.

Now, to my palace and the shrines of home,
I will pass in, and greet you first and fair,
Ye gods, who bade me forth, and home
again —
And long may Victory tarry in my train!

[*Enter* CLYTEMNESTRA, *followed by maidens
bearing purple robes.*]

CLYTEMNESTRA. Old men of Argos,
lieges of our realm,
Shame shall not bid me shrink lest ye
should see
The love I bear my lord. Such blushing
fear
Dies at the last from hearts of human kind.
From mine own soul and from no alien lips,

I know and will reveal the life I bore,
Reluctant, through the lingering livelong
years,
The while my lord beleaguered Ilion's wall.

First, that a wife sat sundered from her
lord,
In widowed solitude, was utter woe —
And woe, to hear how Rumor's many
tongues
All boded evil — woe, when he who came
And he who followed spake of ill on ill,
Keening *Lost, lost, all lost!* thro' hall and
bower.
Had this my husband met so many wounds,
As by a thousand channels Rumor told,
No network e'er was full of holes as he.
Had he been slain, as oft as tidings came
That he was dead, he well might boast him
now
A second Geryon of triple frame,
With triple robe of earth above him laid —
For that below, no matter — triply dead,
Dead by one death for every form he bore.
And thus distraught by news of wrath and
woe,
Oft for self-slaughter had I slung the noose,
But others wrenched it from my neck
away.
Hence haps it that Orestes, thine and mine,
The pledge and symbol of our wedded
troth,
Stands not beside us now, as he should
stand.
Nor marvel thou at this: he dwells with one
Who guards him loyally; 't is Phocis' king,
Strophius, who warned me erst, *Bethink
thee, queen,*
What woes of doubtful issue well may fall!
Thy lord in daily jeopardy at Troy,
While here a populace uncurbed may cry
*"Down with the council, down!" bethink thee
too,*
*'T is the world's way to set a harder heel
On fallen power.*
For thy child's absence, then,
Such mine excuse, no wily afterthought.
For me, long since the gushing fount of
tears
Is wept away; no drop is left to shed.
Dim are the eyes that ever watched till
dawn,

Weeping, the bale-fires, piled for thy re-
turn,
Night after night unkindled. If I slept,
Each sound — the tiny humming of a gnat
Roused me again, again, from fitful dreams
Wherein I felt thee smitten, saw thee slain,
Thrice for each moment of mine hour of
sleep.

All this I bore, and now, released from woe,
I hail my lord as watch-dog of a fold,
As saving stay-rope of a storm-tossed ship,
As column stout that holds the roof aloft,
As only child unto a sire bereaved,
As land beheld, past hope, by crews forlorn,
As sunshine fair when tempest's wrath is
past,
As gushing spring to thirsty wayfarer.
So sweet it is to 'scape the press of pain.
With such salute I bid my husband hail!
Nor Heaven be wroth therewith! for long
and hard
I bore that ire of old.
　　　　　　Sweet lord, step forth,
Step from thy car, I pray — nay, not on
earth
Plant the proud foot, O king, that trod
down Troy!
Women! why tarry ye, whose task it is
To spread your monarch's path with tap-
estry?
Swift, swift, with purple strew his passage
fair,
That justice lead him to a home, at last,
He scarcely looked to see.
　　　　　　For what remains,
Zeal unsubdued by sleep shall nerve my
hand
To work as right and as the gods command.
　　AGAMEMNON. Daughter of Leda, watcher
o'er my home,
Thy greeting well befits mine absence long,
For late and hardly has it reached its end.
Know, that the praise which honor bids us
crave,
Must come from others' lips, not from our
own:
See too that not in fashion feminine
Thou make a warrior's pathway delicate;
Not unto me, as to some Eastern lord,
Bowing thyself to earth, make homage
loud.

Strew not this purple that shall make each
step
An arrogance; such pomp beseems the gods,
Not me. A mortal man to set his foot
On these rich dyes? I hold such pride in
fear,
And bid thee honor me as man, not god.
Fear not — such footcloths and all gauds
apart,
Loud from the trump of Fame my name is
blown
Best gift of Heaven it is, in glory's hour,
To think thereon with soberness: and
thou —
Bethink thee of the adage, *Call none blest
Till peaceful death have crowned a life of
weal.*
'T is said: I fain would fare unvexed by
fear.
　　CLYTEMNESTRA. Nay, but unsay it —
thwart not thou my will!
　　AGAMEMNON. Know, I have said, and
will not mar my word.
　　CLYTEMNESTRA. Was it fear made this
meekness to the gods?
　　AGAMEMNON. If cause be cause, 't is
mine for this resolve.
　　CLYTEMNESTRA. What, think'st thou,
in thy place had Priam done?
　　AGAMEMNON. He surely would have
walked on broidered robes.
　　CLYTEMNESTRA. Then fear not thou the
voice of human blame.
　　AGAMEMNON. Yet mighty is the murmur
of a crowd.
　　CLYTEMNESTRA. Shrink not from envy,
appanage of bliss.
　　AGAMEMNON. War is not woman's part,
nor war of words.
　　CLYTEMNESTRA. Yet happy victors well
may yield therein.
　　AGAMEMNON. Dost crave for triumph in
this petty strife?
　　CLYTEMNESTRA. Yield; of thy grace
permit me to prevail!
　　AGAMEMNON. Then, if thou wilt, let
some one stoop to loose
Swiftly these sandals, slaves beneath my
foot:
And stepping thus upon the sea's rich dye,
I pray, *Let none among the gods look down
With jealous eye on me* — reluctant all,

To trample thus and mar a thing of price,
Wasting the wealth of garments silver-
    worth.
Enough hereof: and, for the stranger maid,
Lead her within, but gently: God on high
Looks graciously on him whom triumph's
    hour
Has made not pitiless. None willingly
Wear the slave's yoke — and she, the prize
    and flower
Of all we won, comes hither in my train,
Gift of the army to its chief and lord.
— Now, since in this my will bows down
    to thine,
I will pass in on purples to my home.
    CLYTEMNESTRA. A Sea there is — and
        who shall stay its springs?
And deep within its breast, a mighty store,
Precious as silver, of the purple dye,
Whereby the dipped robe doth its tint re-
    new.
Enough of such, O king, within thy halls
There lies, a store that cannot fail; but I —
I would have gladly vowed unto the gods
Cost of a thousand garments trodden thus
(Had once the oracle such gift required),
Contriving ransom for thy life preserved.
For while the stock is firm the foliage
    climbs,
Spreading a shade, what time the dog-star
    glows;
And thou, returning to thine hearth and
    home,
Art as a genial warmth in winter hours,
Or as a coolness, when the lord of heaven
Mellows the juice within the bitter grape.
Such boons and more doth bring into a
    home
The present footstep of its proper lord.
Zeus, Zeus, Fulfillment's lord! my vows
    fulfill,
And whatsoe'er it be, work forth thy will!
        [*Exeunt all but* CASSANDRA *and
            the* CHORUS.]
    CHORUS. Wherefore forever on the
        wings of fear
Hovers a vision drear
Before my boding heart? a strain,
Unbidden and unwelcome, thrills mine ear,
Oracular of pain.
Not as of old upon my bosom's throne
Sits Confidence, to spurn

Such fears, like dreams we know not to
    discern.
Old, old and gray long since the time has
    grown,
Which saw the linkèd cables moor
The fleet, when erst it came to Ilion's
    sandy shore;
And now mine eyes and not another's see
Their safe return.
Yet none the less in me
The inner spirit sings a boding song,
Self-prompted, sings the Furies' strain —
And seeks, and seeks in vain,
To hope and to be strong!

Ah! to some end of Fate, unseen, unguessed,
Are these wild throbbings of my heart and
    breast —
Yea, of some doom they tell —
Each pulse, a knell.
Lief, lief I were, that all
To unfulfillment's hidden realm might fall.

Too far, too far our mortal spirits strive,
Grasping at utter weal, unsatisfied —
Till the fell curse, that dwelleth hard be-
    side,
Thrust down the sundering wall. Too fair
    they blow,
The gales that waft our bark on Fortune's
    tide!
Swiftly we sail, the sooner all to drive
Upon the hidden rock, the reef of woe.

Then if the hand of caution warily
Sling forth into the sea
Part of the freight, lest all should sink be-
    low,
From the deep death it saves the bark:
    even so,
Doom-laden though it be, once more may
    rise
His household, who is timely wise.

How oft the famine-stricken field
Is saved by God's large gift, the new year's
    yield!
But blood of man once spilled,
Once at his feet shed forth, and darkening
    the plain, —
Nor chant nor charm can call it back again.
So Zeus hath willed:

Else had he spared the leech Asclepius,
    skilled
To bring man from the dead: the hand di-
    vine
Did smite himself with death — a warning
    and a sign.

Ah me! if Fate, ordained of old,
Held not the will of gods constrained, con-
    trolled,
Helpless to us-ward, and apart —
Swifter than speech my heart
Had poured its presage out!
Now, fretting, chafing in the dark of
    doubt,
'T is hopeless to unfold
Truth, from fear's tangled skein; and,
    yearning to proclaim
Its thought, my soul is prophecy and flame.

[Re-enter CLYTEMNESTRA.]

CLYTEMNESTRA. Get thee within thou
    too, Cassandra, go!
For Zeus to thee in gracious mercy grants
To share the sprinklings of the lustral bowl,
Beside the altar of his guardianship,
Slave among many slaves. What, haughty
    still?
Step from the car; Alcmena's son, 't is said,
Was sold perforce and bore the yoke of old.
Aye, hard it is, but, if such fate befall,
'T is a fair chance to serve within a home
Of ancient wealth and power. An upstart
    lord,
To whom wealth's harvest came beyond
    his hope,
Is as a lion to his slaves, in all
Exceeding fierce, immoderate in sway.
Pass in: thou hearest what our ways will be.
CHORUS. Clear unto thee, O maid, is her
    command,
But thou — within the toils of Fate thou
    art —
If such thy will, I urge thee to obey;
Yet I misdoubt thou dost nor hear nor
    heed.
CLYTEMNESTRA. I wot — unless like
    swallows she doth use
Some strange barbarian tongue from over-
    sea —
My words must speak persuasion to her
    soul.

CHORUS. Obey: there is no gentler way
    than this.
Step from the car's high seat and follow
    her.
CLYTEMNESTRA. Truce to this bootless
    waiting here without!
I will not stay: beside the central shrine
The victims stand, prepared for knife and
    fire —
Offerings from hearts beyond all hope made
    glad.
Thou — if thou reckest aught of my com-
    mand,
'T were well done soon: but if thy sense be
    shut
From these my words, let thy barbarian
    hand
Fulfill by gesture the default of speech.
CHORUS. No native is she, thus to read
    thy words
Unaided: like some wild thing of the wood,
New-trapped, behold! she shrinks and
    glares on thee.
CLYTEMNESTRA. 'T is madness and the
    rule of mind distraught,
Since she beheld her city sink in fire,
And hither comes, nor brooks the bit, until
In foam and blood her wrath be champed
    away.
See ye to her; unqueenly 't is for me,
Unheeded thus to cast away my words.
                    [Exit CLYTEMNESTRA.]
CHORUS. But with me pity sits in anger's
    place.
Poor maiden, come thou from the car; no
    way
There is but this — take up thy servitude.
CASSANDRA. Woe, woe, alas! Earth,
    Mother Earth! and thou
Apollo, Apollo!
CHORUS. Peace! shriek not to the bright
    prophetic god,
Who will not brook the suppliance of woe.
CASSANDRA. Woe, woe, alas! Earth,
    Mother Earth! and thou
Apollo, Apollo!
CHORUS. Hark, with wild curse she calls
    anew on him,
Who stands far off and loathes the voice of
    wail.
CASSANDRA. Apollo, Apollo!
God of all ways, but only Death's to me,

Once and again, O thou, Destroyer named,
Thou hast destroyed me, thou, my love of
   old!
   CHORUS. She grows presageful of her
     woes to come,
Slave tho' she be, instinct with prophecy.
   CASSANDRA. Apollo, Apollo!
God of all ways, but only Death's to me,
O thou Apollo, thou Destroyer named!
What way hast led me, to what evil home?
   CHORUS. Know'st thou it not? The
     home of Atreus' race:
Take these my wo̶ ̶ds for sooth and ask no
   more.
   CASSAND̶ ̶ Home cursed of God!
    ̶ ̶ear witness unto me,
Ye̶ ̶oned woes within —
The blood-stained hands of them that
   smite their kin —
The strangling noose, and, spattered o'er
With human blood, the reeking floor!
   CHORUS. How like a sleuth-hound quest-
     ing on the track,
Keen-scented unto blood and death she
   hies!
   CASSANDRA. Ah! can the ghostly guid-
     ance fail,
Whereby my prophet-soul is onwards led?
Look! for their flesh the specter-children
   wail,
Their sodden limbs on which their father
   fed!
   CHORUS. Long since we knew of thy
     prophetic fame, —
But for those deeds we seek no prophet's
   tongue.
   CASSANDRA. God! 't is another crime —
Worse than the storied woe of olden time,
Cureless, abhorred, that one is plotting
   here —
A shaming death, for those that should be
   dear!
Alas! and far away, in foreign land,
He that should help doth stand!
   CHORUS. I knew th' old tales, the city
     rings withal —
But now thy speech is dark, beyond my
   ken.
   CASSANDRA. O wretch, O purpose fell!
Thou for thy wedded lord
The cleansing wave hast poured —
A treacherous welcome!

          How the sequel tell?
Too soon 't will come, too soon, for now,
   even now,
She smites him, blow on blow!
   CHORUS. Riddles beyond my rede — I
     peer in vain
Thro' the dim films that screen the proph-
   ecy.
   CASSANDRA. God! a new sight! a net, a
     snare of hell,
Set by her hand — herself a snare more fell!
A wedded wife, she slays her lord,
Helped by another hand!
          Ye powers, whose hate
Of Atreus' home no blood can satiate,
Raise the wild cry above the sacrifice ab-
   horred!
   CHORUS. Why biddest thou some fiend,
     I know not whom,
Shriek o'er the house? Thine is no cheering
   word.
Back to my heart in frozen fear I feel
My wanning life-blood run —
The blood that round the wounding steel
Ebbs slow, as sinks life's parting sun —
Swift, swift and sure, some woe comes
   pressing on!
   CASSANDRA. Away, away — keep him
     away —
The monarch of the herd, the pasture's
   pride,
Far from his mate! In treach'rous wrath,
Muffling his swarthy horns, with secret
   scathe
She gores his fenceless side!
Hark! in the brimming bath,
The heavy plash — the dying cry —
Hark — in the laver — hark, he falls by
   treachery!
   CHORUS. I read amiss dark sayings such
     as thine,
Yet something warns me that they tell of ill.
O dark prophetic speech,
Ill tidings dost thou teach
Ever, to mortals here below!
Ever some tale of awe and woe
Thro' all thy windings manifold
Do we unriddle and unfold!
   CASSANDRA. Ah, well-a-day! the cup of
     agony,
Whereof I chant, foams with a draught
   for me.

Ah, lord, ah, leader, thou hast led me
    here —
Was 't but to die with thee whose doom is
    near?
    CHORUS. Distraught thou art, divinely
        stirred,
And wailest for thyself a tuneless lay,
As piteous as the ceaseless tale
Wherewith the brown melodious bird
Doth ever Itys! Itys! wail,
Deep-bowered in sorrow, all its little life-
    time's day!
    CASSANDRA. Ah, for thy fate, O shrill-
        voice nightingale!
Some solace for thy woes did Heaven
    afford,
Clothed thee with soft brown plumes, and
    life apart from wail —
But for my death is edged the double-
    biting sword!
    CHORUS. What pangs are these, what
        fruitless pain,
Sent on thee from on high?
Thou chantest terror's frantic strain,
Yet in shrill measured melody.
How thus unerring canst thou sweep along
The prophet's path of boding song?
    CASSANDRA. Woe, Paris, woe on thee!
        thy bridal joy
Was death and fire upon thy race and
    Troy!
And woe for thee, Scamander's flood!
Beside thy banks, O river fair,
I grew in tender nursing care
From childhood unto maidenhood!
Now not by thine, but by Cocytus' stream
And Acheron's banks shall ring my boding
    scream.
    CHORUS. Too plain is all, too plain!
A child might read aright thy fateful strain.
Deep in my heart their piercing fang
Terror and sorrow set, the while I heard
That piteous, low, tender word,
Yet to mine ear and heart a crushing
    pang.
    CASSANDRA. Woe for my city, woe for
        Ilion's fall!
Father, how oft with sanguine stain
Streamed on thine altar-stone the blood of
    cattle, slain
That Heaven might guard our wall!
But all was shed in vain.

Low lie the shattered towers whereas they
    fell,
And I — ah burning heart! — shall soon
    lie low as well.
    CHORUS. Of sorrow is thy song, of sor-
        row still!
Alas, what power of ill
Sits heavy on thy heart and bids thee tell
In tears of perfect moan thy deadly tale?
Some woe — I know not what — must
    close thy piteous wail.
    CASSANDRA. List! for no more the pres-
        age of my soul,
Bride-like, shall peer from its secluding
    veil;
But as the morning wind blows clear the
    east,
More bright shall blow the wind of proph-
    ecy,
And as against the low bright line of dawn
Heaves high and higher yet the rolling
    wave,
So in the clearing skies of prescience
Dawns on my soul a further, deadlier woe,
And I will speak, but in dark speech no
    more.
Bear witness, ye, and follow at my side —
I scent the trail of blood, shed long ago.
Within this house a choir abidingly
Chants in harsh unison the chant of ill;
Yea, and they drink, for more enhardened
    joy,
Man's blood for wine, and revel in the
    halls,
Departing never, Furies of the home.
They sit within, they chant the primal
    curse,
Each spitting hatred on that crime of old,
The brother's couch, the love incestuous
That brought forth hatred to the ravisher.
Say, is my speech or wild and erring now,
Or doth its arrow cleave the mark, indeed?
They called me once, *The prophetess of lies,*
The wandering hag, the pest of every door —
Attest ye now, *She knows in very sooth*
The house's curse, the storied infamy.
    CHORUS. Yet how should oath — how
        loyally soe'er
I swear it — aught avail thee? In good
    sooth,
My wonder meets thy claim: I stand
    amazed

That thou, a maiden born beyond the seas,
Dost as a native know and tell aright
Tales of a city of an alien tongue.
CASSANDRA. That is my power — a
boon Apollo gave.
CHORUS. God though he were, yearning
for mortal maid?
CASSANDRA. Aye! what seemed shame
of old is shame no more.
CHORUS. Such finer sense suits not with
slavery.
CASSANDRA. He strove to win me, pant-
ing for my love.
CHORUS. Came ye by compact unto
bridal joys?
CASSANDRA. Nay — for I plighted troth,
then foiled the god.
CHORUS. Wert thou already dowered
with prescience?
CASSANDRA. Yea — prophetess to Troy
of all her doom.
CHORUS. How left thee, then, Apollo's
wrath unscathed?
CASSANDRA. I, false to him, seemed
prophet false to all.
CHORUS. Not so — to us at least thy
words seem sooth.
CASSANDRA. Woe for me, woe! Again
the agony —
Dread pain that sees the future all too well
With ghastly preludes whirls and racks my
soul.
Behold ye — yonder on the palace roof
The specter-children sitting — look, such
things
As dreams are made on, phantoms as of
babes,
Horrible shadows, that a kinsman's hand
Hath marked with murder, and their arms
are full —
A rueful burden — see, they hold them up,
The entrails upon which their father fed!

For this, for this, I say there plots revenge
A coward lion, couching in the lair —
Guarding the gate against my master's
foot —
My master — mine — I bear the slave's
yoke now.
And he, the lord of ships, who trod down
Troy,
Knows not the fawning treachery of tongue

Of this thing false and dog-like — how
her speech
Glozes and sleeks her purpose, till she win
By ill fate's favor the desirèd chance,
Moving like Atè to a secret end.
O aweless soul! the woman slays her lord —
Woman? what loathsome monster of the
earth
Were fit comparison? The double snake —
Or Scylla, where she dwells, the seaman's
bane,
Girt round about with rocks? some hag of
hell,
Raving a truceless curse upon her kin?
Hark — even now she cries exultingly
The vengeful cry that tells of battle
turned —
How fain, forsooth, to greet her chief re-
stored!
Nay, then, believe me not: what skills be-
lief
Or disbelief? Fate works its will — and
thou
Wilt see and say in ruth, *Her tale was true.*
CHORUS. Ah — 't is Thyestes' feast on
kindred flesh —
I guess her meaning and with horror thrill,
Hearing no shadow'd hint of th' o'er-true
tale,
But its full hatefulness: yet, for the rest,
Far from the track I roam, and know no
more.
CASSANDRA. 'T is Agamemnon's doom
thou shalt behold.
CHORUS. Peace, hapless woman, to thy
boding words!
CASSANDRA. Far from my speech stands
he who sains and saves.
CHORUS. Aye — were such doom at
hand — which God forbid!
CASSANDRA. Thou prayest idly — these
move swift to slay.
CHORUS. What man prepares a deed of
such despite?
CASSANDRA. Fool! thus to read amiss
mine oracles.
CHORUS. Deviser and device are dark to
me.
CASSANDRA. Dark! all too well I speak
the Grecian tongue.
CHORUS. Aye — but in thine, as in
Apollo's strains,

Familiar is the tongue, but dark the thought.
CASSANDRA. Ah, ah, the fire! it waxes, nears me now —
Woe, woe for me, Apollo of the dawn!

Lo, how the woman-thing, the lioness
Couched with the wolf — her noble mate afar —
Will slay me, slave forlorn! Yea, like some witch,
She drugs the cup of wrath, that slays her lord,
With double death — his recompense for me!
Aye, 't is for me, the prey he bore from Troy,
That she hath sworn his death, and edged the steel!
Ye wands, ye wreaths that cling around my neck,
Ye showed me prophetess yet scorned of all —
I stamp you into death, or e'er I die —
Down, to destruction!
　　　　　Thus I stand revenged —
Go, crown some other with a prophet's woe.
Look! it is he, it is Apollo's self
Rending from me the prophet-robe he gave.
God! while I wore it yet, thou saw'st me mocked
There at my home by each malicious mouth —
To all and each, an undivided scorn.
The name alike and fate of witch and cheat —
Woe, poverty, and famine — all I bore;
And at this last the god hath brought me here
Into death's toils, and what his love had made,
His hate unmakes me now: and I shall stand
Not now before the altar of my home,
But me a slaughter-house and block of blood
Shall see hewn down, a reeking sacrifice.
Yet shall the gods have heed of me who die,
For by their will shall one requite my doom.
He, to avenge his father's blood outpoured,
Shall smite and slay with matricidal hand.

Aye, he shall come — tho' far away he roam,
A banished wanderer in a stranger's land —
To crown his kindred's edifice of ill,
Called home to vengeance by his father's fall:
Thus have the high gods sworn, and shall fulfill.
And now why mourn I, tarrying on earth,
Since first mine Ilion has found its fate
And I beheld, and those who won the wall
Pass to such issue as the gods ordain?
I too will pass and like them dare to die!
[*Turns and looks upon the palace door.*]
Portal of Hades, thus I bid thee hail!
Grant me one boon — a swift and mortal stroke,
That all unwrung by pain, with ebbing blood
Shed forth in quiet death, I close mine eyes.
CHORUS. Maid of mysterious woes, mysterious lore,
Long was thy prophecy: but if aright
Thou readest all thy fate, how, thus unscared,
Dost thou approach the altar of thy doom,
As fronts the knife some victim, heaven-controlled?
CASSANDRA. Friends, there is no avoidance in delay.
CHORUS. Yet who delays the longest, his the gain.
CASSANDRA. The day is come — flight were small gain to me!
CHORUS. O brave endurance of a soul resolved!
CASSANDRA. That were ill praise, for those of happier doom.
CHORUS. All fame is happy, even famous death.
CASSANDRA. Ah sire, ah, brethren, famous once were ye!
[*She moves to enter the house, then starts back.*]
CHORUS. What fear is this that scares thee from the house?
CASSANDRA. Pah!
CHORUS. What is this cry? some dark despair of soul?
CASSANDRA. Pah! the house fumes with stench and spilth of blood.
CHORUS. How? 't is the smell of household offerings.

CASSANDRA. 'T is rank as charnel-scent
from open graves.
CHORUS. Thou canst not mean this
scented Syrian nard?
CASSANDRA. Nay, let me pass within to
cry aloud
The monarch's fate and mine — enough of
life.
Ah, friends!
Bear to me witness, since I fall in death,
That not as birds that shun the bush and
scream
I moan in idle terror. This attest
When for my death's revenge another dies,
A woman for a woman, and a man
Falls, for a man ill-wedded to his curse.
Grant me this boon — the last before I die.
CHORUS. Brave to the last! I mourn thy
doom foreseen.
CASSANDRA. Once more one utterance,
but not of wail,
Though for my death — and then I speak
no more.

Sun! thou whose beam I shall not see again,
To thee I cry, Let those whom vengeance
calls
To slay their kindred's slayers, quit withal
The death of me, the slave, the fenceless prey.

Ah, state of mortal man! in time of weal,
A line, a shadow! and if ill fate fall,
One wet sponge-sweep wipes all our trace
away —
And this I deem less piteous, of the twain.
                    [Exit into the palace.]
CHORUS. Too true it is! our mortal state
With bliss is never satiate,
And none, before the palace high
And stately of prosperity,
Cries to us with a voice of fear,
Away! 't is ill to enter here!

Lo! this our lord hath trodden down,
By grace of Heaven, old Priam's town,
And praised as god he stands once more
On Argos' shore!
Yet now — if blood shed long ago
Cries out that other blood shall flow —
His life-blood, his, to pay again
The stern requital of the slain —
Peace to that braggart's vaunting vain,

Who, having heard the chieftain's tale,
Yet boasts of bliss untouched by bale!
                [A loud cry from within.]
VOICE OF AGAMEMNON. O I am sped —
a deep, a mortal blow.
CHORUS. Listen, listen! who is screaming
as in mortal agaony?
VOICE OF AGAMEMNON. O! O! again,
another, another blow!
CHORUS. The bloody act is over — I
have heard the monarch's cry —
Let us swiftly take some counsel, lest we
too be doomed to die.
ONE OF THE CHORUS. 'T is best, I judge,
aloud for aid to call,
"Ho! loyal Argives! to the palace, all!"
ANOTHER. Better, I deem, ourselves to
bear the aid,
And drag the deed to light, while drips the
blade.
ANOTHER. Such will is mine, and what
thou say'st I say:
Swiftly to act! the time brooks no delay.
ANOTHER. Aye, for 't is plain, this pre-
lude of their song
Foretells its close in tyranny and wrong.
ANOTHER. Behold, we tarry — but thy
name, Delay,
They spurn, and press with sleepless hand
to slay.
ANOTHER. I know not what 't were
well to counsel now —
Who wills to act, 't is his to counsel how.
ANOTHER. Thy doubt is mine: for when
a man is slain,
I have no words to bring his life again.
ANOTHER. What? e'en for life's sake,
bow us to obey
These house-defilers and their tyrant sway?
ANOTHER. Unmanly doom! 't were bet-
ter far to die —
Death is a gentler lord than tyranny.
ANOTHER. Think well — must cry or
sign of woe or pain
Fix our conclusion that the chief is slain?
ANOTHER. Such talk befits us when the
deed we see —
Conjecture dwells afar from certainty.
LEADER OF THE CHORUS. I read one
will from many a diverse word,
To know aright, how stands it with our
lord!

[*The scene opens, disclosing* CLY-
TEMNESTRA, *who comes forward.
The body of* AGAMEMNON *lies,
muffled in a long robe, within a
silver-sided laver; the corpse of*
CASSANDRA *is laid beside him.*]
CLYTEMNESTRA. Ho, ye who heard me
speak so long and oft
The glozing word that led me to my will —
Hear how I shrink not to unsay it all!
How else should one who willeth to requite
Evil for evil to an enemy
Disguised as friend, weave the mesh
straitly round him,
Not to be overleaped, a net of doom?
This is the sum and issue of old strife,
Of me deep-pondered and at length ful-
filled.
All is avowed, and as I smote I stand
With foot set firm upon a finished thing!
I turn not to denial: thus I wrought
So that he could nor flee nor ward his doom.
Even as the trammel hems the scaly shoal,
I trapped him with inextricable toils,
The ill abundance of a baffling robe;
Then smote him, once, again — and at each
wound
He cried aloud, then as in death relaxed
Each limb and sank to earth; and as he lay,
Once more I smote him, with the last third
blow,
Sacred to Hades, savior of the dead.
And thus he fell, and as he passed away,
Spirit with body chafed; each dying breath
Flung from his breast swift bubbling jets of
gore,
And the dark sprinklings of the rain of
blood
Fell upon me; and I was fain to feel
That dew — not sweeter is the rain of
heaven
To cornland, when the green sheath teems
with grain.

Elders of Argos — since the thing stands
so,
I bid you to rejoice, if such your will:
Rejoice or not, I vaunt and praise the deed,
And well I ween, if seemly it could be,
'T were not ill done to pour libations here,
Justly — aye, more than justly — on his
corpse

Who filled his home with curses as with
wine,
And thus returned to drain the cup he filled.
CHORUS. I marvel at thy tongue's
audacity,
To vaunt thus loudly o'er a husband slain.
CLYTEMNESTRA. Ye hold me as a wo-
man, weak of will,
And strive to sway me: but my heart is
stout,
Nor fears to speak its uttermost to you,
Albeit ye know its message. Praise or
blame,
Even as ye list, I reck not of your words.
Lo! at my feet lies Agamemnon slain,
My husband once — and him this hand of
mine,
A right contriver, fashioned for his death.
Behold the deed!
CHORUS. Woman, what deadly birth,
What venomed essence of the earth
Or dark distilment of the wave,
To thee such passion gave,
Nerving thine hand
To set upon thy brow this burning crown,
The curses of thy land?
Our king by thee cut off, hewn down !
Go forth — they cry — *accursèd and forlorn,*
To hate and scorn !
CLYTEMNESTRA. O ye just men, who
speak my sentence now,
The city's hate, the ban of all my realm!
Ye had no voice of old to launch such doom
On him, my husband, when he held as light
My daughter's life as that of sheep or goat,
One victim from the thronging fleecy fold!
Yea, slew in sacrifice his child and mine,
The well-loved issue of my travail-pangs,
To lull and lay the gales that blew from
Thrace.
That deed of his, I say, that stain and
shame,
Had rightly been atoned by banishment;
But ye, who then were dumb, are stern to
judge
This deed of mine that doth affront your
ears.
Storm out your threats, yet knowing this
for sooth,
That I am ready, if your hand prevail
As mine now doth, to bow beneath your
sway:

If God say nay, it shall be yours to learn
By chastisement a late humility.
   CHORUS. Bold is thy craft, and proud
Thy confidence, thy vaunting loud;
Thy soul, that chose a murd'ress' fate,
Is all with blood elate —
Maddened to know
The blood not yet avenged, the damnèd
   spot
Crimson upon thy brow.
But Fate prepares for thee thy lot —
Smitten as thou didst smite, without a
   friend,
To meet thine end!
   CLYTEMNESTRA. Hear then the sanction
   of the oath I swear —
By the great vengeance for my murdered
   child,
By Atè, by the Fury unto whom
This man lies sacrificed by hand of mine,
I do not look to tread the hall of Fear,
While in this hearth and home of mine
   there burns
The light of love — Ægisthus — as of old
Loyal, a stalwart shield of confidence —
As true to me as this slain man was false,
Wronging his wife with paramours at Troy,
Fresh from the kiss of each Chryseis there!
Behold him dead — behold his captive
   prize,
Seeress and harlot — comfort of his bed,
True prophetess, true paramour — I wot
The sea-bench was not closer to the flesh,
Full oft, of every rower, than was she.
See, ill they did, and ill requites them now.
His death ye know: she as a dying swan
Sang her last dirge, and lies, as erst she
   lay,
Close to his side, and to my couch has left
A sweet new taste of joys that know no
   fear.
   CHORUS. Ah, woe and well-a-day! I
   would that Fate —
Not bearing agony too great,
Nor stretching me too long on couch of
   pain —
Would bid mine eyelids keep
The morningless and unawakening sleep!
For life is weary, now my lord is slain,
The gracious among kings!
Hard fate of old he bore and many grievous
   things,

And for a woman's sake, on Ilian land —
Now is his life hewn down, and by a
   woman's hand.

O Helen, O infatuate soul,
Who bad'st the tides of battle roll,
O'erwhelming thousands, life on life,
'Neath Ilion's wall!
And now lies dead the lord of all.
The blossom of thy storied sin
Bears blood's inexpiable stain,
O thou that erst, these halls within,
Wert unto all a rock of strife,
A husband's bane!
   CLYTEMNESTRA. Peace! pray not thou
   for death as though
Thine heart was whelmed beneath this woe,
Nor turn thy wrath aside to ban
The name of Helen, nor recall
How she, one bane of many a man,
Sent down to death the Danaan lords,
To sleep at Troy the sleep of swords,
And wrought the woe that shattered all.
   CHORUS. Fiend of the race! that swoop-
   est fell
Upon the double stock of Tantalus,
Lording it o'er me by a woman's will,
Stern, manful, and imperious —
A bitter sway to me!
Thy very form I see,
Like some grim raven, perched upon the
   slain,
Exulting o'er the crime, aloud, in tuneless
   strain!
   CLYTEMNESTRA. Right was that word
   — thou namest well
The brooding race-fiend, triply fell!
From him it is that murder's thirst,
Blood-lapping, inwardly is nursed —
Ere time the ancient scar can sain,
New blood comes welling forth again.
   CHORUS. Grim is his wrath and heavy on
   our home,
That fiend of whom thy voice has cried,
Alas, an omened cry of woe unsatisfied,
An all-devouring doom!

Ah, woe, ah, Zeus! from Zeus all things
   befall —
Zeus the high cause and finisher of all! —
Lord of our mortal state, by him are willed
All things, by him fulfilled!

Yet ah, my king, my king no more!
What words to say, what tears to pour
Can tell my love for thee?
The spider-web of treachery
She wove and wound, thy life around,
And lo! I see thee lie,
And thro' a coward, impious wound
Pant forth thy life and die!
A death of shame — ah, woe on woe!
A treach'rous hand, a cleaving blow!
    CLYTEMNESTRA. My guilt thou harpest,
       o'er and o'er!
I bid thee reckon me no more
As Agamemnon's spouse.
The old Avenger, stern of mood
For Atreus and his feast of blood,
Hath struck the lord of Atreus' house,
And in the semblance of his wife
The king hath slain. —
Yea, for the murdered children's life,
A chieftain's in requital ta'en.
    CHORUS. Thou guiltless of this murder,
       thou!
Who dares such thought avow?
Yet it may be, wroth for the parent's deed,
The fiend hath holpen thee to slay the son.
Dark Ares, god of death, is pressing on
Thro' streams of blood by kindred shed,
Exacting the accompt for children dead,
For clotted blood, for flesh on which their
    sire did feed.

Yet, ah, my king, my king no more!
What words to say, what tears to pour
Can tell my love for thee?
The spider-web of treachery
She wove and wound, thy life around,
And lo! I see thee lie,
And thro' a coward, impious wound
Pant forth thy life and die!
A death of shame — ah, woe on woe!
A treach'rous hand, a cleaving blow!
    CLYTEMNESTRA. I deem not that the
      death he died
Had overmuch of shame:
For this was he who did provide
Foul wrong unto his house and name:
His daughter, blossom of my womb,
He gave unto a deadly doom,
Iphigenia, child of tears!
And as he wrought, even so he fares.
Nor be his vaunt too loud in hell;

For by the sword his sin he wrought,
And by the sword himself is brought
Among the dead to dwell.
    CHORUS. Ah, whither shall I fly?
For all in ruin sinks the kingly hall;
Nor swift device nor shift of thought have I,
To 'scape its fall.
A little while the gentler rain-drops fail;
I stand distraught — a ghastly interval,
Till on the roof-tree rings the bursting hail
Of blood and doom. Even now Fate whets
    the steel
On whetstones new and deadlier than of old,
The steel that smites, in Justice' hold,
Another death to deal.
O Earth! that I had lain at rest
And lapped forever in thy breast,
Ere I had seen my chieftain fall
Within the laver's silver wall,
Low-lying on dishonored bier!
And who shall give him sepulcher,
And who the wail of sorrow pour?
Woman, 't is thine no more!
A graceless gift unto his shade
Such tribute, by his murd'ress paid!
Strive not thus wrongly to atone
The impious deed thy hand hath done.
Ah who above the god-like chief
Shall weep the tears of loyal grief?
Who speak above his lowly grave
The last sad praises of the brave?
    CLYTEMNESTRA. Peace! for such task is
      none of thine.
By me he fell, by me he died,
And now his burial rites be mine!
Yet from these halls no mourners' train
Shall celebrate his obsequies;
Only by Acheron's rolling tide
His child shall spring unto his side,
And in a daughter's loving wise
Shall clasp and kiss him once again!
    CHORUS. Lo! sin by sin and sorrow
      dogg'd by sorrow —
And who the end can know?
The slayer of to-day shall die to-morrow —
The wage of wrong is woe.
While Time shall be, while Zeus in heaven
    is lord,
His law is fixed and stern;
On him that wrought shall vengeance be
    outpoured —
The tides of doom return.

The children of the curse abide within
These halls of high estate —
And none can wrench from off the home of
    sin
The clinging grasp of Fate.
CLYTEMNESTRA. Now walks thy word
    aright, to tell
This ancient truth of oracle;
But I with vows of sooth will pray
To him, the power that holdeth sway
O'er all the race of Pleisthenes —
Tho' dark the deed and deep the guilt,
With this last blood, my hands have spilt,
I pray thee let thine anger cease !
I pray thee pass from us away
To some new race in other lands,
There, if thou wilt, to wrong and slay
The lives of men by kindred hands.

For me 't is all sufficient meed,
Tho' little wealth or power were won,
So I can say, *'T is past and done.*
The bloody lust and murderous,
The inborn frenzy of our house,
Is ended, by my deed !

[*Enter* ÆGISTHUS.]

ÆGISTHUS. Dawn of the day of rightful
    vengeance, hail!
I dare at length aver that gods above
Have care of men and heed of earthly
    wrongs.
I, I who stand and thus exult to see
This man lie wound in robes the Furies wove,
Slain in requital of his father's craft.
Take ye the truth, that Atreus, this man's
    sire,
The lord and monarch of this land of old,
Held with my sire Thyestes deep dispute,
Brother with brother, for the prize of sway,
And drave him from his home to banishment.
Thereafter, the lorn exile homeward stole
And clung a suppliant to the hearth divine,
And for himself won this immunity —
Not with his own blood to defile the land
That gave him birth. But Atreus, godless
    sire
Of him who here lies dead, this welcome
    planned —
With zeal that was not love he feigned to
    hold
In loyal joy a day of festal cheer,

And bade my father to his board, and set
Before him flesh that was his children once.
First, sitting at the upper board alone,
He hid the fingers and the feet, but gave
The rest — and readily Thyestes took
What to his ignorance no semblance wore
Of human flesh, and ate: behold what curse
That eating brought upon our race and
    name!
For when he knew what all unhallowed
    thing
He thus had wrought, with horror's bitter
    cry
Back-starting, spewing forth the fragments
    foul,
On Pelops' house a deadly curse he spake —
As darkly as I spurn this damnèd food,
So perish all the race of Pleisthenes !
Thus by that curse fell he whom here ye
    see,
And I — who else? — this murder move
    and planned;
For me, an infant yet in swaddling bands,
Of the three children youngest, Atreus sent
To banishment by my sad father's side:
But Justice brought me home once more,
    grown now
To manhood's years; and stranger tho' I
    was,
My right hand reached unto the chieftain's
    life,
Plotting and planning all that malice bade.
And death itself were honor now to me,
Beholding him in Justice' ambush ta'en.
    CHORUS. Ægisthus, for this insolence of
    thine
That vaunts itself in evil, take my scorn.
Of thine own will, thou sayest, thou hast
    slain
The chieftain, by thine own unaided plot
Devised the piteous death: I rede thee well,
Think not thy head shall 'scape, when right
    prevails,
The people's ban, the stones of death and
    doom.
    ÆGISTHUS. This word from thee, this
    word from one who rows
Low at the oars beneath, what time we rule,
We of the upper tier? Thou 'lt know anon,
'T is bitter to be taught again in age,
By one so young, submission at the word.
But iron of the chain and hunger's throes

Can minister unto an o'erswoln pride
Marvelous well, aye, even in the old.
Hast eyes, and seest not this? Peace —
kick not thus
Against the pricks, unto thy proper pain!
CHORUS. Thou womanish man, waiting
till war did cease,
Home-watcher and defiler of the couch,
And arch-deviser of the chieftain's doom!
ÆGISTHUS. Bold words again! but they
shall end in tears.
The very converse, thine, of Orpheus'
tongue:
He roused and led in ecstasy of joy
All things that heard his voice melodious;
But thou as with the futile cry of curs
Wilt draw men wrathfully upon thee.
Peace!
Or strong subjection soon shall tame thy
tongue.
CHORUS. Aye, thou art one to hold an
Argive down —
Thou, skilled to plan the murder of the
king,
But not with thine own hand to smite the
blow!
ÆGISTHUS. That fraudful force was
woman's very part,
Not mine, whom deep suspicion from of old
Would have debarred. Now by his treas-
ure's aid
My purpose holds to rule the citizens.
But whoso will not bear my guiding hand,
Him for his corn-fed mettle I will drive
Not as a trace-horse, light-caparisoned,
But to the shafts with heaviest harness
bound.
Famine, the grim mate of the dungeon dark,
Shall look on him and shall behold him tame.
CHORUS. Thou losel soul, was then thy
strength too slight
To deal in murder, while a woman's hand,
Staining and shaming Argos and its gods,
Availed to slay him? Ho, if anywhere
The light of life smite on Orestes' eyes,
Let him, returning by some guardian fate,
Hew down with force her paramour and her!
ÆGISTHUS. How thy word and act shall
issue, thou shalt shortly understand.
CHORUS. Up to action, O my comrades!
for the fight is hard at hand.

Swift, your right hands to the sword hilt!
bare the weapon as for strife —
ÆGISTHUS. Lo! I too am standing ready,
hand on hilt for death or life.
CHORUS. 'T was thy word and we accept
it: onward to the chance of war!
CLYTEMNESTRA. Nay, enough, enough,
my champion! we will smite and
slay no more.
Already have we reaped enough the har-
vest-field of guilt:
Enough of wrong and murder, let no other
blood be spilt.
Peace, old men! and pass away unto the
homes by Fate decreed,
Lest ill valor meet our vengeance — 't was
a necessary deed.
But enough of toils and troubles — be the
end, if ever, now,
Ere thy talon, O Avenger, deal another
deadly blow.
'T is a woman's word of warning, and let
who will list thereto.
ÆGISTHUS. But that these should loose
and lavish reckless blossoms of the
tongue,
And in hazard of their fortune cast upon
me words of wrong,
And forget the law of subjects, and revile
their ruler's word —
CHORUS. Ruler? but 't is not for Argives,
thus to own a dastard lord!
ÆGISTHUS. I will follow to chastise thee
in my coming days of sway.
CHORUS. Not if Fortune guide Orestes
safely on his homeward way.
ÆGISTHUS. Ah, well I know how exiles
feed on hopes of their return.
CHORUS. Fare and batten on pollution
of the right, while 't is thy turn.
ÆGISTHUS. Thou shalt pay, be well
assurèd, heavy quittance for thy
pride.
CHORUS. Crow and strut, with her to
watch thee, like a cock, his mate
beside!
CLYTEMNESTRA. Heed not thou too
highly of them — let the cur-pack
growl and yell:
I and thou will rule the palace and will
order all things well. [Exeunt.]

ŒDIPUS THE KING

By SOPHOCLES

Translated into English prose by SIR RICHARD CLAVERING JEBB

CHARACTERS

ŒDIPUS, *King of Thebes*
PRIEST OF ZEUS
CREON, *brother of Iocasta*
TEIRESIAS, *the blind prophet*
IOCASTA.
FIRST MESSENGER, *a shepherd from Corinth*
A SHEPHERD, *formerly in the service of Laïus*
SECOND MESSENGER, *from the house*
CHORUS OF THEBAN ELDERS

A train of suppliants (old men, youths, and children). The children ANTIGONE *and* ISMENE, *daughters of* ŒDIPUS *and* IOCASTA

SCENE: *Before the Royal Palace at Thebes*

ŒDIPUS THE KING

ŒDIPUS. My children, latest-born to Cadmus who was of old, why are ye set before me thus with wreathed branches of suppliants, while the city reeks with incense, rings with prayers for health and cries of woe? I deemed it unmeet, my children, to hear these things at the mouth of others, and have come hither myself, I, Œdipus renowned of all.

Tell me, then, thou venerable man — since it is thy natural part to speak for these — in what mood are ye placed here, with what dread or what desire? Be sure that I would gladly give all aid; hard of heart were I, did I not pity such suppliants as these.

PRIEST OF ZEUS. Nay, Œdipus, ruler of my land, thou seest of what years we are who beset thy altars, — some, nestlings still too tender for far flights, — some, bowed with age, priests, as I of Zeus, — and these, the chosen youth; while the rest of the folk sit with wreathed branches in the market-places, and before the two shrines of Pallas, and where Ismenus gives answer by fire.

For the city, as thou thyself seest, is now too sorely vexed, and can no more lift her head from beneath the angry waves of death; a blight is on her in the fruitful blossoms of the land, in the herds among the pastures, in the barren pangs of women; and withal the flaming god, the malign plague, hath swooped on us, and ravages the town; by whom the house of Cadmus is made waste, but dark Hades rich in groans and tears.

It is not as deeming thee ranked with gods that I and these children are suppliants at thy hearth, but as deeming thee first of men, both in life's common chances, and when mortals have to do with more than man: seeing that thou camest to the town of Cadmus, and didst quit us of the tax that we rendered to the hard songstress; and this, though thou knewest nothing from us that could avail thee, nor hadst been schooled; no, by a god's aid, 't is said and believed, didst thou uplift our life.

And now, Œdipus, king glorious in all eyes, we beseech thee, all we suppliants, to find for us some succor, whether by the whisper of a god thou knowest it, or haply as in the power of man; for I see that, when men have been proved in deeds past, the issues of their counsels, too, most often have effect.

On, best of mortals, again uplift our State! On, guard thy fame, — since now this land calls thee savior for thy former zeal; and never be it our memory of thy reign that we were first restored and afterward cast down: nay, lift up this State in such wise that it fall no more!

With good omen didst thou give us that past happiness; now also show thyself the same. For if thou art to rule this land, even as thou art now its lord, 't is better to be lord of men than of a waste: since neither walled town nor ship is anything, if it is void and no men dwell with thee therein.

ŒDIPUS. Oh my piteous children, known, well known to me are the desires wherewith ye have come: well wot I that ye suffer all; yet, sufferers as ye are, there is not one of you whose suffering is as mine. Your pain comes on each one of you for himself alone, and for no other; but my soul mourns at once for the city, and for myself, and for thee.

So that ye rouse me not, truly, as one sunk in sleep: no, be sure that I have wept full many tears, gone many ways in wanderings of thought. And the sole remedy which, well pondering, I could find, this I have put into act. I have sent the son of Menœceus, Creon, mine own wife's brother, to the Pythian house of Phœbus, to learn by what deed or word I might deliver this town. And already, when the lapse of days is reckoned, it troubles me what he doth; for he tarries strangely, beyond the fitting space. But when he comes, then shall I be no true man if I do not all that the god shows.

PRIEST. Nay, in season hast thou spoken; at this moment these sign to me that Creon draws near.

ŒDIPUS. O king Apollo, may he come to us in the brightness of saving fortune, even as his face is bright!

PRIEST. Nay, to all seeming, he brings comfort; else would he not be coming crowned thus thickly with berry-laden bay.

ŒDIPUS. We shall know soon: he is at range to hear. — Prince, my kinsman, son of Menœceus, what news hast thou brought us from the god?

[*Enter* CREON.]

CREON. Good news: I tell thee that even troubles hard to bear, — if haply they find the right issue, — will end in perfect peace.

ŒDIPUS. But what is the oracle? So far, thy words make me neither bold nor yet afraid.

CREON. If thou wouldest hear while these are nigh, I am ready to speak; or else to go within.

ŒDIPUS. Speak before all: the sorrow which I bear is for these more than for mine own life.

CREON. With thy leave, I will tell what I heard from the god. Phœbus our lord bids us plainly to drive out a defiling thing, which (he saith) hath been harbored in this land, and not to harbor it, so that it cannot be healed.

ŒDIPUS. By what rite shall we cleanse us? What is the manner of the misfortune?

CREON. By banishing a man, or by bloodshed in quittance of bloodshed, since it is that blood which brings the tempest on our city.

ŒDIPUS. And who is the man whose fate he thus reveals?

CREON. Laïus, king, was lord of our land before thou wast pilot of this State.

ŒDIPUS. I know it well — by hearsay, for I saw him never.

CREON. He was slain; and the god now bids us plainly to wreak vengeance on his murderers — whosoever they be.

ŒDIPUS. And where are they upon the earth? Where shall the dim track of this old crime be found?

CREON. In this land, — said the god. What is sought for can be caught; only that which is not watched escaps.

ŒDIPUS. And was it in the huse, or in the field, or on strange soil that Laïus met this bloody end?

CREON. 'T was on a visit to Delphi, as he said, that he had left our land; and he came home no more, after he had once set forth.

ŒDIPUS. And was there none to tell? Was there no comrade of his jou. ey who saw the deed, from whom tidings might have been gained, and used?

CREON. All perished, save one who fled in fear, and could tell for certain but one thing of all that he saw.

ŒDIPUS. And what was that? One thing might show the clue to many, could we get but a small beginning for hope.

CREON. He said that robbers met and fell on them, not in one man's might, but with full many hands.

ŒDIPUS. How, then, unless there was some trafficking in bribes from here, should the robber have dared thus far?

CREON. Such things were surmised; but, Laïus once slain, amid our troubles no avenger arose.

ŒDIPUS. But, when royalty had fallen thus, what trouble in your path can have hindered a full search?

CREON. The riddling Sphinx had made us let dark things go, and was inviting us to think of what lay at our doors.

[*Exit* CREON.]

ŒDIPUS. Nay, I will start afresh, and once more make dark things plain. Right worthily hath Phœbus, and worthily hast thou, bestowed this care on the cause of the dead; and so, as is meet, ye shall find me too leagued with you in seeking vengeance for this land, and for the god besides. On behalf of no far-off friend, no, but in mine own cause, shall I dispel this taint. For whoever was the slayer of Laïus might wish to take vengeance on me also with a hand as fierce. Therefore, in doing right to Laïus, I serve myself.

Come, haste ye, my children, rise from the altar-steps, and lift these suppliant boughs; and let some other summon hither the folk of Cadmus, warned that I mean to leave nought untried; for our health (with the god's help) shall be made certain — or our ruin.

PRIEST. My children, let us rise; we came at first to seek what this man promises of himself. And may Phœbus, who sent these oracles, come to us therewith, our savior and deliverer from the pest.

CHORUS. O sweetly speaking message of Zeus, in what spirit hast thou come from golden Pytho unto glorious Thebes? I am on the rack, terror shakes my soul, O thou Delian healer to whom wild cries rise, in holy fear of thee, what thing thou wilt work for me, perchance unknown before, perchance renewed with the revolving years: tell me, thou immortal Voice, born of Golden Hope!

First, call I on thee, daughter of Zeus, divine Athena, and on thy sister, guardian of our land, Artemis, who sits on her throne of fame, above the circle of our Agora, and on Phœbus the far-darter: O shine forth on me, my threefold help against death! If ever aforetime, in arrest of ruin hurrying on the city, ye drove a fiery pest beyond our borders, come now also!

Woe is me, countless are the sorrows that I bear; a plague is on all our host, and thought can find no weapon for defense. The fruits of the glorious earth grow not; by no birth of children do women surmount the pangs in which they shriek; and life on life mayest thou see sped, like bird on nimble wing, aye, swifter than resistless fire, to the shore of the western god.

By such deaths, past numbering, the city perishes: unpitied, her children lie on the ground, spreading pestilence, with none to mourn: and meanwhile young wives, and gray-haired mothers with them, uplift a wail at the steps of the altars, some here, some there, entreating for their weary woes. The prayer to the Healer rings clear, and, blent therewith, the voice of lamentation: for these things, golden daughter of Zeus, send us the bright face of comfort.

And grant that the fierce god of death, who now with no brazen shields, yet amid cries of battle, wraps me in the flame of his onset, may turn his back in speedy flight from our land, borne by a fair wind to the great deep of Amphitritè, or to those waters in which none find haven, even to the Thracian wave; for if night leave aught undone, day follows to accomplish this. O thou who wieldest the powers of the fire-fraught lightning, O Zeus our father, slay him beneath thy thunderbolt!

Lycean King, fain were I that thy shafts also, from thy bent bow's string of woven gold, should go abroad in their might, our champions in the face of the foe; yea, and the flashing fires of Artemis wherewith she glances through the Lycian hills. And I call him whose locks are bound with gold, who is named with the name of this land, ruddy Bacchus to whom Bacchants cry, the comrade of the Mænads, to draw near with the blaze of his blithe torch, our ally against the god unhonored among gods.

ŒDIPUS. Thou prayest: and in answer to thy prayer, — if thou wilt give a loyal welcome to my words and minister to thine own disease, — thou mayest hope to find succor and relief from woes. These words will I speak publicly, as one who has been a stranger to this report, a stranger to the deed; for I should not be far on the track, if I were tracing it alone, without a clue. But as it is, — since it was only after the time of the deed that I was numbered a Theban among Thebans, — to you, the Cadmeans all, I do thus proclaim.

Whosoever of you knows by whom Laïus son of Labdacus was slain, I bid him to declare all to me. And if he is afraid, I tell him to remove the danger of the charge from his path by denouncing himself; for he shall suffer nothing else unlovely, but only leave the land, unhurt. Or if any one knows an alien, from another land, as the assassin, let him not keep silence; for I will pay his guerdon, and my thanks shall rest with him besides.

But if ye keep silence — if any one, through fear, shall seek to screen friend or self from my behest — hear ye what I then shall do. I charge you that no one of this land, whereof I hold the empire and the throne, give shelter or speak word unto that murderer, whosoever he be, — make him partner of his prayer or sacrifice or serve him with the lustral rite; but that all ban him their homes, knowing that *this* is our defiling thing, as the oracle of the Pythian god hath newly shown me. I then am on this wise the ally of the god and of the slain. And I pray solemnly that the slayer, whoso he be, whether his hidden guilt is lonely or hath partners, evilly, as he is evil, may wear out his unblest life. And for myself I pray that if, with my privity, he should become an inmate of my house, I may suffer the same things which even now I called down upon others. And on you I lay it to make all these words good, for my sake, and for the sake of the god, and for our land's thus blasted with barrenness by angry heaven.

For even if the matter had not been urged on us by a god, it was not meet that ye should leave the guilt thus unpurged, when one so noble, and he your king, had perished; rather were ye bound to search it out. And now, since 't is I who hold the powers which once he held, who possess his bed and the wife who bare seed to him; and since, had his hope of issue not been frustrate, children born of one mother would have made ties betwixt him and me — but, as it was, fate swooped upon his head; by reason of these things will I uphold this cause, even as the cause of mine own sire, and will leave nought untried in seeking to find him whose hand shed that blood, for the honor of the son of Labdacus and of Polydorus and elder Cadmus and Agenor who was of old.

And for those who obey me not, I pray that the gods send them neither harvest of the earth nor fruit of the womb, but that they be wasted by their lot that now is, or by one yet more dire. But for all you, the loyal folk of Cadmus to whom these things seem good, may Justice, our ally, and all the gods be with you graciously forever.

CHORUS. As thou hast put me on my oath, on my oath, O king, I will speak. I am not the slayer, nor can I point to him who slew. As for the question, it was for Phœbus, who sent it, to tell us this thing — who can have wrought the deed.

ŒDIPUS. Justly said; but no man on the earth can force the gods to what they will not.

CHORUS. I would fain say what seems to me next best after this.

ŒDIPUS. If there is yet a third course, spare not to show it.

CHORUS. I know that our lord Teiresias is the seer most like to our lord Phœbus, from whom, O king, a searcher of these things might learn them most clearly.

ŒDIPUS. Not even this have I left out of my cares. On the hint of Creon, I have twice sent a man to bring him; and this long while I marvel why he is not here.

CHORUS. Indeed (his skill apart) the rumors are but faint and old.

ŒDIPUS. What rumors are they? I look to every story.

CHORUS. Certain wayfarers were said to have killed him.

ŒDIPUS. I, too, have heard it, but none sees him who saw it.

CHORUS. Nay, if he knows what fear is, he will not stay when he hears thy curses, so dire as they are.

ŒDIPUS. When a man shrinks not from a deed, neither is he scared by a word.

CHORUS. But there is one to convict him. For here they bring at last the god-like prophet, in whom alone of men doth live the truth.

[*Enter* TEIRESIAS, *led by a boy.*]

ŒDIPUS. Teiresias, whose soul grasps all things, the lore that may be told and the unspeakable, the secrets of heaven and the low things of earth, — thou feelest, though thou canst not see, what a plague doth haunt our State, — from which, great prophet, we find in thee our protector and only savior. Now, Phœbus — if indeed thou knowest it not from the messengers — sent answer to our question that the only riddance from this pest which could come was if we should learn aright the slayers of Laïus, and slay them, or send them into exile from our land. Do thou, then, grudge neither voice of birds nor any other way of seer-lore that thou hast, but rescue thyself and the State, rescue me, rescue all that is defiled by the dead. For we are in thy hand; and man's noblest task is to help others by his best means and powers.

TEIRESIAS. Alas, how dreadful to have wisdom where it profits not the wise! Aye, I knew this well, but let it slip out of mind; else would I never have come here.

ŒDIPUS. What now? How sad thou hast come in!

TEIRESIAS. Let me go home; most easily wilt thou bear thine own burden to the end, and I mine, if thou wilt consent.

ŒDIPUS. Thy words are strange, nor kindly to this State which nurtured thee, when thou withholdest this response.

TEIRESIAS. Nay, I see that thou, on thy part, openest not thy lips in season: therefore I speak not, that neither may I have thy mishap.

ŒDIPUS. For the love of the gods, turn not away, if thou hast knowledge: all we suppliants implore thee on our knees.

TEIRESIAS. Aye, for ye are all without knowledge; but never will I reveal my griefs — that I say not thine.

ŒDIPUS. How sayest thou? Thou knowest the secret, and wilt not tell it, but art minded to betray us and to destroy the State?

TEIREISAS. I will pain neither myself nor thee. Why vainly ask these things? Thou wilt not learn them from me.

ŒDIPUS. What, basest of the base, — for thou wouldest anger a very stone, — wilt thou never speak out? Can nothing touch thee? Wilt thou never make an end?

TEIRESIAS. Thou blamest my temper, but seest not that to which thou thyself art wedded: no, thou findest fault with me.

ŒDIPUS. And who would not be angry to hear the words with which thou now dost slight this city?

TEIRESIAS. The future will come of itself, though I shroud it in silence.

ŒDIPUS. Then, seeing that it must come, thou on thy part shouldst tell me thereof.

TEIRESIAS. I will speak no further; rage, then, if thou wilt, with the fiercest wrath thy heart doth know.

ŒDIPUS. Aye, verily, I will not spare — so wroth I am — to speak all my thought. Know that thou seemest to me e'en to have helped in plotting the deed, and to have done it, short of slaying with thy hands. Hadst thou eyesight, I would have said that the doing, also, of this thing was thine alone.

TEIRESIAS. In sooth? — I charge thee that thou abide by the decree of thine own mouth, and from this day speak neither to these nor to me: thou art the accursed defiler of this land.

ŒDIPUS. So brazen with thy blustering taunt? And wherein dost thou trust to escape thy due?

TEIRESIAS. I have escaped: in my truth is my strength.

ŒDIPUS. Who taught thee this? It was not, at least, thine art.

TEIRESIAS. Thou: for thou didst spur me into speech against my will.

ŒDIPUS. What speech? Speak again that I may learn it better.

TEIRESIAS. Didst thou not take my sense before? Or art thou tempting me in talk?

ŒDIPUS. No, I took it not so that I can call it known: — speak again.

TEIRESIAS. I say that thou art the slayer of the man whose slayer thou seekest.

ŒDIPUS. Now thou shalt rue that thou hast twice said words so dire.

TEIRESIAS. Wouldst thou have me say more, that thou mayest be more wroth?

ŒDIPUS. What thou wilt; it will be said in vain.

TEIRESIAS. I say that thou hast been living in unguessed shame with thy nearest kin, and seest not to what woe thou hast come.

ŒDIPUS. Dost thou indeed think that thou shalt always speak thus without smarting?

TEIRESIAS. Yes, if there is any strength in truth.

ŒDIPUS. Nay, there is, — for all save thee; for thee that strength is not, since thou art maimed in ear, and in wit, and in eye.

TEIRESIAS. Aye, and thou art a poor wretch to utter taunts which every man here will soon hurl at thee.

ŒDIPUS. Night, endless night hath thee in her keeping, so that thou canst never hurt me, or any man who sees the sun.

TEIRESIAS. No, thy doom is not to fall by *me:* Apollo is enough, whose care it is to work that out.

ŒDIPUS. Are these Creon's devices, or thine?

TEIRESIAS.. Nay, Creon is no plague to thee; thou art thine own.

ŒDIPUS. O wealth, and empire, and skill surpassing skill in life's keen rivalries, how great is the envy that cleaves to you, if for the sake, yea, of this power which the city hath put into my hands, a gift unsought, Creon the trusty, Creon mine old friend, hath crept on me by stealth, yearning to thrust me out of it, and hath suborned such a scheming juggler as this, a tricky quack, who hath eyes only for his gains, but in his art is blind!

Come, now, tell me, where hast thou proved thyself a seer? Why, when the Watcher was here who wove dark song, didst thou say nothing that could free this folk? Yet the riddle, at least, was not for the first comer to read; there was need of a seer's skill; and none such thou wast found to have, either by help of birds, or as known from any god: no, I came, I, Œdipus the ignorant, and made her mute, when I had seized the answer by my wit, untaught of birds. And it is I whom thou art trying to oust, thinking to stand close to Creon's throne. Methinks thou and the plotter of these things will rue your zeal to purge the land. Nay, didst thou not seem to be an old man, thou shouldst have learned to thy cost how bold thou art.

CHORUS. To our thinking, both this man's words and thine, Œdipus, have been said in anger. Not for such words is our need, but to seek how we shall best discharge the mandates of the god.

TEIRESIAS. King though thou art, the right of reply, at least, must be deemed the same for both; of that I too am lord. Not to thee do I live servant, but to Loxias; and so I shall not stand enrolled under Creon for my patron. And I tell thee — since thou hast taunted me even with blindness —that thou hast sight, yet seest not in what misery thou art, nor where thou dwellest, nor with whom. Dost thou know of what stock thou art? And thou hast been an unwitting foe to thine own kin, in the shades, and on the earth above; and the double lash of thy mother's and thy father's curse shall one day drive thee from this land in dreadful haste, with darkness then on the eyes that now see true.

And what place shall not be harbor to thy shriek, what of all Cithæron shall not ring with it soon, when thou hast learnt the meaning of the nuptials in which, within that house, thou didst find a fatal haven, after a voyage so fair? And a throng of other ills thou guessest not, which shall make thee level with thy true self and with thine own brood.

Therefore heap thy scorns on Creon and on my message: for no one among men shall ever be crushed more miserably than thou.

ŒDIPUS. Are these taunts to be indeed borne from *him?* — Hence, ruin take thee! Hence, this instant! Back! — away! — avaunt thee from these doors!

TEIRESIAS. I had never come, not I, hadst thou not called me.

ŒDIPUS. I knew not that thou wast about to speak folly, or it had been long ere I had sent for thee to my house.

TEIRESIAS. Such am I, — as thou thinkest, a fool; but for the parents who begat thee, sane.

ŒDIPUS. What parents? Stay . . . and who of men is my sire?

TEIRESIAS. This day shall show thy birth and shall bring thy ruin.

ŒDIPUS. What riddles, what dark words thou always speakest!

TEIRESIAS. Nay, art not thou most skilled to unravel dark speech?

ŒDIPUS. Make that my reproach in which thou shalt find me great.

TEIRESIAS. Yet 't was just that fortune that undid thee.

ŒDIPUS. Nay, if I delivered this town, I care not.

TEIRESIAS. Then I will go: so do thou, boy, take me hence.

ŒDIPUS. Aye, let him take thee: while here, thou art a hindrance, thou, a trouble: when thou hast vanished, thou wilt not vex me more.

TEIRESIAS. I will go when I have done mine errand, fearless of thy frown: for thou canst never destroy me. And I tell thee — the man of whom thou hast this long while been in quest, uttering threats, and proclaiming a search into the murder of Laïus — that man is here, — in seeming, an alien sojourner, but anon he shall be found a native Theban, and shall not be glad of his fortune. A blind man, he who now hath sight, a beggar, who now is rich, he shall make his way to a strange land, feeling the ground before him with his staff. And he shall be found at once brother and father of the children with whom he consorts; son and husband of the woman who bore him; heir to his father's bed, shedder of his father's blood.

So go thou in and think on that; and if thou find that I have been at fault, say thenceforth that I have no wit in prophecy. [TEIRESIAS *is led out by the boy.* CEDIPUS *enters the palace.*]

CHORUS. Who is he of whom the divine voice from the Delphian rock hath spoken, as having wrought with red hands horrors that no tongue can tell?

It is time that he ply in flight a foot stronger than the feet of storm-swift steeds: for the son of Zeus is springing on him, all armed with fiery lightnings, and with him come the dread, unerring Fates.

Yea, newly given from snowy Parnassus, the message hath flashed forth to make all search for the unknown man. Into the wild wood's covert, among caves and rocks he is roaming, fierce as a bull, wretched and forlorn on his joyless path, still seeking to put from him the doom spoken at Earth's central shrine: but that doom ever lives, ever flits around him.

Dreadly, in sooth, dreadly doth the wise augur move me, who approve not, nor am able to deny. How to speak, I know not; I am fluttered with forebodings; neither in the present have I clear vision, nor of the future. Never in past days, nor in these, have I heard how the house of Labdacus or the son of Polybus had, either against other, any grief that I could bring as proof in assailing the public fame of CEdipus, and seeking to avenge the line of Labdacus for the undiscovered murder.

Nay, Zeus indeed and Apollo are keen of thought, and know the things of earth; but that mortal seer wins knowledge above mine, of this there can be no sure test; though man may surpass man in lore. Yet, until I see the word made good, never will I assent when men blame CEdipus. Before all eyes, the winged maiden came against him of old, and he was seen to be wise; he bore the test, in welcome service to our State; never, therefore, by the verdict of my heart shall he be adjudged guilty of crime.

[*Enter* CREON.]

CREON. Fellow citizens, having learned that CEdipus the king lays dire charges against me, I am here, indignant. If, in the present troubles, he thinks that he has suffered from *me*, by word or deed, aught that tends to harm, in truth I crave not my full term of years, when I must bear such blame as this. The wrong of this rumor touches me not in one point alone, but has the largest scope, if I am to be called a traitor in the city, a traitor, too, by thee and by my friends.

CHORUS. Nay, but this taunt came under stress, perchance, of anger, rather than from the purpose of the heart.

CREON. And the saying was uttered, that *my* counsels won the seer to utter his falsehoods?

CHORUS. Such things were said — I know not with what meaning.

CREON. And was this charge laid against me with steady eyes and steady mind?

CHORUS. I know not; I see not what my masters do: but here comes our lord forth from the house.

[*Enter* CEDIPUS.]

CEDIPUS. Sirrah, how camest thou here? Hast thou a front so bold that thou hast come to my house, who art the proved assassin of its master, — the palpable robber of my crown? Come, tell me, in the name of the gods, was it cowardice or folly that thou sawest in me, that thou didst plot to do this thing? Didst thou think that I would not note this deed of thine creeping on me by stealth, or, aware, would not ward it off? Now is not thine attempt foolish, - to seek, without followers or friends, throne, — a prize which followers and we th must win?

CREON. Mark me now, — in answer to thy words, hear a fair reply, and then judge for yourself on knowledge.

ŒDIPUS. Thou art apt in speech, but I have a poor wit for thy lessons, since I have found thee my malignant foe.

CREON. Now first hear how I will explain this very thing —

ŒDIPUS. Explain me not one thing — that thou art not false.

CREON. If thou deemest that stubbornness without sense is a good gift, thou art not wise.

ŒDIPUS. If thou deemest that thou canst wrong a kinsman and escape the penalty, thou art not sane.

CREON. Justly said, I grant thee: but tell me what is the wrong that thou sayest thou hast suffered from me.

ŒDIPUS. Didst thou advise, or didst thou not, that I should send for that reverend seer?

CREON. And now I am still of the same mind.

ŒDIPUS. How long is it, then, since Laïus —

CREON. Since Laïus . . .? I take not thy drift . . .

ŒDIPUS. — was swept from men's sight by a deadly violence?

CREON. The count of years would run far into the past.

ŒDIPUS. Was this seer, then, of the craft in those days?

CREON. Yea, skilled as now, and in equal honor.

ŒDIPUS. Made he, then, any mention of me at that time?

CREON. Never, certainly, when I was within hearing.

ŒDIPUS. But held ye not a search touching the murder?

CREON. Due search we held, of course — and learned nothing.

ŒDIPUS. And how was it that this sage did not tell his story *then?*

CREON. I know not; where I lack light, 't is my wont to be silent.

ŒDIPUS. Thus much, at least, thou knowest, and couldst declare with light enough.

CREON. What is that? If I know it, I will not deny.

ŒDIPUS. That, if he had not conferred with thee, he would never have named *my* slaying of Laïus.

CREON. If so he speaks, thou best knowest; but I claim to learn from thee as much as thou hast now from me.

ŒDIPUS. Learn thy fill: I shall never be found guilty of the blood.

CREON. Say, then — thou hast married my sister?

ŒDIPUS. The question allows not of denial.

CREON. And thou rulest the land as she doth, with like sway?

ŒDIPUS. She obtains from me all her desire.

CREON. And rank not I as a third peer of you twain?

ŒDIPUS. Aye, 't is just therein that thou art seen a false friend.

CREON. Not so, if thou wouldst reason with thine own heart as I with mine. And first weigh this, — whether thou thinkest that any one would choose to rule amid terrors rather than in unruffled peace, — granting that he is to have the same powers. Now I, for one, have no yearning in my nature to be a king rather than to do kingly deeds, no, nor hath any man who knows how to keep a sober mind. For now I win all boons from thee without fear; but, were I ruler myself, I should be doing much e'en against mine own pleasure.

How, then, could royalty be sweeter for me to have than painless rule and influence? Not yet am I so misguided as to desire other honors than those which profit. Now, all wish me joy; now, every man has a greeting for me; now, those who have a suit to thee crave speech with me, since therein is all their hope of success. Then why should I resign these things, and take those? No mind will become false, while it is wise. Nay, I am no lover of such policy, and, if another put it into deed, never could I bear to act with him.

And, in proof of this, first, go to Pytho, and ask if I brought thee true word of the oracle; then next, if thou find that I have planned aught in concert with the sooth-sayer, take and slay me, by the sentence not of one mouth, but of twain — by mine own, no less than thine. But make me not guilty in a corner, on unproved surmise. It is not right to adjudge bad men good at random, or good men bad. I count it a like thing for a man to cast off a true friend as to cast away the life in his own bosom, which most he loves. Nay, thou wilt learn these things with sureness in time, for time alone shows a just man; but thou couldst discern a knave even in one day.

CHORUS. Well hath he spoken, O king, for one who giveth heed not to fall: the quick in counsel are not sure.

ŒDIPUS. When the stealthy plotter is moving on me in quick sort, I, too, must be quick with my counterplot. If I await him in repose, his ends will have been gained, and mine missed.

CREON. What wouldst thou, then? Cast me out of the land?

ŒDIPUS. Not so: I desire thy death — not thy banishment — that thou mayest show forth what manner of thing is envy.

CREON. Thou speakest as resolved not to yield or to believe?

CREON. No, for I find thee not sane.

ŒDIPUS. Sane, at least, in mine own interest.

CREON. Nay, thou shouldst be so in mine also.

ŒDIPUS. Nay, thou art false.

CREON. But if thou understandest nought?

ŒDIPUS. Yet must I rule.

CREON. Not if thou rule ill.

ŒDIPUS. Hear him, O Thebes!

CREON. Thebes is for me also — not for thee alone.

CHORUS. Cease, princes; and in good time for you I see Iocasta coming yonder from the house, with whose help ye should compose your present feud.

[*Enter* IOCASTA.]

IOCASTA. Misguided men, why have ye raised such foolish strife of tongues? Are ye not ashamed, while the land is thus sick, to stir up troubles of your own? Come, go thou into the house, — and thou, Creon, to thy home, — and forbear to make much of a petty grief.

CREON. Kinswoman, Œdipus thy lord claims to do dread things unto me, even one or other of two ills, —to thrust me from the land of my fathers, or to slay me amain.

ŒDIPUS. Yea; for I have caught him, lady, working evil, by ill arts, against my person.

CREON. Now may I see no good, but perish accursed, if I have done aught to thee of that wherewith thou chargest me!

IOCASTA. Oh, for the gods' love, believe it, Œdipus — first, for the awful sake of this oath unto the gods, — then for my sake and for theirs who stand before thee?

CHORUS. Consent, reflect, hearken, O my king, I pray thee!

ŒDIPUS. What grace, then, wouldest thou have me grant thee?

CHORUS. Respect him who aforetime was not foolish, and who now is strong in his oath.

ŒDIPUS. Now dost thou know what thou cravest?

CHORUS. Yea.

ŒDIPUS. Declare, then, what thou meanest.

CHORUS. That thou shouldest never use an unproved rumor to cast a dishonoring charge on the friend who has bound himself with a curse.

ŒDIPUS. Then be very sure that, when thou seekest this, for me thou art seeking destruction, or exile from this land.

CHORUS. No, by him who stands in the front of all the heavenly host; no, by the Sun! Unblest, unfriended, may I die by the uttermost doom, if I have that thought! But my unhappy soul is worn by the with-ering of the land, and again by the thought that our old sorrows should be crowned by sorrows springing from you twain.

ŒDIPUS. Then let him go, though I am surely doomed to death, or to be thrust dishonored from the land. Thy lips, not his, move my compassion by their plaint; but he, where'er he be, shall be hated.

CREON. Sullen in yielding art thou seen, even as vehement in the excesses of thy

wrath; but such natures are justly sorest
for themselves to bear.

ŒDIPUS. Then wilt thou not leave me in
peace, and get thee gone?

CREON. I will go my way; I have found
thee undiscerning, but in the sight of these
I am just.   [Exit.]

CHORUS. Lady, why dost thou delay to
take yon man into the house?

IOCASTA. I will do so, when I have learned
what hath chanced.

CHORUS. Blind suspicion, bred of talk,
arose; and, on the other part, injustice
wounds.

IOCASTA. It was on both sides?

CHORUS. Aye.

IOCASTA. And what was the story?

CHORUS. Enough, methinks, enough —
when our land is already vexed — that the
matter should rest where it ceased.

ŒDIPUS. Seest thou to what thou hast
come, for all thy honest purpose, in seeking
to slack and blunt my zeal?

CHORUS. King, I have said it not once
alone — be sure that I should have been
shown a madman, bankrupt in sane counsel, if I put thee away — thee, who gavest
a true course to my beloved country when
distraught by troubles — thee, who now
also art like to prove our prospering guide.

IOCASTA. In the name of the gods, tell
me also, O king, on what account thou hast
conceived this steadfast wrath.

ŒDIPUS. That will I; for I honor thee,
lady, above yonder men: — the cause is
Creon, and the plots that he hath laid
against me.

IOCASTA. Speak on — if thou canst tell
clearly how the feud began.

ŒDIPUS. He says that I stand guilty of
the blood of Laïus.

IOCASTA. As on his own knowledge? Or
on hearsay from another?

ŒDIPUS. Nay, he hath made a rascal
seer his mouthpiece; as for himself, he
keeps his lips wholly pure.

IOCASTA. Then absolve thyself of the
things whereof thou speakest; hearken to
me, and learn for thy comfort that nought
of mortal birth is a sharer in the science
of the seer. I will give thee pithy proof of
that.

An oracle came to Laïus once — I will
not say from Phœbus himself, but from his
ministers — that the doom should overtake
him to die by the hand of his child, who
should spring from him and me.

Now Laïus, — as, at least, the rumor
saith, — was murdered one day by foreign
robbers at a place where three highways
meet. And the child's birth was not three
days past, when Laïus pinned its ankles
together, and had it thrown, by others'
hands, on a trackless mountain.

So, in that case, Apollo brought it not
to pass that the babe should become the
slayer of his sire, or that Laïus should die
— the dread thing which he feared — by
his child's hand. Thus did the messages of
seer-craft map out the future. Regard
them, thou, not at all. Whatsoever needful things the god seeks, he himself will
easily bring to light.

ŒDIPUS. What restlessness of soul, lady,
what tumult of the mind hath just come
upon me since I heard thee speak!

IOCASTA. What anxiety hath startled
thee, that thou sayest this?

ŒDIPUS. Methought I heard this from
thee, — that Laïus was slain where three
highways meet.

IOCASTA. Yea, that was the story; nor
hath it ceased yet.

ŒDIPUS. And where is the place where
this befell?

IOCASTA. The land is called Phocis; and
branching roads lead to the same spot from
Delphi and from Daulia.

ŒDIPUS. And what is the time that hath
passed since these things were?

IOCASTA. The news was published to the
town shortly before thou wast first seen in
power over this land.

ŒDIPUS. O Zeus, what hast thou decreed
to do unto me?

IOCASTA. And wherefore, Œdipus, doth
this thing weigh upon thy soul?

ŒDIPUS. Ask me not yet; but say what
was the stature of Laïus, and how ripe his
manhood.

IOCASTA. He was tall, — the silver just
lightly strewn among his hair; and his form
was not greatly unlike to thine.

ŒDIPUS. Unhappy that I am! Methinks

I have been laying myself even now under a dread curse, and knew it not.

IOCASTA. How sayest thou? I tremble when I look on thee, my king.

ŒDIPUS. Dread misgivings have I that the seer can see. But thou wilt show better if thou wilt tell me one thing more.

IOCASTA. Indeed — though I tremble — I will answer all thou askest, when I hear it.

ŒDIPUS. Went he in small force, or with many armed followers, like a chieftain?

IOCASTA. Five they were in all, — a herald one of them; and there was one carriage, which bore Laïus.

ŒDIPUS. Alas! 'T is now clear indeed. — Who was he who gave you these tidings, lady?

. IOCASTA. A servant — the sole survivor who came home.

ŒDIPUS. Is he haply at hand in the house now?

IOCASTA. No, truly; so soon as he came thence, and found thee reigning in the stead of Laïus, he supplicated me, with hand laid on mine, that I would send him to the fields, to the pastures of the flocks, that he might be far from the sight of this town. And I sent him; he was worthy, for a slave, to win e'en a larger boon than that.

ŒDIPUS. Would, then, that he could return to us without delay!

IOCASTA. It is easy: but wherefore dost thou enjoin this?

ŒDIPUS. I fear, lady, that mine own lips have been unguarded; and therefore am I fain to behold him.

IOCASTA. Nay, he shall come. But I, too, methinks, have a claim to learn what lies heavy on thy heart, my king.

ŒDIPUS. Yea, and it shall not be kept from thee, now that my forebodings have advanced so far. Who, indeed, is more to me than thou, to whom I should speak in passing through such a fortune as this?

My father was Polybus of Corinth, — my mother, the Dorian Meropè; and I was held the first of all the folk in that town, until a chance befell me, worthy, indeed, of wonder, though not worthy of mine own heat concerning it. At a banquet, a man full of wine cast it at me in his cups that I was not the true son of my sire. And I,

vexed, restrained myself for that day as best I might; but on the next I went to my mother and father, and questioned them; and they were wroth for the taunt with him who had let that word fly. So on their part I had comfort; yet was this thing ever rankling in my heart; for it still crept abroad with strong rumor. And, unknown to mother or father, I went to Delphi; and Phœbus sent me forth disappointed of that knowledge for which I came, but in his response set forth other things, full of sorrow and terror and woe; even that I was fated to defile my mother's bed; and that I should show unto men a brood which they could not endure to behold; and that I should be the slayer of the sire who begat me.

And I, when I had listened to this, turned to flight from the land of Corinth, thenceforth wotting of its region by the stars alone, to some spot where I should never see fulfillment of the infamies foretold in mine evil doom. And on my way I came to the regions in which thou sayest that this prince perished. Now, lady, I will tell thee the truth. When in my journey I was near to those three roads, there met me a herald, and a man seated in a carriage drawn by colts, as thou hast described; and he who was in front, and the old man himself, were for thrusting me rudely from the path. Then, in anger, I struck him who pushed me aside — the driver; and the old man, seeing it, watched the moment when I was passing, and, from the carriage, brought his goad with two teeth down full upon my head. Yet was he paid with interest; by one swift blow from the staff in this hand he was rolled right out of the carriage, on his back; and I slew every man of them.

But if this stranger had any tie of kinship with Laïus, who is now more wretched than the man before thee? What mortal could prove more hated of heaven? Whom no stranger, no citizen, is allowed to receive in his house; whom it is unlawful that any one accost; whom all must repel from thei homes! And this — this curse — was la on me by no mouth but mine own! An pollute the bed of the slain man with hands by which he perished. Say, am I vile? Oh, am I not utterly unclean? — seeing that I must be banished, and in banishment see not mine own people, nor set foot in mine own land, or else be joined in wedlock to my mother, and slay my sire, even Polybus, who begat and reared me.

Then would not he speak aright of Œdipus, who judged these things sent by some cruel power above man? Forbid, forbid, ye pure and awful gods, that I should see that day! No, may I be swept from among men, ere I behold myself visited with the brand of such a doom!

CHORUS. To us, indeed, these things, O king, are fraught with fear; yet have hope, until at least thou hast gained full knowledge from him who saw the deed.

ŒDIPUS. Hope, in truth, rests with me thus far alone; I can await the man summoned from the pastures.

IOCASTA. And when he has appeared — what wouldst thou have of him?

ŒDIPUS. I will tell thee. If his story be found to tally with thine, I, at least, shall stand clear of disaster.

IOCASTA. And what of special note didst thou hear from me?

ŒDIPUS. Thou wast saying that he spoke of Laïus as slain by robbers. If, then, he still speaks, as before, of several, I was not the slayer: a solitary man could not be held the same with that band. But if he names one lonely wayfarer, then beyond doubt this guilt leans to me.

IOCASTA. Nay, be assured that thus, at least, the tale was first told; he cannot revoke that, for the city heard it, not I alone. But even if he should diverge somewhat from his former story, never, king, can he show that the murder of Laïus, at least, is truly square to prophecy; of whom Loxias plainly said that he must die by the hand of my child. Howbeit that poor innocent never slew him, but perished first itself. So henceforth, for what touches divination, I would not look to my right hand or my left.

ŒDIPUS. Thou judgest well. But nevertheless send some one to fetch the peasant, and neglect not this matter.

IOCASTA. I will send without delay. But let us come into the house: nothing will I do save at thy good pleasure.

[Exeunt ŒDIPUS and IOCASTA.]

CHORUS. May destiny still find me winning the praise of reverent purity in all words and deeds sanctioned by those laws of range sublime, called into life throughout the high clear heaven, whose father is Olympus alone; their parent was no race of mortal men, no, nor shall oblivion ever lay them to sleep; the god is mighty in them, and he grows not old.

Insolence breeds the tyrant; Insolence, once vainly surfeited on wealth that is not meet nor good for it, when it hath scaled the topmost ramparts, is hurled to a dire doom, wherein no service of the feet can serve. But I pray that the god never quell such rivalry as benefits the State; the god will I ever hold for our protector.

But if any man walks haughtily in deed or word, with no fear of Justice, no reverence for the images of gods, may an evil doom seize him for his ill-starred pride, if he will not win his vantage fairly, nor keep him from unholy deeds, but must lay profaning hands on sanctities.

Where such things are, what mortal shall boast any more that he can ward the arrows of the gods from his life? Nay, if such deeds are in honor, wherefore should we join in the sacred dance?

No more will I go reverently to earth's central and inviolate shrine, no more to Abæ's temple or Olympia, if these oracles fit not the issue, so that all men shall point at them with the finger. Nay, king, — if thou art rightly called, — Zeus all-ruling, may it not escape thee and thine ever-deathless power!

The old prophecies concerning Laïus are fading; already men are setting them at nought, and nowhere is Apollo glorified with honors; the worship of the gods is perishing.

[Enter IOCASTA.]

IOCASTA. Princes of the land, the thought has come to me to visit the shrines of the gods, with this wreathed branch in my hands, and these gifts of incense. For Œdipus excites his soul overmuch with all manner of alarms, nor, like a man of sense, judges the new things by the old, but is at the will of the speaker, if he speak terrors.

Since, then, by counsel I can do no good, to thee, Lycean Apollo, for thou art nearest, I have come, a suppliant with these symbols of prayer, that thou mayest find us some riddance from uncleanness. For now we are all afraid, seeing *him* affrighted, even as they who see fear in the helmsman of their ship.

[*Enter Messenger.*]

MESSENGER. Might I learn from you, strangers, where is the house of the king CEdipus? Or, better still, tell me where he himself is — if ye know.

CHORUS. This is his dwelling, and he himself, stranger, is within; and this lady is the mother of his children.

MESSENGER. Then may she be ever happy in a happy home, since she is his heaven-blest queen.

IOCASTA. Happiness to thee also, stranger! 'T is the due of thy fair greeting. But say what thou hast come to seek or to tell.

MESSENGER. Good tidings, lady, for thy house and for thy husband.

IOCASTA. What are they? And from whom hast thou come?

MESSENGER. From Corinth: and at the message which I will speak anon thou wilt rejoice — doubtless; yet haply grieve.

IOCASTA. And what is it? How hath it thus a double potency?

MESSENGER. The people will make him king of the Isthmian land, as 't was said there.

IOCASTA. How then? Is the aged Polybus no more in power?

MESSENGER. No, verily: for death holds him in the tomb.

IOCASTA. How sayest thou? Is Polybus dead, old man?

MESSENGER. If I speak not the truth, I am content to die.

IOCASTA. O handmaid, away with all speed, and tell this to thy master! O ye oracles of the gods, where stand ye now! This is the man whom CEdipus long feared and shunned, lest he should slay him; and

now this man hath died in the course of destiny, not by his hand.

[*Enter* CEDIPUS.]

CEDIPUS. Iocasta, dearest wife, why hast thou summoned me forth from these doors?

IOCASTA. Hear this man, and judge, as thou listenest, to what the awful oracles of the gods have come.

CEDIPUS. And he — who may he be, and what news hath he for me?

IOCASTA. He is from Corinth, to tell that thy father Polybus lives no longer, but hath perished.

CEDIPUS. How, stranger? Let me have it from thine own mouth.

MESSENGER. If I must first make these tidings plain, know indeed that he is dead and gone.

CEDIPUS. By treachery, or by visit of disease?

MESSENGER. A light thing in the scale brings the aged to their rest.

CEDIPUS. Ah, he died, it seems, of sickness?

MESSENGER. Yea, and of the long years that he had told.

CEDIPUS. Alas, alas! Why, indeed, my wife, should one look to the hearth of the Pythian seer, or to the birds that scream above our heads, on whose showing I was doomed to slay my sire? But he is dead, and hid already beneath the earth; and here am I, who have not put hand to spear. — Unless, perchance, he was killed by longing for me: thus, indeed, I should be the cause of his death. But the oracles as they stand, at least, Polybus hath swept with him to his rest in Hades: they are worth nought.

IOCASTA. Nay, did I not so foretell to thee long since?

CEDIPUS. Thou didst: but I was misled by my fear.

IOCASTA. Now no more lay aught of those things to heart.

CEDIPUS. But surely I must needs fear my mother's bed?

IOCASTA. Nay, what should mortal fear, for whom the decrees of Fortune are supreme, and who hath clear foresight of nothing? 'T is best to live at random, as one may. But fear not thou touching wedlock with thy mother. Many men ere now have so fared in dreams also: but he to whom these things are as nought bears his life most easily.

ŒDIPUS. All these bold words of thine would have been well, were not my mother living; but as it is, since she lives, I must needs fear — though thou sayest well.

IOCASTA. Howbeit thy father's death is a great sign to cheer us.

ŒDIPUS. Great, I know; but my fear is of her who lives.

MESSENGER. And who is the woman about whom ye fear?

ŒDIPUS. Meropè, old man, the consort of Polybus.

MESSENGER. And what is it in her that moves your fear?

ŒDIPUS. A heaven-sent oracle of dread import, stranger.

MESSENGER. Lawful, or unlawful, for another to know?

ŒDIPUS. Lawful, surely. Loxias once said that I was doomed to espouse mine own mother, and to shed with mine own hands my father's blood. Wherefore my home in Corinth was long kept by me afar; with happy event, indeed, — yet still 't is sweet to see the face of parents.

MESSENGER. Was it indeed for fear of this that thou wast an exile from that city?

ŒDIPUS. And because I wished not, old man, to be the slayer of my sire.

MESSENGER. Then why have I not freed thee, king, from this fear, seeing that I came with friendly purpose?

ŒDIPUS. Indeed thou shouldst have guerdon due from me.

MESSENGER. Indeed 't was chiefly for this that I came — that, on thy return home, I might reap some good.

ŒDIPUS. Nay, I will never go near my parents.

MESSENGER. Ah my son, 't is plain enough that thou knowest not what thou doest.

ŒDIPUS. How, old man? For the gods' love, tell me.

MESSENGER. If for these reasons thou shrinkest from going home.

ŒDIPUS. Aye, I dread lest Phœbus prove himself true for me.

MESSENGER. Thou dreadest to be stained with guilt through thy parents?

ŒDIPUS. Even so, old man — this it is that ever affrights me.

MESSENGER. Dost thou know, then, that thy fears are wholly vain?

ŒDIPUS. How so, if I was born of those parents?

MESSENGER. Because Polybus was nothing to thee in blood.

ŒDIPUS. What sayest thou? Was Polybus not my sire?

MESSENGER. No more than he who speaks to thee, but just so much.

ŒDIPUS. And how can my sire be level with him who is as nought to me?

MESSENGER. Nay, he begat thee not, any more than I.

ŒDIPUS. Nay, wherefore, then, called he me his son?

MESSENGER. Know that he had received thee as a gift from my hands of yore.

ŒDIPUS. And yet he loved me so dearly, who came from another's hand?

MESSENGER. Yea, his former childlessness won him thereto.

ŒDIPUS. And thou — hadst thou bought me or found me by chance, when thou gavest me to him?

MESSENGER. Found thee in Cithæron's winding glens.

ŒDIPUS. And wherefore wast thou roaming in those regions?

MESSENGER. I was there in charge of mountain flocks.

ŒDIPUS. What, thou wast a shepherd — a vagrant hireling?

MESSENGER. But thy preserver, my son, in that hour.

ŒDIPUS. And what pain was mine when thou didst take me in thine arms?

MESSENGER. The ankles of thy feet might witness.

ŒDIPUS. Ah me, why dost thou speak of that old trouble?

MESSENGER. I freed thee when thou hadst thine ankles pinned together.

ŒDIPUS. Aye, 't was a dread brand of shame that I took from my cradle.

MESSENGER. Such, that from that fortune thou wast called by the name which still is thine.

ŒDIPUS. Oh, for the gods' love — was the deed my mother's or father's? Speak!

MESSENGER. I know not; he who gave thee to me wots better of that than I.

ŒDIPUS. What, thou hadst me from another? Thou didst not light on me thyself?

MESSENGER. No: another shepherd gave thee up to me.

ŒDIPUS. Who was he? Art thou in case to tell clearly?

MESSENGER. I think he was called one of the household of Laïus.

ŒDIPUS. The king who ruled this country long ago?

MESSENGER. The same: 't was in his service that the man was a herd.

ŒDIPUS. Is he still alive, that I might see him?

MESSENGER. Nay, ye folk of the country should know best. [Exit.]

ŒDIPUS. Is there any of you here present that knows the herd of whom he speaks — that hath seen him in the pastures or the town? Answer! The hour hath come that these things should be finally revealed.

CHORUS. Methinks he speaks of no other than the peasant whom thou wast already fain to see; but our lady Iocasta might best tell that.

ŒDIPUS. Lady, wottest thou of him whom we lately summoned? Is it of him that this man speaks?

IOCASTA. Why ask of whom he spoke? Regard it not . . . waste not a thought on what he said . . . 't were idle.

ŒDIPUS. It must not be that, with such clues in my grasp, I should fail to bring my birth to light.

IOCASTA. For the gods' sake, if thou hast any care for thine own life, forbear this search! My anguish is enough.

ŒDIPUS. Be of good courage; though I be found the son of servile mother, — aye, a slave by three descents, — thou wilt not be proved base-born.

IOCASTA. Yet hear me, I implore thee: do not thus.

ŒDIPUS. I must not hear of not discovering the whole truth.

IOCASTA. Yet I wish thee well — I counsel thee for the best.

ŒDIPUS. These best counsels, then, vex my patience.

IOCASTA. Ill-fated one! Mayst thou never come to know who thou art!

ŒDIPUS. Go, some one, fetch me the herdsman hither, — and leave yon woman to glory in her princely stock.

IOCASTA. Alas, alas, miserable! — that word alone can I say unto thee, and no other word henceforth forever.
[She rushes into the palace.]

CHORUS. Why hath the lady gone, Œdipus, in a transport of wild grief? I misdoubt, a storm of sorrow will break forth from this silence.

ŒDIPUS. Break forth what will! Be my race never so lowly, I must crave to learn it. Yon woman, perchance, — for she is proud with more than a woman's pride — thinks shame of my base source. But I, who hold myself son of Fortune that gives good, will not be dishonored. She is the mother from whom I spring; and the months, my kinsmen, have marked me sometimes lowly, sometimes great. Such being my lineage, never more can I prove false to it, or spare to search out the secret of my birth.

CHORUS. If I am a seer or wise of heart, O Cithæron, thou shalt not fail — by yon heaven, thou shalt not! — to know at tomorrow's full moon that Œdipus honors thee as native to him, as his nurse, and his mother, and that thou art celebrated in our dance and song, because thou art wellpleasing to our prince. O Phœbus to whom we cry, may these things find favor in thy sight!

Who was it, my son, who of the race whose years are many that bore thee in wedlock with Pan, the mountain-roaming father? Or was it a bride of Loxias that bore thee? For dear to him are all the upland pastures. Or perchance 't was Cyllene's lord, or the Bacchants' god, dweller on the hill-tops, that received thee, a newborn joy, from one of the Nymphs of Helicon, with whom he most doth sport.

ŒDIPUS. Elders, if 't is for me to guess, who have never met with him, I think I see the herdsman of whom we have long been in quest; for in his venerable age he tallies with yon stranger's years, and withal I know those who bring him, methinks, as servants of mine own. But perchance thou mayest have the advantage of me in knowledge, if thou hast seen the herdsman before.

CHORUS. Aye, I know him, be sure; he was in the service of Laïus — trusty as any man, in his shepherd's place.

[*The Herdsman is brought in.*]

ŒDIPUS. I ask thee first, Corinthian stranger, is this he whom thou meanest?

MESSENGER. This man whom thou beholdest.

ŒDIPUS. Ho thou, old man — I would have thee look this way, and answer all that I ask thee. — Thou wast once in the service of Laïus?

HERDSMAN. I was — a slave not bought, but reared in his house.

ŒDIPUS. Employed in what labor, or what way of life?

HERDSMAN. For the best part of my life I tended flocks.

ŒDIPUS. And what the regions that thou didst chiefly haunt?

HERDSMAN. Sometimes it was Cithæron, sometimes the neighboring ground.

ŒDIPUS. Then wottest thou of having noted yon man in these parts —

HERDSMAN. Doing what? . . . What man dost thou mean? . . .

ŒDIPUS. This man here — or of having ever met him before?

HERDSMAN. Not so that I could speak at once from memory.

MESSENGER. And no wonder, master. But I will bring clear recollection to his ignorance. I am sure that he well wots of the time when we abode in the region of Cithæron, — he with two flocks, I, his comrade, with one, — three full half-years, from spring to Arcturus; and then for the winter I used to drive my flock to mine own fold, and he took his to the fold of Laïus. Did aught of this happen as I tell, or did it not?

HERDSMAN. Thou speakest the truth — though 't is long ago.

MESSENGER. Come, tell me now — wottest thou of having given me a boy in those days, to be reared as mine own foster-son?

HERDSMAN. What now? Why dost thou ask the question?

MESSENGER. Yonder man, my friend, is he who then was young.

HERDSMAN. Plague seize thee — be silent once for all!

ŒDIPUS. Ha! chide him not, old man — thy words need chiding more than his.

HERDSMAN. And wherein, most noble master, do I offend?

ŒDIPUS. In not telling of the boy concerning whom he asks.

HERDSMAN. He speaks without knowledge — he is busy to no purpose.

ŒDIPUS. Thou wilt not speak with a good grace, but thou shalt on pain.

HERDSMAN. Nay, for the gods' love, misuse not an old man!

ŒDIPUS. Ho, some one — pinion him this instant!

HERDSMAN. Alas, wherefore? what more wouldst thou learn?

ŒDIPUS. Didst thou give this man the child of whom he asks?

HERDSMAN. I did, — and would I had perished that day!

ŒDIPUS. Well, thou wilt come to that, unless thou tell the honest truth.

HERDSMAN. Nay, much more am I lost, if I speak.

ŒDIPUS. The fellow is bent, methinks, on more delays . . .

HERDSMAN. No, no! — I said before that I gave it to him.

ŒDIPUS. Whence hadst thou got it? In thine own house, or from another?

HERDSMAN. Mine own it was not — I had received it from a man.

ŒDIPUS. From whom of the citizens here? From what home?

HERDSMAN. Forbear, for the gods' love, master, forbear to ask more!

ŒDIPUS. Thou art lost if I have to question thee again.

HERDSMAN. It was a child, then, of the house of Laïus.

ŒDIPUS. A slave — or one born of his own race?

HERDSMAN. Ah me — I am on the dreaded brink of speech —

ŒDIPUS. And I of hearing; yet must I hear.

HERDSMAN. Thou must know, then, that 't was said to be his own child — but thy lady within could best say how these things are.

ŒDIPUS. How? She gave it to thee?

HERDSMAN. Yea, O king.

ŒDIPUS. For what end?

HERDSMAN. That I should make away with it.

ŒDIPUS. Her own child, the wretch?

HERDSMAN. Aye, from fear of evil prophecies.

ŒDIPUS. What were they?

HERDSMAN. The tale ran that he must slay his sire.

ŒDIPUS. Why, then, didst thou give him up to this old man?

HERDSMAN. Through pity, master, as deeming that he would bear him away to another land, whence he himself came; but he saved him for the direst woe. For if thou art what this man saith, know that thou wast born to misery.

[Exit Herdsman.]

ŒDIPUS. Oh, oh! All brought to pass — all true! Thou light, may I now look my last on thee — I who have been found accursed in birth, accursed in wedlock, accursed in the shedding of blood!

[He rushes into the palace.]

CHORUS. Alas, ye generations of men, how mere a shadow do I count your life! Where, where is the mortal who wins more of happiness than just the seeming, and, after the semblance, a falling away? Thine is a fate that warns me, — thine, thine, unhappy Œdipus — to call no earthly creature blest.

For he, O Zeus, sped his shaft with peerless skill, and won the prize of an all-prosperous fortune; he slew the maiden with crooked talons who sang darkly; he arose for our land as a tower against death. And from that time, Œdipus, thou hast been called our king, and hast been honored supremely, bearing sway in great Thebes.

But now whose story is more grievous in men's ears? Who is a more wretched captive to fierce plagues and troubles, with all his life reversed?

Alas, renowned Œdipus! The same bounteous place of rest sufficed thee, as child and as sire also, that thou shouldst make thereon thy nuptial couch. Oh, how can the soil wherein thy father sowed, unhappy one, have suffered thee in silence so long?

Time the all-seeing hath found thee out in thy despite: he judgeth the monstrous marriage wherein begetter and begotten have long been one.

Alas, thou child of Laïus, would, would that I had never seen thee! I wail as one who pours a dirge from his lips; sooth to speak, 't was thou that gavest me new life, and through thee darkness hath fallen upon mine eyes.

[Enter Second Messenger from the house.]

SECOND MESSENGER. Ye who are ever most honored in this land, what deeds shall ye hear, what deeds behold, what burden of sorrow shall be yours, if, true to your race, ye still care for the house of Labdacus! For I ween that not Ister nor Phasis could wash this house clean, so many are the ills that it shrouds, or will soon bring to light, — ills wrought not unwittingly, but of purpose. And those griefs smart most which are seen to be of our own choice.

CHORUS. Indeed those which we knew before fall not short of claiming sore lamentation: besides them, what dost thou announce?

SECOND MESSENGER. This is the shortest tale to tell and to hear: our royal lady Iocasta is dead.

CHORUS. Alas, hapless one! From what cause?

SECOND MESSENGER. By her own hand. The worst pain in what hath chanced is not for you, for yours it is not to behold. Nevertheless, so far as mine own memory serves, ye shall learn that unhappy woman's fate.

When, frantic, she had passed within the vestibule, she rushed straight towards her nuptial couch, clutching her hair with the fingers of both hands; once within the chamber, she dashed the doors together at her back; then called on the name of Laïus, long since a corpse, mindful of that son begotten long ago, by whom the sire w' slain, leaving the mother to breed accursed offspring with his own.

And she bewailed the wedlock wherein, wretched, she had borne a twofold brood, husband by husband, children by her child. And how thereafter she perished, is more than I know. For with a shriek Œdipus burst in, and suffered us not to watch her woe unto the end; on him, as he rushed around, our eyes were set. To and fro he went, asking us to give him a sword, — asking where he should find the wife who was no wife, but a mother whose womb had borne alike himself and his children. And, in his frenzy, a power above man was his guide; for 't was none of us mortals who were nigh. And with a dread shriek, as though some one beckoned him on, he sprang at the double doors, and from their sockets forced the bending bolts, and rushed into the room.

There beheld we the woman hanging by the neck in a twisted noose of swinging cords. But he, when he saw her, with a dread, deep cry of misery, loosed the halter whereby she hung. And when the hapless woman was stretched upon the ground, then was the sequel dread to see. For he tore from her raiment the golden brooches wherewith she was decked, and lifted them, and smote full on his own eyeballs, uttering words like these: "No more shall ye behold such horrors as I was suffering and working! long enough have ye looked on those whom ye ought never to have seen, failed in knowledge of those whom I yearned to know — henceforth ye shall be dark!"

To such dire refrain, not once alone but oft struck he his eyes with lifted hand; and at each blow the ensanguined eyeballs bedewed his beard, nor sent forth sluggish drops of gore, but all at once a dark shower of blood came down like hail.

From the deeds of twain such ills have broken forth, not on one alone, but with mingled woe for man and wife. The old happiness of their ancestral fortune was aforetime happiness indeed; but to-day — lamentation, ruin, death, shame, all earthly ills that can be named — all, all theirs.

CHORUS. And hath the sufferer now any respite from pain?

SECOND MESSENGER. He cries for some one to unbar the gates and show to all the Cadmeans his father's slayer, his mother's — the unholy word must not pass my lips, — as purposing to cast himself out of the land, and abide no more, to make the house accursed under his own curse. Howbeit he lacks strength, and one to guide his steps; for the anguish is more than man may bear. And he will show this to thee also; for lo, the bars of the gates are withdrawn, and soon thou shalt behold a sight which even he who abhors it must pity.

[*Enter* Œdipus.]

CHORUS. O dread fate for men to see, O most dreadful of all that have met mine eyes! Unhappy one, what madness hath come on thee? Who is the unearthly foe that, with a bound of more than mortal range, hath made thine ill-starred life his prey?

Alas, alas, thou hapless one! Nay, I cannot e'en look on thee, though there is much that I would fain ask, fain learn, much that draws my wistful gaze, — with such a shuddering dost thou fill me!

Œdipus. Woe is me! Alas, alas, wretched that I am! Whither, whither am I borne in my misery? How is my voice swept abroad on the wings of the air? O my Fate, how far hast thou sprung!

CHORUS. To a dread place, dire in men's ears, dire in their sight.

Œdipus. O thou horror of darkness that enfoldest me, visitant unspeakable, resistless, sped by a wind too fair!

Ay me! and once again, ay me!

How is my soul pierced by the stab of these goads, and withal by the memory of sorrows!

CHORUS. Yea, amid woes so many a twofold pain may well be thine to mourn and to bear.

Œdipus. Ah, friend, thou still art steadfast in thy tendance of me, — thou still hast patience to care for the blind man! Ah me! Thy presence is not hid from me — no, dark though I am, yet know I thy voice full well.

d deeds, how
quench thy
man power

vas he
hese
at
e,
ee,
weet?
as thou

I more
reeting can
aste, lead me
d me hence, the
ccursed, yea, the
of heaven!
alike for thy fortune
ereof, would that I had
known thee!
sh the man, whoe'er he
me in the pastures from the
on my feet, and saved me
and gave me back to life, — a
ed! Had I died then, to my
to mine own soul I had not
a grief.
I also would have had it thus.
So had I not come to shed my
d, nor been called among men
f her from whom I sprang: but
orsaken of the gods, son of a
her, successor to his bed who
ne own wretched being: and if
a woe surpassing woes, it hath
portion of Œdipus.
I know not how I can say that
counseled well: for thou wert
than living and blind.
Show me not at large that these
not best done thus: give me
more. For, had I sight, I know
hat eyes I could e'en have looked
her, when I came to the place of
aye, or on my miserable mother,
st both I have sinned such sins
ng could not punish. But deem
e sight of children, born as mine
, was lovely for me to look upon?
ot lovely to mine eyes forever!
vas this town with its towered

walls, nor the sacred statues of the gods, since I, thrice wretched that I am, — I, noblest of the sons of Thebes, — have doomed myself to know these no more, by mine own command that all should thrust away the impious one, — even him whom gods have shown to be unholy — and of the race of Laïus!

After bearing such a stain upon me, was I to look with steady eyes on this folk? No, verily: no, were there yet a way to choke the fount of hearing, I had not spared to make a fast prison of this wretched frame, that so I should have known nor sight nor sound: for 't is sweet that our thought should dwell beyond the sphere of griefs.

Alas, Cithæron, why hadst thou a shelter for me? When I was given to thee, why didst thou not slay me straightway, that so I might never have revealed my source to men? Ah, Polybus, — ah, Corinth, and thou that wast called the ancient house of my fathers, how seeming-fair was I your nurseling, and what ills were festering beneath! For now I am found evil, and of evil birth. O ye three roads, and thou secret glen, — thou coppice, and narrow way where three paths met — ye who drank from my hands that father's blood which was mine own, — remember ye, perchance, what deeds I wrought for you to see, — and then, when I came hither, what fresh deeds I went on to do?

O marriage-rites, ye gave me birth, and when ye had brought me forth, again ye bore children to your child, ye created an incestuous kinship of fathers, brothers, sons, — brides, wives, mothers, — yea, all the foulest shame that is wrought among men! Nay, but 't is unmeet to name what 't is unmeet to do: — haste ye, for the gods' love, hide me somewhere beyond the land, or slay me, or cast me into the sea, where ye shall never behold me more! Approach, — deign to lay your hands on a wretched man; — hearken, fear not, — my plague can rest on no mortal beside.

CHORUS. Nay, here is Creon, in meet season for thy requests, crave they act or counsel; for he alone is left to guard the land in thy stead.

. ŒDIPUS. Ah me, how indeed shall I

accost him? What claim to credence can be shown on my part? For in the past I have been found wholly false to him.

[*Enter* CREON.]

CREON. I have not come in mockery, Œdipus, nor to reproach thee with any bygone fault. (*To the attendants.*) But ye, if ye respect the children of men no more, revere at least the all-nurturing flame of our lord the Sun, — spare to show thus nakedly a pollution such as this, — one which neither earth can welcome, nor the holy rain, nor the light. Nay, take him into the house as quickly as ye may; for it best accords with piety that kinsfolk alone should see and hear a kinsman's woes.

ŒDIPUS. For the gods' love — since thou hast done a gentle violence to my presage, who hast come in a spirit so noble to me, a man most vile — grant me a boon: — for thy good I will speak, not for mine own.

CREON. And what wish art thou so fain to have of me?

ŒDIPUS. Cast me out of this land with all speed, to a place where no mortal shall be found to greet me more.

CREON. This would I have done, be thou sure, but that I craved first to learn all my duty from the god.

ŒDIPUS. Nay, his behest hath been set forth in full, — to let me perish, the parricide, the unholy one, that I am.

CREON. Such was the purport; yet, seeing to what a pass we have come, 't is better to learn clearly what should be done.

ŒDIPUS. Will ye, then, seek a response on behalf of such a wretch as I am?

CREON. Aye, for thou thyself wilt now surely put faith in the god.

ŒDIPUS. Yea; and on thee lay I this charge, to thee will I make this entreaty: — give to her who is within such burial as thou thyself wouldest; for thou wilt meetly render the last rites to thine own. But for me — never let this city of my sire be condemned to have me dwelling therein, while I live: no, suffer me to abide on the hills, where yonder is Cithæron, famed as mine, — which my mother and sire, while they lived, set for my appointed tomb, — that so I may die by their decree who sought to

slay me. Howbei[t] — that neithe[r] destroy me: from deat[h] doom.

N[...] as [...] Cr[...] th[...] may,[...] But m[...] who ne[...] lacked t[...] all things s[...] thee, care for[...] suffer me to tou[...] and to indulge m[...] grant it, though noble[...] once touch them wit[...] think that they were w[...] I had sight. . . .

[CREON's *attendan[ts]* *children* ANTIGON[E]

Ha? O ye gods, can it be m[...] that I hear sobbing, — can [...] taken pity on me and sent me [...] — my darlings? Am I right?

CREON. Yea: 't is of my co[...] I knew thy joy in them of old [...] that now is thine.

ŒDIPUS. Then blessed be th[...] guerdon of this errand, may he[...] to thee a kinder guardian tha[n] me! My children, where are [...] hither, — hither to the hands o[f] mother was your own, the ha[...] offices have wrought that your [...] bright eyes should be such orb[...] — his, who seeing nought, know[...] became your father by her from[...] sprang! For you also do I weep[...] you I cannot — when I think of[...] life in days to come which men [...] you live. To what company of t[...] will ye go, to what festival, from[...] shall not return home in tears, [...] sharing in the holiday? But wh[...] now come to years ripe for mar[...] shall he be, who shall be the [...] daughters, that will hazard tak[...] him such reproaches as must b[...] alike to my offspring and to yo[u] what misery is wanting? Your sire slew his sire, he had seed of her who bare him, and begat you at the sources of his own being! Such are the taunts that will be cast at you; and who then will wed? The man lives not, no, it cannot be, my children, but ye must wither in barren maidenhood.

Ah, son of Menœceus, hear me — since thou art the only father left to them, for we, their parents, are lost, both of us, — allow them not to wander poor and unwed, who are thy kinswomen, nor abase them to the level of my woes. Nay, pity them, when thou seest them at this tender age so utterly forlorn, save for thee. Signify thy promise, generous man, by the touch of thy hand! To you, my children, I would have given much counsel, were your minds mature; but now I would have this to be your prayer — that ye live where occasion suffers, and that the life which is your portion may be happier than your sire's.

CREON. Thy grief hath had large scope enough: nay, pass into the house.

ŒDIPUS. I must obey, though 't is in no wise sweet.

CREON. Yea: for it is in season that all things are good.

ŒDIPUS. Knowest thou, then, on what conditions I will go?

CREON. Thou shalt name them; so shall I know them when I hear.

ŒDIPUS. See that thou send me to dwell beyond this land.

CREON. Thou askest me for what the god must give.

ŒDIPUS. Nay, to the gods I have become most hateful.

CREON. Then shalt thou have thy wish anon.

ŒDIPUS. So thou consentest?

CREON. 'T is not my wont to speak idly what I do not mean.

ŒDIPUS. Then 't is time to lead me hence.

CREON. Come, then, — but let thy children go.

ŒDIPUS. Nay, take not these from me!

CREON. Crave not to be master in things: for the mastery which thou win hath not followed thee through

CHORUS. Dwellers in our native behold, this is Œdipus, who kn riddle, and was a man m whose fortunes what cit with envy? Behold int of dread trouble he

Therefore, whil destined final happy who i crossed lif from pain.

m I sure,
nt else can
en snatched
some strange

her it will: but
— I pray thee,
hee for my sons;
e they where they
k the means to live.
oor hapless ones,
table spread apart, or
presence, but ever in
y daily bread, — I pray
; and — if thou canst —
ch them with my hands
y grief. Grant it, princ
heart! Ah, could
my hands, ev
th me, ev

MEDEA

By EURIPIDES

Translated into English verse by GILBERT MURRAY

CHARACTERS

MEDEA, *daughter of Aietes, King of Colchis*

JASON, *chief of the Argonauts; nephew of Pelias,*
King of Iolcos in Thessaly

CREON, *ruler of Corinth*

ÆGEUS, *King of Athens*

NURSE *of Medea*

TWO CHILDREN *of Jason and Medea*

ATTENDANT *on the children*

A MESSENGER.

CHORUS *of Corinthian Women, with their* LEADER
Soldiers and Attendants

The Scene is laid in Corinth. The play was first acted when
Pythodorus was Archon, Olympiad 87, year 1 (B.C. 431).
Euphorion was first, Sophocles second, Euripides third, with
Medea, Philoctetes, Dictys, and the Harvesters, a Satyr-play.

MEDEA

[*The Scene represents the front of* MEDEA'S
*house in Corinth. A road to the right leads
toward the royal castle, one on the left to the
harbor. The Nurse is discovered alone.*]

NURSE. Would God no Argo e'er had
    winged the seas
To Colchis through the blue Symplegades:
No shaft of riven pine in Pelion's glen
Shaped that first oar-blade in the hands of
    men
Valiant, who won, to save King Pelias' vow,
The fleece All-golden! Never then, I trow,
Mine own princess, her spirit wounded sore
With love of Jason, to the encastled shore
Had sailed of old Iolcos: never wrought
    not,
The daughters of King Pelias, knowing
To spill their father's life: nor fled in fear,
Hunted for that fierce sin, to Corinth here
With Jason and her babes. This folk at
    need
Stood friend to her, and she in word and
    deed
Served alway Jason. Surely this doth bind,
Through all ill days, the hurts of human-
    kind,
When man and woman in one music move.
    But now, the world is angry, and true
    love
Sick as with poison. Jason doth forsake
My mistress and his own two sons, to make
His couch in a king's chamber. He must
    wed:
Wed with this Creon's child, who now is
    head
And chief of Corinth. Wherefore sore be-
    trayed
Medea calleth up the oath they made,
They two, and wakes the claspèd hands
    again,
The troth surpassing speech, and cries
    amain
On God in heaven to mark the end, and
    how
Jason hath paid his debt.

All fasting now
And cold, her body yielded up to pain,
Her days a waste of weeping, she hath lain,
Since first she knew that he was false. Her
    eyes
Are lifted not; and all her visage lies
In the dust. If friends will speak, she hears
    no more
Than some dead rock or wave that beats
    the shore:
Only the white throat in a sudden shame
May writhe, and all alone she moans the
    name
Of father, and land, and home, forsook that
    day
For this man's sake, who casteth her away.
Not to be quite shut out from home . . .
    alas,
She knoweth now how rare a thing that
    was!
Methinks she hath a dread, not joy, to see
Her children near. 'T is this that maketh
    me
Most tremble, lest she do I know not what.
Her heart is no light thing, and useth not
To brook much wrong. I know that woman,
    aye,
And dread her! Will she creep alone to die
Bleeding in that old room, where still is
    laid
Lord Jason's bed? She hath for that a
    blade
Made keen. Or slay the bridegroom and
    the king,
And win herself God knows what dire
    thing?
'T is a fell spirit. Few, I ween, shall stir
Her hate unscathed, or lightly humble her.
    Ha! 'T is the children from their games
    again,
Restéd and gay; and all their mother's pain
Forgotten! Young lives ever turn from
    gloom!
    [*The Children and their Attendant
    come in.*]

ATTENDANT. Thou ancient treasure of
my lady's room,
What mak'st thou here before the gates
alone,
And alway turning on thy lips some moan
Of old mischances? Will our mistress be
Content, this long time to be left by thee?
NURSE. Gray guard of Jason's children,
a good thrall
Hath his own grief, if any hurt befall
His masters. Aye, it holds one's heart! . . .
Meseems
I have strayed out so deep in evil dreams,
I longed to rest me here alone, and cry
Medea's wrongs to this still Earth and Sky.
ATTENDANT. How? Are the tears yet
running in her eyes?
NURSE. 'T were good to be like thee! . . .
Her sorrow lies
Scarce wakened yet, not half its perils
wrought.
ATTENDANT. Mad spirit! . . . if a man
may speak his thought
Of masters mad. — And nothing in her ears
Hath sounded yet of her last cause for
tears!
    [*He moves towards the house, but
    the Nurse checks him.*]
NURSE. What cause, old man? . . . Nay,
grudge me not one word.
ATTENDANT. 'T is nothing. Best forget
what thou hast heard.
NURSE. Nay, housemate, by thy beard!
Hold it not hid
From me. . . . I will keep silence if thou bid.
ATTENDANT. I heard an old man talking,
where he sate
At draughts in the sun, beside the fountain
gate,
And never thought of me, there standing
still
Beside him. And he said, 'T was Creon's
will,
Being lord of all this land, that she be
sent,
And with her her two sons, to banishment.
Maybe 't is all false. For myself, I know
No further, and I would it were not so.
NURSE. Jason will never bear it — his
own sons
Banished, — however hot his anger runs
Against their mother!

ATTENDANT. Old love burneth low
When new love wakes, men say. He is not
now
Husband nor father here, nor any kin.
NURSE. But this is ruin! New waves
breaking in
To wreck us, ere we are righted from the old!
ATTENDANT. Well, hold thy peace. Our
mistress will be told
All in good time. Speak thou no word
hereof.
NURSE. My babes! What think ye of
your father's love?
God curse him not, he is my master still:
But, oh, to them that loved him, 't is an ill
Friend. . . .
ATTENDANT. And what man on earth is
different? How?
Hast thou lived all these years, and learned
but now
That every man more loveth his own head
Than other men's? He dreameth of the bed
Of this new bride, and thinks not of his
sons.
NURSE. Go: run into the house, my little
ones!
All will end happily! . . . Keep them apart:
Let not their mother meet them while her
heart
Is darkened. Yester night I saw a flame
Stand in her eye, as though she hated them,
And would I know not what. For sure her
wrath
Will never turn nor slumber, till she hath . . .
Go: and if some must suffer, may it be
Not we who love her, but some enemy!
VOICE [*within*]. O shame and pain: O
woe is me!
Would I could die in my misery!
    [*The Children and the Attendant
    go in.*]
NURSE. Ah, children, hark! She moves
again
Her frozen heart, her sleeping wrath.
In, quick! And never cross her path,
Nor rouse that dark eye in its pain;

That fell sea-spirit, and the dire
Spring of a will untaught, unbowed.
Quick, now! — Methinks this weeping
cloud
Hath in its heart some thunder-fire,

Slow gathering, that must flash ere long.
  I know not how, for ill or well,
  It turns, this uncontrollable
Tempestuous spirit, blind with wrong.
  VOICE [within]. Have I not suffered?
    Doth it call
No tears? . . . Ha, ye beside the wall
Unfathered children, God hate you
As I am hated, and him, too,
  That gat you, and this house and all!
  NURSE. For pity! What have they to do,
Babes, with their father's sin? Why call
Thy curse on these? . . . Ah, children, all
These days my bosom bleeds for you.

Rude are the wills of princes: yea,
  Prevailing alway, seldom crossed,
  On fitful winds their moods are tossed:
'T is best men tread the equal way.

Aye, not with glory but with peace
  May the long summers find me crowned:
  For gentleness — her very sound
Is magic, and her usages

All wholesome: but the fiercely great
  Hath little music on his road,
  And falleth, when the hand of God
Shall move, most deep and desolate.
    [During the last words the Leader
      of the Chorus has entered. Other
      women follow her.]
  LEADER. I heard a voice and a moan,
  A voice of the eastern seas:
Hath she found not yet her ease?
  Speak, O agèd one.
For I stood afar at the gate,
  And there came from within a cry,
And wailing desolate.
  Ah, no more joy have I,
For the griefs this house doth see,
And the love it hath wrought in me.
  NURSE. There is no house! 'T is gone.
    The lord
Seeketh a prouder bed: and she
Wastes in her chamber, nor one word
Will hear of care or charity.
  VOICE [within]. O Zeus, O Earth, O
    Light,
  Will the fire not stab my brain?
  What profiteth living? Oh,
  Shall I not lift the slow ·

  Yoke, and let Life go,
As a beast out in the night,
  To lie, and be rid of pain?
  CHORUS — Some Women. (A.) "O Zeus,
    O Earth, O Light":
The cry of a bride forlorn
Heard ye, and wailing born
    Of lost delight?
  (B.) Why weariest thou this day,
  Wild heart, for the bed abhorrèd,
The cold bed in the clay?
Death cometh though no man pray,
  Ungarlanded, unadorèd.
    Call him not thou.
  (C.) If another's arms be now
    Where thine have been,
    On his head be the sin:
Rend not thy brow!
  (D.) All that thou sufferest,
  God seeth: Oh, not so sore
Waste nor weep for the breast
  That was thine of yore.
  VOICE [within]. Virgin of Righteousness,
Virgin of hallowed Troth,
Ye marked me when with an oath
I bound him; mark no less
That oath's end. Give me to see
Him and his bride, who sought
My grief when I wronged her not,
  Broken in misery,
And all her house. . . . O God,
My mother's home, and the dim
Shore that I left for him,
And the voice of my brother's blood. . . .
  NURSE. Oh, wild words! Did ye hear
    her cry
To them that guard man's faith forsworn,
Themis and Zeus? . . . This wrath new-
    born
Shall make mad workings ere it die.
  CHORUS — Other Women. (A.) Would
    she but come to seek
Our faces, that love her well,
And take to her heart the spell
    Of words that speak?
  (B.) Alas for the heavy hate
And anger that burneth ever!
Would it but now abate,
Ah God, I love her yet.
  And surely my love's endeavor
    Shall fail not here.
  (C.) Go: from that chamber drear

Forth to the day
Lead her, and say, Oh, say
　　That we love her dear.
　(D.)　Go, lest her hand be hard
　On the innocent: Ah, let be!
For her grief moves hitherward,
　　Like an angry sea.
　　NURSE. That will I: though what words
　　　of mine
Or love shall move her? Let them lie
With the old lost labors! . . . Yet her
　eye —
Know ye the eyes of the wild kine,

The lion flash that guards their brood?
　So looks she now if any thrall
　Speak comfort, or draw near at all
My mistress in her evil mood.
　　　　　[The Nurse goes into the house.]
　　CHORUS — A Woman. Alas, the bold
　　blithe bards of old
　That all for joy their music made,
For feasts and dancing manifold,
　That Life might listen and be glad.

But all the darkness and the wrong,
　Quick deaths and dim heart-aching
　　things,
Would no man case them with a song
　Or music of a thousand strings?

Then song had served us in our need.
　What profit, o'er the banquet's swell
That lingering cry that none may heed?
　The feast hath filled them: all is well!
　　CHORUS — Others. I heard a song, but it
　　comes no more,
　Where the tears ran over:
A keen cry but tired, tired:
A woman's cry for her heart's desired,
　For a traitor's kiss and a lost lover.
But a prayer, methinks, yet riseth sore
　To God, to Faith, God's ancient daugh-
　　ter —
The Faith that over sundering seas
Drew her to Hellas, and the breeze
Of midnight shivered, and the door
　Closed of the salt unsounded water.
　　　　　[During the last words MEDEA has
　　　　　　come out from the house.]
　　MEDEA. Women of Corinth, I am come
　　to show

My face, lest ye despise me. For I know
Some heads stand high and fail not, even
　　at night
Alone — far less like this, in all men's sight:
And we, who study not our wayfarings
But feel and cry — Oh we are drifting
　things,
And evil! For what truth is in men's eyes,
Which search no heart, but in a flash
　despise
A strange face, shuddering back from one
　that ne'er
Hath wronged them? . . . Sure, far-comers
　anywhere,
I know, must bow them and be gentle.
　Nay,
A Greek himself men praise not, who alway
Should seek his own will recking not. . . .
　But I —
This thing undreamed of, sudden from on
　high,
Hath sapped my soul: I dazzle where I
　stand,
The cup of all life shattered in my hand,
Longing to die — O friends! He, even he,
Whom to know well was all the world to
　me,
The man I loved, hath proved most evil. —
　Oh,
Of all things upon earth that bleed and
　grow,
A herb most bruised is woman. We must
　pay
Our store of gold, hoarded for that one day,
To buy us some man's love; and lo, they
　bring
A master of our flesh! There comes the
　sting
Of the whole shame. And then the jeop-
　ardy,
For good or ill, what shall that master be;
Reject she cannot: and if he but stays
His suit, 't is shame on all that woman's
　days.
So thrown amid new laws, new places, why,
'T is magic she must have, or prophecy —
Home never taught her that — how best to
　guide
Toward peace this thing that sleepeth at
　her side.
And she who, laboring long, shall find some
　way

Whereby her lord may bear with her, nor
    fray
His yoke too fiercely, blessed is the breath
That woman draws! Else, let her pray for
    death.
Her lord, if he be wearied of the face
Withindoors, gets him forth; some merrier
    place
Will ease his heart: but she waits on, her
    whole
Vision enchainèd on a single soul.
And then, forsooth, 't is they that face the
    call
Of war, while we sit sheltered, hid from
    all
Peril! — False mocking! Sooner would I
    stand
Three times to face their battles, shield in
    hand,
Than bear one child.
    But peace! There cannot be
Ever the same tale told of thee and me.
Thou hast this city, and thy father's home,
And joy of friends, and hope in days to
    come:
But I, being citiless, am cast aside
By him that wedded me, a savage bride
Won in far seas and left — no mother near,
No brother, not one kinsman anywhere
For harbor in this storm. Therefore of
    thee
I ask one thing. If chance yet ope to me
Some path, if even now my hand can win
Strength to requite this Jason for his sin,
Betray me not! Oh, in all things but
    this,
I know how full of fears a woman is,
And faint at need, and shrinking from the
    light
Of battle: but once spoil her of her right
In man's love, and there moves, I warn thee
    well,
No bloodier spirit between heaven and hell.
    LEADER. I will betray thee not. It is but
        just,
Thou smite him. — And that weeping in
    the dust
And stormy tears, how should I blame
    them? . . . Stay:
'T is Creon, lord of Corinth, makes his way
Hither, and bears, methinks, some word
    of weight.

[*Enter* CREON, *the King, with armed Atten-
    dants, from the right.*

    CREON. Thou woman sullen-eyed and
        hot with hate
Against thy lord, Medea, I here command
That thou and thy two children from this
    land
Go forth to banishment. Make no delay:
Seeing ourselves, the King, are come this
    day
To see our charge fulfilled; nor shall again
Look homeward ere we have led thy chil-
    dren twain
And thee beyond our realm's last boundary.
    MEDEA. Lost! Lost!
Mine haters at the helm with sail flung free
Pursuing; and for us no beach nor shore
In the endless waters! . . . Yet, though
    stricken sore,
I still will ask thee, for what crime, what
    thing
Unlawful, wilt thou cast me out, O King?
    CREON. What crime? I fear thee,
        woman — little need
To cloak my reasons — lest thou work
    some deed
Of darkness on my child. And in that fear
Reasons enough have part. Thou comest
    here
A wise-woman confessed, and full of lore
In unknown ways of evil. Thou art sore
In heart, being parted from thy lover's
    arms.
And more, thou hast made menace . . . so
    the alarms
But now have reached mine ear . . . on
    bride and groom,
And him who gave the bride, to work thy
    doom
Of vengeance. Which, ere yet it be too late,
I sweep aside. I choose to earn thine hate
Of set will now, not palter with the mood
Of mercy, and hereafter weep in blood.
    MEDEA. 'T is not the first nor second
        time, O King,
That fame hath hurt me, and come nigh to
    bring
My ruin. . . . How can any man, whose
    eyes
Are wholesome, seek to rear his children
    wise

Beyond men's wont? Much helplessness
in arts
Of common life, and in their townsmen's
hearts
Envy deep-set . . . so much their learning
brings!
Come unto fools with knowledge of new
things,
They deem it vanity, not knowledge. Aye,
And men that erst for wisdom were held
high,
Feel thee a thorn to fret them, privily
Held higher than they. So hath it been
with me.
A wise-woman I am; and for that sin
To divers ill names men would pen me in;
A seed of strife; an eastern dreamer; one
Of brand not theirs; one hard to play
upon . . .
Ah, I am not so wondrous wise! And now,
To thee, I am terrible! What fearest thou?
What dire deed? Do I tread so proud a
path —
Fear me not thou! — that I should brave
the wrath
Of princes? Thou: what hast thou ever done
To wrong me? Granted thine own child to
one
Whom thy soul chose. — Ah, *him* out of
my heart
I hate; but thou, meseems, hast done thy
part
Not ill. And for thine houses' happiness
I hold no grudge. Go: marry, and God
bless
Your issues. Only suffer me to rest
Somewhere within this land. Though sore
oppressed,
I will be still, knowing mine own defeat.
CREON. Thy words be gentle: but I fear
me yet
Lest even now there creep some wickedness
Deep hid within thee. And for that the less
I trust thee now than ere these words began.
A woman quick of wrath, aye, or a man,
Is easier watching than the cold and still.
Up, straight, and find thy road! Mock
not my will
With words. This doom is passed beyond
recall;
Nor all thy crafts shall help thee, being
withal

My manifest foe, to linger at my side.
MEDEA (*suddenly throwing herself down
and clinging to* CREON). Oh, by thy knees!
By that new-wedded bride . . .
CREON. 'T is waste of words. Thou
shalt not weaken me.
MEDEA. Wilt hunt me? Spurn me when
I kneel to thee?
CREON. 'T is mine own house that kneels
to me, not thou.
MEDEA. Home, my lost home, how I
desire thee now!
CREON. And I mine, and my child, be-
yond all things.
MEDEA. O Loves of man, what curse is
on your wings!
CREON. Blessing or curse, 't is as their
chances flow.
MEDEA. Remember, Zeus, the cause of
all this woe!
CREON. Oh, rid me of my pains! Up,
get thee gone!
MEDEA. What would I with thy pains?
I have mine own.
CREON. Up: or, 'fore God, my soldiers
here shall fling . . .
MEDEA. Not that! Not that! . . . I do
but pray, O King . . .
CREON. Thou wilt not? I must face the
harsher task?
MEDEA. I accept mine exile. 'T is not
that I ask.
CREON. Why then so wild? Why cling-
ing to mine hand?
MEDEA [*rising*]. For one day only leave
me in thy land
At peace, to find some counsel, ere the
strain
Of exile fall, some comfort for these twain,
Mine innocents; since others take no
thought,
It seems, to save the babes that they begot.
Ah! Thou wilt pity them! Thou also art
A father: thou hast somewhere still a heart
That feels. . . . I reck not of myself: 't is
they
That break me, fallen upon so dire a day.
CREON. Mine is no tyrant's mood. Aye,
many a time
Ere this my tenderness hath marred the
chime
Of wisest counsels. And I know that now

I do mere folly. But so be it! Thou
Shalt have this grace . . . But this I warn
    thee clear,
If once the morrow's sunlight find thee here
Within my borders, thee or child of thine,
Thou diest! . . . Of this judgment not a line
Shall waver nor abate. So linger on,
If thou needs must, till the next risen sun;
No further. . . . In one day there scarce
    can be
Those perils wrought whose dread yet
    haunteth me.
                    [*Exit* CREON *with his suite.*]
    CHORUS. O woman, woman of sorrow,
Where wilt thou turn and flee?
What town shall be thine to-morrow,
    What land of all lands that be,
What door of a strange man's home?
    Yea, God hath hunted thee,
Medea, forth to the foam
    Of a trackless sea.
    MEDEA. Defeat on every side; what
    else? — But oh,
Not here the end is: think it not! I know
For bride and groom one battle yet un-
    tried,
And goodly pains for him that gave the
    bride.
Dost dream I would have groveled to
    this man,
Save that I won mine end, and shaped my
    plan
For merry deeds? My lips had never
    deigned
Speak word with him: my flesh been never
    stained
With touching. . . . Fool, oh, triple fool!
    It lay
So plain for him to kill my whole essay
By exile swift: and, lo, he sets me free
This one long day: wherein mine haters
    three
Shall lie here dead, the father and the bride
And husband — mine, not hers! Oh, I have
    tried
So many thoughts of murder to my turn,
I know not which best likes me. Shall I
    burn
Their house with fire? Or stealing past
    unseen
To Jason's bed — I have a blade made
    keen

For that — stab, breast to breast, that
    wedded pair?
Good, but for one thing. When I am taken
    there,
And killed, they will laugh loud who hate
    me. . . .
    Nay,
I love the old way best, the simple way
Of poison, where we too are strong as men.
    Ah me!
And they being dead — what place shall
    hold me then?
What friend shall rise, with land inviolate
And trusty doors, to shelter from their hate
This flesh? . . . None anywhere! . . . A
    little more
I needs must wait: and, if there ope some
    door
Of refuge, some strong tower to shield me,.
    good:
In craft and darkness I will hunt this blood..
Else, if mine hour be come and no hope
    nigh,
Then sword in hand, full-willed and sure to,
    die,
I yet will live to slay them. I will wend
Man-like, their road of daring to the end.
    So help me She who of all Gods hath.
    been
The best to me, of all my chosen queen
And helpmate, Hecate, who dwells apart,
The flame of flame, in my fire's inmost
    heart:
For all their strength, they shall not stab
    my soul
And laugh thereafter! Dark and full of dole
Their bridal feast shall be, most dark the
    day
They joined their hands, and hunted me
    away.
    Awake thee now, Medea! Whatso plot
Thou hast, or cunning, strive and falter not.
On to the peril-point! Now comes the
    strain
Of daring. Shall they trample thee again?
How? And with Hellas laughing o'er thy
    fall
While this thief's daughter weds, and weds
    withal
Jason? . . . A true king was thy father, yea,
And born of the ancient Sun! . . . Thou
    know'st the way;

And God hath made thee woman, things
    most vain
For help, but wondrous in the paths of
    pain.
       [MEDEA *goes into the house.*]
CHORUS. Back streams the wave on the
    ever-running river:
Life, life is changed and the laws of it
    o'ertrod.
Man shall be the slave, the affrighted, the
    low-liver!
       Man hath forgotten God.
And woman, yea, woman, shall be terrible
    in story:
    The tales too, meseemeth, shall be other
      than of yore.
For a fear there is that cometh out of
    Woman and a glory,
    And the hard hating voices shall encom-
      pass her no more!

The old bards shall cease, and their memory
    that lingers
    Of frail brides and faithless, shall be
      shriveled as with fire.
For they loved us not, nor knew us: and
    our lips were dumb, our fingers
Could wake not the secret of the lyre.
Else, else, O God the Singer, I had sung
    amid their rages
    A long tale of Man and his deeds for
      good and ill.
But the old World knoweth — 't is the
    speech of all his ages —
    Man's wrong and ours: he knoweth and
      is still.
CHORUS — *Some Women.* Forth from
    thy father's home
    Thou camest, O heart of fire,
To the Dark Blue Rocks, to the clashing
    foam,
    To the seas of thy desire:

Till the Dark Blue Bar was crossed;
    And, lo, by an alien river
Standing, thy lover lost,
    Void-armed forever,

Forth yet again, O lowest
    Of landless women, a ranger
Of desolate ways, thou goest,
    From the walls of the stranger.

CHORUS — *Others.* And the great Oath
    waxeth weak;
    And Ruth, as a thing outstriven,
Is fled, fled, from the shores of the Greek,
    Away on the winds of heaven.

Dark is the house afar,
    Where an old king called thee daughter;
All that was once thy star
    In stormy water,

Dark: and, lo, in the nearer
    House that was sworn to love thee,
Another, queenlier, dearer,
    Is thronèd above thee.

       [*Enter* JASON *from the right.*]

JASON. Oft have I seen, in other days
    than these,
How a dark temper maketh maladies
No friend can heal. 'T was easy to have
    kept
Both land and home. It needed but to
    accept
Unstrivingly the pleasure of our lords.
But thou, for mere delight in stormy words,
Wilt lose all! . . . Now thy speech provokes
    not me.
Rail on. Of all mankind let Jason be
Most evil; none shall check thee. But for
    these
Dark threats cast out against the majesties
Of Corinth, count as veriest gain thy path
Of exile. I myself, when princely wrath
Was hot against thee, strove with all good
    will
To appease the wrath, and wished to keep
    thee still
Beside me. But thy mouth would never stay
From vanity, blaspheming night and day
Our masters. Therefore thou shalt fly the
    land.
    Yet, even so, I will not hold my hand
From succoring mine own people. Here
    am I
To help thee, woman, pondering heedfully
Thy new state. For I would not have thee
    flung
Provisionless away — aye, and the young
Children as well; nor lacking aught that
    will
Of mine can bring thee. Many a lesser ill

Hangs on the heels of exile. . . . Aye, and
    though
Thou hate me, dream not that my heart
    can know
Or fashion aught of angry will to thee.
    MEDEA. Evil, most evil! . . . since thou
    grantest me
That comfort, the worst weapon left me
    now
To smite a coward. . . . Thou comest to
    me, thou,
Mine enemy! (*Turning to the Chorus.*) Oh,
    say, how call ye this,
To face, and smile, the comrade whom his
    kiss
Betrayed? Scorn? Insult? Courage? None
    of these:
'T is but of all man's inward sicknesses
The vilest, that he knoweth not of shame,
Nor pity! Yet I praise him that he came . . .
To me it shall bring comfort, once to clear
My heart on thee, and thou shalt wince to
    hear.
    I will begin with that, 'twixt me and thee,
That first befell. I saved thee. I saved
    thee —
Let thine own Greeks be witness, every one
That sailed on Argo — saved thee, sent
    alone
To yoke with yokes the bulls of fiery breath,
And sow that Acre of the Lords of Death;
And mine own ancient Serpent, who did
    keep
The Golden Fleece, the eyes that knew not
    sleep,
And shining coils, him also did I smite
Dead for thy sake, and lifted up the light
That bade thee live. Myself, uncounseled,
Stole forth from father and from home, and
    fled
Where dark Iolcos under Pelion lies,
With thee — Oh, single-hearted more than
    wise!
I murdered Pelias, yea, in agony,
By his own daughters' hands, for sake of
    thee;
I swept their house like War. — And hast
    thou then
Accepted all — O evil yet again! —
And cast me off and taken thee for bride
Another? And with children at thy side!
One could forgive a childless man. But no:

I have borne thee children . . .
    Is sworn faith so low
And weak a thing? I understand it not.
Are the old gods dead? Are the old laws
    forgot,
And new laws made? Since not my passion-
    ing,
But thine own heart, doth cry thee for a
    thing
Forsworn.
      [*She catches sight of her own hand
      which she has thrown out to de-
      nounce him.*]
Poor, poor right hand of mine, whom he
Did cling to, and these knees, so cravingly,
We are unclean, thou and I; we have caught
    the stain
Of bad men's flesh . . . and dreamed our
    dreams in vain.
    Thou comest to befriend me? Give me,
    then,
Thy counsel. 'T is not that I dream again
For good from thee: but, questioned, thou
    wilt show
The viler. Say: now whither shall I go?
Back to my father? Him I did betray,
And all his land, when we two fled away.
To those poor Peliad maids? For them
    't were good
To take me in, who spilled their father's
    blood. . . .
Aye, so my whole life stands! There were
    at home
Who loved me well: to them I am become
A curse. And the first friends who sheltered
    me,
Whom most I should have spared, to pleas-
    ure thee
I have turned to foes. Oh, therefore hast
    thou laid
My crown upon me, blest of many a maid
In Hellas, ow I have won what all did
    crave,
Thee, the world-wondered lover and the
    brave;
Who this day looks and sees me banished,
    thrown
Away with these two babes, all, all, alone . . .
Oh, merry mocking when the lamps are
    red:
"Where go the bridegroom's babes to beg
    their bread

In exile, and the woman who gave all
To save him?''
  O great God, shall gold withal
Bear thy clear mark, to sift the base and
  fine,
And o'er man's living visage runs no sign
To show the lie within, ere all too late?
LEADER. Dire and beyond all healing is
  the hate
When hearts that loved are turned to
  enmity.
  JASON. In speech at least, meseemeth, I
  must be
Not evil; but, as some old pilot goes
Furled to his sail's last edge, when danger
  blows
Too fiery, run before the wind and swell,
Woman, of thy loud storms. — And thus
  I tell
My tale. Since thou wilt build so wondrous
  high
Thy deeds of service in my jeopardy,
To all my crew and quest I know but one
Savior, of gods or mortals one alone,
The Cyprian. Oh, thou hast both brain
  and wit,
Yet underneath . . . nay, all the tale of it
Were graceless telling; how sheer love, a fire
Of poison-shafts, compelled thee with de-
  sire
To save me. But enough. I will not score
That count too close. 'T was good help:
  and therefor
I give thee thanks, howe'er the help was
  wrought.
Howbeit, in my deliverance, thou hast got
Far more than given. A good Greek land
  hath been
Thy lasting home, not barbary. Thou hast
  seen
Our ordered life, and justice, and the long
Still grasp of law not changing with the
  strong
Man's pleasure. Then, all Hellas far and
  near
Hath learned thy wisdom, and in every ear
Thy fame is. Had thy days run by unseen
On that last edge of the world, where then
  had been
The story of great Medea? Thou and I . . .
What worth to us were treasures heapèd
  high

In rich kings' rooms; what worth a voice of
  gold
More sweet than ever rang from Orpheus
  old,
Unless our deeds have glory?
  Speak I so,
Touching the Quest I wrought, thyself did
  throw
The challenge down. Next for thy caviling
Of wrath at mine alliance with a king,
Here thou shalt see I both was wise, and free
From touch of passion, and a friend to thee
Most potent, and my children . . . Nay, be
  still!
  When first I stood in Corinth, clogged
  with ill
From many a desperate mischance, what
  bliss
Could I that day have dreamed of, like to
  this,
To wed with a king's daughter, I exiled
And beggared? Not — what makes thy
  passion wild —
From loathing of thy bed; not overfraught
With love for this new bride; not that I
  sought
To upbuild mine house with offspring: 't is
  enough,
What thou hast borne: I make no word
  thereof:
But, first and greatest, that we all might
  dwell
In a fair house and want not, knowing well
That poor men have no friends, but far
  and near
Shunning and silence. Next, I sought to
  rear
Our sons in nurture worthy of my race,
And, raising brethren to them, in one place
Join both my houses, and be all from now
Prince-like and happy. What more need
  hast thou
Of children? And for me, it serves my star
To link in strength the children that now
  are
With those that shall be.
  Have I counseled ill?
Not thine own self would say it, couldst
  thou still
One hour thy jealous flesh. — 'T is ever so!
Who looks for more in women? When the
  flow

Of love runs plain, why, all the world is
fair:
But, once there fall some ill chance any-
where
To baulk that thirst, down in swift hate
are trod
Men's dearest aims and noblest. Would to
God
We mortals by some other seed could raise
Our fruits, and no blind women block our
ways!
Then had there been no curse to wreck
mankind.

LEADER. Lord Jason, very subtly hast
thou twined
Thy speech: but yet, though all athwart
thy will
I speak, this is not well thou dost, but ill,
Betraying her who loved thee and was true.

MEDEA. Surely I have my thoughts, and
not a few
Have held me strange. To me it seemeth,
when
A crafty tongue is given to evil men
'T is like to wreck, not help them. Their
own brain
Tempts them with lies to dare and dare
again,
Till . . . no man hath enough of subtlety.
As thou — be not so seeming-fair to me
Nor deft of speech. One word will make
thee fall.
Wert thou not false, 't was thine to tell me
all,
And charge me help thy marriage path, as I
Did love thee; not befool me with a lie.

JASON. An easy task had that been!
Aye, and thou
A loving aid, who canst not, even now,
Still that loud heart that surges like the
tide!

MEDEA. That moved thee not. Thine
old barbarian bride,
The dog out of the east who loved thee sore,
She grew gray-haired, she served thy pride
no more.

JASON. Now understand for once! The
girl to me
Is nothing, in this web of sovereignty
I hold. I do but seek to save, even yet,
Thee: and for brethren to our sons beget
Young kings, to prosper all our lives again.

MEDEA. God shelter me from prosperous
days of pain,
And wealth that maketh wounds about my
heart.

JASON. Wilt change that prayer, and
choose a wiser part?
Pray not to hold true sense for pain, nor
rate
Thyself unhappy, being too fortunate.

MEDEA. Aye, mock me; thou hast where
to lay thine head,
But I go naked to mine exile.

JASON. Tread
Thine own path! Thou hast made it all
to be.

MEDEA. How? By seducing and forsak-
ing thee?

JASON. By those vile curses on the royal
halls
Let loose. . . .

MEDEA. On thy house also, as chance
falls,
I am a living curse.

JASON. Oh, peace! Enough
Of these vain wars: I will no more thereof.
If thou wilt take from all that I possess
Aid for these babes and thine own helpless-
ness
Of exile, speak thy bidding. Here I stand
Full-willed to succor thee with stintless
hand,
And send my signet to old friends that
dwell
On foreign shores, who will entreat thee
well.
Refuse, and thou shalt do a deed most
vain.
But cast thy rage away, and thou shalt
gain
Much, and lose little for thine anger's sake.

MEDEA. I will not seek thy friends. I
will not take
Thy givings. Give them not. Fruits of a
stem
Unholy bring no blessing after them.

JASON. Now God in heaven be witness,
all my heart
Is willing, in all ways, to do its part
For thee and for thy babes. But nothing
good
Can please thee. In sheer savageness of
mood

Thou drivest from thee every friend.
Wherefore
I warrant thee, thy pains shall be the more.
[*He goes slowly away.*]
MEDEA. Go: thou art weary for the new
delight
Thou wooest, so long tarrying out of sight
Of her sweet chamber. Go, fulfill thy pride,
O bridegroom! For it may be, such a bride
Shall wait thee, — yea, God heareth me in
this —
As thine own heart shall sicken ere it kiss.
CHORUS. Alas, the Love that falleth like
a flood,
Strong-winged and transitory:
Why praise ye him? What beareth he of good
To man, or glory?
Yet Love there is that moves in gentleness,
Heart-filling, sweetest of all powers that
bless.
Loose not on me, O Holder of man's heart,
Thy golden quiver,
Nor steep in poison of desire the dart
That heals not ever.

The pent hate of the word that cavileth,
The strife that hath no fill;
Where once was fondness; and the mad
heart's breath
For strange love panting still:
O Cyprian, cast me not on these; but sift.
Keen-eyed, of love the good and evil gift,
Make Innocence my friend, God's fairest
star,
Yea, and abate not
The rare sweet beat of bosoms without war,
That love, and hate not.
CHORUS — *Others.* Home of my heart,
land of my own,
Cast me not, nay, for pity,
Out on my ways, helpless, alone,
Where the feet fail in the mire and stone,
A woman without a city.
Ah, not that! Better the end:
The green grave cover me rather,
If a break must come in the days I know,
And the skies be changed and the earth
below;
For the weariest road that man may wend
Is forth from the home of his father.

Lo, we have seen: 't is not a song

Sung, nor learned of another.
For whom hast thou in thy direst wrong
For comfort? Never a city strong
To hide thee, never a brother.
Ah, but the man — cursèd be he,
Cursèd beyond recover,
Who openeth, shattering, seal by seal,
A friend's clean heart, then turns his heel,
Deaf unto love: never in me
Friend shall he know nor lover.
[*While* MEDEA *is waiting downcast,
seated upon her doorstep, there
passes from the left a traveler with
followers. As he catches sight of*
MEDEA, *he stops.*]
ÆGEUS. Have joy, Medea! 'T is the
homeliest
Word that old friends can greet with, and
the best.
MEDEA [*looking up, surprised*]. Oh, joy
on thee, too, Ægeus, gentle king
Of Athens! — But whence com'st thou
journeying?
ÆGEUS. From Delphi now and the old
encaverned stair. . . .
MEDEA. Where Earth's heart speaks in
song? What mad'st thou there?
ÆGEUS. Prayed heaven for children —
the same search alway.
MEDEA. Children? Ah God! Art child-
less to this day?
ÆGEUS. So God hath willed. Childless
and desolate.
MEDEA. What word did Phœbus speak,
to change thy fate?
ÆGEUS. Riddles, too hard for mortal
man to read.
MEDEA. Which I may hear?
ÆGEUS. Assuredly: they need
A rarer wit.
MEDEA. How said he?
ÆGEUS. Not to spill
Life's wine, nor seek for more. . . .
MEDEA. Until?
ÆGEUS. Until
I tread the hearth-stone of my sires of yore.
MEDEA. And what should bring thee
here, by Creon's shore?
ÆGEUS. One Pittheus know'st thou,
high lord of Trozen?
MEDEA. Aye, Pelops' son, a man most
pure of sin.

ÆGEUS. Him I would ask, touching Apollo's will.

MEDEA. Much use in God's ways hath he, and much skill.

ÆGEUS. And, long years back he was my battle-friend,
The truest e'er man had.

MEDEA. Well, may God send
Good hap to thee, and grant all thy desire.

ÆGEUS. But thou . . .? Thy frame is wasted, and the fire
Dead in thine eyes.

MEDEA. Ægeus, my husband is
The falsest man in the world.

ÆGEUS. What word is this?
Say clearly what thus makes thy visage dim?

MEDEA. He is false to me, who never injured him.

ÆGEUS. What hath he done? Show all, that I may see.

MEDEA. Ta'en him a wife; a wife, set over me
To rule his house!

ÆGEUS. He hath not dared to do,
Jason, a thing so shameful?

MEDEA. Aye, 't is true:
And those he loved of yore have no place now.

ÆGEUS. Some passion sweepeth him? Or is it thou
He turns from?

MEDEA. Passion, passion to betray
His dearest!

ÆGEUS. Shame be his, so fallen away
From honor!

MEDEA. Passion to be near a throne,
A king's heir!

ÆGEUS. How, who gives the bride? Say on.

MEDEA. Creon, who o'er all Corinth standeth chief.

ÆGEUS. Woman, thou hast indeed much cause for grief.

MEDEA. 'T is ruin. — And they have cast me out as well.

ÆGEUS. Who? 'T is a new wrong this, and terrible.

MEDEA. Creon the king, from every land and shore. . . .

ÆGEUS. And Jason suffers him? Oh, 't is too sore!

MEDEA. He loveth to bear bravely ills like these!
But, Ægeus, by thy beard, oh, by thy knees,
I pray thee, and I give me for thine own,
Thy suppliant, pity me! Oh, pity one
So miserable. Thou never wilt stand there
And see me cast out friendless to despair.
Give me a home in Athens . . . by the fire
Of thine own hearth! Oh, so may thy desire
Of children be fulfilled of God, and thou
Die happy! . . . Thou canst know not; even now
Thy prize is won! I, I will make of thee
A childless man no more. The seed shall be,
I swear it, sown. Such magic herbs I know.

ÆGEUS. Woman, indeed my heart goes forth to show
This help to thee, first for religion's sake,
Then for thy promised hope, to heal my ache
Of childlessness. 'T is this hath made mine whole
Life as a shadow, and starved out my soul.
But thus it stands with me. Once make thy way
To Attic earth, I, as in law I may,
Will keep thee and befriend. But in this land,
Where Creon rules, I may not raise my hand
To shelter thee. Move of thine own essay
To seek my house, there thou shalt alway stay,
Inviolate, never to be seized again.
But come thyself from Corinth. I would fain
Even in foreign eyes be alway just.

MEDEA. 'T is well. Give me an oath wherein to trust
And all that man could ask thou hast granted me.

ÆGEUS. Dost trust me not? Or what thing troubleth thee?

MEDEA. I trust thee. But so many, far and near,
Do hate me — all King Pelias' house, and here
Creon. Once bound by oaths and sanctities
Thou canst not yield me up for such as these
To drag from Athens. But a spoken word,

No more, to bind thee, which no God hath
    heard. . . .
The embassies, methinks, would come and
    go:
They all are friends to thee. . . . Ah me, I
    know
Thou wilt not list to me! So weak am I,
And they full-filled with gold and majesty.
    ÆGEUS. Methinks 't is a far foresight,
    this thine oath.
Still, if thou so wilt have it, nothing loath
Am I to serve thee. Mine own hand is so
The stronger, if I have this plea to show
Thy persecutors: and for thee withal
The bond more sure. — On what god shall
    I call?
    MEDEA. Swear by the Earth thou tread-
    est, by the Sun,
Sire of my sires, and all the gods as one. . . .
    ÆGEUS. To do what thing or not do?
    Make all plain.
    MEDEA. Never thyself to cast me out
    again.
Nor let another, whatsoe'er his plea,
Take me, while thou yet livest and art free.
    ÆGEUS. Never: so hear me, Earth, and
    the great star
Of daylight, and all other gods that are!
    MEDEA. 'T is well: and if thou falter
    from thy vow . . . ?
    ÆGEUS. God's judgment on the godless
    break my brow!
    MEDEA. Go! Go thy ways rejoicing. —
    All is bright
And clear before me. Go: and ere the night
Myself will follow, when the deed is done
I purpose, and the end I thirst for won.
                    [ÆGEUS and his train depart.]
    CHORUS. Farewell: and Maia's guiding
    Son
Back lead thee to thy hearth and fire,
Ægeus; and all the long desire
That wasteth thee, at last be won:
Our eyes have seen thee as thou art,
A gentle and a righteous heart.
    MEDEA. God, and God's Justice, and ye
    blinding Skies!
At last the victory dawneth! Yea, mine
    eyes
See, and my foot is on the mountain's brow.
Mine enemies! Mine enemies, oh, now
Atonement cometh! Here at my worst hour

A friend is found, a very port of power
To save my shipwreck. Here will I make
    fast
Mine anchor, and escape them at the last
In Athens' wallèd hill. — But ere the end
'T is meet I show thee all my counsel,
    friend:
Take it, no tale to make men laugh withal!
    Straightway to Jason I will send some
    thrall
To entreat him to my presence. Comes he
    here,
Then with soft reasons will I feed his ear,
How *his* will now is *my* will, how all things
Are well, touching this marriage-bed of
    kings
For which I am betrayed — all wise and
    rare
And profitable! Yet will I make one prayer,
That my two children be no more exiled
But stay. . . . Oh, not that I would leave a
    child
Here upon angry shores till those have
    laughed
Who hate me: 't is that I will slay by craft
The king's daughter. With gifts they shall
    be sent,
Gifts to the bride to spare their banishment
Fine robings and a carcanet of gold.
Which raiment let her once but take, and
    fold
About her, a foul death that girl shall die
And all who touch her in her agony.
Such poison shall they drink, my robe and
    wreath!
Howbeit, of that no more. I gnash my
    teeth
Thinking on what a path my feet must
    tread
Thereafter. I shall lay those children
    dead —
Mine, whom no hand shall steal from me
    away!
Then, leaving Jason childless, and the day
As night above him, I will go my road
To exile, flying, flying from the blood
Of these my best-beloved, and having
    wrought
All horror, so but one thing reach me not,
The laugh of them that hate us.
    Let it come!
What profits life to me? I have no home,

No country now, nor shield from any wrong.
That was my evil hour, when down the
   long
Halls of my father out I stole, my will
Chained by a Greek man's voice, who still,
   oh, still,
If God yet live, shall all requited be.
For never child of mine shall Jason see
Hereafter living, never child beget
From his new bride, who this day, desolate
Even as she made me desolate, shall die
Shrieking amid my poisons. . . . Names
   have I
Among your folk? One light? On'o weak
   of hand?
An eastern dreamer? — Nay, but with the
   brand
Of strange suns burnt, my hate, by God
   above,
A perilous thing, and passing sweet my
   love!
For these it is that make life glorious.
   LEADER. Since thou hast bared thy fell
      intent to us,
I, loving thee, and helping in their need
Man's laws, adjure thee, dream not of this
   deed!
   MEDEA. There is no other way. — I par-
      don thee
Thy littleness, who art not wronged like
   me.
   LEADER. Thou canst not kill the fruit
      thy body bore!
   MEDEA. Yes: if the man I hate be pained
      the more.
   LEADER. And thou made miserable,
      most miserable?
   MEDEA. Oh, let it come! All words 'of
      good or ill
Are wasted now.
      [*She claps her hands: the Nurse
      comes out from the house.*]
'Ho, woman; get thee gone
And lead lord Jason hither. . . . There is
   none
Like thee, to work me these high services.
But speak no word of what my purpose is,
As thou art faithful, thou, and bold to try
All succors, and a woman even as I!
                      [*The Nurse departs.*]
   CHORUS. The sons of Erechtheus, the
      olden,

Whom high gods planted of yore
In an old land of heaven upholden,
A proud land untrodden of war:
They are hungered, and, lo, their desire
With wisdom is fed as with meat:
In their skies is a shining of fire,
A joy in the fall of their feet:
And thither, with manifold dowers,
From the North, from the hills, from the
   morn,
The Muses did gather their powers,
That a child of the Nine should be born;
And Harmony, sown as the flowers,
Grew gold in the acres of corn.

And Cephisus, the fair-flowing river —
The Cyprian dipping her hand
Hath drawn of his dew, and the shiver
Of her touch is as joy in the land.
For her breathing in fragrance is written,
And in music her path as she goes,
And the cloud of her hair, it is litten
With stars of the wind-woven rose.
So fareth she ever and ever,
And forth of her bosom is blown,
As dews on the winds of the river,
An hunger of passions unknown,
Strong Loves of all godlike endeavor,
Whom Wisdom shall throne on her
   throne.
   CHORUS — *Some Women.* But Cephisus
      the fair-flowing,
Will he bear thee on his shore?
   Shall the land that succors all, succor
      thee,
Who art foul among thy kind,
With the tears of children blind?
Dost thou see the red gash growing,
   Thine own burden dost thou see?
      Every side, every way,
   Lo, we kneel to thee and pray:
By thy knees, by thy soul, O woman
   wild!
One at least thou canst not slay,
      Not thy child!
   CHORUS — *Others.* Hast thou ice that
      thou shalt bind it
To thy breast, and make thee dead
   To thy children, to thine own spirit's
      pain?
When the hand knows what it dares,
When thine eyes look into theirs,

Shalt thou keep by tears unblinded
   Thy dividing of the slain?
      These be deeds not for thee:
      These be things that cannot be!
      Thy babes — though thine hardi-
         hood be fell,
   When they cling about thy knee,
      'T will be well!

               [*Enter* JASON.]

   JASON. I answer to thy call. Though
      full of hate
Thou be, I yet will not so far abate
My kindness for thee, nor refuse mine ear.
Say in what new desire thou hast called me
   here.
   MEDEA. Jason, I pray thee, for my
      words but now
Spoken, forgive me. My bad moods. . . .
   Oh, thou
At least wilt strive to bear with them!
   There be
Many old deeds of love 'twixt me and thee.
Lo, I have reasoned with myself apart
And chidden: "Why must I be mad, O
   heart
Of mine: and raging against one whose
   word
Is wisdom: making me a thing abhorred
To them that rule the land, and to mine own
Husband, who doth but that which, being
   done,
Will help us all — to wed a queen, and get
Young kings for brethren to my sons? And
   yet
I rage alone, and cannot quit my rage —
What aileth me? — when God sends har-
   borage
So simple? Have I not my children? Know
I not we are but exiles, and must go
Beggared and friendless else?" Thought
   upon thought
So pressed me, till I knew myself full-
   fraught
With bitterness of heart and blinded eyes.
So now — I give thee thanks: and hold
   thee wise
To have caught this anchor for our aid.
   The fool
Was I; who should have been thy friend,
   thy tool;
Gone wooing with thee, stood at thy bedside

Serving, and welcomed duteously thy
   bride.
But, as we are, we are — I will not say
Mere evil — women! Why must thou to-
   day
Turn strange, and make thee like some evil
   thing,
Childish, to meet my childish passioning?
See, I surrender: and confess that then
I had bad thoughts, but now have turned
   again
And found my wiser mind.
                    [*She claps her hands.*]
   Ho, children! Run
Quickly! Come hither, out into the sun,
      [*The Children come from the house,
      followed by their Attendant.*]
And greet your father. Welcome him with
   us,
And throw quite, quite away, as mother
   does,
Your anger against one so dear. Our peace
Is made, and all the old bad war shall cease
Forever. — Go, and take his hand. . . .
      [*As the Children go to* JASON, *she
      suddenly bursts into tears. The
      Children quickly return to her;
      she recovers herself, smiling amid
      her tears.*]
   Ah me,
I am full of hidden horrors! . . . Shall it be
A long time more, my children, that ye live
To reach to me those dear, dear arms? . . .
   Forgive!
I am so ready with my tears to-day,
And full of dread. . . . I sought to smooth
   away
The long strife with your father, and, lo,
   now
I have all drowned with tears this little
   brow!   [*She wipes the child's face.*]
   LEADER. O'er mine eyes too there steal-
      eth a pale tear:
Let the evil rest, O God, let it rest here!
   JASON. Woman, indeed I praise thee
      now, nor say
Ill of thine other hour. 'T is nature's way,
A woman needs must stir herself to wrath,
When work of marriage by so strange a
   path
Crosseth her lord. But thou, thine heart
   doth wend

The happier road. Thou hast seen, ere
    quite the end,
What choice must needs be stronger: which
    to do
Shows a wise-minded woman. . . . And for
    you,
Children; your father never has forgot
Your needs. If God but help him, he hath
    wrought
A strong deliverance for your weakness.
    Yea,
I think you, with your brethren, yet one
    day
Shall be the mightiest voices in this land.
Do you grow tall and strong. Your father's
    hand
Guideth all else, and whatso power divine
Hath alway helped him. . . . Ah, may it be
    mine
To see you yet in manhood, stern of brow,
Strong-armed, set high o'er those that hate
    me. . . .
    How?
Woman, thy face is turned. Thy cheek is
    swept
With pallor of strange tears. Dost not
    accept
Gladly and of good will my benisons?
    MEDEA. 'T is nothing. Thinking of
    these little ones. . . .
    JASON. Take heart, then. I will guard
    them from all ill.
    MEDEA. I do take heart. Thy word I
    never will
Mistrust. Alas, a woman's bosom bears
But woman's courage, a thing born for
    tears.
    JASON. What ails thee? — All too sore
    thou weepest there.
    MEDEA. I was their mother! When I
    heard thy prayer
Of long life for them, there swept over me
A horror, wondering how these things shall
    be.
But for the matter of my need that thou
Should speak with me, part I have said,
    and now
Will finish. — Seeing it is the king's behest
To cast me out from Corinth . . . aye, and
    best,
Far best, for me — I know it — not to
    stay

Longer to trouble thee and those who sway
The realm, being held to all their house a
    foe. . . .
Behold, I spread my sails, and meekly go
To exile. But our children. . . . Could this
    land
Be still their home awhile: could thine own
    hand
But guide their boyhood. . . . Seek the
    king, and pray
His pity, that he bid thy children stay!
    JASON. He is hard to move. Yet surely
    't were well done.
    MEDEA. Bid *her* — for thy sake, for a
    daughter's boon. . . .
    JASON. Well thought! Her I can fashion
    to my mind.
    MEDEA. Surely. She is a woman like her
    kind. . . .
Yet I will aid thee in thy labor; I
Will send her gifts, the fairest gifts that lie
In the hands of men, things of the days of
    old,
Fine robings and a carcanet of gold,
By the boys' hands. — Go, quick, some
    handmaiden,
And fetch the raiment.
        [*A handmaid goes into the house.*]
    Ah, her cup shall then
Be filled indeed! what more should woman
    crave,
Being wed with thee, the bravest of the
    brave,
And girt with raiment which of old the
    sire
Of all my house, the Sun, gave, steeped in
    fire,
To his own fiery race?
        [*The handmaid has returned bear-
        ing the gifts.*]
    Come, children, lift
With heed these caskets. Bear them as
    your gift
To her, being bride and princess and of
    right
Blessed! — I think she will not hold them
    light.
    JASON. Fond woman, why wilt empty
    thus thine hand
Of treasure? Doth King Creon's castle
    stand
In stint of raiment, or in stint of gold?

Keep these, and make no gift. For if she
    hold
Jason of any worth at all, I swear
Chattels like these will not weigh more
    with her.
    MEDEA. Ah, chide me not! 'T is written,
    gifts persuade
The gods in heaven; and gold is stronger
    made
Than words innumerable to bend men's
    ways.
Fortune is hers. God maketh great her
    days:
Young and a crownèd queen! And banish-
    ment   .
For those two babes. . . . I would not gold
    were spent,
But life's blood, ere that come.
    My children, go
Forth into those rich halls, and, bowing
    low,
Beseech your father's bride, whom I obey,
Ye be not, of her mercy, cast away
Exiled: and give the caskets — above all
Mark this! — to none but her, to hold
    withal
And keep. . . . Go quick! And let your
    mother know
Soon the good tiding that she longs for. . . .
    Go!
        [She goes quickly into the house.
        JASON and the Children with
        their Attendant depart.]
    CHORUS. Now I have no hope more of
    the children's living;
No hope more. They are gone forth unto
    death.
The bride, she taketh the poison of their
    giving:
    She taketh the bounden gold and open-
    eth;
And the crown, the crown, she lifteth about
    her brow,
Where the light brown curls are clustering.
    No hope now!

O sweet and cloudy gleam of the garments
    golden!
    The robe, it hath clasped her breast and
    the crown her head.
Then, then, she decketh the bride, as a
—-. . bride, of olden

Story, that goeth pale to the kiss of the
    dead.
For the ring hath closed, and the portion
    of death is there;
And she flieth not, but perisheth unaware.
    CHORUS — Some Women. O bridegroom,
    bridegroom of the kiss so cold,
Art thou wed with princes, art thou girt
    with gold,
    Who know'st not, suing
    For thy child's undoing,
And, on her thou lovest, for a doom un-
    told?
How art thou fallen from thy place of old!
    CHORUS — Others. O Mother, mother,
    what hast thou to reap,
When the harvest cometh, between wake
    and sleep?
    For a heart unslaken,
    For a troth forsaken,
Lo, babes that call thee from a bloody deep:
And thy love returns not. Get thee forth
    and weep!

[Enter the Attendant with the two Children;
    MEDEA comes out from the house.]

    ATTENDANT. Mistress, these children
    from their banishment
Are spared. The royal bride hath mildly
    bent
Her hand to accept thy gifts, and all is now
Peace for the children. — Ha, why standest
    thou
Confounded, when good fortune draweth
    near?
    MEDEA. Ah, God!
    ATTENDANT. This chimes not with the
    news I bear.
    MEDEA. O God, have mercy!
    ATTENDANT. Is some word of wrath
Here hidden that I knew not of? And hath
My hope to give thee joy so cheated me?
    MEDEA. Thou givest what thou givest:
    I blame not thee.
    ATTENDANT. Thy brows are all o'ercast:
    thine eyes are filled. . . .
    MEDEA. For bitter need, old man! The
    gods have willed,
And mine own evil mind, that this should
    come.
    ATTENDANT. Take heart! Thy sons one
    day will bring thee home.

MEDEA. Home? . . . I have others to send home. Woe's me!

ATTENDANT. Be patient. Many a mother before thee
Hath parted from her children. We poor things
Of men must needs endure what fortune brings.

MEDEA. I will endure. — Go thou within, and lay
All ready that my sons may need to-day.

[*The Attendant goes into the house.*]

O children, children mine: and you have found
A land and home, where, leaving me discrowned
And desolate, forever you will stay,
Motherless children! And I go my way
To other lands, an exile, ere you bring
Your fruits home, ere I see you prospering
Or know your brides, or deck the bridal bed,
All flowers, and lift your torches overhead.
     Oh, cursèd be mine own hard heart! 'T was all
In vain, then, that I reared you up, so tall
And fair; in vain I bore you, and was torn
With those long pitiless pains, when you were born.
Ah, wondrous hopes my poor heart had in you,
How you would tend me in mine age, and do
The shroud about me with your own dear hands,
When I lay cold, blessèd in all the lands
That knew us. And that gentle thought is dead!
You go, and I live on, to eat the bread
Of long years, to myself most full of pain.
And never your dear eyes, never again,
Shall see your mother, far away being thrown
To other shapes of life. . . . My babes, my own,
Why gaze ye so? — What is it that ye see?
And laugh with that last laughter? . . .
     Woe is me,
What shall I do?
     Women, my strength is gone,
Gone like a dream, since once I looked upon
Those shining faces. . . . I can do it not.
Good-bye to all the thoughts that burned so hot

Aforetime! I will take and hide them far,
Far, from men's eyes. Why should I seek a war
So blind: by these babes' wounds to sting again
Their father's heart, and win myself a pain
Twice deeper? Never, never! I forget
Henceforward all I labored for.
     And yet,
What is it with me? Would I be a thing
Mocked at, and leave mine enemies to sting
Unsmitten? It must be. O coward heart,
Ever to harbor such soft words! — Depart
Out of my sight, ye twain.
     [*The Children go in.*]
And they whose eyes
Shall hold it sin to share my sacrifice,
On their heads be it! My hand shall swerve not now.

     Ah, Ah, thou Wrath within me! Do not thou,
Do not. . . . Down, down, thou tortured thing, and spare
My children! They will dwell with us, aye, there
Far off, and give thee peace.
     Too late, too late!
By all Hell's living agonies of hate,
They shall not take my little ones alive
To make their mock with! Howsoe'er I strive
The thing is doomed; it shall not escape now
From being. Aye, the crown is on the brow,
And the robe girt, and in the robe that high
Queen dying.
     I know all. Yet . . . seeing that I
Must go so long a journey, and these twain
A longer yet and darker, I would fain
Speak with them, ere I go.
     [*A handmaid brings the Children out again.*]
     Come, children; stand
A little from me. There. Reach out your hand,
Your right hand — so — to mother: and good-bye!
     [*She has kept them hitherto at arm's-length: but at the touch of their hands, her resolution breaks down, and she gathers them passionately into her arms.*]

Oh, darling hand! Oh, darling mouth, and
   eye,
And royal mien, and bright brave faces
   clear,
May you be blessèd, but not here! What
   here
Was yours, your father stole. . . . Ah God,
   the glow
Of cheek on cheek, the tender touch; and
   oh,
Sweet scent of childhood. . . . Go! Go! . . .
   Am I blind? . . .
Mine eyes can see not, when I look to
   find
Their places. I am broken by the wings
Of evil. . . . Yea, I know to what bad
   things
I go, but louder than all thought doth cry
Anger, which maketh man's worst misery.
   [*She follows the Children into the
      house.*]
CHORUS. My thoughts have roamed a
   cloudy land,
And heard a fierier music fall
Than woman's heart should stir withal:
And yet some Muse majestical,
Unknown, hath hold of woman's hand,
Seeking for Wisdom — not in all:
A feeble seed, a scattered band,
Thou yet shalt find in lonely places,
Not dead amongst us, nor our faces
Turned alway from the Muses' call.

And thus my thought would speak: that
   she
Who ne'er hath borne a child nor known
Is nearer to felicity:
Unlit she goeth and alone,
With little understanding what
A child's touch means of joy or woe,
And many toils she beareth not.

But they within whose garden fair
That gentle plant hath blown, they go
Deep-written all their days with care —
To rear the children, to make fast
Their hold, to win them wealth; and
   then
Much darkness, if the seed at last
Bear fruit in good or evil men!
And one thing at the end of all
Abideth, that which all men dread:

The wealth is won, the limbs are bred
To manhood, and the heart withal
Honest: and, lo, where Fortune smiled,
Some change, and what hath fallen? Hark!
'T is death slow winging to the dark,
And in his arms what was thy child.

What therefore doth it bring of gain
To man, whose cup stood full before,
That God should send this one thing more
Of hunger and of dread, a door
Set wide to every wind of pain?
   [MEDEA *comes out alone from the
      house.*]
MEDEA. Friends, this long hour I wait
   on Fortune's eyes,
And strain my senses in a hot surmise
What passeth on that hill. — Ha! even now
There comes . . . 't is one of Jason's men,
   I trow.
His wild-perturbèd breath doth warrant
   me
The tidings of some strange calamity.

   [*Enter Messenger.*]

MESSENGER. O dire and ghastly deed!
   Get thee away,
Medea! Fly! Nor let behind thee stay
One chariot's wing, one keel that sweeps
   the seas. . . .
MEDEA. And what hath chanced, to
   cause such flights as these?
MESSENGER. The maiden princess lieth
   — and her sire,
The king — both murdered by thy poison-
   fire.
MEDEA. Most happy tiding! Which thy
   name prefers
Henceforth among my friends and well-
   wishers.
MESSENGER. What say'st thou? Wom-
   an, is thy mind within
Clear, and not raving? Thou art found in
   sin
Most bloody wrought against the king's
   high head,
And laughest at the tale, and hast no dread?
MEDEA. I have words also that could
   answer well
Thy word. But take thine ease, good friend,
   and tell,
How died they? Hath it been a very foul

Death, prithee? That were comfort to my
soul.
MESSENGER. When thy two children,
hand in hand entwined,
Came with their father, and passed on to
find
The new-made bridal rooms, oh, we were
glad,
We thralls, who ever loved thee well, and
had
Grief in thy grief. And straight there
passed a word
From ear to ear, that thou and thy false
lord
Had poured peace offering upon wrath
foregone.
A right glad welcome gave we them, and
one
Kissed the small hands, and one the shining
hair:
Myself, for very joy, I followed where
The women's rooms are. There our mis-
tress . . . she
Whom now we name so . . . thinking not to
see
Thy little pair, with glad and eager brow
Sate waiting Jason. Then she saw, and
slow
Shrouded her eyes, and backward turned
again,
Sick that thy children should come near
her. Then
Thy husband quick went forward, to en-
treat
The young maid's fitful wrath. "Thou wilt
not meet
Love's coming with unkindness? Nay,
refrain
Thy suddenness, and turn thy face again,
Holding as friends all that to me are dear,
Thine husband. And accept these robes
they bear
As gifts: and beg thy father to unmake
His doom of exile on them — for my sake."
When once she saw the raiment, she could
still
Her joy no more, but gave him all his will.
And almost ere the father and the two
Children were gone from out the room, she
drew
The flowerèd garments forth, and sate her
down

To her arraying: bound the golden crown
Through her long curls, and in a mirror
fair
Arranged their separate clusters, smiling
there
At the dead self that faced her. Then
aside
She pushed her seat, and paced those cham-
bers wide
Alone, her white foot poising delicately —
So passing joyful in those gifts was she! —
And many a time would pause, straight-
limbed, and wheel
Her head to watch the long fold to her heel
Sweeping. And then came something
strange. Her cheek
Seemed pale, and back with crooked steps
and weak
Groping of arms she walked, and scarcely
found
Her old seat, that she fell not to the
ground.
Among the handmaids was a woman old
And gray, who deemed, I think, that Pan
had hold
Upon her, or some spirit, and raised a keen
Awakening shout; till through her lips was
seen
A white foam crawling, and her eyeballs
back
Twisted, and all her face dead pale for lack
Of life: and while that old dame called, the
cry
Turned strangely to its opposite, to die
Sobbing. Oh, swiftly then one woman flew
To seek her father's rooms, one for the new
Bridegroom, to tell the tale. And all the
place
Was loud with hurrying feet.
So long a space
As a swift walker on a measured way
Would pace a furlong's course in, there she
lay
Speechless, with veilèd lids. Then wide her
eyes
She oped, and wildly, as she strove to rise,
Shrieked: for two diverse waves upon her
rolled
Of stabbing death. The carcanet of gold
That gripped her brow was molten in a
dire
And wondrous river of devouring fire.

And those fine robes, the gift thy children
    gave —
God's mercy! — everywhere did lap and
    lave
The delicate flesh; till up she sprang, and
    fled,
A fiery pillar, shaking locks and head
This way and that, seeking to cast the
    crown
Somewhere away. But like a thing nailed
    down
The burning gold held fast the anadem,
And through her locks, the more she scat-
    tered them,
Came fire the fiercer, till to earth she fell
A thing — save to her sire — scarce name-
    able,
And strove no more. That cheek of royal
    mien,
Where was it — or the place where eyes
    had been?
Only from crown and temples came faint
    blood
Shot through with fire. The very flesh, it
    stood
Out from the bones, as from a wounded
    pine
The gum starts, where those gnawing poi-
    sons fine
Bit in the dark — a ghastly sight! And
    touch
The dead we durst not. We had seen too
    much.
    But that poor father, knowing not, had
    sped,
Swift to his daughter's room, and there the
    dead
Lay at his feet. He knelt, and groaning
    low,
Folded her in his arms, and kissed her:
    "Oh,
Unhappy child, what thing unnatural hath
So hideously undone thee? Or what wrath
Of gods, to make this old gray sepulcher
Childless of thee? Would God but lay me
    there
To die with thee, my daughter!" So he
    cried.
But after, when he stayed from tears, and
    tried
To uplift his old bent frame, lo, in the folds
Of those fine robes it held, as ivy holds

Strangling among young laurel boughs.
    Oh, then
A ghastly struggle came! Again, again,
Up on his knee he writhed; but that dead
    breast
Clung still to his: till, wild, like one pos-
    sessed,
He dragged himself half free; and, lo, the
    live
Flesh parted; and he laid him down to
    strive
No more with death, but perish; for the
    deep
Had risen above his soul. And there they
    sleep,
At last, the old proud father and the bride,
Even as his tears had craved it, side by
    side.
    For thee — Oh, no word more! Thyself
    will know
How best to baffle vengeance. . . . Long ago
I looked upon man's days, and found a
    gray
Shadow. And this thing more I surely say,
That those of all men who are counted wise,
Strong wits, devisers of great policies,
Do pay the bitterest toll. Since life began,
Hath there in God's eye stood one happy
    man?
Fair days roll on, and bear more gifts or less
Of fortune, but to no man happiness.
                        [Exit Messenger.]
    CHORUS — Some Women. Wrath upon
            wrath, meseems, this day shall fall
From God on Jason! He hath earned it all.
    CHORUS — Other Women. O miserable
            maiden, all my heart
Is torn for thee, so sudden to depart
From thy king's chambers and the light
    above
To darkness, all for sake of Jason's love!
    MEDEA. Women, my mind is clear. I go
            to slay
My children with all speed, and then, away
From hence; not wait yet longer till they
    stand
Beneath another and an angrier hand
To die. Yea, howsoe'er I shield them, die
They must. And, seeing that they must,
    't is I
Shall slay them, I their mother, touched of
    none

Beside. Oh, up, and get thine armor on,
My heart! Why longer tarry we to win
Our crown of dire inevitable sin?
Take up thy sword, O poor right hand of
   mine,
Thy sword: then onward to the thin-drawn
   line
Where life turns agony. Let there be naught
Of softness now: and keep thee from that
   thought,
"Born of thy flesh," "thine own belovèd."
   Now,
For one brief day, forget thy children: thou
Shalt weep hereafter. Though thou slay
   them, yet
Sweet were they. . . . I am sore unfortu-
   nate.   [She goes into the house.]
   CHORUS — Some Women. O Earth, our
     mother; and thou
     All-seer, arrowy crown
   Of Sunlight, manward now
     Look down, oh, look down!
   Look upon one accurst,
     Ere yet in blood she twine
     Red hands — blood that is thine!
   O Sun, save her first!
   She is thy daughter still,
     Of thine own golden line;
   Save her! Or shall man spill
     The life divine?
   Give peace, O Fire that diest not! Send
     thy spell
   To stay her yet, to lift her afar, afar —
   A torture-changèd spirit, a voice of Hell
   Wrought of old wrongs and war!
   CHORUS — Others. Alas for the mother's
     pain
     Wasted! Alas the dear
     Life that was born in vain!
     Woman, what mak'st thou here,
     Thou from beyond the Gate
     Where dim Symplegades
     Clash in the dark blue seas,
   The shores where death doth wait?
   Why hast thou taken on thee,
     To make us desolate,
   This anger of misery
     And guilt of hate?
For fierce are the smitings back of blood
   once shed
   Where love hath been: God's wrath upon
     them that kill,

And an anguished earth, and the wonder of
   the dead
   Haunting as music still. . . .
       [A cry is heard within.]
   A WOMAN. Hark! Did ye hear? Heard
     ye the children's cry?
   ANOTHER. O miserable woman! O ab-
     horred!
   A CHILD [within]. What shall I do?
     What is it? Keep me fast
From mother!
   THE OTHER CHILD. I know nothing.
     Brother! Oh,
I think she means to kill us.
   A WOMAN. Let me go!
I will — Help! Help! — and save them at
   the last.
   A CHILD. Yes, in God's name! Help
     quickly ere we die!
   THE OTHER CHILD. She has almost
     caught me now. She has a sword.
     [Many of the women are now beat-
     ing at the barred door to get in.
     Others are standing apart.]
   WOMEN [at the door]. Thou stone, thou
     thing of iron! Wilt verily
Spill with thine hand that life, the vintage
   stored
Of thine own agony?
   THE OTHER WOMEN. A mother slew
     her babes in days of yore,
   One, only one, from dawn to eventide,
     Ino, god-maddened, whom the Queen
     of Heaven
     Set frenzied, flying to the dark: and
     she
     Cast her for sorrow to the wide salt
     sea,
     Forth from those rooms of murder
     unforgiven,
Wild-footed from a white crag of the shore,
And clasping still her children twain, she
   died.

O Love of Woman, charged with sorrow sore,
   What hast thou wrought upon us? What
     beside
     Resteth to tremble for?

[Enter hurriedly JASON and Attendants.]

   JASON. Ye women by this doorway clus-
     tering

Speak, is the doer of the ghastly thing
Yet here, or fled? What hopeth she of
    flight?
Shall the deep yawn to shield her? Shall
    the height
Send wings, and hide her in the vaulted
    sky
To work red murder on her lords, and
    fly
Unrecompensed? But let her go! My care
Is but to save my children, not for her.
Let them she wronged requite her as they
    may.
I care not. 'T is my sons I must some
    way
Save, ere the kinsmen of the dead can
    win
From them the payment of their mother's
    sin.
    LEADER. Unhappy man, indeed thou
        knowest not
What dark place thou art come to! Else,
    God wot,
Jason, no word like these could fall from
    thee.
    JASON. What is it? — Ha! The woman
        would kill me?
    LEADER. Thy sons are dead, slain by
        their mother's hand.
    JASON. How? Not the children. . . . I
        scarce understand. . . .
O God, thou hast broken me!
    LEADER. Think of those twain
As things once fair, that ne'er shall bloom
    again.
    JASON. Where did she murder them? In
        that old room?
    LEADER. Open, and thou shalt see thy
        children's doom.
    JASON. Ho, thralls! Unloose me yonder
        bars! Make more
Of speed! Wrench out the jointing of the
    door.
And show my two-edged curse, the chil-
    dren dead,
The woman. . . . Oh, this sword upon her
    head. . . .
        [While the Attendants are still bat-
        tering at the door, MEDEA ap-
        pears on the roof, standing on a
        chariot of winged dragons, in
        which are the children's bodies.]

    MEDEA. What make ye at my gates?
        Why batter ye
With brazen bars, seeking the dead and
    me
Who slew them? Peace! . . . And thou, if
    aught of mine
Thou needest, speak, though never touch
    of thine
Shall scathe me more. Out of his firma-
    ment
My fathers' father, the high Sun, hath sent
This, that shall save me from mine enemies'
    rage.
    JASON. Thou living hate! Thou wife in
        every age
Abhorrèd, blood-red mother, who didst kill
My sons, and make me as the dead: and
    still
Canst take the sunshine to thine eyes, and
    smell
The green earth, reeking from thy deed of
    hell;
I curse thee! Now, oh, now mine eyes can
    see,
That then were blinded, when from sav-
    agery
Of eastern chambers, from a cruel land,
To Greece and home I gathered in mine
    hand
Thee, thou incarnate curse: one that be-
    trayed
Her home, her father, her . . . Oh, God
    hath laid
Thy sins on me! — I knew, I knew, there
    lay
A brother murdered on thy hearth that day
When thy first footstep fell on Argo's
    hull. . . .
Argo, my own, my swift and beautiful!
    That was her first beginning. Then a
        wife
I made her in my house. She bore to life
Children: and now for love, for chambering
And men's arms, she hath murdered them!
    A thing
Not one of all the maids of Greece, not
    one,
Had dreamed of; whom I spurned, and for
    mine own
Chose thee, a bride of hate to me and
    death,
Tigress, not woman, beast of wilder breath

Than Scylla shrieking o'er the Tuscan sea.
Enough! No scorn of mine can reach to thee,
Such iron is o'er thine eyes. Out from my road,
Thou crime-begetter, blind with children's blood!
And let me weep alone the bitter tide
That sweepeth Jason's days, no gentle bride
To speak with more, no child to look upon
Whom once I reared . . . all, all forever gone!

MEDEA. An easy answer had I to this swell
Of speech, but Zeus our father knoweth well,
All I for thee have wrought, and thou for me.
So let it rest. This thing was not to be,
That thou shouldst live a merry life, my bed
Forgotten and my heart uncomforted,
Thou nor thy princess: nor the king that planned
Thy marriage drive Medea from his land,
And suffer not. Call me what thing thou please,
Tigress or Scylla from the Tuscan seas:
My claws have gripped thine heart, and all things shine.

JASON. Thou too hast grief. Thy pain is fierce as mine.

MEDEA. I love the pain, so thou shalt laugh no more.

JASON. Oh, what a womb of sin my children bore!

MEDEA. Sons, did ye perish for your father's shame?

JASON. How? It was not my hand that murdered them.

MEDEA. 'T was thy false wooings, 't was thy trampling pride.

JASON. Thou hast said it! For thy lust of love they died.

MEDEA. And love to women a slight thing should be?

JASON. To women pure! — All thy vile life to thee!

MEDEA. Think of thy torment. They are dead, they are dead!

JASON. No: quick, great God; quick curses round thy head!

MEDEA. The gods know who began this work of woe.

JASON. Thy heart and all its loathliness they know.

MEDEA. Loathe on. . . . But, oh, thy voice. It hurts me sore.

JASON. Aye, and thine me. Wouldst hear me then no more?

MEDEA. How? Show me but the way. 'T is this I crave.

JASON. Give me the dead to weep, and make their grave.

MEDEA. Never! Myself will lay them in a still
Green sepulcher, where Hera by the Hill
Hath precinct holy, that no angry men
May break their graves and cast them forth again
To evil. So I lay on all this shore
Of Corinth a high feast forevermore
And rite, to purge them yearly of the stain
Of this poor blood. And I, to Pallas' plain
I go, to dwell beside Pandion's son,
Ægeus. — For thee, behold, death draweth on,
Evil and lonely, like thine heart: the hands
Of thine old Argo, rotting where she stands,
Shall smite thine head in twain, and bitter be
To the last end thy memories of me.

[*She rises on the chariot and is slowly borne away.*]

JASON. May They that hear the weeping child
Blast thee, and They that walk in blood!

MEDEA. Thy broken vows, thy friends beguiled
Have shut for thee the ears of God.

JASON. Go, thou art wet with children's tears!

MEDEA. Go thou, and lay thy bride to sleep.

JASON. Childless, I go, to weep and weep.

MEDEA. Not yet! Age cometh and long years.

JASON. My sons, mine own!

MEDEA. Not thine, but mine . . .

JASON. . . . Who slew them!

MEDEA. Yes: to torture thee.
JASON. Once let me kiss their lips, once
  twine
Mine arms and touch. . . . Ah, woe is me!
  MEDEA. Wouldst love them and en-
  treat? But now
They were as nothing.
  JASON. At the last,
O God, to touch that tender brow!
  MEDEA. Thy words upon the wind are
  cast.
JASON. Thou, Zeus, wilt hear me. All is
  said
For naught. I am but spurned away
And trampled by this tigress, red
  With children's blood. Yet, come what
  may,
So far as thou hast granted, yea,
  So far as yet my strength may stand,

I weep upon these dead, and say
  Their last farewell, and raise my hand

To all the demons of the air
  In witness of these things; how she
  Who slew them, will not suffer me
To gather up my babes, nor bear
To earth their bodies; whom, O stone
Of women, would I ne'er had known
  Nor gotten, to be slain by thee!
     [*He casts himself upon the earth.*]
  CHORUS. Great treasure halls hath Zeus
    in heaven,
From whence to man strange dooms be
  given,
  Past hope or fear.
And the end men looked for cometh not,
And a path is there where no man thought:
  So hath it fallen here.

THE FROGS

By ARISTOPHANES

Translated in verse by JOHN HOOKHAM FRERE

CHARACTERS

BACCHUS

XANTHIAS, *servant of Bacchus*

HERCULES

CHARON

ÆACUS

EURIPIDES

ÆSCHYLUS

PLUTO

Dead Man

PROSERPINE'S *Servant Maid*

Two Women Sutlers

Mutes

Chorus of Votaries, and Frogs

THE FROGS

[*Enter* BACCHUS *and* XANTHIAS.]

XANTHIAS. Master, shall I begin with
the usual jokes
That the audience always laugh at?
BACCHUS. If you please;
Any joke you please except "being over-
burthen'd."
— Don't use it yet — We've time enough
before us.
XANTHIAS. Well, something else that's
comical and clever?
BACCHUS. I forbid being "overpress'd
and overburthen'd."
XANTHIAS. Well, but the drollest joke
of all —?
BACCHUS. Remember
There's one thing I protest against —
XANTHIAS. What's that?
BACCHUS. Why, shifting off your load to
the other shoulder,
And fidgeting and complaining of the gripes.
XANTHIAS. What then do you mean to
say, that I must not say
That I'm ready to befoul myself?
BACCHUS. By no means —
Except when I take an emetic.
XANTHIAS. What's the use, then,
Of my being burthen'd here with all these
bundles,
If I'm to be deprived of the common jokes
That Phrynichus, and Lycis, and Ameipsias
Allow the servants always in their comedies,
Without exception, when they carry bun-
dles?
BACCHUS. Pray, leave them off — for
those ingenious sallies
Have such an effect upon my health and
spirits
That I feel grown old and dull when I get
home.
XANTHIAS. It's hard for me to suffer in
my limbs,
To be overburthen'd and debarr'd from
joking.

BACCHUS. Well, this is monstrous, quite,
and insupportable!
Such insolence in a servant! When your
master
Is going afoot and has provided you
With a beast to carry ye.
XANTHIAS. What! do I carry nothing?
BACCHUS. You're carried yourself.
XANTHIAS. But I carry bundles, don't I?
BACCHUS. But the beast bears all the
burdens that you carry.
XANTHIAS. Not those that I carry my-
self — 't is I that carry 'em.
BACCHUS. You're carried yourself, I tell
ye.
XANTHIAS. I can't explain it,
But I feel it in my shoulders plainly enough.
BACCHUS. Well, if the beast don't help
you, take and try;
Change places with the ass and carry him.
XANTHIAS [*in a tone of mere disgust*].
Oh, dear! I wish I had gone for a volunteer,
And left you to yourself. I wish I had.
BACCHUS. Dismount, you rascal! Here,
we're at the house
Where Hercules lives. — Hello!   there!
who's within there?

[*Enter* HERCULES.]

HERCULES. Who's there? (He has
bang'd at the door, whoever he is,
With the kick of a centaur.) What's the
matter, there?
BACCHUS [*aside*]. Ha! Xanthias!
XANTHIAS. What?
BACCHUS [*aside*]. Did ye mind how he
was frighten'd?
XANTHIAS. I suppose he was afraid you
were going mad.
HERCULES [*aside*]. By Jove! I shall
laugh outright; I'm ready to burst.
I shall laugh, in spite of myself, upon my life.
BACCHUS. Come hither, friend. — What
ails ye? Step this way;
I want to speak to ye.

HERCULES. But I can't help laughing,
To see the lion's skin with a saffron robe,
And the club with the women's sandals —
altogether —
What's the meaning of it all? Have you
been abroad?
BACCHUS. I've been abroad — in the
Fleet — with Cleisthenes.
HERCULES. You fought —?
BACCHUS. Yes, that we did — we gain'd
a victory;
And we sunk the enemies' ships — thirteen
of 'em.
HERCULES. "So you woke at last and
found it was a dream?"
BACCHUS. But aboard the fleet, as I pur-
sued my studies,
I read the tragedy of Andromeda;
And then such a vehement passion struck
my heart,
You can't imagine.
HERCULES. A small one, I suppose,
My little fellow — a moderate little pas-
sion?
BACCHUS. It's just as small as Molon is
— that's all —
Molon the wrestler, I mean — as small as
he is —
HERCULES. Well, what was it like? what
kind of a thing? what was it?
BACCHUS. No, friend, you must not
laugh; it's past a joke;
It's quite a serious feeling — quite dis-
tressing;
I suffer from it —
HERCULES. Well, explain. What was it?
BACCHUS. I can't declare it at once; but
I'll explain it
Theatrically and enigmatically:
Were you ever seized with a sudden pas-
sionate longing
For a mess of porridge?
HERCULES. Often enough, if that's all.
BACCHUS. Shall I state the matter to
you plainly at once;
Or put it circumlocutorily?
HERCULES. Not about the porridge. I
understand your instance.
BACCHUS. Such is the passion that pos-
sesses me
For poor Euripides, that's dead and
gone;

And it's all in vain people trying to per-
suade me
From going after him.
HERCULES. What, to the shades below?
BACCHUS. Yes, to the shades below, or
the shades beneath 'em.
To the undermost shades of all. I'm quite
determined.
HERCULES. But what's your object?
BACCHUS. Why my object is
That I want a clever poet — "for the good,
The gracious and the good, are dead and
gone;
The worthless and the weak are left alive."
HERCULES. Is not Iophon a good one?
— He's alive sure?
BACCHUS. If he's a good one, he's our
only good one;
But it's a question; I'm in doubt about him.
HERCULES. There's Sophocles; he's
older than Euripides —
If you go so far for 'em, you'd best bring
him.
BACCHUS. No; first I'll try what Iophon
can do,
Without his father, Sophocles, to assist him.
— Besides, Euripides is a clever rascal;
A sharp, contriving rogue that will make a
shift
To desert and steal away with me; the other
Is an easy-minded soul, and always was.
HERCULES. Where's Agathon?
BACCHUS. He's gone and left me too,
Regretted by his friends; a worthy poet —
HERCULES. Gone! Where, poor soul?
BACCHUS. To the banquets of the blest!
HERCULES. But then you've Xenocles —
BACCHUS. Yes! a plague upon him!
HERCULES. Pythangelus too —
XANTHIAS. But nobody thinks of me;
Standing all this while with the bundles on
my shoulder.
HERCULES. But have not you other
young ingenious youths
That are fit to out-talk Euripides ten times
over;
To the amount of a thousand, at least, all
writing tragedy — ?
BACCHUS. They're good for nothing —
"Warblers of the Grove" —
— "Little, foolish, fluttering things" —
poor puny wretches,

That dawdle and dangle about with the
    tragic muse;
Incapable of any serious meaning —
— There's not one hearty poet amongst
    them all
That's fit to risk an adventurous valiant
    phrase.
    HERCULES. How — "hearty?" What do
      you mean by "valiant phrases?"
    BACCHUS. I mean a . . . kind . . . of a
      . . . doubtful, bold expression
To talk about . . . "*The viewless foot of
    Time*" —
And . . . "*Jupiter's Secret Chamber in the
    Skies*" —
And about . . . a person's soul . . . not
    being perjured
When . . . the tongue . . . forswears itself
    . . . in spite of the soul.
    HERCULES. Do you like that kind of
      stuff?
    BACCHUS. I'm crazy after it.
    HERCULES. Why, sure, it's trash and
      rubbish — Don't you think so?
    BACCHUS. "Men's fancies are their own
      — Let mine alone" —
    HERCULES. But, in fact, it seems to me
      quite bad — rank nonsense.
    BACCHUS. You'll tell me next what I
      ought to like for supper.
    XANTHIAS. But nobody thinks of me
      here, with the bundles.
    BACCHUS. — But now to the business
      that I came upon —
(With the apparel that you see — the same
    as yours)
To obtain a direction from you to your
    friends,
(To apply to them — in case of anything —
If anything should occur) the acquaint-
    ances
That received you there — (the time you
    went before
— For the business about Cerberus) — if
    you'd give me
Their names and their directions, and com-
    municate
Any information relative to the country,
The roads, — the streets, — the bridges,
    and the brothels,
The wharfs, — the public walks, — the
    public houses,

The fountains, — aqueducts, — and inns,
    and taverns,
And lodgings, — free from bugs and fleas,
    if possible,
If you know any such —
    XANTHIAS. But nobody thinks of me.
    HERCULES. What a notion! You! Will
      you risk it? Are you mad?
    BACCHUS. I beseech you say no more —
      no more of that,
But inform me briefly and plainly about
    my journey:
The shortest road and the most convenient
    one.
    HERCULES. Well, — which shall I tell
      ye first, now? — Let me see now —
There's a good convenient road by the
    Rope and Noose;
The Hanging Road.
    BACCHUS. No; that's too close and sti-
      fling.
    HERCULES. Then, there's an easy, fair,
      well-beaten track,
As you go by the Pestle and Mortar —
    BACCHUS. What, the Hemlock?
    HERCULES. To be sure —
    BACCHUS. That's much too cold — it
      will never do.
They tell me it strikes a chill to the legs
    and feet.
    HERCULES. Should you like a speedy,
      rapid, downhill road?
    BACCHUS. Indeed I should, for I'm a
      sorry traveler.
    HERCULES. Go to the Keramicus then.
    BACCHUS. What then?
    HERCULES. Get up to the very top of
      the tower.
    BACCHUS. What then?
    HERCULES. Stand there and watch when
      the Race of the Torch begins;
And mind when you hear the people cry
    "*Start! start!*"
Then start at once with 'em.
    BACCHUS. Me? Start? Where from?
    HERCULES. From the top of the tower
      to the bottom.
    BACCHUS. No, not I.
It's enough to dash my brains out! I'll
    not go
Such a road upon any account.
    HERCULES. Well, which way then?

BACCHUS. The way you went yourself.
HERCULES. But it's a long one,
For first you come to a monstrous bottom-
less lake.
BACCHUS. And what must I do to pass?
HERCULES. You'll find a boat there;
A little tiny boat, as big as that,
And an old man that ferries you over in it,
Receiving twopence as the usual fee.
BACCHUS. Ah! that same twopence gov-
erns everything
Wherever it goes. — I wonder how it man-
aged
To find its way there?
HERCULES. Theseus introduced it.
— Next you'll meet serpents, and wild
beasts, and monsters,
Horrific to behold!
BACCHUS. Don't try to fright me;
You'll not succeed, I promise you. — I'm
determined.
HERCULES. Then there's an abyss of
mire and floating filth,
In which the damn'd lie wallowing and
overwhelm'd;
The unjust, the cruel, and the inhospit-
able;
And the barbarous bilking Cullies that
withhold
The price of intercourse with fraud and
wrong;
The incestuous, and the parricides, and the
robbers;
The perjurers, and assassins, and the
wretches
That willfully and presumptuously tran-
scribe
Extracts and trash from Morsimus's plays.
BACCHUS. And, by Jove! Cinesias with
his Pyrrhic dancers
Ought to be there — they're worse, or
quite as bad.
HERCULES. But after this your sense will
be saluted
With a gentle breathing sound of flutes
and voices,
And a beautiful spreading light like ours on
earth,
And myrtle glades and happy quires among,
Of women and men with rapid applause
and mirth.
BACCHUS. And who are all those folks?

HERCULES. The initiated.
XANTHIAS. I won't stand here like a
mule in a procession
Any longer, with these packages and
bundles.
HERCULES. They'll tell you everything
you want to know,
For they're established close upon the
road,
By the corner of Pluto's house — so fare
you well;
Farewell, my little fellow.   [Exit.]
BACCHUS. I wish you better.
[To XANTHIAS.] You, sirrah, take your
bundles up again.
XANTHIAS. What, before I put them
down?
BACCHUS. Yes! now, this moment.
XANTHIAS. Nah! don't insist; there's
plenty of people going
As corpses with the convenience of a car-
riage;
They'd take it for a trifle gladly enough.
BACCHUS. But if we meet with nobody?
XANTHIAS. Then I'll take 'em.
BACCHUS. Come, come, that's fairly
spoken, and in good time;
For there they're carrying a corpse out to
be buried.
        [A funeral, with a corpse on an
        open bier, crosses the stage.]
— Hello! you there — you Deadman —
can't you hear?
Would you take any bundles to hell with
ye, my good fellow?
DEADMAN. What are they?
BACCHUS. These.
DEADMAN. Then I must have two drach-
mas.
BACCHUS. I can't — you must take less.
DEADMAN. Bearers, move on.
BACCHUS. No, stop! we shall settle be-
tween us — you're so hasty.
DEADMAN. It's no use arguing; I must
have two drachmas.
BACCHUS. Ninepence!
DEADMAN. I'd best be alive again at
that rate.   [Exit.]
BACCHUS. Fine airs the fellow gives him-
self — a rascal!
I'll have him punish'd, I vow, for over-
charging.

XANTHIAS. Best give him a good beating: give me the bundles,
I'll carry 'em.
BACCHUS. You're a good, true-hearted fellow;
And a willing servant. — Let's move on to the ferry.

[*Enter* CHARON.]

CHARON. Hoy! Bear a hand, there — Heave ashore.
BACCHUS. What's this?
XANTHIAS. The lake it is — the place he told us of.
By Jove! and there's the boat — and here's old Charon.
BACCHUS. Well, Charon! — Welcome, Charon! — Welcome kindly!
CHARON. Who wants the ferryman? Anybody waiting
To remove from the sorrows of life? A passage anybody?
To Lethe's wharf? — to Cerberus's Reach?
To Tartarus? — to Tænarus? — to Perdition?
BACCHUS. Yes, I.
CHARON. Get in then.
BACCHUS. Tell me, where are you going?
To Perdition really —?
CHARON. Yes, to oblige you, I will
With all my heart — Step in there.
BACCHUS. Have a care!
Take care, good Charon! — Charon, have a care!
Come, Xanthias, come!
CHARON. I take no slaves aboard
Except they've volunteer'd for the naval victory.
XANTHIAS. I could not — I was suffering with sore eyes.
CHARON. You must trudge away then, round by the end of the lake there.
XANTHIAS. And whereabouts shall I wait?
CHARON. At the Stone of Repentance, By the Slough of Despond beyond the Tribulations;
You understand me?
XANTHIAS. Yes, I understand you;
A lucky, promising direction, truly.
CHARON [*to* BACCHUS]. Sit down at the oar — Come quick, if there's more coming!
[*To* BACCHUS *again.*] Hello! what's that you're doing?
BACCHUS. What you told me.
I'm sitting at the oar.
CHARON. Sit *there*, I tell you,
You Fatguts; that's your place.
BACCHUS. Well, so I do.
CHARON. Now ply your hands and arms.
BACCHUS. Well, so I do.
CHARON. You'd best leave off your fooling. Take to the oar,
And pull away.
BACCHUS. But how shall I contrive?
I've never served on board — I'm only a landsman;
I'm quite unused to it —
CHARON. We can manage it.
As soon as you begin you shall have some music
That will teach you to keep time.
BACCHUS. What music's that?
CHARON. A chorus of Frogs — uncommon musical Frogs.
BACCHUS. Well, give me the word and the time.
CHARON. Whooh up, up; whooh up, up.

[*Enter Chorus of Frogs.*]

CHORUS. Brekeke-kesh, koash, koash,
Shall the Choral Quiristers of the Marsh
Be censured and rejected as hoarse and harsh;
And their Chromatic essays
Deprived of praise?
No, let us raise afresh
Our obstreperous Brekeke-kesh;
The customary croak and cry
Of the creatures
At the theaters,
In their yearly revelry,
Brekeke-kesh, koash, koash.
BACCHUS. How I'm maul'd,
How I'm gall'd;
Worn and mangled to a mash —
There they go! *"Koash, koash!"* —
FROGS. Brekeke-kesh, koash, koash.
BACCHUS. Oh, beshrew,
All your crew;
You don't consider how I smart.

FROGS. Now for a sample of the Art!
Brekeke-kesh, koash, koash.
BACCHUS. I wish you hang'd, with all
    my heart.
— Have you nothing else to say?
"*Brekeke-kesh, koash*" all day!
    FROGS. We've a right,
        We've a right;
        And we croak at ye for spite.
        We've a right,
        We've a right;
        Day and night,
        Day and night;
        Night and day,
        Still to creak and croak away.
Phœbus and every Grace
Admire and approve of the croaking race;
And the egregious guttural notes
That are gargled and warbled in their
    lyrical throats.
        In reproof
        Of your scorn
        Mighty Pan
        Nods his horn;
        Beating time
        To the rhyme
        With his hoof,
        With his hoof.
        Persisting in our plan,
        We proceed as we began,
        Breke-kesh, Breke-kesh,
        Kooash, kooash.
    BACCHUS. Oh, the Frogs, consume and
    rot 'em,
I've a blister on my bottom.
Hold your tongues, you tuneful creatures.
    FROGS. Cease with your profane en-
    treaties
All in vain forever striving:
    Silence is against our natures.
With the vernal heat reviving,
    Our aquatic crew repair
From their periodic sleep,
In the dark and chilly deep,
To the cheerful upper air;
Then we frolic here and there
All amidst the meadows fair;
Shady plants of asphodel,
Are the lodges where we dwell;
Chaunting in the leafy bowers
All the livelong summer hours,
Till the sudden gusty showers

Send us headlong, helter, skelter,
To the pool to seek for shelter;
Meager, eager, leaping, lunging,
From the sedgy wharfage plunging
To the tranquil depth below,
There we muster all a-row;
Where, secure from toil and trouble,
With a tuneful hubble-bubble,
Our symphonious accents flow.
Brekeke-kesh, koash, koash.
    BACCHUS. I forbid you to proceed.
    FROGS. That would be severe indeed;
Arbitrary, bold, and rash —
Brekeke-kesh, koash, koash.
    BACCHUS. I command you to desist —
— Oh, my back, there! oh, my wrist!
What a twist!
What a sprain!
    FROGS. Once again —
We renew the tuneful strain.
Brekeke-kesh, koash, koash.
    BACCHUS. I disdain — (Hang the pain!)
All your nonsense, noise, and trash.
Oh, my blister! Oh, my sprain!
    FROGS. Brekeke-kesh, koash, koash.
Friends and Frogs, we must display
All our powers of voice to-day;
Suffer not this stranger here,
With fastidious foreign ear,
To confound us and abash.
Brekeke-kesh, koash, koash.
    BACCHUS. Well, my spirit is not broke,
If it's only for the joke,
I'll outdo you with a croak.
Here it goes — "Koash, koash."
    FROGS. Now for a glorious croaking
    crash,
Brekeke-kesh, koash, koash.
    BACCHUS. I'll disperse you with a splash.
    FROGS. Brekeke-kesh, koash, koash.
    BACCHUS. I'll subdue
Your rebellious, noisy crew —
— Have amongst you there, slap-dash.
    FROGS. Brekeke-kesh, koash, koash.
We defy your oar and you.
    CHARON. Hold! We're ashore just —
    shift your oar. Get out.
— Now pay for your fare.
    BACCHUS. There — there it is — the
    twopence.
    BACCHUS. Ho, Xanthias! Xanthias, I
    say! Where's Xanthias?

XANTHIAS. A-hoy!
BACCHUS. Come here.
XANTHIAS. I'm glad to see you, master.
BACCHUS. What's that before us there?
XANTHIAS. The mire and darkness.
BACCHUS. Do you see the villains and
the perjurers
That he told us of?
XANTHIAS. Yes, plain enough, don't
you?
BACCHUS. Ah! now I see them, indeed,
quite plain — and now too.
Well, what shall we do next?
XANTHIAS. We'd best move forward;
For here's the place that Hercules there
inform'd us
Was haunted by those monsters.
BACCHUS. Oh, confound him!
He vapor'd and talk'd at random to deter
me
From venturing. He's amazingly conceited
And jealous of other people, is Hercules;
He reckon'd I should rival him, and, in fact
(Since I've come here so far), I should
rather like
To meet with an adventure in some shape.
XANTHIAS. By Jove! and I think I hear
a kind of a noise.
BACCHUS. Where? Where?
XANTHIAS. There, just behind us.
BACCHUS. Go behind, then.
XANTHIAS. There! — it's before us now.
— There!
BACCHUS. Go before, then.
XANTHIAS. Ah! now I see it — a mon-
strous beast indeed!
BACCHUS. What kind?
XANTHIAS. A dreadful kind — all kinds
at once.
It changes and transforms itself about
To a mule and an ox, — and now to a
beautiful creature;
A woman!
BACCHUS. Where? Where is she? Let
me seize her.
XANTHIAS. But now she's turned to a
mastiff all of a sudden.
BACCHUS. It's the Weird hag! the
Vampire!
XANTHIAS. Like enough.
She's all of a blaze of fire about the mouth.
BACCHUS. Has she got the brazen foot?

XANTHIAS. Yes, there it is —
By Jove! — and the cloven hoof to the
other leg,
Distinct enough — that's she!
BACCHUS. But what shall I do?
XANTHIAS. And I, too?
BACCHUS. Save me, Priest, protect and
save me,
That we may drink and be jolly together
hereafter.
XANTHIAS. We're ruin'd, Master Her-
cules.
BACCHUS. Don't call me so, I beg:
Don't mention my name, good friend, upon
any account.
XANTHIAS. Well, Bacchus, then!
BACCHUS. That's worse, ten thousand
times.
XANTHIAS. Come, master, move along
— Come, come this way.
BACCHUS. What's happened?
XANTHIAS. Why we're prosperous and
victorious:
The storm of fear and danger has subsided,
And (as the actor said the other day)
"Has only left a gentle *qualm* behind."
The Vampire's vanish'd.
BACCHUS. Has she? Upon your oath?
XANTHIAS. By Jove! she has.
BACCHUS. No, swear again.
XANTHIAS. By Jove!
BACCHUS. Is she, by Jupiter?
XANTHIAS. By Jupiter!
BACCHUS. Oh, dear; what a fright I was
in with the very sight of her:
It turn'd me sick and pale — but see, the
priest here!
He has color'd up quite with the same alarm.
— What has brought me to this pass? —
It must be Jupiter
With his "*Chamber in the Skies*," and the
"*Foot of Time*."
XANTHIAS. Hello, you!
BACCHUS. What?
XANTHIAS. Why, did you not hear?
BACCHUS. Why, what?
XANTHIAS. The sound of a flute.
BACCHUS. Indeed! And there's a smell
too;
A pretty mystical ceremonious smell
Of torches. We'll watch here, and keep
quite quiet.

[Enter Chorus of Votaries.]

CHORUS. Iacchus! Iacchus! Ho!
Iacchus! Iacchus! Ho!
XANTHIAS. There, Master, there they
are, the initiated;
All sporting about as he told us we should
find 'em.
They're singing in praise of Bacchus like
Diagoras.
BACCHUS. Indeed, and so they are; but
we'll keep quiet
Till we make them out a little more distinctly.
CHORUS. Mighty Bacchus! Holy Power!
Hither at the wonted hour
    Come away,
    Come away,
With the wanton holiday,
Where the revel uproar leads
To the mystic holy meads,
Where the frolic votaries fly,
With a tipsy shout and cry;
Flourishing the Thyrsus high,
Flinging forth, alert and airy,
To the sacred old vagary,
The tumultuous dance and song,
Sacred from the vulgar throng;
Mystic orgies, that are known
To the votaries alone —
To the mystic chorus solely —
Secret — unreveal'd — and holy.
XANTHIAS. Oh glorious virgin, daughter
of the goddess!
What a scent of roasted griskin reach'd my
senses.
BACCHUS. Keep quiet — and watch for
a chance of a piece of the haslets.
CHORUS. Raise the fiery torches high!
Bacchus is approaching nigh,
Like the planet of the morn,
Breaking with the hoary dawn,
On the dark solemnity —
There they flash upon the sight;
All the plain is blazing bright,
Flush'd and overflown with light:
Age has cast his years away,
And the cares of many a day,
Sporting to the lively lay —
Mighty Bacchus! march and lead
(Torch in hand toward the mead)
Thy devoted humble Chorus,
Mighty Bacchus — move before us!

Keep silence — keep peace — and let all
    the profane
From our holy solemnity duly refrain;
Whose souls unenlightened by taste, are
    obscure;
Whose poetical notions are dark and
    impure;
Whose theatrical conscience
    Is sullied by nonsense;
Who never were train'd by the mighty
    Cratinus
In mystical orgies poetic and vinous;
Who delight in buffooning and jests out of
    season;
Who promote the designs of oppression and
    treason;
Who foster sedition, and strife, and debate;
All traitors, in short, to the stage and the
    state;
Who surrender a fort, or in private, export
To places and harbors of hostile resort,
Clandestine consignments of cables and
    pitch;
In the way that Thorycion grew to be rich
From a scoundrelly dirty collector of
    tribute:
All such we reject and severely prohibit:
All statesmen retrenching the fees and the
    salaries
Of theatrical bards, in revenge for the rail-
    leries,
And jests, and lampoons, of this holy
    solemnity,
Profanely pursuing their personal enmity,
For having been flouted, and scoff'd, and
    scorn'd,
All such are admonish'd and heartily
    warn'd;
    We warn them once,
    We warn them twice,
    We warn and admonish — we warn them
        thrice,
To conform to the law,
To retire and withdraw;
While the Chorus again with the formal saw
(Fixt and assign'd to the festive day)
Move to the measure and march away.
    March! march! lead forth,
    Lead forth manfully,
    March in order all;
    Bustling, hustling, justling,
    As it may befall;

Flocking, shouting, laughing,
Mocking, flouting, quaffing,
    One and all;
All have had a belly-full
Of breakfast brave and plentiful;
    Therefore
    Evermore
With your voices and your bodies
Serve the goddess,
    And raise
    Songs of praise;
She shall save the country still,
And save it against the traitor's will;
    So she says.
Now let us raise, in a different strain,
The praise of the goddess the giver of grain;
Imploring her favor
With other behavior,
In measures more sober, submissive, and
    graver.
Ceres, holy patroness,
Condescend to mark and bless,
    With benevolent regard,
Both the Chorus and the Bard;
Grant them for the present day
Many things to sing and say,
Follies intermix'd with sense;
Folly, but without offense.
Grant them with the present play
To bear the prize of verse away.
Now call again, and with a different
    measure,
The power of mirth and pleasure;
The florid, active Bacchus, bright and gay,
To journey forth and join us on the way.
O Bacchus, attend! the customary patron
    Of every lively lay;
    Go forth without delay
    Thy wonted annual way,
To meet the ceremonious holy matron:
    Her grave procession gracing,
    Thine airy footsteps tracing
With unlaborious, light, celestial motion;
And here at thy devotion
    Behold thy faithful quire
    In pitiful attire;
    All overworn and ragged,
This jerkin old and jagged,
These buskins torn and burst,
    Though sufferers in the fray,
May serve us at the worst
    To sport throughout the day;

And there within the shades,
I spy some lovely maids;
With whom we romp'd and revel'd,
Dismantled and dishevel'd;
With their bosoms open,
With whom we might be coping.
    XANTHIAS. Well, I was always hearty,
Disposed to mirth and ease,
I'm ready to join the party.
    BACCHUS. And I will, if you please.
[*To the Chorus.*] Prithee, my good fellows,
Would you please to tell us
    Which is Pluto's door,
I'm an utter stranger,
    Never here before.
    CHORUS. Friend, you're out of danger,
    You need not seek it far;
There it stands before ye,
    Before ye, where you are.
    BACCHUS. Take up your bundles,
        Xanthias.
    XANTHIAS. Hang all bundles;
A bundle has no end, and these have none.
    CHORUS. Now we go to dance and sing
    In the consecrated shades;
Round the secret holy ring,
    With the matrons and the maids.
Thither I must haste to bring
    The mysterious early light;
    Which must witness every rite
    Of the joyous happy night.
Let us hasten — let us fly —
Where the lovely meadows lie;
    Where the living waters flow;
    Where the roses bloom and blow.
— Heirs of Immortality,
Segregated, safe and pure,
Easy, sorrowless, secure;
Since our earthly course is run,
We behold a brighter sun.
Holy lives — a holy vow —
Such rewards await them now.
    BACCHUS. Well, how must I knock at
        the door now? Can't ye tell me?
How do the native inhabitants knock at
    doors?
    XANTHIAS. Pah; don't stand fooling
        there; but smite it smartly,
With the very spirit and air of Hercules.
    BACCHUS. Hello!
    ÆACUS. Who's there?
    BACCHUS. 'T is I, the valiant Hercules!

ÆACUS. Thou brutal, abominable, detestable,
Vile, villainous, infamous, nefarious scoundrel!
— How durst thou, villain as thou wert, to seize
Our watchdog, Cerberus, whom I kept and tended
Hurrying him off, half-strangled in your grasp?
— But now, be sure we have you safe and fast,
Miscreant and villain! — Thee, the Stygian cliffs,
With stern adamantine durance, and the rocks
Of inaccessible Acheron, red with gore,
Environ and beleaguer; and the watch,
And swift pursuit of the hideous hounds of hell;
And the horrible Hydra, with her hundred heads,
Whose furious ravening fangs shall rend and tear thee;
Wrenching thy vitals forth, with the heart and midriff;
While inexpressible Tartesian monsters,
And grim Tithrasian Gorgons toss and scatter
With clattering claws, thine intertwined intestines.
To them, with instant summons, I repair,
Moving in hasty march with steps of speed.
  XANTHIAS. Hello, you! What's the matter there —?
  BACCHUS. Oh dear,
I've had an accident.
  XANTHIAS. Poh! poh! jump up!
Come! you ridiculous simpleton! don't lie there,
The people will see you.
  BACCHUS. Indeed I'm sick at heart; la!
  XANTHIAS. Was there ever in heaven or earth such a coward?
  BACCHUS. Me?
A coward! Did not I show my presence of mind —
And call for a sponge and water in a moment?
Would a coward have done that?
  XANTHIAS. What else would he do?

  BACCHUS. He'd have lain there stinking like a nasty coward;
But I jump'd up at once, like a lusty wrestler,
And look'd about, and wiped myself, withal.
  XANTHIAS. Most manfully done!
  BACCHUS. By Jove, and I think it was;
But tell me, wern't you frighten'd with that speech?
— Such horrible expressions!
  XANTHIAS. No, not I;
I took no notice —
  BACCHUS. Well, I'll tell you what,
Since you're such a valiant-spirited kind of fellow,
Do you be Me — with the club and the lion's skin,
Now you're in this courageous temper of mind;
And I'll go take my turn and carry the bundles.
  XANTHIAS. Well — give us hold — I must humor you, forsooth;
Make haste, and now behold the Xanthian Hercules,
And mind if I don't display more heart and spirit.
  BACCHUS. Indeed, and you look the character, completely,
Like that heroic Melitensian hangdog —
Come, now for my bundles. I must mind my bundles.

[Enter PROSERPINE's Servant Maid who immediately addresses XANTHIAS.]

  SERVANT MAID. Dear Hercules. Well, you're come at last. Come in,
For the goddess, as soon as she heard of it, set to work
Baking peck loaves and frying stacks of pancakes,
And making messes of furmety; there's an ox
Besides, she has roasted whole, with a relishing stuffing,
If you'll only just step in this way.
  XANTHIAS. I thank you,
I'm equally obliged.
  SERVANT MAID. No, no, by Jupiter!
We must not let you off, indeed. There's wild fowl

And sweetmeats for the dessert, and the
best of wine;
Only walk in.
XANTHIAS. I thank you. You'll excuse
me.
SERVANT MAID. No, no, we can't excuse
you, indeed we can't;
There are dancing and singing girls besides.
XANTHIAS. What! dancers?
SERVANT MAID. Yes, that there are;
the sweetest, charmingest things
That you ever saw — and there's the cook
this moment
Is dishing up the dinner.
XANTHIAS. Go before then,
And tell the girls — those singing girls you
mentioned —
To prepare for my approach in person
presently.
[*To* BACCHUS.] You, sirrah! follow be-
hind me with the bundles.
BACCHUS. Hello, you! what, do you take
the thing in earnest,
Because, for a joke, I drest you up like
Hercules?
Come, don't stand fooling, Xanthias.
You'll provoke me.
There, carry the bundles, sirrah, when I
bid you.
XANTHIAS. Why, sure? Do you mean to
take the things away
That you gave me yourself of your own
accord this instant?
BACCHUS. I never mean a thing; I do it
at once.
Let go of the lion's skin directly, I tell you.
XANTHIAS. To you, just Gods, I make
my last appeal,
Bear witness!
BACCHUS. What! the gods? — do you
think they mind you?
How could you take it in your head, I
wonder;
Such a foolish fancy for a fellow like you,
A mortal and a slave, to pass for Hercules?
XANTHIAS. There. Take them. — There
— you may have them — but,
please God,
You may come to want my help some time
or other.
CHORUS. Dexterous and wily wits,
Find their own advantage ever;

For the wind where'er it sits,
Leaves a berth secure and clever
To the ready navigator;
That foresees and knows the nature,
Of the wind and weather's drift;
And betimes can turn and shift
To the sheltered easy side;
'T is a practice proved and tried,
Not to wear a formal face;
Fixt in attitude and place,
Like an image on its base;
'T is the custom of the seas,
Which, as all the world agrees,
Justifies Theramenes.
BACCHUS. How ridiculous and strange;
What a monstrous proposition,
That I should condescend to change
My dress, my name, and my condition,
To follow Xanthias, and behave
Like a mortal and a slave;
To be set to watch the door
While he wallow'd with his whore,
Tumbling on a purple bed;
While I waited with submission,
To receive a broken head;
Or be kick'd upon suspicion
Of impertinence and peeping
At the joys that he was reaping.

[*Enter two Women, Sutlers or Keepers of an
eating-house.*]

FIRST WOMAN. What, Platana! Goody
Platana! there! that's he,
The fellow that robs and cheats poor
victualers;
That came to our house and eat those nine-
teen loaves.
SECOND WOMAN. Ay, sure enough that's
he, the very man.
XANTHIAS. There's mischief in the wind
for somebody!
FIRST WOMAN. — And a dozen and a
half of cutlets and fried chops,
At a penny halfpenny apiece —
XANTHIAS. There are pains and penalties
Impending —
FIRST WOMAN. — And all the garlic: such
a quantity
As he swallowed —
BACCHUS. Woman, you're beside your-
self;
You talk you know not what —

SECOND WOMAN. No, no! you reckoned I should not know you again with them there buskins.

FIRST WOMAN. — Good lack! and there was all that fish besides.

Indeed — with the pickle, and all — and the good green cheese That he gorged at once, with the rind, and the rush-baskets; And then, when I called for payment, he looked fierce, And stared at me in the face, and grinned, and roared —

XANTHIAS. Just like him! That's the way wherever he goes.

FIRST WOMAN. — And snatched his sword out, and behaved like mad.

XANTHIAS. Poor souls! you suffered sadly!

FIRST WOMAN. Yes, indeed; And then we both ran off with the fright and terror, And scrambled into the loft beneath the roof; And he took up two rugs and stole them off.

XANTHIAS. Just like him again — but something must be done. Go call me Cleon, he's my advocate.

SECOND WOMAN. And Hyperbolus, if you meet him send him here. He's mine; and we'll demolish him, I warrant.

FIRST WOMAN. How I should like to strike those ugly teeth out With a good big stone, you ravenous greedy villain! You gormandizing villain! that I should — Yes, that I should; your wicked ugly fangs That have eaten up my substance, and devoured me.

BACCHUS. And I could toss you into the public pit With the malefactors' carcasses; that I could, With pleasure and satisfaction; that I could.

FIRST WOMAN. And I should like to rip that gullet out With a reaping hook that swallowed all my tripe, And liver and lights — but I'll fetch Cleon here,

And he shall summon him. He shall settle him, And have it out of him this very day.

[*Exeunt First and Second Woman.*]

BACCHUS. I love poor Xanthias dearly, that I do; I wish I might be hanged else.

XANTHIAS. Yes, I know — I know your meaning — No; no more of that, I won't act Hercules —

BACCHUS. Now pray don't say so, My little Xanthias.

XANTHIAS. How should I be Hercules? A mortal and a slave, a fellow like me? —

BACCHUS. I know you're angry, and you've a right to be angry; And if you beat me for it I'd not complain; But if ever I strip you again, from this time forward, I wish I may be utterly confounded, With my wife, my children, and my family, And the blear-eyed Archedemus into the bargain.

XANTHIAS. I agree then, on that oath, and those conditions.

CHORUS. Now that you revive and flourish In your old attire again, You must rouse afresh and nourish Thoughts of an heroic strain; That exalt and raise the figure, And assume a fire and vigor; And an attitude and air Suited to the garb you wear; With a brow severely bent, Like the god you represent. But beware, Have a care! If you blunder, or betray Any weakness any way; Weakness of the heart or brain, We shall see you once again Trudging in the former track, With the bundles at your back.

XANTHIAS. Friends, I thank you for your care; Your advice was good and fair; Corresponding in its tone With reflections of my own. — Though I clearly comprehend All the upshot and the end

(That if any good comes of it,
Any pleasure any profit —
He, my master, will recede
From the terms that were agreed),
You shall see me, notwithstanding,
Stern, intrepid, and commanding.
Now's the time; for there's a noise!
Now for figure, look, and voice!

[*Enter* ÆACUS.]

ÆACUS. Arrest me there that fellow that
    stole the dog.
There! — Pinion him! — Quick!
BACCHUS. There's somebody in a scrape.
XANTHIAS. Keep off, and be hanged.
ÆACUS. Oh, ho! do you mean to fight
    for it?
Here! Pardokas, and Skeblias, and the rest
    of ye,
Make up to the rogue, and settle him.
    Come, be quick.
BACCHUS. Well, is not this quite mon-
    strous and outrageous,
To steal the dog, and then to make an
    assault
In justification of it.
XANTHIAS. Quite outrageous!
ÆACUS. An aggravated case!
XANTHIAS. Well, now — by Jupiter,
May I die; but I never saw this place
    before —
Nor ever stole the amount of a farthing
    from you:
Nor a hair of your dog's tail — But you
    shall see now,
I'll settle all this business nobly and fairly.
— This slave of mine — you may take and
    torture him;
And if you make out anything against me,
You may take and put me to death for
    aught I care.
ÆACUS. But which way would you
    please to have him tortured?
XANTHIAS. In your own way — with . . .
    the lash — with . . . knots and screws,
With . . . the common usual customary
    tortures.
With the rack — with . . . the water-tor-
    ture — anyway —
With fire and vinegar — all sorts of ways.
There's only one thing I should warn you
    of:

I must not have him treated like a child,
To be whipp'd with fennel, or with lettuce
    leaves.
ÆACUS. That's fair — and if so be . . .
    he's maim'd or crippled
In any respect — the valy shall be paid you.
XANTHIAS. Oh no! — by no means! not
    to me! — by no means!
You must not mention it! — Take him to
    the torture.
ÆACUS. It had better be here, and under
    your own eye.
Come you — put down your bundles and
    make ready.
And mind — let me hear no lies!
BACCHUS. I'll tell you what:
I'd advise people not to torture me;
I give you notice — I'm a deity.
So mind now — you'll have nobody to
    blame
But your own self —
ÆACUS. What's that you're saying
    there?
BACCHUS. Why that I'm Bacchus,
    Jupiter's own son:
That fellow there's a slave.
ÆACUS. Do ye hear?
XANTHIAS. I hear him —
A reason the more to give him a good beat-
    ing;
If he's immortal he need never mind it.
BACCHUS. Why should not you be beat
    as well as I then,
If you're immortal, as you say you are?
XANTHIAS. Agreed — and him, the first
    that you see flinching,
Or seeming to mind it at all, you may set
    him down
For an impostor and no real deity.
ÆACUS. Ah, you're a worthy gentleman,
    I'll be bound for't;
You're all for the truth and the proof.
    Come — Strip there both o' ye.
XANTHIAS. But how can ye put us to
    the question fairly,
Upon equal terms?
ÆACUS. Oh, easily enough,
Conveniently enough — a lash apiece,
Each in your turn; you can have 'em one
    by one.
XANTHIAS. That's right. Now mind if
    ye see me flinch or swerve.

ÆACUS. I've struck.

XANTHIAS. Not you!

ÆACUS. Why it seems as if I had not.
I'll smite this other fellow.

BACCHUS. When will you do it?
Oh dear! Companions of my youthful
years.

XANTHIAS [to ÆACUS]. Did ye hear? he
made an outcry.

ÆACUS. What was that?

BACCHUS. A favorite passage from
Archilochus.

XANTHIAS. O Jupiter! that on the Idean
height;

ÆACUS. Well, after all my pains, I'm
quite at a loss
To discover which is the true, real deity.
By the Holy Goddess — I'm completely
puzzled;
I must take you before Proserpine and
Pluto,
Being gods themselves they're likeliest to
know.

BACCHUS. Why, that's a lucky thought.
I only wish
It had happen'd to occur before you beat
us.

CHORUS. Muse, attend our solemn sum-
mons
And survey the assembled commons,
Congregated as they sit,
An enormous mass of wit,
— Full of genius, taste, and fire,
Jealous pride, and critic ire —
Cleophon among the rest
(Like the swallow from her nest,
A familiar foreign bird),
Chatters loud and will be heard,
(With the accent and the grace
Which he brought with him from Thrace);
But we fear the tuneful strain
Will be turn'd to grief and pain;
He must sing a dirge perforce
When his trial takes its course;
We shall hear him moan and wail,
Like the plaintive nightingale.
It behoves the sacred Chorus, and of right
to them belongs,
To suggest the best advice in their addresses
and their songs,
In performance of our office, we present
with all humility

A proposal for removing groundless fears
and disability.
First that all that were inveigled into
Phrynichus's treason,
Should be suffer'd and received by rules of
evidence and reason
To clear their conduct — Secondly, that
none of our Athenian race
Should live suspected and subjected to loss
of franchise and disgrace,
Feeling it a grievous scandal when a single
naval fight
Renders foreigners and slaves partakers of
the city's right:
— Not that we condemn the measure; we
conceived it wisely done,
As a just and timely measure, and the first
and only one:
— But your kinsmen and your comrades,
those with whom you fought and bore
Danger, hardship, and fatigue, or with their
fathers long before,
Struggling on the land and ocean, laboring
with the spear and oar
— These we think, as they profess repent-
ance for their past behavior,
Might, by your exalted wisdoms, be re-
ceived to grace and favor.
Better it would be, believe us, casting off
revenge and pride,
To receive as friends and kinsmen all that
combat on our side
Into full and equal franchise: on the other
hand we fear,
If your hearts are fill'd with fancies,
haughty, captious, and severe;
While the shock of instant danger threatens
shipwreck to the state,
Such resolves will be lamented and re-
pented of too late.
If the Muse foresees at all
What in future will befall
Dirty Cleigenes the small —
He, the sovereign of the bath,
Will not long escape from scath;
But must perish by and by,
With his potash and his lye;
With his realm and dynasty,
His terraqueous scouring ball,
And his washes, one and all;
Therefore he can never cease
To declaim against a peace.

Often times have we reflected on a similar
    abuse,
In the choice of men for office, and of coins
    for common use;
For your old and standard pieces, valued,
    and approved, and tried,
Here among the Grecian nations, and in all
    the world beside;
Recognized in every realm for trusty stamp
    and pure assay,
Are rejected and abandon'd for the trash
    of yesterday;
For a vile, adulterate issue, drossy, counter-
    feit, and base,
Which the traffic of the city passes current
    in their place!
And the men that stood for office, noted for
    acknowledged worth,
And for manly deeds of honor, and for
    honorable birth;
Train'd in exercise and art, in sacred dances
    and in song,
All are ousted and supplanted by a base
    ignoble throng;
Paltry stamp and vulgar mettle raise them
    to command and place,
Brazen counterfeit pretenders, scoundrels
    of a scoundrel race;
Whom the state in former ages scarce would
    have allow'd to stand,
At the sacrifice of outcasts, as the scape-
    goats of the land.
— Time it is — and long has been, re-
    nouncing all your follies past,
To recur to sterling merit and intrinsic
    worth at last.
— If we rise, we rise with honor; if we fall,
    it must be so!
— But there was an ancient saying, which
    we all have heard and know,
That the wise, in dangerous cases, have
    esteem'd it safe and good
To receive a slight chastisement from *a
wand of noble wood.*

ÆACUS. By Jupiter; but he's a gentleman,
That master of yours.

XANTHIAS. A gentleman! To be sure he is;
Why, he does nothing else but wench and
    drink.

ÆACUS. His never striking you when you
    took his name —
Outfacing him and contradicting him! —

XANTHIAS. It might have been worse for
    him if he had.

ÆACUS. Well, that's well spoken, like a
    true-bred slave.
It's just the sort of language I delight in.

XANTHIAS. You love excuses?

ÆACUS. Yes; but I prefer
Cursing my master quietly in private.

XANTHIAS. Mischief you're fond of?

ÆACUS. Very fond indeed.

XANTHIAS. What think ye of muttering
    as you leave the room
After a beating?

ÆACUS. Why, that's pleasant too.

XANTHIAS. By Jove, is it! But listening
    at the door
To hear their secrets?

ÆACUS. Oh, there's nothing like it.

XANTHIAS. And then the reporting them
    in the neighborhood.

ÆACUS. That's beyond everything. —
    That's quite ecstatic.

XANTHIAS. Well, give me your hand.
    And, there, take mine — and buss me.
And there again — and now for Jupiter's
    sake! —
(For he's the patron of our cuffs and beat-
    ings)
Do tell me what's that noise of people
    quarreling
And abusing one another there within?

ÆACUS. Æschylus and Euripides, only!

XANTHIAS. Heh? — ? —?

ÆACUS. Why, there's a desperate busi-
    ness has broke out
Among these here dead people; — quite a
    tumult.

XANTHIAS. As how?

ÆACUS. First, there's a custom we have
    establish'd
In favor of professors of the arts.
When any one, the first in his own line,
Comes down amongst us here, he stands
    entitled
To privilege and precedence, with a seat
At Pluto's royal board.

XANTHIAS. I understand you.

ÆACUS. So he maintains it, till there
    comes a better
Of the same sort, and then resigns it up.

XANTHIAS. But why should Æschylus
    be disturb'd at this?

ÆACUS. He held the seat for tragedy, as
the master
In that profession.
XANTHIAS. Well, and who's there now?
ÆACUS. He kept it till Euripides ap-
peared;
But he collected audiences about him,
And flourish'd, and exhibited, and ha-
rangued
Before the thieves, and housebreakers, and
rogues,
Cut-purses, cheats, and vagabonds, and
villains,
That make the mass of population here;
And they — being quite transported, and
delighted
With his equivocations and evasions,
His subtleties and niceties and quibbles —
In short — they raised an uproar, and de-
clared him
Archpoet, by a general acclamation.
And he with this grew proud and confident,
And laid a claim to the seat where Æschy-
lus sat.
XANTHIAS. And did not he get pelted for
his pains?
ÆACUS. Why, no — The mob call'd out,
and it was carried,
To have a public trial of skill between them.
XANTHIAS. You mean the mob of scoun-
drels that you mention'd?
ÆACUS. Scoundrels indeed! Ay, scoun-
drels without number.
XANTHIAS. But Æschylus must have
had good friends and hearty?
ÆACUS. Yes; but good men are scarce
both here and elsewhere.
XANTHIAS. Well, what has Pluto settled
to be done?
ÆACUS. To have an examination and a
trial
In public.
XANTHIAS. But how comes it? — Sopho-
cles? —
Why does he not put forth his claim
amongst them?
ÆACUS. No, no! — He's not the kind of
man — not he!
I tell ye; the first moment that he came,
He went up to Æschylus and saluted him
And kiss'd his cheek and took his hand
quite kindly;

And Æschylus edged a little from his seat
To give him room; so now the story goes,
(At least I had it from Cleidemides)
He means to attend there as a stander-by,
Proposing to take up the conqueror;
If Æschylus gets the better, well and good,
He gives up his pretensions — but if not,
He'll stand a trial, he says, against Eurip-
ides.
XANTHIAS. There'll be strange doings.
ÆACUS. That there will — and shortly
— Here — in this place — strange things,
I promise you;
A kind of thing that no man could have
thought of;
Why, you'll see poetry weigh'd out and
measured.
XANTHIAS. What, will they bring their
tragedies to the steel-yards?
ÆACUS. Yes, will they — with their
rules and compasses
They'll measure, and examine, and compare,
And bring their plummets, and their lines
and levels,
To take the bearings — for Euripides
Says that he'll make a survey, word by
word.
XANTHIAS. Æschylus takes the thing to
heart, I doubt.
ÆACUS. He bent his brows and pored
upon the ground; I saw him.
XANTHIAS. Well, but who decides the
business?
ÆACUS. Why, there the difficulty lies —
for judges,
True learned judges, are grown scarce, and
Æschylus
Objected to the Athenians absolutely.
XANTHIAS. Considering them as rogues
and villains mostly.
ÆACUS. As being ignorant and empty
generally;
And in their judgment of the stage partic-
ularly.
In fine, they've fix'd upon that master of
yours,
As having had some practice in the busi-
ness.
But we must wait within — for when our
masters
Are warm and eager, stripes and blows
ensue. [Exit ÆACUS.]

CHORUS. The full-mouth'd master of the
tragic quire,
We shall behold him foam with rage and
ire;
— Confronting in the list
His eager, shrewd, sharp-tooth'd antago-
nist.
Then will his visual orbs be wildly whirl'd
And huge invectives will be hurl'd
Superb and supercilious,
Atrocious, atrabilious,
With furious gesture and with lips of foam,
And lion crest unconscious of the comb;
Erect with rage — his brow's impending
gloom
O'ershadowing his dark eyes' terrific blaze.
The opponent, dexterous and wary,
Will fend and parry:
While masses of conglomerated phrase,
Enormous, ponderous, and pedantic,
With indignation frantic,
And strength and force gigantic,
Are desperately sped
At his devoted head —
Then in different style
The touchstone and the file,
And subtleties of art
In turn will play their part;
Analysis and rule,
And every modern tool;
With critic scratch and scribble,
And nice invidious nibble;
Contending for the important choice,
A vast expenditure of human voice!

[*Enter* EURIPIDES, *and* ÆSCHYLUS.]

EURIPIDES. Don't give me your advice,
I claim the seat
As being a better and superior artist.
BACCHUS. What, Æschylus, don't you
speak? you hear his language.
EURIPIDES. He's mustering up a grand
commanding visage
— A silent attitude — the common trick
That he begins with in his tragedies.
BACCHUS. Come, have a care, my friend
— You'll say too much.
EURIPIDES. I know the man of old —
I've scrutinized
And shown him long ago for what he is,
A rude unbridled tongue, a haughty spirit;
Proud, arrogant, and insolently pompous;

Rough, clownish, boisterous, and overbear-
ing.
ÆSCHYLUS. Say'st thou me so? Thou
bastard of the earth,
With thy patch'd robes and rags of senti-
ment
Raked from the streets and stitch'd and
tack'd together!
Thou mumping, whining, beggarly hypo-
crite!
But you shall pay for it.
BACCHUS. There now, Æschylus,
You grow too warm. Restrain your ireful
mood.
ÆSCHYLUS. Yes; but I'll seize that
sturdy beggar first,
And search and strip him bare of his pre-
tensions.
BACCHUS. Quick! Quick! A sacrifice to
the winds — Make ready;
The storm of rage is gathering. Bring a
victim.
ÆSCHYLUS. — A wretch that has cor-
rupted everything;
Our music with his melodies from Crete;
Our morals with incestuous tragedies.
BACCHUS. Dear, worthy Æschylus, con-
tain yourself,
And as for you, Euripides, move off
This instant, if you're wise; I give you
warning.
Or else, with one of his big thumping
phrases,
You'll get your brains dash'd out, and all
your notions
And sentiments and matter mash'd to
pieces.
— And thee, most noble Æschylus, I be-
seech
With mild demeanor calm and affable
To hear and answer. — For it ill beseems
Illustrious bards to scold like market-
women.
But you roar out and bellow like a fur-
nace.
EURIPIDES. I'm up to it. — I'm re-
solved, and here I stand
Ready and steady — take what course you
will;
Let him be first to speak, or else let me.
I'll match my plots and characters against
him;

My sentiments and language, and what
  not:
Ay! and my music too, my Meleager,
My Æolus and my Telephus and all.
Bacchus. Well, Æschylus, — determine.
  What say you?
Æschylus. I wish the place of trial had
  been elsewhere,
I stand at disadvantage here.
Bacchus. As how?
Æschylus. Because my poems live on
  earth above,
And his died with him, and descended here,
And are at hand as ready witnesses;
But you decide the matter: I submit.
Bacchus. Come — let them bring me
  fire and frankincense,
That I may offer vows and make oblations
For an ingenious critical conclusion
To this same elegant and clever trial —
And you too, — sing me a hymn there. —
  To the Muses.
Chorus. To the Heavenly Nine we pe-
  tition,
Ye, that on earth or in air are forever
  kindly protecting the vagaries of
  learned ambition,
And at your ease from above our sense and
  folly directing (or poetical contests
  inspecting,
Deign to behold for a while as a scene of
  amusing attention, all the struggles
  of style and invention),
Aid, and assist, and attend, and afford to
  the furious authors your refined and
  enlighten'd suggestions;
Grant them ability — force and agility,
  quick recollections, and address in
  their answers and questions,
Pithy replies, with a word to the wise, and
  pulling and hauling, with inordinate
  uproar and bawling,
Driving and drawing, like carpenters saw-
  ing, their dramas asunder:
With suspended sense and wonder,
All are waiting and attending
On the conflict now depending!
Bacchus. Come, say your prayers, you
  two before the trial.
Æschylus. O Ceres, nourisher of my
  soul, maintain me
A worthy follower of thy mysteries.

Bacchus. There, you there, make your
  offering.
Euripides. Well, I will;
But I direct myself to other deities.
Bacchus. Hey, what? Your own? Some
  new ones?
Euripides. Most assuredly!
Bacchus. Well! Pray away, then — to
  your own new deities.
Euripides. Thou foodful Air, the nurse
  of all my notions;
And ye, the organic powers of sense and
  speech,
And keen refined olfactory discernment,
Assist my present search for faults and
  errors.
Chorus. Here beside you, here are we,
Eager all to hear and see
This abstruse and mighty battle
Of profound and learned prattle.
— But, as it appears to me,
Thus the course of it will be;
He, the junior and appellant,
Will advance as the assailant.
Aiming shrewd satyric darts
At his rival's noble parts;
And with sallies sharp and keen
Try to wound him in the spleen,
While the veteran rends and raises
Rifted, rough, uprooted phrases,
Wielded like a threshing staff
Scattering the dust and chaff.
Bacchus. Come, now begin, dispute
  away, but first I give you notice
That every phrase in your discourse must
  be refined, avoiding
Vulgar absurd comparisons, and awkward
  silly joking.
Euripides. At the first outset, I forbear
  to state my own pretensions;
Hereafter I shall mention them, when his
  have been refuted;
After I shall have fairly shown, how he
  befool'd and cheated
The rustic audience that he found, which
  Phrynichus bequeathed him.
He planted first upon the stage a figure
  veil'd and muffled,
An Achilles or a Niobe, that never show'd
  their faces;
But kept a tragic attitude, without a word
  to utter.

BACCHUS. No more they did: 't is very true.

EURIPIDES. — In the meanwhile the Chorus
Strung on ten strophes right-an-end, but they remain'd in silence.

BACCHUS. I liked that silence well enough, as well, perhaps, or better
Than those new talking characters —

EURIPIDES. That's from your want of judgment,
Believe me.

BACCHUS. Why, perhaps it is; but what was his intention?

EURIPIDES. Why, mere conceit and insolence; to keep the people waiting
Till Niobe should deign to speak, to drive his drama forward.

BACCHUS. O what a rascal. Now I see the tricks he used to play me.
— What makes you writhe and winch about? —

EURIPIDES. Because he feels my censures.
— Then having dragg'd and drawl'd along, half-way to the conclusion,
He foisted in a dozen words of noisy boisterous accent,
With lofty plumes and shaggy brows, mere bugbears of the language.
That no man ever heard before. —

ÆSCHYLUS. Alas! alas!

BACCHUS. Have done there!

EURIPIDES. He never used a simple word.

BACCHUS. Don't grind your teeth so strangely.

EURIPIDES. But "Bulwarks and Scamanders" and "Hippogrifs and Gorgons."
"On burnish'd shields emboss'd in brass;" bloody remorseless phrases
Which nobody could understand.

BACCHUS. Well, I confess, for my part, I used to keep awake at night, with guesses and conjectures
To think what kind of foreign bird he meant by griffin-horses.

ÆSCHYLUS. A figure on the heads of ships; you goose, you must have seen them.

BACCHUS. Well, from the likeness, I declare, I took it for Eruxis.

EURIPIDES. So! Figures from the heads of ships are fit for tragic diction.

ÆSCHYLUS. Well then — thou paltry wretch, explain. What were your own devices?

EURIPIDES. Not stories about flying-stags, like yours, and griffin-horses;
Nor terms nor images derived from tapestry Persian hangings.
When I received the Muse from you I found her puff'd and pamper'd
With pompous sentences and terms, a cumbrous huge virago.
My first attention was applied to make her look genteelly;
And bring her to a slighter shape by dint of lighter diet:
I fed her with plain household phrase, and cool familiar salad,
With water-gruel episode, with sentimental jelly,
With moral mincemeat; till at length I brought her into compass;
Cephisophon, who was my cook, contrived to make them relish.
I kept my plots distinct and clear, and, to prevent confusion,
My leading characters rehearsed their pedigrees for prologues.

ÆSCHYLUS. 'T was well, at least, that you forbore to quote your own extraction.

EURIPIDES. From the first opening of the scene, all persons were in action;
The master spoke, the slave replied, the women, young and old ones,
All had their equal share of talk —

ÆSCHYLUS. Come, then, stand forth and tell us,
What forfeit less than death is due for such an innovation?

EURIPIDES. I did it upon principle, from democratic motives.

BACCHUS. Take care, my friend — upon that ground your footing is but ticklish.

EURIPIDES. I taught these youths to speechify.

ÆSCHYLUS. I say so too. — Moreover I say that — for the public good — you ought to have been hang'd first.

EURIPIDES. The rules and forms of rhetoric, — the laws of composition,

To prate — to state — and in debate to
meet a question fairly:
At a dead lift to turn and shift — to make
a nice distinction.
ÆSCHYLUS. I grant it all — I make it all
— my ground of accusation.
EURIPIDES. The whole in cases and concerns occurring and recurring
At every turn and every day domestic and
familiar,
So that the audience, one and all, from
personal experience,
Were competent to judge the piece, and
form a fair opinion
Whether my scenes and sentiments agreed
with truth and nature.
I never took them by surprise to storm
their understandings,
With Memnons and Tydides's and idle
rattle-trappings
Of battle-steeds and clattering shields to
scare them from their senses;
But for a test (perhaps the best) our pupils
and adherents
May be distinguish'd instantly by person
and behavior;
His are Phormisius the rough, Meganetes
the gloomy,
Hobgoblin-headed, trumpet-mouth'd, grim
visaged, ugly-bearded;
But mine are Cleitophon the smooth, —
Theramenes the gentle.
BACCHUS. Theramenes — a clever hand,
a universal genius.
I never found him at a loss in all the turns
of party
To change his watchword at a word or at
a moment's warning.
EURIPIDES. Thus it was that I began,
With a nicer, neater plan;
Teaching men to look about,
Both within doors and without;
To direct their own affairs,
And their house and household wares;
Marking everything amiss —
"Where is that? and — What is this?"
"This is broken — that is gone,"
'T is the modern style and tone.
BACCHUS. Yes, by Jove — and at their
homes
Nowadays each master comes,
Of a sudden bolting in

With an uproar and a din;
Rating all the servants round,
"If it's lost, it must be found.
Why was all the garlic wasted?
There, that honey has been tasted:
And these olives pilfer'd here.
Where's the pot we bought last year?
What's become of all the fish?
Which of you has broke the dish?"
Thus it is, but heretofore,
The moment that they cross'd the door,
They sat them down to doze and snore.
    CHORUS. "Noble Achilles! you see the
    disaster
    The shame and affront, and an enemy
    nigh!"
Oh! bethink thee, mighty master,
    Think betimes of your reply;
Yet beware, lest anger force
Your hasty chariot from the course;
Grievous charges have been heard,
With many a sharp and bitter word,
Notwithstanding, mighty chief,
Let Prudence fold her cautious reef
In your anger's swelling sail;
By degrees you may prevail,
But beware of your behavior
Till the wind is in your favor:
Now for your answer, illustrious architect,
    Founder of lofty theatrical lays!
Patron in chief of our tragical trumperies!
    Open the floodgate of figure and phrase!
ÆSCHYLUS. My spirit is kindled with
    anger and shame,
To so base a competitor forced to reply,
But I needs must retort, or the wretch will
    report
That he left me refuted and foil'd in debate;
Tell me then, What are the principal merits
Entitling a poet to praise and renown?
    EURIPIDES. The improvement of morals,
    the progress of mind,
When a poet, by skill and invention,
Can render his audience virtuous and wise.
    ÆSCHYLUS. But if you, by neglect or
    intention,
Have done the reverse, and from brave
    honest spirits
Depraved, and have left them degraded
    and base,
Tell me, what punishment ought you to
    suffer?

BACCHUS. Death, to be sure! — Take that answer from me.

ÆSCHYLUS. Observe then, and mark, what our citizens were,
When first from my care they were trusted to you;
Not scoundrel informers, or paltry buffoons,
Evading the services due to the state;
But with hearts all on fire, for adventure and war,
Distinguished for hardiness, stature, and strength,
Breathing forth nothing but lances and darts,
Arms, and equipment, and battle array,
Bucklers, and shields, and habergeons, and hauberks,
Helmets, and plumes, and heroic attire.

BACCHUS. There he goes, hammering on with his helmets,
He'll be the death of me one of these days.

EURIPIDES. But how did you manage to make 'em so manly,
What was the method, the means that you took?

BACCHUS. Speak, Æschylus, speak, and behave yourself better,
And don't in your rage stand so silent and stern.

ÆSCHYLUS. A drama, brimful with heroical spirit.

EURIPIDES. What did you call it?

ÆSCHYLUS. "The Chiefs against Thebes,"
That inspired each spectator with martial ambition,
Courage, and ardor, and prowess, and pride.

BACCHUS. But you did very wrong to encourage the Thebans.
Indeed, you deserve to be punish'd, you do,
For the Thebans are grown to be capital soldiers,
You've done us a mischief by that very thing.

ÆSCHYLUS. The fault was your own, if you took other courses;
The lesson I taught was directed to you:
Then I gave you the glorious theme of "the Persians,"
Replete with sublime patriotical strains,
The record and example of noble achievement,

The delight of the city, the pride of the stage.

BACCHUS. I rejoiced, I confess, when the tidings were carried
To old King Darius, so long dead and buried,
And the chorus in concert kept wringing their hands,
Weeping and wailing, and crying, Alas!

ÆSCHYLUS. Such is the duty, the task of a poet,
Fulfilling in honor his office and trust.
Look to traditional history — look
To antiquity, primitive, early, remote:
See there, what a blessing illustrious poets
Conferred on mankind, in the centuries past,
Orpheus instructed mankind in religion,
Reclaim'd them from bloodshed and barbarous rites:
Musæus deliver'd the doctrine of medicine,
And warnings prophetic for ages to come:
Next came old Hesiod, teaching us husbandry,
Ploughing, and sowing, and rural affairs,
Rural economy, rural astronomy,
Homely morality, labor, and thrift:
Homer himself, our adorable Homer,
What was his title to praise and renown?
What, but the worth of the lessons he taught us,
Discipline, arms, and equipment of war?

BACCHUS. Yes, but Pantacles was never the wiser;
For in the procession he ought to have led,
When his helmet was tied, he kept puzzling, and tried
To fasten the crest on the crown of his head.

ÆSCHYLUS. But other brave warriors and noble commanders
Were train'd in his lessons to valor and skill;
Such was the noble heroical Lamachus;
Others besides were instructed by him;
And I, from his fragments ordaining a banquet,
Furnish'd and deck'd with majestical phrase,
Brought forward the models of ancient achievement,
Teucer, Patroclus, and chiefs of antiquity;
Raising and rousing Athenian hearts,

When the signal of onset was blown in their
ear,
With a similar ardor to dare and to do;
But I never allow'd of your lewd Stheno-
bœas,
Or filthy, detestable Phædras — not I —
Indeed, I should doubt if my drama
throughout
Exhibit an instance of woman in love.
EURIPIDES. No, you were too stern for
an amorous turn,
For Venus and Cupid too stern and too
stupid.
ÆSCHYLUS. May they leave me at rest,
and with peace in my breast,
And infest and pursue your kindred and you,
With the very same blow that despatch'd
you below.
BACCHUS. That was well enough said;
with the life that he led,
He himself in the end got a wound from a
friend.
EURIPIDES. But what, after all, is the
horrible mischief ?
My poor Sthenobœas, what harm have
they done?
ÆSCHYLUS. The example is followed, the
practice has gain'd,
And women of family, fortune, and worth,
Bewilder'd with shame in a passionate
fury,
Have poison'd themselves for Bellerophon's
sake.
EURIPIDES. But at least you'll allow that
I never invented it,
Phædra's affair was a matter of fact.
ÆSCHYLUS. A fact, with a vengeance!
but horrible facts
Should be buried in silence, not bruited
abroad,
Nor brought forth on the stage, nor em-
blazon'd in poetry,
Children and boys have a teacher assign'd
them —
The bard is a master for manhood and
youth,
Bound to instruct them in virtue and
truth,
Beholden and bound.
EURIPIDES. But is virtue a sound?
Can any mysterious virtue be found
In bombastical, huge, hyperbolical phrase?

ÆSCHYLUS. Thou dirty, calamitous
wretch, recollect
That exalted ideas of fancy require
To be clothed in a suitable vesture of
phrase;
And that heroes and gods may be fairly
supposed
Discoursing in words of a mightier import,
More lofty by far than the children of man;
As the pomp of apparel assign'd to their
persons,
Produced on the stage and presented to
view,
Surpasses in dignity, splendor, and luster
Our popular garb and domestic attire,
A practice which nature and reason allow,
But which you disannull'd and rejected.
EURIPIDES. As how?
ÆSCHYLUS. When you brought forth
your kings, in a villainous fashion,
In patches and rags, as a claim for com-
passion.
EURIPIDES. And this is a grave misde-
meanor, forsooth!
ÆSCHYLUS. It has taught an example of
sordid untruth;
For the rich of the city, that ought to equip,
And to serve with, a ship, are appealing to
pity,
Pretending distress — with an overworn
dress.
BACCHUS. By Jove, so they do; with a
waistcoat brand new,
Worn closely within, warm and new for the
skin;
And if they escape in this beggarly shape,
You'll meet 'em at market, I warrant 'em
all,
Buying the best at the fishmonger's stall.
ÆSCHYLUS. He has taught every soul to
sophisticate truth;
And debauch'd all the bodies and minds of
the youth;
Leaving them morbid, and pallid, and spare;
And the places of exercise vacant and
bare: —
The disorder has spread to the fleet and
the crew;
The service is ruin'd, and ruin'd by you —
With prate and debate in a mutinous state;
Whereas, in my day, 't was a different way;
Nothing they said, nor knew nothing to say,

But to call for their porridge, and cry,
"Pull away."
BACCHUS. Yes — yes, they knew this,
How to f . . . in the teeth
Of the rower beneath;
And befoul their own comrades,
And pillage ashore;
But now they forget the command of the
    oar: —
Prating and splashing,
Discussing and dashing,
They steer here and there,
With their eyes in the air,
Hither and thither,
Nobody knows whither.
ÆSCHYLUS. Can the reprobate mark in
    the course he has run,
One crime unattempted, a mischief un-
    done?
With his horrible passions, of sisters and
    brothers,
And sons-in-law, tempted by villainous
    mothers,
And temples defiled with a bastardly birth,
And women, divested of honor or worth,
That talk about life "as a death upon
    earth";
And sophistical frauds and rhetorical
    bawds;
Till now the whole state is infested with
    tribes
Of scriveners and scribblers, and rascally
    scribes —
All practice of masculine vigor and pride,
Our wrestling and running, are all laid aside,
And we see that the city can hardly pro-
    vide
For the Feast of the Founder, a racer of
    force
To carry the torch and accomplish a course.
BACCHUS. Well, I laugh'd till I cried
The last festival tide,
At the fellow that ran, —
'T was a heavy fat man,
And he panted and hobbled,
And stumbled and wabbled,
And the pottery people about the gate,
Seeing him hurried, and tired, and late,
Stood to receive him in open rank,
Helping him on with a hearty spank
Over the shoulder and over the flank,
The flank, the loin, the back, the shoulders,

With shouts of applause from all beholders;
While he ran on with a filthy fright,
Puffing his link to keep it alight.
CHORUS. Ere the prize is lost and won
Mighty doings will be done.
Now then — (though to judge aright
Is difficult, when force and might
Are opposed with ready slight,
When the Champion that is cast
Tumbles uppermost at last)
— Since you meet in equal match,
Argue, contradict and scratch,
Scuffle, and abuse and bite,
Tear and fight,
With all your wits and all your might.
— Fear not for a want of sense
Or judgment in your audience,
That defect has been removed;
They're prodigiously improved,
Disciplined, alert and smart,
Drill'd and exercised in art:
Each has got a little book,
In the which they read and look,
Doing all their best endeavor
To be critical and clever;
Thus their own ingenious natures,
Aided and improved by learning,
Will provide you with spectators
Shrewd, attentive, and discerning.
. . . .
EURIPIDES. Proceed — Continue!
BACCHUS. Yes, you must continue,
Æschylus, I command you to continue.
And you, keep a look-out and mark his
    blunders.
ÆSCHYLUS. "From his sepulchral mound
    I call my father
"To listen and hear" —
EURIPIDES. There's a tautology!
"To listen and hear" —
BACCHUS. Why, don't you see, you
    ruffian!
It's a dead man he's calling to — Three
    times
We call to 'em, but they can't be made to
    hear.
ÆSCHYLUS. And you: your prologues,
    of what kind were they?
EURIPIDES. I'll show ye; and if you'll
    point out a tautology,
Or a single word clapped in to botch a
    verse —

That's all! — I 'll give you leave to spit upon me.

BACCHUS. Well, I can't help myself; I 'm bound to attend.

Begin then with these same fine-spoken prologues.

EURIPIDES. "Œdipus was at first a happy man." . . .

ÆSCHYLUS. Not he, by Jove! — but born to misery;

Predicted and predestined by an oracle
Before his birth to murder his own father!
— Could he have been "at first a happy man?"

EURIPIDES. . . . . "But afterwards became a wretched mortal."

ÆSCHYLUS. By no means! he continued to be wretched,
— Born wretched, and exposed as soon as born
Upon a potsherd in a winter's night;
Brought up a foundling with disabled feet;
Then married — a young man to an aged woman,
That proved to be his mother — whereupon
He tore his eyes out.

BACCHUS. To complete his happiness,
He ought to have served at sea with Erasinides.

. . . .

There! — that's enough — now come to music, can't ye?

EURIPIDES. I mean it; I shall now proceed to expose him
As a bad composer, awkward, uninventive,
Repeating the same strain perpetually. —

CHORUS. I stand in wonder and perplext
To think of what will follow next.
Will he dare to criticize
The noble bard, that did devise
Our oldest, boldest harmonies,
Whose mighty music we revere?
Much I marvel, much I fear. —

EURIPIDES. Mighty fine music, truly! I 'll give ye a sample;
It 's every inch cut out to the same pattern.

BACCHUS. I 'll mark — I 've pick'd these pebbles up for counters.

EURIPIDES. Noble Achilles! Forth to the rescue!

Forth to the rescue with ready support!

Hasten and go,
There is havoc and woe,
Hasty defeat,
And a bloody retreat,
Confusion and rout,
And the terrible shout
Of a conquering foe,
Tribulation and woe!

BACCHUS. Whoh hoh there! we 've had woes enough, I reckon;
Therefore I 'll go to wash away my woe
In a warm bath.

EURIPIDES. No, do pray wait an instant,
And let me give you first another strain,
Transferr'd to the stage from music to the lyre.

BACCHUS. Proceed then — only give us no more woes.

EURIPIDES. The supremacy scepter and haughty command
Of the Grecian land — with a flatto-flatto-flatto-thrat —
And the ravenous sphinx, with her horrible brood,
Thirsting for blood — with a flatto-flatto-flatto-thrat,
And armies equipt for a vengeful assault,
For Paris's fault — with a flatto-flatto-flatto-thrat.

BACCHUS. What herb is that same flatto-thrat? Some simple,
I guess, you met with in the field of Marathon:
— But such a tune as this! You must have learned it
From fellows hauling buckets at the well.

ÆSCHYLUS. Such were the strains I purified and brought
To just perfection — taught by Phrynichus,
Not copying him, but culling other flowers
From those fair meadows which the Muses love —
— But he filches and begs, adapts and borrows
Snatches of tunes from minstrels in the street,
Strumpets and vagabonds — the lullabys
Of nurses and old women — jigs and ballads —
I 'll give ye a proof — Bring me a lyre here, somebody.
What signifies a lyre? the castanets

Will suit him better — Bring the castanets,
With Euripides's Muse to snap her fingers
In cadence to her master's compositions.
    BACCHUS. This Muse, I take it, is a
        Lesbian Muse.
    ÆSCHYLUS. Gentle halcyons, ye that
        lave
Your snowy plume,
Sporting on the summer wave;
    Ye too that around the room,
On the rafters of the roof
Strain aloft your airy woof;
Ye spiders, spiders ever spinning,
Never ending, still beginning —
Where the dolphin loves to follow,
Weltering in the surge's hollow,
Dear to Neptune and Apollo;
By the seamen understood
Ominous of harm or good;
In capricious, eager sallies,
Chasing, racing round the galleys.
    ÆSCHYLUS. Well now. Do you see this?
    BACCHUS. I see it —
    ÆSCHYLUS. Such is your music. I shall
        now proceed
To give a specimen of your monodies —
    O dreary shades of night!
    What phantoms of affright
    Have scared my troubled sense
    With saucer eyes immense;
    And huge horrific paws
    With bloody claws!
    Ye maidens haste, and bring
    From the fair spring
A bucket of fresh water; whose clear stream
May purify me from this dreadful dream:
    But oh! my dream is out!
    Ye maidens search about!
O mighty powers of mercy, can it be;
    That Glyke, Glyke, she
(My friend and civil neighbor heretofore),
Has robb'd my henroost of its feather'd
    store?
    With the dawn I was beginning,
    Spinning, spinning, spinning, spinning,
    Unconscious of the meditated crime;
Meaning to sell by yarn at market-time.
    Now tears alone are left me,
    My neighbor hath bereft me,
Of all — of all — of all — all but a tear!
Since he, my faithful trusty chanticleer
    Is flown — is flown! — Is gone — is gone!

— But, O ye nymphs of sacred Ida, bring
Torches and bows, with arrows on the
    string;
    And search around
    All the suspected ground:
And thou, fair huntress of the sky;
Deign to attend, descending from on high—
— While Hecate, with her tremendous
    torch,
Even from the topmost garret to the porch
Explores the premises with search exact,
To find the thief and ascertain the fact —
    BACCHUS. Come, no more songs!
    ÆSCHYLUS. I've had enough of 'em;
For my part, I shall bring him to the
    balance,
As a true test of our poetic merit,
To prove the weight of our respective
    verses.
    BACCHUS. Well then, so be it — if it
        must be so,
That I'm to stand here like a cheesemonger
Retailing poetry with a pair of scales.
    CHORUS. Curious eager wits pursue
Strange devices quaint and new,
Like the scene you witness here,
Unaccountable and queer;
I myself, if merely told it,
If I did not here behold it,
Should have deem'd it utter folly,
Craziness and nonsense wholly.

[*Enter* PLUTO.]

    BACCHUS. Move up; stand close to the
        balance!
    EURIPIDES. Here are we —
    BACCHUS. Take hold now, and each of
        you repeat a verse,
And don't leave go before I call to you!
    EURIPIDES. We're ready.
    BACCHUS. Now, then, each repeat a
        verse.
    EURIPIDES. "I wish that Argo with her
        woven wings."
    ÆSCHYLUS. "O streams of Sperchius,
        and ye pastured plains."
    BACCHUS. Let go! — See now — this
        scale outweighs that other
Very considerably —
    EURIPIDES. How did it happen?
    BACCHUS. He slipp'd a river in, like the
        wool-jobbers,

To moisten his meter — but your line was
    light,
A thing with wings — ready to fly away.
EURIPIDES. Let him try once again then,
    and take hold.
BACCHUS. Take hold once more.
EURIPIDES. We're ready.
BACCHUS. Now repeat.
EURIPIDES. "Speech is the temple and
    altar of persuasion."
ÆSCHYLUS. "Death is a God that loves
    no sacrifice."
BACCHUS. Let go! — See there again!
This scale sinks down;
No wonder that it should, with Death put
    into it,
The heaviest of all calamities.
EURIPIDES. But I put in persuasion
    finely express'd
In the best terms.
BACCHUS. Perhaps so; but persuasion
Is soft and light and silly — Think of some-
    thing
That's heavy and huge, to outweigh him,
    something solid.
EURIPIDES. Let's see — Where have I
    got it? Something solid?
BACCHUS. "Achilles has thrown twice —
    Twice a deuce ace!"
Come now, one trial more; this is the last.
EURIPIDES. "He grasp'd a mighty mace
    of massy weight."
ÆSCHYLUS. "Cars upon cars, and
    corpses heap'd pell mell."
BACCHUS. He has nick'd you again —
EURIPIDES. Why so? What has he done?
BACCHUS. He has heap'd ye up cars and
    corpses, such a load
As twenty Egyptian laborers could not
    carry —
ÆSCHYLUS. Come, no more single lines
    — let him bring all,
His wife, his children, his Cephisophon,
His books and everything, himself to
    boot —
I'll counterpoise them with a couple of
    lines.
BACCHUS. Well, they're both friends of
    mine — I shan't decide
To get myself ill-will from either party;
One of them seems extraordinary clever,
And the other suits my taste particularly.

PLUTO. Won't you decide then, and con-
    clude the business?
BACCHUS. Suppose then I decide; what
    then?
PLUTO. Then take him
Away with you, whichever you prefer,
As a present for your pains in coming down
    here.
BACCHUS. Heaven bless ye — Well —
    let's see now — Can't ye advise me?
This is the case — I'm come in search of
    a poet —
PLUTO. With what design?
BACCHUS. With this design; to see
The City again restored to peace and
    wealth,
Exhibiting tragedies in a proper style.
— Therefore whichever gives the best
    advice
On public matters I shall take him with me.
— First then of Alcibiades, what think ye?
The City is in hard labor with the question.
EURIPIDES. What are her sentiments
    towards him?
BACCHUS. What?
"She loves and she detests and longs to
    have him."
But tell me, both of you, your own opin-
    ions.
EURIPIDES. I hate the man, that in his
    country's service
Is slow, but ready and quick to work her
    harm;
Unserviceable except to serve himself.
BACCHUS. Well said, by Jove! — Now
    you — Give us a sentence.
ÆSCHYLUS. 'T is rash and idle policy to
    foster
A lion's whelp within the city walls,
But when he's rear'd and grown you must
    indulge him.
BACCHUS. By Jove then I'm quite puz-
    zled; one of them
Has answer'd clearly, and the other sen-
    sibly:
But give us both of ye one more opinion;
— What means are left of safety for the
    state?
EURIPIDES. To tack Cinesias like a pair
    of wings
To Cleocritus' shoulders, and dispatch them
From a precipice to sail across the seas.

BACCHUS. It seems a joke; but there's some sense in it.

EURIPIDES. . . . Then being both equipp'd with little cruets
They might coöperate in a naval action,
By sprinkling vinegar in the enemies' eyes.
— But I can tell you and will.

BACCHUS. Speak, and explain then —

EURIPIDES. If we mistrust where present trust is placed,
Trusting in what was heretofore mistrusted —

BACCHUS. How! What? I'm at a loss — Speak it again
Not quite so learnedly — more plainly and simply.

EURIPIDES. If we withdraw the confidence we placed
In these our present statesmen, and transfer it
To those whom we mistrusted heretofore,
This seems I think our fairest chance for safety:
If with our present counselors we fail,
Then with their opposites we might succeed.

BACCHUS. That's capitally said, my Palamedes!
My politician! Was it all your own?
Your own invention?

EURIPIDES. All except the cruets;
That was a notion of Cephisophon's.

BACCHUS. Now you — what say you?

ÆSCHYLUS. Inform me about the city —
What kind of persons has she placed in office?
Does she promote the worthiest?

BACCHUS. No, not she,
She can't abide 'em.

ÆSCHYLUS. Rogues then she prefers?

BACCHUS. Not altogether, she makes use of 'em
Perforce as it were.

ÆSCHYLUS. Then who can hope to save
A state so wayward and perverse, that finds
No sort of habit fitted for her wear?
Drugget or superfine, nothing will suit her!

BACCHUS. Do think a little how she can be saved.

ÆSCHYLUS. Not here; when I return there, I shall speak.

BACCHUS. No, do pray send some good advice before you.

ÆSCHYLUS. When they regard their lands as enemy's ground,
Their enemy's possessions as their own,
Their seamen and the fleet their only safeguard,
Their sole resource hardship and poverty,
And resolute endurance in distress —

BACCHUS. That's well, — but juries eat up everything,
And we shall lose our supper if we stay.

PLUTO. Decide then —

BACCHUS. You'll decide for your own selves,
I'll make a choice according to my fancy.

EURIPIDES. Remember, then, your oath to your poor friend;
And, as you swore and promised, rescue me.

BACCHUS. "It was my tongue that swore" — I fix on Æschylus.

EURIPIDES. O wretch! what have you done?

BACCHUS. Me? Done? What should I?
Voted for Æschylus to be sure — Why not?

EURIPIDES. And after such a villainous act, you dare
To view me face to face — Art not ashamed?

BACCHUS. Why shame, in point of fact, is nothing real:
Shame is the apprehension of a vision
Reflected from the surface of opinion —
— The opinion of the public — they must judge.

EURIPIDES. O cruel! — Will you abandon me to death?

BACCHUS. Why perhaps death is life, and life is death,
And victuals and drink an illusion of the senses;
For what is Death but an eternal sleep?
And does not Life consist in sleeping and eating?

PLUTO. Now, Bacchus, you'll come here with us within.

BACCHUS. What for?

PLUTO. To be received and entertain'd
With a feast before you go.

BACCHUS. That's well imagined,
With all my heart — I've not the least objection.

CHORUS. Happy is the man possessing
The superior holy blessing
Of a judgment and a taste
Accurate, refined and chaste;
As it plainly doth appear
In the scene presented here;
Where the noble worthy Bard
Meets with a deserved reward,
Suffer'd to depart in peace
Freely with a full release,
To revisit once again
His kindred and his countrymen —
Hence moreover
You discover,
That to sit with Socrates,
In a dream of learned ease;
Quibbling, counter-quibbling, prating,
Argufying and debating
With the metaphysic sect,
Daily sinking in neglect,
Growing careless, incorrect,
While the practice and the rules
Of the true poetic Schools
Are renounced or slighted wholly,
Is a madness and a folly.

PLUTO. Go forth with good wishes and
hearty good-will,
And salute the good people on Pallas's
hill;
Let them hear and admire father Æschylus
still
In his office of old which again he must fill:
— You must guide and direct them,
Instruct and correct them,
With a lesson in verse,
For you'll find them much worse;
Greater fools then before, and their folly
much more,
And more numerous far than the block-
heads of yore —
— And give Cleophon this,
And bid him not miss,
But be sure to attend
To the summons I send:
To Nicomachus too,
And the rest of the crew

That devise and invent
New taxes and tribute,
Are summonses sent,
Which you'll mind to distribute.
Bid them come to their graves,
Or, like runaway slaves,
If they linger and fail,
We shall drag them to jail;
Down here in the dark
With a brand and a mark.

ÆSCHYLUS. I shall do as you say;
But the while I'm away,
Let the seat that I held
Be by Sophocles fill'd,
As deservedly reckon'd
My pupil and second
In learning and merit
And tragical spirit —
And take special care;
Keep that reprobate there
Far aloof from the Chair;
Let him never sit in it
An hour or a minute,
By chance or design
To profane what was mine.

PLUTO. Bring forward the torches! —
The Chorus shall wait
And attend on the Poet in triumph and state
With a thundering chant of majestical tone
To wish him farewell, with a tune of his
own.

CHORUS. Now may the powers of the
earth give a safe and speedy departure
To the Bard at his second birth, with a
prosperous happy revival;
And may the city, fatigued with wars and
long revolution,
At length be brought to return to just and
wise resolutions;
Long in peace to remain — Let restless
Cleophon hasten
Far from amongst us here — since wars
are his only diversion,
Thrace his native land will afford him wars
in abundance.

THE CAPTIVES

(CAPTIVI)

By PLAUTUS

Translated in the original meters by EDWARD H. SUGDEN

CHARACTERS

Ergasilus, *a parasite*

Hegio, *an old gentleman*

Philocrates, *an Elian Knight,*⎫
Tyndarus, *son of Hegio*   ⎬ *the prisoners*
                                 ⎭

Aristophontes, *a prisoner*

Philopolemus, *a young man, son of Hegio*

Stalagmus, *a slave*

Overseers of slaves

A boy

THE CAPTIVES

[*The Scene represents the house of* HEGIO *in Ætolia. Before the house are seen standing in chains the two prisoners*, PHILOCRATES *and* TYNDARUS.]

PROLOGUE. You all can see two prisoners standing here,
Standing in bonds; they stand, they do not sit;
In this you'll witness that I speak the truth.
Old Hegio, who lives here, is this one's father;
But how he's come to be his father's slave
My prologue shall inform you, if you'll listen.
This old man had two sons; the one of whom
Was stolen by a slave when four years old.
He ran away to Elis and there sold him
To this one's father.
— Do you see? — That's right!
Yon fellow in the gallery says he does n't?
Let him come nearer, then! What, there's no room?
If there's no room to sit, there's room to walk!
You'd like to send me begging, would you, sir!
Pray, don't suppose I'll crack my lungs for *you!*
You gentlemen of means and noble rank
Receive the rest; I hate to be in debt.
That run-a-way, as I've already said,
When in his flight he'd stolen from his home
His master's son, sold him to this man's father,
Who, having bought him, gave him to his son
To be his valet; for the two lads were
Much of an age. Now he's his father's slave
In his own home, nor does his father know it;
See how the gods play ball with us poor men!
Now then, I've told you how he lost *one* son.
The Ætolians and the Elians being at war,
His *other* son, a not uncommon thing

In war, was taken prisoner; and a doctor
At Elis, called Menarchus, bought him there.
His father then began to buy up Elians,
To see if he could find one to exchange
Against his son, — the one that is a prisoner;
The other, who's at home, he does n't know
Now, only yesterday he heard a rumor
How that an Elian knight of highest rank
And noblest family was taken prisoner;
He spared no cash if he might save his son;
And so, to get him home more readily,
He bought these two from the commissioners.
But they between themselves have laid a plot,
So that the slave may get his lord sent home.
Thus they've exchanged their clothing and their names;
He's called Philocrates, *he* Tyndarus,
And either plays the other's part to-day.
The slave to-day will work this clever dodge,
And get his master set at liberty.
By the same act he'll save his brother too,
And get him brought back free to home and father,
Though all unwitting: oft we do more good
In ignorance than by our best-laid plans.
Well, ignorantly, in their own deceit,
They've so arranged and worked their little trick,
That he shall still remain his father's slave.
For now, not knowing it, he serves his father.
What things of naught are men, when one reflects on 't!
This story's ours to act, and yours to see.
But let me give you one brief word of warning:
It's well worth while to listen to this play.
It's not been treated in a hackneyed fashion,

Nor like the rest of plays; here you 'll not
    find
Verses that are too nasty to be quoted.
Here is no perjured pimp, or crafty girl,
Or braggart captain. — Pray, don't be afraid
Because I said a war was going on
Between the Ætolians and the Elians;
The battles won't take place upon the stage.
We 're dressed for comedy; you can't expect
That we should act a tragedy all at once.
If anybody 's itching for a fight,
Just let him start a quarrel; if he gets
An opposite that 's stronger, I dare bet
He 'll quickly see more fighting than he
    likes,
And never long to see a fight again.
I 'm off. Farewell, ye most judicious judges
At home, most valiant fighters in the field!
                                [Exit Prologue.]

[Enter ERGASILUS *from the town.]*

ERGASILUS. *Grace* is the name the boys
    have given me,
Because I 'm always found *before the meat!*
The wits, I know, say it 's ridiculous;
But so don't I! For at the banquet-table
Your gamester throws the dice and asks for
    grace.
Then is *grace* there or not? Of course she is!
But, more of course, we parasites are there,
Though no one ever asks or summons us!
Like mice we live on other people's food;
In holidays, when folks go out of town,
Our teeth enjoy a holiday as well.
As, when it 's warm, the snails lie in their
    shells,
And, failing dew, live on their native juices;
So parasites lie hid in misery
All through the holidays, living on their
    juices,
Whilst those they feed on jaunt it in the
    country.
During the holidays, we parasites
Are greyhounds; when they 're over, we are
    mastiffs,
Bred out of "Odious" by "Prince of Bores."
Now here, unless your parasite can stand
Hard fisticuffs, and has no strong objection
To have the crockery broken on his pate,
He 'd better go and take a porter's billet
At the Trigeminal gate; which lot, I fear,
Is not at all unlikely to be mine.

My patron has been captured by the foe —
The Ætolians and the Elians are at war,
(This is Ætolia); Philopolemus,
The son of Hegio here, whose house this is,
In Elis lies a prisoner; so this house
A house of lamentation is to me;
As oft as I behold it, I must weep.
Now for his son's sake, he 's begun a trade,
Dishonorable, hateful to himself;
He 's buying prisoners, if perchance he may
Find any to exchange against his son.
O how I pray that he may gain his wish!
Till he 's recovered, I am past recovery.
The other youths are selfish, hopelessly,
And only he keeps up the ancient style.
I 've never flattered him without reward;
And the good father takes after his son!
Now I 'll go see him. Ha! the door is open-
    ing,
Whence I have often come, just drunk with
    gorging.

[Enter from the house HEGIO *and an
    Overseer.]*

HEGIO. Attend to me; those prisoners
    that I bought
A day ago from the Commissioners
Out of the spoil, put lighter fetters on them;
Take off these heavier ones with which
    they 're bound,
And let them walk indoors or out at will;
But watch them with the utmost careful-
    ness.
For when a free man 's taken prisoner,
He 's just like a wild bird; if once he gets
A chance of running off, it 's quite enough;
You need n't hope to catch your man again.
OVERSEER. Why, all of us would rather
    far be free
Than slaves.
HEGIO. Why not take steps, then, to be
    free?
OVERSEER. Shall I give *leg-bail?* I 've
    naught else to give!
HEGIO. I fancy that in that case you
    would *catch it!*
OVERSEER. I 'll be like that wild bird you
    spoke about.
HEGIO. All right; then I will clap you in
    a cage.
Enough of this; do what I said, and go.
                    [Exit Overseer into the house.]

I'll to my brother's, to my other captives,
To see how they've behaved themselves
    last night,
And then I'll come back home again
    straightway.
    ERGASILUS [*aside*]. It grieves me that
    the poor old man should ply
This gaoler's trade to save his hapless son.
But if perchance the son can be brought
    back,
The father may turn hangman: what care I?
    HEGIO. Who speaks there?
    ERGASILUS. One who suffers in your grief.
I'm growing daily thinner, older, weaker!
See, I'm all skin and bones, as lean as lean!
All that I eat at home does me no good;
Only a bite at a friend's agrees with me.
    HEGIO. Ergasilus! hail!
    ERGASILUS. Heav'n bless you, Hegio!
    HEGIO. Don't weep!
    ERGASILUS. Not weep for him? What,
    not bewail
That excellent young man?
    HEGIO. I always knew
You and my son to be the best of friends.
    ERGASILUS. Alas! we don't appreciate
    our blessings
Till we have lost the gifts we once enjoyed.
Now that your son is in the foeman's hands,
I realize how much he was to me!
    HEGIO. Ah, if a stranger feels his loss so
    much,
What must *I* feel? He was my only joy.
    ERGASILUS. A stranger? I a stranger?
    Hegio,
Never say that nor cherish such a thought!
Your only joy he was, but oh! to me
Far dearer than a thousand only joys.
    HEGIO. You're right to make your
    friend's distress your own;
But come, cheer up!
    ERGASILUS. Alas! it pains me here,
That now the feaster's army is discharged.
    HEGIO. And can't you meantime find
    another general
To call to arms this army that's discharged?
    ERGASILUS. No fear! since Philopolemus
    was taken,
Who filled that post, they all refuse to act.
    HEGIO. And it's no wonder they refuse
    to act.
You need so many men of divers races

To work for you; first, those of Bakerton;
And several tribes inhabit Bakerton;
Then men of Breadport and of Biscuitville,
Of Thrushborough and Ortolania,
And all the various soldiers of the sea.
    ERGASILUS. How oft the noblest talents
    lie concealed!
O what a splendid general you would make,
Though now you're serving as a private
    merely.
    HEGIO. Be of good cheer; in a few days, I
    trust,
I shall receive my dear son home again.
I've got a youthful Elian prisoner,
Whom I am hoping to exchange for him,
One of the highest rank and greatest wealth.
    ERGASILUS. May Heaven grant it!
    HEGIO. Where've you been invited
To dine to-day?
    ERGASILUS. Why, nowhere that I know
    of.
Why do you ask?
    HEGIO. Because it is my birthday;
And so, I pray you, come and dine with me.
    ERGASILUS. Well said indeed!
    HEGIO. That is if you're content
With frugal fare.
    ERGASILUS. Well, if it's not *too* frugal;
I get enough of that, you know, at home.
    HEGIO. Well, name your figure!
    ERGASILUS. Done! unless I get
A better offer, and on such conditions
As better suit my partners and myself.
As I am selling you my whole estate,
It's only fair that I should make my terms.
    HEGIO. I fear that this estate you're sell-
    ing me
Has got a bottomless abyss within't!
But if you come, come early.
    ERGASILUS. Now, if you like!
    HEGIO. Go hunt a hare; you've only
    caught a weasel.
The path my guest must tread is full of
    stones.
    ERGASILUS. You won't dissuade me,
    Hegio; don't think it!
I'll get my teeth well shod before I come.
    HEGIO. My table's really coarse.
    ERGASILUS. Do you eat brambles?
    HEGIO. My dinner's from the soil.
    ERGASILUS. So is good pork.
    HEGIO. Plenty of cabbage!

ERGASILUS. Food for invalids!
What more?
HEGIO. Be there in time.
ERGASILUS. I'll not forget.
    [*Exit* ERGASILUS *to the market-*
    place.]
HEGIO. Now I'll go in and look up my
    accounts,
To see what I have lying at my banker's;
Then to my brother's, as I said just now.
    [*Exit* HEGIO *into the house.*]

[*Enter Overseers,* PHILOCRATES *and* TYN-
    DARUS, *each in the other's clothes, and
    other slaves.*]

OVERSEER. Since Heaven has willed it
    should be so,
That you must drink this cup of woe,
Why, bear it with a patient mind,
And so your pain you'll lighter find.
At home, I dare say, you were free;
Now that your lot is slavery,
Just take it as a thing of course,
Instead of making matters worse;
Behave yourselves and don't be queasy
About your lord's commands; 't is easy.
PRISONERS. Oh, oh!
OVERSEER. No need for howls and cries!
I see your sorrow in your eyes.
Be brave in your adversities.
TYNDARUS. But we're ashamed to wear
    these chains.
OVERSEER. My lord would suffer far
    worse pains,
Should he leave you to range at large out of
    his custody,
Or set you at liberty whom he bought yes-
    terday.
TYNDARUS. Oh, he need n't fear that
    he'll lose his gains;
Should he release us, we know what's our
    duty, sir.
OVERSEER. Yes, you'll run off; I know
    that. You're a beauty, sir!
TYNDARUS. Run off ? run off where?
OVERSEER. To the land of your birth.
TYNDARUS. Nay, truly, it never would
    answer
To imitate runaway slaves.
OVERSEER. Well, by Jove!
I'd advise you, if you get a chance, sir.
TYNDARUS. One thing I beg of you.

OVERSEER. What's your petition, sir?
TYNDARUS. Give us a chance of exchang-
    ing a word,
Where there's no fear that we'll be over-
    heard.
OVERSEER. Granted! Go, leave them.
    We'll take our position there.
See that your talk does n't last too long!
TYNDARUS. Oh, that's my intention.
    So, now, come along!
OVERSEER. Go, leave them alone.
TYNDARUS. We ever shall own
We're in your debt for the kindness you've
    shown to us;
You have the power, and you've proved
    yourself bounteous.
PHILOCRATES. Come away farther, as
    far as we can from them;
We must contrive to conceal our fine plan
    from them,
Never disclose any trace of our trickery,
Else we shall find all our dodges a mockery.
    Once they get wind of it,
    There'll be an end of it;
    For if you are my master brave,
    And I pretend to be your slave,
    Then we must watch with greatest care;
    Of eavesdroppers we must beware.
With caution and skill keep your senses all
    waking;
There's no time to sleep; it's a big under-
    taking.
TYNDARUS. So I'm to be master?
PHILOCRATES. Yes, that is the notion.
TYNDARUS. And so for your head (I
    would pray you remark it),
You want me to carry my own head to
    market!
PHILOCRATES. I know.
TYNDARUS. Well, when you've gained
    your wish, remember my devotion.
This is the way that you'll find most men
    treating you;
    Until they have
    The boon they crave,
They're kind as can be; but success makes
    the knave!
When they have got it, they set to work
    cheating you.
Now I have told you the treatment you owe
    to me.
You I regard as a father, you know, to me.

PHILOCRATES. Nay, let us say, — no conventions shall hinder us, —
Next to my own, you're my father, dear Tyndarus.

TYNDARUS. That will do!

PHILOCRATES. Now then, I warn you always to remember this;
I no longer am your master but your slave; don't be remiss.
Since kind Heav'n has shown us plainly that the way ourselves to save
Is for me, who was your master, now to turn into your slave,
Where before I gave you orders, now I beg of you in prayer,
By the changes in our fortune, by my father's kindly care,
By the common fetters fastened on us by the enemy,
Think of who you were and are, and pay no more respect to me
Than I used to pay to you, when you were slave and I was free.

TYNDARUS. Well, I know that I am you and you are me!

PHILOCRATES. Yes, stick to that!
Then I hope that by your shrewdness we shall gain what we are at.

[Enter HEGIO from his house.]

HEGIO [addressing some one inside]. I'll be back again directly when I've looked into the case:
Where are those whom I directed at the door to take their place?

PHILOCRATES. O by Pollux! you've been careful that we shouldn't be to seek;
Thus by bonds and guards surrounded we have had no chance to sneak!

HEGIO. Howsoever careful, none can be as careful as he ought;
When he thinks he's been most careful, oft your careful man is caught.
Don't you think that I've just cause to keep a careful watch on you,
When I've had to pay so large a sum of money for the two?

PHILOCRATES. Truly we've no right to blame you, that you watch and guard us thus;
And if we should get a chance and run away, you can't blame us.

HEGIO. Just like you, my son is held in slavery by your countrymen.

PHILOCRATES. Was he taken prisoner?

HEGIO. Yes.

PHILOCRATES. We were n't the only cowards then.

HEGIO. Come aside here; there is something I would ask of you alone;
And I hope you'll not deceive me.

PHILOCRATES. Everything I know I'll own;
If in aught I'm ignorant, I'll tell you so, upon my life.

[HEGIO and PHILOCRATES go aside; TYNDARUS standing where he can hear their conversation.]

TYNDARUS [aside]. Now the old man's at the barber's; see my master whets his knife!
Why, he has n't even put an apron on to shield his clothes!
Will he shave him close or only cut his hair? Well, goodness knows!
But if he has any sense, he'll crop the old man properly!

HEGIO. Come now, tell me, would you rather be a slave or get set free?

PHILOCRATES. What I want is that which brings me most of good and least of ill.
Though I must confess my slavery was n't very terrible;
Little difference was made between me and my master's son.

TYNDARUS [aside]. Bravo! I'd not give a cent for Thales, the Milesian!
For, compared with this man's cunning, he is but a trifling knave.
Mark how cleverly he talks, as if he'd always been a slave!

HEGIO. Tell me to what family Philocrates belongs?

PHILOCRATES. The Goldings;
That's a family most wealthy both in honors and in holdings.

HEGIO. Is your master there respected?

PHILOCRATES. Highly, by our foremost men.

HEGIO. If his influence amongst them is as great as you maintain,
Are his riches fat?

PHILOCRATES. I guess so! Fat as suet, one might say.

HEGIO, Is his father living?

PHILOCRATES. Well, he *was*, sir, when we came away;

Whether he still lives or not, you'll have to go to hell to see.

TYNDARUS [aside]. Saved again! for now he's adding to his lies philosophy!

HEGIO. What's his name, I pray?

PHILOCRATES. Thensaurocrœsonicochrysides.

HEGIO. I suppose a sort of nickname given to show now rich he is.

PHILOCRATES. Nay, by Pollux! it was given him for his avarice and greed.

Truth to tell you, Theodoromedes is his name indeed.

HEGIO. What is this? His father's grasping?

PHILOCRATES. Grasping? Ay, most covetous!

Just to show you, when he sacrifices to his Genius,

All the vessels that he uses are of Samian crockery,

Lest the Genius should steal them! There's his character, you see.

HEGIO. Come with me then.

Now I'll ask the other what I want to know.

[To TYNDARUS.] Now, Philocrates, your slave has acted as a man should do,

For from him I've learnt your birth; the whole he has confessed to me.

If you will admit the same, it shall to your advantage be;

For your slave has told me all.

TYNDARUS. It was his duty so to do.

All is true that he's confessed; although I must admit to you,

'T was my wish to hide from you my birth, and wealth, and family;

But now, Hegio, that I've lost my fatherland and liberty,

Naturally he should stand in awe of you much more than me,

Since by force of arms our fortunes stand on an equality.

I remember when he durst not speak a word to do me ill;

He may strike me now; so fortune plays with mortals as she will.

I, once free, am made a slave and brought from high to low degree,

And instead of giving orders must obey submissively.

But if I should have a master, such as *I* was when at home,

I've no fear that his commands will prove unjust or burdensome.

Hegio, will you bear from me a word of warning?

HEGIO. Yes, say on.

TYNDARUS. Once I was as free and happy as your own beloved son.

But the force of hostile arms has robbed him of his freedom, too;

He's a slave amongst our people, just as I am here with you.

Certainly there is a God who watches us where'er we be;

He will treat your son exactly as He finds that you treat me.

Virtue sure will be rewarded, vice will e'er bring sorrow on —

I've a father misses me, as much as you your absent son.

HEGIO. Yes, I know. Do you admit, then, what your slave confessed to me?

TYNDARUS. I admit, sir, that my father is a man of property,

And that I'm of noble birth. But I beseech you, Hegio,

Do not let my ample riches cause your avarice to grow,

Lest my father think it better, though I am his only son,

That I should continue serving you and keep your livery on,

Rather than come home a beggar to my infinite disgrace.

HEGIO. Thanks to Heav'n and my forefathers, I've been wealthy all my days;

Nor is wealth, in my opinion, always useful to obtain —

Many a man I've known degraded to a beast by too much gain;

There are times when loss is better far than gain, in every way.

Gold! I hate it! Oh, how many people has it led astray!

Now, attend to me, and I my purpose
plainly will declare:
There in Elis, with your people, is my son a
prisoner.
If you'll bring him back to me, you shall
not pay a single cent:
I'll release you and your slave too; other-
wise I'll not relent.
TYNDARUS. That's the noblest, kindest
offer! All the world can't find your
mate!
But is he in slavery to a private man or to
the State?
HEGIO. To Menarchus, a physician.
TYNDARUS. Ah! my client! all is plain;
Everything will be as easy as the falling of
the rain.
HEGIO. Bring him home as soon as may be.
TYNDARUS. Certainly; but, Hegio —
HEGIO. What's your wish? For I'll do
aught in reason.
TYNDARUS. Listen; you shall know.
I don't ask that I should be sent back until
your son has come.
Name the price you'll take for yonder slave,
to let me send him home,
That he may redeem your son.
HEGIO. Nay, some one else I should pre-
fer,
Whom I'll send when truce is made to go
and meet your father there.
He can take your father any message that
you like to send.
TYNDARUS. It's no use to send a stranger;
all your toil in smoke would end.
Send my slave, he'll do the business just as
soon as he gets there;
You won't hit on anybody you can send
who's trustier,
Or more faithful; he's a man who does his
work with all his heart.
Boldly trust your son to him; and he will
truly play his part.
Don't you fear! at my own peril I'll make
trial of his truth;
For he knows my kindness to him; I can
safely trust the youth.
HEGIO. Well, I'll send him at your risk,
if you consent.
TYNDARUS. Oh, I agree.
HEGIO. Let him start as soon as may be.
TYNDARUS. That will suit me perfectly.

HEGIO. Well, then, if he does n't come
back here you'll pay me fifty pounds;
Are you willing?
TYNDARUS. Certainly.
HEGIO. Then go and loose him from his
bonds;
And the other too.
TYNDARUS. May Heaven ever treat you
graciously!
Since you've shown me so much kindness,
and from fetters set me free.
Ah, my neck's more comfortable, now I've
cast that iron ruff!
HEGIO. Gifts when given to good people
win their gratitude! Enough!
Now, if you are going to send him, teach
and tell him what to say,
When he gets home to your father. Shall I
call him?
TYNDARUS. Do so, pray!
    [HEGIO crosses the stage to PHILO-
    CRATES and addresses him.]
HEGIO. Heav'n bless this project to my
son and me,
And you as well! I, your new lord, desire
That you should give your true and faithful
service
To your old master. I have lent you to him,
And set a price of fifty pounds upon you.
He says he wants to send you to his father
That he may ransom my dear son and make
An interchange between us of our sons.
PHILOCRATES. Well, I'm prepared to
serve either one or t' other;
I'm like a wheel, just twist me as you please!
I'll turn this way or that, as you command.
HEGIO. I'll see that you don't lose by
your compliance;
Since you are acting as a good slave should.
Come on.
Now, here's your man.
TYNDARUS. I thank you, sir,
For giving me this opportunity
Of sending him to bring my father word
About my welfare and my purposes;
All which he'll tell my father as I bid him.
Now, Tyndarus, we've come to an agree-
ment,
That you should go to Elis to my father;
And should you not come back, I've under-
taken
To pay the sum of fifty pounds for you.

PHILOCRATES. A fair agreement! for your
father looks
For me or for some other messenger
To come from hence to him.
TYNDARUS. Then, pray attend,
And I will tell you what to tell my father.
PHILOCRATES. I have always tried to
serve you hitherto, Philocrates,
As you wished me, to the utmost of my
poor abilities.
That I 'll ever seek and aim at, heart and
soul and strength alway.
TYNDARUS. That is right: you know your
duty. Listen now to what I say.
First of all, convey a greeting to my parents
dear from me,
And to other relatives and friends, if any
you should see.
Say I'm well, and held in bondage by this
worthy gentleman,
Who has shown and ever shows me all the
honor that he can.
PHILOCRATES. Oh, you need n't tell me
that, it's rooted in my memory.
TYNDARUS. If I did n't see my keeper, I
should think that I was free.
Tell my father of the bargain I have made
with Hegio,
For the ransom of his son.
PHILOCRATES. Don't stay to tell me that.
I know.
TYNDARUS. He must purchase and re-
store him, then we both shall be set
free.
PHILOCRATES. Good!
HEGIO. Bid him be quick, for your sake
and for mine in like degree.
PHILOCRATES. You don't long to see your
son more ardently than he does his!
HEGIO. Why, each loves his own.
PHILOCRATES. Well, have you any other
messages?
TYNDARUS. Yes; don't hesitate to say
I'm well and happy, Tyndarus;
That no shade of disagreement ever sep-
arated us;
That you've never once deceived me nor
opposed your master's will,
And have stuck to me like wax in spite of all
this flood of ill.
By my side you've stood and helped me in
my sore adversities,

True and faithful to me ever. When my
father hears of this,
Tyndarus, and knows your noble conduct
towards himself and me,
He will never be so mean as to refuse to set
you free;
When I'm back I'll spare no effort that it
may be brought about.
To your toil, and skill, and courage, and
your wisdom, there's no doubt
That I owe my chance of getting to my
father's home again:
For 't was you confessed my birth and
riches to this best of men;
So you set your master free from fetters by
your ready wit.
PHILOCRATES. Yes, I did, sir, as you say;
I'm glad that you remember it.
But indeed, you've well deserved it at my
hands, Philocrates;
For if I should try to utter all your many
kindnesses,
Night would fall before I'd finished; you
have done as much for me
As if you had been my slave.
HEGIO. Good heavens, what nobility
Shines in both their dispositions! I can
scarce refrain from tears
When I see their true affection, and the way
the slave reveres
And commends his master.
TYNDARUS. Truly he has not commended
me
Even a hundredth part as much as he him-
self deserves to be.
HEGIO. Well, as you've behaved so nobly,
now you have a splendid chance
Here to crown your services by doubly
faithful vigilance.
PHILOCRATES. As I wish the thing ac-
complished, so I shall do all I know;
To assure you of it, I call Jove to witness,
Hegio!
That I never will betray Philocrates, I'll
take my oath!
HEGIO. Honest fellow!
PHILOCRATES. I will treat him as myself,
upon my troth!
TYNDARUS. From these loving protesta-
tions, mind you never never swerve.
And if I 've said less about you than your
faithful deeds deserve,

Pray you, don't be angry with me on account of what I've said;
But remember you are going with a price upon your head;
And that both my life and honor I have staked on your return;
When you've left my sight, I pray you, don't forget what you have sworn,
Or when you have left me here in slavery instead of you,
Think that you are free, and so neglect what you are pledged to do,
And forget your solemn promise to redeem this good man's son.
Fifty pounds, remember, is the price that we've agreed upon.
Faithful to your faithful master, do not let your faith be bought;
And I'm well assured my father will do everything he ought.
Keep me as your friend forever, and this good old man as well.
Take my hand in yours, I pray you, swear an oath unbreakable,
That you'll always be as faithful as I've ever been to you.
Mind, you're now my master, aye protector, and my father too!
I commit to you my hopes and happiness.
PHILOCRATES. O that'll do!
Are you satisfied if I can carry this commission through?
TYNDARUS. Yes.
PHILOCRATES. Then I'll return in such a manner as shall please you both.
Is that all, sir?
HEGIO. Come back quickly.
PHILOCRATES. So I will, upon my troth.
HEGIO. Come along then to my banker's; I'll provide you for the way.
Also I will get a passport from the prætor.
TYNDARUS. Passport, eh?
HEGIO. Yes, to get him through the army so that they may let him go.
Step inside.
TYNDARUS. A pleasant journey!
PHILOCRATES. Fare-you-well!
HEGIO. By Pollux, though,
What a blessing that I bought these men from the Commissioners!
So, please Heav'n, I've saved my son from bondage to those foreigners.

Dear! How long I hesitated whether I should buy or not!
Please to take him in, good slaves, and do not let him leave the spot,
When there is no keeper with him; I shall soon be home again.
[*Exeunt* TYNDARUS *and slaves into the house.*]
Now I'll run down to my brother's and inspect my other men.
I'll inquire if any of them is acquainted with this youth.
[*To* PHILOCRATES.] Come along and I'll despatch you. That must be done first, in sooth.
[*Exeunt* HEGIO *and* PHILOCRATES *to the market-place.*]

[*Enter* ERGASILUS *returning from the market-place.*]

ERGASILUS. Wretched he who seeks his dinner, and with trouble gets a haul;
Wretcheder who seeks with trouble, and can't find a meal at all;
Wretchedest who dies for food, and can't get any anyway.
If I could, I'd like to scratch the eyes out of this cursed day!
For it's filled all men with meanness towards me. Oh, I never saw
Day so hungry; why, it's stuffed with famine in its greedy maw.
Never day pursued its purpose in so vacuous a way;
For my gullet and my stomach have to keep a holiday.
Out upon the parasite's profession: it's all gone to pot!
For us impecunious wits the gilded youth don't care a jot.
They no longer want us Spartans, owners of a single chair,
Sons of Smacked-Face, whose whole stock-in-trade is words, whose board is bare.
Those that they invite are fellows who can ask them back in turn.
Then they cater for themselves and us poor parasites they spurn;
You will see them shopping in the market with as little shame
As when, sitting on the bench, the culprit's sentence they proclaim.

For us wits they don't care twopence; keep
    entirely to their set.
When I went just now to market, there a
    group of them I met;
"Hail!" says I; "where shall we go," says
    I, "to lunch?" They all were mum.
"Who speaks first? Who volunteers?" says
    I. And still the chaps were dumb.
Not a smile! "Where shall we dine together?
    Answer." Not a word!
Then I flashed a jest upon them from my
    very choicest hoard,
One that meant a month of dinners in the
    old days, I declare.
No one smiled; and then I saw the whole
    was a got-up affair.
Why, they would n't even do as much as
    any angry cur;
If they could n't smile, they might at least
    have shown their teeth, I swear!
Well, I left the rascals when I saw that they
    were making game;
Went to others; and to others; and to others
    — still the same!
They had formed a ring together, just like
    those who deal in oil
I' the Velabrum. So I left them when I saw
    they mocked my toil.
In the Forum vainly prowling other para-
    sites I saw.
I've resolved that I must try to get my
    rights by Roman law.
As they've formed a plot to rob us of our
    life and victuals too,
I shall summon them and fine them, as a
    magistrate would do.
They shall give me ten good dinners, at a
    time when food is dear!
So I'll do; now to the harbor; there I may
    to dinner steer;
If that fails me, I'll return and try this old
    man's wretched cheer.

    [*Exit* ERGASILUS *to the harbor.*]

[*Enter* HEGIO *from his brother's with*
    ARISTOPHONTES.]

HEGIO. How pleasant it is when you've
    managed affairs
For the good of the public, as yesterday I
    did,
When I bought those two fellows. Why,
    every one stares

And congratulates me on the way I decided.
To tell the plain truth, I am worried with
    standing,
    And weary with waiting;
From the flood of their words I could scarce
    get a landing,
And even at the prætor's it showed no
    abating.
I asked for a passport; and when it had
    come,
    I gave it to Tyndarus; *he* set off home.
When he had departed, for home off I
    started;
Then went to my brother's, to question the
    others,
Whether any among them Philocrates knew.
Then one of them cries, "He's my friend,
    good and true."
    I told him I'd bought him;
He begged he might see him; and so I have
    brought him.
    I bade them loose him from his chains,
And came away. (*To* ARISTOPHONTES.)
Pray follow me;
    Your earnest suit success obtains,
    Your dear old friend you soon shall see.
        [*Exeunt* HEGIO *and* ARISTO-
        PHONTES *into the house;* TYN-
        DARUS *immediately rushes out.*]
    TYNDARUS. Alas! the day has come on
        which I wish I never had been
        born.
My hopes, resources, stratagems, have fled
    and left me all forlorn.
On this sad day no hope remains of saving
    my poor life, t is clear;.
No help or hope remains to me to drive
    away my anxious fear.
No cloak I anywhere can find to cover up
    my crafty lies,
No cloak, I say, comes in my way to hide
    my tricks and rogueries.
There is no pardon for my fibs, and no
    escape for my misdeeds;
My cheek can't find the shelter, nor my
    craft the hiding-place it needs.
All that I hid has come to light; my plans
    lie open to the day;
The whole thing's out, and in this scrape I
    fail to see a single ray
Of hope to shun the doom which I must
    suffer for my master's sake.

This Aristophontes, who's just come, will
surely bring me to the stake;
He knows me, and he is the friend and kinsman of Philocrates.
Salvation could n't save me, if she would;
there is no way but this,
To plan some new and smarter trickeries.
Hang it, *what* ? What shall I do? I *am* just
up a lofty tree,
If I can't contrive some new and quite pre-
posterous foolery.

[*Enter from the house* HEGIO *and*
ARISTOPHONTES.]

HEGIO. Where's the fellow gone whom
we saw rushing headlong from the
house?
TYNDARUS [*aside*]. Now the day of
doom has come; the foe's upon thee,
Tyndarus!
O, what story shall I tell them? What deny
and what confess?
My purposes are all at sea; O, ain't I in a
pretty mess?
O would that Heaven had blasted you be-
fore you left your native land,
You wretch, Aristophontes, who have
ruined all that I had planned.
The game is up if I can't light on some
atrocious villainy!
HEGIO. Ah, there's your man; go speak
to him.
TYNDARUS [*aside*]. What man is wretch-
eder than I?
ARISTOPHONTES. How is this that you
avoid my eyes and shun me, Tyn-
darus?
Why, you might have never known me,
fellow, that you treat me thus!
I'm a slave as much as you, although in
Elis I was free,
Whilst you from your earliest boyhood were
enthralled in slavery.
HEGIO. Well, by Jove! I'm not surprised
that he should shun you, when he
sees
That you call him Tyndarus, not, as you
should, Philocrates.
TYNDARUS. Hegio, this man in Elis was
considered raving mad.
Take no note of anything he tells you either
good or bad.

Why, he once attacked his father and his
mother with a spear;
And the epilepsy takes him in a form that's
most severe.
Don't go near him!
HEGIO. Keep your distance!
ARISTOPHONTES. Rascal! Did I rightly
hear,
That you say I'm mad, and once attacked
my father with a spear?
And that I have got the sickness for which
men are wont to spit?
HEGIO. Never mind! for many men be-
sides yourself have suffered it,
And the spitting was a means of healing
them, and they were glad.
ARISTOPHONTES. What, do you believe
the wretch?
HEGIO. In what respect?
ARISTOPHONTES. That I am mad!
TYNDARUS. Do you see him glaring at
you? Better leave him! O beware!
Hegio, the fit is on him; he'll be raving
soon! Take care!
HEGIO. Well, I thought he was a mad-
man when he called you Tyndarus.
TYNDARUS. Why, he sometimes does n't
know his *own* name. Oh, he's often
thus.
HEGIO. But he said you were his comrade.
TYNDARUS. Ah, no doubt! precisely so!
And Alcmæon, and Orestes, and Lycurgus,
don't you know,
Are my comrades quite as much as he is!
ARISTOPHONTES. Oh, you gallows bird,
Dare you slander me? What, don't I know
you?
HEGIO. Come, don't be absurd.
You don't know him, for you called him
Tyndarus: that's very clear.
You don't know the man you see; you name
the man who is n't here.
ARISTOPHONTES. Nay, he says he is the
man he is n't, not the man he is.
TYNDARUS. O yes! Doubtless you know
better whether I'm Philocrates
Than Philocrates himself does!
ARISTOPHONTES. You'd prove truth it-
self a liar,
As it strikes me. But, I pray you, look at me!
TYNDARUS. As you desire!
ARISTOPHONTES. Are n't you Tyndarus?

TYNDARUS. I'm not.
ARISTOPHONTES. You say you are Philocrates?
TYNDARUS. Certainly.
ARISTOPHONTES. Do you believe him?
HEGIO. Yes, and shall do, if I please.
For the other, who you say he is, went home from here to-day
To the father of this captive.
ARISTOPHONTES. Father? He's a slave.
TYNDARUS. And, pray!
Are you not a slave, though you were free once, as I hope to be,
When I have restored good Hegio's son to home and liberty?
ARISTOPHONTES. What's that, gaol-bird? Do you tell me that you were a freeman born?
TYNDARUS. No! Philocrates, not Freeman, is my name.
ARISTOPHONTES. Pray, mark his scorn!
Hegio, I tell you, you're being mocked and swindled by this knave;
Why, he never had a slave except himself; for he's a slave.
TYNDARUS. Ah, because you're poor yourself, and have no means of livelihood,
You'd wish everybody else to be like you. I know your mood;
All poor men like you are spiteful, envy those who're better off.
ARISTOPHONTES. Hegio, don't believe this fellow; for he's doing naught but scoff;
Sure I am, he'll play some scurvy trick on you before he's done;
I don't like this tale of his about the ransom of your son.
TYNDARUS. You don't like it, I dare say; but I'll accomplish it, you see!
I'll restore him to his father; he in turn releases me.
That's why I've sent Tyndarus to see my father.
ARISTOPHONTES. Come, that's lame!
You are Tyndarus yourself, the only slave who bears that name!
TYNDARUS. Why reproach me with my bondage? I was captured in the fray.
ARISTOPHONTES. Oh, I can't restrain my fury!

TYNDARUS. Don't you hear him? Run away!
He'll be hurling stones at us just now, if you don't have him bound.
ARISTOPHONTES. Oh, damnation!
TYNDARUS. How he glares at us! I hope your ropes are sound.
See, his body's covered over with bright spots of monstrous size!
It's the black bile that afflicts him.
ARISTOPHONTES. Pollux! if this old man's wise,
You will find black pitch afflict you, when it blazes round your breast.
TYNDARUS. Ah, he's wandering now, poor fellow! by foul spirits he's possessed!
HEGIO [to TYNDARUS]. What do you think? Would it be best to have him bound?
TYNDARUS. Yes, so I said.
ARISTOPHONTES. Oh, perdition take it! Would I had a stone to smash his head,
This whipped cur, who says I'm mad! By Jove, sir, I will make you smart!
TYNDARUS. Hear him calling out for stones!
ARISTOPHONTES. Pray, might we have a word apart, Hegio?
HEGIO. Yes, but keep your distance; there's no need to come so close!
TYNDARUS. If, by Pollux, you go any nearer, he'll bite off your nose.
ARISTOPHONTES. Hegio, I beg and pray you, don't believe that I am mad,
Or that I have epilepsy as this shameless fellow said.
But if you're afraid of me, then have me bound; I won't say no,
If you'll bind that rascal too.
TYNDARUS. O no, indeed, good Hegio!
Bind the man who wishes it!
ARISTOPHONTES. Be quiet, you! The case stands thus;
I shall prove Philocrates the false to be true Tyndarus.
What are you winking for?
TYNDARUS. I was n't.
ARISTOPHONTES. He winks before your very face!
HEGIO. What, if I approached this madman?

TYNDARUS. It would be a wild-goose chase.
He'll keep chattering, till you can't make either head or tail of it.
Had they dressed him for the part, you'd say 't was Ajax in his fit.
HEGIO. Never mind, I *will* approach him.
TYNDARUS [aside]. Things are looking very blue.
I'm between the knife and altar, and I don't know what to do.
HEGIO. I attend, Aristophontes, if you 've anything to say.
ARISTOPHONTES. You shall hear that that is true which you 've been thinking false to-day.
First I wish to clear myself of all suspicion that I rave,
Or that I am subject to disease — except that I'm a slave.
So may He who's king of gods and men restore me home again:
He's no more Philocrates than you or I.
HEGIO. But tell me then,
Who he is.
ARISTOPHONTES. The same that I have told you from the very first.
If you find it otherwise, I pray that I may be accursed,
And may suffer forfeit of fatherland and freedom sweet.
HEGIO. What say *you*?
TYNDARUS. That I'm your slave, and you're my master.
HEGIO. That's not it.
Were you free?
TYNDARUS. I was.
ARISTOPHONTES. He was n't. He's just lying worse and worse.
TYNDARUS. How do *you* know? Perhaps it happened that you were my mother's nurse,
That you dare to speak so boldly!
ARISTOPHONTES. Why, I saw you when a lad.
TYNDARUS. Well, I see you when a man to-day! So we are quits, by gad!
Did I meddle with your business? Just let mine alone then, please.
HEGIO. Was his father called Thensaurocrœsonicochrysides?

ARISTOPHONTES. No, he was n't, and I never heard the name before to-day.
Theodoromedes was his master's father.
TYNDARUS [aside]. Deuce to pay!
O be quiet, or go straight and hang yourself, my beating heart!
You are dancing there, whilst I can hardly stand to play my part.
HEGIO. He in Elis was a slave then, if you are not telling lies,
And is not Philocrates?
ARISTOPHONTES. You'll never find it otherwise.
HEGIO. So I've been chopped into fragments and dissected, goodness knows,
By the dodges of this scoundrel, who has led me by the nose.
Are you sure there's no mistake though?
ARISTOPHONTES. Yes, I speak of what I know.
HEGIO. Is it certain?
ARISTOPHONTES. Certain? Nothing could be more entirely so.
Why, Philocrates has been my friend from when he was a boy;
But where is he now?
HEGIO. Ah, that's what vexes me, but gives *him* joy.
Tell me though, what sort of looking man is this Philocrates?
ARISTOPHONTES. Thin i' the face, a sharpish nose, a fair complexion, coal-black eyes,
Reddish, crisp, and curly hair.
HEGIO. Yes, that's the fellow to a T.
TYNDARUS [aside]. Curse upon it, everything has gone all wrong to-day with me.
Woe unto those wretched rods that on my back to-day must die!
HEGIO. So I see that I've been cheated.
TYNDARUS [aside]. Come on, fetters, don't be shy!
Run to me and clasp my legs and I'll take care of you, no fear!
HEGIO. Well, I've been sufficiently bamboozled by these villains here.
T' other said he was a slave, while this pretended to be free;
So I've gone and lost the kernel, and the husk is left to me.

Yes, they've corked my nose most finely!
Don't I make a foolish show?
But this fellow here shan't mock me! Cola-
phus, Corax, Cordalio,
Come out here and bring your thongs.

[*Enter Overseers.*]

OVERSEER. To bind up faggots? Here's
a go!
HEGIO. Come, bind your heaviest
shackles on this wretch.
TYNDARUS. Why, what's the matter?
what's my crime?
HEGIO. Your crime!
You've sowed and scattered ill, now you
shall reap it.
TYNDARUS. Had n't you better say I
harrowed too?
For farmers always harrow first, then sow.
HEGIO. How boldly does he flout me to
my face!
TYNDARUS. A harmless, guiltless man,
although a slave,
Should boldly face his master, of all men.
HEGIO. Tie up his hands as tightly as
you can.
TYNDARUS. You'd better cut them off;
for I am yours.
But what's the matter? Why are you so
angry?
HEGIO. Because my plans, as far as in
you lay,
By your thrice-villainous and lying tricks
You've torn asunder, mangled limb from
limb,
And ruined all my hopes and purposes.
Philocrates escaped me through your guile;
I thought he was the slave, and you the free;
For so you said, and interchanged your names
Between yourselves.
TYNDARUS. Yes, I admit all that.
'T is just as you have said, and cunningly
He's got away by means of my smart work;
But I beseech you, are you wroth at that?
HEGIO. You've brought the worst of tor-
ments on yourself.
TYNDARUS. If not for sin I perish, I don't
care!
But though I perish, and he breaks his
word,
And does n't come back here, my joy is
this:

My deed will be remembered when I'm dead,
How I redeemed my lord from slavery,
And rescued him and saved him from his
foes,
To see once more his father and his home;
And how I rather chose to risk my life,
Than let my master perish in his bonds.
HEGIO. The only fame you'll get will be
in hell.
TYNDARUS. Nay, he who dies for virtue
does n't perish.
HEGIO. When I've expended all my tor-
ments on you,
And given you up to death for your deceits,
People may call it death or perishing
Just as they like; so long as you are dead,
I don't mind if they say that you're alive.
TYNDARUS. By Pollux! if you do so,
you'll repent,
When he comes back as I am sure he will.
ARISTOPHONTES. O Heavens! I see it
now! and understand
What it all means. My friend Philocrates
Is free at home, and in his native land.
I'm glad of that; nothing could please me
more.
But I am grieved I've got *him* into trouble,
Who stands here bound because of what I
said.
HEGIO. Did I forbid you to speak falsely
to me?
TYNDARUS. You did, sir.
HEGIO. Then how durst you tell me lies?
TYNDARUS. Because to tell the truth
would have done hurt
To him I served; he profits by my lie.
HEGIO. But *you* shall smart for it!
TYNDARUS. O that's all right!
I've saved my master and am glad of that,
For I've been his companion from a boy;
His father, my old master, gave me to him.
D' you now think this a crime?
HEGIO. A very vile one.
TYNDARUS. *I* say it's right; I don't agree
with you.
Consider, if a slave had done as much
For your own son, how grateful you would
be!
Would n't you give that slave his liberty?
Would n't that slave stand highest in your
favor?
Answer!

HEGIO. Well, yes.

TYNDARUS. Then why be wroth with
me?

HEGIO. Because you were more faithful
to your master
Than e'er to me.

TYNDARUS. What else could you expect?
Do you suppose that in one night and day
You could so train a man just taken captive,
A fresh newcomer, as to serve you better
Than him with whom he'd lived from ear-
liest childhood?

HEGIO. Then let him pay you for it.
Take him off,
And fit him with the heaviest, thickest
chains;
Thence to the quarries you shall go right
on.
And whilst the rest are hewing eight stones
each,
You shall each day do half as much again,
Or else be nicknamed the Six-hundred-
striper.

ARISTOPHONTES. By gods and men, I
pray you, Hegio,
Do not destroy him.

HEGIO. I'll take care of him!
For in the stocks all night he shall be kept,
And quarry stones all day from out the
ground.
O, I'll prolong his torments day by day.

ARISTOPHONTES. Is this your purpose?

HEGIO. Death is not so sure.
Go take him to Hippolytus the smith;
Tell him to rivet heavy fetters on him.
Then cause him to be led out of the city
To Cordalus, my freedman at the quarries,
And tell him that I wish him to be treated
With greater harshness than the worst slave
there.

TYNDARUS. Why should I plead with
you when you're resolved?
The peril of my life is yours as well
When I am dead I have no ill to fear;
And if I live to an extreme old age,
My time of suffering will be but short.
Farewell! though you deserve a different
wish.
Aristophontes, as you've done to me,
So may you prosper; for it is through you
That this has come upon me.

HEGIO. Take him off.

TYNDARUS. But if Philocrates returns to
you,
Give me a chance of seeing him, I pray.

HEGIO. Come, take him from my sight or
I'll destroy you!

TYNDARUS. Nay, this is sheer assault
and battery!
[Exeunt Overseers and TYNDARUS
to the quarries.]

HEGIO. There, he has gone to prison as
he merits.
I'll give my other prisoners an example,
That none of them may dare repeat his
crime.
Had it not been for him, who laid it bare,
The rascals would have led me in a string.
Never again will I put trust in man.
Once cheated is enough. Alas! I hoped
That I had saved my son from slavery.
My hope has perished. One of my sons I
lost,
Stolen by a slave when he was four years
old;
Nor have I ever found the slave or him.
The elder's now a captive. What's my
crime,
That I beget my children but to lose them?
Follow me, you! I'll take you where you
were.
Since no one pities me, I'll pity none.

ARISTOPHONTES. Under good auspices I
left my chain;
But I must take the auspices again.
[Exeunt ARISTOPHONTES and HE-
GIO to HEGIO's brother's.]

[Enter ERGASILUS from the harbor.]

ERGASILUS. Jove supreme, thou dost
protect me and increase my scanty
store,
Blessings lordly and magnific thou bestow-
est more and more;
Both thanks and gain, and sport and jest,
festivity and holidays,
Processions plenty, lots of drink and heaps
of meat and endless praise.
Ne'er again I'll play the beggar, everything I want I've got;
I'm able now to bless my friends, and send
my enemies to pot.
With such joyful joyfulness this joyful day
has loaded me!

Though it has n't been bequeathed me, I 've
    come into property!
So now I 'll run and find the old man Hegio.
O what a store
Of good I bring to him, as much as ever he
    could ask, and more.
I am resolved I 'll do just what the slaves do
    in a comedy;
I 'll throw my cloak around my neck, that
    he may hear it first from me.
For this good news I hope to get my board
    in perpetuity.

[*Enter* HEGIO *from his brother's.*]

HEGIO. How sad the regrets in my heart
    that are kindled,
As I think over all that has happened to me.
O is n't it shameful the way I 've been
    swindled,
And yet could n't see!
As soon as it 's known, how they 'll laugh
    in the city!
When I come to the market they 'll show
    me no pity,
But chaffing say, "Wily old man up a tree!"
But is this Ergasilus coming? Bless me!
His cloak 's o'er his shoulder. Why, what
    can it be?
ERGASILUS. Come, Ergasilus, act, and
    act vigorously!
Hereby I denounce and threaten all who
    shall obstruct my way;
Any man who dares to do so will have seen
    his life's last day.
I will stand him on his head.
HEGIO. 'Fore me the man begins to spar!
ERGASILUS. I shall do it. Wherefore let
    all passers-by stand off afar;
Let none dare to stand conversing in this
    street, till I 've passed by;
For my fist's my catapult, my arm is my
    artillery,
And my shoulder is my ram; who meets my
    knee, to earth he goes.
Folk will have to pick their teeth up, if
    with me they come to blows.
HEGIO. What's he mean by all this
    threatening? I confess I 'm puzzled
    quite.
ERGASILUS. I 'll take care they don't
    forget this day, this place, my
    mickle might.

He who stops me in my course, will find
    he 's stopped his life as well.
HEGIO. What he 's after with these
    threats and menaces, I cannot tell.
ERGASILUS. I proclaim it first, that none
    may suffer inadvertently;
Stay at home, good people all, and then
    you won't get hurt by me.
HEGIO. Oh, depend on 't, it 's a dinner
    that has stirred his valorous bile.
Woe to that poor wretch whose food has
    given him this lordly style!
ERGASILUS. First, for those pig-breeding
    millers, with their fat and bran-fed
    sows,
Stinking so that one is hardly able to get
    past the house;
If in any public place I catch their pigs
    outside their pen,
With my fists I 'll hammer out the bran
    from those same filthy — men!
HEGIO. Here 's pot-valor with a venge-
    ance! He 's as full as man could
    wish!
ERGASILUS. Then those fishmongers,
    who offer to the public stinking
    fish,
Riding to the market on a jumping, jolting,
    joggling cob,
Whose foul smell drives to the Forum every
    loafer in the mob;
With their fish baskets I 'll deal them on
    their face a few smart blows,
Just to let them feel the nuisance that they
    cause the public nose.
HEGIO. Listen to his proclamations!
    What a royal style they keep!
ERGASILUS. Then the butchers, who
    arrange to steal the youngsters from
    the sheep,
Undertake to kill a lamb, but send you
    home right tough old mutton;
Nickname ancient ram as yearling, sweet
    enough for any glutton;
If in any public street or square that ram
    comes in my view,
I will make them sorry persons — ancient
    ram and butcher, too!
HEGIO. Bravo! he makes rules as if he
    were a mayor and corporation.
Surely he 's been made the master of the
    market to our nation.

ERGASILUS. I'm no more a parasite, but
   kinglier than a king of kings.
Such a stock of belly-timber from the port
   my message brings.
Let me haste to heap on Hegio this good
   news of jollity.
Certainly there's no man living who's more
   fortunate than he.
HEGIO. What's this news of gladness
   which he gladly hastes on me to
   pour?
ERGASILUS. Ho! where are you?
Who is there? Will some one open me this
   door?
HEGIO. Ah! the fellow's come to dinner.
ERGASILUS. Open me the door, I say;
Or I'll smash it into matchwood, if there's
   any more delay.
HEGIO. I'll speak to him. Ergasilus!
ERGASILUS. Who calls my name so
   lustily?
HEGIO. Pray, look my way!
ERGASILUS. You bid me do what For-
   tune never did to me!
Who is it?
HEGIO. Why, just look at me. It's
   Hegio!
ERGASILUS. Ye gods! It's he.
Thou best of men, in nick of time we have
   each other greeted.
HEGIO. You've got a dinner at the port;
   that makes you so conceited.
ERGASILUS. Give me your hand.
HEGIO. My hand?
ERGASILUS. Your hand, I say, at once!
HEGIO. I give it. There!
ERGASILUS. Now rejoice!
HEGIO. Rejoice! but why?
ERGASILUS. 'T is my command. Begone
   dull care!
HEGIO. Nay, the sorrows of my house-
   hold hinder me from feeling joy.
ERGASILUS. Ah, but I will wash you
   clean from every speck that can
   annoy.
Venture to rejoice!
HEGIO. All right, though I've no reason
   to be glad.
ERGASILUS. That's the way. Now or-
   der —
HEGIO. What?
ERGASILUS. To have a mighty fire made.

HEGIO. What, a mighty fire?
ERGASILUS. I said so; have it big
   enough.
HEGIO. What next?
Do you think I'll burn my house down at
   your asking?
ERGASILUS. Don't be vexed!
Have the pots and pans got ready. Is it to
   be done or not?
Put the ham and bacon in the oven, have
   it piping hot.
Send a man to buy the fish —
HEGIO. His eyes are open, but he dreams!
ERGASILUS. And another to buy pork,
   and lamb, and chickens —
HEGIO. Well, it seems
You could dine well, if you'd money.
ERGASILUS. — Perch and lamprey, if
   you please,
Pickled mackerel and sting-ray, then an
   eel and nice soft cheese.
HEGIO. Naming's easy, but for eating
   you won't find facilities
At my house, Ergasilus.
ERGASILUS. Why, do you think I'm
   ordering this
For myself?
HEGIO. Don't be deceived; for you'll eat
   neither much, nor little,
If you've brought no appetite for just your
   ordinary victual.
ERGASILUS. Nay, I'll make you eager
   for a feast though I should urge you
   not.
HEGIO. Me?
ERGASILUS. Yes, you.
HEGIO. Then you shall be my lord.
ERGASILUS. A kind one too, I wot!
Come, am I to make you happy?
HEGIO. Well, I'm not in love with woe.
ERGASILUS. Where's your hand?
HEGIO. There, take it.
ERGASILUS. Heaven's your friend!
HEGIO. But I don't mark it, though.
ERGASILUS. You're not in the *market*,
   that's why you don't *mark it*: come
   now, bid
That pure vessels be got ready for the
   offering, and a kid,
Fat and flourishing, be brought.
HEGIO. What for?
ERGASILUS. To make a sacrifice.

HEGIO. Why, to whom?

ERGASILUS. To me, of course! — I'm
Jupiter in human guise!

Yes, to you I am Salvation, Fortune, Light,
Delight, and Joy.

It's your business to placate my deity
with food, dear boy!

HEGIO. Hunger seems to be your trouble.

ERGASILUS. Well, my hunger is n't
yours.

HEGIO. As you say; so I can bear it.

ERGASILUS. Lifelong habit that en-
sures!

HEGIO. Jupiter and all the gods confound you!

ERGASILUS. Nothing of the sort!

Thanks I merit for reporting such good
tidings from the port.

Now I'll get a meal to suit me!

HEGIO. Idiot, go! you've come too late.

ERGASILUS. If I'd come before I did,
your words would come with greater
weight.

Now receive the joyful news I bring you.
I have seen your son

Philopolemus in harbor safe; and he'll be
here anon.

He was on a public vessel; with him was
that Elian youth

And your slave Stalagmus, he who ran
away — it's naught but truth —

He who stole your little boy when four
years old so cruelly.

HEGIO. Curse you, cease your mocking!

ERGASILUS. So may holy Fulness smile
on me,

Hegio, and make me ever worthy of her
sacred name,

As I saw him.

HEGIO. Saw my son?

ERGASILUS. Your son, my patron: they
're the same.

HEGIO. And the prisoner from Elis?

ERGASILUS. *Oui, parbleu!*

HEGIO. And that vile thief,

Him who stole my younger son, Stalagmus?

ERGASILUS. *Oui, monsieur, par Crieff!*

HEGIO. What, just now?

ERGASILUS. *Par Killiecrankie!*

HEGIO. Has he come?

ERGASILUS. *Oui, par Dundee!*

HEGIO. Are you sure?

ERGASILUS. *Par Auchtermuchtie!*

HEGIO. Certain?

ERGASILUS. *Oui, par Kirkcudbright!*

HEGIO. Why by these barbarian cities
do you swear?

ERGASILUS. Because they're rude,

As you said your dinner was.

HEGIO. That's just like your ingratitude!

ERGASILUS. Ah, I see you won't believe
me though it's simple truth I say.

But what countryman was this Stalagmus,
when he went away?

HEGIO. A Sicilian.

ERGASILUS. Well, but he belongs to
*Color*ado now;

For he's married to a *collar*, and she
squeezes him, I vow!

HEGIO. Tell me, is your story true?

ERGASILUS. It's really true — the very
truth.

HEGIO. O good Heav'ns! if you're not
mocking, I've indeed renewed my
youth.

ERGASILUS. What? Will you continue
doubting when I've pledged my
sacred troth?

As a last resource then, Hegio, if you can't
believe my oath,

Go and see.

HEGIO. Of course I will; go in, prepare
the feast at once;

Everything's at your disposal; you're my
steward for the nonce.

ERGASILUS. If my oracle's a false one,
with a cudgel comb my hide!

HEGIO. You shall have your board forever, if you've truly prophesied.

ERGASILUS. Who will pay?

HEGIO. My son and I.

ERGASILUS. You promise that?

HEGIO. I do indeed.

ERGASILUS. Then I promise you your
son has really come in very deed.

HEGIO. Take the best of everything!

ERGASILUS. May no delay your path
impede!

[*Exit* HEGIO *to the harbor.*]

ERGASILUS. He has gone; and put his
kitchen absolutely in my hands!

Heav'ns! how necks and trunks will be
   dissevered at my stern commands!
What a ban will fall on bacon, and what
   harm on humble ham!
O what labor on the lard, and what calamity on lamb!
Butchers and pork dealers, you shall find
   a deal to do to-day!
But to tell of all who deal in food would
   cause too long delay.
Now, in virtue of my office, I'll give sentence on the lard,
Help those gammons, hung though un-
   condemned — a fate for them too
   hard.
             [*Exit* ERGASILUS *into the house.*]

[*Enter a boy from the house of* HEGIO.]

BOY. May Jupiter and all the gods,
   Ergasilus, confound you quite,
And all who ask you out to dine, and every
   other parasite.
Destruction, ruin, dire distress, have come
   upon our family.
I feared that, like a hungry wolf, he'd
   make a fierce attack on me.
I cast an anxious look at him, he licked his
   lips and glared around;
I shook with dread, by Hercules! he gnashed
   his teeth with fearsome sound.
When he'd got in, he made a raid upon the
   meat-safe and the meats;
He seized a knife — from three fat sows he
   cut away the dainty teats.
Save those which held at least a peck, he
   shattered every pan and pot:
Then issued orders to the cook to get the
   copper boiling hot.
He broke the cupboard doors and searched
   the secrets of the storeroom's hoard.
So kindly watch him if you can, good slaves,
   whilst I go seek my lord.
I'll tell him to lay in fresh stores, if he
   wants any for himself,
For as this fellow's carrying on, there'll
   soon be nothing on the shelf.
             [*Exit boy to the harbor.*]

[*Enter from the harbor* HEGIO, PHILOPOLE-
MUS, PHILOCRATES, *and* STALAGMUS.]

HEGIO. All praise and thanksgiving to
   Jove I would render

For bringing you back to your father again;
For proving my staunch and successful
   defender,
When, robbed of my son, I was tortured
   with pain;
For restoring my runaway slave to my
   hands;
For Philocrates' honor; unsullied it stands.
   PHILOPOLEMUS. Grieved I have enough
   already, I don't want to grow still
   thinner,
And you've told me all your sorrows at the
   harbor, pending dinner.
Now to business!
   PHILOCRATES. Tell me, Hegio, have I
   kept my promises,
And restored your son to freedom?
   HEGIO. Yes, you have, Philocrates.
I can never, never thank you for the serv-
   ices you've done,
As you merit for the way you've dealt with
   me and with my son.
   PHILOPOLEMUS. Yes, you can, dear fa-
   ther, and the gods will give us both
   a chance,
Worthily to recompense the source of my
   deliverance.
And I'm sure, my dearest father, it will be
   a pleasing task.
   HEGIO. Say no more. I have no tongue
   that can deny you aught you ask.
   PHILOCRATES. Then restore to me the
   slave whom, as a pledge, I left be-
   hind.
He has always served me better than him-
   self, with heart and mind.
To reward him for his kindness now shall
   be my earnest care.
   HEGIO. For your goodness he shall be
   restored to you; 't is only fair.
That and aught beside you ask for, you
   shall have. But don't, I pray,
Be enraged with me because in wrath I've
   punished him to-day.
   PHILOCRATES. Ah, what have you done?
   HEGIO. I sent him to the quarries bound
   with chains,
When I found how I'd been cheated.
   PHILOCRATES. Woe is me! he bears these
   pains,
Dear good fellow, for my sake, because he
   gained me my release.

HEGIO. And on that account you shall not pay for him a penny piece.
I will set him free for nothing.

PHILOCRATES. Well, by Pollux! Hegio,
That is kind. But send and fetch him quickly, will you?

HEGIO. Be it so.
[*To a slave.*] Ho, where are you? Run and quickly bid young Tyndarus return.

Now, go in; for from this slave, this whipping-block, I fain would learn
What has happened to my younger son, and if he's living still.
Meanwhile you can take a bath.

PHILOPOLEMUS. Come in, Philocrates.

PHILOCRATES. I will.
[*Exeunt* PHILOPOLEMUS *and* PHILOCRATES *into the house.*]

HEGIO. Now stand forth, my worthy sir, my slave so handsome, good, and wise!

STALAGMUS. What can you expect from *me*, when such a man as *you* tells lies?
For I never was nor shall be fine or handsome, good or true;
If you're building on my goodness, it will be the worse for you.

HEGIO. Well, it is n't hard for you to see which way your interest lies;
If you tell the truth, 't will save you from the harshest penalties.
Speak out, straight and true; although you've not done right and true, I guess.

STALAGMUS. Oh, you need n't think I blush to hear you say what I confess.

HEGIO. I will make you blush, you villain; for a bath of blood prepare!

STALAGMUS. That will be no novelty! you threaten one who's oft been there!
But no more of that; just tell me what you want to ask of me.
Perhaps you'll get it.

HEGIO. You're too fluent; kindly speak with brevity.

STALAGMUS. As you please.

HEGIO. Ah, from a boy he was a supple, flattering knave.

But to business! Pray attend to me, and tell me what I crave.
If you speak the truth, you'll find your interest 't will best subserve.

STALAGMUS. Don't tell me! D' you think that I don't know full well what I deserve?

HEGIO. But you may escape a part if not the whole of your desert.

STALAGMUS. Oh, it's little I'll escape! and much will happen to my hurt:
For I ran away and stole your son from you, and him I sold.

HEGIO. Oh, to whom?

STALAGMUS. To Theodoromedes of the house of Gold
For ten pounds.

HEGIO. Good Heav'ns! Why, that's the father of Philocrates.

STALAGMUS. Yes, I know that quite as well as you do — better, if you please.

HEGIO. Jupiter in Heaven, save me, and preserve my darling son!
On your soul, Philocrates, come out! I want you. Make haste, run!

[*Enter* PHILOCRATES *from the house.*]

PHILOCRATES. Hegio, I am at your service.

HEGIO. This man says he sold my son
To your father there in Elis for ten pounds.

PHILOCRATES. When was this done?

STALAGMUS. Twenty years ago.

PHILOCRATES. O, nonsense! Hegio, he's telling lies.

STALAGMUS. Either you or I am lying; for when you were little boys,
He was given you by your father to be trained along with you.

PHILOCRATES. Well, then, tell me what his name was, if this tale of yours is true.

STALAGMUS. Pægnium at first; in after time you called him Tyndarus.

PHILOCRATES. How is it that I don't know you?

STALAGMUS. Men are oft oblivious,
And forget the names of those from whom they've nothing to expect.

PHILOCRATES. Then this child you sold my father, if your story is correct,

Was bestowed on me as valet. Who was he?
STALAGMUS. My master's son.
HEGIO. Is he living, fellow?
STALAGMUS. Nay, I got the money; then
I'd done.
HEGIO. What say you?
PHILOCRATES. That Tyndarus is your
lost son! I give you joy!
So at least this fellow's statements make
me think; for he's the boy
Who received his education with myself all
through our youth.
HEGIO. Well, I'm fortunate and wretched
all at once, if you speak truth;
Wretched that I treated him so cruelly,
if he's my son;
Oh, alas! I did both more and less than
what I should have done!
How I'm vexed that I chastised him!
Would that I could alter it!
See, he comes! and in a fashion that is any-
thing but fit.

[*Enter* TYNDARUS *from the quarries.*]

TYNDARUS. Well, I've often seen in
pictures all the torments of the
damned;
But I'm certain that you could n't find a
hell that's stuffed and crammed
With such tortures as those quarries. There
they've got a perfect cure
For all weariness; you simply drive it off by
working more.
When I got there, just as wealthy fathers
oft will give their boys
Starlings, goslings, quills to play with in
the place of other toys,
So when I got there, a *crow* was given me as
plaything pretty!
Ah, my lord is at the door; and my old lord
from Elis city
Has returned!
HEGIO. O hail, my long lost son!
TYNDARUS. What means this talk of
"sons"?
Oh, I see why you pretend to be my father;
yes, for once
You have acted like a parent, for you've
brought me to the light.
PHILOCRATES. Hail, good Tyndarus!
TYNDARUS. All hail! for you I'm in this
pretty plight.

PHILOCRATES. Ah! but now you shall be
free and wealthy; for you must be
told,
Hegio's your father. That slave stole you
hence when four years old;
And then sold you to my father for ten
pounds, who gave you me,
When we both were little fellows, that my
valet you might be.
This man whom we brought from Elis has
most certain proofs supplied.
TYNDARUS. What, am I his son?
PHILOCRATES. You are; your brother too
you'll find inside.
TYNDARUS. Then you have brought back
with you his son who was a prisoner?
PHILOCRATES. Yes, and he is in the house.
TYNDARUS. You've done right well and
nobly, sir.
PHILOCRATES. Now you have a father;
here's the thief who stole you when
a boy.
TYNDARUS. Now that I'm grown up,
he'll find that theft will bring him
little joy.
PHILOCRATES. He deserves your venge-
ance.
TYNDARUS. Oh, I'll have him paid for
what he's done.
Tell me though, are you my father really?
HEGIO. Yes, I am, my son.
TYNDARUS. Now at length it dawns
upon me, and I seem, when I re-
flect,
Yes, I seem to call to mind and somewhat
vaguely recollect,
As if looking through a mist, my father's
name was Hegio.
HEGIO. I am he!
PHILOCRATES. Then strike the fetters off
your son and let him go!
And attach them to this villain.
HEGIO. Certainly, it shall be so.
Let's go in, and let the smith be summoned
to strike off your chains,
And to put them on this fellow.
STALAGMUS. Right! For they're my
only gains.
EPILOGUE. Gentlemen, this play's been
written on the lines of modesty;
Here are found no wiles of women, no gay
lovers' gallantry;

Here are no affiliations, and no tricks for
    getting gold;
No young lover buys his mistress whilst his
    father is cajoled.
It's not often nowadays that plays are
    written of this kind,
In which good folk are made better. Now
    then, if it be your mind,
And we've pleased you and not bored you,
    kindly undertake our cause,
And to modesty award the prize with
    heartiest applause.

PHORMIO

By TERENCE

Translated into English prose by MORRIS H. MORGAN

CHARACTERS

DAVOS, *a slave*

GETA, *slave of Demipho*

ANTIPHO, *a young man, son of Demipho*

PHÆDRIA, *a young man, son of Chremes*

DEMIPHO, *an old man*

PHORMIO, *a parasite*

HEGIO,
CRATINUS, } *advisers of Demipho*
CRITO,

DORIO, *a slave-trader*

CHREMES, *an old man, Demipho's brother*

SOPHRONA, *an old nurse*

NAUSISTRATA, *a matron, wife of Chremes*

A Cantor

PHORMIO

ACT I

[SCENE: *A street in Athens, leading on the right to the market-place, on the left to the port. At the back, the houses of* CHREMES (L.), DEMIPHO (C.), *and* DORIO (R.).]

[*Enter* DAVOS, R.]

DAVOS. My particular friend and countryman, Geta, came to see me yesterday. I had been owing him some small balance of cash on account a good while, and he asked me to get it together. I've got it together, and I'm bringing it to him now. The fact is, I'm told that his master's son has got married; it's for the girl, I suppose, that he's scraping this testimonial together. How unfair it is that poor folks should always be adding something to rich people's piles! Now here's Geta; — the poor fellow's been saving up out of his rations a pint at a time, and hardly that, cheating his own belly, and now my lady'll spoil him of it all without ever thinking what a lot of work it took to get it. Then besides they'll strike him for another testimonial when she has a baby; and then another too when the baby has a birthday, and another when it gets initiated. The mother, of course, will walk off with it all, and the child will be only an excuse for the gift. But don't I see Geta?

[*Enter* GETA, *from* DEMIPHO'S.]

GETA [*looking back*]. If e'er a red-head asks for me —

DAVOS. Here he is. That'll do.

GETA. Ha! Why, Davos, you were the very man I wanted to meet.

DAVOS [*handing him the bag*]. There you are! Take it; it's good money. You'll find the total comes to what I owe you.

GETA. Thank you. I'm obliged to you for not forgetting it.

DAVOS. Particularly as things go now-adays. Why, it's come to such a pass that you're expected to feel very much obliged when a man pays you a debt. But what makes you so glum?

GETA. Me? Oh, you don't know what a fright and what danger we are in!

DAVOS. Why! what's the matter?

GETA. You shall hear, — that is, provided you can keep mum.

DAVOS. Get out, will you, you simpleton. When you've seen that a man's to be trusted in a matter of money, are you afraid to trust him with words? Why, what should I gain by deceiving you there?

GETA. Well, then, listen.

DAVOS. I'm at your service.

GETA. Davos, do you know our old gentleman's elder brother Chremes?

DAVOS. Of course I do.

GETA. And his son Phædria?

DAVOS. As well as I know you.

GETA. The two old fellows happened to start out at the same time, — Chremes on a trip to Lemnos, and our governor to Cilicia to see an old friend. He had enticed the old man over by letters, promising him all but mountains of gold.

DAVOS. Him, with already so much and to spare?

GETA. Never mind; it is his nature to.

DAVOS. Oh, if only *I* had been a millionaire!

GETA. Well, when the two old gentlemen set out, they left me here with their sons as a sort of guardian.

DAVOS. O Geta, Geta! No soft job you had there.

GETA. I've found that out — by experience. I see now that my guardian angel was out of sorts with me when I was left behind. I started in by opposition; but, to make a long story short, I found that being true to the old man was the ruination of my back.

DAVOS. Just what I was thinking; it's folly, you know, kicking against the pricks.

GETA. So I began to do everything they wanted, and to comply with all their wishes.

DAVOS. You understand how to carry your pigs to the best market.

GETA. Our fellow did n't make any trouble at first; but Phædria there, — the first thing he did was to pick up a pretty little harp-lady, and he fell desperately in love with her. She belonged to the lowest sort of a slave-trader, and we had n't a penny to give him, — the old gentlemen had looked out for that. So the only thing left for Phædria to do was to feast his eyes on her, tag at her heels, take her down to the singing school, and see her home. My young master and I, having nothing to do, devoted ourselves to Phædria. Now there was a barber's shop just across the street from the school she went to, and there we pretty generally used to wait until it was time for her to go home. One day, as we were sitting there, a young fellow came up, all in a flood of tears. Surprise on our part, — we asked what was up. "I never knew so well before," cried he, "what a wretched, crushing burden it is to be poor. I've just seen near here a poor girl bewailing her dead mother, who lay buried over opposite. She had n't with her a well-wisher or friend or relative helping with the funeral, except one lone woman. It was pitiable. The girl herself was a beauty." In short, he stirred us all up, and Antipho cried out, "Shall we go and see her?" and somebody else, "I move we do, — let's go, — show us the way, please." We start; we're there; we take a look. The girl *was* a beauty, and you could put it all the more strongly because she had n't any artificial fallals to make her so. Hair disheveled — feet bare — she all frowsy — weeping — meanly dressed; in fact, if she had n't been the very essence of beauty, all this would have eclipsed her beauty. The young fellow who was in love with the harp-lady only said, "She's very pretty"; but my young master —

DAVOS. I know without being told; he fell in love with her.

GETA. Rather! See how it turns out. The very next day he went straight to the old woman; begged that he might have her. But she refused, and said he was n't doing the proper thing; "for the girl was an Athenian, a good girl of good stock. If he wanted to marry her, it could be done in the regular legal way; but if he meant anything else, no." My master did n't know what to do; on the one hand he longed to marry the girl, on the other he was afraid of his father, who was gone abroad.

DAVOS. Would n't his father have given him leave when he came home?

GETA. What, he! give leave to marry a girl without a dowry and of unknown family? Never in the world.

DAVOS. Well, what happened in the end?

GETA. What happened? There's a parasite of the name of Phormio — a cheeky fellow — blast him!

DAVOS. Why, what's he been up to?

GETA. He supplied the scheme which I am going to describe. "There's a law," says he, "that orphan girls must marry their next of kin, and by the same law the kinsmen are obliged to marry them. Now, I'll say that you're her kinsman, and I'll bring a suit against you. I'll pretend that I was a friend of the girl's father. We shall come into court. Who her father was, and who her mother, and how she is related to you, I'll make all that up. It will be good and easy for me, for you won't disprove any of the charges, and so of course I shall win. Your father will come home; that means a lawsuit against me. But what do I care for that? The girl will be ours anyhow.

DAVOS. A jolly piece of cheek!

GETA. Antipho agreed — 't was done — off we went — got beaten — he married her.

DAVOS. What *are* you telling me?

GETA. Just what you hear.

DAVOS. Oh, Geta, what will become of you?

GETA. By the powers I don't know that; but one thing I do know, which is, that "bravely we'll bear the burden fortune brings."

Davos, I like that; that's taking it like a little man.

Geta. I've no hope in anybody but myself.

Davos. Good again!

Geta. I suppose I must go to somebody who will beg me off in this style: "Do let him off just this once; but if he is ever guilty again, I won't say a word," — all but adding, "Kill him, for all me, when I've once got away."

Davos. What about the harp-lady's chaperon? How's he getting on?

Geta. So, so. Pretty poorly.

Davos. Has n't much to give, perhaps?

Geta. Nothing at all but unadulterated hope.

Davos. His father home yet or not?

Geta. Not yet.

Davos. Well, how long before you expect your own old man?

Geta. I don't know for sure, but I'm told that a letter has come from him which has been taken to the custom-house; I'll go after it.

Davos. Can't do anything more for you, Geta, can I?

Geta. Only take care of yourself. [Exit Davos, R.] Hi! boy! is nobody ever coming? [Enter a slave.] Take this, and give it to Dorcium. [Gives him the bag, and exit L.]

ACT II

[Enter Antipho and Phædria from the house of Chremes.]

Antipho. Oh, Phædria, to think that it has come to this, that I should be afraid of my own father whenever I think of his coming home! He wishes nothing but my good. If I had n't been so thoughtless, I should be waiting for his coming with joy.

Phædria. Why, what's the matter?

Antipho. Matter, you accomplice in my bold scheme? Oh, how I wish it had never occurred to Phormio to urge me to it, and that he had n't driven me, when I was in the heat of my passion, to take this step, which was the beginning of all my troubles! I should n't have got the girl, of course, and that would have made me wretched for

some days; but still, I should n't be suffering this everlasting anxiety all the time, —

Phædria. Yes, yes.

Antipho. Constantly expecting that he will soon be here to break up this marriage of mine.

Phædria. Other men are wretched because they have n't got the object of their love, but you're unhappy because you've got too much of it. You're embarrassed with bliss, Antipho. But I tell you that your position is one to be coveted and desired. Bless me, for the chance to be so long with her I love I'm ready to pay down my life. Only just reckon up all that I'm suffering from privation and all that you're enjoying in possession! To say nothing of your having got a well-born lady without any expense, and of having the wife of your choice publicly acknowledged, and without any scandal! Here you are perfectly happy except for one thing, — a temper to bear it all with equanimity. If you had to deal with a slave-trader like that one of mine, then you'd find out! But that's the way almost all of us are made; we're dissatisfied with our own lot.

Antipho. On the contrary, Phædria, it seems to me that you are the lucky man. You're still perfectly free to make up your mind to your liking, — to keep your sweetheart or to give her up. But I, unluckily, have got into such a fix that I can neither keep mine nor let her go either. But what's here? Is n't this Geta I see running up this way? It's the very man. Oh, dear me, I'm dreadfully frightened about the news he may be bringing! [They retire up.]

[Enter Geta, hastily from the port.]

Geta. You're done for, Geta, unless you find some way out and mighty quick! Such troubles threaten you all of a sudden and you're so unprepared. I don't see how to dodge them or how to get myself out of this fix. Our reckless doings can't possibly be concealed any longer.

Antipho [aside]. Why in the world is the man come in such a fright?

Geta. Besides, I've only a minute to think of it; master's close by.

Antipho [aside]. What's this trouble?

GETA. Once he's heard of it, how shall I head off his fury? Talk? 'T would set him afire. Silence? Merely egging him on. Clear myself? Might as well wash a brick. Oh, dear me! I'm frightened on my own account, and then I'm in torture when I think of Antipho. He's the man I'm sorry for. I'm afraid for his sake now, and it's he that keeps me here. Why, if it were not for him, I should have seen to myself easily enough, and got even with the old man for his anger. I should just have got some traps together, and then taken to my heels straight out of here.

ANTIPHO [aside]. Why, what's this he's plotting about running away or stealing?

GETA. But where shall I find Antipho? Which way shall I go to look for him?

PHÆDRIA [aside]. He's talking about you.

ANTIPHO [aside]. I dread some great misfortune from this news.

PHÆDRIA [aside]. Oh, dear!

GETA. I'll go on home. That's where he is generally.

PHÆDRIA [aside]. Let's call the fellow back.

ANTIPHO. Stop where you are!

GETA. Ha! pretty peremptory, don't care who you are!

ANTIPHO. Geta!

GETA. It's the very man I wanted to find.

ANTIPHO. Out with your news, for mercy's sake; and, if you can, dispatch it in one word.

GETA. I will.

ANTIPHO. Speak out.

GETA. Just now, down at the post —

ANTIPHO. My —

GETA. You've hit it.

ANTIPHO. I'm a dead man!

PHÆDRIA. Whew!

ANTIPHO. What shall I do?

PHÆDRIA. What's this you say?

GETA. That I saw his father, your uncle.

ANTIPHO. Now how am I to find a way out of this sudden catastrophe, dear, dear me? Why, life isn't worth living, if it's my fate to be torn away from you, Phanium.

GETA. Well, if that's so, Antipho, there's all the more need of being wide awake. Fortune favors the brave.

ANTIPHO. I'm all abroad!

GETA. But that's just where you mustn't be now, Antipho; for your father will think you guilty if he sees you frightened.

PHÆDRIA. That's true.

ANTIPHO. I can't change my nature.

GETA. Suppose you had to do something still harder, what then?

ANTIPHO. As I can't do this, I could do that still less.

GETA. It's no use, Phædria; it's all over. Why waste our time here for nothing? I'm off.

PHÆDRIA. And I too [going].

ANTIPHO. For mercy's sake! Suppose I make believe? Will this do?
[Strikes an attitude.]

GETA. Silly!

ANTIPHO. But just look at my face. There! is that satisfactory?

GETA. No.

ANTIPHO. How about this?

GETA. Pretty fair.

ANTIPHO. And this?

GETA. That will do. Keep that, and look out that you answer him word for word, tit for tat, so that he shan't rout you with harsh language while he's in a passion.

ANTIPHO. I understand.

GETA. Say you were forced into it, against your will.

PHÆDRIA. By the law — by the court.

GETA. Do you catch on? But who's that old man I see down the street? It's the governor!

ANTIPHO. I can't face him.

GETA. Here! what are you doing? Where are you going, Antipho? Wait, say.

ANTIPHO. I know myself and my own fault. I leave Phanium and my own life in your hands. [Runs off, R.]

PHÆDRIA. What's going to be done now, Geta?

GETA. You'll get a wigging pretty soon, and I shall be strung up and whipped, if I'm not mistaken. But we ought to do ourselves, Phædria, just what we were advising Antipho.

PHÆDRIA. None of your "oughts." Just give me your orders what I'm to do.

GETA. Do you remember what you said long ago when we started in with this affair, about protecting ourselves from trouble, — that the other side's case was just, easy, sure to win, the best in the world?

PHÆDRIA. Yes, I remember.

GETA. Well, now's the time for that very plea, or, if possible, for a better and one more cunning still.

PHÆDRIA. I'll do my best.

GETA. You go up to him first, and I'll stay here in ambush as a reserve force, in case you fail.

PHÆDRIA. Very well. [GETA retires up.]

[Enter DEMIPHO, L.]

DEMIPHO. What, what, what! Antipho's got married, has he, without my consent? As for my authority, — well, never mind authority, — but only think of his having no regard even for my displeasure! Not a bit ashamed, either. Oh, what a monstrous thing! Oh, Geta, Geta, you rare advisor!

GETA [aside]. In for it at last!

DEMIPHO. Now what will they say to me? What excuse will they find? I wonder very much.

GETA [aside]. Oh, I shall find one; you need n't worry about that.

DEMIPHO. Is this what he'll say: "I did it against my will; the law forced me to it." Yes, yes; I admit it.

GETA. You old dear!

DEMIPHO. But with his eyes open, without a word, to give up the case to the other side! Did the law force him to that?

PHÆDRIA [aside]. Ah, that's a hard nut!

GETA [aside]. I'll crack it, though; let me alone for that!

DEMIPHO. It's taken me so unawares, — it's so past belief that I can't tell what to do. I'm so much exasperated that I can't compose my mind to think it over. Well, the fact is, when everything is most successful with you, then's the time to reflect how to bear the brunt of trouble, — your son's bad conduct, your wife's death, your daughter's illness; — these things happen to everybody, they can happen to you, so there should n't be anything surprising in them; but everything that surprises you

by ending well, you can set down as so much clear gain.

GETA [aside]. Ha, Phædria! It's past belief how much more of a sage I am than my master. I *have* reflected on all the troubles that master's return will bring upon *me*, — grinding to do at the mill, floggings to get, fetters to wear, set to work on the farm. Not a single one of them will take me by surprise. But everything that surprises me by ending well, I shall set down as so much clear gain. But why don't you step up to him and address him politely to begin with?

DEMIPHO. There's my nephew Phædria, I see, coming to meet me.

PHÆDRIA. How do you do, uncle?

DEMIPHO. How do you do? But where's Antipho?

PHÆDRIA. You've got back safe, —

DEMIPHO. Yes, yes; but answer my question.

PHÆDRIA. He's well — he's here; but has everything gone to your liking?

DEMIPHO. I wish it had, indeed.

PHÆDRIA. Why, what's the matter?

DEMIPHO. What a question, Phædria! This is a fine marriage that you've cooked up here while I was away!

PHÆDRIA. Holloa! are you angry with him for that?

GETA [aside]. Fine acting!

DEMIPHO. And should n't I be angry with him? Why, I'm just aching to get a sight of him, so that he may find out once for all how he's turned his good-natured old father into a perfect savage!

PHÆDRIA. But he has n't done anything to make you angry, uncle.

DEMIPHO. Now just look at that! Birds of a feather! They're all in it! When you know one, you know all.

PHÆDRIA. It is n't so.

DEMIPHO. When A's in trouble, B turns up to make excuses for him; and when it's B, then up comes A. They go partners in it.

GETA [aside]. The old man's drawn a fine sketch of their proceedings without knowing it.

DEMIPHO. If it was n't so, you would n't be taking his part, Phædria.

PHÆDRIA. Well, uncle, if it is a fact that Antipho has done a wrong, regardless of his interests or reputation, I have nothing to say against his suffering as he has deserved. But if somebody took advantage of his own cunning to lay a snare for our youthful innocence and has caught us in it, is it our fault or that of the judges? You know what a habit they have of robbing the rich from envy, and giving to the poor from pity.

GETA [aside]. If I did n't know the case, I should believe that he was telling the truth.

DEMIPHO. Is there a judge alive who can possibly know your rights when you don't answer a word yourself, like that son of mine?

PHÆDRIA. He behaved like a young man of good breeding. When we got into court, he could n't speak his piece; his modesty struck him quite dumb then and there.

GETA [aside]. Bravo, you! but shall I not address the old man at once? [Going forward.] Good-day, master. I'm glad you've got home safe.

DEMIPHO. Ha, ha! fine guardian, good-day, main stay of my house; it was in your charge that I left my son when I went away.

GETA. I've heard you blaming us all for ever so long when we did n't deserve it, and I least of anybody. Why, what would you have had me do in the matter? The laws don't allow a man who's a slave to plead, and he can't give evidence either.

DEMIPHO. I waive all that, and I admit this, too, that the boy was afraid and unsuspecting. I grant that you are a slave. But no matter how near a relative she was, he need n't have married her; no, no. You should have given her a dowry, as the law directs, and let her look out for another husband. On what account, then, did he prefer to bring home a pauper?

GETA. It was n't on account, — it was cash down that was wanted.

DEMIPHO. He should have got it somewhere or other.

GETA. Somewhere or other? Nothing easier to say!

DEMIPHO. On interest, at the worst, if on no other terms.

GETA. Bless my soul! Pretty fine talk! As if anybody would have trusted him, with you alive!

DEMIPHO. No, no; it shan't be so; it can't be. What! let her stay on as his wife a single day? This is no case for kindness. But I want to have that man pointed out to me, or to be shown where he lives.

GETA. You mean Phormio?

DEMIPHO. The woman's next friend.

GETA. I'll bring him here at once.

DEMIPHO. Where's Antipho now?

GETA. Out.

DEMIPHO. Go and look for him, Phædria, and bring him here.

PHÆDRIA. I'll make a bee line.

[Exit to DORIO's.]

GETA [aside]. Yes, to Pamphila's. [Exit R.]

DEMIPHO. As for me, I'll turn in home and pay my respects to my household gods, and then go on 'Change and call some friends to stand by me in this affair, so that I shan't be unprepared in case of Phormio's coming. [Exit to his house.]

ACT III

[Enter PHORMIO and GETA, R.]

PHORMIO. And so you say he's gone off in a fright at his father's return?

GETA. Exactly.

PHORMIO. Phanium left all by herself?

GETA. Just so.

PHORMIO. And the old man boiling.

GETA. Precisely.

PHORMIO. Then, Phormio, the whole responsibility rests on you; you mixed this mess, and now you've got to eat it all yourself. Brace up!

GETA. For mercy's sake, Phormio!

PHORMIO. Supposing he asks —

GETA. You're our only hope!

PHORMIO. See here, what if he retorts —

GETA. You drove the boy to it.

PHORMIO. There, that'll do, I fancy.

GETA. Come to the rescue!

PHORMIO. Trot out your old man, for I've got my plans all marshaled in my head.

GETA. What are you going to do?

PHORMIO. What, indeed, except let Phanium stay here, clear Antipho of this charge, and turn the whole current of the old man's wrath on to myself?

GETA. Oh, you brave, kind man! but what I'm often afraid of, Phormio, is that all this courage may land you in the stocks at last.

PHORMIO. Oh, no, not at all; I've tried it; I know where to set my feet. How many fellows do you think I've beaten to death before to-day? Yet come, did you ever hear of anybody bringing a suit against me for assault and battery?

GETA. How does it come about?

PHORMIO. It's because we never set traps for the hawks and kites that really hurt us; it's only for birds that don't hurt that traps are set. There's something to be made out of them, but on others it's only time thrown away. Other people have their dangers, from one source or another, — people something can be got out of; but everybody knows that I've got nothing to lose. But perhaps you'll say that they'll convict me and take me home to hold me there. Oh, no; they don't want to keep a ravenous fellow like me; they don't want to do good for evil, and that's where they're wise, I think.

GETA. Well, he can't ever thank you as much as you deserve.

PHORMIO. Not quite so. Nobody ever can thank his *patron* as much as he deserves. Think of it! You come scot free to his dinner, all perfumed and shining from the bath, with a heart free from care, when he's drowned with worry and eaten up with expenses. While everything's done to your liking, he's snarling. You can laugh, drink your wine before him, take the higher seat; and then a puzzling banquet's spread.

GETA. What's that?

PHORMIO. That's when you're puzzled what to help yourself to first. Now, when you come to reckon up how nice all this is and how much it costs, are n't you obliged to think your host a god incarnate right before your eyes?

GETA. Here's the old man; mind what you're about; the first onset is always the fiercest. If you stand that, you may afterwards make play as you like.

[*Enter* DEMIPHO *and his advisers*, R.]

DEMIPHO. Did you ever hear of a more insulting piece of injustice done to anybody than this to me? Stand by me, I beg of you.

GETA [*aside*]. He's in a passion.

PHORMIO [*to* GETA *aside*]. Mind your cue now; I'm going to touch him up pretty quick. [*Aloud, to* GETA.] Great heavens! Does Demipho actually *deny* that Phanium's related to him? What! Demipho says this girl's no relation?

GETA. He says not.

PHORMIO. And that he does n't know who her father was?

GETA. He says not.

DEMIPHO. I fancy this is the very man I was talking about. Follow me.

PHORMIO. Because the poor thing is left in poverty, her father is disowned and she herself is abandoned. Only see what avarice does!

GETA. You'll hear what you won't like if you insinuate anything wrong about my master.

DEMIPHO. Oh, what impudence! Why, he's come to take the initiative by accusing me!

PHORMIO. I've no reason at all to be angry with the young fellow for not knowing her father; of course he was a man pretty well along, poor, working for his living, generally keeping in the country, where my father let him have a farm to cultivate. The old fellow used often to tell me how this kinsman of his neglected him. But what a fine man he was! the best *I* ever saw in all my life.

GETA. I hope you'll ever see yourself such as you describe him.

PHORMIO. You be hanged! No; if I had n't esteemed him as I did, I should never have got into a quarrel with your people, all on account of this girl that your master's slighting now in this ungentlemanlike way.

GETA. Will you persist in slandering my master behind his back, you dirty dog?

PHORMIO. Serves him right.

GETA. Still more of it, you jail-bird?

DEMIPHO. Geta —

GETA. You extortioner, you law-shark!

DEMIPHO. Geta!

PHORMIO [aside]. Answer him.

GETA. Whom have we here? Oh!

DEMIPHO. Hold your tongue!

GETA. Why, he's been insulting you all day long behind your back, — insults that don't fit you and do fit him.

DEMIPHO. Avast there! Hold on! Young man [to PHORMIO], to begin with, I want to ask you this, with your kind permission, if you will be good enough to answer me: Explain to me who this friend of yours was you're talking about, and how he said that I was related to him.

PHORMIO. There you are, fishing; as if you did n't know.

DEMIPHO. Did n't know?

PHORMIO. Yes.

DEMIPHO. I say I don't; but you, who say I do, just jog my memory.

PHORMIO. What, man! not know your own cousin?

DEMIPHO. You're killing me. Tell me his name.

PHORMIO. His name; of course.

DEMIPHO. Why don't you speak?

PHORMIO [aside]. By the powers, I'm a goner! I've forgotten the name.

DEMIPHO. What's that you say?

PHORMIO [aside to GETA]. Geta, just prompt me if you recollect the name that was given at the time. [Aloud.] No, I won't tell you. You're here to pump me, as if you did n't know it yourself.

DEMIPHO. What! Pumping you?

GETA [aside to PHORMIO]. Stilpo.

PHORMIO. And then again, what do I care? It's Stilpo.

DEMIPHO. Whom did you say?

PHORMIO. Stilpo, I tell you; you knew him.

DEMIPHO. I did n't know him either, and I never had a relative of such a name.

PHORMIO. So, so? Don't you feel abashed before these gentlemen? Yet if he had left a property worth ten talents —

DEMIPHO. Oh confound you!

PHORMIO. You'd be the very first with a tip-top memory to trace your ancestry all the way from grandfather and great-grandfather.

DEMIPHO. Very likely, as you say. Well, when I came forward I should have stated how she was related to me. Now, you do the same. Come, how is she related?

GETA. Bravo, master, well done! and you, sir, look out for yourself.

PHORMIO. My duty was to explain it to the court, and I did so with perfect clearness. If it was n't true, why did n't your son do it on the spot?

DEMIPHO. You talk to me about my son? Why, I can't find words to describe his stupidity.

PHORMIO. Well, then, you who are so wise, go to the magistrates and make them try the same case all over again for you. For you talk as though you were sole lord paramount in these parts and the only man alive entitled to a second trial of the same case.

DEMIPHO. Though I have been unjustly treated, still, rather than go to law or have to listen to you — here, just as if she really were related, take these five ducats, the dowry that the law directs, and carry her away.

PHORMIO. Ha! ha! ha! you sweety!

DEMIPHO. What's the matter? There's nothing wrong in my demand, is there? Am I not to get the benefit of what is the law of the land?

PHORMIO. Does the law direct you, I'd like to know, to pay her and send her off like a courtesan? Or was it to prevent a freeborn lady from doing anything to disgrace herself through poverty that the law directs to give her to her nearest kinsman to live with him? And that's just what you're preventing.

DEMIPHO. Yes, to her nearest kinsman. But how do we come in, or on what grounds?

PHORMIO. Oh, dear! "don't open a case that's closed," as the saying goes.

DEMIPHO. Don't open it? On the contrary, I'll never rest until I've seen it through.

PHORMIO. Silly of you.

DEMIPHO. You just let me alone.

PHORMIO. In short, Demipho, I've nothing to do with you. It was your son that lost the suit, not you; for your time for marrying was gone long ago.

DEMIPHO. You can take him as saying all that I say now; if he does n't I'll shut him and his wife out of my house.

GETA [aside]. He's in a passion.

PHORMIO. You'd better do the same thing with yourself.

DEMIPHO. So you're ready to take a stand against me in everything, are you, you ill-starred wretch?

PHORMIO [aside to GETA]. He's afraid of us, though he tries hard to conceal it.

GETA [aside to PHORMIO]. Your first moves are well made.

PHORMIO [aloud]. Why not put up with what you must put up with? That will be in keeping with your reputation, and we shall be friends.

DEMIPHO. What! I seek your friendship, or wish to see or hear of you?

PHORMIO. If you make it up with her, you'll have somebody to cheer your old age; think of your time of life.

DEMIPHO. Keep her to cheer yourself.

PHORMIO. Do moderate your angry passions.

DEMIPHO. See here! enough said. If you don't hurry and take that woman away, I'll throw her out of doors. That's my last word, Phormio.

PHORMIO. And if you lay a finger on her in any way unbefitting a lady, I'll bring a smashing suit against you. That's my last word, Demipho. [Aside to GETA.] Here! if you need me for anything, you'll find me at home.

GETA. All right! [Exit PHORMIO, R.]

DEMIPHO. What worry and trouble my son does give me by involving himself and me in this marriage! And he does n't come to let me see him either, so that at least I might know what he has to ___ matter, or what he thinks. ___ see whether he has got hom___

GETA. Yes. [Exit to hous___

DEMIPHO [to his adviser___ what a state things are. ___ to do? Tell me, Hegio.

HEGIO. I? I move Crat___ please.

DEMIPHO. Well, speak, Cratinus.

CRATINUS. Do you mean me?

DEMIPHO. Yes sir.

CRATINUS. I should like to have you act for the interests of your house. Now this is the way it seems to me; it's all right and proper that what your son has done in your absence should be put back entirely as it was, and you will carry that point. That's what I say.

DEMIPHO. Now, Hegio, it's your turn to speak.

HEGIO. I believe that he has spoken advisedly; but this is the way of it; many men of many minds, many birds of many kinds; each man has his own point of view. Now it does n't seem to me that what the law has done can be undone; and it's discreditable to try it.

DEMIPHO. Well, Crito?

CRITO. I vote we take time to think it over; it's important.

HEGIO. We can't do anything more for you, can we?

DEMIPHO. You have done finely. [Exeunt advisers R.] I'm much more bewildered than before.

[Enter GETA, from DEMIPHO's house.]

GETA. They say he has n't come in.

DEMIPHO. I must wait for my brother. I'll follow the advice which he gives me in the matter. I'll go down to the port to find out when he's to come home. [Exit L.]

GETA. And I'll go look for Antipho, so that he may know how things are. But, hallon! I see him coming in the nick of time.

[Enter ANTIPHO, R.]

ANTIPHO. Well, A___
panic have ___
of you___

GETA. And really, master, we too have been finding fault with you behind your back for leaving us.

ANTIPHO. You're the very man I was looking for.

GETA. But for all that we have n't failed you a bit.

ANTIPHO. For heaven's sake, tell me how my fate and fortunes stand. My father has n't got wind of anything?

GETA. Not yet.

ANTIPHO. Any prospect for the future?

GETA. I don't know.

ANTIPHO. Oh, dear!

GETA. But Phædria has never ceased his efforts for you.

ANTIPHO. That's nothing new in him.

GETA. Then Phormio, too, has shown the man of energy in this as in everything else.

ANTIPHO. Why, what has he done?

GETA. He's bluffed the angry old man with his talk.

ANTIPHO. Oh, bravo, Phormio!

GETA. And I did what I could myself.

ANTIPHO. My dear Geta, I'm much obliged to you all.

GETA. The opening moves were made as I have described; all's quiet up to the present time, and your father is going to wait until your uncle comes home.

ANTIPHO. Why for him?

GETA. He said he wanted to act in this case according to his advice.

ANTIPHO. Oh, Geta, how I do dread to see my uncle come home safe and sound! For life and death, I find, depend on his single voice.

GETA. Here comes Phædria.

ANTIPHO. Where, pray?

There, coming out from his play-

_____IA _and_ DORIO, _from_ DORIO'S _house._]

_____en to me, Dorio, for
pity's sa_____

_____alone?
_____ve to

DORIO. No; I'm tired of hearing the same thing a thousand times.

PHÆDRIA. But now I'm going to say something which you will like to hear.

DORIO. Speak out then. I'm listening.

PHÆDRIA. Can't I prevail on you to wait just these three days? Why, where are you going now?

DORIO. I wondered whether you had anything new to bring forward.

ANTIPHO [aside]. Oh, dear! I'm afraid this slave-trader may be —

GETA [aside]. Hoist with his own petar? I'm afraid so, too.

PHÆDRIA. You don't believe me yet, eh?

DORIO. You're a mind reader!

PHÆDRIA. But if I give you my word?

DORIO. Stuff!

PHÆDRIA. You'll have reason to call your kindness a fine investment.

DORIO. Words, words.

PHÆDRIA. Believe me, you'll be glad you did it. It's true, by heaven!

DORIO. Moonshine!

PHÆDRIA. Just try the experiment; it's not for long.

DORIO. Always singing the same old song!

PHÆDRIA. I'll call you my kinsman, — father, — friend —

DORIO. Nonsense!

PHÆDRIA. To think of your being so hard and unbending that neither pity nor prayers can soften you!

DORIO. And to think of your being so unreasonable and impudent, Phædria, as to lead me on with gilded promises, and so get my slave girl for nothing!

ANTIPHO [aside]. What a pity!

PHÆDRIA. Oh, dear me! he's got the better of me.

GETA [aside]. How they both do live up to their own characters.

PHÆDRIA. Think of all this trouble happening to me at the very time when Antipho is full of another worry of his own.

ANTIPHO [coming forward] Why, Phædria, what is all this?

PHÆDRIA. Oh, Antipho, you luckiest of men!

ANTIPHO. I?

PHÆDRIA. Yes; for the girl you love is

in your own keeping, and you've never had occasion to struggle with such a difficulty as mine.

ANTIPHO. In my own keeping? Not quite so; I'm "holding a wolf by the ears," as the old saying is.

DORIO. That's just how I feel about him.

ANTIPHO. Halloa! Act up to your rôle of slave-trader! Has he been doing anything?

PHÆDRIA. He? Been behaving like a barbarian; he's sold my Pamphila.

ANTIPHO. What! sold her?

GETA. You don't say so! sold her?

PHÆDRIA. Yes, he's sold her.

DORIO. What an outrage, to sell a girl bought with my own money!

PHÆDRIA. And I can't prevail on him to wait for me and to put off keeping his promise to the man for only three days, while I am getting the money promised me by my friends. If I don't pay it by that time, you need n't wait for me an hour longer.

DORIO. Still dinning it into me?

ANTIPHO. It's no long time he asks for. Come, consent. He'll return the kindness with a hundred per cent interest.

DORIO. Fine talk!

ANTIPHO. Will you let Pamphila be carried away from this town, and can you bear to see such a pair of lovers torn asunder?

DORIO. Of course I can't any more than you.

GETA. Heaven send you what you deserve!

DORIO. I have been putting up for some months against my will with your promising and not performing and your whimpering; but now I've got the opposite of all this. I have found a man who pays and does n't cry about it. Make way for your betters.

ANTIPHO. But, by heaven, if I remember rightly, there was a day set on which you were to pay him?

PHÆDRIA. There was.

DORIO. I don't deny it, do I?

ANTIPHO. Has it come yet?

DORIO. No, but to-day has come in ahead of it.

ANTIPHO. Are n't you ashamed to be such a fraud?

DORIO. Not a bit of it is for my gain.

GETA. Oh, you dunghill!

PHÆDRIA. Look here, Dorio, is this the right way to behave?

DORIO. It's my way; if you like me, take me as you find me.

ANTIPHO. And you cheat him like this?

DORIO. On the contrary, Antipho, it's he who is cheating me: for he knew all along that I was the sort of man I am; but I supposed that he was different. He's taken me in, but to him I am exactly what I was before. But never mind; this is what I'll do. A soldier man has promised to pay me the money to-morrow morning; now, Phædria, if you bring it to me before he does, I'll follow my regular rule, that he is the better man who is first to come down with the cash. Good-bye.   [Exit, R.]

PHÆDRIA. What shall I do? Where am I to find the money for him in such a hurry, when I've less than nothing myself, poor fellow? It was promised to me, if I could only have begged these three days out of him!

ANTIPHO. Shall we let him be made so unhappy, Geta, after he has just helped me, as you tell me, in such a friendly way? Why not try to return his kindness now when it's needed?

GETA. I know of course it's only the fair thing to do.

ANTIPHO. Come, then, you are the only man who can save him.

GETA. What can I do?

ANTIPHO. Find the money.

GETA. I want to; but where? Tell me that.

ANTIPHO. My father's here.

GETA. I know he is, but what of it?

ANTIPHO. Oh, a word to the wise is quite enough.

GETA. That's it, hey?

ANTIPHO. That's it.

GETA. And a fine suggestion, too, by cracky! Get out, won't you? Is n't it triumph enough if I get off from your marriage with a whole skin without your telling me, when I'm in the stocks already, to try to get hanged for his sake?

ANTIPHO. There's truth in what he says.

PHÆDRIA. What, Geta, am I a mere stranger to all of you?

GETA. I suppose not; but is n't it enough that the old man is so very angry with us all now, without our prodding him still more, so as to leave us no chance to cry off?

PHÆDRIA. And shall another man carry her off to foreign parts before my very eyes? Ah me! Well, then, you two, talk to me and look your fill on me while you may, Antipho, and while I'm here.

ANTIPHO. What do you mean? What are you going to do? Out with it.

PHÆDRIA. Wherever in the world she's carried, I'm resolved to follow, or to die in the attempt.

GETA. Heaven bless your efforts; go slow, though.

ANTIPHO. Do see whether you can help him in any way.

GETA. Any way? But what way?

ANTIPHO. Try to think of something, for mercy's sake. Don't let him do anything, great or small, Geta, that shall make us sorry when it's too late.

GETA. I am trying. [A pause.] Well, he's all right, I think; but really I'm afraid there'll be trouble.

ANTIPHO. Never fear; we'll share it with you, good or bad.

GETA. Tell me; how much money do you need?

PHÆDRIA. Only thirty ducats.

GETA. Thirty? Whew! She's pretty dear, Phædria.

PHÆDRIA. No, not at all; she's cheap.

GETA. Well, well. I'll see that it's found, and give it to you.

PHÆDRIA. Oh, you are a trump!

GETA. Take yourself off.

PHÆDRIA. I need it at once.

GETA. You shall have it at once; but I need Phormio to help me in this business.

ANTIPHO. He's all ready; lay on him boldly any load you like; he'll carry it off. He's a friend indeed to a friend.

GETA. Let's hurry to him then.

ANTIPHO. You don't need any help from me, do you?

GETA. No. You go home and comfort that poor girl, for I know she's in there now half dead with fright. What! waiting?

ANTIPHO. There's nothing I shall be so glad to do. [Exit to DEMIPHO'S.]

PHÆDRIA. How are you going to manage this affair?

GETA. I'll tell you on the way; only take yourself out of this. [Exeunt, R.]

ACT IV

[Enter DEMIPHO and CHREMES, L.]

DEMIPHO. Well, Chremes, did you bring your daughter with you, what you went to Lemnos for?

CHREMES. No.

DEMIPHO. Why not?

CHREMES. Why, when her mother saw that I kept staying and staying on in Athens, and the girl was grown up and could n't be neglected any longer, she set out, they told me, bag and baggage, to come and find me.

DEMIPHO. Then why, I want to know, did you stay there so long when you heard that?

CHREMES. 'Gad, I was kept there by illness.

DEMIPHO. How so? What illness?

CHREMES. What illness? Old age is illness enough in itself. But the skipper who brought them told me that they reached here safe and sound.

DEMIPHO. Have you heard what has happened to my son in my absence, Chremes?

CHREMES. That's just what makes me so undecided in my plans. For if I offer her in marriage to any outsider, I must tell the whole story of how and by whom I came to be her father. As for you, I knew that you were as loyal to me as I am to myself. But if a stranger seeks alliance with me, he will hold his tongue just so long as we are close friends with one another; but if he breaks with me, then he will know more than he ought to know. And I'm afraid my wife may get an inkling of all this. If she does, the only thing left for me to do is to give myself a shake and leave the house; for I'm all I've got in the world.

DEMIPHO. I know that is so; that's what makes me so anxious, and I shall never weary of making every effort to perform my promise for you.

[Enter GETA, R.]

GETA [*aside*]. A shrewder fellow than
Phormio I never saw in my born days. I
went to tell him that money was wanted
and how it was to be got. I had hardly
told him half the story when he understood
it all, — began to laugh, congratulated me,
asked where the old man was. Then he
thanked heaven that now he had a chance
to show that he was as much of a friend to
Phædria as to Antipho. I told the fellow
to wait on 'Change, and said that I would
bring the old man there. Halloa! here he is.
Who's that on the other side? Oh my!
Phædria's father's come home. Lubber
that I am, what was I afraid of? Was it
because I've got two to trick instead of
one? It's handier, I think, to have two
strings to your bow. I'll try to get the
money from the man I meant originally.
If he gives it, all right; if nothing can be
done with him, then I'll attack this newcomer.

[Enter ANTIPHO, *unobserved,* R.]

ANTIPHO [*aside*]. I'm expecting Geta
back every minute. Why, there's my uncle
standing with my father. Dear me! how
I do fear what father may be driven to by
his coming!

GETA. I'll go up. Why! our good friend
Chremes! How do you do?

CHREMES. How do you do, Geta?

GETA. I'm delighted to see you back
safe.

CHREMES. Dare say.

GETA. How goes it? Do you find many
surprises here, as usual when a man comes
home?

CHREMES. A good many.

GETA. To be sure. Have you heard
what's happened to Antipho?

CHREMES. The whole story.

GETA [*to* DEMIPHO.] You told him, then?
What an outrageous thing, Chremes, to be
taken in in this way.

CHREMES. Just what I was telling him.

GETA. But on thinking it all over carefully, by the powers I believe I've found a
way out of it.

CHREMES. What, Geta?

DEMIPHO. What's your way out?

GETA. When I left you I happened to
meet Phormio.

CHREMES. Who's Phormio?

DEMIPHO. The man who was her —

CHREMES. I see.

GETA. I thought I had better find out
his real feelings, so I buttonholed the fellow. "Phormio," says I, "why not try to
settle these matters that are between us
with good feeling, rather than with bad?
My master is a gentleman, and he is shy
of lawsuits. But, by the powers, all his
friends have just been advising him with
one voice to turn the girl out of doors!"

ANTIPHO [*aside*]. Now what can he be
starting on, or how will he end this blessed
day?

GETA. "But, you'll say, won't the law
punish him if he turns her out? He's
looked into that already, and I tell you,
you'll have to sweat for it, if you begin on
a man like him. He's that eloquent! But
come, suppose he is beaten: at the worst
it's only money that's at stake, and not
his life." When I saw that the fellow was
shaken by this talk, "Here we are by ourselves," says I; "come now, say what you
want in cash for yourself to release my
master from this lawsuit, she to make
herself scarce, and you to give no trouble."

ANTIPHO [*aside*]. Can he be in his sober
senses?

GETA. "The fact is, I am certain that if
you name anything that's at all fair and
reasonable, there won't be three words
between you. He's such a kind-hearted
man."

DEMIPHO. Who gave you orders to say
that?

CHREMES. No, no; he couldn't have better brought about just what we want.

ANTIPHO [*aside*]. I'm a dead man!

DEMIPHO. Go on and finish.

GETA. At first the fellow was wild.

CHREMES. Tell us what he asked.

GETA. Oh, a great deal too much.

CHREMES. How much? Speak.

GETA. If you'd offer a great talent —

DEMIPHO. A great big D, you mean!
What! has the fellow no shame?

GETA. Just what I said to him. "Look

here," said I; "suppose he were marrying off an only daughter of his own; he has n't gained much by not having one himself if somebody else's turns up for him to portion." Well, to be brief, and omitting all his silly talk, this was finally his last word: "From the very first," says he, "I have wanted to marry my old friend's daughter myself, as was proper; for I saw how disagreeable it would be for her, a poor girl, married only to be a rich man's slave. But, to tell you the honest truth, I needed a wife who should bring me a little something to pay off what I owe; yes, and even after all that's passed, if Demipho is willing to give as much as I am getting with the girl to whom I am engaged, there's nobody in the world whom I should like better for a wife."

ANTIPHO [aside]. I can't make out whether he's acting from stupidity or mischief, from design or off his guard.

DEMIPHO. But suppose he owes body and soul?

GETA. "My farm," said he, "is mortgaged for ten ducats."

DEMIPHO. Well, well; let him marry her. I'll pay it.

GETA. "Then my house for another ten."

DEMIPHO. Whew! it's too much!

CHREMES. Don't make a row. You can get those ten of me.

GETA. "Then there's a lady's maid to be bought for my wife; then I need a little more furniture, and some cash to spend on the wedding. Put down ten more for this," says he.

DEMIPHO. Then let him bring hundreds and hundreds of lawsuits against me. I won't give him a penny. What! that dirty fellow to get the laugh on me again?

CHREMES. Pray be quiet. I'll pay it myself. All you've got to do is to make your son marry the girl we wish.

ANTIPHO [aside]. Oh, dear me! you've been the death of me, Geta, with your tricks.

CHREMES. She is turned out for my sake, and so it's fair for me to be the loser.

GETA. "Let me know as soon as you can," says he, "if they are going to give her to me, so that I may get rid of this other girl, and not be kept in doubt; for her people have agreed to pay me the dowry down at once."

CHREMES. Let him have the money at once, break the engagement with them, and marry her.

DEMIPHO. Yes, and may bad luck go with her.

CHREMES. Fortunately, I have just brought the money with me now, the rents from my wife's estates in Lemnos. I'll take it out of that, and tell my wife that you needed it.

[Exeunt DEMIPHO and CHREMES to CHREMES'S.]

ANTIPHO [coming forward]. Geta!

GETA. Halloa!

ANTIPHO. What have you done?

GETA. Cleaned the old gentlemen out of their cash.

ANTIPHO. Is that all?

GETA. By the powers, I don't know; it was all I was told to do.

ANTIPHO. What, you rogue! I ask you one thing, and you answer another?

GETA. Why, what are you talking about?

ANTIPHO. What am I talking about? Here I am actually reduced to the rope, and it's all your doing? May all the gods and goddesses up above and down below make the worst sort of an example of you! Well, well; if you want to succeed in a thing, leave it to this fellow, who can bring you out of smooth sailing straight on to a rock! Why, what could have been worse than to lay your finger on this sore and to mention my wife? Here's my father made to hope that he can cast her off. Come now, what follows? Suppose Phormio gets the dowry and has to marry her, what then?

GETA. But he won't marry her.

ANTIPHO. Oh, no! But when they ask the money back, then of course he'll prefer to go to jail for my sake.

GETA. There is n't any story in the world, Antipho, that can't be spoiled in the telling. Now you're leaving out all the good side and telling only the bad. Now, then, hear the other side. Suppose now he gets the money: he will have to marry her, as you say; I admit that;—but they'll give him a little time anyhow to get ready for the wedding, to send out the invitations, and to offer sacrifice. Meanwhile Phædria's friends will give him the money which they have promised, and Phormio will pay back the dowry out of that.

ANTIPHO. On what ground? What can he say?

GETA. What a question! "Since my engagement I've had so many bad omens. A strange black dog trotted straight into my front hall; a snake fell down from the roof through the rain hole; a hen has crowed; the clairvoyant forbade it, the soothsayer won't let me. Besides, to take up anything new before the winter sets in," — that's the strongest reason in the world. That's the way it will be.

ANTIPHO. I only hope it may.

GETA. May? It shall. Look to me for that. There's your father coming out. Go tell Phædria that we've got the money.

[Exit ANTIPHO, R.]

[Enter DEMIPHO *and* CHREMES, *from* CHREMES'S.]

DEMIPHO. Do be quiet, I say. I'll take care he doesn't play me any trick. I'll never let the money go from me helterskelter without having witnesses. I'll have it understood to whom I am giving it and why I give it.

GETA *[aside]*. How cautious he is, where he hasn't any call to be.

CHREMES. That's just what you ought to do; but make haste, while he's still in the mood for it. If that other girl is more pressing, perhaps he'll leave us in the lurch.

GETA *[aside]*. You've hit the very point.

DEMIPHO *[to* GETA]. Take me to him, then.

GETA. I'm ready.

CHREMES. When you have attended to that, go over to my wife's to get her to call on the girl before she goes away. Let her tell the girl, to prevent her from being angry, that we are marrying her to Phormio, and that he is a better match for her, because she knows him better; and that we have done our duty, too, and given her as large a dowry as he asked for.

DEMIPHO. What the plague does that matter to you?

CHREMES. A good deal, Demipho. It's not enough for you to do your duty if the world doesn't approve of what you've done. I want this to take place of her own free will, so that she shan't be saying that we drove her out.

DEMIPHO. Well, I can bring all that about myself.

CHREMES. But a woman's the best hand to deal with a woman.

DEMIPHO. I'll ask her, then.

[Exeunt DEMIPHO *and* GETA, R.]

CHREMES. I wonder now where I can find those women?

[Enter SOPHRONA *from the house of* DEMIPHO.]

SOPHRONA. What shall I do? Where am I to find a friend in my distress? Whom shall I consult? Where get help? I'm afraid my mistress may come to grief from following my advice; the young man's father takes all this so hard, I hear.

CHREMES *[aside]*. Why, who's this old woman that's come out of my brother's house so excited?

SOPHRONA. It was our poverty that drove me to it, though I knew such a marriage was a shaky thing, to provide that at least she might be sure of a living in the mean time.

CHREMES *[aside]*. Upon my word, unless my mind's going or my eyesight's bad, that's my own daughter's nurse that I see there.

SOPHRONA. And we can't track out —

CHREMES *[aside]*. What shall I do?

SOPHRONA. Her father —

CHREMES *[aside]*. Shall I go and speak to her, or stay where I am until I know better what she is saying?

SOPHRONA. If only I could find him, there's nothing I should be afraid of.

CHREMES. It's the very woman. I'll speak to her.

SOPHRONA. Who's this talking here?

CHREMES. Sophrona!

SOPHRONA. Calling me by name, too.

CHREMES. Look at me.

SOPHRONA. Oh, good gracious! can this be Stilpo?

CHREMES. No!

SOPHRONA. What? No?

CHREMES. Come over here a little, away from that door, Sophrona, please, and don't call me by that name any more.

SOPHRONA. Why not? for mercy's sake, are n't you the man you always said you were?

CHREMES. Hush!

SOPHRONA. What is there in this door that you 're afraid of?

CHREMES. I've got a savage wife caged up in there. As for that name, it was a wrong one which I took in those days, so that you should n't let the truth leak out without meaning to, and my wife find it out some way or other.

SOPHRONA. Law me, that's just why we poor women have never been able to find you.

CHREMES. But tell me, what have you to do with the people whose house you just came out from? Where are the ladies?

SOPHRONA. Oh, dear me!

CHREMES. Hey? What's the matter? Are n't they alive?

SOPHRONA. Your daughter is; but her mother, poor thing, died of grief.

CHREMES. Too bad!

SOPHRONA. And so I, being only a lone lorn old woman, whom nobody knew, did my best and got the girl married to the young gentleman who lives in here.

CHREMES. To Antipho?

SOPHRONA. Certainly; the very man.

CHREMES. What! has he got two wives?

SOPHRONA. For pity's sake, no; she's the only one he has.

CHREMES. What about the other who is called his relative?

SOPHRONA. Why, it's she, of course.

CHREMES. What's that you say?

SOPHRONA. It was a put-up job, — the only way by which her lover might get her without a dowry.

CHREMES. Heaven help us! how often things do turn out by haphazard which you'd scarcely dare to wish for! Here I've come home and found my daughter married to the very man I wanted and just as I wanted it! The very thing that we were both trying with all our might to bring about, he has taken the greatest trouble to

do all by himself without any trouble of ours.

SOPHRONA. Well now, just see what's to be done next. The young man's father has arrived, and they say that he is bitterly opposed to it.

CHREMES. There's no danger at all. But, by heaven and earth, don't let anybody find out that she is my daughter.

SOPHRONA. Nobody shall from me.

CHREMES. Follow me; you shall hear the rest inside.   [Exeunt to DEMIPHO'S.]

ACT V

[Enter DEMIPHO and GETA, R.]

DEMIPHO. It's all our own fault that people find it pays them to be rogues; it's because we are too anxious to be called kind and generous. "Enough is as good as a feast," says the proverb. Was n't it enough to be injured by him that we must actually go and throw him a sop in the way of money, to give him something to live on until he can work up some other outrage?

GETA. Perfectly true.

DEMIPHO. Nowadays people who make right wrong get rewarded.

GETA. True enough.

DEMIPHO. So it proves that we've made a stupid mess of it with him!

GETA. Well, if only we get out of it by his marrying her —

DEMIPHO. Why, is there any question about that?

GETA. I swear, I don't know but that he may change his mind, considering the kind of fellow he is.

DEMIPHO. Bless me! What! Change his mind?

GETA. I don't know about it. I'm only saying "supposing."

DEMIPHO. That's what I'll do, what my brother advised: I'll bring his wife here to talk with that girl. Geta, you go ahead and tell her that Nausistrata is coming.

[Exit to CHREMES'S.]

GETA. Phædria's money is found and all's quiet with the lawsuit. We've looked out that the bride shan't be sent off for the present. Now, what next? What's to be done? Sticking in the same rut still? Robbing Peter to pay Paul, Geta? You've put off the evil day for now, but there's a crop of whippings growing if you don't look out ahead. I'll go home and tell Phanium that she must n't be afraid of Phormio or of Nausistrata's talk.   [*Exit to* DEMIPHO'S.]

[*Enter* DEMIPHO *and* NAUSISTRATA *from* CHREMES'S.]

DEMIPHO. Come, then, Nausistrata, with your usual good nature make her feel kindly towards us, so that she may do of her own accord what must be done.

NAUSISTRATA. I will.

DEMIPHO. You'll be aiding me now with your good offices, just as you helped me a while ago with your purse.

NAUSISTRATA. You're quite welcome; and upon my word, it's my husband's fault that I can do less than I might well do.

DEMIPHO. Why, how is that?

NAUSISTRATA. Because he takes wretched care of my father's honest savings; he used regularly to get two silver talents from those estates. How much better one man is than another!

DEMIPHO. Two talents, do you say?

NAUSISTRATA. Yes, two talents, and when prices were much lower than now.

DEMIPHO. Whew!

NAUSISTRATA. What do you think of that?

DEMIPHO. Oh, of course —

NAUSISTRATA. I wish I'd been born a man. I'd soon show you —

DEMIPHO. Oh yes, I'm sure.

NAUSISTRATA. The way —

DEMIPHO. Pray, do save yourself up for her, lest she may wear you out; she's young, you know.

NAUSISTRATA. I'll do as you tell me. But there's my husband coming out of your house.

[*Enter* CHREMES.]

CHREMES. Ha! Demipho, has the money been paid him yet?

DEMIPHO. I saw to it at once.

CHREMES. I wish it had n't been. [*Aside.*] Oh, dear! there's my wife. I had almost said too much.

DEMIPHO. What makes you wish it had n't, Chremes?

CHREMES. No matter now.

DEMIPHO. What have you been about? Have you told her why we are bringing Nausistrata?

CHREMES. I've attended to it.

DEMIPHO. Well, what does she say?

CHREMES. She's not to be taken away.

DEMIPHO. Why is n't she?

CHREMES. Because they're heart to heart.

DEMIPHO. What's that to us?

CHREMES. A good deal. Besides I have found out that she really is related to us.

DEMIPHO. What? You're raving.

CHREMES. You'll find it's so. I'm not speaking at random. I've recollected.

DEMIPHO. Are you in your right mind?

NAUSISTRATA. Oh, for mercy's sake! take care not to hurt a relative.

DEMIPHO. She is n't one.

CHREMES. Don't say that. Her father went by another name; that's how you made a mistake.

DEMIPHO. Did n't she know who her father was?

CHREMES. Oh, yes.

DEMIPHO. What made her call him something else?

CHREMES. Won't you ever stop insisting, and take in what I mean?

DEMIPHO. But if you don't tell me anything?

CHREMES [*aside to* DEMIPHO]. You'll ruin me!

NAUSISTRATA. I wonder what it all is.

DEMIPHO. By heaven, I'm sure I don't know.

CHREMES. Do you want to know the truth? Then, so help me God, there is n't a man in the world nearer of kin to her than you and I.

DEMIPHO. Great heavens! Let's go straight to her. If it's so, I want us all to know it alike — or if it is n't so.

CHREMES. Oh, dear!

DEMIPHO. What's the matter?

CHREMES. To think of your trusting me so little!

DEMIPHO. You want me to believe it, then? You want me to consider it settled?

Very well, have it so. But then, what's to be done with the other girl, *our friend's* daughter?

CHREMES. Oh, that's all right.

DEMIPHO. Shall we drop her, then?

CHREMES. Why not?

DEMIPHO. And this one is to stay?

CHREMES. Yes.

DEMIPHO. You can go, then, Nausistrata.

NAUSISTRATA. Good gracious, I think it is better for all concerned that she should stay, than to have it as you first intended; for she seemed to me a very lady-like thing when I saw her.

[*Exit* NAUSISTRATA *to* CHREMES's.]

DEMIPHO. Now, what is the meaning of this business?

CHREMES. Has she shut the door yet?

DEMIPHO. Yes.

CHREMES. O Lord! heaven does smile on us! I've found my daughter married to your son!

DEMIPHO. Bless me! how can that be?

CHREMES. This place is n't safe enough to tell the story in.

DEMIPHO. Well, come indoors, then.

CHREMES. Look here, I don't want our sons to get an inkling of this.

[*Exeunt to* DEMIPHO's.]

[*Enter* ANTIPHO, R.]

ANTIPHO. However things are going with me, I'm glad that my cousin has succeeded in getting what he wants. What a nice thing it is to conceive such desires that you can satisfy them by simple means when things go wrong! No sooner has he got the money than he's freed from anxiety; but here I am, unable to get out of these troubles by any means whatever, but what I'm in terror if it's kept quiet, and disgraced if it comes out. I should n't be coming home now if there was n't some hope of my having her. But where can I find Geta?

[*Enter* PHORMIO, R.]

PHORMIO. I've received the money and handed it over to the trader. I've taken away the girl and arranged that Phædria may have her for his own; she's been emancipated. Now there's only one thing left

over for me to see to, and that is to get time from the old gentlemen to make a spree of it. I propose to take some days off.

ANTIPHO. Why, there's Phormio. Say!

PHORMIO. Say what?

ANTIPHO. What's Phædria going to do now? How does he propose to spend his honeymoon?

PHORMIO. He's going to take his turn at playing your part.

ANTIPHO. What part is that?

PHORMIO. To run away from his father. And he requests you in return to play his and plead his cause for him. The fact is, he is going to my house for a little spree. I shall tell the old gentlemen that I am going down to Sunium to the fair, to buy that lady's maid that Geta talked about; then they won't think I'm squandering their money when they don't see me here. But there's a noise at your front door.

ANTIPHO. See who is coming out.

PHORMIO. It's Geta.

[*Enter* GETA *from* DEMIPHO's.]

GETA. Oh Fortune! oh Lucky Fortune! With what blessings and how suddenly have you loaded my master Antipho with your kindness to-day!

ANTIPHO [*aside*]. Why, what can he mean?

GETA. And unloaded all us friends of his of fear! But here I am dilly-dallying instead of loading up my shoulder with my cloak and hurrying off to find him, so that he may learn all that's happened.

ANTIPHO [*aside to* PHORMIO]. You can't make out what he is talking about, can you?

PHORMIO [*aside*]. Nor you either?

ANTIPHO [*aside*]. Not a bit.

PHORMIO [*aside*]. No more can I.

GETA. I'll start and go to the slave-trader's; they're there now.

ANTIPHO. Halloa, Geta!

GETA. There you are! Always the way! Called back just when you have started running!

ANTIPHO. Geta!

GETA. Keeping it up, begad! Well, you shan't ever beat me with your insolence.

ANTIPHO. Wait, won't you?

GETA. Oh, go get yourself thrashed!

ANTIPHO. That's just what will happen

to you in a minute if you don't stop, you knave!

GETA. He must know me pretty well — to threaten me with a thrashing. Why, is it the man I am after or not? It is the very man. Up to him on the spot.

ANTIPHO. What's the matter?

GETA. Oh you most blessed man in all the world! I tell you, Antipho, there's no denying that you're the only man whom heaven loves.

ANTIPHO. I should like to be; but I should like to have you tell me why I'm to think so.

GETA. Is it enough if I set you all dripping down with joy?

ANTIPHO. You'll be the death of me.

PHORMIO. Away with your promises and out with your news!

GETA. What! you here too, Phormio?

PHORMIO. Yes, but why don't you go ahead?

GETA. Well, then, listen. After we had paid you the money on 'Change, we started straight home; then master sent me over to see your wife.

ANTIPHO. What for?

GETA. I'll leave that out; it's nothing to do with the case, Antipho. Just as I was entering my lady's chamber, Mida, her slave boy, ran up to me, caught me by the cloak behind and pulled me back. I looked round and asked him what he was stopping me for. He said that there was no admission to his mistress. "Sophrona has just brought in the old man's brother Chremes and he's in there now with the ladies," says he. When I heard that, I went up softly on tiptoe, stood still, held my breath and put my ear against the door; and I began to listen, trying to catch their talk so fashion.

PHORMIO. Bravo, Geta!

GETA. Whereupon I heard a most beautiful piece of business; so much so that by cracky, I nearly shouted for joy.

ANTIPHO. What was it?

GETA. Well, what do you think?

ANTIPHO. I don't know.

GETA. But it's most marvelous! Your uncle has proved to be your wife Phanium's father.

ANTIPHO. What's that you say?

GETA. He lived with her mother at Lemnos unbeknownst.

PHORMIO. You're dreaming! As if the girl would n't know her own father!

GETA. Oh well, depend upon it, Phormio, there's some reason for that; but do you think that I, outside of the door, could understand everything that went on between them inside?

ANTIPHO. Yes, and I have had an inkling of this story, too.

GETA. Yes, and I'll give you something to make you believe still more. After a while your uncle came out here, and soon after that he went in again with your father. They both said that you were allowed to keep her. Finally I was sent to look you up and bring you home.

ANTIPHO. Why don't you drag me off then? What are you waiting for?

GETA. I'll do it mighty quick.

ANTIPHO. Good-bye, my dear Phormio.

PHORMIO. Good-bye, Antipho. God bless me, this is a good thing. I'm glad of it.

[*Exeunt* ANTIPHO *and* GETA *to* DEMIPHO'S.]

PHORMIO. What an unexpected piece of good luck for these boys! And now I have a fine chance to take the old gentlemen in, and to rid Phædria of his worry about the money, so that he shan't have to beg it of any of his fellows. For this very same money, given already, shall be his outright in spite of all their opposition. The facts have shown me how to force them to it. I must now put on a new air and change my expression. I'll withdraw into this alley close by and show myself to them from there when they come out. I shan't go to the fair as I pretended.

[*Withdraws,* R.]

[*Enter* DEMIPHO *and* CHREMES *from* DEMIPHO'S.]

DEMIPHO. I am grateful and thankful to the gods, brother, and they deserve it, since all this has turned out so well for us to-day.

CHREMES. Is n't she a thorough lady though, as I told you?

DEMIPHO. Through and through. We must now find Phormio as soon as possible and get our thirty ducats away from him before he makes ducks and drakes of them.

PHORMIO [coming forward]. I'll just see whether Demipho is at home, so as to —

DEMIPHO. Ah, we were just going to see you, Phormio.

PHORMIO. On the same old errand, perhaps?

DEMIPHO. Yes, to be sure.

PHORMIO. I supposed so. But what made you think it necessary to come?

DEMIPHO. Oh pooh!

PHORMIO. Did you think I would n't do what I had once undertaken? See here, however poor I may be, there's one thing I've always been particular about, and that is to keep my word. And so I came to tell you this, Demipho, that I'm all ready. Give me my wife whenever you wish. I have put off all my other business, and properly enough, too, when I saw how very bent you were upon it.

DEMIPHO. But Chremes here has persuaded me not to give her to you. "Why, what will Mrs. Grundy say," says he, "if you do that? Awhile ago, when you could have done it decently, you did n't release her. To turn her out now, divorced, is an outrage." In fact, his arguments were all pretty much the same that you urged against me yourself awhile ago face to face.

PHORMIO. You 're making game of me in a pretty high and mighty way.

DEMIPHO. How 's that?

PHORMIO. How 's that? Why, because I shan 't be able to marry that other girl now. For how could I have the face to go back to the woman after slighting her?

CHREMES. [aside to DEMIPHO.] "Besides I see that Antipho does n't want to let her leave him" — say that.

DEMIPHO. Besides I see that my son does n't at all want to let the woman leave him. So come over to the bank, please, and have that money transferred to me again, Phormio.

PHORMIO. What! after I have already paid it round among my different creditors?

DEMIPHO. What's to be done then?

PHORMIO. If you will give me the lady as you promised, I will marry her; but if you really want her to stay with you, Demipho, why the dowry must stay with me. It is n't fair that I should be the loser through the means of you two; for it was out of regard for you that I broke off with the other lady who was to bring me just as large a dowry.

DEMIPHO. You be hanged with your high-toned talk, you vagabond! Do you suppose that we don't know you and your doings?

PHORMIO. You're making me angry.

DEMIPHO. So you'd marry her, would you, if we gave her to you?

PHORMIO. Try it on.

DEMIPHO. Yes, so that my son might live with her in your house; that was your scheme.

PHORMIO. What are you talking about, pray?

DEMIPHO. Come, hand over my money.

PHORMIO. Not much; you hand over my wife.

DEMIPHO. Walk straight into court then.

PHORMIO. Look here, if you are going to keep on being troublesome —

DEMIPHO. What are you going to do about it?

PHORMIO. I? Perhaps you two think that I'm the protector of undowried women only; but I'm in the habit of protecting dowried ones too.

CHREMES. What's that to us?

PHORMIO. Oh, nothing. But I knew a woman round here whose husband married —

CHREMES. Ha!

DEMIPHO. What's the matter?

PHORMIO. Another wife at Lemnos —

CHREMES. I'm done for!

PHORMIO. By whom he had a daughter; is bringing her up, too, on the sly.

CHREMES. I'm as good as buried.

PHORMIO. I'm just going to tell her all about it.

CHREMES. For heaven's sake, don't!

PHORMIO. Oh, you were the man, were you?

DEMIPHO. What game he's making of us!

CHREMES. We let you off scot free.

PHORMIO. Oh, bosh!

CHREMES. Well, what would you have? We let you off with the money that you've got.

PHORMIO. Oh, yes! Why the deuce are you making game of me with your silly, childish shilly-shallying? "I won't, I will, and I will, I won't," — one after the other; "take it — give it back" — say a thing and unsay it; make a bargain one minute and break it off the next.

CHREMES [aside]. How or where did he ever come to find this out?

DEMIPHO [aside]. I don't know; but I'm sure I did n't tell anybody.

CHREMES [aside.] A perfect miracle, as I hope to live!

PHORMIO [aside]. I've put a spoke in his wheel.

DEMIPHO. See here, is this rascal going to rob us of all this money and laugh in our very faces? By heaven, I'll die the death first! [Aside to CHREMES.] Make ready to be bold and have your wits about you. You see your little peccadillo has got out and you can't hide it from your wife any longer. The easiest way to get it forgiven, Chremes, is for us to tell her ourselves what she is sure to hear from others. And then we shall be able to revenge ourselves at our ease upon this dirty fellow.

PHORMIO [aside]. My goodness! I'm in a fix if I don't look out for myself. They are making at me with the air of prize-fighters.

CHREMES [aside]. But I'm afraid we can't make her forgive me.

DEMIPHO [aside]. Courage, Chremes! I'll bring you back into her good graces, on the strength of this, that the woman by whom you had this child is out of the way.

PHORMIO. That's the way you deal with me, is it? A cunning attack enough! It's not for his good that you've stirred me up, Demipho, by heaven! Aha! when you've been carrying on abroad after your own sweet will without any regard for yonder noble lady, but on the contrary, insulting her in this strange fashion, would you come now with prayers to wash away your sin? Why, I'll set her so afire against you with this story that you shan't put her out though you actually dissolve away in tears.

DEMIPHO. Was ever a man so impudent! Why does n't the government transport the knave to some desert island?

CHREMES. I'm reduced to such a state that I don't know what to do with him.

DEMIPHO. I do, then. Let's go to law.

PHORMIO. To law? To her, if you don't mind.

CHREMES. Follow him up; hold on to him while I call the slaves out.

DEMIPHO. I can't all by myself; run and help me.

PHORMIO. Here's one suit for assault and battery against you!

DEMIPHO. Go to law, then!

PHORMIO. And another for you, Chremes.

CHREMES. Hurry him off!

PHORMIO. That's it, hey? Why, then, I must use my voice — Nausistrata! Come out here!

CHREMES. Stop his dirty mouth; just see how strong he is.

PHORMIO. I say, Nausistrata!

DEMIPHO. Hold your tongue, won't you?

PHORMIO. Hold my tongue?

DEMIPHO. If he does n't come along, hit him in the belly with your fists.

PHORMIO. Gouge out an eye if you like; but I shall soon have a fine revenge.

[Enter NAUSISTRATA from CHREMES'S.]

NAUSISTRATA. Who's calling me? Why, husband, what's this disturbance about, for mercy's sake?

PHORMIO. Halloa! what's struck you so dumb now?

NAUSISTRATA. Who is this fellow? Won't you answer me?

PHORMIO. He answer you! When by heaven he does n't know who he is himself!

CHREMES. Don't believe anything the fellow says.

PHORMIO. Go and touch him; if he's not cold all over, you may murder me.

CHREMES. It's nothing at all.

NAUSISTRATA. Well, then, what is he talking about?

PHORMIO. You shall soon find out — just listen.

CHREMES. Are you going to believe him?

NAUSISTRATA. For mercy's sake, what should I believe when he has n't said anything?

PHORMIO. The poor wretch is raving mad with fear.

NAUSISTRATA. Upon my word, it's not for nothing that you are so frightened.

CHREMES. I frightened?

PHORMIO. All right, then. As you're afraid of nothing, and as what I say is nothing, just tell her yourself.

DEMIPHO. What! tell it for you, you scoundrel?

PHORMIO. Oho you! you've done finely for your brother, of course!

NAUSISTRATA. Won't you tell me, husband?

CHREMES. But —

NAUSISTRATA. But what?

CHREMES. There's no need of telling.

PHORMIO. Not for you of course, but she ought to know. In Lemnos —

NAUSISTRATA. Ah! what's that you say?

CHREMES. Won't you hold your tongue?

PHORMIO. Behind your back —

CHREMES. Oh dear me!

PHORMIO. He married another wife.

NAUSISTRATA. God forbid, my dear man!

PHORMIO. It's true.

NAUSISTRATA Alas! I'm undone!

PHORMIO. And by her he's already had one daughter, too, without your dreaming of it.

CHREMES. What shall I do?

NAUSISTRATA. Oh heavens! what a wicked, shameful thing!

PHORMIO. Do? You're done for!

NAUSISTRATA. Was there ever anything more infamous! When it comes to their wives, they're old enough, forsooth! Demipho, I appeal to you, for I am sick of talking to this creature. This was the meaning, was it, of all those constant trips and long stays at Lemnos? This was the low prices that reduced our rents there?

DEMIPHO. For my part, Nausistrata, I don't say that he does n't deserve to be blamed in this matter, but it is a fault that may be pardoned.

PHORMIO. Might as well talk to the dead.

DEMIPHO. The fact is, it was not that he did n't care for you or that he disliked you. His affair with this woman was about fifteen years ago, once when he had drunk too much, and that was how this girl came to be born; he never went near the woman afterwards; she is dead and out of the way; that was the only stumbling-block left. And so I beg of you that you will bear this patiently, as you act in other things.

NAUSISTRATA. Patiently — why should I? I certainly do want to have an end of it all, I'm so wretched; but how could I expect that? Can I count on his sinning less as he grows older? He was an old man even then, if it's old age that makes men virtuous. Do my own looks or my years make me more attractive now than I was then, Demipho? Come, what can you offer to make me expect or trust that this won't happen again?

PHORMIO. All who desire to attend the funeral of Chremes, now's the time! That's the way I'll give it to 'em! Now come on, whoever wants to stir up Phormio! I'll ruin him as completely as I have Chremes.

DEMIPHO. Don't be so angry; calm yourself, Nausistrata.

PHORMIO. Yes, yes, let him back into your good graces; he's been punished enough to satisfy me. And she's got something to din into his ears just as long as he lives.

NAUSISTRATA. I deserved it, then, I suppose. Why should I, at this late day, Demipho, rehearse what a wife I've been to him?

DEMIPHO. I know it all as well as you do.

NAUSISTRATA. Do you think I've deserved this treatment?

DEMIPHO. Never in the world. But what's done cannot be undone by reproaches. Do forgive him. He begs pardon, — he owns up, — he offers to atone. What more can you want?

PHORMIO [aside]. Really now, before she pardons him I must look out for myself and Phædria. [Aloud.] See here, Nausistrata, just listen to me before you answer him off-hand.

NAUSISTRATA. What is it?

PHORMIO. I got thirty ducats out of him by a trick, and gave them to your son. He bought his mistress with them from her owner.

CHREMES. Hey! what's that you say?

NAUSISTRATA. Do you think it's so very bad for a young fellow like your son to have one mistress, when here you are yourself with two wives? Have you no sense of shame? How can you have the face to scold him for it? Answer me that.

DEMIPHO. He shall do everything you wish.

NAUSISTRATA. Well, to let you know my decision, I neither pardon him nor promise anything nor make any answer at all, before seeing my son. I leave the whole thing to his judgment. I'll do whatever he tells me.

PHORMIO. You are a wise woman, Nausistrata.

NAUSISTRATA. Does that satisfy you?

DEMIPHO. Certainly.

CHREMES [aside]. Upon my word, I get out of it pretty finely, and better than I expected.

NAUSISTRATA [to PHORMIO]. Please to tell me your name.

PHORMIO. Phormio, a friend of your house, by heaven, and particularly of your son Phædria.

NAUSISTRATA. Well, Phormio, after this I'll do and say for you whatever you like as well as I can, upon my word I will.

PHORMIO. That's very kind of you.

NAUSISTRATA. I'm sure you have deserved it.

PHORMIO. Do you want to begin by giving me a pleasure to day, Nausistrata, and to make your husband's eyes ache at the same time?

NAUSISTRATA. Yes.

PHORMIO. Then invite me to dinner.

NAUSISTRATA. Certainly, I invite you.

DEMIPHO. Let us go in, then.

NAUSISTRATA. Well, but where is Phædria, who is to decide between us?

PHORMIO. I'll bring him here.

CANTOR. Farewell, and give us your applause.

[Exeunt, PHORMIO, R., the others to CHREMES'S.]

THE STAR OF SEVILLE

(LA ESTRELLA DE SEVILLA)

By LOPE DE VEGA

Translated in prose by PHILIP M. HAYDEN

CHARACTERS

King Sancho the Bold

Don Arias, *confidant of the King*

Don Pedro de Guzman, } *chief alcaldes*
Farfan de Rivera,

Don Gonzalo de Ulloa, *the Cid of Cordova*

Fernan Perez de Medina, *Captain*

Don Sancho Ortiz, } *councilors*
Bustos Tabera,

Iñigo Osorio

Don Manuel

Pedro de Caus, *Governor of the Prison of Triana*

Clarindo, *Gracioso, servant to* Don Sancho

Stella, *the Star of Seville*

Teodora, *servant*

Matilde, *slave*

Attendants, Servants, Musicians, People.

THE STAR OF SEVILLE

ACT I

[SCENE I. *A room in the palace.*]

[*Enter the* KING, DON ARIAS, DON PEDRO DE GUZMAN, *and* FARFAN DE RIVERA.]

KING. My welcome in Seville has greatly pleased me, and I perceive I am indeed the sovereign monarch in Castile; my reign dates from this day, since this day Seville receives me and does me honor; for it is clear and evident, and an accepted law, that no man could be king in Castille who did not reign in Seville. I shall not be content if I do not reward the munificence of my reception, and the splendor of my entrance. My court shall have its seat within these walls, and marvel not that the Castilian court should make its seat in Seville, for I shall reign in Castile, while I reign in Seville.

DON PEDRO. We, the chief alcaldes of the city, kiss your feet in gratitude, for we receive your favors in her name. Jurors and councilmen gladly offer you their wealth and loyalty, and the council is in accord, provided only that the chartered rights of this your city do not suffer.

KING. I am much pleased —

DON PEDRO. Grant us your hand to kiss.

KING. — that in receiving me you have borne yourselves like the men you are, and I believe that with your support I shall make myself king of Gibraltar, which sleeps in fancied security upon the Columns, and if fortune favors me I shall make myself remembered.

FARFAN. With loyalty the people of Seville will serve Your Highness in this lofty enterprise, offering their lives as one.

ARIAS. His Majesty feels it so, and is well pleased with you and your desire.

KING. Men of Seville, I believe you and so declare. Go with God.

[*Exeunt the alcaldes.*]

ARIAS. My lord, how like you Seville?

KING. Much; for to-day I am truly king.

ARIAS. She will deserve your favor, Sire, and win it more from day to day.

KING. Surely; for so rich and fair a city, as I live longer in it, will be admired at leisure.

ARIAS. The beauty and the grandeur of its streets — I know not if Augustus saw the like in Rome, or had such wealth.

KING. And her ladies, divinely fair, why do you not mention them? How can you limit or describe their attributes and radiance? Tell me, why are you not aflame in the light of such glories?

ARIAS. Doña Leonor de Ribera seemed heaven itself, for in her countenance shone the light of the springtime sun.

KING. She is too pale. A sun with rays of ice is little worth, for it chills instead of warming. I want a burning sun, not freezing.

ARIAS. The one who threw you roses is Doña Mencia Coronel.

KING. A handsome dame, but I saw others lovelier.

ARIAS. The two lively damsels at the next window were Doña Ana and Doña Beatriz Megia, sisters through whom day gains fresh splendors.

KING. Ana is but a vulgar name for one, and Beatriz for the other, lonely like the phœnix, because unequaled.

ARIAS. Does good fortune or ill attend even upon a name?

KING. In love — and do not wonder at it — names unusual, and indicating quality and breeding, are a magnet to a man.

ARIAS. The pale, auburn-haired. . . .

KING. Tell me not her name. The pale lady with auburn hair will be marble and bronze, and your descriptions weary me as you continue. One I saw there full of grace, whom you have left unmentioned; for you have noted only the blonde, and not the raven-haired. Who is she who on her balcony drew my attention, and to whom I doffed my hat? Who is she whose two eyes flash lightning like Jove's thunder-bolts, and sent their deadly rays into my heart, unknowing of their power? One who, though dark, outshone the sun? In tresses of night she eclipsed the orb of day; her beauty obscured its rays.

ARIAS. I have it, Sire.

KING. Choose the loveliest of them all, for that is she.

ARIAS. They call her the Star of Seville.

KING. If she is fairer than the sun, why slight her thus? But Seville does not esteem her, seeing her daily. Sun she shall be called, since she is a sun that revives and kindles.

ARIAS. Her name is Doña Stella Tabera, and Seville, in homage, calls her its star.

KING. And it might call her its sun.

ARIAS. Her brother hopes to marry her in Seville, as well he may.

KING. Her brother's name?

ARIAS. Bustos Tabera, and he is councilor in Seville, in saying which I bear tribute to his quality.

KING. And is he married?

ARIAS. He is not married, for in the Sevillian firmament he is the sun, if Stella is his sister, and Star and Sun are in conjunction.

KING. My guiding star brought me to Seville, and I find great joy in it, if it is as brilliant as I hope. All will go well with me, under such a star. What means, Don Arias, will you find, for me to see her and to speak with her?

ARIAS. You shall find her a friendly star, in spite of the Sun. Heap honors upon her brother, for the most rigid honor yields to honors. Favor him, for favors can overcome and conquer the impossible. If you give to him, and he receives, he binds himself, and sees himself obliged to requite what you have given; for he graves in bronze who accepts favors.

KING. Let him be summoned, and take measures likewise that the following night I may see Stella in her house. O vision that inflames my inmost soul.   [Exit ARIAS.]

[Enter DON GONZALO, in mourning.]

GONZALO. I kiss your highness' feet.

KING. Rise, Gonzalo. On this day of joy, why do you come so sad?

GONZALO. My father is no more.

KING. I have lost a valiant captain.

GONZALO. And the frontier remains without defender.

KING. Yes, a heroic commander has departed. Grieving I listen to you.

GONZALO. Sire, the frontier of Archidona has suffered a great loss, and since there can be found no equal to his valor, and since I have inherited the honored name of the great general, I implore your majesty not to permit another to receive the post now vacant.

KING. There is sufficient proof that his valor lives again in you. Lament your father's death, and while you are in mourning and in sorrow, rest in my court.

GONZALO. Fernan Perez de Medina comes with the same request, and thinks his services may claim the baton, for in fact he has been ten years captain, and with his sword has stained with ruby hue the pearly walls of Granada. Hence my diligence.

KING. I will consider it; for if I must make this decision, I wish to weigh the matter.

[Enter FERNAN PEREZ DE MEDINA.]

FERNAN. I fear, O king, that I arrive too late. I kiss your feet, and then . . .

KING. You may present your homage, Fernan Perez, with a tranquil mind. The office is still in my hands, and such a post will not be given without consulting first yourself and others of high credit in the kingdom who being bulwarks in themselves will be advisers concerning Archidona. Go, and rest.

GONZALO. This memorial I leave with you, my lord.

FERNAN. And I leave mine, which is the crystal mirror of my valor, in which my nature can be seen, pure, accomplished, loyal.

GONZALO. Mine is crystal too, and shows the clearness of my claim.

[Exeunt FERNAN and GONZALO.]

[*Enter* ARIAS *and* BUSTOS.]

ARIAS. Here, my lord, is Bustos Tabera.

BUSTOS. Perturbed you see me at your feet, my lord, for so it is natural for the vassal to be confused in presence of his king; I am for this reason and by the common lot perturbed, but twice perturbed, because this undreamt-of favor hath further agitated me.

KING. Rise.

BUSTOS. Nay, this is my place. If kings should be adored like saints upon an altar, my place is here.

KING. You are a gallant gentleman.

BUSTOS. Of that I have shown proof in Spain. But, Sire, I crave but such advancement as is due me.

KING. Then cannot I advance you?

BUSTOS. The laws of God and man give power to kings, but forbid the vassal to be presumptuous; for he, my lord, must keep his wishes within bounds. So I, seeing this law transgressed, limit my ambition to my lawful aspirations.

KING. What man ever did not desire to become greater?

BUSTOS. If I were greater, I should be covered now; but if I am Tabera, Tabera must stand uncovered.

KING [*aside to* ARIAS]. A strange philosophy of honor!

ARIAS [*aside to* KING]. A caprice novel and unexampled.

KING. I do not desire, Tabera, upon my life, that you stand covered before I have advanced you, and given you a proof of my affection. And thus it is my will that you cease to be Tabera, and become General of Archidona, for your heroism shall be the defense of that frontier.

BUSTOS. But, Sire, in what war have I ever served you?

KING. Even in the occupations of peace, Bustos, I see you so capable of defending my lands, that I give you preference over these, whose memorials show such services. Here in my presence read and decide: the candidates are three — yourself and these two; see what competitors you have.

BUSTOS [*reads*]: "Most noble King, Don Gonzalo de Ulloa entreats your majesty to grant him the post of captain general of the frontier of Archidona, inasmuch as my father died in battle, after serving you more than fourteen years, rendering notable services to God in behalf of your crown. I implore justice, etc." If Don Gonzalo has inherited the valor of his father, I name him for the place.

KING. Read the other memorial.

BUSTOS [*reads*]: "Most noble king, Fernan Perez de Medina has been a soldier twenty years in the service of your father, and desires to serve you with his arm and sword, on Spanish or on foreign soil. Ten years he has been captain in the plain of Granada, and three years a prisoner, in close confinement, for which reasons, and by his sword, in which he places all his claim, he by this memorial asks the baton of general of the fields of Archidona."

KING. Recite your claims.

BUSTOS. I have no service to relate to second a request, or justify a favor. I could recall the noble exploits of my ancestors, the banners captured, the castles conquered; but, Sire, they had their reward, and I cannot reap the glory for their services. Justice, to deserve the name, must be well ordered, for it is a sacred boon divine, suspended by a hair. Justice requires that this post be given to one of these two men, for if you give it me, you do injustice. Here in Seville, my lord, I have no claim upon you, for in the wars I was a soldier, in peace, a councilor. In truth Fernan Perez de Medina merits the honor, for his age is worthy of the frontier post; Don Gonzalo is young, and a nobleman of Cordova; him you can make a captain.

KING. Then it shall be as you desire.

BUSTOS. I desire only what is right and in accord with justice, to give to those who serve their due reward.

KING. Enough. You put me to shame with your good counsels.

BUSTOS. They are mirrors of truth, and so in them you see your true self.

KING. You are a noble gentleman, and I desire your attendance in my chamber and in my palace, for I wish to have you near me. Are you married?

BUSTOS. My lord, I am the protector of

a sister, and will not marry, until I have given her a husband.

KING. I will give her a better one, Bustos. Her name?

BUSTOS. Doña Stella.

KING. To a star, if she be fair, I know not what husband to give, except the sun.

BUSTOS. I wish only a man, Sire, for Stella. She is not a heavenly star.

KING. I will unite her to one who is worthy of her.

BUSTOS. In her name I thank you, Sire.

KING. I will give her, Bustos, a husband suited to her rank. Inform your sister that her marriage is in my care, and that I shall dower her.

BUSTOS. Now, Sire, I pray you tell me on what business you have called me; for your summons agitated me.

KING. You are right, Tabera, I summoned you for an affair of Seville, and wished to talk with you first before discussing it. But peace and leisure are before us and we will treat it later. From to-day attend me in my chamber and my palace. Go with God.

BUSTOS. I kiss your feet.

KING. I embrace you, noble councilor.

BUSTOS [aside]. Such favor passes my understanding, and I am filled with misgiving. To love me and to honor me without knowing me seems rather to attack my honor than to favor me. [Exit.]

KING. The man is keen of mind; as wise as he is honorable.

ARIAS. I have no patience with these men of honor. How many, Sire, have been so, until occasion meets them! Yes, all are occasionally wise, but not all, my lord, on all occasions. To-day the breath of slander reaches him who denounced another yesterday; and the law which he invoked is invoked anon on him. If he puts his honor in the balance, you can put in the other your favors and your gifts, your praises and your privity.

KING. In secret I intend to see this woman in her house. For she is a sun, and has inflamed me, although she seems a star. Let Spain say what it will, a blinded king, I follow the Star of Seville.

[Exeunt the KING and ARIAS.]

[SCENE II. A room in TABERA'S house.]

[Enter DON SANCHO, DONA STELLA, MATILDE, and CLARINDO.]

SANCHO. Angel of heaven, when will you be mine, when will you free from this restraint the passion that I feel for you? Like a sun you rise, dispensing radiance from coral lips formed for love: — when will you turn the pale dew that drops from my eyes to pearls that may deck the peaceful joys of our souls?

STELLA. If time kept pace with my desires, its giant strides should outstrip the sun; Seville should celebrate my sweet submission, and your happy love should cease to envy the tender turtle dove, which, softly cooing, makes its nest amid a thousand favoring branches.

SANCHO. Ah, how gratefully my heart receives these sighings! My soul yearns for the noblest gifts of fame, to lay them at your feet.

STELLA. I ask only for life, to join it to yours.

SANCHO. Oh, sweet Stella, clothed in love and light!

STELLA. Ah! Can life endure such love?

SANCHO. Oh charms divine, lodestar to my dazzled eyes!

CLARINDO [to MATILDE]. Why should not we, like our masters, utter a few sweet sighs, soft as finest cambric?

SANCHO. Be quiet, knave!

CLARINDO. We're dumb. [To MATILDE.] Ah! Sleek filly! Despair of my existence!

MATILDE. Oh, low-born suitor! Your poetics smack of the currycomb.

CLARINDO. Oh, my love!

MATILDE. Oh, happy man!

CLARINDO. What leper ever heaved such sighs!

SANCHO. What does your brother say?

STELLA. That when the papers are made out and signed, the marriage may proceed; and that there shall be but a few days' delay, while he makes the arrangements.

SANCHO. He'll bring my love to desperation; delay is torment for it. Would we might wed to-day, lest fortune change before to-morrow!

STELLA. If delay continues, speak to my brother.

SANCHO. Speak I will, for I shall die if this persists.

CLARINDO. Bustos Tabera comes.

[Enter BUSTOS.]

BUSTOS. Sancho, my friend!

STELLA. Heavens! What is this?

SANCHO. Such sadness? You?

BUSTOS. Sadness and joy are cause of my dismay. Stella, leave us alone.

STELLA. God help me! Delay has turned against me. [Exit.]

BUSTOS. Sancho Ortiz de las Roelas, . . .

SANCHO. Do you no longer call me brother?

BUSTOS. A steed beyond control sweeps me on unspurred. Know that the king sent for me; God is my witness that I know not why, for though I asked him, yet he told me not. Unasked, he was about to make me general of Archidona, and indeed, had I not resisted, would have given me the royal commission. Finally he made me . . .

SANCHO. Proceed, for all of this is joy. Tell me your sadness, explain your grief.

BUSTOS. He attached me to his suite.

SANCHO. And he did well.

BUSTOS. We come now to the pain.

SANCHO [aside]. I foresee sorrow here for me.

BUSTOS. He told me not to seek a match for Stella; that should be his care; and he preferred that he should dower her, not I, and give to her a husband of his choosing.

SANCHO. You said that you were sad and joyful too, but I alone am sad; for you attain to honors, and I reap only pains. Leave with me your grief, and keep your joy, for in the king's suite, and with a brilliant marriage for your sister, it is natural for you to be merry. But you break the law of friendship, for you should have told the king your sister was already promised.

BUSTOS. It was all so strange, and my head so troubled, that I did not find the chance to say it.

SANCHO. Being so, shall my marriage not take place?

BUSTOS. I will return and inform the king that the agreements and the writings are all made, and the contract will then stand, for his authority will not disregard your just claim.

SANCHO. But if the king should turn the law, who can constrain him if guided by self-interest or pleasure?

BUSTOS. I will speak to him, and you as well; for then, in my confusion, I did not tell him of our agreement.

SANCHO. Would that my griefs might kill me! I said indeed that fortune stands not a moment steadfast, and that sorrow and weeping cast their shadow on our joys. And if the king should wish to do us wrong?

BUSTOS. Sancho Ortiz, the king's the king. Be silent and have patience. [Exit.]

SANCHO. In such a plight, who can have patience, and forbear? Oh, tyrant, come to thwart my happy marriage, applauded though you be in Seville, may your people drive you from your kingdom of Castile! Well do you deserve the name of Sancho the Bold by the acts I learn of now, if you win the name by tyranny! But God will break your plans — may He drive you from your kingdom of Castile! I'll leave Seville, and go to Gibraltar, to seek death in the battle-front.

CLARINDO. Methinks we'll find it nearer than Gibraltar!

SANCHO. Loving Stella the fair, why is my love so ill-starred? But my star is unfavorable, and her influence works my unhappiness!

CLARINDO. A shooting star, mayhap.

SANCHO. May you be banished from your kingdom of Castile! [Exeunt.]

[SCENE III. A street in Seville, showing entrance to TABERA'S house.]

[Enter the KING, DON ARIAS, and Suite.]

KING. Announce that I am here.

ARIAS. They are informed, and Don Bustos Tabera is already at the door to greet you, Sire.

[Enter BUSTOS.]

BUSTOS. What an honor, and what condescension! Your highness in my house!

KING. I was strolling in disguise to see the city, and they told me as we passed, this was your house; and I would see it, for they say it is most beautiful.

BUSTOS. It is the house of a simple esquire.

KING. Let us go in.

BUSTOS. Sire, 't is fit for my humble station, but not for you; for so great a lord it is too small. And it will not be well received in Seville, when they know you came to visit me.

KING. I come not for your house, Tabera, but for you.

BUSTOS. My lord, you do me great honor. But if you come for me, it is not meet that I obey you; for it would be uncourtly, that the king should come to the vassal, and the vassal permit it and consent to it. I am your servant and your vassal, and it is fitting that I come to you in the palace, if you wish to honor me. For favors may become affronts, when open to suspicion.

KING. Suspicion? Of what?

BUSTOS. It will be said, though it be false, you came to my house to see my sister; and her good name, however well established, might come in question; for honor is a crystal clear — a breath may tarnish it.

KING. Since I am here, I wish to speak with you of matters of importance. Let us go in.

BUSTOS. It shall be upon the way, with your permission. My house is not in order.

KING [aside to ARIAS]. He makes great opposition.

ARIAS [aside to the KING]. Take him away, and I will stay behind and speak to her for you.

KING. Speak low, that he may not hear you. The fool puts all his honor in his ears.

ARIAS. The weight will break them.

KING [to BUSTOS]. So be it; I would not see your house against your will.

BUSTOS. Sire, at Stella's marriage you shall see it suitably adorned.

ARIAS. Bring up the coach.

KING. Bustos, you'll ride upon the step.

BUSTOS. I'll go on foot, with your permission.

KING. The coach is mine, and I give orders here.

ARIAS. The carriage waits.

KING. Drive to the palace.

BUSTOS [aside]. Great favors these! The king does me much honor: please God it be for good. [Exeunt. Manet ARIAS.]

[Enter STELLA and MATILDE.]

STELLA. What do you say, Matilde?

MATILDE. It was the king, my lady.

ARIAS. It was he, and it is not the first time a king was guided by a star. He came to your house to do homage to your charms; for if he is king of Castile, you are the queen of beauty. The King Don Sancho, whom for his unconquered prowess, the public, and the Moors who tremble at his name, have called The Bold, saw at a balcony your divine beauty, which rivals Aurora in her palace, when, hailed by drowsy birds mid roses and lilies, and weeping at the wakening, she scatters garlands of pearls. He ordered me to offer you the riches of Castile, though riches be but little for such charms. Accept his will, for if you do accept it, and reward it, you shall be the Sun of Seville, where you have been the Star. He will give you towns and cities, whereof you shall be Duchess, and he will wed you to a Duke, whereby you will crown the glory of your ancestors, and bring honor to the name of Tabera. What say you?

STELLA. What do I say? See!
[She turns her back.]

ARIAS. Hold! Wait!

STELLA. To such ignoble message, my back gives a reply. [Exit.]

ARIAS. A noble pair! I marvel at them both. The austerity of Rome survives in them in Seville. It seems impossible for the king to outwit and conquer them, but strength and persistence level mountains and split rocks. I'll speak to this servant, for gifts are gates to favor with the Portias and Lucrecias. Are you the servant of the house?

MATILDE. Servant I am, by force.

ARIAS. By force?

MATILDE. I am a slave.

ARIAS. A slave!

MATILDE. Deprived of blessed liberty, and subject both to prison and to death.

ARIAS. I'll have the king release you,

and give you with your freedom, a thousand ducats rent, if you will do his will.

MATILDE. For liberty and gold, there is no crime that I'll not undertake. What is there I can do? I'll do it if I can.

ARIAS. You'll give the king admittance to the house to-night.

MATILDE. He shall find the doors all open, if you but keep your promise.

ARIAS. Before he enters, I will give you a letter from the king, in his own hand and signed by him.

MATILDE. Then I'll put him in Stella's very bed to-night.

ARIAS. What time does Bustos come?

MATILDE. Each night he's out till dawn. He has a lady, and this distraction often costs men dear.

ARIAS. What time do you think the king should come?

MATILDE. Let him come at eleven, for then she will be in bed.

ARIAS. Take this emerald as pledge of the favors that await you. [*Exeunt.*]

[SCENE IV. *A room in the palace.*]

[*Enter* IÑIGO OSORIO, BUSTOS TABERA, *and* DON MANUEL, *with golden keys.*]

MANUEL. I congratulate your lordship on the key, and the dignity it represents. May you win the honors you desire.

BUSTOS. Would I might repay his majesty the honor that he does me, undeserved.

IÑIGO. 'T is not beyond your merit. Be assured, the king makes no mistake.

BUSTOS. The key he's given me admits me to his paradise; although thus elevated I fear a fall to earth; for he has granted me abruptly all these honors and I foresee that he who gives thus hastily may change as suddenly.

[*Enter* ARIAS.]

ARIAS. You may retire, gentlemen. The king intends to write.

MANUEL. Let's go and seek amusement for the night. [*Exeunt.*]

[*Enter the* KING.]

KING. You say I shall enjoy her charms to-night, Don Arias?

ARIAS. The little slave is wholly won.

KING. Castile shall raise a statue to her.

ARIAS. You are to give her a document.

KING. Prepare it, Arias. I shall not hesitate to sign, for my love impels it.

ARIAS. In faith, the little slave is useful.

KING. 'T is the sun in heaven she procures for me, in the Star of Seville.

[*Exeunt* KING *and* ARIAS.]

ACT II

[SCENE I. *Street before* TABERA'S *house.*]

[*Enter the* KING, DON ARIAS, *and* MATILDE.]

MATILDE. Alone; it will be safer, for all are now at rest.

KING. And Stella?

MATILDE. She is sleeping, and the room is dark.

KING. Although my promise might suffice, here, woman, is the paper, with your liberty therein. I will give another slave to Bustos.

ARIAS. And the money and all is included in it.

MATILDE. I kiss your feet.

ARIAS. All alike, my lord, yield to their interest.

KING. What joy divine to be a king!

ARIAS. Who can resist it?

KING. To be more secret, I'll go up alone.

ARIAS. You risk yourself alone, my lord?

KING. Now, tell me: although I risk myself, and though it be not safe — is not the king at hand? Begone.

ARIAS. Where shall I wait?

KING. Not in the street; some nook where I can find you.

ARIAS. I'll enter in Saint Mark's.

[*Exit.*]

KING. What time will Bustos come?

MATILDE. He always comes when the birds salute the dawn. And till he comes, the door is open.

KING. My love impels me to this high adventure.

MATILDE. Follow me, your highness; the passage is in darkness. [*Exeunt.*]

[*Enter* Bustos, Don Manuel, *and* Don Iñigo.]

Bustos. Here is my house.

Iñigo. Farewell.

Bustos. It is early for me.

Manuel. You need not go farther.

Bustos. 'T is well.

Iñigo. We two have a certain visit still to make.

Bustos. Did Feliciana please your fancy?

Manuel. To-morrow at the palace, my good friend, we will speak of her, for she is a figure worthy of all praise. [*Exeunt.*]

Bustos. I 'm early home to bed. The house is dark. No page is at the door. Ho! Lujan, Osorio, Juan, Andres! They 're all asleep. Justine! Ines! The maids are sleeping too. Matilde! The slave also has surrendered. Sleep is the god and master of her senses. [*Exit* Bustos.]

[Scene II. *A room in the house.*]

[*Enter* Matilde *and the* King.]

Matilde. I think that was my master calling. I am lost.

King. Did you not say he came at dawn?

Matilde. Woe is me!

[*Enter* Bustos. *The* King *wraps himself in his cloak.*]

Bustos. Matilde!

Matilde. O God! I cannot face him.

King [*aside to* Matilde]. Have no fear. [*Exit* Matilde.]

Bustos. Who 's there?

King. A man.

Bustos. A man, at this hour? And in my house? His name!

King. Stand back.

Bustos. You lack in courtesy, and if you pass, it shall be by the point of this sword; for although this house is sacred, I 'll profane it.

King. Lower your sword.

Bustos. What! Lower it, when my sister's room is thus profaned? Tell me your name, or I will kill you here.

King. I am a person of importance. Let me pass.

Bustos. This house is mine, and I command in it.

King. Let me pass; observe, I am a man of rank, and though I have come to your house, my intent is not to attack your honor, but to increase it.

Bustos. Is honor thus increased?

King. Your honor is in my care.

Bustos. A better defender is this sword. And if you seek my honor, why do you come disguised? Do you conceal yourself to honor me? Do you hide yourself to do me service? Let your fear convince you how true it is that no one who gives honor need bring shame with it. Draw, or by Heaven, I 'll kill you!

King. Rash provocation!

Bustos. I 'll kill you here and now, or you 'll kill me.

King. I 'll tell him who I am. Hold! I am the king.

Bustos. You lie! The king, seeking my shame, alone, disguised, and unattended? It cannot be, and you insult your king, since you accuse him of a fault that is the depth of baseness. What? The king outrage his vassal? This angers me still more. For this I 'll kill you, in spite of all resistance. Offending me, lay not such charges against His Majesty, for well you know the laws of God and man condemn to just chastisement him who fancies or suspects unworthy conduct in his king.

King. What strange persistence! Man, I say I am the king.

Bustos. Still less do I believe it, for the name of king is here, but not the deeds. The king is he who seeks my honor, and you seek my dishonor.

King [*aside*]. He is both fool and boor. What shall I do?

Bustos [*aside*]. It is the king, disguised. There is no doubt. I 'll let him pass, and later learn if he has wronged me. My soul is roused to anger and to fury, for honor is a thing that he who gives may also take away. — Pass, whoever you may be, and next time do not defame the king, nor call yourself the king, wretch, when you have to blush for your acts. Know that the king my master, the dread of Africa, is most Christian and most holy, and you insult his name. He has entrusted to me the key to his house, and could not come without a key to mine, when he has given me his. And do not offend the law; remember that he is an honorable man. This I say to you, and I spare you because you feigned to be the king. Marvel not to see me loyal, though offended, for 't is a vassal's obligation to respect the name. Thus will he learn to be ruler of the honor of his vassals, and cease to wrong them against God's law and man's.

KING. I can no more; I choke with shame and anger. Fool! You let me go because I feigned to be the king? Then let me tell you that because I said so, I 'll go out thus from here. [*He draws.*] For if I win to freedom because I called myself the king, and you respect the name, I 'll act the king, and you 'll respect his deeds. [*They fight.*] Die, villain, for here the name of king gives power to me; the king will kill you.

BUSTOS. My honor rules me mor than any king.

[*Enter servants with lights.*]

SERVANT. What 's this?

KING. I 'll make escape before I 'm recognized. I leave this offended ruffian, but I will have revenge. [*Exit.*]

SERVANT. Your enemy has fled.

BUSTOS. Follow him! Chastise him! . . . No, let him go, we 'll give the enemy a bridge of silver. Give a light to Matilde, and do you withdraw.

[*They give her one and exeunt.*]

BUSTOS [*aside*]. She has betrayed me, for she hangs her head in shame. I will obtain the truth with a cunning lie. — Close the door. I am about to kill you. The king has told me all.

MATILDE. If he has not kept the secret, how can I in my unhappy state do so, my lord? All the king has told you is the truth.

BUSTOS [*aside*]. Now I shall learn the damage to my honor. — So then you gave the king admittance?

MATILDE. He promised me my freedom, and for that I brought him to this place, as you have seen.

BUSTOS. And does Stella know aught of this?

MATILDE. I think her wrath would have consumed me, had she heard my plot.

BUSTOS. That is certain, for if her light were dimmed, she 'd be no star.

MATILDE. Her radiance suffers neither shadow nor eclipse, and her light is clear and bright as of the sun. The king but reached her room, and entered, giving me this paper, and you behind him.

BUSTOS. What? The king gave you this paper?

MATILDE. With a thousand ducats rent, and liberty.

BUSTOS. A noble gift, at the expense of my honor! Well does he honor and advance me! Come with me.

MATILDE. Where do you take me?

BUSTOS. You are going where the king may see you, for thus I fulfill the law and obligation that rests upon me.

MATILDE. Ah, unhappy slave!

BUSTOS. Though the king sought to eclipse her, the fame shall not be lost in Spain of the Star of Seville.

[*Exeunt* BUSTOS *and* MATILDE.]

[SCENE III. *A street leading to the palace.*]

[*Enter the* KING *and* ARIAS.]

KING. And that is what befell me.

ARIAS. You would go in alone.

KING. He was so mad and bold as to insult me; for I know he recognized me. He drew upon me with equivocal words and though I contained myself a time, the natural resentment born in every man broke down the dignity my rank demands. I attacked him, but they came with lights who would have told the truth that they imagined, had I not turned my back fearing to be recognized. And so I come; you see, Arias, what befell me with Bustos Tabera.

ARIAS. Let him pay for his offense with death; behead him, let the rising sun shine on his just punishment, for in the boundaries of Spain there is no law but your desire.

KING. To execute him publicly, Arias, is error great.

ARIAS. You will have sufficient pretext; for he is councilor of Seville, and the wisest and most prudent, Sire, still commits some crime, a prey to power and ambition.

KING. He is so circumspect and prudent, that he has no guilt.

ARIAS. Then have him killed in secret, Sire.

KING. That might be done, but to whom can I entrust the secret?

ARIAS. To me.

KING. I do not wish to endanger you.

ARIAS. Then I will find you a man, courageous and valiant soldier, and distinguished nobleman as well, before whom the Moor has trembled in the strong fortress of Gibraltar, where he has been many times victorious captain, and was never conquered. To-day in Seville they give him first rank among the brave and gallant, for he is the glory of the soldier's trade.

KING. What is his name?

ARIAS. Sancho Ortiz de las Roelas, called besides the Cid of Andalusia.

KING. Summon him to me at once, for dawn approaches.

ARIAS. Come to bed.

KING. What bed can tempt him who is offended, and in love? Call the man at once.

ARIAS. What form is that, that hangs upon the palace, swinging in the wind?

KING. A form, you say? What can it be?

ARIAS. There must be reason for it.

KING. See what it is.

ARIAS. The little slave, with her paper in her hands.

KING. What cruelty!

ARIAS. And what a crime!

KING. I'll kill the brother and the sister, too, if Seville shows sedition.

ARIAS. Have her cut down at once, and secretly give her a decent burial. Such bold effrontery! Tabera must die.

[*Exeunt the* KING *and* ARIAS.]

[SCENE IV. *A room in* TABERA'S *house.*]

[*Enter* BUSTOS *and* STELLA.]

STELLA. What do I hear?

BUSTOS. Close the door.

STELLA. Hardly does the sleepy sun, shod with sapphires, leave the palace of Aurora, and you rouse me from my bed, alone, troubled, and afflicted? You are agitated and perturbed! Tell me, have you seen some fault, in which I am concerned?

BUSTOS. You can tell me if there has been such.

STELLA. I? What do you say? Are you mad? Tell me, have you lost your mind? I, a fault? Nay, you have committed one in saying so, for only to question is a crime against me. Do you not know me? Know you not who I am? In my mouth have you ever heard words not in keeping with the honor with which I guard my tongue? And if you have seen nothing that can testify against me, what fault can I have done?

BUSTOS. I do not speak without occasion.

STELLA. Without occasion?

BUSTOS. Alas! Stella! . . . for this night and in this house . . .

STELLA. Speak, for if I should be guilty, I offer myself at once for punishment. What happened in this house this night?

BUSTOS. This night was the epicycle of the sun, for this night my Stella's star declined.

STELLA. No astrologics in dealing with questions of honor! Speak plainly, and leave the sun in its five zones, for though my name be Stella, the sun does not control me.

BUSTOS. When the discordant tones of the bell of Cuevas sounding in the sky marked the middle of the night, I entered the house, and found in it, and near your very room, the king alone and in disguise.

STELLA. What say you?

BUSTOS. I speak the truth. Ask yourself, Stella, why the king could have come to my house alone at such an hour, if he came not for Stella. Matilde was with him: I heard her step, for then my honor was alert and keen. I drew, and said: "Who's there?" "A man," he answered. I advanced upon him, and he retreating, said he was the king. And although I recognized him at once, I pretended not to know him, for Heaven willed to give me torment. He attacked me like an angry and offended monarch, for a king who attacks in anger fails not in valor. Pages came with lights, and then he turned his back lest he be seen, and was not recognized by any. I questioned the slave, and she, without need of torture, confessed the truth. The king gave her her freedom, signed in a paper that he wrote, chief witness in the case, in which his guilt stood clear. I took her from the house at once, lest her infected breath sow dishonor within these walls. I seized her at the door, and placing her upon my shoulders, made my way to the palace, and for her crime I hanged her from the railings; for I'd have the king know that if he is a Tarquin, I will be a Brutus. Now you know all, Stella. Our honor is in danger. I am forced to leave you, and must give you a husband. Sancho Ortiz it shall be, for in his care you will be delivered from the designs of the king, and I can go my way in peace.

STELLA. Oh, Bustos, give me your hand for the service you have done me.

BUSTOS. It must be to-day, and till I see you wed to him, keep silence, for my honor is at stake.

STELLA. O joy, my love! Thou art mine at last, and shalt not escape again. And yet, who knows the end from the beginning, if between the cup and the lip the sage feared danger?   [*Exeunt* STELLA *and* BUSTOS.]

[SCENE V. *A room in the palace.*]

[*Enter* ARIAS, *and the* KING, *with two papers.*]

ARIAS. Sanchos Ortiz de las Roelas is waiting in the antechamber.

KING. All of love is trickery, and pity takes hold upon me. In this paper I have sealed his name and fate, and in this I say that I command his death: in this fashion the killer will be safeguarded. Have him come in. Then draw the bolt and do you remain without.

ARIAS. Without?

KING. Yes; for I wish him to see that I alone am in the secret. Thus my desire conceives the vengeance more assured.

ARIAS. I'll call him.   [*Exit.*]

KING. I fear this is no glorious or lofty token of my love.

[*Enter* SANCHO ORTIZ.]

SANCHO. I kiss your feet.

KING. Rise, I would not humble you, rise.

SANCHO. My lord.

KING [*aside*]. A noble youth.

SANCHO. My lord, it is not strange that I should be confused, being no courtier, nor yet orator.

KING. Why, tell me: What see you in me?

SANCHO. Majesty and valor; and in fine I see in you God's image, since the king is his embodiment; and I believe in you, as I do in Him. I submit myself here, great king, to your imperial will.

KING. What is your state?

SANCHO. Never so honored as I am to-day.

KING. I applaud your wisdom and your zeal. Now, since you will be anxious, and eager to learn why I have summoned you, I'll tell you, and will see if I have in you as well a valiant soldier. My interest demands the killing of a man, in secret, and this task I mean to trust to you, for I prefer you to all others in the city.

SANCHO. Is he guilty?

KING. He is.

SANCHO. Then, why a secret murder for a culprit? You may, in justice, publicly effect his death, without killing him in secret; for thus you do accuse yourself, accusing him, since men will think you cause his death unjustly. If this poor man has but a slight offense, my lord, I ask you pardon him.

KING. Sancho Ortiz, you are not here as advocate for him, but executioner. And since I order it, hiding the hand that strikes, it must be that it interests my honor to kill him thus. Does he who has attacked my person merit death?

SANCHO. By fire.

KING. And if his crime was that?

SANCHO. My lord, I would demand his death at once, and if 't is so, then I will give it, though he were my brother, and hesitate no more.

KING. Give me your hand upon it.

SANCHO. And with it my soul and faith.

KING. You can kill him, taking him unawares.

SANCHO. My lord, I am Roela and a soldier, would you make me a traitor? I, kill by treachery! Face to face I'll kill him, where Seville may see, in street or market-place. For none can excuse him who kills and does not fight; and he who dies by treachery fares better than the one who kills. He who lives thus proclaims his perfidy to all he meets.

KING. Kill him as you like. You bear this paper signed by me, as guarantee, in which it states that I have pardoned any crime you do. Read. [He gives him a paper.]

SANCHO. It reads thus [reads]: "Sancho Ortiz, At once for me and in my name give death to him this paper indicates. I act through you, and if you be disturbed, I promise you hereby that I shall free you. "I the King." I am amazed Your Majesty should think so meanly of me. I, a promise! a paper! My loyalty trusts more in you than it. If your words have effect to move the hills, and carry out whate'er they say, give me your promise, Sire, and then I need no paper. Destroy it, for without it death is better sought than with it, since to some degree the paper casts discredit on your word. [He tears it.] Without a paper, Sire, we'll pledge ourselves, and promise, I to avenge you, you to protect me. If so it be, we need no documents which are an obstacle. I go at once to execute your will, and only ask you, as reward, the woman whom I choose, as wife.

KING. Be she a duchess of Castile, I give her to you.

SANCHO. May you regain the Moorish throne! May your glorious possessions reach the sea, and even to the pole!

KING. Your excellent service, Sancho, shall be rewarded. In this paper is the name of the man who is to die. [Gives him the paper.] And when you open it, be not dismayed. I have heard it said in Seville, he is brave.

SANCHO. That we shall see hereafter.

KING. We two alone this secret know. I need not say, be prudent, act, and keep your counsel. [Exit.]

[Enter CLARINDO.]

CLARINDO. I have sought you, my lord, bearing good news. I ask a guerdon for your dearest wish fulfilled.

SANCHO. You come in good spirits.

CLARINDO. Does your heart not divine the guerdon? [Gives him a paper.]

SANCHO. From whom is this?

CLARINDO. From Stella, who was fairer and lovelier than the sun. She ordered me to give you this paper and ask a guerdon.

SANCHO. For what?

CLARINDO. For the marriage, which is to take place at once.

SANCHO. What do you say? This joy will kill me. What! Stella will be mine? The glorious radiance of Aurora is for me? And I may hope that the sun's golden rays will bathe in floods of light our former griefs? [Reads:] "My husband: The happy day so long desired has arrived. My brother seeks you, to crown my life, and to reward you. If you accord, seek him at once and lose no time. "Your Stella."

Oh, fairest maid! What height may I not reach with such a star! Advise my steward of the happy bond which I assume. Let him bring forth at once the liveries reserved for this event, and let my servants and pages put on their hats adorned with finest plumes. And if you claim a guerdon, take this hyacinth. I would give even the sun, if it were mounted in a ring.

CLARINDO. May you outlive the very stones, and cling like ivy to your bride! Nay, since I love you so, may you live longer than a fool! [Exit.]

SANCHO. I will seek Bustos, for I am tormented with hope and eagerness. But with this marriage and my joy, I had forgot the king. It was not right. The paper is unsealed; I'll see who is it must be killed. [Reads:] "Sancho, he whom you must kill is Bustos Tabera."

Heaven help me! Is this his will? After joy, disaster! All this life is but a game of chance, the cards ill shuffled and leading to reverse and ruin, for it's all in gains and losses, like a game of cards. I won at first, but now my luck has changed, and turned the card to give me death. Did I read aright? But I should not have read it, if the paper said not so. I'll look again. [Reads.] "Sancho, he whom you must kill is Bustos Tabera." I am undone. What

shall I do? For I have given my promise to
the king, and I shall lose his sister. . . .
Sancho Ortiz, it must not be; Bustos shall
live! — But it is not right that my desire
constrain my honor. Bustos shall die!
Bustos must die! — But hold, fierce hand!
Bustos must live, shall live! — But I cannot obey my honor, if I yield to love. —
But who can resist the force of love? —
'T is better that I die or go away, so that I
serve the king, and he may live. — But
I must do the king's will. [Reads.] " Sancho, he whom you must kill is Bustos Tabera." — But if the king kills him because
of Stella, and seeks to honor her? If for
Stella he kills him! Then he shall not die
because of her. I will offend him and defend her. — But I am a gentleman, and
must not do that which I will, but what I
ought. — What is my duty? To obey the
law that takes precedence. — But there is
no law that forces me to this — But yes,
there is, for though the king be wrong, he is
accountable to God. My mad love must
give way, for though it cost me cruel grief,
to obey the king is right: Bustos must die,
shall die! None may rightly say: Bustos
must live, shall live! Forgive me, beloved
Stella, but O the sacrifice, to renounce you
and become your enemy. What shall I do?
Can I do otherwise?

[Enter BUSTOS TABERA.]

BUSTOS. Brother, I am blessed by fate
in finding you
SANCHO [aside]. And I am cursed by
fate in meeting you, for you seek me to
give me life, but I seek you to kill you.
BUSTOS. Brother, the hour has come for
your desired marriage.
SANCHO [aside]. The hour of all my
grief, I'd better say. O God! Was ever
man in such despair? That I should have
to kill the man I most have loved! to renounce his sister! to lose all that I hold
dear!
BUSTOS. By contract you are already
wed to Stella.
SANCHO. I meant to marry her, but now
it may not be, although you grant it.
BUSTOS. Do you know me, and address
me thus?

SANCHO. Because I know you, I speak
thus, Tabera.
BUSTOS. If you know me to be Tabera,
how dare you use such words?
SANCHO. I speak because I know you.
BUSTOS. You know my birth, my blood,
and valor; and virtue, which is honor, for
without it honor never was: and I am aggrieved, Sancho.
SANCHO. But less than I.
BUSTOS. How so?
SANCHO. To have to speak with you.
BUSTOS. If you cast reflection on my
honor or my faith, you basely lie, and here
I do maintain it. [He draws.]
SANCHO. What have you to maintain,
villain? [Aside.] Forgive me, love; the
king's excess has made me mad, and none
may resist me now. [They fight.]
BUSTOS. You've killed me; stay your
hand.
SANCHO. Ah! I am beside myself and
wounded you unknowing. But now I beg
you, brother, since I have regained my
sense, to kill me. Sheathe your sword
within my breast, and open passage for my
soul.
BUSTOS. Brother, I leave my Stella in
your care. Farewell. [He dies.]
SANCHO. O cruel sword! O bloody, savage murder! Since thou hast taken half my
life, complete thy work, that my soul may
expiate this other wound.

[Enter two alcaldes, PEDRO and FARFAN.]

PEDRO. What's this? Hold your hand.
SANCHO. Why stay me if I've killed one
dear to me?
FARFAN. O what confusion!
PEDRO. What is this?
SANCHO. I have killed my brother. I am
a Cain in Seville, since in cruel vengeance I
killed an innocent Abel. You see him; kill
me here, for since he dies through me I seek
to die through him.

[Enter ARIAS.]

ARIAS. What's this?
SANCHO. A cruel violence, for such is the
effect in man of promises fulfilled, and
purest loyalty. Tell the king my master
that Sevillians keep their promises by acts,

as you see here; and for them they offend
the stars, and know no brother.

PEDRO. Has he killed Bustos Tabera?

ARIAS. O what a rash deed!

SANCHO. Seize me, take me prisoner, for
it is right that he who kills should die. See
what a cruel deed love made me undertake, for it has forced me to kill him, and
has forced me to die. Now through him I
come to ask the death he owes to me.

PEDRO. Take him a prisoner to Triana,
for the city is in confusion.

SANCHO. O Bustos Tabera, my friend!

FARFAN. The man has lost his mind.

SANCHO. Gentlemen, let me bear away
the cold form, bathed in its noble blood,
for so I shall support him, and will give
him for a space the life that I have taken.

PEDRO. He's mad.

SANCHO. If I have violated friendship, I
have kept the law, and that, sir, is to be
king; and that, sir, is not to be king. Understand me, or understand me not, for
I'll be silent. I killed him, there is no denying, but I will not answer why; let another
tell the reason, for I confess I killed him.

[*They take him and exeunt.*]

[SCENE VI. *A room in* TABERA'S *house.*]

[*Enter* STELLA *and* TEODORA.]

STELLA. I know not if I dressed me well,
for I did dress in haste. Give me the mirror, Teodora.

TEODORA. You have but to regard
within yourself, my lady, for there is no
glass that tells such truths, nor shows the
image of such beauty.

STELLA. My face is flushed, my color
warm.

TEODORA. Your blood, my lady, has
mounted to your cheek, 'twixt fear and
modesty, to celebrate your joy.

STELLA. It seems to me already that I
see my husband come, his face all wreathed
in smiles, with soft caress to take my hand;
— I seem to hear him utter a thousand
tender words, and that my soul on hearing leaps into my eyes, and takes possession
of them. O happy day! O my guiding star!

TEODORA. I hear a knock. [*Drops mirror.*] The envious mirror fell. [*She picks it*

up.] The glass within the frame of one
light made a thousand.

STELLA. Did it break?

TEODORA. Yes, my lady.

STELLA. 'T is well, for I await the mirror, Teodora, in which my eyes will see
another self, and since I shall have such a
mirror, let this one break, for I would not
have this serve as mirror when he comes.

[*Enter* CLARINDO *in gala dress.*]

CLARINDO. This dress announces joy
and happiness, for my plumes already proclaim the wedding. I gave the paper to my
master, and he gave this ring for guerdon.

STELLA. Then I will change this guerdon
for you. Give it me, and take this diamond.

CLARINDO. The stone is split in two; it
is for melancholy; they say that hyacinths
have this complaint, although they lose it.
It's split in two.

STELLA. What matter that 't is broken!
The very jewels feel my joy and happiness.
O happy day! O my guiding star!

TEODORA. I hear people in the courtyard.

CLARINDO. I think I hear the guests
upon the stairs.

STELLA. How can I bear my joy? . . .
But what is this?

[*Enter the two alcaldes with* TABERA'S *body.*]

PEDRO. Disaster and sorrow are the lot
of man; for life is a sea of tears. Don
Bustos Tabera is dead.

STELLA. O hostile fate!

PEDRO. One consolation still remains to
you, which is that the murderer, Sancho
Ortiz de las Roelas, is a prisoner, and that
he will suffer the penalty to-morrow without fail.

STELLA. Leave me, O cruel men, for in
your words you bear the torments of hell.
My brother dead, and killed by Sancho
Ortiz! Can one pronounce these words, or
listen to them, and not die? I must be
stone, for I am still alive. O fateful day!
O my guiding star! But if you have human pity, kill me.

PEDRO. Her grief dements her, and well
may.

STELLA. Unhappy is my star! My

brother is dead, and Sancho Ortiz killed him, and broke three hearts in one! Leave me, for I'm lost indeed. [Starts to go.]

PEDRO. She's desperate.

FARFAN. Unhappy maid!

PEDRO. Follow her.

CLARINDO. My lady . . .

STELLA. Leave me, wretch, henchman of that murderer! Now, since all is ended, I'll end my life as well. Unhappy day! O my guiding star! [Exeunt.]

ACT III

[SCENE I. A room in the palace.]

[Enter the KING, the two alcaldes, DON ARIAS.]

PEDRO. He confesses that he killed him, but he will not confess why.

KING. Does he not say what impelled him?

FARFAN. He only answers "I do not know."

ARIAS. Great mystery!

KING. Does he say whether there was provocation?

PEDRO. In no wise, my lord.

ARIAS. What obstinate temerity!

FARFAN. He says he killed him, but he knows not if 't was right. He only confesses that he killed him, because he swore to kill him.

ARIAS. He must have given provocation.

PEDRO. He says not so.

KING. Go back and speak to him for me, and say that I demand his plea. Tell him I am his friend, but I will be his enemy in rigorous punishment. Let him declare on what provocation he killed Bustos Tabera, and give in summary phrase the reason for the crime, rather than meet death in obstinacy. Let him say who ordered him, or on whose account he killed him, or what incitement moved him to this act; that on this condition I will show him mercy, else he must prepare to die.

PEDRO. 'T is that he most desires; his grief has made him mad: after a deed so odious, so barbarous and cruel, he is bereft of reason.

KING. Does he complain of any man?

FARFAN. No, Sire. He takes counsel only of his grief.

KING. Rare and noble courage.

FARFAN. He is silent on the crimes of others, and blames himself alone.

KING. Never in the world were two such men; as I perceive their valor, it astounds me more and more. Tell him from me to name who caused the death or urged him to it; and warn him that he should declare it, though 't were the king. If he do not confess at once, to-morrow on the scaffold he shall serve as warning to Seville.

ARIAS. I go.

[Exeunt alcaldes and ARIAS.]

[Enter DON MANUEL.]

MANUEL. Doña Stella begs permission to kiss your hand.

KING. Who prevents her?

MANUEL. The citizens, my lord.

KING. She measures her act with reason. Give me a chair, and let her enter now.

MANUEL. I'll go for her. [Exit.]

KING. She will come radiant with beauty, like the star that appears in heaven after a storm.

[Enter DON MANUEL, STELLA, and people.]

MANUEL. She is here, beautiful as the sun, but a sun whose summer radiance has turned cold as stone.

STELLA. Don Sancho, most Christian and illustrious monarch of Castile, famous for your exploits, celebrated for virtue: an unhappy star, her bright rays veiled in mourning, in dark clouds gathered by weeping, comes to implore justice; not, however, that you administer it, but that you leave my vengeance in my hands. I would not dry my eyes, for drowned in tears, my grief commands respect. I loved my brother Tabera, whose concerns are now of heaven, where he treads the starry streets of paradise. As a brother he protected me, and I obeyed him as a father, and respected his commands. I lived in happiness with him, and sheltered from the sun, though its beams but rarely assailed my window. Seville envied our mutual affection, and all believed we were twin stars reduced to one. A cruel hunter bends his bow upon my brother, and ends our happiness. I have lost my brother, I have lost my husband, I am left alone. And you do not hasten to your royal duty, from which none has released you! Justice, Sire! Give me the murderer, fulfill the law in this; let me pass judgment on him.

KING. Be comforted, and dry your eyes, else will my palace burst in flame, for stars are tears of the sun, as each of its rays is topaz. Let Aurora gather her riches in them, if the new-born sun gives her the time, and let heaven treasure them, for 't is not right that they be squandered here. Take this ring, it will open the castle of Triana for you. Let them deliver him to you, and be to him the cruel tigress of Hircanian cliffs; — although the storks in flight urge us to pity and to weak compassion, for it is true, surprising though it be, that birds and beasts confound man's savagery.

STELLA. In this case, Sire, severity's a virtue, for if in me were silver and gold, I'd tear them from my head, and cover my face with ugliness, though 't were by burning coals. If one Tabera's dead, another lives, and if Tabera's shame is in my face, my hands shall tear my flesh till it strike terror to the hardest heart.

[*Exeunt all but the* KING.]

KING. If they deliver Sancho Ortiz to her, I believe she'll slay him with her own hands. Can God permit such cruelty to be in form so fair and wonderful! See what a deed mad passion doth commit: I did incite Sancho Ortiz, and now I give him up, for love treads under foot the royal purple and promulgates his decrees at his own pleasure. [*Exit.*]

[SCENE II. *A prison.*]

[*Enter* SANCHO, CLARINDO, *and musicians.*]

SANCHO. Have you not made some verses on my fate, Clarindo?

CLARINDO. Who would write verses, my lord, when poetry is so ill paid? At the festival in the market-place, many asked verses from me, and later seeing me in the streets, would say to me, as if I were a tailor, or repairer, "Is not the compliment finished?" and urged me to more haste than for a mended doublet. And had I not been hungry, I'd have excelled Anaxagoras in silence, and would have made a jest of Greek and Latin genius.

[*Enter the alcaldes and* ARIAS.]

PEDRO. Enter.

CLARINDO. I believe these men have come, my lord, to inform you of your sentence.

SANCHO [*to musicians*]. Then quickly begin a song. Now is death welcome, and I wish by singing to give evidence of my content. Besides, I'd show them my fortitude, and that death itself has no power to move me.

CLARINDO. Admirable courage! What better could a drunken Teuton do, his soul steeped in oldest wine?

MUSICIANS [*sing*].

Since my unhappy fate
Consists in living,
So long as death delays,
It stays my dying.

CLARINDO. An excellent enigma that they sing!

SANCHO. A timely sentiment.

MUSICIANS.

There's naught in life like death
For one who lives a-dying.

PEDRO. Is this a time for music, sir?

SANCHO. Why, what better entertainment in their misery can prisoners have?

FARFAN. Can one be entertained by music when death threatens him hourly, and when he momentarily awaits the sentence of his harsh judgment?

SANCHO. I am a swan, and sing before I die.

FARFAN. The time has come.

SANCHO. I kiss your hands and feet, for the news you give me. O blessed day of my desire!

PEDRO. Sancho Ortiz de las Roelas, do you confess you killed Bustos Tabera?

SANCHO. Yes, I declare it here aloud. Seek barbarous punishments, invent new tortures, that shall make Spain forget Phalaris and Maxentius.

FARFAN. Then did you kill him unprovoked?

SANCHO. I killed him; that I do confess. The cause, since I have kept it secret, if there be any man who knows it, let him tell; for I know not why he died, I only know I killed him without knowing.

PEDRO. It seems a treachery to kill him without cause.

SANCHO. He certainly gave cause, since he is dead.

PEDRO. To whom?

SANCHO. To him who brought me where I am, to this extremity.

PEDRO. Who is it?

SANCHO. I cannot tell, because he charged me secrecy. And if I acted like a king, I will keep silence like one, and to put me to death, you need but know that I have killed him, without demanding why.

ARIAS. Señor Sancho Ortiz, I come to you in the king's name, to ask that you confess, at his request, who caused this mad disorder. If you did it for friends, for women, or for relatives, or for some man in power, some grandee of this realm, and if you have from him some paper, safeguard, or agreement, written or signed by his hand, show it at once, and thereby do your duty.

SANCHO. If I do so, my lord, I shall not do my duty. Say to His Majesty, my friend, that I fulfill my promise, and if he is Don Sancho the Bold I bear the same name. Tell him that I may have had a paper, but he insults me when he asks for papers, having seen them torn. I killed Bustos Tabera, and though I might free myself now, I will not, because I know I break a promise. I keep my promise like a king, and I have done that I did promise, and he should do the same who also promises. Let him now act whose obligation is to speak, for I fulfilled my obligation in action.

ARIAS. If you can justify yourself by a word, 't is madness to refuse it.

SANCHO. I am who I am, and being who I am, I avenge myself by my silence, and I defy one who keeps silence. And who is who he is, let him act as who he is, and so we shall both act as befits us.

ARIAS. I 'll say that to His Majesty.

PEDRO. Sancho Ortiz, you have done a thing most ill advised, and you have acted rashly.

FARFAN. You have offended the municipality of Seville, and exposed your life to her severity, your neck to her just vengeance.

[*Exeunt the alcaldes and* ARIAS.]

CLARINDO. Is it possible that you accept such insults?

SANCHO. I consent that men should punish me, and Heaven confound me: and already, Clarindo, it begins. Do you not hear a confused clamor? The air 's aflame with thunderbolts and lightning: one sweeps upon me like a serpent, describing swift curves of fire.

CLARINDO. I think that he has lost his wits. I 'll follow his humor.

SANCHO. How I burn!

CLARINDO. How I broil!

SANCHO. Did the bolt strike you too?

CLARINDO. Do you not see me in ashes?

SANCHO. God save us!

CLARINDO. Yes, my lord, I am the ashes of a fagot.

SANCHO. We are now in the other world.

CLARINDO. In hell, I think.

SANCHO. In hell, Clarindo? Why say you so?

CLARINDO. Because I see in yonder castle, my lord, a thousand lying tailors.

SANCHO. You rightly say we 're there; for Pride is burning upon yon tower formed of the arrogant and haughty; there I see Ambition drinking a river of fire.

CLARINDO. And farther on there is a legion of cabmen.

SANCHO. If coaches pass through here, they 'll wreck the place. But if this is hell, why do we see no lawyers?

CLARINDO. They won't receive them, lest they bring lawsuits here.

SANCHO. If there are no lawsuits here, hell 's not so bad.

CLARINDO. Aha! There is the tyrant Honor, bearing a crowd of fools, who suffer for honor.

SANCHO. I 'll join them. — Honor, an honorable fool comes to be your servant, for not violating your laws. — Friend, you have done badly, for true honor consists to-day in having none. Dost seek me yonder, and for a thousand centuries I've been dead! Seek wealth, my friend, for wealth is honor. What did you do? — I sought to keep a promise. — You make me laugh. Do you keep promises? You seem a simpleton, for not to keep a promise is a noble act these days. — I promised to kill a man, and raging killed him, though he was my friend. — Bad!

CLARINDO. At least not good!

SANCHO. At least not good. Put him in prison, and condemn him for a fool. — Honor, I lost his sister, and now I suffer in that I did fight him. — No matter.

CLARINDO. God help me! If I let him continue further, he will be mad entirely. I will invent a trick. [He shouts.]

SANCHO. Who calls? Who calls?

CLARINDO. It is the dog Cerberus who calls, the porter of this palace. Do you not know me?

SANCHO. Methinks I do.

CLARINDO. And who are you?

SANCHO. A man of honor.

CLARINDO. What! In here! Begone.

SANCHO. What say you?

CLARINDO. Go out at once; this place is not for men of honor. Seize him, and take him bound to the other world, to the prison of Seville, on the wind, but bandage his eyes, that he may fly without fear. — Now his eyes are covered. — Now let the lame devil on his shoulders take him there at a leap. — At a leap? I am content. — Go, and take also his companion by the hand. [Gives him a whirl, and releases him.] — Now you are in the world, my friend. God be with you, as with me.

SANCHO. God, said he?

CLARINDO. Yes, my lord, for this devil, before he was one, was a baptized Christian, and is a Gallego of Caldefrancos.

SANCHO. It seems to me that I am waking from a trance. God help me! O Stella! How wretched is my fate without you! But since I caused your grief, I deserve my punishment.

[Enter the Governor of the prison and STELLA, veiled.]

STELLA. Deliver me the prisoner at once.

GOVERNOR. Here is the prisoner, my lady, and as the king commands me, I deliver him to your hands. Señor Sancho Ortiz, His Majesty commands us to deliver you to this lady.

STELLA. Sir, come with me.

SANCHO. I welcome your compassion, if it is to kill me, for I desire death.

STELLA. Give me your hand and come.

CLARINDO. Does it not seem enchantment?

STELLA. Let no one follow us. [Exeunt.]

CLARINDO. 'T is well. In faith, we're traveling well, from hell to Seville, and from Seville to hell! Please God this Star reveal herself as Venus! [Exit.]

[SCENE III. Outside the prison.]

[Enter STELLA, covered with her cloak, SANCHO.]

STELLA. Now I have placed you at liberty. Go with God, Sancho Ortiz, and remember that I have been merciful and compassionate. Go with God! Go. You are free. Why do you linger? Why look you so? Why hesitate? He who delays is wasting time. Go, for a horse awaits you on which you can escape; the servant has money for the journey.

SANCHO. Madame, I kiss your feet.

STELLA. Go, for there is no time to lose.

SANCHO. With heavy heart I go. May I not know who has liberated me, that I may give thanks for such mercy?

STELLA. A woman; I wish you well, for I give you liberty, having it in my discretion. Go with God.

SANCHO. I will not pass from here, except you tell me who you are, or let me see your face.

STELLA. I cannot now.

SANCHO. I wish to repay you for my life, and freedom: I must know to whom I owe such obligation, acknowledging this debt.

STELLA. I am a woman of noble birth, and moreover, the one who loves you best, and whom you love least. Go with God.

SANCHO. I will not go if you do not uncover.

STELLA. That you may go, I am . . . [Uncovers.]

SANCHO. Stella, star of my soul!

STELLA. A star I am, that guides you, the omen of your life. Go, for thus does love o'ercome the force of sternness, for as I love you, so am I to you a favoring Star.

SANCHO. You! resplendent and fair, in presence of your mortal enemy! You! Such pity for me! Treat me more cruelly, for here pity is cruelty, for pity is punishment. Have me put to death, seek not so generously to do me harm with good, when good is to my harm. Give liberty to one who killed your brother! It is not right that I should live, since he met death through me. And it is right that one who thus lost a friend should lose you too. In freedom now I thus deliver myself to death, for if I were a prisoner, how should I ask for death?

STELLA. My love is finer and stronger, and so I give you life.

SANCHO. Then I will go to death, since 't is your will to free me, for if you act as who you are, I have to act my part.

STELLA. Why do you die?

SANCHO. To avenge you.

STELLA. For what?

SANCHO. For my treachery.

STELLA. 'T is cruelty.

SANCHO. 'T is justice.

STELLA. There is no plaintiff.

SANCHO. Love is plaintiff.

STELLA. 'T is to offend me.

SANCHO. 'T is to love you.

STELLA. How do you prove it?

SANCHO. By dying.

STELLA. Nay, you insult me.

SANCHO. By living.

STELLA. Hear me.

SANCHO. There is nothing to be said.

STELLA. Where are you going?

SANCHO. I go to die, since by my life I offend you.

STELLA. Go, and leave me.

SANCHO. It is not well.

STELLA. Live, and take your freedom.

SANCHO. It is not right.

STELLA. Why do you die?

SANCHO. It is my pleasure.

STELLA. 'T is cruelty.

SANCHO. 'T is honor, too.

STELLA. Who accuses you?

SANCHO. Your disdain.

STELLA. I have none.

SANCHO. I am unmoved.

STELLA. Are you in your senses?

SANCHO. I am in my honor, and I offend you by living.

STELLA. Then, madman, go and die, for I will also die. [*Exeunt on opposite sides.*]

[SCENE IV. *A room in the palace.*]

[*Enter the* KING *and* ARIAS.]

KING. And so he'll not confess that I commanded him to kill?

ARIAS. I ne'er saw bronze more firm. His whole intent is to deny. He said at last that he has fulfilled his obligation, and that it is right that he to whom he owed the obligation now keep his word.

KING. He hopes to force me by his silence.

ARIAS. Indeed he has constrained you.

KING. He has fulfilled his promise, and I am sore perplexed not to be able to keep the word I gave him in a moment of anger.

ARIAS. You cannot evade a promise given, for if an ordinary man must keep it, in a king's mouth it becomes law, and all must bow before the law.

KING. 'T is true, when the law is interpreted by natural right.

ARIAS. It is an obligation. The vassal does not question the law of the king; the vassal can only execute the law, blindly and unquestioning; and it is for the king to take thought. In this instance you did give it in a paper, and since he executed it without the paper, you are bound to fulfill to him the law you made in ordering him to kill Bustos Tabera; for had it not been by your command, he had not killed him.

KING. Then must I say that I ordered his death, and used such cruelty to one who never offended me? What will the council of Seville say of me, Arias, when it sees I was the cause? And what will be said in Castille when Don Alonso there already calls me tyrant, and the Roman pontiff attacks me with his censure? Perchance he will take up my nephew's claims, and his support assures them. I fail in my desires likewise, I see, if I let Sancho die, and that is baseness. What shall I do?

ARIAS. Your Highness may with flattery win the alcaldes, and ask them that by exile Sancho Ortiz pay for his crime and grievous fault, suppressing greater rigors; thus do you intercede for him. You may make him general on some frontier, and so you reward him with a laurel crown.

KING. You say well; but if Doña Stella, to whom I gave my ring, has already wreaked vengeance on him, what shall we do then?

ARIAS. All shall be put in order. I will go in your name and seize her person alleging your order, and will bring her alone and secretly to the palace. Here you may win her to your design; and to persuade her, you may marry her to some grandee of the court, for her virtue and her rank deserve a noble husband.

KING. How I repent my weakness, Arias! The sage well says that he alone is wise who is upon occasion prudent, as on occasion stern. Go now and take Stella, since by her capture you free me from my perplexity. And to placate her I will marry her to a Duke of Castile, and could I give my throne, would put her in my place, for such a brother and sister merit immortal glory.

ARIAS. The people of this city dim the glory of Rome.   [Exit ARIAS.]

[Enter the Governor of the prison.]

GOVERNOR. I kiss Your Highness' feet.

KING. Pedro de Caus, what occasion brings you to my feet?

GOVERNOR. Sire, this ring, engraved with your arms, is it not Your Majesty's?

KING. Yes, this is pardon and safeguard for any crime you may have done.

GOVERNOR. O mighty king, there came with it to Triana a woman closely veiled, saying that Your Highness ordered Sancho Ortiz be delivered her. I referred your mandate to the guards, together with the ring, and all were of opinion that he be delivered. I released him, but shortly Sancho Ortiz, like a madman, with loud cries, begs that the castle gate be opened. "I will not do the king's command," he said, "and wish to die, for it is right that he who kills should die." I refused admittance, but he shouted so I was obliged to

open. He entered, and in joy he waits for death.

KING. I never saw such noble or such Christian folk as in this city. Bronze, marble, statues, may be silent.

GOVERNOR. The woman says, my lord, she gave him freedom, and he would not accept it, when he knew she was the sister of Bustos Tabera, whom he put to death.

KING. What you say now astounds me all the more, their magnanimity passes nature. She when she should be most vindictive, forgives, and frees him; and he to reward her generous soul, returned to die. If their deeds go further, they will be immortalized in records of eternity. Do you, Pedro de Caus, bring me Don Sancho in my carriage to the palace, with strictest secrecy, avoiding noise or guards.

GOVERNOR. I go to do your bidding.
[Exit.]

[Enter a servant.]

SERVANT. The two chief alcaldes desire to see Your Majesty.

KING. Tell them to enter, with their wands of office. [Exit servant.] Now if I can I'll keep my word to Sancho Ortiz, without revealing my deed of cruelty.

[Enter the alcaldes.]

PEDRO. Sire, the guilt is proved; the case requires sentence.

KING. Pronounce it. I only beg you, since you are the guardians of the state, to consider justice, and clemency oft favors it. Sancho Ortiz is councilor of Seville, and if he who is dead was also councilor, the one claims mercy, if the other calls for vengeance.

FARFAN. Sire, we are alcaldes of Seville, and her confidence and honor repose on us to-day. These staves represent your imperial authority, and if they fail to honor your divine right, they offend your person. Held upright, they look to God, and if they are bent or lowered, they look to man, and deflecting, they lose their heavenly function.

KING. I ask not that you deflect them, but that equity be done in justice.

PEDRO. Sire, the source of our authority

is Your Majesty. On your command depend our hopes. Spare his life; you may pardon him, since kings are accountable to none. God creates kings, and God transfers the crown of sovereignty from Saul to David.

KING. Go in, and weigh the sentence that you give for penalty, and let Sancho Ortiz go to execution as the laws require. [Aside.] You, Pedro de Guzman, listen to a word apart.

PEDRO. What is Your Highness' will?

KING. By putting Sancho to death, my dear Don Pedro, you do not restore life to the dead. May we not avoid the extreme penalty, and exile him to Gibraltar, or Granada, where in my service he may find a voluntary death? What say you?

PEDRO. That I am Don Pedro de Guzman, and I am at your feet. Yours is my life, and my possessions and my sword.

KING. Embrace me, Don Pedro de Guzman. I did expect no less from a noble heart. Go with God; send Farfan de Rivera to me. [Aside.] Flattery levels mountains.

FARFAN. You see me at your feet.

KING. Farfan de Rivera, it grieved me that Sancho Ortiz should die, but now it is proposed that death be changed to exile, and it will be longer, since it will be for life. I need your opinion to decide a matter of so great importance.

FARFAN. Your Highness may command Farfan de Rivera without reserve, for my loyalty has no reserve in serving you.

KING. In truth you are Rivera, in whom the flowers of virtue spring, to adorn and attend you. Go with God. [Exeunt alcaldes.] Well have I labored. Now, Sancho Ortiz escapes death, and my promise is saved without becoming known. I will have him go as general to some frontier, whereby I exile and reward him.

[Reënter alcaldes.]

PEDRO. Now the sentence is signed, and it remains only to submit it to Your Majesty.

KING. Such noble lords as you will have made it, I doubt not, as I desired.

FARFAN. Our boast is loyalty.

KING [reads the sentence]: "Our finding and decision is that he be publicly beheaded." Is this the sentence that you bring me signed? Thus, traitors, do you keep your promise to your king? Zounds!

FARFAN. When this wand is laid aside, the lowest of your subjects, as you see, will keep his promise with his life or arms. But with it in hand, let none commit offense in act or words, for human empire, for earth or heaven.

PEDRO. Give us your orders as subjects, but as chief alcaldes, ask not unjust things, for then we bear our wands; as vassals we're without them. And the Council of Seville is what it is.

KING. Enough; 't is well, for all of you put me to shame.

[Enter ARIAS and STELLA.]

ARIAS. Stella is now here.

KING. Don Arias, what shall I do? What is your counsel in such great confusion?

[Enter the Governor, SANCHO ORTIZ, and CLARINDO.]

GOVERNOR. Sancho Ortiz is before you.

SANCHO. Great king, why do you not end my sufferings with death, my misfortunes with your condemnation? I killed Bustos Tabera, kill me; he who kills must die. Show mercy, Sire, by executing justice.

KING. Wait! Who ordered you to kill him?

SANCHO. A paper.

KING. From whom?

SANCHO. Could the paper speak, 't would tell; that is clear and evident; but papers torn give but confused reply. I only know I killed the man I most did love, because I promised. But here at your feet Stella awaits my death in atonement, and still is her vengeance incomplete.

KING. Stella, I have determined your marriage with a noble of my house, young, gallant, a prince of Castile, and lord of Salva. And in return for this, we ask his pardon, which may not justly be refused.

STELLA. Sire, if I am married, let Sancho Ortiz go free. I renounce my vengeance.

SANCHO. And so you give me pardon, because His Highness marries you?

STELLA. Yes, for that I pardon you.

SANCHO. And are you thus avenged for my offense?

STELLA. And satisfied.

SANCHO. Then that your hopes may be fulfilled, I consent to live, although I wished to die.

KING. Go with God.

FARFAN. Look what you do, my lord, for this is to offend Seville, and he must die.

KING [to ARIAS]. What shall I do? These people anger and dismay me.

ARIAS. Speak.

KING. Men of Seville, put me to death, for I was cause of this murder. I ordered him to kill, and this suffices to discharge him.

SANCHO. My honor awaited only this avowal, for the king ordered me to kill him, and I had not committed an act so cruel, had the king not ordered it.

KING. I declare that this is true.

FARFAN. Then is Seville content, for since you ordered he be put to death, no doubt he gave you cause.

KING. The nobility of Seville leaves me in wonder.

SANCHO. I will depart to exile, when Your Majesty fulfills another promise that you gave me.

KING. I'll keep it.

SANCHO. I said that you should give to me for wife the woman I should ask.

KING. So it was.

SANCHO. I ask for Stella.

STELLA. Sancho Ortiz, I am promised.

SANCHO. Promised?

STELLA. Yes.

SANCHO. Woe is me.

KING. Stella, this was my promise; I am king and must fulfill it. What do you say?

STELLA. Your will be done. I am his.

SANCHO. I am hers.

KING. And now, what lacks?

SANCHO. Harmony.

STELLA. Which we shall never find in life together.

SANCHO. I say the same, and therefore I release you from your word.

STELLA. And I release your word; for always to see the murderer of my brother at my bed and board, would give me too much pain.

SANCHO. And me too much, to be forever with the sister of him I killed unjustly, loving him like my soul.

STELLA. Then we are free?

SANCHO. Yes.

STELLA. So then farewell.

SANCHO. Farewell.

KING. Wait.

STELLA. Sire, I cannot take for husband a man who killed my brother, though I love him and adore him.   [Exit.]

SANCHO. And I, Sire, because I love her, it is not just that I should marry her.

KING. What nobility!

ARIAS. What constancy!

CLARINDO. Madness it seems to me.

KING. I marvel at these people.

PEDRO. Such are the people of Seville.

KING. I intend to give her a husband, and such as she deserves.

CLARINDO. And now Lope consecrates to you this tragedy, giving eternal fame to the Star of Seville, whose marvelous history is writ on tablets of bronze.

LIFE IS A DREAM

(LA VIDA ES SUEÑO)

BY CALDERON

Translated in the original meters by DENIS FLORENCE MAC-CARTHY

CHARACTERS

BASILIUS, *King of Poland*

SIGISMUND, *his son*

ASTOLFO, *Duke of Muscovy*

CLOTALDO, *a nobleman*

ESTRELLA, *a princess*

ROSAURA, *a lady*

CLARIN, *her servant*

Soldiers, Guards, Musicians, Attendants, Ladies, Servants

------

*The Scene is in the Court of Poland, in a fortress at
some distance, and in the open field.*

LIFE IS A DREAM

ACT I

[SCENE I. *At one side a craggy mountain, at the other a tower, the lower part of which serves as the prison of Sigismund. The door facing the spectators is half open. The action commences at nightfall.*]

[ROSAURA *in man's attire appears on the rocky heights and descends to the plain. She is followed by* CLARIN.]

ROSAURA. Wild hippogriff swift speeding,
Thou that dost run, the wingéd winds exceeding,
Bolt which no flash illumes,
Fish without scales, bird without shifting plumes,
And brute while bereft
Of natural instinct, why to this wild cleft,
This labyrinth of naked rocks, dost sweep
Unreined, uncurbed, to plunge thee down the steep?
Stay in this mountain wold,
And let the beasts their Phaëton behold.
For I, without a guide,
Save what the laws of destiny decide,
Benighted, desperate, blind,
Take any path whatever that doth wind
Down this rough mountain to its base,
Whose wrinkled brow in heaven frowns in the sun's bright face.
Ah, Poland! in ill mood
Hast thou received a stranger, since in blood
The name thou writest on thy sands
Of her who hardly here fares hardly at thy hands
My fate may well say so: —
But where shall one poor wretch find pity in her woe?
CLARIN. Say two, if you please;
Don't leave me out when making plaints like these.
For if we are the two
Who left our native country with the view
Of seeking strange adventures, if we be
The two who, madly and in misery,
Have got so far as this, and if we still
Are the same two who tumbled down this hill,
Does it not plainly to a wrong amount,
To put me in the pain and not in the account?
ROSAURA. I do not wish to impart,
Clarin, to thee, the sorrows of my heart;
Mourning for thee would spoil the consolation
Of making for thyself thy lamentation;
For there is such a pleasure in complaining,
That a philosopher I've heard maintaining
One ought to seek a sorrow and be vain of it,
In order to be privileged to complain of it.
CLARIN. That same philosopher
Was an old drunken fool, unless I err:
Oh, that I could a thousand thumps present him,
In order for complaining to content him!
But what, my lady, say,
Are we to do, on foot, alone, our way
Lost in the shades of night? -
For see, the sun descends another sphere to light.
ROSAURA. So strange a misadventure who has seen?
But if my sight deceives me not, between
These rugged rocks, half-lit by the moon's ray
And the declining day,
It seems, or is it fancy? that I see
A human dwelling?
CLARIN. So it seems to me,
Unless my wish the longed-for lodging mocks.
ROSAURA. A rustic little palace 'mid the rocks
Uplifts its lowly roof,
Scarce seen by the far sun that shines aloof.
Of such a rude device
Is the whole structure of this edifice,

That lying at the feet
Of these gigantic crags that rise to greet
The sun's first beams of gold,
It seems a rock that down the mountain
    rolled.
CLARIN. Let us approach more near,
For long enough we've looked at it from
    here;
Then better we shall see
If those who dwell therein will generously
A welcome give us.
ROSAURA. See an open door
(Funereal mouth 't were best the name it
    bore),
From which as from a womb
The night is born, engendered in its gloom.
    [*The sound of chains is heard within.*]
CLARIN. Heavens! what is this I hear?
ROSAURA. Half ice, half fire, I stand
    transfixed with fear.
CLARIN. A sound of chains, is it not?
Some galley-slave his sentence here hath
    got;
My fear may well suggest it so may be.
SIGISMUND [*in the tower*]. Alas! Ah,
    wretched me! Ah, wretched me!
ROSAURA. Oh what a mournful wail!
Again my pains, again my fears prevail.
CLARIN. Again with fear I die.
ROSAURA. Clarin!
CLARIN. My lady!
ROSAURA. Let us turn and fly
The risks of this enchanted tower.
CLARIN. For one,
I scarce have strength to stand, much less
    to run.
ROSAURA. Is not that glimmer there
    afar —
That dying exhalation — that pale star —
A tiny taper, which, with trembling blaze
Flickering 'twixt struggling flames and
    dying rays,
With ineffectual spark
Makes the dark dwelling place appear
    more dark?
Yes, for its distant light,
Reflected dimly, brings before my sight
A dungeon's awful gloom,
Say rather of a living corse, a living tomb;
And to increase my terror and surprise,
Dressed in the skins of beasts a man there
    lies:

A piteous sight,
Chained, and his sole companion this poor
    light.
Since then we cannot fly,
Let us attentive to his words draw nigh,
Whatever they may be.
    [*The doors of the tower open wide,
    and* SIGISMUND *is discovered in
    chains and clad in the skins of
    beasts. The light in the tower
    increases.*]
SIGISMUND. Alas! Ah, wretched me!
    Ah, wretched me!
Heaven, here lying all forlorn,
I desire from thee to know,
Since thou thus dost treat me so,
Why have I provoked thy scorn
By the crime of being born? —
Though for being born I feel
Heaven with me must harshly deal,
Since man's greatest crime on earth
Is the fatal fact of birth —
Sin supreme without appeal.
This alone I ponder o'er,
My strange mystery to pierce through;
Leaving wholly out of view
Germs my hapless birthday bore,
How have I offended more,
That the more you punish me?
Must not other creatures be
Born? If born, what privilege
Can they over me allege
Of which I should not be free?
Birds are born, the bird that sings,
Richly robed by Nature's dower,
Scarcely floats — a feathered flower,
Or a bunch of blooms with wings —
When to heaven's high halls it springs,
Cuts the blue air fast and free,
And no longer bound will be
By the nest's secure control: —
And with so much more of soul,
Must I have less liberty?
Beasts are born, the beast whose skin
Dappled o'er with beauteous spots,
As when the great pencil dots
Heaven with stars, doth scarce begin
From its impulses within —
Nature's stern necessity,
To be schooled in cruelty, —
Monster, waging ruthless war: —
And with instincts better far

Must I have less liberty?
Fish are born, the spawn that breeds
Where the oozy seaweeds float,
Scarce perceives itself a boat,
Scaled and plated for its needs,
When from wave to wave it speeds,
Measuring all the mighty sea,
Testing its profundity
To its depths so dark and chill: —
And with so much freer will,
Must I have less liberty?
Streams are born, a coiled-up snake
When its path the streamlet finds,
Scarce a silver serpent winds
'Mong the flowers it must forsake,
But a song of praise doth wake,
Mournful though its music be,
To the plain that courteously
Opes a path through which it flies: —
And with life that never dies,
Must I have less liberty?
When I think of this I start,
Ætna-like in wild unrest
I would pluck from out my breast
Bit by bit my burning heart: —
For what law can so depart
From all right, as to deny
One lone man that liberty —
That sweet gift which God bestows
On the crystal stream that flows,
Birds and fish that float or fly?

ROSAURA. Fear and deepest sympathy
Do I feel at every word.

SIGISMUND. Who my sad lament has
heard?
What! Clotaldo!

CLARIN [aside to his mistress]. Say 't is
he.

ROSAURA. No, 't is but a wretch (ah,
me!)
Who in these dark caves and cold
Hears the tale your lips unfold.

SIGISMUND. Then you'll die for listen-
ing so,
That you may not know I know
That you know the tale I told. [Seizes her.]
Yes, you'll die for loitering near:
In these strong arms gaunt and grim
I will tear you limb from limb.

CLARIN. I am deaf and could n't hear: —
No!

ROSAURA. If human heart you bear,
'T is enough that I prostrate me.
At thy feet, to liberate me!

SIGISMUND. Strange thy voice can so
unbend me,
Strange thy sight can so suspend me,
And respect so penetrate me!
Who art thou? For though I see
Little from this lonely room,
This, my cradle and my tomb,
Being all the world to me,
And if birthday it could be,
Since my birthday I have known
But this desert wild and lone,
Where throughout my life's sad course
I have lived, a breathing corse,
I have moved, a skeleton;
And though I address or see
Never but one man alone,
Who my sorrows all hath known,
And through whom have come to me
Notions of earth, sky, and sea;
And though harrowing thee again,
Since thou 'lt call me in this den,
Monster fit for bestial feasts,
I'm a man among wild beasts,
And a wild beast amongst men.
But though round me has been wrought
All this woe, from beasts I've learned
Polity, the same discerned
Heeding what the birds had taught,
And have measured in my thought
The fair orbits of the spheres;
You alone, 'midst doubts and fears,
Wake my wonder and surprise —
Give amazement to my eyes,
Admiration to my ears.
Every time your face I see
You produce a new amaze:
After the most steadfast gaze,
I again would gazer be.
I believe some hydropsy
Must affect my sight, I think
Death must hover on the brink
Of those wells of light, your eyes,
For I look with fresh surprise,
And though death result, I drink.
Let me see and die: forgive me;
For I do not know, in faith,
If to see you gives me death,
What to see you not would give me;
Something worse than death would grieve
me,

Anger, rage, corroding care,
Death, but double death it were,
Death with tenfold terrors rife,
Since what gives the wretched life,
Gives the happy death, despair!
   ROSAURA. Thee to see wakes such dismay,
Thee to hear I so admire,
That I'm powerless to inquire,
That I know not what to say:
Only this, that I to-day,
Guided by a wiser will,
Have here come to cure my ill,
Here consoled my grief to see,
If a wretch consoled can be
Seeing one more wretched still.
Of a sage, who roamed dejected,
Poor, and wretched, it is said,
That one day, his wants being fed
By the herbs which he collected,
"Is there one" (he thus reflected)
"Poorer than I am to-day?"
Turning round him to survey,
He his answer got, detecting
A still poorer sage collecting
Even the leaves he threw away.
Thus complaining to excess,
Mourning fate, my life I led,
And when thoughtlessly I said
To myself, "Does earth possess
One more steeped in wretchedness?"
I in thee the answer find.
Since revolving in my mind,
I perceive that all my pains
To become thy joyful gains
Thou hast gathered and entwined.
And if haply some slight solace
By these pains may be imparted,
Hear attentively the story
Of my life's supreme disasters.
I am. . . .
   CLOTALDO [within]. Warders of this tower,
Who, or sleeping or faint-hearted,
Give an entrance to two persons
Who herein have burst a passage . . .
   ROSAURA. New confusion now I suffer.
   SIGISMUND. 'T is Clotaldo, who here guards me;
Are not yet my miseries ended?
   CLOTALDO [within]. Hasten hither, quick! be active!

And before they can defend them,
Kill them on the spot, or capture!
   [Voices within.] Treason!
   CLARIN. Watchguards of this tower,
Who politely let us pass here,
Since you have the choice of killing
Or of capturing, choose the latter.

[Enter CLOTALDO and Soldiers; he with a pistol, and all with their faces covered.]

   CLOTALDO [aside to the Soldiers]. Keep your faces all well covered,
For it is a vital matter
That we should be known by no one,
While I question these two stragglers.
   CLARIN. Are there masqueraders here?
   CLOTALDO. Ye who in your ignorant rashness
Have passed through the bounds and limits
Of this interdicted valley,
'Gainst the edict of the King,
Who has publicly commanded
None should dare descry the wonder
That among these rocks is guarded,
Yield at once your arms and lives,
Or this pistol, this cold aspic
Formed of steel, the penetrating
Poison of two balls will scatter,
The report and fire of which
Will the air astound and startle.
   SIGISMUND. Ere you wound them, ere you hurt them,
Will my life, O tyrant master,
Be the miserable victim
Of these wretched chains that clasp me;
Since in them, I vow to God,
I will tear myself to fragments
With my hands, and with my teeth,
In these rocks here, in these caverns,
Ere I yield to their misfortunes,
Or lament their sad disaster.
   CLOTALDO. If you know that your misfortunes,
Sigismund, are unexampled,
Since before being born you died
By Heaven's mystical enactment;
If you know these fetters are
Of your furies oft so rampant
But the bridle that detains them,
But the circle that contracts them.

[*To the Soldiers.*] Why these idle boasts?
The door
Of this narrow prison fasten;
Leave him there secured.
    SIGISMUND. Ah, heavens,
It is wise of you to snatch me
Thus from freedom! since my rage
'Gainst you had become Titanic,
Since to break the glass and crystal
Gold-gates of the sun, my anger
On the firm-fixed rocks' foundations
Would have mountains piled of marble.
    CLOTALDO. 'T is that you should not so
        pile them
That perhaps these ills have happened.
        [*Some of the Soldiers lead* SIGIS-
        MUND *into his prison, the doors
        of which are closed upon him.*]
    ROSAURA. Since I now have seen how
        pride
Can offend thee, I were hardened
Sure in folly not here humbly
At thy feet for life to ask thee;
Then to me extend thy pity,
Since it were a special harshness
If humility and pride,
Both alike were disregarded.
    CLARIN. If Humility and Pride
Those two figures who have acted
Many and many a thousand times
In the *autos sacramentales*,
Do not move you, I, who am neither
Proud nor humble, but a sandwich
Partly mixed of both, entreat you
To extend to us your pardon.
    CLOTALDO. Ho!
    SOLDIERS. My lord?
    CLOTALDO. Disarm the two,
And their eyes securely bandage,
So that they may not be able
To see whither they are carried.
    ROSAURA. This is, sir, my sword; to thee
Only would I wish to hand it,
Since in fine of all the others
Thou art chief, and I could hardly
Yield it unto one less noble.
    CLARIN. Mine I'll give the greatest
        rascal
Of your troop: [*to a Soldier*] so take it, you.
    ROSAURA. And if I must die, to thank
        thee
For thy pity, I would leave thee

This as pledge, which has its value
From the owner who once wore it;
That thou guard it well, I charge thee,
For although I do not know
What strange secret it may carry,
This I know, that some great mystery
Lies within this golden scabbard,
Since relying but on it
I to Poland here have traveled
To revenge a wrong.
    CLOTALDO [*aside*]. Just heavens!
What is this? Still graver, darker,
Grow my doubts and my confusion,
My anxieties and my anguish. —
Speak, who gave you this?
    ROSAURA. A woman.
    CLOTALDO. And her name?
    ROSAURA. To that my answer
Must be silence.
    CLOTALDO. But from what
Do you now infer, or fancy,
That this sword involves a secret?
    ROSAURA. She who gave it said: "De-
        part hence
Into Poland, and by study,
Stratagem, and skill so manage
That this sword may be inspected
By the nobles and the magnates
Of that land, for you, I know,
Will by one of them be guarded," —
But his name, lest he was dead,
Was not then to me imparted.
    CLOTALDO [*aside*]. Bless me, ⸢Heaven!
        what's this I hear?
For so strangely has this happened,
That I cannot yet determine
If 't is real or imagined.
This is the same sword that I
Left with beauteous Violante,
As a pledge unto its wearer,
Who might seek me out thereafter,
As a son that I would love him,
And protect him as a father.
What is to be done (ah, me!)
In confusion so entangled,
If he who for safety bore it
Bears it now but to dispatch him,
Since condemned to death he cometh
To my feet? How strange a marvel!
What a lamentable fortune!
How unstable! how unhappy!
This must be my son — the tokens

All declare it, superadded
To the flutter of the heart,
That to see him loudly rappeth
At the breast, and not being able
With its throbs to burst its chamber,
Does as one in prison, who,
Hearing tumult in the alley,
Strives to look from out the window;
Thus, not knowing what here passes
Save the noise, the heart uprusheth
To the eyes the cause to examine —
They the windows of the heart,
Out through which in tears it glances.
What is to be done? (O Heavens!)
What is to be done? To drag him
Now before the King were death;
But to hide him from my master,
That I cannot do, according
To my duty as a vassal.
Thus my loyalty and self-love
Upon either side attack me;
Each would win. But wherefore doubt?
Is not loyalty a grander,
Nobler thing than life, than honor?
Then let loyalty live, no matter
That he die; besides, he told me,
If I well recall his language,
That he came to revenge a wrong,
But a wronged man is a lazar, —
No, he cannot be my son,
Not the son of noble fathers.
But if some great chance, which no one
Can be Yree from, should have happened,
Since the delicate sense of honor
Is a thing so fine, so fragile,
That the slightest touch may break it,
Or the faintest breath may tarnish,
What could he do more, do more,
He whose cheek the blue blood mantles,
But at many risks to have come here
It again to reëstablish?
Yes, he is my son, my blood,
Since he shows himself so manly.
And thus then betwixt two doubts
A mid course alone is granted:
'T is to seek the King, and tell him
Who he is, let what will happen.
A desire to save my honor
May appease my royal master;
Should he spare his life, I then
Will assist him in demanding
His revenge; but if the King

Should, persisting in his anger,
Give him death, then he will die
Without knowing I 'm his father. —
Come, then, come then with me, strangers.
[*To* ROSAURA *and* CLARIN.] Do not fear in
    your disasters
That you will not have companions
In misfortune; for so balanced
Are the gains of life or death,
That I know not which are larger.
                                    [*Exeunt.*]

[SCENE II. *A Hall in the Royal Palace.*]

[*Enter at one side* ASTOLFO *and Soldiers,
    and at the other the* INFANTA ESTRELLA
    *and her Ladies. Military music and
    salutes within.*]

ASTOLFO. Struck at once with admira-
        tion
At thy starry eyes outshining,
Mingle many a salutation,
Drums and trumpet-notes combining,
Founts and birds in alternation;
Wondering here to see thee pass,
Music in grand chorus gathers
All her notes from grove and grass:
Here are trumpets formed of feathers,
There are birds that breathe in brass.
All salute thee, fair Señora,
Ordnance as their Queen proclaim thee,
Beauteous birds as their Aurora,
As their Pallas trumpets name thee,
And the sweet flowers as their Flora;
For Aurora sure thou art,
Bright as day that conquers night —
Thine is Flora's peaceful part,
Thou art Pallas in thy might,
And as Queen thou rul'st my heart.
ESTRELLA. If the human voice obeying
Should with human action pair,
Then you have said ill in saying
All these flattering words and fair,
Since in truth they are gainsaying
This parade of victory,
'Gainst which I my standard rear,
Since they say, it seems to me,
Not the flatteries that I hear,
But the rigors that I see.
Think, too, what a base invention
From a wild beast's treachery sprung, —
Fraudful mother of dissension —

Is to flatter with the tongue,
And to kill with the intention.
   ASTOLFO. Ill informed you must have
     been,
Fair Estrella, thus to throw
Doubt on my respectful mien:
Let your ear attentive lean
While the cause I strive show.
King Eustorgius the Fair,
Third so called, died, leaving two
Daughters, and Basilius heir;
Of his sisters I and you
Are the children — I forbear
To recall a single scene
Save what's needful. Clorilene,
Your good mother and my aunt,
Who is now a habitant
Of a sphere of sunnier sheen,
Was the elder, of whom you
Are the daughter; Recisunda,
Whom God guard a thousand years,
Her fair sister (Rosamunda
Were she called if names were true)
Wed in Muscovy, of whom
I was born. 'T is needful now
The commencement to resume.
King Basilius, who doth bow
'Neath the weight of years, the doom
Age imposes, more inclined
To the studies of the mind
Than to women, wifeless, lone,
Without sons, to fill his throne
I and you our way would find.
You, the elder's child, averred,
That the crown you stood more nigh:
I, maintaining that you erred,
Held, though born of the younger, I,
Being a man, should be preferred.
Thus our mutual pretension
To our uncle we related,
Who replied that he would mention
Here, and on this day he stated,
What might settle the dissension.
With this end, from Muscovy
I set out, and with that view,
I to-day fair Poland see,
And not making war on you,
Wait till war you make on me.
Would to love — that God so wise —
That the crowd may be a sure
Astrologue to read the skies,
And this festive truce secure

Both to you and me the prize,
Making you a Queen, but Queen
By my will, our uncle leaving
You the throne we'll share between —
And my love a realm receiving
Dearer than a King's demesne.
   ESTRELLA. Well, I must be generous too,
For a gallantry so fine;
This imperial realm you view,
If I wish it to be mine
'T is to give it unto you.
Though if I the truth confessed,
I must fear your love may fail —
Flattering words are words at best,
For perhaps a truer tale
Tells that portrait on your breast.
   ASTOLFO. On that point complete con-
     tent
Will I give your mind, not here,
For each sounding instrument
               [*Drums are heard.*]
Tells us that the King is near,
With his Court and Parliament.

[*Enter the* KING BASILIUS, *with his retinue.*]

   ESTRELLA. Learned Euclid . . .
   ASTOLFO. Thales wise . . .
   ESTRELLA. The vast Zodiac . . .
   ASTOLFA. The star spaces . . .
   ESTRELLA. Who dost soar to . . .
   ASTOLFO. Who dost rise . . .
   ESTRELLA. The sun's orbit . . .
   ASTOLFO. The stars' places . . .
   ESTRELLA. To describe . . .
   ASTOLFO. To map the skies . . .
   ESTRELLA. Let me humbly interlac-
     ing . . .
   ASTOLFO. Let me lovingly embrac-
     ing . . .
   ESTRELLA. Be the tendril of thy tree.
   ASTOLFO. Bend respectfully my knee.
   BASILIUS. Children, that dear word dis-
     placing
Colder names, my arms here bless;
And be sure, since you assented
To my plan, my love's excess
Will leave neither discontented,
Or give either more or less.
And though I from being old
Slowly may the facts unfold,
Hear in silence my narration,
Keep reserved your admiration,

Till the wondrous tale is told.
You already know — I pray you
Be attentive, dearest children,
Great, illustrious Court of Poland,
Faithful vassals, friends and kinsmen,
You already know — my studies
Have throughout the whole world given me
The high title of " the learnéd,"
Since 'gainst time and time's oblivion
The rich pencils of Timanthes,
The bright marbles of Lysippus,
Universally proclaim me
Through earth's bounds the great Basilius.
You already know the sciences
That I feel my mind most given to
Are the subtle mathematics,
By whose means my clear prevision
Takes from rumor its slow office,
Takes from time its jurisdiction
Of, each day, new facts disclosing;
Since in algebraic symbols
When the fate of future ages
On my tablets I see written,
I anticipate time in telling
What my science hath predicted.
All those circles of pure snow,
All those canopies of crystal,
Which the sun with rays illumines,
Which the moon cuts in its circles,
All those orbs of twinkling diamond,
All those crystal globes that glisten,
All that azure field of stars
Where the zodiac signs are pictured,
Are the study of my life,
Are the books where heaven has written
Upon diamond-dotted paper,
Upon leaves by sapphires tinted,
With light luminous lines of gold,
In clear characters distinctly
All the events of human life,
Whether adverse or benignant.
These so rapidly I read
That I follow with the quickness
Of my thoughts the swiftest movements
Of their orbits and their circles.
Would to heaven, that ere my mind
To those mystic books addicted
Was the comment of their margins
And of all their leaves the index,
Would to heaven, I say, my life
Had been offered the first victim
Of its anger, that my death-stroke

Had in this way have been given me,
Since the unhappy find even merit
Is the fatal knife that kills them,
And his own self-murderer
Is the man whom knowledge injures! —
I may say so, but my story
So will say with more distinctness,
And to win your admiration
Once again I pray you listen. —
Clorilene, my wife, a son
Bore me, so by fate afflicted
That on his unhappy birthday
All Heaven's prodigies assisted.
Nay, ere yet to life's sweet light
Gave him forth her womb, that living
Sepulchre (for death and life
Have like ending and beginning),
Many a time his mother saw
In her dreams' delirious dimness
From her side a monster break,
Fashioned like a man, but sprinkled
With her blood, who gave her death,
By that human viper bitten.
Round his birthday came at last,
All its auguries fulfilling
(For the presages of evil
Seldom fail or even linger):
Came with such a horoscope,
That the sun rushed blood-red tinted
Into a terrific combat
With the dark moon that resisted;
Earth its mighty lists outspread
As with lessening lights diminished
Strove the twin-lamps of the sky.
'T is of all the sun's eclipses
The most dreadful that it suffered
Since the hour its bloody visage
Wept the awful death of Christ.
For o'erwhelmed in glowing cinders
The great orb appeared to suffer
Nature's final paroxysm.
Gloom the glowing noontide darkened,
Earthquake shook the mightiest buildings,
Stones the angry clouds rained down,
And with blood ran red the rivers.
In this frenzy of the sun,
In its madness and delirium,
Sigismund was born, thus early
Giving proofs of his condition,
Since his birth his mother slew,
Just as if these words had killed her,
" I am a man, since good with evil

I repay here from the beginning," —
I, applying to my studies,
Saw in them as 't were forewritten
This, that Sigismund would be
The most cruel of all princes,
Of all men the most audacious,
Of all monarchs the most wicked;
That his kingdom through his means
Would be broken and partitioned,
The academy of the vices,
And the high school of sedition;
And that he himself, borne onward
By his crimes' wild course resistless,
Would even place his feet on me:
For I saw myself down-stricken,
Lying on the ground before him
(To say this what shame it gives me!)
While his feet on my white hairs
As a carpet were imprinted.
Who discredits threatened ill,
Specially an ill previsioned
By one's study, when self-love
Makes it his peculiar business? —
Thus then crediting the fates
Which far off my science witnessed,
All these fatal auguries
Seen though dimly in the distance,
I resolved to chain the monster
That unhappily life was given to,
To find out if yet the stars
Owned the wise man's weird dominion.
It was publicly proclaimed
That the sad ill-omened infant
Was stillborn. I then a tower
Caused by forethought to be builded
'Mid the rocks of these wild mountains
Where the sunlight scarce can gild it,
Its glad entrance being barred
By these rude shafts obeliscal.
All the laws of which you know,
All the edicts that prohibit
Any one on pain of death
That secluded part to visit
Of the mountain, were occasioned
By this cause, so long well hidden.
There still lives Prince Sigismund,
Miserable, poor, in prison.
Him alone Clotaldo sees,
Only tends to and speaks with him;
He the sciences has taught him,
He the Catholic religion
Has imparted to him, being

Of his miseries the sole witness.
Here there are three things: the first
I rate highest, since my wishes
Are, O Poland, thee to save
From the oppression, the affliction
Of a tyrant King, because
Of his country and his kingdom
He were no benignant father
Who to such a risk could give it.
Secondly, the thought occurs
That to take from mine own issue
The plain right that every law
Human and divine hath given him
Is not Christian charity;
For by no law am I bidden
To prevent another proving,
Say, a tyrant, or a villain,
To be one myself: supposing
Even my son should be so guilty,
That he should not crimes commit
I myself should first commit them.
Then the third and last point is,
That perhaps I erred in giving
Too implicit a belief
To the facts foreseen so dimly;
For although his inclination
Well might find its precipices,
He might possibly escape them:
For the fate the most fastidious,
For the impulse the most powerful,
Even the planets most malicious
Only make free will incline,
But can force not human wishes.
And thus 'twixt these different causes
Vacillating and unfixéd,
I a remedy have thought of
Which will with new wonder fill you.
I to-morrow morning purpose,
Without letting it be hinted
That he is my son, and therefore
Your true King, at once to fix him
As King Sigismund (for the name
Still he bears that first was given him)
'Neath my canopy, on my throne,
And in fine in my position,
There to govern and command you,
Where in dutiful submission
You will swear to him allegiance.
My resources thus are triple,
As the causes of disquiet
Were which I revealed this instant.
The first is; that he being prudent,

Careful, cautious, and benignant,
Falsifying the wild actions
That of him had been predicted,
You'll enjoy your natural prince,
He who has so long been living
Holding court amid these mountains,
With the wild beasts for his circle.
Then my next resource is this:
If he, daring, wild, and wicked,
Proudly runs with loosened rein
O'er the broad plain of the vicious,
I will have fulfilled the duty
Of my natural love and pity;
Then his righteous deposition
Will but prove my royal firmness,
Chastisement and not revenge
Leading him once more to prison.
My third course is this: the Prince
Being what my words have pictured,
From the love I owe you, vassals,
I will give you other princes
Worthier of the crown and scepter;
Namely, my two sisters' children,
Who their separate pretensions
Having happily commingled
By the holy bonds of marriage,
Will then fill their fit position.
This is what a king commands you,
This is what a father bids you,
This is what a sage entreats you,
This is what an old man wishes;
And as Seneca, the Spaniard,
Says, a king for all his riches
Is but slave of his Republic,
This is what a slave petitions.
    ASTOLFO. If on me devolves the answer,
As being in this weighty business
The most interested party,
I, of all, express the opinion: —
Let Prince Sigismund appear;
He's thy son, that's all-sufficient.
    ALL. Give to us our natural prince,
We proclaim him king this instant!
    BASILIUS. Vassals, from my heart I
        thank you
For this deference to my wishes: —
Go, conduct to their apartments
These two columns of my kingdom,
On to-morrow you shall see him.
    ALL. Live, long live great King Basilius!
        [Exeunt all, accompanying ESTRELLA
        and ASTOLFO; the King remains.]

[Enter CLOTALDO, ROSAURA, and CLARIN.]
    CLOTALDO. May I speak to you, Sire?
    BASILIUS. Clotaldo,
You are always welcome with me.
    CLOTALDO. Although coming to your feet
Shows how freely I'm admitted,
Still, Your Majesty, this once,
Fate as mournful as malicious
Takes from privilege its due right,
And from custom its permission.
    BASILIUS. What has happened?
    CLOTALDO. A misfortune,
Sire, which has my heart afflicted
At the moment when all joy
Should have overflown and filled it.
    BASILIUS. Pray proceed.
    CLOTALDO. This handsome youth here,
Inadvertently, or driven
By his daring, pierced the tower,
And the Prince discovered in it.
Nay. . . .
    BASILIUS. Clotaldo, be not troubled
At this act, which if committed
At another time had grieved me,
But the secret so long hidden
Having myself told, his knowledge
Of the fact but matters little.
See me presently, for I
Much must speak upon this business,
And for me you much must do
For a part will be committed
To you in the strangest drama
That perhaps the world e'er witnessed.
As for these, that you may know
That I mean not your remissness
To chastise, I grant their pardon.   [Exit.]
    CLOTALDO. Myriad years to my lord be
        given!
[Aside.] Heaven has sent a happier fate;
Since I need not now admit it,
I'll not say he is my son. —
Strangers who have wandered hither,
You are free.
    ROSAURA. I give your feet
A thousand kisses.
    CLARIN. I say misses,
For a letter more or less
'Twixt two friends is not considered.
    ROSAURA. You have given me life, my lord,
And since by your act I'm living,
I eternally will own me
As your slave.

CLOTALDO. The life I've given
Is not really your true life,
For a man by birth uplifted
If he suffers an affront
Actually no longer liveth;
And supposing you have come here
For revenge as you have hinted,
I have not then given you life,
Since you have not brought it with you,
For no life disgraced is life.
[Aside.] (This I say to arouse his spirit.)
ROSAURA. I confess I have it not,
Though by you it has been given me;
But revenge being wreaked, my honor
I will leave so pure and limpid,
All its perils overcome,
That my life may then with fitness
• Seem to be a gift of yours.
CLOTALDO. Take this burnished sword
which hither
You brought with you; for I know,
To revenge you, 't is sufficient,
In your enemy's blood bathed red;
For a sword that once was girded
Round me (I say this the while
That to me it was committed),
Will know how to right you.
ROSAURA. Thus
In your name once more I gird it,
And on it my vengeance swear,
Though the enemy who afflicts me
Were more powerful.
CLOTALDO. Is he so?
ROSAURA. Yes; so powerful, I am hin-
dered
Saying who he is, not doubting
Even for greater things your wisdom
And calm prudence, but through fear
Lest against me your prized pity
Might be turned.
CLOTALDO. 'T will rather be,
By declaring it more kindled;
Otherwise you bar the passage
'Gainst your foe of my assistance. —
[Aside.] (Would that I but knew his name!)
ROSAURA. Not to think I set so little
Value on such confidence,
Know my enemy and my victim
Is no less than Prince Astolfo,
Duke of Muscovy.
CLOTALDO [aside.] Resistance
Badly can my grief supply

Since 't is heavier than I figured.
Let us sift the matter deeper. —
If a Muscovite by birth, then
He who is your natural lord
Could not 'gainst you have committed
Any wrong; reseek your country,
And abandon the wild impulse
That has driven you here.
ROSAURA. I know,
Though a prince, he has committed
'Gainst me a great wrong.
CLOTALDO. He could not,
Even although your face was stricken
By his angry hand. [Aside.] (Oh, heavens!)
ROSAURA. Mine's a wrong more deep
and bitter.
CLOTALDO. Tell it, then; it cannot be
Worse than what my fancy pictures.
ROSAURA. I will tell it; though I know not,
With the respect your presence gives me,
With the affection you awaken,
With the esteem your worth elicits,
How with bold face here to tell you
That this outer dress is simply
An enigma, since it is not
What it seems. And from this hint, then,
If I'm not what I appear,
And Astolfo with this princess
Comes to wed, judge how by him
I was wronged: I've said sufficient.
[Exeunt ROSAURA and CLARIN.]
CLOTALDO. Listen! hear me! wait! oh, stay!
What a labyrinthine thicket
Is all this, where reason gives
Not a thread whereby to issue?
My own honor here is wronged,
Powerful is my foe's position,
I a vassal, she a woman;
Heaven reveal some way in pity,
Though I doubt it has the power;
When in such confused abysses,
Heaven is all one fearful presage,
And the world itself a riddle. [Exit.]

ACT II

[SCENE I. A Hall in the Royal Palace.]

[Enter BASILIUS and CLOTALDO.]

CLOTALDO. Everything has been effected
As you ordered.
BASILIUS. How all happened
Let me know, my good Clotaldo.

CLOTALDO. It was done, Sire, in this manner.
With the tranquilizing draft,
Which was made, as you commanded,
Of confections duly mixed
With some herbs, whose juice extracted
Has a strange tyrannic power,
Has some secret force imparted,
Which all human sense and speech
Robs, deprives, and counteracteth,
And as 't were a living corpse
Leaves the man whose lips have quaffed
　　it
So asleep that all his senses,
All his powers are overmastered. . . .
— No need have we to discuss
That this fact can really happen,
Since, my lord, experience gives us
Many a clear and proved example;
Certain 't is that Nature's secrets
May by medicine be extracted,
And that not an animal,
Not a stone, or herb that's planted,
But some special quality
Doth possess: for if the malice
Of man's heart, a thousand poisons
That give death, hath power to examine,
Is it then so great a wonder
That, their venom being abstracted,
If, as death by some is given,
Sleep by others is imparted?
Putting, then, aside the doubt
That 't is possible this should happen,
A thing proved beyond all question
Both by reason and example . . .
— With the sleeping draft, in fine,
Made of opium superadded
To the poppy and the henbane,
I to Sigismund's apartment —
Cell, in fact — went down, and with him
Spoke awhile upon the grammar
Of the sciences, those first studies
Which mute Nature's gentle masters,
Silent skies and hills, had taught him;
In which school divine and ample,
The bird's song, the wild beast's roar,
Were a lesson and a language.
Then to raise his spirit more
To the high design you planned here,
I discoursed on, as my theme,
The swift flight, the stare undazzled
Of a pride-plumed eagle bold,

Which with back-averted talons,
Scorning the tame fields of air,
Seeks the sphere of fire, and passes
Through its flame a flash of feathers,
Or a comet's hair untangled.
I extolled its soaring flight,
Saying, "Thou at last art master
Of thy house, thou 'rt king of birds,
It is right thou should'st surpass them."
He who needed nothing more
Than to touch upon the matter
Of high royalty, with a bearing
As became him, boldly answered;
For in truth his princely blood
Moves, excites, inflames his ardor
To attempt great things: he said,
"In the restless realm of atoms
Given to birds, that even one
Should swear fealty as a vassal!
I, reflecting upon this,
Am consoled by my disasters,
For, at least, if I obey,
I obey through force: untrammeled,
Free to act, I ne'er will own
Any man on earth my master." —
This, his usual theme of grief,
Having roused him nigh to madness,
I occasion took to proffer
The drugged draft: he drank, but hardly
Had the liquor from the vessel
Passed into his breast, when fastest
Sleep his senses seized, a sweat,
Cold as ice, the life-blood hardened
In his veins, his limbs grew stiff,
So that, knew I not 't was acted,
Death was there, feigned death, his life
I could doubt not had departed.
Then those, to whose care you trust
This experiment, in a carriage
Brought him here, where all things fitting
The high majesty and the grandeur
Of his person are provided.
In the bed of your state chamber
They have placed him, where the stupor
Having spent its force and vanished,
They, as 't were yourself, my lord,
Him will serve as you commanded:
And if my obedient service
Seems to merit some slight largess,
I would ask but this alone
(My presumption you will pardon),
That you tell me, with what object

Have you, in this secret manner,
To your palace brought him here?
BASILIUS. Good Clotaldo, what you ask me
Is so just, to you alone
I would give full satisfaction.
Sigismund, my son, the hard
Influence of his hostile planet
(As you know) doth threat a thousand
Dreadful tragedies and disasters;
I desire to test if Heaven
(An impossible thing to happen)
Could have lied — if having given us
Proofs unnumbered, countless samples
Of his evil disposition,
He might prove more mild, more guarded
At the least, and self-subdued
By his prudence and true valor
Change his character; for 't is man
That alone controls the planets.
This it is I wish to test,
Having brought him to this palace,
Where he 'll learn he is my son,
And display his natural talents.
If he nobly hath subdued him,
He will reign; but if his manners
Show him tyrannous and cruel,
Then his chains once more shall clasp him.
But for this experiment,
Now you probably will ask me
Of what moment was 't to bring him
Thus asleep and in this manner?
And I wish to satisfy you,
Giving all your doubts an answer.
If to-day he learns that he
Is my son, and some hours after
Finds himself once more restored
To his misery and his shackles,
Certain 't is that from his temper
Blank despair may end in madness —
But once knowing who he is,
Can he be consoled thereafter?
Yes, and thus I wish to leave
One door open, one free passage,
By declaring all he saw
Was a dream. With this advantage
We attain two ends. The first
Is to put beyond all cavil
His condition, for on waking
He will show his thoughts, his fancies:
To console him is the second;
Since, although obeyed and flattered,
He beholds himself awhile,

And then back in prison shackled
Finds him, he will think he dreamed.
And he rightly so may fancy,
For, Clotaldo, in this world
All who live but dream they act here.
CLOTALDO. Reasons fail me not to show
That the experiment may not answer;
But there is no remedy now,
For a sign from the apartment
Tells me that he hath awoken
And even hitherward advances.
BASILIUS. It is best that I retire;
But do you, so long his master,
Near him stand; the wild confusions
That his waking sense may darken
Dissipate by simple truth.
CLOTALDO. Then your license you have
    granted
That I may declare it?
BASILIUS. Yes;
For it possibly may happen
That admonished of his danger
He may conquer his worst passions. [*Exit.*]

[Enter CLARIN.]

CLARIN [*aside*]. Four good blows are all
    it cost me
To come here, inflicted smartly
By a red-robed halberdier,
With a beard to match his jacket.
At that price I see the show,
For no window's half so handy
As that which, without entreating
Tickets of the ticket-master,
A man carries with himself;
Since for all the feasts and galas
Cool effrontery is the window
Whence at ease he gazes at them.
CLOTALDO [*aside*]. This is Clarin,
    Heavens! of her,
Yes, I say, of her the valet,
She, who dealing in misfortunes,
Has my pain to Poland carried; —
Any news, friend Clarin?
CLARIN. News?
Yes, sir, since your great compassion
Is disposed Rosaura's outrage
To revenge, she has changed her habit,
And resumed her proper dress.
CLOTALDO. 'T is quite right, lest possible
    scandal
Might arise.

CLARIN. More news: her name
Having changed and wisely bartered
For your niece's name, she now
So in honor has advanced her,
That among Estrella's ladies
She here with her in the palace
Lives.
CLOTALDO. 'T is right that I once more
Should her honor reëstablish.
CLARIN. News; that anxiously she
waiteth
For that very thing to happen,
When you may have time to try it.
CLOTALDO. Most discreetly has she
acted;
Soon the time will come, believe me,
Happily to end this matter.
CLARIN. News, too; that she's well re-
galed,
Feasted like a queen, and flattered
On the strength of being your niece.
And the last news, and the saddest,
Is that I who here came with her
Am with hunger almost famished.
None remember me, or think
I am Clarin, clarion rather,
And that if that clarion sounded,
All the Court would know what passes.
For there are two things, to wit,
A brass clarion and a lackey,
That are bad at keeping secrets;
And it so may chance, if haply
I am forced to break my silence,
They of me may sing this passage:
"Never, when the day is near,
Does clarion sound more clear."
CLOTALDO. Your complaint is too well-
founded;
I will get you satisfaction,
Meanwhile you may wait on me.
CLARIN. See, sir, Sigismund advances.
[*Music and song.* SIGISMUND
enters, lost in amazement. Serv-
ants minister to him, present-
ing costly robes. CLOTALDO *and*
CLARIN.]
SIGISMUND. Help me, Heaven, what's
this I see!
Help me, Heaven, what's this I view!
Things I scarce believe are true,
But, if true, which fright not me.
I in palaces of state?

I 'neath silks and cloth of gold?
I, around me, to behold
Rich-robed servants watch and wait?
I so soft a bed to press
While sweet sleep my senses bowed?
I to wake in such a crowd,
Who assist me even to dress?
'T were deceit to say I dream,
Waking I recall my lot,
I am Sigismund, am I not?
Heaven make plain what dark doth seem!
Tell me, what has phantasy —
Wild, misleading, dream-adept —
So effected while I slept,
That I still the phantoms see?
But let that be as it may,
Why perplex myself and brood?
Better taste the present good,
Come what will some other day.
FIRST SERVANT [*aside to the Second*
Servant, and to CLARIN]. What a
sadness doth oppress him!
SECOND SERVANT. Who in such-like case
would be
Less surprised and sad than he?
CLARIN. I for one.
SECOND SERVANT [*to the First*]. You had
best address him.
FIRST SERVANT [*to* SIGISMUND]. May
they sing again?
SIGISMUND. No, no;
I don't care to hear them sing.
SECOND SERVANT. I conceived the song
might bring
To your thought some ease.
SIGISMUND. Not so;
Voices that but charm the ear
Cannot soothe my sorrow's pain;
'T is the soldier's martial strain
That alone I love to hear.
CLOTALDO. May Your Highness, mighty
Prince,
Deign to let me kiss your hand,
I would first of all this land
My profound respect evince.
SIGISMUND [*aside*]. 'T is my jailer! how
can he
Change his harshness and neglect
To this language of respect?
What can have occurred to me?
CLOTALDO. The new state in which I find
you

Must create a vague surprise,
Doubts unnumbered must arise
To bewilder and to blind you;
I would make your prospect fair,
Through the maze a path would show,
Thus, my lord, 't is right you know
That you are the prince and heir
Of this Polish realm: if late
You lay hidden and concealed
'T was that we were forced to yield
To the stern decrees of fate,
Which strange ills, I know not how,
Threatened on this land to bring
Should the laurel of a king
Ever crown thy princely brow.
Still relying on the power
Of your will the stars to bind,
For a man of resolute mind
Can them bind how dark they lower;
To this palace from your cell
In your lifelong turret keep
They have borne you while dull sleep
Held your spirit in its spell.
Soon to see you and embrace
Comes the King, your father, here —
He will make the rest all clear.
   SIGISMUND. Why, thou traitor vile and
base,
What need I to know the rest,
Since it is enough to know
Who I am my power to show,
And the pride that fills my breast?
Why this treason brought to light
Hast thou to thy country done,
As to hide from the King's son,
'Gainst all reason and all right,
This his rank?
   CLOTALDO. Oh, destiny!
   SIGISMUND. Thou the traitor's part hast
played
'Gainst the law; the King betrayed,
And done cruel wrong to me;
Thus for each distinct offense
Have the law, the King, and I
Thee condemned this day to die
By my hands.
   SECOND SERVANT. Prince . . .
   SIGISMUND. No pretence
Shall undo the debt I owe you.
Catiff, hence! By Heaven! I say,
If you dare to stop my way
From the window I will throw you.

   SECOND SERVANT. Fly, Clotaldo!
   CLOTALDO. Woe to thee,
In thy pride so powerful seeming,
Without knowing thou art dreaming!
                [Exit.]
   SECOND SERVANT. Think . . .
   SIGISMUND. Away! don't trouble me.
   SECOND SERVANT. He could not the
King deny.
   SIGISMUND. Bade to do a wrongful thing
He should have refused the King;
And, besides, his prince was I.
   SECOND SERVANT. 'T was not his affair
to try
If the act was wrong or right.
   SIGISMUND. You're indifferent, black or
white,
Since so pertly you reply.
   CLARIN. What the Prince says is quite
true,
What you do is wrong, I say.
   SECOND SERVANT. Who gave you this
license, pray?
   CLARIN. No one gave; I took it.
   SIGISMUND. Who
Art thou, speak?
   CLARIN. A meddling fellow,
Prating, prying, fond of scrapes,
General of all jackanapes,
And most merry when most mellow.
   SIGISMUND. You alone in this new sphere
Have amused me.
   CLARIN. That's quite true, sir,
For I am the great amuser
Of all Sigismunds who are here.

          [Enter ASTOLFO.]

   ASTOLFO. Thousand times be blest the
day,
Prince, that gives thee to our sight,
Sun of Poland, whose glad light
Makes this whole horizon gay,
As when from the rosy fountains
Of the dawn the stream-rays run,
Since thou issuest like the sun
From the bosom of the mountains!
And though late do not defer
With thy sovereign light to shine;
Round thy brow the laurel twine —
Deathless crown.
   SIGISMUND. God guard thee, sir.
   ASTOLFO. In not knowing me I o'erlook,

But alone for this defect,
This response that lacks respect,
And due honor. Muscovy's Duke
Am I, and your cousin born,
Thus my equal I regard thee.
SIGISMUND. Did there, when I said "God
guard thee,"
Lie concealed some latent scorn? —
Then if so, now having got
Thy big name, and seeing thee vexed,
When thou com'st to see me next
I will say God guard thee not.
SECOND SERVANT [to ASTOLFO]. Think,
Your Highness, if he errs
Thus, his mountain birth's at fault,
Every word is an assault.
[To SIGISMUND.] Duke Astolfo, sir, pre-
fers. . . .
SIGISMUND. Tut! his talk became a bore,
Nay his act was worse than that,
He presumed to wear his hat.
SECOND SERVANT. As grandee.
SIGISMUND. But I am more.
SECOND SERVANT. Nevertheless respect
should be
Much more marked betwixt ye two
Than 'twixt others.
SIGISMUND. And pray who
Asked your meddling thus with me?

[Enter ESTRELLA.]

ESTRELLA. Welcome may Your Highness
be,
Welcomed oft to this thy throne,
Which long longing for its own
Finds at length its joy in thee;
Where, in spite of bygone fears,
May your reign be great and bright,
And your life in its long flight
Count by ages, not by years.
SIGISMUND [to CLARIN]. Tell me, thou,
say, who can be
This supreme of loveliness —
Goddess in a woman's dress —
At whose feet divine we see
Heaven its choicest gifts doth lay? —
This sweet maid? Her name declare.
CLARIN. 'T is your star-named cousin fair.
SIGISMUND. Nay, the sun, 't were best
to say. —
[To ESTRELLA.] Though thy sweet felic-
itation

Adds new splendor to my throne,
'T is for seeing thee alone
That I merit gratulation;
Therefore I a prize have drawn
That I scarce deserved to win,
And am doubly blessed therein: —
Star, that in the rosy dawn
Dimmest with transcendent ray
Orbs that brightest gem the blue,
What is left the sun to do,
When thou risest with the day? —
Give me then thy hand to kiss,
In whose cup of snowy whiteness
Drinks the day delicious brightness.
ESTRELLA. What a courtly speech is this?
ASTOLFO [aside]. If he takes her hand I
feel
I am lost.
SECOND SERVANT [aside]. Astolfo's grief
I perceive, and bring relief: —
Think, my lord, excuse my zeal,
That perhaps this is too free,
Since Astolfo . . .
SIGISMUND. Did I say
Woe to him that stops my way? —
SECOND SERVANT. What I said was just.
SIGISMUND. To me
This is tiresome and absurd.
Nought is just, or good or ill,
In my sight that balks my will.
SECOND SERVANT. Why, my lord, your-
self I heard
Say in any righteous thing
It was proper to obey.
SIGISMUND. You must, too, have heard
me say
Him I would from window throw
Who should tease me or defy?
SECOND SERVANT. Men like me perhaps
might show
That could not be done, sir.
SIGISMUND. No?
Then, by Heaven, at least, I'll try!
[He seizes him in his arms and
rushes to the side. All follow, and
return immediately.]
ASTOLFO. What is this I see? Oh, woe!
ESTRELLA. Oh, prevent him! Follow me!
[Exit.]
SIGISMUND [returning]. From the win-
dow into the sea
He has fallen; I told him so.

ASTOLFO. These strange bursts of savage
malice
You should regulate, if you can;
Wild beasts are to civilized man
As rude mountains to a palace.
SIGISMUND. Take a bit of advice for that:
Pause ere such bold words are said,
Lest you may not have a head
Upon which to hang your hat.
[Exit ASTOLFO.]

[Enter BASILIUS.]

BASILIUS. What's all this?
SIGISMUND. A trifling thing:
One who teased and thwarted me
I have just thrown into the sea.
CLARIN [to SIGISMUND]. Know, my lord,
it is the King.
BASILIUS. Ere the first day's sun hath set,
Has thy coming cost a life?
SIGISMUND. Why he dared me to the
strife,
And I only won the bet.
BASILIUS. Prince, my grief, indeed is
great,
Coming here when I had thought
That admonished thou wert taught
To o'ercome the stars and fate,
Still to see such rage abide
In the heart I hoped was free,
That thy first sad act should be
A most fearful homicide.
How could I by love conducted,
Trust me to thine arms' embracing,
When their haughty interlacing,
Has already been instructed
How to kill? For who could see,
Say, some dagger bare and bloody,
By some wretch's heart made ruddy,
But would fear it? Who is he,
Who may happen to behold
On the ground the gory stain
Where another man was slain
But must shudder? The most bold
Yields at once to Nature's laws;
Thus I, seeing in your arms
The dread weapon that alarms,
And the stain, must fain withdraw;
And though in embraces dear
I would press you to my heart,
I without them must depart,
For, alas! your arms I fear.

SIGISMUND. Well, without them I must
stay,
As I've stayed for many a year,
For a father so severe,
Who could treat me in this way,
Whose unfeeling heart could tear me
From his side even when a child,
Who, a denizen of the wild,
As a monster there could rear me,
And by many an artful plan
Sought my death, it cannot grieve me
Much his arms will not receive me
Who has scarcely left me man.
BASILIUS. Would to God it had not been
Act of mine that name conferred,
Then thy voice I ne'er had heard,
Then thy boldness ne'er had seen.
SIGISMUND. Did you manhood's right
retain,
I would then have nought to say,
But to give and take away
Gives me reason to complain;
For although to give with grace
Is the noblest act 'mongst men,
To take back the gift again
Is the basest of the base.
BASILIUS. This then is thy grateful
mood
For my changing thy sad lot
To a prince's!
SIGISMUND. And for what
Should I show my gratitude!
Tyrant of my will o'erthrown,
If thou hoary art and gray,
Dying, what dost give me? Say,
Dost thou give what's not mine own?
Thou'rt my father and my King,
Then the pomp these walls present
Comes to me by due descent
As a simple, natural thing.
Yes, this sunshine pleaseth me,
But 't is not through thee I bask;
Nay, a reckoning I might ask
For the life, love, liberty
That through thee I've lost so long:
Thine 't is rather to thank me,
That I do not claim from thee
Compensation for my wrong.
BASILIUS. Still untamed and uncon-
trolled; —
Heaven fulfills its word I feel,
I to that same court appeal

'Gainst thy taunts, thou vain and bold,
But although the truth thou'st heard,
And now know'st thy name and race,
And dost see thee in this place,
Where to all thou art preferred,
Yet be warned, and on thee take
Ways more mild and more beseeming,
For perhaps thou art but dreaming,
When it seems that thou'rt awake. [*Exit.*]
SIGISMUND. Is this, then, a phantom
   scene? —
Do I wake in seeming show? —
No, I dream not, since I know
What I am and what I've been.
And although thou should'st repent thee,
Remedy is now too late.
Who I am I know, and fate,
Howsoe'er thou should'st lament thee,
Cannot take from me my right
Of being born this kingdom's heir.
If I saw myself erewhile
Prisoned, bound, kept out of sight,
'T was that never on my mind
Dawned the truth; but now I know
Who I am — a mingled show
Of the man and beast combined.

[*Enter* ROSAURA, *in female attire.*]

ROSAURA [*aside*]. To wait upon Estrella
   I come here,
And lest I meet Astolfo tremble with much
   fear;
Clotaldo's wishes are
The Duke should know me not, and from
   afar
See me, if see he must.
My honor is at stake, he says; my trust
Is in Clotaldo's truth.
He will protect my honor and my youth.
  CLARIN [*to* SIGISMUND]. Of all this palace
   here can boast,
All that you yet have seen, say which has
   pleased you most?
  SIGISMUND. Nothing surprised me, noth-
   ing scared,
Because for everything I was prepared;
But if I felt for aught, or more or less
Of admiration, 't was the loveliness
Of woman; I have read
Somewhere in books on which my spirit fed,
That which caused God the greatest care to
   plan,

Because in him a little world he formed,
   was man;
But this were truer said, unless I err,
Of woman, for a little heaven he made in
   her;
She who in beauty from her birth
Surpasses man as heaven surpasseth earth;
Nay, more, the one I see.
  ROSAURA [*aside*]. The Prince is here; I
   must this instant flee.
  SIGISMUND. Hear, woman! stay;
Nor wed the western with the orient ray,
Flying with rapid tread;
For joined the orient rose and western red,
The light and the cold gloom,
The day will sink untimely to its tomb.
But who is this I see?
  ROSAURA [*aside*]. I doubt and yet be-
   lieve that it is he.
  SIGISMUND [*aside*]. This beauty I have seen
Some other time.
  ROSAURA [*aside*]. This proud, majestic
   mien,
This form I once saw bound
Within a narrow cell.
  SIGISMUND [*aside*]. My life I have
   found. —
[*Aloud.*] Woman, the sweetest name
That man can breathe, or flattering lan-
   guage frame,
Who art thou? for before
I see thee, I believe and I adore;
Faith makes my love sublime,
Persuading me we've met some other time.
Fair woman, speak; my will must be
   obeyed.
  ROSAURA. In bright Estrella's train a
   hapless maid. —
[*Aside.*] He must not know my name.
  SIGISMUND. The sun, say rather, of that
   star whose flame,
However bright its blaze
Is but the pale reflection of thy rays.
In the fair land of flowers,
The realm of sweets that lies in odorous
   bowers,
The goddess rose I have seen
By right divine of beauty reign as queen.
I have seen where brightest shine
Gems, the assembled glories of the mine,
The brilliant throng elect the diamond king
For the superior splendor it doth fling.

Amid the halls of light,
Where the unresting star-crowds meet at
    night,
I have seen fair Hesper rise
And take the foremost place of all the skies.
And in that higher zone
Where the sun calls the planets round his
    throne,
I have seen, with sovereign sway,
That he presides the oracle of the day.
How, then, 'mid flowers of earth or stars of
    air,
'Mid stones or suns, if that which is most
    fair
The preference gains, canst thou
Before a lesser beauty bend and bow,
When thine own charms compose
Something more bright than sun, stone,
    star, or rose?

[*Enter* CLOTALDO.]

CLOTALDO [*aside*]. To calm Prince Sigis-
    mund devolves on me,
Because 't was I who reared him: — What
    do I see?
ROSAURA. Thy favor, sir, I prize;
To thee the silence of my speech replies;
For when the reason's dull, the mind de-
    pressed,
He best doth speak who keeps his silence
    best.
SIGISMUND. You must not leave me. Stay:
What! would you rob my senses of the ray
Your beauteous presence gave?
ROSAURA. That license, from your High-
    ness, I must crave.
SIGISMUND. The violent efforts that you
    make
Show that you do not ask the leave you take.
ROSAURA. I hope to take it, if it is not
    given.
SIGISMUND. You rouse my courtesy to
    rage, by Heaven! —
In me resistance, as it were, distils
A cruel poison that my patience kills.
ROSAURA. Then though that poison may
    be strong,
The source of fury, violence, and wrong,
Potent thy patience to subdue,
It dare not the respect to me that's due.
SIGISMUND. As if to show I may,
You take the terror of your charms away.

For I am but too prone
To attempt the impossible; I to-day have
    thrown
Out of this window one who said, like you,
I dare not do the thing I said I would do.
Now just to show I can,
I may throw out your honor, as the man.
    CLOTALDO [*aside*]. More obstinate doth
        he grow;
What course to take, O Heavens! I do not
    know,
When wild desire, nay, crime,
Perils my honor for the second time.
    ROSAURA. Not vainly, as I see,
This hapless land was warned thy tyranny
In fearful scandals would eventuate,
In wrath and wrong, in treachery, rage and
    hate.
But who in truth could claim
Aught from a man who is but a man in
    name,
Audacious, cruel, cold,
Inhuman, proud, tyrannical and bold,
'Mong beasts a wild beast born? —
    SIGISMUND. It was to save me from such
        words of scorn
So courteously I spoke,
Thinking to bind you by a gentler yoke;
But if I am in aught what you have said,
Then, as God lives, I will be all you dread.
Ho, there! here leave us. See to it at your
    cost,
The door be locked; let no one in.
        [*Exeunt* CLARIN *and the attendants.*]
    ROSAURA. I'm lost!
Consider . . .
    SIGISMUND. I'm a despot, and 't is vain
You strive to move me, or my will restrain.
    CLOTALDO [*aside*]. Oh, what a moment!
        what an agony!
I will go forth and stop him though I die.
        [*He advances.*]
My lord, consider, stay . . .
    SIGISMUND. A second time you dare to
        cross my way,
Old dotard: do you hold
My rage in such slight awe you are so
    bold?
What brought you hither? Speak!
    CLOTALDO. The accents of this voice,
        however weak,
To tell you to restrain

Your passions, if as King you wish to
   reign, —
Not to be cruel, though you deem
Yourself the lord of all, for all may be a
   dream.
SIGISMUND. You but provoke my rage
By these old saws, the unwelcome light of
   age,
In killing you, at least I'll see
If 't is a dream or truth.
      [*As he is about to draw his dagger*
      CLOTALDO *detains it, and throws*
      himself on his knees.]
CLOTALDO. Sole hope for me
To save my life is thus to humbly kneel.
SIGISMUND. Take your audacious hand
From off my steel.
CLOTALDO. Till some kind aid be sent,
Till some one come who may your rage
   prevent,
I will not loose my hold.
ROSAURA. Oh, Heaven!
SIGISMUND. I say,
Loose it, old dotard, grim and gaunt and
   gray,
Or by another death   [*They struggle.*]
I'll crush you in my arms while you have
   breath.
ROSAURA. Quick! quick! they slay
Clotaldo, help! oh, help!   [*Exit.*]

[ASTOLFO *enters at this moment, and* CLO-
   TALDO *falls at his feet; he stands be-*
   tween them.]

ASTOLFO. This strange affray,
What can it mean, magnanimous Prince?
   would you
So bright a blade imbrue
In blood that age already doth congeal?
Back to its sheath return the shining steel.
SIGISMUND. Yes, when it is bathed red
In his base blood.
ASTOLFO. This threatened life hath fled
For sanctuary to my feet;
I must protect it in that poor retreat.
SIGISMUND. Protect your own life, then,
   for in this way,
Striking at it, I will the grudge repay
I owe you for the past.
ASTOLFO. I thus defend
My life; but majesty will not offend.
      [ASTOLFO *draws his sword and they fight.*]

CLOTALDO. Oh! wound him not, my
   lord.

      [*Enter* BASILIUS, ESTRELLA *and*
      Attendants.]

BASILIUS. Swords flashing here! —
ESTRELLA [*aside*]. Astolfo is engaged: —
   Oh, pain severe!
BASILIUS. What caused this quarrel?
   Speak, say why?
ASTOLFO. 'T is nothing now, my lord,
   since thou art by.
SIGISMUND. 'T is much, although thou
   now art by, my lord.
I wished to kill this old man with my sword.
BASILIUS. Did you not then respect
These snow-white hairs?
CLOTALDO. My lord will recollect
They scarce deserved it, being mine.
SIGISMUND. Who dares
To ask of me do I respect white hairs?
Your own some day
My feet may trample in the public way,
For I have not as yet revenged my wrong,
Your treatment so unjust and my sad state
   so long.   [*Exit.*]
BASILIUS. But ere that dawn doth break,
You must return to sleep, where when you
   wake
All that hath happened here will seem —
As is the glory of the world — a dream.
      [*Exeunt the King,* CLOTALDO, *and*
      Attendants.]
ASTOLFO. Ah, how rarely fate doth lie
When it some misfortune threatens!
Dubious when 't is good that's promised,
When 't is evil, ah, too certain! —
What a good astrologer
Would he be, whose art foretelleth
Only cruel things; for, doubtless,
They would turn out true forever!
This in Sigismund and me
Is exemplified, Estrella,
Since between our separate fortunes
Such a difference is presented.
In his case had been foreseen
Murders, miseries, and excesses,
And in all they turned out true,
Since all happened as expected.
But in mine, here seeing, lady,
Rays so rare and so resplendent
That the sun is but their shadow.

And even heaven a faint resemblance,
When fate promised me good fortune,
Trophies, praises, and all blessings,
It spoke ill and it spoke well;
For it was of both oppressive,
When it held out hopes of favor,
But disdain alone effected.

ESTRELLA. Oh, I doubt not these fine speeches
Are quite true, although intended
Doubtless for that other lady,
She whose portrait was suspended
From your neck, when first, Astolfo,
At this Court here you addressed me.
This being so, 't is she alone
Who these compliments deserveth.
Go and pay them to herself,
For like bills that are protested
In the counting-house of love,
Are those flatteries and finesses
Which to other kings and ladies
Have been previously presented.

[*Enter* ROSAURA.]

ROSAURA [*aside*]. Well, thank God, my miseries
Have attained their lowest level,
Since by her who sees this sight
Nothing worse can be expected.

ASTOLFO. Then that portrait from my breast
Shall be taken, that thy perfect
Beauty there may reign instead.
For where bright Estrella enters
Shadow cannot be, or star
Where the sun; I go to fetch it. —
[*Aside.*] Pardon, beautiful Rosaura,
This offense; the absent never,
Man or woman, as this shows,
Faith or plighted vows remember. [*Exit.*]

[ROSAURA *comes forward.*]

ROSAURA [*aside*]. Not a single word I heard,
Being afraid they might observe me.

ESTRELLA. Oh, Astrea!

ROSAURA. My good lady!

ESTRELLA. Nothing could have pleased me better
Than your timely coming here.
I have something confidential
To entrust you with.

ROSAURA. You honor
Far too much my humble service.

ESTRELLA. Brief as is the time, Astrea,
I have known you, you already
Of my heart possess the keys.
'T is for this and your own merits
That I venture to entrust you
With what oft I have attempted
From myself to hide.

ROSAURA. Your slave!

ESTRELLA. Then concisely to express it,
Know, Astolfo, my first cousin
('T is enough that word to mention,
For some things may best be said
When not spoken but suggested),
Soon expects to wed with me,
If my fate so far relenteth,
As that by one single bliss
All past sorrows may be lessened.
I was troubled, the first day
That we met, to see suspended
From his neck a lady's portrait.
On the point I urged him gently,
He so courteous and polite
Went immediately to get it,
And will bring it here. From him
I should feel quite disconcerted
To receive it. You here stay,
And request him to present it
Unto you. I say no more.
You are beautiful and clever,
You must know too what is love. [*Exit.*]

ROSAURA. Would I knew it not! O help me
Now, kind Heaven! for who could be
So prudential, so collected,
As to know how best to act
In so painful a dilemma?
Is there in the world a being,
Is there one a more inclement
Heaven has marked with more misfortunes,
Has 'mid more of sorrow centered? —
What, bewildered, shall I do,
When 't is vain to be expected
That my reason can console me,
Or consoling be my helper?
From my earliest misfortune
Everything that I've attempted
Has been but one misery more —
Each the other's sad successor,

All inheritors of themselves.
Thus, the Phœnix they resemble,
One is from the other born,
New life springs where old life endeth,
And the young are warmly cradled
By the ashes of the elder.
Once a wise man called them cowards,
Seeing that misfortunes never
Have been seen to come alone.
But I call them brave, intrepid,
Who go straight unto their end,
And ne'er turn their backs in terror: —
By the man who brings them with him
Everything may be attempted,
Since he need on no occasion
Have the fear of being deserted.
I may say so, since at all times,
Whatsoever life presented,
I, without them, never saw me,
Nor will they grow weary ever,
Till they see me in death's arms,
Wounded by fate's final weapon.
Woe is me! but what to-day
Shall I do in this emergence? —
If I tell my name, Clotaldo,
Unto whom I am indebted
For my very life and honor,
May be with me much offended;
Since he said my reparation
Must in silence be expected.
If I tell not to Astolfo
Who I am, and he detects me
How can I dissemble then?
For although a feigned resemblance
Eyes and voice and tongue might try,
Ah, the truthful heart would tremble,
And expose the lie. But wherefore
Study what to do? 'T is certain
That however I may study,
Think beforehand how to nerve me,
When at last the occasion comes,
Then alone what grief suggesteth
I will do, for no one holds
In his power the heart's distresses.
And thus what to say or do
As my soul cannot determine,
Grief must only reach to-day
Its last limit, pain be ended,
And at last an exit make
From the doubts that so perplex me
How to act: but until then
Help me, Heaven, oh, deign to help me!

[*Enter* ASTOLFO, *with the portrait.*]

ASTOLFO. Here then is the portrait,
Princess:
But, good God!
ROSAURA. Your Highness trembles;
What has startled, what surprised you?
ASTOLFO. Thee, Rosaura, to see present.
ROSAURA. I Rosaura? Oh, Your High-
ness
Is deceived by some resemblance
Doubtless to some other lady;
I 'm Astrea, one who merits
Not the glory of producing
An emotion so excessive.
ASTOLFO. Ah, Rosaura, thou mayst
feign,
But the soul bears no deception,
And though seeing thee as Astrea,
As Rosaura it must serve thee.
ROSAURA. I, not knowing what Your
Highness
Speaks of, am of course prevented
From replying aught but this,
That Estrella (the bright Hesper
Of this sphere) was pleased to order
That I here should wait expectant
For that portrait, which to me
She desires you give at present:
For some reason she prefers
It through me should be presented —
So Estrella — say, my star —
Wishes — so a fate relentless
Wills — in things that bring me loss —
So Estrella now expecteth.
ASTOLFO. Though such efforts you at-
tempt,
Still how badly you dissemble,
My Rosaura! Tell the eyes
In their music to keep better
Concert with the voice, because
Any instrument whatever
Would be out of tune that sought
To combine and blend together
The true feelings of the heart
With the false words speech expresses.
ROSAURA. I wait only, as I said,
For the portrait.
ASTOLFO. Since you 're bent then
To the end to keep this tone,
I adopt it, and dissemble.
Tell the Princess, then, Astrea,

That I so esteem her message,
That to send to her a copy
Seems to me so slight a present,
How so highly it is valued
By myself, I think it better
To present the original,
And you easily may present it,
Since, in point of fact, you bring it
With you in your own sweet person.

ROSAURA. When it has been undertaken
By a man, bold, brave, determined,
To obtain a certain object,
Though he get perhaps a better,
Still not bringing back the first
He returns despised: I beg, then,
That Your Highness give the portrait;
I, without it, dare not venture.

ASTOLFO. How, then, if I do not give it
Will you get it?

ROSAURA. I will get it
Thus, ungrateful. [She attempts to snatch it.]

ASTOLFO. 'T is in vain.

ROSAURA. It must ne'er be seen, no,
never
In another woman's hands.

ASTOLFO. Thou art dreadful.

ROSAURA. Thou deceptive.

ASTOLFO. Oh, enough, Rosaura mine.

ROSAURA. Thine! Thou liest, base de-
serter. [Both struggle for the portrait.]

[Enter ESTRELLA.]

ESTRELLA. Prince! Astrea! What is
this?

ASTOLFO [aside]. Heavens! Estrella!

ROSAURA [aside]. Love befriend me;
Give me wit enough my portrait
To regain: — [To ESTRELLA.] If thou
would'st learn then
What the matter is, my lady,
I will tell thee.

ASTOLFO [aside to ROSAURA]. Would'st
o'erwhelm me?

ROSAURA. You commanded me to wait
here
For the Prince, and, representing
You, to get from him a portrait.
I remained alone, expecting,
And, as often by one thought
Is some other thought suggested,
Seeing that you spoke of portraits,
I, reminded thus, remembered

That I had one of myself
In my sleeve: I wished to inspect it,
For a person quite alone
Even by trifles is diverted.
From my hand I let it fall
On the ground; the Prince, who entered
With the other lady's portrait,
Raised up mine, but so rebellious
Was he to what you had asked him
That, instead of his presenting
One, he wished to keep the other.
Since he mine will not surrender
To my prayers and my entreaties:
Angry at this ill-timed jesting
I endeavored to regain it,
That which in his hand is held there
Is my portrait, if you see it;
You can judge of the resemblance.

ESTRELLA. Duke, at once, give up the
portrait. [She takes it from his hand.]

ASTOLFO. Princess . . .

ESTRELLA. Well, the tints were blended
By no cruel hand, methinks.

ROSAURA. Is it like me?

ESTRELLA. Like! 'T is perfect.

ROSAURA. Now demand from him the
other.

ESTRELLA. Take your own, and leave
our presence.

ROSAURA [aside]. I have got my portrait
back;
Come what may I am contented. [Exit.]

ESTRELLA. Give me now the other por-
trait;
For — although perhaps I never
May again address or see you —
I desire not, no, to let it
In your hands remain, if only
For my folly in requesting
You to give it.

ASTOLFO [aside]. How escape
From this singular dilemma? —
Though I wish, most beauteous Princess,
To obey thee and to serve thee,
Still I cannot give the portrait
Thou dost ask for, since . . .

ESTRELLA. A wretched
And false-hearted lover art thou.
Now I wish it not presented,
So to give thee no pretext
For reminding me that ever
I had asked it at thy hands. [Exit.]

ASTOLFO. Hear me! listen! wait! remember! —
God, what hast thou done, Rosaura?
Why, or wherefore, on what errand,
To destroy thyself and me
Hast thou Poland rashly entered?   [*Exit.*]

[SCENE II. *Prison of the Prince in the Tower.*]

[SIGISMUND, *as at the commencement, clothed in skins, chained, and lying on the ground;* CLOTALDO, *two Servants, and* CLARIN.]

CLOTALDO. Leave him here on the ground,
Where his day, — its pride being o'er, —
Finds its end too.
A SERVANT. As before
With the chain his feet are bound.
CLARIN. Never from that sleep profound
Wake, O Sigismund, or rise,
To behold with wondering eyes
All thy glorious life o'erthrown,
Like a shadow that hath flown,
Like a bright brief flame that dies!
CLOTALDO. One who can so wisely make
Such reflections on this case
Should have ample time and space,
Even for the Solon's sake,
To discuss it; [*to the Servant*] him you 'll take
To this cell here, and keep bound.
    [*Pointing to an adjoining room.*]
CLARIN. But why me?
CLOTALDO. Because 't is found
Safe, when clarions secrets know,
Clarions to lock up, that so
They may not have power to sound.
CLARIN. Did I, since you treat me thus,
Try to kill my father? No.
Did I from the window throw
That unlucky Icarus?
Is my drink somniferous?
Do I dream? Then why be pent?
CLOTALDO. 'T is a clarion's punishment.
CLARIN. Then a horn of low degree,
Yea, a cornet I will be,
A safe, silent instrument.
    [*They take him away, and* CLO-
    TALDO *remains alone.*]

[*Enter* BASILIUS, *disguised.*]

BASILIUS. Hark, Clotaldo!
CLOTALDO. My lord here?
Thus disguised, Your Majesty?
BASILIUS. Foolish curiosity
Leads me in this lowly gear
To find out, ah, me! with fear,
How the sudden change he bore.
CLOTALDO. There behold him as before
In his miserable state.
BASILIUS. Wretched Prince! unhappy fate!
Birth by baneful stars watched o'er! —
Go and wake him cautiously,
Now that strength and force lie chained
By the opiate he hath drained.
CLOTALDO. Muttering something restlessly,
See he lies.
BASILIUS. Let's listen; he
May some few clear words repeat.
SIGISMUND.   [*Speaking in his sleep.*]
Perfect Prince is he whose heat
Smites the tyrant where he stands,
Yes, Clotaldo dies by my hands,
Yes, my sire shall kiss my feet.
CLOTALDO. Death he threatens in his rage.
BASILIUS. Outrage vile he doth intend.
CLOTALDO. He my life has sworn to end.
BASILIUS. He has vowed to insult my age.
SIGISMUND [*still sleeping*]. On the mighty world's great stage,
'Mid the admiring nations' cheer,
Valor mine, that has no peer,
Enter thou: the slave so shunned
Now shall reign Prince Sigismund,
And his sire his wrath shall fear. —
    [*He awakes.*]
But, ah me! Where am I? Oh! —
BASILIUS. Me I must not let him see.
[*To* CLOTALDO.] Listening I close by will be,
What you have to do you know.
    [*He retires.*]
SIGISMUND. Can it possibly be so?
Is the truth not what it seemed?
Am I chained and unredeemed?
Art not thou my lifelong tomb,
Dark old tower? Yes! What a doom!
God! what wondrous things I've dreamed!

CLOTALDO. Now in this delusive play
Must my special part be taken: —
Is it not full time to waken?
SIGISMUND. Yes, to waken well it may.
CLOTALDO. Wilt thou sleep the livelong
day? —
Since we gazing from below
Saw the eagle sailing slow,
Soaring through the azure sphere,,
All the time thou waited here,
Didst thou never waken?
SIGISMUND. No,
Nor even now am I awake,
Since such thoughts my memory fill,
That it seems I'm dreaming still:
Nor is this a great mistake;
Since if dreams could phantoms make
Things of actual substance seen,
I things seen may phantoms deem.
Thus a double harvest reaping,
I can see when I am sleeping,
And when waking I can dream.
CLOTALDO. What you may have dreamed
of, say.
SIGISMUND. If I thought it only seemed,
I would tell not what I dreamed,
But what I behold, I may.
I awoke, and lo! I lay
(Cruel and delusive thing!)
In a bed whose covering,
Bright with blooms from rosy bowers,
Seemed a tapestry of flowers
Woven by the hand of Spring.
Then a crowd of nobles came,
Who addressed me by the name
Of their prince, presenting me
Gems and robes, on bended knee.
Calm soon left me, and my frame
Thrilled with joy to hear thee tell
Of the fate that me befell,
For though now in this dark den,
I was Prince of Poland then.
CLOTALDO. Doubtless you repaid me
well?
SIGISMUND. No, not well: for, calling thee
Traitor vile, in furious strife
Twice I strove to take thy life.
CLOTALDO. But why all this rage 'gainst
me?
SIGISMUND. I was master, and would be
Well revenged on foe and friend.
Love one woman could defend . . .

That, at least, for truth I deem,
All else ended like a dream,
That alone can never end.
[The King withdraws.]
CLOTALDO [aside]. From his place the
King hath gone,
Touched by his pathetic words: —
[Aloud.] Speaking of the king of birds
Soaring to ascend his throne,
Thou didst fancy one thine own;
But in dreams, however bright,
Thou shouldst still have kept in sight
How for years I tended thee,
For 't were well, whoe'er we be,
Even in dreams to do what's right. [Exit.]
SIGISMUND. That is true: then let's re-
strain
This wild rage, this fierce condition
Of the mind, this proud ambition,
Should we ever dream again:
And we'll do so, since 't is plain,
In this world's uncertain gleam,
That to live is but to dream:
Man dreams what he is, and wakes
Only when upon him breaks
Death's mysterious morning beam.
The king dreams he is a king,
And in this delusive way
Lives and rules with sovereign sway;
All the cheers that round him ring,
Born of air, on air take wing.
And in ashes (mournful fate!)
Death dissolves his pride and state:
Who would wish a crown to take,
Seeing that he must awake
In the dream beyond death's gate?
And the rich man dreams of gold,
Gilding cares it scarce conceals,
And the poor man dreams he feels
Want and misery and cold.
Dreams he too who rank would hold,
Dreams who bears toil's rough-ribbed
hands,
Dreams who wrong for wrong demands,
And in fine, throughout the earth,
All men dream, whate'er their birth,
And yet no one understands.
'T is a dream that I in sadness
Here am bound, the scorn of fate;
'T was a dream that once a state
I enjoyed of light and gladness.
What is life? 'T is but a madness.

What is life? A thing that seems,
A mirage that falsely gleams,
Phantom joy, delusive rest,
Since is life a dream at best,
And even dreams themselves are dreams.

[Exit.]

ACT III

[SCENE I. *Within the Tower.*]

CLARIN. In a strange enchanted tower,
I, for what I know, am prisoned;
How would ignorance be punished,
If for knowledge they would kill me?
What a thing to die of hunger,
For a man who loves good living!
I compassionate myself;
All will say: "I well believe it";
And it well may be believed,
Because silence is a virtue
Incompatible with my name
Clarin, which of course forbids it.
In this place my sole companions,
It may safely be predicted,
Are the spiders and the mice:
What a pleasant nest of linnets! —
Owing to this last night's dream,
My poor head I feel quite dizzy
From a thousand clarionets,
Shawms, and seraphines and cymbals,
Crucifixes and processions,
Flagellants who so well whipped them,
That as up and down they went,
Some even fainted as they witnessed
How the blood ran down the others.
I, if I the truth may whisper,
Simply fainted from not eating,
For I see me in this prison
All day wondering how this Poland
Such a *Hungary* look exhibits,
All night reading in the *Fasti*
By some half-starved poet written.
In the calendar of saints,
If a new one is admitted,
Then St. Secret be my patron,
For I fast upon his vigil;
Though it must be owned I suffer
Justly for the fault committed,
Since a servant to be silent
Is a sacrilege most sinful.

[A sound of drums and trumpets, with voices within.]

[*Soldiers and* CLARIN.]

FIRST SOLDIER [*within*]. He is here
within this tower.
Dash the door from off its hinges;
Enter all.
CLARIN. Good God! 't is certain
That 't is me they seek so briskly,
Since they say that I am here.
What can they require?
FIRST SOLDIER [*within*]. Go in there.

[*Several Soldiers enter.*]

SECOND SOLDIER. Here he is.
CLARIN. He's not.
ALL THE SOLDIERS. Great lord!
CLARIN [*aside*]. Are the fellows mad or
tipsy?
FIRST SOLDIER. Thou art our own
Prince, and we
Will not have, and won't admit of,
Any but our natural Prince;
We no foreign Prince here wish for.
Let us kneel and kiss thy feet.
THE SOLDIERS. Live, long live our best
of Princes!
CLARIN [*aside*]. 'Gad! the affair grows
rather serious.
Is it usual in this kingdom
To take some one out each day,
Make him Prince, and then remit him
To this tower? It must be so,
Since each day that sight I witness.
I must therefore play my part.
SOLDIERS. Thy feet give us!
CLARIN. I can't give them,
As I want them for myself.
For a prince to be a cripple
Would be rather a defect.
SECOND SOLDIER. We have all con-
veyed our wishes
To your father; we have told him
You alone shall be our Prince here,
Not the Duke.
CLARIN. And were you guilty
'Gainst my sire, of disrespect?
FIRST SOLDIER. 'T was the loyalty of
our spirit.
CLARIN. If 't was loyalty, I forgive you.
SECOND SOLDIER. Come, regain thy
lost dominion.
Long live Sigismund!

ALL. Live the Prince.
CLARIN [aside]. Say they Sigismund?
   Good. Admitted.
Sigismund must be the name
Given to all pretended princes.

[Enter SIGISMUND.]

SIGISMUND. Who has named here Sigis-
   mund?
CLARIN [aside]. Ah, I'm but an addled
   prince, then!
FIRST SOLDIER. Who is Sigismund?
SIGISMUND. Who? I.
SECOND SOLDIER [to CLARIN]. How,
   then, didst thou, bold and silly,
Dare to make thee Sigismund?
   CLARIN. I a Sigismund? Thou fib-
   best;
It was you yourselves that thus
Sigismundized me and princed me:
All the silliness and the boldness
Have been by yourselves committed.
   FIRST SOLDIER. Great and brave Prince
   Sigismund
(For thy bearing doth convince us
Thou art he, although on faith
We proclaim thee as our prince here).
King Basilius, thy father,
Fearful of the Heavens fulfilling
A prediction, which declared
He would see himself submitted
At thy victor feet, attempts
To deprive thee of thy birthright,
And to give it to Astolfo,
Muscovy's duke. For this his missives
Summoned all his court: the people
Understanding, by some instinct,
That they had a natural king,
Did not wish a foreign princeling
To rule o'er them. And 't is thus,
That the fate for thee predicted
Treating with a noble scorn,
They have sought thee where imprisoned
Thou dost live, that issuing forth,
By their powerful arms assisted,
From this tower, thy crown and scepter
Thou shouldst thus regain, and quit them
Of a stranger and a tyrant.
Forth! then; for among these cliffs here.
There is now a numerous army,
Formed of soldiers and banditti,
That invoke thee: freedom waits thee;

To the thousand voices listen.
[Voices within.] Long, long live Prince
   Sigismund!
SIGISMUND. Once again, O Heaven!
   wouldst wish me
Once again to dream of greatness
Which may vanish in an instant?
Once again to see the glories,
That a royal throne encircle,
Die in darkness and in gloom,
Like a flame the winds extinguish?
Once again by sad experience
To be taught the dangerous limits
Human power may overleap,
At its birth and while it liveth?
No, it must not, must not be: —
See me now once more submitted
To my fate: and since I know
Life is but a dream, a vision,
Hence, ye phantoms, that assume
To my darkened sense the figure
And the voice of life — although
Neither voice nor form is in them.
I no longer now desire
A feigned majesty, a fictitious
And fantastic pomp — illusions
Which the slightest breath that ripples
The calm ether can destroy,
Even as in the early spring-time,
When the flowering almond tree
Unadvisedly exhibits
All its fleeting bloom of flowers,
The first blast their freshness withers,
And the ornament and grace
Of its rosy locks disfigures.
Now I know ye — know ye all,
And I know the same false glimmer
Cheats the eyes of all who sleep.
Me false shows no more bewilder;
Disabused, I now know well
Life is but a dream — a vision.
   SECOND SOLDIER. If thou thinkest we
   deceive thee,
Turn thine eyes to those proud cliffs
   here,
See the crowds that wait there, willing,
Eager to obey thee.
   SIGISMUND. Yet
Just as clearly and distinctly,
I have seen another time
The same things that now I witness,
And 't was but a dream.

SECOND SOLDIER. At all times
Great events, my lord, bring with them
Their own omens; and thy dream
But the actual fact prefigured.
SIGISMUND. You say well, it was an
omen;
But supposing the bright vision
Even were true, since life is short,
Let us dream, my soul, a little,
Once again, remembering now
With all forethought and prevision
That we must once more awake
At the better time not distant;
That being known, the undeceiving,
When it comes, will be less bitter;
For it takes the sting from evil
To anticipate its visit.
And with this conviction, too,
Even its certainty admitting,
That all power being only lent
Must return unto the Giver,
Let us boldly then dare all. —
For the loyalty you exhibit,
Thanks, my lieges. See in me
One who will this land deliver
From a stranger's alien yoke.
Sound to arms; you soon shall witness
What my valor can effect.
'Gainst my father I have lifted
Hostile arms, to see if Heaven
Has of me the truth predicted.
At my feet I am to see him . . .
[Aside.] But if I, from dreams delivered,
Wake ere then, and nothing happens,
Silence now were more befitting.
ALL. Long live Sigismund, our king!

[Enter CLOTALDO.]

CLOTALDO. Ha! what tumult, heavens!
has risen?
SIGISMUND. Well, Clotaldo.
CLOTALDO. Sire . . . [Aside.] On me
Will his wrath now fall.
CLARIN [aside]. He'll fling him
Headlong down the steep, I'll bet. [Exit.]
CLOTALDO. At your royal feet sub-
mitted
I know how to die.
SIGISMUND. My father,
Rise, I pray, from that position,
Since to you, my guide and polestar,
Are my future acts committed;

All my past life owes you much
For your careful supervision.
Come, embrace me.
CLOTALDO. What do you say?
SIGISMUND. That I dream, and that my
wishes
Are to do what 's right, since we
Even in dreams should do what's fitting.
CLOTALDO. Then, my Prince, if you
adopt
Acting rightly as your symbol,
You will pardon me for asking,
So to act, that you permit me.
No advice and no assistance
Can I give against my king.
Better that my lord should kill me
At his feet here.
SIGISMUND. Oh, ungrateful!
Villain! wretch! [Aside.] But, Heavens!
't is fitter
I restrain myself, not knowing
But all this may be a vision. —
The fidelity I envy
Must be honored and admitted.
Go and serve your lord, the king.
Where the battle rages thickest
We shall meet. — To arms, my friends!
CLOTALDO. Thanks, most generous of
princes. [Exit.]
SIGISMUND. Fortune, we go forth to
reign;
Wake me not if this is vision,
Let me sleep not if 't is true.
But which ever of them is it,
To act right is what imports me.
If 't is true, because it is so;
If 't is not, that when I waken
Friends may welcome and forgive me.
[Exeunt all, drums beating.]

[SCENE II. Hall in the Royal Palace.]

[Enter BASILIUS and ASTOLFO.]

BASILIUS. Who can expect, Astolfo, to
restrain
An untamed steed that wildly turns to
flee?
Who can the current of a stream detain,
That swollen with pride sweeps down to
seek the sea?
Who can prevent from tumbling to the
plain

Some mighty peak the lightning's flash
sets free?
Yet each were easier in its separate way,
Than the rude mob's insensate rage to
stay.
The several bands that throng each green
retreat
This truth proclaim by their disparted
cries;
Astolfo here the echoing notes repeat,
While there 't is *Sigismund* that rends the
skies.
The place where late the land was glad to
greet
The choice we made, a second venture
tries;
And soon will be, as Horror o'er it leans,
The fatal theater of tragic scenes.

ASTOLFO. My lord, let all this joy sus-
pended be,
These plaudits cease, and to another day
Defer the rapture thou hast promised me;
For if this Poland (which I hope to sway)
Resists to-day my right of sovereignty,
'T is that by merit I should win my way.
Give me a steed; to stem this wild revolt
My pride shall be the flash that bears the
bolt. *[Exit.]*
BASILIUS. Slight help there is for what is
fixed by fate,
And much of danger to foresee the blow;
If it must fall, defense is then too late,
And he who most forestalls doth most fore-
know.
Hard law! Stern rule! Dire fact to con-
template!
That he who thinks to fly doth nearer go.
Thus by the very means that I employed,
My country and myself I have destroyed.

[Enter ESTRELLA.]

ESTRELLA. If, mighty lord, thy presence,
which it braves,
The tumult of the crowd cannot defeat —
The frenzy of the multitude that raves
In hostile bands through every square and
street, —
Thou 'lt see thy kingdom swim in crimson
waves,
A purple sea of blood shall round it beat;
For even already in its dismal doom
All is disaster, tragedy, and gloom.

Such is thy kingdom's ruin, so severe
The hard and bloody trial fate hath sent,
Dazed is the eye, and terrified the ear;
Dark grows the sun, and every wind is
spent;
Each stone a mournful obelisk doth rear,
And every flower erects a monument;
A grave seems every house, whence life is
gone, —
Each soldier is a living skeleton.

[Enter CLOTALDO.]

CLOTALDO. Thanks be to God, I reach
thy feet alive.
BASILIUS. What news of Sigismund,
Clotaldo, say?
CLOTALDO. The crowd, whom frenzy
and blind impulse drive,
Into the tower resistless burst their way,
Released the Prince, who seeing thus revive
The honor he had tasted for one day,
Looked brave, declaring, in a haughty tone,
The truth at last that Heaven must now
make known.
BASILIUS. Give me a horse! In person
forth I'll ride
To check the pride of this ungrateful son.
Where Science erred let now the sword
decide;
By my own valor shall my throne be won!
[Exit.]
ESTRELLA. Let me the glory of the fight
divide —
A twinkling star beside that royal sun —
Bellona matched with Mars: for I would
dare
To scale even heaven to rival Pallas there.
[Exit, and they sound to arms.]

[Enter ROSAURA, who detains CLOTALDO.]

ROSAURA. Though the trumpets from afar
Echo in thy valorous breast,
Hear me, list to my request,
For I know that all is war.
Well thou knowest that I came
Poor to Poland, sad, dejected;
And that graciously protected,
Thou thy pity let me claim.
It was thy command, ah, me!
I should live here thus disguised,
Striving, as thy words advised
(Hiding all my jealousy),

To avoid Astolfo's sight;
But he saw me, and though seeing,
With Estrella, he — false being! —
Converse holds this very night
In a garden bower. The key
I have taken, and will show
Where, by entering, with a blow
Thou canst end my misery.
Thus, then, daring, bold, and strong,
Thou my honor wilt restore;
Strike, and hesitate no more,
Let his death revenge my wrong.
  CLOTALDO. It is true, my inclination
Since thou first wert seen by me,
Was to strive and do for thee
(Be thy tears my attestation)
All my life could do to serve thee.
What I first was forced to press,
Was that thou should'st change thy
    dress;
Lest if chancing to observe thee
Masquerading like a page,
By appearances so strong
Led astray, the Duke might wrong
By a thought thy sex and age.
Meanwhile various projects held me
In suspense, oft pondering o'er
How thy honor to restore;
Though (thy honor so compelled me)
I Astolfo's life should take —
Wild design that soon took wing —
Yet, as he was not my king,
It no terror could awake.
I his death was seeking, when
Sigismund with vengeful aim
Sought for mine; Astolfo came,
And despising what most men
Would a desperate peril deem,
Stood in my defense; his bearing,
Nigh to rashness in its daring,
Showed a valor most extreme.
How then, think, could I, whose breath
Is his gift, in murderous strife,
For his giving me my life,
Strive in turn to give him death?
And thus, grateful, yet aggrieved,
By two opposite feelings driven,
Seeing it to thee have given,
And from him have it received,
Doubting this, and that believing,
Half revenging, half forgiving,
If to thee I'm drawn by giving,

I to him am by receiving;
Thus bewildered and beset,
Vainly seeks my love a way,
Since I have a debt to pay,
Where I must exact a debt.
  ROSAURA. It is settled, I believe,
As all men of spirit know,
That 't is glorious to bestow,
But a meanness to receive.
Well, admitting this to be,
Then thy thanks should not be his,
Even supposing that he is
One who gave thy life to thee;
As the gift of life was thine,
And from him the taking came,
In his case the act was shame,
And a glorious act in mine.
Thus by him thou art aggrieved,
And by me even complimented,
Since to me thou hast presented
What from him thou hast received:
Then all hesitation leaving,
Thou to guard my fame shouldst fly,
Since my honor is as high
As is giving to receiving.
  CLOTALDO. Though it seems a generous
    fever
In a noble heart to give,
Still an equal fire may live
In the heart of the receiver.
Heartlessness is something hateful,
I would boast a liberal name;
Thus I put my highest claim
In the fact of being grateful.
Then to me that title leave, —
Gentle birth breeds gentleness;
For the honor is no less
To bestow than to receive.
  ROSAURA. I received my life from
    thee,
But for thee I now were dead;
Still it was thyself that said
No insulted life could be
Called a life: on that I stand;
Nought have I received from thee,
For the life no life could be
That was given me by thy hand.
But if thou wouldst first be just
Ere being generous in this way
(As I heard thyself once say),
Thou wilt give me life I trust,
Which thou hast not yet; and thus

Giving will enhance thee more,
For if liberal before,
Thou wilt then be generous.
    CLOTALDO. Conquered by thy argument,
Liberal I first will be.
I, Rosaura, will to thee
All my property present;
In a convent live; by me
Has the plan been weighed some time,
For escaping from a crime
Thou wilt there find sanctuary;
For so many ills present them
Through the land on every side,
That being nobly born, my pride
Is to strive and not augment them.
By the choice that I have made,
Loyal to the land I'll be,
I am liberal with thee,
And Astolfo's debt is paid;
Choose then, nay, let honor, rather,
Choose for thee, and for us two,
For, by Heaven! I could not do
More for thee were I thy father! —
    ROSAURA. Were that supposition true,
I might strive and bear this blow;
But not being my father, no.
    CLOTALDO. What then dost thou mean
      to do?
    ROSAURA. Kill the Duke.
    CLOTALDO. A gentle dame,
Who no father's name doth know,
Can she so much valor show?
    ROSAURA. Yes.
    CLOTALDO. What drives thee on?
    ROSAURA. My fame.
    CLOTALDO. Think that in the Duke
      thou'lt see . . .
    ROSAURA. Honor all my wrath doth
      rouse.
    CLOTALDO. Soon thy king — Estrella's
      spouse.
    ROSAURA. No, by Heaven! it must not
      be.
    CLOTALDO. It is madness.
    ROSAURA. Yes, I see it.
    CLOTALDO. Conquer it.
    ROSAURA. I can't o'erthrow it.
    CLOTALDO. It will cost thee . . .
    ROSAURA. Yes, I know it.
    CLOTALDO. Life and honor.
    ROSAURA. Well, so be it.

    CLOTALDO. What wouldst have?
    ROSAURA. My death.
    CLOTALDO. Take care!
It is spite.
    ROSAURA. 'T is honor's cure.
    CLOTALDO. 'T is wild fire.
    ROSAURA. That will endure.
    CLOTALDO. It is frenzy.
    ROSAURA. Rage, despair.
    CLOTALDO. Can there then be nothing
      done
This blind rage to let pass by?
    ROSAURA. No.
    CLOTALDO. And who will help thee?
    ROSAURA. I.
    CLOTALDO. Is there then no remedy?
    ROSAURA. None.
    CLOTALDO. Think of other means
      whereby . . .
    ROSAURA. Other means would seal my
      fate.   [*Exit.*]
    CLOTALDO. If 't is so, then, daughter,
      wait,
For together we shall die.   [*Exit.*]

[SCENE III. *The Open Plain.*]

[*Enter* SIGISMUND, *clothed in skins: Soldiers
    marching.* CLARIN. *Drums are heard.*]

    SIGISMUND. If Rome could see me on
      this day
Amid the triumphs of its early sway,
Oh, with what strange delight
It would have seen so singular a sight,
Its mighty armies led
By one who was a savage wild beast bred,
Whose courage soars so high,
That even an easy conquest seems the
    sky!
But let us lower our flight,
My spirit; 't is not thus we should invite
This doubtful dream to stay,
Lest when I wake and it has past away,
I learn to my sad cost,
A moment given, 't was in a moment lost;
Determined not to abuse it,
The less will be my sorrow should I lose it.
               [*A trumpet sounds.*]
    CLARIN. Upon a rapid steed,
(Excuse my painting it; I can't indeed
Resist the inspiration),
Which seems a moving mass of all creation,

Its body being the earth,
The fire the soul that in its heart hath birth,
Its foam the sea, its panting breath the air,
Chaos confused at which I stand and stare,
Since in its soul, foam, body, breath, to
    me
It is a monster made of fire, earth, air, and
    sea;
Its color, dapple gray,
Speckled its skin, and flecked, as well it
    may,
By the impatient spur its flank that dyes,
For lo! it doth not run, the meteor flies;
As borne upon the wind,
A beauteous woman seeks thee.
    SIGISMUND. I'm struck blind!
    CLARIN. Good God, it is Rosaura, oh,
    the pain!   [Retires.]
    SIGISMUND. Heaven has restored her to
    my sight again.

[Enter ROSAURA, in a light corselet, with
    •   sword and dagger.]

    ROSAURA. Noble-hearted Sigismund!
Thou whose hidden light heroic
Issues from its night of shadows
To the great deeds of its morning;
And as heaven's sublimest planet
From the white arms of Aurora
Back restores their beauteous color
To the wild flowers and the roses,
And upon the seas and mountains,
When endiademed glory,
Scatters light, diffuses splendor,
Braids their foam, their hair makes golden;
Thus thou dawnest on the world
Bright auspicious sun of Poland,
Who will help a hapless woman,
She who at thy feet doth throw her,
Help her, since she is unhappy,
And a woman; two good motives
Quite enough to move a man
Who of valor so doth boast him,
Though even one would be sufficient,
Though even one would be all potent.
Thou hast seen me thrice already,
Thrice thou hast not truly known me,
For each time by different dresses
Was I strangely metamorphosed.
First I seemed to thee a man,
When within thy sad and somber
Cell thou sawest me, when thy life

Wiled from me mine own misfortunes.
As a woman next thou sawest me,
Where the splendors of thy throne-room
Vanished like a fleeting vision,
Vain, phantasmal and abortive.
The third time is now, when being
Something monstrous and abnormal,
In a woman's dress thou see'st me
With a warrior's arms adornéd.
And to pity and compassion
That thou may'st be moved more strongly,
Listen to the sad succession
Of my tragical misfortunes.
In the Court of Muscovy
I was born of a noble mother,
Who indeed must have been fair
Since unhappiness was her portion.
Fond and too persuading eyes
Fixed on her, a traitor lover,
Whom, not knowing, I don't name,
Though mine own worth hath informed me
What was his: for being his image,
I sometimes regret that fortune
Made me not a pagan born,
That I might, in my wild folly,
Think he must have been some god,
Such as he was, who in golden
Shower wooed Danae, or as swan
Leda loved, as bull, Europa.
When I thought to lengthen out,
Citing these perfidious stories,
My discourse, I find already
That I have succinctly told thee
How my mother, being persuaded
By the flatteries of love's homage,
Was as fair as any fair,
And unfortunate as all are.
That ridiculous excuse
Of a plighted husband's promise
So misled her, that even yet
The remembrance brings her sorrow.
For that traitor, that Æneas
Flying from his Troy, forgot there,
Or left after him his sword.
By this sheath its blade is covered,
But it shall be naked drawn
Ere this history is over.
From this loosely fastened knot
Which binds nothing, which ties nothing,
Call it marriage, call it crime,
Names its nature cannot alter,
I was born, a perfect image,

A true copy of my mother,
In her loveliness, ah, no!
In her miseries and misfortunes.
Therefore there is little need
To say how the hapless daughter,
Heiress of such scant good luck,
Had her own peculiar portion.
All that I will say to thee
Of myself is, that the robber
Of the trophies of my fame,
Of the sweet spoils of my honor,
Is Astolfo . . . Ah! to name him
Stirs and rouses up the choler
Of the heart, a fitting effort
When an enemy's name is spoken, —
Yes, Astolfo was that traitor,
Who, forgetful of his promise
(For when love has passed away,
Even its memory is forgotten),
Came to Poland, hither called.
From so sweet so proud a conquest,
To be married to Estrella,
Of my setting sun the torch-light.
Who'll believe that when one star
Oft unites two happy lovers,
Now one star, Estrella, comes
Two to tear from one another?
I offended, I deceived,
Sad remained, remained astonished,
Mad, half dead, remained myself;
That's to say, in so much torment,
That my heart was like a Babel
Of confusion, hell, and horror:
I resolving to be mute
(For there are some pains and sorrows
That by feelings are expressed,
Better than when words are spoken),
I by silence spoke my pain,
Till one day being with my mother
Violante, she (oh, Heavens!)
Burst their prison; like a torrent
Forth they rushed from out my breast,
Streaming wildly o'er each other.
No embarrassment it gave me
To relate them, for the knowing
That the person we confide to
A like weakness must acknowledge
Gives as 't were to our confusion
A sweet soothing and a solace,
For at times a bad example
Has its use. In fine, my sorrows
She with pity heard, relating

Even her own grief to console me:
When he has himself been guilty
With what ease the judge condoneth!
Knowing from her own experience
That 't was idle, to slow-moving
Leisure, to swift-fleeting time,
To intrust one's injured honor.
She could not advise me better,
As the cure of my misfortunes,
Than to follow and compel him
By prodigious acts of boldness
To repay my honor's debt:
And that such attempt might cost me
Less, my fortune wished that I
Should a man's strange dress put on me.
She took down an ancient sword,
Which is this I bear: the moment
Now draws nigh I must unsheath it,
Since to her I gave that promise,
When confiding in its marks,
Thus she said, "Depart to Poland,
And so manage that this steel
Shall be seen by the chief nobles
Of that land, for I have hope
That there may be one among them
Who may prove to thee a friend,
An adviser and consoler."
Well, in Poland I arrived;
It is useless to inform thee
What thou knowest already, how
A wild steed resistless bore me
To thy caverned tower, wherein
Thou with wonder didst behold me.
Let us pass, too, how Clotaldo
Passionately my cause supported,
How he asked my life of the King,
Who to him that boon accorded;
How discovering who I am
He persuaded me my proper
Dress to assume, and on Estrella
To attend as maid of honor,
So to thwart Astolfo's love
And prevent the marriage contract.
Let us, too, pass by, that here
Thou didst once again behold me
In a woman's dress, my form
Waking thus a twofold wonder,
And approach the time, Clotaldo
Being convinced it was important
That should wed and reign together
Fair Estrella and Astolfo,
'Gainst my honor, me advised

To forego my rightful project.
But, O valiant Sigismund,
Seeing that the moment cometh
For thy vengeance, since Heaven wishes
Thee to-day to burst the portals
Of thy narrow rustic cell,
Where so long immured, thy body
Was to feeling a wild beast,
Was to sufferance what the rock is,
And that 'gainst thy sire and country
Thou hast gallantly revolted,
And ta'en arms, I come to assist thee,
Intermingling the bright corselet
Of Minerva with the trappings
Of Diana, thus enrobing
Silken stuff and shining steel
In a rare but rich adornment.
On, then, on, undaunted champion!
To us both it is important
To prevent and bring to nought
This engagement and betrothal;
First to me, that he, my husband,
Should not falsely wed another,
Then to thee, that their two staffs
Being united, their jointed forces
Should with overwhelming power
Leave our doubtful victory hopeless.
Woman, I come here to urge thee
To repair my injured honor,
And as man I come to rouse thee
Crown and scepter to recover.
Woman I would wake thy pity
Since here at thy feet I throw me,
And as man, my sword and person
In thy service I devote thee.
But remember, if to-day
As a woman thou should'st court me,
I, as man, will give thee death
In the laudable upholding,
Of my honor, since I am
In this strife of love, this contest,
Woman my complaints to tell thee,
And a man to guard my honor.
　　SIGISMUND [aside]. Heavens! if it is true
　　　I dream,
Memory then suspend thy office,
For 't is vain to hope remembrance
Could retain so many objects.
Help me, God! or teach me how
All these numerous doubts to conquer,
Or to cease to think of any! —
Whoe'er tried such painful problems?

If 't was but a dream, my grandeur,
How then is it, at this moment,
That this woman can refer me
To some facts that are notorious?
Then 't was truth, and not a dream;
But if it was truth (another
And no less confusion), how
Can my life be called in proper
Speech a dream? So like to dreams
Are then all the world's chief glories,
That the true are oft rejected
As the false, the false too often
Are mistaken for the true?
Is there then 'twixt one and the other
Such slight difference, that a question
May arise at any moment
Which is true or which is false?
Are the original and the copy
So alike, that which is which
Oft the doubtful mind must ponder?
If 't is so, and if must vanish,
As the shades of night at morning,
All of majesty and power,
All of grandeur and of glory,
Let us learn at least to turn
To our profit the brief moment
That is given us, since our joy
Lasteth while our dream lasts only.
In my power Rosaura stands,
Thou, my heart, her charms adoreth,
Let us seize then the occasion;
Let love trample in its boldness
All the laws on which relying
She here at my feet has thrown her.
'T is a dream; and since 't is so,
Let us dream of joys, the sorrows
Will come soon enough hereafter.
But with mine own words just spoken,
Let me now confute myself!
If it is a dream that mocks me,
Who for human vanities
Would forego celestial glory?
What past bliss is not a dream?
Who has had his happy fortunes
Who hath said not to himself
As his memory ran o'er them,
"All I saw, beyond a doubt
Was a dream." If this exposeth
My delusion, if I know
That desire is but the glowing
Of a flame that turns to ashes
At the softest wind that bloweth;

Let us seek then the eternal,
The true fame that ne'er reposeth,
Where the bliss is not a dream,
Nor the crown a fleeting glory.
Without honor is Rosaura.
But it is a prince's province
To give honor, not to take it:
Then, by Heaven! it is her honor
That for her I must win back,
Ere this kingdom I can conquer.
Let us fly then this temptation.
'T is too strong: [*To the Soldiers.*] To
    arms! March onward!
For to-day I must give battle,
Ere descending night, the golden
Sunbeams of expiring day
Buries in the dark green ocean.
ROSAURA. Dost thou thus, my lord,
    withdraw thee?
What! without a word being spoken?
Does my pain deserve no pity?
Does my grief so little move thee?
Can it be, my lord, thou wilt not
Deign to hear, to look upon me?
Dost thou even avert thy face?
SIGISMUND. Ah, Rosaura, 't is thy
    honor
That requires this harshness now,
If my pity I would show thee.
Yes, my voice does not respond,
'T is my honor that respondeth;
True I speak not, for I wish
That my actions should speak for me;
Thee I do not look on, no,
For, alas! it is of moment,
That he must not see thy beauty
Who is pledged to see thy honor.
    [*Exit, followed by the Soldiers.*]
ROSAURA. What enigmas, O ye skies!
After many a sigh and tear,
Thus in doubt to leave me here
With equivocal replies!
CLARIN. Madam, is it visiting hour?
ROSAURA. Welcome, Clarin, where have
    you been?
CLARIN. Only four stout walls between
In an old enchanted tower;
Death was on the cards for me,
But amid the sudden strife
Ere the last trump came, my life
Won the trick and I got free.
I ne'er hoped to sound again.

ROSAURA. Why?
CLARIN. Because alone I know
Who you are: and this being so,
Learn, Clotaldo is . . . This strain
Puts me out.   [*Drums are heard.*]
ROSAURA. What can it be?
CLARIN. From the citadel at hand,
Leaguered round, an armed band
As to certain victory
Sallies forth with flags unfurled.
ROSAURA. 'Gainst Prince Sigismund!
    and I,
Coward that I am, not by
To surprise and awe the world,
When with so much cruelty
Each on each the two hosts spring! [*Exit.*]
VOICES OF SOME. Live, long live our vic-
    tor King!
VOICES OF OTHERS. Live, long live our
    liberty!
CLARIN. Live, long live the two, I say!
Me it matters not a pin,
Which doth lose or which doth win,
If I can keep out of the way! —
So aside here I will go,
Acting like a prudent hero,
Even as the Emperor Nero
Took things coolly long ago.
Or if care I cannot shun,
Let it 'bout mine ownself be;
Yes, here hidden I can see
All the fighting and the fun;
What a cozy place I spy
Mid the rocks there! so secure,
Death can't find me out I'm sure,
Then a fig for death I say!
    [*Conceals himself, drums beat and
    the sound of arms is heard.*]

[*Enter* BASILIUS, CLOTALDO, *and* ASTOLFO,
    flying.]

BASILIUS. Hapless king! disastrous
    reign!
Outraged father! guilty son!
CLOTALDO. See thy vanquished forces
    run
In a panic o'er the plain!
ASTOLFO. And the rebel conqueror's
    stay,
Proud, defiant.
BASILIUS. 'T is decreed
Those are loyal who succeed,

Rebels those who lose the day.
Let us then, Clotaldo, flee,
Since the victory he hath won,
From a proud and cruel son.
[*Shots are fired within, and* CLARIN
*falls wounded from his hiding-
place.*]
CLARIN. Heaven protect me!
ASTOLFO. Who can be
This last victim of the fight,
Who struck down in the retreat,
Falls here bleeding at our feet?
CLARIN. I am an unlucky wight,
Who to shun Death's fearful face
Found the thing I would forget:
Flying from him, him I've met.
For there is no secret place
Hid from death; and therefore I
This conclusion hold as clear,
He 'scapes best who goes more near,
He dies first who first doth fly.
Then return, return and be
In the bloody conflict lost;
Where the battle rages most,
There is more security
Than in hills how desolate,
Since no safety can there be
'Gainst the force of destiny,
And the inclemency of fate;
Therefore 't is in vain thou flyest
From the death thou draw'st more nigh,
Oh, take heed for thou must die
If it is God's will thou diest! [*Falls within.*]
BASILIUS. Oh, take heed for thou must
die
If it is God's will thou diest! —
With what eloquence, O Heaven!
Does this body that here lieth,
Through the red mouth of a wound
To profoundest thoughts entice us
From our ignorance and our error!
The red current as it glideth
Is a bloody tongue that teaches
All man's diligence is idle,
When against a greater power,
And a higher cause it striveth.
Thus with me, 'gainst strife and murder
When I thought I had provided,
I but brought upon my country
All the ills I would have hindered.
CLOTALDO. Though, my lord, fate know-
eth well

Every path, and quickly findeth
Whom it seeks; yet still it strikes me
'T is not Christian-like to say
'Gainst its rage that nought suffices.
That is wrong, a prudent man
Even o'er fate victorious rises;
And if thou art not preserved
From the ills that have surprised thee,
From worse ills thyself preserve.
ASTOLFO. Sire, Clotaldo doth address
thee
As a cautious, prudent man,
Whose experience time hath ripened.
I as a bold youth would speak:
Yonder, having lost its rider,
I behold a noble steed
Wandering reinless and unbridled,
Mount and fly with him while I
Guard the open path behind thee.
BASILIUS. If it is God's will I die,
Or if Death for me here lieth
As in ambush, face to face
I will meet it and defy it.

[*Enter* SIGISMUND, ESTRELLA, ROSAURA,
Soldiers and Attendants.]

A SOLDIER. 'Mid the thickets of the
mountain,
'Neath these dark boughs so united,
The King hides.
SIGISMUND. Pursue him then,
Leave no single shrub unrifled,
Nothing must escape your search,
Not a plant, and not a pine tree.
CLOTALDO. Fly, my lord!
BASILIUS. And wherefore fly?
ASTOLFO. Come!
BASILIUS. Astolfo, I'm decided.
CLOTALDO. What to do?
BASILIUS. To try, Clotaldo,
One sole remedy that surviveth.
[*To* SIGISMUND.] If 't is me thou'rt seek-
ing, Prince,
At thy feet behold me lying.   [*Kneeling.*]
Let thy carpet be these hairs
Which the snows of age have whitened.
Tread upon my neck, and trample
On my crown; in base defilement
Treat me with all disrespect;
Let thy deadliest vengeance strike me
Through my honor; as thy slave
Make me serve thee, and in spite of

All precautions let fate be,
Let Heaven keep the word it plighted.
　SIGISMUND. Princes of the Court of Po-
　　land,
Who such numerous surprises
Have astonished seen, attend,
For it is your prince invites ye.
That which heaven has once determined,
That which God's eternal finger
Has upon the azure tablets
Of the sky sublimely written,
Those transparent sheets of sapphire
Superscribed with golden ciphers
Ne'er deceive, and never lie;
The deceiver and the liar
Is he who to use them badly
In a wrongful sense defines them.
Thus, my father, who is present,
To protect him from the wildness
Of my nature, made of me
A fierce brute, a human wild beast;
So that I, who from my birth,
From the noble blood that trickles
Through my veins, my generous nature,
And my liberal condition,
Might have proved a docile child,
And so grew, it was sufficient
By so strange an education,
By so wild a course of living,
To have made my manners wild; —
What a method to refine them!
If to any man 't was said,
"It is fated that some wild beast
Will destroy you," would it be
Wise to wake a sleeping tiger
As the remedy of the ill?
If 't were said, "This sword here hidden
In its sheath, which thou dost wear,
Is the one foredoomed to kill thee,"
Vain precaution it would be
To preserve the threatened victim.
Bare to point it at his breast.
If 't were said, "These waves that ripple
Calmly here for thee will build
Foam-white sepulchers of silver,"
Wrong it were to trust the sea
When its haughty breast is lifted
Into mountain heights of snow,
Into hills of curling crystal.
Well, this very thing has happened
Unto him, who feared a wild beast,
And awoke him while he slept;

Or who drew a sharp sword hidden
Naked forth, or dared the sea
When 't was roused by raging whirlwinds.
And though my fierce nature (hear me)
Was as 't were the sleeping tiger,
A sheathed sword my innate rage,
And my wrath a quiet ripple,
Fate should not be forced by means
So unjust and so vindictive,
For they but excite it more;
And thus he who would be victor
O'er his fortune, must succeed
By wise prudence and self-strictness.
Not before an evil cometh
Can it rightly be resisted
Even by him who hath foreseen it,
For although (the fact's admitted)
By an humble resignation
It is possible to diminish
Its effects, it first must happen,
And by no means can be hindered.
Let it serve as an example
This strange sight, this most surprising
Spectacle, this fear, this horror,
This great prodigy; for none higher
E'er was worked than this we see,
After years of vain contriving,
Prostrate at my feet a father,
And a mighty king submitted.
This the sentence of high Heaven
Which he did his best to hinder
He could not prevent. Can I,
Who in valor and in science,
Who in years am so inferior,
It avert? [To the King.] My lord, forgive
　me,
Rise, sir, let me clasp thy hand;
For since Heaven has now apprized thee
That thy mode of counteracting
Its decree was wrong, a willing
Sacrifice to thy revenge
Let my prostrate neck be given.
　BASILIUS. Son, this noble act of thine
In my heart of hearts reviveth
All my love, thou 'rt there reborn.
Thou art Prince; the bay that bindeth
Heroes' brows, the palm, be thine,
Let the crown thine own deeds give thee.
　ALL. Long live Sigismund our King!
　SIGISMUND. Though my sword must
　　wait a little
Ere great victories it can gain,

I to-day will win the highest,
The most glorious, o'er myself. —
Give, Astolfo, give your plighted
Hand here to Rosaura, since
It is due and I require it.
ASTOLFO. Though 't is true I owe the debt,
Still 't is needful to consider
That she knows not who she is;
It were infamous, a stigma
On my name to wed a woman . . .
CLOTALDO. Stay, Astolfo, do not finish;
For Rosaura is as noble
As yourself. My sword will right her
In the field against the world:
She's my daughter, that's sufficient.
ASTOLFFO. What do you say?
CLOTALDO. Until I saw her
To a noble spouse united,
I her birth would not reveal.
It were now a long recital,
But the sum is, she's my child.
ASTOLFO. That being so, the word I've plighted
I will keep.
SIGISMUND. And that Estrella
May not now be left afflicted,
Seeing she has lost a prince
Of such valor and distinction,
I propose from mine own hand
As a husband one to give her,
Who, if he does not exceed
Him in worth, perhaps may rival,
Give to me thy hand.
ESTRELLA. I gain
By an honor so distinguished.
SIGISMUND. To Clotaldo, who so truly

Served my father, I can give him
But these open arms wherein
He will find whate'er he wishes.
A SOLDIER. If thou honorest those who serve thee,
Thus, to me the first beginner
Of the tumult through the land,
Who from out the tower, thy prison,
Drew thee forth, what wilt thou give?
SIGISMUND. Just that tower: and that you issue
Never from it until death,
I will have you guarded strictly;
For the traitor is not needed
Once the treason is committed.
BASILIUS. So much wisdom makes one wonder.
ASTOLFO. What a change in his condition!
ROSAURA. How discreet! how calm! how prudent!
SIGISMUND. Why this wonder, these surprises,
If my teacher was a dream,
And amid my new aspirings
I am fearful I may wake,
And once more a prisoner find me
In my cell? But should I not,
Even to dream it is sufficient:
For I thus have come to know
That at last all human blisses
Pass and vanish as a dream,
And the time that may be given me
I henceforth would turn to gain:
Asking for our faults forgiveness,
Since to generous, noble hearts
It is natural to forgive them.

THE CID

By PIERRE CORNEILLE

Translated into English blank verse by FLORENCE KENDRICK COOPER

CHARACTERS

FERNAND, *first King of Castile*

URRAQUE, *Infanta of Castile*

DIÈGUE, *father of Roderick*

GOMEZ, *Count of Gormaz, father of Chimène*

RODERICK, *lover of Chimène*

SANCHO, *enamored of Chimène*

ARIAS,
ALONSO, } *Castilian gentlemen*

CHIMÈNE, *daughter of the Count of Gormaz*

LEONORA, *governess of the Infanta*

ELVIRE, *governess of Chimène*

A Page of the Infanta

The Scene is at Seville

THE CID

ACT I

[*Enter* CHIMÈNE *and* ELVIRE.]

CHIMÈNE. Tell me, Elvire, is this a true
report?
In naught dost thou disguise my father's
words?
ELVIRE. My heart thrills with delight
when I recall them.
Your love for Roderick vies with his es-
teem;
Unless I read amiss his inmost soul,
He will command that you return his love.
CHIMÈNE. Repeat, I pray, a second time
the cause
Why thou dost think that he approves my
choice;
What hope he gives me, let me learn anew;
Such welcome news I could forever hear.
Thou canst not with too sure a promise
pledge
The sunlight of his sanction to our love.
What utterance gave he on the secret plot
That Roderick and Sancho made with thee?
Hast thou not made too clear the differ-
ences
Which draw me to my chosen Roderick's
side?
ELVIRE. No, an indifferent heart I pic-
tured yours,
That kindles not, nor blights, the hope of
either,
And, not too stern, nor yet too soft, but
waits
Your father's wish in choosing you a hus-
band.
This filial spirit charmed him, as his lips
And every feature quick assurance gave.
And since your heart demands his very
words
Repeated o'er and o'er — why, here they
are:
"Wisely she waits my choice; they both are
worthy,
Of noble blood, of faithful, valiant soul.

Their youthful faces speak the unbroken
line
Of shining virtues handed proudly down.
In Roderick's glance no slightest trace I see
Of aught but courage high and stainless
honor.
Cradled amid war's trophies was this son,
So many warriors has his house produced.
A marvelous tale of valor and emprise,
His father's glorious acts have long been
told;
And the seamed brow that tells the flight of
years
Speaks clearer still his mighty deeds in arms.
The son will prove fully worthy of the sire;
'T would please me should he win my
daughter's love."
Then to the council-chamber did he haste,
Whose pressing hour an interruption made;
But from his hurried words I think 't is
clear
He leans not strongly to the suit of either.
The king must choose a tutor for his son,
And this high service to your father gives;
The choice is certain, and his valor rare
Admits no fear of question or dispute;
His unmatched gifts ne'er meet a rival
claim,
Whether in royal court or honor's field.
And since your Roderick has his father's
word
To press the marriage, at the council's close,
Your heart may well assure you of his plea,
And in a tender hope will rest content.
CHIMÈNE. My troubled heart in hope
finds little ease,
But, burdened with sad doubt, asks cer-
tainty:
Fate in a moment can reverse her will;
Even this happiness may mean a sorrow.
ELVIRE. Nay, happily that fear shall be
dispelled.
CHIMÈNE. Away! — to wait the issue,
what it be.

[*Exeunt* CHIMÈNE *and* ELVIRE.]

[Enter the INFANTA, LEONORA, *and Page.]*

INFANTA. Page, quickly tell Chimène
    she stays too long
Before her promised coming; my affection
Complains that she neglects the heart that
    loves her.   *[Exit Page.]*
LEONORA. Madam, some longing burns
    within your soul,
For at each meeting anxiously you seek
The daily progress of her lover's suit.
INFANTA. Have I not reason? Her young
    heart is pierced
By darts myself did level at her breast.
Her lover Roderick was my lover first,
And 't is to me she owes his passion deep;
Thus having forged these lovers' lasting
    chains,
I yearn to see the end of all their pains.
LEONORA. Madam, their dear delight in
    mutual love
Finds, as I read your heart, no echo there.
But sorrow weighs your spirit at their
    hopes.
Can your great soul feel grief at others' joy?
Why should your love for them react in
    pain,
And cause you suffering in their hour of
    rapture?
But, pardon, madam, I am overbold.
INFANTA. Concealment deepens sorrow,
    therefore hear
What struggles my too-loving heart has
    borne;
Listen what fierce assault my courage
    braves.
The tyrant Love spares neither high nor
    low; ·
This cavalier whose heart I've given away
I love!
LEONORA. You love him!
INFANTA. Feel my bounding pulse!
Mark what its conqueror's name alone can
    do;
It knows its master.
LEONORA. Madam, pardon me,
I would not fail in gentle courtesy,
And rudely censure you for this affection.
But for a royal princess so to stoop
As to admit a simple cavalier
Within her heart — what would your
    father say?

What all Castile? Yours is the blood of
    kings!
Have you remembered that?
INFANTA. So well, alas!
That I would ope these veins ere I would
    prove
False to the sacred trust of rank and name.
In noble souls, 't is true, worth, worth alone
Should kindle love's bright fires; and did I
    choose
To justify my passion, many a one
As high-born as myself could give me cause.
But honor heeds not Love's excuses fond,
And sense, surprised, makes not my cour-
    age less.
The daughter of a king must mate with
    kings;
No other hand than kingly sues for mine.
To save my heart from well-nigh fatal
    stroke,
With mine own hand I turned the steel
    away.
I drew the bond that binds him to Chimène,
And tuned their notes to love to still my
    own.
No longer wonder that my harassed soul,
With restless haste, will urge their nuptials
    on.
Love lives on hope, and dies when hope is
    dead —
A flame that needs perpetual renewal.
My heart has suffered much; but if this tie
Be consummated with no long delay,
My hope is dead, my wounded spirit healed.
But till that hour I'm rent with varying
    pangs;
I will to lose, yet suffer in my loss;
The love I would resign I still would keep;
And thus the court that to Chimène he pays
Excites the secret pain I cannot hide.
Love moves my sighs for one whose rank I
    scorn.
My mind divided feels a double pang;
My will is strong; my heart is all aflame.
I dare not hope from their united lives
More than a mingled sense of joy and pain.
Honor and Love war on this fatal field;
Neither can wholly conquer, neither yield.
LEONORA. Madam, I blame not, but I
    pity you,
And have no word to utter, save that I
Sigh with your sighs and suffer in your grief.

But since your royal heart, unstained and
strong,
Can front an ill so tempting and so sharp,
And bear it down, your noble spirit soon
Will know again its sweet serenity.
Time is the friend of Virtue; with its aid
You will forget; and Heaven, whose God is
just,
Will not forsake you in this trying hour.

INFANTA. My surest hope is hope's own
swift defeat.

[*Enter Page.*]

PAGE. Chimène awaits Your Highness
at your wish.

INFANTA [*to Leonora*]. Go, entertain her
in the gallery.

LEONORA. Here, brooding o'er your sorrow, will you stay?

INFANTA. No, I but wish to hide my grief
from her,
And to assume a joy I scarce can feel;
I follow soon.

INFANTA [*alone*]. Just Heaven, whence I
must hope alone for aid,
Put to this bitter suffering an end;
Grant me repose; in honor's path be guide;
In others' bliss my own I fain would seek.
Three hearts are waiting for this marriage
bond;
Oh, hasten it, or strengthen my weak soul!
The tie that makes these happy lovers one
Will break my fetters and my anguish end.
But I am lingering; I will seek Chimène;
Her gentle presence will assuage my pain.
[*Exit* INFANTA.]

[*Enter the* COUNT *and* DIÈGUE.]

COUNT. At last you win the prize; the
royal hand
Uplifts you to a place where I should stand.
You are to train the young prince of Castile.

DIÈGUE. His justice and his gratitude
the king
Has blended in this honor to my house.

COUNT. Kings, howsoever great they
be, are men,
And, like us all, they ofttimes strangely err;
All courtiers may, in this, a warning see
That present service meets but poor re-
ward.

DIÈGUE. No longer let us speak upon a
theme
So chafing to your spirit; kindness may
Have turned the balance quite as much as
merit.
But to a king whose power is absolute
'T is due to take, nor question, what he
wills.
An added honor I would ask of you —
The union of our houses and our names.
You have a daughter, I an only son,
Their marriage would forever make us one
In more than friendship's bonds; this favor
grant.

COUNT. To such alliance does this youth
presume?
Will the new splendor of your office serve
To puff his mind with swelling vanity?
Use your new dignity, direct the prince,
Instruct him how a province should be
ruled
So all his subjects tremble 'neath his laws,
And love and terror make his throne secure;
To civic duties add a soldier's life —
To laugh at hardship, ply the trade of Mars
Undaunted and unequaled; pass long days
And nights on horseback; to sleep fully
armed;
To force a stronghold, and, the battle won,
To owe the glory to himself alone.
Instruct him by example; his young eyes
Must in yourself his perfect pattern see.

DIÈGUE. Your envious soul speaks in
your sneering words;
But, for example, he need only turn
The pages of my life; therein he 'll read,
Through a long story of heroic acts,
How to subdue the nations, storm a fort,
Command an army, and to make a name
Whose wide renown shall rest on mighty
deeds.

COUNT. Living examples are the only
guides;
Not from a book a prince his lesson learns.
Your boasted years a single day of mine
Equals not only, but surpasses oft.
Valiant you have been; I am valiant now!
On my strong arm this kingdom rests se-
cure;
When my sword flashes, Aragon retreats,
Granada trembles; by my name of might
Castile is girdled round as by a wall.

Without me you would pass 'neath other
laws,
And soon you'd have your enemies your
kings.
Each day, each flying hour, exalts my fame,
Adds victory unto victory, praise to praise.
Under the guarding shadow of my arm
The prince should prove his mettle on the
field,
Should learn by seeing conquest how to
conquer.
In his young princehood he should early win
The loftiest heights of courage; he should
see —

DIÈGUE. I know! you serve the king,
your master, well;
'Neath my command I've often watched
you fight;
And since the stiffening currents of old age
Have chilled my powers, your prowess
nobly shows —
No more; what I have been, you are to-day.
'T is true, however, that when choice is due,
Our monarch sees a difference 'twixt us still.

COUNT. Nay! you have stolen what was
mine by right!

DIÈGUE. To win an honor is the proof of
merit.

COUNT. He is most worthy who can use
it best.

DIÈGUE. To be refused it is poor proof
of worth.

COUNT. You've used a courtier's wiles,
and won by trick!

DIÈGUE. My fame has been my only par-
tisan.

COUNT. Admit the king but honors your
old age.

DIÈGUE. My years the king but measures by my deeds.

COUNT. If deeds are years, I'm elder far
than you!

DIÈGUE. Who not obtained this honor
not deserved it.

COUNT. I not deserved it? I?

DIÈGUE. Yes, you!

COUNT. Old man,
Thine insolence shall have its due reward.
[Gives him a blow.]

DIÈGUE [drawing his sword]. Quick, run
me through! — the first of all my race
To wear a flush of shame upon my brow.

COUNT. What dost thou hope thine im-
potence can do?

DIÈGUE. O God! my worn-out strength
at need forsakes me.

COUNT. Thy sword is mine, but thou
wouldst be too vain
If I should take this trophy of thy fall.
Adieu! Go read the prince, in spite of
sneers,
For his instruction, thy life's history.
This chastisement of insolent discourse
Will prove, methinks, no slight embellish-
ment.   [Exit COUNT.]

DIÈGUE. Rage and despair! age, my
worst enemy!
Must my great life end with a foul disgrace?
Shall laurels gained with slowly whitening
locks,
In years of warlike toils, fade in a day?
And does the arm all Spain has wondered
at,
Whose might has often saved the king his
throne,
And kept the rod of empire in his grasp,
Betray me now, and leave me unavenged?
O sad remembrance of my vanished glory!
O years of life undone in one short hour!
This new-won height is fatal to my fortune,
A precipice from which my honor falls.
Must the Count's triumph add the final
pang
To death dishonorable, to life disgraced?
The office, Count, is thine; thine the high
place
Of tutor to my prince, for thine own hand,
With envious insult, the king's choice re-
versed,
And leaves me here with hope and honor
gone.
And thou, brave instrument of my exploits,
But useless ornament of feeble age,
Once terror to my enemies, but now
A bauble, not a man's defense at need —
My sword! — go, quit thy now dishonored
master;
Pass, to avenge me, into worthier hands!

[Enter RODERICK.]

DIÈGUE. Hast thou a brave heart, Roderick?

RODERICK. Any man
Except my father soon would prove it so.

DIÈGUE. O pleasing choler! wrath that soothes my hurt!
My own blood speaks in this resentment swift,
And in thy heat my youth comes back to me.
My son, my scion, come, repair my wrong;
Avenge me instantly!
RODERICK. For what? for what?
DIÈGUE. For an affront so cruel, so unjust,
'T is fatal to the honor of our house.
A blow! across my cheek! his life had paid,
Save that my nerveless arm betrayed my will.
This sword, which I again can never wield,
I pass to thee for vengeance to the death.
Against this arrogance thy courage set;
Only in blood such stains are cleansed, and thou
Must kill or die. This man, mine enemy,
Whom thou must meet, is worthy of thy steel;
Begrimed with blood and dust, I've seen him hold
An army terror-stricken at his will,
And break a hundred squadrons by his charge;
And, to say all, more than a leader brave,
More than a warrior great, he is — he is —
RODERICK. In mercy speak!
DIÈGUE. The father of Chimène!
RODERICK. Chimène!
DIÈGUE. Nay, answer not; I know thy love;
But who can live disgraced deserves not life.
Is the offender dear, worse the offense.
Thou know'st my wrong; its quittance lies with thee;
I say no more; avenge thyself and me!
Remember who thy father is — and was!
Weighed down with Fate's misfortunes heaped on me,
I go to mourn them. Do thou fly to vengeance!　　　　　[Exit DIÈGUE.]
RODERICK. My heart's o'erwhelmed with woe.
A mortal stroke that mocks my tender trust
Makes me avenger of a quarrel just,
And wretched victim of an unjust blow.

Though crushed in spirit, still my pride must cope
With that which slays my hope.
So near to love's fruition to be told —
O God, the strange, strange pain! —
My father has received an insult bold,
The offender is the father of Chimène.

'Mid conflicts wild I stand.
I lift my arm to strike my father's foe,
But Love with mighty impulse urges "No!"
Pride fires my heart, affection stays my hand;
I must be deaf to Passion's calls, or face
A life of deep disgrace.
Whate'er I do, fierce anguish follows me —
O God, the strange, strange pain!
Can an affront so base unpunished be?
But can I fight the father of Chimène?

To which allegiance give? —
To tender tyranny or noble bond? —
A tarnished name or loss of pleasures fond?
Unworthy or unhappy must I live.
[To his sword.] Thou dear, stern hope of souls high-born and bold
And fired with love untold,
But enemy of my new dreams of bliss,
Sword, cause of all my pain,
Was 't given me to use for this, for this? —
To save my honor, but to lose Chimène?

I must seek death's dread bourne.
To weigh my duty and my love is vain.
If I avenge his death, her hate I gain,
If I no vengeance take, I win her scorn;
Unfaithful must I prove to hope most sweet,
Or for that hope unmeet.
What heals my honor's wounds augments my grief,
And causes keener pain;
Be strong, my soul! Since death's my sole relief,
I'll die, nor lose the love of my Chimène.

What, die without redress?
Seek death — so fatal to my future fame?
Endure that Spain shall heap on me the shame
Of one who failed in honor's sorest stress?
All for a love whose hope my frenzied heart

Already sees depart?
I'll list no longer to the subtle plea
  Which but renews my pain;
Come, arm of mine, my choice turns now
    to thee,
  Since naught, alas! can give me back
    Chimène.

Yes, love my will misled.
My father — life and name to him I owe —
Whether of grief or from a mortal blow
  I die, my blood all pure and true I'll shed.
Too long I've dallied with a purpose weak;
  Now vengeance swift I seek.
The flush of shame mounts hotly to my
    brow,
  That I can deem it pain
To save my father's house. I haste e'en now
  To seek — woe's me! — the father of
    Chimène.   [*Exit* RODERICK.]

ACT II

[*Enter* ARIAS *and the* COUNT.]

COUNT. I grant you that my somewhat
    hasty blood
Took fire too soon, and carried me too far;
But — what is done, is done: the blow was
    struck.
ARIAS. To the king's will let your proud
    spirit yield.
This moves him deeply, and his anger
    roused
Will make you suffer penalty extreme.
No just defense can you before him plead;
The deed was gross, the aged victim great;
No common rule that serves 'twixt man
    and man
Will meet the high demand exacted here.
COUNT. The king can use my life to suit
    his will.
ARIAS. You add the fault of anger to
    your deed.
The king still loves you well; appease his
    wrath;
You know his wish; you will not disobey?
COUNT. To disobey — a little — were
    no crime,
Should it preserve the fame I most do prize.
But were it such, forsooth, my valiant
    service

More than suffices for o'erlooking it.
ARIAS. For deeds howe'er illustrious and
    high,
A king can ne'er become a subject's debtor.
Better than any other you should know
Who serves his king well does his simple
    duty;
This haughty confidence will cost you dear.
COUNT. I will believe you when I pay
    the price.
ARIAS. You should respect your mon-
    arch's sovereign will.
COUNT. I can outlive a single day's dis-
    pleasure.
Let the whole state be armed to hurl me
    down —
If I be made to suffer, Spain will fall!
ARIAS. What! you, forsooth, defy the
    power supreme!
COUNT. Why should I fear a sceptered
    hand whose grasp
Is weaker than my own? He knows my
    use;
My head, in falling, will shake off his
    crown.
ARIAS. Let reason rule your action; be
    advised.
COUNT. I wish no further counsel: all is
    said.
ARIAS. What message to your king shall
    I report ?
COUNT. That I shall ne'er consent to
    my disgrace.
ARIAS. Remember that you brave a ty-
    rant's power.
COUNT. The die is cast and longer speech
    is vain.
ARIAS. Adieu, then, since I cannot
    change your will.
E'en on your laureled head the bolt may
    strike!
COUNT. I wait it without fear.
ARIAS. 'T will cast you down.
COUNT. Then old Diègue will be well
    satisfied.   [*Exit* ARIAS.]
Who fears not death need surely not fear
    threats.
My proud resolve yields not to weak dis-
    grace;
Though I be stripped of fortune, rank, and
    name,
Myself alone can rob me of my honor.

[*Enter* RODERICK.]

RODERICK. Grant me a word, Count.
COUNT. Speak.
RODERICK. Dost know Diègue?
COUNT. Yes.
RODERICK. Listen, then, and let us softly speak.
Dost also know that his now feeble arm
Was once Spain's chiefest honor, valor, glory?
COUNT. Perhaps!
RODERICK. This fire enkindled in my eyes
Marks the same blood as his; dost thou know that?
COUNT. What matters that to me?
RODERICK. I'll teach you, Count,
At some four paces hence, what matters it.
COUNT. Presumptuous youth!
RODERICK. Speak quietly, I pray.
My years are few, but, Count, in high-born souls,
Valor and youth full oft united are.
COUNT. And thou wouldst stand 'gainst me! thou vain, untried,
Impudent upstart? Cease thy boyish brag!
RODERICK. The temper of my steel will not demand
A second proof; the first will be enough.
COUNT. Know'st thou to whom thou speakest?
RODERICK. I know well!
Another than I am would hear with dread
The mention of thy name: thy crowns of palm
Must mean to me, 't would seem, the stroke of doom.
But bold I meet thine all-victorious arm;
Where courage leads, there force will aye be found.
A father's honor is a triple shield;
Invincible thou art not, though uncon-quered.
COUNT. Thy fearless words a fearless heart reveal.
I've watched thy growing powers from day to day;
In thee the future glory of Castile
I have believed to see, and proud of heart,
Was laying in thine own my daughter's hand.

I know thy love, and charmed am I to learn
That duty is a dearer mistress still,
Nor soft emotions weaken warlike zeal.
Thy manly worth responds to my esteem;
And wishing for my son a noble knight,
I did not err when I made choice of thee.
But pity stirs within me at thy words;
Such boldness ill befits thy youthful form;
Let not thy maiden effort be thy last;
I cannot fight a combat so unequal;
A victory won without a peril braved
Is but inglorious triumph, and for me
Such contest is not fitting. None would dream
Thou couldst withstand an instant, and regret
At thy young, foolish death would e'er be mine.
RODERICK. Thy pity more insults me than thy scorn;
Thou fear'st my arm, but dar'st attack my honor.
COUNT. Withdraw from here!
RODERICK. Let us to deeds, not words!
COUNT. Art tired of life?
RODERICK. Dost thou, then, fear to die?
COUNT. Come on! Thou'rt right. I'll help thee do thy duty!
'T is a base son survives a father's fame!
[*Exeunt* COUNT *and* RODERICK.]

[*Enter the* INFANTA, CHIMÈNE, *and* LEONORA.]

INFANTA. Nay, do not weep! allay thy grief, Chimène!
This sorrow should disclose thy spirit's strength.
After this transient storm a calm will fall,
And happiness, deferred and clouded now,
Will brighter seem in contrast. Do not weep!
CHIMÈNE. My heart, worn out with trouble, has no hope.
A storm so sudden and so terrible,
To my poor bark brings direful threat of wreck.
Ere I set sail upon my smiling sea,
I perish in the harbor. I was loved
By him I fondly loved; our sires approved;
But even while I told my charming story
At that same moment was the quarrel on,
Whose sad recital changed my tale to woe.

O cursed ambition! wrath's insanity!
Pride, to my dearest wishes pitiless,
Whose tyranny the noblest nature rules!
In sighs and tears a heavy price I pay.
INFANTA. Thy fears o'ercome thee; 't is
a hasty word;
The quarrel of a moment dies as soon.
The king already seeks to make a peace;
And I, as well thou knowest, to dry thy
tears
And heal thy grief would try the impos-
sible.
CHIMÈNE. No reconciliation can avail.
Such wounds are mortal and defy all art
Of king or princess, of command or plead-
ing.
And though an outward show of peace be
gained,
The fires of hate, compressed within the
heart,
Burn fiercer, and will break at last in
flame.
INFANTA. When Love has bound Chi-
mène and Roderick
In sacred marriage, hatred will depart;
Their fathers will forget, and happiness
Will silence discord in sweet harmony.
CHIMÈNE. I wish for such an end, but
dare not hope.
'T is a matched combat between two proud
souls;
Neither will yield; I know them; I must
weep!
The past I mourn, the future frightens me.
INFANTA. What fearest thou? an old
man's feebleness?
CHIMÈNE. Brave sires make braver sons;
Roderick is bold.
INFANTA. He is too young.
CHIMÈNE. Such men are born high-
hearted!
INFANTA. Thou shouldst not fear his
boldness overmuch;
He cannot wound thee, whom he loves so
well;
A word from thy sweet lips will check his
wrath.
CHIMÈNE. How shall I speak it? If he
do not yield,
'T is but an added burden to my heart;
And if he do, what will men say of him —
His father's son, to see his father's fall,

Nor lift an arm of vengeance? In this strait
I stand confused, nor know what I would
choose —
His too weak love, or his too stern refusal.
INFANTA. In thy high soul, Chimène, no
thought can live
Unworthy of thee; love but more exalts.
But if, until this trouble be o'erpast,
I make a prisoner of this gallant youth,
Preventing thus the dread results you fear,
Would it offend thy proud and loving heart?
CHIMÈNE. Ah! madam, then my cares
are quieted.

[*Enter the Page.*]

INFANTA. Page, summon Roderick
hither; I would see him.
PAGE. He and the Count de Gormaz —
CHIMÈNE. Heaven, oh, help me!
INFANTA. What? Speak!
PAGE. Together they have left the pal-
ace.
CHIMÈNE. Alone?
PAGE. Yes, and they muttered angrily.
CHIMÈNE. They've come to blows! All
words are useless now;
Madam, forgive this haste — my heart
will break!
                [*Exeunt* CHIMÈNE *and Page.*]
INFANTA. Alas! that such inquietude is
mine;
I weep her griefs, but Roderick still en-
thrals;
My peace is gone; my dying flame revives.
The fate that parts Chimène from him she
loves
Renews alike my sorrow and my hope.
Their separation, cruel though it be,
Excites a secret ecstasy in me.
LEONORA. Surely, the noble virtue of
your soul
Yields not so soon to passion's baser thrall.
INFANTA. Nay, do not name it thus,
since in my heart,
Strong and triumphant, it controls my will·
Respect my love, for it is dear to me;
My nobler pride forbids it — yet I hope.
Ill-guarded 'gainst a madness so bewild'ring,
My heart flies to a love Chimène has lost.
LEONORA. And thus your high resolve
all-powerless fails?
And Reason lays her wonted scepter down?

INFANTA. Ah! Reason has a harsh and rude effect,
When such sweet poison has inflamed the heart;
The patient loves his painful malady,
Nor willingly accepts a healing draught.

LEONORA. Be not beguiled by Love's seductions soft;
That Roderick is beneath you, all well know.

INFANTA. Too well myself must know it, but my heart
Hears subtle words which Love, the flatterer, speaks.
If from this combat Roderick victor comes,
And this great warrior falls beneath his blow,
What other plea need Love, the pleader, use?
Who could withstand that conqueror's conqueror!
My fancy sets no bounds to his exploits;
Whole kingdoms soon would fall beneath his laws;
I see him on Granada's ancient throne;
The subject Moors with trembling do his will;
Proud Aragon acknowledges him king,
And Portugal receives him, while the seas
Bear his high destiny to other lands.
In Afric's blood his laurels shall be dyed,
And all that e'er was said of greatest chief,
I hear of Roderick, this victory won;
Then in his love my highest glory lies.

LEONORA. Nay, madam, 't is your fancy makes you dream
Of conquests whose beginning may not chance.

INFANTA. The count has done the deed
— Roderick enraged —
They have gone forth to combat — needs there more?

LEONORA. E'en should they fight —
since you will have it so —
Will Roderick prove the knight you picture him?

INFANTA. Nay, I am weak; my foolish mind runs wild;
Love spreads its snares for victims such as I.
Come to my chamber; there console my grief,
Nor leave me till this troubled hour is o'er.

[*Exeunt* INFANTA *and* LEONORA.]

[*Enter the* KING, ARIAS, *and* SANCHO.]

KING. Pray, is this haughty count bereft of sense?
Dares he believe his crime can be o'erlooked?

ARIAS. To him I have conveyed your strong desire;
Nothing I gained from long and earnest pleas.

KING. Just Heaven! A subject have I in my realm
So rash that he will disregard my wish?
My oldest, foremost courtier he affronts,
Then aims his boundless insolence at me!
The law, in my own court, he would decree:
Leader and warrior, great howe'er he be,
I'll school his haughty soul with lesson hard.
Were he the god of battles, valor's self,
Obedience to his sovereign he shall pay.
Although his act like chastisement deserved,
It was my will to show him leniency.
Since he abuses mercy, from this hour
He is a prisoner, all resistance vain.

SANCHO. Pray, sire, a brief delay may calm his mind.
Fresh from the quarrel he was first approached,
Boiling with passion. Sire, a soul like his,
So hasty and so bold, belies itself
In its first impulse; soon he'll know his fault,
But cannot yet admit he was the offender.

KING. Be silent, Sancho, and be warned henceforth.
He who defends the guilty shares the guilt.

SANCHO. Yea, sire, I will obey, but grant me grace
To say one further word in his defense.

KING. What can you say for such a reckless man?

SANCHO. Concessions do not suit a lofty soul
Accustomed to great deeds; it can conceive
Of no submission without loss of honor.
He cannot bend his pride to make amends;
Too humble is the part you'd have him play;
He would obey you were he less a man.
Command his arm, nourished 'mid war's alarms,

To right this wrong upon the field of honor.
The boldest champion who his steel will
    face
He will accept and make atonement swift.
KING. You fail in due respect, but youth
    is rash,
And in your ardor I your fault excuse.
A king, whom prudence ever should inform,
Is guardian of his subjects' life and death.
O'er mine I watch with care, and jealously,
Like a great head, I guard my members
    well.
Your reason, then, no reason is for me;
You speak, a soldier; I must act, a king.
Moreover, let the count think what he will,
Obedience to his king ennobles him.
He has affronted me; he rudely stained
The honor of my son's appointed guide.
To strike a blow at him — 't is nothing less
Than to attack with blows the power su-
    preme.
I 'll hear no more. Listen! — there have
    been seen
Ten hostile vessels, with their colors up;
They 've dared approach clear to the riv-
    er's mouth.
    ARIAS. The Moors have learned, per-
    force, to know you well;
Conquered so oft, what courage can they
    feel
To risk themselves against their conqueror?
    KING. They 'll never see, without a jeal-
    ous rage,
My scepter rule o'er Andalusia.
That lovely land, by them too long pos-
    sessed,
Always with envious eye they closely watch.
That was the only cause why Castile's
    throne
In old Seville I placed, now years ago;
I would be near, and ready at demand,
To overthrow uprising or attack.
    ARIAS. They know, at cost of many a
    mighty chief,
That triumph, sire, your presence only
    needs.
Naught can you have to fear.
    KING. Nor to neglect;
For confidence is danger's sure ally.
Well do you know with what an easy sweep
A rising tide may float them to our walls.
'T is but a rumor; let no panic rise,

Nor causeless fears be spread by false
    alarms.
Stir not the city in the hours of night;
But doubly fortify the walls and harbor.
Enough, till more is known.

[*Enter* ALONSO.]

    ALONSO. The count is dead!
Diègue has taken vengeance by his son!
    KING. Soon as the affront I learned, I
    feared revenge.
Would that I might have turned that fatal
    wrath!
    ALONSO. Chimène approaches, bathed
    in bitter tears,
And at your feet would she for justice plead.
    KING. Compassion moves my soul at her
    mishaps;
But the count's deed, methinks, has well
    deserved
This chastisement of his audacity.
And yet, however just may be his doom,
I lose with pain a warrior strong and true,
After long service rendered to our state,
His blood poured out for us a thousand
    times.
His pride excites my anger, but my throne
His loss enfeebles while his death bereaves.

[*Enter* DIÈGUE *and* CHIMÈNE.]

    CHIMÈNE. Justice, sire, justice!
    DIÈGUE. Ah, sire, let me speak!
    CHIMÈNE. Behold me, at your feet!
    DIÈGUE. I clasp your knees!
    CHIMÈNE. 'T is justice I demand!
    DIÈGUE. Hear my defense!
    CHIMÈNE. Punish the insolence of this
    bold youth!
He has struck down your kingdom's chief
    support!
My father he has slain!
    DIÈGUE. To avenge his own!
    CHIMÈNE. A subject's blood demands his
    monarch's justice!
    DIÈGUE. A vengeance just demands no
    punishment.
    KING. Rise, and in calmness let us hear
    of this.
Chimène, my deepest sympathy is stirred;
A grief not less than yours affects my heart.
[*To* DIÈGUE.] You will speak after, nor dis-
    turb her plaint.

CHIMÈNE. My father, sire, is dead; mine eyes have seen
Great drops of blood roll from his noble side;
That blood that oft your walls has fortified;
That blood that many times your fights has won;
That blood which, shed, still holds an angry heat
To be outpoured for other lives than yours.
What in war's deadliest carnage ne'er was spilled,
The hand of Roderick sheds upon your soil.
Breathless and pale, I reached the fatal spot;
I found him lifeless, sire — forgive my tears;
In this sad tale words mock my trembling lips;
My sighs will utter what I cannot speak.
KING. Take courage, child; thy king henceforth shall be
Thy father, in the place of him that's lost.
CHIMÈNE. Such honor, sire, I ask not in my woe;
I said I found him lifeless: open wound
And blood outpoured, and mixed with horrid dust,
Showed me my duty, drove me here in haste;
That dreadful gaping mouth speaks with my voice,
And must be heard by the most just of kings.
O sire, let not such license reign unchecked
Beneath your sovereign sway, before your eyes;
So the most noble may, without restraint,
Suffer the blows of beardless insolence,
And a young braggart triumph o'er their glory,
Bathe in their blood and mock their memory.
This valiant warrior, slain, if unavenged,
Will surely cool the ardor of your knights.
O sire, grant vengeance for my father's death!
Your throne demands it more than my poor heart.
His rank was high, his death will cost you dear;
Pay death with death, and blood with blood avenge.

A victim, not for me, but for your crown,
Your person, and Your Majesty, I beg —
A victim that will show to all the state
The madness of a deed so arrogant.
KING. What say'st, Diègue?
DIÈGUE. Worthy of envy he
Who, losing life's best gift, can part with life!
For age's weakness brings to noble souls
A mournful fate before its closing scene.
I, whose proud 'scutcheon is graved o'er with deeds,
I, whom a victor laurels oft have crowned,
To-day, because too long with life I've stayed,
Affronted, prostrate lie and powerless.
What neither siege nor fight nor ambuscade,
Nor all your foes, nor all my envious friends,
Nor Aragon could do, nor proud Granada,
The count, your subject, jealous of your choice,
Bold in the power which youth has over age,
Has done within your court, beneath your eye.
Thus, sire, these locks, 'neath war's rough harness blanched,
This blood, so gladly lavished in your cause,
This arm, the lifelong terror of your foes,
To a dishonored grave would have descended,
Had not my son proved worthy of his sire,
An honor to his country and his king.
He took his father's sword, he slew the count,
He gave me back my honor cleansed from stain.
If to show courage and resentment deep,
If to avenge a blow, claim punishment,
On me alone should fall your anger's stroke.
When the arm errs, the head must bear the blame.
Whether this be a crime of which we speak,
His was the hand, but mine, sire, was the will.
Chimène names him her father's murderer;
The deed was mine; I longed to take his place.
Spare for your throne the arm of youth and might,
But slay the chief whom Time o'ermasters soon.

If an old soldier's blood will expiate
And satisfy Chimène, 't is hers to shed;
Far from repining at such stern decree,
I 'll glory in an honorable death.
    KING. Of deep and serious import is this
        deed,
And in full council must be gravely met.
Lead the count's daughter home; and you,
    Diègue,
Shall be held prisoner by your word of
    honor.
Let Roderick be brought; I must do justice.
    CHIMÈNE. 'T is justice, sire, a murderer
        should die.
    KING. Allay your grief, my child, and
        take repose.
    CHIMÈNE. When silence urges thought,
        then anguish grows. [*Exeunt omnes.*]

ACT III

[*Enter* RODERICK *and* ELVIRE.]

    ELVIRE. Roderick, what hast thou done?
        why com'st thou here?
    RODERICK. I follow my sad fate's un-
        happy course.
    ELVIRE. Whence hast thou this audacity,
        to come
To places filled with mourning by thy deed?
Com'st here to brave the dead count's very
    shade?
Hast thou not killed him?
    RODERICK. To my shame he lived;
My father's house demanded that he die.
    ELVIRE. But why seek shelter 'neath
        thy victim's roof?
What murderer ever sought retreat so
    strange?
    RODERICK. I come to yield myself up to
        my judge.
No more look on me with astonished eye;
I seek my death in penance for a death.
My love 's my judge, my judge Chimène
    alone.
Sharper than death the knowledge of her
    hate;
That I deserve, and I have come to ask
The sentence of her lips, her hand's death
    blow.
    ELVIRE. Nay, rather flee her sight, her
        passion's force,

Remove thy presence from her fresh de-
    spair.
Flee! shun the promptings of her anguish
    new
Which will but rouse to fury every feeling.
    RODERICK. This dearest object of my
        heart's desire
Cannot too sorely chide me in her wrath;
That is a punishment I well deserve.
In seeking for a death from hand of hers
I shun a hundred others worse to face.
    ELVIRE. Chimène is at the palace,
        drowned in tears,
And will return escorted from the king.
Flee, Roderick, flee! pray add not to my
    cares.
What would be said if here thou shouldst
    be seen!
Wouldst thou that slander, adding to her
    woe,
Charge that she hide her father's murderer?
She 'll soon return! Hark! hark! she comes,
    she 's here!
Hide thyself, then, for her sake; Roderick,
    hide!   [*Exit* RODERICK.]

[*Enter* SANCHO *and* CHIMÈNE.]

    SANCHO. True, madam, blood alone pays
        debts like this;
Your wrath is righteous, and your tears are
    just.
I would not try with weak and foolish words
To calm your anger or console your grief.
But if to serve you I am capable,
My sword is at your service to command;
My love is yours to avenge your father's
    death;
If you I serve, my arm will outmatch his.
    CHIMÈNE. O wretched that I am!
    SANCHO. Accept my sword!
    CHIMÈNE. It would offend the king, who
        pledges justice.
    SANCHO. The march of Justice often is
        so slow
That crime escapes the tardy loiterer.
Her oft uncertain course costs tears and
    pain!
Suffer a knight to avenge you with his
    sword;
The way is sure, the punishment is swift.
    CHIMÈNE. It is the last resort. If come it
        must,

And still my sorrows move your soul to
pity,
You shall be free to avenge my injury.
SANCHO. To that one happiness my soul
aspires,
And hoping this, I leave you, well content.
[*Exit* SANCHO.]
CHIMÈNE. At last, in freedom from a
forced restraint,
I can pour out to thee my poignant woe,
Can give an utterance to my mournful sighs,
And let my soul tell all its many griefs.
My father's dead, Elvire; the maiden thrust
Of Roderick's sword has cut his life-thread
short.
Weep, weep, my eyes, dissolve yourselves
in tears;
One half my heart the other half entombs;
And for this mortal stroke, my heart that
loves
Must vengeance take for that which is no
more.
ELVIRE. Rest, madam, rest.
CHIMÈNE. Nay, mock me not with
words!
In misery like mine to speak of rest!
Whence-ever shall my agony be soothed
Unless I hate the hand that caused my
grief?
What respite can I hope from torment aye,
When love and hate both seek the criminal?
ELVIRE. You still can love the one who
killed your father?
CHIMÈNE. Love is a word too weak for
what I feel;
I do adore him, spite of my resentment;
My lover and my enemy are one.
Still, notwithstanding all my hatred fierce,
Against my father Roderick contends;
My filial love resists his sweet assault,
And struggles, feeble now, and now trium-
phant.
In this rude war of anger and of love,
My heart is rent, but stronger grows my
soul;
I feel Love's power, but duty's deeper
claims
Forbid that I should change or hesitate;
I balance not, nor swerve, when honor leads.
To me is Roderick dear; I weep his fate;
My heart pleads in his favor, yet, alas!
I am my father's daughter; he is dead.

ELVIRE. Shall you pursue it further?
CHIMÈNE. Cruel thought!
And cruel path which I am forced to tread!
I seek his life, yet fear my end to gain;
My death will follow his, yet he must die.
ELVIRE. Nay, madam, quit so terrible a
task,
Nor on yourself impose a law so stern.
CHIMÈNE. My father dead — nay,
snatched from my embrace!
Shall his dear blood unheard for vengeance
cry?
Shall my weak heart, snared by seducing
spells,
With woman's tears alone pay honor's
debt?
Shall guileful love betray my filial duty,
And in a shameful silence still its voice?
ELVIRE. Believe me, madam, there is
much excuse
For cooler counsels toward a loving heart,
Against a lover dear. You've made appeal
Unto the king himself; press not too far
Persistence in this purpose strange and sad.
CHIMÈNE. My word is pledged to ven-
geance; it must fall.
Love would beguile us with sweet subtle-
ties;
To noble souls excuses shameful seem.
ELVIRE. If you love Roderick, he can
not offend you.
CHIMÈNE. 'T is true!
ELVIRE. Then, after all, what will you
do?
CHIMÈNE. I will avenge my father, end
my woe;
I'll follow him, destroy him, then I'll —
die!

[*Enter* RODERICK.]

RODERICK. Nay, madam, you shall find
an easier way;
My life is in your hand; your honor's sure.
CHIMÈNE. Elvire, where are we? Who
is this I see?
Is Roderick in my house? — before my
eyes?
RODERICK. I offer you my life; taste,
when you will,
The sweetness of my death and your re-
venge.
CHIMÈNE. Oh, woe!

RODERICK. Pray, hear me!
CHIMÈNE. Nay, I die!
RODERICK. A moment!
CHIMÈNE. Go; let me die!
RODERICK. I would but speak a word.
You shall reply with sword-thrust at my
    heart.
CHIMÈNE. What! with a blade stained
    with my father's blood?
RODERICK. Chimène!
CHIMÈNE. Remove that object from
    mine eyes!
Its sight recalls thy crime and sues for
    death!
RODERICK. Nay, gaze upon it; 't will
    excite still more
Thy hatred and thy wrath; 't will haste my
    doom.
CHIMÈNE. 'T is tinged with my own
    blood.
RODERICK. Plunge it in mine!
Wash in my veins what it has brought
    from thine.
CHIMÈNE. Oh, cruel steel, which in one
    awful day
A father's and a daughter's life can take.
I cannot live and see it! Take it hence!
Thou did'st me hear, and yet thou strik'st
    me dead!
RODERICK. I do thy will, but cherish
    still the wish
Of ending by thy hand my wretched life.
Not even love of thee works in my soul
Craven repentance for a righteous deed.
The fatal end of wrath too swift and hot
Brought shame upon my father's honored
    head.
The insult of a blow what heart can bear?
The affront was mine, I sought its author
    swift,
And swift avenged the honor of my sire.
Were it again to do, again 't were done!
But even 'gainst the inevitable deed,
My love long struggled for supremacy.
Judge how it ruled my heart, when I could
    pause,
In such an hour of rage, and hesitate
Between my house, my father, and — my
    love,
Compelled to wound thy heart or stand
    disgraced.
Myself I did accuse of haste undue,

Of passions too alive to feel affront.
Thy beauty might have turned the balance
    still,
But for the thought that pressed itself at
    last —
A man disgraced had naught to offer thee,
And vainly would thy heart's voice plead
    for me,
If nobleness were sunk in infamy.
To yield to love, to hearken to its cry,
Proved me unworthy of thy tenderness.
With sighs I tell thee o'er and o'er again,
And with my latest breath I still would say,
With cruel hand I've hurt thee, but naught
    else
Could blot my shame and leave me worthy
    thee.
Now, honor and my father satisfied,
To thee I come, to pay my final debt;
To offer thee my life, I seek thee here.
That duty done, this only rests to do.
Thou need'st not tell me that thy father
    slain
Arms thee against me — see, thy victim
    here!
Shrink not from offering up the blood of
    him
Who shed thy father's nor can mourn the
    deed.
CHIMÈNE. Ah! Roderick, strangely does
    my changeful heart
Defend thee who hast saved thy father's
    fame.
If my distracted mind has cruel seemed,
'T is not with blame for thee, but in despair.
The ardor of a high, unbroken spirit
That cannot brook an insult, well I know.
It was thy duty taught thee, but, alas!
In doing thine, thou teachest me mine own.
The very terror of thy deed compels;
For, as thy father's name thou hast re-
    stored,
Mine also calls upon his child for vengeance
But, oh! my love for thee drives me to mad-
    ness!
My father's loss by other hand had left
The solace of thy presence and thy love,
A consolation sweet in misery.
I still had felt in grief thy sympathy,
And loved the hand that wiped my tears
    away.
But now, in losing him thee too I lose;

This victory o'er my love his fame demands,
And duty, with the face of an assassin,
Drives me to work thy ruin and mine own.
For in my heart no more than in thine own
Must courage yield to luring dreams of love.
My strength must equal thine. In thine offense
Thou hast but proved thy worth. By thine own death
Alone can I be worthy of thy love.

RODERICK. Defer no longer what thy cause demands.
It claims my head; I offer it to thee;
Make me the victim of thy just revenge.
I welcome the decree; I hail the stroke;
The tedious course of Justice to await
Retards thy glory, as my punishment.
'T is welcome fate to die by thy dear hand.

CHIMÈNE. No, not thine executioner am I;
'T is not for me to take thine offered life;
'T is thine to make defense 'gainst my attack.
Some other hand than mine must work my will;
Challenge I must, but punish never, never!

RODERICK. However love constrains thee for my sake,
Thy spirit must be equal to mine own,
Thyself hast said; then wouldst thou borrow arms
To avenge a father's death? Nay, my Chimène,
The soul of vengeance fails. No hand but mine
Could slay thy father; thine must punish me.

CHIMÈNE. O cruelty, to stand upon this point!
Thou didst not need my aid, I need not thine!
I follow thine example, and my spirit
Will never share with thee my glory's task.
My father's fame and I shall nothing owe
To love of thine, or to thy late despair.

RODERICK. 'T is thou that standest on a point of honor.
Shall I ne'er win this mercy at thy hand?
In thy dead father's name, for our love's sake,
In vengeance or in pity, slay me here!

Thy wretched lover keener pain will know
To live and feel thy hate than meet thy blow.

CHIMÈNE. Leave me, I hate thee not.

RODERICK. 'T is my desert.

CHIMÈNE. I cannot.

RODERICK. When my deed is fully known,
And men can say that still thy passion burns,
Dost thou not fear the cruel, stinging words
Of censure and of malice? Silence them;
Save thine own fame by sending me to death.

CHIMÈNE. My fame will shine the brighter for thy life,
The voice of blackest slander will lift up
My honor to the heavens, and mourn my griefs,
Knowing I love thee and yet seek thy life.
Go, vex no longer my poor, troubled soul
By sight of what I love and what I lose.
Hide thy departure in the shade of night;
For calumny may touch me, art thou seen;
The sole occasion for a slanderous word
Is, that I suffer thee within my house.
See that thou guard my virtue, and withdraw.

RODERICK. Oh, let me die!

CHIMÈNE. Depart. -

RODERICK. What wilt thou do?

CHIMÈNE. The fires of wrath burn with the flames of love.
My father's death demands my utmost zeal;
'T is duty drives me with its cruel goad,
And my dear wish is — nothing to achieve.

RODERICK. O miracle of love!

CHIMÈNE. O weight of woe!

RODERICK. We pay our filial debt in suffering!

CHIMÈNE. Roderick, who would have thought —

RODERICK. Or could have dreamed —

CHIMÈNE. That joy so near so soon our grasp would miss?

RODERICK. Or storm so swift, already close to port,
Should shatter the dear bark of all our hope?

CHIMÈNE. Oh, mortal griefs!

RODERICK. Regrets that count for naught!

CHIMÈNE. Pray, leave me now; I cannot
longer hear.
RODERICK. Adieu! I go to drag a dying
life,
Till it is ended at thine own command.
CHIMÈNE. If my dire fate e'er bring that
hour to me,
Thy breath and mine together will depart.
Adieu! and let no eye have sight of thee.
[*Exit* RODERICK.]
ELVIRE. Madam, whatever ills kind
Heaven may send —
CHIMÈNE. Trouble me not; pray, leave
me with my grief.
I long for night's dark silence, and for tears.
[*Exeunt* ELVIRE *and* CHIMÈNE.]

[*Enter* DIÈGUE.]

DIÈGUE. Never a perfect happiness is
ours;
Our best achievements have their bitter
drop;
In each event, whate'er its promise be,
Care troubles still the currents of our peace.
In my rejoicing o'er my honor saved,
An anxious fear now seizes on my soul.
The count whose hand affronted me is dead,
But now I seek in vain my avenger's face.
Hither and yon I strive, with labor vain,
To roam the city, broken as I am;
The remnant of my strength which age has
left
Consumes itself in fruitless hours of search.
Each moment, in each place, I hear his
voice,
I see his form — a shadow of the night.
I would embrace him — lo, he is not
there! —
Till love, deceived, suspicious grows and
fearful.
No marks of hasty flight do I discern,
And that strong troop of friends who served
the count
Affrights me and suggests a thousand ills.
If Roderick lives, he breathes a dungeon's
air. —
Just Heaven! do I deceive myself again?
Or do I see at last my hope, my son?
'T is he! I doubt no more; my vows are
heard,
My fears dispelled, my anxious longings
o'er.

[*Enter* RODERICK.]

DIÈGUE. At last, my Roderick, Heaven
restores thee mine.
RODERICK. Alas!
DIÈGUE. Mar not my new delight with
sighs.
Let me find words to praise thee as I would;
My valor sees in thee no cause to blush,
But marks a kindred spirit; live in thee
The heroes of thy race, bold and renowned.
Thine ancestors are they, my son thou art.
Thine earliest sword-thrust equals all of
mine;
Thine untaught youth, inspired by ardor
great,
By this one effort, touches my renown.
Prop of my age, and crown of all my for-
tune,
On these white hairs lay thy redeeming
hand;
Come, kiss this cheek where still thou canst
behold
The mark of that affront thou hast avenged.
RODERICK. The honor is your due; I
could no less,
Your blood in mine, your care my school of
arms.
Most happy am I that my maiden blow
Did not disgrace the author of my life.
But in your satisfaction do not shun
To grant me, also, what my soul demands.
Your words too long have silenced my de-
spair,
Which bursts anew with every painful
thought.
No mean regret for serving thee I feel;
But canst thou render back the price it
cost?
My arm, for thee, I've raised against my
love,
And with the stroke I cast away my all!
No more, no more; I owed you life itself;
That which I owed I've paid; your cause
is won.
DIÈGUE. Nay, glory in the fruit of vic-
tory;
I gave thee life, life's joy I owe to thee.
By all that honor means to men like me,
Far more than life I owe thee in return.
But spurn this weakness from thy warlike
breast;

Love is a pleasure summoned when thou
wilt;
Thy soul's one rightful master is thine
honor.
. RODERICK. What 's this you teach me?
DIÈGUE. That which thou shouldst
know.
RODERICK. My outraged honor turns
upon myself,
And now thou dar'st to counsel treachery—
Treason to her I love! Baseness is one,
Whether in craven knight or lover false.
Wrong not with breath of doubt my faith-
fulness;
To thee, to her, I would be wholly true.
Bonds such as mine cannot be broken thus;
A promise lives, though hope be dead for
aye.
I cannot leave, nor can I win, Chimène;
In death I find my solace and my pain.
DIÈGUE. This is no time for thee to
prate of death.
Thy country and thy prince demand thine
arm.
The fleet, whose coming has aroused our
fears,
Plots to surprise and pillage all our towns.
The Moors invade, the night's advancing
tide
All silently may float them to our walls.
The court is shaken, and the people tremble;
Terror and tears are seen on every side;
'T is my good fortune, in this hour of need,
To find five hundred followers, ready armed
To avenge my quarrel, knowing my affront.
Their zeal thou hast prevented; now their
hands
They shall dip deep in blood of Moorish
chiefs.
Go, lead their line; assume thy rightful
place.
This valiant band calls thee to be their
head;
Front the assault of these old enemies;
If die thou wilt, seek there a noble death
In service of thy king and war's emprise.
Let the king owe his safety to thy loss.
Nay, but return, far rather, crowned with
bays,
Thy fame not narrowed to a vengeful deed,
But broadened to a kingdom's strong de-
fense.

Win silence from Chimène, grace from the
king.
And if thou still wouldst gain her maiden
heart,
Know that to conquering hero it will yield.
I waste thy time in words. Come, follow
me;
Forth to the fight, and let thy sovereign see
What in the count he 's lost he 's gained in
thee.

[*Exeunt* DIÈGUE *and* RODERICK.]

ACT IV

[*Enter* CHIMÈNE *and* ELVIRE.]

CHIMÈNE. Is this no false report? — art
sure, Elvire?
ELVIRE. Should I repeat how all do
sound his praise,
And bear to heaven the fame of his exploits,
And wonder at his youth, you'd scarce be-
lieve.
The Moors before him met a quick disgrace;
The attack was swift, but swifter still the
flight.
After three hours of combat we had won
Two captive kings and victory secure;
Naught could resist the young chief's onset
fierce.
CHIMÈNE. And Roderick's arm this
miracle has wrought?
ELVIRE. Of his great prowess are two
kings the prize,
Conquered and captured by his hand alone.
CHIMÈNE. How knowest thou the truth
of this strange news?
ELVIRE. The people do extol him to the
skies —
Call him their liberator and their angel,
The author and the guardian of their
peace.
CHIMÈNE. The king, what thinks he of
these mighty deeds?
ELVIRE. Not yet has Roderick braved
the royal eye;
But the two captive kings, in fetters bound,
Still wearing crowns, Diègue with joy
presents,
Entreating of the king, as recompense,
That he will see the conqueror and forgive.
CHIMÈNE. Is Roderick wounded?

ELVIRE. I've heard naught of it.
You lose your color! pray take heart again.
CHIMÈNE. I'll take again my weak
   heart's failing wrath!
Must I forget myself in thought of him!
Shall my lips join in praises of his deeds!
While honor's mute, and duty, dull, con-
   sents?
Be still, my love, and let my anger swell!
What are two conquered kings? My
   father's slain!
This mourning garb, which speaks of my
   distress,
Is the first token of his wondrous might!
Others may call his deeds magnanimous;
Here, every object testifies his crime.
May all this somber pomp which wraps me
   round —
This sweeping veil, these heavy depths of
   crape —
Add force to my resentment, fail it ever;
Nor let my love my honor overcome.
Should fond, alluring passion e'er prevail,
Recall my duty to my wavering mind,
And bid me fearless meet this hero proud.
   ELVIRE. Calm yourself now; the Infanta
   is approaching.

[Enter the INFANTA and LEONORA.]

INFANTA. I come not vainly to console
   thy grief;
Rather my tears to mingle with thine own.
   CHIMÈNE. Ah, madam, thou canst share
   the common joy;
'T is thine to taste this Heaven-sent happi-
   ness;
The right to weep is mine, and mine alone.
The peril Roderick's wisdom could avert,
The public safety by his valor won,
Permit to me alone, to-day, a tear.
The city he has saved, the king has
   served —
His valorous arm brings woe to me alone.
   INFANTA. 'T is true, Chimène, he has
   great marvels wrought.
   CHIMÈNE. This grievous news already
   reaches me;
On every side I hear him loud proclaimed
Noble in war, unfortunate in love.
   INFANTA. Why shouldst thou suffer in
   this generous praise?
But now this youthful Mars delighted thee;

He dwelt within thy heart, he owned thy
   sway;
To tell his praises is to sound thine own.
   CHIMÈNE. Others may boast his deeds;
   't is not for me;
His praises are but torture to my soul;
My anguish deepens with his rising fame;
My loss is greater as he greater grows.
Ah, cruel torture of a heart that loves!
My passion burns the brighter with his
   worth,
While duty, stern defender of my course,
Would follow him to death in love's de-
   spite.
   INFANTA. But yesterday thy duty's
   proud demands
Won from the court an admiration high,
So worthy of thy filial love it seemed;
Thy victory o'er thy passion was sublime;
But now — wilt have a faithful friend's
   advice?
   CHIMÈNE. Not to hear you would show
   me base indeed.
   INFANTA. To-day thy duty wears a dif-
   ferent face;
The chief support of a whole nation's life,
A people's love and hope, is Roderick now.
On him the Moors with hopeless terror
   gaze,
Securely leans on him our loved Castile.
The king himself can never now deny
Thy father's spirit moving in the youth;
Thou seek'st the public ruin in his death.
Thy country was thy father's country first,
And ne'er canst thou to hostile hands be-
   tray it.
Wilt thou pursue thy vengeance though its
   blow
Enwrap the kingdom in a fatal woe?
I plead not for thy lover; let thy heart
Cling to its filial ties; send him away,
And think no more of wedlock, but for us,
Thy country and thy king, preserve his
   life.
   CHIMÈNE. The gift of mercy is not mine
   to grant;
I cannot check the duty driving me;
Though in my heart the voice of love may
   plead,
Though prince and people praise him and
   adore,
Though all heroic souls encircle him —

My cypress-boughs his laurels shall o'er-
    spread.
INFANTA. 'T is noble not to falter, my
    Chimène,
Though to avenge a father stabs our heart;
But 't is a higher nobleness to place
The public good above all private wrong.
Believe me, to exclude him from thy soul
Will be the bitterest pang thou canst be-
    stow.
Yield to the act thy country's weal de-
    mands,
Nor doubt thy king's most willing leni-
    ency.
CHIMÈNE. Whether he hear, I still must
    plead for justice.
INFANTA. Consider well what course you
    now will take.
Adieu! let solitude thy counsel aid.
CHIMÈNE. My father dead! — what
    choice remains for me?
                           [Exeunt omnes.]

[Enter the KING, DIÈGUE, ARIAS, RODER-
    ICK, and SANCHO.]

KING. Bold heir of an illustrious ances-
    try,
Ever the hope and glory of Castile,
Son of a race of valor unexcelled,
Whose best exploits thine own already
    rank,
For due reward my power is all too weak —
What thou hast earned thy king can never
    pay.
Our land set free from barbarous enemy,
My scepter in my hand, by thine secured.
The Moors despatched before the call to
    arms
Had fully warned the people of attack —
Deeds such as these a king must ever find
Beyond the hope of suitable reward.
But thy two royal captives, they, in sooth,
In my own presence recognize thy might.
Their CID they name thee, sovereign, lord,
    and head.
I well might envy thee this title proud,
The highest in their land; but, no, I call
On all to know that thou the CID shalt be.
The CID henceforth art thou. To that great
    name
May every foe succumb! — Granada yield.
Toledo tremble, but on hearing it.

To all my subjects ever shall it show
How great the debt to thee we proudly owe.
    RODERICK. Nay, sire, your words too
    highly speak my praise,
And make me flush with shame before a
    king
Whose generous honor is so undeserved.
The blood within these veins, the air I
    breathe —
All, all, to this great empire do I owe.
Had these been lost, and death alone been
    won,
A subject's duty only had I done.
    KING. E'en duty done is not the whole
    of service;
Its glory is a courage quick and high,
Which, reckoning not with danger or de-
    feat,
Pushes its way to triumph and renown.
Suffer thy praises from a grateful sover-
    eign,
And now relate the story of thy deeds.
    RODERICK. That in this sudden stress
    of peril, sire,
A troop of followers of my father's house
Urged me to be their leader, well you know.
My troubled soul was painfully perplexed—
I dared not lead the band without thy
    word,
But to approach thee was a fatal step.
Pardon the rashness, sire, that dared to act!
I chose to lose my head in serving thee,
Rather than while my followers stood in
    arms.
    KING. The state defended is thy full
    defense,
And thy too heated vengeance I excuse.
Chimène, hereafter, has a cause forlorn;
I hear her but to comfort her; say on.
    RODERICK. I take the lead, and, with
    defiant front,
The little column slowly makes advance;
Five hundred at the starting, but ere long
Three thousand was our number, strong
    and bold.
The frightened gathered courage at the
    sight.
A certain part I hurriedly conceal
In vessels lying at the river's mouth;
The rest, whose numbers every hour in-
    creased,
Impatient for the fray, with me remain.

Close to the ground they crouched, and,
still as death,
They passed the night, nor slept, nor
scarcely breathed.
At my command, pretended, sire, from you,
The guard itself conceals, and aids my plot.
Just as the flow of tide comes rolling in,
By starlight pale, lo! thirty Moorish sails,
Mounting the wave, sweep to the harbor's
mouth.
They enter; all seems tranquil; not a guard,
No soldiers on the quay, none on the walls'
Our ambush is complete, and fearlessly,
Not doubting their attack a full surprise,
They anchor, and debark; suspecting
naught,
They rush into the embraces of their foes.
We spring from every hiding-place, and
loud
A thousand cries of battle rise to heaven.
Then from the ships pour forth our armed
men;
But half have sprung to land when, terror-
struck,
They see the fight is lost ere 't is begun.
They came for pillage; they encounter war.
We press them on the water, on the land;
Their blood, in rivers, flows upon our soil,
While dire disorder hinders all resistance.
But soon their leaders rally them with
shouts,
Their panic is dispelled, their ranks are
formed,
Their terrors are forgotten in their fury.
To die without a struggle were a shame,
And bravely with their sabers they oppose.
On sea, on land, on fleet, within the port,
All was a field of carnage, death its lord.
Their blood and ours in horrid mixture
ran.
Brave deeds were wrought which never
will be known;
The darkness was a veil, 'neath which each
man
Fought as it were alone; nor any knew
How victory inclined. I praised my men,
Placed reënforcements here, changed orders
there,
Nor knew till dawn which side was con-
queror.
But day made clear our gain and their
defeat.

Their courage fails them, with the fear of
death;
And when they see approach a fresh com-
mand,
They seek their ships, cut cables, and their
cries
Of terror and of anguish fill the air.
They wait not to discover if their kings
Are dead or wounded: in a tumult wild,
On the ebb-tide which bore them in at
flood,
They take their desperate flight and quit
our shores.
The kings and others, left without retreat
Or hope of succor, make a valiant stand;
They sell their lives at cost of life in turn,
And fight till nearly every man is dead.
I urge surrender, but they listen not,
Till the last follower falls, when yield they
must.
Then the two kings demand to see the chief;
I tell them who I am, they seek my grace;
I send them straightway to Your Majesty.
So the fight ended, lacking combatants.
'T was in this manner, sire, that for your
cause —

[*Enter* Alonso.]

Alonso. Chimène approaches, sire, to
sue for justice.
King. 'T is sorry news! a duty most un-
timely!
Go, for I would not force thee on her sight;
For sign of gratitude, I send thee hence;
But first receive thy monarch's kind em-
brace.   [*Embraces him.*]
                              [*Exit* Roderick.]
Diègue. Chimène would save him from
her own pursuit.
King. 'T is said she loves him still;
I 'll test her heart;
Assume a mournful air —

[*Enter* Chimène *and* Elvire.]

King. Chimène, your wishes with success are crowned;
Our foes have fallen beneath Roderick's
hand.
Give thanks to Heaven, which hath avenged
you thus.
[*Aside to* Diègue.] Mark how her color
changes at my words.

DIÈGUE. But see, she swoons, a token, sire, most sure,
Of perfect love; this grief the secret tells
Which rules her soul. No longer can you doubt
Her passion's flame still burns with glow unquenched.
CHIMÈNE. Tell me, is Roderick dead?
KING. Nay, nay, he lives,
And still his love unchanged for thee remains.
Forget the anxious grief that mourns for him.
CHIMÈNE. O sire, one swoons from joy as well as grief;
The soul surprised with happiness grows weak;
Too sudden gladness every sense o'erwhelms.
KING. Thou canst not so deceive my watchful eye;
Thy grief, Chimène, too manifest appeared.
CHIMÈNE. Add, then, this deeper pain to my distress;
My swoon but told my disappointment sore;
My righteous wrath has brought me down to this.
His death would snatch him from my just revenge.
From wounds received in battle should he die,
What place remains for my unyielding will!
And end so honorable mocks my aim.
I wish him dead, but not with honor's stroke,
Not in a blaze of glory should he pass,
But on a scaffold, shrouded in disgrace.
Grant him a murderer's, not a patriot's death.
To die for country is a noble fate;
Not that for him, but with a blemished name,
A tarnished 'scutcheon, should his breath depart.
His victory gives me pleasure unalloyed —
The state gains stableness, and I, I gain
A victim worthier still my father's house.
No longer a rash youth, whose violence
Condemns itself; but great, chief among chiefs,

A warrior crowned with laurels, one whose fall
Would vindicate my purpose. But, alas!
My hopes beyond my reason bear me on.
What force is in my tears, which men despise?
The freedom of your empire is his own;
Under your power, he works his wicked will.
He from my feebleness has naught to fear,
O'er me, as o'er his enemies, he triumphs.
To stifle Justice in his victory
Makes a new trophy for this conqueror.
I serve his pomp when, trampling on the law,
He, with his captives, hears me speak his praise,
And from his car of triumph bids me follow.
KING. My child, your words are all too violent;
The scales of justice must not swerve a hair.
Thy father was the aggressor; that thou know'st.
Justice must see that mercy has a claim.
Nay, be not swift to oppose thy monarch's plea;
Consult thy heart; there still thy Roderick lives.
Thy love, though hidden, is a mighty thing,
And will approve this favor from thy king.
CHIMÈNE. Favor to him a cause of thanks from me!
The author of my woes, my bitter foe!
Is anger o'er a father slain, and wrath
For the assassin, such a trifling thing
That I, forsooth, must grateful be to him
Who thinks to aid my cause by mocking it?
Since tears call forth no justice from my king,
Redress by arms I now, sire, will demand.
By arms alone my happiness was wrecked,
By arms alone my vengeance should be wrought.
Of all you cavaliers I ask his head;
To him who brings it, I will give my hand.
Confirm the combat, sire, by your decree;
I wed the man who conquers Roderick.
KING. That ancient custom I would not restore.
The state was oft enfeebled 'neath its rule.
Under the false pretence of righting wrong,

The noblest oft would fall, the base escape.
A life whose import deepens to our state
Shall not be left to Fate's capricious whim;
From that ordeal of arms is Roderick free.
Whatever crime his hasty wrath has wrought
The flying Moors have borne with them afar.

DIÈGUE. What, sire, for him alone reverse the laws
Your court so oft has honored by observance?
What will your people think, or envy say,
If 'neath your arm, a coward, he retreat,
Nor make redress upon the field of honor,
Where men of spirit seek a worthy death?
Such favors would but tarnish his renown.
Nay, let him drain unto the sweetest drops
The draught of triumph. Bravely did he front
The bragging count; he will be brave again.

KING. Since you demand it, let it be;
but know
A thousand warriors will replace the slain
By Roderick conquered; for the offered prize
Will make an eager foe of every knight.
To oppose them all would be a grievous wrong;
Once only shall he enter in the lists.
Choose whom thou wilt, Chimène, but choose with care;
No more reproaches will thy sovereign bear.

DIÈGUE. Let none be overlooked — not those who most
Do tremble at the prowess of his arm.
The deeds of valor wrought by him to-day
Will fright the boldest. Who would dare confront
A warrior so audacious and so keen?

SANCHO. Declare an open field! I enter it.
Rash though I be, I dare confront this knight.
Madam, this favor grant to my devotion;
Your word's fulfillment shall I surely claim.

KING. Chimène, do you accept this champion?

CHIMÈNE. It is a promise, sire.

KING. To-morrow, then.

DIÈGUE. Nay, sire, why should there longer be delay?

The brave are ever ready. Now's the time.

KING. He scarce has quit his battle with the Moors.

DIÈGUE. While in your presence he took breathing space.

KING. An hour or two of respite I impose.
And lest this combat seem to speak my will —
To show the deep reluctance that I feel
In suffering this bloody pass at arms —
I and my court will straight withdraw us hence.
[To ARIAS.] You shall be judge between these combatants;
See that the laws of honor govern them.
The combat ended, lead to me the victor.
Whoe'er he be, the prize is still the same.
With mine own hand Chimène I would present,
And for his guerdon she her faith shall plight.

CHIMÈNE. What, sire, impose on me a law so stern?

KING. Thou murmurest, but thy changeful, loving heart,
If Roderick wins, will gladly take his part.
Cease to complain of such a mild decree;
The victor shall thy husband surely be.
[Exeunt omnes.]

ACT V

[Enter RODERICK, and CHIMÈNE.]

CHIMÈNE. What, Roderick! whence this boldness — to my face?
Go! — this will cost my honor. Leave me, pray.

RODERICK. Madam, to death I go, but ere I die,
To offer you a last farewell I come.
The love that keeps me vassal to your laws
Even in death demands my homage still.

CHIMÈNE. And wilt thou die?

RODERICK. I count the moment blest
That satisfies your hatred with my life.

CHIMÈNE. But wilt thou die? Sancho is not the one
To terrify that dauntless soul of thine!
What renders thee so weak, or him so strong?

Before the combat, Roderick talks of
    death!
He who nor feared my father nor the
    Moors,
Is going to fight one Sancho, and despairs!
Does courage thus desert thee, valorous
    knight?
RODERICK. I haste to punishment, and
    not to combat.
Since you desire my death, what wish
    have I
To keep my life? My courage fails me not;
But my indifferent arm will not preserve
What thou dost find displeasing. Not a
    blow
Could I have struck against the fiery Moors
For wrong of mine alone; 't was for my
    king,
His people, and his kingdom, that I fought.
To poorly guard myself were treachery.
Life is not yet so hateful to my heart
That basely I can sacrifice its claims.
The question now is different. I alone
Am in the balance. You demand my death;
Your sentence I accept, although the hand
You let inflict it should have been your
    own.
He who shall wield your weapon in your
    stead
Shall meet no sword-thrust answering to
    his steel.
I cannot strike the man that fights for you;
I joy to think his blow is from your hand.
Since 't is your honor that his arms main-
    tain,
Unguarded shall I offer every point,
Seeing in his your hand which slays me
    thus.
CHIMÈNE. Let no blind folly lead thee to
    forget
That glory ends with life. Though my just
    wrath
Impels me to a course which I abhor,
And forces me to follow thee to death —
E'en though a sense of honor would de-
    mand
A nerveless arm, an undefended blow —
Remember, all the splendor of thy deeds
Will change to shame when death has con-
    quered thee.
Who will believe thou didst not raise thy
    hand?

Though I am dear, honor is dearer still,
Else I had still my father, and the hope
That fatal blow has cost thee would re-
    main —
The hope of calling me thine own Chimène.
Thou canst not hold so cheap thy high
    renown
To weakly, unresisting yield it up.
What strange inconstancy can valor show!
Thou shouldst have more or else thou
    shouldst have less!
Is it to grieve me only thou art bold,
And courage fails when courage I de-
    mand?
Wilt thou my father's might so disallow
That, conquering him, thou 'lt to a weaker
    yield?
Go, do not will to die, o'ercome my will;
If life no longer charms thee, honor pleads.
    RODERICK. The count is dead, the
        Moors defeated fly —
Still other claims to glory need I prove?
Henceforth, my fame can scorn all self-
    defense.
None would believe this heart of mine
    could quail.
What can I not accomplish? Who will
    doubt
That, honor gone, naught dear to me re-
    mains?
No, doubt it if you will, this fatal fight
Increases not nor lessens my renown.
None e'er will dare my courage to im-
    pugn,
Nor deem that I did meet my conqueror.
"He loved Chimène" — 't is thus the
    court will say —
"He would not live and her resentment
    face.
To the stern hand of Fate that followed
    him —
Her vengeful hand — he yielded up his
    breath.
She sought his life; to his great soul it
    seemed
'T would be ignoble did he care to live.
He lost his love to save his father's name;
He loses life for his dear mistress' sake.
Whate'er of hope his heart had cherished
    still,
Honor for love, and love for life, he chose."
'T will not obscure my glory thus to die,

But brighter will its growing splendor
shine.
My willing death this honor high will win,
No life but mine for thee redress could
make.
CHIMÈNE. Since life and honor feebly
plead my cause,
Nor stay thee from a death unwished by
me,
Let mine old love speak for me, Roderick,
And, in return, shield me from Sancho's
power.
Save me from such a fate as will be mine
If I, the prize, am won by him I hate.
Need I say more? Go, plan a sure defense,
Silence my wrath, my filial duty done.
Then, if thy heart still beats for thy
Chimène,
As conqueror, thou lovest not in vain.
Adieu! my cheek is hot at this avowal.
                              [Exit CHIMÈNE.]
RODERICK. What foe can daunt my
valiant spirit now?
Come on, Navarre, Morocco, and Castile!
Come, all the valor of our kingdom's
might!
In one great host unite to hurl me down!
My arm alone will equal all your force.
Against a hope so sweet, the flower of
Spain
Were all too weak! I fight for my Chimène!
                              [Exit RODERICK.]

[Enter INFANTA.]

INFANTA. Thou pride of birth, which
turns my love to crime,
Thy warning shall I list, or thy sweet
voice
My heart, whose soft constraint compels
revolt
Against that tyrant stern? In worth alone
Thou, Roderick, art mine equal; but thy
blood,
Though brave and pure, flows not from
royal veins.

Unhappy lot, which rudely separates
My duty and my love. Must loyalty
To valor rare condemn to misery
A loving soul? What anguish must I bear
If ne'er I learn, despite my high resolve,
Nor lover to embrace, nor love to quell!

'Twixt love and pride my reason bids me
choose
Though birth's high destiny demand a
throne,
Thou, Roderick, art of kings the conqueror,
And 'neath thy sway with honor shall I
dwell.
The glorious name of Cid that now is thine
Points clearly to the realm where thou
shalt reign.

Worthy is he, but 't is Chimène he loves.
Her father's death so slightly breaks their
bonds,
That, though her duty slays him, she
adores.
No hope to my long grief his crime can
bring.
Alas for me! ordains a wretched fate
That love outlast the bitterness of hate.

[Enter LEONORA.]

INFANTA. Why com'st thou, Leonora?
LEONORA. 'T is to praise thee,
That thou at last hast conquered all thy
pain,
And hast repose.
INFANTA. Repose? whence shall that
come
To a heart burdened with a hopeless woe?
LEONORA. Love lives on hope; without
it, surely dies.
No more can Roderick's image charm your
heart;
For whether in this combat he prevail,
Or whether fall, he is her victim still.
Your hope is dead, your wounded heart is
healed.
INFANTA. That time — how distant
still!
LEONORA. Why mock yourself?
INFANTA. Say, rather, why forbid me
still to hope?
I can invent a thousand happy shifts
This combat's hard conditions to evade.
Love tortures me, but 't is from love I
learn
To use a lover's skillful artifice.
LEONORA. The flame of love, enkindled
in their hearts,
Survives a father slain. What, then, can
you?

No deadly hate inspires Chimène's pur-
suit.
She claims a combat, but she straight ac-
cepts
The combatant who offers first his sword.
None does she choose among the valiant
knights
Whose bold exploits match Roderick's own
renown.
A youth whose steel has never yet been
tried
Suits her cause well — young Sancho is
her choice.
His highest merit is his unskilled blade.
Without a name, no fame has he to save;
And this too easy choice full plainly shows
This combat is but duty's weak pretence.
To Roderick she gives a victim sure,
Whose harmless death her honor seems to
crown.
INFANTA. I read her plan, and still this
restless heart
Rivals Chimène, and loves this conqueror.
Unhappy that I am! what shall I do?
LEONORA. Recall the high conditions of
your birth.
Shall a king's daughter love her father's
subject?
INFANTA. My love has changed its
object; listen, pray!
It is no longer Roderick I love,
A simple gentleman; not so, not so!
I love the author of most noble deeds,
The valorous Cid, the conqueror of two
kings.
But still my love I'll conquer; not in fear,
But lest their sweet devotion I betray.
If for my sake a crown he should receive,
I would not take again the gift I gave.
Since to no doubtful combat he is gone,
Another happy scheme must I employ.
Do thou, the confidant of all my woes,
Help me to finish what I have begun.

[*Exeunt* INFANTA *and* LEONORA.]

[*Enter* CHIMÈNE, *and* ELVIRE.]

CHIMÈNE. Elvire, I suffer — pity, pity
me!
I can but hope, yet everything I fear.
A vow escapes me I would fain withdraw;
A swift repentance follows every wish.
Two rivals for my sake are now at arms;

Of dear success my tears the price will pay.
Though Fate may seem to grant my great
desire,
I still must carry in my heart the pain
Of father unavenged or lover dead.
ELVIRE. Nay, 't is of consolation you
must dream.
Your lover or your vengeance is assured.
Whatever issue destiny decrees,
Your honor and a husband are your own.
CHIMÈNE. What! him I hate, or him
I've wished to slay!
The murderer of my father, or of Roderick?
The victory of either gives to me
A husband stained with blood that I adore.
From this most wretched choice my soul
revolts.
Far more than death I dread this quarrel's
end.
Hence, vengeance, love, disturbers of my
peace!
I can no longer pay your cruel price.
Almighty author of my direful fate,
Bring thou this combat to no certain close —
Let there be neither conqueror nor con-
quered.
ELVIRE. Nay, wish not a result so prof-
itless.
If still you cherish Justice' stern demands,
And still your deep resentment you would
nurse,
Unsatisfied, because your lover lives,
This combat will but torture you anew.
Far rather hope his valor may secure
New bays for him, and silence for your
plaints;
That by the law of combat, still revered,
Your sighs be stifled and your heart con-
soled.
CHIMÈNE. To him, though conqueror,
think'st thou I will yield?
Too strong my duty, and my loss too dear.
No law of combat, nor the king's decree,
Can force a daughter's conscience to be
quiet.
An easy victory he may win in fight,
Chimène will prove an adversary still.
ELVIRE. 'T were well if Heaven prevent
your vengeance just,
To punish pride so strange and impious!
What! will you now the happiness reject
Of silence with your honor reconciled?

What means such duty? Pray, what hope
you for?
Your lover slain, will't give your father
back?
Does one such sorrow not suffice for you, —
Must you heap loss on loss, and grief on
grief?
'T is a caprice of temper you indulge,
Which of your promised lord makes you
unfit.
The wrath of Heaven will snatch him from
your arms,
And leave you as young Sancho's rightful
bride.
CHIMÈNE. Elvire, the conflicts which my
soul endures
Pray deepen not by prophecy malign.
Would Heaven ordain I might escape them
both;
If not, for Roderick all my vows ascend.
Not that my foolish love inclines me
thus,
But Sancho's prize I cannot, cannot be!
That fear o'ermasters every wish besides.
What is 't I see? Undone! — I am undone!

[Enter SANCHO.]

SANCHO. 'T is mine this sword to offer at
your feet.
CHIMÈNE. What! dripping still with
Roderick's life-blood pure?
Perfidious wretch! how dar'st thou show
thyself
To me, of my dear love by thee bereft?
Burst forth, my love! no longer need'st thou
fear!
My father's death restrains thee never-
more;
By one fell blow my honor is assured,
My love set free, my soul plunged in de-
spair.
SANCHO. With calmer mind —
CHIMÈNE. Thou speak'st to me again!
Assassin of a hero I adore!
Away! thou wast a traitor! Well I know
That valiant knight by thee was never
slain
In open combat. Nothing hope from me.
My champion thou! — my death thou'lt
surely be!
SANCHO. What strange illusion! Hear
me, I entreat!

CHIMÈNE. Think'st thou I'll listen to
thy bragging tale —
With patience bear thine insolence which
paints
His fall, my crime, and, chiefest still, thy
valor?

[Enter the KING, DIÈGUE, ARIAS, and
ALONSO.]

CHIMÈNE. Ah, sire, no more need I dis-
simulate
What vainly I have struggled to conceal.
I loved; 't was known to you; but for my
father
I could devote to death so dear a head.
Love, sire, to duty's desperate cause I gave
Now Roderick is dead, my heart is changed
From foe relentless to afflicted lover.
To him who gave me life was vengeance
due;
But now my tears can fall for him I love.
Young Sancho in defending me destroys,
And of his murderous arm I am the prize.
In pity, sire, if pity move a king,
Revoke a law so terrible to me!
As recompense for victory, whose end
To me is loss of all on earth I love,
All that I have is his; myself, I pray,
May to a holy cloister now retire,
Where death shall find me weeping life
away.
DIÈGUE. No longer, sire, it seems to her
a shame
To openly avow her heart's desire.
KING. Be undeceived, Chimène: thy
Roderick lives!
The champion has, though vanquished,
told thee false.
SANCHO. 'T was her too hasty thought
deceived herself.
To tell the issue of the fight I came —
How the brave warrior who her heart en-
chains,
After disarming me, thus nobly spoke:
"Fear naught! I'd leave the combat all
in doubt,
Rather than pierce a heart that loves
Chimène.
My duty summons me at once to court.
Do thou convey to her the final chance,
And lay thy sword, her trophy, at her feet."
This had I done, but seeing me return,

Bearing my sword, she deemed me con-
queror.
Then love and anger, mingled suddenly,
Betrayed her into transports uncontrolled,
Nor could I gain a hearing for my tale.
Vanquished in combat, still I am content,
And gratefully accept my own defeat;
For though I love and lose my love, 't is
· sweet
This perfect love of theirs to consummate.
KING. My child, no flush of shame
should mount thy cheek.
No longer seek to disavow thy flame.
Thy faithful love unmeasured praise shall
win,
Thy honor's safe, thy filial duty done.
Thy father is avenged; to do thy will
Thy Roderick's life thou hast in peril set.
'T was Heaven ordained to save him for
thine own;
Thou hast not shunned thy part; take thy
reward;
Be not rebellious toward my wise decree,
Thy lover in thy loving arms enfold.

[*Enter* RODERICK, INFANTA, *and* LEONORA.]

INFANTA. No longer weep, Chimène.
With joy receive
This noble conqueror from thy princess'
hand.
RODERICK. I crave indulgence, sire, that
love's high claim
Impels me, in thy presence, to her feet. —
To ask no promised prize, Chimène, I
come,
But once again my life to offer thee.
My love cannot for thee obey alone
The code of honor or a sovereign's will.
If still your father's death seem unavenged,
But speak your wish; you shall be satisfied.
A thousand rivals I will yet o'ercome,
To utmost bounds of earth I'll fight my
way.
Alone I'll force a camp, an army rout,
The fame of demigods I'll cast in shade;
Whate'er the deeds my crime to expiate,
All things will I attempt and all achieve.
But if the voice of honor unappeased
Still clamors for the guilty slayer's death,
Arm not against me warrior such as I.
My head is at your feet: strike now the
blow!

You only can o'ercome the invincible;
No other hand than yours can vengeance
take.
One thing I pray: let death end punish-
ment;
From your dear memory ne'er banish me.
Your honor is exalted in my death;
As recompense let my remembrance live.
Say sometimes, thinking of my love for
you,
"He died, because he ne'er could be un-
true."
CHIMÈNE. Nay, Roderick, rise. — Ah,
sire, no more I hide
The feelings which have burst their long
control.
His virtues high compel my heart to love.
A king commands; obedience is his due;
Yet, though my fate is sealed by sentence
stern,
Can you with eye approving give consent?
If duty drive me on to do your will,
Can justice the unnatural act confirm?
For Roderick's service to his monarch's
cause
Must I, the guerdon, though reluctant,
be?
A prey forever to remorseful shame
That in paternal blood my hands I've
stained.
KING. Time changes all; a deed to-day
unmeet,
May seem hereafter lawful and benign.
Thou has been won by Roderick; thou art
his.
This day his valor rightly gained the prize.
But since so freshly from the field he comes,
And still thy heart unreconciled remains,
I well might seem thy fair fame's enemy,
If I so soon reward his victory.
My law decreed no hour for nuptial vows,
Nor does delay show change in royal will.
Let a round year bring solace to thy
heart,
And dry the fountain of a daughter's tears.
For thee, brave knight, wait mighty deeds
of arms:
The Moors on our own borders thou hast
slain,
Their plots confounded, their assaults
repelled;
Now into their own country push the war,

Command my army, plunder all their land.
Thy name of Cid their terrors will inflame;
Themselves have given it — king they'll choose thee now.
Fidelity is valor's noblest crown;
Return yet worthier of this lovely maid.
Let thy great deeds so loudly plead for thee,
That pride and love will join to make her thine.

RODERICK. To win Chimène and serve my glorious king,
My arm is iron and my heart is flame.
Though absence from her eyes I must endure,
I thank you, sire, for hope's unfailing bliss.
KING. Thy valor and my word assure thy hopes;
Her heart already is confessed thine own.
The filial honor that resists thee now,
To time, thy king, and thy high deeds will bow.

CHARACTERS

MADAME PERNELLE, *mother of Orgon*

ORGON, *husband of Elmire*

ELMIRE, *wife of Orgon*

DAMIS, *son of Orgon*

MARIANE, *daughter of Orgon, in love with Valère*

VALÈRE, *in love with Mariane*

CLÉANTE, *brother-in-law of Orgon*

TARTUFFE, *a hypocrite*

DORINE, *Mariane's maid*

M. LOYAL, *a bailiff*

FLIPOTTE, *Madame Pernelle's servant*

A Police Officer

The Scene is at Paris

TARTUFFE

ACT I

[*Enter* MADAME PERNELLE *and* FLIPOTTE, *her servant;* ELMIRE, MARIANE, CLÉ-ANTE, DAMIS, DORINE.]

MADAME PERNELLE. Come, come, Flipotte, and let me get away.

ELMIRE. You hurry so, I hardly can attend you.

MADAME PERNELLE. Then don't, my daughter-in-law. Stay where you are.
I can dispense with your polite attentions.

ELMIRE. We're only paying what is due you, mother.
Why must you go away in such a hurry?

MADAME PERNELLE. Because I can't endure your carryings-on,
And no one takes the slightest pains to please me.
I leave your house, I tell you, quite disgusted;
You do the opposite of my instructions;
You've no respect for anything; each one
Must have his say; it's perfect pandemonium.

DORINE. If . . .

MADAME PERNELLE. You're a servant wench, my girl, and much
Too full of gab, and too impertinent
And free with your advice on all occasions.

DAMIS. But . . .

MADAME PERNELLE. You're a fool, my boy — f, o, o, l
Just spells your name. Let grandma tell you that.
I've said a hundred times to my poor son,
Your father, that you'd never come to good
Or give him anything but plague and torment.

MARIANE. I think . . .

MADAME PERNELLE. O dearie me, his little sister!
You're all demureness, butter would n't melt

In *your* mouth, one would think to look at you.
Still waters, though, they say . . . you know the proverb;
And I don't like your doings on the sly.

ELMIRE. But, mother . . .

MADAME PERNELLE. Daughter, by your leave, your conduct
In everything is altogether wrong;
You ought to set a good example for 'em;
Their dear departed mother did much better.
You are extravagant; and it offends me,
To see you always decked out like a princess.
A woman who would please her husband's eyes
Alone, wants no such wealth of fineries.

CLÉANTE. But, madam, after all . . .

MADAME PERNELLE. Sir, as for you,
The lady's brother, I esteem you highly,
Love, and respect you. But, sir, all the same,
If I were in my son's, her husband's, place,
I'd urgently entreat you not to come
Within our doors. You preach a way of living
That decent people cannot tolerate.
I'm rather frank with you; but that's my way —
I don't mince matters, when I mean a thing.

DAMIS. Mr. Tartuffe, your friend, is mighty lucky . . .

MADAME PERNELLE. He is a holy man, and must be heeded;
I can't endure, with any show of patience,
To hear a scatterbrains like you attack him.

DAMIS. What! Shall I let a bigot criticaster
Come and usurp a tyrant's power here?
And shall we never dare amuse ourselves
Till this fine gentleman deigns to consent?

DORINE. If we must hark to him, and heed his maxims,

There's not a thing we do but what's a crime;
He censures everything, this zealous carper.
MADAME PERNELLE. And all he censures is well censured, too.
He wants to guide you on the way to heaven;
My son should train you all to love him well.
DAMIS. No, madam, look you, nothing
— not my father
Nor anything — can make me tolerate him.
I should belie my feelings not to say so.
His actions rouse my wrath at every turn;
And I foresee that there must come of it
An open rupture with this sneaking scoundrel.
DORINE. Besides, 't is downright scandalous to see
This unknown upstart master of the house —
This vagabond, who had n't, when he came,
Shoes to his feet, or clothing worth six farthings,
And who so far forgets his place, as now
To censure everything, and rule the roost!
MADAME PERNELLE. Eh! Mercy sakes alive! Things would go better
If all were governed by his pious orders.
DORINE. He passes for a saint in your opinion.
In fact, he's nothing but a hypocrite.
MADAME PERNELLE. Just listen to her tongue!
DORINE. I would n't trust him,
Nor yet his Lawrence, without bonds and surety.
MADAME PERNELLE. I don't know what the servant's character
May be; but I can guarantee the master
A holy man. You hate him and reject him
Because he tells home truths to all of you.
'T is sin alone that moves his heart to anger,
And Heaven's interest is his only motive.
DORINE. Of course. But why, especially of late,
Can he let nobody come near the house?
Is Heaven offended at a civil call
That he should make so great a fuss about it?

I'll tell you, if you like, just what I think;
[Pointing to ELMIRE.] Upon my word, he's jealous of our mistress.
MADAME PERNELLE. You hold your tongue, and think what you are saying.
He's not alone in censuring these visits;
The turmoil that attends your sort of people,
Their carriages forever at the door,
And all their noisy footmen, flocked together,
Annoy the neighborhood, and raise a scandal.
I'd gladly think there's nothing really wrong;
But it makes talk; and that's not as it should be.
CLÉANTE. Eh! madam, can you hope to keep folk's tongues
From wagging? It would be a grievous thing
If, for the fear of idle talk about us,
We had to sacrifice our friends. No, no;
Even if we could bring ourselves to do it,
Think you that every one would then be silenced?
Against backbiting there is no defense.
So let us try to live in innocence,
To silly tattle pay no heed at all,
And leave the gossips free to vent their gall.
DORINE. Our neighbor Daphne, and her little husband,
Must be the ones who slander us, I'm thinking.
Those whose own conduct's most ridiculous,
Are always quickest to speak ill of others;
They never fail to seize at once upon
The slightest hint of any love affair,
And spread the news of it with glee, and give it
The character they'd have the world believe in.
By others' actions, painted in their colors,
They hope to justify their own; they think,
In the false hope of some resemblance, either
To make their own intrigues seem innocent,
Or else to make their neighbors share the blame
Which they are loaded with by everybody.

MADAME PERNELLE. These arguments
are nothing to the purpose.
Orante, we all know, lives a perfect life;
Her thoughts are all of heaven; and I have
heard
That she condemns the company you keep.
DORINE. O admirable pattern! Virtu-
ous dame!
She lives the model of austerity;
But age has brought this piety upon her,
And she's a prude, now she can't help her-
self.
As long as she could capture men's atten-
tions
She made the most of her advantages;
But, now she sees her beauty vanishing,
She wants to leave the world, that's leaving
her,
And in the specious veil of haughty virtue
She'd hide the weakness of her worn-out
charms.
That is the way with all your old coquettes,
They find it hard to see their lovers leave
'em;
And thus abandoned, their forlorn estate
Can find no occupation but a prude's.
These pious dames, in their austerity,
Must carp at everything, and pardon noth-
ing.
They loudly blame their neighbors' way of
living,
Not for religion's sake, but out of envy,
Because they can't endure to see another
Enjoy the pleasures age has weaned them
from.
MADAME PERNELLE [to ELMIRE]. There!
That's the kind of rigmarole to
please you,
Daughter-in-law. One never has a chance
To get a word in edgewise, at your house,
Because this lady holds the floor all day;
But none the less, I mean to have my say,
too.
I tell you that my son did nothing wiser
In all his life, than take this godly man
Into his household; Heaven sent him here,
In your great need, to make you all re-
pent;
For your salvation, you must hearken to
him;
He censures nothing but deserves his cen-
sure.

These visits, these assemblies, and these
balls,
Are all inventions of the evil spirit.
You never hear a word of godliness
At them — but idle cackle, nonsense, flim-
flam.
Our neighbor often comes in for a share,
The talk flies fast, and scandal fills the air;
It makes a sober person's head go round,
At these assemblies, just to hear the sound
Of so much gab, with not a word to say;
And as a learned man remarked one day
Most aptly, 't is the Tower of Babylon,
Where all, beyond all limit, babble on.
And just to tell you how this point came
in . . .
[To CLÉANTE]. So! Now the gentleman
must snicker, must he?
Go find fools like yourself to make you
laugh
And don't . . .
[To ELMIRE.] Daughter, good-bye; not one
word more.
As for this house, I leave the half unsaid;
But I shan't soon set foot in it again.
[Cuffing FLIPOTTE.] Come, you! What
makes you dream and stand agape,
Hussy! I'll warm your ears in proper
shape!
March, trollop, march!
[Exeunt all but CLÉANTE, DORINE.]
CLÉANTE. I won't escort her down,
For fear she might fall foul of me again;
The good old lady . . .
DORINE. Bless us! What a pity
She should n't hear the way you speak of
her!
She'd surely tell you you're too "good"
by half,
And that she's not so "old" as all that,
neither!
CLÉANTE. How she got angry with us,
all for nothing!
And how she seems possessed with her
Tartuffe!
DORINE. Her case is nothing, though,
beside her son's!
To see him, you would say he's ten times
worse!
His conduct in our late unpleasantness
Had won him much esteem, and proved his
courage

In service of his king; but now he's like
A man besotted, since he's been so taken
With this Tartuffe. He calls him brother,
    loves him
A hundred times as much as mother, son,
Daughter, and wife. He tells him all his
    secrets
And lets him guide his acts, and rule his
    conscience.
He fondles and embraces him; a sweet-
    heart
Could not, I think, be loved more tenderly;
At table he must have the seat of honor,
While with delight our master sees him eat
As much as six men could; we must give
    up
The choicest tidbits to him; if he belches,
Master exclaims: "God bless you!" —
    Oh, he dotes
Upon him; he's his universe, his hero;
He's lost in constant admiration, quotes
    him
On all occasions, takes his trifling acts
For wonders, and his words for oracles.
The fellow knows his dupe, and makes the
    most on't,
He fools him with a hundred masks of
    virtue,
Gets money from him all the time by
    canting,
And takes upon himself to carp at us.
Even his silly coxcomb of a lackey
Makes it his business to instruct us too;
He comes with rolling eyes to preach at
    us,
And throws away our ribbons, rouge, and
    patches.
The wretch, the other day, tore up a ker-
    chief
That he had found, pressed in the *Golden
    Legend*,
Calling it horrid crime for us to mingle
The devil's finery with holy things.

[*Enter* ELMIRE, MARIANE, DAMIS.]

ELMIRE [*to* CLÉANTE]. You're very
    lucky to have missed the speech
She gave us at the door. I see my husband
Is home again. He hasn't seen me yet,
So I'll go up and wait till he comes in.
CLÉANTE. And I, to save time, will
    await him here;

I'll merely say good-morning, and be gone.
    [*Exeunt* ELMIRE *and* MARIANE.]
DAMIS. I wish you'd say a word to him
    about
My sister's marriage; I suspect Tartuffe
Opposes it, and puts my father up
To all these wretched shifts. You know,
    besides,
How nearly I'm concerned in it myself;
If love unites my sister and Valère,
I love his sister too; and if this marriage
Were to . . .
    DORINE. He's coming. .
                        [*Exit* DAMIS.]

        [*Enter* ORGON.]

ORGON. Ah! Good-morning, brother.
CLÉANTE. I was just going, but am glad
    to greet you.
Things are not far advanced yet, in the
    country?
ORGON. Dorine . . .
[*To* CLÉANTE.] Just wait a bit, please,
    brother-in-law.
Let me allay my first anxiety
By asking news about the family.
[*To* DORINE.] Has everything gone well
    these last two days?
What's happening? And how is every-
    body?
DORINE. Madam had fever, and a split-
    ting headache
Day before yesterday, all day and evening.
ORGON. And how about Tartuffe?
DORINE. Tartuffe? He's well;
He's mighty well; stout, fat, fair, rosy-
    lipped.
ORGON. Poor man!
DORINE. At evening she had nausea
And couldn't touch a single thing for
    supper,
Her headache still was so severe.
ORGON. And how
About Tartuffe?
DORINE. He supped alone, before her,
And unctuously ate up two partridges,
As well as half a leg o' mutton, deviled.
ORGON. Poor man!
DORINE. All night she couldn't get a
    wink
Of sleep, the fever racked her so; and we
Had to sit up with her till daylight.

ORGON. How
About Tartuffe?
DORINE. Gently inclined to slumber,
He left the table, went into his room,
Got himself straight into a good warm bed,
And slept quite undisturbed until next
morning.
ORGON. Poor man!
DORINE. At last she let us all persuade
her,
And got up courage to be bled; and then
She was relieved at once.
ORGON. And how about
Tartuffe?
DORINE. He plucked up courage prop-
erly,
Bravely entrenched his soul against all
evils,
And, to replace the blood that she had lost,
He drank at breakfast four huge draughts
of wine.
ORGON. Poor man!
DORINE. So now they both are doing
well;
And I'll go straightway and inform my
mistress
How pleased you are at her recovery.
[Exit DORINE.]
CLÉANTE. Brother, she ridicules you to
your face;
And I, though I don't want to make you
angry,
Must tell you candidly that she's quite
right.
Was such infatuation ever heard of?
And can a man to-day have charms to
make you
Forget all else, relieve his poverty,
Give him a home, and then . . . ?
ORGON. Stop there, good brother,
You do not know the man you're speaking
of.
CLÉANTE. Since you will have it so, I
do not know him;
But after all, to tell what sort of man
He is . . .
ORGON. Dear brother, you'd be charmed
to know him;
Your raptures over him would have no
end.
He is a man . . . who . . . ah! . . . in fact
. . . a man.

Whoever does his will, knows perfect peace,
And counts the whole world else, as so much
dung.
His converse has transformed me quite; he
weans
My heart from every friendship, teaches
me
To have no love for anything on earth;
And I could see my brother, children,
mother,
And wife, all die, and never care — a snap.
CLÉANTE. Your feelings are humane,
I must say, brother!
ORGON. Ah! If you'd seen him, as I saw
him first,
You would have loved him just as much
as I.
He came to church each day, with con-
trite mien,
Kneeled, on both knees, right opposite my
place,
And drew the eyes of all the congregation,
To watch the fervor of his prayers to
heaven;
With deep-drawn sighs and great ejacula-
tions,
He humbly kissed the earth at every mo-
ment;
And when I left the church, he ran before
me
To give me holy water at the door.
I learned his poverty, and who he was,
By questioning his servant, who is like him,
And gave him gifts; but in his modesty
He always wanted to return a part.
"It is too much," he'd say, "too much by
half;
I am not worthy of your pity." Then,
When I refused to take it back, he'd go,
Before my eyes, and give it to the poor.
At length Heaven bade me take him to my
home,
And since that day, all seems to prosper
here.
He censures everything, and for my sake
He even takes great interest in my wife;
He lets me know who ogles her, and seems
Six times as jealous as I am myself.
You'd not believe how far his zeal can go:
He calls himself a sinner just for trifles;
The merest nothing is enough to shock him;
So much so, that the other day I heard him

Accuse himself for having, while at prayer,
In too much anger caught and killed a flea.
CLÉANTE. Zounds, brother, you are
    mad, I think! Or else
You're making sport of me, with such a
    speech.
What are you driving at with all this non-
    sense . . . ?
ORGON. Brother, your language smacks
    of atheism;
And I suspect your soul's a little tainted
Therewith. I've preached to you a score
    of times
That you'll draw down some judgment on
    your head.
CLÉANTE. That is the usual strain of all
    your kind;
They must have every one as blind as
    they.
They call you atheist if you have good
    eyes;
And if you don't adore their vain grimaces,
You've neither faith nor care for sacred
    things.
No, no; such talk can't frighten me;
    I know
What I am saying; Heaven sees my heart.
We're not the dupes of all your canting
    mummers;
There are false heroes — and false de-
    votees;
And as true heroes never are the ones
Who make much noise about their deeds of
    honor,
Just so true devotees, whom we should
    follow,
Are not the ones who make so much vain
    show.
What! Will you find no difference between
Hypocrisy and genuine devoutness?
And will you treat them both alike, and
    pay
The selfsame honor both to masks and
    faces,
Set artifice beside sincerity,
Confuse the semblance with reality,
Esteem a phantom like a living person,
And counterfeit as good as honest coin?
Men, for the most part, are strange crea-
    tures, truly!
You never find them keep the golden
    mean;

The limits of good sense, too narrow for
    them,
Must always be passed by, in each direc-
    tion;
They often spoil the noblest things, be-
    cause
They go too far, and push them to ex-
    tremes.
I merely say this by the way, good brother.
ORGON. You are the sole expounder of
    the doctrine;
Wisdom shall die with you, no doubt, good
    brother,
You are the only wise, the sole enlight-
    ened,
The oracle, the Cato, of our age.
All men, compared to you, are downright
    fools.
CLÉANTE. I'm not the sole expounder
    of the doctrine,
And wisdom shall not die with me, good
    brother.
But this I know, though it be all my
    knowledge,
That there's a difference 'twixt false and
    true.
And as I find no kind of hero more
To be admired than men of true religion,
Nothing more noble or more beautiful
Than is the holy zeal of true devoutness;
Just so I think there's naught more odious
Than whited sepulchers of outward unc-
    tion,
Those barefaced charlatans, those hireling
    zealots,
Whose sacrilegious, treacherous pretense
Deceives at will, and with impunity
Makes mockery of all that men hold
    sacred;
Men who, enslaved to selfish interests,
Make trade and merchandise of godliness,
And try to purchase influence and office
With false eye-rollings and affected rap-
    tures;
Those men, I say, who with uncommon
    zeal
Seek their own fortunes on the road to
    heaven;
Who, skilled in prayer, have always much
    to ask,
And live at court to preach retirement;
Who reconcile religion with their vices,

Are quick to anger, vengeful, faithless,
    tricky,
And, to destroy a man, will have the bold-
    ness
To call their private grudge the cause of
    Heaven;
All the more dangerous, since in their anger
They use against us weapons men revere,
And since they make the world applaud
    their passion,
And seek to stab us with a sacred sword.
There are too many of this canting kind.
Still, the sincere are easy to distinguish;
And many splendid patterns may be found,
In our own time, before our very eyes.
Look at Ariston, Périandre, Oronte,
Alcidamas, Clitandre, and Polydore;
No one denies their claim to true religion;
Yet they're no braggadocios of virtue,
They do not make insufferable display,
And their religion's human, tractable;
They are not always judging all our ac-
    tions,
They'd think such judgment savored of
    presumption;
And, leaving pride of words to other men,
'T is by their deeds alone they censure ours.
Evil appearances find little credit
With them; they even incline to think the
    best
Of others. No cabalers, no intriguers,
They mind the business of their own right
    living.
They don't attack a sinner tooth and nail,
For sin's the only object of their hatred;
Nor are they overzealous to attempt
Far more in Heaven's behalf than Heaven
    would have 'em.
That is my kind of man, that is true living,
That is the pattern we should set ourselves.
Your fellow was not fashioned on this
    model;
You're quite sincere in boasting of his
    zeal;
But you're deceived, I think, by false pre-
    tenses.

ORGON. My dear good brother-in-law,
    have you quite done?
CLÉANTE. Yes.
ORGON. I'm your humble servant.
                [Starts to go.]
CLÉANTE. Just a word.

We'll drop that other subject. But you
    know
Valère has had the promise of your
    daughter.
ORGON. Yes.
CLÉANTE. You had named the happy
    day.
ORGON. 'T is true.
CLÉANTE. Then why put off the cele-
    bration of it?
ORGON. I can't say.
CLÉANTE. Can you have some other
    plan
In mind?
ORGON. Perhaps.
CLÉANTE. You mean to break your
    word?
ORGON. I don't say that.
CLÉANTE. I hope no obstacle
Can keep you from performing what you've
    promised.
ORGON. Well, that depends.
CLÉANTE. Why must you beat about?
Valère has sent me here to settle matters.
ORGON. Heaven be praised!
CLÉANTE. What answer shall I take
    him?
ORGON. Why, anything you please.
CLÉANTE. But we must know
Your plans. What are they?
ORGON. I shall do the will
Of Heaven.
CLÉANTE. Come, be serious. You've
    given
Your promise to Valère. Now will you keep
    it?
ORGON. Good-bye.   [Exit.]
CLÉANTE [alone]. His love, methinks, has
    much to fear;
I must go let him know what's happening
    here.   [Exit.]

ACT II

[Enter ORGON and MARIANE.]

ORGON. Now, Mariane.
MARIANE. Yes, father?
ORGON. Come: I'll tell you
A secret.
MARIANE. Yes ... What are you look-
    ing for?

ORGON [*looking into a small closet-room*].
To see there's no one there to spy
upon us;
That little closet's mighty fit to hide in.
There! We're all right now. Mariane, in
you
I've always found a daughter dutiful
And gentle. So I've always loved you
dearly.
MARIANE. I'm grateful for your fatherly
affection.
ORGON. Well spoken, daughter. Now,
prove you deserve it
By doing as I wish in all respects.
MARIANE. To do so is the height of my
ambition.
ORGON. Excellent well. What say you
of — Tartuffe?
MARIANE. Who? I?
ORGON. Yes, you. Look to it how you
answer.
MARIANE. Why! I'll say of him — any-
thing you please.

[DORINE *enters quietly, and stands behind
ORGON, so that he does not see her.*]

ORGON. Well spoken. A good girl. Say
then, my daughter,
That all his person shines with noble merit,
That he has won your heart, and you
would like
To have him, by my choice, become your
husband.
Eh?
MARIANE. Eh?
ORGON. What say you?
MARIANE. Please, what did you say?
ORGON. What?
MARIANE. Surely I mistook you, sir?
ORGON. How now?
MARIANE. Who is it, father, you would
have me say
Has won my heart, and I would like to
have
Become my husband, by your choice?
ORGON. Tartuffe.
MARIANE. But, father, I protest it is n't
true!
Why should you make me tell this dread-
ful lie?
ORGON. Because I mean to have it be the
truth.

Let this suffice for you: I've settled it.
MARIANE. What, father, you would . . .
ORGON. Yes, child, I'm resolved
To graft Tartuffe into my family.
So he must be your husband. That I've
settled.
And since your duty . . .
[*Seeing* DORINE.] What are you doing
there?
Your curiosity is keen, my girl,
To make you come eavesdropping on us
so.
DORINE. Upon my word, I don't know
how the rumor
Got started — if 't was guesswork or mere
chance —
But I had heard already of this match,
And treated it as utter stuff and nonsense.
ORGON. What! Is the thing incredible?
DORINE. So much so
I don't believe it even from yourself, sir.
ORGON. I know a way to make you
credit it.
DORINE. No, no, you're telling us a
fairy tale!
ORGON. I'm telling you just what will
happen shortly.
DORINE. Stuff!
ORGON. Daughter, what I say is in good
earnest.
DORINE. There, there, don't take your
father seriously;
He's fooling.
ORGON. But I tell you . . .
DORINE. No. No use.
They won't believe you.
ORGON. If I let my anger . . .
DORINE. Well, then, we do believe you;
and the worse
For you it is. What! Can a grown-up man
With that expanse of beard across his face
Be mad enough to want . . . ?
ORGON. You hark to me:
You've taken on yourself here in this
house
A sort of free familiarity
That I don't like, I tell you frankly, girl.
DORINE. There, there, let's not get
angry, sir, I beg you.
But are you making game of everybody?
Your daughter's not cut out for bigot's
meat;

And he has more important things to
think of.
Besides, what can you gain by such a
match?
How can a man of wealth, like you, go
choose
A wretched vagabond for son-in-law?
ORGON. You hold your tongue. And
know, the less he has,
The better cause have we to honor him.
His poverty is honest poverty;
It should exalt him more than worldly
grandeur,
For he has let himself be robbed of all,
Through careless disregard of temporal
things
And fixed attachment to the things eternal.
My help may set him on his feet again,
Win back his property — a fair estate
He has at home, so I'm informed — and
prove him
For what he is, a true-born gentleman.
DORINE. Yes, so he says himself. Such
vanity
But ill accords with pious living, sir.
The man who cares for holiness alone
Should not so loudly boast his name and
birth;
The humble ways of genuine devoutness
Brook not so much display of earthly
pride.
Why should he be so vain? . . . But I
offend you:
Let's leave his rank, then, — take the man
himself:
Can you without compunction give a man
Like him possession of a girl like her!
Think what a scandal's sure to come of
it!
Virtue is at the mercy of the fates,
When a girl's married to a man she hates;
The best intent to live an honest wo-
man
Depends upon the husband's being hu-
man,
And men whose brows are pointed at afar
May thank themselves their wives are
what they are.
For to be true is more than woman can,
With husbands built upon a certain plan;
And he who weds his child against her
will

Owes Heaven account for it, if she do ill.
Think then what perils wait on your de-
sign.
ORGON [to MARIANE]. So! I must learn
what's what from her, you see!
DORINE. You might do worse than fol-
low my advice.
ORGON. Daughter, we can't waste time
upon this nonsense;
I know what's good for you, and I'm your
father.
True, I had promised you to young Valère;
But, first, they tell me he's inclined to
gamble,
And then, I fear his faith is not quite sound.
I have n't noticed that he's regular
At church.
DORINE. You'd have him run there just
when you do,
Like those who go on purpose to be seen?
ORGON. I don't ask your opinion on the
matter.
In short, the other is in Heaven's best
graces,
And that is riches quite beyond compare.
This match will bring you every joy you
long for;
'T will be all steeped in sweetness and de-
light.
You'll live together, in your faithful loves,
Like two sweet children, like two turtle-
doves;
You'll never fall to quarrel, scold, or
tease,
And you may do with him whate'er you
please.
DORINE. With him? Do naught but
give him horns, I'll warrant.
ORGON. Out on the wench!
DORINE. I tell you he's cut out for 't;
However great your daughter's virtue, sir,
His destiny is sure to prove the stronger.
ORGON. Have done with interrupting.
Hold your tongue.
Don't poke your nose in other people's
business.
DORINE. [She keeps interrupting him,
just as he turns and starts to speak to
his daughter.] If I make bold, sir,
't is for your own good.
ORGON. You're too officious; pray you,
hold your tongue.

DORINE. 'T is love of you . . .

ORGON. I want none of your love.

DORINE. Then I will love you in your own despite.

ORGON. You will, eh?

DORINE. Yes, your honor's dear to me; I can't endure to see you made the butt Of all men's ridicule.

ORGON. Won't you be still?

DORINE. 'T would be a sin to let you make this match.

ORGON. Won't you be still, I say, you impudent viper!

DORINE. What! you are pious, and you lose your temper?

ORGON. I'm all wrought up, with your confounded nonsense; Now, once for all, I tell you hold your tongue.

DORINE. Then mum's the word; I'll take it out in thinking.

ORGON. Think all you please; but not a syllable To me about it, or . . . you understand! [Turning to his daughter.] As a wise father, I've considered all With due deliberation.

DORINE. I'll go mad If I can't speak.
    [She stops the instant he turns his head.]

ORGON. Though he's no lady's man, Tartuffe is well enough . . .

DORINE. A pretty phiz!

ORGON. So that, although you may not care at all For his best qualities . . .

DORINE. A handsome dowry!
    [ORGON turns and stands in front of her, with arms folded, eyeing her.]

Were I in her place, any man should rue it Who married me by force, that's mighty certain; I'd let him know, and that within a week, A woman's vengeance is n't far to seek.

ORGON [to DORINE]. So — nothing that I say has any weight?

DORINE. Eh? What's wrong now? I did n't speak to you.

ORGON. What were you doing?

DORINE. Talking to myself.

ORGON. Oh! Very well. [Aside.] Her monstrous impudence Must be chastised with one good slap in the face.
    [He stands ready to strike her, and, each time he speaks to his daughter, he glances toward her; but she stands still and says not a word.]

ORGON. Daughter, you must approve of my design. . . . Think of this husband . . . I have chosen for you . . . [To DORINE.] Why don't you talk to yourself?

DORINE. Nothing to say.

ORGON. One little word more.

DORINE. Oh, no, thanks. Not now.

ORGON. Sure, I'd have caught you.

DORINE. Faith, I'm no such fool.

ORGON. So, daughter, now obedience is the word; You must accept my choice with reverence.

DORINE [running away]. You'd never catch me marrying such a creature.

ORGON [swinging his hand at her and missing her]. Daughter, you've such a pestilent hussy there I can't live with her longer without sin. I can't discuss things in the state I'm in. My mind's so flustered by her insolent talk, To calm myself, I must go take a walk.
    [Exit.]

DORINE. Say, have you lost the tongue from out your head? And must I speak your rôle from A to Zed? You let them broach a project that's absurd, And don't oppose it with a single word!

MARIANE. What can I do? My father is the master.

DORINE. Do? Everything, to ward off such disaster.

MARIANE. But what?

DORINE. Tell him one does n't love by proxy; Tell him you'll marry for yourself, not him; Since you're the one for whom the thing is done, You are the one, not he, the man must please;

If his Tartuffe has charmed him so, why
    let him
Just marry him himself — no one will hinder.
MARIANE. A father's rights are such,
    it seems to me,
That I could never dare to say a word.
DORINE. Come, talk it out. Valère has
    asked your hand:
Now do you love him, pray, or do you not?
MARIANE. Dorine! How can you wrong
    my love so much,
And ask me such a question? Have I not
A hundred times laid bare my heart to you?
Do you not know how ardently I love him?
DORINE. How do I know if heart and
    words agree,
And if in honest truth you really love him?
MARIANE. Dorine, you wrong me greatly
    if you doubt it;
I've shown my inmost feelings, all too
    plainly.
DORINE. So then, you love him?
MARIANE. Yes, devotedly.
DORINE. And he returns your love, ap-
    parently?
MARIANE. I think so.
DORINE. And you both alike are eager
To be well married to each other?
MARIANE. Surely.
DORINE. Then what's your plan about
    this other match?
MARIANE. To kill myself, if it is forced
    upon me.
DORINE. Good! That's a remedy I
    had n't thought of.
Just die, and everything will be all right.
This medicine is marvelous, indeed!
It drives me mad to hear folk talk such
    nonsense.
MARIANE. Oh, dear, Dorine, you get in
    such a temper!
You have no sympathy for people's troubles.
DORINE. I have no sympathy when folk
    talk nonsense,
And flatten out as you do, at a pinch.
MARIANE. But what can you expect? —
    if one is timid? —
DORINE. But what is love worth, if it
    has no courage?
MARIANE. Am I not constant in my
    love for him?
Is 't not his place to win me from my father?

DORINE. But if your father is a crazy fool,
And quite bewitched, with his Tartuffe?
    And breaks
His bounden word? Is that your lover's
    fault?
MARIANE. But shall I publicly refuse
    and scorn
This match, and make it plain that I'm in
    love?
Shall I cast off for him, whate'er he be,
Womanly modesty and filial duty?
You ask me to display my love in pub-
    lic . . . ?
DORINE. No, no, I ask you nothing.
    You shall be
Mister Tartuffe's; why, now I think of it,
I should be wrong to turn you from this
    marriage.
What cause can I have to oppose your
    wishes?
So fine a match! An excellent good match!
Mister Tartuffe! Oh ho! No mean pro-
    posal!
Mister Tartuffe, sure, take it all in all,
Is not a man to sneeze at — oh, by no
    means!
'T is no small luck to be his happy spouse.
The whole world joins to sing his praise
    already;
He 's noble — in his parish; handsome too;
Red ears, and high complexion — oh, my
    lud!
You'll be too happy, sure, with him for
    husband.
MARIANE. Oh, dear! . . .
DORINE. What joy and pride will fill
    your heart
To be the bride of such a handsome fellow!
MARIANE. Oh, stop, I beg you; try to
    find some way
To help break off the match. I quite
    give in,
I'm ready to do anything you say.
DORINE. No, no, a daughter must obey
    her father,
Though he should want to make her wed
    a monkey.
Besides, your fate is fine. What could be
    better!
You'll take the stage-coach to his little
    village,
And find it full of uncles and of cousins,

Whose conversation will delight you.
Then
You'll be presented in their best society.
You'll even go to call, by way of welcome,
On Mrs. Bailiff, Mrs. Tax-Collector,
Who'll patronize you with a folding-stool.
There, once a year, at carnival, you'll
have —
Perhaps — a ball; with orchestra — two
bag-pipes;
And sometimes a trained ape, and Punch
and Judy;
Though if your husband . . .
MARIANE. Oh, you'll kill me. Please
Contrive to help me out with your advice.
DORINE. I thank you kindly.
MARIANE. Oh! Dorine, I beg you . . .
DORINE. To serve you right, this mar-
riage must go through.
MARIANE. Dear girl!
DORINE. No.
MARIANE. If I say I love Valère . . .
DORINE. No, no. Tartuffe's your man,
and you shall taste him.
MARIANE. You know I've always
trusted you; now help me . . .
DORINE. No, you shall be, my faith!
Tartuffified.
MARIANE. Well, then, since you've no
pity for my fate
Let me take counsel only of despair;
It will advise and help and give me cour-
age;
There's one sure cure, I know, for all my
troubles. [She starts to go.]
DORINE. There, there! Come back. I
can't be angry long.
I must take pity on you, after all.
MARIANE. Oh, don't you see, Dorine, if
I must bear
This martyrdom, I certainly shall die.
DORINE. Now don't you fret. We'll
surely find some way
To hinder this . . . But here's Valère, your
lover.

[Enter VALÈRE.]

VALÈRE. Madam, a piece of news —
quite new to me —
Has just come out, and very fine it is.
MARIANE. What piece of news?
VALÈRE. Your marriage with Tartuffe.

MARIANE. 'T is true my father has this
plan in mind.
VALÈRE. Your father, madam . . .
MARIANE. Yes, he's changed his plans,
And did but now propose it to me.
VALÈRE. What!
Seriously?
MARIANE. Yes, he was serious,
And openly insisted on the match.
VALÈRE. And what's your resolution in
the matter,
Madam?
MARIANE. I don't know.
VALÈRE. That's a pretty answer.
You don't know?
MARIANE. No.
VALÈRE. No?
MARIANE. What do you advise?
VALÈRE. I? My advice is, marry him, by
all means.
MARIANE. That's your advice?
VALÈRE. Yes.
MARIANE. Do you mean it?
VALÈRE. Surely.
A splendid choice, and worthy your ac-
ceptance.
MARIANE. Oh, very well, sir! I shall
take your counsel.
VALÈRE. You'll find no trouble taking
it, I warrant.
MARIANE. No more than you did giving
it, be sure.
VALÈRE. I gave it, truly, to oblige you,
madam.
MARIANE. And I shall take it to oblige
you, sir.
DORINE [withdrawing to the back of the
stage]. Let's see what this affair will
come to.
VALÈRE. So.
That is your love? And it was all deceit
When you . . .
MARIANE. I beg you, say no more of
that.
You told me, squarely, sir, I should accept
The husband that is offered me; and I
Will tell you squarely that I mean to do so,
Since you have given me this good advice.
VALÈRE. Don't shield yourself with
talk of my advice.
You had your mind made up, that's evi-
dent;

And now you're snatching at a trifling
pretext
To justify the breaking of your word.

MARIANE. Exactly so.

VALÈRE. Of course it is; your heart
Has never known true love for me.

MARIANE. Alas!
You're free to think so, if you please.

VALÈRE. Yes, yes,
I'm free to think so; and my outraged
love
May yet forestall you in your perfidy,
And offer elsewhere both my heart and
hand.

MARIANE. No doubt of it; the love your
high deserts
May win . . .

VALÈRE. Good Lord, have done with
my deserts!
I know I have but few, and you have
proved it.
But I may find more kindness in another;
I know of some one, who'll not be ashamed
To take your leavings, and make up my
loss.

MARIANE. The loss is not so great; you'll
easily
Console yourself completely for this
change.

VALÈRE. I'll try my best, that you may
well believe.
When we're forgotten by a woman's heart,
Our pride is challenged; we, too, must
forget;
Or if we cannot, must at least pretend
to.
No other way can man such baseness
prove,
As be a lover scorned, and still in love.

MARIANE. In faith, a high and noble
sentiment.

VALÈRE. Yes; and it's one that all men
must approve.
What! Would you have me keep my love
alive,
And see you fly into another's arms
Before my very eyes; and never offer
To some one else the heart that you had
scorned?

MARIANE. Oh, no, indeed! For my part,
I could wish
That it were done already.

VALÈRE. What! You wish it?

MARIANE. Yes.

VALÈRE. This is insult heaped on injury;
I'll go at once and do as you desire.
[He takes a step or two as if to go
away.]

MARIANE. Oh, very well then.

VALÈRE [turning back]. But remember
this:
'T was you that drove me to this desperate
pass.

MARIANE. Of course.

VALÈRE [turning back again]. And in the
plan that I have formed
I only follow your example.

MARIANE. Yes.

VALÈRE [at the door]. Enough; you shall
be punctually obeyed.

MARIANE. So much the better.

VALÈRE [coming back again]. This is
once for all.

MARIANE. So be it, then.

VALÈRE [going toward the door, but just
as he reaches it, turning around]. Eh?

MARIANE. What?

VALÈRE. You did n't call me?

MARIANE. I? You are dreaming.

VALÈRE. Very well, I'm gone.
Madam, farewell.
[He walks slowly away.]

MARIANE. Farewell, sir.

DORINE. I must say
You've lost your senses and both gone clean
daft!
I've let you fight it out to the end o' the
chapter
To see how far the thing could go. Oho,
there,
Mister Valère!
[She goes and seizes him by the
arm, to stop him. He makes a
great show of resistance.]

VALÈRE. What do you want, Dorine?

DORINE. Come here.

VALÈRE. No, no, I'm quite beside myself.
Don't hinder me from doing as she wishes.

DORINE. Stop!

VALÈRE. No. You see, I'm fixed, resolved, determined.

DORINE. So!

MARIANE [*aside*]. Since my presence pains him, makes him go,
I'd better go myself, and leave him free.
DORINE [*leaving* VALÈRE, *and running after* MARIANE]. Now 't other! Where are you going?
MARIANE. Let me be.
DORINE. Come back.
MARIANE. No, no, it is n't any use.
VALÈRE [*aside*]. 'T is clear the sight of me is torture to her;
No doubt, 't were better I should free her from it.
DORINE [*leaving* MARIANE, *and running after* VALÈRE]. Same thing again! Deuce take you both, I say.
Now stop your fooling; come here, you; and you.
[*She pulls first one, then the other, toward the middle of the stage.*]
VALÈRE [*to* DORINE]. What's your idea?
MARIANE [*to* DORINE]. What can you mean to do?
DORINE. Set you to rights, and pull you out o' the scrape.
[*To* VALÈRE.] Are you quite mad, to quarrel with her now?
VALÈRE. Did n't you hear the things she said to me?
DORINE [*to* MARIANE]. Are you quite mad, to get in such a passion?
MARIANE. Did n't you see the way he treated me?
DORINE. Fools, both of you.
[*To* VALÈRE.] She thinks of nothing else But to keep faith with you, I vouch for it.
[*To* MARIANE.] And he loves none but you, and longs for nothing
But just to marry you, I stake my life on 't.
MARIANE [*to* VALERE]. Why did you give me such advice then, pray?
VALÈRE [*to* MARIANE]. Why ask for my advice on such a matter?
DORINE. You both are daft, I tell you. Here, your hands.
[*To* VALÈRE.] Come, yours.
VALÈRE [*giving* DORINE *his hand*]. What for?
DORINE [*to* MARIANE]. Now, yours.
MARIANE [*giving* DORINE *her hand*]. But what's the use?

DORINE. Oh, quick now, come along. There, both of you —
You love each other better than you think.
[VALÈRE *and* MARIANE *hold each other's hands some time without looking at each other.*]
VALÈRE [*at last turning toward* MARIANE]. Come, don't be so ungracious now about it;
Look at a man as if you did n't hate him.
[MARIANE *looks sideways toward* VALÈRE, *with just a bit of a smile.*]
DORINE. My faith and troth, what fools these lovers be!
VALÈRE [*to* MARIANE]. But come now, have I not a just complaint?
And truly, are you not a wicked creature
To take delight in saying what would pain me?
MARIANE. And are you not yourself the most ungrateful . . . ?
DORINE. Leave this discussion till another time;
Now, think how you'll stave off this plaguey marriage.
MARIANE. Then tell us how to go about it.
DORINE. Well,
We'll try all sorts of ways.
[*To* MARIANE.] Your father's daft;
[*To* VALÈRE.] This plan is nonsense.
[*To* MARIANE.] You had better humor His notions by a semblance of consent,
So that in case of danger, you can still Find means to block the marriage by delay.
If you gain time, the rest is easy, trust me. One day you'll fool them with a sudden illness,
Causing delay; another day, ill omens: You've met a funeral, or broke a mirror,
Or dreamed of muddy water. Best of all, They cannot marry you to any one
Without your saying yes. But now, methinks,
They must n't find you chattering together.
[*To* VALÈRE.] You, go at once and set your friends at work
To make him keep his word to you; while we Will bring the brother's influence to bear,
And get the stepmother on our side, too. Good-bye.

VALÈRE [to MARIANE]. Whatever efforts
we may make,
My greatest hope, be sure, must rest on
you.
MARIANE [to VALÈRE]. I cannot an-
swer for my father's whims;
But no one save Valère shall ever have me.
VALÈRE. You thrill me through with joy!
Whatever comes . . .
DORINE. Oho! These lovers! Never
done with prattling!
Now, go.
VALÈRE [starting to go, and coming back
again]. One last word . . .
DORINE. What a gabble and pother!
Be off! By this door, you. And you, by
t'other.
[She pushes them off, by the
shoulders, in opposite direc-
tions.]

ACT III

[Enter DAMIS and DORINE.]

DAMIS. May lightning strike me dead
this very instant,
May I be everywhere proclaimed a scoun-
drel,
If any reverence or power shall stop me,
And if I don't do straightway something
desperate!
DORINE. I beg you, moderate this tow-
ering passion;
Your father did but merely mention it.
Not all things that are talked of turn to
facts;
The road is long, sometimes, from plans to
acts.
DAMIS. No, I must end this paltry fel-
low's plots,
And he shall hear from me a truth or two.
DORINE. So ho! Go slow now. Just you
leave the fellow —
Your father too — in your stepmother's
hands.
She has some influence with this Tartuffe,
He makes a point of heeding all she says,
And I suspect that he is fond of her.
Would God 't were true! — 'T would be
the height of humor.
Now, she has sent for him, in your behalf,

To sound him on this marriage, to find out
What his ideas are, and to show him plainly
What troubles he may cause, if he persists
In giving countenance to this design.
His man says, he's at prayers, I must n't
see him,
But likewise says, he 'll presently be down.
So off with you, and let me wait for him.
DAMIS. I may be present at this inter-
view.
DORINE. No, no! They must be left
alone.
DAMIS. I won't
So much as speak to him.
DORINE. Go on! We know you
And your high tantrums. Just the way to
spoil things!
Be off.
DAMIS. No, I must see — I'll keep my
temper.
DORINE. Out on you, what a plague!
He's coming. Hide!
[DAMIS goes and hides in the closet
at the back of the stage.]

[Enter TARTUFFE.]

TARTUFFE [speaking to his valet, off the
stage, as soon as he sees DORINE is
there]. Lawrence, put up my hair-
cloth shirt and scourge,
And pray that Heaven may shed its light
upon you.
If any come to see me, say I'm gone
To share my alms among the prisoners.
DORINE [aside]. What affectation and
what showing off!
TARTUFFE. What do you want with me?
DORINE. To tell you . . .
TARTUFFE [taking a handkerchief from
his pocket]. Ah!
Before you speak, pray take this hand-
kerchief.
DORINE. What?
TARTUFFE. Cover up that bosom, which
I can't
Endure to look on. Things like that offend
Our souls, and fill our minds with sinful
thoughts.
DORINE. Are you so tender to tempta-
tion, then,
And has the flesh such power upon your
senses?

I don't know how you get in such a heat;
For my part, I am not so prone to lust,
And I could see you stripped from head to
foot,
And all you hide not tempt me in the least.
TARTUFFE. Show in your speech some
little modesty,
Or I must instantly take leave of you.
DORINE. No, no, I'll leave you to your-
self; I've only
One thing to say: Madam will soon be
down,
And begs the favor of a word with you.
TARTUFFE. Ah! Willingly.
DORINE [aside]. How gentle all at once!
My faith, I still believe I've hit upon it.
TARTUFFE. Will she come soon?
DORINE. I think I hear her now.
Yes, here she is herself; I'll leave you with
her. [Exit.]

[Enter ELMIRE.]

TARTUFFE. May Heaven's overflowing
kindness ever
Give you good health of body and of soul,
And bless your days according to the wishes
And prayers of its most humble votary!
ELMIRE. I'm very grateful for your
pious wishes.
But let's sit down, so we may talk at ease.
TARTUFFE [after sitting down]. And how
are you recovered from your ill-
ness?
ELMIRE [sitting down also]. Quite well;
the fever soon let go its hold.
TARTUFFE. My prayers, I fear, have not
sufficient merit
To have drawn down this favor from on
high;
But each entreaty that I made to Heaven
Had for its object your recovery.
ELMIRE. You're too solicitous on my
behalf.
TARTUFFE. We could not cherish your
dear health too much;
I would have given mine, to help restore it.
ELMIRE. That's pushing Christian char-
ity too far;
I owe you many thanks for so much kind-
ness.
TARTUFFE. I do far less for you than
you deserve.

ELMIRE. There is a matter that I wished
to speak of
In private; I am glad there's no one here
To listen.
TARTUFFE. Madam, I am overjoyed.
'T is sweet to find myself alone with you.
This is an opportunity I've asked
Of Heaven, many a time; till now, in vain.
ELMIRE. All that I wish, is just a word
from you,
Quite frank and open, hiding nothing from
me.
    [DAMIS, without their seeing him,
    opens the closet door halfway.]
TARTUFFE. I too could wish, as Heaven's
especial favor,
To lay my soul quite open to your eyes,
And swear to you, the trouble that I made
About those visits which your charms
attract,
Does not result from any hatred toward
you,
But rather from a passionate devotion,
And purest motives . . .
ELMIRE. That is how I take it,
I think 't is my salvation that concerns you.
TARTUFFE [pressing her finger-tips].
Madam, 't is so; and such is my
devotion . . .
ELMIRE. Ouch! but you squeeze too
hard.
TARTUFFE. Excess of zeal.
In no way could I ever mean to hurt you,
And I'd as soon . . .
    [He puts his hand on her knee.]
ELMIRE. What's your hand doing there?
TARTUFFE. Feeling your gown; the stuff
is very soft.
ELMIRE. Let be, I beg you; I am very
ticklish.
    [She moves her chair away, and
    TARTUFFE brings his nearer.]
TARTUFFE [handling the lace yoke of
ELMIRE's dress]. Dear me, how
wonderful in workmanship
This lace is! They do marvels, nowadays;
Things of all kinds were never better made.
ELMIRE. Yes, very true. But let us come
to business.
They say my husband means to break his
word,
And marry Mariane to you. Is't so?

TARTUFFE. He did hint some such thing;
but truly, madam,
That's not the happiness I'm yearning
after;
I see elsewhere the sweet compelling
charms
Of such a joy as fills my every wish.
ELMIRE. You mean you cannot love
terrestrial things.
TARTUFFE. The heart within my bosom
is not stone.
ELMIRE. I well believe your sighs all
tend to Heaven,
And nothing here below can stay your
thoughts.
TARTUFFE. Love for the beauty of eter-
nal things
Cannot destroy our love for earthly beauty;
Our mortal senses well may be entranced
By perfect works that Heaven has fash-
ioned here.
Its charms reflected shine in such as you,
And in yourself, its rarest miracles;
It has displayed such marvels in your face,
That eyes are dazed, and hearts are rapt
away;
I could not look on you, the perfect crea-
ture,
Without admiring Nature's great Creator,
And feeling all my heart inflamed with
love
For you, His fairest image of Himself.
At first I trembled lest this secret love
Might be the Evil Spirit's artful snare;
I even schooled my heart to flee your
beauty,
Thinking it was a bar to my salvation.
But soon, enlightened, O all lovely one,
I saw how this my passion may be blame-
less,
How I may make it fit with modesty,
And thus completely yield my heart to it.
'T is, I must own, a great presumption in
me
To dare make you the offer of my heart;
My love hopes all things from your perfect
goodness,
And nothing from my own poor weak en-
deavor.
You are my hope, my stay, my peace of
heart;
On you depends my torment or my bliss;

And by your doom of judgment, I shall be
Blest, if you will; or damned, by your
decree.
ELMIRE. Your declaration's turned most
gallantly;
But truly, it is just a bit surprising.
You should have better armed your heart,
methinks,
And taken thought somewhat on such a
matter.
A pious man like you, known every-
where . . .
TARTUFFE. Though pious, I am none the
less a man;
And when a man beholds your heavenly
charms,
The heart surrenders, and can think no
more.
I know such words seem strange, coming
from me;
But, madam, I'm no angel, after all;
If you condemn my frankly made avowal
You only have your charming self to
blame.
Soon as I saw your more than human
beauty,
You were thenceforth the sovereign of my
soul;
Sweetness ineffable was in your eyes,
That took by storm my still resisting heart,
And conquered everything, fasts, prayers,
and tears,
And turned my worship wholly to your-
self.
My looks, my sighs, have spoke a thousand
times;
Now, to express it all, my voice must speak.
If but you will look down with gracious
favor
Upon the sorrows of your worthless slave,
If in your goodness you will give me com-
fort
And condescend unto my nothingness,
I'll ever pay you, O sweet miracle,
An unexampled worship and devotion.
Then too, with me your honor runs no
risk ;
With me you need not fear a public scandal.
These court gallants, that women are so
fond of,
Are boastful of their acts, and vain in
speech;

They always brag in public of their prog-
ress;
Soon as a favor's granted, they'll divulge
it;
Their tattling tongues, if you but trust to
them,
Will foul the altar where their hearts have
worshiped.
But men like me are so discreet in love,
That you may trust their lasting secrecy.
The care we take to guard our own good
name
May fully guarantee the one we love;
So you may find, with hearts like ours
sincere,
Love without scandal, pleasure without
fear.

ELMIRE. I've heard you through —
your speech is clear, at least.
But don't you fear that I may take a fancy
To tell my husband of your gallant passion,
And that a prompt report of this affair
May somewhat change the friendship
which he bears you?

TARTUFFE. I know that you're too good
and generous,
That you will pardon my temerity,
Excuse, upon the score of human frailty,
The violence of passion that offends you,
And not forget, when you consult your
mirror,
That I'm not blind, and man is made of
flesh.

ELMIRE. Some women might do other-
wise, perhaps,
But I am willing to employ discretion,
And not repeat the matter to my husband;
But in return, I'll ask one thing of you:
That you urge forward, frankly and sin-
cerely,
The marriage of Valère to Mariane;
That you give up the unjust influence
By which you hope to win another's rights;
And . . .

DAMIS [coming out of the closet-room where
he had been hiding]. No, I say! This
thing must be made public.
I was just there, and overheard it all;
And Heaven's goodness must have brought
me there
On purpose to confound this scoundrel's
pride

And grant me means to take a signal venge-
ance
On his hypocrisy and arrogance,
And undeceive my father, showing up
The rascal caught at making love to you.

ELMIRE. No, no; it is enough if he reforms,
Endeavoring to deserve the favor shown
him.
And since I've promised, do not you belie
me.
'T is not my way to make a public scandal;
An honest wife will scorn to heed such
follies,
And never fret her husband's ears with
them.

DAMIS. You've reasons of your own for
acting thus;
And I have mine for doing otherwise.
To spare him now would be a mockery;
His bigot's pride has triumphed all too long
Over my righteous anger, and has caused
Far too much trouble in our family.
The rascal all too long has ruled my father,
And crossed my sister's love, and mine as
well.
The traitor now must be unmasked before
him;
And Providence has given me means to do
it.
To Heaven I owe the opportunity,
And if I did not use it now I have it,
I should deserve to lose it once for all.

ELMIRE. Damis . . .

DAMIS. No, by your leave; I'll not be
counseled.
I'm overjoyed. You need n't try to tell me
I must give up the pleasure of revenge.
I'll make an end of this affair at once;
And, to content me, here's my father now.

[Enter ORGON.]

DAMIS. Father, we've news to welcome
your arrival,
That's altogether novel, and surprising.
You are well paid for your caressing care,
And this fine gentleman rewards your love
Most handsomely, with zeal that seeks no
less
Than your dishonor, as has now been proven.
I've just surprised him making to your
wife

The shameful offer of a guilty love.
She, somewhat over gentle and discreet,
Insisted that the thing should be concealed;
But I will not condone such shamelessness,
Nor so far wrong you as to keep it secret.

ELMIRE. Yes, I believe a wife should never trouble
Her husband's peace of mind with such vain gossip;
A woman's honor does not hang on telling;
It is enough if she defend herself;
Or so I think; Damis, you'd not have spoken,
If you would but have heeded my advice. [Exit.]

ORGON. Just Heaven! Can what I hear be credited?

TARTUFFE. Yes, brother, I am wicked, I am guilty,
A miserable sinner, steeped in evil,
The greatest criminal that ever lived.
Each moment of my life is stained with soilures;
And all is but a mass of crime and filth;
Heaven, for my punishment, I see it plainly,
Would mortify me now. Whatever wrong
They find to charge me with, I'll not deny it
But guard against the pride of self-defense.
Believe their stories, arm your wrath against me,
And drive me like a villain from your house;
I cannot have so great a share of shame
But what I have deserved a greater still.

ORGON [to his son]. You miscreant, can you dare, with such a falsehood,
To try to stain the whiteness of his virtue?

DAMIS. What! The feigned meekness of this hypocrite
Makes you discredit . . .

ORGON. Silence, cursèd plague!

TARTUFFE. Ah! Let him speak; you chide him wrongfully;
You'd do far better to believe his tales.
Why favor me so much in such a matter?
How can you know of what I'm capable?
And should you trust my outward semblance, brother,
Or judge therefrom that I'm the better man?
No, no; you let appearances deceive you;
I'm anything but what I'm thought to be,

Alas! and though all men believe me godly,
The simple truth is, I'm a worthless creature.
[To DAMIS.] Yes, my dear son, say on, and call me traitor,
Abandoned scoundrel, thief, and murderer;
Heap on me names yet more detestable,
And I shall not gainsay you; I've deserved them;
I'll bear this ignominy on my knees,
To expiate in shame the crimes I've done.

ORGON [to TARTUFFE]. Ah, brother, 't is too much!
[To his son.] You'll not relent,
You blackguard?

DAMIS. What! His talk can so deceive you . . .

ORGON. Silence, you scoundrel!
[To TARTUFFE.] Brother, rise, I beg you.
[To his son.] Infamous villain!

DAMIS. Can he . . .

ORGON. Silence!

DAMIS. What . . .

ORGON. Another word, I'll break your every bone.

TARTUFFE. Brother, in God's name, don't be angry with him!
I'd rather bear myself the bitterest torture
Than have him get a scratch on my account.

ORGON [to his son]. Ungrateful monster!

TARTUFFE. Stop. Upon my knees
I beg you pardon him . . .

ORGON [throwing himself on his knees too, and embracing TARTUFFE]. Alas!
How can you?
[To his son.] Villain! Behold his goodness!

DAMIS. So . . .

ORGON. Be still,

DAMIS. What! I . . .

ORGON. Be still, I say. I know your motives
For this attack. You hate him, all of you;
Wife, children, servants, all let loose upon him,
You have recourse to every shameful trick
To drive this godly man out of my house;
The more you strive to rid yourselves of him,
The more I'll strive to make him stay with me;
I'll have him straightway married to my daughter,
Just to confound the pride of all of you.

DAMIS. What! Will you force her to accept his hand?

ORGON. Yes, and this very evening, to enrage you,
Young rascal! Ah! I'll brave you all, and show you
That I'm the master, and must be obeyed.
Now, down upon your knees this instant, rogue,
And take back what you said, and ask his pardon.

DAMIS. Who? I? Ask pardon of that cheating scoundrel . . . ?

ORGON. Do you resist, you beggar, and insult him?
A cudgel, here! a cudgel!
[*To* TARTUFFE.] Don't restrain me.
[*To his son.*] Off with you! Leave my house this instant, sirrah,
And never dare set foot in it again.

DAMIS. Yes, I will leave your house, but . . .

ORGON. Leave it quickly.
You reprobate, I disinherit you,
And give you, too, my curse into the bargain.   [*Exit* DAMIS.]
What! So insult a saintly man of God!

TARTUFFE. Heaven forgive him all the pain he gives me!
[*To* ORGON.] Could you but know with what distress I see
Them try to vilify me to my brother!

ORGON. Ah!

TARTUFFE. The mere thought of such ingratitude
Makes my soul suffer torture, bitterly . . .
My horror at it . . . Ah! my heart 's so full
I cannot speak . . . I think I'll die of it.

ORGON [*in tears, running to the door through which he drove away his son*].
Scoundrel! I wish I'd never let you go,
But slain you on the spot with my own hand.
[*To* TARTUFFE.] Brother, compose yourself, and don't be angry.

TARTUFFE. Nay, brother, let us end these painful quarrels.
I see what troublous times I bring upon you,
And think 't is needful that I leave this house.

ORGON. What! You can't mean it?

TARTUFFE. Yes, they hate me here,
And try, I find, to make you doubt my faith.

ORGON. What of it? Do you find I listen to them?

TARTUFFE. No doubt they won't stop there. These same reports
You now reject, may some day win a hearing.

ORGON. No, brother, never.

TARTUFFE. Ah! my friend, a woman
May easily mislead her husband's mind.

ORGON. No, no.

TARTUFFE. So let me quickly go away
And thus remove all cause for such attacks.

ORGON. No, you shall stay; my life depends upon it.

TARTUFFE. Then I must mortify myself. And yet,
If you should wish . . .

ORGON. No, never!

TARTUFFE. Very well then;
No more of that. But I shall rule my conduct
To fit the case. Honor is delicate,
And friendship binds me to forestall suspicion,
Prevent all scandal, and avoid your wife.

ORGON. No, you shall haunt her, just to spite them all.
'T is my delight to set them in a rage;
You shall be seen together at all hours;
And what is more, the better to defy them,
I'll have no other heir but you; and straightway
I'll go and make a deed of gift to you,
Drawn in due form, of all my property.
A good true friend, my son-in-law to be,
Is more to me than son, and wife, and kindred.
You will accept my offer, will you not?

TARTUFFE. Heaven's will be done in everything!

ORGON. Poor man!
We'll go make haste to draw the deed aright,
And then let envy burst itself with spite!
    [*Exeunt.*]

ACT IV

[*Enter* CLÉANTE *and* TARTUFFE.]

CLÉANTE. Yes, it's become the talk of
all the town,
And made a stir that's scarcely to your
credit;
And I have met you, sir, most opportunely,
To tell you in a word my frank opinion.
Not to sift out this scandal to the bottom,
Suppose the worst for us — suppose Damis
Acted the traitor, and accused you falsely;
Should not a Christian pardon this offense,
And stifle in his heart all wish for venge-
ance?
Should you permit that, for your petty
quarrel,
A son be driven from his father's house?
I tell you yet again, and tell you frankly,
Every one, high or low, is scandalized;
If you'll take my advice, you'll make it up,
And not push matters to extremities.
Make sacrifice to God of your resentment;
Restore the son to favor with his father.
TARTUFFE. Alas! So far as I'm con-
cerned, how gladly
Would I do so! I bear him no ill-will;
I pardon all, lay nothing to his charge,
And wish with all my heart that I might
serve him;
But Heaven's interests cannot allow it;
If he returns, then I must leave the house.
After his conduct, quite unparalleled,
All intercourse between us would bring
scandal;
God knows what every one's first thought
would be!
They would attribute it to merest schem-
ing
On my part — say that conscious of my
guilt
I feigned a Christian love for my accuser,
But feared him in my heart, and hoped to
win him
And underhandedly secure his silence.
CLÉANTE. You try to put us off with
specious phrases;
But all your arguments are too far-fetched.
Why take upon yourself the cause of
Heaven?
Does Heaven need our help to punish sin-
ners?

Leave to itself the care of its own venge-
ance,
And keep in mind the pardon it commands
us;
Besides, think somewhat less of men's
opinions,
When you are following the will of Heaven.
Shall petty fear of what the world may
think
Prevent the doing of a noble deed?
No! — let us always do as Heaven com-
mands,
And not perplex our brains with further
questions.
TARTUFFE. Already I have told you I
forgive him;
And that is doing, sir, as Heaven com-
mands.
But after this day's scandal and affront
Heaven does not order me to live with him.
CLÉANTE. And does it order you to lend
your ear
To what mere whim suggested to his father,
And to accept the gift of his estates,
On which, in justice, you can make no
claim?
TARTUFFE. No one who knows me, sir,
can have the thought
That I am acting from a selfish motive.
The goods of this world have no charms for
me;
I am not dazzled by their treacherous
glamor;
And if I bring myself to take the gift
Which he insists on giving me, I do so,
To tell the truth, only because I fear
This whole estate may fall into bad hands,
And those to whom it comes may use it ill
And not employ it, as is my design,
For Heaven's glory and my neighbors'
good.
CLÉANTE. Eh, sir, give up these con-
scientious scruples
That well may cause a rightful heir's com-
plaints.
Don't take so much upon yourself, but let
him
Possess what's his, at his own risk and
peril;
Consider, it were better he misused it,
Than you should be accused of robbing him.
I am astounded that unblushingly

You could allow such offers to be made!
Tell me — has true religion any maxim
That teaches us to rob the lawful heir?
If Heaven has made it quite impossible
Damis and you should live together here,
Were it not better you should live quietly
And honorably withdraw, than let the son
Be driven out for your sake, dead against
All reason? 'T would be giving, sir, be-
lieve me
Such an example of your probity . . .
TARTUFFE. Sir, it is half-past three;
certain devotions
Recall me to my closet; you'll forgive me
For leaving you so soon. [*Exit.*]
CLÉANTE [*alone*]. Ah!

[*Enter* ELMIRE, MARIANE, *and* DORINE.]

DORINE [*to* CLÉANTE]. Sir, we beg you
To help us all you can in her behalf;
She's suffering almost more than heart can
bear;
This match her father means to make to-
night
Drives her each moment to despair. He's
coming.
Let us unite our efforts now, we beg you,
And try by strength or skill to change his
purpose.

[*Enter* ORGON.]

ORGON. So ho! I'm glad to find you all
together.
[*To* MARIANE.] Here is the contract that
shall make you happy,
My dear. You know already what it
means.
MARIANE [*on her knees before* ORGON].
Father, I beg you, in the name of
Heaven
That knows my grief, and by whate'er can
move you,
Relax a little your paternal rights,
And free my love from this obedience!
Oh, do not make me, by your harsh com-
mand,
Complain to Heaven you ever were my
father;
Do not make wretched this poor life you
gave me.
If, crossing that fond hope which I had
formed,

You'll not permit me to belong to one
Whom I have dared to love, at least, I beg
you
Upon my knees, oh, save me from the
torment
Of being possessed by one whom I abhor!
And do not drive me to some desperate act
By exercising all your rights upon me.
ORGON [*a little touched*]. Come, come,
my heart, be firm! no human weak-
ness!
MARIANE. I am not jealous of your love
for him;
Display it freely; give him your estate,
And if that's not enough, add all of mine;
I willingly agree, and give it up,
If only you'll not give him me, your
daughter;
Oh, rather let a convent's rigid rule
Wear out the wretched days that Heaven
allots me.
ORGON. These girls are ninnies! — al-
ways turning nuns
When fathers thwart their silly love-affairs.
Get on your feet! The more you hate to
have him,
The more 't will help you earn your soul's
salvation.
So, mortify your senses by this marriage,
And don't vex me about it any more.
DORINE. But what . . . ?
ORGON. You, hold your tongue, before
your betters.
Don't dare to say a single word, I tell you.
CLÉANTE. If you will let me answer,
and advise . . .
ORGON. Brother, I value your advice
most highly;
'T is well thought out; no better can be
had;
But you'll allow me — not to follow it.
ELMIRE [*to her husband*]. I can't find
words to cope with such a case;
Your blindness makes me quite astounded
at you.
You are bewitched with him, to disbelieve
The things we tell you happened here
to-day.
ORGON. I am your humble servant, and
can see
Things, when they're plain as noses on
folks' faces.

I know you're partial to my rascal son,
And did n't dare to disavow the trick
He tried to play on this poor man; besides,
You were too calm, to be believed; if that
Had happened, you'd have been far more
disturbed.

ELMIRE. And must our honor always
rush to arms
At the mere mention of illicit love?
Or can we answer no attack upon it
Except with blazing eyes and lips of scorn?
For my part, I just laugh away such non-
sense;
I've no desire to make a loud to-do.
Our virtue should, I think, be gentle-na-
tured;
Nor can I quite approve those savage
prudes
Whose honor arms itself with teeth and
claws
To tear men's eyes out at the slightest
word.
Heaven preserve me from that kind of
honor!
I like my virtue not to be a vixen,
And I believe a quiet cold rebuff
No less effective to repulse a lover.

ORGON. I know . . . and you can't
throw me off the scent.

ELMIRE. Once more, I am astounded at
your weakness;
I wonder what your unbelief would answer,
If I should let you see we've told the truth?

ORGON. See it?

ELMIRE. Yes.

ORGON. Nonsense.

ELMIRE. Come! If I should find
A way to make you see it clear as day?

ORGON. All rubbish.

ELMIRE. What a man! But answer me.
I'm not proposing now that you believe
us;
But let's suppose that here, from proper
hiding,
You should be made to see and hear all
plainly;
What would you say then, to your man of
virtue?

ORGON. Why, then, I'd say . . . say
nothing. It can't be.

ELMIRE. Your error has endured too long
already,

And quite too long you've branded me a
liar.
I must at once, for my own satisfaction,
Make you a witness of the things we've told
you.

ORGON. Amen! I take you at your word.
We'll see
What tricks you have, and how you'll keep
your promise.

ELMIRE [to DORINE]. Send him to me.

DORINE [to ELMIRE]. The man's a
crafty codger;
Perhaps you'll find it difficult to catch
him.

ELMIRE [to DORINE]. Oh, no! A lover's
never hard to cheat,
And self-conceit leads straight to self-
deceit.
Bid him come down to me.

[To CLÉANTE and MARIANE.] And you,
withdraw.

[Exeunt CLÉANTE and MARIANE.]

ELMIRE. Bring up this table, and get
under it.

ORGON. What?

ELMIRE. One essential is to hide you
well.

ORGON. Why under there?

ELMIRE. Oh, dear! Do as I say;
I know what I'm about, as you shall see.
Get under, now, I tell you; and once there
Be careful no one either sees or hears you.

ORGON. I'm going a long way to humor
you,
I must say; but I'll see you through your
scheme.

ELMIRE. And then you'll have, I think,
no more to say.

[To her husband, who is now under the
table.] But mind, I'm going to
meddle with strange matters;
Prepare yourself to be in no wise shocked.
Whatever I may say must pass, because
'T is only to convince you, as I promised.
By wheedling speeches, since I'm forced
to do it,
I'll make this hypocrite put off his mask,
Flatter the longings of his shameless pas-
sion,
And give free play to all his impudence.
But, since 't is for your sake, to prove to
you

His guilt, that I shall feign to share his
    love,
I can leave off as soon as you're convinced,
And things shall go no further than you
    choose.
So, when you think they've gone quite far
    enough,
It is for you to stop his mad pursuit,
To spare your wife, and not expose me
    further
Than you shall need, yourself, to undeceive
    you.
It is your own affair, and you must end it
When . . . Here he comes. Keep still,
    don't show yourself.

[*Enter* TARTUFFE.]

TARTUFFE. They told me that you wished
    to see me here.
ELMIRE. Yes. I have secrets for your
    ear alone.
But shut the door first, and look every-
    where
For fear of spies.
        [TARTUFFE *goes and closes the
        door, and comes back.*]
We surely can't afford
Another scene like that we had just now;
Was ever any one so caught before!
Damis did frighten me most terribly
On your account; you saw I did my best
To baffle his design, and calm his anger.
But I was so confused, I never thought
To contradict his story; still, thank
    Heaven,
Things turned out all the better, as it hap-
    pened,
And now we're on an even safer footing.
The high esteem you're held in, laid the
    storm;
My husband can have no suspicion of you,
And even insists, to spite the scandal-
    mongers,
That we shall be together constantly;
So that is how, without the risk of blame,
I can be here locked up with you alone,
And can reveal to you my heart, perhaps
Only too ready to allow your passion.
TARTUFFE. Your words are somewhat
    hard to understand,
Madam; just now you used a different
    style.

ELMIRE. If that refusal has offended you,
How little do you know a woman's heart!
How ill you guess what it would have you
    know,
When it presents so feeble a defense!
Always, at first, our modesty resists
The tender feelings you inspire us with.
Whatever cause we find to justify
The love that masters us, we still must feel
Some little shame in owning it; and strive
To make as though we would not, when we
    would.
But from the very way we go about it,
We let a lover know our heart surrenders,
The while our lips, for honor's sake, oppose
Our heart's desire, and in refusing promise.
I'm telling you my secret all too freely
And with too little heed to modesty.
But — now that I've made bold to speak
    — pray, tell me,
Should I have tried to keep Damis from
    speaking,
Should I have heard the offer of your heart
So quietly, and suffered all your pleading,
And taken it just as I did — remember —
If such a declaration had not pleased me,
And, when I tried my utmost to persuade
    you
Not to accept the marriage that was talked
    of,
What should my earnestness have hinted
    to you
If not the interest that you've inspired,
And my chagrin, should such a match
    compel me
To share a heart I want all to myself?
TARTUFFE. 'T is, past a doubt, the
    height of happiness,
To hear such words from lips we dote upon;
Their honeyed sweetness pours through all
    my senses
Long draughts of suavity ineffable.
My heart employs its utmost zeal to please
    you,
And counts your love its one beatitude;
And yet that heart must beg that you al-
    low it
To doubt a little its felicity.
I well might think these words an honest
    trick
To make me break off this approaching
    marriage;

And if I may express myself quite plainly,
I cannot trust these too enchanting words
Until the granting of some little favor
I sigh for, shall assure me of their truth
And build within my soul, on firm founda-
tions,
A lasting faith in your sweet charity.
ELMIRE [*coughing to draw her husband's
attention*]. What! Must you go so
fast? — and all at once
Exhaust the whole love of a woman's
heart?
She does herself the violence to make
This dear confession of her love, and you
Are not yet satisfied, and will not be
Without the granting of her utmost favors?
TARTUFFE. The less a blessing is de-
served, the less
We dare to hope for it; and words alone
Can ill assuage our love's desires. A fate
Too full of happiness, seems doubtful still;
We must enjoy it ere we can believe it.
And I, who know how little I deserve
Your goodness, doubt the fortunes of my
daring;
So I shall trust to nothing, madam, till
You have convinced my love by something
real.
ELMIRE. Ah! How your love enacts the
tyrant's rôle,
And throws my mind into a strange con-
fusion!
With what fierce sway it rules a conquered
heart,
And violently will have its wishes granted!
What! Is there no escape from your pur-
suit?
No respite even? — not a breathing space?
Nay, is it decent to be so exacting,
And so abuse by urgency the weakness
You may discover in a woman's heart?
TARTUFFE. But if my worship wins your
gracious favor,
Then why refuse me some sure proof
thereof?
ELMIRE. But how can I consent to what
you wish,
Without offending Heaven you talk so
much of?
TARTUFFE. If Heaven is all that stands
now in my way,
I'll easily remove that little hindrance;

Your heart need not hold back for such a
trifle.
ELMIRE. But they affright us so with
Heaven's commands!
TARTUFFE. I can dispel these foolish
fears, dear madam;
I know the art of pacifying scruples.
Heaven forbids, 't is true, some satisfac-
tions;
But we find means to make things right
with Heaven.
There is a science, madam, that instructs
us
How to enlarge the limits of our conscience
According to our various occasions,
And rectify the evil of the deed
According to our purity of motive.
I'll duly teach you all these secrets, madam;
You only need to let yourself be guided.
Content my wishes, have no fear at all;
I answer for 't, and take the sin upon me.
[ELMIRE *coughs still louder.*]
Your cough is very bad.
ELMIRE. Yes, I'm in torture.
TARTUFFE. Would you accept this bit
of licorice?
ELMIRE. The case is obstinate, I find;
and all
The licorice in the world will do no good.
TARTUFFE. 'T is very trying.
ELMIRE. More than words can say.
TARTUFFE. In any case, your scruple's
easily
Removed. With me you're sure of secrecy,
And there's no harm unless a thing is
known.
The public scandal is what brings offense,
And secret sinning is not sin at all.
ELMIRE [*after coughing again*]. So then,
I see I must resolve to yield;
I must consent to grant you everything,
And cannot hope to give full satisfaction,
Or win full confidence, at lesser cost.
No doubt 't is very hard to come to this;
'T is quite against my will I go so far;
But since I must be forced to it, since noth-
ing
That can be said suffices for belief,
Since more convincing proof is still de-
manded,
I must make up my mind to humor people.
If my consent give reason for offense,

So much the worse for him who forced me
    to it;
The fault can surely not be counted mine.
TARTUFFE. It need not, madam; and the
    thing itself . . .
ELMIRE. Open the door, I pray you, and
    just see
Whether my husband's not there, in the
    hall.
TARTUFFE. Why take such care for him?
    Between ourselves,
He is a man to lead round by the nose.
He's capable of glorying in our meetings;
I've fooled him so, he'd see all, and deny
    it.
ELMIRE. No matter; go, I beg you, look
    about,
And carefully examine every corner.
                  [*Exit* TARTUFFE.]
ORGON [*crawling out from under the
    table*]. That is, I own, a man . . .
    abominable!
I can't get over it; the whole thing floors
    me.
ELMIRE. What? You come out so soon?
    You cannot mean it!
Go back under the table; 't is not time
    yet;
Wait till the end, to see, and make quite
    certain,
And don't believe a thing on mere conjec-
    ture.
ORGON. Nothing more wicked e'er came
    out of hell.
ELMIRE. Dear me! Don't go and credit
    things too lightly.
No, let yourself be thoroughly convinced;
Don't yield too soon, for fear you'll be
    mistaken.
    [*As* TARTUFFE *enters, she makes
    her husband stand behind her.*]
TARTUFFE [*not seeing* ORGON]. All things
    conspire toward my satisfaction,
Madam. I've searched the whole apart-
    ment through.
There's no one here; and now my ravished
    soul . . .
| ORGON [*stopping him*]. Softly! You are
    too eager in your amours;
You need n't be so passionate. Ah, ha!
My holy man! You want to put it on
    me!

How is your soul abandoned to temptation!
Marry my daughter, eh? — and want my
    wife, too?
I doubted long enough if this was earnest,
Expecting all the time the tone would
    change;
But now the proof's been carried far
    enough;
I'm satisfied, and ask no more, for my
    part.
ELMIRE [*to* TARTUFFE]. 'T was quite
    against my character to play
This part; but I was forced to treat you
    so.
TARTUFFE. What? You believe . . . ?
ORGON. Come, now, no protestations.
Get out from here, and make no fuss about
    it.
TARTUFFE. But my intent . . .
ORGON. That talk is out of season.
You leave my house this instant.
TARTUFFE. You're the one
To leave it, you who play the master here!
This house belongs to me, I'll have you
    know,
And show you plainly it 's no use to turn
To these low tricks, to pick a quarrel with
    me,
And that you can't insult me at your
    pleasure,
For I have wherewith to confound your
    lies,
Avenge offended Heaven, and compel
Those to repent who talk to me of leaving.
               [*Exit* TARTUFFE.]
ELMIRE. What sort of speech is this?
    What can it mean?
ORGON. My faith, I'm dazed. This is
    no laughing matter.
ELMIRE. What?
ORGON. From his words I see my great
    mistake;
The deed of gift is one thing troubles me.
ELMIRE. The deed of gift . . .
ORGON. Yes, that is past recall.
But I've another thing to make me anx-
    ious.
ELMIRE. What's that?
ORGON. You shall know all. Let's see
    at once
Whether a certain box is still upstairs
                   [*Exeunt.*]

ACT V

[*Enter* ORGON *and* CLÉANTE.]

CLÉANTE. Whither away so fast?

ORGON. How should I know?

CLÉANTE. Methinks we should begin by
taking counsel
To see what can be done to meet the case.

ORGON. I'm all worked up about that
wretched box.
More than all else it drives me to despair.

CLÉANTE. That box must hide some
mighty mystery?

ORGON. Argas, my friend who is in
trouble, brought it
Himself, most secretly, and left it with me.
He chose me, in his exile, for this trust;
And on these documents, from what he
said,
I judge his life and property depend.

CLÉANTE. How could you trust them to
another's hands?

ORGON. By reason of a conscientious
scruple.
I went straight to my traitor, to confide
In him; his sophistry made me believe
That I must give the box to him to keep,
So that, in case of search, I might deny
My having it at all, and still, by favor
Of this evasion, keep my conscience clear
Even in taking oath against the truth.

CLÉANTE. Your case is bad, so far as I
can see;
This deed of gift, this trusting of the
secret
To him, were both — to state my frank
opinion —
Steps that you took too lightly; he can
lead you
To any length, with these for hostages;
And since he holds you at such a disad-
vantage,
You'd be still more imprudent, to provoke
him;
So you must go some gentler way about.

ORGON. What! Can a soul so base, a
heart so false,
Hide 'neath the semblance of such touching
fervor!
I took him in, a vagabond, a beggar! . . .
'T is too much! No more pious folk for
me!

I shall abhor them utterly forever,
And henceforth treat them worse than any
devil.

CLÉANTE. So! There you go again, quite
off the handle!
In nothing do you keep an even temper.
You never know what reason is, but al-
ways
Jump first to one extreme, and then the
other.
You see your error, and you recognize
That you've been cozened by a feignèd
zeal;
But to make up for 't, in the name of rea-
son,
Why should you plunge into a worse mis-
take,
And find no difference in character
Between a worthless scamp, and all good
people?
What! Just because a rascal boldly duped
you
With pompous show of false austerity,
Must you needs have it everybody's like
him,
And no one's truly pious nowadays?
Leave such conclusions to mere infidels;
Distinguish virtue from its counterfeit,
Don't give esteem too quickly, at a ven-
ture,
But try to keep, in this, the golden mean.
If you can help it, don't uphold impos-
ture;
But do not rail at true devoutness, either;
And if you must fall into one extreme,
Then rather err again the other way.

[*Enter* DAMIS.]

DAMIS. What! father, can the scoundrel
threaten you,
Forget the many benefits received,
And in his base abominable pride
Make of your very favors arms against
you?

ORGON. Too true, my son. It tortures
me to think on 't.

DAMIS. Let me alone, I'll chop his ears
off for him.
We must deal roundly with his insolence;
'T is I must free you from him at a blow;
'T is I, to set things right, must strike him
down.

CLÉANTE. Spoke like a true young man.
Now, just calm down,
And moderate your towering tantrums,
will you?
We live in such an age, with such a king,
That violence cannot advance our cause.

[Enter MADAME PERNELLE, ELMIRE,
MARIANE, and DORINE.]

MADAME PERNELLE. What's this? I
hear of fearful mysteries!
ORGON. Strange things, indeed, for my
own eyes to witness;
You see how I'm requited for my kindness.
I zealously receive a wretched beggar,
I lodge him, entertain him like my brother,
Load him with benefactions every day,
Give him my daughter, give him all my
fortune:
And he meanwhile, the villain, rascal,
wretch,
Tries with black treason to suborn my
wife,
And not content with such a foul design,
He dares to menace me with my own
favors,
And would make use of those advantages
Which my too foolish kindness armed him
with,
To ruin me, to take my fortune from me,
And leave me in the state I saved him from.
DORINE. Poor man!
MADAME PERNELLE. My son, I cannot
possibly
Believe he could intend so black a deed.
ORGON. What?
MADAME PERNELLE. Worthy men are
still the sport of envy.
ORGON. Mother, what do you mean by
such a speech?
MADAME PERNELLE. There are strange
goings-on about your house,
And everybody knows your people hate
him.
ORGON. What's that to do with what I
tell you now?
MADAME PERNELLE. I always said, my
son, when you were little:
That virtue here below is hated ever;
The envious may die, but envy never.
ORGON. What's that fine speech to do
with present facts?

MADAME PERNELLE. Be sure, they've
forged a hundred silly lies . . .
ORGON. I've told you once, I saw it all
myself.
MADAME PERNELLE. For slanderers
abound in calumnies . . .
ORGON. Mother, you'd make me damn
my soul. I tell you
I saw with my own eyes his shamelessness.
MADAME PERNELLE. Their tongues for
spitting venom never lack,
There's nothing here below they'll not
attack.
ORGON. Your speech has not a single
grain of sense.
I saw it, harkee, saw it, with these eyes
I saw — d' ye know what saw means? —
must I say it
A hundred times, and din it in your ears?
MADAME PERNELLE. My dear, appear-
ances are oft deceiving,
And seeing should n't always be believing.
ORGON. I'll go mad.
MADAME PERNELLE. False suspicions
may delude,
And good to evil oft is misconstrued.
ORGON. Must I construe as Christian
charity
The wish to kiss my wife!
MADAME PERNELLE. You must, at least,
Have just foundation for accusing people,
And wait until you see a thing for sure.
ORGON. The devil! How could I see any
surer?
Should I have waited till, before my eyes,
He . . . No, you'll make me say things
quite improper.
MADAME PERNELLE. In short, 't is
known too pure a zeal inflames him;
And so, I cannot possibly conceive
That he should try to do what's charged
against him.
ORGON. If you were not my mother, I
should say
Such things! . . . I know not what, I'm so
enraged!
DORINE [to ORGON]. Fortune has paid
you fair, to be so doubted;
You flouted our report, now yours is
flouted.
CLÉANTE. We're wasting time here in
the merest trifling,

Which we should rather use in taking measures
To guard ourselves against the scoundrel's threats.
DAMIS. You think his impudence could go so far?
ELMIRE. For one, I can't believe it possible;
Why, his ingratitude would be too patent.
CLÉANTE. Don't trust to that; he'll find abundant warrant
To give good color to his acts against you;
And for less cause than this, a strong cabal
Can make one's life a labyrinth of troubles.
I tell you once again: armed as he is
You never should have pushed him quite so far.
ORGON. True; yet what could I do? The rascal's pride
Made me lose all control of my resentment.
CLÉANTE. I wish with all my heart that some pretense
Of peace could be patched up between you two.
ELMIRE. If I had known what weapons he was armed with,
I never should have raised such an alarm,
And my . . .
ORGON [to DORINE, seeing MR. LOYAL come in]. Who's coming now? Go quick, find out.
I'm in a fine state to receive a visit!
MR. LOYAL [to DORINE, at the back of the stage]. Good-day, good sister. Pray you, let me see
The master of the house.
DORINE. He's occupied;
I think he can see nobody at present.
MR. LOYAL. I'm not by way of being unwelcome here.
My coming can, I think, nowise displease him;
My errand will be found to his advantage.
DORINE. Your name, then?
MR. LOYAL. Tell him simply that his friend
Mr. Tartuffe has sent me, for his goods . . .
DORINE [to ORGON]. It is a man who comes, with civil manners,
Sent by Tartuffe, he says, upon an errand
That you'll be pleased with.

CLÉANTE [to ORGON]. Surely you must see him,
And find out who he is, and what he wants.
ORGON [to CLÉANTE]. Perhaps he's come to make it up between us;
How shall I treat him?
CLÉANTE. You must not get angry;
And if he talks of reconciliation,
Accept it.
MR. LOYAL [to ORGON]. Sir, good-day. And Heaven send
Harm to your enemies, favor to you.
ORGON [aside to CLÉANTE]. This mild beginning suits with my conjectures
And promises some compromise already.
MR. LOYAL. All of your house has long been dear to me;
I had the honor, sir, to serve your father.
ORGON. Sir, I am much ashamed, and ask your pardon
For not recalling now your face or name.
MR. LOYAL. My name is Loyal. I'm from Normandy.
My office is court-bailiff, in despite
Of envy; and for forty years, thank Heaven
It's been my fortune to perform that office
With honor. So I've come, sir, by your leave,
To render service of a certain writ . . .
ORGON. What, you are here to . . .
MR. LOYAL. Pray, sir, don't be angry.
'T is nothing, sir, but just a little summons: —
Order to vacate, you and yours, this house,
Move out your furniture, make room for others,
And that without delay or putting off,
As needs must be . . .
ORGON. I? Leave this house?
MR. LOYAL. Yes, please, sir.
The house is now, as you well know, of course,
Mr. Tartuffe's. And he, beyond dispute,
Of all your goods is henceforth lord and master
By virtue of a contract here attached,
Drawn in due form, and unassailable.
DAMIS [to MR. LOYAL]. Your insolence is monstrous, and astounding!
MR. LOYAL [to DAMIS]. I have no business, sir, that touches you;
[Pointing to ORGON.] This is the gentleman. He's fair and courteous,

And knows too well a gentleman's behavior
To wish in any wise to question justice.
ORGON. But . . .
MR. LOYAL. Sir, I know you would not
    for a million
Wish to rebel; like a good citizen
You'll let me put in force the court's de-
    cree.
DAMIS. Your long black gown may well,
    before you know it,
Mister Court-bailiff, get a thorough beat-
    ing.
MR. LOYAL [to ORGON]. Sir, make your
    son be silent or withdraw.
I should be loath to have to set things down,
And see your names inscribed in my report.
DORINE [aside]. This Mr. Loyal's looks
    are most disloyal.
MR. LOYAL. I have much feeling for
    respectable
And honest folk like you, sir, and con-
    sented
To serve these papers, only to oblige you,
And thus prevent the choice of any other
Who, less possessed of zeal for you than
    I am,
Might order matters in less gentle fashion.
ORGON. And how could one do worse
    than order people
Out of their house?
MR. LOYAL. Why, we allow you time;
And even will suspend until to-morrow
The execution of the order, sir.
I'll merely, without scandal, quietly,
Come here and spend the night, with half
    a score
Of officers; and just for form's sake, please
You'll bring your keys to me, before retir-
    ing.
I will take care not to disturb your rest,
And see there's no unseemly conduct here.
But by to-morrow, and at early morning,
You must make haste to move your least
    belongings;
My men will help you — I have chosen
    strong ones
To serve you, sir, in clearing out the house.
No one could act more generously, I fancy,
And, since I'm treating you with great in-
    dulgence,
I beg you'll do as well by me, and see
I'm not disturbed in my discharge of duty.

ORGON. I'd give this very minute, and
    not grudge it,
The hundred best gold louis I have left,
If I could just indulge myself, and land
My fist, for one good square one, on his
    snout.
CLÉANTE [aside to ORGON]. Careful! —
    don't make things worse.
DAMIS. Such insolence!
I hardly can restrain myself. My hands
Are itching to be at him.
DORINE. By my faith,
With such a fine broad back, good Mr.
    Loyal,
A little beating would become you well.
MR. LOYAL. My girl, such infamous
    words are actionable,
And warrants can be issued against women.
CLÉANTE [to MR. LOYAL]. Enough of
    this discussion, sir; have done.
Give us the paper, and then leave us,
    pray.
MR. LOYAL. Then au revoir. Heaven
    keep you from disaster!   [Exit.]
ORGON. May Heaven confound you
    both, you and your master!
— Well, mother, am I right or am I not?
This writ may help you now to judge the
    matter.
Or don't you see his treason even yet?
MADAME PERNELLE. I'm all amazed,
    befuddled, and beflustered!
DORINE [to ORGON]. You are quite
    wrong, you have no right to blame
    him;
This action only proves his good inten-
    tions.
Love for his neighbor makes his virtue
    perfect;
And knowing money is a root of evil,
In Christian charity, he'd take away
Whatever things may hinder your salva-
    tion.
ORGON. Be still. You always need to
    have that told you.
CLÉANTE [to ORGON]. Come, let us see
    what course you are to follow.
ELMIRE. Go and expose his bold in-
    gratitude.
Such action must invalidate the contract;
His perfidy must now appear too black
To bring him the success that he expects.

[*Enter* VALÈRE.]

VALÈRE. 'T is with regret, sir, that I
bring bad news;
But urgent danger forces me to do so.
A close and intimate friend of mine, who
knows
The interest I take in what concerns you,
Has gone so far, for my sake, as to break
The secrecy that's due to state affairs,
And sent me word but now, that leaves you
only
The one expedient of sudden flight.
The villain who so long imposed upon you,
Found means, an hour ago, to see the
prince,
And to accuse you (among other things)
By putting in his hands the private strong-
box
Of a state criminal, whose guilty secret,
You failing in your duty as a subject
(He says) have kept. I know no more of it
Save that a warrant's drawn against you,
sir,
And for the greater surety, that same rascal
Comes with the officer who must arrest
you.
CLÉANTE. His rights are armed; and
this is how the scoundrel
Seeks to secure the property he claims.
ORGON. Man is a wicked animal, I'll
own it!
VALÈRE. The least delay may still be
fatal, sir.
I have my carriage, and a thousand louis,
Provided for your journey, at the door.
Let's lose no time; the bolt is swift to
strike,
And such as only flight can save you from.
I'll be your guide to seek a place of safety,
And stay with you until you reach it, sir.
ORGON. How much I owe to your oblig-
ing care!
Another time must serve to thank you fitly;
And I pray Heaven to grant me so much
favor
That I may some day recompense your
service.
Good-bye; see to it, all of you . . .
CLÉANTE. Come, hurry;
We'll see to everything that's needful,
brother.

[*Enter* TARTUFFE *and an Officer.*]

TARTUFFE [*stopping* ORGON]. Softly, sir,
softly; do not run so fast;
You have n't far to go to find your lodg-
ing;
By order of the prince, we here arrest you.
ORGON. Traitor! You saved this worst
stroke for the last;
This crowns your perfidies, and ruins me.
TARTUFFE. I shall not be embittered by
your insults,
For Heaven has taught me to endure all
things.
CLÉANTE. Your moderation, I must
own, is great.
DAMIS. How shamelessly the wretch
makes bold with Heaven!
TARTUFFE. Your ravings cannot move
me; all my thought
Is but to do my duty.
MARIANE. You must claim
Great glory from this honorable act.
TARTUFFE. The act cannot be aught but
honorable,
Coming from that high power which sends
me here.
ORGON. Ungrateful wretch, do you for-
get 't was I
That rescued you from utter misery?
TARTUFFE. I've not forgot some help
you may have given;
But my first duty now is toward my prince.
The higher power of that most sacred
claim
Must stifle in my heart all gratitude;
And to such puissant ties I'd sacrifice
My friend, my wife, my kindred, and my-
self.
ELMIRE. The hypocrite!
DORINE. How well he knows the trick
Of cloaking him with what we most revere!
CLÉANTE. But if the motive that you
make parade of
Is perfect as you say, why should it wait
To show itself, until the day he caught you
Soliciting his wife? How happens it
You have not thought to go inform against
him
Until his honor forces him to drive you
Out of his house? And though I need not
mention

That he's just given you his whole estate,
Still, if you meant to treat him now as
   guilty,
How could you then consent to take his
   gift?
TARTUFFE [to the Officer]. Pray, sir, de-
   liver me from all this clamor;
Be good enough to carry out your order.
THE OFFICER. Yes, I've too long de-
   layed its execution;
'T is very fitting you should urge me to it;
So, therefore, you must follow me at once
To prison, where you'll find your lodging
   ready.
TARTUFFE. Who? I, sir?
THE OFFICER. You.
TARTUFFE. But why to prison?
THE OFFICER. You
Are not the one to whom I owe account.
You, sir [to ORGON], recover from your hot
   alarm.
Our prince is not a friend to double-deal-
   ing,
His eyes can read men's inmost hearts, and
   all
The art of hypocrites cannot deceive him.
His sharp discernment sees things clear and
   true;
His mind cannot too easily be swayed,
For reason always holds the balance even.
He honors and exalts true piety,
But knows the false, and views it with dis-
   gust.
This fellow was by no means apt to fool
   him,
Far subtler snares have failed against his
   wisdom,
And his quick insight pierced immediately
The hidden baseness of this tortuous heart.
Accusing you, the knave betrayed him-
   self,
And by true recompense of Heaven's justice
He stood revealed before our monarch's
   eyes
A scoundrel known before by other names,
Whose horrid crimes, detailed at length,
   might fill
A long-drawn history of many volumes.
Our monarch — to resolve you in a word —
Detesting his ingratitude and baseness,
Added this horror to his other crimes,

And sent me hither under his direction
To see his insolence out-top itself,
And force him then to give you satisfac-
   tion.
Your papers, which the traitor says are his,
I am to take from him, and give you back;
The deed of gift transferring your estate
Our monarch's sovereign will makes null
   and void;
And for the secret personal offense
Your friend involved you in, he pardons
   you:
Thus he rewards your recent zeal, dis-
   played
In helping to maintain his rights, and shows
How well his heart, when it is least ex-
   pected,
Knows how to recompense a noble deed,
And will not let true merit miss its due,
Remembering always rather good than
   evil.
DORINE. Now, Heaven be praised!
MADAME PERNELLE. At last I breathe
   again.
ELMIRE. A happy outcome!
MARIANE. Who'd have dared to hope
   it?
ORGON [to TARTUFFE, who is being led off
   by the Officer]. There, traitor! Now,
   you're . . .
                [Exeunt TARTUFFE and Officer.]
CLÉANTE. Brother, hold ! — and don't
Descend to such indignities, I beg you.
Leave the poor wretch to his unhappy fate,
And let remorse oppress him, but not you.
Hope rather that his heart may now return
To virtue, hate his vice, reform his ways,
And win the pardon of our glorious prince;
While you must straightway go, and on
   your knees
Repay with thanks his noble generous
   kindness.
ORGON. Well said! We'll go, and at his
   feet kneel down,
With joy to thank him for his goodness
   shown;
And this first duty done, with honors due,
We'll then attend upon another, too,
With wedded happiness reward Valère,
And crown a lover noble and sincere.
                [Exeunt omnes.]

PHÆDRA

(PHÈDRE)

By JEAN RACINE

Translated into English blank verse by ROBERT BRUCE BOSWELL

CHARACTERS

THESEUS, *son of Ægeus and King of Athens*

PHÆDRA, *wife of Theseus and daughter of Minos and Pasiphaë*

HIPPOLYTUS, *son of Theseus and Antiope, Queen of the Amazons*

ARICIA, *Princess of the Blood Royal of Athens*

ŒNONE, *nurse of Phædra*

THERAMENES, *tutor of Hippolytus*

ISMENE, *bosom friend of Aricia*

PANOPE, *waiting-woman of Phædra*

Guards

The scene is laid at Trœzen, a town of the Peloponnesus

PHÆDRA

ACT I

[*Enter* HIPPOLYTUS, THERAMENES.]

HIPPOLYTUS. My mind is settled, dear
    Theramenes,
And I can stay not more in lovely Trœzen.
In doubt that racks my soul with mortal
    anguish,
I grow ashamed of such long idleness.
Six months and more my father has been
    gone,
And what may have befallen one so dear
I know not, nor what corner of the earth
Hides him.
    THERAMENES. And where, prince, will
      you look for him?
Already, to content your just alarm,
Have I not cross'd the seas on either side
Of Corinth, ask'd if aught were known of
    Theseus
Where Acheron is lost among the Shades,
Visited Elis, doubled Tœnarus,
And sail'd into the sea that saw the fall
Of Icarus? Inspired with what new hope,
Under what favor'd skies think you to trace
His footsteps? Who knows if the king, your
    father,
Wishes the secret of his absence known?
Perchance, while we are trembling for his
    life,
The hero calmly plots some fresh intrigue,
And only waits till the deluded fair —
    HIPPOLYTUS. Cease, dear Theramenes,
      respect the name
Of Theseus. Youthful errors have been left
Behind, and no unworthy obstacle
Detains him. Phædra long has fix'd a heart
Inconstant once, nor need she fear a rival.
In seeking him I shall but do my duty,
And leave a place I dare no longer see.
    THERAMENES. Indeed! When, prince,
      did you begin to dread
These peaceful haunts, so dear to happy
    childhood,
Where I have seen you oft prefer to stay,

Rather than meet the tumult and the pomp
Of Athens and the court? What danger
    shun you,
Or shall I say what grief?
    HIPPOLYTUS. That happy time
Is gone, and all is changed, since to these
    shores
The gods sent Phædra.
    THERAMENES. I perceive the cause
Of your distress. It is the queen whose sight
Offends you. With a step-dame's spite she
    schemed
Your exile soon as she set eyes on you.
But if her hatred is not wholly vanish'd,
It has at least taken a milder aspect.
Besides, what danger can a dying woman,
One too who longs for death, bring on your
    head?
Can Phædra, sick'ning of a dire disease
Of which she will not speak, weary of life
And of herself, form any plots against you?
    HIPPOLYTUS. It is not her vain enmity I
      fear;
Another foe alarms Hippolytus.
I fly, it must be own'd, from young Aricia,
The sole survivor of an impious race.
    THERAMENES. What! You become her
      persecutor too!
The gentle sister of the cruel sons
Of Pallas shared not in their perfidy;
Why should you hate such charming inno-
    cence?
    HIPPOLYTUS. I should not need to fly, if
      it were hatred.
    THERAMENES. May I, then, learn the
      meaning of your flight?
Is this the proud Hippolytus I see,
Than whom there breathed no fiercer foe to
    love
And to that yoke which Theseus has so oft
Endured? And can it be that Venus,
    scorn'd
So long, will justify your sire at last?
Has she, then, setting you with other mor-
    tals,

Forced e'en Hippolytus to offer incense
Before her? Can you love?
HIPPOLYTUS. Friend, ask me not.
You, who have known my heart from in-
    fancy
And all its feelings of disdainful pride,
Spare me the shame of disavowing all
That I profess'd. Born of an Amazon,
The wildness that you wonder at I suck'd
With mother's milk. When come to riper
    age,
Reason approved what Nature had im-
    planted.
Sincerely bound to me by zealous service,
You told me then the story of my sire,
And know how oft, attentive to your voice,
I kindled when I heard his noble acts,
As you described him bringing consolation
To mortals for the absence of Alcides,
The highways clear'd of monsters and of
    robbers,
Procrustes, Cercyon, Sciro, Sinnis slain,
The Epidaurian giant's bones dispersed,
Crete reeking with the blood of Minotaur.
But when you told me of less glorious
    deeds,
Troth plighted here and there and every-
    where,
Young Helen stolen from her home at
    Sparta,
And Peribœa's tear s in Salamis,
With many another trusting heart deceived
Whose very names have 'scaped his mem-
    ory,
Forsaken Ariadne to the rocks
Complaining, last this Phædra, bound to
    him
By better ties, — you know with what
    regret
I heard and urged you to cut short the tale,
Happy had I been able to erase
From my remembrance that unworthy
    part
Of such a splendid record. I, in turn,
Am I too made the slave of love, and
    brought
To stoop so low? The more contemptible
That no renown is mine such as exalts
The name of Theseus, that no monsters
    quell'd
Have given me a right to share his weak-
    ness.

And if my pride of heart must needs be
    humbled,
Aricia should have been the last to tame it.
Was I beside myself to have forgotten
Eternal barriers of separation
Between us? By my father's stern com-
    mand
Her brethren's blood must ne'er be rein-
    forced
By sons of hers; he dreads a single shoot
From stock so guilty, and would fain with
    her
Bury their name, that, even to the tomb
Content to be his ward, for her no torch
Of Hymen may be lit. Shall I espouse
Her rights against my sire, rashly provoke
His wrath, and launch upon a mad career—
    THERAMENES. The gods, dear prince, if
        once your hour is come,
Care little for the reasons that should
    guide us.
Wishing to shut your eyes, Theseus unseals
    them;
His hatred, stirring a rebellious flame
Within you, lends his enemy new charms.
And, after all, why should a guiltless pas-
    sion
Alarm you? Dare you not essay its sweet-
    ness,
But follow rather a fastidious scruple?
Fear you to stray where Hercules has wan-
    der'd?
What heart so stout that Venus has not
    vanquish'd?
Where would you be yourself, so long her
    foe,
Had your own mother, constant in her scorn
Of love, ne'er glowed with tenderness for
    Theseus?
What boots it to affect a pride you feel not?
Confess it, all is changed; for some time
    past
You have been seldom seen with wild de-
    light
Urging the rapid car along the strand,
Or, skillful in the art that Neptune taught,
Making th' unbroken steed obey the bit;
Less often have the woods return'd our
    shouts;
A secret burden on your spirits cast
Has dimm'd your eye. How can I doubt
    you love?

Vainly would you conceal the fatal wound.
Has not the fair Aricia touch'd your heart?
HIPPOLYTUS. Theramenes, I go to find
my father.
THERAMENES. Will you not see the
queen before you start, ,
My prince?
HIPPOLYTUS. That is my purpose: you
can tell her.
Yes, I will see her; duty bids me do it.
But what new ill vexes her dear Œnone?

[*Enter* ŒNONE.]

ŒNONE. Alas, my lord, what grief was
e'er like mine?
The queen has almost touch'd the gates of
death.
Vainly close watch I keep by day and night,
E'en in my arms a secret malady
Slays her, and all her senses are disorder'd.
Weary yet restless from her couch she rises,
Pants for the outer air, but bids me see
That no one on her misery intrudes.
She comes.
HIPPOLYTUS. Enough. She shall not be
disturb'd,
Nor be confronted with a face she hates.
[*Exeunt* HIPPOLYTUS *and* THERA-
MENES.]

[*Enter* PHÆDRA.]

PHÆDRA. We have gone far enough.
Stay, dear Œnone;
Strength fails me, and I needs must rest
awhile.
My eyes are dazzled with this glaring light
So long unseen, my trembling knees refuse
Support. Ah me!
ŒNONE. Would Heaven that our tears
Might bring relief!
PHÆDRA. Ah, how these cumbrous gauds,
These veils oppress me! What officious
hand
Has tied these knots, and gather'd o'er my
brow
These clustering coils? How all conspires
to add
To my distress!
ŒNONE. What is one moment wish'd,
The next, is irksome. Did you not just now,
Sick of inaction, bid us deck you out,
And, with your former energy recall'd,

Desire to go abroad, and see the light
Of day once more? You see it, and would
fain
Be hidden from the sunshine that you
sought.
PHÆDRA. Thou glorious author of a hap-
less race,
Whose daughter 't was my mother's boast
to be,
Who well may'st blush to see me in such
plight,
For the last time I come to look on thee,
O Sun!
ŒNONE. What! Still are you in love with
death?
Shall I ne'er see you, reconciled to life,
Forego these cruel accents of despair?
PHÆDRA. Would I were seated in the
forest's shade!
When may I follow with delighted eye,
Thro' glorious dust flying in full career,
A chariot —
ŒNONE. Madam?
PHÆDRA. Have I lost my senses?
What said I? and where am I? Whither
stray
Vain wishes? Ah! The gods have made me
mad.
I blush, Œnone, and confusion covers
My face, for I have let you see too clearly
The shame and grief that, in my own de-
spite,
O'erflow these eyes of mine.
ŒNONE. If you must blush,
Blush at a silence that inflames your woes.
Resisting all my care, deaf to my voice,
Will you have no compassion on yourself,
But let your life be ended in mid course?
What evil spell has drain'd its fountain dry?
Thrice have the shades of night obscured
the heav'ns
Since sleep has enter'd thro' your eyes, and
thrice
The dawn has chased the darkness thence,
since food
Pass'd your wan lips, and you are faint and
languid.
To what dread purpose is your heart in-
clined?
How dare you make attempts upon your
life,
And so offend the gods who gave it you,

Prove false to Theseus and your marriage
    vows,
Ay, and betray your most unhappy chil-
    dren,
Bending their necks yourself beneath the
    yoke?
That day, be sure, which robs them of their
    mother,
Will give high hopes back to the stranger's
    son,
To that proud enemy of you and yours,
To whom an Amazon gave birth, I mean
    Hippolytus —
    PHÆDRA. Ye gods!
    ŒNONE. Ah, this reproach
Moves you!
    PHÆDRA. Unhappy woman, to what
    name
Gave your mouth utterance?
    ŒNONE. Your wrath is just.
'T is well that that ill-omen'd name can
    rouse
Such rage. Then live. Let love and duty
    urge
Their claims. Live, suffer not this son of
    Scythia,
Crushing your children 'neath his odious
    sway,
To rule the noble offspring of the gods,
The purest blood of Greece. Make no delay;
Each moment threatens death; quickly
    restore
Your shatter'd strength, while yet the
    torch of life
Holds out, and can be fann'd into a flame.
    PHÆDRA. Too long have I endured its
    guilt and shame!
    ŒNONE. Why? What remorse gnaws at
    your heart? What crime
Can have disturb'd you thus? Your hands
    are not
Polluted with the blood of innocence?
    PHÆDRA. Thanks be to Heav'n, my
    hands are free from stain.
Would that my soul were innocent as they!
    ŒNONE. What awful project have you
    then conceived,
Whereat your conscience should be still
    alarm'd?
    PHÆDRA. Have I not said enough?
    Spare me the rest.
I die to save myself a full confession.

    ŒNONE. Die then, and keep a silence so
    inhuman;
But seek some other hand to close your
    eyes.
Tho' but a spark of life remains within you,
My soul shall go before you to the Shades.
A thousand roads are always open thither;
Pain'd at your want of confidence, I'll
    choose
The shortest. Cruel one, when has my
    faith
Deceived you? Think how in my arms you
    lay
New born. For you, my country and my
    children
I have forsaken. Do you thus repay
My faithful service?
    PHÆDRA. What do you expect
From words so bitter? Were I to break
    silence,
Horror would freeze your blood.
    ŒNONE. What can you say
To horrify me more than to behold
You die before my eyes?
    PHÆDRA. When you shall know
My crime, my death will follow none the
    less,
But with the added stain of guilt.
    ŒNONE. Dear madam,
By all the tears that I have shed for you,
By these weak knees I clasp, relieve my
    mind
From torturing doubt.
    PHÆDRA. It is your wish. Then rise.
    ŒNONE. I hear you. Speak.
    PHÆDRA. Heav'ns! How shall I begin?
    ŒNONE. Dismiss vain fears, you wound
    me with distrust.
    PHÆDRA. O fatal animosity of Venus!
Into what wild distractions did she cast
My mother!
    ŒNONE. Be they blotted from remem-
    brance,
And for all time to come buried in silence.
    PHÆDRA. My sister Ariadne, by what
    love
Were you betray'd to death, on lonely
    shores
Forsaken!
    ŒNONE. Madam, what deep-seated pain
Prompts these reproaches against all your
    kin?

PHÆDRA. It is the will of Venus, and I
    perish,
Last, most unhappy of a family
Where all were wretched.
ŒNONE. Do you love?
PHÆDRA. I feel
All its mad fever.
ŒNONE. Ah! For whom?
PHÆDRA. Hear now
The crowning horror. Yes, I love — my
    lips
Tremble to say his name. .
ŒNONE. Whom?
PHÆDRA. Know you him,
Son of the Amazon, whom I've oppress'd
So long?
ŒNONE. Hippolytus? Great gods!
PHÆDRA. 'T is you
Have named him.
ŒNONE. All my blood within my veins
Seems frozen. O despair! O cursèd race!
Ill-omen'd journey! Land of misery!
Why did we ever reach thy dangerous
    shores?
PHÆDRA. My wound is not so recent.
    Scarcely had I
Been bound to Theseus by the marriage
    yoke,
And happiness and peace seem'd well
    secured,
When Athens show'd me my proud enemy.
I look'd, alternately turn'd pale and
    blush'd
To see him, and my soul grew all distraught;
A mist obscured my vision, and my voice
Falter'd, my blood ran cold, then burn'd
    like fire;
Venus I felt in all my fever'd frame,
Whose fury had so many of my race
Pursued. With fervent vows I sought to
    shun
Her torments, built and deck'd for her a
    shrine,
And there, 'mid countless victims did I
    seek
The reason I had lost; but all for naught,
No remedy could cure the wounds of love!
In vain I offer'd incense on her altars;
When I invoked her name my heart adored
Hippolytus, before me constantly;
And when I made her altars smoke with
    victims,

'T was for a god whose name I dared not
    utter.
I fled his presence everywhere, but found
    him —
O crowning horror! — in his father's fea-
    tures.
Against myself, at last, I raised revolt,
And stirr'd my courage up to persecute
The enemy I loved. To banish him
I wore a step-dame's harsh and jealous
    carriage,
With ceaseless cries I clamor'd for his exile,
Till I had torn him from his father's arms.
I breathed once more, Œnone; in his ab-
    sence
My days flow'd on less troubled than before,
And innocent. Submissive to my husband,
I hid my grief, and of our fatal marriage
Cherish'd the fruits. Vain caution! Cruel
    Fate!
Brought hither by my spouse himself, I saw
Again the enemy whom I had banish'd,
And the old wound too quickly bled afresh.
No longer is it love hid in my heart,
But Venus in her might seizing her prey.
I have conceived just terror for my crime;
I hate my life, and hold my love in horror.
Dying I wish'd to keep my fame unsullied,
And bury in the grave a guilty passion;
But I have been unable to withstand
Tears and entreaties, I have told you all;
Content, if only, as my end draws near,
You do not vex me with unjust reproaches,
Nor with vain efforts seek to snatch from
    death
The last faint lingering sparks of vital
    breath.

[*Enter* PANOPE.]

PANOPE. Fain would I hide from you
    tidings so sad,
But 't is my duty, madam, to reveal them.
The hand of death has seized your peerless
    husband,
And you are last to hear of this disaster.
ŒNONE. What say you, Panope?
PANOPE. The queen, deceived
By a vain trust in Heav'n, begs safe return
For Theseus, while Hippolytus his son
Learns of his death from vessels that are
    now
In port.

PHÆDRA. Ye gods!

PANOPE. Divided counsels sway
The choice of Athens; some would have the
prince,
Your child, for master; others, disregarding
The laws, dare to support the stranger's
son.
'T is even said that a presumptuous faction
Would crown Aricia and the house of
Pallas.
I deem'd it right to warn you of this danger.
Hippolytus already is prepared
To start, and should he show himself at
Athens,
'T is to be fear'd the fickle crowd will all
Follow his lead.

ŒNONE. Enough. The queen, who hears
you,
By no means will neglect this timely warn-
ing. [Exit PANOPE.]
Dear lady, I had almost ceased to urge
The wish that you should live, thinking to
follow
My mistress to the tomb, from which my
voice
Had fail'd to turn you; but this new mis-
fortune
Alters the aspect of affairs, and prompts
Fresh measures. Madam, Theseus is no
more,
You must supply his place. He leaves a
son,
A slave, if you should die, but, if you live,
A king. On whom has he to lean but you?
No hand but yours will dry his tears. Then
live
For him, or else the tears of innocence
Will move the gods, his ancestors, to wrath
Against his mother. Live, your guilt is gone,
No blame attaches to your passion now.
The king's decease has freed you from the
bonds
That made the crime and horror of your
love.
Hippolytus no longer need be dreaded,
Him you may see henceforth without re-
proach.
It may be, that, convinced of your aversion,
He means to head the rebels. Undeceive
him,
Soften his callous heart, and bend his pride.
King of this fertile land, in Trœzen here

His portion lies; but as he knows, the laws
Give to your son the ramparts that Min-
erva
Built and protects. A common enemy
Threatens you both, unite then to oppose
Aricia.

PHÆDRA. To your counsel I consent.
Yes, I will live, if life can be restored,
If my affection for a son has pow'r
To rouse my sinking heart at such a dan-
gerous hour. [Exeunt.]

ACT II

[Enter ARICIA and ISMENE.]

ARICIA. Hippolytus request to see me
here!
Hippolytus desire to bid farewell!
Is 't true, Ismene? Are you not deceived?

ISMENE. This is the first result of The-
seus' death.
Prepare yourself to see from every side
Hearts turn toward you that were kept
away
By Theseus. Mistress of her lot at last,
Aricia soon shall find all Greece fall low,
To do her homage.

ARICIA. 'T is not then, Ismene,
An idle tale? Am I no more a slave?
Have I no enemies?

ISMENE. The gods oppose
Your peace no longer, and the soul of
Theseus
Is with your brothers.

ARICIA. Does the voice of fame
Tell how he died?

ISMENE. Rumors incredible
Are spread. Some say that, seizing a new
bride,
The faithless husband by the waves was
swallow'd.
Others affirm, and this report prevails,
That with Pirithoüs to the world below
He went, and saw the shores of dark Cocy-
tus,
Showing himself alive to the pale ghosts;
But that he could not leave those gloomy
realms,
Which whoso enters there abides forever.

ARICIA. Shall I believe that ere his destined hour

A mortal may descend into the gulf
Of Hades? What attraction could o'er-
    come
Its terrors?
    ISMENE. He is dead, and you alone
Doubt it. The men of Athens mourn his
    loss.
Trœzen already hails Hippolytus
As king. And Phædra, fearing for her son,
Asks counsel of the friends who share her
    trouble,
Here in this palace.
    ARICIA. Will Hippolytus,
Think you, prove kinder than his sire, make
    light
My chains, and pity my misfortunes?
    ISMENE. Yes,
I think so, madam.
    ARICIA. Ah, you know him not
Or you would never deem so hard a heart
Can pity feel, or me alone except
From the contempt in which he holds our
    sex.
Has he not long avoided every spot
Where we resort?
    ISMENE. I know what tales are told
Of proud Hippolytus, but I have seen
Him near you, and have watch'd with curi-
    ous eye
How one esteem'd so cold would bear him-
    self.
Little did his behavior correspond
With what I look'd for; in his face confusion
Appear'd at your first glance, he could not
    turn
His languid eyes away, but gazed on you.
Love is a word that may offend his pride,
But what the tongue disowns, looks can
    betray.
    ARICIA. How eagerly my heart hears
        what you say,
Tho' it may be delusion, dear Ismene!
Did it seem possible to you, who know me,
That I, sad sport of a relentless Fate,
Fed upon bitter tears by night and day,
Could ever taste the maddening draught of
    love?
The last frail offspring of a royal race,
Children of Earth, I only have survived
War's fury. Cut off in the flow'r of youth,
Mown by the sword, six brothers have I
    lost,

The hope of an illustrious house, whose
    blood
Earth drank with sorrow, near akin to his
Whom she herself produced. Since then,
    you know
How thro' all Greece no heart has been
    allow'd
To sigh for me, lest by a sister's flame
The brothers' ashes be perchance rekindled.
You know, besides, with what disdain I
    view'd
My conqueror's suspicions and precau-
    tions,
And how, oppos'd as I have ever been
To love, I often thank'd the king's injustice
Which happily confirm'd my inclination.
But then I never had beheld his son.
Not that, attracted merely by the eye,
I love him for his beauty and his grace,
Endowments which he owes to Nature's
    bounty,
Charms which he seems to know not or to
    scorn.
I love and prize in him riches more rare,
The virtues of his sire, without his faults.
I love, as I must own, that generous pride
Which ne'er has stoop'd beneath the amor-
    ous yoke.
Phædra reaps little glory from a lover
So lavish of his sighs; I am too proud
To share devotion with a thousand others,
Or enter where the door is always open.
But to make one who ne'er has stoop'd be-
    fore
Bend his proud neck, to pierce a heart of
    stone,
To bind a captive whom his chains astonish,
Who vainly 'gainst a pleasing yoke rebels,—
That piques my ardor, and I long for that.
'T was easier to disarm the god of strength
Than this Hippolytus, for Hercules
Yielded so often to the eyes of beauty,
As to make triumph cheap. But, dear
    Ismene,
I take too little heed of opposition
Beyond my pow'r to quell, and you may
    hear me,
Humbled by sore defeat, upbraid the pride
I now admire. What! Can he love? and I
Have had the happiness to bend —
    ISMENE. He comes.
Yourself shall hear him.

[*Enter* HIPPOLYTUS.]

HIPPOLYTUS. Lady, ere I go
My duty bids me tell you of your change
Of fortune. My worst fears are realized;
My sire is dead. Yes, his protracted ab-
    sence
Was caused as I foreboded. Death alone,
Ending his toils, could keep him from the
    world
Conceal'd so long. The gods at last have
    doom'd
Alcides' friend, companion, and successor.
I think your hatred, tender to his virtues,
Can hear such terms of praise without re-
    sentment,
Knowing them due. One hope have I that
    soothes
My sorrow: I can free you from restraint.
Lo, I revoke the laws whose rigor moved
My pity; you are at your own disposal,
Both heart and hand; here, in my heritage,
In Trœzen, where my grandsire Pittheus
    reign'd
Of yore and I am now acknowledged king,
I leave you free, free as myself, — and
    more.
    ARICIA. Your kindness is too great, 't is
    overwhelming.
Such generosity, that pays disgrace
With honor, lends more force than you can
    think
To those harsh laws from which you would
    release me.
    HIPPOLYTUS. Athens, uncertain how to
    fill the throne
Of Theseus, speaks of you, anon of me,
And then of Phædra's son.
    ARICIA. Of me, my lord?
    HIPPOLYTUS. I know myself excluded by
    strict law:
Greece turns to my reproach a foreign
    mother.
But if my brother were my only rival,
My rights prevail o'er his clearly enough
To make me careless of the law's caprice.
My forwardness is check'd by juster claims:
To you I yield my place, or, rather, own
That it is yours by right, and yours the
    scepter,
As handed down from Earth's great son,
    Erechtheus.

Adoption placed it in the hands of Ægeus:
Athens, by him protected and increased,
Welcomed a king so generous as my sire,
And left your hapless brothers in oblivion.
Now she invites you back within her walls;
Protracted strife has cost her groans enough,
Her fields are glutted with your kinsmen's
    blood
Fatt'ning the furrows out of which it sprung
At first. I rule this Trœzen; while the son
Of Phædra has in Crete a rich domain.
Athens is yours. I will do all I can
To join for you the votes divided now
Between us.
    ARICIA. Stunn'd at all I hear, my lord,
I fear, I almost fear a dream deceives me.
Am I indeed awake? Can I believe
Such generosity? What god has put it
Into your heart? Well is the fame deserved
That you enjoy! That fame falls short of
    truth!
Would you for me prove traitor to yourself?
Was it not boon enough never to hate me,
So long to have abstain'd from harboring
The enmity —
    HIPPOLYTUS. To hate you? I, to hate
    you?
However darkly my fierce pride was
    painted,
Do you suppose a monster gave me birth?
What savage temper, what envenom'd
    hatred
Would not be mollified at sight of you?
Could I resist the soul-bewitching charm —
    ARICIA. Why, what is this, sir?
    HIPPOLYTUS. I have said too much
Not to say more. Prudence in vain resists
The violence of passion. I have broken
Silence at last, and I must tell you now
The secret that my heart can hold no longer.
    You see before you an unhappy instance
Of hasty pride, a prince who claims com-
    passion.
I, who, so long the enemy of Love,
Mock'd at his fetters and despised his cap-
    tives,
Who, pitying poor mortals that were ship-
    wreck'd,
In seeming safety view'd the storms from
    land,
Now find myself to the same fate exposed,
Toss'd to and fro upon a sea of troubles!

My boldness has been vanquish'd in a
    moment,
And humbled is the pride wherein I boasted.
For nearly six months past, ashamed,
    despairing,
Bearing where'er I go the shaft that rends
My heart, I struggle vainly to be free
From you and from myself; I shun you,
    present;
Absent, I find you near; I see your form
In the dark forest depths; the shades of
    night,
Nor less broad daylight, bring back to my
    view
The charms that I avoid; all things con-
    spire
To make Hippolytus your slave. For fruit
Of all my bootless sighs, I fail to find
My former self. My bow and javelins
Please me no more, my chariot is forgotten,
With all the Sea God's lessons; and the
    woods
Echo my groans instead of joyous shouts
Urging my fiery steeds.
    Hearing this tale
Of passion so uncouth, you blush perchance
At your own handiwork. With what wild
    words
I offer you my heart, strange captive held
By silken jess! But dearer in your eyes
Should be the offering, that this language
    comes
Strange to my lips; reject not vows ex-
    press'd
So ill, which but for you had ne'er been
    form'd.

[Enter THERAMENES.]

THERAMENES. Prince, the queen comes.
    I herald her approach.
'T is you she seeks.
HIPPOLYTUS. Me?
THERAMENES. What her thought may be
I know not. But I speak on her behalf.
She would converse with you ere you go
    hence.
HIPPOLYTUS. What shall I say to her?
    Can she expect —
ARICIA. You cannot, noble Prince, re-
    fuse to hear her,
Howe'er convinced she is your enemy,
Some shade of pity to her tears is due.

HIPPOLYTUS. Shall we part thus? and
    will you let me go,
Not knowing if my boldness has offended
The goddess I adore? Whether this heart,
Left in your hands —
ARICIA. Go, Prince, pursue the schemes
Your generous soul dictates, make Athens
    own
My scepter. All the gifts you offer me
Will I accept, but this high throne of em-
    pire
Is not the one most precious in my sight.
        [Exeunt ARICIA *and* ISMENE.]
HIPPOLYTUS. Friend, is all ready?
    But the Queen approaches.
Go, see the vessel in fit trim to sail.
Haste, bid the crew aboard, and hoist the
    signal;
Then soon return, and so deliver me
From interview most irksome.
        [Exit THERAMENES.]

[Enter PHÆDRA *and* ŒNONE.]

PHÆDRA *[to* ŒNONE]. There I see him!
My blood forgets to flow, my tongue to
    speak
What I am come to say.
ŒNONE. Think of your son,
How all his hopes depend on you.
PHÆDRA. I hear
You leave us, and in haste. I come to add
My tears to your distress, and for a son
Plead my alarm. No more has he a father,
And at no distant day my son must witness
My death. Already do a thousand foes
Threaten his youth. You only can defend
    him.
But in my secret heart remorse awakes,
And fear lest I have shut your ears against
His cries. I tremble lest your righteous
    anger
Visit on him ere long the hatred earn'd
By me, his mother.
HIPPOLYTUS. No such base resentment,
Madam, is mine.
PHÆDRA. I could not blame you, Prince,
If you should hate me. I have injured you:
So much you know, but could not read my
    heart.
T' incur your enmity has been mine aim:
The selfsame borders could not hold us
    both;

In public and in private I declared
Myself your foe, and found no peace till
   seas
Parted us from each other. I forbade
Your very name to be pronounced before
   me.
And yet if punishment should be propor-
   tion'd
To the offense, if only hatred draws
Your hatred, never woman merited
More pity, less deserved your enmity.
HIPPOLYTUS. A mother jealous of her
   children's rights
Seldom forgives the offspring of a wife
Who reign'd before her. Harassing sus-
   picions
Are common sequels of a second marriage.
Of me would any other have been jealous
No less than you, perhaps more violent.
PHÆDRA. Ah, Prince, how Heav'n has
   from the general law
Made me exempt, be that same Heav'n my
   witness!
Far different is the trouble that devours me!
HIPPOLYTUS. This is no time for self-
   reproaches, madam.
It may be that your husband still beholds
The light, and Heav'n may grant him safe
   return,
In answer to our prayers. His guardian god
Is Neptune, ne'er by him invoked in vain.
PHÆDRA. He who has seen the mansions
   of the dead
Returns not thence. Since to those gloomy
   shores
Theseus is gone, 't is vain to hope that
   Heav'n
May send him back. Prince, there is no
   release
From Acheron's greedy maw. And yet, me-
   thinks,
He lives, and breathes in you. I see him
   still
Before me, and to him I seem to speak;
My heart —
Oh! I am mad; do what I will,
I cannot hide my passion.
HIPPOLYTUS. Yes, I see
The strange effects of love. Theseus, tho'
   dead,
Seems present to your eyes, for in your soul
There burns a constant flame.

PHÆDRA. Ah, yes, for Theseus
I languish and I long, not as the Shades
Have seen him, of a thousand different
   forms
The fickle lover, and of Pluto's bride
The would-be ravisher, but faithful, proud
E'en to a slight disdain, with youthful
   charms
Attracting every heart, as gods are painted,
Or like yourself. He had your mien, your
   eyes,
Spoke and could blush like you, when to the
   isle
Of Crete, my childhood's home, he cross'd
   the waves,
Worthy to win the love of Minos' daughters.
What were you doing then? Why did he
   gather
The flow'r of Greece, and leave Hippolytus?
Oh, why were you too young to have em-
   bark'd
On board the ship that brought thy sire to
   Crete?
At your hands would the monster then have
   perish'd,
Despite the windings of his vast retreat.
To guide your doubtful steps within the
   maze
My sister would have arm'd you with the
   clue.
But no, therein would Phædra have fore-
   stall'd her,
Love would have first inspired me with the
   thought;
And I it would have been whose timely aid
Had taught you all the labyrinth's crooked
   ways.
What anxious care a life so dear had cost me!
No thread had satisfied your lover's fears:
I would myself have wish'd to lead the way,
And share the peril you were bound to face;
Phædra with you would have explored the
   maze,
With you emerged in safety, or have
   perish'd.
HIPPOLYTUS. Gods! What is this I hear?
   Have you forgotten
That Theseus is my father and your hus-
   band?
PHÆDRA. Why should you fancy I have
   lost remembrance
Thereof, and am regardless of mine honor?

HIPPOLYTUS. Forgive me, madam. With
   a blush I own
That I misconstrued words of innocence.
For very shame I cannot bear your sight
Longer. I go —
  PHÆDRA. Ah! cruel Prince, too well
You understood me. I have said enough
To save you from mistake. I love. But
   think not
That at the moment when I love you most
I do not feel my guilt; no weak compliance
Has fed the poison that infects my brain.
The ill-starr'd object of celestial vengeance,
I am not so detestable to you
As to myself. The gods will bear me wit-
   ness,
Who have within my veins kindled this fire,
The gods, who take a barbarous delight
In leading a poor mortal's heart astray.
Do you yourself recall to mind the past:
'T was not enough for me to fly, I chased
   you
Out of the country, wishing to appear
Inhuman, odious; to resist you better,
I sought to make you hate me. All in
   vain!
Hating me more I loved you none the less:
New charms were lent to you by your mis-
   fortunes.
I have been drown'd in tears, and scorch'd
   by fire;
Your own eyes might convince you of the
   truth,
If for one moment you could look at me.
What is 't I say? Think you this vile con-
   fession
That I have made is what I meant to utter?
Not daring to betray a son for whom
I trembled, 't was to beg you not to hate
   him
I came. Weak purpose of a heart too full
Of love for you to speak of aught besides!
Take your revenge, punish my odious
   passion;
Prove yourself worthy of your valiant sire,
And rid the world of an offensive monster!
Does Theseus' widow dare to love his son?
The frightful monster! Let her not escape
   you!
Here is my heart. This is the place to strike.
Already prompt to expiate its guilt,
I feel it leap impatiently to meet

Your arm. Strike home. Or, if it would
   disgrace you
To steep your hand in such polluted blood,
If that were punishment too mild to slake
Your hatred, lend me then your sword, if
   not
Your arm. Quick, giv 't.
  ŒNONE. What, madam, will you do?
Just gods! But some one comes. Go, fly
   from shame,
You cannot 'scape if seen by any thus.
    [*Exeunt* PHÆDRA *and* ŒNONE.]

    [*Enter* THERAMENES.]

THERAMENES. Is that the form of
   Phædra that I see
Hurried away? What mean these signs of
   sorrow?
Where is your sword? Why are you pale,
   confused?
  HIPPOLYTUS. Friend, let us fly. I am,
   indeed, confounded
With horror and astonishment extreme.
Phædra — but no; gods, let this dreadful
   secret
Remain forever buried in oblivion.
  THERAMENES. The ship is ready if you
   wish to sail.
But Athens has already giv'n her vote;
Their leaders have consulted all her tribes;
Your brother is elected, Phædra wins
  HIPPOLYTUS. Phædra?
  THERAMENES. A herald, charged with a
   commission
From Athens, has arrived to place the reins
Of power in her hands. Her son is king.
  HIPPOLYTUS. Ye gods, who know her, do
   ye thus reward
Her virtue?
  THERAMENES. A faint rumor meanwhile
   whispers
That Theseus is not dead, but in Epirus
Has shown himself. But, after all my
   search,
I know too well —
  HIPPOLYTUS. Let nothing be neglected.
This rumor must be traced back to its
   source.
If it be found unworthy of belief,
Let us set sail, and cost whate'er it may,
To hands deserving trust the scepter's
   sway.   [*Exeunt.*]

ACT III

[Enter PHÆDRA *and* ŒNONE.]

PHÆDRA. Ah! Let them take elsewhere
    the worthless honors
They bring me. Why so urgent I should
    see them?
What flattering balm can soothe my
    wounded heart?
Far rather hide me: I have said too much.
My madness has burst forth like streams
    in flood,
And I have utter'd what should ne'er have
    reach'd
His ear. Gods! How he heard me! How
    reluctant
To catch my meaning, dull and cold as
    marble,
And eager only for a quick retreat!
How oft his blushes made my shame the
    deeper!
Why did you turn me from the death I
    sought?
Ah! When his sword was pointed to my
    bosom,
Did he grow pale, or try to snatch it from
    me?
That I had touch'd it was enough for him
To render it forever horrible,
Leaving defilement on the hand that holds
    it.
ŒNONE. Thus brooding on your bitter
    disappointment,
You only fan a fire that must be stifled.
Would it not be more worthy of the blood
Of Minos to find peace in nobler cares,
And, in defiance of a wretch who flies
From what he hates, reign, mount the
    proffer'd throne?
PHÆDRA. I reign! Shall I the rod of
    empire sway,
When reason reigns no longer o'er myself?
When I have lost control of all my senses?
When 'neath a shameful yoke I scarce can
    breathe?
When I am dying?
ŒNONE. Fly.
PHÆDRA. I cannot leave him.
ŒNONE. Dare you not fly from him you
    dared to banish?
PHÆDRA. The time for that is past. He
    knows my frenzy.

I have o'erstepp'd the bounds of modesty,
And blazon'd forth my shame before his
    eyes.
Hope stole into my heart against my will.
Did you not rally my declining pow'rs?
Was it not you yourself recall'd my soul
When fluttering on my lips, and with your
    counsel,
Lent me fresh life, and told me I might love
    him?
ŒNONE. Blame me or blame me not for
    your misfortunes,
Of what was I incapable, to save you?
But if your indignation e'er was roused
By insult, can you pardon his contempt?
How cruelly his eyes, severely fix'd,
Survey'd you almost prostrate at his feet!
How hateful then appear'd his savage pride!
Why did not Phædra see him then as I
Beheld him?
PHÆDRA. This proud mood that you re-
    sent
May yield to time. The rudeness of the
    forests
Where he was bred, inured to rigorous laws,
Clings to him still; love is a word he ne'er
Had heard before. It may be his surprise
Stunn'd him, and too much vehemence was
    shown
In all I said.
ŒNONE. Remember that his mother
Was a barbarian.
PHÆDRA. Scythian tho' she was,
She learned to love.
ŒNONE. He has for all the sex
Hatred intense.
PHÆDRA. Then in his heart no rival
Shall ever reign. Your counsel comes too
    late.
Œnone, serve my madness, not my reason.
His heart is inaccessible to love:
Let us attack him where he has more feel-
    ing.
The charms of sovereignty appear'd to
    touch him;
He could not hide that he was drawn to
    Athens;
His vessels' prows were thither turn'd al-
    ready,
All sail was set to scud before the breeze.
Go you on my behalf, to his ambition
Appeal, and let the prospect of the crown

Dazzle his eyes. The sacred diadem
Shall deck his brow, no higher honor mine
Than there to bind it. His shall be the
    pow'r
I cannot keep; and he shall teach my son
How to rule men. It may be he will deign
To be to him a father. Son and mother
He shall control. Try ev'ry means to move
    him;
Your words will find more favor than can
    mine.
Urge him with groans and tears; show
    Phædra dying,
Nor blush to use the voice of supplication.
In you is my last hope; I'll sanction all
You say; and on the issue hangs my fate.
                          [*Exit* Œnone.]
Phædra [*alone*]. Venus implacable, who
    seest me shamed
And sore confounded, have I not enough
Been humbled? How can cruelty be
    stretch'd
Farther? Thy shafts have all gone home,
    and thou
Hast triumph'd. Would'st thou win a new
    renown?
Attack an enemy more contumacious:
Hippolytus neglects thee, braves thy wrath,
Nor ever at thine altars bow'd the knee.
Thy name offends his proud, disdainful ears.
Our interests are alike: avenge thyself,
Force him to love —
But what is this? Œnone
Return'd already? He detests me then,
And will not hear you.

              [*Enter* Œnone.]

Œnone. Madam, you must stifle
A fruitless love. Recall your former virtue:
The king who was thought dead will soon
    appear
Before your eyes, Theseus has just arrived,
Theseus is here. The people flock to see
    him
With eager haste. I went by your command
To find the prince, when with a thousand
    shouts
The air was rent —
    Phædra. My husband is alive,
That is enough, Œnone. I have own'd
A passion that dishonors him. He lives:
I ask to know no more.

Œnone. What?
    Phædra. I foretold it,
But you refused to hear. Your tears pre-
    vail'd
Over my just remorse. Dying this morn,
I had deserved compassion; your advice
I took, and die dishonor'd.
    Œnone. Die?
    Phædra. Just Heav'ns!
What have I done to-day? My husband
    comes,
With him his son: and I shall see the witness
Of my adulterous flame watch with what
    face
I greet his father, while my heart is big
With sighs he scorn'd, and tears that could
    not move him
Moisten mine eyes. Think you that his re-
    spect
For Theseus will induce him to conceal
My madness, nor disgrace his sire and king?
Will he be able to keep back the horror
He has for me? His silence would be vain.
I know my treason, and I lack the boldness
Of those abandon'd women who can taste
Tranquillity in crime, and show a forehead
All unabash'd. I recognize my madness,
Recall it all. These vaulted roofs, me-
    thinks,
These walls can speak, and, ready to accuse
    me,
Wait but my husband's presence to reveal
My perfidy. Death only can remove
This weight of horror. Is it such misfortune
To cease to live? Death causes no alarm
To misery. I only fear the name
That I shall leave behind me. For my sons
How sad a heritage! The blood of Jove
Might justly swell the pride that boasts
    descent
From Heav'n, but heavy weighs a mother's
    guilt
Upon her offspring. Yes, I dread the scorn
That will be cast on them with too much
    truth,
For my disgrace. I tremble when I think
That, crush'd beneath that curse, they'll
    never dare
To raise their eyes.
    Œnone. Doubt not I pity both;
Never was fear more just than yours. Why,
    then,

Expose them to this ignominy? Why
Will you accuse yourself? You thus de-
    stroy
The only hope that's left; it will be said
That Phædra, conscious of her perfidy,
Fled from her husband's sight. Hippolytus
Will be rejoiced that, dying, you should
    lend
His charge support. What can I answer
    him?
He'll find it easy to confute my tale,
And I shall hear him with an air of triumph
To every open ear repeat your shame.
Sooner than that may fire from heav'n con-
    sume me!
Deceive me not. Say, do you love him still?
How look you now on this contemptuous
    prince?
PHÆDRA. As on a monster frightful to
    mine eyes.
ŒNONE. Why yield him, then, an easy
    victory?
You fear him. Venture to accuse him first,
As guilty of the charge which he may bring
This day against you. Who can say 't is
    false?
All tells against him: in your hands his
    sword
Happily left behind, your present trouble,
Your past distress, your warnings to his
    father,
His exile which your earnest pray'rs ob-
    tain'd.
PHÆDRA. What! Would you have me
    slander innocence?
ŒNONE. My zeal has need of naught
    from you but silence.
Like you I tremble, and am loath to do it;
More willingly I 'd face a thousand deaths.
But since without this bitter remedy
I lose you, and to me your life outweighs
All else, I'll speak. Theseus, howe'er en-
    raged,
Will do no worse than banish him again.
A father, when he punishes, remains
A father, and his ire is satisfied
With a light sentence. But if guiltless blood
Should flow, is not your honor of more
    moment?
A treasure far too precious to be risk'd?
You must submit, whatever it dictates;
For, when our reputation is at stake,

All must be sacrificed, conscience itself.
But someone comes. 'T is Theseus.
    PHÆDRA. And I see
Hippolytus, my ruin plainly written
In his stern eyes. Do what you will; I trust
My fate to you. I cannot help myself.

    [Enter THESEUS, HIPPOLYTUS, and
        THERAMENES.]

THESEUS. Fortune no longer fights
    against my wishes,
Madam, and to your arms restores —
    PHÆDRA. Stay, Theseus!
Do not profane endearments that were once
So sweet, but which I am unworthy now
To taste. You have been wrong'd. Fortune
    has proved
Spiteful, nor in your absence spared your
    wife.
I am unfit to meet your fond caress,
How I may bear my shame my only care
Henceforth.
        [Exeunt PHÆDRA and ŒNONE.]
    THESEUS. Strange welcome for your
        father, this!
What does it mean, my son?
HIPPOLYTUS. Phædra alone
Can solve this mystery. But if my wish
Can move you, let me never see her more;
Suffer Hippolytus to disappear
Forever from the home that holds your
    wife.
    THESEUS. You, my son! Leave me?
    HIPPOLYTUS. 'T was not I who sought
        her:
'T was you who led her footsteps to these
    shores.
At your departure you thought meet, my
    lord,
To trust Aricia and the queen to this
Trœzenian land, and I myself was charged
With their protection. But what cares
    henceforth
Need keep me here? My youth of idleness
Has shown its skill enough o'er paltry foes
That range the woods. May I not quit a
    life
Of such inglorious ease, and dip my spear
In nobler blood? Ere you had reach'd my
    age
More than one tyrant, monster more than
    one

Had felt the weight of your stout arm.
   Already,
Successful in attacking insolence,
You had removed all dangers that infested
Our coasts to east and west. The traveler
   fear'd
Outrage no longer. Hearing of your deeds,
Already Hercules relied on you,
And rested from his toils. While I, un-
   known
Son of so brave a sire, am far behind
Even my mother's footsteps. Let my cour-
   age
Have scope to act, and if some monster yet
Has 'scaped you, let me lay the glorious
   spoils
Down at your feet; or let the memory
Of death faced nobly keep my name alive,
And prove to all the world I was your son.
   THESEUS. Why, what is this? What
      terror has possess'd
My family to make them fly before me?
If I return to find myself so fear'd,
So little welcome, why did Heav'n release
   me
From prison? My sole friend, misled by
   passion,
Was bent on robbing of his wife the tyrant
Who ruled Epirus. With regret I lent
The lover aid, but Fate had made us blind,
Myself as well as him. The tyrant seized
   me
Defenseless and unarm'd. Pirithoüs
I saw with tears cast forth to be devour'd
By savage beasts that lapp'd the blood of
   men.
Myself in gloomy caverns he enclosed,
Deep in the bowels of the earth, and nigh
To Pluto's realms. Six months I lay ere
   Heav'n
Had pity, and I 'scaped the watchful eyes
That guarded me. Then did I purge the
   world
Of a foul foe, and he himself has fed
His monsters. But when with expectant
   joy
To all that is most precious I draw near
Of what the gods have left me, when my
   soul
Looks for full satisfaction in a sight
So dear, my only welcome is a shudder,
Embrace rejected, and a hasty flight.

Inspiring, as I clearly do, such terror,
Would I were still a prisoner in Epirus!
Phædra complains that I have suffer'd out-
   rage.
Who has betray'd me? Speak. Why was I
   not
Avenged? Has Greece, to whom mine arm
   so oft
Brought useful aid, shelter'd the criminal?
You make no answer. Is my son, mine own
Dear son, confederate with mine enemies?
I 'll enter. This suspense is overwhelming.
I 'll learn at once the culprit and the crime,
And Phædra must explain her troubled
   state.   [Exit.]
   HIPPOLYTUS. What do these words por-
      tend, which seem'd to freeze
My very blood? Will Phædra, in her frenzy,
Accuse herself, and seal her own destruc-
   tion?
What will the king say? Gods! What fatal
   poison
Has love spread over all his house! Myself,
Full of a fire his-hatred disapproves,
How changed he finds me from the son he
   knew!
With dark forebodings is my mind alarm'd,
But innocence has surely naught to fear.
Come, let us go, and in some other place
Consider how I best may move my sire
To tenderness, and tell him of a flame
Vex'd but not vanquish'd by a father's
   blame.   [Exeunt.]

ACT IV

[Enter THESEUS and ŒNONE.]

   THESEUS. Ah! What is this I hear?
      Presumptuous traitor!
And would he have disgraced his father's
   honor?
With what relentless footsteps Fate pur-
   sues me!
Whither I go I know not, nor where now
I am. O kind affection ill repaid!
Audacious scheme! Abominable thought!
To reach the object of his foul desire
The wretch disdain'd not to use violence.
I know this sword that served him in his
   fury,
The sword I gave him for a nobler use.

Could not the sacred ties of blood restrain
    him?
And Phædra — was she loath to have him
    punish'd?
She held her tongue. Was that to spare the
    culprit?
    ŒNONE. Nay, but to spare a most un-
    happy father.
O'erwhelm'd with shame that her eyes
    should have kindled
So infamous a flame and prompted him
To crime so heinous, Phædra would have
    died.
I saw her raise her arm, and ran to save her.
To me alone you owe it that she lives;
And, in my pity both for her and you,
Have I against my will interpreted
    Her tears.
    THESEUS. The traitor! He might well
    turn pale.
'T was fear that made him tremble when he
    saw me.
I was astonish'd that he show'd no pleasure;
His frigid greeting chill'd my tenderness.
But was this guilty passion that devours
    him
Declared already ere I banish'd him
From Athens?
    ŒNONE. Sire, remember how the queen
Urged you. Illicit love caused all her hatred.
    THESEUS. And then this fire broke out
    again at Trœzen?
    ŒNONE. Sire, I have told you all. Too
    long the queen
Has been allow'd to bear her grief alone.
Let me now leave you and attend to her.
                         [*Exit.*]

    [*Enter* HIPPOLYTUS.]

    THESEUS. Ah! There he is. Great gods!
    That noble mien
Might well deceive an eye less fond than
    mine!
Why should the sacred stamp of virtue
    gleam
Upon the forehead of an impious wretch!
Ought not the blackness of a traitor's heart
To show itself by sure and certain signs?
    HIPPOLYTUS. My father, may I ask what
    fatal cloud
Has troubled your majestic countenance?
Dare you not trust this secret to your son?

    THESEUS. Traitor, how dare you show
    yourself before me?
Monster, whom Heaven's bolts have spared
    too long!
Survivor of that robber crew whereof
I cleansed the earth. After your brutal lust
Scorn'd even to respect my marriage bed,
You venture — you, my hated foe — to
    come
Into my presence, here, where all is full
Of your foul infamy, instead of seeking
Some unknown land that never heard my
    name.
Fly, traitor, fly! Stay not to tempt the
    wrath
That I can scarce restrain, nor brave my
    hatred.
Disgrace enough have I incurr'd forever
In being father of so vile a son,
Without your death staining indelibly
The glorious record of my noble deeds.
Fly, and unless you wish quick punishment
To add you to the criminals cut off
By me, take heed this sun that lights us
    now
Ne'er see you more set foot upon this soil.
I tell you once again, — fly, haste, return
    not,
Rid all my realms of your atrocious pres-
    ence.
    To thee, to thee, great Neptune, I appeal;
If erst I clear'd thy shores of foul assassins,
Recall thy promise to reward those efforts,
Crown'd with success, by granting my first
    pray'r.
Confined for long in close captivity,
I have not yet call'd on thy pow'rful aid,
Sparing to use the valued privilege
Till at mine utmost need. The time is
    come,
I ask thee now. Avenge a wretched father!
I leave this traitor to thy wrath; in blood
Quench his outrageous fires, and by thy
    fury
Theseus will estimate thy favor tow'rds him.
    HIPPOLYTUS. Phædra accuses me of law-
    less passion!
This crowning horror all my soul con-
    founds;
Such unexpected blows, falling at once,
O'erwhelm me, choke my utterance, strike
    me dumb.

THESEUS. Traitor, you reckon'd that in
timid silence
Phædra would bury your brutality.
You should not have abandon'd in your
flight
The sword that in her hands helps to con-
demn you
Or rather, to complete your perfidy,
You should have robb'd her both of speech
• and life.
HIPPOLYTUS. Justly indignant at a lie so
black
I might be pardon'd if I told the truth;
But it concerns your honor to conceal it.
Approve the reverence that shuts my
mouth;
And, without wishing to increase your woes,
Examine closely what my life has been.
Great crimes are never single, they are
link'd
To former faults. He who has once trans-
gress'd
May violate at last all that men hold
Most sacred; vice, like virtue, has degrees
Of progress; innocence was never seen
To sink at once into the lowest depths
Of guilt. No virtuous man can in a day
Turn traitor, murderer, an incestuous
wretch.
The nursling of a chaste, heroic mother,
I have not proved unworthy of my birth.
Pittheus, whose wisdom is by all esteem'd,
Deign'd to instruct me when I left her
hands.
It is no wish of mine to vaunt my merits,
But, if I may lay claim to any virtue,
I think beyond all else I have display'd
Abhorrence of those sins with which I'm
charged.
For this Hippolytus is known in Greece,
So continent that he is deem'd austere.
All know my abstinence inflexible:
The daylight is not purer than my heart.
How, then, could I, burning with fire pro-
fane —
THESEUS. Yes, dastard, 't is that very
pride condemns you.
I see the odious reason of your coldness:
Phædra alone bewitch'd your shameless
eyes;
Your soul, to others' charms indifferent,
Disdain'd the blameless fires of lawful love.

HIPPOLYTUS. No, father, I have hidden
it too long,
This heart has not disdain'd a sacred
flame.
Here at your feet I own my real offense:
I love, and love in truth where you forbid
me;
Bound to Aricia by my heart's devotion,
The child of Pallas has subdued your son.
A rebel to your laws, her I adore,
And breathe forth ardent sighs for her
alone.
THESEUS. You love her? Heav'ns! Heav'ns!
But no, I see the trick.
You feign a crime to justify yourself.
HIPPOLYTUS. Sir, I have shunn'd her for
six months, and still
Love her. To you yourself I came to tell it,
Trembling the while. Can nothing clear
your mind
Of your mistake? What oath can reassure
you?
By heav'n and earth and all the pow'rs of
nature —
THESEUS. The wicked never shrink from
perjury.
Cease, cease, and spare me irksome protes-
tations,
If your false virtue has no other aid.
HIPPOLYTUS. Tho' it to you seem false
and insincere,
Phædra has secret cause to know it true.
THESEUS. Ah, how your shamelessness
excites my wrath!
HIPPOLYTUS. What is my term and place
of banishment?
THESEUS. Were you beyond the Pillars
of Alcides,
Your perjured presence were too near me
yet.
HIPPOLYTUS. What friends will pity me,
when you forsake
And think me guilty of a crime so vile?
THESEUS. Go, look you out for friends
who hold in honor
Adultery and clap their hands at incest,
Low, lawless traitors, steep'd in infamy,
The fit protectors of a knave like you.
HIPPOLYTUS. Are incest and adultery
the words
You cast at me? I hold my tongue. Yet
think

What mother Phædra had; too well you
    know
Her blood, not mine, is tainted with those
    horrors.
THESEUS. What! Does your rage before
    my eyes lose all
Restraint? For the last time — out of my
    sight!
Hence, traitor! Wait not till a father's
    wrath
Force thee away 'mid general execration.
                [Exit HIPPOLYTUS.]
THESEUS [alone]. Wretch! Thou must
    meet inevitable ruin.
Neptune has sworn by Styx — to gods
    themselves
A dreadful oath — and he will execute
His promise. Thou canst not escape his
    vengeance.
I loved thee; and, in spite of thine offense,
My heart is troubled by anticipation
For thee. But thou hast earn'd thy doom
    too well.
Had father ever greater cause for rage?
Just gods, who see the grief that over-
    whelms me,
Why was I cursed with such a wicked son?

[Enter PHÆDRA.]

PHÆDRA. My lord, I come to you, fill'd
    with just dread.
Your voice raised high in anger reach'd
    mine ears,
And much I fear that deeds have follow'd
    threats.
Oh, if there yet is time, spare your own
    offspring,
Respect your race and blood, I do beseech
    you.
Let me not hear that blood cry from the
    ground;
Save me the horror and perpetual pain
Of having caused his father's hand to shed
    it.
THESEUS. No, madam, from that stain
    my hand is free,
But, for all that, the wretch has not es-
    caped me.
The hand of an Immortal now is charged
With his destruction. 'T is a debt that
    Neptune
Owes me, and you shall be avenged.

PHÆDRA. A debt
Owed you? Pray'rs made in anger —
THESEUS. Never fear
That they will fail. Rather join yours to
    mine.
In all their blackness paint for me his
    crimes,
And fan my tardy passion to white heat.
But yet you know not all his infamy;
His rage against you overflows in slan-
    ders;
Your mouth, he says, is full of all deceit,
He says Aricia has his heart and soul,
That her alone he loves.
PHÆDRA. Aricia?
THESEUS. Aye,
He said it to my face: an idle pretext!
A trick that gulls me not! Let us hope
    Neptune
Will do him speedy justice. To his altars
I go, to urge performance of his oaths.
                      [Exit.]
PHÆDRA [alone]. Ah, he is gone! What
    tidings struck mine ears?
What fire, half smother'd, in my heart re-
    vives?
What fatal stroke falls like a thunder-
    bolt?
Stung by remorse that would not let me
    rest,
I tore myself out of Œnone's arms,
And flew to help Hippolytus with all
My soul and strength. Who knows if that
    repentance
Might not have moved me to accuse my-
    self?
And, if my voice had not been choked with
    shame,
Perhaps I had confess'd the frightful truth.
Hippolytus can feel, but not for me!
Aricia has his heart, his plighted troth.
Ye gods, when, deaf to all my sighs and
    tears,
He arm'd his eye with scorn, his brow with
    threats,
I deem'd his heart, impregnable to love,
Was fortified 'gainst all my sex alike.
And yet another has prevail'd to tame
His pride, another has secured his favor.
Perhaps he has a heart easily melted;
I am the only one he cannot bear!
And shall I charge myself with his defense?

[*Enter* Œnone.]

PHÆDRA. Know you, dear nurse, what I have learn'd just now?

ŒNONE. No; but I come in truth with trembling limbs. I dreaded with what purpose you went forth. The fear of fatal madness made me pale.

PHÆDRA. Who would have thought it, nurse? I had a rival.

ŒNONE. A rival?

PHÆDRA. Yes, he loves. I cannot doubt it.
This wild untamable Hippolytus,
Who scorn'd to be admired, whom lovers' sighs
Wearied, this tiger, whom I fear'd to rouse,
Fawns on a hand that has subdued his pride:
Aricia has found entrance to his heart.

ŒNONE. Aricia?

PHÆDRA. Ah! anguish as yet untried!
For what new tortures am I still reserved?
All I have undergone, transports of passion,
Longings and fears, the horrors of remorse,
The shame of being spurn'd with contumely,
Were feeble foretastes of my present torments.
They love each other! By what secret charm
Have they deceived me? Where, and when, and how
Met they? You knew it all. Why was I cozen'd?
You never told me of those stolen hours
Of amorous converse. Have they oft been seen
Talking together? Did they seek the shades
Of thickest woods? Alas! full freedom had they
To see each other. Heav'n approved their sighs;
They loved without the consciousness of guilt;
And every morning's sun for them shone clear,
While I, an outcast from the face of Nature,
Shunn'd the bright day, and sought to hide myself.
Death was the only god whose aid I dared
To ask: I waited for the grave's release.
Water'd with tears, nourish'd with gall, my woe
Was all too closely watch'd; I did not dare
To weep without restraint. In mortal dread
Tasting this dangerous solace, I disguised
My terror 'neath a tranquil countenance,
And oft had I to check my tears, and smile.

ŒNONE. What fruit will they enjoy of their vain love?
They will not see each other more.

PHÆDRA. That love
Will last forever. Even while I speak,
Ah, fatal thought, they laugh to scorn the madness
Of my distracted heart. In spite of exile
That soon must part them, with a thousand oaths
They seal yet closer union. Can I suffer
A happiness, Œnone, which insults me?
I crave your pity. She must be destroy'd.
My husband's wrath against a hateful stock
Shall be revived, nor must the punishment
Be light: the sister's guilt passes the brothers'.
I will entreat him in my jealous rage.
What am I saying? Have I lost my senses?
Is Phædra jealous, and will she implore
Theseus for help? My husband lives, and yet
I burn. For whom? Whose heart is this I claim
As mine? At every word I say, my hair
Stands up with horror. Guilt henceforth has pass'd
All bounds. Hypocrisy and incest breathe
At once thro' all. My murderous hands are ready
To spill the blood of guileless innocence.
Do I yet live, wretch that I am, and dare
To face this holy Sun from whom I spring?
My father's sire was king of all the gods;
My ancestors fill all the universe.
Where can I hide? In the dark realms of Pluto?
But there my father holds the fatal urn;
His hand awards th' irrevocable doom:
Minos is judge of all the ghosts in hell.
Ah! how his awful shade will start and shudder

When he shall see his daughter brought be-
fore him,
Forced to confess sins of such varied dye,
Crimes it may be unknown to hell itself!
What wilt thou say, my father, at a sight
So dire? I think I see thee drop the urn,
And, seeking some unheard-of punishment,
Thyself become my executioner.
Spare me! A cruel goddess has destroy'd
Thy race; and in my madness recognize
Her wrath. Alas! My aching heart has
reap'd
No fruit of pleasure from the frightful crime
The shame of which pursues me to the
grave,
And ends in torment life-long misery.
  ŒNONE. Ah, madam, pray dismiss a
groundless dread:
Look less severely on a venial error.
You love. We cannot conquer destiny.
You were drawn on as by a fatal charm.
Is that a marvel without precedent
Among us? Has love triumph'd over you,
And o'er none else? Weakness is natural
To man. A mortal, to a mortal's lot
Submit. You chafe against a yoke that
others
Have long since borne. The dwellers in
Olympus,
The gods themselves, who terrify with
threats
The sins of men, have burn'd with lawless
fires.
  PHÆDRA. What words are these I hear?
What counsel this
You dare to give me? Will you to the end
Pour poison in mine ears? You have de-
stroy'd me.
You brought me back when I should else
have quitted
The light of day, made me forget my duty
And see Hippolytus, till then avoided.
What hast thou done? Why did your
wicked mouth
With blackest lies slander his blameless
life?
Perhaps you've slain him, and the impious
pray'r
Of an unfeeling father has been answer'd.
No, not another word! Go, hateful mon-
ster;
Away, and leave me to my piteous fate.

May Heav'n with justice pay you your
deserts!
And may your punishment forever be
A terror to all those who would, like you,
Nourish with artful wiles the weaknesses
Of princes, push them to the brink of ruin
To which their heart inclines, and smooth
the path
Of guilt. Such flatterers doth the wrath of
Heav'n
Bestow on kings as its most fatal gift. [Exit.]
  ŒNONE [alone]. O gods! to serve her
what have I not done?
This is the due reward that I have won.
            [Exit.]

ACT V

[Enter HIPPOLYTUS and ARICIA.]

  ARICIA. Can you keep silent in this mor-
tal peril?
Your father loves you. Will you leave him
thus
Deceived? If in your cruel heart you scorn
My tears, content to see me nevermore,
Go, part from poor Aricia; but at least,
Going, secure the safety of your life.
Defend your honor from a shameful stain.
And force your father to recall his pray'rs.
There yet is time. Why out of mere caprice
Leave the field free to Phædra's calumnies?
Let Theseus know the truth.
  HIPPOLYTUS. Could I say more,
Without exposing him to dire disgrace?
How should I venture, by revealing all,
To make a father's brow grow red with
shame?
The odious mystery to you alone
Is known. My heart has been outpour'd
to none
Save you and Heav'n. I could not hide
from you
(Judge if I love you) all I fain would hide
E'en from myself. But think under what
seal
I spoke. Forget my words, if that may be;
And never let so pure a mouth disclose
This dreadful secret. Let us trust to
Heav'n
My vindication, for the gods are just;
For their own honor will they clear the
guiltless;

Sooner or later punish'd for her crime,
Phædra will not escape the shame she
    merits.
I ask no other favor than your silence;
In all besides I give my wrath free scope.
Make your escape from this captivity,
Be bold to bear me company in flight;
Linger not here on this accursèd soil,
Where virtue breathes a pestilential air.
To cover your departure take advantage
Of this confusion, caused by my disgrace.
The means of flight are ready, be assured;
You have as yet no other guards than mine.
Pow'rful defenders will maintain our quar-
    rel;
Argos spreads open arms, and Sparta calls
    us.
Let us appeal for justice to our friends,
Nor suffer Phædra, in a common ruin
Joining us both, to hunt us from the throne,
And aggrandize her son by robbing us.
Embrace this happy opportunity:
What fear restrains? You seem to hesitate.
Your interest alone prompts me to urge
Boldness. When I am all on fire, how
    comes it
That you arc ice? Fear you to follow then
A banish'd man?
    ARICIA. Ah, dear to me would be
Such exile! With what joy, my fate to yours
United, could I live, by all the world
Forgotten! But not yet has that sweet tie
Bound us together. How then can I steal
Away with you? I know the strictest honor
Forbids me not out of your father's hands
To free myself; this is no parent's home,
And flight is lawful when one flies from
    tyrants.
But you, sir, love me; and my virtue
    shrinks —
    HIPPOLYTUS. No, no, your reputation is
    to me
As dear as to yourself. A nobler purpose
Brings me to you. Fly from your foes, and
    follow
A husband. Heav'n, that sends us these
    misfortunes,
Sets free from human instruments the
    pledge
Between us. Torches do not always light
The face of Hymen.
At the gates of Trœzen,

'Mid ancient tombs where princes of my
    race
Lie buried, stands a temple ne'er approach'd
By perjurers, where mortals dare not make
False oaths, for instant punishment befalls
The guilty. Falsehood knows no stronger
    check
Than what is present there — the fear of
    death
That cannot be avoided. Thither then
We'll go, if you consent, and swear to love
Forever, take the guardian god to witness
Our solemn vows, and his paternal care
Entreat. I will invoke the name of all
The holiest Pow'rs; chaste Dian, and the
    Queen
Of Heav'n, yea all the gods who know my
    heart
Will guarantee my sacred promises.
    ARICIA. The king draws near. Depart —
    make no delay.
To mask my flight, I linger yet one moment.
Go you; and leave with me some trusty
    guide,
To lead my timid footsteps to your side.
                    [*Exit* HIPPOLYTUS.]

[*Enter* THESEUS *and* ISMENE.]

    THESEUS. Ye gods, throw light upon my
    troubled mind,
Show me the truth which I am seeking here.
    ARICIA [*aside to* ISMENE]. Get ready, dear
    Ismene, for our flight.
                    [*Exit* ISMENE.]
    THESEUS. Your color comes and goes,
    you seem confused,
Madam! What business had my son with
    you?
    ARICIA. Sire, he was bidding me farewell
    forever.
    THESEUS. Your eyes, it seems, can tame
    that stubborn pride;
And the first sighs he breathes are paid to
    you.
    ARICIA. I can't deny the truth; he has
    not, sire,
Inherited your hatred and injustice;
He did not treat me like a criminal.
    THESEUS. That is to say, he swore eter-
    nal love.
Do not rely on that inconstant heart;
To others has he sworn as much before.

ARICIA. He, sire?

THESEUS. You ought to check his roving
taste
How could you bear a partnership so vile?

ARICIA. And how can you endure that
vilest slanders
Should make a life so pure as black as pitch?
Have you so little knowledge of his heart?
Do you so ill distinguish between guilt
And innocence? What mist before your eyes
Blinds them to virtue so conspicuous?
Ah! 't is too much to let false tongues de-
fame him.
Repent; call back your murderous wishes,
sire;
Fear, fear lest Heav'n in its severity
Hate you enough to hear and grant your
pray'rs.
Oft in their wrath the gods accept our
victims,
And oftentimes chastise us with their gifts.

THESEUS. No, vainly would you cover
up his guilt.
Your love is blind to his depravity.
But I have witness irreproachable:
Tears have I seen, true tears, that may be
trusted.

ARICIA. Take heed, my lord. Your
hands invincible
Have rid the world of monsters numberless;
But all are not destroy'd, one you have left
Alive — Your son forbids me to say more;
Knowing with what respect he still regards
you,
I should too much distress him if I dared
Complete my sentence. I will imitate
His reverence, and, to keep silence, leave
you. [Exit.]

THESEUS [alone]. What is there in her
mind? What meaning lurks
In speech begun but to be broken short?
Would both deceive me with a vain pre-
tense?
Have they conspired to put me to the
torture?
And yet, despite my stern severity,
What plaintive voice cries deep within my
heart?
A secret pity troubles and alarms me.
Œnone shall be questioned once again,
I must have clearer light upon this crime.
Guards, bid Œnone come, and come alone.

[Enter PANOPE.]

PANOPE. I know not what the queen in-
tends to do,
But from her agitation dread the worst.
Fatal despair is painted on her features;
Death's pallor is already in her face.
Œnone, shamed and driven from her sight,
Has cast herself into the ocean depths.
None knows what prompted her to deed so
rash;
And now the waves hide her from us for-
ever.

THESEUS. What say you?

PANOPE. Her sad fate seems to have
added
Fresh trouble to the queen's tempestuous
soul.
Sometimes, to soothe her secret pain, she
clasps
Her children close, and bathes them with
her tears;
Then suddenly, the mother's love forgot-
ten,
She thrusts them from her with a look of
horror.
She wanders to and fro with doubtful steps;
Her vacant eye no longer knows us. Thrice
She wrote, and thrice did she, changing her
mind,
Destroy the letter ere 't was well begun.
Vouchsafe to see her, sire: vouchsafe to help
her. [Exit.]

THESEUS. Heav'ns! Is Œnone dead, and
Phædra bent
On dying too? Oh, call me back my son!
Let him defend himself, and I am ready
To hear him. Be not hasty to bestow
Thy fatal bounty, Neptune; let my pray'rs
Rather remain ever unheard. Too soon
I lifted cruel hands, believing lips
That may have lied! Ah! What despair
may follow!

[Enter THERAMENES.]

THESEUS. Theramenes, is 't thou? Where
is my son?
I gave him to thy charge from tenderest
childhood.
But whence these tears that overflow thine
eyes?
How is it with my son?

THERAMENES. Concern too late!
Affection vain! Hippolytus is dead.
THESEUS. Gods!
THERAMENES. I have seen the flow'r of
all mankind
Cut off, and I am bold to say that none
Deserved it less.
THESEUS. What! My son dead! When I
Was stretching out my arms to him, has
Heav'n
Hasten'd his end? What was this sudden
stroke?
THERAMENES. Scarce had we pass'd out
of the gates of Trœzen,
He silent in his chariot, and his guards,
Downcast and silent too, around him
ranged;
To the Mycenian road he turn'd his steeds,
Then, lost in thought, allow'd the reins to
lie
Loose on their backs. His noble chargers,
erst
So full of ardor to obey his voice,
With head depress'd and melancholy eye
Seem'd now to mark his sadness and to
share it.
A frightful cry, that issues from the deep,
With sudden discord rends the troubled
air;
And from the bosom of the earth a groan
Is heard in answer to that voice of terror.
Our blood is frozen at our very hearts;
With bristling manes the list'ning steeds
stand still.
Meanwhile upon the watery plain there
rises
A mountain billow with mighty crest
Of foam, that shoreward rolls, and, as it
breaks,
Before our eyes vomits a furious monster.
With formidable horns its brow is arm'd,
And all its body clothed with yellow scales,
In front a savage bull, behind a dragon
Turning and twisting in impatient rage.
Its long continued bellowings make the
shore
Tremble; the sky seems horror-struck to
see it;
The earth with terror quakes; its poisonous
breath
Infects the air. The wave that brought it
ebbs

In fear. All fly, forgetful of the courage
That cannot aid, and in a neighboring
temple
Take refuge — all save bold Hippolytus.
A hero's worthy son, he stays his steeds,
Seizes his darts, and, rushing forward, hurls
A missile with sure aim that wounds the
monster
Deep in the flank. With rage and pain it
springs
E'en to the horses' feet, and, roaring, falls,
Writhes in the dust, and shows a fiery
throat
That covers them with flames, and blood,
and smoke.
Fear lends them wings; deaf to his voice for
once,
And heedless of the curb, they onward fly.
Their master wastes his strength in efforts
vain;
With foam and blood each courser's bit is
red.
Some say a god, amid this wild disorder,
Is seen with goads pricking their dusty
flanks.
O'er jaggèd rocks they rush urged on by
terror;
Crash! goes the axle-tree. Th' intrepid
youth
Sees his car broken up, flying to pieces;
He falls himself entangled in the reins.
Pardon my grief. That cruel spectacle
Will be for me a source of endless tears.
I saw thy hapless son, I saw him, sire,
Dragg'd by the horses that his hands had
fed,
Pow'rless to check their fierce career, his
voice
But adding to their fright, his body soon
One mass of wounds. Our cries of anguish
fill
The plain. At last they slacken their swift
pace,
Then stop, not far from those old tombs
that mark
Where lie the ashes of his royal sires.
Panting I thither run, and after me
His guard, along the track stain'd with
fresh blood
That reddens all the rocks; caught in the
briers
Locks of his hair hang dripping, gory spoils!

I come, I call him. Stretching forth his
hand,
He opes his dying eyes, soon closed again.
"The gods have robb'd me of a guiltless
life,"
I hear him say: "Take care of sad Aricia
When I am dead. Dear friend, if e'er my
father
Mourn, undeceived, his son's unhappy fate
Falsely accused; to give my spirit peace,
Tell him to treat his captive tenderly,
And to restore —" With that the hero's
breath
Fails, and a mangled corpse lies in my arms,
A piteous object, trophy of the wrath
Of Heav'n — so changed, his father would
not know him.
    THESEUS. Alas, my son! Dear hope for-
ever lost!
The ruthless gods have served me but too
well.
For what a life of anguish and remorse
Am I reserved!
    THERAMENES. Aricia at that instant,
Flying from you, comes timidly, to take
him
For husband, there, in presence of the gods.
Thus drawing nigh, she sees the grass all
red
And reeking, sees (sad sight for lover's
eye!)
Hippolytus stretch'd there, pale and dis-
figured.
But, for a time doubtful of her misfortune,
Unrecognized the hero she adores,
She looks, and asks — "Where is Hippoly-
tus?"
Only too sure at last that he lies there
Before her, with sad eyes that silently
Reproach the gods, she shudders, groans,
and falls,
Swooning and all but lifeless, at his feet.
Ismene, all in tears, kneels down beside her,
And calls her back to life — life that is
naught
But sense of pain. And I, to whom this
light
Is darkness now, come to discharge the
duty
The hero has imposed on me, to tell thee
His last request — a melancholy task.
But hither comes his mortal enemy.

[*Enter* PHÆDRA, PANOPE, *and Guards.*]

    THESEUS. Madam, you 've triumph'd,
and my son is kill'd!
Ah, but what room have I for fear! How
justly
Suspicion racks me that in blaming him
I err'd! But he is dead; accept your victim;
Rightly or wrongly slain, let your heart
leap
For joy. My eyes shall be forever blind:
Since you accuse him, I 'll believe him
guilty.
His death affords me cause enough for tears,
Without a foolish search for further light
Which, pow'rless to restore him to my grief,
Might only serve to make me more un-
happy.
Far from this shore and far from you I 'll
fly,
For here the image of my mangled son
Would haunt my memory and drive me
mad.
From the whole world I fain would banish
me,
For all the world seems to rise up in judg-
ment
Against me; and my very glory weights
My punishment; for, were my name less
known,
'T were easier to hide me. All the favors
The gods have granted me I mourn and
hate,
Nor will I importune them with vain
pray'rs
Henceforth forever. Give me what they
may,
What they have taken will all else out-
weigh.
    PHÆDRA. Theseus, I cannot hear you
and keep silence:
I must repair the wrong that he has suf-
fer'd —
Your son was innocent.
    THESEUS. Unhappy father!
And it was on your word that I condemn'd
him!
Think you such cruelty can be excused —
    PHÆDRA. Moments to me are precious;
hear me, Theseus.
'T was I who cast an eye of lawless passion
On chaste and dutiful Hippolytus.

Heav'n in my bosom kindled baleful fire,
And vile Œnone's cunning did the rest.
She fear'd Hippolytus, knowing my mad-
ness,
Would make that passion known which he
regarded
With horror; so advantage of my weakness
She took, and hasten'd to accuse him first.
For that she has been punish'd, tho' too
mildly;
Seeking to shun my wrath she cast herself
Beneath the waves. The sword ere now had
cut
My thread of life, but slander'd innocence
Made its cry heard, and I resolved to die
In a more lingering way, confessing first
My penitence to you. A poison, brought
To Athens by Medea, runs thro' my veins.
Already in my heart the venom works,
Infusing there a strange and fatal chill;

Already as thro' thickening mists I see
The spouse to whom my presence is an out-
rage;
Death, from mine eyes veiling the light of
heav'n,
Restores its purity that they defiled.
PANOPE. She dies, my lord!
THESEUS. Would that the memory
Of her disgraceful deed could perish with
her!
Ah, disabused too late! Come, let us go,
And with the blood of mine unhappy son
Mingle our tears, clasping his dear remains,
In deep repentance for a pray'r detested.
Let him be honor'd as he well deserves;
And, to appease his sore offended ghost,
Be her near kinsmen's guilt whate'er it
may,
Aricia shall be held my daughter from to-
day.   [Exeunt omnes.]

THE BARBER OF SEVILLE

(LE BARBIER DE SEVILLE)

By BEAUMARCHAIS

Translated by ARTHUR B. MYRICK

CHARACTERS

Count Almaviva, *a grandee of Spain, the unknown lover of Rosine*

Bartholo, *a physician, guardian of Rosine*

Rosine, *a young lady of noble birth, and the ward of Bartholo*

Figaro, *a barber of Seville*

Don Bazile, *organist, and singing-master to Rosine*

La Jeunesse, *an old domestic of Bartholo*

L'Eveillé, *another servant of Bartholo, a simpleton and sluggard*

A Notary

An Alclade and a Justice

Policemen and Servants with torches

The scene is laid in Seville in the first act, in the street, and under the windows of Rosine: the remainder of the piece is in the house of Doctor Bartholo.

THE BARBER OF SEVILLE

ACT I

[*The stage represents a street in Seville: windows looking upon the street are barred. The* COUNT *in a heavy brown cloak and broad-brimmed hat. He looks at his watch as he walks back and forth.*]

COUNT. The morning is not so far advanced as I thought; the hour at which she usually shows herself behind her blinds is still far off. No matter; I would far rather arrive too soon than miss the one moment when I may see her. If any of my amiable friends at court could see me one hundred leagues from Madrid, lingering beneath the window of a lady to whom I have never spoken, they would certainly take me for a Spaniard of Isabella's time. Why not? Every one seeks his own happiness. Mine I find in the heart of Rosine. What! follow a lady to Seville, when Madrid and the court everywhere offer pleasures so easily attained! That itself is the thing I shun. I am weary to death of conquests which self-interest, convenience, or vanity are yielding me every day. Ah! 't is so sweet to be loved for one's self alone! And if I could be perfectly sure that under this disguise ... The devil take this unseasonable rascal!

[*Enter* FIGARO, *with a guitar slung across his back by a broad ribbon, paper and pencil in hand.*]

FIGARO [*singing gayly*].

Away with sorrow consuming!
Without the fire of good liquor inspiring,
Without enlivening pleasure,
All men would live in a stupor,
With very good prospects of dying.

Really, that's not so bad, so far, is it?

With very good prospects of dying.
Generous wine and idleness
Shall e'er dispute my heart.

Well, no! they do not dispute; they reign together peaceably enough. . . .

Shall ever share my heart.

Shall I say *se partagent?* Well, thank goodness, we writers of comic operas are not so particular about style. Nowadays, what is scarcely worth saying, we sing.

[*Sings.*]

Generous wine and idleness
Shall ever share my heart.

I should like to finish with something fine, brilliant, sparkling, which would really look like an idea.

[*Kneels and writes as he sings.*]

Shall ever share my heart.
If one enjoys my tenderness. . . .
The other is my joy.

Pshaw! that's flat. It is not that. . . . I need an antithesis: —

If one be my mistress,
The other . . .

There! I have it. . . .

The other shall be my slave.

Well done, Master Figaro.

[*Writes and sings.*]

Generous wine and idleness
Shall ever share my heart.
If one be my mistress,
The other shall be my slave,
The other shall be my slave,
The other shall be my slave!

There, how is that? When we have the accompaniments, we shall see now, gentlemen of the cabal, if I know what I am talking about. [*He perceives the* COUNT.] I have seen that priest somewhere.

[*He rises.*]

COUNT [*aside*]. I am sure I know this fellow.

FIGARO. No, he's no priest. His proud and noble bearing . . .

COUNT. That grotesque figure . . .

FIGARO. I was right. Count Almaviva.

COUNT. I think this rascal must be Figaro.

FIGARO. The very same, my lord.

COUNT. You knave! If you say one word . . .

FIGARO. Yes, I recognize you; the same familiar kindness with which you have always honored me.

COUNT. I did not recognize you at all. You were so tall and stout . . .

FIGARO. What would you have, my lord? 't is hard times.

COUNT. Poor fellow! what are you doing in Seville? Not long since I recommended you to a position in the government.

FIGARO. I received my appointment, my lord, and my gratitude . . .

COUNT. Call me Lindor. Don't you see, by my disguise, that I wish to be unknown?

FIGARO. I will leave you.

COUNT. On the contrary. I await the issue of a certain affair, and two men chatting together are less suspect than one pacing back and forth. Let us appear to be chatting. Now, this position.

FIGARO. The minister, having considered your excellency's recommendation, forthwith appointed me apothecary's boy.

COUNT. In the army hospitals?

FIGARO. No, indeed; in the Andalusian studs.

COUNT [laughing]. Truly, a fine beginning!

FIGARO. The position was not a bad one; for, having the dressings and the drugs in my charge, I often sold the men the best of horse medicines . . .

COUNT. Which killed the king's loyal subjects?

FIGARO. Ha! ha! There is no universal remedy which has not failed sometimes to cure Galicians, Catalans, or Auvergnats.

COUNT. Why, then, did you resign it?

FIGARO. Resign it! Faith, I was removed. Some one maligned me to the powers. "Envy with crooked fingers, with visage pale and livid."

COUNT. For pity's sake, my friend! Do you also make verses? I saw you scratching away there on your knee, and singing this very morning.

FIGARO. That is really the cause of my misfortune, your excellency. When they reported to the minister that I was making, if I may so, some very fair garlands of verses to Cloris, that I was sending riddles to the journals, that madrigals of my composition were the fashion, — in short, when he found out that I was everywhere in print, — he took the matter tragically, and had me dismissed the service, on the pretext that a love of letters is quite incompatible with the spirit of business.

COUNT. Powerfully reasoned! And you failed to represent to him . . .

FIGARO. I thought myself only too happy to be forgotten; for I am persuaded that a grandee does us good enough when he does us no harm.

COUNT. You do not tell the whole story. I remember that in my service you were something of a rascal.

FIGARO. Good Heavens! my lord, you would have a poor fellow absolutely faultless.

COUNT. Lazy, dissolute . . .

FIGARO. In comparison with the virtues demanded of a domestic, does your excellency know of many masters worthy of being valets?

COUNT [laughing]. Not so bad. And you retired to this city?

FIGARO. No, not immediately.

COUNT [stopping him]. One moment . . . I thought 't was she. . . . Keep on talking, I can hear you well enough.

FIGARO. On my return to Madrid, I tried my literary talents again; and the theater seemed to me a field of honor . . .

COUNT. Ah! God help you there!

FIGARO [while he replies, the COUNT gazes attentively in the direction of the blind]. Truly I know not why I had not the greatest success; for I had filled the pit with the most excellent workers, with hands like paddles; I had forbidden gloves, canes, and everything else which produces only dull applause, and, on my honor, before the piece was played, the café seemed to be perfectly well-disposed toward us. But the efforts of the cabal . . .

COUNT. Ah! the cabal! The last refuge of our fallen author.

FIGARO. I may say that as well as another; why not? They hissed me, but if I could ever get them together again . . .

COUNT. You would take your revenge by boring them to death.

FIGARO. Ah! how I lay it up against them! Zounds!

COUNT. You swear! Do you know that in the courts you have only twenty-four hours in which to curse your judges?

FIGARO. You have twenty-four years in the theater; life is only too short to exhaust such resentment.

COUNT. Your merry anger delights me. But you have not told me what caused you to leave Madrid.

FIGARO. My good angel, your excellency, since I am happy enough to find my old master. Recognizing that, at Madrid, the republic of letters is the republic of wolves, continually at each others' throats, and that, delivered up to the contempt to which this ridiculous obstinacy leads them, all the insects, gnats, mosquitoes and critics, all the envious, journalists, booksellers, censors, and, in fact, everything able to cling to the hide of the unhappy man of letters, succeeded in lacerating and sucking the little substance left to them; worn out with writing, weary of myself, disgusted with others, overwhelmed with debts, and innocent of cash; finally convinced that the tangible revenue from my razor is preferable to the empty honors of the pen, I left Madrid, my baggage slung upon my shoulder, philosophically wandering through the two Castiles, la Mancha, Estremadura, Sierra Morena, and Andalusia; welcomed in one town, imprisoned in the next, and everywhere superior to events; praised by some, blamed by others, making the best of good weather and enduring the bad; mocking the foolish and braving the wicked; laughing in my misery and shaving all; you see me finally established in Seville and ready to serve your excellency in anything you may be pleased to order.

COUNT. Who, then, has endowed you with so gay a philosophy?

FIGARO. Continual misfortune. I always hasten to laugh at everything for fear that I may be obliged to weep. What are you staring at over there?

COUNT. Let us hide.

FIGARO. Why?

COUNT. Come, you blockhead! You will be my destruction. [*They conceal themselves.*]

[*The blind in the first story opens, and* BARTHOLO *and* ROSINE *appear at the window.*]

ROSINE. What a pleasure it is to breathe the fresh air! This blind is so rarely opened . . .

BARTHOLO. What is that paper?

ROSINE. These are a few couplets from *The Useless Precaution*, which my singing master gave me yesterday.

BARTHOLO. What is this *Useless Precaution?*

ROSINE. 'T is a new comedy.

BARTHOLO. Some new play! Some new sort of folly!

ROSINE. I know nothing about it.

BARTHOLO. Well, the journals and the authorities will avenge us. Barbarous age . . . !

ROSINE. You are always criticizing our poor century.

BARTHOLO. Pardon the liberty that I take! What has it produced that we should praise it? Follies of all sorts; liberty of thought, gravitation, electricity, religious toleration, inoculation, quinine, the encyclopædia, and plays . . .

ROSINE [*as the paper drops from her hand and falls into the street*]. Oh! my song! My song dropped from my hand as I was listening to you. . . . Run, run, sir, — my song — it will be lost!

BARTHOLO. Confound it! When you had it why did you not hold it?

[*Leaves the balcony.*]

ROSINE [*glances about the room and signals to the* COUNT *in the street*]. Sh! [*The* COUNT *appears.*] Pick it up quickly, make your escape. [*The* COUNT *seizes the paper and retreats to his hiding-place.*]

BARTHOLO [*appears in the street and searches for the song*]. Where is it? I cannot find it.

ROSINE. Under the balcony, at the foot of the wall.

BARTHOLO. You have sent me upon a fine errand. Has any one passed by?

Rosine. I have seen no one.

Bartholo [aside]. And I, who have been so simple as to search . . . Bartholo, my friend, you are indeed a simpleton. This should teach you never to open the blinds. [He reënters the house.]

Rosine [in the balcony]. My excuse lies in my unhappiness; alone, ill, and a butt for the persecutions of an odious man, is it a crime to try to escape the bonds of slavery?

Bartholo [appearing in the balcony]. Go in, young lady; it is my fault that you have lost your song; but this misfortune will never overtake you again; I swear it. [Carefully locks the blind.]

Count. Now that they have gone in, let us examine this song, in which a mystery surely lies hidden. Ah, it is a note!

Figaro. He asked what The Useless Precaution was!

Count [reading excitedly]. "Your devotion excites my curiosity. As soon as my guardian has gone out, sing carelessly to the well-known air of these couplets, a few words which shall tell me the name, the rank, and the intentions of the gentleman who appears so desperately attached to the unfortunate Rosine."

Figaro [imitating Rosine's voice]. My song, I have lost my song; run, quickly. [Laughing.] Ha! ha! Oh! these women! Would you teach cunning to the most unsophisticated? Just shut her up.

Count. My dear Rosine!

Figaro. My lord, I am at no more trouble for the motives for your masquerade; you are making love here in prospective.

Count. I see that you know how the land lies; but if you chatter . . .

Figaro. I, chatter! To reassure you I shall employ none of the high-sounding phrases of honor and devotion which are continually abused. I have only one word to say; my interest will answer for my loyalty; weigh everything in that balance, and . . .

Count. Very well! Know, then, that six months ago I met, by chance, in the Prado, a young lady of such beauty . . . Well, you have just seen her. I have sought her in vain through all Madrid. It was only

a few days ago that I discovered that her name is Rosine, that she is of noble blood, an orphan, and married to an old physician of that city, one Bartholo.

Figaro. A fine bird, by my faith! — and a hard one to root out! But who told you that she is the doctor's wife?

Count. Everybody.

Figaro. That is a story invented by him on his arrival from Madrid, to give the slip to the gallants, and put them off the scent. She is still only his ward, but soon . . .

Count [passionately]. Never! Ah! what news! I was resolved to dare everything to express my disappointment, and now I find her free! There's not a moment to lose; I must win her love, and snatch her from the unworthy husband to whom she is destined. Do you know her guardian?

Figaro. As well as my mother.

Count. What sort of man is he?

Figaro [vivaciously]. He is a fine big, short, young old man, dapple gray, crafty, well-shaven, blasé, peeping and prying, grumbling and moaning, all at once.

Count [impatiently]. Ah! I have seen him. And his character?

Figaro. Brutal, avaricious, and absurdly jealous of his ward, who hates him with a deadly hatred.

Count. So his power to please is . . .

Figaro. Zero.

Count. So much the better! His honesty?

Figaro. He is quite honest enough to escape hanging.

Count. So much the better! To punish a rascal while at the same moment I find my happiness . . .

Figaro. Is to do a public and private good; really, a masterpiece of morality, my lord!

Count. You say that fear of the gallants makes him keep his doors closed upon her?

Figaro. Upon every one if he could stop up the cracks in it. . . .

Count. The devil! So much the worse! Do you happen to have access to his house?

Figaro. Have I! The house that I occupy belongs to the doctor, who lodges me there gratis.

Count. Ha! ha!

Figaro. Yes, indeed! And I, in my gratitude, promise him ten gold pistoles a year also *gratis*.

Count [*impatiently*]. You are his tenant?

Figaro. Much more; his barber, his surgeon, his apothecary; there is not a stroke of the razor, the lancet, or the syringe in his house which does not proceed from the hand of your humble servant.

Count [*embracing him*]. Ah, Figaro, my friend! you shall be my savior and my guardian angel.

Figaro. The plague! How soon has my usefulness shortened the distance between us! Talk to me of men with a passion!

Count. Fortunate Figaro! You shall see my Rosine! you shall see her! Can you imagine your good fortune?

Figaro. That's the usual lover's talk! I do not adore her. I wish that you could take my place.

Count. Ah, if we could only dodge these vigilant fellows!

Figaro. That's what I was thinking of.

Count. For but a single day.

Figaro. By setting the servants to look out for their own interests, we shall prevent them from interfering with the interests of others.

Count. Doubtless. Well?

Figaro [*reflecting*]. I shall rack my brains to see whether *materia medica* will not furnish some innocent means . . .

Count. Scoundrel!

Figaro. Am I going to hurt them? They all need my ministrations. It is only a question of how to treat them all at once.

Count. But this doctor may grow suspicious?

Figaro. We shall have to set to work so quickly that he will have no time to suspect. I have an idea. The regiment of the heir-apparent has just arrived in the city.

Count. The colonel is one of my friends.

Figaro. Good. Go to the doctor's in a trooper's uniform with your billet; he will be obliged to lodge you; and I will look after the rest.

Count. Excellent!

Figaro. It would be still better if you appeared a trifle intoxicated . . .

Count. Why?

Figaro. And treat him a bit cavalierly, for you have an excellent excuse for being unreasonable.

Count. Again I ask you why?

Figaro. So that he will take no offense, and think you more in a hurry to go to bed than carry on intrigues in his house.

Count. Beautifully planned! But why do you not figure in it?

Figaro. I, indeed! We shall be fortunate enough if he does not recognize you whom he has never seen. And how should I introduce you afterward?

Count. You are right.

Figaro. It is because you may not be able to act this difficult part. Cavalier . . . the worse for wine . . .

Count. You are laughing at me. [*Imitating the speech of a drunkard.*] Is this the house of Doctor Bartholo, my friend?

Figaro. Truly, not bad, only a little more unsteady in the legs. [*In a more drunken voice.*] Is this the house of Doctor Bartholo . . .

Count. Shame upon you! 'T is a low and vulgar drunkenness.

Figaro. A good one and a pleasant one.

Count. The door opens.

Figaro. Our man: let us make off until he is gone. [*They hide.*]

Bartholo [*coming out, speaking to some one in the house*]. I shall return instantly, let no one enter the house. How foolish I was to come down. As soon as she asked me, I should have suspected. . . . Why is Bazile so late? He was to arrange everything for my secret marriage to-morrow: and no news! Let us go and find out what may have delayed him. [*Exit.*]

Count. What did I hear? To-morrow he marries Rosine secretly!

Figaro. My lord, the difficulties in the way of success only add to the necessity of the undertaking.

Count. What sort of a man is this Bazile who is meddling with this marriage?

Figaro. A poor devil who teaches music to the doctor's ward, infatuated with his art, a bit of a rascal, always needy, on his knees before a crown-piece, who, in short,

will be very easy to manage, my lord . . .
[*Glancing at the blind.*] There she is! there
she is!

COUNT. Who?

FIGARO. Behind the blind, — there she
is! there she is! Don't look! Don't look!

COUNT. Why?

FIGARO. Did she not write: "Sing carelessly"? — that is to say, sing . . . as if
you were singing . . . only for the sake of
singing. Oh! there she is! there she is!

COUNT. Since I have begun to interest
her without being known to her, I shall
keep the name of Lindor which I have assumed; my triumph will have a greater
charm. [*He unfolds the paper which* ROSINE
has thrown out of the window.] But how
shall I sing to this music. I cannot make
verses.

FIGARO. Every verse that occurs to you,
my lord, will be excellent: in love, the heart
assists the productions of the mind . . .
And take my guitar.

COUNT. What shall I do with it? I play
so badly!

FIGARO. Can a man like you be ignorant
of anything? With the back of the hand:
tum, tum tum. . . . To sing without a
guitar in Seville! You would soon be recognized; faith, you would soon be hunted
out.

[FIGARO *stands close to the wall
under the balcony.*]

COUNT [*singing, walking back and forth,
and accompanying himself on the guitar*].

Thou shalt know my name, since to command
　　is thine;
Unknown to thee, I dared to show my adora-
　　tion;
My name once known, I've nought but des-
　　peration.
What matters it? My master's will is mine.

FIGARO [*in a low voice*]. Fine, upon my
word! Courage, my lord!

COUNT.

Lindor am I, of common birth and nation;
A simple student's life is all I claim:
Alas! why bear I not some knight's exalted
　　name,
To offer you his brilliant rank and station?

FIGARO. Deuce take it! I, who pique
myself on my verses, could do no better.

COUNT.

Here, with a tender voice will I
My hopeless love proclaim, each morning
　　bright,
My pleasures shall be bounded by thy sight;
Each morning here with tender notes and long
Will I my hopeless love of thee proclaim!
To see thee . . . this shall be my joy, my
　　flame,
And mayest thou pleasure find to list my
　　song!

FIGARO. Oh! my word! this last one! . . .
　　[*Approaches his master and kisses
　　the hem of his cloak.*]

COUNT. Figaro!

FIGARO. Your excellency?

COUNT. Do you think she heard me?

ROSINE [*within singing:*] —

All tells me now of Lindor's charms,
Whom I must love with constancy . . .

　　[*They hear the window closed noisily.*]

FIGARO. Now, do you think that she
heard you?

COUNT. She has closed her window;
some one has apparently entered the room.

FIGARO. Ah! poor little thing! how she
trembles as she sings! She is caught, my
lord.

COUNT. She avails herself of the very
means which she pointed out to me: —

All tells me now of Lindor's charm.
What grace! what a pretty wit.

FIGARO. What cunning! what love!

COUNT. That is enough! I am Rosine's
. . . forever.

FIGARO. You forget, my lord, that she
cannot hear you now.

COUNT. Master Figaro! I have but one
word to say; she will be my wife, and if you
further my plan by refusing to disclose my
name to her . . . you understand me, you
know me . . .

FIGARO. I agree. Come, Figaro, your
fortune is made, my boy.

COUNT. Let us retire, for fear of exciting
suspicion.

FIGARO [*vivaciously*]. I shall enter this
house, where by means of my art, with a
single stroke of my wand, I shall put vigilance to sleep, awake love, banish jealousy,
mislead intrigue, and overcome all obstacles. You, my lord, my house, a soldier's

uniform, the billet, and gold in your pockets.

COUNT. Gold for whom?

FIGARO [*impatiently*]. Gold, for Heaven's sake, gold! it is the sinews of intrigue!

COUNT. Calm yourself, Figaro, I shall bring plenty of it.

FIGARO [*going off*]. I shall rejoin you in a short time.

COUNT. Figaro!

FIGARO. What is it?

COUNT. Your guitar?

FIGARO. I have forgotten my guitar! I am losing my wits! [*Exit.*]

COUNT. And your house, stupid!

FIGARO [*returning*]. Ah! really, I am astonished! My shop is a few steps away; 't is painted blue, has leaden window frames, three cups in the air, an eye in a hand, with a motto, *Consilio manuque*. [*Exit.*]

ACT II

[*The apartments of* ROSINE. *The casement at the rear of the stage is closed by a barred shutter.*]

[*Enter* ROSINE *alone, a candle in her hand. She takes some paper and sits down to the table to write.*]

ROSINE. Marcelline is ill, all the servants are busy, and no one sees me writing. I know not whether these walls have eyes and ears, or whether my Argus commands some evil genius who is always warning him at precisely the wrong moment; but I cannot say one word, take one step, that he does not immediately guess its purpose. . . . Ah! Lindor! [*She seals the letter.*] Well, I must seal my letter, though I know not when or how I may deliver it. As I looked through my blind, I saw him talking for a long time to the barber Figaro. The good fellow has sometimes shown some pity for me; if I could only speak to him for a moment . . .

[*Enter* FIGARO.]

ROSINE [*in surprise*]. Ah! Master Figaro, how glad I am to see you!

FIGARO. Your health, madame?

ROSINE. Not too good, Master Figaro, I am dying of *ennui*.

FIGARO. I believe you; only fools fatten upon it.

ROSINE. With whom were you talking so earnestly down there? I did not hear; but . . .

FIGARO. With a young bachelor, a relation of mine, a young man of fine parts, full of wit, sentiment, and talent, and gifted, moreover, with a most attractive countenance.

ROSINE. Oh! most excellent, I assure you! and his name? . . .

FIGARO. Lindor. He has nothing; but had he not left Madrid in such a hurry, he might have found some good position there.

ROSINE [*thoughtlessly*]. He will find one, Master Figaro, he will find one. Such a man as he whose portrait you have painted is not born to remain unknown.

FIGARO [*aside*]. Very well. [*Aloud.*] But he has one great fault which will always stand in the way of his advancement.

ROSINE. A fault, Master Figaro! A fault! you are quite sure?

FIGARO. He is in love.

ROSINE. He is in love! and you call that a fault?

FIGARO. In truth, 't is none but in regard to his poor fortune.

ROSINE. Ah! how unjust is Fate! And has he told you whom he loves? I am curious . . .

FIGARO. You are the last, madame, to whom I should like to entrust such a secret as this.

ROSINE [*beseechingly*]. Why, Master Figaro? I am discreet; the young man is your relation, he interests me greatly . . . tell me, then.

FIGARO [*with a sly glance*]. Imagine the prettiest little darling, sweet, tender, gentle-mannered, fresh as the rose, provoking one's appetite, with a dainty foot, a figure agile and slender, plump arms, a rosy mouth, and hands! cheeks! teeth! eyes! . . .

ROSINE. Does she live in this city?

FIGARO. In this quarter of it.

ROSINE. On this street, perhaps?

FIGARO. Not two feet away from me.

ROSINE. Ah! how charming! . . . for your relation. And this person is? . . .

FIGARO. Have I not named her?

ROSINE [excitedly]. It is the only thing that you have forgotten, Master Figaro. Tell me, please tell me quickly; if any one should come in, I might never know . . .

FIGARO. Do you really wish to know, madame? Well! this person is . . . your guardian's ward.

ROSINE. Ward?

FIGARO. Doctor Bartholo's: yes, madame.

ROSINE [with emotion]. Ah, Master Figaro! . . . I do not believe it, I assure you.

FIGARO. And that is what he is himself dying to convince you of.

ROSINE. You make me tremble, Master Figaro.

FIGARO. Shame, tremble, indeed! a bad plan, madame; when one yields to the fear of suffering, one suffers from fear. Besides, I have come to rid you of all your watchers until to-morrow.

ROSINE. If he loves me, he must prove it to me by remaining absolutely quiet.

FIGARO. Indeed, madame! May love and repose dwell side by side in the same heart? Poor youth is so unfortunate, nowadays, that it has but this terrible choice, love without repose, or repose without love.

ROSINE [dropping her eyes]. Repose without love . . . seems . . .

FIGARO. Ah! very languid, indeed. It seems, in fact, that love without repose cuts a much better figure; and, as for myself, if I were a woman . . .

ROSINE [in embarrassment]. It is quite certain that a young lady cannot prevent a good man from esteeming her.

FIGARO. So my relation loves you to distraction.

ROSINE. But if he should be guilty of any imprudence, Master Figaro, he would ruin us.

FIGARO [aside]. He would ruin us . . . [Aloud.] If you would forbid him expressly in a little note . . . a note has a great deal of power.

ROSINE [gives him the letter which she has just written]. I have no time to write this over again, but when you give it to him, tell him . . . well, tell him . . . [Listens.]

FIGARO. No one, madame.

ROSINE. That all that I do is out of pure friendship.

FIGARO. That speaks for itself. God-a-mercy! Love sets us another pace!

ROSINE. Only out of pure friendship, you understand? All that I fear is, that, discouraged by difficulties . . .

FIGARO. As if his passion were only a will-o'-the-wisp. Remember, madame, that the gust which blows out a light will light a brazier, and that, often enough, we are the brazier. Speaking of that only, he breathes out such a flame, that he has made me almost delirious with his passion, I who have nothing to do with the whole matter!

ROSINE. Good Heaven! I hear my guardian. If he should find you here . . . Go out through the music-room, and go down as softly as you can.

FIGARO. Be easy about that. [Aside, holding up the letter.] This is worth more than all my observations. [Exit.]

ROSINE [alone]. I am beside myself with anxiety until he has left the house . . . How I like him, that good Figaro! He is a very honest fellow, a good relation! Ah! There is my tyrant, I must take up my work.

[She blows out the candle, sits down, and takes up some embroidery.]

[Enter BARTHOLO.]

BARTHOLO [in a rage]. Ah! curses upon that villain, that piratical rogue, Figaro! Zounds! I cannot leave my house one moment, and be sure when I return . . .

ROSINE. What makes you so angry, sir?

BARTHOLO. That damned barber who just crippled my whole household in a jiffy! He has given Eveillé a sleeping powder, La Jeunesse something to make him sneeze, he has bled Marcelline in the foot; even down to my mule; he has put a poultice over the eyes of a poor blind beast! Because he owes me one hundred crowns, he is in haste to balance his account. Ah! let him bring them! And no one in the anteroom! one might enter this apartment as easily as the parade-ground.

ROSINE. And who but yourself, sir?

BARTHOLO. I would rather have unreasonable fears than expose myself without precautions. There are bold and daring fellows everywhere . . . This very morning, did not some one quickly pick up your song while I was going down to get it? Oh! I . . .

ROSINE. That is giving importance to everything just for the pleasure of it! The wind may have carried it off, or the first passer-by, how do I know?

BARTHOLO. The wind, the first passer-by! . . . There is no wind, madame, there is no first passer-by in the world; it is always some one waiting there on purpose to pick up all the papers which any woman affects to drop by mistake.

ROSINE. Affects, sir?

BARTHOLO. Yes, madame, affects.

ROSINE [aside]. Oh! the wicked old fellow!

BARTHOLO. But it will never happen again, because I am going to have this blind locked.

ROSINE. Do better than that; wall up all the windows; between a prison and a cell there is very little choice.

BARTHOLO. As for those which look out upon the street, it would not be a bad idea, perhaps . . . At least, that barber has not been here?

ROSINE. Is he also an object of your jealousy?

BARTHOLO. Just as much as any other.

ROSINE. How civilly you answer me!

BARTHOLO. Ah! Trust in everybody, and you will soon have in your house a wife to deceive you, good friends to spirit her off, and good servants to help them do it.

ROSINE. What! You will not grant, indeed, that one has principles against the seduction of Master Figaro?

BARTHOLO. Who the devil knows anything about the peculiarities of women? And how many of these high and mighty virtues have I seen . . .

ROSINE [angrily]. But, sir, if one must only be a man to please us, why is it, then, that you are so repulsive to me?

BARTHOLO [in amazement]. Why? . . . Why? . . . You do not answer my question about that barber?

ROSINE [provoked]. Yes, then! Yes, that man came into my room, I saw him, I spoke to him, I will not conceal from you, even, that I found him very agreeable, and may you die of vexation! [Exit.]

BARTHOLO [alone]. Ah! the Jews! those dogs of servants! Jeunesse! Eveillé! that damned Eveillé!

[Enter EVEILLÉ, yawning, and half awake.]

EVEILLÉ. Aah, aah, ah, ah . . .

BARTHOLO. Where were you, you confounded idiot, when that barber entered the house?

EVEILLÉ. Sir, I was . . . ah, aah, ah . . .

BARTHOLO. Hatching out some trick, no doubt? And you did not see him?

EVEILLÉ. Certainly I saw him, because he found me very ill, as he said; and it must have been very true, because I commenced to have pains in all my limbs, just hearing him talk . . . ah, ah, aah . . .

BARTHOLO [mimics him]. Just hearing him talk . . . Where is that good-for-nothing Jeunesse? To drug this little fellow without my prescription! There is some rascality in it.

[Enter JEUNESSE like an old man, leaning upon a cane; he sneezes several times.]

EVEILLÉ [still yawning]. Jeunesse!

BARTHOLO. You will sneeze Sunday.

JEUNESSE. That's more than fifty . . . fifty times . . . in a minute. [Sneezes.] I am exhausted.

BARTHOLO. I ask you twice if any one entered Rosine's apartment, and you tell me only that barber . . .

EVEILLÉ [still yawning]. Is Master Figaro any one? aah, ah . . .

BARTHOLO. I would wager that the sly fellow has an understanding with him.

EVEILLÉ [weeping foolishly]. I! . . . I, have an understanding! . . .

JEUNESSE [sneezing]. But sir, is there any justice . . . is there any justice?

BARTHOLO. Justice! Justice for you, you wretches! I am your master, who is always right.

JEUNESSE [sneezing]. But, now, when a thing is true . . .

BARTHOLO. When a thing is true. If I do

not wish it to be true, I claim that it is not true. If you would only allow all these rascals to be right, you would soon see what would become of authority.

JEUNESSE [*sneezing*]. You may as well give me my dismissal. It's a terrible position and a devilish row all the time.

EVEILLÉ [*weeping*]. A poor respectable fellow is treated like a wretch.

BARTHOLO. Out with you, you poor respectable fellow! [*Mimics them.*] T'chew! t'chew! One sneezes and the other yawns in my face.

JEUNESSE. Ah, sir! I swear that without Miss Rosine there would be no way of getting on in the house.   [*Exit sneezing.*]

BARTHOLO. In what a plight has Figaro left them all! See what's the matter; the villain wants to pay me my hundred crowns without opening his purse.

[*Enter* DON BAZILE. FIGARO, *hidden in the cabinet, appears from time to time and listens.*]

BARTHOLO. Ah, Don Bazile! have you come to give Rosine her music-lesson?

BAZILE. That is the least part of my haste.

BARTHOLO. I went to see you without finding you at home.

BAZILE. I had gone out on your business. I have learned some sorry news.

BARTHOLO. For yourself?

BAZILE. No, for you. Count Almaviva is in this city.

BARTHOLO. Speak lower. The one who had Rosine sought for throughout the whole city of Madrid?

BAZILE. He is lodging in a house on the Plaza, and comes out every day in disguise.

BARTHOLO. He has designs upon me, that's certain. What shall I do?

BAZILE. If he were a private citizen, we might soon get him out of the way.

BARTHOLO. Yes, we might ambush him in the evening, with sword and buckler . . .

BASILE. *Bone-Deus!* Compromise ourselves! To start a nasty affair, that is fine, and meanwhile slander him to the utmost *concedo!*

BARTHOLO. That is a singular way of getting rid of a man.

BAZILE. Slander, sir? You hardly know what you despise. I have seen the best of men nearly crushed under it. Believe me that there is no vulgar wickedness, no horror, no absurd story, that one cannot fasten upon the idle residents of a great city if he go about it in the right way, and we have some pretty skillful fellows here! At first, a slight rumor, skimming the ground like the swallow before the storm, *pianissimo*, it murmurs, and twists and leaves behind it its poisonous trail. So-and-So hears it and *piano piano* slips it gracefully into your ear. The evil is done, it sprouts, crawls, travels on, and *rinforzando* from mouth to mouth, it goes on at the deuce of a pace; then, suddenly, I know not how, you see slander arising, hissing, swelling, and visibly growing. It rushes forward, extends its flight, whirls, envelops, tears, bursts, and thunders, and becomes, thank Heaven, a general cry, a public *crescendo*, a universal chorus of hate and denunciation. Who the deuce could withstand it?

BARTHOLO. What old wives' tale are you telling me? And what connection may this *piano-crescendo* have with my situation?

BAZILE. What! — what connection! What one does everywhere to put his enemy out of the way, must now be done to prevent yours from further approach.

BARTHOLO. Approach? I intend to marry Rosine before she knows that this count even exists.

BAZILE. In that case, you have not a moment to lose.

BARTHOLO. Why don't you hasten, Bazile? I entrusted all the details of this affair to you.

BAZILE. Yes, but you skimped on the expenses; and in the harmony of good order, an unequal marriage, a wicked judgment, and evident injustice are discords that we must always watch for and prevent, by the perfect accord of gold.

BARTHOLO [*giving him money*]. Well, we shall have to give in to you; but to continue . . .

BAZILE. That's what I call talking. It will be all over to-morrow; it is for you to prevent any one from warning your ward to-day.

BARTHOLO. Trust to me. Are you coming this evening?

BAZILE. Do not count upon me. Your marriage alone will keep me busy the whole day; do not count upon me.

BARTHOLO [*accompanying him to the door*]. Your servant.

BAZILE. No ceremony, doctor.

BARTHOLO. No, indeed. I wish to close the street door after you.   [*Exeunt.*]

FIGARO [*alone, issuing from the cabinet*]. Oh! a good precaution, indeed! Close your street door, then, and I shall open it again for the count as I go out. What a great rogue is that Bazile! Luckily he is even more foolish than rascally. One needs station, family, name, rank, and, in short, the regard of the world, to make any sensation in the world as a slanderer. But a Bazile! His lies would never pass current.

[*Enter* ROSINE, *in haste.*]

ROSINE. What! You are still there, Master Figaro?

FIGARO. Luckily for you, miss. Your guardian and your singing-master, thinking that they were here alone, have spoken very clearly. . . .

ROSINE. And you listened to them, Master Figaro? Do you know that that is very wrong?

FIGARO. To listen? That is the very best way to hear well. Know, then, that your guardian is preparing to wed you to-morrow.

ROSINE. Ah! great Heaven!

FIGARO. Fear nothing; we shall give him so much to do that he will have no time to think of that.

ROSINE. He is returning; go out by the little staircase. You terrify me.

[*Exit* FIGARO.]

[*Enter* BARTHOLO.]

ROSINE. You were here with some one, sir?

BARTHOLO. Don Bazile, whom I have just accompanied to the door, and with good reason. You would have preferred that it was Master Figaro?

ROSINE. I assure you, it's all the same to me.

BARTHOLO. I should like to know what that barber was so anxious to tell you.

ROSINE. Must we talk seriously? He gave me an account of Marcelline's condition, and, so he says, she is none too well.

BARTHOLO. Give you an account? I will wager that he was commissioned to hand you some letter.

ROSINE. And from whom, if you please?

BARTHOLO. Oh, from whom! From some one whom women never name. How should I know? Perhaps the answer to the paper that dropped from the window.

ROSINE [*aside*]. He is perfectly right, to be sure. [*Aloud.*] It would serve you right if it was.

BARTHOLO [*examining* ROSINE'S *hand*]. That is it. You have been writing.

ROSINE [*in embarrassment*]. You will be skillful indeed to make me acknowledge it.

BARTHOLO [*taking her right hand*]. I? Not at all! But your finger is stained with ink. . . . What do you make of that, you sly miss?

ROSINE. What a cursed man!

BARTHOLO [*still holding her hand*]. A woman always thinks that she is safe when she is alone.

ROSINE. Ah! No doubt. . . . A fine proof! . . . Stop, sir, you are twisting my arms. I burned myself with the candle, and I have always been told that you must immediately dip it in ink; that is what I did.

BARTHOLO. That is what you did? Let us see if the second witness will corroborate the deposition of the first. I am certain that there were six sheets in this package of paper, for I have counted them every morning as well as to-day.

ROSINE [*aside*]. Oh! what a fool! . . .

BARTHOLO [*counting*]. Three, four, five! . . .

ROSINE. The sixth . . .

BARTHOLO. I see very clearly that there is no sixth.

ROSINE [*dropping her eyes*]. The sixth? I used it to make a bag for some bon-bons which I sent to little Mistress Figaro.

BARTHOLO. Little Mistress Figaro? And the pen, which was brand-new, how did that become black? Was it in writing her address?

ROSINE. This man has a genius for jealousy! . . . [*Aloud.*] I used it to sketch a faded flower on the jacket which I am embroidering.

BARTHOLO. How edifying that is! In order to be believed, my child, you should not blush when concealing the truth so fast; but you do not know that yet.

ROSINE. What! Who would not blush, sir, to see such damaging deductions drawn from the most innocent circumstances?

BARTHOLO.. Certainly I am wrong; to burn one's finger, dip it in the ink, to make bon-bon bags for Mistress Figaro, and to sketch an embroidery design! What more innocent! But how many lies told to conceal a single fact! *I am alone, I am not observed, I may lie as I please:* but the end of her finger is still black, the pen is soiled, and the paper is missing! Of course, we could not think of everything. Indeed, my young lady, when I go out into the city, a good double lock shall answer for you.

COUNT [*entering in a cavalry uniform, feigning intoxication and singing:*]

Let 's wake her, etc.

BARTHOLO. What does this fellow wish of us? A soldier! Go into your room, young lady.

COUNT [*singing*].

Let's wake her,

[*Advancing toward* ROSINE.] Which of you two ladies is named Doctor Balordo? [*Aside to* ROSINE.] I am Lindor.

BARTHOLO. Bartholo!

ROSINE. He speaks of Lindor.

COUNT. Balordo, Barque-à-l'eau, I don't care which, only I must know which of the two. . . . [*To* ROSINE, *showing her a paper.*] Take this letter.

BARTHOLO. Which! You see very well that it is I! Which, forsooth! Retire to your room, Rosine, this man seems to be drunk!

ROSINE. But you are alone, sir. A woman sometimes inspires a little respect.

BARTHOLO. Off with you; I am not timid. [*Exit* ROSINE.]

COUNT. Oh! I recognized you immediately by your description.

BARTHOLO [*to the* COUNT, *who is folding up the letter*]. What are you hiding in your pocket?

COUNT. I am hiding this in my pocket so that you will not know what it is.

BARTHOLO. My description! Those fellows are forever believing that they are talking to soldiers!

COUNT. Do you think that it is such a hard matter to describe you?
The nodding head, the bald and polished crown,
The wall-eyed, blear, and savage-squinting frown,
The manners like a fierce Algonquin chief,
The heavy figure, warped beyond belief,
The crooked shoulder and swarthy skin,
As black as any Moorish child of sin,
The nose, moreover, like a baldaquin,
The bent and twisted leg, forever flexed,
The hangman's voice, confused with words perplexed,
And all his vicious appetites declare
This man 's the pearl of doctors, rich and rare!

BARTHOLO. What do you mean? Have you come here to insult me? Clear out this moment!

COUNT. Clear out! Ah, pshaw! That's a churlish speech. Can you read, doctor . . . Barbe-à-l'eau?

BARTHOLO. Another silly question.

COUNT. Oh! don't let that worry you; for I, who am at least as much of a doctor as yourself . . .

BARTHOLO. What is that?

COUNT. Am I not horse-doctor to the regiment? That is why they have lodged me with a colleague.

BARTHOLO. He dares to compare a farrier! . . .

COUNT. No, doctor, I will not proclaim
That this our art can put to shame
Old Hippocrates and his crew;
Your knowledge, comrade, it is true,
Hath a success of wider sway,
The ill it may not bear away,
Yet bear off patients not a few.
Do I not speak you fairly?

BARTHOLO. It becomes you well, you ignorant manipulator, so to revile the first, the greatest, and the most useful of the arts!

COUNT. Useful, indeed, for those who practice it.

BARTHOLO. An art honoring the sun which shines upon its successes!

COUNT. And whose blunders the earth makes haste to cover.

BARTHOLO. I see very well, you saucy fellow, that you are only accustomed to talk to horses.

COUNT. Talk to horses! Ah, doctor! a poor wit for a witty doctor. . . . Is it not notorious that the farrier always cures his patients without speaking to them, though, on the contrary, the physician talks much to his. . . .

BARTHOLO. Without curing them, you mean?

COUNT. You have said so.

BARTHOLO. Who the devil sends us this cursed drunkard?

COUNT. My dear fellow, I think that you are firing epigrams at me!

BARTHOLO. Well, what would you have? what do you want?

COUNT [feigning a rage]. Well, then! What do I want? Don't you see?

ROSINE [entering in haste]. Master soldier, do not get angry, I beg you! [To BARTHOLO.] Speak to him gently, sir: an unreasonable man . . .

COUNT. You are right; he is unreasonable; but we are reasonable! I, polite, you, pretty . . . that's enough. To tell the truth, I wish to have dealings with no one in this house but you.

ROSINE. What can I do to serve you, sir?

COUNT. A mere trifle, my child. If there is any obscurity in my words . . .

ROSINE. I shall understand their meaning.

COUNT [showing her the letter]. Now, confine yourself to the letter, to the letter. It is only this . . . that you give me a bed to-night.

BARTHOLO. Nothing but that?

COUNT. No more. Read the note which our quartermaster has written you.

BARTHOLO. Let us see. [The COUNT hides the letter and gives him another paper. BARTHOLO reads.] "Doctor Bartholo will receive, feed, lodge, and bed . . . "

COUNT [leaning over his shoulder]. Bed!

BARTHOLO. "For one night only, one Lindor called the Scholar, trooper in the regiment."

ROSINE. It is he, it is he!

BARTHOLO [quickly to ROSINE]. What is that?

COUNT. Well, am I wrong now, Doctor Bartholo?

BARTHOLO. One might say that this man takes a malicious pleasure in belaboring me in every possible way. To the devil with your Barbaro, Barbe-à-l'eau! and tell your impertinent quartermaster that since my journey to Madrid I am exempt from lodging soldiers.

COUNT [aside]. O Heaven! What a vexatious misfortune!

BARTHOLO. Ha! ha! my friend, that puts you out a little? Clear out this very moment.

COUNT [aside]. I nearly betrayed myself. [Aloud.] Be off! If you are exempt from men of war, you are not exempt from politeness! Decamp! Show me your exemption warrant; although I cannot read, I shall soon see . . .

BARTHOLO. What has that to do with it? It is in this bureau . . .

COUNT [as he approaches it says without moving]. Ah! my fair Rosine!

ROSINE. What, Lindor, is it you?

COUNT. At all events, take this letter.

ROSINE. Take care, he has his eyes upon us.

COUNT. Take out your handkerchief, I will drop the letter. [He approaches.]

BARTHOLO. Gently, gently, sir soldier, I do not like my wife looked at so closely.

COUNT. Is she your wife?

BARTHOLO. And what then?

COUNT. I took you for her grandfather, paternal, maternal, eternal. There are at least three generations between her and yourself.

BARTHOLO [reading from a parchment]. "In consideration of good and faithful testimony proffered us . . ."

COUNT [striking the parchments from his hand to the floor]. Do I need this string of words?

BARTHOLO. You know very well, soldier, that if I call my people, I will have you treated forthwith as you deserve.

COUNT. A fight! Ah, willingly! that is my trade [showing a pistol in his belt] and here is something to throw powder in their eyes. Perhaps you have never seen a battle, madame?

ROSINE. Nor do I wish to see one.

COUNT. Nothing, however, is as gay as a battle! Imagine [pushing the doctor], in the first place, that the enemy is on one side of the ravine, and the friends on the other. [To ROSINE, showing her the letter.] Now take out your handkerchief. [Spits on the floor.] That's the ravine, you understand.

[ROSINE takes out her handkerchief. The COUNT drops his letter between them.]

BARTHOLO [stooping]. Ha! ha!

COUNT. There! . . . I was going to teach you all the secrets of my trade. . . . Truly, a very discreet lady! Has she not just dropped a note from her pocket?

BARTHOLO. Give it to me.

COUNT. Softly, papa! No meddling, if you please. If a prescription for rhubarb had fallen out of yours? . . .

ROSINE [reaching for it]. Ah! I know what it is, master soldier.

[She takes the letter and hides it in the little pocket of her apron.]

BARTHOLO. Are you going to get out?

COUNT. Well, I will go. Good-bye, doctor; no bitterness. A little compliment, my dear fellow: pray Death to forget me for a few more campaigns: life has never been so dear to me.

BARTHOLO. Never mind, if I had so much credit with Death . . .

COUNT. With Death! Are you not a physician? You do so much for Death, that he can refuse you nothing.   [Exit.]

BARTHOLO [watching him out]. He is gone at last. [Aside.] Let us dissemble.

ROSINE. Now confess, sir, that he is a very gay fellow, this young soldier! Despite his drunkenness, I can see that he does not lack wit, nor a certain amount of education.

BARTHOLO. Fortunate, my love, that we have been able to get rid of him! But are you not a little anxious to read me the paper that he handed you?

ROSINE. What paper?

BARTHOLO. The one that he pretended to pick up to hand to you.

ROSINE. Good! that is a letter from my cousin the officer, which had dropped from my pocket.

BARTHOLO. I had an idea that he got it out of his own.

ROSINE. I recognized it easily.

BARTHOLO. What does it cost to look at it.

ROSINE. I do not know what I have done with it.

BARTHOLO [pointing to her pocket]. You put it there.

ROSINE. Oh, yes! absent-mindedly.

BARTHOLO. Oh! certainly. You will probably see that it is some piece of foolishness.

ROSINE [aside]. There is no way of refusing him without making him angry.

BARTHOLO. Give it to me, my dear.

ROSINE. But what do you mean, sir, by insisting? Do you distrust me?

BARTHOLO. But why are you so unwilling to show it to me?

ROSINE. I repeat, sir, that this paper is no other than a letter from my cousin, which you delivered to me yesterday unsealed; and in regard to that, I will tell you frankly that your liberties displease me exceedingly.

BARTHOLO. I do not understand you.

ROSINE. Shall I examine every paper addressed to you? Why do you take it upon you to examine everything addressed to me? If it is jealousy, it insults me; if it is the abuse of a power usurped, I am even more disgusted.

BARTHOLO. What, disgusted! You have never before spoken to me in this fashion.

ROSINE. If I have been moderate until to-day, it was not to give you any right to offend me with impunity.

BARTHOLO. What offense are you talking about?

ROSINE. It is unheard of to permit any one to open one's letters.

BARTHOLO. Not even your wife's?

ROSINE. I am not yet your wife. But why should she be made the object of an indignity that you would not offer to every one?

BARTHOLO. You are trying to put me off the scent, and divert my attention from the note, which is, no doubt, a missive from some lover! But I shall see it, I assure you.

ROSINE. You shall not see it. If you approach me, I flee this house, and I shall ask refuge of the first comer.

BARTHOLO. Who will not receive you.

ROSINE. We shall see about that.

BARTHOLO. We are not in France, where they always give way to women; but in order to destroy your illusion, I shall lock the door.

ROSINE [as he departs to do so]. Ah! Heaven! What shall I do? Let us quickly exchange it for my cousin's letter, and give him a chance to find it.

[She makes the exchange, puts her cousin's letter in her pocket, so that it protrudes a trifle.]

BARTHOLO [returning]. Ah! now I expect to see it.

ROSINE. By what right, if you please?

BARTHOLO. By the right most universally recognized, the right of might.

ROSINE. You may kill me before you get it from me.

BARTHOLO [stamping with vexation]. Madame! madame! . . .

ROSINE [falling into an arm-chair and feigning illness]. Oh! what an outrage! . . .

BARTHOLO. Give me that letter, or you will have reason to fear my anger.

ROSINE [falling backward]. Unfortunate Rosine!

BARTHOLO. What is the matter with you?

ROSINE. What a terrible future.

BARTHOLO. Rosine!

ROSINE. I am choking with anger.

BARTHOLO. She is ill.

ROSINE. I am fainting. . . . I am dying.

BARTHOLO [feeling her pulse and saying aside]. Heavens! the letter! Let us read it before she knows it.

[He continues to feel her pulse, and seizes the letter, which he tries to read by turning aside a little.]

ROSINE [still reclining]. Ah! unfortunate! . . .

BARTHOLO [dropping his arm and saying aside]. How mad are we to learn what we always fear to know.

ROSINE. Ah! poor Rosine!

BARTHOLO. The use of perfumes produces spasmodic affections.

[He reads behind the armchair as he feels her pulse. ROSINE rises a little, gazes at him fixedly, nods, and falls back without a word.]

BARTHOLO [aside]. O Heaven! it is her cousin's letter. Cursed anxiety! Now, how shall I appease her? At least, let her not know that I have read it!

[He pretends to raise her up and slips the letter into her pocket.]

ROSINE [sighs]. Ah! . . .

BARTHOLO. Well! it is nothing, my child, a slight attack of the vapors, that is all; for your pulse has not varied one beat.

[He turns to take a flask from the table.]

ROSINE [aside]. He has replaced my letter! very well.

BARTHOLO. My dear Rosine, a little of these spirits.

ROSINE. I wish nothing from you; leave me alone.

BARTHOLO. I confess that I was a little too rough about the note.

ROSINE. He is still talking of the note! It is your manner of asking for things which is disgusting.

BARTHOLO [on his knees]. Your pardon. I soon saw that I was quite wrong; you see me at your feet, ready to make reparation.

ROSINE. Yes, pardon indeed! when you believe that this letter does not come from my cousin.

BARTHOLO. Whether it comes from him or any one else, I ask for no explanation.

ROSINE [presenting him the letter]. You see that by decent behavior you may obtain anything of me. Read it.

BARTHOLO. This open manner would dissipate my suspicions if I were unfortunate enough to have any.

ROSINE. Read it, sir.

BARTHOLO [drawing back]. God forbid that I should offer you such an insult!

ROSINE. You would displease me by refusing it.

BARTHOLO. Receive as a recompense

this mark of my perfect confidence. I am going to see poor Marcelline, whom that Figaro has, for some odd reason, bled in the foot; will you not come also?

ROSINE. I will go up in a moment.

BARTHOLO. Since we have made peace, my darling, give me your hand. If you could only love me, how happy you might be!

ROSINE [dropping her eyes]. If you would only please me, ah! how I should love you!

BARTHOLO. I will please you, I will please you! and when I say that I will please you! . . . [Exit.]

ROSINE [watching him go out]. Ah, Lindor! He says that he will please me! . . . Let us read this letter which has almost caused me so much sorrow. [She reads and cries out:] Ah! . . . I am too late, he asks me to start an open quarrel with my guardian. I had such a good opportunity and I let it escape me! When I received the letter I felt that I blushed to the eyes. Ah! my guardian is right, I am far from having that acquaintance with the world which, he oftens tell me, assures the manners of women on every occasion! But an unjust man would succeed in making an intriguer of innocence itself. [Exit.]

ACT III

BARTHOLO [alone and in despair]. What caprices! what caprices! She seemed quite satisfied . . . There! I wish some one could tell me who the devil has put it into her head not to wish any more lessons from Don Bazile! She knows that he has something to do with my marriage . . . [A knock at the door.] Do everything in the world to please a woman. If you omit one single point . . . one only . . . [Another knock.] Let's see who it is.

[Enter the COUNT as a student.]

COUNT. May peace and joy forever dwell herein.

BARTHOLO [shortly]. Never was wish in better season.

COUNT. I am Alonzo, bachelor, licentiate . . .

BARTHOLO. I have no need of a tutor.

COUNT. The pupil of Don Bazile, organist to the grand convent, who has the honor to teach music to madame, your . . .

BARTHOLO. Bazile! organist! who has the honor! I know it! Yes, indeed!

COUNT [aside]. What a man! [Aloud.] A sudden illness which forces him to keep his bed . . .

BARTHOLO. Keep his bed! Bazile! He has done well to send me word, I will go to see him this moment.

COUNT [aside]. Oh! the devil! [Aloud.] When I say his bed, sir, I . . . I . . . I mean his room.

BARTHOLO. Even if it be only a trifling illness . . . Go ahead, I will follow you.

COUNT [in embarrassment]. Sir, I was charged . . . Nobody can hear us?

BARTHOLO [aside]. He is some rogue. [Aloud.] No, master mysterious! Speak without fear, if you can.

COUNT [aside]. Confounded old man! [Aloud.] Don Bazile charged me to tell you . . .

BARTHOLO. Speak louder, I am deaf in one ear.

COUNT [raising his voice]. Ah! willingly . . . that Count Almaviva, who was lodging in the Plaza . . .

BARTHOLO [in terror]. Speak lower, speak lower.

COUNT [louder] . . . has moved away this morning. As it was through me that he knew Count Almaviva . . .

BARTHOLO. Not so loud, I beg you.

COUNT [in the same tone] . . . was in this city, and that I have discovered that Miss Rosine has written to him . . .

BARTHOLO. Has written to him? My dear friend, not so loud, I beg you! There, let us sit down, and have a friendly chat. You have discovered, you say, that Rosine . . .

COUNT [anxiously]. Assuredly. Bazile, disturbed on your account about this correspondence, has asked me to show you the letter; but the way in which you take things . . .

BARTHOLO. Goodness! I take them well. But can't you speak in a lower voice?

COUNT. You are deaf in one ear, you say.

BARTHOLO. Pardon, Master Alonzo, if you found me suspicious and harsh; but I am so completely surrounded by intriguers and plots; . . . and then your appearance, your age, your air . . . Your pardon. Well! you have the letter.

COUNT. In good time! If you take it this way, sir . . . But I am afraid lest some one may be eavesdropping.

BARTHOLO. Who do you think? All my servants are laid out! Rosine, in a rage, shut up in her room! The devil has entered my house. I will go to make sure . . .

[He opens ROSINE'S door softly.]

COUNT [aside]. I have got into trouble by being too much in a hurry . . . Shall I keep the letter for the present? I shall have to take myself off; I might as well have stayed away . . . Show it to him . . . If I can put Rosine upon her guard, to show it is a master-stroke.

BARTHOLO [returning upon tiptoe]. She is sitting near the window with her back turned toward the door, reading over a letter from her cousin, an officer, which I had unsealed . . . Let 's see hers.

COUNT [hands him ROSINE'S letter]. Here it is. [Aside.] It is my letter which she is reading.

BARTHOLO [reads]. "Since you have told me your name and rank" . . . Ah! the wretch! It is, indeed, her hand.

COUNT [in terror]. It is your turn to speak lower.

BARTHOLO. What an obligation, my dear fellow!

COUNT. When everything is done, if you think that you owe anything for it, you will be free to reward me. After a work which Don Bazile is at present carrying on with a lawyer . . .

BARTHOLO. With a lawyer, for my marriage?

COUNT. Would I have stopped without telling you that? He charged me to tell you that all would be ready for to-morrow. Then, if she resists . . .

BARTHOLO. She will resist.

COUNT [tries to regain the letter from Bartholo, who keeps it in his possession]. That is the time when I may be able to serve you; we will show her her letter, and if it is necessary [more mysteriously] I shall go so far as to tell her that I had it from a woman to whom the Count had given it. You see that anxiety, shame, and spite may drive her immediately . . .

BARTHOLO [laughing]. Calumny! Now, indeed do I see that you really come from Bazile! But in order that all this may not appear to be a plot, would it not be well for her to know you beforehand?

COUNT [represses a start of joy]. That was Don Bazile's opinion. But how shall we do it? It is late . . . In the little time which remains . . .

BARTHOLO. I will tell her that you are coming in his place. Will you not give her a lesson?

COUNT. There is nothing that I would not do to please you. But bear in mind that all these stories of alleged masters are old dodges, comedy tricks. If she suspects . . .

BARTHOLO. If you are introduced by me, there is no likelihood of it. You look more like a disguised lover than an obliging friend.

COUNT. Really! Do you think that my appearance will add to the deceit?

BARTHOLO. I will leave the solution of that to some one cleverer than I. She is in a horrible humor this evening. But if she would only see you . . . Her harpsichord is in this cabinet. Amuse yourself while you wait; I am going to try the impossible in bringing her to you.

COUNT. Take care not to speak of the letter.

BARTHOLO. Before the decisive moment? That would destroy all its effect. You need not tell me things twice. [Exit.]

COUNT [alone]. Saved! Phew! How hard this devilish fellow is to handle! Figaro knows him well. I could see myself as I lied; it surely made me look flat and stupid, and he has eyes! My word, if it had not been for the sudden inspiration of the letter, I must confess, I would have gone on like a fool. O Heaven! they are disputing in there. If she should refuse to come! Let 's listen . . . She refuses to come out of her room, and I have lost all the advantage that I had gained. [He listens again.] Here she is; let us not appear at first.

[He enters the cabinet.]

[*Enter* ROSINE *and* BARTHOLO.]

ROSINE [*with an affected anger*]. All that you may say, sir, is useless; I have decided, I wish to hear nothing more about music.

BARTHOLO. Listen, my child; it is Master Alonzo, the pupil and friend of Don Bazile, chosen by him to be one of our witnesses. Music will calm you, I assure you.

ROSINE. Oh! as for that, you may give up that notion. You want me to sing this evening! Where is this master whom you are afraid to send away? I will send him about his business, and Bazile's too. [*She sees her lover and utters a cry.*] Ah! . . .

BARTHOLO. What is the matter?

ROSINE [*clasping her hands upon her breast*]. Ah! sir! . . . Ah, sir! . . .

BARTHOLO. She is ill again, Master Alonzo!

ROSINE. No, I am not ill . . . but, as I turned . . . Ah!

COUNT. You turned your ankle, madame?

ROSINE. Ah, yes! I turned my ankle. It gave me a terrible pain.

COUNT. I perceived that it did.

ROSINE [*gazing at the* COUNT]. It struck me to the heart.

BARTHOLO. A chair, a chair. Not an armchair here! [*Goes to seek one.*]

COUNT. Ah, Rosine!

ROSINE. What an imprudence!

COUNT. I have a thousand things to tell you.

ROSINE. He will not leave us.

COUNT. Figaro will come to our assistance.

BARTHOLO [*bringing an easy chair*]. There, darling, sit down. It is quite improbable, master bachelor, that she will take a lesson this evening; you will have to wait until another day. Farewell.

ROSINE [*to the* COUNT]. No, wait; my pain is a little eased. [*To* BARTHOLO.] I see that I was wrong with you, sir; I will follow your example by repairing immediately . . .

BARTHOLO. Ah! what good little dispositions women have! But after enduring such pain, my child, I will not allow you to make the least effort. Farewell, farewell, master bachelor.

ROSINE [*to the* COUNT]. One moment, sir, if you please! [*To* BARTHOLO.] I will think, sir, that you do not like to oblige me, if you prevent me from showing my regret by taking the lesson.

COUNT [*aside to* BARTHOLO]. Do not oppose her, if you wish to take my advice.

BARTHOLO. That is enough, my dear. I am so far from trying to displease you, that I shall remain here while you are taking your lesson.

ROSINE. Oh, no, sir, I know that music has no attraction for you.

BARTHOLO. I assure you that I shall be enchanted this evening.

ROSINE [*aside to the* COUNT]. He puts me to the torment.

COUNT [*taking up a sheet of music*]. Will you sing that, madame?

ROSINE. Yes, it is a very pretty piece from *The Useless Precaution*.

BARTHOLO. *The Useless Precaution* again!

COUNT. It is the newest thing of the day. It is a picture of Spring in a very lively *genre*. Does madame wish to try it?

ROSINE [*gazing at the* COUNT]. With great pleasure; a picture of Spring will enchant me; it is the youth of Nature. After the winter, it seems as if the heart reaches a higher degree of sensibility, as a slave who has long been confined enjoys to the full the charm of liberty which has just been offered him.

BARTHOLO [*to the* COUNT *in a low voice*]. Her head is forever full of these romantic ideas.

COUNT [*in a low voice*]. Do you see the point of it?

BARTHOLO. Zounds!

[*Seats himself in the chair which* ROSINE *has been occupying.*]

ROSINE [*sings*].

When o'er the plain
Love once again
   Doth bring
The lovers' cherished Spring,
   Then everything
   With new life thrills;
The flowers it fills
And maketh young hearts sing.

The flocks are seen
Upon the green,
And all the hills
With the young lambs' cries resound.
They frisk and bound —
All things be growing,
All blossoms blowing.
And grazing sheep
The faithful watchdogs keep,
But Lindor, passion-moved,
Thinks none the less
But of the joy of being loved
By his fair shepherdess.

Far from her mother, with a blithesome song,
Our shepherdess doth trip along
To tryst her waiting lover.
By this device doth Love entice
And snare the pretty rover.
Will song protection give her?
The piping reeds
She lists and heeds,
Birds' sweet alarms,
Her swelling charms,
Her fifteen years —
All that she sees,
All that she hears
Fills her with fears
And vague malease.

From his retreat
Lindor discreet
Doth meet perchance
The maid's advance.
The youth has just embraced her.
The maid though pleased
Doth feign a sudden anger
In order to be teased.

Refrain.

Now sighs
And sweet alarms and many a fond caress,
Now amorous vows and lively tenderness,
Bright eyes
Dear dalliance and swift repartee
All come in play, and now, perdie,
Right soon our gentle shepherdess
Feels her just rage grow less;
And if some jealous swain
Dare trouble such sweet pain,
Our lovers in accord,
With every act and word
Their highest joys conceal,
For when we love indeed
Restraint can naught but feed
The fires of love we feel.

[*As he listens,* BARTHOLO *falls asleep. The* COUNT, *during the*

refrain, ventures to seize her hand, which he covers with kisses. In her emotion the song dies away, until it ceases in the middle of the cadence at the last word. The orchestra follows the movement of the singer, and is silent with her. The absence of the sounds which had put BARTHOLO *to sleep awakes him. The* COUNT *rises,* ROSINE *and the orchestra quickly continue the air.*]

COUNT. Truly it is a charming piece, and madame sings it with a degree of understanding . . .

ROSINE. You flatter me, sir; the praise belongs entirely to the master.

BARTHOLO [*yawning*]. I think that I must have slept a little during this charming piece. I have my little weaknesses. I go and come, I become a little giddy, and as soon as I sit down, my poor legs . . .

[*He rises and pushes away the chair.*]

ROSINE [*whispers to the* COUNT]. Figaro does not come.

COUNT. Let us try to kill time.

BARTHOLO. But, master bachelor, I have already said so to that old Bazile; is there no way of making her study something more lively than all these grand *arias*, which go up and down, rolling along with a hi, ho, a, a, a, a, and which seem to me like so many funerals? Now, some of those little airs that they used to sing in my youth, and which all remembered so easily. I used to know some of them . . . For example . . .

[*During the prelude he scratches his head and sings, snapping his fingers and dancing with his knees bent in the mánner of old men.*]

Dost thou, my Rosinette,
Elect to get
A spouse, the prince of men? . . .

[*To the* COUNT, *laughing.*] There is a Fanchonette in the song, but I substituted Rosinette for her, to make it more pleasing to her, and to make it fit the circumstances. Ha! ha! ha! ha! Pretty good, is n't it?

COUNT [*laughing*]. Ha! ha! ha! ha! yes, capital.

[*Enter* FIGARO, *who remains at the back.*]

BARTHOLO [*sings*].

Dost thou, my Rosinette,
Elect to get
A spouse, the prince of men?
No Thyrsis I — yet when
The shadows fall, at ending of the day,
I still am worth my fee,
For in obscurity
The bravest cats are merely somber gray.

[*He repeats the refrain dancing.*
FIGARO, *behind him, imitates
his movements.*]

No Thyrsis I, etc.

[*Perceiving* FIGARO.] Ah! enter master
barber: come in, you are charming!

FIGARO [*salutes*]. Sir, it is true that my
mother used to tell me so: but I am somewhat deformed since that time. [*Aside to
the* COUNT.] Bravo, my lord.

[*During this whole scene, the*
COUNT *makes numerous at-
tempts to speak to* ROSINE, *but
the restless and vigilant eye of
her guardian prevents him, which
produces a sort of dumb show of
all the actors not taking part in
the discussion between the doctor
and* FIGARO.]

BARTHOLO. Have you come again to
bleed, drug, and prostrate my whole household?

FIGARO. Feast days, sir, come only once
a year; but, without counting my daily attentions, you may have seen, sir, that when
they need them, my zeal does not wait
upon command . . .

BARTHOLO. Your zeal does not wait!
What have you to say, master zealot, to
that wretch who yawns and sleeps, though
wide awake? and the other, who, for the last
three hours, has been sneezing enough to
crack his cranium, or blow out his brains!
What have you to say to that?

FIGARO. What have I to say to that?

BARTHOLO. Yes!

FIGARO. Well, I should say . . . I should
say to him who sneezes, *God bless you:* and
Go to bed, to him who yawns. It is not that,
sir, which will increase the bill.

BARTHOLO. Truly, no: but it is bleed-
ings and medicines which would increase it
if I would stand it. Is it due to your zeal
also that you bandaged my mule's eyes?
And will your bandage return its sight?

FIGARO. If it does not bring back the
sight, it will no longer prevent it from seeing.

BARTHOLO. Wait till I find it in the bill!
. . . I will not stand such extravagance!

FIGARO. Faith, sir, there being little to
choose between stupidity and folly, in
which I see no profit, I wish at least to find
some pleasure, and long live joy! Who
knows if the world will last three weeks
longer?

BARTHOLO. You would do much better,
master reasoner, to pay me my hundred
crowns and the interest, without any nonsense: I warn you.

FIGARO. Do you doubt my honesty,
sir? Your hundred crowns! I would rather
owe them to you all my life than deny them
to you for a single moment.

BARTHOLO. And tell me how Mistress
Figaro liked the bon-bons that you took
her.

FIGARO. What bon-bons? What do you
mean?

BARTHOLO. Yes, those bon-bons, in the
bag made from a sheet of this letter paper
. . . this morning.

FIGARO. The devil fly away with me
if . . .

ROSINE [*interrupting him*]. Did you
take care to tell her that they were from
me, Master Figaro? I told you to do so.

FIGARO. Ah, yes! this morning's bon-
bons! How stupid I am! I had quite forgotten that . . . Oh! excellent, madame,
admirable!

BARTHOLO. Excellent! admirable! Yes,
doubtless, Master Figaro, you are retrac-
ing your steps! That is a fine business, sir,
that you ply. . . .

FIGARO. What is the matter with it, sir?

BARTHOLO. Which will acquire a fine
reputation for you, sirrah.

FIGARO. I will try to live up to it, sir.

BARTHOLO. Say that you will live it
down, sirrah.

FIGARO. As you please, sir.

BARTHOLO. You ride a high horse, sirrah. Know that when I dispute with a fool, I never yield to him.

FIGARO [*turning his back upon him*]. We differ in that, sir, for I always yield to him.

BARTHOLO. Hey! What does he mean by that, bachelor?

FIGARO. That you think that you have to do with some village barber, who only knows how to handle the razor. Learn, sir, that I have labored with my pen at Madrid, and that were it not for the envious . . .

BARTHOLO. Why did you not stay there, without coming here to change your profession!

FIGARO. We do what we can; put yourself in my place.

BARTHOLO. Put myself in your place! Ah! zounds! I would say a fine lot of stupidities!

FIGARO. Sir, you do not begin badly; I appeal to your colleague, who is dreaming there. . . .

COUNT [*turning to him*]. I . . . I am not his colleague.

FIGARO. No? Seeing you here in consultation, I thought that you were pursuing the same object.

BARTHOLO [*angrily*]. Well, what brings you here? Is it to bring madame another letter this evening? Speak; must I retire?

FIGARO. How harshly you treat the poor world! Zounds, sir, I come to shave you, that 's all. Is not to-day your day?

BARTHOLO. You may return later.

FIGARO. Ah, yes, return! The whole garrison takes medicine to-morrow morning. I obtained the contract through some friends of mine. Consider, then, how much time I have to lose! Will you go into your room, sir?

BARTHOLO. No, I will not. But . . . why can't you shave me here?

ROSINE [*contemptuously*]. You are polite! And why not in my apartments?

BARTHOLO. You are angry? Pardon, my child; you may finish taking your lesson; it is in order not to lose for a moment the pleasure of hearing you.

FIGARO [*whispers to the* COUNT]. We cannot get him out of here! [*Aloud.*] Come, Eveillé! Jeunesse! the basin, the water, everything master needs!

BARTHOLO. That 's right, call them! Fatigued, harassed, belabored at your hands, did they not need to go to bed?

FIGARO. Well! I will go and look for everything; is it not in your room? [*To the* COUNT *aside.*] I am going to coax him out.

BARTHOLO [*unfastens his bunch of keys and says reflectively:*] No, no, I will go myself. [*Whispers to the* COUNT *as he goes out:*] Keep your eyes on them, I beg you.
[*Exit.*]

FIGARO. Oh! what a great opportunity we have missed! He was going to give me the keys. Was not the key of the blind among them?

ROSINE. It was the newest of them all.

BARTHOLO [*returning*]. [*Aside.*] Good! I do not know what I am doing in having this cursed barber here. [*To* FIGARO.] Here. [*Gives him the keys.*] In my dressing-room, under the bureau; touch nothing else.

FIGARO. The plague! It would be good enough for you, suspicious as you are! [*Aside, going off.*] See how Heaven protects innocence! [*Exit.*]

BARTHOLO [*whispers to the* COUNT]. He is the knave who took the letter to the Count.

COUNT [*in a low voice*]. He looks like a rogue to me.

BARTHOLO. He will not catch me again.

COUNT. I think that as far as that goes, the worst is over.

BARTHOLO. Everything considered, I thought it more prudent to send him to my room than leave him with her.

COUNT. They could not have said a word without my being a third party to it.

ROSINE. It is very polite, gentlemen, to whisper continually! And my lesson? [*They hear a noise as of dishes upset.*]

BARTHOLO [*with a cry*]. What do I hear! That cruel barber must have dropped everything downstairs, and the finest pieces in my dressing-case!
[*He runs out.*]

COUNT. Let us profit by the moments which Figaro's intelligence has secured us. Grant me, this evening, I beg you, madame, one moment's converse, which is absolutely necessary to save you from the slavery to which you are destined.

ROSINE. Ah, Lindor!

Count. I can climb to your blind; and as for the letter which I received from you this morning, I found myself forced . . .

[*Enter* Bartholo *and* Figaro.]

Bartholo. I was not mistaken; everything is broken, smashed.

Figaro. It must be a great calamity to make so much noise! You can't see at all on the stairs. [*He shows the key to the* Count.] As I came upstairs I stumbled upon a key . . .

Bartholo. You should take care what you are doing. Stumble upon a key! The clever man!

Figaro. My faith, sir, you may look for a cleverer.

[*Enter* Don Bazile.]

Rosine [*aside in terror*]. Don Bazile! . . .

Count [*aside*]. Good Heaven!

Figaro [*aside*]. 'T is the devil!

Bartholo [*advancing to meet him*]. Ah! Bazile, my friend, you are soon cured. Your accident has had no bad consequences? Truly, Master Alonzo had frightened me considerably about you; ask him; I was going out to see you, and if he had not restrained me . . .

Bazile [*in astonishment*]. Master Alonzo? . . .

Figaro [*stamps his foot*]. What! More bad places? Two hours for one poor beard. Confound such a customer!

Bazile [*looking at all*]. Will you be kind enough to tell me, sirs? . . .

Figaro. You may speak to him when I am gone.

Bazile. But why should that be necessary, anyway?

Count. You should be silent, Bazile. Do you think to teach him something which he does not know? I told him that you had requested me to come to give a music lesson in your place.

Bazile [*in greater astonishment*]. The music lesson! . . . Alonzo! . . .

Rosine [*aside to* Bazile]. Come! Will you be still?

Bazile. And she, too!

Count [*in a low voice to* Bartholo]. Whisper to him that we have all agreed.

Bartholo [*aside to* Bazile]. Don't give us the lie, Bazile, by saying that he is not your pupil; you would spoil everything.

Bazile. Ha! ha!

Bartholo [*aloud*]. Truly, Bazile, no one has more talent than your scholar.

Bazile [*in astonishment*]. Than my scholar! . . . [*Whispers.*] I was coming to tell you that the Count has moved.

Bartholo [*in a low voice*]. Silence, I know it.

Bazile [*lowering his voice*]. Who told you?

Bartholo [*whispers*]. He, of course!

Count [*whispers*]. Certainly I: if you would only listen.

Rosine [*in a whisper to* Bazile]. Is it so difficult to keep still?

Figaro [*the same*]. Hum! your great hippogriff! He is deaf!

Bazile [*aside*]. Who the devil is it that they are fooling here? Every one seems to be in the secret.

Bartholo [*aloud*]. Well! Bazile, your lawyer?

Figaro. You have the whole evening to talk about your lawyer.

Bartholo [*to* Bazile]. One word only; tell me if you are really satisfied with the lawyer?

Bazile [*in a fright*]. With the lawyer?

Count [*smiling*]. Did n't you see your lawyer?

Bazile [*impatiently*]. No, I did not see the lawyer.

Count [*aside to* Bartholo]. You don't want him to explain before her, do you? Send him off.

Bartholo [*in a whisper to the* Count]. You are right. [*To* Bazile.] But what made you ill so suddenly?

Bazile [*angrily*]. I don't understand you.

Count [*aside, puts a purse into his hand*]. Yes, he has just asked you what you expect to do here in your present state of illness.

Figaro. He is as pale as death.

Bazile. Ah! I understand . . .

Count. Go to bed, my dear Bazile: you are not well and you give us a terrible fright. Go to bed!

FIGARO. He looks very much upset. Go to bed! . . .

BARTHOLO. Upon my word! You could tell a league away that he has the fever. Go to bed!

ROSINE. Why did you come out? They say that it is catching. Go to bed!

BAZILE [completely astonished]. I, go to bed?

All. Oh! certainly.

BAZILE [gazing at them all]. In fact, I do believe that I would not do ill to retire; I feel as if I were a little out of sorts.

BARTHOLO. To-morrow, again, if you are better.

COUNT. Bazile, I shall be at your house very early to-morrow.

FIGARO. Believe me, keep yourself warm in your bed.

ROSINE. Good-evening, Master Bazile.

BAZILE [aside]. The devil fly away with me if I understand anything about it; and if it were not for this purse . . .

All. Good-evening, Bazile, good-evening.

BAZILE [exit]. Well! Good-evening, then, good-evening.

[They accompany him with a burst of laughter.]

BARTHOLO [with an important air]. That man is not at all well.

ROSINE. His eyes are wild.

COUNT. He has probably caught a chill.

FIGARO. You saw how he talked to himself? How easy it is for us to fall ill! [To BARTHOLO.] Now, are you going to decide this time?

[He pushes an easy chair to some distance from the COUNT and hands him the linen.]

COUNT. Before we finish, madame, I must tell you one thing which is very essential for progress in the art which I have the honor to teach you.

[He approaches her and whispers in her ear.]

BARTHOLO [to FIGARO]. Come, now! It seems as if it were on purpose that you approach me, and stand in front of me to prevent me from seeing . . .

COUNT [in a low voice to ROSINE]. We have the key to the blind, and we shall be here at midnight.

FIGARO [ties the napkin around BARTHOLO's neck]. See what? If it were a dancing lesson, we might let you look at it; but a singing lesson! . . . Dear me!

BARTHOLO. What's that?

FIGARO. I do not know what has got into my eye.

[He brings his head nearer.]

BARTHOLO. Don't rub so hard.

FIGARO. That's the left. Would you try to breathe a little harder for me?

[BARTHOLO seizes FIGARO's head, looks over it, pushes him away roughly, and steals behind the lovers to listen to their conversation.]

COUNT [in a low voice, to ROSINE]. And as for your letter, I soon found myself so hard put to it for an excuse to stay here . . .

FIGARO [at a distance to warn them]. Hem! . . . Hem! . . .

COUNT. In despair also at seeing my disguise useless . . .

BARTHOLO [slipping between them]. Your disguise useless!

ROSINE [terrified]. Oh! . . .

BARTHOLO. Very well, madame, do not trouble yourself. What! under my very eyes, in my presence, you dare to outrage me in that fashion!

COUNT. What is the matter with you, sir?

BARTHOLO. Perfidious Alonzo!

COUNT. Master Bartholo, if you often have whims like that of which chance has made me a witness, I no longer wonder at the disgust which the young lady shows at the prospect of becoming your wife.

ROSINE. His wife! I! Pass my days in the company of a jealous old man, who, for its one joy, offers my youth an abominable slavery!

BARTHOLO. Ah! what do I hear?

ROSINE. Yes, I tell you so to your face: I will give my heart and my hand to him who is able to release me from this horrible prison, where my person and my property are detained in defiance of all justice.

[Exit ROSINE.]

BARTHOLO. I am choking with anger.

COUNT. In short, sir, for a young woman . . .

FIGARO. Yes, a young woman and old age, that's what troubles the heads of old men.

BARTHOLO. What! When I catch them in the act! Infernal barber! I have a mind . . .

FIGARO. I am going to retire; he is mad.

COUNT. And I also; upon my word, he is mad.

FIGARO. He is mad; he is mad. . . .

[Exit both.]

[BARTHOLO, alone, pursues them.]

BARTHOLO. I am mad! Infamous bribers! Emissaries of the devil, whose errands you are doing here, and may the devil fly away with you all! . . . I am mad! . . . I saw them as clearly as I see this desk . . . and to brazen it out so! . . . Ah! Bazile is the only one who can explain it all. Yes, let's send for him. Holloa, somebody! . . . Ah! I forget that I have nobody . . . A neighbor, the first comer; no matter who. It is enough to make me lose my mind! . . . It is enough to make me lose my mind!

ACT IV

The stage is darkened.

[*Enter* BARTHOLO *and* DON BAZILE, *a paper lantern in his hand.*]

BARTHOLO. What, Bazile, you do not know him? Is it possible that you have just told me the truth?

BAZILE. If you should ask me one hundred times, I should always give you the same answer. If he handed over to you Rosine's letter, he is doubtless one of the Count's emissaries. But from the magnificence of the present which he made me, it might very well be the Count himself.

BARTHOLO. Not very likely. But à propos of that present . . . why did you take it?

BAZILE. Both of you seemed to have an agreement; I knew nothing about it; and in all these cases which are hard to decide, a purse of gold always seems to me an unanswerable argument. And then, as the proverb says, what is good to take . . .

BARTHOLO. I understand, is good . . .

BAZILE. To keep.

BARTHOLO [*in surprise*]. Ha! ha!

BAZILE. Yes, I have arranged several little proverbs like that with variations. But let us come to the point: what are your plans?

BARTHOLO. If you were in my place, Bazile, would you not make the most determined efforts to keep her in your power?

BAZILE. No, upon my word, doctor. In all sorts of property, possession amounts to little; it is their enjoyment which renders one happy; my opinion is that marrying a woman who does not love you is only to expose yourself . . .

BARTHOLO. You would fear mischances?

BAZILE. Ha, ha, sir! . . . we see many of them this year. I would not do violence to her heart.

BARTHOLO. Your servant, Bazile. It is much better for her to weep in the possession of myself, than for me to die of grief at not having her.

BAZILE. Oh, it is a matter of life and death? Marry, doctor, marry.

BARTHOLO. I shall do so, and this very night.

BAZILE. Farewell, then. Remember, when you speak to your ward, to paint them all blacker than hell.

BARTHOLO. You are right.

BAZILE. Calumny, doctor, calumny! You must always use that.

BARTHOLO. Here is Rosine's letter which that Alonzo handed over to me, and he showed me, unwillingly, the use which I must make of it in dealing with her.

BAZILE. Farewell; we shall all be here at four o'clock.

BARTHOLO. Why not sooner?

BAZILE. Impossible; the notary is engaged.

BARTHOLO. For a marriage?

BAZILE. Yes, at the barber Figaro's; his niece is going to be married.

BARTHOLO. His niece? He has none.

BAZILE. That is what they told the notary.

BARTHOLO. That rascal is in the plot: what the devil! . . .

BAZILE. Would you think? . . .

BARTHOLO. My word, those fellows are so alert! Look here, my friend, I am uneasy. Go to the notary's. Tell him to return with you immediately.

BAZILE. It rains, the weather is infernal; but nothing will stop me in your service. What are you doing?

BARTHOLO. I will lead you. Have they not put that Figaro up to crippling all my servants! I am alone here.

BAZILE. I have my lantern.

BARTHOLO. There, Bazile, there is my pass-key: I will wait, I will watch for you; and, come who will, none but the notary and yourself will get in to-night.

BAZILE. With these precautions, you are sure of your case. [*Exeunt*.]

[ROSINE, *alone, coming out of her room*.]

ROSINE. It seemed to me that I heard talking. It has just struck midnight; Lindor has not come! This bad weather was the very thing to help him. Sure not to meet a soul . . . Ah, Lindor! If you have deceived me! . . . What noise do I hear? . . . Heaven! It is my guardian. Let us get back.

[BARTHOLO *returns*.]

BARTHOLO [*holding up the light*]. Ah, Rosine! since you have not yet retired to your apartments . . .

ROSINE. I am going to retire.

BARTHOLO. In this horrible weather you will not get any repose, and I have many important things to tell you.

ROSINE. What will you have, sir? Is it not enough to be tormented by day?

BARTHOLO. Rosine, listen to me.

ROSINE. To-morrow I will listen to you.

BARTHOLO. One moment, if you please!

ROSINE [*aside*]. If he would only come!

BARTHOLO [*showing her the letter*]. Do you recognize this letter?

ROSINE [*recognizing it*]. Ah! Great Heaven! . . .

BARTHOLO. My intention, Rosine, is not to reproach you: at your age one may err; but I am your best friend: listen to me.

ROSINE. I am overwhelmed.

BARTHOLO. That letter which you wrote to Count Almaviva. . .

ROSINE [*astounded*]. To Count Almaviva! . . .

BARTHOLO. Now see what a terrible fellow this Count is: as soon as he received it he made a trophy of it; I have it from a woman to whom he gave it.

ROSINE. Count Almaviva! . . .

BARTHOLO. You can hardly persuade yourself that it is so horrible. Inexperience, Rosine, makes your sex confiding and credulous; but learn into what a trap they were enticing you. That woman has warned me of everything, apparently in order to put out of the way a rival so dangerous as yourself. I shudder at the thought! The most abominable plot, between Almaviva, Figaro, and that Alonzo, that pretended scholar of Bazile's, who bears another name and is only a vile agent of the Count, was going to drag you down into an abyss from which nothing could have drawn you out.

ROSINE [*overwhelmed*]. How horrible! . . . What! Lindor? . . . what! that young man . . .

BARTHOLO [*aside*]. Ah! it is Lindor.

ROSINE. It is for Count Almaviva . . . It is for another . . .

BARTHOLO. That is what they said when they gave me your letter.

ROSINE [*angrily*]. Ah! what an indignity! He will be punished for it. Sir, you desire to marry me?

BARTHOLO. You know the depth of my feelings.

ROSINE. If you can still feel so, I am yours.

BARTHOLO. Well, the notary will come this very evening.

ROSINE. That is not all; O Heaven! am I sufficiently humiliated! . . . Know that in a little while the traitor will dare to enter through this blind, whose key they have artfully stolen from you.

BARTHOLO [*glancing at his bunch of keys*]. Oh, the rascals! . . . My child, I will leave you no more.

ROSINE [*in terror*]. Oh, sir! and if they should be armed?

BARTHOLO. You are right: I would lose my revenge. Go up to Marcelline: lock yourself in her room with a double bolt. I am going to call the police, and wait for him near the house. Arrested as a thief, we shall have the pleasure of being at once avenged and delivered from him! And remember that my love will repay you . . .

ROSINE [*in despair*]. Only forget my errors. [*Aside*.] Ah! I am sufficiently punished for it!

BARTHOLO [*going out*]. Let us go to set our trap. At last I have her. [*Exit*.]

ROSINE. His love will repay me. . . . Wretch that I am! . . . [*She takes her handkerchief and gives way to her tears*.] What shall I do? . . . He will come. I will remain and dissemble with him, to contemplate him for a moment in all his blackness. The baseness of his actions will be my preserver. Ah! I have great need of one. What a noble figure! what a gentle air! what a tender voice! and they are only the vile agents of a corrupter. Ah! unfortunate! unfortunate! . . . Heaven! some one is opening the blind! [*She runs out*.]

[*The* COUNT, FIGARO *wrapped in a mantle, appear at the window*.]

FIGARO [*speaking from the outside*]. Some one has just rushed out; shall I enter?

COUNT [*outside*]. A man?

FIGARO. No.

COUNT. It is Rosine, whom your hideous figure has probably put to flight.

FIGARO [*leaping into the room*]. My word, I believe you. . . . Here we are at last, despite the rain, the thunder, and the lightning.

COUNT [*wrapped in a long mantle*]. Give me your hand. [*Also leaps in*.] Victory!

FIGARO [*throwing off his mantle*]. We are quite drenched. Charming weather to go on love quests. My lord, how do you like this evening?

COUNT. Superb for a lover.

FIGARO. Yes, but for the confidant? . . . And suppose some one should surprise us here?

COUNT. Are you not with me? I have other anxieties: that is, to persuade her to leave her guardian's house immediately.

FIGARO. You have in your interest three passions very powerful over the fair sex: love, hatred, and fear.

COUNT [*gazing into the darkness*]. How shall I tell her abruptly that the notary is waiting at your house to unite us? She will

think my plan a very bold one. She will call me audacious.

FIGARO. If she calls you audacious, you may call her cruel. Women are much pleased to be called cruel. At the most, if her love is as strong as you hope, you may tell her who you are: she will no longer doubt you.

[*Enter* ROSINE. FIGARO *lights all the candles on the table*.]

COUNT. Here she is! My fair Rosine! . . .

ROSINE [*very calmly*]. I began, sir, to fear that you were not coming.

COUNT. Charming anxiety! . . . I should not take advantage of circumstances to ask you to share the lot of an unfortunate man; but whatever asylum you should choose, I swear upon my honor . . .

ROSINE. Sir, if the gift of my hand had not had to follow instantly that of my heart, you would not be here. May necessity justify whatever irregularity there is in this interview!

COUNT. You, Rosine! the companion of an unfortunate without fortune, without birth! . . .

ROSINE. Birth, fortune! Let us put aside such attendants on chance, and if you will assure me that your intentions are pure . . .

COUNT [*at her feet*]. Ah, Rosine! I adore you! . . .

ROSINE [*indignantly*]. Stop, you wretch! You dare to profane! You adore me! . . . Go! You are no longer dangerous to me; I was waiting for this word only to detest you. But before I abandon you to the remorse which awaits you, [*weeping*] learn that I did love you; learn that it made me happy to think of sharing your poor lot. Miserable Lindor! I was going to leave everything to follow you, but the cowardly abuse which you have made of my kindness, and the baseness of that horrible Count Almaviva, to whom you sold me, have brought me this evidence of my weakness. Do you recognize this letter?

COUNT [*excitedly*]. Which your guardian gave you?

ROSINE [*proudly*]. Yes, I am obliged to him for it.

COUNT. Heaven! how glad I am! He had it from me. In my embarrassment, yesterday, I made use of it to draw him out, and I have been unable to find a favorable moment to tell you of it. Ah, Rosine! it is true, then, that you love me truly!

FIGARO. My lord, you sought a woman who should love you for yourself.

ROSINE. My lord! what is he saying?

COUNT [*throwing aside his heavy mantle, appears magnificently clothed*]. O most beloved of women! I must no longer deceive you: the happy man whom you see at your feet is not Lindor: I am Count Almaviva, who loves you to distraction and who has sought for you in vain for the last six months.

ROSINE [*falling into the arms of the* COUNT]. Ah! . . .

COUNT [*frightened*]. Figaro?

FIGARO. Don't be uneasy, my lord: the sweet emotion of joy never has sorrowful consequences. There, she is coming to her senses; my word! how beautful she is!

ROSINE. Ah, Lindor! . . . Ah, sir! how guilty I am! I was going to yield to my guardian this very night.

COUNT. You, Rosine?

ROSINE. Only see how I am punished: I would have passed my life in detesting you. Ah, Lindor! is it not a most frightful punishment to hate, when you feel impelled to love?

FIGARO [*looking out of the window*]. My lord, our escape is cut off, the ladder is taken away!

COUNT. Taken away!

ROSINE [*in anxiety*]. Yes, it is I . . . it is the doctor. That is the fruit of my credulity. He deceived me. I confessed everything, betrayed everything: he knows that you are here, and will come with the police.

FIGARO [*looking out again*]. My lord, they are opening the street door.

ROSINE [*hastening to the arms of the* COUNT *in terror*]. Ah, Lindor!

COUNT [*firmly*]. Rosine, you love me! I fear no one, and you shall be my wife. I shall have the pleasure of punishing the odious old fellow as I please.

ROSINE. No, no, pardon him, dear Lindor! My heart is so full that vengeance can find no place there.

[*Enter the Notary and* DON BAZILE.]

FIGARO. My lord, it is our notary.

COUNT. And friend Bazile with him!

BAZILE. Ah! what do I see?

FIGARO. By what chance, my friend? . . .

BAZILE. By what chance, sirs? . . .

NOTARY. Are these the betrothed?

COUNT. Yes, sir. You were to unite Señora Rosine and myself to-night, at the house of the barber Figaro; but we preferred this house for reasons which you will know later. Have you our contract?

NOTARY. I have the honor, then, to speak to His Excellency Count Almaviva?

FIGARO. Precisely.

BAZILE [*aside*]. If that is the reason that he gave me his pass-key . . .

NOTARY. I have two marriage contracts here, my lord; let us not confuse them: here is yours, and here is Bartholo's with Señora . . . Rosine too? These ladies, apparently, are two sisters who bear the same name?

COUNT. Let us sign quickly. Don Bazile will be willing to serve as the second witness. [*They sign.*]

BAZILE. But, Your Excellency . . . I don't understand . . .

COUNT. Master Bazile, a trifle confuses you, and all astonishes you.

BAZILE. But, my lord . . . if the doctor . . .

COUNT [*throwing him a purse*]. You are acting like a child! Sign quickly.

BAZILE [*astonished*]. Ha! ha!

FIGARO. Why do you make a difficulty of signing?

BAZILE [*weighing the purse*]. There is no further difficulty; but it is because, when I have once given my word, I need reasons of great weight . . . [*He signs.*]

[*Enter* BARTHOLO, *a Justice of the Peace, Policemen, Servants with torches.*]

BARTHOLO [*sees the* COUNT *kissing* ROSINE'S *hand, and* FIGARO *grotesquely embracing* DON BAZILE; *he cries out, seizing the Notary by the throat*]. Rosine with these rascals! Arrest them all. I have one of them by the collar.

NOTARY. I am your notary.

BAZILE. He is your notary. Are you fooling?

BARTHOLO. Ah, Don Bazile! how is it that you are here?

BAZILE. Rather, why were you not here?

JUSTICE [pointing out FIGARO]. One moment; I know this fellow. What are you doing in this house at such an unheard-of hour?

FIGARO. Unheard-of hour? You see very well that it is quite as near morning as evening. Besides, I am a retainer of His Excellency my Lord Count Almaviva.

BARTHOLO. Almaviva!

JUSTICE. They are not robbers, then?

BARTHOLO. Let us drop that. Everywhere else, Count Almaviva, I am Your Excellency's servant; but you understand that superiority of rank is useless here. If you please, have the kindness to retire.

COUNT. Yes, rank must be useless here; but what is more powerful, however, is the preference to you which the young lady has just shown me, by voluntarily giving herself to me.

BARTHOLO. What is he saying, Rosine?

ROSINE. He is telling you the truth. What causes your astonishment? Was I not this very night to be avenged of a deceiver? I am.

BAZILE. When I told you that it was the Count himself, doctor?

BARTHOLO. What does that matter to me? This is a ridiculous marriage! Where are the witnesses?

NOTARY. There is nothing lacking. I have been assisted by these two gentlemen.

BARTHOLO. What, Bazile! ... You signed?

BAZILE. What would you have? This devil of a fellow always has his pockets full of irresistible arguments.

BARTHOLO. I despise your arguments. I shall make use of my authority.

COUNT. You have lost it by abusing it.

BARTHOLO. The young lady is a minor.

FIGARO. She has just come of age.

BARTHOLO. Who is speaking to you, you rascal?

COUNT. The young lady is noble and beautiful; I am a man of rank, young and rich; she is my wife: does any one wish to dispute me this title which honors us both.

BARTHOLO. You shall never take her from my hands.

COUNT. She is no longer in your power. I will put her under the protection of the law; and this gentleman, whom you have summoned yourself, will protect her from any violence which you may wish to offer her. True magistrates are the protectors of all the oppressed.

JUSTICE. Certainly. And this useless resistance to a most honorable marriage shows well enough how frightened he is over the ill-administration of his ward's property, of which he will have to render an account.

COUNT. Ah! let him consent to all, and I shall ask nothing further of him.

FIGARO. But my quittance for my hundred crowns. Let us not lose our heads.

BARTHOLO [angrily]. They were all against me ... I have thrust my head into a scrape.

BAZILE. What scrape? Remember, doctor, that although you cannot have the woman, you have the money — yes, you have the money.

BARTHOLO. Oh! leave me alone, Bazile! You think only of money. Much do I care for money! Of course I shall keep it, but do you think that is the reason which decides me? [He signs.]

FIGARO [laughing]. Ha! ha! ha! my lord, they are of the same family.

NOTARY. But, gentlemen, I do not quite understand. Are there not two young ladies who bear the same name?

FIGARO. No, sir, there is only one.

BARTHOLO [in despair]. And it was I who brought them the ladder in order that the marriage should be more certain! Ah! I have defeated myself for lack of precautions.

FIGARO. Lack of good sense. But to tell you the truth, doctor, when youth and love have agreed to deceive an old man, all that he does to prevent it may well be called The Useless Precaution.

HERNANI

By VICTOR HUGO

Translated into English blank verse by MRS. NEWTON CROSLAND

CHARACTERS

Hernani

Don Carlos

Don Ruy Gomez de Silva

Doña Sol de Silva

The King of Bohemia

The Duke of Bavaria

The Duke of Gotha

The Baron of Hohenbourg

The Duke of Lutzelbourg

Don Sancho

Don Matias

Don Ricardo

Don Garcia Suarez

Don Francisco

Don Juan de Haro

Don Pedro Gusman de Lara

Don Gil Tellez Giron

Doña Josefa Duarte

Jaquez

A Mountaineer

A Lady

First Conspirator

Second Conspirator

Third Conspirator

Conspirators of the Holy League, Germans and Spaniards, Mountaineers,
Nobles, Soldiers, Pages, Attendants, etc.

HERNANI

ACT I

[*Saragossa. A Chamber. Night: a lamp on the table.*]

[*Enter* DOÑA JOSEFA DUARTE, *an old woman dressed in black, with body of her dress worked in jet in the fashion of Isabella the Catholic. She draws the crimson curtains of the window, and puts some armchairs in order. A knock at a little secret door on the right. She listens. A second knock.*]

DOÑA JOSEFA. Can it be he already?
[*Another knock.*] 'T is, indeed,
At th' hidden stairway. [*A fourth knock.*] I
must open quick.
[*She opens the concealed door.*]

[*Enter* DON CARLOS, *his face muffled in his cloak, and his hat drawn over his brows.*

Good-evening to you, sir!
[*She ushers him in. He drops his cloak and reveals a rich dress of silk and velvet in the Castilian style of 1519. She looks at him closely, and recoils astonished.*]

What now? — not you,
Signor Hernani! Fire! fire! Help, oh, help!
DON CARLOS [*seizing her by the arm*]. But
two words more, duenna, and you die!
[*He looks at her intently. She is frightened into silence.*]
Is this the room of Doña Sol, betrothed
To her old uncle, Duke de Pastrana?
A very worthy lord he is — senile,
White-hair'd and jealous. Tell me, is it true
The beauteous Doña loves a smooth-faced youth,
All whiskerless as yet, and sees him here
Each night, in spite of envious care? Tell me,
Am I informed aright?
[*She is silent. He shakes her by the arm.*]
Will you not speak?
DOÑA JOSEFA. You did forbid me, sir, to
speak two words.

DON CARLOS. One will suffice. I want a
yes, or no.
Say, is thy mistress Doña Sol de Silva?
DOÑA JOSEFA. Yes, why?
DON CARLOS. No matter why. Just at
this hour
The venerable lover is away?
DOÑA JOSEFA. He is.
DON CARLOS. And she expects the young
one now?
DOÑA JOSEFA. Yes.
DON CARLOS. Oh, that I could die!
DOÑA JOSEFA. Yes.
DON CARLOS. Say, duenna,
Is this the place where they will surely meet?
DOÑA JOSEFA. Yes.
DON CARLOS. Hide me somewhere here.
DOÑA JOSEFA. You?
DON CARLOS. Yes, me.
DOÑA JOSEFA. Why?
DON CARLOS. No matter why.
DOÑA JOSEFA. I hide you here!
DON CARLOS. Yes, here.
DOÑA JOSEFA. No, never!
DON CARLOS [*drawing from his girdle a purse and a dagger*]. Madam, condescend to choose
Between a purse and dagger.
DOÑA JOSEFA [*taking the purse*]. Are you,
then,
The devil?
DON CARLOS. Yes, duenna.
DOÑA JOSEFA [*opening a narrow cupboard in the wall*]. Go — go in.
DON CARLOS [*examining the cupboard*].
This box!
DOÑA JOSEFA [*shutting up the cupboard.*]
If you don't like it, go away.
DON CARLOS [*reopening cupboard*]. And
yet! [*Again examining it.*] Is this
the stable where you keep
The broom-stick that you ride on?
[*He crouches down in the cupboard with difficulty.*]
Oh! Oh! Oh!
DOÑA JOSEFA [*joining her hands and looking ashamed*]. A man here!

Don Carlos [*from the cupboard, still open*]. And was it a woman, then, Your mistress here expected?
Doña Josefa. Heavens! I hear The step of Doña Sol! Sir, shut the door! Quick — quick!
[*She pushes the cupboard door, which closes.*]
Don Carlos [*from the closed cupboard*]. Remember, if you breathe a word You die!
Doña Josefa [*alone*]. Who is this man? If I cry out,
Gracious! there's none to hear. All are asleep
Within the palace walls — madam and I Excepted. Pshaw! The other'll come. He wears
A sword; 't his affair. And Heav'n keep us
From powers of hell. [*Weighing the purse in her hand.*] At least no thief he is.

[*Enter* Doña Sol *in white.* Doña Josefa *hides the purse.*]

Doña Sol. Josefa!
Doña Josefa. Madam?
Doña Sol. I some mischief dread,
For 't is full time Hernani should be here.
[*Noises of steps at the secret door.*]
He's coming up; go — quick! at once, undo
Ere he has time to knock.
[Josefa *opens the little door.*]

[*Enter* Hernani *in large cloak and large hat; underneath, costume of mountaineer of Aragon — gray, with a cuirass of leather; a sword, a dagger, and a horn at his girdle.*]

Doña Sol [*going to him*]. Hernani! Oh!
Hernani. Ah, Doña Sol! It is yourself at last
I see — your voice it is I hear. Oh, why Does cruel fate keep you so far from me? I have such need of you to help my heart Forget all else!
Doña Sol [*touching his clothes*]. Oh! Heav'ns! Your cloak is drench'd! The rain must pour!
Hernani. I know not.
Doña Sol. And the cold — You must be cold!

Hernani. I feel it not.
Doña Sol. Take off This cloak, then, pray.
Hernani. Doña, beloved, tell me, When night brings happy sleep to you, so pure
And innocent — sleep that half opes your mouth,
Closing your eyes with its light finger-touch —
Does not some angel show how dear you are
To an unhappy man, by all the world Abandoned and repulsed?
Doña Sol. Sir, you are late; But tell me, are you cold?
Hernani. Not near to you.
Ah! when the raging fire of jealous love Burns in the veins, and the true heart is riven
By its own tempest, we feel not the clouds
O'erhead, though storm and lightning they fling forth!
Doña Sol. Come, give me now the cloak, and your sword too.
Hernani [*his hand on his sword*]. No. 'T is my other love, faithful and pure.
The old Duke, Doña Sol, — your promised spouse,
Your uncle, — is he absent now?
Doña Sol. Oh, yes; This hour to us belongs.
Hernani. And that is all! Only this hour! And then comes after-wards! —
What matter! For I must forget or die! Angel! One hour with thee — with whom I would
Spend life, and afterwards eternity!
Doña Sol. Hernani!
Hernani. It is happiness to know The Duke is absent. I am like a thief Who forces doors. I enter — see you — rob
An old man of an hour of your sweet voice
And looks. And I am happy, though, no doubt
He would deny me e'en one hour, although He steals my very life.

Doña Sol. Be calm. [*Giving the cloak to the duenna.*] Josefa! This wet cloak take and dry it.

[*Exit* Josefa.]

[*She seats herself, and makes a sign for* Hernani *to draw near.*]

Now, come here.

Hernani [*without appearing to hear her*]. The Duke, then, is not in the mansion now?

Doña Sol. How grand you look!

Hernani. He is away?

Doña Sol. Deaɪ one, Let us not think about the Duke.

Hernani. Madam, But let us think of him, the grave old man Who loves you — who will marry you! How now? He took a kiss from you the other day. Not think of him!

Doña Sol. Is 't that which grieves you thus? A kiss upon my brow — an uncle's kiss — Almost a father's.

Hernani. No, not so; it was A lover's, husband's, jealous kiss. To him To him it is that you will soon belong. Think'st thou not of it! Oh, the foolish dotard, With head drooped down to finish out his days! Wanting a wife, he takes a girl; himself Most like a frozen specter. Sees he not, The senseless one! that while with one hand he Espouses you, the other mates with Death! Yet without shudder comes he 'twixt our hearts! Seek out the grave-digger, old man, and give Thy measure. Who is it that makes for you This marriage? You are forced to it, I hope?

Doña Sol. They say the King desires it.

Hernani. King! This king! My father on the scaffold died condemned By his; and, though one may have aged since then, — For e'en the shadow of that king, his son, His widow, and for all to him allied, My hate continues fresh. Him dead, no more

We count with; but while still a child I swore That I 'd avenge my father on his son. I sought him in all places — Charles the King Of the Castiles. For hate is rife between Our families. The fathers wrestled long And without pity, and without remorse, For thirty years! Oh, 't is in vain that they Are dead; their hatred lives. For them no peace Has come; their sons keep up the duel still. Ah! then I find 't is thou who hast made up This execrable marriage! Thee I sought — Thou comest in my way!

Doña Sol. You frighten me!

Hernani. Charged with the mandate of anathema, I frighten e'en myself; but listen now: This old, old man, for whom they destine you, This Ruy de Silva, Duke de Pastrana, Count and grandee, rich man of Aragon, In place of youth can give thee, oh! young girl, Such store of gold and jewels that your brow Will shine 'mong royalty's own diadems; And for your rank and wealth, and pride and state, Queens many will perhaps envy you. See, then, Just what he is. And now consider me. My poverty is absolute, I say. Only the forest, where I ran barefoot In childhood, did I know. Although perchance I too can claim illustrious blazonry, That 's dimm'd just now by rusting stain of blood. Perchance I 've rights, though they are shrouded still, And hid 'neath ebon folds of scaffold cloth, Yet which, if my attempt one day succeeds, May, with my sword from out their sheath leap forth. Meanwhile, from jealous Heaven I 've received But air, and light, and water — gifts bestowed On all. Now, wish you from the Duke, or me,

To be delivered? You must choose 'twixt
us,
Whether you marry him, or follow me.
DOÑA SOL. You, I will follow!
HERNANI. 'Mong companions rude,
Men all proscribed, of whom the headsman
knows
The names already. Men whom neither
steel
Nor touch of pity softens; each one urged
By some blood feud that's personal. Wilt
thou
Then come? They'd call thee mistress of
my band,
For know you not that I a bandit am?
When I was hunted throughout Spain,
alone
In thickest forests, and on mountains steep,
'Mong rocks which but the soaring eagle
spied,
Old Catalonia like a mother proved.
Among her hills — free, poor, and stern —
I grew;
And now, to-morrow if this horn should
sound,
Three thousand men would rally at the
call.
You shudder, and should pause to ponder
well.
Think what 't will prove to follow me
through woods
And over mountain paths, with comrades
like
The fiends that come in dreams! To live in
fear,
Suspicious of a sound, of voices, eyes:
To sleep upon the earth, drink at the
stream,
And hear at night, while nourishing per-
chance
Some wakeful babe, the whistling musket
balls.
To be a wanderer with me proscribed,
And when my father I shall follow — then,
E'en to the scaffold, you to follow me!
DOÑA SOL. I'll follow you.
HERNANI. The Duke is wealthy, great
And prosperous, without a stain upon
His ancient name. He offers you his hand,
And can give all things — treasures, digni-
ties,
And pleasure —

DOÑA SOL. We'll set out to-morrow.
Oh!
Hernani, censure not th' audacity
Of this decision. Are you angel mine
Or demon? Only one thing do I know,
That I'm your slave. Now, listen: where-
soe'er
You go, I go — pause you or move I'm
yours.
Why act I thus? Ah! that I cannot tell;
Only I want to see you evermore.
When sound of your receding footstep dies
I feel my heart stops beating; without you
Myself seems absent, but when I detect
Again the step I love, my soul comes back,
I breathe — I live once more.
HERNANI [embracing her]. Oh! angel
mine!
DOÑA SOL. At midnight, then, to-mor-
row, clap your hands
Three times beneath my window, bringing
there
Your escort. Go! I shall be strong and
brave.
HERNANI. Now know you who I am?
DOÑA SOL. Only my lord.
Enough — what matters else? — I follow
you.
HERNANI. Not so. Since you, a woman
weak, decide
To come with me, 't is right that you should
know
What name, what rank, what soul, per-
chance what fate
There hides beneath the low Hernani here.
Yes, you have willed to link yourself for
aye
With brigand — would you still with out-
law mate?
DON CARLOS [opening the cupboard].
When will you finish all this history?
Think you 't is pleasant in this cupboard
hole?
[HERNANI recoils, astonished.
DOÑA SOL screams and takes
refuge in HERNANI's arms, look-
ing at DON CARLOS with fright-
ened gaze.]
HERNANI [his hand on the hilt of his sword].
Who is this man?
DOÑA SOL. Oh, Heavens, help!
HERNANI. Be still,

My Doña Sol! you'll wake up dangerous
eyes.
Never — whatever be — while I am near,
Seek other help than mine.
[*To* DON CARLOS.] What do you here?
    DON CARLOS. I? — Well, I am not rid-
ing through the wood,
That you should ask.
    HERNANI. He who affronts, then jeers,
May cause his heir to laugh.
    DON CARLOS. Each, sir, in turn.
Let us speak frankly. You the lady love,
And come each night to mirror in her eyes
Your own. I love her, too, and want to
know
Who 't is I have so often seen come in
The window way, while I stand at the door.
    HERNANI. Upon my word, I'll send you
out the way
I enter.
    DON CARLOS. As to that we'll see. My
love
I offer unto madam. Shall we, then,
Agree to share it? In her beauteous soul
I've seen so much of tenderness, and love,
And sentiment, that she, I'm very sure,
Has quite enough for ardent lovers twain.
Therefore, to-night, wishing to end sus-
pense
On your account, I forced an entrance,
hid,
And — to confess it all — I listened too.
But I heard badly, and was nearly choked;
And then I crumpled my French vest —
and so,
By Jove! come out I must!
    HERNANI. Likewise my blade
Is not at ease, and hurries to leap out.
    DON CARLOS [*bowing*]. Sir, as you please.
    HERNANI [*drawing his sword*]. Defend
yourself!
        [DON CARLOS *draws his sword.*]
    DOÑA SOL. Oh, Heaven!
    DON CARLOS. Be calm, señora.
    HERNANI [*to* DON CARLOS]. Tell me, sir,
your name.
    DON CARLOS. Tell me yours!
    HERNANI. It is a fatal secret,
Kept for my breathing in another's ear,
Some day when I am conqueror, with my
knee
Upon his breast, and dagger in his heart.

    DON CARLOS. Then tell to me this
other's name.
    HERNANI. To thee
What matters it? On guard! Defend thyself!
        [*They cross swords.* DOÑA SOL
        *falls trembling into a chair. They
        hear knocks at the door.*]
    DOÑA SOL [*rising in alarm*]. Oh, Heav-
ens! There's some one knocking at
the door!
        [*The champions pause.*]
[*Enter* JOSEFA, *at the little door, in a frightened state.*]
    HERNANI [*to* JOSEFA]. Who knocks in
this way?
    DOÑA JOSEFA [*to* DOÑA SOL]. Madam, a
surprise!
An unexpected blow. It is the Duke
Come home.
    DOÑA SOL [*clasping her hands*]. The
Duke. Then every hope is lost!
    DOÑA JOSEFA [*looking round*]. Gracious!
— the stranger out! — and swords,
and fighting
Here's a fine business!
        [*The two combatants sheathe their
        swords.* DON CARLOS *draws his
        cloak round him, and pulls his
        hat down on his forehead. More
        knocking.*]
    HERNANI. What is to be done?
        [*More knocking.*]
    A VOICE [*without*]. Doña Sol, open to me.
        [DONA JOSEFA *is going to the door,
        when* HERNANI *stops her.*]
    HERNANI. Do not open.
    DOÑA JOSEFA [*pulling out her rosary*].
Holy St. James! Now draw us
through this broil!
        [*More knocking.*]
    HERNANI [*pointing to the cupboard*]. Let's
hide!
    DON CARLOS. What! in the cupboard?
    HERNANI. Yes, go in;
I will take care that it shall hold us both.
    DON CARLOS. Thanks. No; it is too
good a joke.
    HERNANI [*pointing to secret door*]. Let's
fly
That way.

Don Carlos. Good-night! But as for
me I stay
Here.
Hernani. Fire and fury, sir, we will be
quits
For this.
[*To* Doña Sol.] What if I firmly barr'd
the door?
Don Carlos [*to* Josefa]. Open the door.
Hernani. What is it that he says?
Don Carlos [*to* Josefa, *who hesitates be-
wildered*]. Open the door, I say.
[*More knocking.* Josefa *opens the
door, trembling.*]
Doña Sol. Oh, I shall die!

[*Enter* Don Ruy Gomez de Silva, *in black;
white hair and beard. Servants with
lights.*]

Don Ruy Gomez. My niece with two
men at this hour of night!
Come all! The thing is worth exposing
here.
[*To* Doña Sol.] Now, by St. John of Avila,
I vow
That we three with you, madam, are by two
Too many.
[*To the two young men.*] My young sirs,
what do you here?
When we'd the Cid and Bernard — giants
both
Of Spain and of the world — they traveled
through
Castile protecting women, honoring
Old men. For them steel armor had less
weight
Than your fine velvets have for you. These
men
Respected whitened beards, and when they
loved,
Their love was consecrated by the Church.
Never did such men cozen or betray,
For reason that they had to keep unflawed
The honor of their house. Wished they to
wed,
They took a stainless wife in open day,
Before the world, with sword, or axe, or
lance
In hand. But as for villains such as you,
Who come at eve, peeping behind them oft,
To steal away the honor of men's wives
In absence of their husbands, I declare,

The Cid, our ancestor, had he but known
Such men, he would have plucked away
from them
Nobility usurped, have made them kneel,
While he with flat of sword their blazon
dashed.
Behold what were the men of former
times
Whom I, with anguish, now compare with
these
I see to-day! What do you here? Is it
To say, a white-haired man's but fit for
youth
To point at when he passes in the street,
And jeer at there? Shall they so laugh at
me,
Tried soldier of Zamora? At the least
Not yours will be that laugh.
   Hernani. But, Duke —
Don Ruy Gomez. Be still!
What! You have sword and lance, falcons,
the chase,
And songs to sing 'neath balconies at night,
Festivals, pleasures, feathers in your hats,
Raiment of silk — balls, youth, and joy of
life;
But wearied of them all, at any price
You want a toy, and take an old man for it.
Ah, though you've broke the toy, God
wills that it
In bursting should be flung back in your
face!
Now follow me!
   Hernani. Most noble Duke —
Don Ruy Gomez. Follow —
Follow me, sirs. Is this alone a jest?
What! I've a treasure, mine to guard with
care,
A young girl's character, a family's fame.
This girl I love — by kinship to me bound,
Pledged soon to change her ring for one
from me.
I know her spotless, chaste, and pure. Yet
when
I leave my home one hour, I — Ruy
Gomez
De Silva — find a thief who steals from
me
My honor, glides unto my house. Back,
back,
Make clean your hands, oh, base and soul-
less men,

Whose presence, brushing by, must serve
    to taint
Our women's fame! But no, 't is well.
    Proceed.
Have I not something more?
[*Snatches off his collar.*] Take, tread it now
Beneath your feet. Degrade my Golden
    Fleece.
[*Throws off his hat.*] Pluck at my hair, in-
    sult me every way,
And then, to-morrow through the town
    make boast
That lowest scoundrels in their vilest sport
Have never shamed a nobler brow, nor soiled
More whitened hair.
    DOÑA SOL. My lord —
    DON RUY GOMEZ [*to his servants*]. A
    rescue! grooms!
Bring me my dagger of Toledo, axe,
And dirk.
[*To the young men.*] Now, follow — follow
    me — ye two.
    DON CARLOS [*stepping forward a little*].
    Duke, this is not the pressing thing
    just now;
First we've to think of Maximilian dead,
The Emperor of Germany.
        [*Opens his cloak, and shows his face,
        previously hidden by his hat.*]
    DON RUY GOMEZ. Jest you!
Heavens, the King!
    DOÑA SOL. The King!
    HERNANI. The King of Spain!
    DON CARLOS [*gravely*]. Yes, Charles, my
    noble Duke, are thy wits gone?
The Emperor, my grandsire, is no more.
I knew it not until this eve, and came
At once to tell it you and counsel ask,
Incognito, at night, knowing you well
A loyal subject that I much regard.
The thing is very simple that has caused
This hubbub.
        [DON RUY GOMEZ *sends away
        servants by a sign, and ap-
        proaches* DON CARLOS. DOÑA
        SOL *looks at the King with fear
        and surprise.* HERNANI *from a
        corner regards him with flashing
        eyes.*]
    DON RUY GOMEZ. But oh, why was it
    the door
Was not more quickly opened?

    DON CARLOS. Reason good.
Remember all your escort. When it is
A weighty secret of the state I bear
That brings me to your palace, it is not
To tell it to thy servants.
    DON RUY GOMEZ. Highness, oh!
Forgive me, some appearances —
    DON CARLOS. Good father,
Thee Governor of the Castle of Figuère
I've made. But whom thy governor shall
    I make?
    DON RUY GOMEZ. Oh, pardon —
    DON CARLOS. 'T is enough. We'll say no
    more
Of this. The Emperor is dead.
    DON RUY GOMEZ. Your Highness's
Grandfather dead!
    DON CARLOS. Aye! Duke, you see me
    here
In deep affliction.
    DON RUY GOMEZ. Who'll succeed to
    him?
    DON CARLOS. A Duke of Saxony is
    named. The throne
Francis the First of France aspires to
    mount.
    DON RUY GOMEZ. Where do the Electors
    of the Empire meet?
    DON CARLOS. They say at Aix-la-Cha-
    pelle, or at Spire,
Or Frankfort.
    DON RUY GOMEZ. But our King, whom
    God preserve!
Has he not thought of Empire?
    DON CARLOS. Constantly.
    DON RUY GOMEZ. To you it should re-
    vert.
    DON CARLOS. I know it, Duke.
    DON RUY GOMEZ. Your father was
    Archduke of Austria.
I hope 't will be remembered that you are
Grandson to him, who but just now has
    changed
Th' imperial purple for a winding-sheet.
    DON CARLOS. I am, besides, a citizen of
    Ghent.
    DON RUY GOMEZ. In my own youth
    your grandfather I saw.
Alas! I am the sole survivor now
Of all that generation past. All dead!
He was an Emperor magnificent
And mighty.

DON CARLOS. Rome is for me.
DON RUY GOMEZ. Valiant, firm,
And not tyrannical, this head might well
Become th' old German body.
        [*He bends over the King's hands
                and kisses them.*]
Yet so young.
I pity you, indeed, thus plunged in such
A sorrow.
    DON CARLOS. Ah! the Pope is anxious
        now
To get back Sicily — the isle that's mine;
'T is ruled that Sicily cannot belong
Unto an Emperor; therefore it is
That he desires me Emperor to be made;
And then, to follow that, as docile son
I give up Naples too. Let us but have
The Eagle, and we'll see if I allow
Its wings to be thus clipp'd!
    DON RUY GOMEZ. What joy 't would be
For this great veteran of the throne to see
Your brow, so fit, encircled by his crown!
Ah, Highness, we together weep for him,
The Christian Emperor, so good, so great!
    DON CARLOS. The Holy Father's clever.
        He will say —
This isle unto my States should come;
        't is but
A tatter'd rag that scarce belongs to Spain.
What will you do with this ill-shapen isle
That's sewn upon the Empire by a thread?
Your Empire is ill-made; but quick, come
        here,
The scissors bring, and let us cut away! —
Thanks, Holy Father, but if I have luck
I think that many pieces such as this
Upon the Holy Empire will be sewn!
And if some rags from me are ta'en, I
        mean
With isles and duchies to replace them all.
    DON RUY GOMEZ. Console yourself, for
        we shall see again
The dead more holy and more great. There
        is
An Empire of the Just.
    DON CARLOS. Francis the First
Is all ambition. The old Emperor dead,
Quick he'll turn wooing. Has he not fair
        France
Most Christian? 'Tis a place worth hold-
        ing fast.
Once to King Louis did my grandsire say —

If I were God, and had two sons, I'd make
The elder God, the second, King of France.
[*To* DON RUY GOMEZ.] Think you that
        Francis has a chance to win?
    DON RUY GOMEZ. He is a victor.
    DON CARLOS. There'd be all to change —
The golden bull doth foreigners exclude.
    DON RUY GOMEZ. In a like manner,
        Highness, you would be
Accounted King of Spain.
    DON CARLOS. But I was born
A citizen of Ghent.
    DON RUY GOMEZ. His last campaign
Exalted Francis mightily.
    DON CARLOS. The Eagle
That soon perchance upon my helm will
        gleam
Knows also how to open out its wings.
    DON RUY GOMEZ. And knows Your
        Highness Latin?
    DON CARLOS. Ah, not much.
    DON RUY GOMEZ. A pity that. The
        German nobles like
The best those who in Latin speak to them.
    DON CARLOS. With haughty Spanish
        they will be content,
For trust King Charles, 't will be of small
        account,
When masterful the voice, what tongue it
        speaks.
To Flanders I must go. Your King, dear
        Duke,
Must Emperor return. The King of France
Will stir all means. I must be quick to win.
I shall set out at once.
    DON RUY GOMEZ. Do you, then, go,
Oh, Highness, without clearing Aragon
Of those fresh bandits who, among the
        hills,
Their daring insolence show everywhere?
    DON CARLOS. To the Duke D'Arcos I
        have orders given
That he should quite exterminate the
        band.
    DON RUY GOMEZ. But is the order given
        to its chief
To let the thing be done?
    DON CARLOS. Who is this chief —
His name?
    DON RUY GOMEZ. I know not. But the
        people say
That he's an awkward customer.

Don Carlos. Pshaw! I know
That now he somewhere in Galicia hides;
With a few soldiers, soon we'll capture him.
Don Ruy Gomez. Then it was false, the
rumor which declared
That he was hereabouts?
Don Carlos. Quite false. Thou canst
Accommodate me here to-night?
Don Ruy Gomez [*bowing to the ground*].
Thanks! Thanks!
Highness! [*He calls his servants.*] You'll
do all honor to the King,
My guest.
[*The servants reënter with lights.
The Duke arranges them in two
rows to the door at the back.
Meanwhile* Doña Sol *ap-
proaches* Hernani *softly. The
King observes them.*]
Doña Sol [*to* Hernani]. To-morrow,
midnight, without fail
Beneath my window clap your hands three
times.
Hernani [*softly*]. To-morrow night.
Don Carlos [*aside*]. To-morrow!
[*Aloud to* Doña Sol, *whom he approaches
with politeness.*] Let me now
Escort you hence, I pray.
[*He leads her to the door. She goes
out.*]
Hernani [*his hand in his breast on dagger
hilt*]. My dagger true!
Don Carlos [*coming back, aside*]. Our
man here has the look of being
trapped. [*He takes* Hernani *aside.*]
I've crossed my sword with yours; that
honor, sir,
I've granted you. For many reasons I
Suspect you much, but to betray you now
Would shame the King; go therefore
freely. E'en
I deign to aid your flight.
Don Ruy Gomez [*coming back, and
pointing to* Hernani]. This lord —
who's he?
Don Carlos. One of my followers,
who'll soon depart.
[*They go out with servants and
lights, the Duke preceding with
waxlight in his hand.*]
Hernani. One of thy followers! I am,
O King!

Well said. For night and day and step by
step
I follow thee, with eye upon thy path
And dagger in my hand. My race in me
Pursues thy race in thee. And now, behold
Thou art my rival! For an instant I
'Twixt love and hate was balanced in the
scale.
Not large enough my heart for her and
thee;
In loving her oblivious I became
Of all my hate of thee. But since 't is thou
That comes to will I should remember it,
I recollect. My love it is that tilts
Th' uncertain balance, while it falls entire
Upon the side of hate. Thy follower!
'T is thou hast said it. Never courtier yet
Of thy accursed court, or noble, fain
To kiss thy shadow — not a seneschal
With human heart abjured in serving thee;
No dog within the palace, trained the King
To follow, will thy steps more closely
haunt
And certainly than I. What they would
have,
These famed grandees, is hollow title, or
Some toy that shines — some golden sheep
to hang
About the neck. Not such a fool am I.
What I would have is not some favor vain,
But 't is thy blood, won by my conquering
steel —
Thy soul from out thy body forced — with
all
That at the bottom of thy heart was
reached
After deep delving. Go — you are in
front —
I follow thee. My watchful vengeance
walks
With me, and whispers in mine ear. Go
where
Thou wilt I'm there to listen and to spy,
And noiselessly my step will press on thine.
No day, should'st thou but turn thy head,
O King,
But thou wilt find me, motionless and
grave,
At festivals; at night, should'st thou look
back,
Still wilt thou see my flaming eyes behind.
[*Exit by the little door.*

ACT II

Saragossa. A square before the palace of SILVA. *On the left the high walls of the palace, with a window and a balcony. Below the window a little door. To the right, at the back, houses of the street. Night. Here and there are a few windows still lit up, shining in the front of the houses.*

[*Enter* DON CARLOS, DON SANCHO SAN- CHEZ DE ZUÑIGA, COUNT DE MON- TEREY, DON MATIAS CENTURION, MARQUIS D'ALMUNAN, DON RICARDO DE ROXAS, LORD OF CASAPALMA, DON CARLOS *at the head, hats pulled down, and wrapped in long cloaks, which their swords inside raise up.*]

DON CARLOS [*looking up at the balcony*]. Behold! We're at the balcony — the door.
My heart is bounding.
[*Pointing to the window, which is dark.*] Ah, no light as yet.
　　[*He looks at the windows where light shines.*]
Although it shines just where I'd have it not,
While where I wish for light is dark.

DON SANCHO. Your Highness,
Now let us of this traitor speak again.
And you permitted him to go!

DON CARLOS. 'T is true.

DON MATIAS. And he, perchance, was major of the band.

DON CARLOS. Were he the major or the captain e'en,
No crown'd king ever had a haughtier air.

DON SANCHO. Highness, his name?

DON CARLOS [*his eyes fixed on the win- dow*]. Muñoz — Fernan —
[*With gesture of a man suddenly recollect- ing.*] A name
In *i*.

DON SANCHO. Perchance Hernani?

DON CARLOS. Yes.

DON SANCHO. 'T was he.

DON MATIAS. The chief, Hernani!

DON SANCHO. Cannot you recall
His speech?

DON CARLOS. Oh, I heard nothing in the vile
And wretched cupboard.

DON SANCHO. Wherefore let him slip
When there you had him?

DON CARLOS [*turning round gravely and looking him in the face*]. Count de Monterey,
You question me!
　　[*The two nobles step back, and are silent.*]
Besides, it was not he
Was in my mind. It was his mistress, not
His head, I wanted. Madly I'm in love
With two dark eyes, the loveliest in the world,
My friends! Two mirrors, and two rays! two flames!
I heard but of their history these words:
"To-morrow come at midnight." 'T was enough.
The joke is excellent! For while that he,
The bandit lover, by some murd'rous deed
Some grave to dig, is hindered and de- layed,
I softly take his dove from out its nest.

DON RICARDO. Highness, 't would make the thing far more complete
If we, the dove in gaining, killed the kite.

DON CARLOS. Count, 't is most capital advice. Your hand
Is prompt.

DON RICARDO [*bowing low*]. And by what title will it please
The King that I be count?

DON SANCHO. 'T was a mistake.

DON RICARDO [*to* DON SANCHO]. The King has called me count.

DON CARLOS. Enough — enough!
[*To* DON RICARDO.] I let the title fall; but pick it up.

DON RICARDO [*bowing again*]. Thanks, Highness.

DON SANCHO. A fine count — count by mistake!
　　[*The King walks to the back of the stage, watching eagerly the lighted windows. The two lords talk together at the front.*]

DON MATIAS [*to* DON SANCHO]. What think you that the King will do, when once
The beauty's taken?

DON SANCHO [*looking sideways at* DON RICARDO]. Countess she'll be made;

Lady of honor afterwards, and then,
If there's a son, he will be King.
DON MATIAS. How so? —
My lord! a bastard! Let him be a count.
Were one His Highness, would one choose
    as king
A countess' son?
DON SANCHO. He'd make her marchion-
    ess
Ere then, dear marquis.
DON MATIAS. Bastards — they are kept
For conquer'd countries. They for viceroys
    serve.
    [DON CARLOS *comes forward.*]
DON CARLOS [*looking with vexation at the
    lighted windows*]. Might one not say
    they're jealous eyes that watch?
Ah! there are two which darken; we shall
    do.
Weary the time of expectation seems —
Sirs, who can make it go more quickly?
DON SANCHO. That
Is what we often ask ourselves within
The palace.
DON CARLOS. 'T is the thing my people
    say
Again with you.
[*The last window light is extinguished.*] The
    last light now is gone.
    [*Turning toward the balcony of
    DOÑA SOL, still dark.*]
Oh, hateful window! When wilt thou light
    up?
The night is dark; come, Doña Sol, and
    shine
Like to a star!
[*To DON RICARDO.*] Is't midnight yet?
DON RICARDO. Almost.
DON CARLOS. Ah! we must finish, for
    the other one
At any moment may appear.
    [*A light appears in DOÑA SOL'S
    chamber. Her shadow is seen
    through the glass.*]
My friends!
A lamp! and she herself seen through the
    pane!
Never did daybreak charm me as this
    sight.
Let's hasten with the signal she expects.
We must clap hands three times. An in-
    stant more

And you will see her. But our number,
    perhaps,
Will frighten her. Go, all three out of
    sight
Beyond there, watching for the man we
    want.
'Twixt us, my friends, we'll share the lov-
    ing pair,
For me the girl — the brigand is for you.
DON RICARDO. Best thanks.
DON CARLOS. If he appear from am-
    buscade,
Rush quickly, knock him down, and, while
Recovers from the blow, it is for me
To carry safely off the darling prize.
We'll laugh anon. But kill him not out-
    right,
He's brave, I own; — killing's a grave
    affair.
    [*The lords bow and go.* DON
    CARLOS *waits till they are quite
    gone, then claps his hands twice.
    At the second time the window
    opens, and* DOÑA SOL *appears
    on the balcony.*]
DOÑA SOL [*from the balcony*]. Hernani,
    is that you?
DON CARLOS [*aside*]. The devil! We
    must
Not parley! [*He claps his hands again.*]
DOÑA SOL. I am coming down.
    [*She closes the window, and the
    light disappears. The next min-
    ute the little door opens, and she
    comes out, the lamp in her hand,
    and a mantle over her shoulders.*]
DOÑA SOL. Hernani!
    [DON CARLOS *pulls his hat down
    on his face, and hurries toward
    her.*]
DOÑA SOL [*letting her lamp fall*].
    Heavens! 'T is not his footstep!
    [*She attempts to go back, but* DON
    CARLOS *runs to her and seizes
    her by the arm.*]
DON CARLOS. Doña Sol!
DOÑA SOL. 'T is not his voice! Oh,
    misery!
DON CARLOS. What voice
Is there that thou could'st hear that would
    be more

A lover's? It is still a lover here,
And King for one.
    Doña Sol. The King!
' Don Carlos. Ah! wish, command,
A kingdom waits thy will; for he whom
    thou
Hast vanquish'd is the King, thy lord —
    't is Charles,
Thy slave!
    Doña Sol [trying to escape from him].
To the rescue! Help, Hernani!
    Help!
    Don Carlos. Thy fear is maidenly, and
    worthy thee.
'T is not thy bandit — 't is thy King that
    holds
Thee now!
    Doña Sol. Ah, no. The bandit's you.
    Are you
Not 'shamed? The blush unto my own
    cheek mounts
For you. Are these the exploits to be
    noised
Abroad? A woman thus at night to seize!
My bandit's worth a hundred of such
    kings!
I do declare, if man were born at level
Of his soul, and God made rank propor-
    tional
To his heart, he would be king and prince,
    and you
The robber be!
    Don Carlos [trying to entice her].
    Madam! —
    Doña Sol. Do you forget
My father was a count?
    Don Carlos. And you I'll make
A duchess.
    Doña Sol [repulsing him]. Cease! All
    this is shameful; — go!
        [She retreats a few steps.]
Nothing, Don Carlos, can there 'twixt us
    be.
My father for you freely shed his blood.
I am of noble birth, and heedful ever
Of my name's purity. I am too high
To be your concubine — too low to be
Your wife.
    Don Carlos. Princess!
    Doña Sol. Carry to worthless girls,
King Charles, your vile addresses. Or, if
    me

You treat insultingly, I'll show you well
That I'm a woman, and a noble dame.
    Don Carlos. Well, then but come, and
    you shall share my throne,
My name — you shall be Queen and Em-
    press —
    Doña Sol. No.
It is a snare. Besides, I frankly speak,
Since, Highness, it concerns you. I avow
I'd rather with my king, Hernani, roam,
An outcast from the world and from the
    law —
Know thirst and hunger, wandering all the
    year,
Sharing the hardships of his destiny —
Exile and warfare, mourning hours of
    terror,
Than be an Empress with an Emperor!
    Don Carlos. Oh, happy man is he!
    Doña Sol. What! poor, proscribed!
    Don Carlos. 'T is well with him,
    ' though poor, proscribed he be,
For he's beloved! — an angel watches him!
I'm desolate. You hate me, then?
    Doña Sol. I love
You not.
    Don Carlos [seizing her violently]. Well,
    then, it matters not to me
Whether you love me, or you love me not!
You shall come with me — yes, for that
    my hand's
The stronger, and I will it! And we'll see
If I for nothing am the King of Spain
And of the Indies!
    Doña Sol [struggling]. Highness! Pity
    me!
You're King, you only have to choose
    among
The countesses, the duchesses, the great
Court ladies, all have love prepared to
    meet
And answer yours; but what has my pro-
    scribed
Received from niggard fortune? You
    possess
Castile and Aragon — Murcia and Léon,
Navarre, and still ten kingdoms more.
    Flanders,
And India with the mines of gold you own,
An empire without peer, and all so vast
That ne'er the sun sets on it. And when
    you,

The King, have all, would you take me, poor girl,
From him who has but me alone.
*[She throws herself on her knees.
He tries to draw her up.]*
DON CARLOS. Come — come!
I cannot listen. Come with me. I'll give
Of Spain a fourth part unto thee. Say, now,
What wilt thou? Choose.
DOÑA SOL *[struggling in his arms].* For
mine own honor's sake
I'll only from Your Highness take this dirk.
*[She snatches the poniard from his
girdle.]*
Approach me now but by a step!
DON CARLOS. The beauty!
I wonder not she loves a rebel now.
*[He makes a step towards her. She
raises the dirk.]*
DOÑA SOL. Another step, I kill you —
and myself.
*[He retreats again. She turns and
cries loudly.]*
Hernani! Oh, Hernani!
DON CARLOS. Peace!
DOÑA SOL. One step,
And all is finished.
DON CARLOS. Madam, to extremes
I'm driven. Yonder there I have three men
To force you — followers of mine.
HERNANI *[coming suddenly behind him].*
But one
You have forgotten.
[The King turns, and sees HERNANI
*motionless behind him in the
shade, his arms crossed under the
long cloak which is wrapped
round him, and the brim of his
hat raised up.* DOÑA SOL *makes
an exclamation and runs to him.]*
HERNANI *[motionless, his arms still
crossed, and his fiery eyes fixed on the
King].* Heaven my witness is,
That far from here it was I wished to seek
him.
DOÑA SOL. Hernani! Save me from him.
HERNANI. My dear love,
Fear not.
DON CARLOS. Now, what could all my
friends in town
Be doing, thus to let pass by the chief
Of the Bohemians? Ho! Monterey!

HERNANI. Your friends are in the hands
of mine just now,
So call not on their powerless swords; for
three
That you might claim, sixty to me would
come
Each one worth four of yours. So let us
now
Our quarrel terminate. What! You have
dared
To lay a hand upon this girl! It was
An act of folly, great Castilian King,
And one of cowardice!
DON CARLOS. Sir Bandit, hold!
There must be no reproach from you to me!
HERNANI. He jeers! Oh, I am not a
king; but when
A king insults me, and above all jeers,
My anger swells and surges up, and lifts
Me to his height. Take care! When I'm
offended,
Men fear far more the reddening of my
brow
Than helm of king. Foolhardy, therefore,
you
If still you're lured by hope. *[Seizes his
arm.]* Know you what hand
Now grasps you? Listen. 'T was your
father who
Was death of mine. I hate you for it. You
My title and my wealth have taken. You
I hate. And the same woman now we love.
I hate — hate — from my soul's depths
you I hate.
DON CARLOS. That's well.
HERNANI. And yet this night my hate
was lull'd.
Only one thought, one wish, one want I
had —
'T was Doña Sol! And I, absorbed in love,
Came here to find you daring against her
To strive, with infamous design! You —
you,
The man forgot — thus in my pathway
placed!
I tell you, King, you are demented! Ah!
King Charles, now see you're taken in the
snare
Laid by yourself: and neither flight nor
help
For thee is possible. I hold thee fast,
Besieged, alone, surrounded by thy foes,

Bloodthirsty ones, — what wilt thou do?
DON CARLOS [*proudly*]. Dare you
To question me!
HERNANI. Pish! pish! I would not wish
An arm obscure should strike thee. 'T is
    not so
My vengeance should have play. 'T is I
    alone
Must deal with thee. Therefore defend
    thyself.   [*He draws his sword.*]
DON CARLOS. I am your lord, the King.
Strike! but no duel.
HERNANI. Highness, thou may'st re-
    member yesterday
Thy sword encountered mine.
DON CARLOS. I yesterday
Could do it. I your name knew not, and
    you
Were ignorant of my rank. Not so to-day.
You know who I am, I who you are now.
HERNANI. Perchance.
DON CARLOS. No duel. You can murder.
    Do.
HERNANI. Think you that kings to me
    are sacred? Come,
Defend thyself.
DON CARLOS. You will assassinate
Me, then?
        [HERNANI *falls back. The King
        looks at him with eagle eyes.*]
Ah, bandits, so you dare to think
That your most vile brigades may safely
    spread
Through towns — ye blood-stained, mur-
    derous, miscreant crew —
But that you'll play at magnanimity!
As if we'd deign th' ennobling of your dirks
By touch of our own swords — we victims
    duped.
No, crime enthralls you — after you it
    trails.
Duels with you! Away! and murder me.
        [HERNANI, *morose and thoughtful,
        plays for some instants with the
        hilt of his sword, then turns
        sharply toward the King and
        snaps the blade on the pavement.*]
HERNANI. Go, then.
        [*The King half turns toward him
        and looks at him haughtily.*]
We shall have fitter meetings. Go.
Get thee away.

DON CARLOS. 'T is well. I go, sir,
    soon
Unto the ducal palace. I, your King,
Will then employ the magistrate. Is there
Yet put a price upon your head?
HERNANI. Oh, yes.
DON CARLOS. My master, from this day
    I reckon you
A rebel, trait'rous subject; you I warn.
I will pursue you everywhere, and make
You outlaw from my kingdom.
HERNANI. That I am
Already.
DON CARLOS. That is well.
HERNANI. But France is near
To Spain. There's refuge there.
DON CARLOS. But I shall be
The Emperor of Germany, and you
Under the Empire's ban shall be.
HERNANI. Ah, well!
I still shall have the remnant of the world,
From which to brave you — and with
    havens safe
O'er which you'll have no power.
DON CARLOS. But when I've gain'd
The world?
HERNANI. Then I shall have the grave.
DON CARLOS. Your plots
So insolent I shall know how to thwart.
HERNANI. Vengeance is lame, and comes
    with lagging steps,
But still it comes.
DON CARLOS [*with a half laugh of dis-
    dain*]. For touch of lady whom
The bandit loves!
HERNANI [*with flashing eyes*]. Dost thou
    remember, King,
I hold thee still? Make me not recollect
O future Roman Cæsar, that despised
I have thee in my all too loyal hand,
And that I only need to close it now
To crush the egg of thy Imperial Eagle!
DON CARLOS. Then do it.
HERNANI. Get away.
        [*He takes off his cloak, and throws
        it on the shoulders of the King.*]
Go, fly, and take
This cloak to shield thee from some knife
    I fear
Among our ranks.
        [*The King wraps himself in the cloak.*] At
        present safely go,

My thwarted vengeance for myself I keep.
It makes 'gainst every other hand thy life
Secure.

DON CARLOS. And you who've spoken
thus to me
Ask not for mercy on some future day.

[*Exit* DON CARLOS.]

DOÑA SOL [*seizing* HERNANI'S *hand*].
Now, let us fly — be quick.

HERNANI. It well becomes
You, loved one, in the trial hour to prove
Thus strong, unchangeable, and willing
e'er
To th' end and depth of all to cling to me;
A noble wish, worthy a faithful soul!
But thou, O God, dost see that to accept
The joy that to my cavern she would
bring —
The treasure of a beauty that a king
Now covets — and that Doña Sol to me
Should all belong — that she with me
should 'bide,
And all our lives be joined — that this
should be
Without regret, remorse — it is too late.
The scaffold is too near.

DOÑA SOL. What is 't you say?

HERNANI. This king, whom to his face
just now I braved,
Will punish me for having dared to show
Him mercy. He already, perhaps, has
reached
His palace, and is calling round him guards
And servants, his great lords, his heads-
men —

DOÑA SOL. Heavens!
Hernani! Oh, I shudder. Never mind,
Let us be quick and fly together, then.

HERNANI. Together! No; the hour has
passed for that.
Alas! When to my eyes thou didst reveal
Thyself, so good and generous, deigning
e'en
To love me with a helpful love, I could
But offer you — I, wretched one! — the
hills,
The woods, the torrents, bread of the
proscribed,
The bed of turf, all that the forest gives;
Thy pity then emboldened me — but now
To ask of thee to share the scaffold! No,
No, Doña Sol. That is for me alone.

DOÑA SOL. And yet you promised even
that!

HERNANI [*falling on his knees*]. Angel!
At this same moment, when perchance
from out
The shadow Death approaches, to wind
up
All mournfully a life of mournfulness,
I do declare that here a man proscribed,
Enduring trouble great, profound, — and
rock'd
In blood-stained cradle, — black as is the
gloom
Which spreads o'er all my life, I still de-
clare
I am a happy, to-be-envied man,
For you have loved me, and your love have
owned!
For you have whispered blessings on my
brow
Accursed!

DOÑA SOL [*leaning over his head*]. Hernani!

HERNANI. Praiséd be the fate
Sweet and propitious that for me now sets
This flower upon the precipice's brink!
[*Raising himself.*] 'T is not to you that I
am speaking thus;
It is to Heaven that hears, and unto God.

DOÑA SOL. Let me go with you.

HERNANI. Ah, 't would be a crime
To pluck the flower while falling in the
abyss.
Go: I have breathed the perfume — 't is
enough.
Remould your life, by me so sadly marred.
This old man wed; 't is I release you now.
To darkness I return. Be happy thou —
Be happy and forget.

DOÑA SOL. No, I will have
My portion of thy shroud. I follow thee.
I hang upon thy steps.

HERNANI [*pressing her in his arms*]. Oh,
let me go
Alone! Exiled — proscribed — a fearful
man
Am I.

[*He quits her with a convulsive
movement, and is going.*]

DOÑA SOL [*mournfully, and clasping her
hands*]. Hernani, do you fly from
me!

HERNANI [*returning*]. Well, then, no, no.
You will it, and I stay.
Behold me! Come into my arms. I'll wait
As long as thou wilt have me. Let us
rest,
Forgetting them. [*He seats her on a bench.*]
Be seated on this stone.
[*He places himself at her feet.*]
The liquid light of your eyes inundates
Mine own. Sing me some song, such as
sometimes
You used at eve to warble, with the tears
In those dark orbs. Let us be happy now,
And drink; the cup is full. This hour is
ours,
The rest is only folly. Speak and say,
Enrapture me. Is it not sweet to love,
And know that he who kneels before you
loves?
To be but two alone? Is it not sweet
To speak of love in stillness of the night
When Nature rests? Oh, let me slumber
now,
And on thy bosom dream. Oh, Doña Sol,
My love, my darling!
[*Noise of bells in the distance.*]
DOÑA SOL [*starting up frightened*].
Tocsin! — dost thou hear?
The tocsin!
HERNANI [*still kneeling at her feet*]. Eh!
No, 't is our bridal bell
They're ringing.
[*The noise increases. Confused
cries. Lights at all the windows,
on the roofs, and in the streets.*]
DOÑA SOL. Rise — oh, fly — great God!
the town
Lights up!
HERNANI [*half rising*]. A torchlight wed-
ding for us 't is!
DOÑA SOL. The nuptials these of Death,
and of the tombs!
[*Noise of swords and cries.*]
HERNANI [*lying down on the stone bench*].
Let us to sleep again.
A MOUNTAINEER [*rushing in, sword in
hand*]. The runners, sir.
The alcaldes rush out in cavalcades
With mighty force. Be quick — my Cap-
tain, — quick. [HERNANI *rises*.]
DOÑA SOL [*pale*]. Ah, thou wert right!
THE MOUNTAINEER. Oh, help us!

HERNANI [*to Mountaineer*]. It is well —
I'm ready.
[*Confused cries outside.*] Death to the
bandit!
HERNANI [*to Mountaineer*]. Quick, thy
sword —
[*To* DOÑA SOL]. Farewell!
DOÑA SOL. 'T is I have been thy ruin!
Oh,
Where canst thou go?
[*Pointing to the little door.*] The door is free.
Let us
Escape that way.
HERNANI. Heavens! Desert my friends!
What dost thou say?
DOÑA SOL. These clamors terrify.
Remember, if thou diest I must die.
HERNANI [*holding her in his arms*]. A
kiss!
DOÑA SOL. Hernani! Husband! Master
mine!
HERNANI [*kissing her forehead*]. Alas! it
is the first!
DOÑA SOL. Perchance the last!
[*Exit* HERNANI. *She falls on the
bench.*]

ACT III

*The Castle of Silva in the midst of the
mountains of Aragon. The gallery of family
portraits of Silva; a great hall of which these
portraits — surrounded with rich frames,
and surmounted by ducal coronets and gilt
escutcheons — form the decoration. At the
back a lofty Gothic door. Between the portraits complete panoplies of armor of different centuries.* DOÑA SOL, *pale, and standing near a table.* DON RUY GOMEZ DE
SILVA, *seated in his great carved oak chair.*

DON RUY GOMEZ. At last the day has
come! — and in an hour
Thou'lt be my duchess, and embrace me!
Not
Thine uncle then! But hast thou pardoned
me?
That I was wrong I own. I raised thy
blush,
I made thy cheek turn pale. I was too
quick
With my suspicions — should have stayed
to hear

Before condemning; but appearances
Should take the blame. Unjust we were.
    Certes
The two young handsome men were there.
    But then —
No matter — well I know that I should not
Have credited my eyes. But, my poor child,
What would'st thou with the old?
    DOÑA SOL [seriously, and without moving].
    You ever talk
Of this. Who is there blames you?
    DON RUY GOMEZ. I myself,
I should have known that such a soul as
    yours
Never has gallants; when 't is Doña Sol,
And when good Spanish blood is in her
    veins.
    DOÑA SOL. Truly, my Lord, 't is good
    and pure; perchance
'T will soon be seen.
    DON RUY GOMEZ [rising, and going
    toward her]. Now list. One cannot
    be
The master of himself, so much in love
As I am now with thee. And I am old
And jealous, and am cross — and why?
    Because
I'm old; because the beauty, grace, or
    youth
Of others frightens, threatens me. Be-
    cause,
While jealous thus of others, of myself
I am ashamed. What mockery! that this
    love
Which to the heart brings back such joy
    and warmth,
Should halt, and but rejuvenate the soul,
Forgetful of the body. When I see
A youthful peasant, singing blithe and gay,
In the green meadows, often then I muse—
I, in my dismal paths, and murmur low:
Oh, I would give my battlemented towers,
And ancient ducal donjon, and my fields
Of corn, and all my forest lands, and
    flocks
So vast which feed upon my hills, my name
And all my ancient titles — ruins mine,
And ancestors who must expect me soon,
All — all I'd give for his new cot, and brow
Unwrinkled. For his hair is raven black,
And his eyes shine like yours. Beholding
    him

You might exclaim: A young man this!
    And then
Would think of me so old. I know it well.
I am named Silva. Ah, but that is not
Enough; I say it, see it. Now behold
To what excess I love thee. All I'd give
Could I be like thee — young and hand-
    some now!
Vain dream! that I were young again, who
    must
By long, long years precede thee to the
    tomb.
    DOÑA SOL. Who knows?
    DON RUY GOMEZ. And yet, I pray you,
    me believe,
The frivolous swains have not so much of
    love
Within their hearts as on their tongues.
    A girl
May love and trust one; if she dies for him,
He laughs. The strong-winged and gay-
    painted birds
That warble sweet, and in the thicket trill,
Will change their loves as they their plum-
    age moult.
They are the old, with voice and color gone,
And beauty fled, who have the resting
    wings
We love the best. Our steps are slow, and
    dim
Our eyes. Our brows are furrowed, — but
    the heart
Is never wrinkled. When an old man loves
He should be spared. The heart is ever
    young,
And always it can bleed. This love of mine
Is not a plaything made of glass to shake
And break. It is a love severe and sure,
Solid, profound, paternal, — strong as is
The oak which forms my ducal chair. See,
    then,
How well I love thee — and in other ways
I love thee — hundred other ways, e'en as
We love the dawn, and flowers, and
    heaven's blue!
To see thee, mark thy graceful step each
    day,
Thy forehead pure, thy brightly beaming
    eye,
I'm joyous — feeling that my soul will
    have
Perpetual festival!

Doña Sol. Alas!

Don Ruy Gomez. And then,
Know you how much the world admires,
   applauds,
A woman, angel pure, and like a dove,
When she an old man comforts and con-
   soles
As he is tott'ring to the marble tomb,
Passing away by slow degrees as she
Watches and shelters him, and condescends
To bear with him, the useless one, that
   seems
But fit to die? It is a sacred work
And worthy of all praise — effort supreme
Of a devoted heart to comfort him
Unto the end, and without loving, perhaps,
To act as if she loved. Ah, thou to me
Wilt be this angel with a woman's heart
Who will rejoice the old man's soul again
And share his latter years, and by respect
A daughter be, and by your pity like
A sister prove.

Doña Sol. Far from preceding me,
'T is likely me you'll follow to the grave.
My lord, because that we are young is not
A reason we should live. Alas! I know
And tell you, often old men tarry long,
And see the young go first, their eyes shut
   fast
By sudden stroke, as on a sepulcher
That still was open falls the closing stone.

Don Ruy Gomez. Oh, cease, my child,
   such saddening discourse,
Or I shall scold you. Such a day as this
Sacred and joyous is. And, by-the-bye,
Time summons us. Are you not ready yet
For chapel when we're called? Be quick to
   don
The bridal dress. Each moment do I count.

Doña Sol. There is abundant time.

Don Ruy Gomez. Oh, no, there's not.

[Enter a Page.]

What want you?

The Page. At the door, my lord, a
   man —
A pilgrim — beggar — or I know not what,
Is craving here a shelter.

Don Ruy Gomez. Let him in
Whoever he may be. Good enters with
The stranger that we welcome. What's
   the news

From th' outside world? What of the
   bandit chief
That filled our forests with his rebel band?

The Page. Hernani, Lion of the mountains, now
Is done for.

Doña Sol *[aside]*. God!

Don Ruy Gomez *[to the Page]*. How so?

The Page. The troop's destroyed.
The King himself has led the soldiers on.
Hernani's head a thousand crowns is worth
Upon the spot; but now he's dead, they
   say.

Doña Sol *[aside]*. What! Without me,
   Hernani!

Don Ruy Gomez. And thank Heaven!
So he is dead, the rebel! Now, dear love,
We can rejoice; go then and deck thyself,
My pride, my darling. Day of double joy.

Doña Sol. Oh, mourning robes!
                    [Exit Doña Sol.]

Don Ruy Gomez *[to the Page]*. The
   casket quickly send
That I'm to give her.
          [He seats himself in his chair.]
'T is my longing now
To see her all adorned Madonna like,
With her bright eyes, and aid of my rich
   gems,
She will be beautiful enough to make
A pilgrim kneel before her. As for him
Who asks asylum, bid him enter here,
Excuses from us offer; run, be quick.
             [The Page bows and exit.]
'T is ill to keep a guest long waiting thus.
          [The door at the back opens.]

[Hernani *appears disguised as a Pilgrim.
   The Duke rises.* Hernani *pauses at
   the threshold of the door.*]

Hernani. My lord, peace and all happiness be yours!

Don Ruy Gomez *[saluting him with his
   hand]*. To thee be peace and happiness, my guest!

[Hernani *enters. The Duke reseats
   himself.*]

Art thou a pilgrim?

Hernani *[bowing]*. Yes.

Don Ruy Gomez. No doubt you come
From Armillas?

HERNANI. Not so. I hither came
By other road, there was some fighting
    there.
DON RUY GOMEZ. Among the troop of
    bandits, was it not?
HERNANI. I know not.
DON RUY GOMEZ. What's become of
    him — the chief
They call Hernani? Dost thou know?
HERNANI. My lord,
Who is this man?
DON RUY GOMEZ. Dost thou not know
    him, then?
For thee so much the worse! Thou wilt not
    gain
The good round sum. See you a rebel he
That has been long unpunished. To Madrid
Should you be going, perhaps you'll see
    him hanged.
HERNANI. I go not there.
DON RUY GOMEZ. A price is on his
    head
For any man who takes him.
HERNANI [aside]. Let one come!
DON RUY GOMEZ. Whither, good pil-
    grim, goest thou?
HERNANI. My lord,
I'm bound for Saragossa.
DON RUY GOMEZ. A vow made
In honor of a saint, or of Our Lady?
HERNANI. Yes, of Our Lady, Duke.
DON RUY GOMEZ. Of the Pillar?
HERNANI. Of the Pillar.
DON RUY GOMEZ. We must be soulless
    quite
Not to acquit us of the vows we make
Unto the saints. But thine accomplished,
    then
Hast thou not other purposes in view?
Or is to see the Pillar all you wish?
HERNANI. Yes. I would see the lights
    and candles burn,
And at the end of the dim corridor
Our Lady in her glowing shrine, with cope
All golden — then would satisfied return.
DON RUY GOMEZ. Indeed, that's well.
Brother, what is thy name?
Mine, Ruy de Silva is.
HERNANI [hesitating]. My name —
DON RUY GOMEZ. You can
Conceal it if you will. None here has right
To know it. Cam'st thou to asylum ask?

HERNANI. Yes, Duke.
DON RUY GOMEZ. Remain, and know
    thou'rt welcome here.
For nothing want; and as for what thou'rt
    named,
But call thyself my guest. It is enough
Whoever thou may'st be. Without demur
I'd take in Satan if God sent him me.
    [The folding doors at the back open.]

[Enter DOÑA SOL in nuptial attire. Behind
    her Pages and Lackeys, and two women
    carrying on a velvet cushion a casket of
    engraved silver, which they place upon
    a table, and which contains a jewel
    case, with duchess' coronet, necklaces
    bracelets, pearls, and diamonds in pro-
    fusion. HERNANI, breathless and scared,
    looks at DOÑA SOL with flaming eyes
    without listening to the Duke.]

DON RUY GOMEZ [continuing]. Behold
    my blessed Lady — to have prayed
To her will bring thee happiness.
    [He offers his hand to DOÑA SOL,
        still pale and grave.]
Come, then,
My bride. What! not thy coronet, nor
    ring!
HERNANI [in a voice of thunder]. Who
    wishes now a thousand golden
    crowns
To win?
    [All turn to him astonished. He
        tears off his pilgrim's robe, and
        crushes it under his feet, reveal-
        ing himself in the dress of a
        mountaineer.]
I am Hernani.
DOÑA SOL [joyfully]. Heavens! Oh,
He lives!
HERNANI [to the Lackeys]. See! I'm the
    man they seek.
[To the Duke.] You wished
To know my name — Diego or Perez?
No, no! I have a grander name — Her-
nani.
Name of the banished, the proscribed. See
    you
This head? 'T is worth enough of gold to
    pay
For festival.
[To the Lackeys.] I give it to you all.

Take; tie my hands, my feet. But there's
    no need,
The chain that binds me's one I shall not
    break.
Doña Sol [aside]. Oh, misery!
Don Ruy Gomez. Folly! This my guest
    is mad —
A lunatic!
Hernani. Your guest a bandit is.
Doña Sol. Oh, do not heed him.
Hernani. What I say is truth.
Don Ruy Gomez. A thousand golden
    crowns — the sum is large.
And, sir, I will not answer now for all
My people.
Hernani. And so much the better,
    should
A willing one be found.
[To the Lackeys.] Now seize, and sell me!
Don Ruy Gomez [trying to silence him].
    Be quiet, or they'll take you at
    your word.
Hernani. Friends, this your opportun-
    ity is good.
I tell you, I'm the rebel — the proscribed
Hernani!
Don Ruy Gomez. Silence!
Hernani. I am he!
Doña Sol [in a low voice to him]. Be
    still!
Hernani [half turning to Doña Sol].
    There's marrying here! My spouse
    awaits me too.
[To the Duke.] She is less beautiful, my
    lord, than yours,
But not less faithful. She is Death.
[To the Lackeys.] Not one
Of you has yet come forth!
Doña Sol [in a low voice]. For pity's
    sake!
Hernani [to the Lackeys]. A thousand
    golden crowns. Hernani here!
Don Ruy Gomez. This is the demon!
Hernani [to a young Lackey]. Come!
    thou'lt earn this sum,
Then rich, thou wilt from lackey change
    again
To man.
[To the other Lackeys, who do not stir.] And
    also you — you waver. Ah,
Have I not misery enough?
Don Ruy Gomez. My friend,

To touch thy life they'd peril each his
    own.
Wert thou Hernani, or a hundred times
As bad, I must protect my guest, — were
    e'en
An Empire offered for his life — against
The King himself; for thee I hold from
    God.
If hair of thine be injured, may I die.
[To Doña Sol.] My niece, who in an hour
    will be my wife,
Go to your room. I am about to arm
The Castle — shut the gates.
                [Exit, followed by servants.]
Hernani [looking with despair at his
    empty girdle]. Not e'en a knife!
    [Doña Sol, after the departure of
    the Duke, takes a few steps, as if
    to follow her women, then pauses,
    and when they are gone, comes
    back to Hernani with anxiety.
    Hernani looks at the nuptial
    jewel-case with a cold and appar-
    ently indifferent gaze; then he
    tosses back his head, and his
    eyes light up.]
Accept my 'gratulations! Words tell not
How I'm enchanted by these ornaments.
                [He approaches the casket.]
This ring is in fine taste, — the coronet
I like, — the necklace shows surpassing
    skill.
The bracelet's rare — but oh, a hundred
    times
Less so than she, who 'neath a forehead
    pure
Conceals a faithless heart.
                [Examining the casket again.]
What for all this
Have you now given? Of your love some
    share?
But that for nothing goes! Great God! to
    thus
Deceive, and still to live and have no
    shame!   [Looking at the jewels.]
But after all, perchance, this pearl is false,
And copper stands for gold, and glass and
    lead
Make out sham diamonds — pretended
    gems!
Are these false sapphires and false jewels
    all?

If so, thy heart is like them, Duchess false,
Thyself but only gilded. [*He returns to the casket.*] Yet no, no!
They all are real, beautiful, and good,
He dares not cheat, who stands so near the tomb.
Nothing is wanting.
[*He takes up one thing after another.*]
Necklaces are here,
And brilliant earrings, and the Duchess' crown
And golden ring. Oh, marvel! Many thanks
For love so certain, faithful and profound.
The precious box!
   DoÑa Sol [*going to the casket, feeling in it, and drawing forth a dagger*]. You have not reached its depths.
This is the dagger which, by kindly aid
Of patron saint, I snatched from Charles the King
When he made offer to me of a throne,
Which I refused for you, who now insult me.
   Hernani [*falling at her feet*]. Oh, let me on my knees arrest those tears,
The tears that beautify thy sorrowing eyes.
Then after thou canst freely take my life.
   DoÑa Sol. I pardon you, Hernani. In my heart
There is but love for you.
   Hernani. And she forgives —
And loves me still! But who can also teach
Me to forgive myself, that I have used
Such words? Angel, for heaven reserved,
say where
You trod, that I may kiss the ground.
   DoÑa Sol. My love!
   Hernani. Oh, no, I should to thee be odious.
But listen. Say again — I love thee still!
Say it, and reassure a heart that doubts.
Say it, for often with such little words
A woman's tongue hath cured a world of woes.
   DoÑa Sol [*absorbed, and without hearing him*]. To think my love had such short memory!
That all these so ignoble men could shrink
A heart, where his name was enthroned, to love
By them thought worthier.

   Hernani. Alas! I have
Blasphemed! If I were in thy place I should
Be weary of the furious madman, who
Can only pity after he has struck.
I'd bid him go. Drive me away, I say,
And I will bless thee, for thou hast been good
And sweet. Too long thou hast myself endured,
For I am evil; I should blacken still
Thy days with my dark nights. At last it is
Too much; thy soul is lofty, beautiful,
And pure; if I am evil, is't thy fault?
Marry the old Duke, then, for he is good
And noble. By the mother's side he has
Olmédo, by his father's Alcala.
With him be rich and happy by one act.
Know you not what this generous hand of mine
Can offer thee of splendor? Ah, alone
A dowry of misfortune, and the choice
Of blood or tears. Exile, captivity
And death, and terrors that environ me.
These are thy necklaces and jeweled crown.
Never elated bridegroom to his bride
Offered a casket filled more lavishly,
But 't is with misery and mournfulness.
Marry the old man — he deserves thee well!
Ah, who could ever think my head proscribed
Fit mate for forehead pure? What looker-on
That saw thee calm and beautiful, me rash
And violent — thee peaceful, like a flower
Growing in shelter, me by tempests dash'd
On rocks unnumber'd — who could dare to say
That the same law should guide our destinies?
No, God, who ruleth all things well, did not
Make thee for me. No right from Heav'n above
Have I to thee; and I'm resigned to fate.
I have thy heart; it is a theft! I now
Unto a worthier yield it. Never yet
Upon our love has Heaven smiled; 't is false
If I have said thy destiny it was.
To vengeance and to love I bid adieu!
My life is ending; useless I will go,

And take away with me my double dream,
Ashamed I could not punish, nor could
   charm.
I have been made for hate, who only
   wished
To love. Forgive and fly me, these my
   prayers
Reject them not, since they will be my last.
Thou livest — I am dead. I see not why
Thou should'st immure thee in my tomb.
   DOÑA SOL. Ingrate!
   HERNANI. Mountains of old Aragon!
   Galicia!
Estremadura! Unto all who come
Around me I bring misery!
The best, without remorse I've ta'en to
   fight,
And now behold them dead! The bravest
   brave
Of all Spain's sons, lie, soldier-like, upon
The hills, their backs to earth, the living
   God
Before; and if their eyes could ope they'd
   look
On heaven's blue. See what I do to all
Who join me! Is it fortune any one
Should covet? Doña Sol, oh! take the
   Duke,
Take hell, or take the King — all would be
   well,
All must be better than myself, I say.
No longer have I friend to think of me,
And it is fully time that thy turn comes,
For I must be alone. Fly from me, then,
From my contagion. Make not faithful
   love
A duty of religion! Fly from me,
For pity's sake. Thou think'st me, per-
   haps, a man
Like others, one with sense, who knows the
   end
At which he aims, and acts accordingly.
Oh, undeceive thyself. I am a force
That cannot be resisted — agent blind
And deaf of mournful mysteries! A soul
Of misery made of gloom. Where shall I
   go?
I cannot tell. But I am urged, compelled
By an impetuous breath and wild decree;
I fall, and fall, and cannot stop descent.
If sometimes breathless I dare turn my
   head,

A voice cries out, "Go on!" and the abyss
Is deep, and to the depths I see it red
With flame or blood! Around my fearful
   course
All things break up — all die. Woe be to
   them
Who touch me. Fly, I say! Turn thee
   away
From my so fatal path. Alas! without
Intending I should do thee ill.
   DOÑA SOL. Great God!
   HERNANI. My demon is a formidable
   one.
But there's a thing impossible to it —
My happiness. For thee is happiness.
Therefore, go seek another lord, for thou
Art not for me. If Heaven, that my fate
Abjures, should smile on me, believe it not:
It would be irony. Marry the Duke!
   DOÑA SOL. 'T was not enough to tear
   my heart, but you
Must break it now! Ah me! no longer, then
You love me!
   HERNANI. Oh! my heart — its very life
Thou art! The glowing hearth whence all
   warmth comes
Art thou! Wilt thou, then, blame me that
   I fly
From thee, adored one?
   DOÑA SOL. No, I blame thee not,
Only I know that I shall die of it.
   HERNANI. Die! And for what? For me?
   Can it then be
That thou should'st die for cause so small?
   DOÑA SOL [bursting into tears]. Enough.
      [She falls into a chair.]
   HERNANI [seating himself near her]. And
   thou art weeping; and 't is still my
   fault!
And who will punish me? for thou I know
Wilt pardon still! Who, who can tell thee
   half
The anguish that I suffer when a tear
Of thine obscures and drowns those radiant
   eyes
Whose luster is my joy. My friends are
   dead!
Oh, I am crazed — forgive me — I would
   love
I know not how. Alas! I love with love
Profound. Weep not — the rather let us
   die!

Oh that I had a world to give to thee!
Oh, wretched, miserable man I am!
DOÑA SOL [*throwing herself on his neck*].
You are my lion, generous and superb!
I love you.
HERNANI. Ah, this love would be a good
Supreme, if we could die of too much love!
DOÑA SOL. Thou art my lord! I love thee and belong
To thee!
HERNANI [*letting his head fall on her shoulder*]. How sweet would be a poniard stroke
From thee!
DONA SOL [*entreatingly*]. Fear you not
God will punish you
For words like these?
HERNANI [*still leaning on her shoulder*].
Well, then, let Him unite us!
I have resisted; thou would'st have it thus.
[*While they are in each other's arms, absorbed and gazing with ecstasy at each other,* DON RUY GOMEZ *enters by the door at the back of the stage. He sees them, and stops on the threshold as if petrified.*]
DON RUY GOMEZ [*motionless on the threshold, with arms crossed*]. And this is the requital that I find
Of hospitality!
DOÑA SOL. Oh, Heavens — the Duke!
[*Both turn as if awakening with a start.*]
DON RUY GOMEZ [*still motionless*]. This then's the recompense from thee, my guest?
Good Duke, go see if all thy walls be high,
And if the door is closed, and archer placed
Within his tower, and go the castle round
Thyself for us; seek in thine arsenal
For armor that will fit — at sixty years
Resume thy battle-harness — and then see
The loyalty with which we will repay
Such service! Thou for us do thus, and we
Do this for thee! Oh, blessed saints of Heaven!
Past sixty years I've lived, and met sometimes
Unbridled souls; and oft my dirk have drawn

From out its scabbard, raising on my path
The hangman's game birds: murd'rers I have seen
And coiners, traitorous varlets poisoning
Their masters; and I've seen men die without
A prayer, or sight of crucifix. I've seen
Sforza and Borgia; Luther still I see,
But never have I known perversity
So great that feared not thunderbolt, its host
Betraying! 'T was not of my age — such foul
Black treason, that at once could petrify
An old man on the threshold of his door,
And make the master, waiting for his grave,
Look like his statue ready for his tomb.
Moors and Castilians! Tell me, who's this man?
[*He raises his eyes and looks round on the portraits on the wall.*]
Oh, you, the Silvas who can hear me now,
Forgive if, in your presence by my wrath
Thus stirr'd, I say that hospitality
Was ill advised.
HERNANI [*rising*]. Duke —
DON RUY GOMEZ. Silence!
[*He makes three steps into the hall looking at the portraits of the SILVAS.*]
Sacred dead!
My ancestors! Ye men of steel, who know
What springs from heav'n or hell, reveal I say,
Who is this man? No, not Hernani he,
But Judas is his name — oh, try to speak
And tell me who he is!
[*Crossing his arms.*] In all your days
Saw you aught like him? No.
HERNANI. My lord —
DON RUY GOMEZ [*still addressing the portraits*]. See you
The shameless miscreant? He would speak to me,
But better far than I you read his soul.
Oh, heed him not! he is a knave — he'd say
That he foresaw that in the tempest wild
Of my great wrath I brooded o'er some deed

Of gory vengeance shameful to my roof.
A sister deed to that they call the feast
Of Seven Heads. He'll tell you he's pro-
scribed,
He'll tell you that of Silva they will talk
E'en as of Lara. Afterwards he'll say
He is my guest and yours. My lords, my
sires,
Is the fault mine? Judge you between us
now.

HERNANI. Ruy Gomez de Silva, if ever
'neath
The heavens clear a noble brow was raised,
If ever heart was great and soul was high,
Yours are, my lord; and oh, my noble host,
I, who now speak to you, alone have sinn'd.
Guilty most damnably am I, without
Extenuating word to say. I would
Have carried off thy bride — dishonor'd
thee.
'T was infamous. I live; but now my life
I offer unto thee. Take it. Thy sword
Then wipe, and think no more about the
deed.

DOÑA SOL. My lord, 't was not his fault
— strike only me.

HERNANI. Be silent, Doña Sol. This
hour supreme
Belongs alone to me; nothing I have
But it. Let me explain things to the Duke.
Oh, Duke, believe the last words from my
mouth,
I swear that I alone am guilty. But
Be calm and rest assured that she is pure,
That's all. I guilty and she pure. Have
faith
In her. A sword or dagger thrust for me.
Then throw my body out of doors, and have
The flooring washed, if you should will it so.
What matter?

DOÑA SOL. Ah! I only am the cause
Of all; because I love him.

[DON RUY *turns round trembling
at these words, and fixes on* DOÑA
SOL *a terrible look. She throws
herself at his feet.*]

Pardon! Yes,
My lord, I love him!

DON RUY GOMEZ. Love him — you love
him.

[*To* HERNANI.] Tremble! [*Noise of trumpets outside.*]

[*Enter a Page.*]

What is this noise?

THE PAGE. It is the King,
My lord, in person, with a band complete
Of archers, and his herald, who now sounds.

DOÑA SOL. Oh, God! This last fatality
— the King!

THE PAGE [*to the Duke*]. He asks the
reason why the door is closed,
And order gives to open it.

DON RUY GOMEZ. Admit
The King. [*The Page bows and exit.*]

DOÑA SOL. He's lost!

[DON RUY GOMEZ *goes to one of
the portraits — that of himself
and the last on the left; he presses
a spring, and the portrait opens
out like a door, and reveals a
hiding-place in the wall. He
turns to* HERNANI.]

DON RUY GOMEZ. Come hither, sir.

HERNANI. My life
To thee is forfeit; and to yield it up
I'm ready. I thy prisoner am.

[*He enters the recess.* DON RUY
*again presses the spring, and
the portrait springs back to its
place looking as before.*]

DOÑA SOL. My lord,
Have pity on him!

THE PAGE [*entering*]. His Highness the
King!

[DOÑA SOL *hurriedly lowers her
veil. The folding-doors open.*]

[*Enter* DON CARLOS *in military attire, followed by a crowd of gentlemen equally
armed with halberds, arquebuses, and
cross-bows.* DON CARLOS *advances
slowly, his left hand on the hilt of his
sword, his right hand in his bosom, and
looking at the Duke with anger and defiance. The Duke goes before the King
and bows low. Silence. Expectation and
terror on all. At last the King, coming
opposite the Duke, throws back his head
haughtily.*]

DON CARLOS. How comes it, then, my
cousin, that to-day
Thy door is strongly barr'd? By all the
saints

I thought your dagger had more rusty
grown,
And know not why, when I'm your visitor,
It should so haste to brightly shine again
All ready to your hand.
[Don Ruy Gomez *attempts to
speak, but the King continues
with an imperious gesture.*]
Late in the day
It is for you to play the young man's part!
Do we come turban'd? Tell me, are we
named
Boabdil or Mahomet, and not Charles,
That the portcullis 'gainst us you should
lower
And raise the drawbridge?
Don Ruy Gomez [*bowing*]. Highness —
Don Carlos [*to his gentlemen*]. Take the
keys
And guard the doors.
[*Two officers exeunt. Several others
arrange the soldiers in a triple
line in the hall from the King to
the principal door. Don Carlos
turns again to the Duke.*]
Ah! you would wake to life
Again these crushed rebellions. By my
faith,
If you, ye dukes, assume such airs as these
The King himself will play his kingly part,
Traverse the mountains in a warlike mode,
And in their battlemented nests will slay
The lordlings!
Don Ruy Gomez [*drawing himself up*].
Ever have the Silvas been,
Your Highness, loyal.
Don Carlos [*interrupting him*]. With-
out subterfuge
Reply, or to the ground I'll raze thy towers
Eleven! Of extinguished fire remains
One spark — of brigands dead the chief
survives,
And who conceals him? It is thou, I say!
Hernani, rebel ringleader, is here,
And in thy castle thou dost hide him
now.
Don Ruy Gomez. Highness, it is quite
true.
Don Carlos. Well, then, his head
I want — or if not, thine. Dost under-
stand,
My cousin?

Don Ruy Gomez. Well, then, be it so.
You shall
Be satisfied.
[Doña Sol *hides her face in her
hands and sinks into the armchair.*]
Don Carlos [*a little softened*]. Ah! you
repent. Go seek
Your prisoner.
[*The Duke crosses his arms, lowers
his head, and remains some
moments pondering. The King
and* Doña Sol, *agitated by contrary emotions, observe him in
silence. At last the Duke looks up,
goes to the King, takes his hand,
and leads him with slow steps
toward the oldest of the portraits,
which is where the gallery commences to the right of the spectator.*]
Don Ruy Gomez [*pointing out the old
portrait to the King*]. This is the
eldest one,
The great forefather of the Silva race,
Don Silvius our ancestor, three times
Was he made Roman consul.
[*Passing to the next portrait.*] This is he —
Don Galceran de Silva — other Cid!
They keep his body still at Toro, near
Valladolid; a thousand candles burn
Before his gilded shrine. 'T was he who
freed
Leon from tribute o' the hundred virgins.
[*Passing to another.*] Don Blas — who, in
contrition for the fault
Of having ill-advised the king, exiled
Himself of his own will.
[*To another.*] This Christoval!
At fight of Escalon, when fled on foot
The King Don Sancho, whose white plume
was mark
For general deadly aim, he cried aloud,
Oh, Christoval! And Christoval assumed
The plume, and gave his horse.
[*To another.*] This is Don Jorge,
Who paid the ransom of Ramire, the King
Of Aragon.
Don Carlos [*crossing his arms and look-
ing at him from head to foot*]. By
Heavens, now, Don Ruy,
I marvel at you! But go on.

Don Ruy Gomez. Next comes
Don Ruy Gomez Silva; he was made
Grand Master of St. James, and Calatrava.
His giant armor would not suit our heights.
He took three hundred flags from foes, and
won
In thirty battles. For the King Motril
He conquer'd Antequera, Suez,
Nijar; and died in poverty. Highness,
Salute him.
> [*He bows, uncovers, and passes to
> another portrait. The King
> listens impatiently, and with
> increasing anger.*]

Next him is his son, named Gil,
Dear to all noble souls. His promise worth
The oath of royal hands.
[*To another.*] Don Gaspard this,
The pride alike of Mendocé and Silva.
Your Highness, every noble family
Has some alliance with the Silva race.
Sandoval has both trembled at, and wed
With us. Manrique is envious of us: Lara
Is jealous. Alencastre hates us. We
All dukes surpass, and mount to kings.
Don Carlos. Tut! tut!
You're jesting.
Don Ruy Gomez. Here behold Don
Vasquez, called
The Wise. Don Jayme surnamed the
Strong. One day
Alone he stopped Zamet and five score
Moors.
I pass them by, and some the greatest.
> [*At an angry gesture of the King he
> passes by a great number of por-
> traits, and speedily comes to the
> three last at the left of the audi-
> ence.*]

This,
My grandfather, who lived to sixty years,
Keeping his promised word even to Jews.
[*To the last portrait but one.*] This venerable
form my father is,
A sacred head. Great was he, though he
comes
The last. The Moors had taken prisoner
His friend Count Alvar Giron. But my sire
Set out to seek him with six hundred men
To war inured. A figure of the count
Cut out of stone by his decree was made
And dragged along behind the soldiers, he,

By patron saint, declaring that until
The count of stone itself turned back and
fled,
He would not falter; on he went and saved
His friend.
Don Carlos. I want my prisoner.
Don Ruy Gomez. This was
A Gomez de Silva. Imagine — judge
What in this dwelling one must say who
sees
These heroes —
Don Carlos. Instantly — my prisoner!
> [Don Ruy Gomez *bows low before
> the King, takes his hand, and
> leads him to the last portrait,
> which serves for the door of*
> Hernani's *hiding-place.* Doña
> Sol *watches him with anxious
> eyes. Silence and expectation in
> all.*]

Don Ruy Gomez. This portrait is my
own. Mercy! King Charles!
For you require that those who see it
here
Should say, "This last, the worthy son of
race
Heroic, was a traitor found, that sold
The life of one he sheltered as a guest!"
> [*Joy of* Doña Sol. *Movement of
> bewilderment in the crowd. The
> King, disconcerted, moves away
> in anger, and remains some
> moments with lips trembling and
> eyes flashing.*]

Don Carlos. Your castle, Duke, an-
noys me, I shall lay
It low.
Don Ruy Gomez. Thus, Highness,
you'd retaliate,
Is it not so?
Don Carlos. For such audacity
Your towers I'll level with the ground, and
have
Upon the spot the hemp-seed sown.
Don Ruy Gomez. I'd see
The hemp spring freely up where once my
towers
Stood high, rather than stain should eat
into
The ancient name of Silva.
[*To the portraits.*] Is't not true?
I ask it of you all.

DON CARLOS. Now, Duke, this head,
'T is ours, and thou hast promised it to
me.
DON RUY GOMEZ. I promised one or
other.
[*To the portraits.*] Was 't not so?
I ask you all?
[*Pointing to his head.*] This one I give. [*To
the King.*] Take it.
DON CARLOS. Duke, many thanks; but
't would not do. The head
I want is young; when dead the headsman
must
Uplift it by the hair. But as for thine,
In vain he 'd seek, for thou hast not enough
For him to clutch.
DON RUY GOMEZ. Highness, insult me
not.
My head is noble still, and worth far more
Than any rebel's poll. The head of Silva
You thus despise!
DON CARLOS. Give up Hernani!
DON RUY GOMEZ. I
Have spoken, Highness.
DON CARLOS [*to his followers*]. Search
you everywhere
From roof to cellar, that he takes not
wing —
DON RUY GOMEZ. My keep is faithful
as myself; alone
It shares the secret which we both shall
guard
Right well.
DON CARLOS. I am the King!
DON RUY GOMEZ. Out of my house
Demolished stone by stone, they 'll only
make
My tomb, — and nothing gain.
DON CARLOS. Menace I find
And prayer alike are vain. Deliver up
The bandit, Duke, or head and castle both
Will I beat down.
DON RUY GOMEZ. I 've said my word.
DON CARLOS. Well, then,
Instead of one head I 'll have two.
[*To the* DUKE D'ALCALA.] You, Jorge,
Arrest the Duke.
DOÑA SOL [*plucking off her veil and
throwing herself between the King,
the Duke, and the Guards*]. King
Charles, an evil king
Are you!

DON CARLOS. Good Heavens! Is it
Doña Sol I see?
DOÑA SOL. Highness! Thou hast no
Spaniard's heart!
DON CARLOS [*confused*]. Madam, you
are severe upon the King.
[*He approaches her, and speaks low.*]
'T is you have caused the wrath that 's in
my heart.
A man approaching you perforce becomes
An angel or a monster. Ah, when we
Are hated, swiftly we malignant grow!
Perchance, if you had willed it so, young
girl,
I 'd noble been — the lion of Castile;
A tiger I am made by your disdain.
You hear it roaring now. Madam, be still!
[DOÑA SOL *looks at him. He bows.*]
However, I 'll obey. [*Turning to the Duke.*]
Cousin, may be
Thy scruples are excusable, and I
Esteem thee. To thy guest be faithful still,
And faithless to thy King. I pardon thee.
'T is better that I only take thy niece
Away as hostage.
DON RUY GOMEZ. Only!
DOÑA SOL. Highness! Me!
DON CARLOS. Yes, you.
DON RUY GOMEZ. Alone! Oh, wondrous
clemency!
Oh, generous conqueror, that spares the
head
To torture thus the heart! What mercy
this!
DON CARLOS. Choose 'twixt the traitor
and the Doña Sol;
I must have one of them.
DON RUY GOMEZ. The master you!
[DON CARLOS *approaches* DOÑA
SOL *to lead her away. She flies
toward the Duke.*]
DOÑA SOL. Save me, my lord!
[*She pauses. — Aside.*] Oh, misery! and
yet
It must be so. My uncle's life, or else
The other's! — rather mine!
[*To the King.*] I follow you.
DON CARLOS [*aside*]. By all the saints!
the thought triumphant is!
Ah, in the end you 'll soften, princess mine!
[DOÑA SOL *goes with a grave and
steady step to the casket, opens*

*it, and takes from it the dagger,
which she hides in her bosom.
DON CARLOS comes to her and
offers his hand.]*
DON CARLOS. What is 't you 're taking
thence?
DOÑA SOL. Oh, nothing!
DON CARLOS. Is 't
Some precious jewel?
DOÑA SOL. Yes.
DON CARLOS [*smiling*]. Show it to me.
DOÑA SOL. Anon you 'll see it.
*[She gives him her hand and pre-
pares to follow him. DON RUY
GOMEZ, who has remained mo-
tionless and absorbed in thought,
advances a few steps crying out.]*
DON RUY GOMEZ. Heavens, Doña Sol!
Oh, Doña Sol! Since he is merciless,
Help! Walls and armor come down on us
now!
[He runs to the King.] Leave me my child!
I have but her, O King!
DON CARLOS [*dropping DOÑA SOL's
hand*]. Then yield me up my pris-
oner.
*[The Duke drops his head, and
seems the prey of horrible inde-
cision. Then he looks up at the
portraits with supplicating hands
before them.]*
DON RUY GOMEZ. Oh, now
Have pity on me all of you!
*[He makes a step toward the hiding-
place. DOÑA SOL watching him
anxiously. He turns again to
the portraits.]*
Oh, hide
Your faces! They deter me.
*[He advances with trembling steps
toward his own portrait, then
turns again to the King.]*
Is 't your will?
DON CARLOS. Yes.
*[The Duke raises a trembling hand
toward the spring.]*
DOÑA SOL. O God!
DON RUY GOMEZ. No!
*[He throws himself on his knees be-
fore the King.]*
In pity take my life!
DON CARLOS. Thy niece!

DON RUY GOMEZ [*rising*]. Take her, and
leave me honor, then.
DON CARLOS [*seizing the hand of the
trembling DOÑA SOL*]. Adieu, Duke.
DON RUY GOMEZ. Till we meet again!
*[He watches the King, who retires
slowly with DOÑA SOL. Afterwards he puts his hand on his
dagger.]*
May God
Shield you!
*[He comes back to the front of the
stage panting, and stands motionless, with vacant stare, seeming neither to see nor hear anything, his arms crossed on his
heaving chest. Meanwhile the
King goes out with DOÑA SOL, the
suite following two by two according to their rank. They speak in
a low voice among themselves.]*
[*Aside*]. Whilst thou go 'st joyous from my
house,
O King, my ancient loyalty goes forth
From out my bleeding heart.
*[He raises his head, looks all round,
and sees that he is alone. Then
he takes two swords from a
panoply by the wall, measures
them, and places them on a table.
This done, he goes to the portrait,
touches the spring, and the hid-
den door opens.]*
Come out.
*[HERNANI appears at the door of
the hiding-place. DON RUY
GOMEZ points to the two swords
on the table.]*
Now, choose.
Choose, for Don Carlos has departed now,
And it remains to give me satisfaction.
Choose, and be quick. What, then! trem-
bles thy hand?
HERNANI. A duel! Oh, it cannot be, old
man,
'Twixt us.
DON RUY GOMEZ. Why not? Is it thou
art afraid?
Or that thou art not noble? So or not,
All men who injure me, by Hell, I count
Noble enough to cross their swords with
mine.

HERNANI. Old man —

DON RUY GOMEZ. Come forth, young man, to slay me, else
To be the slain.

HERNANI. To die, ah, yes! Against
My will thyself hast saved me, and my life
Is yours. I bid you take it.

DON RUY GOMEZ. This you wish?
[*To the portraits.*] You see he wills it.
[*To* HERNANI.] This is well. Thy prayer
Now make.

HERNANI. It is to thee, my lord, the last
I make.

DON RUY GOMEZ. Pray to the other
Lord.

HERNANI. No, no,
To thee. Strike me, old man, — dagger or sword, —
Each one for me is good, — but grant me first
One joy supreme. Duke, let me see her ere
I die.

DON RUY GOMEZ. See her!

HERNANI. Or at the least I beg
That you will let me hear her voice once more —
Only this one last time!

DON RUY GOMEZ. Hear her!

HERNANI. Ah, well,
My lord, I understand thy jealousy,
But death already seizes on my youth.
Forgive me. Grant me — tell me that without
Beholding her, if it must be, I yet
May hear her speak, and I will die to-night.
I'll grateful be to hear her. But in peace
I'd calmly die, if thou would'st deign that ere
My soul is freed, it sees once more the soul
That shines so clearly in her eyes. To her
I will not speak. Thou shalt be there to see,
My father, and canst slay me afterwards.

DON RUY GOMEZ [*pointing to the recess still open*]. Oh, saints of Heaven!
Can this recess, then, be
So deep and strong that he has nothing heard?

HERNANI. No, I have nothing heard.

DON RUY GOMEZ. I was compelled
To yield up Doña Sol or thee.

HERNANI. To whom?

DON RUY GOMEZ. The King.

HERNANI. Madman! He loves her.

DON RUY GOMEZ. Loves her! He!

HERNANI. He takes her from us! He our rival is!

DON RUY GOMEZ. Curses be on him!
Vassals! all to horse —
To horse! Let us pursue the ravisher!

HERNANI. Listen! The vengeance that is sure of foot
Makes on its way less noise than this would do.
To thee I do belong. Thou hast the right
To slay me. Wilt thou not employ me first
As the avenger of thy niece's wrongs?
Let me take part in this thy vengeance due;
Grant me this boon, and I will kiss thy feet,
If so must be. Let us together speed
The King to follow. I will be thine arm.
I will avenge thee, Duke, and after-wards
The life that's forfeit thou shalt take.

DON RUY GOMEZ. And then,
As now, thou'lt ready be to die?

HERNANI. Yes, Duke.

DON RUY GOMEZ. By what wilt thou swear this?

HERNANI. My father's head.

DON RUY GOMEZ. Of thine own self wilt thou remember it?

HERNANI [*giving him the horn which he takes from his girdle*]. Listen! Take you this horn, and whatsoe'er
May happen — what the place, or what the hour —
Whenever to thy mind it seems the time
Has come for me to die, blow on this horn
And take no other care; all will be done.

DON RUY GOMEZ [*offering his hand*].
Your hand! [*They press hands.*]
[*To the portraits.*] And all of you are witnesses.

ACT IV

The Tomb, Aix-la-Chapelle. The vaults which enclose the Tomb of Charlemagne at Aix-la-Chapelle. Great arches of Lombard architecture, with semicircular columns, having capitals of birds and flowers. At the right a small bronze door, low and curved. A single lamp suspended from the crown of the vault shows the inscription: CAROLVS MAGNVS. *It is night. One cannot see to the end of the vaults, the eye loses itself in the intricacy of arches, steps, and columns which mingle in the shade.*

[*Enter* Don Carlos, Don Ricardo de Roxas, Count de Casapalma, *lanterns in hand, and wearing large cloaks and slouched hats.*]

Don Ricardo [*hat in hand*]. This is the place.

Don Carlos. Yes, here it is the League
Will meet; they that together in my power
So soon shall be. Oh, it was well, my Lord
Of Trèves th' Elector — it was well of you
To lend this place; dark plots should prosper best
In the dank air of catacombs, and good
It is to sharpen daggers upon tombs.
Yet the stake 's heavy — heads are on the game,
Ye bold assassins, and the end we'll see.
By Heaven, 't was well a sepulcher to choose
For such a business, since the road will be
Shorter for them to traverse.
[*To* Don Ricardo.] Tell me now
How far the subterranean way extends?

Don Ricardo. To the strong fortress.

Don Carlos. Farther than we need.

Don Ricardo. And on the other side it reaches quite
The Monastery of Altenheim.

Don Carlos. Ah, where
Lothaire was overcome by Rodolf. Once
Again, Count, tell me o'er their names and wrongs.

Don Ricardo. Gotha.

Don Carlos. Ah, very well I know why 't is
The brave Duke is conspirator: he wills
For Germany, a German Emperor.

Don Ricardo. Hohenbourg.

Don Carlos. Hohenbourg would better like
With Francis hell, than heaven itself with me.

Don Ricardo. Gil Tellez Giron.

Don Carlos. Castile and our Lady!
The scoundrel! — to be traitor to his king!

Don Ricardo. One evening it is said
that you were found
With Madam Giron. You had just before
Made him a baron; he revenges now
The honor of his dear companion.

Don Carlos. This, then, the reason he revolts 'gainst Spain?
What name comes next?

Don Ricardo. The Reverend Vasquez,
Avila's Bishop.

Don Carlos. Pray does he resent
Dishonor of his wife!

Don Ricardo. Then there is named
Guzman de Lara, who is discontent,
Claiming the collar of your order.

Don Carlos. Ah!
Guzman de Lara! If he only wants
A collar he shall have one.

Don Ricardo. Next the Duke
Of Lutzelbourg. As for his plans, they say —

Don Carlos. Ah! Lutzelbourg is by the head too tall.

Don Ricardo. Juan de Haro — who
Astorga wants.

Don Carlos. These Haros! Always they the headsman's pay
Have doubled.

Don Ricardo. That is all.

Don Carlos. Not by my count.
These make but seven.

Don Ricardo. Oh, I did not name
Some bandits, probably engaged by Trèves
Or France.

Don Carlos. Men without prejudice of course,
Whose ready daggers turn to heaviest pay,
As truly as the needle to the pole.

Don Ricardo. However, I observed
two sturdy ones
Among them, both new comers — one was young,
The other old.

DON CARLOS. Their names?
[DON RICARDO *shrugs his shoulders in sign of ignorance.*]
Their age, then, say?
DON RICARDO. The younger may be twenty.
DON CARLOS. Pity, then.
DON RICARDO. The elder must be sixty, quite.
DON CARLOS. One seems
Too young — the other, over-old; so much
For them the worse 't will be. I will take care —
Myself will help the headsman, be there need.
My sword is sharpened for a traitor's block,
I 'll lend it him if blunt his axe should grow,
And join my own imperial purple on
To piece the scaffold cloth, if it must be
Enlarged that way. But shall I Emperor prove?
DON RICARDO. The College at this hour deliberates.
DON CARLOS. Who knows? Francis the first, perchance, they 'll name,
Or else their Saxon Frederick the Wise.
Ah, Luther, thou art right to blame the times
And scorn such makers-up of royalty,
That own no other rights than gilded ones.
A Saxon heretic! Primate of Trèves,
A libertine! Count Palatine, a fool!
As for Bohemia's king, for me he is.
Princes of Hesse, all smaller than their states!
The young are idiots, and the old debauched,
Of crowns a plenty — but for heads we search
In vain! Council of dwarfs ridiculous,
That I in lion's skin could carry off
Like Hercules; and who of violet robes
Bereft, would show but heads more shallow far
Than Triboulet's. See'st thou I want three votes
Or all is lost, Ricardo? Oh! I 'd give
Toledo, Ghent, and Salamanca too,
Three towns, my friends, I 'd offer to their choice
For their three voices — cities of Castile
And Flanders. Safe I know to take them back
A little later on.
[DON RICARDO *bows low to the King, and puts on his hat.*]
You cover, sir!
DON RICARDO. Sire, you have called me thou [*bowing again*]. And thus I 'm made
Grandee of Spain.
DON CARLOS [*aside*]. Ah, how to piteous scorn
You rouse me! Interested brood devour'd
By mean ambition. Thus across my plans
Yours struggle. Base the court where without shame
The King is plied for honors, and he yields,
Bestowing grandeur on the hungry crew.
[*Musing.*] God only, and the Emperor are great,
Also the Holy Father! For the rest,
The kings and dukes, of what account are they?
DON RICARDO. I trust that they Your Highness will elect.
DON CARLOS. Highness — still Highness! Oh, unlucky chance!
If only King I must remain.
DON RICARDO [*aside*]. By Jove,
Emperor or King, Grandee of Spain I am.
DON CARLOS. When they 've decided who shall be the one
They choose for Emperor of Germany,
What sign is to announce his name?
DON RICARDO. The guns.
A single firing will proclaim the Duke
Of Saxony is chosen Emperor;
Two if 't is Francis; for Your Highness three.
DON CARLOS. And Doña Sol! I 'm crossed on every side.
If, Count, by turn of luck, I 'm Emperor made,
Go seek her; she by Cæsar might be won.
DON RICARDO [*smiling*]. Your Highness pleases.
DON CARLOS [*haughtily*]. On that subject peace!
I have not yet inquired what 's thought of me.
But tell me when will it be truly known
Who is elected?

DON RICARDO. In an hour or so,
At latest.
DON CARLOS. Ah, three votes; and only
three!
But first this trait'rous rabble we must
crush,
And then we'll see to whom the Empire
falls,
[*He counts on his fingers and
stamps his foot.*]
Always by three too few! Ah, they hold
power.
Yet did Cornelius know all long ago:
In Heaven's ocean thirteen stars he saw
Coming full sail toward mine, all from the
north.
Empire for me — let's on! But it is said,
On other hand, that Jean Trithème Francis
Predicted! Clearer should I see my fate
Had I some armament the prophecy
To help. The sorcerer's predictions come
Most true when a good army — with its
guns
And lances, horse and foot, and martial
strains,
Ready to lead the way where Fate alone
Might stumble — plays the midwife's part
to bring
Fulfillment of prediction. That's worth
more
Than our Cornelius Agrippa or
Trithème. He, who by force of arms ex-
pounds
His system, and with sharpen'd point of
lance
Can edge his words, and uses soldiers'
swords
To level rugged fortune — shapes events
At his own will to match the prophecy.
Poor fools! who with proud eyes and
haughty mien
Only look straight to Empire, and declare
"It is my right!" They need great guns in
files
Whose burning breath melts towns; and
soldiers, ships,
And horsemen. These they need their ends
to gain
O'er trampled peoples. Pshaw! At the
crossroads
Of human life, where one leads to a throne,
Another to perdition, they will pause

In indecision, — scarce three steps will
take
Uncertain of themselves, and in their
doubt
Fly to the necromancer for advice
Which road to take.
[*To* DON RICARDO.] Go now, 't is near the
time
The trait'rous crew will meet. Give me the
key.
DON RICARDO [*giving key of tomb*]. Sire,
't was the guardian of the tomb, the
Count
De Limbourg, who to me confided it,
And has done everything to pleasure you.
DON CARLOS. Do all, quite all that I
commanded you.
DON RICARDO [*bowing*]. Highness, I go
at once.
DON CARLOS. The signal, then,
That I await is cannon firing thrice?
[DON RICARDO *bows and exit.*
DON CARLOS *falls into a deep
reverie, his arms crossed, his
head drooping; afterwards he
raises it, and turns to the tomb.*]
Forgive me, Charlemagne! Oh, this lonely
vault
Should echo only unto solemn words.
Thou must be angry at the babble vain
Of our ambition at your monument.
Here Charlemagne rests! How can the
somber tomb
Without a rifting spasm hold such dust!
And art thou truly here, colossal power,
Creator of the world? And canst thou now
Crouch down from all thy majesty and
might?
Ah, 't is a spectacle to stir the soul
What Europe was, and what by thee 't was
made.
Mighty construction with two men su-
preme
Elected chiefs to whom born kings submit.
States, duchies, kingdoms, marquisates
and fiefs —
By right hereditary most are ruled,
But nations find a friend sometimes in
Pope
Or Cæsar; and one chance another chance
Corrects; thus even balance is maintained
And order opens out. The cloth-of-gold

Electors, and the scarlet cardinals.
The double, sacred senate, unto which
Earth bends, are but paraded outward
    show,
God's fiat rules it all. One day He wills
A thought, a want, should burst upon the
    world,
Then grow and spread, and mix with every-
    thing,
Possess some man, win hearts, and delve a
    groove
Though kings may trample on it, and may
    seek
To gag; — only that they some morn may
    see
At diet, conclave, this the scorned idea,
That they had spurned, all suddenly ex-
    pand
And soar above their heads, bearing the
    globe
In hand, or on the brow tiara. Pope
And Emperor, they on earth are all in all,
A mystery supreme dwells in them both,
And Heaven's might, which they still rep-
    resent,
Feasts them with kings and nations, hold-
    ing them
Beneath its thunder-cloud, the while they
    sit
At table with the world served out for
    food.
Alone they regulate all things on earth,
Just as the mower manages his field.
All rule and power are theirs. Kings at
    the door
Inhale the odor of their savory meats.
Look through the window, watchful on
    tiptoe,
But weary of the scene. The common
    world
Below them groups itself on ladder-rungs.
They make and all unmake. One can re-
    lease,
The other surely strike. The one is Truth,
The other Might. Each to himself is law,
And is, because he is. When — equals they
The one in purple, and the other swathed
In white like winding-sheet — when they
    come out
From sanctuary, the dazzled multitude
Look with wild terror on these halves of
    God,

The Pope and Emperor. Emperor! oh, to
    be
Thus great! Oh, anguish, not to be this
    Power
When beats the heart with dauntless
    courage fill'd!
Oh, happy he who sleeps within this tomb!
How great, and oh! how fitted for his time!
The Pope and Emperor were more than
    men,
In them two Romes in mystic Hymen joined
Prolific were, giving new form and soul
Unto the human race, refounding realms
And nations, shaping thus a Europe new,
And both remoulding with their hands the
    bronze
Remaining of the great old Roman world.
What destiny! And yet 't is here he lies?
Is all so little that we come to this!
What then? To have been Prince and
    Emperor,
And King — to have been sword, and also
    law;
Giant, with Germany for pedestal —
For title Cæsar — Charlemagne for name:
A greater to have been than Hannibal
Or Attila — as great as was the world.
Yet all rests here! For Empire strive and
    strain
And see the dust that makes an Emperor!
Cover the earth with tumult, and with
    noise
Know you that one day only will remain —
Oh, madd'ning thought — a stone! For
    sounding name
Triumphant, but some letters 'graved to
    serve
For little children to learn spelling by.
How high soe'er ambition made thee soar,
Behold the end of all! Oh, Empire, power,
What matters all to me! I near it now
And like it well. Some voice declares to
    me
Thine — thine — it will be thine. Heavens,
    were it so!
To mount at once the spiral height su-
    preme
And be alone — the keystone of the arch,
With states beneath, one o'er the other
    ranged,
And kings for mats to wipe one's sandal'd
    feet!

To see 'neath kings the feudal families,
Margraves and cardinals, and doges —
        dukes,
Then bishops, abbés — chiefs of ancient
        clans,
Great barons — then the soldier class and
        clerks,
And know yet farther off — in the deep
        shade
At bottom of th' abyss there is Mankind —
That is to say a crowd, a sea of men,
A tumult — cries, with tears, and bitter
        laugh
Sometimes. The wail wakes up and scares
        the earth
And reaches us with leaping echoes, and
With trumpet tone. Oh, citizens, oh, men!
The swarm that from the high church
        towers seems now
To sound the tocsin!
[*Musing.*] Wondrous human base
Of nations, bearing on your shoulders
        broad
The mighty pyramid that has two poles,
The living waves that ever straining hard
Balance and shake it as they heave and roll,
Make all change place, and on the highest
        heights
Make stagger thrones, as if they were but
        stools.
So sure is this, that ceasing vain debates
Kings look to Heaven! Kings look down
        below,
Look at the people! — Restless ocean, there
Where nothing's cast that does not shake
        the whole;
The sea that rends a throne, and rocks a
        tomb —
A glass in which kings rarely look but ill.
Ah, if upon this gloomy sea they gazed
Sometimes, what Empires in its depths
        they'd find!
Great vessels wrecked that by its ebb and
        flow
Are stirr'd — that wearied it — known now
        no more!
To govern this — to mount so high if
        called,
Yet know myself to be but mortal man!
To see the abyss — if not that moment
        struck
With dizziness bewildering every sense.

Oh, moving pyramid of states and kings
With apex narrow, — woe to timid step!
What shall restrain me? If I fail when there
Feeling my feet upon the trembling world,
Feeling alive the palpitating earth,
Then when I have between my hands the
        globe
Have I the strength alone to hold it fast,
To be an Emperor? O God, 't was hard
And difficult to play the kingly part.
Certes, no man is rarer than the one
Who can enlarge his soul to duly meet
Great Fortune's smiles, and still increasing
        gifts.
But I! Who is it that shall be my guide,
My counselor, and make me great?
[*Falls on his knees before the tomb.*] 'T is
        thou,
Oh, Charlemagne! And since 't is God for
        whom
All obstacles dissolve, who takes us now
And puts us face to face — from this
        tomb's depths
Endow me with sublimity and strength.
Let me be great enough to see the truth
On every side. Show me how small the
        world
I dare not measure — me this Babel show
Where, from the hind to Cæsar mounting
        up,
Each one, complaisant with himself, re-
        gards
The next with scorn that is but half re-
        strained.
Teach me the secret of thy conquests all,
And how to rule. And show me certainly
Whether to punish, or to pardon, be
The worthier thing to do.
Is it not fact
That in his solitary bed sometimes
A mighty shade is wakened from his sleep,
Aroused by noise and turbulence on earth;
That suddenly his tomb expands itself,
And bursts its doors — and in the night
        flings forth
A flood of light? If this be true, indeed,
Say, Emperor! what can after Charlemagne
Another do! Speak, though thy sovereign
        breath
Should cleave this brazen door. Or rather
        now
Let me thy sanctuary enter lone!

Let me behold thy veritable face,
And not repulse me with a freezing breath.
Upon thy stony pillow elbows lean,
And let us talk. Yes, with prophetic voice
Tell me of things which make the forehead
    pale,
And clear eyes mournful. Speak, and do not
    blind
Thine awe-struck son, for doubtlessly thy
    tomb
Is full of light. Or if thou wilt not speak,
Let me make study in the solemn peace
Of thee, as of a world, thy measure take,
O giant, for there's nothing here below
So great as thy poor ashes. Let them teach,
Failing thy spirit.
    [*He puts the key in the lock.*] Let us enter
    now.
[*He recoils.*] O God, if he should really
    whisper me!
If he be there and walks with noiseless tread,
And I come back with hair in moments
    bleached!
I'll do it still.   [*Sound of footsteps.*]
Who comes? who dares disturb
Besides myself the dwelling of such dead!
                [*The sound comes nearer.*]
My murderers! I forgot! Now, enter we.
    [*He opens the door of the tomb,
    which shuts upon him.*]

[*Enter several men walking softly, disguised
    by large cloaks and hats. They take
    each others' hands, going from one to
    another and speaking in a low tone.*]

FIRST CONSPIRATOR [*who alone carries
    a lighted torch*]. Ad augusta.
SECOND CONSPIRATOR. Per angusta.
FIRST CONSPIRATOR. The saints
Shield us.
    THIRD CONSPIRATOR. The dead assist
    us.
FIRST CONSPIRATOR. Guard us, God!
                [*Noise in the shade.*]
FIRST CONSPIRATOR. Who's there?
A VOICE. Ad augusta.
SECOND CONSPIRATOR. Per angusta.

[*Enter fresh Conspirators — noise of
    footsteps.*]

FIRST CONSPIRATOR [*to* THIRD]. See!
there is some one still to come.

THIRD CONSPIRATOR. Who's there?
VOICE [*in the darkness*]. Ad augusta.
THIRD CONSPIRATOR. Per angusta.

[*Enter more Conspirators, who exchange
    signs with their hands with the others.*]

FIRST CONSPIRATOR. 'T is well.
All now are here. Gotha, to you it falls
To state the case. Friends, darkness waits
    for light
    [*The Conspirators sit in a half-
    circle on the tombs. The* FIRST
    CONSPIRATOR *passes before them,
    and from his torch each one
    lights a wax taper which he holds
    in his hand. Then the* FIRST
    CONSPIRATOR *seats himself in
    silence on a tomb a little higher
    than the others in the center of
    the circle.*]
DUKE OF GOTHA [*rising*]. My friends!
This Charles of Spain, by mother's
    side
A foreigner, aspires to mount the throne
Of Holy Empire.
    FIRST CONSPIRATOR. But for him the
    grave.
DUKE OF GOTHA [*throwing down his
    light and crushing it with his foot*].
    Let it be with his head as with this
    flame.
ALL. So be it.
FIRST CONSPIRATOR. Death unto him.
DUKE OF GOTHA. Let him die.
ALL. Let him be slain.
DON JUAN DE HARO. German his father
    was.
DUKE DE LUTZELBOURG. His mother
    Spanish.
DUKE OF GOTHA. Thus you see that he
Is no more one than other. Let him die.
A CONSPIRATOR. Suppose th' Electors
    at this very hour
Declare him Emperor!
    FIRST CONSPIRATOR. Him! oh, never
    him!
DON GIL TELLEZ GIRON. What signifies?
Let us strike off the head,
The Crown will fall.
    FIRST CONSPIRATOR. But if to him be-
    longs
The Holy Empire, he becomes so great

And so august, that only God's own hand
Can reach him.
DUKE OF GOTHA. All the better reason
    why
He dies before such power august he gains.
FIRST CONSPIRATOR. He shall not be
    elected.
ALL. Not for him
The Empire.
FIRST CONSPIRATOR. Now, how many
    hands will't take
To put him in his shroud?
ALL. One is enough.
FIRST CONSPIRATOR. How many strokes
    to reach his heart?
ALL. But one.
FIRST CONSPIRATOR. Who, then, will
    strike?
ALL. All! All!
FIRST CONSPIRATOR. The victim is
A traitor proved. They would an Emperor
    choose,
We've a high-priest to make. Let us draw
    lots.
    [All the Conspirators write their
    names on their tablets, tear out
    the leaf, roll it up, and one after
    another throw them into the urn
    on one of the tombs.]
Now, let us pray.   [All kneel.]
Oh, may the chosen one
Believe in God, and like a Roman strike,
Die as a Hebrew would, and brave alike
The wheel and burning pincers, laugh at
    rack,
And fire, and wooden horse, and be re-
    signed
To kill and die. He might have all to do.
    [He draws a parchment from the
    urn.]
ALL. What name?
FIRST CONSPIRATOR [in low voice]. Her-
    nani!
HERNANI [coming out from the crowd of
    Conspirators]. I have won, yes,
    won!
I hold thee fast! Thee I've so long pur-
    sued
With vengeance.
DON RUY GOMEZ [piercing through the
    crowd and taking HERNANI aside].
    Yield — oh, yield this right to me.

HERNANI. Not for my life! Oh, signor,
    grudge me not
This stroke of fortune — 't is the first I've
    known.
DON RUY GOMEZ. You nothing have!
    I'll give you houses, lands,
A hundred thousand vassals shall be yours
In my three hundred villages, if you
But yield the right to strike to me.
HERNANI. No — no.
DUKE OF GOTHA. Old man, thy arm
    would strike less sure a blow.
DON RUY GOMEZ. Back! I have strength
    of soul, if not of arm.
Judge not the sword by the mere scab-
    bard's rust.
[To HERNANI.] You do belong to me.
HERNANI. My life is yours,
As his belongs to me.
DON RUY GOMEZ [drawing the horn from
    his girdle]. I yield her up,
And 'will return the horn.
HERNANI [trembling]. What life! My life
And Doña Sol! No, I my vengeance
    choose.
I have my father to revenge — yet more,
Perchance I am inspired by God in this.
DON RUY GOMEZ. I yield thee Her —
    and give thee back the horn!
HERNANI. No!
DON RUY GOMEZ. Boy, reflect.
HERNANI. Oh, Duke, leave me my prey.
DON RUY GOMEZ. My curses on you for
    depriving me
Of this my joy.
FIRST CONSPIRATOR [to HERNANI]. Oh,
    brother, ere they can
Elect him — 't would be well this very
    night
To watch for Charles.
HERNANI. Fear nought, I know the way
To kill a man.
FIRST CONSPIRATOR. May every treason
    fall
On traitor, and may God be with you now.
We Counts and Barons, let us take the
    oath
That if he fall, yet slay not, we go on
And strike by turn unflinching till Charles
    dies.
ALL [drawing their swords]. Let us all
    swear.

DUKE OF GOTHA [*to* FIRST CONSPIRATOR].
My brother, let's decide
On what we swear.
DON RUY GOMEZ [*taking his sword by
the point and raising it above his
head*]. By this same cross,
ALL [*raising their swords*]. And this
That he must quickly die impenitent. ¹
[*They hear a cannon fired afar off.
All pause and are silent. The
door of the tomb half opens, and
DON CARLOS appears at the
threshold. A second gun is fired,
then a third. He opens wide the
door and stands erect and motionless without advancing.*]
DON CARLOS. Fall back, ye gentlemen
— the Emperor hears.
[*All the lights are simultaneously
extinguished. A profound silence. DON CARLOS advances a
step in the darkness, so dense,
that the silent, motionless Conspirators can scarcely be distinguished.*]
Silence and night! From darkness sprung,
the swarm
Into the darkness plunges back again!
Think ye this scene is like a passing dream,
And that I take you, now your lights are
quenched,
For men's stone figures seated on their
tombs?
Just now, my statues, you had voices loud,
Raise, then, your drooping heads, for
Charles the Fifth
Is here. Strike. Move a pace or two and
show
You dare. But no, 't is not in you to dare.
Your flaming torches, blood-red 'neath
these vaults,
My breath extinguished; but now turn
your eyes
Irresolute, and see that, if I thus
Put out the many, I can light still more.
[*He strikes the iron key on the
bronze door of the tomb. At the
sound all the depths of the cavern
are filled with soldiers bearing
torches and halberts. At their
head the DUKE D'ALCALA, the
MARQUIS D'ALMUÑAN, etc.*]

Come on, my falcons! I've the nest — the
prey.
[*To Conspirators.*] I can make blaze of
light, 't is my turn now,
Behold!
[*To the Soldiers.*] Advance — for flagrant
is the crime.
HERNANI [*looking at the Soldiers*]. Ah.
well! At first I thought 't was
Charlemagne,
Alone he seemed so great — but after all
'T is only Charles the Fifth.'
DON CARLOS [*to the DUKE D'ALCALA*].
Come, Constable
Of Spain.
[*To MARQUIS D'ALMUÑAN.*] And you Cas-
tilian Admiral,
Disarm them all.
[*The Conspirators are surrounded
and disarmed.*]
DON RICARDO [*hurrying in and bowing
almost to the ground*]. Your Majesty!
DON CARLOS. Alcalde
I make you of the palace.
DON RICARDO [*again bowing*]. Two
Electors,
To represent the Golden Chamber, come
To offer to Your Sacred Majesty
Congratulations now.
DON CARLOS. Let them come forth.
[*Aside to DON RICARDO.*] The Doña Sol.
[RICARDO *bows and exit.*]

[*Enter with flambeaux and flourish of
trumpets the KING OF BOHEMIA and the
DUKE OF BAVARIA, both wearing cloth
of gold, and with crowns on their heads.
Numerous followers. German nobles
carrying the banner of the Empire,
the double-headed Eagle, with the
escutcheon of Spain in the middle of it.
The Soldiers divide, forming lines between which the Electors pass to the
Emperor, to whom they bow low. He
returns the salutation by raising his
hat.*]

DUKE OF BAVARIA. Most Sacred
Majesty
Charles, of the Romans King, and Emperor,
The Empire of the world is in your hands —
Yours is the throne to which each king
aspires!

The Saxon Frederick was elected first,
But he judged you more worthy, and de-
clined.
Now, then, receive the crown and globe,
    O King —
The Holy Empire doth invest you now,
Arms with the sword, and you indeed are
    great.
Don Carlos. The College I will thank
    on my return.
But go, my brother of Bohemia,
And you, Bavarian cousin. — Thanks; but
    now
I do dismiss you — I shall go myself.
King of Bohemia. Oh! Charles, our
    ancestors were friends. My sire
Loved yours, and their two fathers were
    two friends —
So young! exposed to varied fortunes! say,
Oh, Charles, may I be ranked a very chief
Among thy brothers? I cannot forget
I knew you as a little child.
Don Carlos. Ah, well —
King of Bohemia, you presume too much.
    [He gives him his hand to kiss, also
       the Duke of Bavaria, both
       bow low.]
Depart.
    [Exeunt the two Electors with
       their followers.]
The Crowd. Long live the Emperor!
Don Carlos [aside]. So 't is mine,
All things have helped, and I am Em-
    peror—
By the refusal, though, of Frederick
Surnamed the Wise!

    [Enter Doña Sol led by Ricardo.]

Doña Sol. What, soldiers! — Emperor!
Hernani! Heaven, what an unlooked-for
    chance!
Hernani. Ah! Doña Sol!
Don Ruy Gomez [aside to Hernani].
    She has not seen me.
    [Doña Sol runs to Hernani, who
       makes her recoil by a look of dis-
       dain.]
Hernani. Madam!
Doña Sol [drawing the dagger from her
    bosom]. I still his poniard have!
Hernani [taking her in his arms]. My
    dearest one!

Don Carlos. Be silent all.
    [To the Conspirators.] Is 't you remorseless
      are?
I need to give the world a lesson now,
The Lara of Castile, and Gotha, you
Of Saxony — all — all — what were your
    plans
Just now? I bid you speak.
Hernani. Quite simple, Sire,
The thing, and we can briefly tell it you.
We 'graved the sentence on Belshazzar's
    wall.
    [He takes out a poniard and
       brandishes it.]
We render unto Cæsar Cæsar's due.
Don Carlos. Silence!
    [To Don Ruy Gomez.] And you! You too
      are traitor, Silva!
Don Ruy Gomez. Which of us two is
    traitor, Sire?
Hernani [turning toward the Conspira-
    tors]. Our heads
And Empire — all that he desires he has.
    [To the Emperor.] The mantle blue of kings
      encumbered you;
The purple better suits — it shows not
    blood.
Don Carlos [to Don Ruy Gomez].
    Cousin of Silva, this is felony,
Attainting your baronial rank. Think well,
Don Ruy — high treason!
Don Ruy Gomez. Kings like Roderick
Count Julians make.
Don Carlos [to the Duke d'Alcala].
    Seize only those who seem
The nobles, — for the rest! —
    [Don Ruy Gomez, the Duke de
      Lutzelbourg, the Duke of
      Gotha, Don Juan de Haro,
      Don Guzman de Lara, Don
      Tellez Giron, the Baron of
      Hohenbourg separate them-
      selves from the group of Con-
      spirators, among whom is Her-
      nani. The Duke d'Alcala
      surrounds them with guards.]
Doña Sol [aside]. Ah, he is saved!
Hernani [coming from among the Con-
    spirators]. I claim to be included!
[To Don Carlos.] Since to this
It comes, the question of the axe — that
    now

Hernani, humble churl, beneath thy feet
Unpunished goes, because his brow is not
At level with thy sword — because one
    must
Be great to die, I rise. God, who gives
    power,
And gives to thee the scepter, made me
    Duke
Of Segorbe and Cardona, Marquis too
Of Monroy, Albaterra's Count, of Gor
Viscount, and Lord of many places, more
Than I can name. Juan of Aragon
Am I, Grand Master of Avis — the son
In exile born, of murder'd father slain
By king's decree, King Charles, which me
    proscribed,
Thus death 'twixt us is family affair;
You have the scaffold — we the poniard
    hold.
Since Heaven a duke has made me, and
    exile
A mountaineer, — since all in vain I've
    sharpen'd
Upon the hills my sword, and in the tor-
    rents
Have tempered it.   [He puts on his hat.]
[To the Conspirators.] Let us be covered
    now,
Us the Grandees of Spain.   [They cover.]
[To Don Carlos.] Our heads, O King,
Have right to fall before thee covered
    thus.
[To the Prisoners.] Silva, and Haro —
    Lara — men of rank
And race make room for Juan of Ara-
    gon.
Give me my place, ye dukes and counts —
    my place.
[To the Courtiers and Guards.] King, heads-
    men, varlets — Juan of Aragon
Am I. If all your scaffolds are too small
Make new ones.
                [He joins the group of nobles.]
    Doña Sol. Heavens!
    Don Carlos. I had forgotten quite
This history.
    Hernani. But they who bleed remember
Far better. Th' evil that wrong-doer thus
So senselessly forgets, forever stirs
Within the outraged heart.
    Don Carlos. Therefore, enough
For me to bear this title, that I'm son

Of sires, whose power dealt death to an-
    cestors
Of yours!
    Doña Sol [falling on her knees before the
        Emperor]. Oh, pardon — pardon!
    Mercy, Sire,
Be pitiful, or strike us both, I pray,
For he my lover is, my promised spouse,
In him it is alone I live — I breathe;
Oh, Sire, in mercy us together slay.
Trembling — oh, Majesty! — I trail my-
    self
Before your sacred knees. I love him,
    Sire,
And he is mine — as Empire is your
    own.
Have pity!
        [Don Carlos looks at her without
            moving.]
Oh, what thought absorbs you?
    Don Carlos. Cease.
Rise — Duchess of Segorbe — Marchioness
Of Monroy — Countess Albaterra —
    and —
[To Hernani.] Thine other names, Don
    Juan?
    Hernani. Who speaks thus,
The King?
    Don Carlos. No, 't is the Emperor.
    Doña Sol. Just Heav'n!
    Don Carlos [pointing to her]. Duke
    Juan, take your wife.
    Hernani [his eyes raised to heaven,
        Doña Sol in his arms]. Just God!
    Don Carlos [to Don Ruy Gomez]. My
    cousin,
I know the pride of your nobility,
But Aragon with Silva well may mate.
    Don Ruy Gomez [bitterly]. 'T is not a
    question of nobility.
    Hernani [looking with love on Doña Sol
        and still holding her in his arms].
    My deadly hate is vanishing away.
                [Throws away his dagger.]
    Don Ruy Gomez [aside, and looking at
        them]. Shall I betray myself? Oh,
    no, — my grief,
My foolish love would make them pity
    cast
Upon my venerable head. Old man
And Spaniard! Let the hidden fire con-
    sume,

And suffer still in secret. Let heart break
But cry not; — they would laugh at
    thee.
Doña Sol [still in Hernani's arms].
    My Duke!
Hernani. Nothing my soul holds now
    but love!
Doña Sol. Oh, joy!
Don Carlos [aside, his hand in his
    bosom]. Stifle thyself, young heart
    so full of flame,
Let reign again the better thoughts which
    thou
So long hast troubled. Henceforth let thy
    loves,
Thy mistresses, alas! — be Germany
And Flanders — [looking at the banner]
    Spain.
The Emperor is like
The Eagle his companion, in the place
Of heart, there's but a 'scutcheon.
Hernani. Cæsar you!
Don Carlos. Don Juan, of your ancient
    name and race
Your soul is worthy [pointing to Doña
    Sol] — worthy e'en of her.
Kneel, Duke.
    [Hernani kneels. Don Carlos
    unfastens his own Golden Fleece
    and puts it on Hernani's neck.]
Receive this collar.
    [Don Carlos draws his sword and
    strikes him three times on the
    shoulder.]
Faithful be,
For by St. Stephen now I make thee
    Knight.
    [He raises and embraces him.]
Thou hast a collar softer and more
    choice;
That which is wanting to my rank su-
    preme, —
The arms of loving woman, loved by
    thee.
Thou wilt be happy — I am Emperor.
[To Conspirators.] Sirs, I forget your names.
    Anger and hate
I will forget. Go — go — I pardon you.
This is the lesson that the world much
    needs.

The Conspirators. Glory to Charles!
Don Ruy Gomez [to Don Carlos]. I
    only suffer, then!
Don Carlos. And I!
Don Ruy Gomez. But I have not like
    Majesty
Forgiven!
Hernani. Who is't has worked this
    wondrous change?
All, Nobles, Soldiers, Conspirators.
    Honor to Charles the Fifth, and
    Germany!
Don Carlos [turning to the tomb].
    Honor to Charlemagne! Leave us
    now together.
    [Exeunt all. Don Carlos, alone,
    bends toward the tomb.]
Art thou content with me, O Charle-
    magne!
Have I the kingship's littleness stripped
    off?
Become as Emperor another man?
Can I Rome's miter add unto my helm?
Have I the right the fortunes of the world
To sway? Have I a steady foot that safe
Can tread the path, by Vandal ruins
    strewed,
Which thou has beaten by thine armies
    vast?
Have I my candle lighted at thy flame?
Did I interpret right the voice that spake
Within this tomb? Ah, I was lost — alone
Before an Empire — a wide howling world
That threatened and conspired! There
    were the Danes
To punish, and the Holy Father's self
To compensate — with Venice — Soliman,
Francis, and Luther — and a thousand
    dirks
Gleaming already in the shade — snares —
    rocks;
And countless foes; 'a score of nations
    each
Of which might serve to awe a score of
    kings.
Things ripe, all pressing to be done at
    once.
I cried to thee — with what shall I begin?
And thou didst answer — Son, by clem-
    ency!

ACT V

Saragossa. A terrace of the palace of Aragon. At the back a flight of steps leading to the garden. At the right and left, doors on to a terrace which shows at the back of the stage a balustrade surmounted by a double row of Moorish arches, above and through which are seen the palace gardens, fountains in the shade, shrubberies and moving lights, and the Gothic and Arabic arches of the palace illuminated. It is night. Trumpets afar off are heard. Masks and Dominoes, either singly or in groups, cross the terrace here and there. At the front of the stage a group of young lords, their masks in their hands, laugh and chat noisily.

[*Enter* DON SANCHO SANCHEZ DE ZUÑIGA, COUNT DE MONTERET, DON MATIAS CENTURION, MARQUIS D'ALMUÑAN, DON RICARDO DE ROXAS, COUNT DE CASAPALMA, DON FRANCISCO DE SOTOMAYOR, COUNT DE VALALCAZAR, DON GARCIA SUAREZ DE CARBAJAL, COUNT DE PENALVER.]

DON GARCIA. Now to the bride long life
— and joy — I say!
DON MATIAS [*looking to the balcony*]. All
Saragossa at its windows shows.
DON GARCIA. And they do well. A
torchlight wedding ne'er
Was seen more gay than this, nor lovelier
night,
Nor handsomer married pair.
DON MATIAS. Kind Emp'ror!
DON SANCHO. When we went with him
in the dark that night
Seeking adventure, Marquis, who'd have
thought
How it would end?
DON RICARDO [*interrupting*]. I, too, was
there. [*To the others.*] Now, list.
Three gallants, one a bandit, his head due
Unto the scaffold; then a duke, a king,
Adoring the same woman, all laid siege
At the same time. The onset made — who
won?
It was the bandit.
DON FRANCISCO. Nothing strange in
that,
For love and fortune, in all other lands
As well as Spain, are sport of the cogg'd
dice.
It is the rogue who wins.
DON RICARDO. My fortune grew
In seeing the love-making. First a count
And then grandee, and next an alcalde
At court. My time was well spent, though
without
One knowing it.
DON SANCHO. Your secret, sir, appears
To be the keeping close upon the heels
O' the King.
DON RICARDO. And showing that my
conduct's worth
Reward.
DON GARCIA. And by a chance you
profited.
DON MATIAS. What has become of the
old Duke? Has he
His coffin ordered?
DON SANCHO. Marquis, jest not thus
At him! For he a haughty spirit has;
And this old man loved well the Doña Sol.
His sixty years had turned his hair to gray,
One day has bleached it.
DON GARCIA. Not again, they say,
Has he been seen in Saragossa.
DON SANCHO. Well?
Wouldst thou that to the bridal he should
bring
His coffin?
DON FRANCISCO. What's the Emperor
doing now?
DON SANCHO. The Emperor is out of
sorts just now,
Luther annoys him.
DON RICARDO. Luther! — subject fine
For care and fear! Soon would I finish him
With but four men-at-arms!
DON MATIAS. And Soliman
Makes him dejected.
DON GARCIA. Luther — Soliman —
Neptune — the devil — Jupiter! What are
They all to me? The women are most
fair,
The masquerade is splendid, and I've said
A hundred foolish things!
DON SANCHO. Behold you now
The chief thing.
DON RICARDO. Garcia's not far wrong,
I say,
Not the same man am I on festal days.

When I put on the mask in truth I think
Another head it gives me.
Don Sancho [apart to Don Matias].
Pity 't is
That all days are not festivals!
Don Francisco. Are those
Their rooms?
Don Garcia [with a nod of his head].
Arrive they will, no doubt, full soon.
Don Francisco. Dost think so?
Don Garcia. Most undoubtedly!
Don Francisco. 'T is well.
The bride is lovely!
Don Ricardo. What an Emperor!
The rebel chief, Hernani, to be pardoned —
Wearing the Golden Fleece! and married
too!
Ah, if the Emperor had been by me
Advised, the gallant should have had a
bed
Of stone, the lady one of down.
Don Sancho [aside to Don Matias].
How well
I'd like with my good sword this lord to
smash,
A lord made up of tinsel coarsely joined;
Pourpoint of count filled out with bailiff's
soul!
Don Ricardo [drawing near]. What are
you saying?
Don Matias [aside to Don Sancho].
Count, no quarrel here!
[To Don Ricardo.] He was reciting one of
Petrarch's sonnets
Unto his lady love.
Don Garcia. Have you not seen
Among the flowers and women, and dresses
gay
Of many hues, a figure specter-like,
Whose domino all black, upright against
A balustrade, seems like a spot upon
The festival?
Don Ricardo. Yes, by my faith!
Don Garcia. Who is 't?
Don Ricardo. By height and mien I
judge that it must be —
The Admiral — the Don Prancasio.
Don Franciso. Oh, no.
Don Garcia. He has not taken off his
mask.
Don Francisco. There is no need; it is
the Duke de Soma,

Who likes to be observed. 'T is nothing
more.
Don Ricardo. No; the Duke spoke to
me.
Don Garcia. Who, then, can be
This Mask? But see — he's here.
[Enter a Black Domino, who slowly crosses
the back of the stage. All turn and
watch him without his appearing to
notice them.]
Don Sancho. If the dead walk,
That is their step.
Don Garcia [approaching the Black
Domino]. Most noble Mask —
[The Black Domino stops and
turns. Garcia recoils.]
I swear,
Good sirs, that I saw flame shine in his eyes.
Don Sancho. If he's the devil, he'll
find one he can
Address.
[He goes to the Black Domino, who
is still motionless.]
Ho, Demon! Comest thou from hell?
The Mask. I come not thence — 't is
thither that I go.
[He continues his walk and disap-
pears at the balustrade of the
staircase. All watch him with a
look of horrified dismay.]
Don Matias. Sepulchral is his voice,
as can be heard.
Don Garcia. Pshaw! What would
frighten elsewhere, at a ball
We laugh at.
Don Sancho. Silly jesting 't is!
Don Garcia. Indeed,
If Lucifer is come to see us dance,
Waiting for lower regions, let us dance!
Don Sancho. Of course it's some buf-
foonery.
Don Matias. We'll know
To-morrow.
Don Sancho [to Don Matias]. Look
now what becomes of him,
I pray you!
Don Matias [at the balustrade of the
terrace]. Down the steps he's gone.
That's all.
Don Sancho. A pleasant jester he!
[Musing.] 'T is strange.

Don Garcia [to lady passing]. Marquise,
Let us pray dance this time.
　　[He bows and offers his hand.]
The Lady. You know, dear sir,
My husband will my dances with you all
Count up.
Don Garcia. All the more reason.
Pleased is he
To count, it seems, and it amuses him.
He calculates — we dance.
　　[The lady gives her hand. Exeunt.]
Don Sancho [thoughtfully]. In truth,
't is strange!
Don Matias. Behold the married pair!
Now, silence all!

[Enter Hernani and Doña Sol hand in
hand. Doña Sol in magnificent bridal
dress. Hernani in black velvet and with
the Golden Fleece hanging from his
neck. Behind them a crowd of Masks
and of ladies and gentlemen who form
their retinue. Two halberdiers in rich
liveries follow them, and four pages
precede them. Every one makes way for
them and bows as they approach. Flourish of trumpets.]

Hernani [saluting]. Dear friends!
Don Ricardo [advancing and bowing].
Your Excellency's happiness
Makes ours.
Don Francisco [looking at Doña Sol].
Now, by St. James, 't is Venus' self
That he is leading.
Don Matias. Happiness is his!
Don Sancho [to Don Matias]. 'T is late
now, let us leave.
　　[All salute the married pair and
retire — some by the door, others
by the stairway at the back.]
Hernani [escorting them]. Adieu!
Don Sancho [who has remained to the last,
and pressing his hand]. Be happy!
　　[Exit Don Sancho. Hernani and
Doña Sol remain alone. The
sound of voices grows fainter and
fainter till it ceases altogether.
During the early part of the following scene the sound of trumpets grows fainter, and the lights
by degrees are extinguished —
till night and silence prevail.]

Doña Sol. At last they all are gone.
Hernani [seeking to draw her to his arms].
Dear love!
Doña Sol [drawing back a little]. Is't
late? —
At least to me it seems so.
Hernani. Angel, dear,
Time ever drags till we together are.
Doña Sol. This noise has wearied me.
Is it not true,
Dear lord, that all this mirth but stifling is
To happiness?
Hernani. Thou sayest truly, love,
For happiness is serious, and asks
For hearts of bronze on which to 'grave
　　itself.
Pleasure alarms it, flinging to it flowers;
Its smile is nearer tears than mirth.
Doña Sol. Thy smile's
Like daylight in thine eyes.
[Hernani seeks to lead her to the door.] Oh,
　　presently.
Hernani. I am thy slave; yes, linger if
　　thou wilt,
Whate'er thou dost is well. I'll laugh and
　　sing
If thou desirest that it should be so.
Bid the volcano stifle flame, and 't will
Close up its gulfs, and on its sides grow
　　flowers,
And grasses green.
Doña Sol. How good you are to me,
My heart's Hernani!
Hernani. Madam, what name's that?
I pray in pity speak it not again!
Thou call'st to mind forgotten things. I
　　know
That he existed formerly in dreams,
Hernani, he whose eyes flashed like a
　　sword,
A man of night and of the hills, a man
Proscribed, on whom was seen writ every-
　　where
The one word vengeance. An unhappy
　　man
That drew down malediction! I know not
The man they called Hernani. As for me,
I love the birds and flowers, and woods —
　　and song
Of nightingale. I'm Juan of Aragon,
The spouse of Doña Sol — a happy man!
Doña Sol. Happy am I!

HERNANI. What does it matter now,
The rags I left behind me at the door!
Behold, I to my palace desolate
Come back. Upon the threshold-sill there
    waits
For me an angel; I come in and lift
Upright the broken columns, kindle fire,
And ope again the windows; and the grass
Upon the courtyard I have all pluck'd
    up;
For me there is but joy, enchantment, love,
Let them give back my towers, and don-
    jon-keep,
My plume, and seat at the Castilian board
Of council, comes my blushing Doña Sol,
Let them leave us — the rest forgotten is.
Nothing I've seen, nor said, nor have I
    done.
Anew my life begins, the past effacing.
Wisdom or madness, you I have and love,
And you are all my joy!
    DOÑA SOL. How well upon
The velvet black the golden collar shows!
    HERNANI. You saw it on the King ere
    now on me.
    DOÑA SOL. I did not notice. Others,
    what are they
To me? Besides, the velvet is it, or
The satin? No, my Duke, it is thy neck
Which suits the golden collar. Thou art
    proud
And noble, my own lord.
[He seeks to lead her indoors.] Oh, presently,
A moment! See you not, I weep with joy?
Come look upon the lovely night. [She
    goes to the balustrade.] My Duke,
Only a moment — but the time to breathe
And gaze. All now is o'er, the torches
    out,
The music done. Night only is with us.
Felicity most perfect! Think you not
That now while all is still and slumber-
    ing,
Nature, half waking, watches us with love?
No cloud is in the sky. All things like us
Are now at rest. Come, breathe with me
    the air
Perfumed by roses. Look, there is no light,
Nor hear we any noise. Silence prevails.
The moon just now from the horizon rose
E'en while you spoke to me; her trembling
    light

And thy dear voice together reached my
    heart.
Joyous and softly calm I felt, oh, thou
My lover! And it seemed that I would
    then
Most willingly have died.
    HERNANI. Ah, who is there
Would not all things forget when listening
    thus
Unto this voice celestial! Thy speech
But seems a chant with nothing human
    mixed,
And as with one, who gliding down a
    stream
On summer eve, sees pass before his eyes
A thousand flowery plains, my thoughts
    are drawn
Into thy reveries!
    DOÑA SOL. This silence is
Too deep, and too profound the calm. Say,
    now,
Wouldst thou not like to see a star shine
    forth
From out the depths — or hear a voice of
    night,
Tender and sweet, raise suddenly its song?
    HERNANI [smiling]. Capricious one! Just
    now you fled away
From all the songs and lights.
    DOÑA SOL. Ah, yes, the ball!
But yet a bird that in the meadow sings,
A nightingale in moss or shadow lost,
Or flute far off. For music sweet can pour
Into the soul a harmony divine,
That like a heavenly choir wakes in the
    heart
A thousand voices! Charming would it be!
    [They hear the sound of a horn from
    the shade.]
My prayer is heard.
    HERNANI [aside, trembling]. Oh, miser-
    able man!
    DOÑA SOL. An angel read my thought
    — 't was thy good angel
Doubtless?
    HERNANI [bitterly]. Yes, my good angel!
    [Aside.] There, again!
    DOÑA SOL [smiling]. Don Juan, I rec-
    ognize your horn.
    HERNANI. Is 't so?
    DOÑA SOL. The half this serenade to
    you belongs?

HERNANI. The half, thou hast declared it.

DOÑA SOL. Ah, the ball
Detestable! Far better do I love
The horn that sounds from out the woods!
And since
It is your horn 't is like your voice to me.
[*The horn sounds again.*]

HERNANI [*aside*]. It is the tiger howling
for his prey!

DOÑA SOL. Don Juan, this music fills
my heart with joy.

HERNANI [*drawing himself up and looking terrible*]. Call me Hernani! call
me it again!
For with that fatal name I have not done.

DOÑA SOL [*trembling*]. What ails you?

HERNANI. The old man!

DOÑA SOL. O God, what looks!
What is it ails you?

HERNANI. That old man who in
The darkness laughs. Can you not see him
there?

DOÑA SOL. Oh, you are wand'ring! Who
is this old man?

HERNANI. The old man!

DOÑA SOL. On my knees I do entreat
Thee, say what is the secret that afflicts
Thee thus?

HERNANI. I swore it!

DOÑA SOL. Swore!
[*She watches his movements with
anxiety. He stops suddenly and
passes his hand across his brow.*]

HERNANI [*aside*]. What have I said?
Oh, let me spare her. [*Aloud.*] I — nought.
What was it
I said?

DOÑA SOL. You said —

HERNANI. No, no, I was disturbed —
And somewhat suffering I am. Do not
Be frightened.

DOÑA SOL. You need something? Order
me,
Thy servant.   [*The horn sounds again.*]

HERNANI [*aside*]. Ah, he claims! He
claims the pledge!
He has my oath. [*Feeling for his dagger.*]
Not there. It must be done!
Ah! —

DOÑA SOL. Suff'rest thou so much?

HERNANI. 'T is an old wound

That I thought healed — it has reopened
now.
[*Aside.*] She must be got away. [*Aloud.*]
My best beloved,
Now, listen; there's a little box that in
Less happy days I carried with me —

DOÑA SOL. Ah,
I know what 't is you mean. Tell me your
wish.

HERNANI. It holds a flask of an elixir
which
Will end my sufferings. — Go!

DOÑA SOL. I go, my lord.
[*Exit by the door to their apartments.*]

HERNANI [*alone*]. This, then, is how my
happiness must end!
Behold the fatal finger that doth shine
Upon the wall! My bitter destiny
Still jests at me.
[*He falls into a profound yet convulsive reverie. Afterwards he
turns abruptly.*]
Ah, well! I hear no sound.
Am I myself deceiving? —
[*The Mask in black domino appears at the balustrade of the steps.
HERNANI stops petrified.*]

THE MASK. "Whatsoe'er
May happen, what the place, or what the
hour,
Whenever to thy mind it seems the time
Has come for me to die — blow on this horn
And take no other care. All will be done."
This compact had the dead for witnesses.
Is it all done?

HERNANI [*in a low voice*]. 'T is he!

THE MASK. Unto thy home
I come, I tell thee that it is the time.
It is my hour. I find thee hesitate.

HERNANI. Well, then, thy pleasure say.
What wouldest thou
Of me?

THE MASK. I give thee choice 'twixt
poison draught
And blade. I bear about me both. We
shall
Depart together.

HERNANI. Be it so.

THE MASK. Shall we
First pray?

HERNANI. What matter?

THE MASK. Which of them wilt thou?

HERNANI. The poison.
THE MASK. Then hold out your hand.
[He gives a vial to HERNANI, who
pales at receiving it.]
Now drink,
That I may finish.
[HERNANI lifts the vial to his lips,
but recoils.]
HERNANI. Oh, for pity's sake,
Until to-morrow wait! If thou hast heart
Or soul, if thou art not a specter just
Escaped from flame, if thou art not a soul
Accursed, forever lost; if on thy brow
Not yet has God inscribed his "never." Oh,
If thou hast ever known the bliss supreme
Of loving, and at twenty years of age
Of wedding the beloved; if ever thou
Hast clasped the one thou lovedst in thine
arms,
Wait till to-morrow. Then thou canst come
back!
THE MASK. Childish it is for you to jest
this way!
To-morrow! Why, the bell this morning
toll'd
Thy funeral! And I should die this night,
And who would come and take thee after
me!
I will not to the tomb descend alone,
Young man, 't is thou must go with me!
HERNANI. Well, then,
I say thee nay; and, demon, I from thee
Myself deliver. I will not obey.
THE MASK. As I expected. Very well.
On what,
Then, didst thou swear? Ah, on a trifling
thing,
The mem'ry of thy father's head. With
ease
Such oath may be forgotten. Youthful
oaths
Are light affairs.
HERNANI. My father! — father! Oh
My senses I shall lose!
THE MASK. Oh, no, — 't is but
A perjury and treason.
HERNANI. Duke!
THE MASK. Since now
The heirs of Spanish houses make a jest
Of breaking promises, I 'll say Adieu!
[He moves as if to leave.]
HERNANI. Stay!

THE MASK. Then —
HERNANI. Oh, cruel man! [He raises the
vial.] Thus to return
Upon my path at heaven's door!

[Reënter DOÑA SOL without seeing the Mask,
who is standing erect near the balustrade
of the stairway at the back of the stage.]

DOÑA SOL. I've failed
To find that little box.
HERNANI [aside]. O God! 't is she!
At such a moment here!
DOÑA SOL. What is 't, that thus
I frighten him, — e'en at my voice he
shakes!
What hold'st thou in thy hand? What fear-
ful thought!
What hold'st thou in thy hand? Reply to
me.
[The DOMINO unmasks; she utters
a cry in recognizing DON RUY.]
'T is poison!
HERNANI. Oh, great Heaven!
DOÑA SOL [to HERNANI]. What is it
That I have done to thee? What mystery
Of horror? I'm deceived by thee, Don
Juan!
HERNANI. Ah, I had thought to hide it
all from thee.
My life I promised to the Duke that time
He saved it. Aragon must pay this debt
To Silva.
DOÑA SOL. Unto me you do belong,
Not him. What signify your other oaths?
[To DON RUY GOMEZ.] My love it is which
gives me strength, and, Duke,
I will defend him against you and all
The world.
DON RUY GOMEZ [unmoved]. Defend
him if you can against
An oath that's sworn.
DOÑA SOL. What oath?
HERNANI. Yes, I have sworn.
DOÑA SOL. No, no; naught binds thee;
it would be a crime,
A madness, an atrocity — no, no,
It cannot be.
DON RUY GOMEZ. Come, Duke.
[HERNANI makes a gesture to obey.
DOÑA SOL tries to stop him.]
HERNANI. It must be done.
Allow it, Doña Sol. My word was pledged

To the Duke, and to my father now in
    heaven!

DoÑa Sol [*to* Don Ruy Gomez]. Better
    that to a tigress you should go
And snatch away her young, than take
    from me
Him whom I love. Know you at all what
    is
This Doña Sol? Long time I pitied you,
And, in compassion for your age, I seemed
The gentle girl, timid and innocent,
But now see eyes made moist by tears of
    rage.
    [*She draws a dagger from her bosom.*]
See you this dagger? Old man imbecile!
Do you not fear the steel when eyes flash
    threat?
Take care, Don Ruy! I'm of thy family.
Listen, mine uncle! Had I been your child
It had been ill for you, if you had laid
A hand upon my husband!
    [*She throws away the dagger, and
      falls on her knees before him.*]
At thy feet
I fall! Mercy! Have pity on us both.
Alas! my lord, I am but woman weak,
My strength dies out within my soul, I fail
So easily; 't is at your knees I plead,
I supplicate — have mercy on us both!

Don Ruy Gomez. Doña Sol!

DoÑa Sol. Oh, pardon! With us
    Spaniards
Grief bursts forth in stormy words, you
    know it.
Alas! you used not to be harsh! My uncle,
Have pity, you are killing me indeed
In touching him! Mercy, have pity now,
So well I love him!

Don Ruy Gomez [*gloomily*]. You love
    him too much!

Hernani. Thou weepest!

DoÑa Sol. No, my love, no, no, it must
Not be. I will not have you die.
[*To* Don Ruy.] To-day
Be merciful, and I will love you well,
You also.

Don Ruy Gomez. After him; the dregs
    you'd give,
The remnants of your love, and friendliness.
Still less and less. — Oh, think you thus to
    quench
The thirst that now devours me?

[*Pointing to* Hernani.] He alone
Is everything. For me kind pityings!
With such affection, what, pray, could I
    do?
Fury! 't is he would have your heart, your
    love,
And be enthroned, and grant a look from
    you
As alms; and if vouchsafed a kindly word
'T is he would tell you, — say so much, it is
Enough, — cursing in heart the greedy one
The beggar, unto whom he's forced to fling
The drops remaining in the emptied glass.
Oh, shame! derision! No, we'll finish.
    Drink!

Hernani. He has my promise, and it
    must be kept.

Don Ruy Gomez. Proceed.
    [Hernani *raises the vial to his
      lips;* DoÑa Sol *throws herself on
      his arm.*]

DoÑa Sol. Not yet. Deign both of you
    to hear me.

Don Ruy Gomez. The grave is open and
    I cannot wait.

DoÑa Sol. A moment only, — Duke,
    and my Don Juan, —
Ah! both are cruel! What is it I ask?
An instant! That is all I beg from you.
Let a poor woman speak what's in her
    heart,
Oh, let me speak —

Don Ruy Gomez. I cannot wait.

DoÑa Sol. My lord,
You make me tremble! What, then, have
    I done?

Hernani. His crime is rending him.

DoÑa Sol [*still holding his arm*]. You see
    full well
I have a thousand things to say.

Don Ruy Gomez [*to* Hernani]. Die —
    die
You must.

DoÑa Sol [*still hanging on his arm*]. Don
    Juan, when all's said, indeed,
Thou shalt do what thou wilt.
[*She snatches the vial.*] I have it now!
    [*She lifts the vial for* Hernani *and
      the old man to see.*]

Don Ruy Gomez. Since with two
    women I have here to deal,
It needs, Don Juan, that I elsewhere go

In search of souls. Grave oaths you took
to me,
And by the race from which you sprang.
I go
Unto your father, and to speak among
The dead. Adieu.
[*He moves as if to depart.* HER-
NANI *holds him back.*]
HERNANI. Stay, Duke.
[*To* DOÑA SOL.] Alas! I do
Implore thee. Wouldst thou wish to see in
me
A perjured felon only, and e'erwhere
I go "a traitor" written on my brow?
In pity give the poison back to me.
'T is by our love I ask it, and our souls
Immortal —
DOÑA SOL [*sadly*]. And thou wilt? [*She
drinks.*] Now, take the rest.
DON RUY GOMEZ [*aside*]. 'T was, then,
for her!
DOÑA SOL [*returning the half-emptied vial
to* HERNANI]. I tell thee, take.
HERNANI [*to* DON RUY]. See'st thou,
Oh, miserable man!
DOÑA SOL. Grieve not for me,
I've left thy share.
HERNANI [*taking the vial*]. O God!
DOÑA SOL. Not thus would'st thou
Have left me mine. But thou! Not thine
the heart
Of Christian wife! Thou knowest not to
love
As Silvas do — but I've drunk first —
made sure.
Now, drink it, if thou wilt!
HERNANI. What hast thou done,
Unhappy one?
DOÑA SOL. 'T was thou who willed it so.
HERNANI. It is a frightful death!
DOÑA SOL. No — no — why so?
HERNANI. This philter leads unto the
grave.
DOÑA SOL. And ought
We not this night to rest together? Does
It matter in what bed?
HERNANI. My father, thou
Thyself avengest upon me, who did
Forget thee!
[*He lifts the vial to his mouth.*]
DOÑA SOL [*throwing herself on him*].
Heavens, what strange agony!

Ah, throw this philter far from thee! My
reason
Is wand'ring. Stop! Alas! oh, my Don
Juan,
This drug is potent, in the heart it wakes
A hydra with a thousand tearing teeth
Devouring it. I knew not that such pangs
Could be! What is the thing? 'T is liquid
fire.
Drink not! For much thou'dst suffer!
HERNANI [*to* DON RUY]. Ah, thy soul
Is cruel! Could'st thou not have found for
her
Another drug?
[*He drinks and throws the vial away.*]
DOÑA SOL. What dost thou?
HERNANI. What thyself
Hast done.
DOÑA SOL. Come to my arms, young
lover, now.
[*They sit down close to each other.*]
Does not one suffer horribly?
HERNANI. No, no.
DOÑA SOL. These are our marriage rites!
But for a bride
I'm very pale, say am I not?
HERNANI. Ah me!
DON RUY GOMEZ. Fulfilled is now the
fatal destiny!
HERNANI. Oh, misery and despair to
know her pangs!
DOÑA SOL. Be calm. I'm better. —
Toward new brighter light
We now together open out our wings.
Let us with even flight set out to reach
A fairer world. Only a kiss — a kiss!
[*They embrace.*]
DON RUY GOMEZ. Oh, agony supreme!
HERNANI [*in a feeble voice*]. Oh, bless'd
be Heav'n
That will'd for me a life by specters fol-
lowed,
And by abysses yawning circled still,
Yet grants, that weary of a road so rough,
I fall asleep my lips upon thy hand.
DON RUY GOMEZ. How happy are they!
HERNANI [*in voice growing weaker and
weaker*]. Come — come, Doña Sol,
All's dark. Dost thou not suffer?
DOÑA SOL [*in a voice equally faint*].
Nothing now.
Oh, nothing.

HERNANI. Seest thou not fires in the gloom?

DOÑA SOL. Not yet.

HERNANI [*with a sigh*]. Behold —

[*He falls.*]

DON RUY GOMEZ [*raising the head, which falls again*]. He's dead!

DOÑA SOL [*disheveled and half raising herself on the seat*]. Oh, no, we sleep. He sleeps. It is my spouse that here you see.

We love each other — we are sleeping thus. It is our bridal. [*In a failing voice.*] I entreat you not To wake him, my Lord Duke of Meudocé, For he is weary.

[*She turns round the face of* HERNANI.] Turn to me, my love.

More near — still closer —

[*She falls back.*]

DON RUY GOMEZ. Dead! Oh, I am damn'd! [*He kills himself.*]

THE SON–IN–LAW OF M. POIRIER

(LE GENDRE DE M. POIRIER)

By EMILE AUGIER AND JULES SANDEAU

Translated by BARRETT H. CLARK

CHARACTERS

Poirier

Gaston, *Marquis de Presles*

Hector, *Duke de Montmeyran*

Verdelet

Antoinette

Salomon,

Chevassus, } *creditors*

Cogne,

Vatel

The Porter

A Servant

The action takes place in the home of M. Poirier, at Paris.

THE SON-IN-LAW OF M. POIRIER

ACT I

A very richly furnished drawing-room. There are doors on either side, and windows at the back, looking out upon the garden. There is a fireplace in which a fire is burning.

[*As the curtain rises, a Servant and the DUKE are discovered.*]

SERVANT. I repeat, Corporal, Monsieur le Marquis cannot possibly receive. He is not up yet.

DUKE. At nine o'clock! [*Aside.*] Ha, the sun rises slowly during the honeymoon. — What time is breakfast served here?

SERVANT. At eleven; but what business is that of yours?

DUKE. You will lay another place.

SERVANT. For your colonel?

DUKE. Yes, for my colonel. Is this to-day's paper?

SERVANT. Yes: February 15, 1846.

DUKE. Give it to me.

SERVANT. I have n't read it yet.

DUKE. You refuse to let me have it? Well, you see, don't you, that I can't wait? Announce me.

SERVANT. Who are you?

DUKE. The Duke de Montmeyran.

SERVANT. You're joking!

[*Enter GASTON.*]

GASTON. Why, it's you! [*They embrace.*]

SERVANT [*aside*]. The devil! I've put my foot in it!

DUKE. My dear Gaston!

GASTON. My dear Hector! I'm so glad to see you!

DUKE. And I you!

GASTON. You could n't possibly have arrived at a better time.

DUKE. How do you mean?

GASTON. Let me tell you — but, my poor fellow, the way you're rigged up!

Who would recognize under that tunic one of the princes of youth, the perfect model of prodigal sons?

DUKE. Next to you, old man. We've both settled down: you have married, I have become a soldier, and whatever you think of my uniform, I prefer my regiment to yours.

GASTON [*looking at the DUKE's uniform*]. Thank you!

DUKE. Yes, look at the tunic. It's the only costume that can keep me from boring myself to death. And this little decoration which you pretend not to notice —

[*He shows his corporal's stripes.*]

GASTON. Stripes!

DUKE. Which I picked up on the field of Isly, old man —

GASTON. And when will you get the star for bravery?

DUKE. My dear fellow, please let's not joke about those things. It was all very well in the past, but to-day the Cross is my one ambition. I would willingly shed a pint of my blood for it.

GASTON. You are a real soldier, I see!

DUKE. Yes — I love my profession. It's the only one for a ruined gentleman. I have but one regret: that I did not enter it long ago. This active and adventurous life is infinitely attractive. Even discipline has its peculiar charm: it's healthy, it calms the mind — this having one's life arranged for one in advance, without any possible discussion, and consequently, without hesitation and without regret. That's why I can feel so care-free and happy. I know my duty, I do it, and I am content.

GASTON. Without very great cost on your part.

DUKE. And then, old man, those patriotic ideas we used to make fun of at the *Café de Paris* and call chauvinism, make our hearts swell when we face the enemy.

The first cannon-shot knocks forever the last vestige of that nonsense out of our minds; the flag then is no longer a bit of cloth at the end of a stick: it is the very vesture of the *patrie*.

GASTON. That's all very well, but this enthusiasm for a flag which is not your own —

DUKE. Nonsense, you can't see the color in the midst of the powder smoke.

GASTON. Well, the important point is that you are satisfied. Are you going to stay in Paris for some time?

DUKE. Just a month. You know how I've arranged my manner of living?

GASTON. No — tell me.

DUKE. Did n't I? It's really very clever: before leaving, I put the remains of my fortune with a certain banker: about a hundred thousand francs, the income from which allows me during a month in the year to live as I used to live. So that I live for one month at a six thousand francs' rate, and for the rest of the year I live on six sous a day. Naturally, I have chosen carnival season for my prodigalities. It began yesterday, but my first visit has been to you.

GASTON. Thanks! But, you understand, I shan't hear of your staying anywhere but with me.

DUKE. But I don't want to be in the way.

GASTON. You won't: there's a small pavilion here, at the end of the garden.

DUKE. To be perfectly frank, I'm not afraid of you, but of myself. You see — you lead a family life here: there's your wife, your father-in-law —

GASTON. Ah, you imagine that, simply because I have married the daughter of a retired dry-goods merchant, my home is a temple of boredom, that my wife brought with her a heap of bourgeois virtues, that all that remains for me to do is write an inscription over my door: "Here lies Gaston, Marquis de Presles." Make no mistake, I live like a prince even, race my horses, gamble like the devil, buy pictures, have the finest chef in Paris, — the fellow pretends he's a direct descendant of Vatel, and takes his art ever so seriously, — I invite whom I like to meals (by the way,

you'll dine with all my friends to-morrow, and you'll see how I treat them). In short, marriage has not changed me in the least — except it has done away with creditors.

DUKE. So your wife and your father-in-law leave you free rein?

GASTON. Absolutely. My wife is a nice little boarding-school miss, rather pretty, somewhat awkward, timid, still wide-eyed with wonder at the sudden change in her station in life, who passes the greater part of her time, I'll warrant, looking at the Marquise de Presles in her mirror. As to Monsieur Poirier, my father-in-law, he is worthy of his name. Modest and nutritious like all fruit-trees, he was born to play the part of a wall fruit-tree. His highest ambition is to serve as a gentleman's dessert: that ambition is now satisfied.

DUKE. Come now, do such bourgeois still exist?

GASTON. In a word, he is Georges Dandin become a father-in-law. But, really, I've made a magnificent match of it.

DUKE. I can well believe that you had good reasons for contracting this misalliance.

GASTON. Judge for yourself. You know the desperate straits I was in? I was an orphan at the age of fifteen, master of a fortune at twenty. I quickly spent my patrimony, and was rapidly running up a capital of debts, worthy the nephew of my uncle. Now, at the very moment when that capital reached the figure of five hundred thousand francs, thanks to my activities, what did my seventy-year-old uncle do but marry a young girl who had fallen in love with him? Corvisart said that at seventy one always has children. I did n't count on cousins — well, I was then forced to do so.

DUKE. And you then occupied the position of honorary nephew.

GASTON. I thought of taking a position in the rank of active sons-in-law. At that time Heaven sent Monsieur Poirier across my path.

DUKE. How did you happen to meet him?

GASTON. He had some money he wanted to invest — it was the merest matter of chance, and we met. I lacked sufficient guarantee as a debtor, but I offered him enough as a son-in-law. I made inquiries about his person, assured myself that his fortune had been honorably acquired, and then, by Jove, I married his daughter.

DUKE. Who brought you — ?

GASTON. The old fellow had four millions; now he has only three.

DUKE. A dowry of a million?

GASTON. Better still: you'll see. He agreed to pay my debts. By the way, to-day a visible proof of the phenomenon can be seen, I believe. It was a matter of five hundred thousand francs. The day we signed the contract he gave me stock which will net me an income of twenty-five thousand francs: five hundred thousand francs more!

DUKE. There's your million. And then?

GASTON. Then? He insisted on not being separated from his daughter and agreed to defray all household expenses so long as we lived in his home with him. So, after receiving lodging, heat, carriages, and board, I still have an income of twenty-five thousand francs for my wife and myself.

DUKE. Very neat.

GASTON. Wait a moment.

Duke. Something else?

GASTON. He bought back the Château de Presles, and I expect that any day I shall find the deeds under my plate at breakfast.

DUKE. What a delightful father-in-law!

GASTON. Wait a moment!

DUKE. What? More?

GASTON. As soon as the contract was signed, he came to me, took my hands in his, and made any number of excuses for being no more than sixty years old; but he assured me that he would hurry on to the age of eighty. But I'm in no great haste — he's not in the way, the poor man. He knows his place, goes to bed with the chickens, rises at cock-crow, keeps his accounts, and is ready to satisfy my every whim. He is a steward who does not rob me; I should have to look long to find a better.

DUKE. Really, you are the most fortunate of men.

GASTON. And wait — you might imagine

that my marriage has lessened me in the eyes of the world, that it has "taken the shine out of me," as Monsieur Poirier says. Never worry, I still hold my place in the social world. I still lead in matters of fashion. The women have forgiven me. As I was saying, you have arrived in the nick of time.

DUKE. Why?

GASTON. Don't you understand — you, my born second?

DUKE. A duel?

GASTON. Yes, a nice little duel, the kind we used to have, in the days of our youth. Well, what do you say? Is the old Marquis de Presles dead? Are you thinking of burying him yet?

DUKE. Whom are you fighting with, and why?

GASTON. The Viscount de Pontgrimaud — a gambling quarrel.

DUKE. Gambling quarrel? Can't it be decided otherwise?

GASTON. Is that the way you are taught to regulate affairs of honor in the regiment?

DUKE. Yes, in the regiment. There we are taught what use to make of our blood. But you can't persuade me that you must shed it over a gambling quarrel?

GASTON. But what if this particular quarrel were only a pretext? What if there be something else — behind it?

DUKE. A woman!

GASTON. That's it.

DUKE. An intrigue — so soon? That's bad!

GASTON. How could I help it? A last year's passion I had imagined dead of the cold, and which, a month after my marriage, had its Indian Summer. You see, there's nothing serious in it, and no cause for worry.

DUKE. And might I know — ?

GASTON. I can have no secrets from you: the Countess de Montjay.

DUKE. My compliments, but the matter is serious. I once thought of making love to her, but I retired before the dangers of such a liaison — that sort of danger has little enough of chivalry in it. You know, of course, that the Countess has no money of her own?

GASTON. That she is waiting for the fortune of her aged husband; that he would have the bad taste to disinherit her in case he discovered her guilt? I know all that.

DUKE. And out of sheer lightness of heart have you imposed that bond on yourself?

GASTON. Habit, a certain residue of my former love, the temptation of forbidden fruit, the pleasure of cutting out that little fool Pontgrimaud, whom I detest —

DUKE. Why, you're doing him an honor!

GASTON. What else can I do? He gets on my nerves, the little imp; he imagines that he is a noble by reason of his knightly achievements, simply because his grandfather, Monsieur Grimaud, supplied arms to the Government. He's a Viscount, Heaven knows how or why, and he imagines that he belongs to a nobility older than our own. He never loses an opportunity to pose as champion of the nobility, and tries to make people believe for that very reason that he represents it. If a Montmorency is scratched, he howls as if he himself had been hit. I tell you there was a quarrel brewing between us, and last night it came to a head over a game of cards. I'll let him off with a scratch — the first in the history of his family.

DUKE. Has he sent his seconds to you?

GASTON. I expect them at any moment. You and Grandlieu will help me.

DUKE. Very well.

GASTON. Of course, you will stay here with me?

DUKE. Delighted.

GASTON. Though this is carnival season, you don't intend to parade about as a hero, do you?

DUKE. No, I wrote beforehand to my tailor —

GASTON. Sh! I hear some one talking. It's my father-in-law. You'll now have an opportunity of seeing him, with his old friend Verdelet, a former partner. You're in luck —

[Enter POIRIER and VERDELET.]

GASTON. How are you, Monsieur Verdelet?

VERDELET. Your servant, messieurs.

GASTON. A dear friend of mine, my dear Monsieur Poirier: the Duke de Montmeyran.

DUKE. Corporal of the African Cavalry.

VERDELET [aside]. Indeed!

POIRIER. Most honored, Monsieur le Duc!

GASTON. More honored than you think, dear Monsieur Poirier: for Monsieur le Duc has been good enough to accept the hospitality which I have offered him.

VERDELET [aside]. Another rat in the cheese!

DUKE. I beg your pardon, monsieur, for accepting an invitation which my friend Gaston has possibly been a trifle too hasty in offering.

POIRIER. Monsieur le Marquis, my son-in-law, need never feel obliged to consult me before inviting his friends to stay with him here. The friends of our friends —

GASTON. Very well, Monsieur Poirier. Hector will stay in the garden pavilion. Is it ready for him?

POIRIER. I shall see to it at once.

DUKE. I am very sorry, monsieur, to cause you any annoyance —

GASTON. None at all; Monsieur Poirier will be only too happy —

POIRIER. Too happy —

GASTON. And you will of course give orders that the little blue coupé be placed at his disposal?

POIRIER. The one I usually use — ?

DUKE. Oh, I positively refuse —

POIRIER. But I can easily hire one; there is a stand at the end of the street.

VERDELET [aside]. Fool! Idiot!

GASTON [to the DUKE]. Now, let us take a look at the stables. Yesterday I got a superb Arabian — you can tell me what you think of him. Come.

DUKE [to POIRIER]. With your permission, monsieur. Gaston is impatient to show me his luxurious surroundings. I don't blame him. He can then tell me more about you.

POIRIER. Monsieur le Duc is well acquainted with my son-in-law's delicate nature and tastes.

GASTON [aside to the DUKE]. You'll spoil my father-in-law! [Going toward the door, *and stopping.*] By the way, Monsieur Poirier, you know I am giving a grand dinner party to-morrow night. Will you give us the pleasure of your company?

POIRIER. No, thank you — I am dining with Verdelet.

GASTON. Ah, Monsieur Verdelet, I am very angry with you for carrying off my father-in-law every time I have company here.

VERDELET [*aside*]. Impertinent!

POIRIER. A man of my age would only be in the way!

VERDELET [*aside*]. You old Géronte!

GASTON. As you please, Monsieur Poirier. [*He goes out with the* DUKE.]

VERDELET. I tell you, that son-in-law of yours is mighty obsequious with you. You warned me beforehand: you'd know how to make him respect you.

POIRIER. I'm doing what pleases me. I prefer to be loved than feared.

VERDELET. You've not always thought that way. Well, you've succeeded: your son-in-law is on a more familiar footing with you than with the other servants.

POIRIER. I can do without your clever remarks, and I advise you to mind your own business.

VERDELET. This is my own business, I tell you! Are n't we partners? Why, we're a little like the Siamese twins. Now, when you grovel before that marquis, I have a hard time keeping my temper.

POIRIER. Grovel? As if — ? That marquis! Do you think I am dazzled by his title? I've always been more of a Liberal than you, and I still am. I don't care a snap of my finger for the nobility! Ability and virtue are the only social distinctions that I recognize and before which I bow down.

VERDELET. Is your son-in-law virtuous?

POIRIER. You make me tired. Do you want me to make him feel that he owes everything to me?

VERDELET. Oh, oh; you have become very considerate in your old age — the result of your economical habits, doubtless. Look here, Poirier, I never did approve of this marriage; you know that I always wanted my dear goddaughter to marry a man from our own class. But you refused to listen to reason —

POIRIER. Ha, ha! Listen to monsieur! That's the last straw!

VERDELET. Well, why not?

POIRIER. Oh, Monsieur Verdelet, you are most clever and you have the noblest ideals; you have read amusing books, you have your own ideas on every subject, but in the matter of common sense, I can give you enormous odds.

VERDELET. Oh, as to common sense — you mean business sense. I don't deny that: you've piled up four millions, while I've barely made forty thousand a year.

POIRIER. And that you owe to me.

VERDELET. I don't deny it. What I have I owe to you. But it is all going eventually to your daughter, after your son-in-law has ruined you.

POIRIER. Ruined me?

VERDELET. Yes — within ten years.

POIRIER. You're crazy.

VERDELET. At the rate he's going now, you know only too well how long it will take him to run through his money.

POIRIER. Well, that's my business.

VERDELET. If you were the only one concerned, I'd never open my lips.

POIRIER. Why not? Don't you take any interest in my welfare? You don't care, then, if I am ruined? I, who have made your fortune?

VERDELET. What is the matter with you?

POIRIER. I don't like ungrateful people.

VERDELET. The devil! You're taking out your son-in-law's familiarities on me. I was going to say, if you were the only one concerned, I could at least be patient about it: you are n't my godson, but it happens that your daughter is my god-daughter.

POIRIER. I was a fool to give you that right over her.

VERDELET. You might easily have found some one who loved her less.

POIRIER. Yes, yes, I know — you love her more than I do — I know, you claim that — and you've even persuaded her —

VERDELET. Are we going to quarrel about that again? For Heaven's sake, then, go ahead!

POIRIER. I will go ahead! Do you think I like to see myself left out, pushed aside by a stranger? Have I no place in my own daughter's heart?

VERDELET. She has the tenderest affection for you —

POIRIER. That's not so: you've taken my place. All her secrets, all her nice pleasing little ways are for you.

VERDELET. Because I don't make her afraid. How can you expect the little one to be confidential with an old bear like you? She can never find an opening, you're always so crabbed.

POIRIER. Well, you are the one who has made me play the part of a kill-joy, while you usurp that of a sugar-plum father. It's not right to make up to children by giving in to all their wishes, and forgetting what's good for them. That's loving them for your own sake, instead of for theirs.

VERDELET. Now, Poirier, you know very well that when the real interests of your daughter were at stake, her whims were opposed by me, and by me alone. Heaven knows, I went against poor Toinon's wishes in this marriage, while you were ass enough to urge her on.

POIRIER. She was in love with the Marquis. — Let me read my paper.

[He sits down and runs his eyes over the "Constitutionnel."]

VERDELET. It's all very well for you to say the child was in love: you forced her into it. You brought the Marquis de Presles here.

POIRIER [rising]. Another one has arrived at the top! Monsieur Michaud, the ironmaster, has just been appointed a peer of France.

VERDELET. What do I care?

POIRIER. What do you care! Does it make no difference to you to see a man of our class arrive at the top? To see the Government honor industry in calling one of her representatives into its midst? Don't you think it admirable that we live in a country and an age in which labor opens every door? You have a right to look forward to becoming a peer some day, and you ask, "What do I care?"

VERDELET. Heaven preserve me from aspiring to the pecrage! And Heaven preserve my country when I become a peer!

POIRIER. But why? Can't Monsieur Michaud fill his position?

VERDELET. Monsieur Michaud is not only a business man, but a man of great personal merit. Molière's father was an upholsterer, but that is no reason why every upholsterer's son should believe himself a poet.

POIRIER. I tell you, commerce is the true school for statesmen. Who shall lay his hand on the wheel unless it is those who have first learned to steer their own barks?

VERDELET. A bark is not a ship, and a little captain is not necessarily a true pilot, and France is no commercial house. I can hardly restrain myself when I see this mania taking root in people's minds. I declare, you might imagine that statesmanship in this country was nothing more than a pastime for people who have nothing else to do! A business man like you or me attends to his own little concerns for thirty years; he makes his fortune, and one fine day closes his shop and sets up business as a statesman. With no more effort than that! Very simple receipt! Good Lord, messieurs, you might just as well say, "I have measured so many yards of cloth, and I therefore know how to play the violin!"

POIRIER. I don't exactly see what connection — ?

VERDELET. Instead of thinking about governing France, learn to govern your own home. Don't marry off your daughters to ruined marquesses who imagine they are doing you an honor in allowing you to pay off their debts with your own hard cash —

POIRIER. Are you saying that for me —?

VERDELET. No; for myself!

[Enter ANTOINETTE.]

ANTOINETTE. How are you, father? How is everything? Hello, godfather. Are you going to have lunch with us? How nice you are!

POIRIER. He is nice. But what am I, I who invited him?

ANTOINETTE. You are charming.

POIRIER. But only when I invite Verdelet. Agreeable for me!

ANTOINETTE. Where is my husband?
POIRIER. In the stable. Where else would he be?
ANTOINETTE. Do you blame him for liking horses? Is n't it natural for a gentleman to like horses and arms — ?
POIRIER. Oh, yes, but I wish he cared for something else.
ANTOINETTE. He is very fond of the arts: poetry, painting, music.
POIRIER. Huh, the agreeable arts! Pleasures!
VERDELET. Would you expect him to care for unpleasant arts? Would you want him to play the piano?
POIRIER. There you are again, taking his part before Toinon. You're trying to get into her good graces. [To ANTOINETTE.] He was just telling me that your husband was ruining me. Did n't you?
VERDELET. Yes, but all you have to do is to pull tight your purse-strings.
POIRIER. It would be much simpler if the young man had some occupation.
VERDELET. It seems to me that he is very much occupied as it is.
POIRIER. Yes: spending money from morning till night. I'd prefer a more lucrative occupation.
ANTOINETTE. What, for instance? He can't sell cloth.
POIRIER. He would n't be able to. I don't ask for so very much, after all. Let him take a position that befits his rank: an embassy, for instance.
VERDELET. An embassy? You don't take an embassy the way you take cold.
POIRIER. When a man is called the Marquis de Presles, he can aspire to anything.
ANTOINETTE. But on the other hand, father, he need not aspire to anything.
VERDELET. That's true. Your son-in-law has his own ideas —
POIRIER. Only one: to be lazy.
ANTOINETTE. That's not fair, father: my husband has very fine ideals.
VERDELET. At least, if he has n't, he possesses that chivalrous obstinacy of his rank. Do you think for one moment that your son-in-law is going to give up the traditions of his family, just for the sake of changing his lazy life?

POIRIER. You don't know my son-in-law, Verdelet; I have studied him thoroughly — I did that before giving my daughter to him. He's hare-brained, and the lightness of his character prevents his being obstinate. As to his family traditions, — well, if he had thought very much of them he would never have married Mademoiselle Poirier.
VERDELET. That makes no difference. It would have been much wiser to have sounded him on this subject before the marriage.
POIRIER. What a fool you are! It would have looked as if I were making a bargain with him, and he would have refused point-blank. You can't get things of that sort unless you go about it in the right way, slowly, tenaciously, perseveringly. He has been living here this past three months on the fat of the land.
VERDELET. I see: you wanted to make it pleasant for him before you came down to business.
POIRIER. Exactly. [To ANTOINETTE.] A man is always indulgent toward his wife during the honeymoon. Now, if you ask him in a nice way — in the evening — when you're taking down your hair —?
ANTOINETTE. Oh, father —!
POIRIER. That's the way Madame Poirier used to get me to promise to take her to the Opéra — I always took her the next day. See?
ANTOINETTE. But I'd never dare speak to my husband on so serious a subject.
POIRIER. Your dowry will surely give you a good enough right to speak.
ANTOINETTE. He would only shrug his shoulders, and not answer.
VERDELET. Does he do that when you talk with him?
ANTOINETTE. No, but —
VERDELET. Ah, you look away! So your husband treats you a little —? I've been afraid of that.
POIRIER. Have you any reason to complain of him?
ANTOINETTE. No, father.
POIRIER. Does n't he love you?
ANTOINETTE. I don't say that.
POIRIER. Then what do you say?

ANTOINETTE. Nothing.

VERDELET. Come, dear, you should speak frankly with your old friends. Our whole object in life is to look after your happiness. Whom have you left to confide in unless it's your father and your godfather? Are you unhappy?

ANTOINETTE. I have n't the right to be: my husband is very kind and good.

POIRIER. Well, then?

VERDELET. But is that enough? He's kind and good, but he pays no more attention to you than to some pretty doll, does he?

ANTOINETTE. It's my fault. I'm so timid with him; I've never dared open my heart to him. I'm sure he thinks me a little boarding-school miss who wanted to become a marquise.

POIRIER. The fool!

VERDELET. Why don't you explain to him?

ANTOINETTE. I tried to more than once, but the tone of his first answer was so different from what I thought it should be, that I could n't continue. There are certain kinds of intimacy that must be encouraged — the heart has a reticence of its own. You ought to be able to understand that, dear Tony?

POIRIER. Well, what about me? Don't I understand, too?

ANTOINETTE. You, too, father. How can I tell Gaston that it was n't his title that pleased me, but his manners, his mind, his knightly bearing, his contempt for the pettinesses of life? How can I tell him that he is the man of my dreams — how can I do that if he stops me at once with some joke?

POIRIER. That shows the boy is in a good humor.

VERDELET. No: it's because his wife bores him.

POIRIER [to ANTOINETTE]. Do you bore your husband?

ANTOINETTE. I'm afraid I do!

POIRIER. I tell you it is n't you, but his own confounded laziness that bores him. A husband does n't love his wife very long when he has nothing else to do but to love her.

ANTOINETTE. Is that true, Tony?

POIRIER. I'm telling you! You need n't ask Verdelet.

VERDELET. Yes, I do believe that passion is soon exhausted unless it is managed like a fortune: economically.

POIRIER. Every man wants to be actively engaged in some pursuit. When his way is barred, that desire is wasted, lost.

VERDELET. A wife should be the preoccupation, not the occupation, of her husband.

POIRIER. Why did I always adore your mother? Because I never had time to think about her.

VERDELET. Your husband has twenty-four hours a day to love you —

POIRIER. That's twelve too many.

ANTOINETTE. You're opening my eyes.

POIRIER. Let him take a position and everything will turn out satisfactorily.

ANTOINETTE. What do you say, Tony?

VERDELET. Possibly! The difficulty is in making him take the position.

POIRIER. Leave that to me. Leave the matter in my hands.

VERDELET. Are you going to attack the question at once?

POIRIER. No, but I shall after lunch. I have noticed that the Marquis is in splendid humor after his meals.

[Enter GASTON and the DUKE.]

GASTON [introducing the DUKE to his wife]. My dear Antoinette, Monsieur de Montmeyran, who is not entirely unknown to you.

ANTOINETTE. Gaston has told me so much about you, monsieur, that I seem to be shaking hands with an old friend.

DUKE. You are not mistaken, madame; you have made me feel that only a moment was necessary to resume, as it were, a former friendship. [Aside to the MARQUIS.] Your wife is charming!

GASTON [aside to the DUKE]. Yes, she is nice. [To ANTOINETTE.] I have some good news for you: Hector is going to stay with us during his leave.

ANTOINETTE. How good of you, monsieur! I trust your leave is a long one?

DUKE. One month, after which I return to Africa.

VERDELET. You afford us a noble example, Monsieur le Duc: *you* do not consider laziness as a family inheritance.

GASTON [*aside*]. Aha! Monsieur Verdelet.

[*Enter a Servant, carrying a picture.*]

SERVANT. This picture has just come for Monsieur le Marquis.

GASTON. Lay it on that chair, by the window. There — good. [*The Servant goes out.*] Just look at it, Montmeyran.

DUKE. Charming — beautiful evening effect! Don't you think so, madame?

ANTOINETTE. Yes — charming — and how real it is! And how calm and quiet. You feel as if you would like to walk about in that silent landscape.

POIRIER [*aside to* VERDELET]. Peer of France!

GASTON. Just look at that strip of greenish light, running between the orange tones of the horizon, and that cold blue of the rest of the sky. Splendid technique!

DUKE. Then the foreground! And the coloring, the handling of the whole thing!

GASTON. Then the almost imperceptible reflection of that little spot of water behind the foliage — charming!

POIRIER. Let's take a look at it, Verdelet. [POIRIER *and* VERDELET *go to look at the picture.*] Well? What does it represent?

VERDELET. It represents some fields at nine o'clock at night.

POIRIER. The subject is n't interesting; it does n't *tell* anything. In my room I have an engraving showing a dog on the seashore barking at a sailor's hat. There now, you can understand that: it's clever, and simple, and touching.

GASTON. My dear Monsieur Poirier, if you like touching pictures, let me have one made for you; the subject I take from nature: on the table is a little onion, cut in quarters, a poor little white onion. The knife lies beside it. Nothing at all, and yet it brings tears to the eyes!

VERDELET [*aside to* POIRIER]. He's making fun of you.

POIRIER [*aside to* VERDELET]. Very well — let him!

DUKE. Who painted this landscape?

GASTON. Poor devil — lots of talent — but he has n't a sou.

POIRIER. What did you pay for the picture?

GASTON. Fifty louis.

POIRIER. Fifty louis? For the picture of an unknown painter who is dying of hunger! If you'd gone around at mealtime you could have got it for twenty-five francs.

ANTOINETTE. Oh, father!

POIRIER. A fine example of misplaced generosity!

GASTON. Then you don't think that the arts should be protected?

POIRIER. Protect the arts as much as you like, but not the artists — they're all rascals or debauchees. Why, the stories they tell about them are enough to raise the hair on your head, things I could n't repeat to my own daughter.

VERDELET [*aside to* POIRIER]. What?

POIRIER [*aside to* VERDELET]. They say, old man, that —

[*He takes* VERDELET *to one side and whispers to him*].

VERDELET. And do you believe things of that kind?

POIRIER. The people who told me knew what they were talking about.

[*Enter a Servant.*]

SERVANT. Dinner is served.

POIRIER [*to the Servant*]. Bring up a bottle of 1811 Pomard. [*To the* DUKE.] The year of the comet, Monsieur le Duc — fifteen francs a bottle! The king drinks no better. [*Aside to* VERDELET.] You must n't drink any — neither will I!

GASTON [*to the* DUKE]. Fifteen francs a bottle, to be returned when empty!

VERDELET [*aside to* POIRIER]. Are you going to allow him to make fun of you like that?

POIRIER [*aside to* VERDELET]. In matters of this sort, you must take your time.

[*They all go out.*]

ACT II

[*The scene is the same. As the curtain rises*, VERDELET, POIRIER, GASTON, *the* DUKE, *and* ANTOINETTE *enter from the dining-room.*]

GASTON. Well, Hector, what do you say? This is the house, and this is what we do every mortal day. Can you imagine a happier man on earth than myself?

DUKE. I must confess that you make me very envious; you almost reconcile me to the idea of marriage.

ANTOINETTE [*aside to* VERDELET]. Charming young man, that Duke de Montmeyran, is n't he?

VERDELET [*aside to* ANTOINETTE]. Yes, I like him.

GASTON. Monsieur Poirier, I must say, you are an excellent soul. Believe me, I'm not in the least ungrateful to you.

POIRIER. Oh, Monsieur le Marquis!

GASTON. Come, now, call me Gaston. Ah, Monsieur Verdelet, I am delighted to see you.

ANTOINETTE. He is a member of the family, dear.

GASTON. Shake hands, uncle!

VERDELET [*shaking hands with* GASTON — *aside*]. He's not so bad after all!

GASTON. You can't deny, Hector, that I'm downright lucky. Monsieur Poirier, something has been weighing on my conscience. You know, you think of nothing but how to make my existence one long series of good times. Will you never give me a chance to repay you? Try, now, I beg you, to think of something I might do for you in return — anything in my power.

POIRIER. Well, since you're in so good a humor, let me have a quarter of an hour's conversation with you — a serious conversation.

DUKE. I shall be glad to retire —

POIRIER. Oh, please don't, monsieur; be good enough to stay with us. This is going to be a kind of family council. You are not at all in the way, any more than is Monsieur Verdelet.

GASTON. What the devil, father-in-law! A family council! Are you going to have me out under a legal adviser?

POIRIER. Far from it, my dear Gaston. Let us sit down.

[*They all seat themselves.*]

GASTON. Monsieur Poirier has the floor.

POIRIER. You say you are happy, my dear Gaston. That is the finest recompense I could have.

GASTON. I ask nothing better than to increase my gratitude twofold.

POIRIER. You have spent three months of your honeymoon in the lap of idleness and luxury, and I think that that part of the romance is enough. It's now time to give your attention to hard facts.

GASTON. You talk like a book, I do declare! Very well, let us give our attention to history.

POIRIER. What do you intend to do?

GASTON. To-day?

POIRIER. And to-morrow — in the future. You surely have some idea?

GASTON. Of course: to-day I intend to do what I did yesterday; to-morrow what I did to-day. I'm not capricious, even though I may appear light-hearted. So long as the future promises to be as bright as the present, I am content.

POIRIER. And yet you are far too reasonable a man to believe that the honeymoon can last forever.

GASTON. Exactly; too reasonable, and too well posted on astronomy — but, of course, you have read Heinrich Heine?

POIRIER. You have, have n't you, Verdelet?

VERDELET. I admit I have.

POIRIER. Yes; he passed his school-days playing truant.

GASTON. Well, when Heinrich Heine was asked what became of all the full moons, he replied that they were broken in pieces and made into stars.

POIRIER. I don't quite see —

GASTON. When our honeymoon grows old, we shall break it up, and there will remain enough fragments to make a whole Milky Way.

POIRIER. Very pretty idea, I suppose.

DUKE. The sole merit of which is its extreme simplicity.

POIRIER. But, seriously, son-in-law, does n't this lazy life you are leading seem to threaten the happiness of a young household?

GASTON. Not in the least.

VERDELET. A man of your ability should n't be always condemned to a life of inactivity.

GASTON. Ah, but one can resign himself to —

ANTOINETTE. Are n't you afraid that in time you may be bored, dear — ?

GASTON. You fail to do yourself justice, my dear.

ANTOINETTE. I am not vain enough to believe that I can be everything in your life, and I must confess that I should be very happy to see you follow Monsieur de Montmeyran's example.

GASTON. Do you mean that I should enlist?

ANTOINETTE. Oh, no.

GASTON. Then, what — ?

POIRIER. We want you to take a position worthy of your name.

GASTON. There are but three: in the army, the church, and agriculture. Choose.

POIRIER. We all owe our services to France: she is our mother.

VERDELET. I can readily understand the sorrow of a son who sees his mother remarry; I can sympathize with his not joining in the wedding festivities; but if he is honest and sincere, he will not blame the mother. And if the second husband makes the mother happy, the son cannot with a good conscience help offering the second husband his hand.

POIRIER. The nobility won't always keep away as it does now; it's even beginning to recognize the fact already. More than one great noble has given a good example: Monsieur de Valchevrière, Monsieur de Chazerolles, Monsieur de Mont-Louis.

GASTON. Those gentlemen did what they thought best. I am not judging them, but I cannot emulate them.

ANTOINETTE. Why not, dear?

GASTON. Ask Montmeyran.

VERDELET. Monsieur le Duc's uniform answers for him.

DUKE. Allow me, monsieur: the soldier has but one idea, to obey; but one adversary, the enemy.

POIRIER. Still, monsieur, I might answer that —

GASTON. Let us drop the subject, Monsieur Poirier; this is not a question of politics. We may discuss opinions, never sentiments. I am bound by gratitude: my fidelity is that of a servant and of a friend. Let us say no more about this. [To the DUKE.] I beg your pardon, my dear fellow, but this is the first time we have talked politics here, and I promise it will be the last.

DUKE [aside to ANTOINETTE]. You have been led into an indiscretion, madame!

ANTOINETTE [aside to the DUKE]. I realize it — only too late!

GASTON. I bear you no malice, Monsieur Poirier. I have been a trifle direct, but I am dreadfully thin-skinned on that subject, and, doubtless without intending it, you have scratched me. I don't blame you, however. Shake hands.

POIRIER. You're only too good!

VERDELET [aside to POIRIER]. This is a pretty mess!

POIRIER [aside to VERDELET]. First attack repulsed, but I'm not lifting the siege.

[Enter a Servant.]

SERVANT. There are some people in the small waiting-room who say they have an appointment with Monsieur Poirier.

POIRIER. Very well. Ask them to wait a moment. I'll be there directly. [The Servant goes out.] Your creditors, son-in-law.

GASTON. Yours, my dear father-in-law. I have given them to you.

DUKE. For a wedding present.

VERDELET. Good-bye, Monsieur le Marquis.

GASTON. Are you leaving us so soon?

VERDELET. Very good of you. Antoinette has asked me to do something for her.

POIRIER. Well! What?

VERDELET. It's a secret between us.

GASTON. You know, if I were inclined to be jealous —

ANTOINETTE. But you are not.

GASTON. Is that a reproach? Very well, Monsieur Verdelet. I have made up my mind to be jealous, and I ask you in the name of the law to unveil the mystery!

VERDELET. You are the last person in the world whom I should think of telling!

GASTON. And why, please?

VERDELET. You are Antoinette's right hand, and the right hand should not know what —

GASTON. The left gives. You are right; I am indiscreet. Allow me to pay my indemnity. [*He gives his purse to* ANTOINETTE.] Put this with your own, my dear child.

ANTOINETTE. Thank you on behalf of my poor.

POIRIER [*aside*]. He *is* mighty generous!

DUKE. Will you allow me, too, madame, to steal a few blessings from you? [*He also gives her his purse.*] It is not heavy, but it is the corporal's mite.

ANTOINETTE. Offered from the heart of a true duke.

POIRIER [*aside*]. Has n't a sou to his name, and he gives to charity!

VERDELET. Are n't you going to add something, Poirier?

POIRIER. I've already given a thousand francs to the charity organization.

VERDELET. I see. Good-day, messieurs. Your names won't appear on the lists, but your charity won't be less welcome.

[*He goes out with* ANTOINETTE.]

POIRIER. See you later, Monsieur le Marquis; I'm going to pay your creditors.

GASTON. Now, Monsieur Poirier, simply because those fellows have lent me money is no reason why you should think you must be polite with them. They're unconscionable rascals. You must have had something to do with them. Hector, — old Père Salomon, Monsieur Chevassus, Monsieur Cogne?

DUKE. Did I! They're the first Arabs I ever had anything to do with. Lent me money at fifty per cent.

POIRIER. Highway robbery! And you were fool enough — I beg your pardon, Monsieur le Duc, — I beg your pardon!

DUKE. What else could I do? Ten thousand francs at two per cent is better than nothing at all at five per cent.

POIRIER. But, monsieur, there is a law against usury.

DUKE. Which the usurers respect and obey; they take only legal interest, but you get only one half the face value of the note in cash, you see.

POIRIER. And the other half?

DUKE. Stuffed lizards, as in Molière's time. Usurers do not progress: they were born perfect.

GASTON. Like the Chinese.

POIRIER. I hope, son-in-law, that you have n't borrowed at any such outrageous rate?

GASTON. I hope so too, father-in-law.

POIRIER. At fifty per cent!

GASTON. No more, no less.

POIRIER. And did you get stuffed lizards?

GASTON. Any number.

POIRIER. Why did n't you tell me sooner? I could have come to an agreement with them before the marriage.

GASTON. That is precisely what I did not want. Would it not be fine to see the Marquis de Presles buying back his pledged word, insulting his noble name!

POIRIER. But if you owe only half the amount — ?

GASTON. I received only half, but I owe the whole. I don't owe the money to those thieves, but to my own signature.

POIRIER. Allow me, Monsieur le Marquis, — I believe I may say that I am an honest man; I have never cheated any one out of a single sou, and I am incapable of advising you to do something underhand, but it appears to me that in paying back those scoundrels their principal at six per cent, you will have acted in an honorable and scrupulous way.

GASTON. This is not a question of honesty, but of honor.

POIRIER. What difference do you see between the two?

GASTON. Honor is a gentleman's honesty.

POIRIER. So, virtues change names when you want to put them into practice? You polish up their vulgarity in order to use them for yourself? I'm surprised at only one thing: that the nose of a nobleman deigns to be called by the same name when it happens to be on a tradesman's face!

GASTON. That is because all noses are similar.

DUKE. Within six inches!

POIRIER. Then don't you think that men are?

GASTON. It's a question.

POIRIER. Which was decided long ago, Monsieur le Marquis.

DUKE. Our rights and privileges have been abolished, but not our duties. Of all that remains to us there are but two words, but they are words which nothing can snatch from us: *Noblesse oblige!* No matter what happens, we shall abide by a code more severe than the law, that mysterious code which we call honor.

POIRIER. Well, Monsieur le Marquis, it is very fortunate for your honor that my honesty pays your debts. Only, as I am not a gentleman, I warn you that I shall do my best to get out of this fix as cheaply as I can.

GASTON. You must be very clever, indeed, to make any sort of compromise with those highway robbers: they are masters of the situation.

[*Reënter* ANTOINETTE.]

POIRIER. We'll see, we'll see. [*Aside.*] I have an idea: I'm going to play my own little game. [*Aloud.*] I'll go at once, so that they shan't get impatient.

DUKE. No, don't wait; they will devour you if you do.   [POIRIER *goes out.*]

GASTON. Poor Monsieur Poirier, I feel sorry for him. This latest revelation takes away all his pleasure in paying my debts.

DUKE. Listen to me: there are very few people who know how to be robbed. It is an art worthy a great lord.

[*Enter a Servant.*]

SERVANT. Messieurs de Ligny and de Chazerolles would like to speak to Monsieur le Marquis on behalf of Monsieur de Pontgrimaud.

GASTON. Very well. [*The Servant goes out.*] You receive the gentlemen, Hector. You don't need me to help you arrange the party.

ANTOINETTE. A party — ?

GASTON. Yes, I won a good deal of money from Pontgrimaud and I promised him a chance to take revenge. [*To* HECTOR.] To-morrow, some time in the morning, will be satisfactory for me.

DUKE [*aside to* GASTON]. When shall I see you again?

GASTON [*aside to* HECTOR]. Madame de Montjay is expecting me. At three, then, here.   [*The* DUKE *goes out.*]

GASTON [*sitting on a sofa, opens a magazine, yawns, and says to his wife*]. Would you like to go to the *Italiens* to-night?

ANTOINETTE. Yes, if you are going.

GASTON. I am. What gown are you going to wear?

ANTOINETTE. Any one you like.

GASTON. It makes no difference to me — I mean, you look very pretty in any of them.

ANTOINETTE. But you have such excellent taste, dear; you ought to advise me.

GASTON. I am not a fashion magazine, my dear child; and then, all you have to do is to watch the great ladies, make them your models: Madame de Nohan, Madame de Villepreux —

ANTOINETTE. Madame de Montjay —

GASTON. Why Madame de Montjay, rather than any one else?

ANTOINETTE. Because she pleases you more.

GASTON. Where did you get that idea?

ANTOINETTE. The other evening at the Opéra you paid her a rather long visit in her box. She is very pretty. Is she clever too?

GASTON. Very.   [*A pause.*]

ANTOINETTE. Why don't you tell me when I do something that does n't please you?

GASTON. I have never failed to do so.

ANTOINETTE. You never said you were displeased.

GASTON. Because you never gave me the occasion.

ANTOINETTE. Why, just a few moments ago, when I insisted that you take some position, I know I displeased you.

GASTON. I'd forgotten about that — it does n't matter.

ANTOINETTE. If I had had any notion what your ideas on that subject were, do you think for an instant that I should have —?

GASTON. Truly, my dear, it almost seems as if you were making excuses.

ANTOINETTE. That is because I am afraid you will think me childish and vain —

GASTON. What if you were a little proud? Is that a crime?

ANTOINETTE. I swear I have n't an ounce of pride.

GASTON [rising]. My dear, you have n't a single fault. And do you know that you have quite won the admiration of Montmeyran? You ought to be proud of that. Hector is difficult to please.

ANTOINETTE. Less so than you.

GASTON. Do you think me difficult to please? You see, you have some vanity — I've caught you in the act!

ANTOINETTE. I have no illusions about myself: I know very well what I need in order to be worthy of you. But if you will only take the trouble to guide me, tell me something about the ideas of the world you know, I love you so much that I would completely change myself.

GASTON [kissing her hand]. I could not but lose by the change, madame, and furthermore, I am only a middling teacher. There is but one school in which to learn what you think you lack: society. Study it.

ANTOINETTE. Very well, then, I shall study Madame de Montjay.

GASTON. Again! Are you doing me the honor to be jealous? Take care, my dear, that failing is distinctly bourgeois. You must learn, since you allow me to be your guide, that in our circle marriage does not necessarily mean a home and a household; only the noble and elegant things in life do we have in common among ourselves. When I am not with you, pray do not worry about what I am doing; merely say to yourself, "He is dissipating his imperfections in order that he may bring to me one hour of perfection, or nearly so."

ANTOINETTE. I think that your greatest imperfection is your absence.

GASTON. Neatly turned. Thank you. Who's this? My creditors!

[Enter the Creditors.]

GASTON. You here, messieurs! You have mistaken the door: the servants' entrance is on the other side.

SALOMON. We did n't want to leave without seeing you, Monsieur le Marquis.

GASTON. I can dispense with your thanks.

COGNE. We have come to ask for yours.

CHEVASSUS. You've treated us long enough as usurers.

COGNE. Leeches.

SALOMON. Blood-suckers.

CHEVASSUS. We're delighted to have this occasion to tell you that we are honest men.

GASTON. I fail to see the joke?

COGNE. This is not a joke, monsieur. We have loaned you money at six per cent.

GASTON. Have my notes not been acquitted in full?

SALOMON. There's a trifle lacking: some two hundred and eighteen thousand francs.

GASTON. What's that?

CHEVASSUS. We were obliged to submit to that!

SALOMON. And your father-in-law insisted on your being sent to the debtors' prison.

GASTON. My father-in-law insisted that —?

COGNE. Yes; it seems that you have been playing some underhanded trick with him, the poor fellow!

SALOMON. It'll teach him better next time!

COGNE. But meantime, we must bear the burden.

GASTON [to ANTOINETTE]. Your father, madame, has behaved in a very undignified way. [To the Creditors.] I confess myself in your debt, messieurs, but I have an income of only twenty-five thousand francs.

SALOMON. You know very well you can't touch the principal without your wife's consent. We have seen your marriage contract.

COGNE. You're not making your wife very happy —

GASTON. Leave the house!

SALOMON. You can't kick honest people

out of the house like dogs — people who've helped you [ANTOINETTE *has meantime sat down and is now writing*] — people who believed that the signature of the Marquis de Presles was worth something.

COGNE. And who were mistaken!

CREDITORS. Yes, mistaken!

ANTOINETTE [*handing SALOMON a check which she has written*]. You are not mistaken, messieurs: you are paid in full.

GASTON [*taking the check, he glances at it, and hands it back to SALOMON*]. Now that you really are thieves — leave the house! Rascals! Hurry up, or we'll have you swept out!

CREDITORS. Too good of you, Monsieur le Marquis! A thousand thanks!
[*They go out.*]

GASTON. You dear! I adore you!
[*He takes her in his arms and kisses her vehemently.*]

ANTOINETTE. Dear Gaston!

GASTON. Where in the world did your father find the heart he gave you?

ANTOINETTE. Don't judge my father too severely, dear. He is good and generous, but his ideas are narrow. He can't see beyond his own individual rights. It's the fault of his mind, not his heart. Now, if you consider that I have done my duty, forgive my father for that one moment of agony —

GASTON. I should be very ungrateful to refuse you anything.

ANTOINETTE. You really won't blame him, will you?

GASTON. No, since you wish it, Marquise, — Marquise, you hear?

ANTOINETTE. Call me your wife — the only title of which I am proud!

GASTON. You do love me a little?

ANTOINETTE. Have n't you noticed it, ungrateful man?

GASTON. Oh, yes, but I like to hear you say it — especially at this moment. [*The clock strikes three.*] Three o'clock! [*Aside.*] The devil! Madame de Montjay is expecting me!

ANTOINETTE. You are smiling — what are you thinking about?

GASTON. Would you like to take a ride with me in the Bois?

ANTOINETTE. Well — I'm not dressed.

GASTON. Just throw a shawl over your shoulders. Ring for your maid. [ANTOINETTE *rings.*]

[*Enter POIRIER.*]

POIRIER. Well, son-in-law, have you seen your creditors?

GASTON [*with evident ill-humor*]. Yes, monsieur —

ANTOINETTE [*aside to GASTON, as she takes his arm*]. Remember your promise.

GASTON [*amiably*]. Yes, my dear father-in-law, I have seen them.

[*Enter the Maid.*]

ANTOINETTE [*to the Maid*]. Bring me my shawl and hat and have the horses hitched.
[*The Maid goes out.*]

GASTON [*to POIRIER*]. Allow me to congratulate you on your good stroke of business; you did play them a very clever trick. [*Aside to ANTOINETTE.*] Am I not nice?

POIRIER. You take it better than I thought you would; I was prepared for any number of objections on the score of your "honor."

GASTON. I am reasonable, father-in-law. You have acted according to your own ideas. I have so little objection to that: we have acted according to *our* ideas.

POIRIER. What's that?

GASTON. You gave those rascals only the actual sum of money borrowed from them: we have paid the rest.

POIRIER [*to ANTOINETTE*]. What! Did you sign away — ? [ANTOINETTE *nods.*] Good God, what have you done!

ANTOINETTE. I beg your pardon, father —

POIRIER. I've moved heaven and earth in order to give you a good round sum and you throw it out of the window! Two hundred and eighteen thousand frances!

GASTON. Don't worry about that, Monsieur Poirier; we are the ones who lose: you receive the benefit.

[*Reënter the Maid, with a hat and shawl.*]

ANTOINETTE. Good-bye, father, we are going to the Bois.

GASTON. Your arm, wife! [*They go out.*]

POIRIER. He gets on my nerves, that son-in-law of mine. I can see very well that I can never get any satisfaction out of him. He's an incurable gentleman! He refuses to do anything — he's good for nothing — he's a frightful expense — he is master of my own house. This has got to end. [*He rings. A moment later —*]

[*Enter a Servant.*]

Have the porter and the cook come here. [*The servant goes out.*] We'll see, son-in-law. I've been too soft and kind and generous. So you won't give in, my fine friend? Very well, do as you please! Neither will I: you remain a marquis, and I shall remain a bourgeois. I'll at least have the consolation of living as I want to live.

[*Enter the Porter.*]

Did monsieur ask for me?

POIRIER. Yes, François, monsieur did ask for you. Put up a sign on the house at once.

PORTER. A sign?

POIRIER. "To let, a magnificent apartment on the first floor, with stables and appurtenances."

PORTER. Monsieur le Marquis's apartment?

POIRIER. Exactly, François.

PORTER. But Monsieur le Marquis gave me no orders about this?

POIRIER. Idiot, who is master here? Who owns this house?

PORTER. You, monsieur.

POIRIER. Then, do as I tell you. I can dispense with your opinions.

PORTER. Very well, monsieur.

[*The Porter goes out.*]

[*Enter VATEL.*]

Hurry, François.— Come here, Monsieur Vatel. You are preparing a grand dinner for to-morrow?

VATEL. Yes, monsieur, and I may even say that the menu would be no disgrace to my illustrious ancestor. It will be a veritable work of art. Monsieur Poirier will be astonished —

POIRIER. Have you the menu with you?

VATEL. No, monsieur, it is being copied, but I know it by heart.

POIRIER. Be good enough to recite it to me.

VATEL. *Potage aux ravioles à l'Italienne* and *potage à l'orge à la Marie Stuart.*

POIRIER. Instead of those two unknown soups you will have ordinary vegetable soup.

VATEL. What, monsieur?

POIRIER. It is my will. Continue.

VATEL. After the soup: *Carpe du Rhin à la Lithuanienne, poulardes à la Godard, filet de bœuf braisé aux raisins à la Napolitaine,* Westphalian ham, Madeira sauce.

POIRIER. Here's an easier and much healthier after-soup course for you: Brill with caper sauce; Bayonne ham with spinach; larded veal with gooseberries; and rabbit.

VATEL. But, Monsieur Poirier, I shall never consent to —

POIRIER. I am master here, do you understand? Continue.

VATEL. Entrées: *Filets de volaille à la concordat — croustades de truffes garnies de foie à la royale;* stuffed pheasants *à la Montpensier,* red partridges *farcis à la bohémienne.*

POIRIER. Instead of these entrées we'll have nothing at all. Let's proceed at once to the roasts. That's the important part.

VATEL. But this is against all the precepts of the art.

POIRIER. I'll take the responsibility for that. Now, what are your roasts?

VATEL. There is no use going any further, monsieur; my ancestor thrust a sword through his heart for a lesser insult. I resign.

POIRIER. I was just going to ask you to do that, old man. Of course, you still have a week here, while I can look for another servant —

VATEL. A servant! Monsieur, I am a chef!

POIRIER. I am going to replace you by a woman-cook. Meantime, during the week when you are in my service, you will be good enough to execute my orders.

VATEL. I would rather blow my brains out than be false to my name!

POIRIER [*aside*]. Another stickler for his name! [*Aloud.*] Blow your brains out, Monsieur Vatel, but be careful not to burn my sauces. Good-day to you. [VATEL *goes out.*] And now I'm going to invite some of my old friends from the Rue des Bourdonnais. Monsieur le Marquis de Presles, we are going to make you come down a few pegs!

[*He goes out humming the first verse of "Monsieur et Madame Denis."*]

ACT III

[*The scene is the same.* GASTON *and* ANTOINETTE *are present.*]

GASTON. What a delightful ride! Charming spring weather. You might almost think it was April!

ANTOINETTE. Really, were n't you too bored?

GASTON. With you, my dear? As a matter of fact, you are the most charming woman I know.

ANTOINETTE. Compliments, Monsieur?

GASTON. Oh, no: the truth in its most brutal form. And what a delightful journey I made into your mind and heart. How many undiscovered points I have found. Why, I have been living near you without knowing you, like a Parisian in Paris.

ANTOINETTE. And I don't displease you too much?

GASTON. It is my place to ask you that question. I feel like a peasant who has been entertaining a disguised queen: all at once the queen puts on her crown and the peasant feels embarrassed and makes excuses for not having been more attentive and hospitable.

ANTOINETTE. Be assured, good peasant, that your queen blamed nothing except her own incognito.

GASTON. For having kept it so long, cruel queen? Was it out of sheer coquetry, and to have another honeymoon? You have succeeded. Hitherto I have been only your husband; now I want to become your lover.

ANTOINETTE. No, my dear Gaston, remain my husband. I think that a woman can cease to love her lover, never her husband.

GASTON. Ah, so you are not romantic?

ANTOINETTE. I am, but in my own way. My ideas on the subject are perhaps not fashionable, but they are deeply rooted in me, like childhood impressions. When I was a little girl, I could never understand how it was that my father and mother were n't related, and ever since then marriage has seemed to me as the tenderest and closest of all relationships. To love a man who is not my husband seems contrary to nature.

GASTON. The ideas rather of a Roman matron, my dear Antoinette, but keep them, for the sake of my honor and my happiness.

ANTOINETTE. Take care! There is another side: I am jealous, I warn you. If there is only one man in the world whom I can love, I must have all his love. The day I discover that this is not so, I shall make no complaint or reproach, but the link will be broken. At once my husband will become a stranger to me — I should consider myself a widow.

GASTON [*aside*]. The devil! [*Aloud.*] Fear nothing, dear Antoinette, we shall live like two lovers, like Philemon and Baucis — with the exception of the hut — you don't insist on the hut, do you?

ANTOINETTE. Not in the least.

GASTON. I am going to hold a brilliant celebration of our wedding, and I want you to eclipse all the other women and make all the men envious of me.

ANTOINETTE. Must we proclaim our happiness so loud?

GASTON. Don't you like entertainments?

ANTOINETTE. I like everything that you like. Are we going to have company at dinner to-day?

GASTON. No — to-morrow. To-day we have only Montmeyran. Why did you ask?

ANTOINETTE. Should I dress?

GASTON. Yes, because I want you to make married life attractive to Hector. Go now, my dear child. I shan't forget this happy day!

ANTOINETTE. How happy I am!
[*She goes out.*]
GASTON. There is no denying the fact:
she is prettier than Madame de Montjay.
Devil take me if I am not falling in love
with my wife! Love is like good fortune:
while we seek it afar, it is waiting for us at
home.

[*Enter* POIRIER.]

Well, my dear father-in-law, how are you
taking your little disappointment? Are you
still angry on account of the money? Have
you decided to do something?
POIRIER. I have.
GASTON. Something violent?
POIRIER. Something necessary.
GASTON. Might I be so indiscreet as to
inquire what?
POIRIER. On the contrary, monsieur, I
even owe you an explanation. When I
gave you my daughter together with a million francs dowry, I never for a moment
thought that you would refuse to take a
position.
GASTON. Please let's drop that subject.
POIRIER. I merely wanted to remind
you. I confess I was wrong in thinking that
a gentleman would ever consent to work
like a man; I own my mistake. As a result
of that mistake, however, I have allowed
you to run my house on a scale which I
don't myself keep up with; and since it is
understood that our fortune alone is our
only source of income, it seems to me just,
reasonable, and necessary, to cut down,
because I see I have no hope of any further
increase in revenue. I have therefore
thought of making a few reforms, which
you will undoubtedly approve.
GASTON. Proceed, Sully! Go on, Turgot!
Cut, slash. You find me in splendid humor!
Take advantage of the fact.
POIRIER. I am most delighted at your
condescension. I have, I say, decided,
resolved, commanded —
GASTON. I beg your pardon, father-in-
law, but if you have decided, resolved,
commanded, it seems quite superfluous for
you to consult me.
POIRIER. I am not consulting you; I
am merely telling you the facts.

GASTON. So you are not consulting me?
POIRIER. Are you surprised?
GASTON. A little, but, as I told you, I
am in splendid humor.
POIRIER. Well, the first reform, my
dear boy —
GASTON. You mean, your dear Gaston,
I think? A slip of the tongue!
POIRIER. Dear Gaston, dear boy — all
the same. Some familiarity between
father-in-law and son-in-law is allowed,
doubtless?
GASTON. And on your part, Monsieur
Poirier, it flatters and honors me. You
were about to say that your first reform — ?
POIRIER. That you, monsieur, do me the
favor to stop making fun of me. I'm tired
of being the butt of all your jokes.
GASTON. Now, now, Monsieur Poirier,
don't be angry.
POIRIER. I know very well that you
think I'm of little account, that I'm not
very intelligent, but —
GASTON. Where did you get that idea?
POIRIER. But let me tell you, there is
more brains in my little finger than there
is in your whole body.
GASTON. This is ridiculous —
POIRIER. *I'm* no marquis!
GASTON. Hush! Not so loud! Some one
might believe it!
POIRIER. It makes no difference to me
whether they do or not. I don't pretend to
be a gentleman, thank God! It's not worth
troubling my mind about.
GASTON. Not worth troubling about?
POIRIER. No, monsieur, no! I'm an old
dyed-in-the-wool Liberal, that's what I
am, and I judge men on their merits, and
not according to their titles. I laugh at
the mere accident of birth. The nobility
don't dazzle me: I think no more of them
than I do of the Judgment Day. I'm delighted to have this occasion of telling
you so.
GASTON. Do you think I have merits?
POIRIER. No, monsieur, I do not.
GASTON. No? Then, why did you give
me your daughter?
POIRIER. Why did I — ?
GASTON. Possibly you had some afterthought?

POIRIER [*embarrassed*]. Afterthought?

GASTON. Allow me: your daughter did not love me when you brought me to your home; and certainly it was not my debts which appealed to you, and which caused the honor of your choice to fall upon me. Now, since it was not my title either, I am forced to assume that you must have had some afterthought.

POIRIER. And what of it, monsieur? What if I did try to combine my own interest with my daughter's happiness? Where would be the harm? Who could blame me, I who gave a million right out of my pocket, for choosing a son-in-law who could in some way pay me back for my sacrifice — My daughter loved you, did n't she? I thought of her first: that was my duty, in fact my right.

GASTON. I don't contest that, Monsieur Poirier; I only say that you were wrong in one respect: not to have had confidence in me.

POIRIER. Well, you are not a very encouraging sort of man.

GASTON. Are you blaming me for my occasional jokes at your expense? Possibly I am not the most respectful son-in-law in the world; I admit it; only allow me to state that in serious matters I know how to be serious. It is only right that you were looking for the support which I have found in you.

POIRIER [*aside*]. Can he really have understood the situation?

GASTON. Look here, my dear father-in-law, can I help you in any way? That is, if I am good for anything?

POIRIER. Well, I once dreamed of being introduced at court.

GASTON. Ah, so you still have that desire to dance at court?

POIRIER. It's not a matter of dancing. Do me the honor of thinking me not quite so frivolous as that. I am not vain or trivial.

GASTON. Then, in the name of Heaven, what are you? Explain yourself.

POIRIER [*piteously*]. I am ambitious.

GASTON. Why, you're not blushing, are you? Why? With all the experience you have acquired in the realm of business, you might well aspire to any heights? Commerce is the true school for statesmanship.

POIRIER. That's what Verdelet was telling me only this morning.

GASTON. That is where one can obtain a high and grand view of things, and stand detached from the petty interests which — that is the sort of condition from which your Richelieus and Colberts sprang.

POIRIER. Oh, I don't pretend — !

GASTON. Now, my good Monsieur Poirier, what would suit you? A prefecture? Nonsense! Council of State? No! Diplomatic service? Let me see, the Turkish Embassy is vacant at present —

POIRIER. I'm a stay-at-home — and then I don't understand Turkish.

GASTON. Wait! [*Striking* POIRIER *on the shoulder.*] The peerage — it would fit you to a T.

POIRIER. Oh! Do you really think so?

GASTON. That's the trouble: you don't fall into any category, you see. The Institute? No. You're not a member of the Institute?

POIRIER. Oh, don't worry about that. I'll pay — three thousand francs, if necessary — direct contributions. I have three millions now at the bank; they await only a word from you to be put to good use.

GASTON. Ah, Machiavelli! Sixtus V! You'll outstrip them all!

POIRIER. Yes, I think I will!

GASTON. But I sincerely hope your ambition will not stop there? You must have a title.

POIRIER. Oh, I don't insist on such vain baubles. I 'm an old Liberal, as I told you.

GASTON. All the more reason. A Liberal must despise only the nobility of the old régime; now, the new nobility, which has no ancestors —

POIRIER. The nobility that owes everything to itself —!

GASTON. You might be a count.

POIRIER. No, I'll be reasonable about it: a baronetcy would suffice.

GASTON. Baron Poirier! Sounds well!

POIRIER. Yes, Baron Poirier !

GASTON [*looks at* POIRIER *and then bursts out laughing*]. I beg your pardon! But —

really — this is too funny! Baron — !
Monsieur Poirier! Baron de Catillard — !
POIRIER [aside]. He's been making fun
of me!
GASTON [calling]. Come here, Hector!

[Enter the DUKE.]

Come here! Do you know why Jean
Gaston de Presles received three wounds
from an arquebuse at the battle of Ivry?
Do you know why François Gaston de
Presles led the attack on La Rochelle?
Why Louis Gaston de Presles was blown to
pieces at La Hogue? Why Philippe Gaston
de Presles captured two flags at Fontenoy?
Why my grandfather gave up his life at
Quiberon? It was all in order that some
day Monsieur Poirier might be peer of
France and a baron!
DUKE. What do you mean?
GASTON. This is the secret of that little
attack on me this morning.
DUKE [aside]. I see!
POIRIER. And do you know, Monsieur
de Duc, why I have worked fourteen hours
a day for thirty years? Why I heaped up,
sou by sou, four millions of cash, while I
deprived myself of everything but bare necessities? It was all in order that some day
Monsieur le Marquis Gaston de Presles,
who died neither at Quiberon, nor at Fontenoy, nor at La Hogue, nor anywhere
else, might die of old age on a feather bed,
after having spent his life doing nothing
at all.
DUKE. Well said, monsieur!
GASTON. You are cut out for an orator!

[Enter a Servant.]

SERVANT. There are some gentlemen
here who would like to see the apartment.
GASTON. What apartment?
SERVANT. Monsieur le Marquis's —
GASTON. Do they think this a natural
history museum?
POIRIER [to the Servant]. Tell the gentlemen to call again. [The Servant goes out.]
Pardon me, son-in-law, I was so carried
away by your gayety, that I forgot to
mention that I am renting the first floor
of my house.
GASTON. What's that?

POIRIER. That is one of the little re-
forms I was speaking about.
GASTON. And where do you intend to
lodge me?
POIRIER. On the floor above: the apart-
ment is large enough for us all.
GASTON. A Noah's Ark!
POIRIER. Of course, it goes without
saying that I am renting the stables and
carriages, too.
GASTON. And my horses — are you
going to lodge them on the second floor?
POIRIER. You will sell them.
GASTON. And go on foot?
DUKE. It will do you good; you don't do
half enough walking.
POIRIER. I shall, however, keep my own
blue coupé. I'll lend it to you when you
need it.
DUKE. When the weather is nice!
GASTON. Now, see here, Monsieur
Poirier, this is — !

[Enter a Servant.]

SERVANT. Monsieur Vatel would like to
speak a word with Monsieur le Marquis.
GASTON. Tell him to come in.

[Enter VATEL, dressed in black.]

What does this mean, Monsieur Vatel?
Are you going to a funeral? And on the
eve of battle!
VATEL. The position in which I have
been placed is such that I am forced to
desert in order to escape dishonor. Will
Monsieur le Marquis kindly cast his eyes
over the menu which Monsieur Poirier has
imposed upon me!
GASTON. Monsieur Poirier imposed on
you? Let us see. [Reading.] "Lapin
sauté!"
POIRIER. My old friend Ducaillou's
favorite dish.
GASTON. "Stuffed turkey and chest-
nuts!"
POIRIER. My old comrade Groschenet
is very fond of it.
GASTON. Are you entertaining the whole
Rue des Bourdonnais?
POIRIER. Together with the Faubourg
Saint-Germain.
GASTON. I accept your resignation,

Monsieur Vatel. [VATEL *goes out*.] So, to-morrow my friends are to have the honor of meeting yours?

POIRIER. Exactly; they will have that honor. Monsieur le Duc will not, I hope, feel humiliated at having to eat soup — my soup — as he sits between Monsieur and Madame Pincebourde?

DUKE. Not at all. This little debauch is not in the least displeasing. Undoubtedly Madame Pincebourde will sing during the dessert?

GASTON. And after dinner we shall have a game of piquet, too?

DUKE. Or lotto.

POIRIER. Pope Joan also.

GASTON. And I trust we shall repeat the debauch from time to time?

POIRIER. My home will be open every evening, and your friends will always find a welcome there.

GASTON. Really, Monsieur Poirier, your home will soon become a center of marvelous pleasures, a miniature Capua. But I am afraid I should become a slave of luxury and I shall, therefore, leave no later than to-morrow.

POIRIER. I am sorry to hear it, but my home is not a prison. What career do you intend to follow? Medicine or Law?

GASTON. Who said anything about a career?

POIRIER. Or will you enter the Department of Roads and Bridges? For you will certainly be unable to keep up your rank on nine thousand francs income?

GASTON. Nine thousand francs income?

POIRIER. Well, the account is easy to make out: you received five hundred thousand francs as my daughter's dowry. The wedding and installation took about a hundred thousand. You have just given two hundred and eighteen thousand to your creditors; you have, therefore, one hundred and eighty-two thousand left, which, at the usual interest, will yield you nine thousand francs income. You see? On that can you supply your friends with *Carpe à la Lithuanienne* and *Volailles à la concordat?* Take my word for it, my dear Gaston, stay with me; you will be more comfortable than in a home of your own.

Think of your children, who will not be sorry some day to find in the pockets of the Marquis de Presles the savings of old man Poirier. Good-bye, son-in-law, I'm going to settle accounts with Monsieur Vatel.

[POIRIER *goes out*.]

GASTON [*as he and the* DUKE *exchange glances and the* DUKE *bursts into peals of laughter*]. You think it funny, do you?

DUKE. Indeed I do! So this is the modest and generous fruit-tree of a father-in-law! This Georges Dandin! At last you've found your master, old man. In the name of Heaven, don't look so miserable! See there, you look like a prince starting on a crusade, turning back because of the rain! Smile a little; this is n't so tragic after all!

GASTON. You are right. Monsieur Poirier, you are rendering me a great service that you little dream of!

DUKE. A service?

GASTON. Yes, my dear fellow. I was about to make a fool of myself: fall in love with my wife. Fortunately, Monsieur Poirier has put a stop to that.

DUKE. Your wife is not to blame for the stupidity of her father. She is charming!

GASTON. Nonsense! She's just like her father!

DUKE. Not the least bit, I tell you!

GASTON. There is a family resemblance — I insist! I could n't kiss her without thinking of the old fool. Now I *did* want to sit at home with my wife by the fireside, but the moment it is to be a kitchen fireside — [*He takes out his watch.*] Good-evening!

DUKE. Where are you going?

GASTON. To Madame de Montjay's; she's been waiting two hours already.

DUKE. Gaston, don't go.

GASTON. They want to make my life a hardship for me here, make me feel penitent —

DUKE. Listen to me!

GASTON. You can't persuade me.

DUKE. What about your duel?

GASTON. That's so — I'd forgotten about that.

DUKE. You are going to fight to-morrow at two in the Bois de Vincennes.

GASTON. Very well. With this humor on me, Pontgrimaud is going to spend a nice fifteen minutes to-morrow!

[*Enter* VERDELET *and* ANTOINETTE.]

ANTOINETTE. Are you going out, dear?

GASTON. Yes, madame, I am going out.
[*He goes out.*]

VERDELET. Well, Toinon, his humor is n't quite so charming as you described it?

ANTOINETTE. I don't understand why—?

DUKE. Very serious things are happening, madame.

ANTOINETTE. What?

DUKE. Your father is ambitious.

VERDELET. Poirier ambitious?

DUKE. He was counting on his son-in-law's title to —

VERDELET. Get into the peerage — like Monsieur Michaud! [*Aside.*] Old fool!

DUKE. He's adopted childish measures in retaliation after Gaston refused to help him. I'm afraid it is you, however, who will bear the expenses of the war.

ANTOINETTE. How do you mean?

VERDELET. It's only too simple: if your father is making the house disagreeable to your husband, he will seek distraction elsewhere.

ANTOINETTE. Distraction elsewhere?

DUKE. Monsieur Verdelet has put his finger on the spot. You, madame, are the only person who can prevent a disaster. If your father loves you, you must stand between him and Gaston. Make a truce between them at once. There is no harm done yet, and everything can be as it was.

ANTOINETTE. No harm done yet? Everything can be as it was? You make me very much afraid. Against whom am I to defend myself?

DUKE. Against your father.

ANTOINETTE. No: you are not telling me everything. What my father has done is not enough to take my husband from me in the space of a single day. He's making love to some woman, is he not?

DUKE. No, madame, but —

ANTOINETTE. Please, Monsieur le Duc, don't try to hide the truth. I have a rival!

DUKE. Do calm yourself!

ANTOINETTE. I feel it. I know it! He is with her now!

DUKE. No, madame: he loves you.

ANTOINETTE. But he has just come to know me since an hour ago. Ha, it was n't to me that he felt he must tell of his anger — he went elsewhere with his troubles!

VERDELET. Now, now, Toinon, don't get so excited. He went out for a walk, that's all. That was what I always did when Poirier made me angry.

[*Enter a Servant carrying a letter on a silver plate.*]

SERVANT. A letter for Monsieur le Marquis.

ANTOINETTE. He has gone out. Lay it there. [*The Servant lays the letter on a table.* ANTOINETTE *looks at it, and says, aside:*] A woman's hand! [*Aloud.*] From whom does this come?

SERVANT. Madame de Montjay's footman brought it.   [*He goes out.*]

ANTOINETTE [*aside*]. Madame de Montjay!

DUKE. I shall see Gaston before you, madame. Would you like me to give him the letter?

ANTOINETTE. Are you afraid I might open it?

DUKE. Oh, madame!

ANTOINETTE. It must have crossed Gaston.

VERDELET. The idea! Your husband's mistress would never dare write him here!

ANTOINETTE. She must despise me, if she would dare to write to him here. But I don't say she is his mistress. I only say that he is making love to her. I say that because I am positive.

DUKE. But I swear, madame —

ANTOINETTE. Would you dare swear, — seriously swear, — Monsieur le Duc?

DUKE. My oath would prove nothing, for a gentleman has the right to lie in a case of this sort. No matter what the truth is, I have warned you of the danger and suggested a means of escape. I have done my duty as a friend and an honorable man. Do not ask anything else of me.

[*He goes out.*]

ANTOINETTE. I have just lost everything I had won in Gaston's affection. An hour ago he called me Marquise, and my father has just brutally reminded him that I was Mademoiselle Poirier.

VERDELET. Well, is it impossible for any one to love Mademoiselle Poirier?

ANTOINETTE. Possibly my own devotion might have touched him, my own love have awakened his. That was already beginning, but my father has stopped it. His mistress! She can't be that yet, can she, Tony? You don't really believe she is, do you?

VERDELET. Certainly not!

ANTOINETTE. I understand how he might have been making love to her for the last few days. But if he is really her lover, then he must have begun the day after our marriage. That would be vile!

VERDELET. Yes, my dear child.

ANTOINETTE. Of course, he did n't marry me with the idea that he would never love me — he should n't have condemned me so soon.

VERDELET. No, of course he should n't.

ANTOINETTE. You don't seem to be very sure. You must be mad to suspect a thing of that sort! You know very well my husband would n't be capable of it! Tell me — there's no doubt, is there? You don't think him so low?

VERDELET. No!

ANTOINETTE. Then you can swear he is innocent! Swear it, dear Tony, swear it!

VERDELET. I swear it! I swear it!

ANTOINETTE. Why is she writing a letter to him?

VERDELET. It's an invitation, probably, to a party of some sort.

ANTOINETTE. It must be very important, if she sends it by a footman. To think that the secret of my whole future life is in that envelope. Let's go — that letter tempts me —

[She lays the letter, which she has meanwhile picked up, on the table and stands fixedly looking at it.]

VERDELET. Come, then, you are right.
[She does not move.]

[Enter POIRIER.]

POIRIER. Why, Antoinette — [To VERDELET.] What is she looking at? A letter? [He picks up the letter.]

ANTOINETTE. Leave it there, father, it is addressed to Monsieur de Presles.

POIRIER [looking at the address]. Pretty handwriting! [He sniffs the letter.] Does n't smell of tobacco! It's from a woman!

ANTOINETTE. Yes, I know; it's from Madame de Montjay.

POIRIER. How excited you are! You're feverish, are n't you? [He takes her hand.] You are!

ANTOINETTE. No, father.

POIRIER. Yes, you are. What's the matter? Tell me.

ANTOINETTE. Nothing, I tell you.

VERDELET [aside to POIRIER]. Don't worry her. She's jealous.

POIRIER. Are you jealous? Is the Marquis unfaithful to you? By God, if that's so —

ANTOINETTE. Father, dear, if you love me, don't —

POIRIER. If I love you — !

ANTOINETTE. Don't torment Gaston.

POIRIER. Who's tormenting him? I'm just economizing, that's all.

VERDELET. You irritate the Marquis, and your daughter suffers for it.

POIRIER. You mind your own business. [To ANTOINETTE.] What has that man done to you? I must know.

ANTOINETTE [frightened]. Nothing — nothing. Don't quarrel with him, for Heaven's sake!

POIRIER. Then, why are you jealous? Why are you looking at that letter, eh? [He takes the letter.] Do you think that Madame de Montjay — ?

ANTOINETTE. No, no!

POIRIER. She does, does n't she, Verdelet?

VERDELET. Well, she thinks —

POIRIER. It's very easy to find out — [He breaks the seal.]

ANTOINETTE. Father! A letter is sacred.

POIRIER. There is nothing so sacred to me as your happiness.

VERDELET. Take care, Poirier. What will your son-in-law say?

POIRIER. I don't care a hang about my son-in-law. [*He opens the letter.*]

ANTOINETTE. Please, don't read that letter.

POIRIER. I will read it. If it is n't my right, it is my duty. [*Reading:*] " Dear Gaston —" The blackguard!

[*He drops the letter.*]

ANTOINETTE. She is his mistress! Oh, God! [*She falls into a chair.*]

POIRIER [*taking* VERDELET *by the coat collar*]. You allowed me to arrange this marriage!

VERDELET. Oh — this is too much!

POIRIER. When I asked for your advice, why did n't you oppose me? Why did n't you warn me what was going to happen?

VERDELET. I told you twenty times — but, no, monsieur was ambitious!

POIRIER. Much good it did me!

VERDELET. She's fainting!

POIRIER. Good God!

VERDELET [*kneeling before* ANTOINETTE]. Toinon, my child, come to yourself!

POIRIER. Get out! You don't know what to say to her! [*Kneeling before* ANTOINETTE.] Toinon, my child, come to yourself!

ANTOINETTE. It was nothing — I'm well, father.

POIRIER. Don't worry, I'll get rid of the monster for you.

ANTOINETTE. What have I done to deserve this! And after three months of marriage! Why — the day after, the day after — ! He was n't faithful to me for a single day. He ran to her from my arms. Did n't he feel my heart beating? He did n't understand that I was giving myself and my love completely up to him. The wretch! I can't live — after this!

POIRIER. Can't live! You must! What would become of me without you? The scoundrel! Where are you going?

ANTOINETTE. To my room.

POIRIER. Do you want me to come with you?

ANTOINETTE. Thank you, father, — no.

VERDELET [*to* POIRIER]. Leave her to cry alone. Tears will make her feel better. [ANTOINETTE *goes out.*]

POIRIER. What a marriage! What a marriage!

[*He strides back and forth, striking his breast as he walks.*]

VERDELET. Calm yourself, Poirier, everything can be arranged again. At present our duty is to bring these two hearts together again.

POIRIER. I know my duty and I am going to do it. [*He picks up the letter.*]

VERDELET. Please, now, don't do anything foolish!

[*Enter* GASTON.]

POIRIER. Are you looking for something, monsieur?

GASTON. Yes: a letter.

POIRIER. From Madame de Montjay. You need n't look for it, it is in my pocket.

GASTON. Have you by any chance opened it?

POIRIER. Yes, monsieur, I have.

GASTON. You have? Do you realize, monsieur, that that is an infamous trick? The act of a dishonest and dishonorable man?

VERDELET. Monsieur le Marquis! — Poirier!

POIRIER. There is only one dishonorable man here, and that is you!

GASTON. Let us drop that! In stealing from me the secret of my fault, you have forfeited the right to judge it. There is but one thing more sacred than the lock of a safe, monsieur, and that is the seal of a letter — because *it* cannot defend itself.

VERDELET [*to* POIRIER]. What did I tell you?

POIRIER. This is ridiculous! Do you mean to tell me that a father has n't the right — ? Why, I'm doing you a great favor even to answer you! You'll explain in court, Monsieur le Marquis.

VERDELET. In court!

POIRIER. Do you think a man can bring despair and sin into our family and not be punished? I'll have a divorce, monsieur!

GASTON. Will you drag all this into court? — Where that letter will be read?

POIRIER. In public. Yes, monsieur, in public.

VERDELET. You're crazy, Poirier. Think of the scandal!

GASTON. Of course, you're forgetting: a woman will lose her reputation!

POIRIER. Now, say something about her honor! Yes, I expected that!

GASTON. Yes, her honor, and if that is n't enough to dissuade you, her ruin —

POIRIER. So much the better! I'm delighted! She will get all she deserves, the — !

GASTON. Monsieur — !

POIRIER. She 'll get no sympathy! To take a husband from his poor young wife, after three months of marriage!

GASTON. She is less to blame than I. I am the only one you should accuse —

POIRIER. You need n't worry: I despise you as the lowest of the low! Are n't you ashamed of yourself? To sacrifice a charming woman like Antoinette! Has she ever given you cause for complaint? Find a single fault, a single one, in order to excuse yourself! She has a heart of gold — and what eyes! And her education! You know what it cost me, Verdelet?

VERDELET. Do keep calm, Poirier!

POIRIER. I am, am I not? If I only — No, there is justice — I'm going to see my lawyer at once.

GASTON. Please wait until to-morrow, monsieur, I beg you. Just take time to think it over.

POIRIER. I have thought it over.

GASTON [to VERDELET]. Please help me to prevent him from committing an irreparable blunder, monsieur.

VERDELET. Ah, you don't know him.

GASTON [to POIRIER]. Take care, monsieur. It is my duty to save that woman, save her at any price. Let me tell you that I am responsible for everything.

POIRIER. I know that very well.

GASTON. You have no idea how desperate I can be.

POIRIER. So you're threatening?

GASTON. Yes, I am threatening. Give me that letter. You are not going to leave this room until I have it.

POIRIER. Violence, eh? Must I ring for the servants?

GASTON. That's so — I'm losing my head. At least, listen to me. You are not naturally mean; you are just angry. And now your sorrow makes you so excited that you have no idea what you are doing.

POIRIER. I have a right to be angry, and my sorrow is decent and fitting.

GASTON. I have told you, monsieur, I confess I am to blame; I am sorry. But if I promised you never to see Madame de Montjay again, if I swore that I would spend my life in trying to make your daughter happy —?

POIRIER. It would merely be the second time you have sworn! Let's stop this nonsense!

GASTON. Very well. You were right this morning: it is lack of an occupation that has been my ruin.

POIRIER. Ah, now, you admit it!

GASTON. Well, what if I took a position?

POIRIER. You —? A position?

GASTON. You have the right to doubt my word, that is true, but I ask you to keep that letter, and if I fail to keep my promise, you can always —

VERDELET. That's a good guarantee, Poirier.

POIRIER. A guarantee of what?

VERDELET. That he will stand by his promise: that he will never see that lady again, that he will take a position, that he will make your daughter happy. What more can you ask?

POIRIER. I see; but what assurance can I have?

VERDELET. The letter! What the devil, the letter!

POIRIER. That's so, yes, that's so.

VERDELET. Well, do you accept? Anything is better than a divorce.

POIRIER. I don't quite agree with that, but if you insist — [To the MARQUIS.] For my part, monsieur, I am willing to accept your offer. Now we have only to consult my daughter.

VERDELET. She will surely not want any scandal.

POIRIER. Let's go and find her. [To GASTON.] Believe me, monsieur, my only object in all this is to assure my daughter's happiness. And the proof of my own sincerity is that I expect nothing from you, that I will receive no favor from your hands, that I am firmly decided to remain the same plain business man I have always been.

VERDELET. Good, Poirier!

POIRIER [to VERDELET]. So long, at least, as he does n't make my daughter so happy that — [They go out.]

GASTON. Blame it on yourself, Marquis de Presles. What humiliations! Ah, Madame de Montjay! This is the hour of my fate. What are they going to do with me? Condemn me, or that unfortunate woman? Shame or remorse? And it has all been because of one caprice — a single day! Blame it on yourself, Marquis de Presles — you have no one else to blame.

[He stands plunged in thought.]

[Enter the DUKE, who comes up to GASTON and slaps him on the shoulder.]

DUKE. What 's the matter?

GASTON. You know what my father-in-law asked me this morning?

DUKE. Yes.

GASTON. What if I told you I was going to accede to his wishes?

DUKE. I should say, Impossible!

GASTON. And yet it's a fact: I am.

DUKE. Are you crazy? You said yourself that if there was one man who had not the right —

GASTON. It must be. My father-in-law has opened a letter to me from Madame de Montjay. He was so angry that he declared he would take it to a lawyer. In order to stop that, I had to offer to accept his conditions.

DUKE. Poor fellow! You are in a difficult situation!

GASTON. Pontgrimaud would be rendering me a great service if he were to kill me to-morrow.

DUKE. Come, come, put that idea out of your head.

GASTON. That would be a solution.

DUKE. You are only twenty-five — you still have a happy life before you.

GASTON. Life? Look at my situation: I am ruined, I am the slave of a father-in-law whose despotism makes capital of my faults, husband of a wife whom I have cruelly wounded, and who will never forget. You say that I may have a happy life before

me, but I tell you I am disgusted with life and with myself! My cursed foolishness, my caprices, have brought me to a point where I have lost everything: liberty, domestic happiness, the esteem of the world, self-respect. How horrible!

DUKE. Courage, my friend. Don't lose hope!

GASTON [rising]. Yes, I am a coward. A gentleman may lose everything except his honor.

DUKE. What are you going to do?

GASTON. What you would do in my place.

DUKE. I should not kill myself! No!

GASTON. You see, then, you have guessed! — Sh-h! I have only my name now, and I want to keep that intact. Some one 's coming!

[Enter POIRIER, ANTOINETTE, and VERDELET.]

ANTOINETTE. No, father, no. It's impossible. All is over between Monsieur de Presles and me!

VERDELET. I can't believe it's you speaking, my dear child.

POIRIER. But I tell you, he is going to take a position! He has promised never to see that woman again. He's going to make you happy!

ANTOINETTE. Happiness is no longer possible for me. If Monsieur de Presles has not been able to love me of his own accord, do you think he can ever love me when he is forced to?

POIRIER [to the MARQUIS]. Speak, monsieur.

ANTOINETTE. Monsieur de Presles says nothing, because he knows I will not believe him. He is well aware, too, that every bond which held us together has been broken, and that he can never be anything but a stranger to me. Let us each, therefore, take what liberty the law allows us. I want a separation, father. Give me that letter: it is mine and mine alone, to make what use of I please. Give it to me.

POIRIER. Please, my child, think of the scandal. It will affect us all.

ANTOINETTE. It will harm only those who are guilty.

VERDELET. Think of that woman whom you will ruin —

ANTOINETTE. Did she have pity on me? Father, give me the letter. It is not as your daughter that I ask for it, but as the outraged Marquise de Presles.

POIRIER. There. — But I tell you he is willing to take a position —

ANTOINETTE. Give it to me. [To the MARQUIS.] Here is my revenge, monsieur; I have you absolutely in my power. You placed your own honor at stake in order to save your mistress; I absolve you in this way.

[She tears up the letter and throws it into the fireplace.]

POIRIER. Well —! What's she done?

ANTOINETTE. My duty.

VERDELET. Dear child! [He kisses her.]

DUKE. Noble heart!

GASTON. Ah, madame, how can I hope to express to you —? I was so haughty and proud — I thought I had made a misalliance, but I see that you bear my name better than I! My whole life will not suffice to make up for the evil I have done you.

ANTOINETTE. I am a widow, monsieur — [She takes VERDELET'S arm, and starts to leave, as the curtain falls.]

ACT IV

[The scene is the same. ANTOINETTE is seated between VERDELET and POIRIER.]

VERDELET. I tell you you still love him.

POIRIER. I tell you you hate him.

VERDELET. No, no, Poirier —

POIRIER. Yes, I say! Evidently what happened yesterday is not enough for you! I suppose you'd like to see that good-for-nothing carry her off now?

VERDELET. I don't want Antoinette's whole life ruined, but from the way you go about things I —

POIRIER. I go about things the way I want to, Verdelet. It's all very well and easy to play the part of mediator, but you're not at swords' points with the Marquis. Once let him carry her off and you'd

be always with her, while I'd be sitting alone in my hole like an old screech-owl — that's what you'd like! I know you! You're selfish, like all old bachelors!

VERDELET. Take care, Poirier! Are you positive that while you're pushing things to extremes, you yourself are not acting selfishly —?

POIRIER. Ha, so I'm the selfish one, am I? Because I'm trying to safeguard my girl's happiness? Because I have no intention of allowing that blackguardly son-in-law of mine to take my child from me and make her life a torture! [To ANTOINETTE.] Say something, can't you? It concerns you more than it does us!

ANTOINETTE. I don't love him any more, Tony. He crushed out of my heart everything that made me love him.

POIRIER. You see!

ANTOINETTE. I don't hate him, father; I am simply indifferent to him. I don't know him any more.

POIRIER. That's enough for me.

VERDELET. But, my poor Toinon, you are just beginning life. Have you ever thought what would become of a divorced woman? Did you ever consider —?

POIRIER. Verdelet, never mind your sermons! She won't have a very hard time of it with her good old father, who is going to spend all his time loving her and taking care of her. You'll see, dearie, what a lovely life we'll lead, we two [indicating VERDELET] — we three! And I'm worth more than you, you selfish brute! You'll see how we'll love you, and do everything in the world for you. We won't leave you alone here and run after countesses! Now, smile at your father, and say that you're happy with him.

ANTOINETTE. Yes, father, very happy.

POIRIER. Hear that, Verdelet?

VERDELET. Yes, yes.

POIRIER. Now, as for your rascal of a husband — why, you've been much too good to him. We have him in our power at last. I'll allow him a thousand crowns a year, and he can go hang himself.

ANTOINETTE. Let him take everything that I have.

POIRIER. Oh, no!

ANTOINETTE. I ask only one thing: never to see him again.

POIRIER. He'll hear from me before long. I've just delivered a last blow.

ANTOINETTE. What have you done?

POIRIER. Offered the Château de Presles for sale, the château of his worthy ancestors.

ANTOINETTE. Havé you done that? And would you allow him, Tony?

VERDELET [aside to ANTOINETTE]. Don't worry.

POIRIER. Yes, I have. The land speculators know their business, and I hope in a month's time that that vestige of feudalism will have disappeared and no longer soil the land of a free people. They'll plant beets over the site. From the old materials they will build huts for workingmen, useful farmers, and vine-growers. The park of his fathers will be cut down and the wood sawed into little pieces, which will be burned in the fireplaces of good bourgeois, who have earned the money to buy firewood for themselves. And I myself will buy a cord or two for my own use.

ANTOINETTE. But he will think this is all revenge.

POIRIER. He will be perfectly right.

ANTOINETTE. He will think it is I who —

VERDELET [aside to ANTOINETTE]. Don't worry, my dear.

POIRIER. I'm going to see if the signs are ready. They're going to be huge, huge enough to cover the great walls all over Paris. " For sale, the Château de Presles"!

VERDELET. Perhaps it's already sold!

POIRIER. Since last evening? Nonsense! I'm going to the printer's. [He goes out.]

VERDELET. Your father is absurd. If we let him have his way, he'd make reconciliation impossible between you and your husband.

ANTOINETTE. But what can you possibly hope for, poor Tony? My love has fallen from too great a height to be able ever to rise again. You have no idea how much Monsieur de Presles meant to me —

VERDELET. Oh, indeed I do.

ANTOINETTE. He was not only a husband, but a master whose slave I was proud

to be. I not only loved him, I admired him as a great representative of a former age. Oh, Tony, what a horrible awakening I've had!

[Enter a Servant.]

SERVANT. Monsieur le Marquis asks whether madame will see him?

ANTOINETTE. No.

VERDELET. See him, dear. [To the Servant.] Monsieur le Marquis may come in.   [The Servant goes out.]

ANTOINETTE. What good can come of it?

[Enter GASTON.]

GASTON. You need have no apprehension, madame; I shall not trouble you long with my company. You said yesterday that you considered yourself a widow, and I am far too guilty not to feel that your decision is irrevocable. I have come to say goodbye to you.

VERDELET. What's this, monsieur?

GASTON. Yes; I am going to do the only honorable thing that remains. You should be able to understand that.

VERDELET. But, monsieur —?

GASTON. I understand. Fear nothing for the future, and reassure Monsieur Poirier. There is one position I can take, that of my father: in the army. I am leaving to-morrow for Africa with Monsieur de Montmeyran, who has been good enough to sacrifice his leave of absence for my sake.

VERDELET [aside to ANTOINETTE]. What a splendid fellow!

ANTOINETTE [aside to VERDELET]. I never said he was a coward!

VERDELET. Now, my dear children, don't do anything extreme. Monsieur le Marquis, you are very much at fault, but I am sure that you ask nothing better than to make amends.

GASTON. If there were anything I could do —! [A pause.] There is nothing — I know! [To ANTOINETTE.] I leave you my name, madame; I am sure you will keep it spotless. I carry away with me the remorse of having troubled your existence, but you are still young and beautiful. And war carries with it happy chances —

[*Enter the* DUKE.]

DUKE. I have come to get him.

GASTON. Come. [*Offering his hand to* VERDELET.] Good-bye, Monsieur Verdelet. [*They embrace.*] Good-bye, madame, — for always.

DUKE. For always! He loves you, madame.

GASTON. Hush!

VERDELET. He loves you desperately. The moment he emerged from the black abyss from which you have helped him, his eyes were opened. He has seen you as you really are.

ANTOINETTE. Mademoiselle Poirier has triumphed over Madame de Montjay. How admirable!

VERDELET. You are cruel!

GASTON. She is only doing justice, monsieur. She deserved the purest sort of love, and I married her for her money. I made a bargain, a bargain which I was not honest enough to abide by. [*To* ANTOINETTE.] Yes, the very day after our marriage I sacrificed you, out of pure viciousness, for a woman who is far beneath you. Your youth, your charm, your purity, were not enough; no, in order to bring light to this darkened heart it was necessary for you to save my honor twice on the same day! How low I was to resist such devotion, and what does my love now prove? Can it possibly reinstate me in your eyes? When I loved you, I did what any man in my place would have done; in blinding myself to your virtues and your splendid qualities, I did what no one else would have done. You are right, madame, to despise a man who is utterly unworthy of you. I have lost all, even the right to pity myself — I don't pity myself. — Come, Hector.

DUKE. Wait. Do you know where he is going, madame? To fight a duel.

VERDELET *and* ANTOINETTE. To fight a duel?

GASTON. What are you saying?

DUKE. Well, if your wife does n't love you any longer, there is no reason for hiding the truth. — Yes, madame, he is going to fight a duel.

ANTOINETTE. Oh, Tony, his life is in danger — !

DUKE. What difference does that make to you, madame? Is it possible that everything is not over between you, then?

ANTOINETTE. Oh, no: everything is over. Monsieur de Presles may dispose of his life as he thinks best — he owes me nothing —

DUKE [*to* GASTON]. Come, then — [*They go as far as the door.*]

ANTOINETTE. Gaston!

DUKE. You see, she still loves you!

GASTON [*throwing himself at her feet*]. Oh, madame, if that is true, if I still have a place in your affection, say some word — give me the wish to live.

[*Enter* POIRIER.]

POIRIER. What are you doing there, Monsieur le Marquis?

ANTOINETTE. He is going to fight a duel!

POIRIER. A duel! And are you the least bit surprised? Mistresses, duels — that's to be expected. He who has land has war.

ANTOINETTE. What do you mean, father? Do you imagine — ?

POIRIER. I'd wager my head on it.

ANTOINETTE. That's not true, is it, monsieur? You don't answer?

POIRIER. Do you think he would be honest enough to admit it?

GASTON. I cannot lie, madame. This duel is the last remnant of an odious past.

POIRIER. He's a fool to confess it! The impudence!

ANTOINETTE. And I was led to understand that you still loved me! I was even ready to forgive you — while you were on the point of fighting a duel for your mistress! Why, this was a trap for my weakness. Ah, Monsieur le Duc!

DUKE. He has already told you, madame, that this duel was the remnant of a past which he detests and wants to lay at rest and obliterate.

VERDELET [*to the* MARQUIS]. Very well, monsieur, then I have a simple plan: If you don't love Madame de Montjay any longer, then don't fight for her.

GASTON. What, monsieur, make excuses?

VERDELET. You must give Antoinette a proof of your sincerity, and this is the only one which you can give. Then did n't you just now ask for something to do as an expiation? Time was the only proof she could impose. Are n't you happy that you now have a chance, and that you can give that proof at once? I know it's a great sacrifice, but if it were any less, could it be a real expiation?

POIRIER [aside]. The fool! He's going to patch up matters!

GASTON. I would gladly sacrifice my life, but my honor — the Marquise de Presles would never accept that sort of sacrifice.

ANTOINETTE. What if you were mistaken, monsieur? What if I would accept it?

GASTON. What, madame, would you ask me — ?

ANTOINETTE. To do for me almost as much as you would for Madame de Montjay? Yes, monsieur. For her sake you consented to forget the past of your family, and now would you refuse to forget a duel, a duel which is most offensive to me? How can I believe in your love, if it is less strong than your pride?

POIRIER. Then what good would a sword-scratch do you? Take my word for it, prudence is the mother of safety.

VERDELET [aside]. Old fool!

GASTON. See? That is what people will say.

ANTOINETTE. Who would doubt your courage? Have n't you given ample proofs of it?

POIRIER. And then what do you care for the opinion of a lot of know-nothings? You will have the respect of my friends, and that ought to be enough —

GASTON. You see, madame, people would laugh at me, and you could not love a ridiculous man very long.

DUKE. No one would laugh at you. Let me take your excuses to the ground, and I promise you that there will be no levity.

GASTON. What! Do you, too, think that — ?

DUKE. Yes, my friend. Your affair is not one of those that can't possibly be arranged. The sacrifice your wife is asking affects only your own personal pride.

GASTON. But to make excuses on the ground — ?

POIRIER. I would!

VERDELET. Really, Poirier, one might think you were trying to make him fight!

POIRIER. I'm doing all in my power to prevent him.

DUKE. Come, Gaston, you have no right to refuse this proof to your wife.

GASTON. Well — no! It's out of the question!

ANTOINETTE. That is the price of my forgiveness.

GASTON. Then I refuse it, madame. I shan't carry my sorrow very long.

POIRIER. Nonsense. Don't listen to him, dearie. Wait till he has his sword in his hand: he'll defend himself, I tell you. It would be like an expert swimmer trying to drown himself: once in the water, the devil himself could n't keep him from saving himself.

ANTOINETTE. If Madame de Montjay objected to your fighting, you would give in to her. Good-bye.

GASTON. Antoinette, for God's sake — !

DUKE. She is exactly right.

GASTON. Excuses! I offer excuses!

ANTOINETTE. I see, you are thinking only of your own pride!

DUKE. Gaston! Give in! I swear I would do the same thing in your place.

GASTON. Very well — but to Pontgrimaud! — Go without me, then.

DUKE [to ANTOINETTE]. Madame, are you now satisfied with him?

ANTOINETTE. Yes, Gaston, you have now made up for everything. I have nothing else to forgive you; I believe in you, I am happy, and I love you. [The MARQUIS stands still, his head bowed. ANTOINETTE goes to him, takes his head in her hands, and kisses his forehead.] Now, go and fight! Go!

GASTON. My dearest wife, you have my mother's heart!

ANTOINETTE. No, my mother's, monsieur —

POIRIER [*aside*]. What idiots women are!

GASTON [*to the* DUKE]. Quick, or we shall be late.

ANTOINETTE. You are a good swordsman, are you not?

DUKE. He's as good as St. George, madame, and he has a wrist of steel. Monsieur Poirier, pray for Pontgrimaud!

ANTOINETTE [*to* GASTON]. Please don't kill the young man.

GASTON. I'll let him off with a scratch — because you love me. Come, Hector.

[*Enter a Servant with a letter on a silver plate.*]

ANTOINETTE. Another letter?

GASTON. Open it yourself.

ANTOINETTE. It will be the first of yours that I have opened.

GASTON. I am sure of that.

ANTOINETTE [*opening the letter*]. It is from Monsieur de Pontgrimaud.

GASTON. Bah!

ANTOINETTE [*reading*]. "My dear Marquis —"

GASTON. Snob!

ANTOINETTE. "We have both proved our valor —"

GASTON. In different ways, however! -

ANTOINETTE. "I therefore have no hesitation in telling you that I regret having for a moment lost my head —"

GASTON. *I* was the one who lost mine!

ANTOINETTE. "You are the only man in the world to whom I should think of making excuses —"

GASTON. You flatter me, monsieur.

ANTOINETTE. "And I have no doubt that you will accept them as gallantly as they are offered —"

GASTON. Exactly!

ANTOINETTE. "With all my heart, Viscount de Pontgrimaud."

DUKE. He is not a viscount, and he has no heart.[1] Otherwise his letter is most appropriate.

VERDELET [*to* GASTON]. Everything has turned out splendidly, my dear boy. I hope you have learned your lesson.

[1] Here follows a pun on "Pont"—"bridge"— and "grimaud"—"scribbler."—Tr.

GASTON. For the rest of my life, dear Monsieur Verdelet. From this day on I begin a serious and calm existence. In order to break definitely with the follies of my past, I ask you for a place in your office.

VERDELET. In my office! You! A gentleman!

GASTON. Have I not my wife to support?

DUKE. You will do as the Breton nobles did, when they laid down their swords in Parliament in order to enter the field of commerce, and took them up again after having set their houses in order.

VERDELET. Very good, Monsieur le Marquis.

POIRIER [*aside*]. It's now my turn to give in. [*Aloud.*] My dear son-in-law, that is a most liberal sentiment; you really deserve to be a bourgeois. Now that we can understand each other, let us make peace. Stay with me.

GASTON. I ask for nothing better than to make my peace with you, monsieur. But as to staying with you, that is another matter. You have made me understand the happiness which the wood-chopper feels when he is master of his own home. I do not blame you, but I cannot help remembering.

POIRIER. Are you going to take away my daughter? Are you going to leave me alone?

ANTOINETTE. I'll come to see you often, father.

GASTON. And you will always be welcome.

POIRIER. So my daughter is going to be the wife of a tradesman!

VERDELET. No, Poirier, your wife will be mistress of the Château de Presles. The château was sold this morning, and, with the permission of your husband, Toinon, it will be my wedding present.

ANTOINETTE. Dear Tony! May I accept it, Gaston?

GASTON. Monsieur Verdelet is one of those to whom it is a pleasure to be grateful.

VERDELET. I am retiring from business, and, if you will allow me, I shall come and live with you, Monsieur le Marquis. We

shall cultivate your land together. That is
a gentleman's profession.

POIRIER. Well, what about me, then?
Are n't you going to invite me? All children
are ungrateful — yes, my poor father was
right.

VERDELET. Buy some neighboring land,
and live near us.

POIRIER. That's an idea!

VERDELET. That's all you have to do;
and besides — you're cured of your ambition, are n't you? I think you are.

POIRIER. Yes, yes. [Aside.] Let me see:
this is 1846. I'll be deputy of the arron-
dissement of Presles in forty-seven, and peer
of France in forty-eight!

THE OUTER EDGE OF SOCIETY

(LE DEMI-MONDE)

By ALEXANDRE DUMAS Fils

Translated by BARRETT H. CLARK

CHARACTERS

Olivier de Jalin

Raymond de Nanjac

Hippolyte Richond

De Thonnerins

First Servant

Second Servant

Third Servant

Baroness Suzanne d'Ange

Viscountess de Vernières

Valentine de Santis

Marcelle

A Chambermaid

The action takes place at Paris; the first and fifth acts in the home of Olivier, the second in that of the Viscountess, the third and fourth, in that of Suzanne.

THE OUTER EDGE OF SOCIETY

ACT I

A drawing-room in the home of OLIVIER
DE JALIN.

[*As the curtain rises, the* VISCOUNTESS *and*
OLIVIER *are discovered.*]

VISCOUNTESS. Then you promise that
the affair will go no further?

OLIVIER. It cannot.

VISCOUNTESS. I wanted to come myself
and ask you, even at the risk of being found
in your home with Heaven knows whom!

OLIVIER. Do I keep evil company?

VISCOUNTESS. People say so.

OLIVIER. People are mistaken. No
women except those who are your intimate
friends come here.

VISCOUNTESS. That's flattering to my
friends!

OLIVIER. But your presence here is
quite explicable. Two friends of yours,
Monsieur de Maucroix and Monsieur de
Latour, were playing cards at your home
and had a little misunderstanding. An explanation became necessary; that explanation should be made in this place. I am
Monsieur de Maucroix's second; you have
come to ask me to arrange the affair —
what more natural?

VISCOUNTESS. I see that clearly enough,
but I should n't like it known that I came
here, because I prefer all Paris not to know
that I gamble at home. If anything serious
happens, there will be a trial, and no respectable woman should appear in court,
even as witness, and have her name appear
in the papers. Please do your best to come
to an amicable arrangement, or, if that is
impossible, for the sake of my friendship,
make the cause of the duel something with
which I am not connected, even indirectly.
I open my house to gambling in order that
people may amuse themselves, not quarrel.

OLIVIER. I understand.

VISCOUNTESS. Well, as Madame de
Santis has n't come yet, I must go.

OLIVIER. Is Madame de Santis to do me
the honor —?

VISCOUNTESS. When she learned that I
was coming to see you she said to me:
"I'll come and call for you. I shan't be
sorry to see him either, the naughty man!"
But she's so careless she may have forgotten all about it. I can't wait an instant
longer. Good-bye. Let me remind you
that you have n't asked after my niece,
who was nice enough to ask me to convey
to you all sorts of things.

OLIVIER. Pleasant things?

VISCOUNTESS. Of course.

OLIVIER. Very kind of her.

VISCOUNTESS. Certainly it is kind; she
did n't have to do it: she knows very well
that you are not going to marry her.

OLIVIER. Oh, no!

VISCOUNTESS. My dear friend, you
might happen upon some one much worse.

OLIVIER. One never *happens* on any one
worth while.

VISCOUNTESS. But we're better off than
you.

OLIVIER. Are you sure?

VISCOUNTESS. You are of the petty
nobility — and, you're not rich?

OLIVIER. I have thirty thousand.

VISCOUNTESS. Dividends?

OLIVIER. Land.

VISCOUNTESS. Not bad. You have a
family?

OLIVIER. One always has a family. But
my family consists only of a mother —
remarried; as I had to sue her husband
when I came of age in order to get my
father's fortune, we see each other very
rarely. I don't think she cares very much
for me. A widowed mother ought never to
remarry. When she casts aside her husband's name, she becomes practically a
stranger to her family. That is how, my

dear Viscountess, I was thrown so much on my own resources at an early age; that is why I have sown my wild oats, and contracted debts which I have since paid, and why to-day I am far too reasonable a man to marry your niece, in spite of the fact that I think her charming, that she appeals to me as an orphan, and that at one time I was afraid I might marry her.

VISCOUNTESS. You—?

OLIVIER. Yes, I! I actually fell deeply in love with her, and if I had continued to visit your home, as I am an honest and upright man, I should have ended by asking you for her hand, which would have been absurd—

VISCOUNTESS. Because she has no money?

OLIVIER. That made no difference to me; I am not the man to marry for money. No, there is another reason.

VISCOUNTESS. What is that?

OLIVIER. We men of the world are not such fools as we may appear to be. When we marry, we choose in our wives what we have been unable to find in the wives of others, and the longer we live the more insistent we are that our wives know nothing of life. Those little ladies who have ready-made reputations for wit and independence before marriage, make a very sorry showing as wives. Look at Madame de Santis!

VISCOUNTESS. But Marcelle has n't Valentine's character.

OLIVIER. Which does not prevent Madame de Santis, who is separated from an unknown husband,—a woman who is compromised and who compromises,—from having as her bosom friend Mademoiselle de Sancenaux, your niece. Tell me, now, is Madame de Santis a fit companion for a girl of twenty?

VISCOUNTESS. Why not? Marcelle has very few amusements, and I have no fortune. Madame de Santis likes the theater, and owns a carriage. Marcelle is merely taking advantage of all that. The poor girl must have some distractions. She is keeping out of mischief, after all.

OLIVIER. She does keep out of mischief, but she gives people the idea that she does n't, and she will end by getting into it.

VISCOUNTESS. My dear Olivier!

OLIVIER. You are wrong! Do you know what you ought to have done? Sent your niece to the Marquis de Thonnerins three years ago, when she left boarding-school. He wanted to have her with him for his own daughter's sake. To-day Marcelle would be living in respectable society, and would have married or been able to marry as she should. Now, I doubt whether she will ever be able to do that.

VISCOUNTESS. I loved her so much that I could n't think of being separated from her.

OLIVIER. That was selfishness, which you will later regret, and for which she will some day blame you.

VISCOUNTESS. No; because if she wishes, she may marry in two months' time. She'll make a charming wife: women are what their husbands make them—

OLIVIER. But husbands are also what their wives make them—and the compensation is not sufficient. Whom are you going to marry her to this time?

VISCOUNTESS. A young man.

OLIVIER. Who is in love with Mademoiselle de Sancenaux and who is loved by her?

VISCOUNTESS. No, but that makes little difference. In marriage if there is love, it is killed by familiarity, and when it does not exist, it gives birth to it.

OLIVIER. You talk like La Rochefoucauld. Where did you find the young man?

VISCOUNTESS. Monsieur de Latour introduced him to her.

OLIVIER. Introduced by Monsieur de Latour, specialist in shoddy: half string, half cotton!

VISCOUNTESS. Listen to me: I know good respectable men when I see them, and I tell you this man is one. He's exactly the husband for Marcelle. He's young, he looks imposing, he's not over thirty-two at the outside, in the army, decorated, no family, with the exception of a young sister who is a widow and lives a retired life in the depths of her Faubourg Saint-Germain; he has twenty thousand francs' income, is free to do as he likes, may marry to-morrow. The only people he knows in

Paris are Monsieur de Latour, Marcelle, and me. This is a splendid chance — I could n't hope for a finer. You 'll be the first to admit it when you 've seen the man.

OLIVIER. Oh, I am to meet him, then?

VISCOUNTESS. To-day: he is Monsieur de Latour's second.

OLIVIER. Then he 's that Monsieur de Nanjac who left his card here yesterday, and who is going to call to-day at three?

VISCOUNTESS. Yes. Now, be nice; you can when you want to be. If Monsieur de Nanjac takes to you, there 's nothing out of the way in that, and if he speaks to you about Marcelle, try not to say too many of those stupid things you referred to a few moments ago.

[Enter a Servant.]

SERVANT. Madame de Santis.

[He goes out.]

[Enter VALENTINE.]

VISCOUNTESS. Come here, my dear child! Where have you been?

VALENTINE. Don't speak about it — I thought I 'd never get away! [To OLIVIER.] How are you?

OLIVIER. Splendid, thanks.

VALENTINE. Just think! My dress-maker came and I had to try on some dresses. You 'll see the one I 'm having made for the races to-morrow. Then I went to hire a coach with two horses. I made them show me the coachman first — he 's English — very nice. Then I went to see my landlord — you know I 'm moving. What rent do you pay here —?

OLIVIER. Three thousand francs.

VALENTINE. You 're in a new neighborhood, a real desert. You might be murdered here and no one would ever know. I 'd die of boredom. I found the dearest little apartment on the third floor — it 's in the Rue de la Paix — seven thousand five hundred a year — landlord will re-paper. The drawing-room is to be decorated in red and gold, the bedroom in yellow, the boudoir in blue satin. I 'm getting new furniture for it — it 'll be lovely!

OLIVIER. How can you afford all that?

VALENTINE. How, you ask? Have n't I my dowry?

OLIVIER. You can't have very much of it left, at the pace you are living?

VALENTINE. I have about thirty thousand. [To the VISCOUNTESS.] My dear, if you ever need money, don't forget my agent: Monsieur Michel. I did n't have time to wait for the sale of some property of mine in Touraine, so I let him have the deeds, and he advanced me five thousand cash at once — interest at eight per cent — that is n't too high. From here I 'm going straight to him and get the rest of the money.

OLIVIER. Is n't that Michel a thin little fellow with a mustache, who wears embroidered shirts, and enameled buttons on his waistcoat?

VALENTINE. He 's very nice-looking.

OLIVIER. That depends on where you see him. You know, he is a thief. I know him: he loaned me money before I became of age. If you 're in the hands of that man, your thirty thousand francs won't last long. When they are gone, then what are you going to do?

VALENTINE. There 's still my husband. He must give me an allowance. Or if he does n't, I can always return to him.

OLIVIER. What luck for him! And to think that at this moment he has n't the slightest inkling of the happiness that awaits him! But what if he were to refuse?

VALENTINE. He can't — our separation is n't a judicial one. I have the right to return to my home whenever I like; he 's forced to receive me. But I know, he 'd ask for nothing better than to take me back: he 's still in love with me.

OLIVIER. I 'd be very curious to know how that comes out.

VALENTINE. You 'll see — I 've got to decide soon. Now — where else have I been? That 's all! I came back by way of the Champs-Élysées — what crowds of people there were! I met heaps of my men friends: little de Bonchamp, the Count de Bryade, Monsieur de Casavaux. I invited them to tea to-morrow. Will you come, too?

OLIVIER. Thank you, no.

VALENTINE. I reserved a box at the theater for to-night, a stage-box downstairs. I paid my bill at the modiste's. I'm leaving her: she works now only for actresses. That's what I've done to-day. [*To the* VISCOUNTESS.] Oh, by the way, we dine Tuesday at Monsieur de Calvillot's — a house-warming. What a charming apartment he has! He asked me to invite the ladies. You'll come with Marcelle, won't you? We'll have a very gay time.

OLIVIER [*looking at her*]. Poor woman!

VALENTINE. What's the matter?

OLIVIER. Nothing — I pity you.

VALENTINE. Why?

OLIVIER. Because you deserve to be pitied. If you can't understand, then I shan't waste time trying to explain.

VALENTINE. By the way, I knew I wanted to ask you something!

OLIVIER. She did n't even hear what I said! — Can she have anything at all in her brain? — And what did you want to know?

VALENTINE. Have you heard anything of Madame d'Ange?

OLIVIER. Why do you ask?

VALENTINE. Did n't she write you from Baden?

OLIVIER. No.

VALENTINE. And you tell that to *me*, to me who — [*She laughs.*]

OLIVIER. To you who — ?

VALENTINE. Who mailed her letters for her. I can keep a secret, though I may look like a fool. She wrote you some charming letters. [*She laughs again.*]

OLIVIER. Why do you laugh?

VALENTINE. Because you tried to appear discreet with me, and because I know more about it all than you do.

OLIVIER. I have n't heard from her for two weeks.

VALENTINE. Exactly: not since I left.

OLIVIER. Did n't she write to you, either?

VALENTINE. She never writes.
                    [*She laughs in his face.*]

OLIVIER [*looking into the whites of her eyes*]. What have you — there?

VALENTINE. Where do you mean?

VISCOUNTESS. He wants to make you angry.

OLIVIER. It's all black around your eyes.

VALENTINE. You're just like all the others: you're going to tell me that I paint my eyebrows and lashes. When I think that fully half my friends believe I paint — !

OLIVIER. And the other half are sure!

VALENTINE. The idea!

OLIVIER. Don't you use powder?

VALENTINE. The way every woman does —

OLIVIER. And rouge?

VALENTINE. Never.

OLIVIER. Never?

VALENTINE. Just a touch, in the evenings — sometimes.

OLIVIER. And don't you touch up a little around the eyes?

VALENTINE. It's the fashion.

OLIVIER. Not among decent women, anyway.

VALENTINE. If it's becoming, what's the difference? So long as people know I'm decent, too —

OLIVIER. It is evident.

VISCOUNTESS. What a gossip you are, dear! We must go now!

VALENTINE [*to the* VISCOUNTESS]. Would you like to come with me to my apartment?

VISCOUNTESS. Delighted — I have n't anything to do.

VALENTINE [*to* OLIVIER]. Come with us: you can advise me about shades.

OLIVIER. I can't go: I am waiting for some one.

VALENTINE. For whom?

OLIVIER. A friend of mine.

VALENTINE. What's his name?

OLIVIER. How can that interest you?

VALENTINE [*feigning indifference*]. I just asked —

OLIVIER. His name is Hippolyte Richond. He's been traveling a good deal during the past ten years. He returned to Paris about a week ago. He's the son of a rich merchant of Marseille, who is now dead; he was in the oil business. Are you satisfied? Do you know him?

VALENTINE [*troubled*]. No.

VISCOUNTESS. Is he married?

OLIVIER. Yes, so you need n't trouble —

VALENTINE. Do you know his wife?

OLIVIER. And his son, too.

VALENTINE [astonished]. He has a son?

OLIVIER. Five or six years old. Why are you surprised? You say you don't know him?

VALENTINE. And this Monsieur Richond lives at — ?

OLIVIER. Number seven, Rue de Lille. Would you care to see him? Wait a moment, I'll introduce you.

VALENTINE. No, no, I don't want to see him.

OLIVIER. What's the matter?

VALENTINE. Nothing! Good-bye!

[Enter a Servant.]

SERVANT. Monsieur Hippolyte Richond.   [He goes out.]

OLIVIER [to VALENTINE]. Won't you — ?

VALENTINE. Don't try to persuade me—
[She lets down her veil, and, as HIPPOLYTE enters, turns her head to one side. She goes out with the VISCOUNTESS.]

OLIVIER. How are you?

HIPPOLYTE. Very well. And you?

OLIVIER. Splendid. How's your wife?

HIPPOLYTE. Everybody is very well. — Who is that woman?

OLIVIER. Her name is Madame de Santis.

HIPPOLYTE. Valentine!

OLIVIER. You know her?

HIPPOLYTE. Not personally, but I knew her husband intimately.

OLIVIER. Is she really married?

HIPPOLYTE. As much married as a person can possibly be.

OLIVIER. Really? She claims that her husband has greatly wronged her.

HIPPOLYTE. True: first he did wrong to marry her, for it seems she'd lost all sense of modesty.

OLIVIER. Not quite.

HIPPOLYTE. Do you know her very well?

OLIVIER. Yes. She has just been here for that old lady whom you saw with her. When I mentioned your name to her, her expression changed. Yet she denied knowing you.

HIPPOLYTE. We have never exchanged a word; but she must know that I am well acquainted with every detail of her life.

OLIVIER. And where is Monsieur de Santis?

HIPPOLYTE. Her husband's name is not de Santis; she got that name from her mother, and used it just after she was separated. Her husband refused to allow her to use his.

OLIVIER. What cause for complaint did he have against her?

HIPPOLYTE. She deceived him — vilely. He was madly in love with her. I must say, she was charming: every one called her the beautiful Mademoiselle de Santis. She didn't have a sou to her name. Her suitor was rich, very much in love, young, very timid, he didn't dare ask for her hand. A friend of his, who first introduced him to the family, offered to make the proposal on his behalf, and the man accepted. The girl took the offer, and the friend was one of the two witnesses at the ceremony.

OLIVIER. And you were the other?

HIPPOLYTE. Yes. Six months after the wedding the husband came to me: he had incontrovertible proof that his wife was the mistress of the scoundrel who had brought about their marriage. He fought a duel with the fellow, killed him, and went away, leaving his wife the stipulated dowry of two hundred thousand francs, but forbidding her to use his name, or even to say that she ever knew him. Since that time they have not seen each other. That was ten years ago.

OLIVIER. And where is the husband now?

HIPPOLYTE. He lives abroad. I met him in Germany two months ago.

OLIVIER. Does he still love his wife?

HIPPOLYTE. I don't think so.

OLIVIER. Yet she maintains that he loves her as much as ever, and that it rests with her whether or not she shall return to him.

HIPPOLYTE. She is mistaken. — Who is that old lady she went out with?

OLIVIER. The remains of a woman of quality whom the need for luxury and pleasure has gradually dragged into a rather free-and-easy social circle. She ruined her husband, who took it into his head to die ten or twelve years ago. She has a few old friends, some few shares which are given her at par and which she sells at a premium, a few scattered fragments of her fortune which the wind casts up from time to time — those are her sole resources. She has a very pretty niece, upon whose marriage she counts to regild her 'scutcheon; the only trouble is that the husband is not yet forthcoming. Meantime, she struggles on as best she is able; gives parties at which you instinctively feel that the coffers are empty, and that the day after, she will have to pawn some jewel or sell something in order to pay for the pink candles, the punch and the ices. The young people whom she invites drink the punch, send bonbons on New Year's, marry girls in real society, and just tip their hats to the Viscountess and her niece when they meet them, in order not to have to invite them to meet their mothers and wives.

HIPPOLYTE. And is Madame de Santis a friend of that woman?

OLIVIER. In what other social circle would she move?

HIPPOLYTE. That's true! — Well, you wrote that you had a favor to ask me. What is it?

OLIVIER. What time is it?

HIPPOLYTE. Two o'clock.

OLIVIER [ringing]. Let me finish something I have to do, then we can talk at our ease.

HIPPOLYTE. Please! I have plenty of time.

[Enter a Servant.]

OLIVIER [to the Servant, as he hands him a letter]. Take this letter to Monsieur le Comte de Lornan. You know him, of course. In case he is not at home, give the letter to Madame la Comtesse. That will do. [The Servant goes out.]

HIPPOLYTE. So you write letters that can be opened by both — ?

OLIVIER. No! I wrote a letter that can be read only by the wife, but, in order not to compromise her, I address it to the husband.

HIPPOLYTE. But what if it is handed to the husband?

OLIVIER. Stupid! The husband is in the country.

HIPPOLYTE. Very ingenious, I declare!

OLIVIER. I recommend it to you, in case you should ever need to make use of it. This is the first and the last time that I employ the means — it is only for the sake of the lady.

HIPPOLYTE. Are you sure of that?

OLIVIER. Here's the story — it's very simple, you see. I'll mention the people, in order to show you that the husband has nothing to fear from the wife, and the wife nothing to fear from me. Last autumn — that's a dangerous season, especially in the country, where the solitude gives rein to the imagination, where each leaf that falls is a ready-made elegy, where one feels the need of becoming a consumptive in order to be in closer harmony with melancholy and fading nature —

HIPPOLYTE. See Millevoye, The Falling of the Leaves, volume one, page twenty-one. I know that! I've suffered from consumption myself.

OLIVIER. Who has n't? Consumption and the mounted National Guard of 1830 — every one has been in both. Well, last autumn I was introduced to the Countess de Lornan, who was spending the month of October in the country with the mother of one of my friends — why, de Maucroix's mother, it was! We were just speaking of him. She's a blonde, very distinguished-looking, poetic, sentimental, always in the clouds, — her husband was away, — you know, the usual situation! I made love to her, and now I believe I am in love with her. On our return to Paris she introduces me to her husband.

HIPPOLYTE. Who is a fool?

OLIVIER. Charming fellow of forty, who took to me, and for whom I feel deep affection. At the end of two weeks I became his intimate friend and forgot all about the woman — absolutely. Now, there was a woman who gave me no hopes whatsoever, and who, between you and me, was no more intended for love affairs and intrigues than — [He tries to find the word.]

HIPPOLYTE. Never mind: you'll find the comparison some other time.

OLIVIER. Her pride was hurt; she believed I had been trifling with her. Well, yesterday she wrote me that her husband had gone away for a few days, and that she wanted an explanation from me, that she was waiting for me to-day at two o'clock. I burned her letter, and instead of having an altogether unnecessary explanation with her, I have just written the truth: that I want to become her friend, that I don't love her enough, or rather that I care too much for her to do the other thing. She will blame me a little, but, good Heavens! it will be something to be proud of to have saved the good name of a woman —

HIPPOLYTE. Splendid, I say!

OLIVIER. And I decided that without any afterthought, I swear! Granted that I have had a great deal of experience, I am an honest man, and I have decided not to commit any more of those petty infamies for which love is only too often the excuse. To go to a man's home, accept his friendship and hospitality, call him friend, and then take his wife, — well, so much the worse for those who don't agree with me, — but I think that it is shameful, repugnant, disgusting.

HIPPOLYTE. You're really magnificent!

OLIVIER. Well — yes!

HIPPOLYTE. You must be in love with some one else.

OLIVIER. Skeptic!

HIPPOLYTE. Confess it!

OLIVIER. Well, it's a fact that —

HIPPOLYTE. I was saying to myself: "There's a gay fellow who's playing the Joseph — he must have good reasons —" Do I know the fair lady?

OLIVIER. No. She went to take the waters before you arrived at Paris. But I should never have mentioned her name to you: I don't want to compromise her. She is a woman of the world.

HIPPOLYTE. Nonsense!

OLIVIER. She says so. Meantime, she is free, she pretends to be a widow, she is no more than twenty. She's wonderful, clever, and knows how to keep up appearances.

There's no danger at present, no possibility of remorse in the future; she is the sort of woman who can foresee every eventuality of a *liaison* and who lead their love with ready-made phrases and a smile on the lips, along past every relay, up to the point where it is necessary to change horses. I entered this *liaison* as a traveler would who is in no particular hurry, and who prefers to take the post-chaise instead of the railroad. It's much more amusing, and I can get out whenever I like.

HIPPOLYTE. And this has been going on for how long?

OLIVIER. For six months.

HIPPOLYTE. And it will last — ?

OLIVIER. As long as she wishes it.

HIPPOLYTE. Until you marry!

OLIVIER. I shall never marry.

HIPPOLYTE. You say so, but some fine day —

[Enter a Servant.]

SERVANT. Monsieur.

OLIVIER. Yes? What is it?

SERVANT [*in an undertone*]. The lady who was away.

OLIVIER [*pointing to a door*]. Tell her to go in there; I shall be with her in a moment. [*The Servant goes out.*]

HIPPOLYTE. Is it she?

OLIVIER. Yes.

HIPPOLYTE. I'm going.

OLIVIER. When shall I see you again?

HIPPOLYTE. Whenever you say.

OLIVIER. Well?

HIPPOLYTE. Well, what?

OLIVIER. Are you running off like this?

HIPPOLYTE. How else should I?

OLIVIER. But what about Maucroix? We've been talking about everything else except his affair.

HIPPOLYTE. That's so. We forgot. What fools we are!

OLIVIER. Use the singular, please!

HIPPOLYTE. Very well. What a fool you are!

OLIVIER. Is monsieur pleased to be clever?

HIPPOLYTE. Sometimes.

OLIVIER. This is the case, then: Monsieur de Maucroix had a quarrel at cards with Monsieur de Latour; it took place at the home of the Madame de Vernières, whom you saw here. De Latour is going to send his second here at three o'clock. Now, the moment he sends me a second, I know that the matter can be arranged. But, if this is out of the question, we must have another meeting, with two seconds for each side. That meeting will doubtless take place this evening. We might as well have it over with as soon as possible. Where can I find you in case I need you?

HIPPOLYTE. At my home, up to six, and from six to eight at the Café Anglais. Will you have dinner with me there?

OLIVIER. Good! Come for me at six; this is not out of your way.

[HIPPOLYTE goes out. As soon as the door at the back has closed, OLIVIER goes to the side door, which has opened meantime.]

[Enter SUZANNE.]

OLIVIER. What! It's you!

[He offers his hand to her.]

SUZANNE [shaking hands and smiling]. Yes it's I.

OLIVIER. I thought you were dead.

SUZANNE. You see, I'm very well.

OLIVIER. When did you come from Baden?

SUZANNE. A week ago.

OLIVIER. A week ago!

SUZANNE. Yes.

OLIVIER. Well, well, and to-day I see you for the first time! There must be some news to tell?

SUZANNE. Possibly. [A pause.] Are you as clever as ever?

OLIVIER. More so.

SUZANNE. Since when?

OLIVIER. Since your return.

SUZANNE. That's almost a compliment.

OLIVIER. Almost.

SUZANNE. So much the better.

OLIVIER. Why?

SUZANNE. Because on my return from Baden, I'm not at all sorry to talk over a number of things.

OLIVIER. Don't people talk at Baden?

SUZANNE. No — they just speak!

OLIVIER. Well, it seems that you

were n't any too anxious to talk this last week. Otherwise you would have come to see me sooner.

SUZANNE. I've been in the country. I've come to Paris to-day for the first time, and no one knows I'm here. You were saying that you were as clever as ever?

OLIVIER. Yes.

SUZANNE. We'll see.

OLIVIER. What are you driving at?

SUZANNE. One point: a question. Will you marry me?

OLIVIER. You?

SUZANNE. Don't be too surprised — that would be most impolite.

OLIVIER. What an idea!

SUZANNE. Then you won't? Don't say any more about it. Well, my dear Olivier, I must now let you know that we shall never see each other again. I'm going away.

OLIVIER. For long?

SUZANNE. Yes, for long.

OLIVIER. Where are you going?

SUZANNE. Far away.

OLIVIER. I'm puzzled.

SUZANNE. It's very simple. People talk; you find them everywhere. It was for such people that carriages and steamboats were invented.

OLIVIER. That's true. Well, what about me?

SUZANNE. You?

OLIVIER. Yes.

SUZANNE. You? You stay here at Paris, I imagine.

OLIVIER. Ah!

SUZANNE. At least — unless you want to go away, too?

OLIVIER. With you?

SUZANNE. Oh, no.

OLIVIER. Then — it's all over?

SUZANNE. What?

OLIVIER. We don't love each other any more?

SUZANNE. Have we ever done so?

OLIVIER. I once thought it.

SUZANNE. I did all in power to believe it.

OLIVIER. Really?

SUZANNE. I have spent my life wanting to love. Up to now, it has been impossible.

OLIVIER. Thank you!

SUZANNE. I'm not referring to you alone.

OLIVIER. Thank you on *our* behalf, then!

SUZANNE. You must know that when I left for Baden, I went there less as a woman who wanted to be lazy than as one who wanted time to reflect — like a sensible woman. At a distance, one can better realize what one truly feels and thinks. Possibly you were of more importance to me than I had wanted to believe. I went away in order to see whether I could do without you.

OLIVIER. Well?

SUZANNE. Well, I can. You did not follow me; and the most that can be said of your letters is that they were clever. Two weeks after I left, you were completely indifferent to me.

OLIVIER. Your words possess the inestimable advantage of being absolutely clear.

SUZANNE. My first idea on returning here was not even to see you and have that explanation, but to wait until chance should bring us together. But then I knew that we were both sensible people, and that in place of trying to escape that situation, it was a much more dignified proceeding to try to have it over with at once. And here I am, asking you whether you wish to make out of our false love a true friendship? [OLIVIER *smiles*.] Why are you smiling?

OLIVIER. Because, except for the form, I said or rather wrote the same thing not two hours ago.

SUZANNE. To a woman?

OLIVIER. Yes.

SUZANNE. To the beautiful Charlotte de Lornan?

OLIVIER. I don't know the lady.

SUZANNE. Toward the end of my last stay in Paris you did not come to see me so regularly as you used to. I very soon saw that the excuses you gave me for not coming, or rather the pretexts you made before not coming, were hiding some mystery. That mystery could be nothing other than a woman. One day when you were leaving my home, after saying that you were to meet some man friend, I followed you to the house where you were going; I gave the porter twenty francs, and learned that Madame de Lornan lived there, and that you went to see her every day. That's how simple it was. Then I understood that I did n't love you: I did my best to be jealous, and I failed.

OLIVIER. And how does it happen that you have not spoken to me before about Madame de Lornan?

SUZANNE. If I had, I should have had to ask you to choose between that woman and me. As she was more recent than I, I should have been sacrificed for her, and my pride would have suffered cruelly. I did n't want to speak to you.

OLIVIER. But you were mistaken. I did go to see Madame de Lornan, but I declare she has never been, is not, and never will be, any other than a good friend of mine.

SUZANNE. That is nothing to me. You are free to love whom you like. All I ask is your friendship; may I have it?

OLIVIER. What is the use, since you are going away?

SUZANNE. Exactly. Friends are rare and more precious at a distance than near at hand.

OLIVIER. Tell me the whole truth.

SUZANNE. What truth?

OLIVIER. Why are you going away?

SUZANNE. Merely in order to — get away.

OLIVIER. Is there no other reason?

SUZANNE. No other.

OLIVIER. Then stay.

SUZANNE. No, there are reasons to prevent that.

OLIVIER. Don't you want to tell me?

SUZANNE. To ask for a secret in exchange for one's friendship is not friendship, it's a venal transaction.

OLIVIER. You are logic incarnate. And what are you going to do before you leave?

SUZANNE. Stay in the country. I know you are bored to death with the country, and that is why I am not asking you to come.

OLIVIER. Very well. Then this is a dismissal in good form. Well, my task as friend will not be difficult.

SUZANNE. It will be more difficult than you imagine. I don't mean by that word friendship one of those banal traditional affairs that every lover offers to every other when the two separate; that is nothing more than the mite of a reciprocal indifference. What I want is an intelligent friendship, a useful attachment, a form of devotion and protection, if need be, and above all, of discretion. You will doubtless have but one occasion, and that lasting five minutes, to prove your friendship. But that will be a sufficient proof. Do you accept?

OLIVIER. I do.

[*Enter a Servant.*]

SERVANT. Monsieur Raymond de Nanjac asks whether monsieur can see him. Here is his card. He has come on behalf of Monsieur le Comte de Latour, and says that monsieur is awaiting him.

OLIVIER. That's so. I shall see him in a moment.

SUZANNE [*to the Servant*]. Wait a moment! Let me see that card.

OLIVIER [*handing her the card*]. Here.

SUZANNE. Good. Monsieur de Nanjac is a friend of yours, is n't he?

OLIVIER. I have never set eyes on him.

SUZANNE. How is it that he is here to see you?

OLIVIER. He is acting as second to Monsieur de Latour, who had a quarrel with a friend of mine.

SUZANNE. What strange coincidences there are!

OLIVIER. What is it?

SUZANNE. Where can I escape without being seen?

OLIVIER. You know very well. How agitated you are! Do you know Monsieur de Nanjac?

SUZANNE. I was introduced to him at Baden — I spoke to him two or three times.

OLIVIER. Oh! I'm getting warm, I think, as little children say when they are playing games. Is Monsieur de Nanjac—?

SUZANNE. You're dreaming!

OLIVIER. Hm! Hm!

SUZANNE. Well, if you insist that Monsieur de Nanjac see me in your apartment, ask him in.

OLIVIER. I should n't think of it.

SUZANNE [*regaining control over herself*]. No, ask him in. That's better.

OLIVIER [*motioning to the Servant*]. I don't understand, now?

SERVANT [*announcing*]. Monsieur Raymond de Nanjac.

[*Enter* RAYMOND.]

OLIVIER [*going to greet him at the door*]. Pardon my having made you wait, monsieur.

[RAYMOND *bows, then looks at* SUZANNE *in astonishment. He is deeply moved.*]

SUZANNE. Don't you recognize me, Monsieur de Nanjac?

RAYMOND. I thought I did, madame, but I was not quite sure.

SUZANNE. When did you come from Baden?

RAYMOND. The day before yesterday I thought I should have the honor of paying you a visit to-day, but it is likely I shall be prevented from doing so by certain things which have happened, contrary to all expectation.

SUZANNE. Whenever you would like to call, I shall be only too delighted to see you. Good-bye, my dear Olivier, and don't forget our agreement.

OLIVIER. I am less inclined to do so now than ever before.

SUZANNE [*to* RAYMOND]. Good-bye, monsieur. I hope to see you again.

[*She goes out.*]

OLIVIER. Now, monsieur, I am at your service. [*He motions* RAYMOND *to a seat.*]

RAYMOND [*sitting down — dryly*]. Monsieur, the matter is most simple. Monsieur de Latour, a friend of mine —

OLIVIER. Pardon me, monsieur, for interrupting: is Monsieur de Latour a friend of yours?

RAYMOND. Yes, monsieur. Why do you ask?

OLIVIER. Because sometimes — Are you a soldier, monsieur?

RAYMOND. Yes, monsieur.

OLIVIER. Because sometimes a soldier believes himself in honor bound not to refuse to act as second to a person whom he scarcely knows, or even whom he does not know at all.

RAYMOND. True, we rarely refuse. But as a matter of fact, I do know Monsieur de Latour; I like him and consider him as a friend. Does he not deserve the title? Is that what you mean to convey?

OLIVIER. Not in the least, monsieur. Continue, please.

RAYMOND. Well, Monsieur de Latour was the day before yesterday at the home of the Viscountess de Vernières. I was there with him; they were playing *lansquenet*. A young man, Monsieur Georges de Maucroix —

OLIVIER. A friend of mine.

RAYMOND. Monsieur de Maucroix "had the hand." I believe that is the term — I am not acquainted with the technical expressions used in cards. I have never played.

OLIVIER. That is the expression which has been consecrated by time.

RAYMOND. Monsieur de Maucroix had "passed" three or four times, and there were twenty-five louis on the table. Monsieur de Latour's turn came next, but as he had lost a great deal during the evening, he found that he had n't any money left, and told Monsieur de Maucroix that he would take the hand and owe the money: give his *word* for it. At that, Monsieur de Maucroix, who was about to lay down his cards, handed them to his right-hand neighbor, and said: "I pass." Monsieur de Latour was pleased to see in this simple occurrence a refusal to accept his word about the money. He believed that he had been offended, and demanded an explanation from Monsieur de Maucroix, who replied that the place where they were was not suitable for that sort of discussion. He mentioned your name and address. Monsieur de Latour has asked me to come and receive the explanation from you which your friend thought he could not make in person.

OLIVIER. The explanation is very simple, monsieur, and in this affair there will result, I hope, one advantage for me: the pleasure of making your acquaintance. Georges had no intention of offending Monsieur de Latour: he "passed," as any one may when he does not wish to risk losing on one hand all that he had won.

RAYMOND. But it was Monsieur de Maucroix's place to decide that before beginning the hand with Monsieur de Latour.

OLIVIER. He merely reconsidered.

RAYMOND. He would have played the hand with any one else; of that I am firmly convinced. He would have played it if Monsieur de Latour's money had been on the table.

OLIVIER. Allow me to say that we cannot know that, monsieur. We can discuss only the visible and known fact. I have the honor of repeating what Monsieur de Maucroix himself said to me: that he did nothing but what he had often done, and which every one does. For my part, I can say that if I had been in Monsieur de Latour's place, I should never have noticed that detail.

RAYMOND. It is possible, monsieur, that in ordinary society it might be as you say, but in military circles —

OLIVIER. I beg your pardon, monsieur, but I was not aware that Monsieur de Latour was in the army.

RAYMOND. But I am.

OLIVIER. Allow me to remark, monsieur, that in this matter neither of *us* is concerned; this is between Monsieur de Latour and Monsieur de Maucroix, neither of whom is in the army.

RAYMOND. But the moment Monsieur de Latour chooses me to represent him, I treat the matter as if it were my own.

OLIVIER. Let me tell you, monsieur, that you are making a mistake. I grant that the seconds should be as careful of the honor of the principals as they would be of their own, but they ought in their discussions to adopt a conciliatory manner or at least a certain impartiality, which will, in case of a tragic outcome, relieve them of responsibility. It is surely sufficient to discuss facts, without making suppositions — *those* should be made only by the principals. Monsieur, believe me, there are not two kinds of honor — one for the uniform you wear, one for the clothes I wear — the same heart beats under each. You see, a man's life appears so serious a matter to me that it deserves serious discussion, and only when no other course is open should one cold-bloodedly bring two men face to face on the dueling-ground. If you like, monsieur, let us have another meeting, for, if you will allow me to speak frankly, you seem in a rather irritable humor, and your friend and mine cannot come to a satisfactory agreement, unless for some reason which I cannot guess (for this is the first time I have had the honor of meeting you) we are ourselves two adversaries needing seconds, and not seconds trying to conciliate two adversaries.

RAYMOND [with a change of tone and manner]. You are right, monsieur; it was personal feeling which led me to speak as I did. Pardon me, and allow me at the same time to speak freely with you.

OLIVIER. Speak, monsieur.

RAYMOND. I am very frank — the way soldiers usually are — and I ask you to be frank in return.

OLIVIER. Very well.

RAYMOND. We are both men of honor; about the same age; we move in similar circles; and if I had not been living like a bear in Africa for the past ten years, we should undoubtedly have met and become friends long ago. You agree with me, do you not?

OLIVIER. I am now beginning to.

RAYMOND. I ought to have begun in this tone, instead of allowing myself to go on in that ill-humored manner, and receiving the little lesson which you so cleverly and delightfully administered to me not long ago. If I had happened upon a man of my own disposition, instead of a man of sense like you, we should now have been at each other's throats — which would have been ridiculous. Now, let me ask you a few delicate questions which only an old friend would ordinarily have the right to ask. I give you my word that not a syllable will go farther than this room.

OLIVIER. Proceed.

RAYMOND. Thank you. This conversation may have the greatest influence over my life.

OLIVIER. I am listening.

RAYMOND. What is the name of the woman who was here when I came in?

OLIVIER. Baroness d'Ange.

RAYMOND. In society?

OLIVIER. Yes.

RAYMOND. Widow?

OLIVIER. Yes.

RAYMOND. What are the relations — answer me, monsieur, on your honor, as I should if you asked me the same question — what are the relations between her and you?

OLIVIER [after a pause]. Simple friendship.

RAYMOND. You are simply her friend?

OLIVIER [emphasizing the word "am"]. I am simply her friend.

RAYMOND. Thank you, monsieur. One word more: how did it happen that Madame d'Ange was here? Surely a friend — ?

OLIVIER. May not a respectable woman visit a respectable man? Why not? And the proof that Madame d'Ange's business here was nothing that she need be ashamed of is that, although she might have left here by that door unseen, she waited, talked with you, and went quite openly.

RAYMOND. That's so. Well, I needed this explanation. Now, as I wish to fulfill my obligations to you for your frankness, let me tell you everything. I am an officer in an African regiment; three months ago I was rather severely wounded, so that I obtained a leave of absence during my convalescence. Two weeks ago I arrived at Baden. I saw Madame d'Ange, and obtained an introduction; she produced an instantaneous and profound impression on me. I followed her to Paris, and I am desperately in love with her. She has never in any way encouraged my passion. She is young and beautiful, and I wondered whether she were in love with some one, because her behavior at Baden was irreproachable. Now you can easily understand how excited I was when I found her here. You will understand my very natural fears, all my suppositions, my ill-humor which was dissipated by your own good common sense, and finally this explanation which I so frankly asked for and which you so courteously gave me. I hope, monsieur, that we shall have occasion to see each other again. Please consider me among your friends; if ever I can help you, remember that I am at your service.

OLIVIER. I have already told you what I had to tell you, monsieur. Good luck to you!

RAYMOND. I believe that this duel affair can be satisfactorily settled.

OLIVIER. I believe so, too.

RAYMOND. We'll outline our conference, give copies to our friends, and nothing more need be done about it.

OLIVIER. Exactly. Shall I see you tomorrow? I shall come to you. I have your address on this card here. At the same hour?

RAYMOND. Very well. Until to-morrow, monsieur.

[*They shake hands, then* RAYMOND *goes out.* HIPPOLYTE *opens the door and looks through.*]

HIPPOLYTE. May I come in?

OLIVIER [*bowing to* RAYMOND, *who is in the hallway — aside*]. Poor fellow!

HIPPOLYTE. What's happening?

OLIVIER. A great deal, my dear man.

HIPPOLYTE. What about Monsieur de Maucroix's affair?

OLIVIER. Settled —

HIPPOLYTE. Good. And the lady who came from Baden?

OLIVIER. All my plans for the future have crumbled. Harlequin proposed beautifully, but Columbine disposed in her own way.

HIPPOLYTE. That makes two ruptures in a single day.

OLIVIER. One before, one after. If Titus were in my place, he would be able to retire early, and he would not have misspent his day.

HIPPOLYTE. Well, something has happened to me, too.

OLIVIER. What?

HIPPOLYTE. I have just received the following invitation from Madame de Vernières: "Madame la Vicomtesse de Vernières has the honor to ask Monsieur Hippolyte Richond to spend the evening with her next Wednesday —" the address follows. But guess what was written at the bottom of the page? "On behalf of Madame

de Santis, who sends her compliments." Madame de Santis wants to talk to me about her husband, no doubt.

OLIVIER. What did you answer?

HIPPOLYTE. Nothing, as yet, but I am going to accept.

OLIVIER. I'll go with you.

HIPPOLYTE. Were you invited, too?

OLIVIER. An invitation is not necessary at Madame de Vernières.' Then I am sure there is some intrigue afoot with those people, and I prefer to be present while it is in process of incubation rather than after it is hatched. — Are you hungry?

HIPPOLYTE. Oh, yes!

OLIVIER. Then let's go to dinner.

ACT II

[*The drawing-room at* MADAME DE VERNIÈRES'. *As the curtain rises, the* VISCOUNTESS *is speaking to a Servant.*]

VISCOUNTESS. Light up the boudoir and my bedroom.

SERVANT [*just as he is leaving, announces*]. Madame la Baronne d'Ange.

[*He goes out.*]

[*Enter* SUZANNE.]

SUZANNE. I'm not as prompt as I wanted to be, my dear Viscountess, but you know when one lives in the country, one cannot always be punctual. I dressed at home, at Paris, but everything was upside down there, as if I'd been away. But to-morrow everything will be in order again.

VISCOUNTESS. You are not late.

SUZANNE. One is always late when one comes to do a favor.

VISCOUNTESS. How good of you! You received my letter, did n't you? You don't blame me too much for my indiscretion, do you?

SUZANNE. But we're friends! Here is what you asked me for. [*She gives the* VISCOUNTESS *a bank-note.*] If that is not enough —

VISCOUNTESS. Thank you, that will be plenty — and I needed it to-day!

SUZANNE. Why did n't you ask for it yesterday?

VISCOUNTESS. Because up to the last moment I thought I could get it from Madame de Santis's broker; he promised me. But at noon he told me it would be impossible. Valentine is very hard-pressed, too, and I could n't ask her. Now I can tell you: I'm being sued. I had good reason to believe that my goods would have been seized to-morrow. I wanted to avoid that scandal.

SUZANNE. You are quite right. You must pay the bailiff to-night.

VISCOUNTESS. There are two.

SUZANNE. Then, the bailiffs.

VISCOUNTESS. I'm going to send my maid with the money.

SUZANNE. Don't take servants into your confidence in matters of that sort.

VISCOUNTESS. But I can't wait until to-morrow. Those men might come the first thing in the morning.

SUZANNE. Then go yourself.

VISCOUNTESS. What about my guests?

SUZANNE. I'll receive them for you. You can be back before the first one arrives. Who are coming?

VISCOUNTESS. Valentine; a Monsieur Richond whom she wanted me to ask — a friend of her husband; Monsieur de Nanjac (oh, if that were only a match! I'm counting on you for that — if it materializes, we'll be saved!); Marcelle; you; I; and then the Marquis de Thonnerins. I'm counting on these. I don't know whether Monsieur de Maucroix and Monsieur de Latour are coming, even though their quarrel has been settled.

SUZANNE. Did n't you invite Monsieur de Jalin?

VISCOUNTESS. He never comes.

SUZANNE. Will the Marquis de Thonnerins come?

VISCOUNTESS. He sent no reply, which means he is coming.

SUZANNE. Quick now, attend to your affairs — I'll wait for you.

VISCOUNTESS. I'll take a cab and be back in twenty minutes. You're going to be bored — or shall I leave Marcelle with you? I don't think she need go with me.

SUZANNE. What has she to do with it?

VISCOUNTESS. I'll tell you: my affairs are in such confusion that the only way I can hope to save a few little odds and ends is by putting them under some one else's name. I have made Marcelle legally independent; you know her mother left her a little money, of which I was made a trustee. You see, she can claim what I still have: it's her only guarantee. Now, that will protect me from further persecution. Still, I think possibly she may have to sign something.

SUZANNE. Then take her with you.

[*Enter a Servant.*]

SERVANT. Monsieur le Marquis de Thonnerins. [*He goes out.*]

SUZANNE. I'll talk with the Marquis while I'm waiting for you.

VISCOUNTESS. Good. I'll go now before he comes; otherwise I could n't get away. Tell him about Marcelle and Monsieur de Nanjac, he might be of use to us.

[*She goes out.*]

[*Enter the* MARQUIS.]

MARQUIS. Who just left?

SUZANNE. The mistress of the house, who has an errand to do. She will be back soon.

MARQUIS. Oh — never mind! I probably shan't see her.

SUZANNE. Are n't you going to spend the evening with us?

MARQUIS. No: I have only a short time to spare. My daughter has just returned from the country, and I am going to take her to my brother's to-day. I came here only because you wrote.

SUZANNE. I wished to speak with you, but I did not want to make you come out to the country — that would be taking advantage of you. Is Mademoiselle de Thonnerins well?

MARQUIS. Very well.

SUZANNE. Are n't you ever going to let me see her? You know, I'd so like to, even at a distance, because you might never bring her.

MARQUIS. My dear Suzanne, I think I've made that matter clear once for all. Why open the discussion again? You have something to tell me; I am listening.

SUZANNE. You once told me that no matter what might happen, I should always find you ready to help me.

MARQUIS. True, and I repeat it.

SUZANNE. Yes, but so distantly that I am not sure whether it would be discreet of me to count on your promise.

MARQUIS. I don't remember ever having made you a promise which I did not keep. The way in which I spoke is because of my age. The time has come when I should remember that I am no longer a young man of twenty, or even of forty. I should be ridiculous if I pretended to be anything but what I am: an old man who is happy if he can be of service, if possible, to those whom he has occasionally bored, and who have been generous enough not to make him aware of the fact.

SUZANNE. Then let me answer in the same way. I owe everything to you, Monsieur le Marquis. Perhaps you have forgotten that, because you are the benefactor; I have not, because I am the recipient of your favors. You might have had for me only a passing fancy; you honored me with a little love.

MARQUIS. Suzanne —!

SUZANNE. I was nothing, and you made something of me. Thanks to you, I have attained a position on the social ladder which might be considered a descent for women who started at the top, but which is for me, who started at the bottom, the apex. Now, you can readily understand that since I have risen through you — to this position — which I should never otherwise have dared aspire to, I cannot help having certain ambitions; they are inevitable under the circumstances. Things being as they are, I must either fall lower than where I began, or rise to the very top. Marriage is my only salvation.

MARQUIS. Marriage?

SUZANNE. Yes.

MARQUIS. You are ambitious.

SUZANNE. Do not discourage me. I said to myself, as you seem to say now, that it was out of the question, because I had to find a man who had enough confidence to believe in me, was strong and fine enough to force society to accept me, brave enough to defend me, sufficiently in love to devote his whole life to me; young enough, handsome enough, to believe that he is loved and that I *shall* love him.

MARQUIS. Have you found this confident, noble, and loving husband?

SUZANNE. Yes.

MARQUIS. Is he young enough to believe he is loved?

SUZANNE. He is young enough for me to love him.

MARQUIS. Do you love him?

SUZANNE. Yes. What of it? No one is perfect!

MARQUIS. Is he going to marry you?

SUZANNE. I have only a word to say, and he will ask me.

MARQUIS. Why have n't you said it?

SUZANNE. Because I wanted to speak to you first. It was the least I could do.

MARQUIS. Well, there is this to fear, you know: that this man, who appears so splendid to you, may be merely speculating. He may know your past and, believing you to be rich, he may be offering to sell you a name as a final resource for saving yourself. That is very often the case.

SUZANNE. He left France ten years ago, and he knows nothing of my life. If he were to find out the slightest detail, he would leave me at once. He has an income of twenty or twenty-five thousand francs, and he need not sell, because he is able to buy. When you hear his name —

MARQUIS. I don't want, nor have I a right, to know it. My interest in your welfare may lead me so far as to wish to see your desires fulfilled, but I really cannot help you in an affair of the heart of this sort, no matter how honorable your motives may be. If by chance you should mention the name of a man I know, you would be placing me in a situation where I should have either to deceive a man of honor, or betray you.

SUZANNE. Of course, people of honor must stand by one another.

MARQUIS. What have you decided to do?

SUZANNE. I am going away, that's the wisest course, but I must be able to be absolute mistress of my life: I must be able to leave France, Europe, even, if need be, and never return. My marriage must not for an instant appear to my husband as being in any way the result of material calculation. To do this I must have a fortune of about the same size as his — I must have it in two hours' time. You are my guardian, and you know how much I have: tell me.

MARQUIS. Just at present your income is fifteen thousand francs.

SUZANNE. Yes?

MARQUIS. Which means a capital of three hundred thousand, figured at five per cent.

SUZANNE. And this capital — ?

MARQUIS. A word to my solicitor, — he has charge of your affairs, too, — and he will hand you over all your papers.

SUZANNE. You are a wonderful man!

MARQUIS. I am merely rendering you your account.

SUZANNE. I owe everything to you, even the happiness I am about to get from another.

MARQUIS. A clever woman never owes anything to any one.

SUZANNE. That is an indirect reproach.

MARQUIS. No: merely a receipt of "paid in full." [He kisses her hand.] Please offer my excuses to the Viscountess.

[He goes out.]

[Enter a Servant.]

SERVANT. Monsieur Raymond de Nanjac. [He goes out.]

[Enter RAYMOND.]

RAYMOND. I have just come from your apartment. I had hoped we might spend a few moments together before coming to the Viscountess's, and I was looking forward to the pleasure of accompanying you.

SUZANNE. I received a note from Madame de Vernières, who asked me to come a little earlier. There was a favor to do.

RAYMOND. That would be an excuse if you needed her. Were you speaking to the Viscountess when I came?

SUZANNE. No: with the Marquis de Thonnerins.

RAYMOND. Has he not a sister?

SUZANNE. Yes: the Duchess d'Haubeney.

RAYMOND. My sister knows her intimately, and ever since I arrived, she has been tormenting me to have me introduced at this house. But I always refused — what was the use?

SUZANNE. The Marquis has a charming daughter.

RAYMOND. What is that to me?

SUZANNE. Whose dowry will amount to four or five millions.

RAYMOND. What difference can that make to me? I don't want to marry her.

SUZANNE. Why not?

RAYMOND. How can I think of Mademoiselle de Thonnerins, or any one else, when I love you?

SUZANNE. How ridiculous! You scarcely know me.

RAYMOND. The day a man sees for the first time the woman he is going to love, he already loves her. Perhaps he even loved her the day before he meets her. Love comes; it is not reasoned about. It is sure and instantaneous, or else it never comes. It seems I have known you for ten years.

SUZANNE. That may be, but if love takes no time in being born, it must take time to live, and while we women do not believe in the permanence of these sudden passions which we inspire, still we want to believe in the durability of true love. Now, you say you love me, and yet you are going to leave in six weeks, and will probably never return. Do I seem to you like one of those women whose amorous' caprices hardly outlast a month? If you have imagined that, you have done me a grave injustice.

RAYMOND. What did I tell you yesterday?

SUZANNE. Nonsense — that you did not want to leave — that you wanted to marry me. A night has passed since then, and night brings counsel.

RAYMOND. I am not going away. I sent in my resignation to-day.

SUZANNE. Really? That was madness! You will surely regret the sacrifice you are making for me — in a year's time, in a month, perhaps. I'm talking to you as a true friend. Think, I'm an old woman compared with you: I am twenty-eight. At twenty-eight, a woman is older than a man of thirty. I must be reasonable for both of us.

RAYMOND. But is it necessary to have lived, as you say, to have worn out one's heart in the banal and vulgar intrigues of what masquerades under the name of love, in order to have the right to give one's self up to a true passion at thirty? I thank God for having granted me since my early youth an active life, for keeping intact all my feelings and energies, until I should be old enough to respond to the call of a true passion! You treat me as you would a child! I was only ten, Suzanne, when I lost a mother whom I worshiped. No matter how soon one loses his mother, that event makes him old all at once. Can't you see that the camp-life I have led, the long days spent in the silent solitudes by the sea, the memory of my dearest friends having fallen at my side — can't you see that all this has matured me and made me live two years in one? I have gray hair, Suzanne; I am an old man; love me.

SUZANNE. But if I love you and if you continue to be suspicious of me, as you were when you saw me at Monsieur de Jalin's (I went there to speak about you); if I must continually struggle against your doubts, your jealousy, what will become of me?

RAYMOND. What I told Olivier proved my love. Is there a man who really loves who can harbor a single suspicion about the woman he loves? There can be no true love without respect and esteem.

SUZANNE. That's true. I can understand this jealousy of yours; I might even feel it myself; perhaps I do. What I like in you is that you have never loved. If I were to become your wife I should want to hide my love and my happiness from every one. I want to forget this society in which I live, to forget that it ever existed, because it is full of women who are younger and more beautiful than I, whom you might some day come to love. Marriage, in my opinion, is being always alone with one's husband.

RAYMOND. Suzanne, that is the way I love you, that is the way I want to be loved. We shall go away as soon as you like — tomorrow, if you say — and never come back.

SUZANNE. But what will your sister say?

RAYMOND. She will say: "If you love her, and if she loves you and is worthy of you, marry her."

SUZANNE. She does not know me, dear. She thinks I am young and beautiful; she imagines that I belong to a family to which she might belong. She does not know that I am alone in the world, and that my marriage will separate her from you — because we must leave. If she knew all that, she would give you the same sort of advice as I gave you not long ago. You love her, and you will end by believing her.

RAYMOND. My sister will live near us; she has no attachments anywhere.

SUZANNE. Let me become acquainted with her first. I want her to like me; I want to win her respect and her affection; I want her to wish to have me for a sister, to want our marriage instead of merely accepting it.

RAYMOND. I shall do as you wish.

SUZANNE. How about the friends whose advice you are going to ask?

RAYMOND. I have no friends.

SUZANNE. Monsieur de Jalin?

RAYMOND. He is the only one. You must admit that he is worthy. He has a loyal heart.

SUZANNE. He has. Just think by how slender a thread our reputation is suspended! You speak of marriage, and yet, if for some reason or other it should not take place, just see in what a false and ridiculous a position I should be! If I should ever cause you pain, you may tell Olivier; otherwise, keep our secret to yourself. The real and true happiness is that of which no one else knows.

RAYMOND. You are right; you always are right. Although Olivier practically deserves this confidence, although we have scarcely been apart during the past four days, he never questioned me, nor was your name once mentioned. Well, I promise to say nothing either to my sister or to Olivier. Is that satisfactory?

SUZANNE. Yes.
RAYMOND. How I love you!
SUZANNE. Here comes some one.

[Enter a Servant.]

SERVANT. Monsieur Olivier de Jalin. Monsieur Hippolyte Richon.

[He goes out.]

SUZANNE [aside]. Olivier! What can he want here?

[Enter HIPPOLYTE and OLIVIER.]

OLIVIER. What! Is the Viscountess not here? And she calls this "receiving"!
SUZANNE. The Viscountess will soon return.
OLIVIER. In any event, she could not have chosen a better representative. Since you are doing the honors, Baroness, allow me to present my friend Monsieur Hippolyte Richond.
HIPPOLYTE [bowing]. Madame.
SUZANNE [likewise bowing]. Monsieur.
OLIVIER. And how are you to-day, my dear Raymond?
RAYMOND. Very well, thank you.
SUZANNE [to OLIVIER and RAYMOND]. How pleasant it is to see two men who have n't been acquainted over a week on terms of such intimacy!
OLIVIER. Between upright and honorable people, my dear Baroness, there exists a mysterious bond which unites them even before they become acquainted, and which very shortly after their meeting takes shape as true friendship. — My dear Raymond, let me introduce you to one of my best friends — I have two now — to Monsieur Hippolyte Richond, who has traveled widely, who has likewise been in Africa. You may chat about it together.
RAYMOND. Ah, monsieur, so you know that beautiful country about which so much evil is spoken!

[They draw aside and converse.]

OLIVIER [to SUZANNE]. I thought you were in the country?
SUZANNE. I returned this evening.
OLIVIER. Oh, have you anything new of interest to tell me?
SUZANNE. Absolutely nothing.
OLIVIER. Then let me tell you some news.

SUZANNE. What?
OLIVIER. Monsieur de Nanjac is in love with you.
SUZANNE. You're joking!
OLIVIER. Has n't he spoken to you?
SUZANNE. No.
OLIVIER. That's strange. He spoke to me.
SUZANNE. He went about it indirectly.
OLIVIER. You may expect a proposal.
SUZANNE. Thank you for preparing me.
OLIVIER. Why?
SUZANNE. Because I'm going to let him know as soon as possible that he would be wasting his time.
OLIVIER. Don't you love Monsieur de Nanjac?
SUZANNE. I? The idea!
OLIVIER. Not even a little?
SUZANNE. Not even a great deal!
OLIVIER. Nor passionately. Then, not at all?
SUZANNE. Not at all, as you say.
OLIVIER. Then I've been very much mistaken, but I am very glad to hear what you tell me.
SUZANNE. Why?
OLIVIER. I'll tell you when we're alone together.
SUZANNE. Tell me soon, because you know I'm going away.
OLIVIER. You have n't gone yet.
SUZANNE. Who can prevent my going?
OLIVIER. I — I hope.
SUZANNE. Take care, or I shall ask Madame de Lornan to protect me.
OLIVIER. Madame de Lornan has nothing to do with me. I've called there daily for the past three days, and she has refused to see me each time.
SUZANNE. Do you want me to see her and make it up between you?
OLIVIER. You — ?
SUZANNE. Yes.
OLIVIER. Do you think she would re-receive you and not me?
SUZANNE. Perhaps. People receive me when I want them to — At your service!

[She turns and goes away.]

OLIVIER [to himself]. That looks like a threat. We'll see.

[*Enter the* VISCOUNTESS *and* MARCELLE.]

VISCOUNTESS. I hope you will excuse me, gentlemen?

SUZANNE [*to the* VISCOUNTESS]. Well?

VISCOUNTESS. Everything is arranged. Thanks.

MARCELLE [*to* SUZANNE]. I hope you are well, madame?

SUZANNE. And you, my dear?

MARCELLE. Well, I'm sorry to say. When a woman is always well, no one is interested in her.

SUZANNE. But I have occasionally heard you cough when we passed the night together.

MARCELLE. That does n't count: I've had colds as long as I can remember. I must have had a cold when I was born.

VISCOUNTESS [*to* HIPPOLYTE, *to whom* OLIVIER *has meantime introduced her*]. It's very good of you, monsieur, to accept my invitation, although it was sent in a rather irregular fashion. Madame de Santis, whose husband you know —

HIPPOLYTE. Yes, madame.

VISCOUNTESS. Madame de Santis was very anxious to consult you on a matter of some importance, and is not yet settled in her own home. She complimented me by believing and saying that you would come here. I think the world of Valentine, and my dearest wish is that she may realize her dreams.

HIPPOLYTE. If that depends on me, madame, she shall.

MARCELLE. Did n't Monsieur de Thonnerins come?

SUZANNE. Yes, but he asked me to offer you his excuses. He called to say that he could not be present: his sister is receiving this evening.

MARCELLE. I wish I might have seen him!

VISCOUNTESS. By the way, Monsieur de Nanjac, did n't you promise me you would bring your sister?

RAYMOND. Yes, madame, but you know she is still in mourning, and is ailing a little at present. As soon as she is better, I shall be delighted to introduce her.

OLIVIER [*to* RAYMOND]. Tell me — ?

RAYMOND. Yes?

MARCELLE. Monsieur de Nanjac?

OLIVIER [*to* RAYMOND]. I'll ask you later.

RAYMOND. Mademoiselle?

MARCELLE [*to* OLIVIER]. Monsieur Olivier, lend me Monsieur de Nanjac a moment; I'll give him back. [*To* RAYMOND.] I have something to talk to you about, but beforehand, please take this pin out of my hat.

HIPPOLYTE [*to* OLIVIER]. That young lady seems very clever.

OLIVIER. She's only a girl. How could you think she was anything more?

MARCELLE. Tell me, Monsieur de Nanjac, do you know that there is a conspiracy hatching against us?

RAYMOND. Really, mademoiselle?

MARCELLE. Yes: they are trying to get you to marry me.

RAYMOND. But —

MARCELLE. Oh, don't try to be gallant, now! You don't any more want to be my husband than I ought to be your wife. You are in love with a woman who is much better than I; I have guessed that, but I shan't say any more about it. Now that you have nothing to fear, come with me, and my aunt will believe you are making love to me. She'll be so pleased. One must do something for one's relatives. But I'm a good girl, and I thought it best to warn unfortunate people of what is in store for them. Now, take care not to spoil my hat; it's the only one I have, and I don't think it's paid for yet.

[*She goes out laughing, with* RAYMOND.]

VISCOUNTESS [*to* SUZANNE]. What did I tell you? Everything is going splendidly.

HIPPOLYTE. That Monsieur de Nanjac seems a fine fellow.

OLIVIER. He is charming. I am going to try to save him, too, even at the risk of repenting later.

[*Enter a Servant.*]

SERVANT. Madame de Santis.

[*He goes out.*]

OLIVIER. This is your affair.

[*Enter* VALENTINE.]

VISCOUNTESS. You are the last to arrive.

VALENTINE [*aside to the* VISCOUNTESS]. Monsieur de Latour did n't want to let me go; I had an awful time getting away; he does n't know I am here. — Is Monsieur Richond here?

VISCOUNTESS. He's talking with Olivier over there.

VALENTINE. Oh, how my heart's beating!

SUZANNE. Courage!

OLIVIER [*going to* VALENTINE]. How are you?

VALENTINE. Very well, thank you.

OLIVIER. You're dressed like a simple little middle-class housekeeper. Suits you beautifully! Let me introduce you to my friend Richond. You had him asked, so that I imagine you would like to meet him?

VALENTINE. Yes. Introduce me.

OLIVIER [*introducing her to* HIPPOLYTE]. Monsieur Hippolyte Richond — Madame de Santis.

HIPPOLYTE. Madame.

VALENTINE [*bowing*]. I have been wanting to meet you for ever so long, monsieur.

HIPPOLYTE. Very good of you, madame, to say so. I have been away from France during the past ten years.

VALENTINE [*after making sure that she will not be overheard* — *to* HIPPOLYTE]. Tell me, now, Hippolyte, what are you going to do with me?

HIPPOLYTE. With you, madame?

VALENTINE. Yes!

HIPPOLYTE. Why — what I have been doing so far!

VALENTINE. But I tell you my situation is impossible.

HIPPOLYTE. Why?

VALENTINE. You ask that! We have n't spoken to each other for ten years. I am still your wife.

HIPPOLYTE. Yes — legally.

VALENTINE. You once loved me.

HIPPOLYTE. Deeply. I nearly died — luckily, I escaped death.

VALENTINE. And now — ?

HIPPOLYTE. Now I don't even think of you any more; you are as indifferent to me as if you had never lived.

VALENTINE. And yet you came here, knowing you would see me. If I were indifferent to you, you would not have come.

HIPPOLYTE. You are mistaken: I came precisely because I had nothing to fear in seeing you again.

VALENTINE. Then will you never forgive me?

HIPPOLYTE. Never!

VALENTINE. Your home will never be open to me?

HIPPOLYTE. I hope it never will.

VALENTINE. Is it true what people have told me?

HIPPOLYTE. What have you been told?

VALENTINE. That your home is — occupied?

HIPPOLYTE. Yes: by people for whom I care a great deal.

VALENTINE. But whom I might drive out.

HIPPOLYTE. You know very well that only one of us two has the right to threaten, and that is I. Don't forget that. Even after three years of sorrow, despair, loneliness, during which, if your heart had found a single word of regret, if you had shed a single tear of repentence, I would have forgiven you, — because I loved you. But now I think I have earned the right to feel and live as I think best. It is in the bosom of a family happened upon by chance, at a borrowed hearth, as it were, that I have found the happiness which you did not think fit to give me. Just see the strange situation into which a wife's sin can bring an honest man. I know everything you have done since our separation, and I know that to-day is the first time you have thought of returning to me. You have wasted your fortune in laziness and luxury, and now that you are at the end of your resources, you say to yourself: "Let's see whether my husband will take me back!" Never has a single word come straight from your heart. No, madame, no, everything is over between us: you are dead to me.

VALENTINE. So — you don't care what becomes of me?

HIPPOLYTE. You may do what you like; I have no more love for you. You cannot make me suffer any more. I am an upright man, and you cannot render me ridiculous.

VALENTINE. That is all I wanted to know. You can blame yourself now for whatever happens to me.

HIPPOLYTE. Good-bye, then. We shall never see each other again.

MARCELLE [who has entered meanwhile and is anxious to speak with HIPPOLYTE]. Are you going, monsieur?

HIPPOLYTE. Yes, mademoiselle. [To VALENTINE.] Madame. [He bows to her.]

VALENTINE [bowing]. Monsieur.

VISCOUNTESS. Are you leaving us so soon, monsieur? That's not at all nice!

HIPPOLYTE. I promised to return early.

VISCOUNTESS. Why did n't you bring Madame Richond?

HIPPOLYTE. Madame de Santis did not ask her.

VISCOUNTESS. I am at home every Wednesday, monsieur, and whenever you and Madame Richond wish to give me the pleasure of your company at tea, I shall be glad to receive you.

HIPPOLYTE [to OLIVIER]. I shall see you to-morrow; I want to talk to you.
[He bows and goes out.]

MARCELLE. You can never count on these married men!

RAYMOND [to OLIVIER]. You had something to say to me awhile ago?

OLIVIER. Yes. Tell me, my dear Raymond, you have never, since that once, referred to Madame d'Ange. What has become of your consuming passion?

RAYMOND. I have given it up.

OLIVIER. So soon?

RAYMOND. Yes: I was only wasting my time.

OLIVIER. You came to that conclusion at once?

RAYMOND. What else could I do?

OLIVIER. That's so. Do you know, you are becoming quite Parisian: you are more reasonable than I had thought. I congratulate you. You have also encouraged me to give you some advice.

RAYMOND. What?

OLIVIER. You promised the Viscountess, did you not, that you would introduce her to your sister?

RAYMOND. Yes.

OLIVIER. Don't bring her here.

RAYMOND. Why not? Is the Viscountess's home not quite respectable?

OLIVIER. I don't say that, only the best homes are not necessarily those which present the best appearance. If you scratch the surface, you will see what lies just beneath. — Listen! [Aloud.] Are we not to have the pleasure of seeing Monsieur de Latour?

VISCOUNTESS. He wrote asking to be excused — urgent business —

MARCELLE. If the person who invented those two words, "urgent business," had taken out a patent, he would have made a mint of money.

OLIVIER. Perhaps Monsieur de Latour is not lying: once, by chance, he might be telling the truth.

MARCELLE. What has he done to you? You invariably speak ill of him, and he never speaks anything but good of you.

OLIVIER. He is only doing his duty.

VALENTINE. He is most charming, very respectable, distinguished - looking, and well-bred; you can't make the same reproach to every one.

OLIVIER. Very well, then, everything is in his favor; he squanders his money —

VALENTINE. That's true enough.

OLIVIER. Yes, true for what it costs him to make: he gambles every night and invariably wins.

VISCOUNTESS. I suppose you will say he cheats?

OLIVIER. No, only that he is lucky at play, and one does not always have luck as one has a paunch — without having it purposely.

RAYMOND. My dear Olivier, don't forget that I was once a second for Monsieur de Latour.

OLIVIER. Whose acquaintance you made at the hotel in Baden. You are a man of honor, my dear Raymond, and you imagine that every one else is like yourself. That is very dangerous. I tell you, I should never have consented to the duel which Monsieur de Latour appears to have provoked.

SUZANNE. Do you deny that he's brave? He fought his first duel when he was eighteen, and killed his adversary.

VISCOUNTESS. A very good beginning in life!

OLIVIER. The life of other people! I don't question Monsieur de Latour's courage; I only say that a man of honor like Monsieur de Maucroix ought no more to fight with Monsieur de Latour than a man of honor like Monsieur de Nanjac to serve as his second.

SUZANNE. But, my dear Olivier, surely Monsieur de Latour is as fine a man as Monsieur de Maucroix?

OLIVIER. No, because Monsieur de Latour, who calls himself Count, is the son of a little money-lender of Marais who left him fifty thousand francs, with the aid of which his son, thanks to cards, nets an income of forty thousand francs.

VALENTINE. Nonsense! He comes of an excellent family.

OLIVIER. What family?

VALENTINE. The Latour of Auvergne.

OLIVIER. Hm! . . . [1] I am astonished that women who claim to belong to society —

VISCOUNTESS. Who *do*, my dear friend.

OLIVIER. Who do, if you like, should receive so readily a man whom no one else receives, and who will end by forcing every decent man to stay away. I am positive that if Monsieur de Briade or Monsieur de Bonchamp, or any of those gentlemen, as Madame de Santis calls them, have not come here to-day, it was for fear of meeting Monsieur de Latour.

VISCOUNTESS. Let us not discuss the matter any further.   [*A pause.*]

OLIVIER. Madame de Santis! Madame de Santis!

VALENTINE. Well?

OLIVIER. Has the lease of your apartment in the Rue de la Paix expired yet?

VALENTINE. What is that to you? I don't think you came very often.

[1] An untranslatable pun on "Latour d' Auvergne" and "Latour prends garde." — Tr.

OLIVIER. Thank you — and your husband?

VALENTINE. My husband?

OLIVIER. He has expired, I know very well. My friend Richond has just given me news of him. Has he swallowed the reconciliation bait? Is he going to pay for the blue-and-yellow rooms?

VALENTINE. My husband? He'll hear from me!

OLIVIER. That will please him.

VALENTINE. I'm going to sue him.

OLIVIER. That's an idea. But is it a good one? Why sue him?

VALENTINE. You'll see why. I know some very interesting facts about him; I leave the rest with my lawyer. I am his wife, after all.

OLIVIER. The lawyer's?

VALENTINE. My dear, you are witty once a week, and yesterday was your day. Keep still now!

OLIVIER. Rather good, you know.

MARCELLE. Let him talk, Valentine, dear. You have the right on your side, and you'll win your case — take my word for it. You don't say anything more, Monsieur Olivier?

OLIVIER. No, mademoiselle: *you* have begun. I speak only of things I know about, and since I know nothing of dolls or lunches, I never converse with little girls.

MARCELLE. Is that for my benefit?

OLIVIER. Yes, mademoiselle.

MARCELLE. But I speak of the same things as you do. When grand people speak of certain things before little girls, the little girls have a right to join in the conversation. And then — well, I'm no longer a little girl.

OLIVIER. Then what are you, mademoiselle?

MARCELLE. I am a woman, and I speak like a woman!

OLIVIER. You might even say, "like a man!"

MARCELLE. Monsieur!

VALENTINE. I thought you would end with some impertinence!

VISCOUNTESS [*taking* MARCELLE *aside*]. You are going a little too far, Monsieur de

Jalin; that child never harmed you. If, in the future, you feel the need of saying disagreeable things to some one, you may do so to me, when you are in my home, and to me alone. — Come, Marcelle. — Are you coming with us, Monsieur de Nanjac?

RAYMOND. One moment, please.

[*The women go out.*]

OLIVIER. You heard that, my dear Raymond? Are you going to bring your sister to Madame de Vernières'?

RAYMOND. Then everything you said is true?

OLIVIER. Absolutely.

RAYMOND. And this Monsieur de Latour —?

OLIVIER. An unprincipled rascal.

RAYMOND. And Madame de Santis?

OLIVIER. A creature without heart and brain, who would be dishonoring her husband's name if he had not forbidden her the use of it.

RAYMOND. And Mademoiselle de Sancenaux?

OLIVIER. A little girl looking for a husband: a new product of our present-day society.

RAYMOND. But what *is* this society? I must confess, I can't understand a thing about it.

OLIVIER. My dear fellow, you must live for a long time, as I have, in the intimate circles of Parisian society in order to understand the various shades of this particular stratum. It is not easy to explain. — Do you like peaches?

RAYMOND [*surprised*]. Peaches? Yes.

OLIVIER. Well, go to a large fruit dealer, Chevet's, say, or Potel's, and ask for his best peaches. He will show you a basket of magnificent ones, each one separated from the other by leaves, in order to keep them from touching, from decaying by the contact. Ask him the price, and he will tell you: "Thirty sous each," I imagine. Look about you then and you will not fail to see another basket filled with peaches looking at first sight exactly like the others, but they are packed closer together; only one side is visible. The dealer did not offer you these. Ask him their price, and he will reply: "Fifteen sous." You will naturally ask

why these peaches, as large, as beautiful, and as ripe as the others, are cheaper in price. Then he will pick one up, with the tips of his fingers, as delicately as he can, and turn it around, and show you on the bottom side a tiny black speck. That is the explanation of the lower price. Well, my dear fellow, you are now in the fifteen-sous peach basket. Each woman here has some blot in her past life, some stain; they are crowded close to one another in order that these blots may be noticed as little as possible. Although they have the same origin, the same appearance, and the same prejudices as women of society, they do not belong to it: they constitute the "Demimonde," or "Half-world," a veritable floating island on the ocean of Paris, which calls to itself, welcomes, accepts, everything that falls, that emigrates, everything that escapes from *terra firma* — not to mention those who have been shipwrecked or who come from God knows where.

RAYMOND. And has this social stratum any particular visible characteristics?

OLIVIER. You see it everywhere, but rather indistinctly; a Parisian can recognize it at a glance.

RAYMOND. How?

OLIVIER. By the absence of husbands. It is full of married women whose husbands are never seen.

RAYMOND. But what is the origin of this strange social world?

OLIVIER. It is a modern creation. In former times adultery, as we now think of it, did not exist: morals were much more lax; there was a word much more trivial to denote what is now thought of as adultery. Molière made frequent use of it, and made rather the husband ridiculous than the wife to blame. But since the husband, aided by the law, has acquired the right to expel the erring wife from his home, a modification of the manner of looking at such things has come, and this modification has created a new society. What was to become of all these compromised and repudiated wives? The first who saw herself sent from the conjugal roof went into distant retirement somewhere to hide her grief and shame;

but — the second? The second followed the first, and the two gave the name of misfortune to what was really a fault; an error, what was actually a crime. They began to console and excuse each other. With the advent of a third, they invited one another to lunch; with the fourth, they had a dance. Then, about this nucleus came in turn young girls who have "made a slip," false widows, women who bear the name of the man they are living with, some truly-married couples who made their *début* in a *liaison* of many years' standing; finally, the women who think they have done something of importance and who do not want to appear what they really are. To-day this irregular society functions regularly; this bastard society holds charms for the younger generation. " Love" is more easily obtained than higher up, and cheaper than at the bottom.

RAYMOND. Where do these people go?

OLIVIER. It's impossible to say. Only, beneath the brilliant surface, gilded by youth, beauty, money, under this social fabric of laces, smiles, fêtes, and passion, dark and tragic dramas are played, dramas of expiation, scandal, ruin, of the dishonor of whole families, law-suits, children separated from their mothers, children who are forced to forget them at an early age in order not to curse them later on. Then youth passes away and lovers disappear, and out of the past come regrets, remorse, abandonment, and solitude. Among these women are some who attach themselves to men who have been fools enough to take them seriously; they ruin the lives of these men as they have ruined their own; others disappear, and no one ever troubles to find out where they have gone. Some cling to this society — like the Viscountess de Vernières — and die not knowing whether they prefer to rise or fear to fall; others, either because they sincerely repent or because they fear the desert about them, pray, in the name of their children or on behalf of the good of the family, to be taken back by their husbands. Then common friends intervene, and a few good reasons are set forth: the wife is old, people will not gossip about her. The ruined marriage is patched up again, the façade is given a new coat of paint, the couple go to the country for a year or two; they return, society closes its eyes, and allows from time to time those who publicly went out by the front door to creep in at the small back door.

RAYMOND. What, is all that true? How delighted the Baroness would be if she heard this!

OLIVIER. Why so?

RAYMOND. Because she has already told me the same thing.

OLIVIER. She did? *She!*

RAYMOND. Yes, but not so cleverly, I must admit.

OLIVIER. Ah! [*Aside.*] Very clever of her to do it. [*Aloud.*] But since the Baroness knows this section of society so well, why does she frequent it?

RAYMOND. I asked her that, and she replied that the early friends she made brought her here from time to time: Madame de Santis, for instance, is a childhood friend. And then she is interested in Mademoiselle de Sancenaux, whom she wants to extricate from. the unpleasant situation in which she now is. But she is not going to remain here long.

OLIVIER. What?

RAYMOND. It's a secret, but in a week you will hear great news.

[*Enter* MARCELLE.]

MARCELLE. Monsieur de Nanjac, Madame d'Ange would like to see you; she has something she wants to say to you. [RAYMOND *goes out.*] Don't go, Monsieur de Jalin, I want to say something to you.

OLIVIER. At your service, mademoiselle.

MARCELLE. You were very hard on me a little while ago: you made me cry. What have I done to you?

OLIVIER. Why, nothing at all.

MARCELLE. And this isn't the first time you've not treated me nicely. I know you have a bad opinion of me — I've been told so.

OLIVIER. You have not been told the truth.

MARCELLE. And yet you didn't use to be that way with me: you used to say pleasant things occasionally. I even thought you considered me a friend. You were n't happy in your home-life; you told me that; I, too, had my own troubles: there should have been a bond of sympathy between us. Why are n't you nice to me now? What have I done?

OLIVIER. I feel that bond of sympathy, mademoiselle, as I used to, only —

MARCELLE. Oh, tell me — !

OLIVIER. Well — a young girl must be a young girl, and she should only have to do with those things which are befitting her age. Now, there are times when your conversation actually makes me blush, me, a man! And I can't think what answer to make to you. I sometimes regret that you have been brought up in this evil society, and that you can speak as you did, not long ago.

MARCELLE. Then you were purposely severe? Thank you. But what can I do? I can't leave this society in which I live: I have no parents; the conversation I indulge in is the kind I have heard for many years. But, after all, perhaps, it's not so great a misfortune that I have lived in this atmosphere? When I see every day of my life what is happening to women who have erred for the first time, I have learned not to err myself.

OLIVIER. That's true.

MARCELLE. But that's not enough, it seems, especially in view of the future. Since you have been kind enough to take an interest in me, Monsieur Olivier, I'm going to ask your advice.

OLIVIER. What is it, mademoiselle?

MARCELLE. If a young girl like me, without money, without a family, with no other protector than a relative like Madame de Vernières, a girl who has been brought up in a society like this, wants to escape the evil influences, the possible scandal, the nasty advice, the discouragement, how is she to go about it? [A pause.] You don't answer? I see: you blame me, you even pity me, but you cannot advise me. Can I say now that I am no longer a young girl?

OLIVIER [touched]. Forgive me!

MARCELLE. I do more than forgive you, I thank you for having opened my eyes before it was too late. But I am going to beg you, no matter what happens, to defend me a little, and in return I promise to find a way of remaining a decent woman. Perhaps I shall some day find an honorable man who will be grateful to me for that. Good-bye, Monsieur Olivier, good-bye and thank you.

[She shakes hands with OLIVIER.]

[Enter SUZANNE.]

SUZANNE. I am delighted to see that peace is once more established.

MARCELLE. Yes, and I am very happy.
[She goes out.]

OLIVIER. Strange girl!

SUZANNE. She is in love with you.

OLIVIER. With me!

SUZANNE. She has been for ever so long.

OLIVIER. Well, one learns strange things every day!

SUZANNE. Yes: for instance, I have just learned that your pledged word is not to be taken seriously.

OLIVIER. And why?

SUZANNE. Because you have not been a friend to me as you promised.

OLIVIER. What have I done?

SUZANNE. Monsieur de Nanjac has just repeated your conversation to me.

OLIVIER. I did not speak of you.

SUZANNE. That's too subtle for me. In saying what you said to Monsieur de Nanjac, you spoke evil of me and harmed me — or would have if I had not taken the reins in my hands.

OLIVIER. What difference can it possibly make to you, if you don't love Monsieur de Nanjac?

SUZANNE. What do you know about that?

OLIVIER. Do you love him?

SUZANNE. I'm not forced to tell you.

OLIVIER. Perhaps you are!

SUZANNE. Then, it's — war?

OLIVIER. Very well: war!

SUZANNE. You have letters of mine; please return them.

OLIVIER. To-morrow I shall do so in person.

SUZANNE. Until to-morrow, then.

OLIVIER. Until to-morrow!
[He goes out.]

ACT III

[*The drawing-room in the home of* Suzanne. Suzanne *and* Sophie *are present.*]

Suzanne. Has my solicitor called yet?
Sophie. No, madame.
Suzanne. I am going out. If any one
comes, ask him to wait.
Sophie [*opening the door, ready to leave*].
Mademoiselle de Sancenaux.
Suzanne. Tell her to come in.
[Sophie *goes out.*]

[*Enter* Marcelle.]

Suzanne. My dear child, to what do I
owe this lovely visit?
Marcelle. Am I keeping you from
something?
Suzanne. You never do that. You
know how much I think of you, and that
I'm always ready to do anything I can for
you. What is it, now?
Marcelle. You can do a great deal for
my future.
Suzanne. Yes? What is it?
Marcelle. You have a great deal of
influence with Monsieur de Thonnerins,
have n't you?
Suzanne. He is good enough to count
me among his friends.
Marcelle. Four or five years ago he
offered my aunt to take me to live in his
home and bring me up with his daughter;
he wanted a companion of her own age for
her.
Suzanne. He told me about it at the
time. But your aunt refused.
Marcelle. Unfortunately. If she had
consented, I should n't have been in the
situation I now am.
Suzanne. What's the trouble?
Marcelle. I don't want to blame my
aunt: it is n't her fault if the meager fortune my parents left me was soon eaten up
in household expenses. If we balanced accounts, I should be in her debt, because
there are cares and affection which cannot
be repaid. However, the continual fight
for money often hardens the kindest
hearts. After you went yesterday we had
a rather sharp discussion, when I told her
I did n't love Monsieur de Nanjac, and

that I refused to make any effort to become
his wife.
Suzanne. Especially as you love some
one else!
Marcelle. Possibly! When we had
stopped discussing, my aunt gave me to
understand that if I was not ready to do as
she directed, I could no longer count on
her help. I did n't sleep a wink, because I
was trying to think of some plan whereby
I should not have to trouble her any
further. Then I happened to remember
Monsieur de Thonnerins' offer, and I decided to come to you, who have always
been so kind to me, and ask you to ask the
Marquis to do for me to-day what he was
willing to do four years ago. Mademoiselle
de Thonnerins won't marry for another
year or two; she lives a very lonely life, and
I'm sure I'll like her extremely well. I'm
positive, too, that she will like me. Even
after she marries, I don't doubt that she'll
have me with her then. And I'm certain
that if you stand sponsor for me, my little
scheme will succeed, and I'll owe you, if
not for a brilliant career, at least for one
that's all I could desire: independent, obscure, and quiet.
Suzanne. I shall see the Marquis to-
day.
Marcelle. Really?
Suzanne. I must go out now, and I'll
call on my way.
Marcelle. How good you are!
Suzanne. Write me a letter to give him.
Marcelle. I'll go home, then, and send
it to you.
Suzanne. No, write it here; it's much
easier — while I'm putting on my hat and
cloak. Bring it to me in my bedroom, and
then wait for the answer; I shall return in
an hour. [*She rings the bell.*]
Marcelle. I'll go back to see my aunt
while you are gone. I went out with the
maid without telling her where I was going, and she might worry.

[*Enter a Servant.*]

Suzanne [*to the Servant*]. If Monsieur
de Jalin comes, ask him to wait. The
same with Monsieur de Nanjac, too. [*The
Servant goes out.* — *To* Marcelle.] I'll go

to my room and wait: we might be delayed by visitors. [*She goes out.*]

MARCELLE [*as she is writing the letter*]. That was a splendid inspiration! He will protect me — [*Meanwhile,* OLIVIER *has come in. He stands watching* MARCELLE *for a few moments. She rises, seals the letter and, turning round, catches sight of* OLIVIER.] Oh!

OLIVIER. Did I frighten you, mademoiselle?

MARCELLE. I did n't expect to see you there — so suddenly.

OLIVIER. You seem very happy this morning.

MARCELLE. Yes, I'm so hopeful, and now I'm very glad to see you. You know, I owe this great feeling of hope to you. Since yesterday, the future has taken on an entirely different aspect.

OLIVIER. What has happened to you?

MARCELLE. I'll tell you later. Could I hold secrets from you, my best friend? I'll see you later.

OLIVIER. Are you going so soon?

MARCELLE. I'm coming back in an hour. You'll still be here: I'll tell the Baroness, whom I'm going to see now, to keep you. [*Taking his hand.*] Please always be as frank as you were yesterday.

[*She goes out.*]

OLIVIER. Possibly some day some one will explain a woman's heart, but the man who can decipher that of a young girl — ! God knows what I thought about that child yesterday, and God knows what she will make me think to-day! [*Taking a packet of letters from his pocket.*] Meantime, let us put an epitaph on this dead past; may the earth lie light over it! [*Writing.*] "To Madame la Baronne d'Ange —"

[*Enter* RAYMOND.]

Raymond! the devil! [*He puts the letters back into his pocket.*] Ah, so it's you! My dear Raymond! I felt sure I was going to see you: I was speaking of you only a short while ago.

RAYMOND. Where?

OLIVIER. With de Maucroix, Senior, with whom I lunched. When I say, "I was speaking of you," I mean, "He was speaking of you."

RAYMOND. Does Monsieur de Maucroix, Senior, know me?

OLIVIER. Not personally, but he knows the Minister of War, and as de Maucroix knows that I know you, and as he is an old soldier, he takes an interest in those who, like you, wear the uniform and honor it. He asked me if I knew why you resigned from the service. I said that, so far was I from knowing the reason, I was ignorant of the very fact. I added that I doubted it, but he said that the Minister himself had vouchsafed the information.

RAYMOND. Well, it is a fact, and if I have not yet spoken to you —

OLIVIER. Your secrets are your own, my dear Raymond. I consider that my friendship can go as far as interest in you, not indiscretion. If you have resigned, though it is a serious step, you must have had very compelling reasons, reasons which a friend could not have combated. You are well, are you not?

RAYMOND. Perfectly well. — Are you going?

OLIVIER. Yes, the Baroness does not seem to come.

RAYMOND. Then let us wait for her together?

OLIVIER. I have n't time; I have a call to make —

RAYMOND. Shall I deliver some message to her from you?

OLIVIER [*after a pause*]. If you will, please tell her that I brought what she asked me for.

RAYMOND. What a mysterious message! Are you annoyed with me?

OLIVIER. Why should I be? Good Lord!

RAYMOND. It's only natural. You are a friend, you have the right to be surprised and even to blame me for concealing something from you. Forgive me! I have promised silence, promised it to some one whom I could not refuse. Not only have I not told you the truth, but yesterday I told you a little lie. I confess it. Now I am going to tell you everything, because, since yesterday, I had been very much worried. I am ashamed to have deceived you.

OLIVIER. I had just as soon that you told me nothing. I even beg you not to say a word.

RAYMOND. Now, that's a touch of childish spite, my dear Olivier; men of our age should be above such things, especially as I was going to call on you to-day and ask a favor.

OLIVIER. A favor?

RAYMOND. I am going to be married.

OLIVIER. You!

RAYMOND. Yes, I.

OLIVIER. And you are marrying —?

RAYMOND. Guess.

OLIVIER. How can I?

RAYMOND. When we met for the first time I told you that the information I asked for might have the greatest possible influence over my life. I am going to marry Madame d'Ange.

OLIVIER. Suzanne! [*Quickly.*] The Baroness?

RAYMOND. Yes.

OLIVIER. You're joking!

RAYMOND. I am not joking.

OLIVIER. You mean it, then?

RAYMOND. I mean it seriously.

OLIVIER. Was the marriage her idea?

RAYMOND. It was mine.

OLIVIER. Oh! — my compliments, Raymond!

RAYMOND. The news seems to surprise you?

OLIVIER. I don't deny that it's unexpected. I rather suspected, though you tried to throw me off the scent yesterday, that you were still in love with Madame d'Ange; I thought, too, that you gave up your commission in order to be with her as long as possible, but I never thought for a second, I must say, that it might be a question of marriage.

RAYMOND. Why not?

OLIVIER. Because, according to my notion, marriage is a serious matter, and when one is going to pledge his life with a single word, he ought to reflect much longer than you have.

RAYMOND. But I think, for my part, my dear friend, that when one believes he has found true happiness, he should lose no time in seizing it. I am free, I have no family, and I have never loved before. Madame d'Ange is free — she is a widow — she is a woman of the world (you told

me that yourself); I love her, she loves me, and we are going to marry. That's all very natural, is n't it?

OLIVIER. Perfectly. And when is the wedding to take place?

RAYMOND. As soon as the law allows. But don't breathe a word of this to any one; the Baroness does n't want it even suspected. We are going to live alone some place; she even wanted the ceremony performed away from Paris. But I insisted on its taking place here, on your account.

OLIVIER. My account?

RAYMOND. Yes; I must have witnesses and I felt sure you would do me the favor.

OLIVIER. I a witness of your marriage with the Baroness? It's impossible.

RAYMOND. You refuse?

OLIVIER. I am going away to-morrow.

RAYMOND. But you never said a word of this! Why, my dear Olivier, what's the matter? You seem so embarrassed — you have for the past few moments.

OLIVIER. It *is* very embarrassing.

RAYMOND. What is it? Tell me.

OLIVIER. Raymond, are you willing to believe that if I were to advise you in a serious situation, the advice could not but be for your good?

RAYMOND. Yes.

OLIVIER. Then, take my advice, delay this wedding — there is still time.

RAYMOND. What do you mean?

OLIVIER. I mean that no matter how deeply in love you are, there is no need of your marrying — when you can do otherwise.

RAYMOND. When I told you that I was in love with Madame d'Ange, my dear Olivier, I doubtless neglected to say that I respected and esteemed her.

OLIVIER. Very well, then, let us say no more about it. Good-day!

RAYMOND. Are n't you going to wait for the Baroness?

OLIVIER. No; I'll return later.

RAYMOND. Olivier!

OLIVIER. Raymond?

RAYMOND. You have something on your mind?

OLIVIER. Nothing.

RAYMOND. Yes, you have.

OLIVIER. My dear fellow, you are not like other men —

RAYMOND. What is there unusual about me?

OLIVIER. I don't seem able to talk with you; you always turn the good to evil. At the slightest word, you ignite like powder, you reason like a cannon-ball of '48, which shatters one's arms and legs. I tell you, it's discouraging. I advise you as a friend; I think it my duty, and you stop the words on my lips with one of those marble answers that no one else but you can make. We Parisians are not familiar with those characters which lack subtlety and cannot understand half-uttered phrases. You make me afraid.

RAYMOND. My dear fellow, the profession of soldier has not altogether crushed out of me all common sense and intelligence. I am still aware that a situation — that is doubtless what you mean? — can have two sides, a serious and a comic. Up to the present, I have taken my situation seriously; now, if it is comic, and I can't see that side of it, it is because I am inexperienced, and it is the right and the duty of a friend to tell me. And, take my word for it, the moment I see the point, I promise I shall be the first to laugh.

OLIVIER. So you say, but you won't laugh.

RAYMOND. You don't know me — a man can be mistaken every day of his life. I tell you, the day a man is shown his mistake, the best he can do is to see the humor of it and laugh. Everything or nothing! That is my motto!

OLIVIER. Word of honor?

RAYMOND. Word of honor!

OLIVIER. Then, my dear fellow, let us laugh.

RAYMOND. Have I been on the wrong track?

OLIVIER. Exactly.

RAYMOND. Doesn't she love me?

OLIVIER. I don't say that. On the contrary, I think she loves you deeply, but, between you and me, that is no good reason for your marrying. She has another reason in mind. Husbands like you are not found every day, and when you are, you must be played for.

RAYMOND. What — ? You mean the Baroness — ? Tell me.

OLIVIER. It would take too long, and then other people's affairs do not concern me. All that I have a right to tell you is, do not marry Madame d'Ange.

RAYMOND. Truly?

OLIVIER. Only your recent arrival from Africa could allow such an idea to creep into your head.

RAYMOND. You are opening my eyes! Now I understand why she wanted me to say nothing about the marriage, why she wanted to be married far from Paris, and why she told me to be on my guard against you.

OLIVIER. She knew that I thought too much of you to allow you to do a thing of this sort, without giving you a little information.

RAYMOND. You know, the woman is very clever! She had me bound hand and foot, body and heart.

OLIVIER. She is most seductive, I will admit; she has a charming personality, and she is far above the women about her, because the mere fact of her being introduced into their society and holding the place there she does, is a proof of her superiority. Don't marry Suzanne, but love her: she is well worth your while.

RAYMOND. You know something about this?

OLIVIER. I? No.

RAYMOND. Why be so discreet at this point? This isn't the same sort of situation as when we first met. That day you were discreet; that was most natural, because you didn't know me.

OLIVIER. I have told you the truth.

RAYMOND. Come, now!

OLIVIER. Word of honor! You said to me: "You are only a friend of Madame d'Ange?" and I replied: "Yes"; that was true, I was only her friend. Then, I did not know you, as you say; you came here ready to kill, right and left, and I had no very good reasons for being interested in your welfare. I said to myself: "There's a young man who is in love with the Baroness; he is or will soon be her lover; he will leave here two months hence with the firm conviction that he has been loved by a woman of the world, and he will then blow his brains out. *Bon voyage!*" But, now that I have come to know and value your open heart, your frankness, to appreciate your character — now you tell me that you are on the point of giving this woman your name! The devil! That's another matter, and silence on my part would be treason, for which you would later on have every right to call me to account. I shan't hide anything now. Things have followed their natural order. You're not blaming me, are you?

RAYMOND. Blame you, my dear friend? Are you mad? Believe me — on the contrary — I shall never forget what you are doing for me, as long as I live.

OLIVIER. You never know just how people in love will behave —

RAYMOND. I don't love that woman now.

OLIVIER. You understand, of course, that everything I say is in strict confidence?

RAYMOND. Of course. Now, what do you advise me to do?

OLIVIER. This concerns *you* —

RAYMOND. It's not easy, and it's going to be embarrassing. Things have gone so far — I must have a good reason.

OLIVIER. In a case of this sort, all reasons are good reasons. At the psychological moment, you are sure to have an inspiration. But, you see, at that moment, she will be forced to confess her situation to you. That will give you a reason.

RAYMOND. What situation?

OLIVIER. In order to become a widow, there must have been a husband — and that husband must be dead; now, a dead husband is harder to obtain than a living one.

RAYMOND. Then she is not a widow?

OLIVIER. She was never married.

RAYMOND. Are you sure?

OLIVIER. I am. No one has ever seen the Baron d'Ange! If you want authentic information about her, see the Marquis de Thonnerins: his sister knows her. There's a man who must know a great deal about her. But don't refer to me. This is the sort of favor a friend does for another

friend, but it is quite useless to speak of the matter to a third party. And now, good-bye; I prefer not to be found here: she would suspect something, and she must not know of this conversation.

RAYMOND. I understand. Then there is no use of my giving her the message you spoke of?

OLIVIER. What message?

RAYMOND. Didn't you ask me to tell her that you were going to bring later what you brought her this morning?

OLIVIER. Say nothing about it.

RAYMOND. What did you bring?

OLIVIER. Some papers.

RAYMOND. Business papers?

OLIVIER. Yes.

RAYMOND. About her income?

OLIVIER. Yes. Good-bye.

RAYMOND. My dear Olivier, to-day is not the first day we have met, and I think it's wrong of you not to be quite frank with me. Those "papers" are letters — don't deny it. [*A pause.*] Come, while we're on the point: the more you tell me, the better it will be.

OLIVIER. Well, yes, they are letters.

RAYMOND. Which she wrote you, and which she, intending to marry, wants back. Now, do your duty.

OLIVIER. How?

RAYMOND. Prove that you are really a friend.

OLIVIER. What must I do?

RAYMOND. Give me the letters.

OLIVIER. You?

RAYMOND. Yes.

OLIVIER. You know that is impossible.

RAYMOND. Why?

OLIVIER. Because one doesn't give away a woman's letters.

RAYMOND. That depends.

OLIVIER. On what?

RAYMOND. On the situation in which the person who asks happens to be placed.

OLIVIER. A woman's letters are sacred, no matter who the woman is.

RAYMOND [*very seriously*]. I think it's a little late to come forth with maxims of that sort, my dear Olivier.

OLIVIER. You think so?

RAYMOND. Yes, because when you once begin a confidential conversation of this sort, you ought to carry it through to the bitter end.

OLIVIER. My dear Raymond, I see that I have made a grave blunder; I ought to say nothing more.

RAYMOND. Why?

OLIVIER. Because you are not in a laughing mood; because you love Madame d'Ange more than you confessed you did; because that mask of gayety you assumed a few moments ago was only in order to make me speak. You are more clever than I thought you. Good-morning.

RAYMOND. Olivier, in the name of our friendship, give me those letters!

OLIVIER. Why, that's out of the question. I tell you it would be unworthy of both of us. I am surprised at your asking.

RAYMOND. I merely ask for a proof of what you have told me —

OLIVIER. You may doubt it all, if you like.

RAYMOND. I would willingly do it for your sake.

OLIVIER. Swear to me on your honor —

RAYMOND. I — [He stops.]

OLIVIER. You see?

RAYMOND. You are right. Well, I swear on my honor not to read the letters. Give them to me, and I promise to hand them to Madame d'Ange to-day.

OLIVIER. No!

RAYMOND. Do you doubt my word?

OLIVIER. Good Heavens, no!

RAYMOND. Well, then — ?

OLIVIER. Listen to me, Raymond: you will never forgive me for having told you the truth. I cannot repent, because I have acted as I believe I ought to have acted. I could not hesitate between a silent complicity for Madame d'Ange's sake, and giving you the information I have given. Between men like you and me, an explanation of this sort ought to be sufficient. I see it is not; let us therefore say no more about the matter. I came here to-day to give to Madame d'Ange, or leave for her in case she was not in, some papers which belonged to her the moment she asked for them. Here they are, in this sealed en-velope. Madame d'Ange is out; I leave the papers on the table, where she will find them on her return. I shall be back in half an hour to see whether she has them. And now, my dear Raymond, do as you think best! I was your friend; I will continue to be such so long as you wish me to be. Good-bye — or — au revoir.

[He goes out.]

RAYMOND. Olivier! [He makes for the letters, which OLIVIER has left on the table.] After all, that woman's past belongs to me, because I am giving her my name. I shall read the letters. [He picks up, then lays down the envelope.] He is right: it is impossible!

[Enter SUZANNE.]

SUZANNE. I've been out long, my dear, have n't I?

RAYMOND. No. Then, I was n't alone.

SUZANNE. Who was here?

RAYMOND. Monsieur de Jalin.

SUZANNE. Why did n't he wait?

RAYMOND. He seemed to be in a hurry.

SUZANNE. Is he coming back?

RAYMOND. Yes, in half an hour. Where have you been, dear Suzanne?

SUZANNE. I've been on some tiresome errands. I don't complain, because they were for you.

RAYMOND. For me?

SUZANNE. Yes, for you, monsieur. When a person marries, he must put all his affairs in order, must n't he? I should n't complain at all — unless you happened to change your mind —

RAYMOND. Not yet!

SUZANNE. Is there any chance of it?

RAYMOND. That will depend on you.

SUZANNE. Then I have nothing to fear. Do you still love me?

RAYMOND. Always, more than you can know. Now, Suzanne, you have been — ?

SUZANNE. To see my solicitor. My husband ought to know the state of my finances.

RAYMOND. Never mind that.

SUZANNE. I have just got my birth-certificate. See, I did n't lie: I'm an old woman of twenty-eight. There's no denying facts. [She reads:] "Infant; sex, feminine; born February 4, 1818, at 11 o'clock in the evening; daughter of Jean-Hyacinthe, Count de Berwach, and of Joséphine-Henriette de Crousserolles, his wife." You see, I come of a good family! This is all that remains of the first two love affairs of my life: an almost illegible scrap of paper, an official document, cold and dry as the epitaph on a tombstone. Here is my marriage-contract. I was n't in a happy mood that day, Raymond dear, because I did n't love my husband; I was simply giving in to the wishes of my parents. But I can't reproach the Baron, he was as good as he could be to me; he came of an old family, and was the last of the line. And here is my husband's death-certificate: that is to say, my right to love you before all the world. You see, I have been a widow for eight years. The past is over and laid at rest; we have only the future to think of. What's the matter? You seem so preoccupied?

RAYMOND. Will you let me have those documents?

SUZANNE. Certainly, but don't lose them.

RAYMOND. You may be sure I shan't; I'll put them with my own, as soon as I get them. Is that all you've done this morning?

SUZANNE. Oh, no, I went to see my guardian, the Marquis de Thonnerins; Mademoiselle de Sancenaux, you know, begged me to ask him for something. I was not successful, and I'm very much put out about it. The poor child is coming here for her answer, and I don't know how to tell her.

RAYMOND. There is a way.

SUZANNE. How?

RAYMOND. Write to her before she comes. Is n't that the best way to break bad news?

SUZANNE. Yes, but it's such a bother to write!

RAYMOND. It depends: to those we love, for instance!

SUZANNE. That's different!

RAYMOND. But you never wrote to me.

SUZANNE. I have seen you every day; what did I have to write? But you've lost nothing: I write a fearful hand.

RAYMOND. Let me see a sample?

SUZANNE. Do you really wish to?

RAYMOND. Yes.

SUZANNE. Very well. [*She writes:*] "My dear child —" Horrid pen! "I have been to see Monsieur de Thonnerins, as I promised, but I did not find our old friend in the frame of mind I had expected —" [*To* RAYMOND, *who is watching closely what she writes.*] Can hardly read it, can you?

RAYMOND. Hardly. Let me have the beginning of the letter, please.

SUZANNE. Why?

RAYMOND. Give it to me.

SUZANNE. There.

RAYMOND [*after having examined the letter*]. My dear Suzanne, I forgot to tell you that Monsieur de Jalin left a little package for you.

SUZANNE. What is it?

RAYMOND. Letters.

SUZANNE. Letters? What letters?

RAYMOND. Letters which you asked him for.

SUZANNE. I?

RAYMOND. Yes, you.

SUZANNE. From whom are they?

RAYMOND. From you!

SUZANNE. From me! I don't understand. Where are they?

RAYMOND. Here.

SUZANNE. Give them to me.

RAYMOND. I beg your pardon, Suzanne, dear, but I'm going to ask your permission to open the package.

SUZANNE. Did Monsieur de Jalin bring these for me?

RAYMOND. I told you that he did.

SUZANNE. Very well, then, open it and read the letters if you wish. If you wanted to see anything in them, you need n't have waited until I came home. Only, after you have seen what you wanted to see, I am going to ask you the meaning of all this, for I don't understand in the least.

RAYMOND. I shall explain everything, I promise; or, rather, *we* shall explain.

[*He opens the package, takes one of the letters and compares it with the one which* SUZANNE *has just written to* MARCELLE.]

SUZANNE. Well?

RAYMOND. Suzanne, some one is being deceived somewhere.

SUZANNE. I, I think, for I hope to die if I can guess a word of the riddle!

RAYMOND. Look at those letters.

SUZANNE. They are from a woman.

RAYMOND. Read them.

SUZANNE [glancing through a few]. Love-letters, or nearly so — the expressions are not particularly tender. But they might pass for love-letters. Well?

RAYMOND. Don't you know who wrote those letters?

SUZANNE. How should I know? They're not signed.

RAYMOND. Are they not in your handwriting?

SUZANNE. What! My handwriting? Are you mad? Is my handwriting like that? I wish it were! That woman writes very nicely.

RAYMOND. Then why Olivier's lie? He seemed so sure!

SUZANNE. What lie? Tell me, what does this mean? Did Monsieur de Jalin say that these letters were from me?

RAYMOND. Yes.

SUZANNE [indignantly]. Then, Monsieur de Jalin must have been my lover?

RAYMOND. So it appears.

SUZANNE. Did he tell you that?

RAYMOND. He gave me to understand —

SUZANNE. Please — where is the joke?

RAYMOND. Monsieur de Jalin was not joking.

SUZANNE. He was making fun of you. You lied to him yesterday, and to-day he is merely taking his revenge. I have known Monsieur de Jalin longer than you have; I know he is incapable of doing anything cowardly. You are now accusing him of something that is. He made love to me at one time, and wrote letters to me, which I can show you. I think he is rather hurt that I am marrying, because it takes his last hope from him. But there's a vast gulf between trying to prevent the marriage and inventing a calumny of that kind. I have no idea what has actually occurred, but I am positive that Monsieur de Jalin is incapable of committing an act like that.

RAYMOND. We shall see.

SUZANNE. Have you any doubts, yourself?

RAYMOND. This matter is between him and me. Will you swear that what Monsieur de Jalin told me was false?

SUZANNE. Do you want me to swear? So, it's something more than a joke, or even a libel on Monsieur de Jalin's part: it is treason on yours, monsieur.

RAYMOND. Treason!

SUZANNE. Yes, you are already beginning to regret the promises you made me. Why did n't you tell me frankly rather than resort to such means, which really do more honor to your cleverness than to your delicacy.

RAYMOND. Suzanne, you are accusing me of something infamous.

SUZANNE. What am I accusing you of?

RAYMOND. Monsieur de Jalin is coming here shortly; let us clear matters up in his presence.

SUZANNE. What! Must you await Monsieur de Jalin's permission to believe that I am telling the truth? I am going to have Monsieur de Jalin himself tell you that he was never my lover; you will believe me only then. Whom do you take me for? I loved you, Raymond, but I must say, this suspicion and jealousy in you terrifies me. That is why I hesitated to become your wife. I at least thought that you respected and honored me. I have no intention of looking into the reasons or causes for this sudden outbreak, but I declare you have put me to a humiliating test, me and my love for you and my dignity. You have doubted me. Everything is over between us now.

RAYMOND. My jealousy is only a proof of my love. I love you so deeply, Suzanne!

SUZANNE. I don't want to be loved that way!

RAYMOND. I swear —

SUZANNE. Please!

RAYMOND. Suzanne!

[Enter SOPHIE.]

SOPHIE. Mademoiselle de Sancenaux wishes to know if madame will see her?

SUZANNE. Ask her to come in.

[SOPHIE goes out.]

RAYMOND. I shall stay with you.

[*Enter* MARCELLE.]

MARCELLE. It's I, madame.

SUZANNE. I'm so glad to see you, dear child. [*To* RAYMOND.] Please excuse us, Monsieur de Nanjac, mademoiselle and I wish to be alone.

RAYMOND. When shall I have the pleasure of seeing you again, madame?

SUZANNE. On my return: I'm leaving to-night, and I shan't see any one in the meantime.

[RAYMOND *bows and goes out, as* SUZANNE *rings.*]

[*Enter a Servant.*]

[*To the Servant*]. If Monsieur de Nanjac calls again to-day, tell him I am not at home; if he insists, add that I refuse to see him. Go! [*The Servant goes out.*] I have seen the Marquis, and I have bad news to report, my poor dear: Monsieur de Thonnerins is interested in you, but —

MARCELLE. But he refuses.

SUZANNE. He would like to do what you ask —

MARCELLE. Only — worldly considerations prevent him. I have thought a good deal since I last saw you, and I came to the conclusion that perhaps it would not be right of him to have as a companion for his daughter a person who is in so exceptional a position as I am. Mademoiselle de Thonnerins is very fortunate in having a father to protect and care for her. Thank you, dear madame, and forgive me for having troubled you so.

SUZANNE. I do wish I had been successful. The Marquis is very fond of you, and he told me he would do what he could to help you, and that if you found some fine young man whom you could love, and if there were no other obstacle except in the matter of fortune, he would see to it that that obstacle were removed.

MARCELLE. I asked for help, not alms.

SUZANNE. That is n't at all kind. Why do you get so discouraged, my dear? How do you know that the man you love may not some day return your love? Perhaps he loves you even now? If he does, what is there to prevent your becoming his wife?

MARCELLE. I don't love any one.

SUZANNE. Oh, very well, Marcelle, I'm not asking for any secrets.

MARCELLE. Did n't I hear you say you were going away to-night?

SUZANNE. Yes.

MARCELLE. Perhaps we shan't see each other again, but I shall never forget how good you have been to me.

SUZANNE. I'll let you know where I am. Write me, and no matter how far away I am, I shall do everything in my power to help you.

MARCELLE. Thank you. [*She kisses* SUZANNE.] Good-bye.

SUZANNE. Good-bye — and courage!

[*Enter a Servant.*]

SERVANT. Monsieur Olivier de Jalin.

[MARCELLE *makes ready to go, as the Servant leaves.*]

[*Enter* OLIVIER.]

OLIVIER. Am I sending you away, mademoiselle!

MARCELLE. No, monsieur, I was going anyway.

OLIVIER. How sad you look. What's the matter?

MARCELLE. One hour follows another, and not one resembles another. I was too quick to hope: life is more difficult than I had imagined, when one is alone to struggle with it.

OLIVIER. But — when there are two? Am I not your friend? I don't want you to be sad any longer. Will you let me come to see you? Then you'll tell me all your troubles!

MARCELLE. I will do everything you tell me.

OLIVIER. I shall see you soon, possibly in a very short while.

[*He shakes hands with her, and she goes out.*]

SUZANNE. It's touching, is n't it? I should very much like to see you marry Mademoiselle de Sancenaux, after what you have said about her.

OLIVIER. I did not know her then, now I do.

SUZANNE. All of which goes to show that

it is never wise to speak evil of people before you know! By the way, you and I have an account to balance.

OLIVIER. What?

SUZANNE. Now pretend not to understand! You told Monsieur de Nanjac that it would be wrong of him to marry me.

OLIVIER. That is true.

SUZANNE. Did you tell him why it would be wrong?

OLIVIER. Yes.

SUZANNE. You are at least frank. However, that is no excuse for your having committed a — What is it? There is a word for such things —

OLIVIER [appearing to be searching for the word]. A blunder?

SUZANNE. No.

OLIVIER. Something tactless?

SUZANNE. Not altogether. Something — er —

OLIVIER. Cowardly? Say it; it burns your lips.

SUZANNE. Exactly: something cowardly!

OLVIER. And why did I do it?

SUZANNE. Because a man of honor keeps such things to himself.

OLIVIER. Which proves that you and I do not agree on the question of honor, fortunately!

SUZANNE. You have nothing more to add?

OLIVIER. Nothing.

SUZANNE. And did you imagine that Monsieur de Nanjac would fail to repeat your conversation to me?

OLIVIER. I did, because he gave me his word of honor.

SUZANNE. But you gave me your word of honor, my friend!

OLIVIER. To be your friend, yes, but not your accomplice.

SUZANNE. "Accomplice" is rather brutal. [She laughs.] Tell me, Olivier?

OLIVIER. Yes?

SUZANNE. You know, what you have done has turned out to my advantage.

OLIVIER. So much the better! Well, I have done my duty on the one hand, and done you a favor on the other.

SUZANNE. He loves me more than ever.

OLIVIER. Indeed?

SUZANNE. I really can't be angry with you. And you pretend to be a clever man! Why, can't you see that you've been caught in a trap?

OLIVIER. Caught in a trap?

SUZANNE. Of course, you poor dear! You are trying to deal with a woman! Have n't you yet learned that the stupidest of women — and I am not that by a long way — is a hundred times more resourceful than the cleverest man? I rather suspected yesterday, after your conversation with Monsieur de Nanjac, that your great friendship for me would end, and that the moment there was any question of my marriage, your loyal self would declare war on me. You had to strike a final blow and lay low the truth so emphatically, that any lies or calumnies could not afterward have the slightest chance. Then I asked you to bring me those letters to-day. That should have opened your eyes! Do you think I am the sort of woman who asks for her letters? But of course you did n't suspect a thing, and you were so nice as to come here this morning, with your little letters in your pocket! A short while before you were due here, I went out in order to leave you alone with Monsieur de Nanjac and you did your duty as an honest man. You told Monsieur de Nanjac what you had been to me, and you found means of giving him my letters. I returned, he did not know my handwriting, so he asked me to give him a sample of it before his very eyes; then he compared the two hands —

OLIVIER. And?

SUZANNE. And as they bear no resemblance to each other, he is convinced that I am the victim of a libelous story. He loves me more than ever, and he has only one thought: to cut your throat. The idea! To think that, at your age, you don't yet know that the very best way to fall out with a friend is to speak evil of the woman he loves, even when the evil can be proved. And can you prove it? I sent him away because he dared entertain such suspicions. I told him I did n't want to see him any more, that I was going away to-day — and any number of other things: everything that an intelligent woman says under similar circumstances. I told him I could never think of becoming his wife. He will be here in ten minutes, and in a week's time we shall be married. I owe all this to you, my dear. You have lost, you see, and you owe me a forfeit.

OLIVIER. Have you two samples of the handwriting?

SUZANNE. I have only one, but that is enough.

OLIVIER. Then how does it happen that — ?

SUZANNE. I shall tell you everything, because at bottom I am obliging, and I have nothing against you. My dear friend, when a woman like me has spent ten years in building up her life, piece by piece, her first care must be to get out of her way every possible chance of danger. Now, among these chances, in the first place, there is the desire to write. Out of a hundred compromised women, two thirds have met their ruin through letters which they have written. Women's letters seem destined to be lost by those to whom they are sent, returned to those who wrote them, intercepted by the one person who ought never to see them, stolen by servants, and shown to the whole world. In matters of love, it is dangerous to write, not to say useless. Consequently, I have made it a rule never to write a compromising letter, and for the last ten years I have adhered to that rule.

OLIVIER. Then the letters you wrote me — ?

SUZANNE. Were dictated to Madame de Santis, the greatest known letter-writer. She has a pen in her hand from morning to night; that is her great passion. She was with me all the time at Baden, and I made use of her mania occasionally, asking her to answer letters from you, which I never read. She writes a lovely English hand, long, delicate, aristocratic, like a lady of high rank taking a walk. And she was so well brought up! So you see, my dear, you were corresponding with Valentine. But you need n't worry; I shan't breathe a word to your friend Monsieur Richond; you might fall out with him!

OLIVIER [bowing]. I have nothing more to say. You are a most powerful —

SUZANNE. Now, let us talk seriously. By what right have you behaved the way you did? In what way can you reproach me? If Monsieur de Nanjac were an old friend of yours, a childhood comrade, or a brother, I might see, but you have known him scarcely a week or ten days. If you were disinterested, too, I might understand, but are you quite sure that you have n't been prompted by a feeling of wounded pride? I know you don't love me, but a man always rather resents being told by a woman who once loved him that she no longer does so. Simply because you happened to make love to me, and because I was confiding enough to believe you, because I thought you an honorable man, because I loved you, perhaps, are you therefore going to be an obstacle to the happiness of my whole life? Did I compromise you? Did I ruin you? Did I even deceive you? I will admit, — I must admit, because it is true — that I am not worthy on morals grounds, of the name and position I aspire to; but is it your place — you helped make me unworthy! — to close to me the honorable path I have chosen to tread? No, my dear Olivier, it's not right; when a person has himself succumbed to certain weaknesses, he ought not to forge weapons and use them against those with whom he has sinned. A man who has been loved, no matter how little, and provided the love was based on neither interest nor calculation, is under an eternal obligation to the woman, and he should remember that no matter how much he does for her, he can never hope to repay her.

OLIVIER. You are right: perhaps I did give in to an evil impulse, to jealousy, thinking I was prompted by honor. Still, there is no honest man who would not have acted likewise in my place. For Raymond's sake, I was right in speaking; for yours, I should have said nothing. The Arabian proverb is right: " Speech is silver, but silence is golden."

SUZANNE. That is all I wanted to hear from you. Now —

OLIVIER. Now?

SUZANNE [seeing SOPHIE enter]. Nothing. [To SOPHIE.] What is it?

SOPHIE. Monsieur de Nanjac has called.

SUZANNE. I have already given my orders —

SOPHIE. He insisted on seeing Madame la Baronne. I told him that Madame la Baronne was not receiving. He asked whether Monsieur de Jalin was with madame, and told me, if he was, to ask him to step out and see him.

SUZANNE. Tell Monsieur de Nanjac to come in.

OLIVIER. Are you going to see him?

SUZANNE. No, but you will, and you will please tell him what you think you ought to tell him. Only remember that he loves me, that I love him, and that what I want, I want. *Au revoir*, my dear Olivier.
[*She goes out.*]

OLIVIER. Well, I'll get this over with at once.

[*Enter* RAYMOND.]

You wished to see me, my dear Raymond? The Baroness is not present — we are alone. I am listening.

RAYMOND. I don't wish to forget that I once called you friend, but —

OLIVIER. But?

RAYMOND. You have deceived me.

OLIVIER [*staccato*]. I have not.

RAYMOND. Listen to me: I have decided not to consider proofs; furthermore, Madame d'Ange proved that what you told me was not so. You said that she was never married; I have seen the marriage contract, seen it with my own eyes. Are you going to tell me that the document is a forgery?

OLIVIER. No.

RAYMOND. You told me that she was not a widow; I have seen her husband's death-certificate. Are you going to tell me that that document is an invention?

OLIVIER. No.

RAYMOND. I have just come from the Marquis de Thonnerins, whom I have questioned, and who said that he knew nothing about the Baroness. And, finally, these letters that you told me were written by Madame d'Ange —

OLIVIER. Are not from her, I now know: one of her friends wrote them for her, and I was led to believe they were her own.

Both of them were making game of me. But it was not I who deceived you, I myself have been deceived. I believed I had the right to warn you, but I did not have the right. I felt positive that I had incontrovertible proofs against the Baroness, but even my own stupidity did n't furnish one. When I tried to prove that I was truly your friend, I succeeded only in proving that I was a fool. I have been beautifully deceived, take my word for it.

RAYMOND. So you take back everything you said?

OLIVIER. Everything. She comes of a good family, she was married, she is a baroness, a widow, she loves you, she was never any more than a stranger to me; she is worthy of you. Whoever denies this is a defamer, because any one is a defamer who speaks evil which he cannot prove. Goodbye, Raymond; after what has happened, I can't show my face to the Baroness again. I shan't see her again until she asks for me, and I hardly think she will do that very soon. Please don't think of me as being anything but clumsy. Good-bye.

RAYMOND. Good-bye. [OLIVIER *goes out.*] I must hear the final word from that man!

[*Enter a Servant.*]

SERVANT. Monsieur knows, of course, that Madame la Baronne has gone out, and will not return until late?

RAYMOND [*sitting down*]. Very well, I shall wait.

ACT IV

The scene is the same. SUZANNE *is present.*

[*Enter a Servant, who announces:*]

SERVANT. Monsieur le Marquis de Thonnerins.   [*He goes out.*]

[*Enter the* MARQUIS.]

MARQUIS. How do you do, Baroness!

SUZANNE. To what do I owe the pleasure of your visit, my dear Marquis?

MARQUIS. I have come to learn, my dear Suzanne, if my solicitor has given you what he was to give you?

SUZANNE. He gave me everything, thank you.

MARQUIS. And then I wanted to find out how you were getting on?

SUZANNE. Very well.

MARQUIS. And your marriage?

SUZANNE. My marriage?

MARQUIS. Yes; is it going to take place?

SUZANNE. That's so — I have n't seen you for a long time. Have n't you heard?

MARQUIS. I have heard nothing.

SUZANNE [with a sigh]. You are right, Monsieur le Marquis, I was too ambitious: some things are impossible.

MARQUIS. You admit it?

SUZANNE. I must.

MARQUIS. Tell me about it.

SUZANNE. Some one told!

MARQUIS. Who?

SUZANNE. Some one in whom I had too great confidence: Monsieur de Jalin.

MARQUIS. And did he tell Monsieur de Nanjac —?

SUZANNE. You know his name?

MARQUIS. Yes. And what did Monsieur de Nanjac do?

SUZANNE. He believed Monsieur de Jalin; then, because he loved me, he believed me.

MARQUIS. And now?

SUZANNE. Now he still loves me — only jealously, and without confidence in me. There's no end of questions, suspicions, spying; and I declare I have n't the strength to endure such a life. And it used to be my ambition! To be incessantly trembling for fear the past should tumble down on our heads, start each morning of my life with some new lie which I have to confess every night, and at the same time love sincerely and loyally — I tell you it's out of the question. I have already used up not only my strength in the struggle, but my love as well. I don't love Monsieur de Nanjac any longer.

MARQUIS. Is that true?

SUZANNE. You are the only person to whom I never lie.

MARQUIS. You don't love Monsieur de Nanjac?

SUZANNE. I love no one.

MARQUIS. Then the marriage will not take place?

SUZANNE. No; I'm going to remain free. I'm going to Italy; they rarely ask where a woman comes from there, and so long as she has money, and is not too homely, they believe everything she says. I am going to buy a house on the shores of Lake Como; I'll powder and rouge like Madame de Santis, and wander about the lake in the light of the stars, write poetry à la Byron, pose as a misunderstood woman, receive and protect artists, and some day, if I like, marry a ruined Italian prince of questionable title, who will squander my fortune, keep a dancing-girl, and beat me besides. Don't you think I'd be doing what I ought, and that a woman like me has n't anything better to look forward to?

MARQUIS. So you're going away?

SUZANNE. In three or four days.

MARQUIS. Alone?

SUZANNE. With my maid.

MARQUIS. Does Monsieur de Nanjac know you are going?

SUZANNE. He has no suspicion of it.

MARQUIS. Are you not going to let him know where you will be?

SUZANNE. If I wanted to continue to see him, I might better remain in Paris. No; I am leaving in order to escape from an unbearable situation, one which cannot but become worse as time goes on.

MARQUIS. Well, I congratulate you. Your common sense is leading you to do what necessity would have forced on your later.

SUZANNE [distractedly]. How is that?

MARQUIS. Chance is a very clumsy bungler in what does not concern it. Now, chance had it that Monsieur de Nanjac's sister is a friend of my own sister. Monsieur de Nanjac did not hide his plans from his sister, who came to see my sister. That was how I heard the name which I had no wish to learn from you. But that is not all: Monsieur de Nanjac himself came to ask me some questions about you. I told him nothing, because, as a man of honor, I preferred to allow you to extricate yourself from this delicate situation with all the honors of war. To-day I have come to tell you what I have told you once before: namely, that the day I should meet (by chance, of course) the man whom you wish to marry, I should tell him the whole truth. I have waited a little, and I am glad, because I see you have decided not to marry now. It's all for the best, if you mean what you say —

SUZANNE. I do. To-morrow Monsieur de Nanjac will be freed from all obligations, and you will be at perfect liberty, if you like, to give him to Mademoiselle de Thonnerins as a husband.

MARQUIS. My daughter has nothing to do in all this, my dear Suzanne; remember that. Everything I have said is in sober earnest.

SUZANNE. Sober earnest, yes.

MARQUIS. Be happy; that is my last wish. Good-bye, Baroness, and remember!

SUZANNE. I shall never forget.

[*The* MARQUIS *goes out as* VALENTINE *enters. They bow to each other.*]

VALENTINE [*who wears a traveling dress, looks at the door through which the* MARQUIS *has gone*]. Was that the Marquis de Thonnerins?

SUZANNE. Yes.

VALENTINE. He's always a little brusque, is n't he?

SUZANNE. Where are you going? You're dressed for traveling?

VALENTINE. I'm going away.

SUZANNE. When?

VALENTINE. In an hour.

SUZANNE. Where?

VALENTINE. To London, and from there to Belgium, and then Germany.

SUZANNE. With — ?

VALENTINE. Yes, some one is going with me.

SUZANNE. But your law-suit?

VALENTINE. I'm not going to sue. I applied — but I lost. When I told the judge of my troubles he said: "Believe me, madame, you had better not bother your husband. That's the best thing you can do." So, I'm going away.

SUZANNE. I have n't seen you for a long time.

VALENTINE. Oh, the things I have to buy for the trip! It seems one can't get anything in England. And I must do some-

thing about my apartment in the Rue de la Paix. I paid a year's rent to the landlord, who let me go; I gave an indemnity to the upholsterer, who took back his furniture, and now I'm free as the winds of heaven.

SUZANNE. But you did n't find time to bring me the answer I asked you for.

VALENTINE. I've written it. Did n't you get my note?

SUZANNE. Yes, only —

VALENTINE. I'll tell you the whole thing; it's much simpler.

SUZANNE. Very well.

VALENTINE. I sent Madame de Lornan an anonymous letter.

SUZANNE. Good.

VALENTINE. I was careful to disguise my hand. I told her that a woman who takes the greatest interest in her welfare, but who must remain unnamed, insists upon speaking with her. I gave her to understand that the matter concerned Monsieur de Jalin. I advised her to be very discreet, and suggested that we meet: the day before yesterday, in the evening.

SUZANNE. Did she come?

VALENTINE. Yes. We met in the Tuileries; it was dusk, and I was thickly veiled. She could n't possibly have seen my face, but I saw hers: she is beautiful.

SUZANNE. What did you say to her?

VALENTINE. Exactly what we agreed I should say: that Olivier was deceiving her, that he was in love with Mademoiselle de Sancenaux, whom he wants to marry; I told her how foolish it was of him, how tragic it would be, because the girl is not at all worthy of him. I pretended to think that Madame de Lornan was no more than a friend of Olivier's. As a matter of fact, she *is* only a friend, but she loves him and is fearfully jealous.

SUZANNE. Did you mention me?

VALENTINE. She was the first to speak of you. I told her I knew you, that you knew all about the matter, and that she and you together might prevent the marriage; it would be rendering a service to Monsieur de Jalin. All she would have to do would be to see you and come to an understanding. She hesitated for a long time, and made me promise that you would be alone when she came. I promised and, as I wrote you, she will be here at two o'clock. The poor woman does n't know where she is. Who would ever believe that that Monsieur de Jalin could inspire such passion? Have you heard from him?

SUZANNE. Yes.

VALENTINE. On what sort of terms is he with Monsieur de Nanjac?

SUZANNE. Bad; but Olivier wrote me —

VALENTINE. What does he say?

SUZANNE. That he loves me, that if he wished to prevent my marriage, it was for that reason —

VALENTINE. That may be true —

SUZANNE. Who knows? Perhaps; but the chances are it is not, because he asks me to call on him. He wants to explain something which, it seems, he cannot explain here.

VALENTINE. There is some trick in this.

SUZANNE. But I am certain that he and Monsieur de Nanjac are not on speaking terms.

VALENTINE. If Monsieur de Nanjac could only give him one good sword-thrust and teach him not to meddle in what does n't concern him! I can't bear this Monsieur de Jalin; he's the one who set Hippolyte against me. Now, my dear, if you want to play him a turn, go ahead, I'll be only too glad to help you.

SUZANNE. Never worry, I shan't forget. What is the use of offending, so long as the offenses are forgiven? Among other things, Monsieur de Jalin remarked that it was wrong to introduce a respectable woman into our society; well, to-day he will be found at my home in the company of Madame de Lornan; that will possibly force him to modify his ideas a little.

VALENTINE. Is he coming?

SUZANNE. Yes.

VALENTINE. He'll be furious — What if he were to get angry with you?

SUZANNE. The idea! The first angry word would mean a duel with Monsieur de Nanjac, and he does n't want that. He will learn his lesson and hold his tongue henceforth.

VALENTINE. Is n't it too bad I have to go away? Well, good-bye. Write me to London, general delivery, care of Mademoiselle Rose — that's my maid's name. Until I'm quite safe, I don't want my husband to know where I am. It's funny to see me leaving Paris: this is the only place where one can enjoy one's self, but I must go. Good-bye.

SUZANNE. You'll let me hear from you, won't you?

VALENTINE. I shan't fail to. Goodbye. Remember, in Mademoiselle Rose's name.

[*Enter* RAYMOND *through one door, as* VALENTINE *disappears through another.*]

SUZANNE. Another woman I shan't receive after I marry! [*To* RAYMOND.] I've been so anxious to see you!

RAYMOND. Everything is ready.

SUZANNE. The contract?

RAYMOND. We shall sign it to-morrow.

SUZANNE. And we leave — ?

RAYMOND. Whenever you like.

SUZANNE. Will you always love me?

RAYMOND. And will you, Suzanne?

SUZANNE. Can you doubt it now? Have n't I given you every proof I was able to? Oh, yes, I love you!

RAYMOND. Tell me, have you seen Monsieur de Jalin again?

SUZANNE. No. Why?

RAYMOND. Well, I saw him not long ago, coming in this direction with his friend Monsieur Richond.

SUZANNE. Yes; he is coming here.

RAYMOND. I thought you were n't to see him any more. I asked you not to; you promised me.

SUZANNE. He wrote that he had to speak to me, and I am going to receive him as if nothing had happened. I shall even pretend that nothing has happened, and I advise you to forget, too.

RAYMOND. Please give your final orders about the signing of the contract to-morrow. I want our marriage officially announced to all our friends, including Monsieur de Jalin, whom I shall receive; I wish to be the first person he sees here. I want him to understand how he is to behave in your home. I shall be with you shortly.

[*She goes out.*]

[*Enter a Servant.*]

SERVANT. Monsieur Olivier de Jalin. Monsieur Hippolyte Richond. [*He goes out.*]

[*Enter* OLIVIER *and* HIPPOLYTE.]

RAYMOND [*bowing formally*]. Messieurs!

OLIVIER. How are you, Raymond?

RAYMOND. In the best of health, thank you.

OLIVIER. Is the Baroness in?

RAYMOND. She asked me to beg you to wait for her; she will be here in a few moments. Messieurs —
[*He bows and goes out.*]

OLIVIER. What a face!

HIPPOLYTE. You might have expected it when you decided to come here. Why did you come? You were clear of all this intriguing; why return to it? You have done your duty. Monsieur de Nanjac is determined to marry the woman; if he insists on seeing no obstacle, like Guzman, leave him alone. After all, it does n't concern you.

OLIVIER. You are perfectly right, and, as a matter of fact, I did make up my mind to have nothing further to do with it all, in spite of the fact that I believe there are certain people who are well worth saving from themselves; but women are extremists, and Suzanne has just dealt me a blow and provoked me to continue. It's not my fault.

HIPPOLYTE. You have been waiting only for a pretext to return to her.

OLIVIER. Possibly; but that is only another reason why you ought not to furnish me with this pretext.

HIPPOLYTE. Tell me what she did.

OLIVIER. Your wife wrote an anonymous letter to Madame de Lornan.

HIPPOLYTE. My wife?

OLIVIER. Yes; the handwriting was disguised, but I recognized it. The letter asked Madame de Lornan for a meeting; her housekeeper showed it to me (she knows the interest I have in her mistress, though Charlotte still refuses to receive me). I know Suzanne is at the bottom of this, but I warn her to take care! If what I believe is true, if she makes the slightest move against Madame de Lornan, I don't know just how I shall go about it, but I declare I will so ruin her prospects of marriage that I'm hanged if she even finds the tiniest fragment!

HIPPOLYTE. What if I tried to stop her? So long as she confined herself to wronging me, it was n't so bad, but the moment she touches others —

OLIVIER. I'll attend to it myself. The moment I heard of these new goings-on, I wrote Suzanne asking her to come to see me, but she took good care not to accept. She replied that she would see me if I called on her to-day. Just allow me to cast my line where I want, and don't make any noise; in an hour, the fish will bite.

[*Enter the* VISCOUNTESS, *very agitated.*]

VISCOUNTESS. Where is the Baroness?

OLIVIER. What is the trouble, my dear Viscountess? You come in like a tempest?

VISCOUNTESS. I'm perfectly furious!

OLIVIER. I'm not at all sorry to see you that way. It changes one.

VISCOUNTESS. I am in no mood for joking.

OLIVIER. Then let me answer your question: the Baroness is with Monsieur de Nanjac; we are now waiting for her.

VISCOUNTESS [*taking* OLIVIER *to one side, as she says to* HIPPOLYTE]. Pardon me, monsieur. [*To* OLIVIER.] Do you know what Marcelle has done?

OLIVIER. She told Monsieur de Nanjac to his face that she would n't marry him.

VISCOUNTESS. Yes.

OLIVIER. Because she does not love him.

VISCOUNTESS. A fine reason! But that is n't all: when I went to Marcelle's room this morning, she was n't there.

OLIVIER. She must have left a letter?

VISCOUNTESS. Yes; she said she had found a means of not being a burden to me any more, that I should fear nothing, and that I should never have reason to be ashamed of her.

OLIVIER. And added that she was going back to the school where she was educated, eh?

VISCOUNTESS. Have you seen her?

OLIVIER. Not long ago.

VISCOUNTESS. Where?

OLIVIER. At her school.

VISCOUNTESS. How did that happen?

OLIVIER. She wrote.

VISCOUNTESS. To you?

OLIVIER. To me.

VISCOUNTESS. Why?

OLIVIER. I advised her to do as she did.

VISCOUNTESS. What business is it of yours?

OLIVIER. It *is* my business.

VISCOUNTESS. It was you, too, doubtless, who advised her to leave Paris?

OLIVIER. Yes; she is going to-morrow. The head of the school has found her a position.

VISCOUNTESS. A position?

OLIVIER. With an excellent family at Besançon. Mademoiselle de Sancenaux will give lessons in English and music to a little girl. She will receive eight hundred francs a year, with board and lodging. It will hardly be amusing, but she considers it more honorable than to stay in Paris, fail to get married, play cards, and compromise herself. And I agree with her.

VISCOUNTESS. Well, you have done a splendid thing! Do you know what I am going to do? Write and tell her at least to change her name. To think of having a Sancenaux, my own brother's daughter, compromise her family like that! A Sancenaux teaching! Why not make her a chambermaid?

OLIVIER. Is that what you call compromising her family? My dear Viscountess, the person who sold you your logic, cheated you shamelessly! It must have been Monsieur de Latour.

VISCOUNTESS. What hope has she of marriage, after a scandal like that?

OLIVIER. She will doubtless marry sooner than if she stayed with you.

VISCOUNTESS. She's not taking the right road.

OLIVIER. All roads lead to Rome, and the longest is more frequently the surest.

VISCOUNTESS. We'll see. I've done all I could for her. She is only my niece, after all.

[*Enter* SUZANNE.]

SUZANNE. How are you, Viscountess?

VISCOUNTESS. How are you, dear?

SUZANNE. What's the matter?

VISCOUNTESS. I'll tell you later. I've returned what you were good enough to lend me.

SUZANNE. There's no hurry.

VISCOUNTESS. Oh, thank you, but I have fallen heir to a little money.

SUZANNE [*to* HIPPOLYTE]. Very good of you, monsieur, to pay me this little visit with Monsieur de Jalin.

HIPPOLYTE. I hesitated for fear of being indiscreet, but Olivier —

SUZANNE. The friends of Monsieur de Jalin are my friends.

HIPPOLYTE. Thank you, madame.

SUZANNE [*to* OLIVIER]. So you are here?

OLIVIER. Yes, I am. You wrote me to come.

SUZANNE. In order to find out what you had to say to me.

OLIVIER. I wrote you that.

SUZANNE. Do you love me?

OLIVIER. I love you.

SUZANNE. So that was why you wanted me to come to you? Hm! Yes, in order that Monsieur de Nanjac might know, and see me go into your home! Really, you're waging a child's war, using wooden cannons and bullets made of bread-crumbs. Do you intend to disarm me?

OLIVIER. Don't you believe me?

SUZANNE. No!

OLIVIER. Very well. Good-bye.

SUZANNE. Don't go; I want to show you something.

OLIVIER. What?

SUZANNE. I can't tell you; it's a surprise.

[*During this conversation*, RAYMOND *has entered and begun speaking with the Viscountess and* HIPPOLYTE. *He says aloud to the former:*]

RAYMOND. My dear Viscountess, you surely know Madame de Lornan, do you not?

VISCOUNTESS. I used to, but we have since drifted apart.

SUZANNE. She is said to be very virtuous.

VISCOUNTESS. That's true.

SUZANNE. She is most particular as to what homes she visits.

VISCOUNTESS. She sees very few people.

SUZANNE. She is coming here. I'll introduce her to you, my dear Monsieur de Nanjac; you'll see, she's most charming.

OLIVIER. If she comes!

SUZANNE. That's so; you know Madame de Lornan very well, don't you, dear Monsieur de Jalin?

OLIVIER. That is why I am willing to wager that she is not coming, or at least, if she does, that she will not enter the house.

SUZANNE. How much will you wager?

OLIVIER. Whatever you like, whatever a respectable woman can wager: a box of candy or a bouquet.

SUZANNE. I accept [seeing a Servant enter], and I think I am going to win immediately. [To the Servant.] What is it?

SERVANT. A lady who would like to speak with Madame la Baronne.

SUZANNE. Her name?

SERVANT. She would not tell me.

SUZANNE. Tell the lady that I do not receive people who refuse to give their names. [The Servant goes out.]

OLIVIER [aside to RAYMOND]. Raymond, for the sake of our former friendship, prevent Madame de Lornan's entering this room.

RAYMOND. Why?

OLIVIER. Because her coming here may have dire results.

RAYMOND. For whom?

OLIVIER. For several people.

RAYMOND. I have no rights in the home of Madame d'Ange.

OLIVIER. Very well.

SERVANT [opening the door]. Madame de Lornan asks whether Madame la Baronne will receive her?

SUZANNE. Ask her to come in.

OLIVIER. Poor woman!

[He hastens out.]

HIPPOLYTE. God grant that you never regret what you are doing, madame!

SUZANNE. I have never regretted anything I ever did. [To RAYMOND, who is about to leave.] Don't go! Monsieur de

Jalin is going to offer his arm to Madame de Lornan. He has lost his wager, and he is doing the best thing he can do.

[RAYMOND goes toward the door. The moment he gets there, it opens, and OLIVIER appears.]

RAYMOND. Where have you been, monsieur?

OLIVIER. I have just told Madame de Lornan that I object to her coming in here.

RAYMOND. By what right?

OLIVIER. By the right of an honest man who wishes to prevent an honest woman's losing her good name.

SUZANNE. Especially when that honest woman is the mistress of that honest man.

OLIVIER. You lie, madame!

RAYMOND. Monsieur, you are insulting a woman.

OLIVIER. During the past week, monsieur, you have been trying to pick a quarrel with me, but allow me to tell you, I did not come here to give you an opportunity to do so. You believe that a sword-thrust can extricate you from the situation you are now in; very well, I am at your service.

RAYMOND. In an hour's time, monsieur, my seconds will pay you a call.

OLIVIER. I shall await him.

RAYMOND. They have only the conditions to fix; the cause should remain unknown. [The men prepare to go.]

SUZANNE. Raymond!

RAYMOND. Wait for me, Suzanne; I shall return at once. [He goes out.]

OLIVIER. Come, Hippolyte.

[They bow, and go out, opposite.]

VISCOUNTESS. My dear, a provocation to a duel in your home, between two men who were such good friends a few days ago! How could it happen?

SUZANNE. I know nothing about it.

VISCOUNTESS. But you surely won't allow it?

SUZANNE. Oh, no; I've done more difficult things than that.

VISCOUNTESS. Can't I help you?

SUZANNE. No, thank you.

VISCOUNTESS. Then I'll go; you have none too much time. Keep me posted on developments.

SUZANNE. I shan't fail. Come back later in the day, or else I'll drop in to see you.

VISCOUNTESS. I'll see you soon again. [*As she goes.*] What does it all mean?

[*She leaves.*]

SUZANNE. Really, Olivier is braver than I had thought him. He's a splendid, upright man. Olivier is not in love with that Madame de Lornan — but what if he were?

[*Enter a Servant.*]

SERVANT. A letter for Madame la Baronne.

[*He gives her the letter and goes out.*]

SUZANNE. Very well. That will do. [*She opens the letter.*] From the Marquis! [*Reading:*] "You have deceived me: you have seen Monsieur de Nanjac again, and you insist on marrying, in spite of the fact that I forbade your so doing. I give you one hour in which to break it off. If by the end of that time you have not found the means, I shall tell everything to Monsieur de Nanjac." — Oh, this past of mine, that keeps crumbling before me, fragment by fragment! Shall I never be able to bury it? Confess everything? No; I am going to fight it out to the bitter end. [*She rings.*] I must gain time, that's the principal thing. [*She writes a note, and gives it to* SOPHIE, *who enters.*] Take this letter to Monsieur de Thonnerins, and deliver it to him yourself. — Close this door.

[SOPHIE *goes to the door, and as she is about to close it, announces:*]

SOPHIE. Madame, Monsieur de Nanjac.

SUZANNE [*closing her writing-portfolio, as she says in a loud voice to* SOPHIE]. Very well. Never mind, Sophie, you may do that errand later. [SOPHIE *goes out as* RAYMOND *enters.* — *To* RAYMOND.] Well, dear?

RAYMOND. I have just been to see two officers, old comrades of mine, and asked them to act as seconds for me. They were not in, but I left word for them.

SUZANNE. Raymond, this duel cannot take place.

RAYMOND. You must be mad, Suzanne. I may allow compromises between Monsieur de Latour and Monsieur de Mau-croix, but not for my own duels. Monsieur de Jalin is right: I hate him.

SUZANNE. Give me up, Raymond: I have done you nothing but harm so far.

RAYMOND. I have sworn that you are to be my wife, and you will be! Now, I may be killed: in a duel one man is as good as another, and Monsieur de Jalin is no coward; he will do his best to defend himself. I do not want to die without having kept my promise.

[*He sits by the table and starts to open the writing-portfolio.*]

SUZANNE [*with an involuntary start*]. What are you going to do?

RAYMOND. Ask my solicitor to come here. Please have this letter taken to him.

SUZANNE. Never mind.

RAYMOND. What's the matter? Did n't we agree — ?

SUZANNE. Yes, but you have plenty of time.

RAYMOND. Not at all; I have very little.

SUZANNE. I'll give you pens and paper.

RAYMOND. Here is everything I need.

SUZANNE. No.

RAYMOND. You're mistaken — why, you were writing here when I came in.

SUZANNE. Raymond, I ask you not to open that.

RAYMOND. I shan't, then, if you have been writing things I have no business seeing.

SUZANNE. Do you suspect something else?

RAYMOND. No, dear Suzanne, no: if you have any secrets, I shall respect them.

SUZANNE. Then open it and read.

RAYMOND. Will you allow me?

SUZANNE. Yes. [RAYMOND *is on the point of opening the portfolio, when she stops him.*] So you defy me?

RAYMOND. I? You should not accuse me of that! This is not defiance, but merely curiosity. You have given me permission, and I am going to look.

SUZANNE. Do you promise not to make fun of me?

RAYMOND. I promise.

SUZANNE. If you only knew what it's about!

RAYMOND. We shall soon see.

SUZANNE. You will know so much more when you see the list of things I have ordered for our trip —

RAYMOND. What have you ordered?

SUZANNE. Dresses, skirts, silk gowns with figured corsages, and — How interesting those details must be to a man!

RAYMOND. Is that the whole secret?

SUZANNE. Yes.

RAYMOND. So you were writing to your dressmaker?

SUZANNE. Yes.

RAYMOND. While I was seeing the seconds for my duel, you were ordering dresses. Really, Suzanne, do you think I am a fool?

SUZANNE. Raymond!

RAYMOND. I want to know whom you were writing to!

SUZANNE. Oh ho, well, I won't tell you! [She opens the writing-portfolio and takes out a letter.]

RAYMOND. Take care!

SUZANNE. Threats! And by what right? Thank God, I am not your wife yet. I am here in my own home, free, mistress of my own actions, as I leave you free to do as you like. Do I ask you questions? Do I search through your private papers?

RAYMOND [seizing her wrist]. Let me see that letter!

SUZANNE. You shall not see it, I tell you! I have never given in to violence. I have told you the truth; you may now believe and suspect whatever you like.

RAYMOND. I believe that you are deceiving me.

SUZANNE. Very well!

RAYMOND [menacingly]. Suzanne — !

SUZANNE. That will do, monsieur! I release you of all your obligations, and I take back my promise. You and I are now nothing to each other.

RAYMOND. You have once before made use of that trick, madame, but this time I shall stay here.

SUZANNE. What sort of man are you?

RAYMOND. A man who asked nothing of you in exchange for an honorable name, except one moment's sincerity; a man who has sworn that you had nothing with which to reproach yourself; a man who to-morrow is going to fight a duel with a man of honor who had cast a slur on your good name; a man who, for the past two weeks, has had to deal with lies and deceptions, with no other help than loyalty, frankness, and confidence; a man who is determined to know the whole truth at any cost. If that letter does not contain all of it, I imagine from your excitement that it contains a part. I must see that letter; give it to me or I will take it!

SUZANNE [crumpling the letter in her hand and trying to tear it]. You are not going to have it.

RAYMOND [shaking her by the arm]. The letter!

SUZANNE. You dare use violence with a woman!

RAYMOND [getting more and more excited]. That letter!

SUZANNE. I don't love you! I never loved you! I did deceive you. Now, go!

RAYMOND. That letter! [He tries to force open her hand.]

SUZANNE. Raymond, I'll tell you everything — you're hurting me — I'm not to blame. Please, for God's sake! [He snatches the letter from her.] Oh, you — ! [She falls exhausted into a chair.] All right — read it — I'll have my revenge, I swear!

RAYMOND [reading, as his voice quivers with emotion]. "I beg you, don't ruin me. I must see you; I shall explain everything to you. I will do as you say. It is not my fault if Monsieur de Nanjac loves me: I love him, that is my excuse. I depend on you. Please be generous and forgive me. If he knew the truth, I should die of shame. I promise you I shall never marry him, but you must never let him know. Wait till I am free, I —" And I still doubted! [He hides his face in his hands.] What did I ever do to you, Suzanne? Why did you deceive me? Here is your letter. Goodbye. [He starts to go out, but falls into a chair and bursts out crying.]

SUZANNE [seeing that he is overcome, says, timidly]. Raymond?

RAYMOND. You have made a man cry who has not cried since his mother's death. I thank you — it has done me good.

SUZANNE [softly and reproachfully]. You hurt my arms and hands cruelly, Raymond.

RAYMOND. I am sorry; forgive me; it was cowardly. But I did so love you!

SUZANNE [going toward him]. I loved you, too.

RAYMOND. If you had loved me, you would not have lied to me.

SUZANNE [still nearer to him]. There is not a woman who would have confessed what you asked me to confess. I loved you; I respected you; I wanted to be loved and respected in turn. Let me tell you about my life. There is one thing I should keep from you, but only one. Ah, if you only knew: I am not so much to blame as I may seem to be; I had no one to advise or help me. I ought to have told you everything; you are generous, and you would have forgiven me. Now, you can't believe me any longer. But, if I am not pure enough to become the wife of a man like you, I love you enough to deserve your love in return. There is nothing now to force me to tell you. [She falls to her knees and takes RAYMOND's hand.] Raymond, believe in me: I love you!

RAYMOND. To whom were you going to send that letter?

SUZANNE. You would want to challenge him if you knew his name.

RAYMOND. I shan't say a word about it to him, but tell me his name!

SUZANNE. That man has no rights over me; you see, I wrote that I loved you.

RAYMOND. Then why does he forbid you to become my wife?

SUZANNE. I will tell you all, if you promise to be calm.

RAYMOND [rising]. Good-bye.

SUZANNE [retaining him]. I'll tell you everything.

RAYMOND. Well?

SUZANNE. I was going to send that letter to —

RAYMOND. To Olivier?

SUZANNE [forcefully]. No, I swear that! But promise me you won't challenge him.

RAYMOND. I promise.

SUZANNE. To the Marquis de Thonnerins. [RAYMOND makes a gesture of surprise and anger.] Raymond, put yourself in the place of a woman who has been cast off by every one, who had at last found an un-

hoped-for though secret protector. I owe everything to the Marquis! If you only realized — I never had any family!

RAYMOND. Then your marriage — ?

SUZANNE. A lie!

RAYMOND. But the documents you showed me?

SUZANNE. Belonged to a young woman who died abroad — she had no friends or relatives.

RAYMOND. But your fortune?

SUZANNE. Comes from Monsieur de Thonnerins.

RAYMOND. And you were prepared to exchange that shame for my confidence and love? Instead of confessing everything to me, frankly, nobly, you were about to bring me a stolen name and a fortune acquired at the price of your honor! You did not see that, after I had become your husband, had I found out about this infamous bargain, the only thing I could do would have been to kill you, and then myself. You not only did not love me, Suzanne, but you did not respect me.

SUZANNE. I am the lowest of creatures, I know; I don't deserve your love, not even that you should remember me. Leave me, Raymond, and forget me.

RAYMOND. This is not all, doubtless? Please continue; what else have you to confess?

SUZANNE. Nothing.

RAYMOND. What about Olivier? Neither misery nor loneliness could have led you to go to him. If that man was ever your lover, it means that you have loved him, and that love is what I can never forgive!

SUZANNE. Olivier has never been anything to me. He told you that himself, and you know it very well.

RAYMOND. Will you swear to that?

SUZANNE [calmly]. I swear.

RAYMOND. Do you love me?

SUZANNE. Do you think I would have confessed unless I did?

RAYMOND. Well, Suzanne, I ask for only one proof of that love.

SUZANNE. What?

RAYMOND. Return to Monsieur de Thonnerins everything you have from him.

SUZANNE [*ringing*]. At once! [*She takes some papers from a drawer, wraps them up and seals them. To the Servant, who enters.*] Take these papers at once to Monsieur de Thonnerins; there is no answer.

SERVANT. Monsieur le Marquis de Thonnerins is just this moment coming up the stairs.

SUZANNE. He is — !

RAYMOND [*to the Servant*]. Ask Monsieur le Marquis to wait! [*The Servant goes out.— To* SUZANNE.] Give me those papers; I shall give them to him myself.

SUZANNE. You frighten me!

RAYMOND. Don't be afraid. There is still time, Suzanne. Choose! Keep these papers; I shall go away, for always; or, if you decide to make those promises again, and in case I am not killed to-morrow, I shall hold you to account only from this moment on. We may then go away together.

SUZANNE. I have told you the truth.

RAYMOND. Oh, Suzanne, I had no idea myself how much I loved you!

[*He goes out.*]

SUZANNE. I am staking my whole life, past and future! Olivier is the only one now who can ruin or save me! If he loves me as he says he does — it would be strange. [*She puts on her cloak and hat.*] We shall see! [*She goes out.*]

ACT V

[*The scene is the same as in the First Act. As the curtain rises,* OLIVIER *is writing. A moment later, enter* HIPPOLYTE.]

HIPPOLYTE [*touching* OLIVIER *on the shoulder*]. It's I.

OLIVIER [*as he seals the letter*]. Well?

HIPPOLYTE. Well, I have done everything.

OLIVIER. Have you seen Madame de Lornan?

HIPPOLYTE. Yes, but through the agency of her housekeeper, because her husband has returned. That is why Madame de Lornan wrote you asking for news. She can't leave her house now. I told her that the duel was not going to take place.

OLIVIER. And that in no event would her name be mentioned? Undoubtedly, she cares more about that than about anything else?

HIPPOLYTE. She cares something about it, but she is most anxious that nothing should happen to you. You wanted to save her, and you succeeded; you ought to be the last one to blame her for refusing to compromise herself even for your sake. She received a good lesson, and she will profit by it. I reassured her. It was not very difficult, because I felt very sure myself.

OLIVIER. How do you mean?

HIPPOLYTE. The duel will not take place, I tell you.

OLIVIER. Why?

HIPPOLYTE. Because I have seen the Marquis; there is something new.

OLIVIER. There can't be anything new which can prevent us, Monsieur de Nanjac and I, from fighting this duel: we have gone too far — unless, that is, he makes excuses to me, which is not likely.

HIPPOLYTE. That depends on you alone.

OLIVIER. Tell me what you mean.

HIPPOLYTE. I have seen the Marquis.

OLIVIER. Does he refuse to act as my second?

HIPPOLYTE. Yes.

OLIVIER. I rather thought he would. He is afraid of compromising himself — he, too.

HIPPOLYTE. He is, and he is right. Things of this sort do not go with his years or his position. For his daughter's sake, his name ought not to be dragged into the affair. But he has seen Monsieur de Nanjac, who knows the whole truth.

OLIVIER. The whole truth?

HIPPOLYTE. So far as the Marquis is concerned. He found a letter that Suzanne had written to Monsieur de Thonnerins. There was a violent quarrel between Raymond and Madame d'Ange. Suzanne was forced to tell about her relations with the Marquis. Raymond forgave her, on the condition that she restore to the Marquis everything that he had given her.

OLIVIER. Did she do it?

HIPPOLYTE. So it seems.

OLIVIER. I am surprised; but, tell me, how can this prevent the duel?

HIPPOLYTE. Monsieur de Nanjac gave back everything himself, and Monsieur de Thonnerins, who was told of the provocation, informed Monsieur de Nanjac that the marriage, like the duel, was out of the question; that Madame d'Ange was not worthy of him, and that your conduct throughout was that of a gallant man and a good friend. You know what a man in love is like when he finds himself in a false position: the more violently the woman is attacked, the more he believes it due his dignity to defend her. Monsieur de Nanjac took it all in a high-handed way and replied: "The moment I restore what Madame d'Ange has received from you, monsieur, it means that I wish to forget everything in Madame d'Ange's life in which you have played a part. As to Monsieur de Jalin, who began by telling me he was no more than a friend to Madame d'Ange, and ended by relating the exact opposite; as to Monsieur de Jalin, who I once thought was my friend, and who was not enough of a friend either to affirm or to deny anything outright, let him say to me, 'I give you my word of honor that I have been that woman's lover,' — that is what he ought to do if he ever cared anything at all for me, — I give him my word of honor, to make excuses to him, to offer him my hand as I used to, and never see Madame d'Ange again." You see now how senseless a duel would be?

OLIVIER. Are you through?

HIPPOLYTE. Yes.

OLIVIER. Well, my poor Hippolyte, I thank you for your splendid intentions; but we have been wasting good time.

HIPPOLYTE. Why?

OLIVIER. Because Madame d'Ange has nothing to do with the question. I do not know and I cannot know anything but one fact: that there is reason for a duel between Monsieur de Nanjac and me, and that any effort to prevent a duel, the basis of which is an insult to a woman (even if it is true), would be undignified and unworthy a man of honor. Monsieur de Nanjac is a soldier,

I belong to what is called the middle-class. What would be said if the duel were stopped? Let us allow things to follow their natural course. Monsieur de Nanjac is more to be pitied than I, but I can understand his conduct. I want to grasp his hand, but I am perhaps on the point of killing him. Such is the false logic of our social code of honor. I did not make that code, but I am forced to submit to it.

HIPPOLYTE. It's not very amusing to kill a man. When I look at my wife and remember that I killed a man for her sake — well, you know what my wife did, don't you?

OLIVIER. No.

HIPPOLYTE. I have just found out, myself. She has run away with Monsieur de Latour, who leaves a deficit of 400,000 francs at the Bourse. She was bound to do that some day, though she has not yet reached the end. She is one of those women whom nothing can stop; once they start going down, they must continue straight to the bottom, without having, as those who are at the bottom of the ladder have, the excuse of evil example, misery, and ignorance.

OLIVIER. I'm sorry, but it is now half-past two.

HIPPOLYTE. That's true. After Monsieur de Thonnerins refused to be your second, I went to see Monsieur de Maucroix, and he and I went to see Monsieur de Nanjac. We meet at three o'clock. We still have three quarters of an hour.

OLIVIER. Where is it to take place?

HIPPOLYTE. In the fields behind your home; they are large and always deserted. No one will disturb us — and then we shall be only a step from where you live. In case of accident, we shall have a safe place to carry the wounded.

OLIVIER. What weapons?

HIPPOLYTE. The seconds left the choice to us.

OLIVIER. Did you refuse?

HIPPOLYTE. Yes, because you told us that you wanted no concessions; we drew lots, and the choice fell to us.

OLIVIER. What did you decide on?

HIPPOLYTE. Swords.

OLIVIER. If anything should happen to me, you will find a letter in this drawer; please have it sent to Mademoiselle de Sancenaux at once, because she is going away to-night. This letter will prevent her leaving.

HIPPOLYTE. Is that all?

OLIVIER. Yes.

HIPPOLYTE. Nothing for Madame d'Ange?

OLIVIER. No, nothing — she is coming.

HIPPOLYTE. Did she send word?

OLIVIER. No; but she is brave and proud only when she is victorious; if she knows that I have to say only a word in order to break off her marriage, she will stop at nothing in order to obtain my silence. She will come.

HIPPOLYTE. Do you know what I am thinking of?

OLIVIER. Tell me.

HIPPOLYTE. That you were more in love with Suzanne than you let any one see, and that perhaps you still are, more than you will admit.

OLIVIER [smiling]. Who knows? The heart of man is so strange!

[Enter a Servant.]

SERVANT. There is a young lady below in a carriage who would like to speak with monsieur.

OLIVIER. Who is it?

SERVANT. She wrote this note.

[He hands OLIVIER a note.]

OLIVIER [reading]. "Marcelle"! Ask the lady to come in. [The Servant goes out. — To HIPPOLYTE.] Go into my room. I am to see some one who does not want to be seen. When the time comes for us to leave, rap on the door, and I shall join you.

HIPPOLYTE. You have only half an hour.

OLIVIER. Don't worry; we shall be on time. [HIPPOLYTE goes out; OLIVIER goes toward the door. Enter MARCELLE.] You here, Marcelle? How imprudent!

MARCELLE. No one saw me come in, and then I don't care what any one may think. I am going away to-night; perhaps I shall never come back. I did n't want to go without seeing you.

OLIVIER. I should have called on you before you went.

MARCELLE. That might not have been possible, perhaps? Or did n't you think of that?

OLIVIER. Is that a reproach?

MARCELLE. What right have I to reproach you? Am I a friend of yours? Am I worthy of your confidence? If your are in trouble, do you come to me? If you are in danger, would you even think of saying good-bye to me before exposing yourself? How miserable I am!

OLVIIER. What is the trouble, Marcelle?

MARCELLE. You are going to fight; perhaps you will be killed! Do you expect me to be calm? And you ask what's the trouble?

OLIVIER. Who told you I was going to fight?

MARCELLE. My aunt, who came to see me after she had been to see Madame d'Ange; she told me everything, and gave me the name of the woman for whose sake you are fighting: Madame de Lornan.

OLIVIER. She was mistaken.

MARCELLE. No. If something had happened to you, I should have heard about it the way every one else did — that you were killed! Not to have a single memory or souvenir of you in the moment of danger — ! How ungrateful of you! I declare, if I were in danger, you would be the only person I would ask to help me! You might at least do for me what I would do for you. But, never mind: I am going to stop the duel.

OLIVIER. How?

MARCELLE. You see — you don't deny it! I'm going to report you to the first police officer I can find.

OLIVIER. By what right?

MARCELLE. By the right of a woman who wants to save the life of the man she loves.

OLIVIER. Do you love me?

MARCELLE. You know I do.

OLIVIER. Marcelle!

MARCELLE. Who else could have induced me, by a word, to change my whole life? Who made me leave the society where I was living? For whose sake would I have been willing to bury myself in the provinces to make a living in sadness and obscurity? For whose sake am I going away, with no other consolation but the thought that I was respected and perhaps would soon be forgotten by you? And, at last, for whose sake does a woman change herself in this way, unless it is for the sake of the man she loves? Deep down in my heart I was taking one hope with me; I said to myself: " Perhaps he is trying to test me? When he sees that I am making an honest effort to live a respectable life, and after he has made of me the woman he wants me to be, who knows but that some day he may come to love me?" I dreamed that — and now I suddenly hear that you are fighting a duel for another woman. Do you think I'm going to allow that? Let her allow it, the woman you love; very well; but I, I who love you? Never!

OLIVIER. Listen to me, Marcelle; I swear if you attempt in any way to stop this duel — and dishonor me, as it surely will, because it will be said that I made a woman my excuse to avoid fighting — I swear, Marcelle, I will not survive the dishonor.

MARCELLE. I shan't say a word; I shall only pray.

OLIVIER. Now, Marcelle, you must go home. I shall see you soon.

MARCELLE. You're sending me away because the duel is going to take place to-day.

OLIVIER. No — perhaps, even, it will not take place at all. Now that I know you love me, I want to live. There is a way out of it all.

MARCELLE. Will you promise that you are not going to fight to-day?

OLIVIER. I promise. [HIPPOLYTE's knock is heard.] Very well — one moment.

MARCELLE. What's that?

OLIVIER. A friend of mine who wants me.

MARCELLE. One of your seconds!

OLIVIER. Yes.

MARCELLE. To take you to the duelingground. Olivier, I'm not going to leave you.

OLIVIER. My seconds are already here: they are having a conference with Monsieur de Nanjac's seconds. They must see me. That is why Hippolyte wants to speak to me.

MARCELLE. I'm so afraid!

OLIVIER. Listen, Marcelle: I, too, perhaps, have dreamed your dream. I was happy and proud to have something to do with developing those good qualities which I felt sure were within you. Some mysterious instinct for happiness has urged me toward you. I was unable to say why I wanted you to be worthy of every one's respect — I see now, it was a basic need in my own heart. That is all I can tell you, because a man whose life is in imminent danger has no right to speak of hope and the future.

MARCELLE. Olivier!

OLIVIER. Everything will have been decided in one hour; then I can explain. Meantime, you must not be seen here. Go back to the Viscountess and wait for me there. We shall meet again, I promise. I shall be there, and when I leave, it will be only to see you. Courage!

[He goes out.]

MARCELLE. O God, protect me!

[She makes ready to leave, as SUZANNE enters.]

SUZANNE. Marcelle!

MARCELLE [turning round]. You, madame!

SUZANNE. How does it happen that you are here?

MARCELLE. I came the moment I heard of the duel.

SUZANNE. Have you seen Olivier?

MARCELLE. Yes.

SUZANNE. When does it take place?

MARCELLE. I hope it won't take place.

SUZANNE. How is that?

MARCELLE. There is one means of stopping it.

SUZANNE. What means?

MARCELLE. I don't know, but Olivier told me that he would make use of it.

SUZANNE. That means is infamous!

MARCELLE. Do you know what it is?

SUZANNE. Yes; and I tell you Olivier would not compromise any woman in order to avoid fighting. He deceived you.

MARCELLE. He did!

SUZANNE. Tell me; what did you tell him when you came here?

MARCELLE. That I didn't want the duel to take place.

SUZANNE. And that you loved him?

MARCELLE. Yes.

SUZANNE. That if he persisted, you would not leave him?

MARCELLE. How do you know that?

SUZANNE. I know what a woman would say under like circumstances. Then did he promise to come to an understanding with his opponent?

MARCELLE. Yes.

SUZANNE. He said, too, that he loved you?

MARCELLE. I could see that.

SUZANNE. He deceived you. He wanted to gain time. He then went out to fight.

MARCELLE. No: he is in there.

SUZANNE. Are you sure?

MARCELLE. If I call he will come.

SUZANNE. Call him.

MARCELLE [calling]. Olivier! Olivier!

SUZANNE [opening the door]. No one! Now are you convinced?

MARCELLE. It's — impossible!

SUZANNE [ringing]. Do you still doubt? [To the Servant, who enters.] Has your master gone out?

SERVANT. Yes, madame.

SUZANNE. Alone?

SERVANT. With Monsieur Richond and Monsieur de Maucroix, who came to get him.

SUZANNE. Did he leave any word either for mademoiselle or for me?

SERVANT. Nothing, madame.

SUZANNE. That will do. [The Servant goes out. — To MARCELLE.] Where are you going?

MARCELLE. I must find him and save him!

SUZANNE. Where? Do you know where he is? How can you save him? Wait! That is all we can do — everything rests on chance. Olivier and Raymond are now fighting, that is sure. They are both brave men, they hate each other, and one of them is sure to be killed.

MARCELLE. My God!

SUZANNE. Now, listen to me: Olivier has lied both to you and to me — he told me, too, that he loved me.

MARCELLE. You? When?

SUZANNE. Two hours ago. I may lose love, fortune, future, in one second. If Raymond survives, I am saved; if he dies, then Olivier's love is my last resource. He must love me, otherwise I should die of shame. You ought to know the truth: the same man has told us both that he loved us. It is our right to know whether he does love us. If he is the one who survives, he must find only one of us here — you understand that, of course? He would never explain before us both. One of us will meet him, the other will remain hidden behind this door, and hear everything: I'll do that, if you like. If he persists in telling you that he loves you, I will sacrifice myself, and go away without saying a word. Tell me — ?

MARCELLE. I don't understand, madame; I don't know what you are saying. How calm you are — it's frightful!

SUZANNE. Listen!

MARCELLE. What?

SUZANNE. A carriage!

MARCELLE. It's he!

SUZANNE. Something has happened! Go in there!

MARCELLE. I must see him.

SUZANNE. Go in there, I tell you! It's he — Olivier!

MARCELLE. He is saved! He is living! Now, O God, let me suffer!

SUZANNE [pushing her toward the door at the left]. Go in! [MARCELLE goes out.]

[Enter OLIVIER.]

OLIVIER [feebly]. Is that you, Suzanne?

SUZANNE. You didn't expect to see me?

OLIVIER. No, I didn't.

SUZANNE. Are you wounded?

OLIVIER. It's nothing!

SUZANNE. But Raymond?

OLIVIER [whose voice grows stronger]. Suzanne, was I in the right? Did I deceive him?

SUZANNE. No. Well — ?

OLIVIER. Did I do my duty as an honest man? Answer me.

SUZANNE. Yes. Well — ?

OLIVIER. When you forced us to fight, whom did you consider was right?

SUZANNE. You.

OLIVIER. Then his death is only a misfortune, and not a crime?

SUZANNE. His death!

OLIVIER. Yes, his death. Listen, Suzanne. The day you came to tell me that you did not love me any longer, a great jealousy was born in me. I wanted to behave generously, and I wore a smile, but my love for you was the strange, fatal sort which you inspire in all who love you: in Monsieur de Thonnerins, that old man who for a moment forgot his daughter for your sake; in Raymond, whom nothing could convince, who believed no one but you, who *would* believe no one but you, who preferred trying to kill me than to be convinced by me. If I wanted to prevent this marriage, if I told Raymond all I did tell him, if on the dueling-ground I forgot that he was a friend, if I — I — killed the man who was dear to me only a week ago — it was not because of any offense, it was because I did n't want you to belong to him, because I loved you — because I love you! In a single moment I have made you lose everything; but in a single moment I can restore everything to you. I can't think of any one but you; you must be mine. Don't leave me! Let us go away together!

SUZANNE [*after looking him straight in the eyes*]. Yes, let us go!

OLIVIER [*clasping her to him*]. At last! — [*He bursts out laughing.*] Oh! It *was* such trouble!

SUZANNE. What!

OLIVIER. You have lost, my dear. You owe me a forfeit! Look!

SUZANNE [*seeing* RAYMOND *appear, followed by* HIPPOLYTE]. Raymond!

[*Enter* MARCELLE, *who throws herself into* OLIVIER'S *arms*.]

MARCELLE. Oh!

OLIVIER. Forgive me, dear child; I had to save a friend.

RAYMOND [*to* OLIVIER]. Thank you, Olivier. I must have been mad. You have taken my honor into your hands; nothing

stopped your attempts to convince me — not even my own blindness, my unjust hatred, or even this wound, which is, luckily, only a slight one. Everything is over between madame and me, except a few material matters, which I shall ask you to regulate. [*He gives him a slip of paper.*] I don't wish to have to speak with her.

[MARCELLE *goes to* RAYMOND, *who takes her hands in his in an amicable manner.* OLIVIER *goes to* SUZANNE.]

SUZANNE. You are a blackguard!

OLIVIER. Careful, please! When one implicates the life and honor of two men, and loses, he should bow to Fate with good grace. It seems I had to receive a swordthrust in order to prove the truth of my assertions. I am not preventing your marriage; reason, common sense, and justice are, and the social law which requires that an honest man marry none but an honest woman. You have lost, but you know you have a consolation prize?

SUZANNE. What?

OLIVIER. In this document, Raymond gives you back the fortune he made you abdicate.

SUZANNE [*playing her last card*]. Give it to me! [*She destroys the document as she looks at* RAYMOND.] What I wanted from him was his name, not his fortune. I shall leave Paris in an hour, on my way to a foreign country.

[RAYMOND *pretends not to hear.*]

OLIVIER. But you have nothing to live on! You returned everything to the Marquis.

SUZANNE. I don't know what it was, but I was so agitated when I gave those documents to Monsieur de Nanjac that I found most of the deeds and so forth on my table after he left. Good-bye, Olivier.

[*She goes out.*]

OLIVIER. And to think that all that woman needed to turn her bad into good was a small proportion of the intelligence she used in doing evil!

RAYMOND [*to* MARCELLE]. You are going to be happy, mademoiselle: you are marrying the finest man I know!

THE MISTRESS OF TIIE INN

(LA LOCANDIERA)

By CARLO GOLDONI

Translated by MERLE PIERSON

CHARACTERS

The Cavalier di Ripafratta

The Marquis di Forlipopoli

The Count D'Albafiorita

Mirandolina, *the Mistress of the Inn*

Fabricius, *serving-man in the Inn*

Servant of the Cavalier

Servant of the Count

The scene is placed in Florence in the Inn of Mirandolina.

THE MISTRESS OF THE INN

ACT I

The public room of the hotel.

[*Enter the* Marquis di Forlipopoli *and the* Count D'Albafiorita.]

Marquis. There is quite a distinction between you and me.

Count. As far as the inn goes my money is as good as yours.

Marquis. But if the mistress of the inn shows me certain marks of consideration, it's because I deserve them more than you.

Count. For what reason?

Marquis. I am the Marquis di Forlipopoli.

Count. And I the Count d'Albafiorita.

Marquis. Yes, count of a purchased county.

Count. I purchased my county when you sold your marquisate.

Marquis. Enough! I am who I am and must be shown respect.

Count. Who's wanting in respect? You speak with over-much boldness. . . .

Marquis. I am in this inn, because I love its mistress. All know it and all ought to respect a young woman who pleases my fancy.

Count. O, that's a good one! You want to keep me from loving Mirandolina. Why do you think I'm in Florence? Why do you think I'm in this particular hotel?

Marquis. Oh, well! You won't accomplish anything at all.

Count. I shall not, and you will?

Marquis. I shall and you will not. I am who I am. Mirandolina needs my protection.

Count. Mirandolina needs money, but not protection.

Marquis. Money? . . . That's not lacking.

Count. I spend ten shillings a day, Marquis, and I'm always giving her gifts.

Marquis. But I'm not telling what I do.

Count. You don't say anything about it, but everybody knows it.

Marquis. All is not known.

Count. Indeed, my dear Marquis, but it is. The waiters are talking about it. A shilling a day!

Marquis. Speaking of waiters there is this waiter here, who's called Fabricius. I don't exactly like that fellow. It seems to me that our hostess looks upon him altogether too favorably.

Count. Perhaps she wants to marry him. It wouldn't be a bad thing. Her father has been dead six months. A young girl alone at the head of an inn will find herself embarrassed. For my part, if she should marry, I have promised her one hundred pounds.

Marquis. If she marries, I am her protector and I shall . . . I know what I'll do.

Count. Come here. As good friends let's arrange the affair. Let us give her a hundred pounds apiece.

Marquis. What I do, I do secretly, and I don't boast of it. I am who I am. [*Calls.*] Who's there?

Count [*aside*]. Ruined, poor, and proud.

[*Enter* Fabricius.]

Fabricius. At your service, sir.

Marquis. Sir? Who taught you your manners?

Fabricius. Pardon me.

Count [*to* Fabricius]. Tell me: how is your mistress?

Fabricius. She is very well, your lordship.

Marquis. Is she up yet?

Fabricius. Yes, your lordship.

Marquis. Ass!

Fabricius. Why, your lordship?

Marquis. Don't lordship me!

Fabricius. It's the title I gave to the other gentleman too.

MARQUIS. There is some distinction between him and me.

COUNT [to FABRICIUS]. Just listen to him.

FABRICIUS [in a low tone to the COUNT]. He speaks the truth. There is a difference. I notice it in the bills.

MARQUIS. Tell your mistress to come to my room; that I want to speak with her.

FABRICIUS. Yes, your excellency. I did n't make a mistake this time, did I?

MARQUIS. All right. You have known it three months. You are an insolent fellow.

FABRICIUS. As you wish, your excellency.

COUNT. Do you want to see the difference between the Marquis and me?

MARQUIS. What do you mean?

COUNT. See here. I'm giving you ten shillings. Make him give you the same.

FABRICIUS [to the COUNT]. Thanks, your lordship. [To the MARQUIS]. Your excellency . . .

MARQUIS. I don't throw away my money as madmen do. Go!

FABRICIUS [to the COUNT]. Your lordship, Heaven bless you. [Aside.] Your excellency! Played out! Outside of your own country you don't have to have titles to be esteemed, you have to have money.

[Exit FABRICIUS.]

MARQUIS. You think you can outdo me with your gifts, but you can't do anything of the sort. My rank is worth more than all your money.

COUNT. I don't care what a thing's worth, what I like is something I can spend.

MARQUIS. You are spending only to break your neck. Mirandolina does n't have any esteem for you at all.

COUNT. Well, do you think that with all that fine nobility of yours she really esteems you? There has to be money.

MARQUIS. How money? She wants protection — she wants some one who can do her a favor in a pinch.

COUNT. Yes, some one who can lend her in a pinch a hundred pounds.

MARQUIS. A man must make himself respected.

COUNT. When there's no lack of money, every one respects you.

MARQUIS. You don't know what you're talking about.

COUNT. I understand better than you do.

[Enter the CAVALIER DI RIPAFRATTA from his room.]

CAVALIER. Friends, what's all this noise about? Are you two quarreling?

COUNT. There's a very fine point in dispute.

MARQUIS [ironically]. The Count and I are at issue on the merit of nobility.

COUNT. I don't deny nobility merit; but I do maintain that there has to be money to satisfy one's caprices.

CAVALIER. Really, my dear Marquis. . . .

MARQUIS. Come now, let's talk about something else.

CAVALIER. How did you come to get into such a quarrel?

COUNT. For the silliest reason in the world.

MARQUIS. Bravo! The Count always ridicules everything.

COUNT. The Marquis loves our hostess here; I too love her — more than he. He claims reciprocal feeling on her part as a tribute to his rank. I hope for it as a recompense for my attentions. Does n't the question seem ridiculous to you?

MARQUIS. You must know with what great difficulty I have been protecting her.

COUNT [to CAVALIER]. He protects her, and I spend the money.

CAVALIER. Indeed, one can't dispute about anything that deserves it less. A woman changes you, a woman upsets you? A woman? What queer things one hears nowadays! As far as I am concerned there is n't any danger that I'll get into a dispute with any one about women. I have never loved them, I have never had any use for them, and I have always thought that woman is an unbearable infirmity for man.

MARQUIS. As far as that goes Mirandolina has extraordinary worth.

COUNT. Up to this point the Marquis has reason on his side. The mistress of our inn is truly an adorable person.

MARQUIS. Now, when I love her you must think there is something fine in her.

CAVALIER. Indeed, you make me laugh. What can she have that's out of the ordinary and not common to all other women?

MARQUIS. She has a noble manner that charms.

COUNT. She is beautiful, she speaks well, she dresses nicely, and she has the best taste imaginable.

CAVALIER. All these things are n't worth a fig. I have been in this hotel three days and I don't see anything especially remarkable about her.

COUNT. Watch her, and perhaps you may find some good in her.

CAVALIER. Nonsense. I have taken a good look at her. She is a woman just like the others.

MARQUIS. She is n't like the others, she has something more in her. I, who have been in the society of the first ladies of the land, have never found a woman who knows how to unite as she does, politeness and decorum.

COUNT. Great Cæsar! I have always been accustomed to be much in the society of women. I know their defects and their weaknesses. And yet with her, in spite of my long courtship, and the great hopes I have had, I have n't been able to touch as much as a finger.

CAVALIER. Art, exquisite art. Poor simpletons. You believe in her, ah? Now, that would n't have happened to me. Women? Away with all of them.

COUNT. You have never been in love?

CAVALIER. No, and I never will be. They have done their best to give me a wife, but I have never wanted one.

MARQUIS. But you are the only one left of your house; don't you have to think of the succession?

CAVALIER. I have thought of it often, but when I consider that to have children I would have to endure a wife my desire suddenly vanishes.

COUNT. What are you going to do with your riches?

CAVALIER. I shall enjoy the little I have with my friends.

MARQUIS. Fine, Cavalier, fine; we shall enjoy ourselves.

COUNT. And you don't want to give anything at all to women?

CAVALIER. Absolutely nothing. They certainly don't get anything out of me.

COUNT. See, our hostess! Look at her and see if she is n't adorable.

CAVALIER. What an idea! For my part I value a fine hunting dog four times as much as I do her.

MARQUIS. If you don't esteem her, I do.

CAVALIER. I'd leave her to you even if she were more beautiful than Venus.

[*Enter* MIRANDOLINA.]

MIRANDOLINA. My respects to the gentlemen. Which of you has asked for me?

MARQUIS. I have a request to make of you, but not here.

MIRANDOLINA. Where do you mean, your excellency?

MARQUIS. In my room.

MIRANDOLINA. In your room? If you need anything, the waiter will come and serve you.

MARQUIS [*aside to the* CAVALIER]. What do you say to that modesty?

CAVALIER [*aside to the* MARQUIS]. What you call modesty I'd call forwardness and impertinence.

COUNT. Dear Mirandolina, I shall speak to you in public; I'll not put you to the inconvenience of coming to my room. You see these earrings. Do you like them?

MIRANDOLINA. Beautiful.

COUNT. They are diamonds; do you know that?

MIRANDOLINA. Oh, I recognize them. I, too, understand diamonds.

MARQUIS. They are at your service.

CAVALIER [*softly to the* COUNT]. My dear friend, you're throwing them away.

MIRANDOLINA. Why do you want to give me these earrings?

MARQUIS. A fine present, indeed, they would make! She has some twice as handsome.

COUNT. These are set in the latest style. I beg you to take them with my love.

CAVALIER [*aside*]. What a madman.

MIRANDOLINA. No, of course not, sir.

Count. If you don't take them, you'll displease me.

Mirandolina. I don't know what to say. . . . It's to my interest to keep on good terms with the patrons of my inn. So as not to displease you, Count, I'll take them.

Cavalier [aside]. Oh, the wretch!

Count [to the Cavalier]. What do you say to this vivacity?

Cavalier [aside]. Splendid vivacity! She takes them from you, and without a word of thanks either.

Marquis. Really, Count, you've made yourself highly esteemed. Out of vanity to give gifts to a woman in public! Mirandolina! I must speak to you privately; I am a gentleman.

Mirandolina [aside]. What penury! He does n't give any one presents. — If the gentlemen desire nothing further of me I shall go.

Cavalier [with displeasure]. Look here, mistress! The linen you gave me is n't to my taste. If you have n't any better, I shall have to provide it myself.

Mirandolina. Sir, you shall have better. It will be brought up; but it seems to me you might ask with a little politeness.

Cavalier. Where I spend my money, I don't need to stand on ceremony.

Count [to Mirandolina]. Excuse him. He is an implacable woman-hater.

Cavalier. Eh! I don't need her indulgence.

Mirandolina. Poor women! What have they done? Why thus cruel to us, Sir Cavalier?

Cavalier. That's enough. You are n't going to get any deeper in my confidence. Change the linen for me. I shall send my valet for it. Friends, your humble servant.
[Exit the Cavalier.]

Mirandolina. What a savage man! I have never seen his like.

Count. Dear Mirandolina, every one does n't appreciate your merits.

Mirandolina. Indeed, I'm so disgusted with his bad behavior, that I shall dismiss him this very moment directly.

Marquis. Yes, do; and if he does n't want to go, tell me and I'll make him leave immediately. Pray make use of my protection.

Count. And whatever money you lose, I'll make good and pay everything. Listen, send away the Marquis, too, and I'll pay you for that.

Mirandolina. Thank you, gentlemen. I have spirit enough to tell a guest that I don't want him; and as regards business, my inn never has a room vacant.

[Enter Fabricius.]

Fabricius [to the Count]. Your lordship, there is some one asking for you.

Count. Do you know who it is?

Fabricius. I think it's a man who sets jewels. [Softly to Mirandolina.] Mirandolina, discretion; this is n't a proper place for you. [Exit.]

Count. Oh, yes; he has a jewel to show me. Mirandolina, I want to match these earrings.

Mirandolina. Oh, no, Count.

Count. You deserve something good, and I don't care anything about the money. I'm going to see this jewel. Adieu, Mirandolina; Sir Marquis, I must take my leave of you. [Exit the Count.]

Marquis [aside]. The accursed Count! He bores me to death with that money of his.

Mirandolina. Indeed, the Count puts himself to too much trouble.

Marquis. People like that have twopence and they spend them through vanity and vainglory. I know them; I know the way of the world.

Mirandolina. Ah, I, too, know the way of the world.

Marquis. They think that women of your kind can be conquered with gifts.

Mirandolina. Presents are never repugnant to any one.

Marquis. I should think I was insulting you by trying to put you under obligations with gifts.

Mirandolina. Oh, certainly, the Marquis has never insulted me.

Marquis. And he never will.

Mirandolina. I sincerely believe you.

Marquis. But wherever I can, I am at your service.

MIRANDOLINA. I should have to know in what you can help me.

MARQUIS. In everything. Try me.

MIRANDOLINA. But, for instance, in what?

MARQUIS. By Jove. You have a wonderful charm.

MIRANDOLINA. Many, many thanks, your excellency.

MARQUIS. Ah, I would make an almost unbecoming remark. I would almost call down curses on my title.

MIRANDOLINA. Why so, sir?

MARQUIS. Sometimes, I wish I were in the count's position.

MIRANDOLINA. Perhaps, because of his money?

MARQUIS. Eh! How money? I don't care a rap about it. If I were a ridiculous Count like him —

MIRANDOLINA. What would you do?

MARQUIS. The deuce. . . . I would marry you. [*Exit the* MARQUIS.]

MIRANDOLINA. Oh, what has he said! Marquis Empty Pockets, that fine fellow, wants to marry me? Yes, if you wanted to you'd find a little difficulty. I'd stand in the way. I like the good things of life, but have no use for the disagreeable. If all who said they wanted me, had married me, oh, how many husbands I'd have had. Every one who has come to this inn has fallen in love with me, every one has made desperate love to me, and many and many a one has offered to marry me on the spot. And as to that Cavalier, who is as rough as a bear, why does he treat me so brusquely? He's the first guest who's come to my inn who hasn't been delighted to be in my society. I don't say that every one has fallen in love at first sight, but to despise me so, is something that makes me angry. He a woman-hater? He can't bear the sight of them? Poor fool! Probably he hasn't found the one who knows how to handle him. But he shall find her. He shall. And who knows that he hasn't found her. I'm going to enter the lists with him. Those who run after me, soon bore me. Nobility has no weight with me. I value riches, but not nobility. My whole delight is in seeing myself served, desired, and adored. That

is my weakness, as it is the weakness of almost all women. I'm not thinking of marrying any one; I don't need any one; I live honestly and I enjoy my freedom. I treat every one well, but I'll never fall in love with any one. I like to make fun of those exaggerated ardent lovers, and I want to use all my skill to conquer, strike down and shake to their depths these cruel and hard hearts which are the enemies of us who are the best thing that beautiful Mother Nature has produced in this world.

[*Enter* FABRICIUS.]

FABRICIUS. Look here, mistress.

MIRANDOLINA. What is it?

FABRICIUS. The guest who has the middle room finds fault with the linen; he says it's commonplace, and he doesn't want it.

MIRANDOLINA. I know it, I know it; he said the same thing to me, and I want his commands to be carried out.

FABRICIUS. Very well. Come, then, and lay out the things so that I can take them to him.

MIRANDOLINA. Never mind, never mind. I shall take them to him.

FABRICIUS. You wish to take them to him.

MIRANDOLINA. Yes, I do.

FABRICIUS. You must be greatly interested in that guest.

MIRANDOLINA. I'm interested in every one. Mind your own business.

FABRICIUS [*aside*]. Indeed, I'm sure of it. Our affair won't amount to anything. She's just flattering me and nothing will come of it.

MIRANDOLINA [*aside*]. Poor fool. He has aspirations. I want to keep him hoping, because he has served me faithfully.

FABRICIUS. It has always been customary for me to serve strangers.

MIRANDOLINA. You are a little too rough with the guests.

FABRICIUS. And you a little too kind.

MIRANDOLINA. I know what I'm doing; I don't need advisers.

FABRICIUS. Very well, very well. Get another waiter.

MIRANDOLINA. Why, Fabricius? Are you displeased with me?

FABRICIUS. Do you remember what your father said to us two before he died? MIRANDOLINA. Yes, when I decide to marry I shall remember what my father told me. FABRICIUS. But I am sensitive; there are certain things I can't endure. MIRANDOLINA. But what do you think I am? A gossip? A flirt? A fool? I'm astonished at you. What do I care about guests who come and go. If I treat them well I do it for my own interest, to keep my inn in good repute. I don't need gifts. One's enough to court me, and this one's not lacking. I know who is deserving and I know what's proper. And when I want to marry . . . I shall remember my father. And he who has served me well can't complain of me. I am grateful. I recognize merit . . . but I am not appreciated. Enough, Fabricius, understand me, if you can.   [Exit MIRANDOLINA.]

FABRICIUS. He's a smart fellow who can understand her. One moment it seems that she wants me, the next that she does n't. She says that she is n't a flirt, but she wants to do as she pleases. I don't know what to say. We shall see. She pleases me, I am fond of her and would join my interests to hers throughout my life. Ah. One has to close one's eyes and let some things slide. After all, guests come and go, but I always remain. I shall have the best advantage after all.   [Exit FABRICIUS.]

[Enter the CAVALIER and a Servant.]

SERVANT. Your lordship, I have brought you this letter. CAVALIER. Bring me a cup of chocolate. [Exit the Servant; the CAVALIER opens the letter.] "Sienna, first of January, 1753." Who's writing? Horace Taccagni, my dear friend. "The tender friendship which binds me to you, makes me anxious to warn you of the necessity of your return to your native land. The Count Manna is dead." . . . Poor fellow! I'm sorry. "He has left one daughter, of marriageable age, heiress to thirty thousand pounds. All your friends would like such a fortune to fall to you and are busy arranging it." They need n't take that trouble for me because I don't want to know anything of it. And they know that I don't want women about me. And this dear friend of mine whom I know better than any one else bores me worst of all. [Tears up the letter.] What do I care about thirty thousand pounds? As long as I'm alone, less is enough. If I were married, a great deal more would n't suffice. A wife for me! Rather a thousand times a quartan fever.

[Enter the MARQUIS.]

MARQUIS. My friend, will you let me stay a little while with you? CAVALIER. You honor me. MARQUIS. At least you and I can talk confidentially; but that ass of a Count is n't good enough to be in our society. CAVALIER. My dear Marquis, excuse me; but respect others, if you want to be respected. MARQUIS. You know my character. I am courteous to every one; but I can't stand that fellow. CAVALIER. You can't endure him merely because he is your rival in love. Shame on you! A gentleman of your station in love with an innkeeper. The idea of a man as intelligent as you running after women! MARQUIS. My dear Cavalier, she has bewitched me. CAVALIER. Oh! Nonsense; folly. What enchantments has she? Why don't women bewitch me? Their witcheries consist in their personal charms, and in their flatteries; and he who stands afar off as I do, is in no danger of being unduly influenced. MARQUIS. Enough! Sometimes I think so, and then again I don't. What's annoying and disturbing me now is the steward of my country-house. CAVALIER. Has he done you some mean trick? MARQUIS. He has n't lived up to his word.

[Enter the Servant with the chocolate.]

CAVALIER [to Servant]. I don't like it. Get me another, right away. SERVANT. At present there is n't any other in the house, your lordship. CAVALIER. You must get it. [To the

MARQUIS]. If you would be so good as to accept this. . . .

MARQUIS [takes the chocolate and drinks it without ceremony, keeping on talking and drinking at the same time]. This overseer of mine, as I told you . . . [drinks] . . .

CAVALIER [aside]. And I shall go without.

MARQUIS. He promised to send me by post . . . [drinks] . . . ten pounds . . .

CAVALIER [aside]. Now he comes with a second thrust.

MARQUIS. And he has not sent it to me . . . [drinks]. The point is . . . the point is . . . [finishes drinking] . . . Here! [giving the glass to the Servant]. The point is that I'm in great difficulty, and I don't know what to do.

CAVALIER. A week more, a week less —

MARQUIS. But you, who are a gentleman, know what it means to keep one's word. I am in difficulties, and by Jove! I am utterly powerless.

CAVALIER. I'm sorry to see you unhappy. [Aside.] If I knew how to get out of it honorably.

MARQUIS. It would put you out, would it, to do me the favor for a week?

CAVALIER. Dear Marquis, if I could, I would help you out willingly; if I had it, I would offer it at once. I'm expecting some, but I don't happen to have any now.

MARQUIS. You would n't have me think you are without money.

CAVALIER [showing a sequin and some small change of various denominations]. See. Behold all my riches. They don't amount to two sequins.

MARQUIS. That is a gold sequin.

CAVALIER. Yes, it's my last; I have n't any more.

MARQUIS. Lend it to me and meanwhile I'll see . . .

CAVALIER. But then I —

MARQUIS. What are you afraid of? I'll pay you back.

CAVALIER [giving him the sequin]. I don't know what to say; help yourself.

MARQUIS [taking the sequin and going]. I have some pressing business, friend; I am bound at present; I'll meet you again at dinner.

CAVALIER. Fine! The Marquis wanted to extort twenty sequins from me and then he is contented with one. After all it does n't matter much if I do lose a sequin, and if he did n't pay it back he would n't bore me any more. What displeases me most is that he drank my chocolate. What impudence. And then, "I am who I am, I am a gentleman." Oh, most polite gentleman!

[Enter MIRANDOLINA with the linen.]

MIRANDOLINA [entering with some constraint]. May I come in, your lordship?

CAVALIER [harshly]. What do you want?

MIRANDOLINA [coming forward a little]. Look, here is some better linen.

CAVALIER [indicating the table]. Very well. Put it down here.

MIRANDOLINA. I beg you to be so good as to see if it is to your liking.

CAVALIER. What kind of stuff is it?

MIRANDOLINA [coming forward a little more]. The sheets are of fine linen.

CAVALIER. Fine linen?

MIRANDOLINA. Yes, sir; ten shillings a yard. Look at it.

CAVALIER. I did n't want anything so nice as all that. It would have been enough so long as it was something better than you gave me at first.

MIRANDOLINA. I made these pieces for people of rank and merit; for those who know how to appreciate them; and indeed, your lordship, I'll let you have them, seeing it's you. I would n't give them to any one else.

CAVALIER. Seeing it's you. The usual compliment.

MIRANDOLINA. Look at the table service.

CAVALIER. Oh! This Flanders linen, when it's washed, is very much spoiled. It is n't necessary to soil them on my account.

MIRANDOLINA. With a gentleman of your quality I don't consider such little things. I have several of these napkins and I shall keep them for your lordship.

CAVALIER [aside]. I can't deny that she's an obliging woman.

MIRANDOLINA [aside]. Indeed, he has a surly face which shows that women don't attract him.

CAVALIER. Give my linen to my valet, or put it down some place there. It is n't necessary that you put yourself out on my account.

MIRANDOLINA. Oh, I'm never putting myself out, when I serve gentlemen of such distinguished merit.

CAVALIER. Well, well, I don't need anything more. [Aside.] She wants to flatter me. Women! Every one of them is just like this.

MIRANDOLINA. I'll put it in the alcove?

CAVALIER [seriously]. Yes, wherever you please.

MIRANDOLINA. Oh, this is a hard proposition! I'm afraid I'll accomplish nothing. [Goes to put away the linen.]

CAVALIER [aside]. Simpletons hear these fine words, they believe those who say them, and they fall.

MIRANDOLINA [returning without the linen]. What would you like to order for dinner?

CAVALIER. I'll eat whatever there is.

MIRANDOLINA. I would like to know your preference. If you like one thing better than another, speak up.

CAVALIER. If I wish anything, I'll tell the waiter.

MIRANDOLINA. But in these matters men don't have the care and patience we women do. If a little ragout, any sauce would please you, be so kind as to tell me.

CAVALIER. Thank you; but by talking this way you are n't going to succeed in doing with me what you have done with the Count and the Marquis.

MIRANDOLINA. Why mention the folly of those two gentlemen? They come to my inn to lodge and then they claim they want to court the mistress of the inn. I have other things to do besides paying attention to their idle talk. I'm trying to act according to my best interests. If I humor them I do it to keep their custom, and then, to cap the climax, when I see how they're taken in, I laugh like a mad woman.

CAVALIER. Good. Your frankness delights me.

MIRANDOLINA. Oh! I don't have any other good qualities?

CAVALIER. But notwithstanding, you know how to pretend with those who pay you attention.

MIRANDOLINA. I pretend? Heaven help me. Ask these two gentlemen, who are infatuated with me, if I have ever given them a sign of affection; if I have ever jested with them in such a way that they could with reason be flattered. I don't treat them rudely, because my interests won't allow it, but I don't come far from it. I can't bear the sight of these effeminate men; I abhor them just as I do women who run after men. Do you see? I am not a girl. I am several years old; I am not beautiful, but I have had some good chances; and yet I have never married, because I thoroughly value my freedom.

CAVALIER. Oh, yes, freedom is a splendid treasure.

MIRANDOLINA. And so many lose it foolishly.

CAVALIER. I know very well what I'm about. Enough!

MIRANDOLINA. Has your lordship a wife?

CAVALIER. Heaven, no, nor children. I'm not fond of women.

MIRANDOLINA. Good. May you always keep that attitude. Women, sir — But then, it is n't just the thing for me to speak ill of them.

CAVALIER. On the contrary you are the first I ever heard speak so.

MIRANDOLINA. I'll say it: we innkeepers see and hear a good deal; and indeed I pity the men who fear our sex.

CAVALIER [aside]. She is a queer piece.

MIRANDOLINA [pretends she wants to go]. With your excellency's permission.

CAVALIER. You are in a hurry to go?

MIRANDOLINA. I would n't want to be troublesome.

CAVALIER. Oh, no, you please and amuse me.

MIRANDOLINA. Do you see, sir? I act just the same with the others. I stay a few minutes; I am rather merry, I make a few little jests to amuse them and all at once they think . . . I meant it; and they make desperate love to me.

CAVALIER. That happens, because you have good manners.

MIRANDOLINA [*with a curtsy*]. You are too kind, your lordship.

CAVALIER. And do they fall in love?

MIRANDOLINA. Just see what weakness! To fall suddenly in love with a woman!

CAVALIER. That's something I've never been able to comprehend.

MIRANDOLINA. What splendid strength! What splendid manliness.

CAVALIER. What frailty! Oh, degenerate human race!

MIRANDOLINA. That is the way men should think. Sir Cavalier, give me your hand.

CAVALIER. Why do you want that?

MIRANDOLINA. Be so kind if you will condescend; see, I'm clean.

CAVALIER. Here it is.

MIRANDOLINA. This is the first time I've had the honor of taking the hand of a man who thought truly as a man.

CAVALIER [*withdrawing his hand*]. Come, enough!

MIRANDOLINA. Now, just see here. If I'd taken the hand of one of those silly gentlemen, he would have thought at once that I was infatuated with him. He would have fainted. I should n't allow them the slightest liberty for all the gold in the world. They don't know how to live. What a fine thing it is to express one's thoughts freely, without affectation, without hard feelings, and without so much foolishness. Your excellency, pardon my impertinence; where I can serve you, command me freely; and I shall have in those services for you something I have never had in serving any other person in this world.

CAVALIER. Why have you taken such a great liking to me?

MIRANDOLINA. Because, besides your worth, besides your station in life, I am at least sure that I can converse with you freely, without any suspicion that I'm trying to make a bad use of my attentions, and that you look at me as a servant, without bothering me with ridiculous pretensions, with grotesque affectations.

CAVALIER [*aside*]. I don't understand that extraordinary character of hers.

MIRANDOLINA [*aside*]. The satyr will gradually become tamed.

CAVALIER. Come, now, if you have some other things to look after, don't stay on my account.

MIRANDOLINA. Yes, sir, I'm going to see to the housework. It's my love and my pastime. If you wish anything, I'll send the waiter.

CAVALIER. Very well. . . . If sometime you should come, too, I'd willingly see you.

MIRANDOLINA. Indeed, I don't go into the guests' rooms, but I'll come sometime to yours.

CAVALIER. To mine . . . why?

MIRANDOLINA. Because, your lordship, you please me very much.

CAVALIER. I please you?

MIRANDOLINA. You please me because you are n't effeminate, because you are n't one of those who fall in love. [*Aside.*] May my nose drop off, if he does n't fall in love before to-morrow. [*Exit* MIRANDOLINA.]

CAVALIER [*alone*]. Eh! I know what I'm doing. Women? Away with them. She would be one of those who could make me love her more than any one else. That truth, that freedom of speech is a thing too little found. She has something or other out of the ordinary about her, but I would n't let myself fall in love with her for that reason. For a little amusement I'd rather be in her company than in any one else's. But to court her? To lose my freedom? But there's no danger. Fools, fools, those people who fall in love with women. [*Exit the* CAVALIER.]

[*Enter* MIRANDOLINA *and the* MARQUIS.]

MARQUIS. May I come in? May I?

[*The* MARQUIS *pulls out of his pocket a fine silk handkerchief, unfolds it, and pretends to wipe his forehead.*]

MIRANDOLINA. A fine handkerchief, Marquis!

MARQUIS. Ah. What do you think of it? Is n't it beautiful? Have n't I good taste?

MIRANDOLINA. Certainly the best taste.

MARQUIS. Have you ever seen any so beautiful?

MIRANDOLINA. It is superb. I have never seen its like.

MARQUIS. It comes from London.

MIRANDOLINA. It is beautiful; it pleases me very much.

MARQUIS. Then I have good taste? I tell you the Count does n't know how to spend. He throws his money away and he never buys a present that's in good taste.

MIRANDOLINA. The Marquis is a connoisseur, he can distinguish, understand, see, appreciate.

MARQUIS [folding the handkerchief carefully]. One must fold this well so as not to spoil it. This sort of thing has to be taken great care of. Here, take it.

[He gives it to MIRANDOLINA.]

MIRANDOLINA. You want me to put it in your room?

MARQUIS. No; put it in yours.

MIRANDOLINA. Why in mine?

MARQUIS. Because . . . I'm giving it to you.

MIRANDOLINA. Your lordship, pardon me —

MARQUIS. No matter, I give it you. . . .

MIRANDOLINA. But I don't want it.

MARQUIS. Don't make me angry.

MIRANDOLINA. Oh, if that's the case, the Marquis knows my disposition; I don't want to displease any one. So as not to make you angry, I'll take it.

[Enter the COUNT.]

COUNT. I was looking for you.

MIRANDOLINA. I'm here.

MARQUIS [aside to MIRANDOLINA]. Look here. Show the Count the handkerchief.

MIRANDOLINA [showing the handkerchief to the COUNT]. See, Sir Count, the beautiful gift the Marquis has made me.

COUNT. Congratulations! Bravo, Marquis!

MARQUIS. Oh, it's nothing at all, nothing at all. Mere nothings. Put it back, away; I don't want you to mention it. I don't want people to know what I do.

MIRANDOLINA [aside]. He does n't want people to know and yet he makes me show it. His pride vies with his poverty.

COUNT [to MIRANDOLINA]. By your leave, I'd like to say a word.

MIRANDOLINA. Pray, speak freely.

MARQUIS. You'll spoil that handkerchief if you put it in your pocket.

MIRANDOLINA. Oh, I shall put it in a wrapper, so it won't be soiled.

COUNT [to MIRANDOLINA]. See this little jewel set with diamonds.

MIRANDOLINA. Very beautiful.

COUNT. It's the companion to the earrings I gave you.

MIRANDOLINA. Certainly it's like them, but it's more beautiful too.

MARQUIS [aside]. The Count be hanged with his diamonds and his money, and may the deuce take him.

COUNT [to MIRANDOLINA]. Now, that you may have an ornament to match, I'm going to give you the jewel.

MIRANDOLINA. I absolutely won't take it.

COUNT. Don't treat me so discourteously.

MIRANDOLINA. Oh, I never do that. So as not to displease you, I'll take it. [To the MARQUIS.] Ah, what do you think of it, Marquis? Is n't it elegant?

MARQUIS. Of its kind the handkerchief is in much better taste.

COUNT. Yes, but between kind and kind there is quite a distance.

MARQUIS. A fine thing! To boast in public of your great outlay.

COUNT. Yes, yes, you give your gifts in secret.

MIRANDOLINA [aside]. I can well say and with truth that where there are two litigants the third person gets the profit.

MARQUIS. Count, Count, you'll pay me for this.

COUNT. What are you complaining about?

MARQUIS. I am who I am, and I won't be treated so. Enough . . . a handkerchief of that kind! Mirandolina hold it dear. Handkerchiefs of that kind you don't run across every day. Diamonds you may get, but handkerchiefs of that kind you won't get. [Exit the MARQUIS.]

MIRANDOLINA [aside]. Oh, what a fool!

COUNT. Dear Mirandolina, you are n't displeased with what I do.

MIRANDOLINA. Not at all, sir.

COUNT. I do it for your sake. I do it in

order to bring profit and customers. Besides, I am yours; yours is my heart, and yours are my riches, and I place them all freely at your disposal. [*Exit the* COUNT.]
MIRANDOLINA [*alone*]. With all his riches, with all his gifts he'll never succeed in making me love him; and much less will the Marquis with his ridiculous protection. If I had to attach myself to one of these two it would certainly be to the one who spends the most money. But the one does n't concern me any more than the other. I am bound to make the Cavalier di Ripafratta fall in love with me, and a jewel twice as fine as this would n't give me half so much pleasure. I'll try; I know I have n't skill, but I'll try. The Count and the Marquis meanwhile will leave me in peace and I'll have leisure to be in the Cavalier's society. Suppose he does n't yield! Ah, but who can resist a woman when he gives her time to use her art. Who runs away does n't have to fear conquest; but he who loiters, who listens and is pleased, must sooner or later fall in spite of himself.
[*Exit* MIRANDOLINA.]

ACT II

The CAVALIER'S *room with table laid for dinner, and chairs.*

[*Enter the* CAVALIER, *who walks about with a book. Servant.* FABRICIUS *enters and puts the soup on the table.*]

FABRICIUS [*to the Servant*]. Tell your master, if he is ready for dinner, that the soup is on the table.
SERVANT [*to* FABRICIUS]. You might just as well tell him.
FABRICIUS. He's such a queer fellow, that I don't say anything to him unless I have to.
SERVANT. And yet he is n't so bad. Of course he can't bear the sight of women; but on the other hand he's most agreeable to men.
FABRICIUS [*aside*]. He can't bear the sight of women. Poor fool! He does n't know what's good when he sees it.
[*Exit* FABRICIUS.]

SERVANT. Your lordship, if you please, dinner is served.
[*The* CAVALIER *puts away the book and goes and sits down at the table.*]
CAVALIER [*to the Servant*]. This morning dinner seemed to be served much earlier than usual.
[*The Servant stands behind the* CAVALIER'S *chair with a napkin under his arm*].
SERVANT. This room has been served first. The Count d'Albafiorita grumbled because he wanted to be served first, but the mistress wanted your lordship to be served first.
CAVALIER. I am much obliged for the attentions she shows me.
SERVANT. She is a very accomplished woman, your lordship. In all the world I've seen, I've never found a politer innkeeper than she.
CAVALIER [*turning a little backward*]. She pleases you, then, eh?
SERVANT. If it were n't for wronging my master, I would like to enter her service as a waiter.
CAVALIER. Poor fool! What would you want her to do yith you?
[*Gives him the plate and he changes it*].
SERVANT. A woman of that sort, I'd like to serve like a little dog.
[*Goes for a dish.*]
CAVALIER. By Jove. She bewitches them all. It would be funny if she should bewitch me too. Cheer up; to-morrow I'm going to Leghorn. Let her do her worst for to-day, but she will discover I'm not so weak. It takes more than that to overcome my dislike for women.
SERVANT [*entering with the boiled meat and another dish*]. The mistress said that if you did n't like the fowl, she would send in a pigeon.
CAVALIER. This is all right. What's that you've got?
SERVANT. The mistress told me that I should tell her whether this sauce suited your lordship, for she made it with her own hands.
CAVALIER. This woman is becoming

more and more obliging. [*Tastes it.*] It is delicious. Tell her that I like it and I thank her.

SERVANT. I'll tell her, your lordship.

CAVALIER. Go, tell her at once.

SERVANT. At once. [*Aside.*] What a miracle? He sends a compliment to a woman! [*Exit Servant.*]

CAVALIER [*alone*]. It is a delicious sauce. I have never tasted a better. [*Goes on eating.*] Certainly, if Mirandolina always does this she will always have patrons. Good table, good linen. And then I can't deny that she is kind; but what I esteem more in her is her frankness. Oh, what a splendid thing is frankness! Why can't I bear the sight of women? Because they are false, wheedling. But that fine frankness! Ah, me . . .

[*Enter the Servant.*]

SERVANT. The mistress thanks you for your kindness in appreciating her humble efforts.

CAVALIER. Bravo, master of ceremonies, bravo.

SERVANT. Now she is making another dish with her hands, but I don't know what it is.

CAVALIER. She is making it?

SERVANT. Yes, sir.

CAVALIER. Give me something to drink.

SERVANT. Yes, sir. [*Goes to get the liquor.*]

CAVALIER. Well, now, I'll have to reciprocate generously. She is overly polite; I'll have to pay double. I must treat her well, but I must go away soon. [*The Servant gives him the liquor.*] Tell me, is the Marquis at the table?

SERVANT. He has gone out, and hasn't been seen.

CAVALIER [*indicating he wants plate changed*]. Here.

SERVANT. Yes, sir.

[*Enter* MIRANDOLINA *with a plate in her hand.*]

MIRANDOLINA. May I come in?

CAVALIER. Who is here?

MIRANDOLINA. At your service.

CAVALIER. Take that plate from her.

MIRANDOLINA. Pardon me. Let me have the honor of putting it on the table with my own hands. [*Puts the food on the table.*]

CAVALIER. That is n't your duty.

MIRANDOLINA. Oh, sir, who am I; some fine lady? I am only the servant of whoever desires to come to my inn.

CAVALIER. What humility!

MIRANDOLINA. Of course, it would n't be difficult to serve all the tables, but I don't do it for certain reasons; I don't know whether you catch my meaning or not. As far as you are concerned, I come without scruples, and frankly.

CAVALIER. Thank you. What dish is that?

MIRANDOLINA. It is a little *ragout* I made with my own hands.

CAVALIER. It will be good. If you have made it, it must be good.

MIRANDOLINA. Oh, you are exceedingly kind, sir. I don't know how to do anything well. But I would like to know how to suit so accomplished a gentleman.

CAVALIER [*aside*]. To-morrow to Leghorn. — If you have anything to do, don't put yourself out for me.

MIRANDOLINA. Not at all, sir. The house is well provided with cooks and servants. I would like it if you would see if the dish is to your taste.

CAVALIER. Gladly. At once. [*He tastes it.*] Splendid. Delicious. Oh, what a flavor! I don't know what it is.

MIRANDOLINA. Oh, I have some special secrets. These hands know how to make some fine things.

CAVALIER [*to the Servant with some passion*]. I would like something to drink.

MIRANDOLINA. You should drink a good wine after that dish.

CAVALIER [*to Servant*]. Give me some Burgundy.

MIRANDOLINA. Fine! Burgundy is delicious. In my opinion it is the best wine one can drink with food.

[*The Servant puts the bottle on the table with a glass.*]

CAVALIER. Your taste is good in everything.

MIRANDOLINA. Indeed, I have been mistaken few times.

CAVALIER. And yet you are mistaken this time.

MIRANDOLINA. In what, sir?

CAVALIER. In believing I deserve special favor at your hands.

MIRANDOLINA [sighing]. Oh, Sir Cavalier, . . .

CAVALIER [changing his tone]. What's the matter? Why these sighs?

MIRANDOLINA. I'll tell you. I am just as attentive to every one and it makes me feel bad when I think that some are ungrateful.

CAVALIER [complacently]. I won't be ungrateful.

MIRANDOLINA. I don't pretend to acquire merit in your eyes, merely by doing my duty.

CAVALIER. No, no, I understand very well. I am not so uncouth as you think me. You won't have to complain of me. [Turns the wine into the glass.]

MIRANDOLINA. But, — sir, — I don't understand.

CAVALIER [drinks]. To your health.

MIRANDOLINA. Very much obliged. You do me exceeding honor.

CAVALIER. This wine is delicious.

MIRANDOLINA. Burgundy is my passion.

CAVALIER [offering the wine]. It is at your service.

MIRANDOLINA. Oh, thanks, sir.

CAVALIER. Have you dined?

MIRANDOLINA. Yes, your lordship.

CAVALIER. Don't you want a little glass?

MIRANDOLINA. I don't deserve these attentions.

CAVALIER. Indeed, I give it to you willingly.

MIRANDOLINA. I don't know what to say. I accept your politeness.

CAVALIER [to the Servant]. Get a glass.

MIRANDOLINA [taking the CAVALIER'S glass]. No, no, if I may, I'll take this.

CAVALIER. I beg you, I have been served from it.

MIRANDOLINA. I shall drink to your beauty.

[Laughing, the Servant puts the other glass in the saucer.]

CAVALIER [aside]. Eh, rascal! [Pours out the wine.]

MIRANDOLINA. But it is some time since I have eaten; I am afraid it will hurt me.

CAVALIER. There is no danger.

MIRANDOLINA. If you could favor me with a small bit of bread.

CAVALIER. Gladly. [Gives her a bit of bread.] Here!

[MIRANDOLINA, with the cup in one hand and the bread in the other, makes a pretense of being ill at ease and does not know what to do with the bread and wine.]

CAVALIER. You are ill at ease. Don't you want to sit down.

MIRANDOLINA. I don't deserve so much, sir.

CAVALIER. Come, come, we are alone. [To the Servant.] Get her a chair.

SERVANT [aside]. My master must be going to die; he has never acted like that before. [Goes to get the chair.]

MIRANDOLINA. If the Count and the Marquis should know, poor me!

CAVALIER. Why?

MIRANDOLINA. A hundred times they have wanted me to oblige them by eating or drinking, and I have never wanted to do it.

CAVALIER. Come, now, sit down.

MIRANDOLINA. To obey you. [Sits down and dips her bread in the wine.]

CAVALIER [aside to Servant]. Listen! Don't tell any one that the innkeeper is sitting at my table.

SERVANT. Don't worry. [Aside.] This new aspect of his surprises me.

MIRANDOLINA. To the health of everything which pleases the Cavalier.

CAVALIER. Thank you, my polite hostess . . .

MIRANDOLINA. This toast does n't refer to women.

CAVALIER. No? Why?

MIRANDOLINA. Because I know you can't bear the sight of them.

CAVALIER. It is true; I have never been able to.

MIRANDOLINA. May you always be of that mind.

CAVALIER. I would not wish. . . [He looks at the Servant.]

MIRANDOLINA. What, sir?

CAVALIER. Listen. [He whispers in her ear.] I would n't want you to make me change my nature.

MIRANDOLINA. I, sir? How?

CAVALIER [to the Servant]. Go away.

SERVANT. Is something wanted?

CAVALIER. Have two eggs cooked for me and when they are done, bring them in.

SERVANT. How do you want them?

CAVALIER. As you please, but hurry up.

SERVANT. I understand. [Exit Servant.]

CAVALIER. Mirandolina, you are a polite young woman.

MIRANDOLINA. Ah, sir, you're making fun of me.

CAVALIER. Listen. I want to say something true, very true, which will redound to your glory.

MIRANDOLINA. I will listen gladly.

CAVALIER. You are the first woman in this world whose society I could endure with pleasure for any length of time.

MIRANDOLINA. I shall tell you, Sir Cavalier, my worth, indeed, is little, but at times there exist these kindred natures which meet. This sympathy, this affinity, lives, too, between persons who don't know each other. I, too, feel for you what I have never felt for another.

CAVALIER. I fear that you wish to destroy my peace of mind.

MIRANDOLINA. Come, sir, if you are a wise man, act like one. Don't fall into the weaknesses of others. Indeed, if I know it, I can't come here again. Besides, I feel something or other in me which I have never felt before, but I don't want to lose my senses over the men, and much less over one who hates women, and who, perhaps to try me, and then make fun of me, comes with a new style of talk to tempt me. Sir, favor me with a little Burgundy.

CAVALIER. Enough —

[Pours the wine into a glass.]

MIRANDOLINA. He is on the very point of falling.

CAVALIER. Here.

[Gives her the glass with the wine.]

MIRANDOLINA. Much obliged. But are n't you going to drink with me?

CAVALIER. Yes, I shall. [Aside.] It would be better if I should get drunk. One devil would drive out the other.

[Turns the wine into his glass.]

MIRANDOLINA [coyly]. Cavalier . . .

CAVALIER. What is it?

MIRANDOLINA. Clink. [She makes her glass clink against his.] Here's to good friends.

CAVALIER [a little tenderly]. Here's to them.

MIRANDOLINA. Here's to those — who like each other — sincerely. Clink.

CAVALIER. Here's to you.

[Enter the MARQUIS.]

MARQUIS. I'm here, too. Who's health is it?

CAVALIER [in a different tone]. What, Marquis?

MARQUIS. Excuse me, friend. I called. There is no one here?

MIRANDOLINA [trying to leave]. With your permission.

CAVALIER [to MIRANDOLINA]. Stay. [To the MARQUIS.] I don't take so much liberty with you.

MARQUIS. Begging your pardon. We are friends. I thought you were alone. I am glad to see you beside our adorable mistress. Ah, what do you say, Is n't she a masterpiece?

MIRANDOLINA. Sir, I was here to serve the Cavalier. I felt a little ill and he braced me up with a glass of Burgundy.

MARQUIS [to the CAVALIER]. Is that Burgundy?

CAVALIER. Yes, it is.

MARQUIS. But, the real thing?

CAVALIER. At least, I paid for such.

MARQUIS. I understand wines. Let me taste it, and I'll tell you whether it's genuine or not.

CAVALIER [calling]. Look here!

[Enter the Servant with the eggs.]

CAVALIER [to Servant]. A little glass for the Marquis.

MARQUIS. Not such a little glass either. Burgundy is n't a cordial. To judge it one has to drink enough of it.

SERVANT. Here are the eggs.

[About to place them on the table.]

CAVALIER. I don't want anything more.

MARQUIS. What dish is that?

CAVALIER. Eggs. I don't want them.

[The Servant takes them away.]

MIRANDOLINA. Marquis, with the permission of the Cavalier, taste this little *ragout* I made with my own hands.

MARQUIS. Oh, yes. Look here! A chair.

[*The Servant brings him a chair and he puts the glass in the saucer*]. A fork.

CAVALIER. Go, get him a cover.

[*The Servant goes to get it.*]

MIRANDOLINA. Sir, I am better, I'm going.

MARQUIS. Do me the pleasure of staying a little while.

MIRANDOLINA. But, sir, I have to attend to my business, and then the Cavalier . . .

MARQUIS [*to the* CAVALIER]. You don't mind if she stays a little while?

CAVALIER. What do you want of her?

MARQUIS. I wish to have you drink a little glass of Cyprian wine which — as long as you are in the world — you'll never taste its like. I want Mirandolina to taste it, too, and give her opinion.

CAVALIER [*to* MIRANDOLINA]. Come, to please the Marquis, stay.

MIRANDOLINA. The Marquis will excuse me.

MARQUIS. You don't want to taste it?

MIRANDOLINA. Some other time, your excellency.

CAVALIER. Come, stay.

MIRANDOLINA [*to the* CAVALIER]. You bid me?

CAVALIER. I tell you to stay.

MIRANDOLINA [*sitting*]. I obey.

CAVALIER [*aside*]. She is always putting me under more and more obligations.

MARQUIS [*eating*]. Oh, what a dish! Oh, what a *ragout!* Oh, what savor! Oh, what taste!

CAVALIER [*aside to* MIRANDOLINA]. The Marquis will be jealous because you are near me.

MIRANDOLINA [*aside to the* CAVALIER]. It does n't make the slightest difference to me.

CAVALIER [*aside to* MIRANDOLINA]. You are a man-hater?

MIRANDOLINA [*aside to the* CAVALIER]. As you are a woman-hater.

CAVALIER [*aside to* MIRANDOLINA]. These enemies of mine are avenging themselves on me.

MIRANDOLINA [*aside to the* CAVALIER]. How, sir?

CAVALIER [*aside to* MIRANDOLINA]. Eh, rogue! You will see very well.

MARQUIS. Friend, to your health.

[*Drinks the Burgundy.*]

CAVALIER. Well, how is it?

MARQUIS. With your leave, it is n't worth anything at all. You should taste my Cyprian wine.

CAVALIER. But where is your Cyprian wine?

MARQUIS. I have it here. I have brought it with me. I want us all to enjoy it. See.

[*Draws out a very small bottle.*]

MIRANDOLINA. Judging from what I see, you don't want the wine to go to our heads.

MARQUIS. That? If you drink it by drops, it is like cordial. [*Opens the bottle.*] Look here! The glasses.

[*Servant carries some glasses for the Cyprian wine.*]

MARQUIS [*covering the bottle with his hand*]. They are altogether too large. Have n't you any smaller?

CAVALIER [*to Servant*]. Bring those used for cordial.

MIRANDOLINA. I think it would be enough to smell it.

MARQUIS. Ah, fine! It has a comforting odor. [*He puts his nose to it.*]

[*Servant brings in three little glasses in the saucer.*]

MARQUIS [*pours very slowly and does not fill the glasses; he pours out for the* CAVALIER, MIRANDOLINA, *and himself, corking the bottle well*]. What nectar! What ambrosia! What distilled manna! [*Drinks.*]

CAVALIER [*aside to* MIRANDOLINA]. What does this miserable stuff seem like to you?

MIRANDOLINA [*aside to the* CAVALIER]. Rinsings of the flask.

MARQUIS [*to the* CAVALIER]. Ah. What are you saying?

CAVALIER. Good! Splendid!

MARQUIS. Are you pleased with it, Mirandolina?

MIRANDOLINA. For my part, sir, I cannot dissimulate. I don't like it; I find it bad and I can't say it's good. I compliment the man who knows how to pretend.

But he who can pretend in one thing will know how to pretend in another also.

CAVALIER [aside]. She rebukes me; I don't see why.

MARQUIS. Mirandolina, you don't understand this kind of wine. I pity you. Indeed, you appreciated the handkerchief I gave you and you were pleased with it, but you don't appreciate my Cyprian wine. [Finishes drinking.]

MIRANDOLINA [aside to the CAVALIER]. You see how he boasts.

CAVALIER [aside to MIRANDOLINA]. I would n't do that.

MIRANDOLINA [aside to the CAVALIER]. Your boast is in despising women.

CAVALIER [aside to MIRANDOLINA]. And yours in conquering all men.

MIRANDOLINA [coyly aside to the CAVALIER]. All, no.

CAVALIER [with some passion aside to MIRANDOLINA]. All, yes!

MARQUIS [to the Servant, who brings them to him on a saucer]. Look here. Three clean glasses.

MIRANDOLINA. I don't care for any more.

MARQUIS. No, no. Don't be afraid. I'm not doing this for you. [Pours the Cyprian wine into the three little glasses.] My good man, with the permission of your master, go to the Count d'Albafiorita and tell him from me in a loud tone of voice, so that every one can hear, that I ask him to taste a little of my Cyprian wine.

SERVANT. At your service. [Aside.] He certainly won't get drunk on it.
[Exit Servant.]

CAVALIER. Marquis, you are exceedingly generous.

MARQUIS. I? Ask Mirandolina.

MIRANDOLINA. Oh, certainly.

MARQUIS [to MIRANDOLINA]. Has the Cavalier seen the handkerchief?

MIRANDOLINA. No, he has n't.

MARQUIS [to the CAVALIER]. You should see it. [Putting back the bottle with a little wine left.] This little bit of balm I'll keep for this evening.

MIRANDOLINA. Take care that it does n't make you ill, Marquis.

MARQUIS [to MIRANDOLINA]. Ah, that does n't, but do you know what does?

MIRANDOLINA. What?

MARQUIS. Your beautiful eyes.

MIRANDOLINA. Really?

MARQUIS. My dear Cavalier, I'm desperately in love with her.

CAVALIER. You displease me.

MARQUIS. You have never had any experience in loving women. Oh, if you had, you would pity me.

CAVALIER. Yes, yes, I pity you.

MARQUIS. And I am as jealous as a beast. I let her stand near you, because I know what you are. With any other man I would n't allow it for a million pounds.

CAVALIER [aside]. This fellow begins to bore me.

[Enter the Servant with a bottle in a saucer.]

SERVANT [to the MARQUIS]. The Count thanks your excellency and sends you a bottle of Canary.

MARQUIS. Oh, oh. He would like to compare his Canary with my Cyprus. Let's see. Poor fool! It is miserable stuff; I know it by the smell.
[He gets up and takes the bottle in his hand.]

CAVALIER [to the MARQUIS]. You taste it first.

MARQUIS. I don't want to taste it at all. This is an impertinence that the Count has done me, just like so many others. He wants to outdo me, to make me angry, to make me do some bit of folly. But I swear by Heaven, I shall do one such act which will do for a hundred. Mirandolina, if you don't turn him out, something will happen. Some fine things will happen. He is a hot-headed fellow. I am who I am and I don't want to have to endure like insults.
[Exit the MARQUIS, taking away the bottle.]

CAVALIER. The poor Marquis is a madman.

MIRANDOLINA. Fearing lest his anger should ever make him ill, he's carried away the bottle to return it.

CAVALIER. He is a madman, I tell you. And you have made him such.

MIRANDOLINA. I am one of those who makes men mad?

CAVALIER [*troubled*]. Yes, indeed, you are. . . .

MIRANDOLINA. Sir, with your permission. [*Rises.*]

CAVALIER. Stay.

MIRANDOLINA [*going*]. Pardon me, I don't make any one mad.

CAVALIER. Listen.

[*Gets up, but remains at the table.*]

MIRANDOLINA. Pardon me.

CAVALIER [*in a commanding tone*]. Stay, I tell you.

MIRANDOLINA [*haughtily turning around*]. What do you want of me?

CAVALIER [*perplexed*]. Nothing. Drink another glass of Burgundy.

MIRANDOLINA. Come, now, sir, quick, quick, for I must be going.

CAVALIER. Sit down.

MIRANDOLINA. Standing up, standing up.

CAVALIER [*giving her the glass tenderly*]. Here.

MIRANDOLINA. I'll give a toast and then I must go immediately. A toast my grandmother taught me —

Live, thou Bacchus, live, thou love;
Ye do both us cheer, console,
One doth pass through throat to goal,
Other runs from eye to soul.
Drink I wine; those eyes of mine —
Them I use as thou dost thine.

[*Exit* MIRANDOLINA.]

CAVALIER. Bravo! Come here! Ah, rogue! She has fled. She has escaped and left me a hundred devils to torture me.

SERVANT [*to the* CAVALIER]. Do you wish the fruit to be served?

CAVALIER. Go to the devil.

[*Exit the Servant.*]

[*Alone.*]

" Drink I wine, those eyes of mine —
Them I use as thou dost —"

What mysterious sort of a toast is that? Ah, wretch, I know you. You want to strike me down, to assassinate me. But she does it with such grace! She knows well how to ingratiate herself. Devil, devil, you would make me endure the sight of her? No, I will go to Leghorn. I would n't

want ever to meet her again. She'll never cross my path again. Cursed women! I swear I'll never go where there are women any more. When I can, I'll insult women with the greatest pleasure in the world. Nevertheless, I have n't been able to insult Mirandolina. She has conquered me with civility, so that I find myself almost obliged to love her. But she is a woman; I don't want to trust myself. I must go away. I must go away to-morrow. But if I wait till to-morrow? If I come and sleep in the house this evening, who can assure me Mirandolina won't finish ruining me? [*Thinks.*] Yes, I must act resolutely like a man.

[*Reënter the Servant.*]

SERVANT. Sir.

CAVALIER. What do you want?

SERVANT. The Marquis is in the public room and awaits you, because he desires to speak to you.

CAVALIER. What does that fool want? He can't get money out of me. Let him wait, and when he's tired of waiting, he will go away. Go to the waiter of the inn and tell him to bring my bill at once.

SERVANT [*on the point of departure*]. Yes, sir.

CAVALIER. Listen. Have everything packed in two hours.

SERVANT. You want to leave, perhaps?

CAVALIER. Yes. Bring me my sword and my hat without letting the Marquis see.

SERVANT. But if he sees me pack the trunks?

CAVALIER. Tell him what you will. Understand?

SERVANT [*aside*]. Oh, how much it pains me to leave Mirandolina.

[*Exit Servant.*]

CAVALIER [*alone*]. And yet it is true. I feel in leaving here a new uneasiness which I have never experienced before. It is so much worse for me to remain here. I must go away all the sooner. Yes, women, I shall always speak ill of you; yes, you have always done evil to us, even when you wished to do good.

[*Enter* FABRICIUS.]

FABRICIUS. Is it true, sir, that you wish your bill?

CAVALIER. Yes; have you made it out yet?

FABRICIUS. The mistress is doing it now.

CAVALIER. She makes out the bills?

FABRICIUS. Ah, always. Even when her father was living. She writes and knows how to keep accounts better than any clerk.

CAVALIER [*aside*]. What a singular woman she is!

FABRICIUS. But you wish to go away at once?

CAVALIER. Yes, my affairs are pressing.

FABRICIUS. I beg you remember the waiter.

CAVALIER. Bring me the bill, and I know what I ought to do.

FABRICIUS. Do you wish your account to be brought here?

CAVALIER. I want it here; I shan't go to the public room for the present.

FABRICIUS. You do well; that bore of a Marquis is in the public room. Good soul. He is in love with the innkeeper, but that's all the satisfaction he'll get. Mirandolina is to be my wife.

CAVALIER [*changing his tone*]. The bill.

FABRICIUS. Yes, sir, at once.

[*Exit* FABRICIUS.]

CAVALIER [*alone*]. Every one is smitten with Mirandolina. It is no wonder that I have begun to feel myself affected. But I will go away. I will overcome this strange power. Whom do I see? Mirandolina? What does she want of me? She has a sheet of paper in her hand. She's bringing me my bill. What shall I do? I must endure this last attack. I'll be gone from here in two hours.

[*Enter* MIRANDOLINA *with a sheet of paper in her hand.*]

MIRANDOLINA [*sadly*]. Sir!

CAVALIER. What is it, Mirandolina?

MIRANDOLINA [*standing in the background*]. Pardon me.

CAVALIER. Come here.

MIRANDOLINA. You asked for your bill; I have brought it.

CAVALIER. Give it here.

MIRANDOLINA. Here it is.

[*She wipes her eyes with her apron in giving the bill.*]

CAVALIER. What is the matter? Are you crying?

MIRANDOLINA. No, sir, the smoke got into my eyes.

CAVALIER. Smoke in your eyes? Oh, well. — How much does my bill come to? [*Reads.*] Ten shillings. For such generous hospitality for four days only ten shillings?

MIRANDOLINA. That is the bill.

CAVALIER. And the two special dishes you gave me this morning; they are not in the bill?

MIRANDOLINA. Pardon me. Whatever I give, I don't put in the bill.

CAVALIER. You make me a present of them?

MIRANDOLINA. Pardon the liberty. Accept them as an act of . . .

[*She covers her face making a pretense of crying.*]

CAVALIER. What is the matter?

MIRANDOLINA. I don't know whether it is the smoke or some sort of running of the eyes.

CAVALIER. I would not have had you suffer, cooking those two delicious dishes for me.

MIRANDOLINA. If it were that, I would suffer — gladly . . .

[*Pretending to be trying to keep from crying*].

CAVALIER [*aside*]. Oh, if I don't get away pretty soon! — Come, now, there's three pounds. Enjoy them for love of me and have pity on me — [*He becomes confused.*]

[MIRANDOLINA *without speaking falls as though she has fainted on a chair.*]

CAVALIER. Mirandolina. Alas! Mirandolina! She's fainted. Can it be that she is in love with me? But so soon? And why not? Am I not in love with her? Dear Mirandolina. . . . "Dear"? I say dear to a woman. But she fainted on my account. Oh, how beautiful you are! If I only had something to make her come to. I am not much in the society of women; I haven't got smelling-salts or vials. Who's there? There's no one? Quick — I'll go. Poor little girl. Blessings on you.   [*Goes out.*]

MIRANDOLINA. Now, then, he has given in at last. The weapons we use to conquer men are many. But when they are obstinate, the final blow, that's sure to win them, is fainting. He's coming back. He's coming back.   [*She lies as before.*]

CAVALIER [*returning with a jug of water*]. Look. Look. She has n't come to yet. Oh, certainly she loves me. Sprinkling water in her face ought to revive her. [*He sprinkles the water and she moves.*] Courage, courage. I am here, dear. I'll never leave you now.

[*Enter the Servant with the sword and hat.*]

SERVANT [*to the* CAVALIER]. Here are your sword and your hat.

CAVALIER [*to Servant*]. Go away.

SERVANT. The trunks . . .

CAVALIER. Go away; curse you.

SERVANT. Mirandolina.

CAVALIER. Go before I split your head. [*He threatens with the jug; the Servant goes.*] She has n't come to yet? Her forehead perspires. Come, dear Mirandolina, take courage, open your eyes. Speak to me freely.

[*Enter the* MARQUIS *and the* COUNT.]

MARQUIS. Cavalier?

COUNT. Friend?

CAVALIER [*aside*]. Curses!

MARQUIS [*becoming angry*]. Mirandolina?

MIRANDOLINA [*getting up*]. Alas!

MARQUIS. I have made her recover.

COUNT. I rejoice, Sir Cavalier.

MARQUIS. Fine for the gentleman who can't bear the sight of women.

CAVALIER. What impertinence!

COUNT. Have you given in?

CAVALIER. Go to the devil, all of you. [*He throws the jug down in the direction of the* COUNT *and the* MARQUIS *and breaks it. Exit the* CAVALIER *in a rage.*]

COUNT. The Cavalier has become a madman.   [*Exit the* COUNT.]

MARQUIS. I want satisfaction for this insult.   [*Exit the* MARQUIS.]

MIRANDOLINA. My task is done. His heart is on fire, in flames, in ashes. All I have to do is to complete my victory, to make my triumph public to the discomforture of presumptuous men, and to the honor of my sex.   [*Exit* MIRANDOLINA.]

ACT III

SCENE I. MIRANDOLINA'S *room with a little table and linen ready to iron.*

[*Enter* MIRANDOLINA.]

MIRANDOLINA. Now the time's past for amusing myself. I want to look after my business now. First I want to iron this linen, if it is dry. Oh, Fabricius.

FABRICIUS. Madam.

MIRANDOLINA. Do me a favor. Get me the hot flat-iron.

FABRICIUS. Yes, ma'am.
        [*With serious mien on the point of leaving.*]

MIRANDOLINA. Excuse me, if I bother you.

FABRICIUS [*offering to go*]. Not at all, madam. While I eat your bread I am under obligations to serve you.

MIRANDOLINA. Wait. Listen; you are not bound to help me in these things; but I know that you do it gladly for me and I — enough, I won't say anything more.

FABRICIUS. I would move heaven and earth for you. But I see that everything is thrown away.

MIRANDOLINA. Why thrown away? Perhaps I am ungrateful?

FABRICIUS. You don't pay any attention to poor men. The nobility pleases you overly much.

MIRANDOLINA. Ah, poor fool! If I could tell you everything! Go, go; get me the iron.

FABRICIUS. But I have seen it with these eyes of mine.

MIRANDOLINA. Go, go; less idle talk. Get me the iron.

FABRICIUS [*going*]. I'm going, I'm going, I will serve you for but little reward.

MIRANDOLINA [*pretending to speak to herself, but really so that she may be heard*]. With these men the better one likes them the worse one treats them.

FABRICIUS [*tenderly, turning around*]. What did you say?

MIRANDOLINA. Come, are you going to get me that iron?

FABRICIUS. Yes, I'll get it. [*Aside.*] I don't understand it at all. Now she lifts me up, now she throws me down. I don't understand it at all.   [*Exit* FABRICIUS.]

MIRANDOLINA [*alone*]. Poor fool! He can't help serving me in spite of himself. I almost burst out laughing to think of making men act according to my will. And that Cavalier who was such a woman-hater, now, if I wished I could make him do any little bit of folly I wanted to.

SERVANT [*entering*]. Mirandolina.

MIRANDOLINA. What is it, friend?

SERVANT. My master sends you his greetings. He told me to ask you how you are.

MIRANDOLINA. Tell him I am very well.

SERVANT. He says you should drink a little of this cordial which will make you feel ever so much better.

[*He gives her a little gold flask*].

MIRANDOLINA. This flask is gold?

SERVANT. Yes, madam, gold; I know it positively.

MIRANDOLINA. Why did n't he give me the cordial when that terrible faint came on?

SERVANT. He did n't have this flask then.

MIRANDOLINA. And how did he get it now?

SERVANT. Listen! In confidence! He sent me to call a goldsmith and he bought it and paid six pounds for it, and then he sent me to an apothecary to buy the spirits.

MIRANDOLINA. Ha! Ha! Ha!

SERVANT. You're laughing.

MIRANDOLINA. I'm laughing because he sends me the medicine after I have recovered from my illness.

SERVANT. It will be good for another time.

MIRANDOLINA. Come, I'll drink a little now for a preventive. [*Drinks.*] Here. [*She offers to give him the flask.*] Thank him.

SERVANT. Oh! The flask is yours.

MIRANDOLINA. How mine?

SERVANT. It's this way. My master bought it purposely for you.

MIRANDOLINA. Purposely for me?

SERVANT. For you; but hush.

MIRANDOLINA. Take him his flask and tell him that I thank him.

SERVANT. Ah, come.

MIRANDOLINA. I tell you to take it to him, that I don't want it.

SERVANT. You want to give him this insult?

MIRANDOLINA. Less idle talk. Do your duty. Take it.

SERVANT. I don't need anything more said to me. I'll carry it to him. [*Aside.*] What a woman. Refuses six pounds. I have never found one like her and it would be some trouble to do so.   [*Exit Servant.*]

MIRANDOLINA [*alone*]. Oh, he's cooked, done brown, twice baked. But just as what I've done with him, I've not done for my own interest; I want him to confess the power of women without being able to say that they are self-seeking and venial.

FABRICIUS [*entering; self-contained, with iron in his hand*]. Here's your iron.

MIRANDOLINA. Is it good and hot?

FABRICIUS. Yes, madam, it is.

MIRANDOLINA. What news is there?

FABRICIUS. This Cavalier sends embassies; he sends gifts. His servant told me so.

MIRANDOLINA. Yes, sir, he sent me a little gold flask and I sent it back to him.

FABRICIUS. You've sent it back?

MIRANDOLINA. That — Fabricius — that he may not say — Now, don't let us talk any more about it.

FABRICIUS. Dear Mirandolina, pardon me.

MIRANDOLINA. Go away, let me iron.

FABRICIUS. I'm not hindering you.

MIRANDOLINA. Go, get another iron ready and when it's hot bring it to me.

FABRICIUS. Yes, I'll go. Believe me, when I say . . .

MIRANDOLINA. Don't talk any more. You make me angry.

FABRICIUS. I'll keep still. [*Aside.*] She is a queer little body, but I am fond of her.

[*Exit* FABRICIUS.]

MIRANDOLINA [*alone*]. This too is fine. I'm acquiring merit in the eyes of Fabricius by having refused the Cavalier's gold flask. That is to say — I know how to live,

to act, to profit by everything, with good grace, nicely, and freely. As regards tact I don't need to say I wrong my sex.
[*Goes on ironing.*]

[*Enter the* CAVALIER.]

CAVALIER [*to himself in the background*]. See here. I did n't want to come here, but the devil dragged me.

MIRANDOLINA [*aside*]. See him. See him.
[*She looks out of the corner of her eyes and irons.*]

CAVALIER. Mirandolina?

MIRANDOLINA. Oh, Sir Cavalier! Your most humble servant. [*Ironing.*]

CAVALIER. How are you?

MIRANDOLINA. Very well, thank you.
[*Ironing without looking at him.*]

CAVALIER. I have reason to complain of you.

MIRANDOLINA. Why, sir?
[*Looking at him a little.*]

CAVALIER. Because you refused a little flask I sent you.

MIRANDOLINA. What did you want me to do with it? [*Ironing.*]

CAVALIER. Make use of it at need.

MIRANDOLINA. Thank Heaven, I'm not subject to fainting spells. What happened to-day never happened to me before.
[*Ironing.*]

CAVALIER. Dear Mirandolina, I hope I was n't the occasion of that disastrous accident.

MIRANDOLINA. Yes, I'm afraid you were precisely the cause of it.

CAVALIER [*passionately*]. I! Why?

MIRANDOLINA. You made me drink that cursed Burgundy and it made me ill.
[*Ironing angrily.*]

CAVALIER [*mortified*]. What? Is it possible?

MIRANDOLINA. It is certainly true. I'll never go into your room again. [*Ironing.*]

CAVALIER. I understand. You will never come into my room again. I understand the mystery. Yes, I understand it. But come there, and you will consider yourself happy.

MIRANDOLINA. This iron is n't very hot. [*In a loud tone of voice.*] Oh, Fabricius. If the other iron is hot, bring it in.

CAVALIER. Do me this favor, take this flask.

MIRANDOLINA. Indeed, sir, I'm not in the habit of taking gifts.
[*Ironing with displeasure.*]

CAVALIER. Yet you have taken them from the Count d'Albafiorita.

MIRANDOLINA. I had to in order not to displease him. [*Ironing.*]

CAVALIER. And yet you would wrong me and displease me?

MIRANDOLINA. What does it matter to one whom all womankind displeases? Indeed, he can't bear the sight of women.

CAVALIER. Oh, Mirandolina, I can't say that now.

MIRANDOLINA. Cavalier, has the moon affected your senses?

CAVALIER. My change is not dependent on the moon, I'm not a lunatic. That is a miracle caused by your beauty and your grace.

MIRANDOLINA Ha! Ha! Ha!
[*Laughs loudly and irons.*]

CAVALIER. You are laughing?

MIRANDOLINA. Don't you want me to laugh? You make fun of me and you don't want me to laugh?

CAVALIER. Ah, you little rogue! I make fun of you, eh? Come, take this bottle.

MIRANDOLINA. Thanks, thanks.
[*Ironing.*]

CAVALIER. Take it or you'll make me angry.

MIRANDOLINA [*calling loudly in an exaggerated way*]. Fabricius, the iron.

CAVALIER [*changing his voice*]. Will you take it, or won't you take it?

MIRANDOLINA. Fury, fury.
[*Takes the flask and with displeasure throws it into the clothes-basket.*]

CAVALIER. You throw it away in that fashion.

MIRANDOLINA [*calling loudly*]. Fabricius.

[*Enter* FABRICIUS *with iron.*]

FABRICIUS [*seeing the* CAVALIER, *he becomes jealous*]. I am here.

MIRANDOLINA [*taking the iron*]. Is the iron good and hot?

FABRICIUS [self-contained]. Yes, madam.

MIRANDOLINA [tenderly to FABRICIUS]. What is the matter that you seem so disturbed?

FABRICIUS. Nothing at all, mistress, nothing at all.

MIRANDOLINA [tenderly]. You are ill?

FABRICIUS. Give me the other iron if you want me to put it on the fire.

MIRANDOLINA [tenderly]. Indeed, I fear you are ill.

CAVALIER. Come, give him the iron and let him go.

MIRANDOLINA. I am fond of him, do you know that? He is my trusty waiter.

CAVALIER [angrily to himself]. I can stand no more.

MIRANDOLINA [giving the iron to FABRICIUS]. Here, my dear, heat it.

FABRICIUS [tenderly]. Mistress.

MIRANDOLINA. Come, come, quick.
[She turns him out.]

FABRICIUS [aside]. What way of acting is this? I feel I can't stand any more.
[Exit FABRICIUS.]

CAVALIER. Fine manners, fine manners, madam, to your waiter.

MIRANDOLINA. As for that, what would you have me say?

CAVALIER. It seems as if you were smitten with him.

MIRANDOLINA. I in love with a waiter? You make fine compliments, sir; I am not of such bad taste. When I wish to fall in love, I won't throw away my time so unprofitably. [Ironing.]

CAVALIER. You deserve the love of a king.

MIRANDOLINA. The king of spades or the king of diamonds. [Ironing.]

CAVALIER. Let us talk seriously and lay jesting aside.

MIRANDOLINA. You talk and I'll listen.
[Ironing.]

CAVALIER. Can't you stop ironing for a while?

MIRANDOLINA. Oh, pardon me. I must get this linen carefully prepared for tomorrow.

CAVALIER. Then this linen concerns you more than I do.

MIRANDOLINA. Surely. [Ironing.]

CAVALIER. And you even repeat it?

MIRANDOLINA. Of course, because I have to use this linen, but I can't count on you in any way.

CAVALIER. On the contrary, you may dispose of me freely.

MIRANDOLINA. Oh. You cannot bear the sight of women.

CAVALIER. Don't torment me any more. You have been avenged enough. I esteem you. I esteem women who are of your stamp, if there are any. I esteem you, I love you, and I ask you to pity me.

MIRANDOLINA. Yes, sir, we'll tell them all about it.
[Ironing hastily, lets fall a cuff.]

CAVALIER [picking up the cuff and giving it to her]. Believe me —

MIRANDOLINA. Don't put yourself out.

CAVALIER. You deserve to be served.

MIRANDOLINA [laughing loudly]. Ha! Ha! Ha!

CAVALIER. Are you laughing?

MIRANDOLINA. I'm laughing because you are making fun of me.

CAVALIER. Mirandolina, I can stand no more.

MIRANDOLINA. Do you feel ill?

CAVALIER. Yes, I feel faint.

MIRANDOLINA [giving his flask to him with displeasure]. Take your cordial.

CAVALIER. Don't treat me so harshly. Believe me ; I love you, I swear it. [Tries to take her hand and she burns him with the iron]. Ouch!

MIRANDOLINA. Excuse me, I didn't do it purposely.

CAVALIER. Patience! That is nothing. You have given me a far worse burn.

MIRANDOLINA. Where, sir?

CAVALIER. In my heart.

MIRANDOLINO [calling laughingly]. Fabricius?

CAVALIER. For mercy sakes, don't call that fellow.

MIRANDOLINA. But I need another iron.

CAVALIER. Wait — but no — I shall call my servant.

MIRANDOLINA. Oh! Fabricius —

CAVALIER. I swear by Heaven that if that fellow comes I'll split his head.

MIRANDOLINA. Oh, this is a fine state of affairs. I can't make use of my own servants?

CAVALIER. Call some one else; I can't stand him.

MIRANDOLINA. It seems to me you go a little too far, Cavalier. [*She goes away from the table with the iron in her hand.*]

CAVALIER. Excuse me. — I am beside myself.

MIRANDOLINA. I'll go into the kitchen and you'll be satisfied then.

CAVALIER. No, dear, stay.

MIRANDOLINA [*walking about*]. This is a queer thing.

CAVALIER [*walking after her*]. Excuse me.

MIRANDOLINA [*she walks about*]. I can't call whom I wish?

CAVALIER. I confess. I am jealous of him. [*He goes after her.*]

MIRANDOLINA [*aside*]. He comes after me just like a little dog.

CAVALIER. This is the first time that I have experienced what love is.

MIRANDOLINA [*walking to and fro*]. No one ever ordered me about so.

CAVALIER. I had no intent of commanding you; I beg you. [*He follows her.*]

MIRANDOLINA [*turning haughtily*]. What do you want of me?

CAVALIER. Love, compassion, pity.

MIRANDOLINA. A man, who this morning could n't bear the sight of women, now asks for love and pity. [*Aside.*] I won't pay any attention to him; it cannot be; I don't believe him. Burst, explode, and learn not to despise women.

[*Exit* MIRANDOLINA.]

CAVALIER [*alone*]. Oh, cursed be the moment I first saw her. I have fallen into the snare and there is n't any help now.

[*Enter the* MARQUIS.]

MARQUIS. Sir Cavalier, you have insulted me.

CAVALIER. Excuse me, it was an accident.

MARQUIS. I'm astonished at you.

CAVALIER. After all the jug did n't hit you.

MARQUIS. A little drop of water stained my clothing.

CAVALIER. I repeat, excuse me.

MARQUIS. That is an impertinence.

CAVALIER. I did nothing purposely. For the third time, I say excuse me.

MARQUIS. I wish satisfaction.

CAVALIER. If you don't want to excuse me, if you want satisfaction, I am here. I'm not afraid of you.

MARQUIS [*changing his tone*]. I fear this stain won't go away. That is what makes me furious.

CAVALIER [*disdainfully*]. When a gentleman asks to be excused, what more do you want?

MARQUIS. If you did n't do it out of malice, I will let you off.

CAVALIER. I tell you that I am capable of giving you any kind of satisfaction.

MARQUIS. Come, let's say no more about it.

CAVALIER. Low-born fellow.

MARQUIS. Oh, that's fine. My anger is all gone and you try to make it come again.

CAVALIER. A fine humor you've found me in just now.

MARQUIS. I pardon you; I know what trouble you are having.

CAVALIER. I don't meddle with your affairs.

MARQUIS. How you have fallen, sir enemy of women!

CAVALIER. I? How?

MARQUIS. Yes, you are in love . . .

CAVALIER. I am, am I? Go to the devil.

MARQUIS. What's the use trying to hide it?

CAVALIER. Let me alone, or I swear to Heaven I'll make you sorry for this.

[*Exit the* CAVALIER.]

MARQUIS [*alone*]. He is in love, he is ashamed of himself, and he does n't want any one to know it. But perhaps he does n't want me to know it because he is afraid of me. He fears to declare himself my rival. I am very much displeased on account of this spot; if I only knew how to take it away. These women usually have some sort of powder to take away stains. [*Looks on the table and in the basket.*] This beautiful flask. Is it gold or brass? It must be brass; if it were gold it would not be left here. If there were some regina water in it, it would be good to take away this stain. [*Opens it, smells it, and tastes it.*] It is cordial. At any rate, it will do that much good. I want to try it.

[*Puts it in his pocket.*]

[*Enter the* CAVALIER'S *Servant.*]

SERVANT [*looking on the table*]. Where the deuce is that flask?

MARQUIS. What are you looking for, my good man.

SERVANT. I'm looking for a flask of cordial. Mirandolina wants it. She says she left it here, but can't find it.

MARQUIS. Was it a little brass flask?

SERVANT. No, sir, it was gold.

MARQUIS. Gold?

SERVANT. Yes, it was gold. I saw it bought for six pounds.

MARQUIS [*aside*]. Oh poor me! But how did she come to leave a gold flask around?

SERVANT. She left it here, but I can't find it.

MARQUIS. And yet it seems impossible that it should be gold.

SERVANT. It was gold, I tell you. Perhaps you have seen it, your excellency?

MARQUIS. I haven't seen anything.

SERVANT. That's enough. I'll tell her I can't find it. It's her loss. She ought to have put it in her pocket.

[*Exit Servant.*]

MARQUIS [*alone*]. Oh, the poor Marquis di Forlipopoli! How must I act in so important a case? If Mirandolina ever finds out I have it, my dignity is in danger. I am a gentleman. I must pay her for it. But I haven't got the money.

[*Enter the* COUNT.]

COUNT. What do you say, Marquis, of this fine bit of news?

MARQUIS. What's happened?

COUNT. The savage Cavalier, the scorner of women, is in love with Mirandolina.

MARQUIS. I'm glad of it. I want him to recognize in spite of himself the merit of this woman, and to see that I'm not smitten with one who does not deserve my love; and may he suffer and burst for his impertinence.

COUNT. But suppose Mirandolina reciprocates his affections?

MARQUIS. That can't be. She wouldn't torture me so. I am who I am. She knows what I have done for her.

COUNT. I have done more for her than you. But everything was thrown away. Mirandolina lured on the Cavalier di Ripafratta; she bestowed attentions on him she never did on you or me; but it is evident that with women the more you do for them, the less you merit; they adore him who makes fun of them, they run after him who disdains them.

MARQUIS. If that were true — but it can't be.

COUNT. Why can't it?

MARQUIS. Would you want to compare the Cavalier with me?

COUNT. Haven't you seen her yourself seated at his table? Has she ever treated us with such confidence? For him, specially fine linen. His table is the first to be served. With her own hands she makes dishes for him. The servants see everything and they talk. Fabricius groans with jealousy. And then that swooning, real or feigned, isn't it a manifest sign of love?

MARQUIS. How? She made him savory *ragouts*, but for me tough beef and thin rice broth. Yes, it is true; this is an insult to my rank, and to my station in life.

COUNT. And I who have spent so much on her?

MARQUIS. And I who gave her gifts continually. I even gave her a drink of that delicious Cyprian wine of mine. The Cavalier couldn't have done for her the smallest part of what we have done.

COUNT. Be sure that he, too, has lavished gifts upon her.

MARQUIS. So? What did he give her?

COUNT. A gold bottle with cordial.

MARQUIS [*aside*]. Alas! — How do you know?

COUNT. His servant told mine.

MARQUIS [*aside*]. Worse and worse. I'm getting into trouble with the Cavalier.

COUNT. I see that she is ungrateful. I

wish to leave her absolutely; I wish to leave this unworthy inn before an hour is up.

MARQUIS. Yes, yes; you do well; go.

COUNT. And you, who are a gentleman of such honor ought to go with me.

MARQUIS. But — where ought we to go?

COUNT. I shall find you a stopping-place. Leave that to me.

MARQUIS. This inn — it will be, for instance . . .

COUNT. We will go into a house of one of my fellow townsmen. We won't spend anything.

MARQUIS. Enough; you are such a good friend of mine, that I can't say no.

COUNT. Let us go and take vengeance on this ungrateful woman.

MARQUIS. Yes, let us go. [Aside.] How about the flask, then? I am a gentleman. I can't do a base action.

COUNT. Don't hesitate, Marquis. Let's get away from here. Do me this favor and then I'm your humble servant wherever I can serve you.

MARQUIS. I shall tell you in confidence — don't tell any one — my steward has delayed my remittance for some time —

COUNT. You perhaps have a bill to settle?

MARQUIS. Yes, six pounds.

COUNT. Six pounds? It must be two months that you have not paid.

MARQUIS. It is true. I owe her six pounds. I can't go without paying her. If you would do me the favor —

COUNT [drawing out his purse]. Gladly. Here are six pounds.

MARQUIS. Wait. Now that I remember it is six pounds, ten. [Aside.] I want to return the Cavalier his ten shillings.

COUNT. Six pounds, or more, it is the same to me. Here.

MARQUIS. I shall return it as soon as possible.

COUNT. Help yourself as far as you please. I don't lack for money, and to get even with her, I would spend two thousand pounds.

MARQUIS. Indeed, she is ungrateful. I spent money on her and she treats me so.

COUNT. I want to ruin her inn; it's thus I'll get even with her. After that, the Cavalier, who has concealed his true motives in order to betray me, will have to give me satisfaction of a different sort.

[Exit the COUNT.]

SCENE II. Room with three doors.

[Enter MIRANDOLINA.]

MIRANDOLINA [alone]. Ah, poor me! I am in a horrid fix. If the Cavalier comes to me, a pretty mess. He is confoundedly furious. I hope the devil does n't tempt him to come here. I must close this door. [She locks the door through which she came.] Now I almost begin to repent of what I have done. It is true that I have been very much amused in having such a proud fellow, such a despiser of women, run so madly after me, but now that the satyr is furious, I see my honor in danger and my life itself. I must make some coup d'état. I am alone. I need some one to look out for my interests. It cannot be any other than that good man Fabricius who in case of need can help me. I shall promise to marry him. But — promises, more promises; he will grow tired of believing me. It would be almost better if I married him. After all, with such a marriage I could hope to protect my honor without detriment to my freedom.

[The CAVALIER knocks at the door from within.]

MIRANDOLINA. Some one is knocking at the door; who ever can it be?

[She approaches it.]

CAVALIER [from within]. Mirandolina?

MIRANDOLINA. Here he is again.

CAVALIER [from within]. Mirandolina, open for me.

MIRANDOLINA [aside]. Open. I am not such a simpleton. — What do you wish, sir?

CAVALIER [from within]. Open the door.

MIRANDOLINA. Do me the favor of going to your room and waiting for me until I am disengaged.

CAVALIER [from within]. Why don't you want to open it?

MIRANDOLINA. Some guests have come. Do me this favor, and wait for me. I'll be with you presently.

CAVALIER [*leaving the door*]. I'll go; but if you don't come, I pity you.

MIRANDOLINA [*aside*]. "If you don't come, I pity you." I pity myself, if I should go. The matter is becoming worse. I would remedy matters, if I could. Has he gone? [*Looks through the keyhole.*] Yes, yes, he's gone; but I'm not going to him. [*At another door.*] Oh, Farbricius? Oh, it would be fine now if Fabricius should be avenged on me and did not intend to — Oh, there is no danger. I have certain manners, certain alluring ways, which make men give in even if they are of stone. [*Calls at the other door.*] Fabricius?

FABRICIUS. You called?

MIRANDOLINA. Come here; I have something confidential to tell you.

FABRICIUS. I am here.

MIRANDOLINA. You know that the Cavalier Ripafratta has shown that he is in love with me.

FABRICIUS. Hum, I noticed it.

MIRANDOLINA. Yes? You noticed it! I in truth was never aware of it.

FABRICIUS. Poor simpleton! You never knew it? You did n't see the grimaces he made when you were ironing — that he was jealous of me?

MIRANDOLINA. I take things indifferently, when I act without malice. It is enough. Just now he said certain words which, indeed, made me blush.

FABRICIUS. You see. He dares to say this because you are a woman alone, without father, without mother, without any one. If you were married, it would not be so.

MIRANDOLINA. Come, now; I understand perfectly what you say; I have thought of marrying.

FABRICIUS. Remember your father.

MIRANDOLINA. Yes, I shall remember him.

[*The* CAVALIER *knocks at the door as before.*]

MIRANDOLINA [*to* FABRICIUS]. Some one is knocking.

FABRICIUS [*in a loud voice toward the door*]. Who is that knocking?

CAVALIER [*from within*]. Open it.

MIRANDOLINA [*to* FABRICIUS]. The Cavalier!

FABRICIUS. What do you want?
                    [*Goes to open it.*]

MIRANDOLINA. Wait until I go.

FABRICIUS. Of what are you afraid?

MIRANDOLINA. Dear Fabricius, I don't know, I'm afraid for myself.
                    [*Exit* MIRANDOLINA.]

FABRICIUS. Don't worry, I'll defend you.

CAVALIER [*from within*]. Open, I swear by Heaven!

FABRICIUS. What do you want, sir? What noise is this? People don't act so in a respectable inn.

CAVALIER. Open that door.
        [*He tries to break open the door.*]

FABRICIUS. The deuce! I would not want to go too far. Help! Who is there? Is n't there any one?

[*Enter the* MARQUIS *and the* COUNT *from the center door.*]

COUNT [*at the door*]. What is that?

MARQUIS [*at the door*]. What noise is that?

FABRICIUS [*aside so that the* CAVALIER *should n't hear him*]. Sirs, I beg you; the Cavalier di Ripafratta wants to smash this door.

CAVALIER [*from within*]. Open it, or I'll throw it down.

MARQUIS [*to the* COUNT]. Has he gone mad? Let us go.

COUNT [*to* FABRICIUS]. Open it. I want to speak with him.

FABRICIUS. I shall open it, but I beg you —

COUNT. Don't hesitate. We are here.

MARQUIS [*aside*]. If I see the least little thing, I'll beat a retreat.

[FABRICIUS *opens the door and the* CAVALIER *enters.*]

CAVALIER. I swear to Heaven, where is she?

FABRICIUS. For whom are you looking, sir?

CAVALIER. Where is Mirandolina?

FABRICIUS. I don't know.

MARQUIS [*aside*]. He is angry with Mirandolina. It is nothing at all.

CAVALIER. Base woman, I shall find her.
        [*He walks about and discovers the* COUNT *and then the* MARQUIS.]

COUNT [to the CAVALIER]. With whom are you angry?

MARQUIS. Cavalier, we are friends.

CAVALIER [aside]. Alas! I would n't want this weakness of mine to be known for all the gold in the world.

FABRICIUS. What do you want, sir, of the mistress?

CAVALIER. I am not responsible to you. When I give orders, I want them obeyed. I pay my money for this, and I swear to Heaven that she will have to settle with me.

FABRICIUS. Your excellency pays his money to be obeyed in legitimate and honest things, but you can't pretend, pardon me, that an honest woman —

CAVALIER. What are you saying? Who are you? I know what I ordered from her.

FABRICIUS. You ordered her to come to your room.

CAVALIER. Come, come, knave, before I break your skull.

FABRICIUS. I am astonished at you.

MARQUIS [to FABRICIUS]. Hush.

COUNT [to FABRICIUS]. Go away from here.

CAVALIER [to FABRICIUS]. Go away from here.

FABRICIUS [becoming angry]. I tell you, sirs, —

MARQUIS. Away.

COUNT. Away.   [They turn him out.]

FABRICIUS [aside]. By Jove! I want to do something reckless!

[Exit FABRICIUS.]

CAVALIER [aside]. Worthless woman. To make me wait in my room!

MARQUIS [aside to the COUNT]. What the deuce is the matter with him?

COUNT [aside to the MARQUIS]. Don't you see? He is in love with Mirandolina.

CAVALIER. And she is with Fabricius and speaks with him about marriage?

COUNT [aside]. Now is the time to avenge myself. — Cavalier, it is n't fitting for one to laugh at the weaknesses of another, when one has a heart as easily broken as yours.

CAVALIER [to the MARQUIS]. Do you know what he is talking about?

MARQUIS. Friend, I don't know anything at all.

COUNT. I'm talking about you, who under the pretext of not being able to endure women have attempted to steal Mirandolina's heart from me, which was already my conquest.

CAVALIER [angrily to the MARQUIS]. I?

MARQUIS. I'm not talking.

COUNT. Turn to me, and answer me. Are n't you ashamed of having acted so basely?

CAVALIER. I am ashamed to listen to you, without telling you that you lie.

COUNT. You give me the lie?

MARQUIS [aside]. The matter is growing worse.

CAVALIER [angrily to the MARQUIS]. On what basis can you say — the Count does n't know what he is saying.

MARQUIS. But I don't want to get mixed up in it.

COUNT. You are a liar.

MARQUIS. I'm going away.

[Wants to go.]

CAVALIER. Stay.   [Holds him by force.]

COUNT. You'll pay me for this.

CAVALIER [to the MARQUIS]. Yes, yes, I'll pay you. — Give me your sword.

MARQUIS. Oh, come, calm yourselves both of you. Dear Count, what difference does it make to you if the Cavalier does love Mirandolina?

CAVALIER. I love her? It is not true; he lies that says it.

MARQUIS. Lies? The lie is n't any of mine. I am not the one that says it.

CAVALIER. Who, then?

COUNT. I say it, and I maintain it, and I'm not afraid of you.

CAVALIER [to the MARQUIS]. Give me that sword.

MARQUIS. No, I say.

CAVALIER. You are my enemy, too?

MARQUIS. I am the friend of all.

COUNT. These actions are unworthy.

CAVALIER. I swear to Heaven!

[He takes the sword from the MARQUIS, but it remains fixed and he pulls the scabbard out of the belt.]

MARQUIS. Don't be wanting in respect.

CAVALIER [to the MARQUIS]. If you consider yourself insulted, I'll give you satisfaction too.

MARQUIS. Come, you are too excited. [*Grieving to himself.*] I don't like this —
COUNT. I wish satisfaction.
CAVALIER. I'll give it to you.
[*He tries to draw away the scabbard, and cannot.*]
MARQUIS. That sword does n't suit you.
CAVALIER. Curses!
[*He tries hard to draw it out.*]
MARQUIS. Cavalier, you are n't accomplishing anything at all.
COUNT. I have n't any more patience.
CAVALIER. See. [*Draws out the sword and sees that the blade is broken off.*] What's this?
MARQUIS. You have ruined my sword.
CAVALIER. Where is the rest? There is n't anything there in the scabbard.
MARQUIS. Yes, that's so, I ruined it in my last duel. I did n't remember it.
CAVALIER [*to the* COUNT]. Let me get a sword.
COUNT. I swear by Heaven, you shan't escape from my clutches.
CAVALIER. What, flee? I am not afraid to face you even with this bit of blade.
MARQUIS. It's a Spanish blade. It knows no fear.
COUNT. Not so much bravado, Sir Boaster.
CAVALIER. Yes, with this blade —
[*He rushes upon the* COUNT.]
COUNT. Back.
[*He puts himself on guard.*]

[*Enter* MIRANDOLINA, FABRICIUS.]

FABRICIUS. Stop, stop, gentlemen.
MIRANDOLINA. Stop, gentlemen, stop.
CAVALIER [*aside, seeing* MIRANDOLINA]. Oh, curses!
MIRANDOLINA. Poor me! With swords?
MARQUIS. Do you see? For your sake.
MIRANDOLINA. For my sake?
COUNT. See the Cavalier, he is in love with you.
CAVALIER. I in love? It is n't true; you lie.
MIRANDOLINA. The Cavalier in love with me? Oh, no, Count, you are mistaken. I can assure you that you are mistaken.
COUNT. And you have an understanding as well —

MARQUIS. It's known, and evident —
CAVALIER. What's known? What's evident?
MARQUIS. I say, when it is so, it's known, — when it is n't so, it's not evident.
MIRANDOLINA. The Cavalier in love with me? He denies it, and denying it in my presence he mortifies, humiliates me, and makes me recognize his strength and my weakness. I confess the truth: if I had succeeded in making him fall in love with me, I would think I had done the greatest act of prowess in the world. A man, who cannot bear the sight of women, who despises them, who has a poor idea of them, I cannot hope to make him love me. My good sirs, I am a woman, who is frank and sincere; when I ought to speak, I speak; and I can't conceal the truth. I tried to make the Cavalier fall in love with me, but all to no purpose. Is n't it true, sir! I have done my best, but I have accomplished nothing.
CAVALIER [*aside*]. Ah. I can't speak.
COUNT [*to* MIRANDOLINA]. Do you see? He is perplexed.
MARQUIS [*to* MIRANDOLINA]. He has n't the courage to say no.
CAVALIER [*to the* MARQUIS, *angrily*]. You don't know what you are talking about.
MIRANDOLINA. Oh the Cavalier is n't in love. He knows women's wiles, he knows women's roguishness; he does n't believe everything they say; he does n't put any confidence in tears. He even laughs when they faint.
CAVALIER. Then women's tears are false, and their fainting but pretense?
MIRANDOLINA. What? Don't you know that, or are you pretending not to know?
CAVALIER. I swear by Heaven. Such deceit deserves a dagger in the heart.
MIRANDOLINA. Cavalier, don't get angry, or these gentlemen will say that you're really in love.
COUNT. Yes, he is; he can't hide it.
MARQUIS. It's perfectly evident.
CAVALIER [*angrily to the* MARQUIS]. No, I am not.
MARQUIS. It is always with me that he's angry.

MIRANDOLINA. No sir, he is not in love. I say it, I maintain it, and I am ready to prove it.

CAVALIER [aside]. I cannot stand any more. Count, another time you will find me provided with a sword.

[He throws away the broken half of the MARQUIS's sword.]

MARQUIS. See here! The hilt costs money. [He takes it from the ground.]

MIRANDOLINA. Stop, Cavalier, your reputation is at stake. These gentlemen believe you are in love; they must be undeceived.

CAVALIER. There is n't any need of it.

MIRANDOLINA. Oh, yes, sir; stay a moment.

CAVALIER [aside]. What does that woman intend to do?

MIRANDOLINA. Sirs, the surest sign of love is jealousy and the man who is n't jealous, is n't in love. If the Cavalier loved me, he could n't bear that I should be another's, but he will bear it, and you shall see —

CAVALIER. To whom does this refer?

MIRANDOLINA. He for whom my father destined me.

FABRICIUS [to MIRANDOLINA]. Perhaps you're speaking of me?

MIRANDOLINA. Yes, dear Fabricius, and I wish, in the presence of these gentlemen, to give my hand to you in token of betrothal.

CAVALIER [aside, acting nervously]. Alas! With that fellow? I can't bear it.

COUNT [aside]. If she marries Fabricius, she does n't love the Cavalier. — Yes, marry and I promise you a hundred pounds.

MARQUIS. Mirandolina, an egg to-day is better than a hen to-morrow. Marry now and I'll give you six pounds.

MIRANDOLINA. Thanks, sirs, I don't need a dowry. I am a poor woman without charm, without vivacity, incapable of making persons of consideration love me. But Fabricius wishes me well, and therefore I'll marry him in the presence of you all.

CAVALIER. Yes, curse you, marry whom you will. I know you deceived me, I know you are exulting within yourself at having

humiliated me, and I see that you wish to put my tolerance to the test. You deserve to be paid for your deception with a dagger in your heart, you deserve to have your heart torn out, and held up as an example of feminine flatterers, of feminine deceivers. But that would be to humiliate myself twice over. I flee from your eyes; I curse your flattery, your tears, your deceit; you have made me see what baleful power your sex has over us, and you have taught me to my cost that it is n't enough to despise it — we men must flee from it.

[Exit the CAVALIER.]

COUNT. Say now that he is n't in love.

MARQUIS. If he gives me the lie again, on the word of a gentleman, I challenge him.

MIRANDOLINA. Hush, gentlemen, hush. He has gone away, and if he does n't return, and if the matter passes over this way, I can say I'm lucky. I have succeeded only too well in making him fall in love with me, and I am thus placed in a precarious condition. I don't want to know anything more of him. Fabricius, come here, dear; give me your hand.

FABRICIUS. Your hand? Not so fast, madam. You find pleasure in making people fall in love with you this way, and you expect me to want to marry you?

MIRANDOLINA. Oh, come, fool! It was a joke, a whim, a little bit of pique. I was a girl; I had no one to order my ways. When I am married, I know what I'll do.

FABRICIUS. What?

[Enter the CAVALIER'S Servant.]

SERVANT. Madame, before leaving I have come to pay my respects.

MIRANDOLINA. Are you going away?

SERVANT. Yes, my master has gone to the stage-coach office, he's making them harness up. He's waiting for me with the things, and we are going to Leghorn.

MIRANDOLINA. Pardon me, if I have ever done you . . .

SERVANT. I have n't time to stay. Thank you, and au revoir.

[Exit Servant.]

MIRANDOLINA. Thank Heavens, he is gone. I have some remorse yet; certainly he left with little satisfaction. I'll never try any more of these jokes.

COUNT. Mirandolina, married or single, I shall always be the same to you.

MARQUIS. Bank on my protection.

MIRANDOLINA. Now, I am married, gentlemen, I don't need protectors, I don't need lovers, I don't need gifts. Up to this time, I have been amusing myself, I have done wrong, and I have taken too many risks, but I shan't do it any more; this is my husband.

FABRICIUS. But, madam, not so fast.

MIRANDOLINA. Why slow? What is it? What difficulty is there? Come, now. Give me that hand.

FABRICIUS. I would like to make our agreements first.

MIRANDOLINA. What agreement? The agreement is this, — either give me your hand or go home.

FABRICIUS. I will give my hand — but then —

MIRANDOLINA. But then, dear, everything will be yours; don't hesitate. I shall always love you, you will always be my soul.

FABRICIUS [giving her his hand]. Here, dear, I can't resist any more.

MIRANDOLINA [aside]. Then this is done.

COUNT. Mirandolina, you are a fine woman, you have the power of leading men where you will.

MARQUIS. Your manner puts us under infinite obligations to you.

MIRANDOLINA. If it is true that I can hope for favors from you, I ask for one last one.

COUNT. Then pray say it.

MARQUIS. Speak.

FABRICIUS [aside]. Whatever will she ask for now?

MIRANDOLINA. I beg you as a favor to change your lodgings.

FABRICIUS [aside]. Fine; now I see she is well disposed toward me.

COUNT. Yes, yes, I understand, and I compliment you. I shall go, but wherever I am, be assured of my esteem.

MARQUIS. Tell me; did you lose a little gold flask?

MIRANDOLINA. Yes, sir.

MARQUIS. Here it is. I found it and I'm going to return it. I shall leave to please you, but in every place, pray, bank on my protection.

MIRANDOLINA. These words will be dear to me in the bounds of decorum and honesty. Changing my state, I wish to change my way of life; and may you gentlemen profit by what you have seen, to the advantage and well-being of your hearts; and whenever you may find yourselves hesitating as to whether you ought to yield or give in, may you think of the tricks you have learned, and remember the Mistress of the Inn.

MINNA VON BARNHELM

By LESSING

Translated by ERNEST BELL

CHARACTERS

MAJOR VON TELLHEIM, *a discharged officer*

MINNA VON BARNHELM

COUNT VON BRUCHSAL, *her uncle*

FRANZISKA, *her lady's maid*

JUST, *servant to the Major*

PAUL WERNER, *an old sergeant of the Major's*

THE LANDLORD *of an inn*

RICCAUT DE LA MARLINIÈRE

A Lady

An Orderly

---

*The Scene alternates between the parlor of an inn
and a room adjoining it.*

MINNA VON BARNHELM

ACT I

JUST [*sitting in a corner, and talking while asleep*]. Rogue of a landlord! You treat us so? On, comrade! Hit hard! [*He strikes with his fist, and wakes through the exertion.*] Ha! There he is again! I cannot shut an eye without fighting with him. I wish he got but half the blows. Why, it is morning! I must look for my poor master at once; if I can help it, he shall not set foot in the cursed house again. I wonder where he has passed the night?

[*Enter* LANDLORD.]

LANDLORD. Good-morning, Herr Just; good-morning! What, up so early! Or shall I say — up so late?

JUST. Say which you please.

LANDLORD. I say only — good-morning! And that deserves, I suppose, that Herr Just should answer, "Many thanks."

JUST. Many thanks.

LANDLORD. One is peevish, if one can't have one's proper rest. What will you bet the Major has not returned home, and you have been keeping watch for him?

JUST. How the man can guess everything!

LANDLORD. I surmise, I surmise.

JUST [*turning round to go*]. Your servant!

LANDLORD [*stopping him*]. Not so, Herr Just!

JUST. Very well, then, not your servant!

LANDLORD. What, Herr Just, I do hope you are not still angry about yesterday's affair! Who would keep his anger over-night?

JUST. I; and over a good many nights.

LANDLORD. Is that like a Christian?

JUST. As much so as to turn an honorable man who cannot pay to a day, out of doors, into the street.

LANDLORD. Fie! Who would be so wicked?

JUST. A Christian innkeeper. — My master! Such a man! Such an officer!

LANDLORD. I thrust him from the house into the streets? I have far too much respect for an officer to do that, and far too much pity for a discharged one! I was obliged to have another room prepared for him. Think no more about it, Herr Just. [*Calls.*] Hullo! I will make it good in another way. [*A lad comes.*] Bring a glass; Herr Just will have a drop; something good.

JUST. Do not trouble yourself, Mr. Landlord. May the drop turn to poison, which — But I will not swear; I have not yet breakfasted.

LANDLORD [*to the lad, who brings a bottle of spirits and a glass*]. Give it here. Go! Now, Herr Just; something quite excellent; strong, delicious, and wholesome. [*Fills and holds it out to him.*] That can set an overtaxed stomach to rights again!

JUST. I hardly ought! — And yet why should I let my health suffer on account of his incivility? [*Takes it and drinks.*]

LANDLORD. May it do you good, Herr Just!

JUST [*giving the glass back*]. Not bad! But, Landlord, you are nevertheless an ill-mannered brute!

LANDLORD. Not so, not so! — Come, another glass; one cannot stand upon one leg.

JUST [*after drinking*]. I must say so much — it is good, very good! Made at home, Landlord?

LANDLORD. At home, indeed! True Dantzig, real double distilled!

JUST. Look ye, Landlord; if I could play the hypocrite, I would do so for such stuff as that; but I cannot, so it must out. — You are an ill-mannered brute all the same.

LANDLORD. Nobody in my life ever told me that before. — But another glass, Herr Just; three is the lucky number!

JUST. With all my heart! [*Drinks.*] Good stuff, indeed, capital! But truth is good also, and indeed, Landlord, you are an ill-mannered brute all the same!

LANDLORD. If I was, do you think I should let you say so?

JUST. Oh, yes; a brute seldom has spirit.

LANDLORD. One more, Herr Just; a four-stranded rope is the strongest.

JUST. No, enough is as good as a feast! And what good will it do you, Landlord? I shall stick to my text till the last drop in the bottle. Shame, Landlord, to have such good Dantzig, and such bad manners! To turn out of his room, — in his absence, — a man like my master, who has lodged at your house above a year; from whom you have had already so many shining thalers; who never owed a heller in his life, — because he let payment run for a couple of months, and because he does not spend quite so much as he used.

LANDLORD. But suppose I really wanted the room and saw beforehand that the Major would willingly have given it up if we could only have waited some time for his return! Should I let strange gentlefolk like them drive away again from my door? Should I willfully send such a prize into the clutches of another innkeeper? Besides, I don't believe they could have got a lodging elsewhere. The inns are all now quite full. Could such a young, beautiful, amiable lady remain in the street? Your master is much too gallant for that. And what does he lose by the change? Have not I given him another room?

JUST. By the pigeon-house, at the back, with a view between a neighbor's chimneys.

LANDLORD. The view was uncommonly fine, before the confounded neighbor obstructed it. The room is otherwise very nice, and is papered —

JUST. Has been!

LANDLORD. No, one side is so still. And the little room adjoining, — what is the matter with that? It has a chimney which, perhaps, smokes somewhat in the winter —

JUST. But does very nicely in the summer. I believe, Landlord, you are mocking us in the bargain!

LANDLORD. Come, come; Herr Just, Herr Just —

JUST. Don't make Herr Just's head hot —

LANDLORD. I make his head hot? It is the Dantzig does that.

JUST. An officer, like my master! Or do you think that a discharged officer is not an officer, who may break your neck for you? Why were you all, you landlords, so civil during the war? Why was every officer an honorable man then, and every soldier a worthy, brave fellow? Does this bit of a peace make you so bumptious?

LANDLORD. What makes you fly out so, Herr Just?

JUST. I will fly out.

MAJOR VON TELLHEIM [*entering*]. Just!

JUST [*supposing the* LANDLORD *is still speaking*]. Just? Are we so intimate?

MAJOR VON TELLHEIM. Just!

JUST. I thought I was "Herr Just" with you.

LANDLORD [*seeing the* MAJOR]. Hist! Hist! Herr Just, Herr Just, look round; your master —

MAJOR VON TELLHEIM. Just, I think you are quarreling! What did I tell you?

LANDLORD. Quarrel, your honor? God forbid! Would your most humble servant dare to quarrel with one who has the honor of being in your service?

JUST. If I could but give him a good whack on that cringing cat's back of his!

LANDLORD. It is true Herr Just speaks up for his master, and rather warmly; but in that he is right. I esteem him so much the more: I like him for it.

JUST. I should like to knock his teeth out for him!

LANDLORD. It is only a pity that he puts himself in a passion for nothing. For I feel quite sure that your honor is not displeased with me in this matter, since — necessity — made it necessary —

MAJOR VON TELLHEIM. More than enough, sir! I am in your debt; you turn out my room in my absence. You must be paid, I must seek a lodging elsewhere. Very natural.

LANDLORD. Elsewhere? You are not going to quit, honored sir? Oh, unfortunate stricken man that I am! No, never! Sooner shall the lady give up the apartments again. The Major cannot and will not let her have his room. It is his; she must go; I cannot help it. I will go, honored sir —

MAJOR VON TELLHEIM. My friend, do not make two foolish strokes instead of one. The lady must retain possession of the room —

LANDLORD. And your honor could suppose that from distrust, from fear of not being paid, I — As if I did not know that your honor could pay me as soon as you pleased. The sealed purse — five hundred thalers in louis d'ors marked on it — which your honor had in your writing-desk — is in good keeping.

MAJOR VON TELLHEIM. I trust so; as the rest of my property. Just shall take them into his keeping, when he has paid your bill —

LANDLORD. Really, I was quite alarmed when I found the purse. I always considered your honor a methodical and prudent man, who never got quite out of money — but still, had I supposed there was ready money in the desk —

⟩ MAJOR VON TELLHEIM. You would have treated me rather more civilly. I understand you. Go, sir; leave me. I wish to speak with my servant.

LANDLORD. But, honored sir —

MAJOR VON TELLHEIM. Come, Just; he does not wish to permit me to give my orders to you in his house.

LANDLORD. I am going, honored sir! My whole house is at your service. [Exit.]

⟩ JUST [stamping with his foot and spitting after the LANDLORD]. Ugh!

MAJOR VON TELLHEIM. What is the matter?

JUST. I am choking with rage.

MAJOR VON TELLHEIM. That is as bad as from plethora.

JUST. And for you, sir, I hardly know you any longer. May I die before your eyes, if you do not encourage this malicious, unfeeling wretch! In spite of gallows, axe, and torture I could — yes, I could have throttled him with these hands, and torn him to pieces with these teeth!

MAJOR VON TELLHEIM. You wild beast!

JUST. Better a wild beast than such a man!

MAJOR VON TELLHEIM. But what is it that you want?

JUST. I want you to perceive how much he insults you.

MAJOR VON TELLHEIM. And then —

JUST. To take your revenge — No, the fellow is beneath your notice!

MAJOR VON TELLHEIM. But to commission you to avenge me? That was my intention from the first. He should not have seen me again, but have received the amount of his bill from your hands. I know that you can throw down a handful of money with a tolerably contemptuous mien.

JUST. Oh! A pretty sort of revenge!

MAJOR VON TELLHEIM. Which, however, we must defer. I have not one heller of ready money, and I know not where to raise any.

JUST. No money! What is that purse, then, with five hundred dollars' worth of louis d'ors, which the Landlord found in your desk?

MAJOR VON TELLHEIM. That is money given into my charge.

JUST. Not the hundred pistoles which your old sergeant brought you four or five weeks back?

MAJOR VON TELLHEIM. The same. Paul Werner's; right.

JUST. And you have not used them yet? Yet, sir, you may do what you please with them. I will answer for it that —

MAJOR VON TELLHEIM. Indeed!

JUST. Werner heard from me, how they had treated your claims upon the War Office. He heard —

MAJOR VON TELLHEIM. That I should certainly be a beggar soon, if I was not one already. I am much obliged to you, Just. And the news induced Werner to offer to share his little all with me. I am very glad that I guessed this. Listen, Just; let me have your account, directly, too; we must part.

JUST. How! What!

MAJOR VON TELLHEIM. Not a word. There is some one coming.

[*Enter Lady in mourning.*]

LADY. I ask your pardon, sir.

MAJOR VON TELLHEIM. Whom do you seek, madam?

LADY. The worthy gentleman with whom I have the honor of speaking. You do not know me again. I am the widow of your late captain.

MAJOR VON TELLHEIM. Good Heavens, madam, how you are changed!

LADY. I have just risen from a sick-bed, to which grief on the loss of my husband brought me. I am troubling you at a very early hour, Major von Tellheim, but I am going into the country, where a kind, but also unfortunate, friend has for the present offered me an asylum.

MAJOR VON TELLHEIM [*to* JUST]. Leave us. [*Exit* JUST.] — Speak freely, madam! You must not be ashamed of your bad fortune before me. Can I serve you in any way?

LADY. Major —

MAJOR VON TELLHEIM. I pity you, madam! How can I serve you? You know your husband was my friend; my friend, I say, and I have always been sparing of this title.

LADY. Who knows better than I do how worthy you were of his friendship — how worthy he was of yours? You would have been in his last thoughts, your name would have been the last sound on his dying lips, had not natural affection, stronger than friendship, demanded this sad prerogative for his unfortunate son and his unhappy wife.

MAJOR VON TELLHEIM. Cease, madam! I could willingly weep with you; but I have no tears to-day. Spare me! You come to me at a time when I might easily be misled to murmur against Providence. Oh, honest Marloff! Quick, madam, what have you to request? If it is in my power to assist you, if it is in my power —

LADY. I cannot depart without fulfilling his last wishes. He recollected, shortly before his death, that he was dying a debtor to you, and he conjured me to discharge his debt with the first ready money I should have. I have sold his carriage, and come to redeem his note.

MAJOR VON TELLHEIM. What, madam? Is that your object in coming?

LADY. It is. Permit me to count out the money to you.

MAJOR VON TELLHEIM. No, madam. Marloff a debtor to me! That can hardly be. Let us look, however. [*Takes out a pocketbook and searches.*] I find nothing of the kind.

LADY. You have doubtless mislaid his note; besides, it is nothing to the purpose. Permit me —

MAJOR VON TELLHEIM. No, madam; I am careful not to mislay such documents. If I have not got it, it is a proof that I never had it, or that it has been honored and already returned by me.

LADY. Major!

MAJOR VON TELLHEIM. Without doubt, madam; Marloff does not owe me anything — nor can I remember that he ever did owe me anything. This is so, madam. He has much rather left me in his debt. I have never been able to do anything to repay a man who shared with me good and ill luck, honor and danger, for six years. I shall not forget that he has left a son. He shall be my son, as soon as I can be a father to him. The embarrassment in which I am at present —

LADY. Generous man! But do not think so meanly of me. Take the money, Major, and then at least I shall be at ease.

MAJOR VON TELLHEIM. What more do you require to tranquilize you than my assurance that the money does not belong to me? Or do you wish that I should rob the young orphan of my friend? Rob, madam; for that it would be in the true meaning of the word. The money belongs to him; invest it for him.

LADY. I understand you; pardon me if I do not yet rightly know how to accept a kindness. Where have you learned that a mother will do more for her child than for the preservation of her own life? I am going —

MAJOR VON TELLHEIM. Go, madam, and may you have a prosperous journey! I do not ask you to let me hear from you. Your news might come to me when it might be of little use to me. There is yet one thing, madam; I had nearly forgotten that which is of most consequence. Marloff also had claims upon the chest of our old regiment. His claims are as good as mine. If my demands are paid, his must be paid also. I will be answerable for them.

LADY. Oh, sir, — but what can I say? Thus to purpose future good deeds is, in the eyes of Heaven, to have performed them already. May you receive its reward, as well as my tears. [*Exit.*]

MAJOR VON TELLHEIM. Poor, good woman! I must not forget to destroy the bill. [*Takes some papers from his pocketbook and destroys them.*] Who would guarantee that my own wants might not some day tempt me to make use of it?

[*Enter* JUST.]

MAJOR VON TELLHEIM. Is that you, Just?

JUST [*wiping his eyes*]. Yes.

MAJOR VON TELLHEIM. You have been crying?

JUST. I have been writing out my account in the kitchen, and the place is full of smoke. Here it is, sir.

MAJOR VON TELLHEIM. Give it to me.

JUST. Be merciful with me, sir. I know well that they have not been so with you; still —

MAJOR VON TELLHEIM. What do you want?

JUST. I should sooner have expected my death than my discharge.

MAJOR VON TELLHEIM. I cannot keep you any longer: I must learn to manage without servants. [*Opens the paper, and reads.*] "What my master, the Major, owes me: Three months and a half wages, 6 thalers per month, is 21 thalers. During the first part of this month, laid out in sundries — 1 thaler 7 groschen 9 pfennigs. Total, 22 thalers 7 groschen 9 pfennigs." Right; and it is just that I also pay your wages for the whole of the current month.

JUST. Turn over, sir.

MAJOR VON TELLHEIM. Oh! More? [*Reads.*] "What I owe my master, the Major: Paid for me to the army surgeon, 25 thalers. Attendance and nurse during my cure, paid for me, 39 thalers. Ad-

vanced, at my request, to my father, — who was burned out of his house and robbed, — without reckoning the two horses of which he made him a present, 50 thalers. Total, 114 thalers. Deduct the above 22 thalers 7 groschen 9 pfennigs; I remain in debt to my master, the Major, 91 thalers 16 groschen 3 pfennigs." — You are mad, my good fellow!

JUST. I willingly grant that I owe you much more; but it would be wasting ink to write it down. I cannot pay you that: and if you take my livery from me too, which, by the way, I have not yet earned — I would rather you had let me die in the workhouse.

MAJOR VON TELLHEIM. For what do you take me? You owe me nothing; and I will recommend you to one of my friends, with whom you will fare better than with me.

JUST. I do not owe you anything, and yet you turn me away!

MAJOR VON TELLHEIM. Because I do not wish to owe you anything.

JUST. On that account? Only on that account? As certain as I am in your debt, as certain as you can never be in mine, so certainly shall you not turn me away now. Do what you will, Major, I remain in your service; I must remain.

MAJOR VON TELLHEIM. With your obstinacy, your insolence, your savage boisterous temper toward all who you think have no business to speak to you, your malicious pranks, your love of revenge —

JUST. Make me as bad as you will, I shall not think worse of myself than of my dog. Last winter I was walking one evening at dusk along the river, when I heard something whine. I stooped down, and reached in the direction whence the sound came, and when I thought I was saving a child, I pulled a dog out of the water. That is well, thought I. The dog followed me; but I am not fond of dogs, so I drove him away — in vain. I whipped him away — in vain. I shut him out of my room at night; he lay down before the door. If he came too near me, I kicked him; he yelped, looked up at me, and wagged his tail. I have never yet given him a bit of bread with my own hand; and yet I am the only person whom he will obey, or who dare touch him. He jumps about me, and shows off his tricks to me, without my asking for them. He is an ugly dog, but he is a good animal. If he carries it on much longer, I shall at last give over hating him. MAJOR VON TELLHEIM [aside]. As I do him. No, there is no one perfectly inhuman. Just, we will not part.

JUST. Certainly not! And you wanted to manage without servants! You forget your wounds, and that you only have the use of one arm. Why, you are not able to dress alone. I am indispensable to you; and I am, — without boasting, Major, — I am a servant who, if the worst comes to the worst, can beg and steal for his master.

MAJOR VON TELLHEIM. Just, we will part.

JUST. All right, sir!

[Enter Servant.]

SERVANT. I say, comrade!

JUST. What is the matter?

SERVANT. Can you direct me to the officer who lodged yesterday in that room? [Pointing to the one out of which he is coming.]

JUST. That I could easily do. What have you got for him?

SERVANT. What we always have, when we have nothing — compliments. My mistress hears that he has been turned out on her account. My mistress knows good manners, and I am therefore to beg his pardon.

JUST. Well, then, beg his pardon; there he stands.

SERVANT. What is he? What is his name?

MAJOR VON TELLHEIM. I have already heard your message, my friend. It is unnecessary politeness on the part of your mistress, which I beg to acknowledge duly. Present my compliments to her. What is the name of your mistress?

SERVANT. Her name! We call her my lady.

MAJOR VON TELLHEIM. The name of her family?

SERVANT. I have not heard that yet, and it is not my business to ask. I manage so that I generally get a new master every six weeks. Hang all their names!

JUST. Bravo, comrade!

SERVANT. I was engaged by my present mistress a few days ago, in Dresden. I believe she has come here to look for her lover.

MAJOR VON TELLHEIM. Enough, friend. I wished to know the name of your mistress, not her secrets. Go!

SERVANT. Comrade, he would not do for my master. [Exit.]

MAJOR VON TELLHEIM. Just, see that we get out of this house directly! The politeness of this strange lady affects me more than the churlishness of the host. Here, take this ring — the only thing of value which I have left — of which I never thought of making such a use. Pawn it! Get eighty louis d'ors for it: our host's bill can scarcely amount to thirty. Pay him, and remove my things. — Ah, where? Where you will. The cheaper the inn, the better. You will find me in the neighboring coffee-house. I am going; you will see to it all properly?

JUST. Have no fear, Major!

MAJOR VON TELLHEIM [coming back]. Above all things, do not let my pistols be forgotten, which hang beside the bed.

JUST. I will forget nothing.

MAJOR VON TELLHEIM [coming back again]. Another thing: bring your dog with you too. Do you hear, Just? [Exit MAJOR VON TELLHEIM.]

JUST. The dog will not stay behind, he will take care of that. Hem! My master still had this valuable ring and carried it in his pocket instead of on his finger! My good landlord, we are not yet so poor as we look. To him himself, I will pawn you, you beautiful little ring! I know he will be annoyed that you will not all be consumed in his house. Ah! —

[Enter PAUL WERNER.]

JUST. Hullo, Werner! Good-day to you, Werner. Welcome to the town.

WERNER. The accursed village! I can't manage to get at home in it again. Merry, my boys, merry; I have got some more money! Where is the Major?

JUST. He must have met you; he just went downstairs.

WERNER. I came up the back stairs. How is he? I should have been with you last week, but —

JUST. Well, what prevented you?

WERNER. Just, did you ever hear of Prince Heraclius?

JUST. Heraclius? Not that I know of.

WERNER. Don't you know the great hero of the East?

JUST. I know the wise men of the East well enough, who go about with the stars on New Year's Eve.

WERNER. Brother, I believe you read the newspapers as little as the Bible. You do not know Prince Heraclius? Not know the brave man who seized Persia, and will break into the Ottoman Porte in a few days? Thank God, there is still war somewhere in the world! I have long enough hoped it would break out here again. But there they sit and take care of their skins. No, a soldier I was, and a soldier I must be again! In short [looking round carefully, to see if any one is listening], between ourselves, Just, I am going to Persia, to have a few campaigns against the Turks, under his Royal Highness Prince Heraclius.

JUST. You?

WERNER. I myself. Our ancestors fought bravely against the Turks; and so ought we, too, if we would be honest men and good Christians. I allow that a campaign against the Turks cannot be half so pleasant as one against the French; but then it must be so much the more beneficial in this world and the next. The swords of the Turks are all set with diamonds.

JUST. I would not walk a mile to have my head split with one of their sabers. You will not be so mad as to leave your comfortable little farm!

WERNER. Oh! I take that with me. Do you see? The property is sold.

JUST. Sold?

WERNER. Hist! Here are a hundred ducats, which I received yesterday toward the payment: I am bringing them for the Major.

JUST. What is he to do with them?

WERNER. What is he to do with them?

Spend them; play them, or drink them away, or whatever he pleases. He must have money, and it is bad enough that they have made his own so troublesome to him. But I know what I would do, were I in his place. I would say — "The deuce take you all here; I will go with Paul Werner to Persia!" Hang it! Prince Heraclius must have heard of Major von Tellheim, if he has not heard of Paul Werner, his late sergeant. Our affair at Katzenhäuser —

JUST. Shall I give you an account of that?

WERNER. You give me! I know well that a fine battle array is beyond your comprehension. I am not going to throw my pearls before swine. Here, take the hundred ducats; give them to the Major: tell him, he may keep these for me too. I am going to the market now. I have sent in a couple of loads of rye; what I get for them he can also have.

JUST. Werner, you mean it well; but we don't want your money. Keep your ducats; and your hundred pistoles you can also have back safe, as soon as you please.

WERNER. What, has the Major money still?

JUST. No.

WERNER. Has he borrowed any?

JUST. No.

WERNER. On what does he live, then?

JUST. We have everything put down in the bill; and when they won't put anything more down, and turn us out of the house, we pledge anything we may happen to have, and go somewhere else. I say, Paul, we must play this landlord here a trick.

WERNER. If he has annoyed the Major, I am ready.

JUST. What if we watch for him in the evening, when he comes from his club, and give him a good thrashing?

WERNER. In the dark! Watch for him! Two to one! No, that won't do.

JUST. Or if we burn his house over his head?

WERNER. Fire and burn! Why, Just, one hears that you have been baggage-boy and not soldier. Shame!

JUST. Or if we ruin his daughter? But she is cursedly ugly.

WERNER. She has probably been ruined long ago. At any rate, you don't want any help there. But what is the matter with you? What has happened?

JUST. Just come with me, and you shall hear something to make you stare.

WERNER. The devil must be loose here, then?

JUST. Just so; come along.

WERNER. So much the better! To Persia, then; to Persia.

ACT II

SCENE: Minna's *Room.*

MINNA [*in morning dress, looking at her watch*]. Franziska, we have risen very early. The time will hang heavy on our hands.

FRANZISKA. Who can sleep in these abominable large towns? The carriages, the watchmen, the drums, the cats, the soldiers, never cease to rattle, to call, to roll, to mew, and to swear; just as if the last thing the night is intended for was for sleep. Have a cup of tea, my lady!

MINNA. I don't care for tea.

FRANZISKA. I will have some chocolate made.

MINNA. For yourself, if you like.

FRANZISKA. For myself! I would as soon talk to myself as drink by myself. Then the time will, indeed, hang heavy. For very weariness we shall have to make our toilets, and try on the dress in which we intend to make the first attack?

MINNA. Why do you talk of attacks, when I have only come to require that the capitulation be ratified?

FRANZISKA. But the officer whom we have dislodged, and to whom we have apologized, cannot be the best-bred man in the world, or he might at least have begged the honor of being allowed to wait upon you.

MINNA. All officers are not Tellheims. To tell you the truth, I only sent him the message in order to have an opportunity of inquiring from him about Tellheim. Franziska, my heart tells me my journey will be a successful one and that I shall find him.

FRANZISKA. The heart, my lady! One must not trust to that too much. The heart echoes to us the words of our tongues. If the tongue was as much inclined to speak the thoughts of the heart, the fashion of keeping mouths under lock and key would have come in long ago.

MINNA. Ha, ha! Mouths under lock and key! That fashion would just suit me.

FRANZISKA. Rather not show the most beautiful set of teeth than let the heart be seen through them every moment.

MINNA. What, are you so reserved?

FRANZISKA. No, my lady; but I would willingly be more so. People seldom talk of the virtue they possess, and all the more often of that which they do not possess.

MINNA. Franziska, you made a very just remark there.

FRANZISKA. Made! Does one make it, if it occurs to one?

MINNA. And do you know why I consider it so good? It applies to my Tellheim.

FRANZISKA. What would not, in your opinion, apply to him?

MINNA. Friend and foe say he is the bravest man in the world. But who ever heard him talk of bravery? He has the most upright mind; but uprightness and nobleness of mind are words never on his tongue.

FRANZISKA. Of what virtues does he talk, then?

MINNA. He talks of none, for he is wanting in none.

FRANZISKA. That is just what I wished to hear.

MINNA. Wait, Franziska; I am wrong. He often talks of economy. Between ourselves, I believe he is extravagant.

FRANZISKA. One thing more, my lady. I have often heard him mention truth and constancy toward you. What, if he be inconstant?

MINNA. Miserable girl! But do you mean that seriously?

FRANZISKA. How long is it since he wrote to you?

MINNA. Alas, he has only written to me once since the peace.

FRANZISKA. What! A sigh on account of the peace? Surprising! Peace ought only to make good the ill which war causes; but it seems to disturb the good which the latter, its opposite, may have occasioned. Peace should not be so capricious! — How long have we had peace? The time seems wonderfully long, when there is so little news. It is no use the post going regularly again; nobody writes, for nobody has anything to write about.

MINNA. "Peace has been made," he wrote to me, "and I am approaching the fulfillment of my wishes." But since he only wrote that to me once, only once —

FRANZISKA. And since he compels us to run after this fulfillment of his wishes ourselves — If we can but find him, he shall pay for this! Suppose, in the mean time, he may have accomplished his wishes, and we should learn here that —

MINNA [anxiously]. That he is dead?

FRANZISKA. To you, my lady; and married to another.

MINNA. You tease, you! Wait, Franziska, I will pay you out for this! But talk to me, or I shall fall asleep. His regiment was disbanded after the peace. Who knows into what a confusion of bills and papers he may thereby have been brought? Who knows into what other regiment, or to what distant station, he may have been sent? Who knows what circumstances — There's a knock at the door.

FRANZISKA. Come in!

LANDLORD [putting his head in at the door]. Am I permitted, your ladyship?

FRANZISKA. Our landlord? — Come in!

LANDLORD [a pen behind his ear, a sheet of paper and an inkstand in his hand]. I am come, your ladyship, to wish you a most humble good-morning. [To FRANZISKA.] And the same to you, my pretty maid.

FRANZISKA. A polite man!

MINNA. We are obliged to you.

FRANZISKA. And wish you also a good-morning.

LANDLORD. May I venture to ask how your ladyship has passed the first night under my poor roof?

FRANZISKA. The roof is not so bad, sir; but the beds might have been better.

LANDLORD. What do I hear! Not slept well! Perhaps the over-fatigue of the journey —

MINNA. Perhaps.

LANDLORD. Certainly, certainly, for otherwise — Yet, should there be anything not perfectly comfortable, my lady, I hope you will not fail to command me.

FRANZISKA. Very well, Mr. Landlord, very well! We are not bashful; and least of all should one be bashful at an inn. We shall not fail to say what we may wish.

LANDLORD. I next come to —
[Taking the pen from behind his ear.]

FRANZISKA. Well?

LANDLORD. Without doubt, my lady, you are already acquainted with the wise regulations of our police.

MINNA. Not in the least, sir.

LANDLORD. We landlords are instructed not to take in any stranger, of whatever rank or sex he may be, for four-and-twenty hours, without delivering, in writing, his name, place of abode, occupation, object of his journey, probable stay, and so on, to the proper authorities.

MINNA. Very well.

LANDLORD. Will your ladyship then be so good —
[Going to the table, and making ready to write.]

MINNA. Willingly. My name is —

LANDLORD. One minute! [He writes.] "Date, 22d August, A.D., etc.; arrived at the King of Spain Hotel." Now your name, my lady.

MINNA. Fräulein von Barnhelm.

LANDLORD [writes]. "Von Barnhelm." Coming from — where, your ladyship?

MINNA. From my estate in Saxony.

LANDLORD [writes]. "Estate in Saxony." Saxony! Indeed, indeed! In Saxony, your ladyship? Saxony?

FRANZISKA. Well, why not? I hope it is no sin in this country to come from Saxony!

LANDLORD. A sin? Heaven forbid! That would be quite a new sin! From Saxony, then? Yes, yes, from Saxony, a delightful country, Saxony! But if I am right, your ladyship, Saxony is not small, and has several — how shall I call them? — districts, provinces. Our police are very particular, your ladyship.

MINNA. I understand. From my estate in Thuringia, then.

LANDLORD. From Thuringia! Yes, that is better, your ladyship; that is more exact. [*Writes and reads.*] "Fräulein von Barnhelm, coming from her estate in Thuringia, together with her lady in waiting and two menservants."

FRANZISKA. Lady in waiting! That means me, I suppose!

LANDLORD. Yes, my pretty maid.

FRANZISKA. Well, Mr. Landlord, instead of "lady in waiting," write "maid in waiting." You say, the police are very exact; it might cause a misunderstanding, which might give me trouble some day when my banns are read out. For I really am still unmarried, and my name is Franziska, with the family name of Willig: Franziska Willig. I also come from Thuringia. My father was a miller, on one of my lady's estates. It is called Little Rammsdorf. My brother has the mill now. I was taken very early to the manor, and educated with my lady. We are of the same age — one-and-twenty next Candlemas. I learned everything my lady learned. I should like the police to have a full account of me.

LANDLORD. Quite right, my pretty maid; I will bear that in mind, in case of future inquiries. — But now, your ladyship, your business here?

MINNA. My business here?

LANDLORD. Have you any business with His Majesty the King?

MINNA. Oh, no.

LANDLORD. Or at our courts of justice?

MINNA. No.

LANDLORD. Or —

MINNA. No, no. I have come here solely on account of my own private affairs.

LANDLORD. Quite right, your ladyship; but what are those private affairs?

MINNA. They are — Franziska, I think we are undergoing an examination.

FRANZISKA. Mr. Landlord, the police surely do not ask to know a young lady's secrets!

LANDLORD. Certainly, my pretty maid; the police wish to know everything, and especially secrets.

FRANZISKA. What is to be done, my lady? — Well, listen, Mr. Landlord — but take care that it does not go beyond ourselves and the police.

MINNA. What is the simpleton going to tell him?

FRANZISKA. We come to carry off an officer from the king.

LANDLORD. How? What? My dear girl!

FRANZISKA. Or to let ourselves be carried off by the officer. It is all one.

MINNA. Franziska, are you mad? The saucy girl is laughing at you.

LANDLORD. I hope not! With your humble servant, indeed, she may jest as much as she pleases; but with the police —

MINNA. I tell you what; I do not understand how to act in this matter. Suppose you postpone the whole affair till my uncle's arrival. I told you yesterday why he did not come with me. He had an accident to his carriage ten miles from here, and did not wish that I should remain a night longer on the road, so I had to come on. I am sure he will not be more than four-and-twenty hours after us.

LANDLORD. Very well, madam, we will wait for him.

MINNA. He will be able to answer your questions better. He will know to whom, and to what extent, he must give an account of himself — what he must relate respecting his affairs, and what he may withhold.

LANDLORD. So much the better! Indeed, one cannot expect a young girl [*looking at* FRANZISKA *in a marked manner*] to treat a serious matter with serious people in a serious manner.

MINNA. And his rooms are in readiness, I hope?

LANDLORD. Quite, your ladyship, quite; except the one —

FRANZISKA. Out of which, I suppose, you will have to turn some other honorable gentleman!

LANDLORD. The waiting maids of Saxony, your ladyship, seem to be very compassionate.

MINNA. In truth, sir, that was not well done. You ought rather to have refused us.

LANDLORD. Why so, your ladyship, why so?

MINNA. I understand that the officer who was driven out on our account —

LANDLORD. Is only a discharged officer, your ladyship.

MINNA. Well, what then?

LANDLORD. Who is almost done for.

MINNA. So much the worse! He is said to be a very deserving man.

LANDLORD. But I tell you he is discharged.

MINNA. The king cannot be acquainted with every deserving man.

LANDLORD. Oh, doubtless he knows them; he knows them all.

MINNA. But he cannot reward them all.

LANDLORD. They would have been rewarded if they had lived so as to deserve it. But they lived during the war as if it would last forever; as if the words "yours" and "mine" were done away with altogether. Now all the hotels and inns are full of them, and a landlord has to be on his guard with them. I have come off pretty well with this one. If he had no more money, he had at any rate money's worth; and I might, indeed, have let him remain quiet two or three months longer. However, it is better as it is. By the by, your ladyship, you understand about jewels, I suppose?

MINNA. Not particularly.

LANDLORD. Of course your ladyship must. I must show you a ring — a valuable ring. I see you have a very beautiful one on your finger; and the more I look at it, the more I am astonished at the resemblance it bears to mine. There! Just look, just look! [Taking the ring from its case, and handing it to her.] What brilliancy! The diamond in the middle alone weighs more than five carats.

MINNA [looking at it]. Good Heavens! What do I see? This ring —

LANDLORD. Is honestly worth fifteen hundred thalers.

MINNA. Franziska! Look!

LANDLORD. I did not hesitate for a moment to advance eighty pistoles on it.

MINNA. Do not you recognize it, Franziska?

FRANZISKA. The same! Where did you get that ring, Mr. Landlord?

LANDLORD. Come, my girl! You surely have no claim to it?

FRANZISKA. We have no claim to this ring! My mistress's monogram must be on it, on the inner side of the setting. — Look at it, my lady.

MINNA. It is! It is! How did you get this ring?

LANDLORD. I! In the most honorable way in the world. You do not wish to bring me into disgrace and trouble, your ladyship! How do I know where the ring properly belongs? During the war many a thing often changed masters, both with and without the knowledge of its owner. War was war. Other rings will have crossed the borders of Saxony. Give it me again, your ladyship; give it me again!

FRANZISKA. When you have said from whom you got it.

LANDLORD. From a man whom I cannot think capable of such things; in other respects a good man —

MINNA. From the best man under the sun, if you have it from its owner. Bring him here directly! It is himself, or, at any rate, he must know him.

LANDLORD. Who? Who, your ladyship?

FRANZISKA. Are you deaf? Our Major!

LANDLORD. Major! Right! He is a Major, who had this room before you, and from whom I received it.

MINNA. Major von Tellheim!

LANDLORD. Yes, Tellheim. Do you know him?

MINNA. Do I know him! He is here! Tellheim here! He had this room! He! He pledged this ring with you! What has brought him into this embarrassment? Where is he? Does he owe you anything? — Franziska, my desk here! Open it! [FRANZISKA puts it on the table and opens it.] — What does he owe you? To whom else does he owe anything? Bring me all his creditors! Here is gold; here are notes. It is all his!

LANDLORD. What is this?

MINNA. Where is he? Where is he?

LANDLORD. An hour ago he was here.

MINNA. Detested man! How could you act so rudely, so hardly, so cruelly toward him?

LANDLORD. Your ladyship must pardon —

MINNA. Quick! Bring him to me.

LANDLORD. His servant is perhaps still here. Does your ladyship wish that he should look for him?

MINNA. Do I wish it? Begone, run! For this service alone I will forget how badly you have behaved to him.

FRANZISKA. Now, then, quick, Mr. Landlord! Be off! Fly! Fly!

[*Pushes him out.*]

MINNA. Now I have found him again, Franziska! Do you hear? Now I have found him again! I scarcely know where I am for joy! Rejoice with me, Franziska. But why should you? And yet you shall; you must rejoice with me. Come, I will make you a present, that you may be able to rejoice with me. Say, Franziska, what shall I give you? Which of my things would please you? What would you like? Take what you will; only rejoice with me. I see you will take nothing. Stop! [*Thrusts her hand into the desk.*] There, Franziska [*gives her money*], buy yourself what you like. Ask for more, if it be not sufficient; but rejoice with me you must. It is so melancholy to be happy alone! There, take it, then.

FRANZISKA. It is stealing it from you, my lady. You are intoxicated, quite intoxicated with joy.

MINNA. Girl, my intoxication is of a quarrelsome kind. Take it, or [*forcing money into her hand*] — and if you thank me — Stay, it is well that I think of it. [*Takes more money from the desk.*] Put that aside, Franziska, for the first poor wounded soldier who accosts us.

[*Enter* LANDLORD.]

Well, is he coming?

LANDLORD. The cross, unmannered fellow!

MINNA. Who?

LANDLORD. His servant. He refuses to go for him.

FRANZISKA. Bring the rascal here, then.

I know all the Major's servants. Which of them was it?

MINNA. Bring him here directly. When he sees us he will go fast enough.

[*Exit* LANDLORD.]

I cannot bear this delay. But, Franziska, how cold you are still! Why will you not share my joy with me?

FRANZISKA. I would from my heart, if only —

MINNA. If only what?

FRANZISKA. We have found him again. But how have we found him? From all we hear, it must go badly with him. He must be unfortunate. That distresses me.

MINNA. Distresses you! Let me embrace you for that, my dear playmate! I shall never forget this of you. I am only in love, you are good.

[*Enter* LANDLORD *and* JUST.]

LANDLORD. With great difficulty I have brought him.

FRANZISKA. A strange face! I do not know him.

MINNA. Friend, do you live with Major von Tellheim?

JUST. Yes.

MINNA. Where is your master?

JUST. Not here.

MINNA. But you could find him?

JUST. Yes.

MINNA. Will you fetch him quickly?

JUST. No.

MINNA. You will be doing me a favor.

JUST. Indeed!

MINNA. And your master a service.

JUST. Perhaps not.

MINNA. Why do you suppose that?

JUST. You are the strange lady who sent your compliments to him this morning, I think?

MINNA. Yes.

JUST. Then I am right.

MINNA. Does your master know my name?

JUST. No; but he likes over-civil ladies as little as over-uncivil landlords.

LANDLORD. That is meant for me, I suppose?

JUST. Yes.

LANDLORD. Well, do not let the lady

suffer for it then; but bring him here directly.

MINNA [to FRANZISKA]. Franziska, give him something —

FRANZISKA [trying to put some money into JUST's hand]. We do not require your services for nothing.

JUST. Nor I your money without services.

FRANZISKA. One in return for the other.

JUST. I cannot. My master has ordered me to pack up. That I am now about, and I beg you not to hinder me further. When I have finished, I will take care to tell him that he may come here. He is close by, at the coffee-house; and if he finds nothing better to do there, I suppose he will come. [Going.]

FRANZISKA. Wait a moment! My lady is the Major's — sister.

MINNA. Yes, yes, his sister.

JUST. I know better; the Major has not a sister. He has sent me twice in six months to his family in Courland. It is true there are different sorts of sisters —

FRANZISKA. Insolent!

JUST. One must be so to get the people to let one alone. [Exit.]

FRANZISKA. That is a rascal!

LANDLORD. So I said. But let him go! I know now where his master is. I will fetch him instantly myself. I only beg your ladyship, most humbly, that you will make an excuse for me to the Major, that I have been so unfortunate as to offend a man of his merit against my will.

MINNA. Pray go quickly. I will set all that right again. [Exit LANDLORD.] — Franziska, run after him, and tell him not to mention my name! [Exit FRANZISKA.] — I have found him again! — Am I alone? — I will not be alone to no purpose. [Clasping her hands.] Yet I am not alone! [Looking upward.] One single grateful thought toward Heaven is the most perfect prayer! I have found him! [With outstretched arms.] I am joyful and happy! What can please the Creator more than a joyful creature! [FRANZISKA returns.] Have you returned, Franziska? You pity him! I do not pity him. Misfortune too is useful. Perhaps Heaven deprived him of

everything — to give him all again, through me!

FRANZISKA. He may be here any moment. — You are still in your morning dress, my lady. Ought you not to dress yourself quickly?

MINNA. Not at all. He will now see me more frequently so than dressed out.

FRANZISKA. Oh! You know, my lady, how you look best.

MINNA [after a pause]. Truly, girl, you have hit it again.

FRANZISKA. I think women who are beautiful are most so when unadorned.

MINNA. Must we then be beautiful? Perhaps it is necessary that we should think ourselves so. Enough for me if only I am beautiful in his eyes. Franziska, if all women feel as I now feel, we are — strange things. Tender-hearted, yet proud; virtuous, yet vain; passionate, yet innocent. I dare say you do not understand me. I do not rightly understand myself. Joy tu ns my head.

FRANZISKA. Compose yourself, my lady. I hear footsteps.

MINNA. Compose myself! What! receive him composedly?

[Enter MAJOR VON TELLHEIM and LANDLORD.]

MAJOR VON TELLHEIM [walks in, and the moment he sees MINNA rushes toward her]. Ah! my Minna!

MINNA [springing toward him]. Ah! my Tellheim!

MAJOR VON TELLHEIM [starts suddenly, and draws back]. I beg your pardon, Fräulein von Barnhelm; but to meet you here —

MINNA. Cannot surely be so very unexpected! [Approaching him, while he draws back still more.] Am I to pardon you because I am still your Minna? Heaven pardon you, that I am still Fräulein von Barnhelm!

MAJOR VON TELLHEIM. Fräulein — [Looks fixedly at the LANDLORD, and shrugs his shoulders.]

MINNA [seeing the LANDLORD, and making a sign to FRANZISKA]. Sir —

MAJOR VON TELLHEIM. If we are not both mistaken —

FRANZISKA. Why, Landlord, whom have you brought us here? Come, quick, let us go and look for the right man.

LANDLORD. Is he not the right one? Surely!

FRANZISKA. Surely not! Come, quick! I have not yet wished your daughter good-morning.

LANDLORD. Oh! you are very good.

[*Still does not stir.*]

FRANZISKA [*taking hold of him*]. Come, and we will make the bill of fare. Let us see what we shall have.

LANDLORD. You shall have first of all —

FRANZISKA. Stop, I say, stop! If my mistress knows now what she is to have for dinner, it will be all over with her appetite. Come, we must talk that over in private.

[*Drags h m off.*]

MINNA. Well, are we still both mistaken?

MAJOR VON TELLHEIM. Would to Heaven it were so! — But there is only one Minna, and you are that one.

MINNA. What ceremony! The world might hear what we have to say to one another.

MAJOR VON TELLHEIM. You here? What do you want here, madam?

MINNA. Nothing now. [*Going to him with open arms.*] I have found all that I wanted.

MAJOR VON TELLHEIM [*drawing back*]. You seek a prosperous man, and one worthy of your love; and you find — a wretched one.

MINNA. Then do you love me no longer? Do you love another?

MAJOR VON TELLHEIM. Ah! He never loved you, who could love another afterward.

MINNA. You draw but one dagger from my breast; for if I have lost your heart, what matters whether indifference or more powerful charms than mine have robbed me of it? You love me no longer; neither do you love another? Wretched man, indeed, if you love nothing!

MAJOR VON TELLHEIM. Right; the wretched must love nothing. He merits his misfortunes, if he cannot achieve this victory over himself — if he can allow the woman he loves to take part in his misfortune — Oh! how difficult is this victory! — Since reason and necessity have commanded me to forget Minna von Barnhelm, what pains have I taken! I was just beginning to hope that my trouble would not forever be in vain — and you appear.

MINNA. Do I understand you right? Stop, sir! Let us see what we mean, before we make further mistakes. Will you answer me one question?

MAJOR VON TELLHEIM. Any one.

MINNA. But will you answer me without shift or subterfuge? With nothing but a plain "Yes," or "No"?

MAJOR VON TELLHEIM. I will — if I can.

MINNA. You can. Well, notwithstanding the pains that you have taken to forget me, do you love me still, Tellheim?

MAJOR VON TELLHEIM. Madam, that question —

MINNA. You have promised to answer Yes, or No.

MAJOR VON TELLHEIM. And added, if I can.

MINNA. You can. You must know what passes in your heart. Do you love me still, Tellheim? Yes, or No?

MAJOR VON TELLHEIM. If my heart —

MINNA. Yes, or No?

MAJOR VON TELLHEIM. Well, yes!

MINNA. Yes?

MAJOR VON TELLHEIM. Yes, yes! Yet —

MINNA. Patience! You love me still; that is enough for me. Into what a mood have we fallen! — an unpleasant, melancholy, infectious mood! I assume my own again. Now, my dear unfortunate, you love me still, and have your Minna still, and you are unhappy? Hear what a conceited, foolish thing your Minna was — is. She allowed — allows herself, to imagine that she makes your whole happiness. Declare all your misery at once. She would like to try how far she can outweigh it. — Well?

MAJOR VON TELLHEIM. Madam, I am not accustomed to complain.

MINNA. Very well. I know nothing in a soldier, after boasting, that pleases me less than complaining. But there is a certain cold, careless way of speaking of bravery and misfortune —

MAJOR VON TELLHEIM. Which at the bottom is still boasting and complaining.

MINNA. You disputant! You should not have called yourself unhappy at all, then. You should have told the whole, or kept quiet. Reason and necessity commanded you to forget me? I am a great stickler for reason; I have a great respect for necessity. But let me hear how reasonable this reason, and how necessary this necessity may be.

MAJOR VON TELLHEIM. Listen then, madam. You call me Tellheim; the name is correct. But you suppose I am that Tellheim whom you knew at home; the prosperous man, full of just pretensions, with a thirst for glory; the master of all his faculties, both of body and mind; before whom the lists of honor and prosperity stood open; who, if he was not then worthy of your heart and your hand, dared to hope that he might daily become more nearly so. This Tellheim I am now, as little as I am my own father. They both have been. Now I am Tellheim the discharged, the suspected, the cripple, the beggar. To the former, madam, you promised your hand; do you wish to keep your word?

MINNA. That sounds very tragic. — Yet, Major Tellheim, until I find the former one again — I am quite foolish about the Tellheims — the latter will have to help me in my dilemma. Your hand, dear beggar! [Taking his hand.]

MAJOR VON TELLHEIM [holding his hat before his face with the other hand, and turning away from her]. This is too much! — What am I? — Let me go, madam. Your kindness tortures me! Let me go.

MINNA. What is the matter? Where would you go?

MAJOR VON TELLHEIM. From you!

MINNA. From me? [Drawing his hand to her heart.] Dreamer!

MAJOR VON TELLHEIM. Despair will lay me dead at your feet.

MINNA. From me?

MAJOR VON TELLHEIM. From you. Never, never to see you again. Or at least determined, fully determined, never to be guilty of a mean action; never to cause you to commit an imprudent one. Let me go, Minna. [Tears himself away, and exit.]

MINNA [calling after him]. Let you go, Minna? Minna, let you go? Tellheim! Tellheim!

ACT III

SCENE: *The Parlor.*

[*Enter* JUST, *with a letter in his hand.*]

JUST. Must I come again into this cursed house! A note from my master to her ladyship that would be his sister. I hope nothing will come of this, or else there will be no end to letter-carrying. I should like to be rid of it; but yet I don't wish to go into the room. The women ask so many questions, and I hate answering. — Ah, the door opens. Just what I wanted, the waiting puss!

FRANZISKA [calling through the door by which she has just entered]. Fear not; I will watch. [Observing JUST.] See! I have met with something immediately. But nothing is to be done with that brute.

JUST. Your servant.

FRANZISKA. I should not like such a servant.

JUST. Well, well, pardon the expression! There is a note from my master to your mistress — her ladyship — his sister, was n't it? — sister.

FRANZISKA. Give it me!
[Snatches it from his hand.]

JUST. You will be so good, my master begs, as to deliver it. Afterward you will be so good, my master begs, as not to think I ask for anything!

FRANZISKA. Well?

JUST. My master understands how to manage the affair. He knows that the way to the young lady is through her maid, methinks. The maid will therefore be so good, my master begs, as to let him know whether he may not have the pleasure of speaking with the maid for a quarter of an hour.

FRANZISKA. With me?

JUST. Pardon me, if I do not give you your right title. Yes, with you. Only for one quarter of an hour; but alone, quite alone, in private, tête-à-tête. He has something very particular to say to you.

FRANZISKA. Very well! I have also much to say to him. He may come; I shall be at his service.

JUST. But when can he come? When is it most convenient for you, young woman? In the evening?

FRANZISKA. What do you mean? Your master can come when he pleases; and now be off.

JUST. Most willingly! [*Going.*]

FRANZISKA. I say! — one word more! Where are the rest of the Major's servants?

JUST. The rest? Here, there, and everywhere.

FRANZISKA. Where is William?

JUST. The valet? He has let him go for a trip.

FRANZISKA. Oh! — and Philip, where is he?

JUST. The huntsman? Master has found him a good place.

FRANZISKA. Because he does not hunt now, of course. But Martin?

JUST. The coachman? He is off on a ride.

FRANZISKA. And Fritz?

JUST. The footman? He is promoted.

FRANZISKA. Where were you, then, when the Major was quartered in Thuringia with us last winter? You were not with him, I suppose!

JUST. Oh, yes, I was groom; but I was in the hospital.

FRANZISKA. Groom! and now you are —

JUST. All in all; valet and huntsman, footman and groom.

FRANZISKA. Well, I never! To turn away so many good, excellent servants, and to keep the very worst of all! I should like to know what your master finds in you!

JUST. Perhaps he finds that I am an honest fellow.

FRANZISKA. Oh! One is precious little if one is nothing more than honest. William was another sort of a man! So your master has let him go for a trip?

JUST. Yes, he — let him — because he could not prevent him.

FRANZISKA. How so?

JUST. Oh! William will do well on his travels. He took master's wardrobe with him.

FRANZISKA. What! He did not run away with it?

JUST. I cannot say that exactly; but when we left Nürnberg, he did not follow us with it.

FRANZISKA. Oh, the rascal!

JUST. He was the right sort! He could curl hair and shave — and chatter — and flirt — could n't he?

FRANZISKA. At any rate, I would not have turned away the huntsman, had I been in the Major's place. If he did not want him any longer as huntsman, he was still a useful fellow. Where has he found him a place?

JUST. With the Commandant of Spandau.

FRANZISKA. The fortress! There cannot be much hunting within the walls either.

JUST. Oh! Philip does not hunt there.

FRANZISKA. What does he do then?

JUST. He rides — on the treadmill.

FRANZISKA. The treadmill!

JUST. But only for three years. He made a bit of a plot among master's company, to get six men through the outposts.

FRANZISKA. I am astonished; the knave!

JUST. Ah, he was a useful fellow; a huntsman who knew all the footpaths and byways for fifty miles round, through forests and bogs. And he could shoot!

FRANZISKA. It is lucky the Major has still got the honest coachman.

JUST. Has he got him still?

FRANZISKA. I thought you said Martin was off on a ride: of course he will come back!

JUST. Do you think so?

FRANZISKA. Well, where has he ridden to?

JUST. It is now going on for ten weeks since he rode master's last and only horse — to water.

FRANZISKA. And has not he come back yet? Oh, the rascal!

JUST. The water may have washed the honest coachman away. Oh, he was a famous coachman! He had driven ten years in Vienna. My master will never get such another again. When the horses were in full gallop, he only had to say "Whoa!" and there they stood, like a wall. Moreover, he was a finished horse-doctor!

FRANZISKA. I begin now to be anxious about the footman's promotion.

JUST. No, no; there is no occasion for that. He has become a drummer in a garrison regiment.

FRANZISKA. I thought as much!

JUST. Fritz chummed up with a scamp, never came home at night, made debts everywhere in master's name, and a thousand rascally tricks. In short, the Major saw that he was determined to rise in the world [pantomimically imitating the act of hanging], so he put him in the right road.

FRANZISKA. Oh, the stupid!

JUST. Yet a perfect footman, there is no doubt of that. In runng, my master could not catch him on his best horse if he gave him fifty paces; but on the other hand, Fritz could give the gallows a thousand paces, and, I bet my life, he would overhaul it. They were all great friends of yours, eh, young woman? — William and Philip, Martin and Fritz! Now, Just wishes you good-day. [Exit.]

FRANZISKA [looking after him seriously]. I deserve the hit! Thank you, Just. I undervalued honesty. I will not forget the lesson. Ah, our unfortunate Major!

[Turns round to enter her mistress's room, when the LANDLORD comes.]

LANDLORD. Wait a bit, my pretty maid.

FRANZISKA. I have not time now, Mr. Landlord.

LANDLORD. Only half a moment! No further tidings of the Major? That surely could not possibly be his leave-taking!

FRANZISKA. What could not?

LANDLORD. Has not her ladyship told you? When I left you, my pretty maid, below in the kitchen, I returned accidentally into this room —

FRANZISKA. Accidentally — with a view to listen a little.

LANDLORD. What, girl! How can you suspect me of that? There is nothing so bad in a landlord as curiosity. I had not

been here long, when suddenly her ladyship's door burst open: the Major dashed out; the lady after him; both in such a state of excitement; with looks — in attitudes — that must be seen to be understood. She seized hold of him; he tore himself away; she seized him again — "Tellheim." "Let me go, madam." "Where?" Thus he drew her as far as the staircase. I was really afraid he would drag her down; but he got away. The lady remained on the top step; looked after him; called after him; wrung her hands. Suddenly she turned round; ran to the window; from the window to the staircase again; from the staircase into the room, backward and forward. There I stood; she passed me three times without seeing me. At length it seemed as if she saw me; but Heaven defend us! I believe the lady took me for you. "Franziska," she cried, with her eyes fixed upon me, "am I happy now?" Then she looked straight up to the ceiling, and said again, "Am I happy now?" Then she wiped the tears from her eyes, and smiled, and asked me again, "Franziska, am I happy now?" I really felt, I know not how. Then she ran to the door of her room, and turned round again toward me, saying, "Come, Franziska, whom do you pity now?" And with that she went in.

FRANZISKA. Oh! Mr. Landlord, you dreamed that.

LANDLORD. Dreamed! No, my pretty maid; one does not dream so minutely. Yes, what would not I give — I am not curious: but what would not I give — to have the key to it!

FRANZISKA. The key? Of our door? Mr. Landlord, that is inside; we take it in at night; we are timid.

LANDLORD. Not that sort of key; I mean, my dear girl, the key — the explanation, as it were; the precise connection of all that I have seen.

FRANZISKA. Indeed! Well, good-bye, Mr. Landlord. Shall we have dinner soon?

LANDLORD. My dear girl, not to forget what I came to say —

FRANZISKA. Well? In as few words as possible.

LANDLORD. Her ladyship has my ring still. I call it mine —

FRANZISKA. You shall not lose it.

LANDLORD. I have no fear on that account: I merely put you in mind. Do you see, I do not wish to have it again at all. I can guess pretty well how she knew the ring, and why it was so like her own. It is best in her hands. I do not want it any more; and I can put them down — the hundred pistoles which I advanced for it, to the lady's bill. Will not that do, my pretty maid?

[*Enter* PAUL WERNER.]

WERNER. There he is!

FRANZISKA. A hundred pistoles? I thought it was only eighty.

LANDLORD. True, only ninety, only ninety. I will do so, my pretty maid, I will do so.

FRANZISKA. All that will come right, Mr. Landlord.

WERNER [*coming from behind, and tapping* FRANZISKA *on the shoulder*]. Little woman — little woman.

FRANZISKA [*frightened*]. Oh! dear!

WERNER. Don't be alarmed! I see you are pretty, and a stranger, too. And strangers who are pretty must be warned. Little woman! Little woman! I advise you to beware of that fellow!

[*Pointing to the* LANDLORD.]

LANDLORD. Ah! What an unexpected pleasure! Herr Werner! Welcome, welcome! Yes, you are just the same jovial, joking, honest Werner! — So you are to beware of me, my pretty maid. Ha, ha, ha!

WERNER. Keep out of his way everywhere!

LANDLORD. My way? Am I such a dangerous man? Ha, ha, ha! — Hear him, my pretty maid! A good joke, is n't it?

WERNER. People like him always call it a joke, if one tells them the truth.

LANDLORD. The truth. Ha, ha, ha! Better and better, my pretty maid, is n't it? He knows how to joke! I dangerous? I? Twenty years ago there might have been something in it. Yes, yes, my pretty maid, then I was a dangerous man; many a one knew it; but now —

WERNER. Oh, the old fool!

LANDLORD. There it is! When we get old, danger is at an end! It will be so with you too, Herr Werner!

WERNER. You utter old fool! — Little woman, you will give me credit for enough common sense not to speak of danger from him. That one devil has left him, but seven others have entered into him.

LANDLORD. Oh, hear him! How cleverly he can turn things about! Joke upon joke, and always something new! Ah, he is an excellent man, Paul Werner is. [*To* FRANZISKA, *as if whispering.*] A well-to-do man, and a bachelor still. He has a nice little freehold three miles from here. He made prize-money in the war, and was a sergeant to the Major. Yes, he is a real friend of the Major's; he is a friend who would give his life for him.

WERNER. Yes. [*Pointing to the* LANDLORD.] And that is a friend of the Major's — that is a friend — whose life the Major ought to take.

LANDLORD. How! What! No, Herr Werner, that is not a good joke. I no friend of the Major! I don't understand that joke.

WERNER. Just has told me pretty things.

LANDLORD. Just! Ah! I thought Just was speaking through you. Just is a nasty, ill-natured man. But here on the spot stands a pretty maid — she can speak, she can say if I am no friend of the Major's — if I have not done him good service. And why should not I be his friend? Is not he a deserving man? It is true, he has had the misfortune to be discharged; but what of that? The king cannot be acquainted with all deserving officers; and if he knew them, he could not reward them all.

WERNER. Heaven put those words into your mouth. But Just — certainly there is nothing remarkable about Just, but still Just is no liar; and if what he has told me be true —

LANDLORD. I don't want to hear anything about Just. As I said, this pretty maid here can speak. [*Whispering to her.*] You know, my dear; the ring! Tell Herr Werner about it. Then he will learn better

what I am. And that it may not appear as if she only said what I wish, I will not even be present. — I will go; but you shall tell me after, Herr Werner, you shall tell me, whether Just is not a foul slanderer.
[*Exit.*]
WERNER. Little woman, do you know my Major?
FRANZISKA. Major von Tellheim? Yes, indeed, I do know that good man.
WERNER. Is he not a good man? Do you like him?
FRANZISKA. From the bottom of my heart.
WERNER. Indeed! I tell you what, little woman, you are twice as pretty now as you were before. But what are the services which the Landlord says he has rendered our Major?
FRANZISKA. That is what I don't know; unless he wished to take credit to himself for the good result which fortunately has arisen from his knavish conduct.
WERNER. Then what Just told me is true? [*Toward the side where the* LANDLORD *went off.*] A lucky thing for you that you are gone! He did really turn him out of his room? — To treat such a man so, because the donkey fancied that he had no more money! The Major no money! FRANZISKA. What! Has the Major any money?
WERNER. By the load. He does n't know how much he has. He does n't know who is in his debt. I am his debtor, and have brought him some old arrears. Look, little woman, in this purse [*drawing it out of one pocket*] are a hundred louis d'ors; and in this packet [*drawing it out of another pocket*] a hundred ducats. All his money!
FRANZISKA. Really! Why, then, does the Major pawn his things? He pledged a ring, you know —
WERNER. Pledged! Don't you believe it. Perhaps he wanted to get rid of the rubbish.
FRANZISKA. It is no rubbish; it is a very valuable ring; which, moreover, I suspect, he received from a loving hand.
WERNER. That will be the reason. From a loving hand! Yes, yes; such a thing often puts one in mind of what one

does not wish to remember, and therefore one gets rid of it.
FRANZISKA. What!
WERNER. Odd things happen to the soldier in winter quarters. He has nothing to do then, so he amuses himself, and to pass the time he makes acquaintances, which he only intends for the winter, but which the good soul with whom he makes them, looks upon for life. Then, presto! a ring is suddenly conjured on to his finger; he hardly knows himself how it gets there; and very often he would willingly give the finger with it, if he could only get free from it again.
FRANZISKA. Oh! And do you think this has happened to the Major?
WERNER. Undoubtedly. Especially in Saxony. If he had had ten fingers on each hand, he might have had all twenty full of rings.
FRANZISKA [*aside*]. That sounds important, and deserves to be inquired into. Mr. Freeholder, or Mr. Sergeant —
WERNER. Little woman, if it makes no difference to you, I like "Mr. Sergeant" best.
FRANZISKA. Well, Mr. Sergeant, I have a note from the Major to my mistress. I will carry it in, and be here again in a moment. Will you be so good as to wait? I should like very much to have a little talk with you.
WERNER. Are you fond of talking, little woman? Well, with all my heart. Go quickly. I am fond of talking too; I will wait.
FRANZISKA. Yes, please wait. [*Exit.*]
WERNER. That is not at all a bad little woman. But I ought not to have promised her that I would wait, for it would be most to the purpose, I suppose, to find the Major. He will not have my money, but rather pawns his property. That is just his way. A little trick occurs to me. When I was in the town, a fortnight back, I paid a visit to Captain Marloff's widow. The poor woman was ill, and was lamenting that her husband had died in debt to the Major for four hundred thalers, which she did not know how to pay. I went to see her again to-day; I intended to tell her that I could

lend her five hundred thalers, when I had received the money for my property; for I must put some of it by, if I do not go to Persia. But she was gone; and no doubt she has not been able to pay the Major. Yes, I'll do that; and the sooner the better. The little woman must not take it ill of me; I cannot wait.

[*Is going, thoughtfully, and almost runs against the* MAJOR, *who meets him.*]

MAJOR VON TELLHEIM. Why so thoughtful, Werner?

WERNER. Oh, that is you! I was just going to pay you a visit in your new quarters, Major.

MAJOR VON TELLHEIM. To fill my ears with curses against the Landlord of my old one. Do not remind me of it.

WERNER. I should have done that by the way; yes. But more particularly, I wished to thank you for having been so good as to take care of my hundred louis d'ors. Just has given them to me again. I should have been very glad if you would have kept them longer for me. But you have got into new quarters, which neither you nor I know much about. Who knows what sort of place it is? They might be stolen, and you would have to make them good to me; there would be no help for it. So I cannot ask you to take them again.

MAJOR VON TELLHEIM [*smiling*]. When did you begin to be so careful, Werner?

WERNER. One learns to be so. One cannot now be careful enough of one's money. I have also a commission for you, Major, from Frau Marloff; I have just come from her. Her husband died four hundred thalers in your debt; she sends you a hundred ducats here, in part payment. She will forward you the rest next week. I believe I am the cause that she has not sent you the whole sum. For she also owed me about eighty thalers, and she thought I was come to dun her for them — which, perhaps, was the fact — so she gave them me out of the roll which she had put aside for you. You can spare your hundred thalers for a week longer, better than I can spare my few groschens. There, take it! [*Hands him the ducats.*]

MAJOR VON TELLHEIM. Werner!

WERNER. Well! Why do you stare at me so? Take it, Major!

MAJOR VON TELLHEIM. Werner!

WERNER. What is the matter with you? What annoys you?

MAJOR VON TELLHEIM [*angrily striking his forehead, and stamping with his foot*]. That — the four hundred thalers are not all there.

WERNER. Come! Major, did not you understand me?

MAJOR VON TELLHEIM. It is because I did understand you! Alas, that the best men should to-day distress me most!

WERNER. What do you say?

MAJOR VON TELLHEIM. This only applies partly to you. Go, Werner!

[*Pushing back* WERNER'S *hand with the money in it.*]

WERNER. As soon as I have got rid of this.

MAJOR VON TELLHEIM. Werner, suppose I tell you that Frau Marloff was here herself early this morning —

WERNER. Indeed?

MAJOR VON TELLHEIM. That she owes me nothing now —

WERNER. Really?

MAJOR VON TELLHEIM. That she has paid me every penny — What will you say then?

WERNER [*thinks for a minute*]. I shall say that I have told a lie, and that lying is a low thing, because one may be caught at it.

MAJOR VON TELLHEIM. And you will be ashamed of yourself?

WERNER. And what of him who compels me to lie? Should not he be ashamed, too? Look ye, Major; if I was to say that your conduct has not vexed me, I should tell another lie, and I won't lie any more.

MAJOR VON TELLHEIM. Do not be annoyed, Werner. I know your heart, and your affection for me. But I do not require your money.

WERNER. Not require it! Rather sell, rather pawn, and get talked about!

MAJOR VON TELLHEIM. Oh! People may know that I have nothing more. One must not wish to appear richer than one is.

WERNER. But why poorer? A man has something as long as his friend has.

MAJOR VON TELLHEIM. It is not proper that I should be your debtor.

WERNER. Not proper! On that summer day which the sun and the enemy made hot for us, when your groom, who had your canteen, was not to be found, and you came to me and said, "Werner, have you nothing to drink?" and I gave you my flask, you took it and drank, did you not? Was that proper? Upon my life, a mouthful of dirty water at that time was often worth more than such filth. [*Taking the purse also out of his pocket, and holding out both to him.*] Take them, dear Major! Fancy it is water. God has made this, too, for all.

MAJOR VON TELLHEIM. You torment me: don't you hear? I will not be your debtor.

WERNER. At first, it was not proper; now you will not. Ah! that is a different thing. [*Rather angrily.*] You will not be my debtor? But suppose you are already, Major? Or, are you not a debtor to the man who once warded off the blow that was meant to split your head; and, at another time, knocked off the arm which was just going to pull and send a ball through your breast? How can you become a greater debtor to that man? Or, is my neck of less consequence than my money? If that is a noble way of thinking, by my soul, it is a very silly one, too!

MAJOR VON TELLHEIM. To whom do you say that, Werner? We are alone, and therefore I may speak; if a third person heard us, it might sound like boasting. I acknowledge with pleasure that I have to thank you for twice saving my life. Do you not think, friend, that if an opportunity occurred, I would have done as much for you, eh?

WERNER. If an opportunity occurred! Who doubts it, Major? Have I not seen you risk your life a hundred times for the lowest soldier, when he was in danger?

MAJOR VON TELLHEIM. Well!

WERNER. But —

MAJOR VON TELLHEIM. Why cannot you understand me? I say, it is not proper that I should be your debtor; I will not be your debtor. That is, not in the circumstances in which I now am.

WERNER. Oh, so you would wait till better times! You will borrow money from me another time, when you do not want any; when you have some yourself, and I perhaps none!

MAJOR VON TELLHEIM. A man ought not to borrow, when he has not the means of repaying.

WERNER. A man like yourself cannot always be in want.

MAJOR VON TELLHEIM. You know the world — Least of all should a man borrow from one who wants his money himself.

WERNER. Oh, yes; I am such a one! Pray, what do I want it for? When they want a sergeant, they give him enough to live on.

MAJOR VON TELLHEIM. You want it, to become something more than a sergeant — to be able to get forward in that path in which even the most deserving, without money, may remain behind.

WERNER. To become something more than a sergeant! I do not think of that. I am a good sergeant; I might easily make a bad captain, and certainly a worse general.

MAJOR VON TELLHEIM. Do not force me to think ill of you, Werner! I was very sorry to hear what Just has told me. You have sold your farm, and wish to rove about again. Do not let me suppose that you do not love the profession of arms so much as the wild, dissolute way of living which is unfortunately connected with it. A man should be a soldier for his own country, or from love of the cause for which he fights. To serve without any purpose — to-day here, to-morrow there — is only traveling about like a butcher's apprentice, nothing more.

WERNER. Well, then, Major, I will do as you say. You know better what is right. I will remain with you. But, dear Major, do take my money in the mean time. Sooner or later your affairs must be settled. You will get money in plenty then; and then you shall repay me with interest. I only do it for the sake of the interest.

MAJOR VON TELLHEIM. Do not talk of it.

WERNER. Upon my life, I only do it for

the sake of the interest. Many a time I have thought to myself: "Werner, what will become of you in your old age, when you are crippled, when you will have nothing in the world, when you will be obliged to go and beg?" And then I thought again: "No, you will not be obliged to beg; you will go to Major Tellheim; he will share his last penny with you; he will feed you till you die; and with him you can die like an honest fellow."

MAJOR VON TELLHEIM [*taking* WERNER'S *hand*]. And, comrade, you do not think so still?

WERNER. No; I do not think so any longer. He who will not take anything from me, when he is in want, and I have to give, will not give me anything when he has to give, and I am in want. So be it.
[*Is going.*]

MAJOR VON TELLHEIM. Man, do not drive me mad! Where are you going? [*Detains him.*] If I assure you now, upon my honor, that I still have money — if I assure you, upon my honor, that I will tell you when I have no more — that you shall be the first and only person from whom I will borrow anything — will that content you?

WERNER. I suppose it must. Give me your hand on it, Major.

MAJOR VON TELLHEIM. There, Paul! And now enough of that. I came here to speak with a certain young woman.

FRANZISKA [*entering*]. Are you there still, Mr. Sergeant? [*Seeing* TELLHEIM.] And you there, too, Major? I will be at your service instantly.
[*Goes back quickly into the room.*]

MAJOR VON TELLHEIM. That was she! But it seems you know her, Werner.

WERNER. Yes, I know her.

MAJOR VON TELLHEIM. Yet, if I remember rightly, when I was in Thuringia you were not with me.

WERNER. No; I was seeing after the uniforms in Leipzig.

MAJOR VON TELLHEIM. Where did you make her acquaintance, then?

WERNER. Our acquaintance is very young. Not a day old. But young friendship is warm.

MAJOR VON TELLHEIM. Have you seen her mistress, too?

WERNER. Is her mistress a young lady? She told me you are acquainted with her mistress.

MAJOR VON TELLHEIM. Did not you hear? She comes from Thuringia.

WERNER. Is the lady young?

MAJOR VON TELLHEIM. Yes.

WERNER. Pretty?

MAJOR VON TELLHEIM. Very pretty.

WERNER. Rich?

MAJOR VON TELLHEIM. Very rich.

WERNER. Is the mistress as fond of you as the maid is? That would be capital!

MAJOR VON TELLHEIM. What do you mean?

FRANZISKA [*entering with a letter in her hand*]. Major —

MAJOR VON TELLHEIM. Franziska, I have not yet been able to give you a "Welcome" here.

FRANZISKA. In thought, I am sure that you have done it. I know you are friendly to me; so am I to you. But it is not at all kind to vex those who are friendly to you so much.

WERNER [*aside*]. Ah, now I see it! It is so!

MAJOR VON TELLHEIM. My destiny, Franziska! Did you give her the letter?

FRANZISKA. Yes; and here I bring you—
[*Holding out a letter.*]

MAJOR VON TELLHEIM. An answer!

FRANZISKA. No, your own letter again.

MAJOR VON TELLHEIM. What! She will not read it!

FRANZISKA. She would have liked, but — we can't read writing well.

MAJOR VON TELLHEIM. You are joking!

FRANZISKA. And we think that writing was not invented for those who can converse with their lips whenever they please.

MAJOR VON TELLHEIM. What an excuse! She must read it. It contains my justification — all the grounds and reasons —

FRANZISKA. My mistress wishes to hear them all from you yourself, not to read them.

MAJOR VON TELLHEIM. Hear them from me myself! That every look, every word of hers, may embarrass me; that I may feel in every glance the greatness of my loss.

FRANZISKA. Without any pity! Take it. [*Giving him his letter.*] She expects you at three o'clock. She wishes to drive out and see the town; you must accompany her.

MAJOR VON TELLHEIM. Accompany her!

FRANZISKA. And what will you give me to let you drive out by yourselves? I shall remain at home.

MAJOR VON TELLHEIM. By ourselves!

FRANZISKA. In a nice close carriage.

MAJOR VON TELLHEIM. Impossible!

FRANZISKA. Yes, yes, in the carriage, Major. You will have to submit quietly; you cannot escape there! And that is the reason. In short, you will come, Major, and punctually at three — [*Looking at* WERNER.] Well, you wanted to speak to me, too, alone. What have you to say to me? Oh, we are not alone.

MAJOR VON TELLHEIM. Yes, Franziska; as good as alone. But as your mistress has not read my letter, I have nothing now to say to you.

FRANZISKA. As good as alone! Then you have no secrets from the Sergeant?

MAJOR VON TELLHEIM. No, none.

FRANZISKA. And yet I think you should have some from him.

MAJOR VON TELLHEIM. Why so?

WERNER. How so, little woman?

FRANZISKA. Particularly secrets of a certain kind — All twenty, Mr. Sergeant? [*Holding up both her hands, with open fingers.*]

WERNER. Hist! Hist! Girl!

MAJOR VON TELLHEIM. What is the meaning of that?

FRANZISKA. Presto! — conjured on to his finger, Mr. Sergeant. [*As if she was putting a ring on her finger.*]

MAJOR VON TELLHEIM. What are you talking about?

WERNER. Little woman, little woman, don't you understand a joke?

MAJOR VON TELLHEIM. Werner, you have not forgotten, I hope, what I have often told you: that one should not jest beyond a certain point with a young woman!

WERNER. Upon my life I may have forgotten it! — Little woman, I beg —

FRANZISKA. Well, if it was a joke, I will forgive you this once.

MAJOR VON TELLHEIM. Well, if I must come, Franziska, see that your mistress reads my letter beforehand? That will spare me the pain of thinking again — of talking again, of things which I would willingly forget. There, give it to her! [*He turns the letter in giving it to her, and sees that it has been opened.*] But do I see aright? Why, it has been opened!

FRANZISKA. That may be. [*Looks at it.*] True, it is open. Who can have opened it? But really we have not read it, Major; really not. And we do not wish to read it, because the writer is coming himself. Come; and I tell you what, Major! Don't come as you are now — in boots, and with such a head. You are excusable, you do not expect us. Come in shoes, and have your hair fresh dressed. You look too soldierlike, too Prussian for me as you are.

MAJOR VON TELLHEIM. Thank you, Franziska.

FRANZISKA. You look as if you had been bivouacking last night.

MAJOR VON TELLHEIM. You may have guessed right.

FRANZISKA. We are going to dress, directly, too, and then have dinner. We would willingly ask you to dinner, but your presence might hinder our eating; and observe, we are not so much in love that we have lost our appetites.

MAJOR VON TELLHEIM. I will go. Prepare her somewhat, Franziska, beforehand, that I may not become contemptible in her eyes, and in my own. — Come, Werner, you shall dine with me.

WERNER. At the table d'hôte here in the house? I could not eat a bit there.

MAJOR VON TELLHEIM. With me, in my room.

WERNER. I will follow you directly. One word first with the little woman.

MAJOR VON TELLHEIM. I have no objection to that. [*Exit.*]

FRANZISKA. Well, Mr. Sergeant!

WERNER. Little woman, if I come again, shall I too come smartened up a bit?

FRANZISKA. Come as you please; my eyes will find no fault with you. But my ears will have to be so much the more on their guard. Twenty fingers, all full of rings. Ah! Ah! Mr. Sergeant!

WERNER. No, little woman; that is just what I wished to say to you. I only rattled on a little. There is nothing in it. One ring is quite enough for a man. Hundreds and hundreds of times I have heard the Major say, "He must be a rascally soldier who can mislead a young girl." So think I, too, little woman. You may trust to that! I must be quick and follow him. A good appetite to you! [Exit.]

FRANZISKA. The same to you! I really believe I like that man!

[Going in, she meets MINNA coming out.]

MINNA. Has the Major gone already, Franziska? I believe I should have been sufficiently composed again now to have detained him here.

FRANZISKA. And I will make you still more composed.

MINNA. So much the better! His letter! Oh, his letter! Each line spoke the honorable, noble man. Each refusal to accept my hand declared his love for me. I suppose he noticed that we had read his letter. I don't mind that, if he does but come. But are you sure he will come? There only seems to me to be a little too much pride in his conduct. For not to be willing to be indebted for his good fortune, even to the woman he loves, is pride, unpardonable pride! If he shows me too much of this, Franziska —

FRANZISKA. You will discard him!

MINNA. See there! Do you begin to pity him again already? No, silly girl, a man is never discarded for a single fault. No; but I have thought of a trick — to pay him off a little for this pride, with pride of the same kind.

FRANZISKA. Indeed, you must be very composed, my lady, if you are thinking of tricks again.

MINNA. I am so; come. You will have a part to play in my plot.

ACT IV

SCENE: *Minna's Room.* MINNA, *dressed handsomely and richly, but in good taste, and* FRANZISKA *have just risen from a table, which a servant is clearing.*

FRANZISKA. You cannot possibly have eaten enough, my lady.

MINNA. Don't you think so, Franziska? Perhaps I had no appetite when I sat down.

FRANZISKA. We had agreed not to mention him during dinner. We should have resolved likewise not to think of him.

MINNA. Indeed, I have thought of nothing but him.

FRANZISKA. So I perceived. I began to speak of a hundred different things, and you made wrong answers to each. [Another servant brings coffee.] Here comes a beverage more suited to fancies — sweet, melancholy coffee.

MINNA. Fancies! I have none. I am only thinking of the lesson I will give him. Did you understand my plan, Franziska?

FRANZISKA. Oh, yes; but it would be better if he spared us the putting it in execution.

MINNA. You will see that I know him thoroughly. He who refuses me now, with all my wealth, will contend for me against the whole world, as soon as he hears that I am unfortunate and friendless.

FRANZISKA [seriously]. That must tickle the most refined self-love.

MINNA. You moralist! First you convict me of vanity — now of self-love. Let me do as I please, Franziska. You, too, shall do as you please with your Sergeant.

FRANZISKA. With my Sergeant?

MINNA. Yes. If you deny it altogether, then it is true. I have not seen him yet; but from all you have said respecting him, I foretell your husband for you.

[Enter RICCAUT DE LA MARLINIÈRE.]

RICCAUT [before he enters]. Est-il permis, Monsieur le Major?

FRANZISKA. Who is that? Any one for us? [Going to the door.]

RICCAUT. Parbleu! I am wrong. Mais non — I am not wrong. C'est la chambre —

FRANZISKA. Without doubt, my lady, this gentleman expects to find Major von Tellheim here still.

RICCAUT. Oui, dat is it! Le Major de Tellheim; juste, ma belle enfant, c'est lui que je cherche. Où est-il?

FRANZISKA. He does not lodge here any longer.

RICCAUT. Comment? Dere is four-and-twenty hour ago he did lodge here, and not lodge here any more? Where lodge he den?

MINNA [going up to him]. Sir —

RICCAUT. Ah! Madame, mademoiselle, pardon, lady.

MINNA. Sir, your mistake is quite excusable, and your astonishment very natural. Major von Tellheim has had the kindness to give up his apartments to me, as a stranger, who was not able to get them elsewhere.

RICCAUT. Ah! Voilà de ses politesses! C'est un très-galant homme que ce Major!

MINNA. Where has he gone now? — truly I am ashamed that I do not know.

RICCAUT. Madame not know? C'est dommage; j'en suis fâché.

MINNA. I certainly ought to have inquired. Of course his friends will seek him here.

RICCAUT. I am vary great his friend, madame.

MINNA. Franziska, do you not know?

FRANZISKA. No, my lady.

RICCAUT. It is vary nécessaire dat I speak him. I come and bring him a nouvelle, of which he will be vary much at ease.

MINNA. I regret it so much the more. But I hope to see him perhaps shortly. If it is a matter of indifference from whom he hears this good news, I would offer, sir —

RICCAUT. I comprehend. Mademoiselle parle français? Mais sans doute; telle que je la vois! La demande était bien impolie; vous me pardonnerez, mademoiselle.

MINNA. Sir —

RICCAUT. No! You not speak French, madame?

MINNA. Sir, in France I would endeavor to do so; but why here? I perceive that you understand me, sir; and I, sir, shall doubtless understand you; speak as you please.

RICCAUT. Good, good! I can also explain me in your langue. Sachez donc, mademoiselle, you must know, madame, dat I come from de table of de ministre, ministre de, ministre de — What is le ministre out dere, in de long street, on de broad place?

MINNA. I am a perfect stranger here.

RICCAUT. Si, le ministre of de war departement. Dere I have eat my dinner; I ordinary dine dere, and de conversation did fall on Major Tellheim; et le ministre m'a dit en confidence, — car Son Excellence est mio ami, et il n'y a point de mystères entre nous — Son Excellence, I say, has trust to me, dat l'affaire from our Major is on de point to end, and to end good. He has made a rapport to de king, and de king has resolved et tout à fait en faveur du Major. "Monsieur," m'a dit Son Excellence, "vous comprenez bien, que tout dépend de la manière, dont on fait envisager les choses au roi, et vous me connaissez. Cela fait un très-joli garçon que ce Tellheim, et ne sais-je pas que vous l'aimez? Les amis de mes amis sont aussi les miens. Il coûte un peu cher au roi ce Tellheim, mais est-ce que l'on sert les rois pour rien? Il faut s'entr'aider en ce monde; et quand il s'agit de pertes, que ce soit le roi qui en fasse, et non pas un honnête homme de nous autres. Voilà le principe, dont je ne me dépars jamais." But what say madame to it? N'est pas, dat is a fine fellow? Ah, que Son Excellence a le cœur bien placé! He assure me au reste, if de Major has not reçu already une lettre de la main, — a royal letter, — dat to-day infailliblement must he receive one.

MINNA. Certainly, sir, this news will be most welcome to Major von Tellheim. I should like to be able to name the friend to him who takes such an interest in his welfare.

RICCAUT. Madame, you wish my name? Vous voyez en moi — you see, lady, in me, le Chevalier Riccaut de la Marlinière, Seigneur de Prêt-au-val, de la branche de Prens d'or. You remain astonished to hear me from so great, great a family, qui est véritablement du sang royal. Il faut le dire; je suis sans doute le cadet le plus aventureux que la maison n'a jamais eu.

I serve from my eleven year. Une affaire
d'honneur make me flee. Den I serve de
holy Papa of Rome, den de Republic St.
Marino, den de Poles, den de States-
General, till enfin I am brought here. Ah,
mademoiselle, que je voudrais n'avoir
jamais vu ce pays-ci! Had one left me in
de service of de States-General, should I
be now at least colonel. But here always
to remain capitaine, and now also a discharged capitaine.

MINNA. That is ill luck.

RICCAUT. Oui, mademoiselle, me voilà
réformé, et par là mis sur le pavé!

MINNA. I am very sorry for you.

RICCAUT. Vous êtes bien bonne, mademoiselle — No, merit have no reward here.
Réformer a man, like me! A man who also
have ruin himself in dis service! I have
lost in it so much as twenty thousand
livres. What have I now? Tranchons le
mot; je n'ai pas le sou, et me voilà exacte-
ment vis-à-vis de rien.

MINNA. I am exceedingly sorry.

RICCAUT. Vous êtes bien bonne, mademoiselle. But as one say — misfortune
never come alone! qu'un malheur ne vient
jamais seul: so it arrive with me. What
ressource rests for an honnête homme of
my extraction, but play? Now, I always
played with luck, so long I not need her.
Now I very much need her, je joue avec un
guignon, mademoiselle, qui surpasse toute
croyance. For fifteen days, not one is
passed, dat I always am broke. Yesterday
I was broke dree times. Je sais bien, qu'il
y avait quelque chose de plus que le jeu.
Car parmi mes pontes se trouvaient cer-
taines dames. I will not speak more. One
must be very galant to les dames. Dey
have invite me again to-day, to give me
revanche; mais — vous m'entendez, mademoiselle — one must first have to live, before one can have to play.

MINNA. I hope, sir —

RICCAUT. Vous êtes bien bonne, mademoiselle.

MINNA [taking FRANZISKA aside]. Franziska, I really feel for the man. Would he
take it ill if I offer him something?

FRANZISKA. He does not look to me like
a man who would.

MINNA. Very well! — Sir, I perceive
that — you play, that you keep the bank;
doubtless in places where something is to
be won. I must also confess that I — am
very fond of play.

RICCAUT. Tant mieux, mademoiselle,
tant mieux! Tous les gens d'esprit aiment
le jeu à la fureur.

MINNA. That I am very fond of winning; that I like to trust my money to a
man who — knows how to play. Are you
inclined, sir, to let me join you? To let me
have a share in your bank?

RICCAUT. Comment, mademoiselle, vous
voulez être de moitié avec moi? De tout
mon cœur.

MINNA. At first, only with a trifle.
[Opens her desk and takes out some
money.]

RICCAUT. Ah, mademoiselle, que vous
êtes charmante!

MINNA. Here is what I won a short
time back; only ten pistoles. I am ashamed,
so little —

RICCAUT. Donnez toujours, mademoiselle, donnez. [Takes it.]

MINNA. Without doubt, your bank, sir,
is very considerable.

RICCAUT. Oh, yes, vary considerable.
Ten pistoles! You shall have, madame, an
interest in my bank for one third, pour le
tiers. Yes, one third part it shall be —
something more. With a beautiful lady
one must not be too exac. I rejoice myself,
to make by that a liaison with madame, et
de ce moment je recommence à bien au-
gurer de ma fortune.

MINNA. But I cannot be present, sir,
when you play.

RICCAUT. For why it nécessaire dat you
be present? We other players are honorable people between us.

MINNA. If we are fortunate, sir, you will
of course bring me my share. If we are unfortunate —

RICCAUT. I come to bring recruits, n'est
pas, madame?

MINNA. In time recruits might fail.
Manage our money well, sir.

RICCAUT. What does madame think
me? A simpleton, a stupid devil?

MINNA. I beg your pardon.

RICCAUT. Je suis des bons, mademoiselle. Savez vous ce que cela veut dire? I am of the quite practiced —

MINNA. But still, sir —

RICCAUT. Je sais monter un coup —

MINNA [amazed]. Could you?

RICCAUT. Je file la carte avec une adresse.

MINNA. Never!

RICCAUT. Je fais sauter la coupe avec une dextérité.

MINNA. You surely would not, sir! —

RICCAUT. What not, madame; what not? Donnez moi un pigeonneau à plumer, et —

MINNA. Play false! Cheat!

RICCAUT. Comment, mademoiselle? Vous appelez cela cheat? Corriger la fortune, l'enchaîner sous ses doigts, être sûr de son fait, dat you call cheat? Cheat! Oh, what a poor tongue is your tongue! What an awkward tongue!

MINNA. No, sir, if you think so —

RICCAUT. Laissez-moi faire, mademoiselle, and be tranquille! What matter to you how I play? Enough! to-morrow, madame, you see me again or with hundred pistol, or you see me no more. Votre très-humble, mademoiselle, votre très-humble. [Exit quickly.]

MINNA [looking after him with astonishment and displeasure]. I hope the latter, sir.

FRANZISKA [angrily]. What can I say? Oh! How grand! How grand!

MINNA. Laugh at me; I deserve it. [After reflecting, more calmly.] No, do not laugh; I do not deserve it.

FRANZISKA. Excellent! You have done a charming act — set a knave upon his legs again.

MINNA. It was intended for an unfortunate man.

FRANZISKA. And what is the best part of it, the fellow considers you like himself. Oh! I must follow him, and take the money from him. [Going.]

MINNA. Franziska, do not let the coffee get quite cold; pour it out.

FRANZISKA. He must return it to you; you have thought better of it; you will not play in partnership with him. Ten pistoles! You heard, my lady, that he was a beggar! [MINNA pours out the coffee herself.] Who would give such a sum to a beggar? And to endeavor, in the bargain, to save him the humiliation of having begged for it! The charitable woman who, out of generosity, mistakes the beggar, is in return mistaken by the beggar. It serves you right, my lady, if he considers your gift as — I know not what. [MINNA hands a cup of coffee to FRANZISKA.] Do you wish to make my blood boil still more? I do not want any. [MINNA puts it down again.] "Parbleu, madame, merit have no reward here." [Imitating the Frenchman.] I think not, when such rogues are allowed to walk about unhanged.

MINNA [coldly and slowly, while sipping her coffee]. Girl, you understand good men very well; but when will you learn to bear with the bad? And yet they are also men; and frequently not so bad as they seem. One should look for their good side. I fancy this Frenchman is nothing worse than vain. Through mere vanity he gives himself out as a false player; he does not wish to appear under an obligation to one; he wishes to save himself the thanks. Perhaps he may now go, pay his small debts, live quietly and frugally on the rest as far as it will go, and think no more of play. If that be so, Franziska, let him come for recruits whenever he pleases. [Gives her cup to FRANZISKA.] There, put it down! But, tell me, should not Tellheim be here by this time?

FRANZISKA. No, my lady, I can neither find out the bad side in a good man, nor the good side in a bad man.

MINNA. Surely he will come!

FRANZISKA. He ought to remain away! You remark in him — in him, the best of men — a little pride; and therefore you intend to tease him so cruelly!

MINNA. Are you at it again? Be silent! I will have it so. Woe to you if you spoil this fun of mine — if you do not say and do all, as we have agreed. I will leave you with him alone; and then — but here he comes.

[PAUL WERNER *comes in, carrying himself very erect as if on duty.*]

FRANZISKA. No, it is only his dear Sergeant.

MINNA. Dear Sergeant! Whom does the "dear" refer to?

FRANZISKA. Pray, my lady, do not make the man embarrassed. — Your servant, Mr. Sergeant; what news do you bring us?

WERNER [*goes up to* MINNA, *without noticing* FRANZISKA]. Major von Tellheim begs to present, through me, Sergeant Werner, his most respectful compliments to Fräulein von Barnhelm, and to inform her that he will be here directly.

MINNA. Where is he, then?

WERNER. Your ladyship will pardon him; we left our quarters before it began to strike three: but the paymaster met us on the way; and because conversation with those gentlemen has no end, the Major made me a sign to report the case to your ladyship.

MINNA. Very well, Mr. Sergeant. I only hope the paymaster may have good news for him.

WERNER. Such gentlemen seldom have good news for officers. — Has your ladyship any orders? [*Going.*]

FRANZISKA. Why, where are you going again, Mr. Sergeant? Had not we something to say to each other?

WERNER [*in a whisper to* FRANZISKA, *and seriously*]. Not here, little woman; it is against respect, against discipline. — Your ladyship —

MINNA. Thank you for your trouble. I am glad to have made your acquaintance. Franziska has spoken in high praise of you to me.

[WERNER *makes a stiff bow, and goes.*]

MINNA. So that is your Sergeant, Franziska?

FRANZISKA [*aside*]. I have not time to reproach her for that jeering *your*. [*Aloud.*] Yes, my lady, that is my Sergeant. You think him, no doubt, somewhat stiff and wooden. He also appeared so to me just now; but I observed, he thought he must march past you as if on parade. And when

soldiers are on parade, they certainly look more like wooden dolls than men. You should see and hear him when he is himself.

MINNA. So I should, indeed!

FRANZISKA. He must still be in the next room; may I go and talk with him a little?

MINNA. I refuse you this pleasure unwillingly: but you must remain here, Franziska. You must be present at our conversation. Another thing occurs to me. [*Takes her ring from her finger.*] There, take my ring; keep it for me, and give me the Major's in the place of it.

FRANZISKA. Why so?

MINNA [*while* FRANZISKA *is fetching the ring*]. I scarcely know, myself; but I fancy I see, beforehand, how I may make use of it. — Some one is knocking. Give it to me, quickly. [*Puts the ring on.*] It is he.

[*Enter* MAJOR VON TELLHEIM, *in the same coat, but otherwise as* FRANZISKA *advised.*]

MAJOR VON TELLHEIM. Madam, you will excuse the delay.

MINNA. Oh! Major, we will not treat each other in quite such a military fashion. You are here now; and to await a pleasure, is itself a pleasure. Well [*looking at him and smiling*], dear Tellheim, have we not been like children?

MAJOR VON TELLHEIM. Yes, madam; like children, who resist when they ought to obey quietly.

MINNA. We will drive out, dear Major, to see a little of the town, and afterward meet my uncle.

MAJOR VON TELLHEIM. What!

MINNA. You see, we have not yet had an opportunity of mentioning the most important matters even. He is coming here to-day. It was accident that brought me here without him, a day sooner.

MAJOR VON TELLHEIM. Count von Bruchsal! Has he returned?

MINNA. The troubles of the war drove him into Italy: peace has brought him back again. Do not be uneasy, Tellheim; if we formerly feared on his part the greatest obstacle to our union —

MAJOR VON TELLHEIM. To our union!

MINNA. He is now your friend. He has

heard too much good of you from too many people, not to become so. He longs to become personally acquainted with the man whom his heiress has chosen. He comes as uncle, as guardian, as father, to give me to you.

MAJOR VON TELLHEIM. Ah, dear lady, why did you not read my letter? Why would you not read it?

MINNA. Your letter! Oh, yes, I remember you sent me one. — What did you do with that letter, Franziska? Did we, or did we not read it? — What was it you wrote to me, dear Tellheim?

MAJOR VON TELLHEIM. Nothing but what honor commands me.

MINNA. That is, not to desert an honorable woman who loves you. Certainly that is what honor commands. Indeed, I ought to have read your letter. But what I have not read, I shall hear, shall not I?

MAJOR VON TELLHEIM. Yes, you shall hear it.

MINNA. No, I need not even hear it. It speaks for itself. As if you could be guilty of such an unworthy act, as not to take me! Do you know that I should be pointed at for the rest of my life? My countrywomen would talk about me, and say, "That is she, that is the Fräulein von Barnhelm, who fancied that because she was rich she could marry the noble Tellheim; as if such men were to be caught with money." That is what they would say, for they are all envious of me. That I am rich, they cannot deny; but they do not wish to acknowledge that I am also a tolerably good girl, who would prove herself worthy of her husband. Is that not so, Tellheim?

MAJOR VON TELLHEIM. Yes, yes, madam, that is like your countrywomen. They will envy you exceedingly a discharged officer, with sullied honor, a cripple, and a beggar.

MINNA. And are you all that? If I mistake not, you told me something of the kind this forenoon. Therein are good and evil mixed. Let us examine each charge more closely. You are discharged? So you say. I thought your regiment was only drafted into another. How did it happen that a man of your merit was not retained?

MAJOR VON TELLHEIM. It has happened, as it must happen. The great ones are convinced that a soldier does very little through regard for them, not much more from a sense of duty, but everything for his own advantage. What, then, can they think they owe him? Peace has made a great many, like myself, superfluous to them; and at last we shall all be superfluous.

MINNA. You talk as a man must talk, to whom in return the great are quite superfluous. And never were they more so than now. I return my best thanks to the great ones that they have given up their claims to a man whom I would very unwillingly have shared with them. I am your sovereign, Tellheim; you want no other master. To find you discharged is a piece of good fortune I dared scarcely dream of! But you are not only discharged; you are more. And what are you more? A cripple, you say! Well [looking at him from head to foot], the cripple is tolerably whole and upright — appears still to be pretty well and strong. Dear Tellheim, if you expect to go begging on the strength of your limbs, I prophesy that you will be relieved at very few doors; except at the door of a good-natured girl like myself.

MAJOR VON TELLHEIM. I only hear the joking girl now, dear Minna.

MINNA. And I only hear the "dear Minna" in your chiding. I will not joke any longer; for I recollect that after all you are something of a cripple. You are wounded by a shot in the right arm; but, all things considered, I do not find much fault with that. I am so much the more secure from your blows.

MAJOR VON TELLHEIM. Madam!

MINNA. You would say, you are so much the less secure from mine. Well, well, dear Tellheim, I hope you will not drive me to that.

MAJOR VON TELLHEIM. You laugh, madam. I only lament that I cannot laugh with you.

MINNA. Why not? What have you to

say against laughing? Cannot one be very serious even while laughing? Dear Major, laughter keeps us more rational than vexation. The proof is before us. Your laughing friend judges of your circumstances more correctly than you do yourself. Because you are discharged, you say your honor is sullied; because you are wounded in the arm, you call yourself a cripple. Is that right? Is that no exaggeration? And is it my doing that all exaggerations are so open to ridicule? I dare say, if I examine your beggary that it will also be as little able to stand the test. You may have lost your equipage once, twice, or thrice; your deposits in the hands of this or that banker may have disappeared together with those of other people; you may have no hope of seeing this or that money again which you may have advanced in the service; but are you a beggar on that account? If nothing else remained to you but what my uncle is bringing for you —

MAJOR VON TELLHEIM. Your uncle, madam, will bring nothing for me.

MINNA. Nothing but the two thousand pistoles which you so generously advanced to our Government.

MAJOR VON TELLHEIM. If you had but read my letter, madam!

MINNA. Well, I did read it. But what I read in it, on this point, is a perfect riddle. It is impossible that any one should wish to turn a noble action into a crime. But explain to me, dear Major.

MAJOR VON TELLHEIM. You remember, madam, that I had orders to collect the contribution for the war most strictly in cash in the districts in your neighborhood. I wished to forego this severity, and advanced the money that was deficient myself.

MINNA. I remember it well. I loved you for that deed before I had seen you.

MAJOR VON TELLHEIM. The Government gave me their bill, and I wished, at the signing of the peace, to have the sum entered among the debts to be repaid by them. The bill was acknowledged as good, but my ownership of the same was disputed. People looked incredulous, when I declared that I had myself advanced the

amount in cash. It was considered as bribery, as a *douceur* from the Government, because I at once agreed to take the smallest sum with which I could have been satisfied in a case of the greatest exigency. Thus the bill went from my possession, and if it be paid, will certainly not be paid to me. Hence, madam, I consider my honor to be suspected! Not on account of my discharge, which, if I had not received, I should have applied for. You look serious, madam! Why do you not laugh? Ha, ha, ha! I am laughing.

MINNA. Oh! Stifle that laugh, Tellheim, I implore you! It is the terrible laugh of misanthropy. No, you are not the man to repent of a good deed, because it may have had a bad result for yourself. Nor can these consequences possibly be of long duration. The truth must come to light. The testimony of my uncle, of our Government —

MAJOR VON TELLHEIM. Of your uncle! Of your Government! Ha, ha, ha!

MINNA. That laugh will kill me, Tellheim. If you believe in virtue and Providence, Tellheim, do not laugh so! I never heard a curse more terrible than that laugh! But, viewing the matter in the worst light, if they are determined to mistake your character here, with us you will not be misunderstood. No, we cannot, we will not, misunderstand you, Tellheim. And if our Government has the least sentiment of honor, I know what it must do. But I am foolish; what would that matter? Imagine, Tellheim, that you have lost the two thousand pistoles on some gay evening. The king was an unfortunate card for you: the queen [*pointing to herself*] will be so much the more favorable. Providence, believe me, always indemnifies a man of honor — often even beforehand. The action which was to cost you two thousand pistoles gained you me. Without that action, I never should have been desirous of making your acquaintance. You know I went uninvited to the first party where I thought I should meet you. I went entirely on your account. I went with a fixed determination to love you — I loved you already! With the fixed determination to make you mine, if I should find you as dark and ugly as the Moor of Venice. So dark and ugly you are not; nor will you be so jealous. But, Tellheim, Tellheim, you are yet very like him! Oh, the unmanageable, stubborn man, who always keeps his eye fixed upon the phantom of honor, and becomes hardened against every other sentiment! Your eyes this way! Upon me — me, Tellheim! [*He remains thoughtful and immovable, with his eyes fixed on one spot.*] Of what are you thinking? Do you not hear me?

MAJOR VON TELLHEIM [*absently*]. Oh, yes; but tell me, how came the Moor into the service of Venice? Had the Moor no country of his own? Why did he hire his arm and his blood to a foreign land?

MINNA [*alarmed*]. Of what are you thinking, Tellheim? It is time to break off. Come [*taking him by the hand*]. — Franziska, let the carriage be brought round.

MAJOR VON TELLHEIM [*disengaging his hand, and following* FRANZISKA]. No, Franziska; I cannot have the honor of accompanying your mistress. — Madam, let me still retain my senses unimpaired for to-day, and give me leave to go. You are on the right way to deprive me of them. I resist it as much as I can. But hear, while I am still myself, what I have firmly determined, and from which nothing in the world shall turn me. If I have not better luck in the game of life; if a complete change in my fortune does not take place; if —

MINNA. I must interrupt you, Major. — We ought to have told him that at first, Franziska. You remind me of nothing. — Our conversation would have taken quite a different turn, Tellheim, if I had commenced with the good news which the Chevalier de la Marlinière brought just now.

MAJOR VON TELLHEIM. The Chevalier de la Marlinière! Who is he?

FRANZISKA. He may be a very honest man, Major von Tellheim, except that —

MINNA. Silence, Franziska! Also a discharged officer from the Dutch service, who —

MAJOR VON TELLHEIM. Ah! Lieutenant Riccaut!

MINNA. He assured us he was a friend of yours.

MAJOR VON TELLHEIM. I assure you that I am not his.

MINNA. And that some minister or other had told him, in confidence, that your business was likely to have the very best termination. A letter from the king must now be on its way to you.

MAJOR VON TELLHEIM. How came Riccaut and a minister in company? Something certainly must have happened concerning my affair; for just now the paymaster of the forces told me that the king had set aside all the evidence offered against me, and that I might take back my promise, which I had given in writing, not to depart from here until acquitted. But that will be all. They wish to give me an opportunity of getting away. But they are wrong, I shall not go. Sooner shall the utmost distress waste me away before the eyes of my calumniators, than —

MINNA. Obstinate man!

MAJOR VON TELLHEIM. I require no favor; I want justice. My honor —

MINNA. The honor of such a man —

MAJOR VON TELLHEIM [*warmly*]. No, madam, you may be able to judge of any other subject, but not of this. Honor is not the voice of conscience, not the evidence of a few honorable men —

MINNA. No, no, I know it well. Honor is — honor.

MAJOR VON TELLHEIM. In short, madam — You did not let me finish. — I was going to say, if they keep from me so shamefully what is my own; if my honor be not perfectly righted — I cannot, madam, ever be yours, for I am not worthy, in the eyes of the world, of being yours. Minna von Barnhelm deserves an irreproachable husband. It is a worthless love which does not scruple to expose its object to scorn. He is a worthless man who is not ashamed to owe a woman all his good fortune; whose blind tenderness —

MINNA. And is that really your feeling, Major? [*Turning her back suddenly.*] — Franziska!

MAJOR VON TELLHEIM. Do not be angry.

MINNA [*aside to* FRANZISKA]. Now is

the time! What do you advise me, Franziska?

FRANZISKA. I advise nothing. But certainly he goes rather too far.

MAJOR VON TELLHEIM [approaching to interrupt them]. You are angry, madam.

MINNA [ironically]. I? Not in the least.

MAJOR VON TELLHEIM. If I loved you less —

MINNA [still in the same tone]. Oh! certainly, it would be a misfortune for me. And hear, Major, I also will not be the cause of your unhappiness. One should love with perfect disinterestedness. It is as well that I have not been more open! Perhaps your pity might have granted to me what your love refuses.

[Drawing the ring slowly from her finger.]

MAJOR VON TELLHEIM. What does this mean, madam?

MINNA. No, neither of us must make the other either more or less happy. True love demands it. I believe you, Major; and you have too much honor to mistake love.

MAJOR VON TELLHEIM. Are you jesting, madam?

MINNA. Here! Take back the ring with which you plighted your troth to me. [Gives him the ring.] Let it be so! We will suppose we have never met.

MAJOR VON TELLHEIM. What do I hear?

MINNA. Does it surprise you? Take it, sir. You surely have not been pretending only!

MAJOR VON TELLHEIM [taking the ring from her]. Heavens! Can Minna speak thus!

MINNA. In one case you cannot be mine; in no case can I be yours. Your misfortune is probable; mine is certain. Farewell! [Is going.]

MAJOR VON TELLHEIM. Where are you going, dearest Minna?

MINNA. Sir, you insult me now by that term of endearment.

MAJOR VON TELLHEIM. What is the matter, madam? Where are you going?

MINNA. Leave me. I go to hide my tears from you, deceiver! [Exit.]

MAJOR VON TELLHEIM. Her tears! And I am to leave her. [Is about to follow her.]

FRANZISKA [holding him back]. Surely not, Major. You would not follow her into her own room!

MAJOR VON TELLHEIM. Her misfortune? Did she not speak of misfortune?

FRANZISKA. Yes, truly; the misfortune of losing you, after —

MAJOR VON TELLHEIM. After? After what? There is more in this. What is it, Franziska? Tell me! Speak!

FRANZISKA. After, I mean, she has made such sacrifices on your account.

MAJOR VON TELLHEIM. Sacrifices for me!

FRANZISKA. Well, listen. It is a good thing for you, Major, that you are freed from your engagement with her in this manner. — Why should I not tell you? It cannot remain a secret long. We have fled from home. Count von Bruchsal has disinherited my mistress, because she would not accept a husband of his choice. On that every one deserted and slighted her. What could we do? We determined to seek him, whom —

MAJOR VON TELLHEIM. Enough! Come, and let me throw myself at her feet.

FRANZISKA. What are you thinking about? Rather go, and thank your good fortune.

MAJOR VON TELLHEIM. Pitiful creature! For what do you take me? Yet no, my dear Franziska, the advice did not come from your heart. Forgive my anger!

FRANZISKA. Do not detain me any longer. I must see what she is about. How easily something might happen to her! Go now, and come again, if you like.

[Follows MINNA.]

MAJOR VON TELLHEIM. But, Franziska! Oh! I will wait your return here. — No, that is more torturing! — If she is in earnest, she will not refuse to forgive me. — Now I want your aid, honest Werner! — No, Minna, I am no deceiver!

[Rushes off.]

ACT V

[Enter MAJOR VON TELLHEIM from one side, WERNER from the other.]

MAJOR VON TELLHEIM. Ah, Werner! I have been looking for you everywhere. Where have you been?

WERNER. And I have been looking for you, Major; that is always the way. — I bring you good news.

MAJOR VON TELLHEIM. I do not want your news now; I want your money. Quick, Werner, give me all you have; and then raise as much more as you can.

WERNER. Major! Now, upon my life, that is just what I said — "He will borrow money from me, when he has got it himself to lend."

MAJOR VON TELLHEIM. You surely are not seeking excuses!

WERNER. That I may have nothing to upbraid you with, take it with your right hand, and give it me again with your left.

MAJOR VON TELLHEIM. Do not detain me, Werner. It is my intention to repay you; but when and how, God knows!

WERNER. Then you do not know yet that the Treasury has received an order to pay you your money? I just heard it at —

MAJOR VON TELLHEIM. What are you talking about? What nonsense have you let them palm off on you? Do you not see that if it were true, I should be the first person to know it? In short, Werner, money! money!

WERNER. Very well, with pleasure. Here is some! A hundred louis d'ors there, and a hundred ducats there.

[Gives him both.]

MAJOR VON TELLHEIM. Werner, go and give Just the hundred louis d'ors. Let him redeem the ring again, on which he raised the money this morning. But whence will you get some more, Werner? I want a good deal more.

WERNER. Leave that to me. The man who bought my farm lives in the town. The date for payment is a fortnight hence, certainly; but the money is ready, and by a reduction of one half per cent —

MAJOR VON TELLHEIM. Very well, my dear Werner! You see that I have had recourse to you alone — I must also confide all to you. The young lady you have seen is in distress —

WERNER. That is bad!

MAJOR VON TELLHEIM. But to-morrow she shall be my wife.

WERNER. That is good!

MAJOR VON TELLHEIM. And the day after, I leave this place with her. I can go; I will go. I would sooner throw over everything here! Who knows where some good luck may be in store for me? If you will, Werner, come with us. We will serve again.

WERNER. Really? But where there is war, Major!

MAJOR VON TELLHEIM. To be sure. Go, Werner, we will speak of this again.

WERNER. Oh, my dear Major! The day after to-morrow! Why not to-morrow? I will get everything ready. In Persia, Major, there is a famous war; what do you say?

MAJOR VON TELLHEIM. We will think of it. Only go, Werner!

WERNER. Hurrah! Long live Prince Heraclius! [Exit.]

MAJOR VON TELLHEIM. How do I feel! — My whole soul has acquired a new impulse. My own unhappiness bowed me to the ground; made me fretful, short-sighted, shy, careless: her unhappiness raises me. I see clearly again, and feel myself ready and capable of undertaking anything for her sake. Why do I tarry?

[Is going toward MINNA'S room, when FRANZISKA comes out of it.]

FRANZISKA. Is it you? I thought I heard your voice. What do you want, Major?

MAJOR VON TELLHEIM. What do I want! What is she doing? Come!

FRANZISKA. She is just going out for a drive.

MAJOR VON TELLHEIM. And alone? Without me? Where to?

FRANZISKA. Have you forgotten, Major?

MAJOR VON TELLHEIM. How silly you are, Franziska! I irritated her, and she was angry. I will beg her pardon, and she will forgive me.

FRANZISKA. What! After you have taken the ring back, Major!

MAJOR VON TELLHEIM. Ah! I did that in my confusion. I had forgotten about the ring. Where did I put it? [Searches for it.] Here it is.

FRANZISKA. Is that it? — [Aside, as he puts it again in his pocket.] If he would only look at it closer!

MAJOR VON TELLHEIM. She pressed it

upon me so bitterly. But I have forgotten that. A full heart cannot weigh words. She will not for one moment refuse to take it again. And have I not hers?

FRANZISKA. She is now waiting for it in return. Where is it, Major? Show it to me, do!

MAJOR VON TELLHEIM [embarrassed]. I have — forgotten to put it on. Just — Just will bring it directly.

FRANZISKA. They are something alike, I suppose; let me look at that one. I am very fond of such things.

MAJOR VON TELLHEIM. Another time, Franziska. Come now.

FRANZISKA [aside]. He is determined not to be drawn out of his mistake.

MAJOR VON TELLHEIM. What do you say? Mistake!

FRANZISKA. It is a mistake, I say, if you think that my mistress is still a good match. Her own fortune is far from considerable; by a few calculations in their own favor her guardians may reduce it to nothing. She expected everything from her uncle; but this cruel uncle —

MAJOR VON TELLHEIM. Let him go! Am I not man enough to make it all good to her again?

FRANZISKA. Do you hear? She is ringing; I must go in again.

MAJOR VON TELLHEIM. I will accompany you.

FRANZISKA. For Heaven's sake, no! She forbade me expressly to speak with you. Come in, at any rate, a little time after me.
                                    [Goes in.]

MAJOR VON TELLHEIM [calling after her]. Announce me! Speak for me, Franziska! I shall follow you directly. — What shall I say to her? Yet where the heart can speak, no preparation is necessary. There is one thing only which may need a studied turn — this reserve, this scrupulousness of throwing herself, unfortunate as she is, into my arms; this anxiety to make a false show of still possessing that happiness which she has lost through me. How she is to exculpate herself to herself — for by me it is already forgiven — for this distrust in my honor, in her own worth. — Ah! here she comes.

MINNA [speaking as she comes out, as if not aware of the MAJOR'S presence]. The carriage is at the door, Franziska, is it not? My fan!

MAJOR VON TELLHEIM [advancing to her]. Where are you going, madam?

MINNA [with forced coldness]. I am going out, Major. I guess why you have given yourself the trouble of coming back; to return me my ring. Very well, Major von Tellheim, have the goodness to give it to Franziska. — Franziska, take the ring from Major von Tellheim! — I have no time to lose.   [Is going.]

MAJOR VON TELLHEIM [stepping before her]. Madam! Ah, what have I heard? I was unworthy of such love.

MINNA. So, Franziska, you have —

FRANZISKA. Told him all.

MAJOR VON TELLHEIM. Do not be angry with me, madam. I am no deceiver. You have, on my account, lost much in the eyes of the world, but not in mine. In my eyes you have gained beyond measure by this loss. It was too sudden. You feared it might make an unfavorable impression on me; at first you wished to hide it from me. I do not complain of this mistrust. It arose from the desire to retain my affection. That desire is my pride. You found me in distress; and you did not wish to add distress to distress. You could not divine how far your distress would raise me above any thoughts of my own.

MINNA. That is all very well, Major, but it is now over. I have released you from your engagement; you have, by taking back the ring —

MAJOR VON TELLHEIM. Consented to nothing! On the contrary, I now consider myself bound more firmly than ever. You are mine, Minna, mine forever. [Takes off the ring.] Here, take it for the second time — the pledge of my fidelity.

MINNA. I take that ring again! That ring?

MAJOR VON TELLHEIM. Yes, dearest Minna, yes.

MINNA. What are you asking me? That ring?

MAJOR VON TELLHEIM. You received it for the first time from my hand, when our positions were similar and the circumstances propitious. They are no longer propitious, but are again similar. Equality is always the strongest tide of love. Permit me, dearest Minna!

[*Seizes her hand to put on the ring.*]

MINNA. What, by force, Major! No, there is no power in the world that shall compel me to take back that ring! Do you think that I am in want of a ring? Oh, you may see [*pointing to her ring*] that I have another here which is in no way inferior to yours.

FRANZISKA [*aside*]. Well, if he does not see it now!

MAJOR VON TELLHEIM [*letting fall her hand*]. What is this? I see Fräulein von Barnhelm, but I do not hear her. — You are pretending. — Pardon me, that I use your own words.

MINNA [*in her natural tone*]. Did those words offend you, Major?

MAJOR VON TELLHEIM. They grieved me much.

MINNA [*affected*]. They were not meant to do that, Tellheim. Forgive me, Tellheim.

MAJOR VON TELLHEIM. Ah, that friendly tone tells me you are yourself again, Minna; that you still love me.

FRANZISKA [*exclaims*]. The joke will soon have gone a little too far.

MINNA [*in a commanding tone*]. Franziska, you will not interfere in our affairs, I beg.

FRANZISKA [*aside, in a surprised tone*]. Not enough yet!

MINNA. Yes, sir; it would only be womanish vanity in me to pretend to be cold and scornful. No! Never! You deserve to find me as sincere as yourself. I do love you still, Tellheim, I love you still; but notwithstanding —

MAJOR VON TELLHEIM. No more, dearest Minna, no more!

[*Seizes her hand again, to put on the ring.*]

MINNA [*drawing back her hand*]. Notwithstanding, so much the more am I determined that that shall never be — never! — Of what are you thinking, Major? — I thought your own distress was sufficient. You must remain here; you must obtain by obstinacy — no better phrase occurs to me at the moment — the most perfect satisfaction, obtain it by obstinacy — And that even though the utmost distress should waste you away before the eyes of your calumniators —

MAJOR VON TELLHEIM. So I thought, so I said, when I knew not what I thought or said. Chagrin and stifling rage had enveloped my whole soul; love itself, in the full blaze of happiness, could not illumine it. But it has sent its daughter, Pity, more familiar with gloomy misfortune, and she has dispelled the cloud, and opened again all the avenues of my soul to sensations of tenderness. The impulse of self-preservation awakes, when I have something more precious than myself to support, and to support through my own exertions. Do not let the word "pity" offend you. From the innocent cause of our distress we may hear the term without humiliation. I am this cause; through me, Minna, have you lost friends and relations, fortune and country. Through me, in me, must you find them all again, or I shall have the destruction of the most lovely of her sex upon my soul. Let me not think of a future in which I must detest myself. — No, nothing shall detain me here longer. From this moment I will oppose nothing but contempt to the injustice which I suffer. Is this country the world? Does the sun rise here alone? Where can I not go? In what service shall I be refused? And should I be obliged to seek it in the most distant clime, only follow me with confidence, dearest Minna — we shall want for nothing. I have a friend who will assist me with pleasure.

[*Enter an Orderly.*]

FRANZISKA [*seeing the Orderly*]. Hist, Major!

MAJOR VON TELLHEIM [*to the Orderly*]. Whom do you want?

ORDERLY. I am looking for Major von Tellheim. Ah, you are the Major, I see. I have to give you this letter from His Majesty the King.

[*Taking one out of his bag.*]

MAJOR VON TELLHEIM. To me?

ORDERLY. According to the direction.

MINNA. Franziska, do you hear? The Chevalier spoke the truth, after all.

ORDERLY [*while* TELLHEIM *takes the letter*]. I beg your pardon, Major; you should properly have had it yesterday, but I could not find you out. I learned your address this morning only from Lieutenant Riccaut, on parade.

FRANZISKA. Do you hear, my lady? — That is the Chevalier's minister. "What is the name of de ministre out dere, on de broad place?"

MAJOR VON TELLHEIM. I am extremely obliged to you for your trouble.

ORDERLY. It is my duty, Major.
[*Exit.*]

MAJOR VON TELLHEIM. Ah! Minna, what is this? What does this contain?

MINNA. I am not entitled to extend my curiosity so far.

MAJOR VON TELLHEIM. What! You would still separate my fate from yours? — But why do I hesitate to open it? It cannot make me more unhappy than I am: no, dearest Minna, it cannot make us more unhappy — but perhaps more happy! Permit me.

[*While he opens and reads the letter, the* LANDLORD *comes stealthily on the stage.*]

LANDLORD [*to* FRANZISKA]. Hist! my pretty maid! A word!

FRANZISKA [*to the* LANDLORD]. Mr. Landlord, we do not yet know ourselves what is in the letter.

LANDLORD. Who wants to know about the letter? I come about the ring. The lady must give it to me again, directly. Just is there, and wants to redeem it.

MINNA [*who in the mean time has approached the* LANDLORD]. Tell Just that it is already redeemed; and tell him by whom — by me.

LANDLORD. But —

MINNA. I take it upon myself. Go!
[*Exit* LANDLORD.]

FRANZISKA. And now, my lady, make it up with the poor Major.

MINNA. Oh, kind intercessor! As if the difficulties must not soon explain themselves.

MAJOR VON TELLHEIM [*after reading the letter with much emotion*]. Ah! Nor has he herein belied himself! Oh! Minna, what justice! what clemency! This is more than I expected; more than I deserve! — My fortune, my honor, all is reëstablished! — Do I dream? [*Looking at the letter, as if to convince himself.*] No, no delusion born of my own desires! Read it yourself, Minna; read it yourself!

MINNA. I would not presume, Major.

MAJOR VON TELLHEIM. Presume! The letter is to me; to your Tellheim, Minna. It contains — what your uncle cannot take from you. You must read it! Do read it.

MINNA. If it affords you pleasure, Major. [*Takes the letter and reads.*] "*My dear Major von Tellheim,*

"I hereby inform you that the business which caused me some anxiety on account of your honor has been cleared up in your favor. My brother had a more detailed knowledge of it, and his testimony has more than proved your innocence. The Treasury has received orders to deliver again to you the bill in question, and to reimburse the sum advanced. I have also ordered that all claims which the Paymaster's Office brings forward against your accounts be nullified. Please to inform me whether your health will allow of your taking active service again. I can ill spare a man of your courage and sentiments. I am your gracious KING," etc.

MAJOR VON TELLHEIM. Now, what do you say to that, Minna?

MINNA [*folding up and returning the letter*]. I? Nothing.

MAJOR VON TELLHEIM. Nothing?

MINNA. Stay — yes. That your king, who is a great man, can also be a good man. — But what is that to me? He is not my king.

MAJOR VON TELLHEIM. And do you say nothing more? Nothing about ourselves?

MINNA. You are going to serve again. From Major, you will become Lieutenant-Colonel, perhaps Colonel. I congratulate you with all my heart.

MAJOR VON TELLHEIM. And you do not know me better? No, since fortune restores me sufficient to satisfy the wishes of a reasonable man, it shall depend upon my Minna alone, whether for the future I shall belong to any one else but her. To her service alone my whole life shall be devoted! The service of the great is dangerous, and does not repay the trouble, the restraint, the humiliation which it costs. Minna is not among those vain people who love nothing in their husbands beyond their titles and positions. She will love me for myself; and for her sake I will forget the whole world. I became a soldier from party feeling — I do not myself know on what political principles — and from the whim that it is good for every honorable man to try the profession of arms for a time, to make himself familiar with danger, and to learn coolness and determination. Extreme necessity alone could have compelled me to make this trial a fixed mode of life, this temporary occupation a profession. But now that nothing compels me, my whole and sole ambition is to be a peaceful and a contented man. This with you, dearest Minna, I shall infallibly become; this in your society I shall unchangeably remain. Let the holy bond unite us to-morrow; and then we will look round us, and in the whole wide habitable world seek out the most peaceful, the brightest, most smiling nook which wants but a happy couple to be a Paradise. There we will dwell; there shall each day — What is the matter, Minna?

[MINNA *turns away uneasily, and endeavors to hide her emotion*.]

MINNA [*regaining her composure*]. It is cruel of you, Tellheim, to paint such happiness to me, when I am forced to renounce it. My loss —

MAJOR VON TELLHEIM. Your loss! Why name your loss? All that Minna could lose is not Minna. You are still the sweetest, dearest, loveliest, best creature under the sun; all goodness and generosity, innocence and bliss! Now and then a little petulant; at times somewhat willful — so much the better! So much the better! Minna would otherwise be an angel, whom I should honor with trepidation, but not dare to love. [*Takes her hand to kiss it*.]

MINNA [*drawing away her hand*]. Not

so, sir. Why this sudden change? Is this flattering, impetuous lover the cold Tellheim! — Could his returning good fortune alone create this ardor in him? He will permit me during his passionate excitement to retain the power of reflection for us both. When he could himself reflect, I heard him say, "It is a worthless love which does not scruple to expose its object to scorn." — True; and I aspire to as pure and noble a love as he himself. Now, when honor calls him, when a great monarch solicits his services, shall I consent that he shall give himself up to love-sick dreams with me? that the illustrious warrior shall degenerate into a toying swain? No, Major, follow the call of your higher destiny.

MAJOR VON TELLHEIM. Well! If the busy world has greater charms for you, Minna, let us remain in the busy world! How mean, how poor is this busy world! You now only know its gilded surface. Yet certainly, Minna, you will — But let it be so! Until then! Your charms shall not want admirers, nor will my happiness lack enviers.

MINNA. No, Tellheim, I do not mean that! I send you back into the busy world, on the road of honor, without wishing to accompany you. Tellheim will there require an irreproachable wife! A fugitive Saxon girl who has thrown herself upon him —

MAJOR VON TELLHEIM [*starting up, and looking fiercely about him*]. Who dare say that? Ah! Minna, I feel afraid of myself, when I imagine that any one but yourself could have spoken so. My anger against him would know no bounds.

MINNA. Exactly! That is just what I fear. You would not endure one word of calumny against me, and yet you would have to put up with the very bitterest every day. In short, Tellheim, hear what I have firmly determined, and from which nothing in the world shall turn me —

MAJOR VON TELLHEIM. Before you proceed, I implore you, Minna, reflect for one moment that you are about to pronounce a sentence of life or death upon me!

MINNA. Without a moment's reflection!

— As certainly as I have given you back the ring with which you formerly pledged your troth to me, as certainly as you have taken back that same ring, so certainly shall the unfortunate Minna never be the wife of the fortunate Tellheim!

MAJOR VON TELLHEIM. And herewith you pronounce my sentence.

MINNA. Equality is the only sure bond of love. The happy Minna only wished to live for the happy Tellheim. Even Minna in misfortune would have allowed herself to be persuaded either to increase or to assuage the misfortune of her friend through herself — He must have seen, before the arrival of that letter, which has again destroyed all equality between us, that in appearance only I refused.

MAJOR VON TELLHEIM. Is that true? I thank you, Minna, that you have not yet pronounced the sentence. You will only marry Tellheim when unfortunate? You may have him. [Coolly.] I perceive now that it would be indecorous in me to accept this tardy justice; that it will be better if I do not seek again that of which I have been deprived by such shameful suspicion. Yes; I will suppose that I have not received the letter. Behold my only answer to it! [About to tear it up.]

MINNA [stopping him]. What are you going to do, Tellheim?

MAJOR VON TELLHEIM. Obtain your hand.

MINNA. Stop!

MAJOR VON TELLHEIM. Madam, it is torn without fail if you do not quickly recall your words. — Then we will see what else you may have to object to in me.

MINNA. What! In such a tone? Shall I, must I, thus become contemptible in my own eyes? Never! She is a worthless creature who is not ashamed to owe her whole happiness to the blind tenderness of a man!

MAJOR VON TELLHEIM. False! Utterly false!

MINNA. Can you venture to find fault with your own words when coming from my lips?

MAJOR VON TELLHEIM. Sophistry! Does the weaker sex dishonor itself by every action which does not become the stronger? Or can a man do everything which is proper in a woman? Which is appointed by nature to be the support of the other?

MINNA. Be not alarmed, Tellheim! — I shall not be quite unprotected if I must decline the honor of your protection. I shall still have as much as is absolutely necessary. I have announced my arrival to our Ambassador. I am to see him to-day. I hope he will assist me. Time is flying. Permit me, Major —

MAJOR VON TELLHEIM. I will accompany you, madam.

MINNA. No, Major; leave me.

MAJOR VON TELLHEIM. Sooner shall your shadow desert you! Come, madam, where you will, to whom you will, everywhere, to friends and strangers, will I repeat in your presence — repeat a hundred times each day — what a bond binds you to me, and with what cruel caprice you wish to break it —

[Enter JUST.]

JUST [impetuously]. Major! Major!

MAJOR VON TELLHEIM. Well!

JUST. Here quick! Quick!

MAJOR VON TELLHEIM. Why? Come to me. Speak! What is the matter?

JUST. What do you think?

[Whispers to him.]

MINNA [aside to FRANZISKA]. Do you notice anything, Franziska?

FRANZISKA. Oh, you merciless creature! I have stood here on thorns!

MAJOR VON TELLHEIM [to JUST]. What do you say? — That is not possible! — You? [Looking fiercely at MINNA.] Speak it out; tell it to her face. — Listen, madam.

JUST. The Landlord says that Fräulein von Barnhelm has taken the ring which I pledged to him; she recognized it as her own, and would not return it.

MAJOR VON TELLHEIM. Is that true, madam? No, that cannot be true!

MINNA [smiling]. And why not, Tellheim? Why can it not be true?

MAJOR VON TELLHEIM [vehemently]. Then it is true! — What terrible light suddenly breaks in upon me! — Now I know you — false, faithless one!

MINNA [alarmed]. Who, who is faithless?
MAJOR VON TELLHEIM. You, whom I
will never more name!
MINNA. Tellheim!
MAJOR VON TELLHEIM. Forget my
name — You came here with the intention
of breaking with me — It is evident! —
Oh, that chance should thus delight to assist the faithless! It brought your ring into
your possession. Your craftiness contrived
to get my own back into mine!
MINNA. Tellheim, what visions are you
conjuring up? Be calm, and listen to me.
FRANZISKA [aside]. Now she will catch it!

[Enter WERNER, with a purse full of gold.]

WERNER. Here I am already, Major!
MAJOR VON TELLHEIM [without looking
at him]. Who wants you?
WERNER. I have brought more money!
A thousand pistoles!
MAJOR VON TELLHEIM. I do not want
them!
WERNER. And to-morrow, Major, you
can have as many more.
MAJOR VON TELLHEIM. Keep your
money!
WERNER. It is your money, Major —
I do not think you see whom you are speak-
ing to!
MAJOR VON TELLHEIM. Take it away, I
say!
WERNER. What is the matter with you?
— I am Werner.
MAJOR VON TELLHEIM. All goodness is
dissimulation; all kindness, deceit.
WERNER. Is that meant for me?
MAJOR VON TELLHEIM. As you please!
WERNER. Why, I have only obeyed
your commands.
MAJOR VON TELLHEIM. Obey once more,
and be off!
WERNER. Major! [Vexed.] I am a
man —
MAJOR VON TELLHEIM. So much the
better!
WERNER. Who can also be angry.
MAJOR VON TELLHEIM. Anger is the
best thing we possess.
WERNER. I beg you, Major.
MAJOR VON TELLHEIM. How often must
I tell you? I do not want your money!

WERNER [in a rage]. Then take it, who
will! [Throws the purse on the ground,
and goes to the side.]
MINNA [to FRANZISKA]. Ah! Franziska,
I ought to have followed your advice. I
have carried the jest too far. — Still, when
he hears me — [Going to him.]
FRANZISKA [without answering MINNA,
goes up to WERNER]. Mr. Sergeant —
WERNER [pettishly]. Go along!
FRANZISKA. Ah, what men these are!
MINNA. Tellheim! Tellheim! [TELL-
HEIM, biting his fingers with rage, turns away
his face, without listening.] No, this is too
bad — Only listen! — You are mistaken!
— A mere misunderstanding. Tellheim,
will you not hear your Minna? Can you
have such a suspicion? — I break my engagement with you? I came here for that
purpose? — Tellheim!

[Enter two Servants, running into the room
from different sides.]

FIRST SERVANT. Your ladyship, His Ex-
cellency the Count!
SECOND SERVANT. He is coming, your
ladyship!
FRANZISKA [running to the window]. It is!
It is he!
MINNA. Is it? Now, Tellheim, quick!
MAJOR VON TELLHEIM [suddenly recovering himself]. Who — who comes? Your
uncle, madam! This cruel uncle! — Let
him come; just let him come! — Fear not!
— He shall not hurt you even by a look.
He shall have to deal with me — You do
not, indeed, deserve it of me.
MINNA. Quick, Tellheim! One embrace
and forget all.
MAJOR VON TELLHEIM. Ah! Did I but
know that you could regret —
MINNA. No, I can never regret having
obtained a sight of your whole heart! —
Ah, what a man you are! — Embrace
your Minna, your happy Minna: and in
nothing more happy than in the possession
of you. [Embracing.] And now to meet
him!
MAJOR VON TELLHEIM. To meet whom?
MINNA. The best of your unknown
friends.
MAJOR VON TELLHEIM. What!

MINNA. The Count, my uncle, my father, your father — My flight, his displeasure, my loss of property — do you not see that all is a fiction, credulous knight?

MAJOR VON TELLHEIM. Fiction! But the ring? — the ring?

MINNA. Where is the ring that I gave back to you?

MAJOR VON TELLHEIM. You will take it again? Ah! Now I am happy — Here, Minna.   [Taking it from his pocket.]

MINNA. Look at it first! — Oh! how blind are those who will not see! — What ring is that? — the one you gave me? — or the one I gave to you? Is it not the one which I did not like to leave in the Landlord's possession?

MAJOR VON TELLHEIM. Heavens! What do I see! What do I hear!

MINNA. Shall I take it again now? Shall I? Give it to me! Give it! [Takes it from him, and then puts it on his finger herself.] There, now all is right!

MAJOR VON TELLHEIM. Where am I? [Kissing her hand.] Oh, malicious angel, to torture me so!

MINNA. As a proof, my dear husband, that you shall never play me a trick without my playing you one in return — Do you suppose that you did not torture me also?

MAJOR VON TELLHEIM. Oh, you actresses! But I ought to have known you.

FRANZISKA. Not I, indeed; I am spoiled for acting. I trembled and shook, and was obliged to hold my lips together with my hand.

MINNA. Nor was mine an easy part. — But come, now —

MAJOR VON TELLHEIM. I have not recovered myself yet. How happy, yet how anxious, I feel! It is like awaking suddenly from a frightful dream.

MINNA. We are losing time — I hear him coming now.

[Enter COUNT VON BRUCHSAL, accompanied by several servants and the LANDLORD.]

COUNT. She arrived in safety, I hope?

MINNA [running to meet him]. Ah, my father!

COUNT. Here I am, dear Minna. [Embracing her.] But what, girl [seeing TELLHEIM], only four-and-twenty hours here, and friends — company already!

MINNA. Guess who it is?

COUNT. Not your Tellheim, surely!

MINNA. Who else! — Come, Tellheim.
[Introducing him.]

COUNT. Sir, we have never met; but at the first glance I fancied I recognized you. I wished it might be Major von Tellheim. — Your hand, sir; you have my highest esteem; I ask for your friendship. My niece, my daughter loves you.

MINNA. You know that, my father! — And was my love blind?

COUNT. No, Minna, your love was not blind; but your lover — is dumb.

MAJOR VON TELLHEIM [throwing himself in the COUNT's arms]. Let me recover myself, my father!

COUNT. Right, my son. I see your heart can speak, though your lips cannot. I do not usually care for those who wear this uniform. But you are an honorable man, Tellheim; and one must love an honorable man, in whatever garb he may be.

MINNA. Ah, did you but know all!

COUNT. Why should I not hear all? — Which are my apartments, Landlord?

LANDLORD. Will Your Excellency have the goodness to walk this way?

COUNT. Come, Minna! — Pray come, Major!
[Exit with the LANDLORD and servants.]

MINNA. Come, Tellheim!

MAJOR VON TELLHEIM. I will follow you in an instant, Minna. One word first with this man.   [Turning to WERNER.]

MINNA. And a good word, methinks, it should be. — Should it not, Franziska?
[Exit.]

MAJOR VON TELLHEIM [pointing to the purse which WERNER had thrown down]. Here, Just, pick up the purse, and carry it home. Go!   [JUST takes it up and goes.]

WERNER [still standing, out of humor, in a corner, and absent till he hears the last words]. Well, what now?

MAJOR VON TELLHEIM [in a friendly tone while going up to him]. Werner, when can I have the other two thousand pistoles?

WERNER [*in a good humor again instantly*]. To-morrow, Major, to-morrow.

MAJOR VON TELLHEIM. I do not need to become your debtor; but I will be your banker. All you good-natured people ought to have guardians. You are in a manner spendthrifts. — I irritated you just now, Werner.

WERNER. Upon my life you did! But I ought not to have been such a dolt. Now I see it all clearly. I deserve a hundred lashes. You may give them to me, if you will, Major. Only no more ill-will, dear Major!

MAJOR VON TELLHEIM. Ill-will! [*Shaking him by the hand.*] Read in my eyes all that I cannot say to you. — Ah, let me see the man with a better wife and a more trusty friend than I shall have. — Eh! Franziska? [*Exit.*]

FRANZISKA [*aside*]. Yes, indeed, he is more than good! — Such a man will never fall in my way again. — It must come out. [*Approaching* WERNER *bashfully.*] Mr. Sergeant!

WERNER [*wiping his eyes*]. Well!

FRANZISKA. Mr. Sergeant —

WERNER. What do you want, little woman?

FRANZISKA. Look at me, Mr. Sergeant.

WERNER. I can't yet; there is something, I don't know what, in my eyes.

FRANZISKA. Now, do look at me!

WERNER. I am afraid I have looked at you too much already, little woman! — There, now I can see you. What then?

FRANZISKA. Mr. Sergeant — don't you want a Mrs. Sergeant?

WERNER. Do you really mean it, little woman?

FRANZISKA. Really I do.

WERNER. And would you go with me to Persia even?

FRANZISKA. Wherever you please.

WERNER. You will? — Hullo, Major, no boasting! At any rate, I have got as good a wife, and as trusty a friend, as you. — Give me your hand, my little woman! It's a match! In ten years' time you shall be a general's wife, or a widow!

GOETZ VON BERLICHINGEN

WITH THE IRON HAND

By J. W. VON GOETHE

Translated by SIR WALTER SCOTT

CHARACTERS

MAXIMILIAN, *Emperor of Germany*

GOETZ VON BERLICHINGEN, *a free knight of the Empire*

ELIZABETH, *his wife*

MARIA, *his sister*

CHARLES, *his son — a boy*

GEORGE, *his page*

BISHOP OF BAMBERG

ADELBERT VON WEISLINGEN, *a free German knight of the Empire*

ADELAIDE VON WALLDORF, *widow of the* COUNT VON WALLDORF

LIEBTRAUT, *a courtier of the Bishop's*

ABBOT OF FULDA, *residing at the Bishop's court*

OLEARIUS, *a doctor of laws*

BROTHER MARTIN, *a monk*

HANS VON SELBITZ,
FRANZ VON SICKINGEN, } *free knights, in alliance with* GOETZ

LERSE, *a trooper*

FRANCIS, *esquire to* WEISLINGEN

Female Attendant on ADELAIDE

President, Accuser, and Avenger of the Secret Tribunal

METZLER,
SIEVERS,
LINK, } *leaders of the insurgent peasantry*
KOHL,
WILD,

Imperial Commissioners

Two Merchants of Nuremberg

Magistrates of Heilbronn

MAXIMILIAN STUMF, *a vassal of the Palsgrave*

An unknown

Bride's father,
Bride, } *peasants*
Bridegroom,

Gypsy captain

Gypsy mother and women

STICKS *and* WOLF, *gypsies*

Imperial captain

Imperial officers

Innkeeper

Sentinel

Sergeant-at-arms

Imperial Soldiers — *Troopers belonging to* GOETZ, *to* SELBITZ, *to* SICKINGEN, *and to* WEISLINGEN — *Peasants* — *Gypsies* — *Judges of the Secret Tribunal* — *Gaolers* — *Courtiers, etc., etc., etc.*

GOETZ VON BERLICHINGEN

ACT I

SCENE I. *An inn at Schwarzenberg in Franconia.*

[METZLER *and* SIEVERS, *two Swabian peasants, are seated at a table. At the fire, at some distance from them, are two troopers from Bamberg. The Innkeeper.*]

SIEVERS. Hänsel! Another cup of brandy — and Christian measure.

INNKEEPER. Thou art a Never-enough.

METZLER [*apart to* SIEVERS]. Repeat that again about Berlichingen. The Bambergers there are so angry they are almost black in the face.

SIEVERS. Bambergers! What are they about here?

METZLER. Weislingen has been two days up yonder at the castle with the Earl — they are his attendants — they came with him, I know not whence; they are waiting for him — he is going back to Bamberg.

SIEVERS. Who is that Weislingen?

METZLER. The bishop of Bamberg's right hand! — a powerful lord, who is lying in wait to play Goetz some trick.

SIEVERS. He had better take care of himself.

METZLER [*aside*]. Prithee go on! [*Aloud.*] How long is it since Goetz had a new dispute with the Bishop? I thought all had been agreed and squared between them.

SIEVERS. Aye! Agreement with priests! When the Bishop saw he could do no good, and always got the worst of it, he pulled in his horns, and made haste to patch up a truce — and honest Berlichingen yielded to an absurd extent, as he always does when he has the advantage.

METZLER. God bless him! — a worthy nobleman.

SIEVERS. Only think! Was it not shameful? They fell upon a page of his, to his no small surprise; but they will soon be mauled for that.

METZLER. How provoking that his last stroke should have missed. He must have been plaguily annoyed.

SIEVERS. I don't think anything has vexed him so much for a long time. Look you, all had been calculated to a nicety: the time the Bishop would come from the bath, with how many attendants, and which road; and had it not been betrayed by some traitor, Goetz would have blessed his bath for him, and rubbed him dry.

FIRST TROOPER. What are you prating there about our Bishop; do you want to pick a quarrel?

SIEVERS. Mind your own affairs; you have nothing to do with our table.

SECOND TROOPER. Who taught you to speak disrespectfully of our Bishop?

SIEVERS. Am I bound to answer *your* questions? Look at the fool!

[*The First Trooper boxes his ears.*]

METZLER. Smash the rascal!

[*They attack each other.*]

SECOND TROOPER [*to* METZLER]. Come on if you dare —

INNKEEPER [*separating them*]. Will you be quiet? Zounds! Take yourself off if you have any scores to settle; in my house I will have order and decency. [*He pushes the Troopers out of doors.*] And what are you about, you jackasses?

METZLER. No bad names, Hänsel, or your sconce shall pay for it. Come, comrade, we'll go and thrash those blackguards.

[*Enter two of* BERLICHINGEN'S *Troopers.*]

FIRST TROOPER. What's the matter?

SIEVERS. Ah! Good-day, Peter! — Good-day, Veit! — Whence come you?

SECOND TROOPER. Mind you don't let out whom we serve.

SIEVERS [*whispering*]. Then your master Goetz isn't far off?

FIRST TROOPER. Hold your tongue! — Have you had a quarrel?

SIEVERS. You must have met the fellows without — they are Bambergers.

FIRST TROOPER. What brings them here?

SIEVERS. They escort Weislingen, who is up yonder at the castle with the Earl.

FIRST TROOPER. Weislingen!

SECOND TROOPER [aside to his companion]. Peter, that is grist to our mill. How long has he been here?

METZLER. Two days — but he is off today, as I heard one of his fellows say.

FIRST TROOPER [aside]. Did I not tell you he was here? — We might have waited yonder long enough — Come, Veit —

SIEVERS. Help us first to drub the Bambergers.

SECOND TROOPER. There are already two of you — We must away. Farewell!

[Exeunt both Troopers.]

SIEVERS. Scurvy dogs, these troopers! They won't strike a blow without pay.

METZLER. I could swear they have something in hand. — Whom do they serve?

SIEVERS. I am not to tell — They serve Goetz.

METZLER. So! — Well, now we'll cudgel those fellows outside While I have a quarter-staff I care not for their spits.

SIEVERS. If we durst but once serve the princes in the same manner, who drag our skins over our ears! [Exeunt.]

SCENE II. A cottage in a thick forest.

[GOETZ VON BERLICHINGEN discovered walking among the trees before the door.]

GOETZ. Where linger my servants? I must walk up and down, or sleep will overcome me. Five days and nights already on the watch. It is hardly earned, this bit of life and freedom. But when I have caught thee, Weislingen, I shall take my ease. [Fills a glass of wine and drinks; looks at the flask.] Again empty. — George! — While this and my courage last, I can laugh at the ambition and chicanery of princes! — George! — You may send round your obsequious Weislingen to your uncles and cousins to calumniate my character. Be it

so. I am on the alert. Thou hast escaped me, Bishop; then thy dear Weislingen shall pay the score. — George! — Does n't the boy hear? — George! George!

GEORGE [entering in the cuirass of a full-grown man]. Worshipful sir.

GOETZ. What kept you? Were you asleep? — What in the devil's name means this masquerade? — Come hither; you don't look amiss. Be not ashamed, boy; you look bravely. Ah! if you could but fill it! — Is it Hans's cuirass?

GEORGE. He wished to sleep a little, and unbuckled it.

GOETZ. He takes things easier than his master.

GEORGE. Do not be angry! I took it quietly away and put it on, then fetched my father's old sword from the wall, ran to the meadow, and drew it —

GOETZ. And laid about you, no doubt? Rare times for the brambles and thorns! — Is Hans asleep?

GEORGE. He started up and cried out to me when you called. I was trying to unbuckle the cuirass when I heard you twice or thrice.

GOETZ. Go, take back his cuirass, and tell him to be ready with his horses.

GEORGE. I have fed them well and they are ready bridled; you may mount when you will.

GOETZ. Bring me a stoup of wine. Give Hans a glass too, and tell him to be on the alert — there is good cause; I expect the return of my scouts every moment.

GEORGE. Ah, noble sir!

GOETZ. What's the matter?

GEORGE. May I not go with you?

GOETZ. Another time, George! when we waylay merchants and seize their wagons —

GEORGE. Another time! — You have said that so often. — Oh, this time, this time! I will only skulk behind; just keep on the lookout. I will gather up all the spent arrows for you.

GOETZ. Next time, George! — You must first have a doublet, a steel cap, and a lance.

GEORGE. Take me with you now! — Had I been with you last time, you would not have lost your crossbow.

GOETZ. Do you know about that?

GEORGE. You threw it at your antagonist's head; one of his followers picked it up, and off with it he went. — Don't I know about it?

GOETZ. Did my people tell you?

GEORGE. Oh yes: and for that, I whistle them all sorts of tunes while we dress the horses, and teach them merry songs, too.

GOETZ. Thou art a brave boy.

GEORGE. Take me with you to prove myself so.

GOETZ. The next time, I promise you! You must not go to battle unarmed as you are. There is a time coming which will also require men. I tell thee, boy, it will be a dear time. Princes shall offer their treasures for a man whom they now hate. Go, George, give Hans his cuirass again, and bring me wine. [Exit GEORGE.] — Where can my people be? It is incomprehensible! — A monk! What brings him here so late?

[Enter Brother MARTIN.]

GOETZ. Good-evening, reverend father! Whence come you so late? Man of holy rest, thou shamest many knights.

MARTIN. Thanks, noble sir! I am at present but an unworthy brother, if we come to titles. My cloister name is Augustin, but I like better to be called by my Christian name, Martin.

GOETZ. You are tired, Brother Martin, and doubtless thirsty.

[Enter GEORGE with wine.]

GOETZ. Here, in good time, comes wine!

MARTIN. For me a draught of water. I dare not drink wine.

GOETZ. Is it against your vow?

MARTIN. Noble sir, to drink wine is not against my vow; but because wine is against my vow, therefore I drink it not.

GOETZ. How am I to understand that?

MARTIN. 'T is well for thee that thou dost not understand it. Eating and drinking nourish man's life.

GOETZ. Well!

MARTIN. When thou hast eaten and drunken, thou art as it were newborn, stronger, bolder, fitter for action. Wine rejoices the heart of man, and joyousness is the mother of every virtue. When thou hast drunk wine, thou art double what thou shouldst be! — twice as ingenious, twice as enterprising, and twice as active.

GOETZ. As I drink it, what you say is true.

MARTIN. 'T is when thus taken in moderation that I speak of it. But we — [GEORGE brings water.]

GOETZ [aside to GEORGE]. Go to the road which leads to Daxbach; lay thine ear close to the earth, and listen for the tread of horses. Return immediately.

MARTIN. But we, on the other hand, when we have eaten and drunken, are the reverse of what we should be. Our sluggish digestion depresses our mental powers; and in the indulgence of luxurious ease, desires are generated which grow too strong for our weakness.

GOETZ. One glass, Brother Martin, will not disturb your sleep. You have traveled far to-day. [Raises his glass.] Here's to all fighting men!

MARTIN. With all my heart! [They ring their glasses.] I cannot abide idle people — yet will I not say that all monks are idle; they do what they can: I am just come from St. Bede, where I slept last night. The prior took me into the garden; that is their hive. Excellent salad, cabbages in perfection, and such cauliflowers and artichokes as you will hardly find in Europe.

GOETZ. So that is not the life for you?

[Goes out and looks anxiously after the boy. Returns.]

MARTIN. Would that God had made me a gardener, or day laborer, I might then have been happy! My convent is Erfurt in Saxony; my Abbot loves me; he knows I cannot remain idle, and so he sends me round the country, wherever there is business to be done. I am on my way to the Bishop of Constance.

GOETZ. Another glass. Good speed to you!

MARTIN. The same to you.

GOETZ. Why do you look at me so steadfastly, brother?

MARTIN. I am in love with your armor.

GOETZ. Would you like a suit? It is heavy and toilsome to the wearer.

MARTIN. What is not toilsome in this world? — But to me nothing is so much so as to renounce my very nature! Poverty, chastity, obedience — three vows, each of which taken singly seems the most dreadful to humanity — so insupportable are they all; — and to spend a lifetime under this burden, or to groan despairingly under the still heavier load of an evil conscience — Ah! Sir Knight, what are the toils of your life compared to the sorrows of a state, which, from a mistaken desire of drawing nearer to the Deity, condemns as crimes the best impulses of our nature, impulses by which we live, grow, and prosper!

GOETZ. Were your vow less sacred, I would give you a suit of armor and a steed, and we would ride out together.

MARTIN. Would to Heaven my shoulders had strength to bear armor, and my arm to unhorse an enemy! — Poor weak hand, accustomed from infancy to swing censers, to bear crosses and banners of peace, how couldst thou manage the lance and falchion? My voice, tuned only to *aves* and *halleluiahs*, would be a herald of my weakness to the enemy, while yours would overpower him; otherwise no vows should keep me from entering an order founded by the Creator himself.

GOETZ. To your happy return! [*Drinks*.]

MARTIN. I drink that only in compliment to you! A return to my prison must ever be unhappy. When you, Sir Knight, return to your castle, with the consciousness of your courage and strength, which no fatigue can overcome; when you, for the first time, after a long absence, stretch yourself unarmed upon your bed, secure from the attack of enemies, and resign yourself to a sleep sweeter than the draught after a long thirst — then can you speak of happiness.

GOETZ. And accordingly it comes but seldom!

MARTIN [*with growing ardor*]. But when it does come, it is a foretaste of paradise. — When you return home laden with the spoils of your enemies, and, remember, " such a one I struck from his horse ere he could discharge his piece — such another I overthrew, horse and man "; then you ride to your castle, and —

GOETZ. And what?

MARTIN. And your wife — [*Fills a glass.*] To her health! [*He wipes his eyes.*] You have one?

GOETZ. A virtuous, noble wife!

MARTIN. Happy the man who possesses a virtuous wife, his life is doubled. This blessing was denied me, yet was woman the glory or crown of creation.

GOETZ [*aside*]. I grieve for him. The sense of his condition preys upon his heart.

[*Enter* GEORGE, *breathless*.]

GEORGE. My lord, my lord, I hear horses in full gallop! — two of them — 'T is they for certain.

GOETZ. Bring out my steed; let Hans mount. Farewell, dear brother, God be with you. Be cheerful and patient. He will give you ample scope.

MARTIN. Let me request your name.

GOETZ. Pardon me — farewell!
[*Gives his left hand.*]

MARTIN. Why do you give the left? Am I unworthy of the knightly right hand?

GOETZ. Were you the Emperor, you must be satisfied with this. My right hand, though not useless in combat, is unresponsive to the grasp of affection. It is one with its mailed gauntlet — You see, it is *iron!*

MARTIN. Then art thou Goetz of Berlichingen. I thank thee, Heaven, who hast shown me the man whom princes hate, but to whom the oppressed throng! [*He takes his right hand.*] Withdraw not this hand; let me kiss it.

GOETZ. You must not!

MARTIN. Let me, let me — thou hand, more worthy even than the saintly relic through which the most sacred blood has flowed! Lifeless instrument, quickened by the noblest spirit's faith in God.

[GOETZ *adjusts his helmet, and takes his lance.*]

MARTIN. There was a monk among us about a year ago, who visited you when your hand was shot off at the siege of Landshut. He used to tell us what you suffered, and your grief at being disabled for your profession of arms; till you remembered having heard of one who had also lost a hand, and yet served long as a gallant knight — I shall never forget it.

[*Enter the two Troopers. They speak apart with* GOETZ.]

MARTIN [*continuing*]. I shall never forget his words uttered in the noblest, the most childlike trust in God: "If I had twelve hands, what would they avail me without thy grace? Then may I with only one —"

GOETZ. In the wood of Haslach, then. [*Turns to* MARTIN.] Farewell, worthy brother! [*Embraces him.*]

MARTIN. Forget me not, as I shall never forget thee! [*Exeunt* GOETZ *and his Troopers.*]

MARTIN. How my heart beat at the sight of him. He spoke not, yet my spirit recognized his. What rapture to behold a great man!

GEORGE. Reverend sir, you will sleep here?

MARTIN. Can I have a bed?

GEORGE. No, sir! I know of beds only by hearsay; in our quarters there is nothing but straw.

MARTIN. It will serve. What is thy name?

GEORGE. George, reverend sir.

MARTIN. George! Thou hast a gallant patron saint.

GEORGE. They say he was a trooper; that is what I intend to be!

MARTIN. Stop! [*Takes a picture from his breviary and gives it to him.*] There, behold him — follow his example; be brave, and fear God. [*Exit into the cottage.*]

GEORGE. Ah! what a splendid gray horse! If I had but one like that — and the golden armor. There is an ugly dragon. At present I shoot nothing but sparrows. O St. George! Make me but tall and strong; give me a lance, armor, and such a horse, and then let the dragons come! [*Exit.*]

SCENE III. *An apartment in Jaxthausen, the castle of Goetz von Berlichingen.*

[ELIZABETH, MARIA, *and* CHARLES *discovered.*]

CHARLES. Pray now, dear aunt, tell me again that story about the good child; it is so pretty —

MARIA. Do you tell it to me, little rogue! that I may see if you have paid attention.

CHARLES. Wait, then, till I think. — "There was once upon" — yes — "There was once upon a time a child, and his mother was sick; so the child went —"

MARIA. No, no! — "Then his mother said, 'Dear child' —"

CHARLES. "'I am sick —'"

MARIA. "'And cannot go out.'"

CHARLES. "And gave him money and said, 'Go and buy yourself a breakfast.' There came a poor man —"

MARIA. "The child went. There met him an old man who was —" Now, Charles!

CHARLES. "Who was — old —"

MARIA. Of course. "Who was hardly able to walk, and said, 'Dear child —'"

CHARLES. "'Give me something; I have eaten not a morsel yesterday or to-day.' Then the child gave him the money —"

MARIA. "That should have bought his breakfast."

CHARLES. "Then the old man said —"

MARIA. "Then the old man took the child by the hand —"

CHARLES. "By the hand, and said — and became a fine beautiful saint — and said — 'Dear child —'"

MARIA. "'The holy Virgin rewards thee for thy benevolence through me: whatever sick person thou touchest —'"

CHARLES. "'With thy hand —'" It was the right hand, I think.

MARIA. Yes.

CHARLES. "'He will get well directly.'"

MARIA. "Then the child ran home, and could not speak for joy —"

CHARLES. "And fell upon his mother's neck and wept for joy."

MARIA. "Then the mother cried, 'What is this?' and became —" Now, Charles.

CHARLES. "Became — became —"

MARIA. You do not attend — "and became well. And the child cured kings and emperors, and became so rich that he built a great abbey."

ELIZABETH. I cannot understand why my husband stays. He has been away five days and nights, and he hoped to have finished his adventure so quickly.

MARIA. I have long felt uneasy. Were I married to a man who continually incurred such danger, I should die within the first year.

ELIZABETH. I thank God that He has made me of firmer stuff!

CHARLES. But must my father ride out, if it is so dangerous?

MARIA. Such is his good pleasure.

ELIZABETH. He must, indeed, dear Charles!

CHARLES. Why?

ELIZABETH. Do you not remember the last time he rode out, when he brought you those nice things?

CHARLES. Will he bring me anything now?

ELIZABETH. I believe so. Listen: There was a tailor at Stutgard who was a capital archer, and had gained the prize at Cologne.

CHARLES. Was it much?

ELIZABETH. A hundred dollars; and afterwards they would not pay him.

MARIA. That was naughty, eh, Charles?

CHARLES. Naughty people!

ELIZABETH. The tailor came to your father and begged him to get his money for him. Then your father rode out and intercepted a party of merchants from Cologne, and kept them prisoners till they paid the money. Would you not have ridden out too?

CHARLES. No; for one must go through a dark thick wood, where there are gypsies and witches —

ELIZABETH. You're a fine fellow; afraid of witches!

MARIA. Charles, it is far better to live at home in your castle, like a quiet Christian knight. One may find opportunities enough of doing good on one's own lands. Even the worthiest knights do more harm than good in their excursions.

ELIZABETH. Sister, you know not what you are saying. — God grant our boy may become braver as he grows up, and not take after that Weislingen, who has dealt so faithlessly with my husband.

MARIA. We will not judge, Elizabeth. — My brother is highly incensed, and so are you; I am only a spectator in the matter, and can be more impartial.

ELIZABETH. Weislingen cannot be defended.

MARIA. What I have heard of him has interested me. — Even your husband relates many instances of his former goodness and affection. — How happy was their youth when they were both pages of honor to the Margrave!

ELIZABETH. That may be. But only tell me, how can a man ever have been good who lays snares for his best and truest friend; who has sold his services to the enemies of my husband; and who strives, by invidious misrepresentations, to poison the mind of our noble emperor, who is so gracious to us? [*A horn is heard.*]

CHARLES. Papa! papa! The warder sounds his horn! Joy! joy! Open the gate!

ELIZABETH. There he comes with booty!

[*Enter* PETER.]

PETER. We have fought — we have conquered! — God save you, noble ladies!

ELIZABETH. Have you captured Weislingen?

PETER. Himself, and three followers.

ELIZABETH. How came you to stay so long?

PETER. We lay in wait for him between Nuremberg and Bamberg, but he would not come, though we knew he had set out. At length we heard of his whereabouts; he had struck off sideways, and was staying quietly with the Earl at Schwarzenberg.

ELIZABETH. They would also fain make the Earl my husband's enemy.

PETER. I immediately told my master. — Up and away we rode into the forest of Haslach. And it was curious, that while we were riding along that night, a shepherd was watching, and five wolves fell upon the flock and attacked them stoutly. Then my master laughed, and said, "Good luck to us all, dear comrades, both to you and us!" And the good omen overjoyed us. Just then Weislingen came riding toward us with four attendants —

MARIA. How my heart beats!

PETER. My comrade and I, as our master had commanded, threw ourselves suddenly on him, and clung to him as if we had grown together, so that he could not move, while my master and Hans fell upon the servants, and overpowered them. They were all taken, except one who escaped.

ELIZABETH. I am curious to see him. Will he arrive soon?

PETER. They are riding through the valley, and will be here in a quarter of an hour.

MARIA. He is, no doubt, cast down and dejected?

PETER. He looks gloomy enough.

MARIA. It will grieve me to see his distress! ·

ELIZABETH. Oh! I must get food ready. You are, no doubt, all hungry?

PETER. Hungry enough, in truth.

ELIZABETH [to MARIA]. Take the cellar keys and bring the best wine. They have deserved it. [Exit ELIZABETH.]

CHARLES. I'll go, too, aunt.

MARIA. Come, then, boy.
[Exeunt CHARLES and MARIA.]

PETER. He'll never be his father, else he would have gone with me to the stable.

[Enter GOETZ, WEISLINGEN, HANS, and other Troopers.]

GOETZ [laying his helmet and sword on a table]. Unbuckle my armor, and give me my doublet. Ease will refresh me. Brother Martin, thou saidst truly. You have kept us long on the watch, Weislingen!

[WEISLINGEN paces up and down in silence.]

Be of good cheer! Come, unarm yourself! Where are your clothes? I hope nothing has been lost. [To the attendants.] Go, ask his servants; open the baggage, and see that nothing is missing. Or I can lend you some of mine.

WEISLINGEN. Let me remain as I am — it is all one.

GOETZ. I can give you a handsome doublet, but it is only of linen; it has grown too tight for me. I wore it at the marriage of my lord the Palsgrave, when your Bishop was so incensed at me. About a fortnight before I had sunk two of his vessels upon the Maine. — I was going upstairs in the Stag at Heidelberg, with Franz von Sickingen. Before you get quite to the top, there is a landing-place with iron rails —

there stood the Bishop, and gave his hand to Franz as he passed, and to me also as I followed close behind him. I laughed in my sleeve, and went to the Landgrave of Hanau, who was always a kind friend to me, and said, "The Bishop has given me his hand, but I'll wager he did not know me." The Bishop heard me, for I was speaking on purpose. He came to us angrily, and said, "True, I gave thee my hand, because I knew thee not." To which I answered, "I know that, my lord; and so here you have your shake of the hand back again!" The manikin grew red as a Turkey cock with spite, and he ran up into the room and complained to the Palsgrave Lewis and the Prince of Nassau. We have laughed over the scene again and again.

WEISLINGEN. I wish you would leave me to myself.

GOETZ. Why so? I entreat you be of good cheer. You are my prisoner, but I will not abuse my power.

WEISLINGEN. I have no fear of that. That is your duty as a knight.

GOETZ. And you know how sacred it is to me.

WEISLINGEN. I am your prisoner — the rest matters not.

GOETZ. You should not say so. Had you been taken by a prince, fettered and cast into a dungeon, your jailer directed to drive sleep from your eyes —

[Enter Servants with clothes. WEISLINGEN unarms himself. Enter CHARLES.]

CHARLES. Good-morrow, papa!

GOETZ [kisses him]. Good-morrow, boy! How have you been this long time?

CHARLES. Very well, father! Aunt says I am a good boy.

GOETZ. Does she?

CHARLES. Have you brought me anything?

GOETZ. Nothing this time.

CHARLES. I have learned a great deal.

GOETZ. Aye!

CHARLES. Shall I tell you about the good child?

GOETZ. After dinner.

CHARLES. I know something else, too.

GOETZ. What may that be?

CHARLES. "Jaxthausen is a village and castle on the Jaxt, which has appertained in property and heritage for two hundred years to the Lords of Berlichingen —"

GOETZ. Do you know the Lord of Berlichingen? [CHARLES *stares at him. Aside.*] His learning is so abstruse that he does not know his own father. To whom does Jaxthausen belong?

CHARLES. "Jaxthausen is a village and castle upon the Jaxt —"

GOETZ. I did not ask that. I knew every path, pass, and ford about the place, before ever I knew the name of the village, castle, or river. — Is your mother in the kitchen?

CHARLES. Yes, papa! They are cooking a lamb and turnips.

GOETZ. Do you know that, too, Jack Turnspit?

CHARLES. And my aunt is roasting an apple for me to eat after dinner —

GOETZ. Can't you eat it raw?

CHARLES. It tastes better roasted.

GOETZ. You must have a tit-bit, must you? — Weislingen, I will be with you immediately. I must go and see my wife. — Come, Charles!

CHARLES. Who is that man?

GOETZ. Bid him welcome. Tell him to be merry.

CHARLES. There's my hand for you, man! Be merry — for the dinner will soon be ready.

WEISLINGEN [*takes up the child and kisses him*]. Happy boy, that knowest no worse evil than the delay of dinner. May you live to have much joy in your son, Berlichingen!

GOETZ. Where there is most light the shades are deepest. Yet I should thank God for it. We'll see what they are about.

[*Exit with* CHARLES *and Servants.*]

WEISLINGEN. Oh, that I could but wake and find this all a dream! In the power of Berlichingen! — from whom I had scarcely detached myself — whose remembrance I shunned like fire — whom I hoped to overpower! And he still the old true-hearted Goetz! Gracious God, what will be the end of it? O Adelbert! Led back to the very hall where we played as children; when thou didst love and prize him as thy soul!

Who can know him and hate him? Alas! I am so thoroughly insignificant here. Happy days, ye are gone. There, in his chair by the chimney, sat old Berlichingen, while we played around him, and loved each other like cherubs! How anxious the Bishop and all my friends will be! Well, the whole country will sympathize with my misfortune. But what avails it? Can they give me the peace after which I strive?

[*Reënter* GOETZ *with wine and goblets.*]

GOETZ. We'll take a glass while dinner is preparing. Come, sit down, — think yourself at home! Fancy you've come once more to see Goetz. It is long since we have sat and emptied a flagon together. [*Lifts his glass.*] Come: a light heart!

WEISLINGEN. Those times are gone by.

GOETZ. God forbid! To be sure, we shall hardly pass more pleasant days than those we spent together at the Margrave's court, when we were inseparable night and day. I think with pleasure on my youth. Do you remember the scuffle I had with the Polander, whose pomaded and frizzled hair I chanced to rub with my sleeve?

WEISLINGEN. It was at table; and he struck at you with a knife.

GOETZ. I gave it him, however; and you had a quarrel upon that account with his comrades. We always stuck together like brave fellows, and were the admiration of every one. [*Raises his glass.*] Castor and Pollux! It used to rejoice my heart when the Margrave so called us.

WEISLINGEN. The Bishop of Würzburg first gave us the name.

GOETZ. That Bishop was a learned man, and withal so kind and gentle. I shall remember as long as I live how he used to caress us, praise our friendship, and say, "Happy is the man who is his friend's twin-brother."

WEISLINGEN. No more of that.

GOETZ. Why not? I know nothing more delightful after fatigue than to talk over old times. Indeed, when I recall to mind how we bore good and bad fortune together, and were all in all to each other, and how I thought this was to continue forever. Was not that my sole comfort when my hand was shot away at Landshut, and you nursed and tended me like a brother? I hoped Adelbert would in future be my right hand. And now —

WEISLINGEN. Alas!

GOETZ. Hadst thou but listened to me when I begged thee to go with me to Brabant, all would have been well. But then that unhappy turn for court-dangling seized thee, and thy coquetting and flirting with the women. I always told thee, when thou wouldst mix with these lounging, vain court sycophants, and entertain them with gossip about unlucky matches and seduced girls, scandal about absent friends, and all such trash as they take interest in — I always said, "Adelbert, thou wilt become a rogue!"

WEISLINGEN. To what purpose is all this?

GOETZ. Would to God I could forget it, or that it were otherwise! Art thou not free and nobly born as any in Germany; independent, subject to the Emperor alone; and dost thou crouch among vassals? What is the Bishop to thee? Granted, he is thy neighbor, and can do thee a shrewd turn; hast thou not power and friends to requite him in kind? Art thou ignorant of the dignigy of a free knight, who depends only upon God, the Emperor, and himself, that thou degradest thyself to be the courtier of a stubborn, jealous priest?

WEISLINGEN. Let me speak!

GOETZ. What hast thou to say?

WEISLINGEN. You look upon the princes as the wolf upon the shepherd. And can you blame them for defending their territories and property? Are they a moment secure from the unruly knights, who plunder their vassals even upon the highroads, and sack their castles and villages? Upon the other hand, our country's enemies threaten to overrun the lands of our beloved Emperor, yet, while he needs the princes' assistance, they can scarce defend their own lives; is it not our good genius which at this moment leads them to devise means of procuring peace for Germany, of securing the administration of justice, and giving to great and small the blessings of quiet? And can you blame us, Berlichingen, for securing the protection of the powerful princes, our neighbors, whose assistance is at hand, rather than relying on that of the Emperor, who is so far removed from us, and is hardly able to protect himself?

GOETZ. Yes, yes, I understand you. Weislingen, were the princes as you paint them, we should all have what we want. Peace and quiet! No doubt! Every bird of prey naturally likes to eat its plunder undisturbed. The general weal! If they would but take the trouble to study that. And they trifle with the Emperor shamefully. Every day some new tinker or other comes to give his opinion. The Emperor means well, and would gladly put things to rights; but because he happens to understand a thing readily, and by a single word, can put a thousand hands into motion, he thinks everything will be as speedily and as easily accomplished. Ordinance upon ordinance is promulgated, each nullifying the last, while the princes obey only those which serve their own interest, and prate of peace and security of the Empire, while they are treading under foot their weaker neighbors. I will be sworn, many a one thanks God in his heart that the Turk keeps the Emperor fully employed!

WEISLINGEN. You view things your own way.

GOETZ. So does every one. The question is, which is the right way to view them? And your plans at least shun the day.

WEISLINGEN. You may say what you will; I am your prisoner.

GOETZ. If your conscience is free, so are you. How was it with the general tranquillity? I remember going as a boy of sixteen with the Margrave to the Imperial Diet. What harangues the princes made! And the clergy were the most vociferous of all. Your Bishop thundered into the Emperor's ears his regard for justice, till one thought it had become part and parcel of his being. And now he has imprisoned a page of mine, at a time when our quarrels were all accommodated, and I had buried them in oblivion. Is not all settled between us? What does he want with the boy?

WEISLINGEN. It was done without his knowledge.

GOETZ. Then, why does he not release him?

WEISLINGEN. He did not conduct himself as he ought.

GOETZ. Not conduct himself as he ought? By my honor, he performed his duty, as surely as he has been imprisoned both with your knowledge and the Bishop's! Do you think I am come into the world this very day, that I cannot see what all this means?

WEISLINGEN. You are suspicious, and do us wrong.

GOETZ. Weislingen, shall I deal openly with you? Inconsiderable as I am, I am a thorn in your side, and Selbitz and Sickingen are no less so, because we are firmly resolved to die sooner than to thank any one but God for the air we breathe, or pay homage to any one but the Emperor. This is why they worry me in every possible way, blacken my character with the Emperor, and among my friends and neighbors, and spy about for advantage over me. They would have me out of the way at any price; that was your reason for imprisoning the page whom you knew I had dispatched for intelligence: and now you say he did not conduct himself as he should do, because he would not betray my secrets. And you, Weislingen, are their tool!

WEISLINGEN. Berlichingen!

GOETZ. Not a word more. I am an enemy to long explanations; they deceive either the maker or the hearer, and generally both.

[*Enter* CHARLES.]

CHARLES. Dinner is ready, father!

GOETZ. Good news! Come, I hope the company of my women-folk will amuse you. You always liked the girls. Aye, aye, they can tell many pretty stories about you. Come!   [*Exeunt.*]

SCENE IV. *The Bishop of Bamberg's palace.*

[*The Bishop, the Abbot of Fulda,* OLEARIUS, LIEBTRAUT, *and Courtiers at table. The dessert and wine before them.*]

BISHOP. Are there many of the German nobility studying at Bologna?

OLEARIUS. Both nobles and citizens; and, I do not exaggerate in saying that they acquire the most brilliant reputation. It is a proverb in the university, "As studious as a German noble." For while the citizens display a laudable diligence, in order to compensate by learning for their want of birth, the nobles strive, with praiseworthy emulation, to enhance their ancestral dignity by superior attainments.

ABBOT. Indeed!

LIEBTRAUT. What may one not live to hear! We live and learn, as the proverb says. "As studious as a German noble." I never heard that before.

OLEARIUS. Yes, they are the admiration of the whole university. Some of the oldest and most learned will soon be coming back with their doctor's degree. The Emperor will doubtless be happy to entrust to them the highest offices.

BISHOP. He cannot fail to do so.

ABBOT. Do you know, for instance, a young man — a Hessian? —

OLEARIUS. There are many Hessians with us.

ABBOT. His name is — is — Does nobody remember it? His mother was a von — Oh! his father had but one eye, and was a marshal —

LIEBTRAUT. Von Wildenholz!

ABBOT. Right. Von Wildenholz.

OLEARIUS. I know him well. A young man of great abilities. He is particularly esteemed for his talent in disputation.

ABBOT. He has that from his mother.

LIEBTRAUT. Yes: but his father would never praise her for that quality.

BISHOP. How call you the Emperor who wrote your *Corpus Juris?*

OLEARIUS. Justinian.

BISHOP. A worthy prince: — here's to his memory!

OLEARIUS. To his memory:
                    [*They drink.*]

ABBOT. That must be a fine book.

OLEARIUS. It may be called a book of books; a digest of all laws; there you find the sentence ready for every case, and where the text is antiquated or obscure, the deficiency is supplied by notes, with which the most learned men have enriched this truly admirable work.

ABBOT. A digest of all laws! — Indeed! — Then the Ten Commandments must be in it.

OLEARIUS. *Implicite;* not *explicite.*

ABBOT. That's what I mean; plainly set down, without any explication.

BISHOP. But the best is, you tell us that a state can be maintained in the most perfect tranquillity and subordination, by receiving and rightly following that statute-book.

OLEARIUS. Doubtless.

BISHOP. All doctors of laws!

[They drink.]

OLEARIUS. I'll tell them of this abroad. *[They drink.]* Would to Heaven that men thought thus in my country.

ABBOT. Whence come you, most learned sir?

OLEARIUS. From Frankfort, at your eminence's service!

BISHOP. You gentlemen of the law, then, are not held in high estimation there? — How comes that?

OLEARIUS. It is strange enough — when I last went there to collect my father's effects, the mob almost stoned me, when they heard I was a lawyer.

ABBOT. God bless me!

OLEARIUS. It is because their tribunal, which they hold in great respect, is composed of people totally ignorant of the Roman law. An intimate acquaintance with the internal condition of the town, and also of its foreign relations, acquired through age and experience, is deemed a sufficient qualification. They decided according to certain established edicts of their own, and some old customs recognized in the city and neighborhood.

ABBOT. That's very right.

OLEARIUS. But far from sufficient. The life of man is short, and in one generation cases of every description cannot occur; our statute-book is a collection of precedents, furnished by the experience of many centuries. Besides, the wills and opinions of men are variable; one man deems right today, what another disapproves to-morrow; and confusion and injustice are the inevitable results. Law determines absolutely, and its decrees are immutable.

ABBOT. That's certainly better.

OLEARIUS. But the common people won't acknowledge that; and, eager as they are after novelty, they hate any innovation in their laws, which leads them out of the beaten track, be it ever so much for the better. They hate a jurist as if he were a cut-purse or a subverter of the state, and become furious, if one attempts to settle among them.

LIEBTRAUT. You come from Frankfort? — I know the place well — we tasted your good cheer at the Emperor's coronation. You say your name is Olearius — I know no one in the town of your name.

OLEARIUS. My father's name was Oilman. But after the example, and with the advice of many jurists, I have latinized the name to Olearius for the decoration of the title-page of my legal treatises.

LIEBTRAUT. You did well to translate yourself: a prophet is not honored in his own country — in your native guise you might have shared the same fate.

OLEARIUS. That was not the reason.

LIEBTRAUT. All things have two reasons.

ABBOT. A prophet is not honored in his own country.

LIEBTRAUT. But do you know why, most reverend sir?

ABBOT. Because he was born and bred there.

LIEBTRAUT. Well, that may be one reason. The other is, because, upon a nearer acquaintance with these gentlemen, the halo of glory and honor shed around them by the distant haze totally disappears; they are then seen to be nothing more than tiny rushlights!

OLEARIUS. It seems you are placed here to tell pleasant truths.

LIEBTRAUT. As I have wit enough to discover them, I do not lack courage to utter them.

OLEARIUS. Yet you lack the art of applying them well.

LIEBTRAUT. It is no matter where you place a cupping-glass, provided it draws blood.

OLEARIUS. Barbers are known by their dress, and no one takes offense at their scurvy jests. Let me advise you as a precaution to bear the badge of your order — a cap and bells!

LIEBTRAUT. Where did you take your degree? I only ask, so that, should I ever take a fancy to a fool's cap, I could at once go to the right shop.

OLEARIUS. You carry face enough.

LIEBTRAUT. And you paunch.

[*The Bishop and Abbot laugh.*]

BISHOP. Not so warm, gentlemen! — Some other subject. At table all should be fair and quiet. Choose another subject, Liebtraut.

LIEBTRAUT. Opposite Frankfort lies a village, called Sachsenhausen —

OLEARIUS [*to the Bishop*]. What news of the Turkish expedition, your excellency?

BISHOP. The Emperor has most at heart, first of all, to restore peace to the Empire, put an end to feuds, and secure the strict administration of justice: then, according to report, he will go in person against the enemies of his country and of Christendom. At present internal dissensions give him enough to do; and the Empire, despite half a hundred treaties of peace, is one scene of murder. Franconia, Swabia, the Upper Rhine, and the surrounding countries are laid waste by presumptuous and reckless knights. — And here, at Bamberg, Sickingen, Selbitz with one leg, and Goetz with the iron hand, scoff at the imperial authority.

ABBOT. If His Majesty does not exert himself, these fellows will at last thrust us into sacks.

LIEBTRAUT. He would be a sturdy fellow, indeed, who should thrust the winebutt of Fulda into a sack!

BISHOP. Goetz especially has been for many years my mortal foe, and annoys me beyond description. But it will not last long, I hope. The Emperor holds his court at Augsburg. We have taken our measures, and cannot fail of success. — Doctor, do you know Adelbert von Weislingen?

OLEARIUS. No, your eminence.

BISHOP. If you stay till his arrival, you will have the pleasure of seeing a most noble, accomplished, and gallant knight.

OLEARIUS. He must be an excellent man, indeed, to deserve such praises from such a mouth.

LIEBTRAUT. And yet he was not bred at any university.

BISHOP. We know that. [*The attendants throng to the window.*] What's the matter?

ATTENDANT. Färber, Weislingen's servant, is riding in at the castle gate.

BISHOP. See what he brings. He most likely comes to announce his master.

[*Exit* LIEBTRAUT. — *They stand up and drink.*]

[LIEBTRAUT *reënters.*]

BISHOP. What news?

LIEBTRAUT. I wish another had to tell it — Weislinger is a prisoner.

BISHOP. What?

LIEBTRAUT. Berlichingen has seized him and three troopers near Haslach — one is escaped to tell you.

ABBOT. A Job's messenger!

OLEARIUS. I grieve from my heart.

BISHOP. I will see the servant; bring him up — I will speak with him myself. Conduct him into my cabinet. [*Exit Bishop.*]

ABBOT [*sitting down*]. Another draught, however. [*The Servants fill round.*]

OLEARIUS. Will not your reverence take a turn in the garden? "*Post cœnam stabis, seu passus mille meabis.*"

LIEBTRAUT. In truth, sitting is unhealthy for you. You might get an apoplexy. [*The Abbot rises. Aside.*] Let me but once get him out of doors, I will give him exercise enough! [*Exeunt.*]

SCENE V. *Jaxthausen.*

[MARIA, WEISLINGEN.]

MARIA. You love me, you say. I willingly believe it and hope to be happy with you, and make you happy also.

WEISLINGEN. I feel nothing but that I am entirely thine. [*Embraces her.*]

MARIA. Softly! — I gave you one kiss for earnest, but you must not take possession of what is only yours conditionally.

WEISLINGEN. You are too strict, Maria! Innocent love is pleasing in the sight of Heaven, instead of giving offense.

MARIA. It may be so. But I think differently; for I have been taught that caresses are, like fetters, strong through their union, and that maidens, when they love, are weaker than Samson after the loss of his locks.

WEISLINGEN. Who taught you so?

MARIA. The abbess of my convent. Till my sixteenth year I was with her — and it is only with you that I enjoy happiness like that her company afforded me. She had loved, and could tell — She had a most affectionate heart. Oh! she was an excellent woman!

WEISLINGEN. Then you resemble her. [*Takes her hand.*] What will become of me when I am compelled to leave you?

MARIA [*withdrawing her hand*]. You will feel some regret, I hope, for I know what my feelings will be. But you must away!

WEISLINGEN. I know it, dearest! and I will — for well I feel what happiness I shall purchase by this sacrifice! Now, blessed be your brother, and the day on which he rode out to capture me!

MARIA. His heart was full of hope for you and himself. "Farewell!" he said, at his departure, "I go to recover my friend."

WEISLINGEN. That he has done. Would that I had studied the arrangement and security of my property, instead of neglecting it, and dallying at that worthless court! — then couldst thou have been instantly mine.

MARIA. Even delay has its pleasures.

WEISLINGEN. Say not so, Maria, else I shall fear that thy heart is less warm than mine. True, I deserve punishment, but what hopes will brighten every step of my journey! To be wholly thine, to live only for thee and thy circle of friends, — far removed from the world, in the enjoyment of all the raptures which two hearts can mutually bestow. What is the favor of princes, what the applause of the universe, to such simple, yet unequaled felicity? Many have been my hopes and wishes; but this happiness surpasses them all.

[*Enter* GOETZ.]

GOETZ. Your page has returned. He can scarcely utter a word for hunger and fatigue. My wife has ordered him some refreshment. Thus much I have gathered: the Bishop will not give up my page —

imperial commissioners are to be appointed, and a day named, upon which the matter may be adjusted. Be that as it may, Adelbert, you are free. Pledge me but your hand that you will for the future give neither open nor secret assistance to my enemies.

WEISINGEN. Here I grasp thy hand. From this moment be our friendship and confidence, firm and unalterable as a primary law of nature! Let me take this hand also [*takes* MARIA'S *hand*], and with it the possession of this most noble lady.

GOETZ. May I say yes for you?

MARIA [*timidly*]. If — if it is your wish —

GOETZ. Happily our wishes do not differ on this point. Thou need'st not blush — the glance of thine eye betrays thee. Well then, Weislingen, join hands, and I say, Amen! My friend and brother! I thank thee, sister; thou canst do more than spin flax, for thou hast drawn a thread which can fetter this wandering bird of paradise. Yet you look not quite at your ease, Adelbert. What troubles you? *I* am perfectly happy! What I but hoped in a dream, I now see with my eyes, and feel as though I was still dreaming. Now my dream is explained. I thought last night that, in token of reconciliation, I gave you this iron hand, and that you held it so fast that it broke away from my arm; I started, and awoke. Had I but dreamed a little longer, I should have seen how you gave me a new living hand. You must away this instant, to put your castle and property in order. That cursed court has made you neglect both. I must call my wife. — Elizabeth!

MARIA. How overjoyed my brother is!

WEISLINGEN. Yet I am still more so.

GOETZ [*to* MARIA]. You will have a pleasant residence.

MARIA. Franconia is a fine country.

WEISLINGEN. And I may venture to say that my castle lies in the most fertile and delicious part of it.

GOETZ. That you may, and I can confirm it. Look you, here flows the Maine, around a hill clothed with cornfields and vineyards, its top crowned with a Gothic castle; then the river makes a sharp turn, and glides round behind the rock on which the castle is built. The windows of the great hall look perpendicularly down upon the river, and command a prospect of many miles in extent.

[*Enter* ELIZABETH.]

ELIZABETH. What wouldst thou?

GOETZ. You, too, must give your hand, and say, God bless you! They are a pair.

ELIZABETH. So soon?

GOETZ. But not unexpectedly.

ELIZABETH. May you ever adore her as ardently as while you sought her hand. And then, as your love, so be your happiness!

WEISLINGEN. Amen! I seek no happiness but under this condition.

GOETZ. The bridegroom, my love, must leave us for a while; for this great change will involve many smaller ones. He must first withdraw himself from the Bishop's court, in order that their friendship may gradually cool. Then he must rescue his property from the hands of selfish stewards, and — But come, sister; come, Elizabeth; let us leave him; his page has, no doubt, private messages for him.

WEISLINGEN. Nothing but what you may hear.

GOETZ. 'T is needless. Franconians and Swabians! Ye are now more closely united than ever. Now we shall be able to keep the princes in check.

[*Exeunt* GOETZ, ELIZABETH, MARIA.]

WEISLINGEN [*alone*]. God in heaven! And canst Thou have reserved such happiness for one so unworthy? It is too much for my heart. How meanly I depended upon wretched fools, whom I thought I was governing, upon the smile of princes, upon the homage of those around me! Goetz, my faithful Goetz, thou hast restored me to myself, and thou, Maria, hast completed my reformation. I feel free, as if brought from a dungeon into the open air. Bamberg will I never see more — will snap all the shameful bonds that have held me beneath myself. My heart expands, and never more will I degrade myself by struggling for a greatness that is denied me. He alone is great and happy who fills his own station of independence, and has neither to command nor to obey.

[*Enter* FRANCIS.]

FRANCIS. God save you, noble sir! I bring you so many salutations that I know not where to begin. Bamberg, and ten miles round, cry with a thousand voices, God save you!

WEISLINGEN. Welcome, Francis! Bring'st thou aught else?

FRANCIS. You are held in such consideration at court that it cannot be expressed.

WEISLINGEN. That will not last long.

FRANCIS. As long as you live; and after your death it will shine with more luster than the brazen characters on a monument. How they took your misfortune to heart!

WEISLINGEN. And what said the Bishop?

FRANCIS. His eager curiosity poured out question upon question, without giving me time to answer. He knew of your accident already; for Färber, who escaped from Haslach, had brought him the tidings. But he wished to hear every particular. He asked so anxiously whether you were wounded. I told him you were whole, from the hair of your head to the nail of your little toe.

WEISLINGEN. And what said he to the proposals?

FRANCIS. He was ready at first to give up the page and a ransom to boot for your liberty. But when he heard you were to be dismissed without ransom, and merely to give your parole that the boy should be set free, he was for putting off Berlichingen with some pretense. He charged me with a thousand messages to you, more than I can ever utter. Oh, how he harangued! It was a long sermon upon the text, "I cannot live without Weislingen!"

WEISLINGEN. He must learn to do so.

FRANCIS. What mean you? He said "Bid him hasten; all the court waits for him."

WEISLINGEN. Let them wait on. I shall not go to court.

FRANCIS. Not go to court! My gracious lord, how comes that? If you knew what I know; could you but dream what I have seen —

WEISLINGEN. What ails thee?

FRANCIS. The bare remembrance takes away my senses. Bamberg is no longer

Bamberg. An angel of heaven, in semblance of woman, has taken up her abode there, and has made it a paradise.

WEISLINGEN. Is that all?

FRANCIS. May I become a shaven friar, if the first glimpse of her does not drive you frantic!

WEISLINGEN. Who is it, then?

FRANCIS. Adelaide von Walldorf.

WEISLINGEN. Indeed! I have heard much of her beauty.

FRANCIS. Heard! You might as well say I have *seen* music. So far is the tongue from being able to rehearse the slightest particle of her beauty, that the very eye which beholds her cannot drink it all in.

WEISLINGEN. You are mad.

FRANCIS. That may well be. The last time I was in her company I had no more command over my senses than if I had been drunk, or, I may rather say, I felt like a glorified saint enjoying the angelic vision! All my senses exalted, more lively and more perfect than ever, yet not one at its owner's command.

WEISLINGEN. That is strange!

FRANCIS. As I took leave of the Bishop, she sat by him; they were playing at chess. He was very gracious; gave me his hand to kiss, and said much, of which I heard not a syllable, for I was looking on his fair antagonist. Her eye was fixed upon the board, as if meditating a bold move. — A touch of subtle watchfulness around the mouth and cheek. — I could have wished to be the ivory king. The mixture of dignity and feeling on her brow — and the dazzling luster of her face and neck, heightened by her raven tresses —

WEISLINGEN. The theme has made you quite poetical.

FRANCIS. I feel at this moment what constitutes poetic inspiration — a heart altogether wrapped in one idea. As the Bishop ended, and I made my obeisance, she looked up and said, "Offer to your master the best wishes of an unknown. Tell him he must come soon. New friends await him; he must not despise them, though he is already so rich in old ones." I would have answered, but the passage betwixt my heart and my tongue was closed,

and I only bowed. I would have given all I had for permission to kiss but one of her fingers! As I stood thus, the Bishop let fall a pawn, and in stooping to pick it up, I touched the hem of her garment. Transport thrilled through my limbs, and I scarce know how I left the room.

WEISLINGEN. Is her husband at court?

FRANCIS. She has been a widow these four months, and is residing at the court of Bamberg to divert her melancholy. You will see her; and to meet her glance is to bask in the sunshine of spring.

WEISLINGEN. She would not make so strong an impression on me.

FRANCIS. I hear you are as good as married.

WEISLINGEN. Would I were really so! My gentle Maria will be the happiness of my life. The sweetness of her soul beams through her mild blue eyes, and, like an angel of innocence and love, she guides my heart to the paths of peace and felicity! Pack up, and then to my castle. I will not to Bamberg, though St. Bede came in person to fetch me. [*Exit* WEISLINGEN.]

FRANCIS [*alone*]. Not to Bamberg! Heavens forbid! But let me hope the best. Maria is beautiful and amiable, and a prisoner or an invalid might easily fall in love with her. Her eyes beam with compassion and melancholy sympathy; but in thine, Adelaide, is life, fire, spirit. I would — I am a fool; one glance from her has made me so. My master must to Bamberg, and I also, and either recover my senses or gaze them quite away.

ACT II

SCENE I. *Bamberg. A hall.*

[*The Bishop and* ADELAIDE, *playing at chess,* LIEBTRAUT *with a guitar, Ladies and Courtiers standing in groups.*]

LIEBTRAUT [*plays and sings*].
Armed with quiver and bow,
With his torch all a-glow,
Young Cupid comes winging his flight.
Courage glows in his eyes,
As adown from the skies,
He rushes, impatient for fight.

Up! up!
On! on!
Hark! the bright quiver rings!
Hark! the rustle of wings!
All hail to the delicate sprite!

They welcome the urchin —;
Ah, maidens, beware!
He finds every bosom
Unguarded and bare.
In the light of his flambeau
He kindles his darts; —
They fondle and hug him
And press to their hearts.

ADELAIDE. Your thoughts are not in your game. Check to the king!

BISHOP. There is still a way of escape.

ADELAIDE. You will not be able to hold out long. Check to the king!

LIEBTRAUT. Were I a great prince, I would not play at this game, and would forbid it at court, and throughout the whole land.

ADELAIDE. 'T is indeed a touchstone of the brain.

LIEBTRAUT. Not on that account. I would rather hear a funeral bell, the cry of the ominous bird, the howling of that snarling watch-dog, conscience; rather would I hear these through the deepest sleep, than from bishops, knights, and such beasts, the eternal — Check to the king!

BISHOP. Into whose head could such an idea enter?

LIEBTRAUT. A man's, for example, endowed with a weak body and a strong conscience, which, for the most part, indeed, accompany each other. Chess is called a royal game, and is said to have been invented for a king, who rewarded the inventor with a mine of wealth. If this be so, I can picture him to myself. He was a minor, either in understanding or in years, under the guardianship of his mother or his wife; had down upon his chin, and flaxen hair around his temples; was pliant as a willow-shoot, and liked to play at draughts with women, not from passion, God forbid! — only for pastime. His tutor, too active for a scholar, too intractable for a man of the world, invented the game, *in usum Delphini*, that was so homogeneous with his majesty — and so on.

ADELAIDE. Checkmate! You should fill up the chasms in our histories, Liebtraut. [*They rise.*]

LIEBTRAUT. To supply those in our family registers would be more profitable. The merits of our ancestors being available for a common object with their portraits, namely, to cover the naked sides of our chambers and of our characters, one might turn such an occupation to good account.

BISHOP. He will not come, you say!

ADELAIDE. I beseech you, banish him from your thoughts.

BISHOP. What can it mean?

LIEBTRAUT. What! The reasons may be told over like the beads of a rosary. He has been seized with a fit of compunction, of which I could soon cure him.

BISHOP. Do so; ride to him instantly.

LIEBTRAUT. My commission —

BISHOP. Shall be unlimited. Spare nothing to bring him back.

LIEBTRAUT. May I venture to use your name, gracious lady?

ADELAIDE. With discretion.

LIEBTRAUT. That's a vague commission.

ADELAIDE. Do you know so little of me, or are you so young as not to understand in what tone you should speak of me to Weislingen?

LIEBTRAUT. In the tone of a fowler's whistle, I think.

ADELAIDE. You will never be reasonable.

LIEBTRAUT. Does one ever become so, gracious lady?

BISHOP. Go! Go! Take the best horse in my stable; choose your servants, and bring him hither.

LIEBTRAUT. If I do not conjure him hither, say that an old woman who charms warts and freckles knows more of sympathy than I.

BISHOP. Yet, what will it avail? Berlichingen has wholly gained him over. He will no sooner be here than he will wish to return.

LIEBTRAUT. He will wish it, doubtless; but can he go? A prince's squeeze of the hand and the smiles of a beauty, from these no Weislingen can tear himself away. I have the honor to take my leave.

BISHOP. A prosperous journey!

ADELAIDE. Adieu!   [*Exit* LIEBTRAUT.]

BISHOP. When he is once here, I must trust to you.

ADELAIDE. Would you make me your lime-twig?

BISHOP. By no means.

ADELAIDE. Your call-bird, then?

BISHOP. No; that is Liebtraut's part. I beseech you do not refuse to do for me what no other can.

ADELAIDE. We shall see.   [*Exeunt.*]

SCENE II. *Jaxthausen. A hall in Goetz's castle.*

[*Enter* GOETZ *and* HANS VON SELBITZ.]

SELBITZ. Every one will applaud you for declaring feud against the Nurembergers.

GOETZ. It would have eaten my very heart away had I remained longer their debtor. It is clear that they betrayed my page to the Bambergers. They shall have cause to remember me.

SELBITZ. They have an old grudge against you.

GOETZ. And I against them. I am glad they have begun the fray.

SELBITZ. These free towns have always taken part with the priests.

GOETZ. They have good reason.

SELBITZ. But we will cook their porridge for them!

GOETZ. I reckon upon you. Would that the Burgomaster of Nuremberg, with his gold chain round his neck, fell in our way, we'd astonish him with all his cleverness.

SELBITZ. I hear Weislingen is again on your side. Does he really join in our league?

GOETZ. Not immediately. There are reasons which prevent his openly giving us assistance; but for the present it is quite enough that he is not against us. The priest without him is what the stole would be without the priest!

SELBITZ. When do we set forward?

GOETZ. To-morrow or next day. There are merchants of Bamberg and Nuremberg returning from the fair of Frankfort. We may strike a good blow.

SELBITZ. Let us hope so!

SCENE III. *The Bishop's palace at Bamberg.*

[ADELAIDE *and her Waiting-Maid.*]

ADELAIDE. He is here, sayest thou? I can scarce believe it.

MAID. Had I not seen him myself, I should have doubted it.

ADELAIDE. The Bishop should frame Liebtraut in gold for such a masterpiece of skill.

MAID. I saw him as he was about to enter the palace. He was mounted on a gray charger. The horse started when he came on the bridge, and would not move forward. The populace thronged up the street to see him. They rejoiced at the delay of the unruly horse. He was greeted on all sides, and he thanked them gracefully all round. He sat the curveting steed with an easy indifference, and by threats and soothing brought him to the gate, followed by Liebtraut and a few servants.

ADELAIDE. What do you think of him?

MAID. I never saw a man who pleased me so well. [*Pointing to a picture.*] He is as like that portrait of the Emperor as if he were his son. His nose is somewhat smaller, but just such gentle light-brown eyes, just such fine light hair, and such a figure! A half-melancholy expression on his face, I know not how, but he pleased me so well.

ADELAIDE. I am curious to see him.

MAID. He would be the husband for you!

ADELAIDE. Foolish girl!

MAID. Children and fools —

[*Enter* LIEBTRAUT.]

LIEBTRAUT. Now, gracious lady, what do I deserve?

ADELAIDE. Horns from your wife! — for judging from the present sample of your persuasive powers, you have certainly endangered the honor of many a worthy family.

LIEBTRAUT. Not so, be assured, gracious lady.

ADELAIDE. How did you contrive to bring him?

LIEBTRAUT. You know how they catch snipes, and why should I detail my little stratagems to you? — First, I pretended to have heard nothing, did not understand the reason of his behavior, and put him upon the disadvantage of telling me the whole story at length. Then I saw the matter in quite a different light to what he did — could not find — could not see, and so forth. Then I gossiped things great and small about Bamberg, and recalled to his memory certain old recollections; and when I had succeeded in occupying his imagination, I knitted together many a broken association of ideas. He knew not what to say — felt a new attraction toward Bamberg — he would, and he would not. When I found him begin to waver, and saw him too much occupied with his own feelings to suspect my sincerity, I threw over his head a halter, woven of the three powerful cords, beauty, court favor, and flattery, and dragged him hither in triumph.

ADELAIDE. What said you of me?

LIEBTRAUT. The simple truth — that you were in perplexity about your estates, and had hoped, as he had so much influence with the Emperor, all would be satisfactorily settled.

ADELAIDE. 'T is well.

LIEBTRAUT. The Bishop will introduce him to you.

ADELAIDE. I expect them. [*Exit* LIEBTRAUT.] And with such feelings have I seldom expected a visitor.

SCENE IV. *The Spessart.*

[*Enter* SELBITZ, GOETZ, *and* GEORGE *in the armor and dress of a trooper.*]

GOETZ. So, thou didst not find him, George?

GEORGE. He had ridden to Bamberg the day before, with Liebtraut and two servants.

GOETZ. I cannot understand what this means.

SELBITZ. I see it well — your reconciliation was almost too speedy to be lasting. Liebtraut is a cunning fellow, and has no doubt inveigled him over.

GOETZ. Think'st thou he will become a traitor?

SELBITZ. The first step is taken.

GOETZ. I will never believe it. Who knows what he may have to do at court — his affairs are still unarranged. Let us hope for the best.

SELBITZ. Would to Heaven he may deserve of your good opinion, and may act for the best!

GOETZ. A thought strikes me! — We will disguise George in the spoils of the Bamberg trooper, and furnish him with the password — he may then ride to Bamberg, and see how matters stand.

GEORGE. I have long wished to do so.

GOETZ. It is thy first expedition. Be careful, boy; I should be sorry if ill befell thee.

GEORGE. Never fear. I care not how many of them crawl about me; I think no more of them than of rats and mice.

[*Exeunt.*]

SCENE V. *The Bishop's palace. His cabinet.*

[*The Bishop and* WEISLINGEN.]

BISHOP. Then thou wilt stay no longer?

WEISLINGEN. You would not have me break my oath.

BISHOP. I could have wished thou hadst not sworn it. — What evil spirit possessed thee? — Could I not have procured thy release without that? Is my influence so small in the imperial court?

WEISLINGEN. The thing is done; — excuse it as you can.

BISHOP. I cannot see that there was the least necessity for taking such a step — to renounce me? Were there not a thousand other ways of procuring thy freedom? Had we not his page? And would I not have given gold enough to boot? — and thus satisfied Berlichingen. Our operations against him and his confederates could have gone on — But, alas! I do not reflect that I am talking to his friend, who has joined him against me, and can easily counterwork the mines he himself has dug.

WEISLINGEN. My gracious lord —

BISHOP. And yet — when I again look on thy face, again hear thy voice — it is impossible — impossible!

WEISLINGEN. Farewell, good my lord!

BISHOP. I give thee my blessing — formerly when we parted, I was wont to say, "Till we meet again!" — Now Heaven grant we meet no more!

WEISLINGEN. Things may alter.

BISHOP. Perhaps I may live to see thee appear as an enemy before my walls, carrying havoc through the fertile plains which now owe their flourishing condition to thee.

WEISLINGEN. Never, my gracious lord!

BISHOP. You cannot say so. My temporal neighbors all have a grudge against me — but while thou wert mine — Go, Weislingen! — I have no more to say — Thou hast undone much. Go —

WEISLINGEN. I know not what to answer.   [*Exit Bishop.*]

[*Enter* FRANCIS.]

FRANCIS. The Lady Adelaide expects you. She is not well — but she will not let you depart without bidding her adieu.

WEISLINGEN. Come.

FRANCIS. Do we go, then, for certain?

WEISLINGEN. This very night.

FRANCIS. I feel as if I were about to leave the world —

WEISLINGEN. I, too, and as if besides I knew not whither to go.

SCENE VI. *Adelaide's apartment.*

[ADELAIDE *and Waiting-Maid.*]

MAID. You are pale, gracious lady!

ADELAIDE. I love him not, yet I wish him to stay — for I am fond of his company, though I should dislike him for my husband.

MAID. Does your ladyship think he will go?

ADELAIDE. He is even now bidding the Bishop farewell.

MAID. He has yet a severe struggle to undergo.

ADELAIDE. What meanest thou?

MAID. Why do you ask, gracious lady? The barb'd hook is in his heart — ere he tear it away he must bleed to death.

[*Enter* WEISLINGEN.]

WEISLINGEN. You are not well, gracious lady?

ADELAIDE. That must be indifferent to you — you leave us, leave us forever: what matters it to you whether we live or die?

WEISLINGEN. You do me injustice.

ADELAIDE. I judge you as you appear.

WEISLINGEN. Appearances are deceitful.

ADELAIDE. Then you are a chameleon.

WEISLIGEN. Could you but see my heart —

ADELAIDE. I should see fine things there.

WEISLINGEN. Undoubtedly ! — You would find your own image —

ADELAIDE. Thrust into some dark corner, with the pictures of defunct ancestors! I beseech you, Weislingen, consider with whom you speak — false words are of value only when they serve to veil our actions — a discovered masquerader plays a pitiful part. You do not disown your deeds, yet your words belie them; what are we to think of you?

WEISLINGEN. What you will — I am so agonized at reflecting on what I am, that I little reck for what I am taken.

ADELAIDE. You came to say farewell.

WEISLINGEN. Permit me to kiss your hand, and I will say adieu! — You remind me — I did not think — but I am troublesome —

ADELAIDE. You misinterpret me. Since you will depart, I only wished to assist your resolution.

WEISLINGEN. Oh, say rather, I must! — were I not compelled by my knightly word — my solemn engagement —

ADELAIDE. Go to! Talk of that to maidens who read the tale of Theuerdanck, and wish that they had such a husband. — Knightly word! — Nonsense!

WEISLINGEN. You do not think so?

ADELAIDE. On my honor, you are dissembling. What have you promised, and to whom? You have pledged your alliance to a traitor to the Emperor, at the very moment when he incurred the ban of the Empire by taking you prisoner. Such an agreement is no more binding than an extorted, unjust oath. And do not our laws release you from such oaths? Go, tell that to children, who believe in Rübezahl. There is something behind all this. — To become an enemy of the Empire — a disturber of public happiness and tranquillity, an enemy of the Emperor, the associate of a robber! — Thou, Weislingen, with thy gentle soul!

WEISLINGEN. Did but you know him?

ADELAIDE. I would deal justly with Goetz. He has a lofty, indomitable spirit, and woe to thee, therefore, Weislingen. Go, and persuade thyself thou art his companion. Go, and receive his commands. Thou art courteous, gentle —

WEISLINGEN. And he, too.

ADELAIDE. But thou art yielding, and he is stubborn. Imperceptibly will he draw thee on. Thou wilt become the slave of a baron; thou that mightest command princes! — Yet it is cruel to make you discontented with your future position.

WEISLINGEN. Did you but know what kindness he showed me.

ADELAIDE. Kindness! — Do you make such a merit of that? It was his duty. And what would you have lost had he acted otherwise? I would rather he had done so. An overbearing man like —

WEISLINGEN. You speak of your enemy.

ADELAIDE. I speak for your freedom; yet I know not why I should take so much interest in it. Farewell!

WEISLINGEN. Permit me, but a moment. [*Takes her hand. A pause.*]

ADELAIDE. Have you aught to say?

WEISLINGEN. I must hence.

ADELAIDE. Then, go.

WEISLINGEN. Gracious lady, I cannot.

ADELAIDE. You must.

WEISLINGEN. And is this your parting look?

ADELAIDE. Go, I am unwell, very inopportunely.

WEISLINGEN. Look not on me thus!

ADELAIDE. Wilt thou be our enemy, and yet have us smile upon thee — go!

WEISLINGEN. Adelaide!

ADELAIDE. I hate thee!

[*Enter* FRANCIS.]

FRANCIS. Noble sir, the Bishop inquires for you.

ADELAIDE. Go! go!

FRANCIS. He begs you to come instantly.

ADELAIDE. Go! go!

WEISLINGEN. I do not say adieu: I shall see you again.

[*Exeunt* WEISLINGEN *and* FRANCIS.]

ADELAIDE. Thou wilt see me again? We must provide for that. Margaret, when he comes, refuse him admittance. Say I am ill, have a headache, am asleep, anything. If this does not detain him, nothing will. [*Exeunt.*]

SCENE VII. *An anteroom.*

[WEISLINGEN *and* FRANCIS.]

WEISLINGEN. She will not see me!

FRANCIS. Night draws on; shall we saddle?

WELISINGEN. She will not see me!

FRANCIS. Shall I order the horses?

WEISLINGEN. It is too late; we stay here.

FRANCIS. God be praised! [*Exit.*]

WEISLINGEN [*alone*]. Thou stayest! Be on thy guard — the temptation is great. My horse started at the castle gate. My good angel stood before him, he knew the danger that awaited me. Yet it would be wrong to leave in confusion the various affairs entrusted to me by the Bishop, without at least so arranging them, that my successor may be able to continue where I left off. That I can do without breach of faith to Berlichingen, and when it is done no one shall detain me. Yet it would have been better that I had never come. But I will away — to-morrow — or next day: — 'T is decided! [*Exit.*]

SCENE VIII. *The Spessart.*

[*Enter* GOETZ, SELBITZ, *and* GEORGE.]

SELBITZ. You see it has turned out as I prophesied.

GOETZ. No, no, no.

GEORGE. I tell you the truth, believe me. I did as you commanded, took the dress and password of the Bamberg trooper, and escorted some peasants of the Lower Rhine, who paid my expenses for my convoy.

SELBITZ. In that disguise? It might have cost thee dear.

GEORGE. So I begin to think, now that it's over. A trooper who thinks of danger beforehand, will never do anything great.

I got safely to Bamberg, and in the very first inn I heard them tell how the Bishop and Weislingen were reconciled, and how Weislingen was to marry the widow of Von Walldorf.

GOETZ. Mere gossip!

GEORGE. I saw him as he led her to table. She is lovely, by my faith, most lovely! We all bowed — she thanked us all. He nodded, and seemed highly pleased. They passed on, and everybody murmured, "What a handsome pair!"

GOETZ. That may be.

GEORGE. Listen further. The next day as he went to mass, I watched my opportunity; he was attended only by his squire; I stood at the steps and whispered to him as he passed, "A few words from your friend Berlichingen." He started — I marked the confession of guilt in his face. He had scarcely the heart to look at me — me, a poor trooper's boy!

SELBITZ. His evil conscience degrades him more than thy condition does thee.

GEORGE. "Art thou of Bamberg?" said he. "The Knight of Berlichingen greets you," said I, "and I am to inquire —" "Come to my apartment to-morrow morning," quoth he, "and we will speak further."

GOETZ. And you went?

GEORGE. Yes, certainly, I went, and waited in his antechamber a long — long time — and his pages, in their silken doublets, stared at me from head to foot. Stare on, thought I. At length I was admitted. He seemed angry. But what cared I? I gave my message. He began blustering like a coward who wants to look brave. He wondered that you should take him to task through a trooper's boy. That angered me. "There are but two sorts of people," said I, "true men and scoundrels, and I serve Goetz of Berlichingen." Then he began to talk all manner of nonsense, which all tended to one point, namely, that you had hurried him into an agreement, that he owed you no allegiance, and would have nothing to do with you.

GOETZ. Hast thou that from his own mouth?

GEORGE. That, and yet more. He threatened me —

GOETZ. It is enough. He is lost forever. Faith and confidence, again have ye deceived me. Poor Maria! How am I to break this to you?

SELBITZ. I would rather lose my other leg than be such a rascal.

SCENE IX. *Hall in the Bishop's palace at Bamberg.*

[ADELAIDE *and* WEISLINGEN *discovered.*]

ADELAIDE. Time begins to hang insupportably heavy here. I dare not speak seriously, and I am ashamed to trifle with you. *Ennui,* thou art worse than a slow fever.

WEISLINGEN. Are you tired of me already?

ADELAIDE. Not so much of you as of your society. I would you had gone when you wished, and that we had not detained you.

WEISLINGEN. Such is woman's favor! At first she fosters with maternal warmth our dearest hopes; and then, like an inconstant hen, she forsakes the nest, and abandons the infant brood to death and decay.

ADELAIDE. Yes, you may rail at women. The reckless gambler tears and curses the harmless cards which have been the instruments of his loss. But let me tell you something about *men.* What are you that talk about fickleness? You that are seldom even what you would wish to be, never what you should be. Princes in holiday garb! the envy of the vulgar. Oh, what would a tailor's wife not give for a necklace of the pearls on the skirt of your robe, which you kick back contemptuously with your heels.

WEISLINGEN. You are severe.

ADELAIDE. It is but the antistrophe to your song. Ere I knew you, Weislingen, I felt like the tailor's wife. Hundred-tongued rumor, to speak without metaphor, had so extolled you, in quack-doctor fashion, that I was tempted to wish — Oh, that I could but see this quintessence of manhood, this phœnix, Weislingen! My wish was granted.

WEISLINGEN. And the phœnix turned out a dunghill cock.

ADELAIDE. No, Weislingen, I took an interest in you.

WEISLINGEN. So it appeared.

ADELAIDE. So it *was* — for you really surpassed your reputation. The multitude prize only the reflection of worth. For my part, I do not care to scrutinize the character of those whom I esteem; so we lived on for some time. I felt there was a deficiency in you, but knew not what I missed; at length my eyes were opened — I saw instead of the energetic being who gave impulse to the affairs of a kingdom, and was ever alive to the voice of fame — who was wont to pile princely project on project, till, like the mountains of the Titans, they reached the clouds — instead of all this, I saw a man as querulous as a love-sick poet, as melancholy as a slighted damsel, and more indolent than an old bachelor. I first ascribed it to your misfortune which still lay at your heart, and excused you as well as I could; but now that it daily becomes worse, you must really forgive me if I withdraw my favor from you. You possess it unjustly: I bestowed it for life on a hero who cannot transfer it to you.

WEISLINGEN. Dismiss me, then.

ADELAIDE. Not till all chance of recovery is lost. Solitude is fatal in your distemper. Alas, poor man, you are as dejected as one whose first love has proved false, and therefore I won't give you up. Give me your hand, and pardon what affection has urged me to say.

WEISLINGEN. Couldst thou but love me, couldst thou but return the fervor of my passion with the least glow of sympathy — Adelaide, thy reproaches are most unjust. Couldst thou but guess the hundredth part of my sufferings, thou wouldst not have tortured me so unmercifully with encouragement, indifference, and contempt. You smile. To be reconciled to myself after the step I have taken must be the work of more than one day. How can I plot against the man who has been so recently and so vividly restored to my affection?

ADELAIDE. Strange being! Can you love him whom you envy? It is like sending provisions to an enemy.

WEISLINGEN. I well know that here there must be no dallying. He is aware that I am again Weislingen; and he will watch his advantage over us. Besides, Ade-laide, we are not so sluggish as you think. Our troopers are reinforced and watchful, our schemes are proceeding, and the Diet of Augsburg will, I hope, soon bring them to a favorable issue.

ADELAIDE. You go there?

WEISLINGEN. If I could carry a glimpse of hope with me.   [*Kisses her hand.*]

ADELAIDE. Oh, ye infidels! Always signs and wonders required. Go, Weislingen, and accomplish the work! The interest of the Bishop, yours, and mine, are all so linked together, that were it only for policy's sake —

WEISLINGEN. You jest.

ADELAIDE. I do not jest. The haughty duke has seized my property. Goetz will not be slow to ravage yours; and if we do not hold together, as our enemies do, and gain over the Emperor to our side, we are lost.

WEISLINGEN. I fear nothing. Most of the princes think with us. The Emperor needs assistance against the Turks, and it is therefore just that he should help us in his turn. What rapture for me to rescue your fortune from rapacious enemies; to crush the mutinous chivalry of Swabia; to restore peace to the bishopric, and then —

ADELAIDE. One day brings on another, and fate is mistress of the future.

WEISLINGEN. But we must lend our endeavors.

ADELAIDE. We do so.

WEISLINGEN. But seriously.

ADELAIDE. Well, then, seriously. Do but go —

WEISLINGEN. Enchantress!   [*Exeunt.*]

SCENE X. *An inn. The bridal of a peasant.*

[*The Bride's Father, Bride, Bridegroom, and other Country-folks,* GOETZ VON BER-LICHINGEN, *and* HANS VON SELBITZ *all discovered at table. Troopers and Peasants attend.*]

GOETZ. It was the best way thus to settle your lawsuit by a merry bridal.

BRIDE'S FATHER. Better than ever I could have dreamed of, noble sir, — to spend my days in quiet with my neighbor, and have a daughter provided for to boot.

BRIDEGROOM. And I to get the bone of contention and a pretty wife into the bargain! Aye, the prettiest in the whole village. Would to Heaven you had consented sooner.

GOETZ. How long have you been at law?

BRIDE'S FATHER. About eight years. I would rather have the fever for twice that time than go through with it again from the beginning. For these periwigged gentry never give a decision till you tear it out of their very hearts; and after all, what do you get for your pains? The Devil fly away with the assessor Sapupi for a damned swarthy Italian!

BRIDEGROOM. Yes, he's a pretty fellow; I was before him twice.

BRIDE'S FATHER. And I thrice; and look ye, gentlemen, we got a judgment at last, which set forth that he was as much in the right as I, and I as much as he; so there we stood like a couple of fools, till a good Providence put it into my head to give him my daughter, and the ground besides.

GOETZ [drinks]. To your better understanding for the future.

BRIDE'S FATHER. With all my heart! But come what may, I'll never go to law again as long as I live. What a mint of money it costs! For every bow made to you by a procurator, you must come down with your dollars.

SELBITZ. But there are annual imperial visitations.

BRIDE'S FATHER. I have never heard of them. Many an extra dollar have they contrived to squeeze out of me. The expenses are horrible.

GOETZ. How mean you?

BRIDE'S FATHER. Why, look you, these gentlemen of the law are always holding out their hands. The assessor alone, God forgive him, eased me of eighteen golden guilders.

BRIDEGROOM. Who?

BRIDE'S FATHER. Why, who else but Sapupi?

GOETZ. That is infamous.

BRIDE'S FATHER. Yes, he asked twenty; and there I had to pay them in the great hall of his fine country-house. I thought my heart would burst with anguish. For look you, my lord, I am well enough off with my house and little farm, but how could I raise the ready cash? I stood there, God knows how it was with me. I had not a single farthing to carry me on my journey. At last I took courage and told him my case: when he saw I was desperate, he flung me back a couple of guilders, and sent me about my business.

BRIDEGROOM. Impossible! Sapupi?

BRIDE'S FATHER. Aye, he himself! — What do you stare at?

BRIDEGROOM. Devil take the rascal! He took fifteen guilders from me, too!

BRIDE'S FATHER. The deuce he did!

SELBITZ. They call us robbers, Goetz!

BRIDE'S FATHER. Bribed on both sides! That's why the judgment fell out so queer. — Oh! the scoundrel!

GOETZ. You must not let this pass unnoticed.

BRIDE'S FATHER. What can we do?

GOETZ. Why, go to Spire where there is an imperial visitation: make your complaint; they must inquire into it, and help you to your own again.

BRIDEGROOM. Does your honor think we shall succeed?

GOETZ. If I might take him in hand, I could promise it you.

SELBITZ. The sum is worth an attempt.

GOETZ. Aye; many a day have I ridden out for the fourth part of it.

BRIDE'S FATHER [to Bridegroom]. What think'st thou?

BRIDEGROOM. We'll try, come what may.

[Enter GEORGE.]

GEORGE. The Nurembergers have set out.

GOETZ. Whereabouts are they?

GEORGE. If we ride off quietly, we shall just catch them in the wood betwixt Berheim and Mühlbach.

SELBITZ. Excellent!

GOETZ. Well, my children, God bless you, and help every man to his own!

BRIDE'S FATHER. Thanks, gallant sir! Will you not stay to supper?

GOETZ. I cannot. Adieu!

[Exeunt GOETZ, SELBITZ, and Troopers.]

ACT III

SCENE I. *A garden at Augsburg.*

[*Enter two Merchants of Nuremberg.*]

FIRST MERCHANT. We'll stand here, for the Emperor must pass this way. He is just coming up the long avenue.

SECOND MERCHANT. Who is that with him?

FIRST MERCHANT. Adelbert of Weislingen.

SECOND MERCHANT. The Bishop's friend. That's lucky!

FIRST MERCHANT. We'll throw ourselves at his feet.

SECOND MERCHANT. See! they come.

[*Enter the* EMPEROR *and* WEISLINGEN.]

FIRST MERCHANT. He looks displeased.

EMPEROR. I am disheartened, Weislingen. When I review my past life, I am ready to despair. So many half — aye, and wholly ruined undertakings — and all because the pettiest feudatory of the Empire thinks more of gratifying his own whims than of seconding my endeavors.

[*The Merchants throw themselves at his feet.*]

FIRST MERCHANT. Most mighty! Most gracious!

EMPEROR. Who are ye? What seek ye?

FIRST MERCHANT. Poor merchants of Nuremberg, Your Majesty's devoted servants, who implore your aid. Goetz von Berlichingen and Hans von Selbitz fell upon thirty of us as we journeyed from the fair of Frankfort, under an escort from Bamberg; they overpowered and plundered us. We implore your imperial assistance to obtain redress, else we are all ruined men, and shall be compelled to beg our bread.

EMPEROR. Good Heavens! What is this? The one has but one hand, the other but one leg; if they both had two hands and two legs, what would you do, then?

FIRST MERCHANT. We most humbly beseech Your Majesty to cast a look of compassion upon our unfortunate condition.

EMPEROR. How is this? — If a merchant loses a bag of pepper, all Germany is to rise in arms; but when business is to be done, in which the imperial majesty and the Empire are interested, should it concern dukedoms, principalities, or kingdoms, there is no bringing you together.

WEISLINGEN. You come at an unseasonable time. Go, and stay at Augsburg for a few days.

MERCHANTS. We make our most humble obeisance. [*Exeunt Merchants.*]

EMPEROR. Again new disturbances; they multiply like the hydra's heads!

WEISLINGEN. And can only be extirpated with fire and sword.

EMPEROR. Do you think so?

WEISLINGEN. Nothing seems to me more advisable, could Your Majesty and the princes but accommodate your other unimportant disputes. It is not the body of the state that complains of this malady — Franconia and Swabia alone glow with the embers of civil discord; and even there many of the nobles and free barons long for quiet. Could we but crush Sickingen, Selbitz — and — and — and Berlichingen, the others would fall asunder; for it is the spirit of these knights which quickens the turbulent mulitude.

EMPEROR. Fain would I spare them; they are noble and hardy. Should I be engaged in war, they would follow me to the field.

WEISLINGEN. It is to be wished they had at all times known their duty; moreover, it would be dangerous to reward their mutinous bravery by offices of trust. For it is exactly this imperial mercy and forgiveness which they have hithertó so grievously abused, and upon which the hope and confidence of their league rests, and this spirit cannot be quelled till we have wholly destroyed their power in the eyes of the world, and taken from them all hope of ever recovering their lost influence.

EMPEROR. You advise severe measures, then?

WEISLINGEN. I see no other means of quelling the spirit of insurrection which has seized upon whole provinces. Do we not already hear the bitterest complaints from the nobles, that their vassals and serfs rebel against them, question their authority, and threaten to curtail their hereditary prerogatives? A proceeding which would involve the most fearful consequences.

EMPEROR. This were a fair occasion for proceeding against Berlichingen and Selbitz; but I will not have them personally injured. Could they be taken prisoners, they should swear to renounce their feuds, and to remain in their own castles and territories upon their knightly parole. At the next session of the Diet we will propose this plan.

WEISLINGEN. A general exclamation of joyful assent will spare Your Majesty the trouble of particular detail. [*Exeunt.*]

SCENE II. *Jaxthausen.*

[*Enter* GOETZ *and* FRANZ VON SICKINGEN.]

SICKINGEN. Yes, my friend, I come to beg the heart and hand of your noble sister.

GOETZ. I would you had come sooner. Weislingen, during his imprisonment, obtained her affections, proposed for her, and I gave my consent. I let the bird loose, and he now despises the benevolent hand that fed him in his distress. He flutters about to seek his food, God knows upon what hedge.

SICKINGEN. Is this so?

GOETZ. Even as I tell you.

SICKINGEN. He has broken a double bond. 'T is well for you that you were not more closely allied with the traitor.

GOETZ. The poor maiden passes her life in lamentation and prayer.

SICKINGEN. I will comfort her.

GOETZ. What! Could you make up your mind to marry a forsaken? —

SICKINGEN. It is to the honor of you both, to have been deceived by him. Should the poor girl be caged in a cloister because the first man who gained her love proved a villain? Not so; I insist on it. She shall be mistress of my castles!

GOETZ. I tell you he was not indifferent to her.

SICKINGEN. Do you think I cannot efface the recollection of such a wretch? Let us go to her. [*Exeunt.*]

SCENE III. *The camp of the party sent to execute the imperial mandate.*

[*Imperial Captain and Officers discovered.*]

CAPTAIN. We must be cautious, and spare our people as much as possible. Besides, we have strict orders to overpower and take him alive. It will be difficult to obey; for who will engage with him hand to hand?

FIRST OFFICER. 'T is true. And he will fight like a wild boar. Besides, he has never in his whole life injured any of us, so each will be glad to leave to the other the honor of risking life and limb to please the Emperor.

SECOND OFFICER. 'T were shame to us should we not take him. Had I him once by the ears, he should not easily escape.

FIRST OFFICER. Don't seize him with your teeth, however, he might chance to run away with your jawbone. My good young sir, such men are not taken like a runaway thief.

SECOND OFFICER. We shall see.

CAPTAIN. By this time he must have had our summons. We must not delay. I mean to dispatch a troop to watch his motions.

SECOND OFFICER. Let me lead it.

CAPTAIN. You are unacquainted with the country.

SECOND OFFICER. I have a servant who was born and bred here.

CAPTAIN. That will do. [*Exeunt.*]

SCENE IV. *Jaxthausen.*

SICKINGEN [*alone*]. All goes as I wish! She was somewhat startled at my proposal, and looked at me from head to foot; I'll wager she was comparing me with her gallant. Thank Heaven, I can stand the scrutiny! She answered little and confusedly. So much the better! Let it work for a time. A proposal of marriage does not come amiss after such a cruel disappointment.

[*Enter* GOETZ.]

SICKINGEN. What news, brother?

GOETZ. They have laid me under the ban.

SICKINGEN. How?

GOETZ. There, read the edifying epistle. The Emperor has issued an edict against me, which gives my body for food to the beasts of the earth and the fowls of the air.

SICKINGEN. They shall first furnish them with a dinner themselves. I am here in the very nick of time.

GOETZ. No, Sickingen, you must leave me. Your great undertakings might be ruined, should you become the enemy of the Emperor at so unseasonable a time. Besides, you can be of more use to me by remaining neutral. The worst that can happen is my being made prisoner; and then your good word with the Emperor, who esteems you, may rescue me from the misfortune into which your untimely assistance would irremediably plunge us both. To what purpose should you do otherwise? These troops are marching against me; and if they knew we were united, their numbers would only be increased, and our position would consequently be no better. The Emperor is at the fountain-head; and I should be utterly ruined were it as easy to inspire soldiers with courage as to collect them into a body.

SICKINGEN. But I can privately reinforce you with a score of troopers.

GOETZ. Good. I have already sent George to Selbitz, and to my people in the neighborhood. My dear brother, when my forces are collected, they will be such a troop as few princes can bring together.

SICKINGEN. It will be small against the multitude.

GOETZ. One wolf is too many for a whole flock of sheep.

SICKINGEN. But if they have a good shepherd?

GOETZ. Never fear! They are all hirelings; and then even the best knight can do but little if he cannot act as he pleases. It happened once, that to oblige the Palsgrave, I went to serve against Conrad Schotten; they then presented me with a paper of instructions from the chancery, which set forth — thus and thus must you proceed. I threw down the paper before the magistrates, and told them I could not act according to it; that something might happen unprovided for in my instructions, and that I must use my own eyes and judge what was best to be done.

SICKINGEN. Good luck, brother! I will hence, and send thee what men I can collect in haste.

GOETZ. Come first to the women. I left them together. I would you had her consent before you depart! Then send me the troopers, and come back in private to carry away my Maria; for my castle, I fear, will shortly be no abode for women.

SICKINGEN. We will hope for the best. [Exeunt.]

SCENE V. Bamberg. Adelaide's chamber.

[ADELAIDE and FRANCIS.]

ADELAIDE. They have already set out to enforce the ban against both?

FRANCIS. Yes; and my master has the happiness of marching against your enemies. I would gladly have gone also, however rejoiced I always am at being dispatched to you. But I will away instantly, and soon return with good news; my master has allowed me to do so.

ADELAIDE. How is he?

FRANCIS. He is well, and commanded me to kiss your hand.

ADELAIDE. There! — Thy lips glow.

FRANCIS [aside, pressing his breast]. Here glows something yet more fiery. [Aloud.] Gracious lady, your servants are the most fortunate of beings!

ADELAIDE. Who goes against Berlichingen?

FRANCIS. The Baron von Sirau. Farewell! Dearest, most gracious lady, I must away. Forget me not!

ADELAIDE. Thou must first take some rest and refreshment.

FRANCIS. I need none, for I have seen you! I am neither weary nor hungry.

ADELAIDE. I know thy fidelity.

FRANCIS. Ah, gracious lady!

ADELAIDE. You can never hold out; you must repose and refresh yourself.

FRANCIS. You are too kind to a poor youth. [Exit.]

ADELAIDE. The tears stood in his eyes. I love him from my heart. Never did man attach himself to me with such warmth of affection. [Exit.]

SCENE VI. *Jaxthausen.*

[GOETZ *and* GEORGE.]

GEORGE. He wants to speak with you in person. I do not know him — he is a tall, well-made man, with keen dark eyes.

GOETZ. Admit him. [*Exit* GEORGE.]

[*Enter* LERSE.]

GOETZ. God save you! What bring you?

LERSE. Myself: not much, but such as it is, it is at your service.

GOETZ. You are welcome, doubly welcome! A brave man, and at a time when, far from expecting new friends, I was in hourly fear of losing the old. Your name?

LERSE. Franz Lerse.

GOETZ. I thank you, Franz, for making me acquainted with a brave man!

LERSE. I made you acquainted with me once before, but then you did not thank me for my pains.

GOETZ. I have no recollection of you.

LERSE. I should be sorry if you had. Do you recollect when, to please the Palsgrave, you rode against Conrad Schotten, and went through Hassfurt on an Allhallow eve?

GOETZ. I remember it well.

LERSE. And twenty-five troopers encountered you in a village by the way?

GOETZ. Exactly. I at first took them for only twelve. I divided my party, which amounted but to sixteen, and halted in the village behind the barn, intending to let them ride by. Then I thought of falling upon them in the rear, as I had concerted with the other troop.

LERSE. We saw you, however, and stationed ourselves on a height above the village. You drew up beneath the hill and halted. When we perceived that you did not intend to come up to us we rode down to you.

GOETZ. And then I saw for the first time that I had thrust my hand into the fire. Five-and-twenty against eight is no jesting business. Everard Truchsess killed one of my followers, for which I knocked him off his horse. Had they all behaved like him and one other trooper, it would have been all over with me and my little band.

LERSE. And that trooper —

GOETZ. Was as gallant a fellow as I ever saw. He attacked me fiercely; and when I thought I had given him enough and was engaged elsewhere, he was upon me again, and laid on like a fury: he cut quite through my armor, and wounded me in the arm.

LERSE. Have you forgiven him?

GOETZ. He pleased me only too well.

LERSE. I hope, then, you have cause to be contented with me, since the proof of my valor was on your own person.

GOETZ. Art thou he? Oh, welcome! welcome! Canst thou boast, Maximilian, that amongst thy followers, thou hast gained one after this fashion?

LERSE. I wonder you did not sooner hit upon me.

GOETZ. How could I think that the man would engage in my service who did his best to overpower me?

LERSE. Even so, my lord. From my youth upwards I have served as a trooper, and have had a tussle with many a knight. I was overjoyed when we met you; for I had heard of your prowess, and wished to know you. You saw I gave way, and that it was not from cowardice, for I returned to the charge. In short, I learn to know you, and from that hour I resolved to enter your service.

GOETZ. How long wilt thou engage with me?

LERSE. For a year, without pay.

GOETZ. No; thou shalt have as the others; nay, more, as befits him who gave me so much work at Remlin.

[*Enter* GEORGE.]

GEORGE. Hans von Selbitz greets you. To-morrow he will be here with fifty men.

GOETZ. 'T is well.

GEORGE. There is a troop of Imperialists riding down the hill, doubtless to reconnoiter.

GOETZ. How many?

GEORGE. About fifty?

GOETZ. Only fifty! Come, Lerse, we'll have a slash at them, so that when Selbitz comes he may find some work done to his hand.

LERSE. 'T will be capital practice.

GOETZ. To horse! [*Exeunt.*]

SCENE VII. *A wood, on the borders of a morass.*

[*Two Imperialist Troopers meeting.*]

FIRST IMPERIALIST. What dost thou here?

SECOND IMPERIALIST. I have leave of absence for ten minutes. Ever since our quarters were beat up last night, I have had such violent attacks that I can't sit on horseback for two minutes together.

FIRST IMPERIALIST. Is the party far advanced?

SECOND IMPERIALIST. About three miles into the wood.

FIRST IMPERIALIST. Then, why are you playing truant here?

SECOND IMPERIALIST. Prithee, betray me not. I am going to the next village to see if I cannot get some warm bandages, to relieve my complaint. But whence comest thou?

FIRST IMPERIALIST. I am bringing our officer some wine and meat from the nearest village.

SECOND IMPERIALIST. So, so! He stuffs himself under our very noses, and we must starve — a fine example!

FIRST IMPERIALIST. Come back with me, rascal.

SECOND IMPERIALIST. Call me a fool, if I do! There are plenty in our troop who would gladly fast, to be as far away as I am. [*Trampling of horses heard.*]

FIRST IMPERIALIST. Hear'st thou? — Horses!

SECOND IMPERIALIST. Oh, dear! Oh, dear!

FIRST IMPERIALIST. I'll get up into this tree.

SECOND IMPERIALIST. And I'll hide among the rushes. [*They hide themselves.*]

[*Enter on horseback,* GOETZ, LERSE, GEORGE, *and Troopers, all completely armed.*]

GOETZ. Away into the wood, by the ditch on the left, — then we have them in the rear. [*They gallop off.*]

FIRST IMPERIALIST [*descending*]. This is a bad business — Michael! — He answers not — Michael, they are gone! [*Goes toward the marsh.*] Alas, he is sunk! — Michael! — He hears me not: he is suffocated. — Poor coward, art thou done for? We are slain — enemies! Enemies on all sides!

[*Reënter* GOETZ *and* GEORGE *on horseback.*]

GOETZ. Yield thee, fellow, or thou diest!

IMPERIALIST. Spare my life!

GOETZ. Thy sword! — George, lead him to the other prisoners, whom Lerse is guarding yonder in the wood. I must pursue their fugitive leader. [*Exit.*]

IMPERIALIST. What has become of the knight, our officer?

GEORGE. My master struck him head over heels from his horse, so that his plume stuck in the mire. His troopers got him up and off they were as if the Devil were behind them. [*Exeunt.*]

SCENE VIII. *Camp of the Imperialists.*

[*Captain and First Officer.*]

FIRST OFFICER. They fly from afar toward the camp.

CAPTAIN. He is most likely hard at their heels. Draw out fifty as far as the mill; if he follows up the pursuit too far, you may perhaps entrap him. [*Exit Officer.*]

[*The Second Officer is borne in.*]

CAPTAIN. How now, my young sir, — have you got a cracked headpiece?

OFFICER. A plague upon you! The stoutest helmet went to shivers like glass. The demon! He ran upon me as if he would strike me into the earth!

CAPTAIN. Thank God, that you have escaped with your life.

OFFICER. There is little left to be thankful for; two of my ribs are broken — Where's the surgeon? [*He is carried off.*]

SCENE IX. *Jaxthausen.*

[*Enter* GOETZ *and* SELBITZ.]

GOETZ. And what say you to the ban, Selbitz?

SELBITZ. 'T is a trick of Weislingen's.

GOETZ. Do you think so?

SELBITZ. I do not think — I know it.

GOETZ. How so?

SELBITZ. He was at the Diet, I tell thee, and near the Emperor's person.

GOETZ. Well, then, we shall frustrate another of his schemes.

SELBITZ. I hope so.

GOETZ. We will away and course these hares.

SCENE X. *The imperial camp.*

[*Captain, Officers, and Followers.*]

CAPTAIN. We shall gain nothing at this work, sirs! He beats one troop after another; and whoever escapes death or captivity, would rather fly to Turkey than return to the camp. Thus our force diminishes daily. We must attack him once for all, and in earnest. I will go myself, and he shall find with whom he has to deal.

OFFICER. We are all content; but he is so well acquainted with the country, and knows every path and ravine so thoroughly, that he will be as difficult to find as a rat in a barn.

CAPTAIN. I warrant you we'll ferret him out. On toward Jaxthausen! Whether he like it or not, he must come to defend his castle.

OFFICER. Shall our whole force march?

CAPTAIN. Yes, certainly — do you know that a hundred of us are melted away already?

OFFICER. Then, let us away with speed, before the whole snowball dissolves; for this is warm work, and we stand here like butter in the sunshine.

[*Exeunt — a march sounded.*]

SCENE XI. *Mountains and a wood.*

[GOETZ, SELBITZ, *and Troopers.*]

GOETZ. They are coming in full force. It was high time that Sickingen's troopers joined us.

SELBITZ. We will divide our party — I will take the left hand by the hill.

GOETZ. Good — and do thou, Lerse, lead fifty men straight through the wood on the right. They are coming across the heath. I will draw up opposite to them. George, stay by me — when you see them attack me, then fall upon their flank: we'll beat the knaves into a mummy — they little think we can face them [*Exeunt.*]

SCENE XII. *A heath — on one side an eminence, with a ruined tower, on the other the forest.*

[*Enter marching, the Captain of the Imperialists with Officers and his Squadron — Drums and standards.*]

CAPTAIN. He halts upon the heath! That's too impudent. He shall smart for it. What! Not fear the torrent that threatens to overwhelm him!

OFFICER. I had rather you did not head the troops; he looks as if he meant to plant the first that comes upon him in the mire with his head downmost. Prithee ride in the rear.

CAPTAIN. Not so.

OFFICER. I entreat you. You are the knot which unites this bundle of hazel twigs; loose it, and he will break them separately like so many reeds.

CAPTAIN. Sound, trumpeter — and let us blow him to hell!

[*A charge sounded — exeunt in full career.*]

[SELBITZ, *with his Troopers, comes from behind the hill, galloping.*]

SELBITZ. Follow me! They shall wish that they could multiply their hands.

[*They gallop across the stage, et exeunt.*]

[*Loud alarm —* LERSE *and his party sally from the wood.*]

LERSE. Ho! to the rescue! Goetz is almost surrounded. — Gallant Selbitz, thou hast cut thy way — we will sow the heath with these thistle heads. [*Gallop off.*]

[*A loud alarm, with shouting and firing for some minutes.*]

[SELBITZ *is borne in wounded by two Troopers.*]

SELBITZ. Leave me here, and hasten to Goetz.

FIRST TROOPER. Let us stay, sir, — you need our aid.

SELBITZ. Get one of you on the watch-tower, and tell me how it goes.

FIRST TROOPER. How shall I get up?

SECOND TROOPER. Mount upon my shoulders — you can then reach the ruined part, and thence scramble up to the opening. [*First Trooper gets up into the tower.*]

FIRST TROOPER. Alas, sir!

SELBITZ. What seest thou?

FIRST TROOPER. Your troopers fly toward the hill.

SELBITZ. Rascally cowards; — I would that they stood their ground, and I had a ball through my head. Ride, one of you, full speed — curse and thunder them back to the field. Seest thou Goetz?

[*Exit Second Trooper.*]

TROOPER. I see his three black feathers floating in the midst of the wavy tumult.

SELBITZ. Swim, brave swimmer — I lie here.

TROOPER. A white plume — whose is that?

SELBITZ. The captain's.

TROOPER. Goetz gallops upon him — crash! Down he goes!

SELBITZ. The captain?

TROOPER. Yes, sir.

SELBITZ. Hurrah! hurrah!

TROOPER. Alas! alas! I see Goetz no more.

SELBITZ. Then, die, Selbitz!

TROOPER. A dreadful tumult where he stood — George's blue plume vanishes too.

SELBITZ. Come down! Dost thou not see Lerse?

TROOPER. No; — everything is in confusion.

SELBITZ. No more. Come down. — How do Sickingen's men bear themselves?

TROOPER. Well. One of them flies to the wood — another — another — a whole troop. Goetz is lost!

SELBITZ. Come down.

TROOPER. I cannot. Hurrah! hurrah! I see Goetz, I see George.

SELBITZ. On horseback?

TROOPER. Aye, aye, high on horseback — Victory! victory! — they fly.

SELBITZ. The Imperialists?

TROOPER. Yes, standard and all, Goetz behind them. They disperse, — Goetz reaches the ensign, — he seizes the standard; he halts. A handful of men rally round him. My comrade reaches him — they come this way.

[*Enter* GOETZ, GEORGE, LERSE, *and Troopers, on horseback.*]

SELBITZ. Joy to thee, Goetz! — victory!

GOETZ [*dismounting*]. Dearly, dearly bought. Thou art wounded, Selbitz!

SELBITZ. But thou dost live and hast conquered! I have done little; and my dogs of troopers! How hast thou come off?

GOETZ. For the present, well! And here I thank George, and thee, Lerse, for my life. I unhorsed the captain, they stabbed my horse, and pressed me hard. George cut his way to me, and sprang off his horse. I threw myself like lightning upon it, and he appeared suddenly like a thunderbolt upon another. How camest thou by thy steed?

GEORGE. A fellow struck at you from behind: as he raised his cuirass in the act, I stabbed him with my dagger. Down he came; and so I rid you of an enemy, and helped myself to a horse.

GOETZ. There we held together till Francis here came to our help; and thereupon we mowed our way out.

LERSE. The hounds whom I led were to have mowed their way in, till our scythes met, but they fled like Imperialists.

GOETZ. Friend and foe all fled, except this little band who protected my rear. I had enough to do with the fellows in front, but the fall of their captain dismayed them: they wavered, and fled. I have their banner, and a few prisoners.

SELBITZ. The captain has escaped you?

GOETZ. They rescued him in the scuffle. Come, lads; come, Selbitz. — Make a litter of lances and boughs. Thou canst not mount a horse, come to my castle. They are scattered, but we are very few; and I know not what troops they may have in reserve. I will be your host, my friends. Wine will taste well after such an action.

[*Exeunt, carrying* SELBITZ.]

SCENE XIII. *The camp.*

[*The Captain and Imperialists.*]

CAPTAIN. I could kill you all with my own hand. — What! to turn tail! He had not a handful of men left. To give way before one man! No one will believe it but those who wish to make a jest of us. Ride round the country, you, and you, and you: collect our scattered soldiers, or cut them down wherever you find them. We must grind these notches out of our blades, even should we spoil our swords in the operation. [*Exeunt.*]

SCENE XIV. *Jaxthausen.*

[GOETZ, LERSE, *and* GEORGE.]

GOETZ. We must not lose a moment. My poor fellows, I dare allow you no rest. Gallop round and strive to enlist troopers, appoint them to assemble at Weilern, where they will be most secure. Should we delay a moment, they will be before the castle. [*Exeunt* LERSE *and* GEORGE.] I must send out a scout. This begins to grow warm. — If we had but brave foemen to deal with! But these fellows are only formidable through their number. [*Exit.*]

[*Enter* SICKINGEN *and* MARIA.]

MARIA. I beseech thee, dear Sickingen, do not leave my brother! His horsemen, your own, and those of Selbitz, all are scattered; he is alone. Selbitz has been carried home to his castle wounded. I fear the worst.

SICKINGEN. Be comforted, I will not leave him.

[*Enter* GOETZ.]

GOETZ. Come to the chapel, the priest waits; in a few minutes you shall be united.

SICKINGEN. Let me remain with you.

GOETZ. You must come now to the chapel.

SICKINGEN. Willingly! — and then —

GOETZ. Then you go your way.

SICKINGEN. Goetz!

GOETZ. Will you not to the chapel?

SICKINGEN. Come, come! [*Exeunt.*]

SCENE XV. *Camp.*

[*Captain and Officers.*]

CAPTAIN. How many are we in all?

OFFICER. A hundred and fifty —

CAPTAIN. Out of four hundred. — That is bad. Set out for Jaxthausen at once, before he collects his forces and attacks us on the way.

SCENE XVI. *Jaxthausen.*

[GOETZ, ELIZABETH, MARIA, *and* SICKINGEN.]

GOETZ. God bless you, give you happy days, and keep those for your children which he denies to you!

ELIZABETH. And may they be virtuous as you — then let come what will.

SICKINGEN. I thank you. — And you, my Maria! As I led you to the altar, so shall you lead me to happiness.

MARIA. Our pilgrimage will be together toward that distant and promised land.

GOETZ. A prosperous journey!

MARIA. That was not what I meant — We do not leave you.

GOETZ. You must, sister.

MARIA. You are very harsh, brother.

GOETZ. And you more affectionate than prudent.

[*Enter* GEORGE.]

GEORGE [*aside to* GOETZ]. I can collect no troopers. One was inclined to come, but he changed his mind and refused.

GOETZ [*aside to* GEORGE]. 'T is well, George. Fortune begins to look coldly on me. I foreboded it, however. [*Aloud.*] Sickingen, I entreat you, depart this very evening. Persuade Maria — you are her husband — let her feel it. When women come across our undertakings, our enemies are more secure in the open field, than they would else be in their castles.

[*Enter a Trooper.*]

TROOPER [*aside to* GOETZ]. The Imperial squadron is in full and rapid march hither.

GOETZ. I have roused them with stripes of the rod! How many are they?

TROOPER. About two hundred. They can scarcely be six miles from us.

GOETZ. Have they passed the river yet?

TROOPER. No, my lord.

GOETZ. Had I but fifty men, they should not cross it. Hast thou seen Lerse?

TROOPER. No, my lord.

GOETZ. Tell all to hold themselves ready. — We must part, dear friends. Weep on, my gentle Maria. Many a moment of happiness is yet in store for thee. It is better thou shouldst weep on thy wedding-day than that present joy should be the forerunner of future misery. — Farewell, Maria! — Farewell, brother!

MARIA. I cannot leave you, sister. Dear brother, let us stay. Dost thou value my husband so little as to refuse his help in thy extremity?

GOETZ. Yes — it is gone far with me. Perhaps my fall is near. You are but beginning life, and should separate your lot from mine. I have ordered your horses to be saddled: you must away instantly.

MARIA. Brother! brother!

ELIZABETH [to SICKINGEN]. Yield to his wishes. Speak to her.

SICKINGEN. Dear Maria! We must go.

MARIA. Thou, too? My heart will break!

GOETZ. Then, stay. In a few hours my castle will be surrounded.

MARIA [weeping bitterly]. Alas! alas!

GOETZ. We will defend ourselves as long as we can.

MARIA. Mother of God, have mercy upon us!

GOETZ. And at last we must die or surrender. Thy tears will then have involved thy noble husband in the same misfortune with me.

MARIA. Thou torturest me!

GOETZ. Remain! Remain! We shall be taken together! Sickingen, thou wilt fall into the pit with me, out of which I had hoped thou shouldst have helped me.

MARIA. We will away — sister — sister!

GOETZ. Place her in safety, and then think of me.

SICKINGEN. Never will I repose a night by her side till I know thou art out of danger.

GOETZ. Sister, dear sister! [Kisses her.]

SICKINGEN. Away! Away!

GOETZ. Yet one moment! I shall see you again. Be comforted, we shall meet again. [Exeunt SICKINGEN and MARIA.] I urged her to depart — yet when she leaves me, what would I not give to detain her! Elizabeth, thou stayest with me. [Exit.]

ELIZABETH. Till death!

GOETZ. Whom God loves, to him may He give such a wife.

[Enter GEORGE.]

GEORGE. They are near! I saw them from the tower. The sun is rising, and I perceived their lances glitter. I cared no more for them than a cat would for a whole army of mice. 'T is true we play the mice at present.

GOETZ. Look to the fastenings of the gates; barricade them with beams and stones. [Exit GEORGE.] We'll exercise their patience, and they may chew away their valor in biting their nails. [A trumpet from without. GOETZ goes to the window.] Aha! Here comes a red-coated rascal to ask me whether I will be a scoundrel! What says he? [The voice of the Herald is heard indistinctly, as from a distance. GOETZ mutters to himself.] A rope for thy throat! [Voice again.] "Offended majesty!" — Some priest has drawn up that proclamation. [Voice concludes, and GOETZ answers from the window.] Surrender — surrender at discretion. With whom speak you? Am I a robber? Tell your captain, that for the Emperor I entertain, as I have ever done, all due respect; but as for him, he may — [Shuts the window with violence.]

SCENE XVII. The kitchen.

[ELIZABETH preparing food. Enter GOETZ.]

GOETZ. You have hard work, my poor wife!

ELIZABETH. Would it might last! But you can hardly hold out long.

GOETZ. We have not had time to provide ourselves.

ELIZABETH. And so many people as you have been wont to entertain. The wine is well-nigh finished.

GOETZ. If we can but hold out a certain time, they must propose a capitulation. We are doing them some damage, I promise you. They shoot the whole day, and only wound our walls and break our windows. Lerse is a gallant fellow. He slips about with his gun: if a rogue comes too nigh — pop! there he lies! [Firing.]

[Enter Trooper.]

TROOPER. We want live coals, gracious lady!

GOETZ. For what?

TROOPER. Our bullets are spent; we must cast some new ones.

GOETZ. How goes it with the powder?

TROOPER. There is as yet no want: we save our fire.

[Firing at intervals. Exeunt GOETZ and ELIZABETH.]

[Enter LERSE with a bullet-mould. Servants with coals.]

LERSE. Set them down, and then go and seek for lead about the house; meanwhile I will make shift with this. [Goes to the window, and takes out the leaden frames.] Everything must be turned to account. So it is in this world — no one knows what a thing may come to: the glazier who made these frames little thought that the lead here was to give one of his grandsons his last headache; and the father that begot me little knew whether the fowls of heaven or the worms of the earth would pick my bones.

[Enter GEORGE with a leaden spout.]

GEORGE. Here's lead for thee! If you hit with only half of it, not one will return to tell His Majesty, "Thy servants have sped ill!"

LERSE [cutting it down]. A famous piece!

GEORGE. The rain must seek some other way. I'm not afraid of it — a brave trooper and a smart shower will always find their road. [They cast balls.]

LERSE. Hold the ladle. [Goes to the window.] Yonder is a fellow creeping about with his rifle; he thinks our fire is spent. He shall have a bullet warm from the pan. [He loads his rifle.]

GEORGE [puts down the mould]. Let me see.

LERSE [fires]. There lies the game!

GEORGE. He fired at me as I stepped out on the roof to get the lead. He killed a pigeon that sat near me; it fell into the spout. I thanked him for my dinner, and went back with the double booty.

[They cast balls.]

LERSE. Now, let us load, and go through the castle to earn our dinner.

[Enter GOETZ.]

GOETZ. Stay, Lerse, I must speak with thee. I will not keep thee, George, from the sport. [Exit GEORGE.]

GOETZ. They offer terms.

LERSE. I will go and hear what they have to say.

GOETZ. They will require me to enter myself into ward in some town on my knightly parole.

LERSE. That won't do. Suppose they allow us free liberty of departure? — for we can expect no relief from Sickingen. We will bury all the valuables, where no divining-rod shall find them; leave them the bare walls, and come out with flying colors.

GOETZ. They will not permit us.

LERSE. It is worth the asking. We will demand a safe-conduct, and I will sally out.

SCENE XVIII. *A hall.*

[GOETZ, ELIZABETH, GEORGE, *and Troopers at table.*]

GOETZ. Danger unites us, my friends! Be of good cheer; don't forget the bottle! The flask is empty. Come, another, dear wife! [ELIZABETH *shakes her head.*] is there no more?

ELIZABETH [aside]. Only one, which I have set apart for you.

GOETZ. Not so, my love! Bring it out; they need strengthening more than I, for it is my quarrel.

ELIZABETH. Fetch it from the cupboard.

GOETZ. It is the last, and I feel as if we need not spare it. It is long since I have been so merry. [*They fill.*] To the health of the Emperor!

ALL. Long live the Emperor!

GOETZ. Be it our last word when we die! I love him, for our fate is similar; but I am happier than he. To please the princes, he must direct his imperial squadrons against mice, while the rats gnaw his possessions. — I know he often wishes himself dead, rather than to be any longer the soul of such a crippled body. [*They fill.*] It will just go once more round. And when our blood runs low, like this flask; when we pour out its last ebbing drop [*empties the wine drop by drop into his goblet*], what then shall be our cry?

GEORGE. Freedom forever!

GOETZ. Freedom forever!

ALL. Freedom forever!

GOETZ. And if that survive us we can die happy; for our spirits shall see our children's children, and their Emperor happy! Did the servants of princes show the same filial attachment to their masters as you to me — did their masters serve the Emperor as I would serve him —

GEORGE. Things would be widely different.

GOETZ. Not so much so as it would appear. Have I not known worthy men among the princes? And can the race be extinct? Men, happy in their own minds and in their subjects, who could bear a free, noble brother in their neighborhood without harboring either fear or envy; whose hearts expanded when they saw their table surrounded by their free equals, and who did not think the knights unfit companions till they had degraded themselves by courtly homage.

GEORGE. Have you known such princes?

GOETZ. Aye, truly. As long as I live I shall recollect how the Landgrave of Hanau made a grand hunting-party, and the princes and free feudatories dined under the open heaven, and the country people all thronged to see them; it was no selfish masquerade instituted for his own private pleasure or vanity. — To see the great round-headed peasant lads and the pretty brown girls, the sturdy hinds, and the venerable old men, a crowd of happy faces, all

as merry as if they rejoiced in the splendor of their master, which he shared with them under God's free sky!

GEORGE. He must have been as good a master as you.

GOETZ. And may we not hope that many such will rule together some future day, to whom reverence to the Emperor, peace and friendship with their neighbors, and the love of their vassals, shall be the best and dearest family treasure handed down to their children's children? Every one will then keep and improve his own, instead of reckoning nothing as gain that is not stolen from his neighbors.

GEORGE. And should we have no more forays?

GOETZ. Would to God there were no restless spirits in all Germany! — We should still have enough to do! We would clear the mountains of wolves, and bring our peaceable laborious neighbor a dish of game from the wood, and eat it together. Were that not full employment, we would join our brethren, and, like cherubims with flaming swords, defend the frontiers of the Empire against those wolves the Turks, and those foxes the French, and guard for our beloved Emperor both extremities of his extensive Empire. That would be a life, George! To risk one's head for the safety of all Germany. [GEORGE *springs up.*] Whither away?

GEORGE. Alas! I forgot we were besieged — besieged by the very Emperor; and before we can expose our lives in his defense, we must risk them for our liberty.

GOETZ. Be of good cheer.

[*Enter* LERSE.]

LERSE. Freedom! Freedom! The cowardly poltroons — the hesitating, irresolute asses. You are to depart with men, weapons, horses, and armor; provisions you are to leave behind.

GOETZ. They will hardly find enough to exercise their jaws.

LERSE [*aside to* GOETZ]. Have you hidden the plate and money?

GOETZ. No! Wife, go with Lerse; he has something to tell thee. [*Exeunt.*]

SCENE XIX. *The court of the castle.*

GEORGE [*in the stable: sings*].

An urchin once, as I have heard,
    Ha! ha!
Had caught and caged a little bird,
    Sa! sa!
    Ha! ha!
    Sa! sa!
He viewed the prize with heart elate,
    Ha! ha!
Thrust in his hand — ah, treacherous fate!
    Sa! sa!
    Ha! ha!
    Sa! sa!
Away the titmouse wing'd its flight,
    Ha! ha!
And laugh'd to scorn the silly wight,
    Sa! sa!
    Ha! ha!
    Sa! sa!

[*Enter* GOETZ.]

GOETZ. How goes it?

GEORGE [*brings out his horse*]. All saddled!

GOETZ. Thou art quick.

GEORGE. As the bird escaped from the cage.

[*Enter all the besieged.*]

GOETZ. Have you all your rifles? Not yet! Go, take the best from the armory, 't is all one; we'll ride on in advance.

GEORGE [*sings*].

    Ha! ha!
    Sa! sa!
    Ha! ha!

SCENE XX. *The armory.*

[*Two Troopers choosing guns.*]

FIRST TROOPER. I'll have this one.

SECOND TROOPER. And I this — but yonder's a better.

FIRST TROOPER. Never mind — make haste. [*Tumult and firing without.*]

SECOND TROOPER. Hark!

FIRST TROOPER [*springs to the window*]. Good Heavens, they are murdering our master! He is unhorsed! George is down!

SECOND TROOPER. How shall we get off? Over the wall by the walnut tree, and into the field. [*Exit.*]

FIRST TROOPER. Lerse keeps his ground; I will to him. If they die, I will not survive them. [*Exit.*]

ACT IV

SCENE I. *An inn in the city of Heilbronn.*

[GOETZ, *solus.*]

GOETZ. I am like the evil spirit whom the Capuchin conjured into a sack. I fret and labor, but all in vain. The perjured villains!

[*Enter* ELIZABETH.]

What news, Elizabeth, of my dear, my trusty followers?

ELIZABETH. Nothing certain: some are slain, some are prisoners; no one could or would tell me further particulars.

GOETZ. Is this the reward of fidelity, of filial obedience? — "That it may be well with thee, and that thy days may be long in the land!"

ELIZABETH. Dear husband, murmur not against our heavenly Father. They have their reward. It was born with them — a noble and generous heart. Even in the dungeon they are free. Pay attention to the imperial commissioners; their heavy gold chains become them —

GOETZ. As a necklace becomes a sow! I should like to see George and Lerse in fetters!

ELIZABETH. It were a sight to make angels weep.

GOETZ. I would not weep— I would clench my teeth, and gnaw my lip in fury. What! in fetters! Had ye but loved me less, dear lads! I could never look at them enough — What! to break their word pledged in the name of the Emperor!

ELIZABETH. Put away these thoughts. Reflect; you must appear before the Council — you are in no mood to meet them, and I fear the worst.

GOETZ. What harm can they do me?

ELIZABETH. Here comes the sergeant.

GOETZ. What! The ass of justice that carries the sacks to the mill and the dung to the field? What now?

[*Enter Sergeant.*]

SERGEANT. The lords commissioners are at the Council-House, and require your presence.

GOETZ. I come.

SERGEANT. I am to escort you.

GOETZ. Too much honor.

ELIZABETH. Be but cool.

GOETZ. Fear nothing.   [*Exeunt.*]

SCENE II. *The Council-House at Heilbronn.*

[*The Imperial Commissioners seated at a table. The Captain and the Magistrates of the city attending.*]

MAGISTRATE. In pursuance of your order, we have collected the stoutest and most determined of our citizens. They are at hand, in order, at a nod from you, to seize Berlichingen.

COMMISSIONER. We shall have much pleasure in communicating to His Imperial Majesty the zeal with which you have obeyed his illustrious commands. — Are they artisans?

MAGISTRATE. Smiths, coopers, and carpenters, men with hands hardened by labor; and resolute here.

[*Points to his breast.*]

COMMISSIONER. 'T is well.

[*Enter Sergeant.*]

SERGEANT. Goetz von Berlichingen waits without.

COMMISSIONER. Admit him.

[*Enter GOETZ.*]

GOETZ. God save you, sirs! What would you with me?

COMMISSIONER. First, that you consider where you are; and in whose presence.

GOETZ. By my faith, I know you right well, sirs.

COMMISSIONER. You acknowledge allegiance.

GOETZ. With all my heart.

COMMISSIONER. Be seated.

[*Points to a stool.*]

GOETZ. What, down there? I'd rather stand. That stool smells so of poor sinners, as, indeed, does the whole apartment.

COMMISSIONER. Stand, then.

GOETZ. To business, if you please.

COMMISSIONER. We shall proceed in due order.

GOETZ. I am glad to hear it. Would you had always done so.

COMMISSIONER. You know how you fell into our hands, and are a prisoner at discretion.

GOETZ. What will you give me to forget it?

COMMISSIONER. Could I give you modesty, I should better your affairs.

GOETZ. Better my affairs! Could you but do that! To repair is more difficult than to destroy.

SECRETARY. Shall I put all this on record?

COMMISSIONER. Only what is to the purpose.

GOETZ. As far as I'm concerned you may print every word of it.

COMMISSIONER. You fell into the power of the Emperor, whose paternal goodness got the better of his justice, and, instead of throwing you into a dungeon, ordered you to repair to his beloved city of Heilbronn. You gave your knightly parole to appear, and await the termination in all humility.

GOETZ. Well; I am here, and await it.

COMMISSIONER. And we are here to intimate to you His Imperial Majesty's mercy and clemency. He is pleased to forgive your rebellion, to release you from the ban and all well-merited punishment; provided you do, with becoming humility, receive his bounty, and subscribe to the articles which shall be read unto you.

GOETZ. I am His Majesty's faithful servant, as ever. One word, ere you proceed. My people — where are they? What will be done with them?

COMMISSIONER. That concerns you not.

GOETZ. So may the Emperor turn his face from you in the hour of your need. They were my comrades, and are so now. What have you done with them?

COMMISSIONER. We are not bound to account to you.

GOETZ. Ah! I forgot that you are not even pledged to perform what you have promised, much less —

COMMISSIONER. Our business is to lay the articles before you. Submit yourself to the Emperor, and you may find a way to petition for the life and freedom of your comrades.

GOETZ. Your paper.

COMMISSIONER. Secretary, read it.

SECRETARY [reads]. "I, Goetz of Berlichingen, make public acknowledgment, by these presents, that I, having lately risen in rebellion against the Emperor and Empire —"

GOETZ. 'T is false! I am no rebel, I have committed no offense against the Emperor, and with the Empire I have no concern.

COMMISSIONER. Be silent, and hear further.

GOETZ. I will hear no further. Let any one arise and bear witness. Have I ever taken one step against the Emperor, or against the House of Austria? Has not the whole tenor of my conduct proved that I feel better than any one else what all Germany owes to its head; and especially what the free knights and feudatories owe to their liege lord the Emperor? I should be a villain could I be induced to subscribe that paper.

COMMISSIONER. Yet we have strict orders to try and persuade you by fair means, or, in case of your refusal, to throw you into prison.

GOETZ. Into prison! — Me?

COMMISSIONER. Where you may expect your fate from the hands of justice, since you will not take it from those of mercy.

GOETZ. To prison! You abuse the imperial power! To prison! That was not the Emperor's command. What, ye traitors, to dig a pit for me, and hang out your oath, your knightly honor as the bait! To promise me permission to ward myself on parole, and then again to break your treaty!

COMMISSIONER. We owe no faith to robbers.

GOETZ. Wert thou not the representative of my sovereign, whom I respect even in the vilest counterfeit, thou should swallow that word, or choke upon it. I was engaged in an honorable feud. Thou mightest thank God, and magnify thyself before the world, hadst thou ever done as gallant a deed as that with which I now stand charged. [The Commissioner makes a sign to the Magistrate of Heilbronn, who rings a bell.] Not for the sake of paltry gain, not to wrest followers or lands from the weak and the defenseless, have I sallied forth. To rescue my page and defend my own person — see ye any rebellion in that? The Emperor and his magnates, reposing on their pillows, would never have felt our need. I have, God be praised, one hand left, and I have done well to use it.

[Enter a party of Artisans armed with halberds and swords.]

GOETZ. What means this?

COMMISSIONER. You will not listen. — Seize him!

GOETZ. Let none come near me who is not a very Hungarian ox. One salutation from my iron fist shall cure him of headache, toothache, and every other ache under the wide heaven! [They rush upon him. He strikes one down; and snatches a sword from another. They stand aloof.] Come on! Come on! I should like to become acquainted with the bravest among you.

COMMISSIONER. Surrender!

GOETZ. With a sword in my hand! Know ye not that it depends but upon myself to make way through all these hares and gain the open field? But I will teach you how a man should keep his word. Promise me but free ward, and I will give up my sword, and am again your prisoner.

COMMISSIONER. How! Would you treat with the Emperor, sword in hand?

GOETZ. God forbid! — only with you and your worthy fraternity! You may go home, good people; you are only losing your time, and here there is nothing to be got but bruises.

COMMISSIONER. Seize him! What! Does not your love for the Emperor supply you with courage?

GOETZ. No more than the Emperor supplies them with plaster for the wounds their courage would earn them.

[Enter Sergeant, hastily.]

OFFICER. The warder has just discovered from the castle-tower, a troop of more than two hundred horsemen hastening toward the town. Unperceived by us, they have pressed forward from behind the hill, and threaten our walls.

COMMISSIONER. Alas! alas! What can this mean?

[*A Soldier enters.*]

SOLDIER. Francis of Sickingen waits at the drawbridge, and informs you that he has heard how perfidiously you have broken your word to his brother-in-law, and how the Council of Heilbronn have aided and abetted in the treason. He is now come to insist upon justice, and if refused it, threatens, within an hour, to fire the four quarters of your town, and abandon it to be plundered by his vassals.

GOETZ. My gallant brother!

COMMISSIONER. Withdraw, Goetz. [*Exit Goetz.*] What is to be done?

MAGISTRATE. Have compassion upon us and our town! Sickingen is inexorable in his wrath; he will keep his word.

COMMISSIONER. Shall we forget what is due to ourselves and the Emperor?

CAPTAIN. If we had but men to enforce it; but situated as we are, a show of resistance would only make matters worse. It is better for us to yield.

MAGISTRATE. Let us apply to Goetz to put in a good word for us. I feel as though I saw the town already in flames.

COMMISSIONER. Let Goetz approach.

[*Enter Goetz.*]

GOETZ. What now?

COMMISSIONER. Thou wilt do well to dissuade thy brother-in-law from his rebellious interference. Instead of rescuing thee, he will only plunge thee deeper in destruction, and become the companion of thy fall!

GOETZ [*sees Elizabeth at the door, and speaks to her aside*]. Go; tell him instantly to break in and force his way hither, but to spare the town. As for these rascals, if they offer any resistance, let him use force. I care not if I lose my life, provided they are all knocked on the head at the same time.

SCENE III. *A large hall in the Council-House, beset by Sickingen's troops.*

[*Enter Sickingen and Goetz.*]

GOETZ. That was help from Heaven. How camest thou so opportunely and unexpectedly, brother?

SICKINGEN. Without witchcraft. I had dispatched two or three messengers to learn how it fared with thee; when I heard of the perjury of these fellows, I set out instantly, and now we have them safe.

GOETZ. I ask nothing but knightly ward upon my parole.

SICKINGEN. You are too noble. Not even to avail yourself of the advantage which the honest man has over the perjurer! They are in the wrong, and we will not give them cushions to sit upon. They have shamefully abused the imperial authority, and, if I know anything of the Emperor, you might safely insist upon more favorable terms. You ask too little.

GOETZ. I have ever been content with little.

SICKINGEN. And therefore that little has always been denied thee. My proposal is, that they shall release your servants, and permit you all to return to your castle on parole — you can promise not to leave it till the Emperor's pleasure be known. You will be safer there than here.

GOETZ. They will say my property is escheated to the Emperor.

SICKINGEN. Then we will answer thou canst dwell there, and keep it for his service till he restores it to thee again. Let them wriggle like eels in the net, they shall not escape us! They may talk of the imperial dignity — of their commission. We will not mind that. I know the Emperor, and have some influence with him. He has ever wished to have thee in his service. You will not be long in your castle without being summoned to serve him.

GOETZ. God grant it, ere I forget the use of arms!

SICKINGEN. Valor can never be forgotten, as it can never be learned. Fear nothing! When thy affairs are settled, I will repair to court, where my enterprises begin to ripen. Good fortune seems to smile on them. I want only to sound the Emperor's mind. The towns of Triers and Pfalz as soon expect that the sky should fall as that I shall come down upon their heads. But I will come like a hailstorm! And if I am successful, thou shalt soon be brother to an elector. I had hoped for thy assistance in this undertaking.

GOETZ [*looks at his hand*]. Oh! That explains the dream I had the night before I promised Maria to Weislingen. I thought he vowed eternal fidelity, and held my iron hand so fast that it loosened from the arm. Alas! I am at this moment more defenseless than when it was shot away. Weislingen! Weislingen!

SICKINGEN. Forget the traitor! We will thwart his plans, and undermine his authority, till shame and remorse shall gnaw him to death. I see, I see the downfall of our enemies. — Goetz — only half a year more!

GOETZ. Thy soul soars high! I know not why, but for some time past no fair prospects have dawned upon me. I have been ere now in sore distress — I have been a prisoner before — but never did I experience such a depression.

SICKINGEN. Fortune gives courage. Come, let us to the bigwigs. They have had time enough to deliberate, let us take the trouble upon ourselves. [*Exeunt.*]

SCENE IV. *The castle of Adelaide, Augsburg.*

[ADELAIDE *and* WEISLINGEN *discovered.*]

ADELAIDE. This is detestable.

WEISLINGEN. I have gnashed my teeth. So good a plan — so well followed out — and after all to leave him in possession of his castle! That cursèd Sickingen!

ADELAIDE. The Council should not have consented.

WEISLINGEN. They were in the net. What else could they do? Sickingen threatened them with fire and sword, — the haughty, vindictive man! I hate him! His power waxes like a mountain torrent — let it but gain a few brooks, and others come pouring to its aid.

ADELAIDE. Have they no Emperor?

WEISLINGEN. My dear wife, he waxes old and feeble; he is only the shadow of what he was. When he heard what had been done, and I and the other counselors murmured indignantly — "Let them alone!" said he; "I can spare my old Goetz his little fortress, and if he remains quiet there, what have you to say against him?" We spoke of the welfare of the state — "Oh," said he, "that I had always had counselors who would have urged my restless spirit to consult more the happiness of individuals!"

ADELAIDE. He has lost the spirit of a prince!

WEISLINGEN. We inveighed against Sickingen — "He is my faithful servant," said he; "and if he has not acted by my express order, he has performed what I wished better than my plenipotentiaries, and I can ratify what he has done as well after as before."

ADELAIDE. 'T is enough to drive one mad.

WEISLINGEN. Yet I have not given up all hope. Goetz is on parole to remain quiet in his castle. 'T is impossible for him to keep his promise, and we shall soon have some new cause of complaint.

ADELAIDE. That is the more likely, as we may hope that the old Emperor will soon leave the world, and Charles, his gallant successor, will display a more princely mind.

WEISLINGEN. Charles! He is neither chosen nor crowned.

ADELAIDE. Who does not expect and hope for that event?

WEISLINGEN. You have a great idea of his abilities; one might almost think you looked on him with partial eyes.

ADELAIDE. You insult me, Weislingen. For what do you take me?

WEISLINGEN. I do not mean to offend; but I cannot be silent upon the subject. Charles's marked attentions to you disquiet me.

ADELAIDE. And do I receive them as —

WEISLINGEN. You are a woman; and no woman hates those who pay their court to her.

ADELAIDE. This from you?

WEISLINGEN. It cuts me to the heart — the dreadful thought — Adelaide.

ADELAIDE. Can I not cure thee of this folly?

WEISLINGEN. If thou wouldst — thou canst leave the court.

ADELAIDE. But upon what pretense? Art thou not here? Must I leave you and all my friends, to shut myself up with the owls in your solitary castle? No, Weislingen, that will never do; be at rest, thou knowest I love thee.

WEISLINGEN. That is my anchor so long as the cable holds. [Exit.]

ADELAIDE. Ah! It is come to this? This was yet wanting. The projects of my bosom are too great to brook the interruption. Charles — the great, the gallant Charles — the future Emperor — shall he be the only man unrewarded by my favor? Think not, Weislingen, to hinder me — else shalt thou to earth; my way lies over thee!

[Enter FRANCIS, with a letter.]

FRANCIS. Here, gracious lady.

ADELAIDE. Hadst thou it from Charles's own hand?

FRANCIS. Yes.

ADELAIDE. What ails thee? Thou look'st so mournful!

FRANCIS. It is your pleasure that I should pine away, and waste my fairest years in agonizing despair.

ADELAIDE [aside]. I pity him; and how little would it cost me to make him happy. [Aloud.] Be of good courage, youth! I know thy love and fidelity, and will not be ungrateful.

FRANCIS [with stifled breath]. If thou wert capable of ingratitude, I could not survive it. There boils not a drop of blood in my veins but what is thine own — I have not a single feeling but to love and to serve thee!

ADELAIDE. Dear Francis!

FRANCIS. You flatter me. [Bursts into tears.] Does my attachment deserve only to be a stepping-stool to another — to see all your thoughts fixed upon Charles?

ADELAIDE. You know not what you wish, and still less what you say.

FRANCIS [stamping with vexation and rage]. No more will I be your slave, your go-between!

ADELAIDE. Francis, you forget yourself.

FRANCIS. To sacrifice my beloved master and myself —

ADELAIDE. Out of my sight!

FRANCIS. Gracious lady!

ADELAIDE. Go; betray to thy beloved master the secret of my soul! Fool that I was to take thee for what thou art not.

FRANCIS. Dear lady! You know how I love you.

ADELAIDE. And thou, who wast my friend — so near my heart — go; betray me.

FRANCIS. Rather would I tear my heart from my breast! Forgive me, gentle lady! My heart is too full, my senses desert me.

ADELAIDE. Thou dear, affectionate boy! [She takes him by both hands, draws him toward her and kisses him. He throws himself weeping upon her neck.] Leave me!

FRANCIS [his voice choked by tears]. Heavens!

ADELAIDE. Leave me! The walls are traitors. Leave me! [Breaks from him.] Be but steady in fidelity and love, and the fairest reward is thine. [Exit.]

FRANCIS. The fairest reward! Let me but live till that moment — I could murder my father, were he an obstacle to my happiness! [Exit.]

SCENE V. Jaxthausen.

[GOETZ seated at a table with writing materials. ELIZABETH beside him with her work.]

GOETZ. This idle life does not suit me. My confinement becomes more irksome every day. I would I could sleep, or persuade myself that quiet is agreeable.

ELIZABETH. Continue writing the account of thy deeds which thou hast commenced. Give into the hands of thy friends evidence to put thine enemies to shame; make a noble posterity acquainted with thy real character.

GOETZ. Alas! Writing is but busy idleness; it wearies me. While I am writing what I have done, I lament the misspent time in which I might do more.

ELIZABETH [*takes the writing*]. Be not impatient. Thou hast come to thy first imprisonment at Heilbronn.

GOETZ. That was always an unlucky place to me.

ELIZABETH [*reads*]. "There were even some of the confederates who told me that I had acted foolishly in appearing before my bitterest enemies, who, as I might suspect, would not deal justly with me." And what didst thou answer? Write on.

GOETZ. I said, "Have I not often risked life and limb for the welfare and property of others, and shall I not do so for the honor of my knightly word?"

ELIZABETH. Thus does fame speak of thee.

GOETZ. They shall not rob me of my honor. They have taken all else from me — property — liberty — everything.

ELIZABETH. I happened once to stand in an inn near the Lords of Miltenberg and Singlingen, who knew me not. Then I was joyful as at the birth of my first-born; for they extolled thee to each other, and said, — "He is the mirror of knighthood, noble and merciful in prosperity, dauntless and true in misfortune."

GOETZ. Let them show me the man to whom I have broken my word. Heaven knows, my ambition has ever been to labor for my neighbor more than for myself, and to acquire the fame of a gallant and irreproachable knight, rather than principalities or power; and, God be praised! I have gained the meed of my labor.

[*Enter* GEORGE *and* LERSE *with game.*]

GOETZ. Good luck to my gallant huntsmen!

GEORGE. Such have we become from gallant troopers. Boots can easily be cut down into buskins.

LERSE. The chase is always something — 't is a kind of war.

GEORGE. Yes; if we were not always crossed by these imperial gamekeepers. Don't you recollect, my lord, how you prophesied we should become huntsmen when the world was turned topsy-turvy? We are become so now without waiting for that.

GOETZ. 'T is all the same, we are pushed out of our sphere.

GEORGE. These are wonderful times! For eight days a dreadful comet has been seen — all Germany fears that it portends the death of the Emperor, who is very ill.

GOETZ. Very ill! Then our career draws to a close.

LERSE. And in the neighborhood there are terrible commotions; the peasants have made a formidable insurrection.

GOETZ. Where?

LERSE. In the heart of Swabia; they are plundering, burning, and slaying. I fear they will sack the whole country.

GEORGE. It is a horrible warfare! They have already risen in a hundred places, and daily increase in number. A hurricane, too, has lately torn up whole forests; and in the place where the insurrection began, two fiery swords have been seen in the sky crossing each other.

GOETZ. Then some of my poor friends and neighbors, no doubt, suffer innocently.

GEORGE. Alas! that we are pent up thus!

ACT V

SCENE I. *A village plundered by the insurgent peasantry. Shrieks and tumult. Women, old men, and children fly across the stage.*

OLD MAN. Away! Away! Let us fly from the murdering dogs.

WOMAN. Sacred Heaven! How blood-red is the sky! How blood-red the setting sun!

ANOTHER. That must be fire.

A THIRD. My husband! My husband!

OLD MAN. Away! Away! To the wood!
[*Exeunt.*]

[*Enter* LINK *and Insurgents.*]

LINK. Whoever opposes you, down with him! The village is ours. Let none of the booty be injured, none be left behind. Plunder clean and quickly. We must soon set fire —

[*Enter* METZLER, *coming down the hill.*]

METZLER. How do things go with you, Link?

LINK. Merrily enough, as you see; you are just in time for the fun. — Whence come you?

METZLER. From Weinsberg. There was a jubilee. •

LINK. How so?

METZLER. We stabbed them all, in such heaps, it was a joy to see it!

LINK. All whom?

METZLER. Dietrich von Weiler led up the dance. The fool! We were all raging round the church steeple. He looked out and wished to treat with us. — Baf! A ball through his head! Up we rushed like a tempest, and the fellow soon made his exit by the window.

LINK. Huzza!

METZLER [to the Peasants]. Ye dogs, must I find you legs? How they gape and loiter, the asses!

LINK. Set fire! Let them roast in the flames! Forward! Push on, ye dolts.

METZLER. Then we brought out Helfenstein, Eltershofen, thirteen of the nobility — eighty in all. They were led out on the plain before Heilbronn. What a shouting and jubilee among our lads as the long row of miserable sinners passed by. They stared at each other, and, heaven and earth! We surrounded them before they were aware, and then dispatched them all with our pikes.

LINK. Why was I not there?

METZLER. Never in all my life did I see such fun.

LINK. On! On! Bring all out!

PEASANT. All's clear.

LINK. Then fire the village at the four corners.

METZLER. 'T will make a fine bonfire! Hadst thou but seen how the fellows tumbled over one another, and croaked like frogs! It warmed my heart like a cup of brandy. One Rexinger was there, a fellow, with a white plume, and flaxen locks, who, when he went out hunting, used to drive us before him like dogs, and with dogs. I had not caught sight of him all the while, when suddenly his fool's visage looked me full in the face. Push! went the spear between his ribs, and there he lay stretched on all-fours above his companions. The fellows lay kicking in a heap like the hares that used to be driven together at their grand hunting-parties.

LINK. It smokes finely already!

METZLER. Yonder it burns! Come, let us with the booty to the main body.

LINK. Where do they halt?

METZLER. Between this and Heilbronn. They wish to choose a captain whom every one will respect, for we are after all only their equals; they feel this, and turn restive.

LINK. Whom do they propose?

METZLER. Maximilian Stumf, or Goetz von Berlichingen.

LINK. That would be well. 'T would give the thing credit should Goetz accept it. He has ever been held a worthy independent knight. Away, away! We march toward Heilbronn! Pass the word.

METZLER. The fire will light us a good part of the way. Hast thou seen the great comet?

LINK. Yes, it is a dreadful ghastly sign! As we march by night we can see it well. It rises about one o'clock.

METZLER. And is visible but for an hour and a quarter, like an arm brandishing a sword, and bloody red!

LINK. Didst thou mark the three stars at the sword's hilt and point?

METZLER. And the broad haze-colored stripe illuminated by a thousand streamers like lances, and between them little swords.

LINK. I shuddered with horror. The sky was pale red streaked with ruddy flames, and among them grisly figures with shaggy hair and beards.

METZLER. Did you see them too? And how they all swam about as though in a sea of blood, and struggled in confusion, enough to turn one's brain.

LINK. Away! Away!   [Exeunt.]

SCENE II. Open country. In the distance two villages and an abbey are burning.

[KOHL, WILD, MAXIMILIAN STUMF, Insurgents.]

STUMF. You cannot ask me to be your leader; it were bad for you and for me: I am a vassal of the Palsgrave, and how shall I make war against my liege lord? Besides, you would always suspect I did not act from my heart.

KOHL. We knew well thou wouldst make some excuse.

[*Enter* GEORGE, LERSE, *and* GOETZ.]

GOETZ. What would you with me?

KOHL. You must be our captain.

GOETZ. How can I break my knightly word to the Emperor. I am under the ban: I cannot quit my territory.

WILD. That's no excuse.

GOETZ. And were I free, and you wanted to deal with the lords and nobles as you did at Weinsberg, laying waste the country round with fire and sword, and should wish me to be an abettor of your shameless, barbarous doings, rather than be your captain, you should slay me like a mad dog!

KOHL. What has been done cannot be undone.

STUMF. That was just the misfortune, that they had no leader whom they honored, and who could bridle their fury. I beseech thee, Goetz, accept the office! The princes will be grateful; all Germany will thank thee. It will be for the weal and prosperity of all. The country and its inhabitants will be preserved.

GOETZ. Why dost not thou accept it?

STUMF. I have given them reasons for my refusal.

KOHL. We have no time to waste in useless speeches. Once for all! Goetz, be our chief, or look to thy castle and thy head! Take two hours to consider it. Guard him!

GOETZ. To what purpose? I am as resolved now as I shall ever be. Why have ye risen up in arms? If to recover your rights and freedom, why do you plunder and lay waste the land? Will you abstain from such evil doings, and act as true men who know what they want? Then will I be your chief for eight days, and help you in your lawful and orderly demands.

WILD. What has been done was done in the first heat, and thy interference is not needed to prevent it for the future.

KOHL. Thou must engage with us at least for a quarter of a year.

STUMF. Say four weeks, that will satisfy both parties.

GOETZ. Then be it so.

KOHL. Your hand!

GOETZ. But you must promise to send the treaty you have made with me in writing to all your troops, and to punish severely those who infringe it.

WILD. Well, it shall be done.

GOETZ. Then I bind myself to you for four weeks.

STUMF. Good fortune to you! In whatever thou doest, spare our noble lord the Palsgrave.

KOHL [*aside*]. See that none speak to him without our knowledge.

GOETZ. Lerse, go to my wife. Protect her; you shall soon have news of me.

[*Exeunt* GOETZ, STUMF, GEORGE, LERSE, *and some Peasants.*]

[*Enter* METZLER, LINK, *and their followers.*]

METZLER. Who talks of a treaty? What's the use of a treaty?

LINK. It is shameful to make any such bargain.

KOHL. We know as well what we want as you; and we may do or let alone what we please.

WILD. This raging, and burning, and murdering must have an end some day or other; and by renouncing it just now, we gain a brave leader.

METZLER. How? An end? Thou traitor! Why are we here but to avenge ourselves on our enemies, and enrich ourselves at their expense? Some prince's slave has been tampering with thee.

KOHL. Come, Wild, he is like a brute-beast. [*Exeunt* WILD *and* KOHL.]

METZLER. Aye, go your way, no band will stick by you. The villains! Link, we'll set on the others to burn Miltenberg yonder; and if they begin a quarrel about the treaty, we'll cut off the heads of those that made it.

LINK. We have still the greater body of peasants on our side.

[*Exeunt with Insurgents.*]

SCENE III. *A hill and prospect of the country. In the flat scene a mill. A body of horsemen.*

[WEISLINGEN *comes out of the mill, followed by* FRANCIS *and a Courier.*]

WEISLINGEN. My horse! Have you announced it to the other nobles?

COURIER. At least seven standards will meet you in the wood behind Miltenberg. The peasants are marching in that direction. Couriers are dispatched on all sides; the entire confederacy will soon be assembled. Our plan cannot fail; and they say there is dissension among them.

WEISLINGEN. So much the better. Francis!

FRANCIS. Gracious sir!

WEISLINGEN. Discharge thine errand punctually. I bind it upon thy soul. Give her the letter. She shall from the court to my castle instantly. Thou must see her depart, and bring me notice of it.

FRANCIS. Your commands shall be obeyed.

WEISLINGEN. Tell her she *shall* go. [*To the Courier.*] Lead us by the nearest and best road.

COURIER. We must go round; all the rivers are swollen with the late heavy rains.

SCENE IV. *Jaxthausen.*

[ELIZABETH *and* LERSE.]

LERSE. Gracious lady, be comforted!

ELIZABETH. Alas! Lerse, the tears stood in his eyes when he took leave of me. It is dreadful, dreadful!

LERSE. He will return.

ELIZABETH. It is not that. When he went forth to gain honorable victories, never did grief sit heavy at my heart. I then rejoiced in the prospect of his return, which I now dread.

• LERSE. So noble a man.

ELIZABETH. Call him not so. There lies the new misery. The miscreants! They threatened to murder his family and burn his castle. Should he return, gloomy, most gloomy shall I see his brow. His enemies will forge scandalous accusations against him, which he will be unable to refute.

LERSE. He will and can.

ELIZABETH. He has broken his parole: — canst thou deny that?

LERSE. No! He was constrained. What reason is there to condemn him?

ELIZABETH. Malice seeks not reasons, but pretexts. He has become an ally of rebels, malefactors, and murderers: — he has become their chief. Say No to that.

LERSE. Cease to torment yourself and me. Have they not solemnly sworn to abjure all such doings as those at Weinsberg? Did I not myself hear them say, in remorse, that, had not that been done already, it never should have been done? Must not the princes and nobles return him their best thanks for having undertaken the dangerous office of leading these unruly people, in order to restrain their rage, and to save so many lives and possessions?

ELIZABETH. Thou art an affectionate advocate. Should they take him prisoner, deal with him as with a rebel, and bring his gray hairs — Lerse, I should go mad!

LERSE. Send sleep to refresh her body, dear Father of mankind, if Thou deniest comfort to her soul!

ELIZABETH. George has promised to bring news, but he will not be allowed to do so. They are worse than prisoners. Well I know they are watched like enemies. — The gallant boy! He would not leave his master.

LERSE. The very heart within me bled as I left him. — Had you not needed my help, all the terrors of grisly death should not have separated us.

ELIZABETH. I know not where Sickingen is. — Could I but send a message to Maria!

LERSE. Write, then: — I will take care that she receives it.   [*Exit.*]

SCENE V. *A village.*

[*Enter* GOETZ *and* GEORGE.]

GOETZ. To horse, George! Quick! I see Miltenberg in flames. Is it thus they keep the treaty? — Ride to them, tell them my purpose. — The murderous incendiaries — I renounce them. Let them make a thieving gypsy their captain, not me! — Quick, George! [*Exit* GEORGE.] Would that I were a thousand miles hence, at the bottom of the deepest dungeon in Turkey! — Could I but come off with honor from them! I have thwarted them every day, and told them the bitterest truths, in the hope they might weary of me and let me go.

[*Enter an Unknown.*]

UNKNOWN. God save you, gallant sir!
GOETZ. I thank you! What is your errand? Your name?
UNKNOWN. My name does not concern my business. I come to tell you that your life is in danger. The insurgent leaders are weary of hearing from you such harsh language, and are resolved to rid themselves of you. Speak them fair, or endeavor to escape from them; and God be with you!
[*Exit.*]
GOETZ. To quit life in this fashion, Goetz, to end thus? But be it so. My death will be the clearest proof to the world that I have had nothing in common with the miscreants.

[*Enter Insurgents.*]

FIRST INSURGENT. Captain, they are prisoners, they are slain!
GOETZ. Who?
SECOND INSURGENT. Those who burned Miltenberg; a troop of confederate cavalry suddenly charged upon them from behind the hill.
GOETZ. They have their reward. Oh, George! George! They have taken him prisoner with the caitiffs. My George! My George!

[*Enter Insurgents in confusion.*]

LINK. Up, Sir Captain, up! — There is no time to lose. The enemy is at hand, and in force.
GOETZ. Who burned Miltenberg?
METZLER. If you mean to pick a quarrel, we'll soon show you how we'll end it.
KOHL. Look to your own safety and ours. Up!
GOETZ [*to* METZLER]. Darest thou threaten me, thou scoundrel. — Thinkest thou to awe me, because thy garments are stained with the Count of Helfenstein's blood?

METZLER. Berlichingen!
GOETZ. Thou mayest call me by my name, and my children will not be ashamed to hear it.
METZLER. Out upon thee, coward! — Prince's slave!
[GOETZ *strikes him down. The others interpose.*]
KOHL. Ye are mad! — The enemy are breaking in on all sides, and you quarrel!
LINK. Away! Away!
[*Cries and tumult — The Insurgents fly across the stage.*]

[*Enter* WEISLINGEN *and Troopers.*]

WEISLINGEN. Pursue! Pursue! They fly! — Stop neither for darkness nor rain. — I hear Goetz is among them; look that he escape you not. Our friends say he is sorely wounded. [*Exeunt Troopers.*] And when I have caught thee — it will be merciful secretly to execute the sentence of death in prison. Thus he perishes from the memory of man, and then, foolish heart, thou mayst beat more freely.

SCENE VI. *The front of a gypsy-hut in a wild forest. Night. A fire before the hut, at which are seated the Mother of the Gypsies and a girl.*

MOTHER. Throw some fresh straw upon the thatch, daughter. There'll be heavy rain again to-night.

[*Enter a Gypsy Boy.*]

BOY. A dormouse, mother! And look! — two field-mice!
MOTHER. I'll skin them and roast them for thee, and thou shalt have a cap of their skins. Thou bleedest!
BOY. Dormouse bit me.
MOTHER. Fetch some dead wood, that the fire may burn bright when thy father comes; he will be wet through and through.

[*Another Gypsy Woman with a child at her back.*]

FIRST WOMAN. Hast thou had good luck?
SECOND WOMAN. Ill enough. The whole country is in an uproar; one's life is not

safe a moment. Two villages are in a blaze.

FIRST WOMAN. Is it fire that glares so yonder? I have been watching it long. One is so accustomed now to fiery signs in the heavens.

[*The Captain of the Gypsies enters with three of his gang.*]

CAPTAIN. Heard ye the wild huntsman?

FIRST WOMAN. He is passing over us now.

CAPTAIN. How the hounds give tongue! Wow! Wow!

SECOND MAN. How the whips crack!

THIRD MAN. And the huntsmen cheer them — Hallo — ho!

MOTHER. 'T is the Devil's chase.

CAPTAIN. We have been fishing in troubled waters. The peasants rob each other; there's no harm in our helping them.

SECOND WOMAN. What hast thou got, Wolf?

WOLF. A hare and a capon, a spit, a bundle of linen, three spoons, and a bridle.

STICKS. I have a blanket and a pair of boots, also a flint and tinder-box.

MOTHER. All wet as mire; I'll dry them; give them here! [*Trampling without.*]

CAPTAIN. Hark! — A horse! Go see who it is.

[*Enter GOETZ on horseback.*]

GOETZ. I thank thee, God! I see fire — they are gypsies. — My wounds bleed sorely — my foes are close behind me! — Great God, this is a fearful end!

CAPTAIN. Is it in peace thou comest?

GOETZ. I crave help from you. My wounds exhaust me — assist me to dismount!

CAPTAIN. Help him! — A gallant warrior in look and speech.

WOLF [*aside*]. 'T is Goetz von Berlichingen!

CAPTAIN. Welcome! Welcome! — All that we have is yours.

GOETZ. Thanks, thanks!

CAPTAIN. Come to my hut!

[*Exeunt to the hut.*]

SCENE VII. *Inside the hut.*

[*Captain, Gypsies, and* GOETZ.]

CAPTAIN. Call our Mother — tell her to bring bloodwort and bandages. [GOETZ *unarms himself.*] Here is my holiday doublet.

GOETZ. God reward you!

[*The Mother binds his wounds.*]

CAPTAIN. I rejoice that you are come.

GOETZ. Do you know me?

CAPTAIN. Who does not know you, Goetz? Our lives and heart's blood are yours.

[*Enter STICKS.*]

STICKS. Horsemen are coming through the wood. They are confederates.

CAPTAIN. Your pursuers! They shall not harm you. Away, Sticks, call the others: we know the passes better than they. We shall shoot them ere they are aware of us.

[*Exeunt Captain and Men Gypsies with their guns.*]

GOETZ [*alone*]. O Emperor! Emperor! Robbers protect thy children. [*A sharp firing.*] The wild foresters! Steady and true!

[*Enter Women.*]

WOMEN. Flee, flee! The enemy has overpowered us.

GOETZ. Where is my horse?

WOMEN. Here!

GOETZ [*girds on his sword and mounts without his armor*]. For the last time shall you feel my arm. I am not so weak yet.

[*Exit. — Tumult.*]

WOMEN. He gallops to join our party.

[*Firing.*]

[*Enter WOLF.*]

WOLF. Away! Away! All is lost. — The Captain is shot! — Goetz a prisoner!

[*The Women scream and fly into the wood.*]

SCENE VIII. *Adelaide's bedchamber.*

[*Enter ADELAIDE with a letter.*]

ADELAIDE. He or I! The tyrant — to threaten me! We will anticipate him. Who glides through the antechamber? [*A low knock at the door.*] Who is there?

FRANCIS [*in a low voice*]. Open, gracious lady!

ADELAIDE. Francis! He well deserves that I should admit him. [*Opens the door.*]

FRANCIS [*throws himself on her neck*]. My dear, my gracious lady!

ADELAIDE. What audacity! If any one should hear you?

FRANCIS. Oh — all — all are asleep.

ADELAIDE. What wouldst thou?

FRANCIS. I cannot rest. The threats of my master, — your fate, — my heart.

ADELAIDE. He was incensed against me when you parted from him?

FRANCIS. He was as I have never seen him. — "To my castle," said he, "she must — she *shall* go."

ADELAIDE. And shall we obey?

FRANCIS. I know not, dear lady!

ADELAIDE. Thou foolish, infatuated boy! Thou dost not see where this will end? Here he knows I am in safety. He has long had designs on my freedom, and therefore wishes to get me to his castle — there he will have power to use me as his hate shall dictate.

FRANCIS. He shall not!

ADELAIDE. Wilt thou prevent him?

FRANCIS. He shall not!

ADELAIDE. I foresee the whole misery of my fate. He will tear me forcibly from his castle to immure me in a cloister.

FRANCIS. Hell and damnation!

ADELAIDE. Wilt thou rescue me?

FRANCIS. Anything! Everything!

ADELAIDE [*throws herself weeping upon his neck*]. Francis! Oh save me!

FRANCIS. He shall fall. I will plant my foot upon his neck.

ADELAIDE. No violence! You shall carry a submissive letter to him announcing obedience — then give him this vial in his wine.

FRANCIS. Give it me! Thou shalt be free!

ADELAIDE. Free! — And then no more shalt thou need to come to my chamber trembling and in fear. No more shall I need anxiously to say, "Away, Francis! the morning dawns."

SCENE IX. *Street before the prison at Heilbronn.*

[ELIZABETH *and* LERSE.]

LERSE. Heaven relieve your distress, gracious lady! Maria is come.

ELIZABETH. God be praised! Lerse, we have sunk into dreadful misery. My worst forebodings are realized! A prisoner — thrown as an assassin and malefactor into the deepest dungeon.

LERSE. I know all.

ELIZABETH. Thou knowest nothing. Our distress is too — too great! His age, his wounds, a slow fever — and, more than all, the despondency of his mind, to think that this should be his end.

LERSE. Aye, and that Weislingen should be commissioner!

ELIZABETH. Weislingen?

LERSE. They have acted with unheard-of severity. Metzler has been burned alive — hundreds of his associates broken upon the wheel, beheaded, quartered, and impaled. All the country round looks like a slaughterhouse, where human flesh is cheap.

ELIZABETH. Weislingen commissioner! O Heaven! A ray of hope! Maria shall go to him: he cannot refuse her. He had ever a compassionate heart, and when he sees her whom he once loved so much, whom he has made so miserable — Where is she?

LERSE. Still at the inn.

ELIZABETH. Take me to her. She must away instantly. I fear the worst.

[*Exeunt.*]

SCENE X. *An apartment in Weislingen's castle.*

[WEISLINGEN, *alone.*]

WEISLINGEN. I am so ill, so weak — all my bones are hollow — this wretched fever has consumed their very marrow. No rest, no sleep, by day or night! And when I slumber, such fearful dreams! Last night methought I met Goetz in the forest. He drew his sword, and defied me to combat. I grasped mine, but my hand failed me. He darted on me a look of contempt, sheathed his weapon, and passed on. He is a prisoner; yet I tremble to think of him.

Miserable man! Thine own voice has condemned him, yet thou tremblest like a malefactor at his very shadow. And shall he die? Goetz! Goetz! We mortals are not our own masters. Fiends have empire over us, and shape our actions after their own hellish will, to goad us to perdition. [*Sits down.*] Weak! Weak! Why are my nails so blue? A cold, clammy, wasting sweat drenches every limb. Everything swims before my eyes. Could I but sleep! Alas!

[*Enter* MARIA.]

WEISLINGEN. Mother of God! Leave me in peace — leave me in peace! This specter was yet wanting. Maria is dead, and she appears to the traitor. Leave me, blessed spirit! I am wretched enough.

MARIA. Weislingen, I am no spirit. I am Maria.

WEISLINGEN. It is her voice!

MARIA. I came to beg my brother's life of thee. He is guiltless, however culpable he may appear.

WEISLINGEN. Hush! Maria — Angel of heaven as thou art, thou bringest with thee the torments of hell! Speak no more!

MARIA. And must my brother die? Weislingen, it is horrible that I should have to tell thee he is guiltless; that I should be compelled to come as a suppliant to restrain thee from a most fearful murder. Thy soul to its inmost depths is possessed by evil powers. Can this be Adelbert?

WEISLINGEN. Thou seest — the consuming breath of the grave hath swept over me — my strength sinks in death — I die in misery, and thou comest to drive me to despair — Could I but tell thee all, thy bitterest hate would melt to sorrow and compassion. O Maria! Maria!

MARIA. Weislingen, my brother is pining in a dungeon — the anguish of his wounds — his age — oh, hadst thou the heart to bring his gray hairs — Weislingen, we should despair.

WEISLINGEN. Enough! —

[*Rings a hand-bell.*]

[*Enter* FRANCIS, *in great agitation.*]

FRANCIS. Gracious sir.

WEISLINGEN. Those papers, Francis.

[*He gives them.* WEISLINGEN *tears open a packet and shows* MARIA *a paper.*] Here is thy brother's death-warrant signed!

MARIA. God in heaven!

WEISLINGEN. And thus I tear it. He shall live! But can I restore what I have destroyed? Weep not so, Francis! Dear youth, my wretchedness lies deeply at thy heart.

[FRANCIS *throws himself at his feet, and clasps his knees.*]

MARIA [*apart*]. He is ill — very ill. The sight of him rends my heart. I loved him! And now that I again approach him, I feel how dearly —

WEISLINGEN. Francis, arise and cease to weep — I may recover! While there is life, there is hope.

FRANCIS. You cannot! You must die!

WEISLINGEN. Must?

FRANCIS [*beside himself*]. Poison! poison! — from your wife! I — I gave it.

[*Rushes out.*]

WEISLINGEN. Follow him, Maria — he is desperate. [*Exit* MARIA.] Poison from my wife! Alas! Alas! I feel it. Torture and death!

MARIA [*within*]. Help! help!

WEISLINGEN [*attempts in vain to rise*]. God! I cannot.

MARIA [*returning*]. He is gone! He threw himself desperately from a window of the hall into the river.

WEISLINGEN. It is well with him! — Thy brother is out of danger! The other commissioners, especially Seckendorf, are his friends. They will readily allow him to ward himself upon his knightly word. Farewell, Maria! Now, go.

MARIA. I will stay with thee — thou poor forsaken one!

WEISLINGEN. Poor and forsaken, indeed! O God, Thou art a terrible avenger! My wife!

MARIA. Remove from thee that thought. Turn thy soul to the Throne of Mercy.

WEISLINGEN. Go, thou gentle spirit! Leave me to my misery! Horrible! Even thy presence, Maria, even the attendance of my only comforter, is agony.

MARIA [*aside*]. Strengthen me, Heaven! My soul droops with his.

WEISLINGEN. Alas! Alas! Poison from my wife! My Francis seduced by the wretch! She waits — listens to every horse's hoof for the messenger who brings her the news of my death. And thou, too, Maria, wherefore art thou come to awaken every slumbering recollection of my sins? Leave me, leave me that I may die!

MARIA. Let me stay! Thou art alone: think I am thy nurse. Forget all. May God forgive thee as freely as I do!

WEISLINGEN. Thou spirit of love! Pray for me! Pray for me! My heart is seared.

MARIA. There is forgiveness for thee. — Thou art exhausted.

WEISLINGEN. I die! I die! And yet I cannot die. In the fearful contest between life and death lie the torments of hell.

MARIA. Heavenly Father, have compassion upon him. Grant him but one token of Thy love, that his heart may be opened to comfort, and his soul to the hope of eternal life, even in the agony of death!

SCENE XI. *A narrow vault dimly illuminated.*

[*The Judges of the Secret Tribunal discovered seated, all muffled in black cloaks.*]

ELDEST JUDGE. Judges of the Secret Tribunal, sworn by the cord and the steel to be inflexible in justice, to judge in secret, and to avenge in secret, like the Deity! Are your hands clean and your hearts pure? Raise them to heaven, and cry, — Woe upon evil-doers!

ALL. Woe! Woe!

ELDEST JUDGE. Crier, begin the diet of judgment.

CRIER. I cry, I cry for accusation against evil-doers! He whose heart is pure, whose hands are clean to swear by the cord and the steel, let him lift up his voice and call upon the steel and the cord for Vengeance! Vengeance! Vengeance!

ACCUSER [*comes forward*]. My heart is pure from misdeed, and my hands are clean from innocent blood: God pardon my sins of thought, and prevent their execution. I raise my hand on high, and cry for Vengeance! Vengeance! Vengeance!

ELDEST JUDGE. Vengeance upon whom?

ACCUSER. I call upon the cord and the steel for vengeance against Adelaide of Weislingen. She has committed adultery and murder. She has poisoned her husband by the hands of her servant — the servant hath slain himself — the husband is dead.

ELDEST JUDGE. Dost thou swear by the God of truth, that thy accusation is true?

ACCUSER. I swear!

ELDEST JUDGE. Dost thou invoke upon thine own head the punishment of murder and adultery, should thy accusation be found false?

ACCUSER. On my head be it.

ELDEST JUDGE. Your voices?

[*They converse a few minutes in whispers.*]

ACCUSER. Judges of the Secret Tribunal, what is your sentence upon Adelaide of Weislingen, accused of murder and adultery?

ELDEST JUDGE. She shall die! — She shall die a bitter and twofold death! By the double doom of the steel and the cord shall she expiate the double crime. Raise your hands to heaven and cry, Woe, woe upon her! Be she delivered into the hands of the avenger.

ALL. Woe! Woe!

ELDEST JUDGE. Woe! Avenger, come forth. [*A man advances.*] Here, take thou the cord and the steel! Within eight days shalt thou blot her out from before the face of Heaven: wheresoever thou findest her, down with her into the dust. Judges, ye that judge in secret and avenge in secret like the Deity, keep your hearts from wickedness, and your hands from innocent blood!

SCENE XII. *The court of an inn.*

[LERSE *and* MARIA.]

MARIA. The horses have rested long enough; we will away, Lerse.

LERSE. Stay till to-morrow; this is a dreadful night.

MARIA. Lerse, I cannot rest till I have seen my brother. Let us away: the weather is clearing up — we may expect a fair morning.

LERSE. Be it as you will.

SCENE XIII. *The prison at Heilbronn.*

[GOETZ *and* ELIZABETH.]

ELIZABETH. I entreat thee, dear husband, speak to me. Thy silence alarms me; thy spirit consumes thee, pent up within thy breast. Come, let me see thy wounds; they mend daily. In this desponding melancholy I know thee no longer!

GOETZ. Seekest thou Goetz? He is long since gone! Piece by piece have they robbed me of all I held dear — my hand, my property, my freedom, my good name! My life! Of what value is it to me? What news of George? Is Lerse gone to seek him?

ELIZABETH. He is, my love! Be of good cheer; things may yet take a favorable turn.

GOETZ. He whom God hath stricken lifts himself up no more! I best know the load I have to bear. — To misfortune I am inured. — But now it is not Weislingen alone, not the peasants alone, not the death of the Emperor, nor my wounds — it is the whole united — My hour is come! I had hoped it should have been like my life. But his will be done!

ELIZABETH. Wilt thou not eat something?

GOETZ. Nothing, my love! See how the sun shines yonder!

ELIZABETH. It is a fine spring day!

GOETZ. My love, wilt thou ask the keeper's permission for me to walk in his little garden for half an hour, that I may look upon the clear face of heaven, the pure air, and the blessed sun?

ELIZABETH. I will — and he will readily grant it.

SCENE XIV. *The prison garden.*

[LERSE *and* MARIA.]

MARIA. Go in, and see how it stands with them. [*Exit* LERSE.]

[*Enter* ELIZABETH *and Keeper.*]

ELIZABETH [*to the Keeper*]. God reward your kindness and attention to my husband! [*Exit Keeper.*] — Maria, how hast thou sped?

MARIA. My brother is safe! But my heart is torn asunder. Weislingen is dead — poisoned by his wife. My husband is in danger — the princes are becoming too powerful for him: they say he is surrounded and besieged.

ELIZABETH. Believe not the rumor; and let not Goetz hear it.

MARIA. How is it with him?

ELIZABETH. I feared he would not survive till thy return: the hand of the Lord is heavy on him. And George is dead!

MARIA. George! The gallant boy!

ELIZABETH. When the miscreants were burning Miltenberg, his master sent him to check their villainy. A body of cavalry charged upon them. Had they all behaved as George, they must all have had as clear a conscience. Many were killed, and George among them; he died the death of a warrior.

MARIA. Does Goetz know it?

ELIZABETH. We conceal it from him. He questions me ten times a day concerning him, and sends me as often to see what is become of him. I fear to give his heart this last wound.

MARIA. O God! What are the hopes of this world?

[*Enter* GOETZ, LERSE, *and Keeper.*]

GOETZ. Almighty God! How lovely it is beneath Thy heaven! How free! The trees put forth their buds, and all the world awakes to hope — Farewell, my children! My roots are cut away, my strength totters to the grave.

ELIZABETH. Shall I not send Lerse to the convent for thy son, that thou may'st once more see and bless him?

GOETZ. Let him be; he needs not my blessing, he is holier than I. — Upon our wedding-day, Elizabeth, could I have thought I should die thus! — My old father blessed us, and prayed for a succession of noble and gallant sons. — God, Thou hast not heard him. I am the last — Lerse, thy countenance cheers me in the hour of death, more than in our most daring fights: then, my spirit encouraged all of you; now, thine supports me — Oh, that I could but once more see George, and sun myself in his look! You turn away and weep. He is dead? George is dead? Then, die, Goetz! Thou hast outlived thyself, outlived the noblest of thy servants — How died he? Alas! they took him among the incendiaries, and he has been executed?

ELIZABETH. No! He was slain at Miltenberg, while fighting like a lion for his freedom.

GOETZ. God be praised! He was the kindest youth under the sun, and one of the bravest — Now, release my soul. My poor wife! I leave thee in a wicked world. Lerse, forsake her not! Lock your hearts more carefully than your doors. The age of fraud is at hand; treachery will reign unchecked. The worthless will gain the ascendancy by cunning, and the noble will fall into their net. Maria, may God restore thy husband to thee! May he not fall the deeper for having risen so high! Selbitz is dead, and the good Emperor, and my George — Give me a draught of water! — Heavenly air! Freedom! Freedom! [He dies.]

ELIZABETH. Freedom is above — above — with thee! The world is a prison-house.

MARIA. Noble man! Woe to this age that rejected thee!

LERSE. And woe to the future, that shall misjudge thee!

WILLIAM TELL

By SCHILLER

Translated into English verse by SIR THEODORE MARTIN

CHARACTERS

HERMANN GESSLER, *the Governor of Schwytz and Uri*

WERNER, *Baron of Attinghausen, free noble of Switzerland*

ULRICH VON RUDENZ, *his nephew*

WERNER STAUFFACHER,
CONRAD HUNN,
HANS AUF DER MAUER,
JORG IM HOFE,   } *people of Schwytz*
ULRICH DER SCHMIDT,
JOST VON WEILER,
ITEL REDING,

WALTER FÜRST,
WILLIAM TELL,
RÖSSELMANN, *the Priest*,
PETERMANN, *Sacristan*,   } *of Uri*
KUONI, *herdsman*,
WERNI, *huntsman*,
RUODI, *fisherman*,

ARNOLD OF MELCHTHAL,
CONRAD BAUMGARTEN,
MEYER VON SARNEN,
STRUTH VON WINKELRIED,   } *of Unterwald*
KLAUS VON DER FLUE,
BURKHART AM BUHEL,
ARNOLD VON SEWA,

PFEIFFER OF LUCERNE

KUNZ OF GERSAU

JENNI, *fisherman's son*

SEPPI, *herdsman's son*

GERTRUDE, *Stauffacher's wife*

HEDWIG, *wife of Tell, daughter of Fürst*

BERTHA OF BRUNECK, *a rich heiress*

ARMGART,
MECHTHILD, } *peasant women*
ELSBETH,

HILDEGARD

WALTER,
} *Tell's sons*
WILLIAM,

FRIESSHARDT,
} *soldiers*
LEUTHOLD,

RUDOLPH DER HARRAS, *Gessler's master of the horse*

JOHANNES PARRICIDA, *Duke of Swabia*

STUSSI, *Overseer*

THE MAYOR OF URI

A Courier

Master Stonemason, Companions, and Workmen

Taskmaster

A Crier

Monks of the Order of Charity

Horsemen of GESSLER *and* LANDENBERG

Many Peasants — Men and Women from the Waldstetten

WILLIAM TELL

ACT I

SCENE I: *A high rocky shore of the Lake of Lucerne opposite Schwytz. The lake makes a bend into the land; a hut stands at a short distance from the shore; the fisher boy is rowing about in his boat. Beyond the lake are seen the green meadows, the hamlets and farms of Schwytz, lying in the clear sunshine. On the left are observed the peaks of The Hacken, surrounded with clouds; to the right, and in the remote distance, appear the glaciers. The Ranz des Vaches, and the tinkling of cattle bells, continue for some time after the rising of the curtain.*

[*Enter Fisher Boy, singing in his boat.*]

Melody of the Ranz des Vaches

The smile-dimpled lake wooed to bathe in its
   deep,
A boy on its green shore had laid him to sleep;
     Then heard he a melody
       Floating along,
     Sweet as the notes
       Of an angel's song.
And as thrilling with pleasure he wakes from
   his rest,
The waters are rippling over his breast;
     And a voice from the deep cries,
       "With me thou must go,
     I charm the young shepherd,
       I lure him below."

[*Herdsman, on the mountains.*]

Air. — Variation of the Ranz des Vaches

   Farewell, ye green meadows,
   Farewell, sunny shore,
   The herdsman must leave you,
     The summer is o'er.
We go to the hills, but you'll see us again,
   When the cuckoo calls, and the merry birds
     sing,
When the flowers bloom afresh in glade and
   in glen,
   And the brooks sparkle bright in the sun-
     shine of spring.

   Farewell, ye green meadows,
   Farewell, sunny shore,
   The herdsman must leave you,
   The summer is o'er.

[*Chamois-Hunter, appearing on the top of a cliff.*]

Second variation of the Ranz des Vaches

On the heights peals the thunder, and
   trembles the bridge,
The huntsman bounds on by the dizzying
   ridge.
     Undaunted he hies him
       O'er ice-covered wild,
     Where leaf never budded,
       Nor Spring ever smiled;
And beneath him an ocean of mist, where his
   eye
No longer the dwellings of man can espy;
     Through the parting clouds only
       The earth can be seen,
     Far down 'neath the vapor
       The meadows of green.

[*A change comes over the landscape. A rumbling, cracking noise is heard among the mountains. Shadows of clouds sweep across the scene.*]

[RUODI, *the fisherman, comes out of his cottage.* WERNI, *the huntsman, descends from the rocks.* KUONI, *the shepherd, enters, with a milk pail on his shoulders, followed by* SEPPI, *his assistant.*]

RUODI. Come, Jenni, bustle; get the
   boat on shore.
The grizzly Vale-King comes, the Glaciers
   moan,
The Mytenstein is drawing on his hood,
And from the Stormcleft chilly blows the
   wind;
The storm will burst, before we know
   what's what.
   KUONI. 'T will rain ere long; my sheep
   browse eagerly,

And Watcher there is scraping up the earth.

WERNI. The fish are leaping, and the water-hen
Keeps diving up and down. A storm is brewing.

KUONI [to his boy]. Look, Seppi, if the beasts be all in sight.

SEPPI. There goes brown Liesel, I can hear her bells.

KUONI. Then all are safe; she ever ranges farthest.

RUODI. You've a fine chime of bells there, master herdsman.

WERNI. And likely cattle, too. Are they your own?

KUONI. I'm not so rich. They are the noble lord's
Of Attinghaus, and told off to my care.

RUODI. How gracefully yon heifer bears her ribbon!

KUONI. Aye, well she knows she's leader of the herd,
And, take it from her, she'd refuse to feed.

RUODI. You're joking now. A beast devoid of reason —

WERNI. Easily said. But beasts have reason, too —
And that we know, we chamois-hunters, well.
They never turn to feed — sagacious creatures! —
Till they have placed a sentinel ahead,
Who pricks his ears whenever we approach,
And gives alarm with clear and piercing pipe.

RUODI [to the Shepherd]. Are you for home?

KUONI. The Alp is grazed quite bare.

WERNI. A safe return, my friend!

KUONI. The same to you!
Men come not always back from tracks like yours.

RUODI. But who comes here, running at topmost speed?

WERNI. I know the man; 't is Baumgart of Alzellen.

CONRAD BAUMGARTEN [rushing in breathless]. For God's sake, ferryman, your boat!

RUODI. How now?
Why all this haste?

BAUMGARTEN. Cast off! My life's at stake!
Set me across!

KUONI. Why, what's the matter, friend.

WERNI. Who are pursuing you? First tell us that.

BAUMGARTEN [to the Fisherman]. Quick, quick, man, quick! They're close upon my heels!
It is the Viceroy's men are after me;
If they should overtake me, I am lost.

RUODI. Why are the troopers in pursuit of you?

BAUMGARTEN. First make me safe and then I'll tell you all.

WERNI. There's blood upon your garments — how is this?

BAUMGARTEN. The Imperial Seneschal, who dwelt at Rossberg —

KUONI. How! What! The Wolfshot!
Is it he pursues you?

BAUMGARTEN. He'll ne'er hurt man again; I've settled him.

ALL [starting back]. Now, God forgive you! What is this you've done?

BAUMGARTEN. What every free man in my place had done.
Mine own good household right I have enforced
'Gainst him that would have wronged my wife — my honor.

KUONI. How! Wronged you in your honor, did he so?

BAUMGARTEN. That he did not fulfill his foul desire,
Is due to God and to my trusty axe.

WERNI. And you have cleft his skull, then, with your axe?

KUONI. Oh, tell us all! You've time enough, and more,
While he is getting out the boat there from the beach.

BAUMGARTEN. When I was in the forest felling timber,
My wife came running out in mortal fear.
"The Seneschal," she said, "was in my house,
Had ordered her to get a bath prepared,
And thereupon had ta'en unseemly freedoms,

From which she rid herself, and flew to me."
Armed as I was, I sought him, and my axe
Has given his bath a bloody benison.
WERNI. And you did well; no man can blame the deed.
KUONI. The tyrant! Now he has his just reward!
We men of Unterwald have owed it long.
BAUMGARTEN. The deed got wind, and now they're in pursuit.
Heavens! while we speak, the time is flying fast. [*It begins to thunder.*]
KUONI. Quick, ferryman, and set the good man over.
RUODI. Impossible! A storm is close at hand.
Wait till it pass! You must.
BAUMGARTEN. Almighty Heavens!
I cannot wait; the least delay is death.
KUONI [*to the Fisherman*]. Push out —
God with you! We should help our neighbors;
The like misfortune may betide us all.
[*Thunder and the roaring of the wind.*]
RUODI. The south wind's up! See how the lake is rising!
I cannot steer against both wind and wave.
BAUMGARTEN [*clasping him by the knees*].
God so help you as now you pity me!
WERNI. His life's at stake. Have pity on him, man!
KUONI. He is a father: has a wife and children.
[*Repeated peals of thunder.*]
RUODI. What! And have I not, then, a life to lose,
A wife and child at home as well as he?
See how the breakers foam, and toss, and whirl,
And the lake eddies up from all its depths!
Right gladly would I save the worthy man,
But 't is impossible, as you must see.
BAUMGARTEN [*still kneeling*]. Then must I fall into the tyrant's hands,
And with the shore of safety close in sight!
Yonder it lies! My eyes can see it clear,
My very voice can echo to its shores.
There is the boat to carry me across,
Yet must I lie here helpless and forlorn.
KUONI. Look! Who comes here?
RUODI. 'T is Tell, aye, Tell, of Bürglen.

[*Enter TELL with a crossbow.*]

TELL. What man is he that here implores for aid?
KUONI. He is from Alzellen, and to guard his honor
From touch of foulest shame, has slain the Wolfshot,
The Imperial Seneschal, who dwelt at Rossberg.
The Viceroy's troopers are upon his heels;
He begs the ferryman to take him over,
But frightened at the storm he says he won't.
RUODI. Well, there is Tell can steer as well as I.
He'll be my judge, if it be possible.
[*Violent peals of thunder — the lake becomes more tempestuous.*]
Am I to plunge into the jaws of hell?
I should be mad to dare the desperate act.
TELL. The brave man thinks upon himself the last.
Put trust in God, and help him in his need!
RUODI. Safe in the port, 't is easy to advise.
There is the boat, and there the lake! Try you!
TELL. The lake may pity, but the Viceroy never.
Come, risk it, man!
SHEPHERD AND HUNTSMAN. Oh, save him! Save him! Save him!
RUODI. Though 't were my brother, or my darling child,
I would not go. 'T is Simon and Jude's day,
The lake is up, and calling for its victim.
TELL. Naught's to be done with idle talking here.
Each moment's precious; the man must be helped;
Say, boatman, will you venture?
RUODI. No; not I.
TELL. In God's name, then, give me the boat! I will,
With my poor strength, see what is to be done!
KUONI. Ha, gallant Tell!
WERNI. That's like a huntsman true.
BAUMGARTEN. You are my angel, my preserver, Tell.

TELL. I may preserve you from the Viceroy's power,
But from the tempest's rage another must.
Yet better 't is you fall into God's hands,
Than into those of men. [*To the Herdsman.*] Herdsman, do thou
Console my wife if I should come to grief.
I could not choose but do as I have done.
[*He leaps into the boat.*]

KUONI [*to the Fisherman*]. A pretty man to keep a ferry, truly!
What Tell could risk, you dared not venture on.

RUODI. Far better men would never cope with Tell.
There's no two such as he 'mong all our hills.

WERNI [*who has ascended a rock*]. Now he is off. — God help thee, gallant sailor!
Look how the little boat reels on the waves!

KUONI [*on the shore*]. There! they have swept clean over it. And now
'T is out of sight. Yet, stay, there 't is again!
Stoutly he stems the breakers, noble fellow!

SEPPI. Here come the troopers hard as they can ride!

KUONI. Heavens! So they do! Why, that was help, indeed.

[*Enter a troop of Horsemen.*]

FIRST HORSEMAN. Give up the murderer! You have him here!

SECOND HORSEMAN. This way he came! 'T is useless to conceal him!

RUODI AND KUONI. Whom do you mean?

FIRST HORSEMAN [*discovering the boat*]. The devil! What do I see?

WERNI [*from above*]. Is 't he in yonder boat ye seek? Ride on;
If you lay to, you may o'ertake him yet.

SECOND HORSEMAN. Curse on you, he's escaped!

FIRST HORSEMAN [*to the Shepherd and Fisherman*]. You helped him off,
And you shall pay for it! — Fall on their herds!
Down with the cottage! Burn it! Beat it down! [*They rush off.*]

SEPPI [*hurrying after them*]. Oh, my poor lambs!

KUONI [*following him*]. Unhappy me, my herds!

WERNI. The tyrants!

RUODI [*wringing his hands*]. Righteous Heaven! Oh, when will come
Deliverance to this doom-devoted land?
[*Exeunt severally.*]

SCENE II: *A lime tree in front of* STAUFFACHER'S *house at Steinen, in Schwytz, upon the public road, near a bridge.*

[WERNER STAUFFACHER *and* PFEIFFER, *of Lucerne, enter into conversation.*]

PFEIFFER. Aye, aye, friend Stauffacher, as I have said,
Swear not to Austria, if you can help it.
Hold by the Empire stoutly as of yore,
And God preserve you in your ancient freedom!
[*Presses his hand warmly and is going.*]

STAUFFACHER. Wait till my mistress comes. Now, do! You are
My guest in Schwytz — I in Lucerne am yours.

PFEIFFER. Thanks! Thanks! But I must reach Gersau to-day.
Whatever grievances your rulers' pride
And grasping avarice may yet inflict,
Bear them in patience — soon a change may come.
Another Emperor may mount the throne.
But Austria's once, and you are hers forever. [*Exit.*]
[STAUFFACHER *sits down sorrowfully upon a bench under the lime tree.*]

[GERTRUDE, *his wife, enters, and finds him in this posture. She places herself near him, and looks at him for some time in silence.*]

GERTRUDE. So sad, my love! I scarcely know thee now.
For many a day in silence I have marked
A moody sorrow furrowing thy brow.
Some silent grief is weighing on thy heart.
Trust it to me. I am thy faithful wife,
And I demand my half of all thy cares.
[STAUFFACHER *gives her his hand and is silent.*]

Tell me what can oppress thy spirits thus?
Thy toil is blest — the world goes well with
thee —
Our barns are full — our cattle, many a
score;
Our handsome team of well-fed horses, too,
Brought from the mountain pastures
safely home,
To winter in their comfortable stalls.
There stands thy house — no nobleman's
more fair!
'T is newly built with timber of the best,
All grooved and fitted with the nicest skill;
Its many glistening windows tell of com-
fort!
'T is quartered o'er with scutcheons of all
hues,
And proverbs sage, which passing travelers
Linger to read, and ponder o'er their
meaning.

STAUFFACHER. The house is strongly
built, and handsomely,
But, ah, the ground on which we built it
quakes.

GERTRUDE. Tell me, dear Werner, what
you mean by that?

STAUFFACHER. No later gone than yes-
terday, I sat
Beneath this linden, thinking with delight
How fairly all was finished, when from
Küssnacht
The Viceroy and his men came riding by.
Before this house he halted in surprise:
At once I rose, and, as beseemed his rank,
Advanced respectfully to greet the lord,
To whom the Emperor delegates his power,
As judge supreme within our canton here.
"Who is the owner of this house?" he
asked,
With mischief in his thoughts, for well he
knew.
With prompt decision, thus I answered
him:
"The Emperor, your grace — my lord and
yours,
And held by me in fief." On this he
answered,
"I am the Emperor's viceregent here,
And will not that each peasant churl should
build
At his own pleasure, bearing him as freely
As though he were the master in the land.

I shall make bold to put a stop to this!"
So saying, he, with menaces, rode off,
And left me musing with a heavy heart
On the fell purpose that his words betrayed.

GERTRUDE. My own dear lord and hus-
band! Wilt thou take
A word of honest counsel from thy wife?
I boast to be the noble Iberg's child,
A man of wide experience. Many a time,
As we sat spinning in the winter nights,
My sisters and myself, the people's chiefs
Were wont to gather round our father's
hearth,
To read the old imperial charters, and
To hold sage converse on the country's
weal.
Then heedfully I listened, marking well
What now the wise man thought, the good
man wished,
And garnered up their wisdom in my heart.
Hear, then, and mark me well; for thou
wilt see,
I long have known the grief that weighs
thee down.
The Viceroy hates thee, fain would injure
thee,
For thou hast crossed his wish to bend the
Swiss
In homage to this upstart house of princes,
And kept them stanch, like their good sires
of old,
In true allegiance to the Empire. Say,
Is't not so, Werner? Tell me, am I wrong?

STAUFFACHER. 'T is even so. For this
doth Gessler hate me.

GERTRUDE. He burns with envy, too, to
see thee living
Happy and free on thine ancestral soil,
For he is landless. From the Emperor's
self
Thou hold'st in fief the lands thy fathers
left thee.
There's not a prince i' the Empire that can
show
A better title to his heritage;
For thou hast over thee no lord but one,
And he the mightiest of all Christian kings.
Gessler, we know, is but a younger son,
His only wealth the knightly cloak he
wears;
He therefore views an honest man's good
fortune

With a malignant and a jealous eye.
Long has he sworn to compass thy destruc-
tion.
As yet thou art uninjured. Wilt thou wait,
Till he may safely give his malice vent?
A wise man would anticipate the blow.
STAUFFACHER. What's to be done?
GERTRUDE. Now, hear what I advise.
Thou knowest well, how here with us in
Schwytz
All worthy men are groaning underneath
This Gessler's grasping, grinding tyranny.
Doubt not the men of Unterwald as well,
And Uri, too, are chafing like ourselves,
At this oppressive and heart-wearying
yoke.
For there, across the lake, the Landenberg
Wields the same iron rule as Gessler here —
No fishing-boat comes over to our side,
But brings the tidings of some new en-
croachment,
Some fresh outrage, more grievous than the
last.
Then it were well, that some of you — true
men —
Men sound at heart, should secretly devise
How best to shake this hateful thralldom
off.
Full sure I am that God would not desert
you,
But lend his favor to the righteous cause.
Hast thou no friend in Uri, one to whom
Thou frankly may'st unbosom all thy
thoughts?
STAUFFACHER. I know full many a gal-
lant fellow there,
And nobles, too, — great men, of high
repute,
In whom I can repose unbounded trust.
[*Rising.*] Wife! What a storm of wild and
perilous thoughts
Hast thou stirred up within my tranquil
breast!
The darkest musings of my bosom thou
Hast dragged to light, and placed them
full before me;
And what I scarce dared harbor e'en in
thought,
Thou speakest plainly out with fearless
tongue.
But hast thou weighed well what thou
urgest thus?

Discord will come, and the fierce clang of
arms,
To scare this valley's long-unbroken peace,
If we, a feeble shepherd race, shall dare
Him to the fight, that lords it o'er the
world.
Even now they only wait some fair pretext
For setting loose their savage warrior
hordes,
To scourge and ravage this devoted land,
To lord it o'er us with the victor's rights,
And, 'neath the show of lawful chastise-
ment,
Despoil us of our chartered liberties.
GERTRUDE. You, too, are men; can
wield a battle-axe
As well as they. God ne'er deserts the
brave.
STAUFFACHER. Oh, wife! A horrid, ruth-
less fiend is war,
That smites at once the shepherd and his
flock.
GERTRUDE. Whate'er great Heaven in-
flicts, we must endure;
But wrong is what no noble heart will bear.
STAUFFACHER. This house — thy pride
— war, unrelenting war
Will burn it down.
GERTRUDE. And did I think this heart
Enslaved and fettered to the things of
earth,
With my own hand I'd hurl the kindling
torch.
STAUFFACHER. Thou hast faith in hu-
man kindness, wife; but war
Spares not the tender infant in its cradle.
GERTRUDE. There is a Friend to inno-
cence in heaven.
Send your gaze forward, Werner, — not
behind.
STAUFFACHER. We men may die like
men, with sword in hand;
But oh, what fate, my Gertrude, may be
thine?
GERTRUDE. None are so weak, but one
last choice is left.
A spring from yonder bridge and I am free!
STAUFFACHER [*embracing her*]. Well may
he fight for hearth and home, that
clasps
A heart so rare as thine against his own!
What are the host of emperors to him?

Gertrude, farewell! I will to Uri straight.
There lives my worthy comrade, Walter
Fürst;
His thoughts and mine upon these times
are one.
There, too, resides the noble Banneret
Of Attinghaus. High though of blood he
be,
He loves the people, honors their old cus-
toms.
With both of these I will take counsel how
To rid us bravely of our country's foe.
Farewell! And while I am away, bear thou
A watchful eye in management at home.
The pilgrim journeying to the house of God,
And holy friar, collecting for his cloister,
To these give liberally from purse and
garner.
Stauffacher's house would not be hid.
Right out
Upon the public way it stands, and offers
To all that pass a hospitable roof.
[*They retire.*]

[TELL *enters with* BAUMGARTEN.]

TELL. Now, then, you have no further
need of me.
Enter yon house. 'T is Werner Stauf-
facher's,
A man that is a father to distress.
See, there he is, himself! Come, follow me.
[*They retire up.*]

SCENE III: *A common near Altdorf. On
an eminence in the background a castle in
progress of erection, and so far advanced that
the outline of the whole may be distinguished.
The back part is finished: men are working
at the front. Scaffolding, on which the workmen are going up and down. A slater is seen
upon the highest part of the roof. All is bustle
and activity.*

[*Enter Taskmaster, Mason, Workmen, Laborers.*]

TASKMASTER [*with a stick, urging on the
workmen*]. Up, up! You've rested
long enough. To work!
The stones here! Now the mortar, and the
lime!
And let his lordship see the work advanced,

When next he comes. These fellows crawl
like snails!
[*To two Laborers, with loads.*]
What! Call ye that a load? Go, double it.
Is this the way ye earn your wages, lag-
gards?
FIRST WORKMAN. 'T is very hard that
we must bear the stones,
To make a keep and dungeon for ourselves!
TASKMASTER. What's that you mutter?
'T is a worthless race,
For nothing fit but just to milk their cows,
And saunter idly up and down the hills.
OLD MAN [*sinks down exhausted*]. I can
no more.
TASKMASTER [*shaking him*]. Up, up, old
man, to work!
FIRST WORKMAN. Have you no bowels
of compassion, thus
To press so hard upon a poor old man,
That scarce can drag his feeble limbs along?
MASTER MASON AND WORKMEN. Shame,
shame upon you — shame! It cries
to Heaven.
TASKMASTER. Mind your own business.
I but do my duty.
FIRST WORKMAN. Pray, master, what's
to be the name of this
Same castle, when 't is built?
TASKMASTER. The Keep of Uri;
For by it we shall keep you in subjection.
WORKMAN. The Keep of Uri?
TASKMASTER. Well, why laugh at that?
SECOND WORKMAN. Keep Uri, will you,
with this paltry place!
FIRST WORKMAN. How many molehills
such as that must first
Be piled up each on each, ere you make
A mountain equal to the least in Uri?
[*Taskmaster retires up the stage.*]
MASTER MASON. I'll drown the mallet
in the deepest lake,
That served my hand on this accursed
pile.

[*Enter TELL and STAUFFACHER.*]

STAUFFACHER. O that I had not lived
to see this sight!
TELL. Here 't is not good to be. Let us
proceed.
STAUFFACHER. Am I in Uri — Uri, freedom's home?

MASTER MASON. Oh, sir, if you could only see the vaults
Beneath these towers! The man that tenants them
Will ne'er hear cock crow more.
STAUFFACHER. O God! O God!
MASON. Look at these ramparts and these buttresses,
That seem as they were built to last forever.
TELL. What hands have built, my friend, hands can destroy.
                    [Pointing to the mountains.]
That home of freedom God hath built for us.   [A drum is heard.]

[People enter bearing a cap upon a pole, followed by a crier. Women and children thronging tumultuously after them.]

FIRST WORKMAN. What means the drum? Give heed!
MASON. Why, here's a mumming!
And look, the cap — what can they mean by that?
CRIER. In the Emperor's name, give ear!
WORKMAN. Hush! silence! hush!
CRIER. Ye men of Uri, ye do see this cap!
It will be set upon a lofty pole
In Altdorf, in the market-place: and this
Is the Lord Governor's good will and pleasure;
The cap shall have like honor as himself,
All do it reverence with bended knee,
And head uncovered; thus the King will know
Who are his true and loyal subjects here;
His life and goods are forfeit to the Crown
That shall refuse obedience to the order.
        [The people burst out into laughter. The drum beats and the procession passes on.]
FIRST WORKMAN. A strange device to fall upon, indeed:
Do reverence to a cap! A pretty farce!
Heard ever mortal anything like this?
MASTER MASON. Down to a cap on bended knee, forsooth!
Rare jesting this with men of sober sense!
FIRST WORKMAN. Nay, an it were the imperial crown! A cap!
Merely the cap of Austria! I've seen it

Hanging above the throne in Gessler's hall.
MASON. The cap of Austria? Mark that! A snare
To get us into Austria's power, by Heaven!
WORKMAN. No freeborn man will stoop to such disgrace.
MASTER MASON. Come — to our comrades, and advise with them!
                    [They retire up.]
TELL [to STAUFFACHER]. You see how matters stand. Farewell, my friend!
STAUFFACHER. Whither away? Oh, leave us not so soon.
TELL. They look for me at home. So fare ye well.
STAUFFACHER. My heart's so full, and has so much to tell you!
TELL. Words will not make a heart that's heavy light.
STAUFFACHER. Yet words may possibly conduct to deeds.
TELL. Endure in silence! We can do no more.
STAUFFACHER. But shall we bear what is not to be borne?
TELL. Impetuous rulers have the shortest reigns.
When the fierce south wind rises from his chasms,
Men cover up their fires, the ships in haste
Make for the harbor, and the mighty spirit
Sweeps o'er the earth, and leaves no trace behind.
Let every man live quietly at home;
Peace to the peaceful rarely is denied.
STAUFFACHER. And is it thus you view our grievances?
TELL. The serpent stings not till it is provoked.
Let them alone; they'll weary of themselves,
When they shall see we are not to be roused.
STAUFFACHER. Much might be done — did we stand fast together.
TELL. When the ship founders, he will best escape
Who seeks no other's safety but his own.
STAUFFACHER. And you desert the common cause so coldly?
TELL. A man can safely count but on himself!

STAUFFACHER. Nay, even the weak
grow strong by union.
TELL. But the strong man is strongest
when alone.
STAUFFACHER. So, then, your country
cannot count on you,
If in despair she rise against her foes.
TELL. Tell rescues the lost sheep from
yawning gulfs:
Is he a man, then, to desert his friends?
Yet, whatsoe'er you do, spare me from
council!
I was not born to ponder and select;
But when your course of action is resolved,
Then call on Tell: you shall not find him
fail.
> [*Exeunt severally. A sudden tu-*
> *mult is heard around the scaf-*
> *folding.*]

MASON [*running in*]. What's wrong?
FIRST WORKMAN [*running forward*]. The
slater's fallen from the roof.
BERTHA [*rushing in*]. Heavens! Is he
dashed to pieces? Save him, help!
If help be possible, save him! Here is gold.
> [*Throws her trinkets among the*
> *people.*]

MASON. Hence with your gold — your
universal charm,
And remedy for ill! When you have torn
Fathers from children, husbands from their
wives,
And scattered woe and wail throughout the
land,
You think with gold to compensate for all.
Hence! Till we saw you, we were happy
men;
With you came misery and dark despair.
BERTHA [*to the Taskmaster, who has re-
turned*]. Lives he?
> [*Taskmaster shakes his head.*]
Ill-omened towers, with curses built,
And doomed with curses to be tenanted!
> [*Exit.*]

SCENE IV: *The house of* WALTER FÜRST.

[WALTER FÜRST *and* ARNOLD VON MELCH-
THAL *enter simultaneously at different
sides.*]

MELCHTHAL. Good Walter Fürst.
FÜRST. If we should be surprised!
Stay where you are. We are beset with
spies.
MELCHTHAL. Have you no news for me
from Unterwald?
What of my father? 'T is not to be borne,
Thus to be pent up like a felon here!
What have I done so heinous that I must
Skulk here in hiding, like a murderer?
I only laid my staff across the fists
Of the pert varlet, when before my eyes,
By order of the Governor, he tried
To drive away my handsome team of oxen.
FÜRST. You are too rash by far. He
did no more
Than what the Governor had ordered him.
You had transgressed, and therefore should
have paid
The penalty, however hard, in silence.
MELCHTHAL. Was I to brook the fel-
low's saucy gibe,
"That if the peasant must have bread to
eat,
Why, let him go and draw the plough him-
self!"
It cut me to the very soul to see
My oxen, noble creatures, when the knave
Unyoked them from the plough. As
though they felt
The wrong, they lowed and butted with
their horns.
On this I could contain myself no longer,
And, overcome by passion, struck him
down.
FÜRST. Oh, we old men can scarce com-
mand ourselves!
And can we wonder youth breaks out of
bounds?
MELCHTHAL. I'm only sorry for my
father's sake!
To be away from him, that needs so much
My fostering care! The Governor detests
him,
Because, whene'er occasion served, he has
Stood stoutly up for right and liberty.
Therefore they'll bear him hard — the
poor old man!
And there is none to shield him from their
grip.
Come what come may, I must go home
again.
FÜRST. Compose yourself, and wait in
patience till

We get some tidings o'er from Unterwald.
Away! Away! I hear a knock! Perhaps
A message from the Viceroy! Get thee in!
You are not safe from Landenberger's arm
In Uri, for these tyrants pull together.
MELCHTHAL. They teach us Switzers
what we ought to do.
FÜRST. Away! I'll call you when the
coast is clear.
[MELCHTHAL *retires.*]
Unhappy youth! I dare not tell him all
The evil that my boding heart predicts! —
Who's there? The door ne'er opens but I
look
For tidings of mishap. Suspicion lurks
With darkling treachery in every nook.
Even to our inmost rooms they force their
way,
These myrmidons of power; and soon we'll
need
To fasten bolts and bars upon our doors.
[*He opens the door and steps back
in surprise as* WERNER STAUF-
FACHER *enters.*]
What do I see? You, Werner? Now, by
Heaven!
A valued guest, indeed. No man e'er set
His foot across this threshold, more es-
teemed,
Welcome! Thrice welcome, Werner, to my
roof!
What brings you here? What seek you
here in Uri?
STAUFFACHER [*shakes* FÜRST *by the hand*].
The olden times and olden Switzer-
land.
FÜRST. You bring them with you. See
how glad I am!
My heart leaps at the very sight of you.
Sit down — sit down, and tell me how you
left
Your charming wife, fair Gertrude? Iberg's
child,
And clever as her father. Not a man,
That wends from Germany, by Meinrad's
Cell,
To Italy, but praises far and wide
Your house's hospitality. But say,
Have you come here direct from Flüelen,
And have you noticed nothing on your way,
Before you halted at my door?
STAUFFACHER [*sits down*]. I saw

A work in progress, as I came along,
I little thought to see — that likes me ill.
FÜRST. O friend! you've lighted on my
thought at once.
STAUFFACHER. Such things in Uri ne'er
were known before.
Never was prison here in man's remem-
brance,
Nor ever any stronghold but the grave.
FÜRST. You name it well. It is the
grave of freedom.
STAUFFACHER. Friend, Walter Fürst,
I will be plain with you.
No idle curiosity it is
That brings me here, but heavy cares. I
left
Thralldom at home, and thralldom meets
me here.
Our wrongs, e'en now, are more than we
can bear,
And who shall tell us where they are to
end?
From eldest time the Switzer has been free,
Accustomed only to the mildest rule.
Such things as now we suffer ne'er were
known,
Since herdsman first drove cattle to the
hills.
FÜRST. Yes, our oppressions are un-
paralleled!
Why, even our own good lord of Atting-
haus,
Who lived in olden times, himself declares
They are no longer to be tamely borne.
STAUFFACHER. In Unterwalden yonder
't is the same;
And bloody has the retribution been.
The Imperial Seneschal, the Wolfshot, who
At Rossberg dwelt, longed for forbidden
fruit —
Baumgarten's wife, that lives at Alzellen,
He tried to make a victim to his lust,
On which the husband slew him with his
axe.
FÜRST. Oh, Heaven is just in all its
judgments still!
Baumgarten, say you? A most worthy
man.
Has he escaped, and is he safely hid?
STAUFFACHER. Your son-in-law con-
veyed him o'er the lake,
And he lies hidden in my house at Steinen.

He brought the tidings with him of a thing
That has been done at Sarnen, worse than
all,
A thing to make the very heart run blood!
FÜRST [attentively]. Say on. What is it?
STAUFFACHER. There dwells in Melch-
thal, then,
Just as you enter by the road from Kerns,
An upright man, named Henry of the
Halden,
A man of weight and influence in the Diet.
FÜRST. Who knows him not? But
what of him? Proceed.
STAUFFACHER. The Landenberg, to pun-
ish some offense
Committed by the old man's son, it seems,
Had given command to take the youth's
best pair
Of oxen from his plough; on which the lad
Struck down the messenger and took to
flight.
FÜRST. But the old father — tell me,
what of him?
STAUFFACHER. The Landenberg sent
for him, and required
He should produce his son upon the spot;
And when the old man protested, and
with truth,
That he knew nothing of the fugitive,
The tyrant called his torturers.
FÜRST [springs up and tries to lead him
to the other side]. Hush! no more!
STAUFFACHER [with increasing warmth].
"And though thy son," he cried,
"has 'scaped me now,
I have thee fast, and thou shalt feel my
vengeance."
With that they flung the old man to the
ground,
And plunged the pointed steel into his eyes.
FÜRST. Merciful Heaven!
MELCHTHAL [rushing out]. Into his eyes,
his eyes?
STAUFFACHER [addresses himself in as-
tonishment to WALTER FÜRST].
Who is this youth?
MELCHTHAL [grasping him convulsively].
Into his eyes? Speak, speak!
FÜRST. Oh, miserable hour!
STAUFFACHER. Who is it, tell me!
[STAUFFACHER makes a sign to
him.]

It is his son! All-righteous Heaven!
MELCHTHAL. And I
Must be from thence! What! Into both
his eyes?
FÜRST. Be calm, be calm; and bear it
like a man!
MELCHTHAL. And all for me — for my
mad, willful folly!
Blind, did you say? Quite blind — and
both his eyes?
STAUFFACHER. Ev'n so. The fountain
of his sight is quenched,
He ne'er will see the blessed sunshine
more.
FÜRST. Oh, spare his anguish!
MELCHTHAL. Never, never more!
[Presses his hands upon his eyes
and is silent for some moments;
then, turning from one to the
other, speaks in a subdued tone,
broken by sobs.]
Oh, the eye's light, of all the gifts of
Heaven,
The dearest, best! From light all beings
live —
Each fair created thing — the very plants
Turn with a joyful transport to the light;
And he — he must drag on through all his
days
In endless darkness! Never more for him
The sunny meads shall glow, the flow'rets
bloom;
Nor shall he more behold the roseate tints
Of the iced mountain-top! To die is noth-
ing.
But to have life, and not have sight — oh,
that
Is misery, indeed! Why do you look
So piteously at me? I have two eyes,
Yet to my poor blind father can give
neither!
No, not one gleam of that great sea of
light,
That with its dazzling splendor floods my
gaze.
STAUFFACHER. Ah, I must swell the
measure of your grief,
Instead of soothing it. The worst, alas!
Remains to tell. They've stripped him of
his all;
Naught have they left him, save his staff,
on which,

Blind, and in rags, he moves from door to
door.

MELCHTHAL. Naught but his staff to
the old eyeless man!
Stripped of his all — even of the light of
day,
The common blessing of the meanest
wretch?
Tell me no more of patience, of conceal-
ment!
Oh, what a base and coward thing am I,
That on mine own security I thought,
And took no care of thine! Thy precious
head
Left as a pledge within the tyrant's grasp!
Hence, craven-hearted prudence, hence!
And all
My thoughts be vengeance, and the des-
pot's blood!
I 'll seek him straight — no power shall
stay me now —
And at his hands demand my father's eyes.
I 'll beard him 'mid a thousand myrmi-
dons!
What 's life to me, if in his heart's best
blood
I cool the fever of this mighty anguish?
[He is going.]
FÜRST. Stay; this is madness, Melch-
thal! What avails
Your single arm against his power? He sits
At Sarnen high within his lordly keep,
And, safe within its battlemented walls,
May laugh to scorn your unavailing rage.
MELCHTHAL. And though he sat within
the icy domes
Of yon far Schreckhorn — aye, or higher,
where,
Veiled since eternity, the Jungfrau soars,
Still to the tyrant would I make my way;
With twenty comrades minded like myself,
I 'd lay his fastness level with the earth!
And if none follow me, and if you all,
In terror for your homesteads and your
herds,
Bow in submission to the tyrant's yoke,
Round me I 'll call the herdsmen on the
hills,
And there beneath heaven's free and
boundless roof,
Where men still feel as men, and hearts are
true,

Proclaim aloud this foul enormity!
STAUFFACHER [to FÜRST]. The meas-
ure's full — and are we then to wait
Till some extremity —
MELCHTHAL. Peace! What extremity
Remains for us to dread? What, when our
eyes
No longer in their sockets are secure?
Heavens! Are we helpless? Wherefore did
we learn
To bend the crossbow — wield the battle-
axe?
What living creature but in its despair
Finds for itself a weapon of defense?
The baited stag will turn, and with the
show
Of his dread antlers hold the hounds at
bay;
The chamois drags the huntsman down th'
abyss;
The very ox, the partner of man's toil,
The sharer of his roof, that meekly bends
The strength of his huge neck beneath the
yoke,
Springs up, if he 's provoked, whets his
strong horn,
And tosses his tormentor to the clouds.
FÜRST. If the three cantons thought as
we three do,
Something might then be done, with good
effect.
STAUFFACHER. When Uri calls, when
Unterwald replies,
Schwytz will be mindful of her ancient
league.
MELCHTHAL. I 've many friends in
Unterwald, and none
That would not gladly venture life and
limb,
If fairly backed and aided by the rest.
Oh, sage and reverend fathers of this land,
Here do I stand before your riper years,
An unskilled youth, who in the Diet must
Into respectful silence hush his voice.
Yet do not, for that I am young, and want
Experience, slight my counsel and my
words.
'T is not the wantonness of youthful
blood
That fires my spirit; but a pang so deep
That e'en the flinty rocks must pity me.
You, too, are fathers, heads of families,

And you must wish to have a virtuous son,
To reverence your gray hairs, and shield
your eyes
With pious and affectionate regard.
Do not, I pray, because in limb and fortune
You still are unassailed, and still your eyes
Revolve undimmed and sparkling in their
spheres —
Oh, do not, therefore, disregard our wrongs!
Above you, also, hangs the tyrant's sword.
You, too, have striven to alienate the land
From Austria. This was all my father's
crime:
You share his guilt, and may his punish-
ment.
STAUFFACHER [to FÜRST]. Do thou re-
solve! I am prepared to follow.
FÜRST. First let us learn what steps the
noble lords
Von Sillinen and Attinghaus propose.
Their names would rally thousands to the
cause.
MELCHTHAL. Is there a name within the
Forest Mountains
That carries more respect than yours —
and yours?
On names like these the people build their
trust
In time of need — such names are house-
hold words.
Rich was your heritage of manly worth,
And richly have you added to its stores.
What need of nobles? Let us do the work
Ourselves. Yes, though we have to stand
alone,
We shall be able to maintain our rights.
STAUFFACHER. The nobles' wrongs are
not so great as ours.
The torrent, that lays waste the lower
grounds,
Hath not ascended to the uplands yet.
But let them see the country once in arms,
They'll not refuse to lend a helping hand.
FÜRST. Were there an umpire 'twixt
ourselves and Austria,
Justice and law might then decide our
quarrel.
But our oppressor is our Emperor too,
And judge supreme. 'T is God must help
us, then,
And our own arm! Be yours the task to
rouse

The men of Schwytz; I'll rally friends in
Uri.
But whom are we to send to Unterwald?
MELCHTHAL. Thither send me. Whom
should it more concern?
FÜRST. No, Melchthal, no; you are my
guest, and I
Must answer for your safety.
MELCHTHAL. Let me go.
I know each forest-track and mountain-
path;
Friends, I'll find, be sure, on every
hand,
To give me willing shelter from the foe.
STAUFFACHER. Nay, let him go; no
traitors harbor there:
For tyranny is so abhorred in Unterwald,
No tools can there be found to work her
will.
In the low valleys, too, the Alzeller
Will gain confederates, and rouse the
country.
MELCHTHAL. But how shall we com-
municate, and not .
Awaken the suspicion of the tyrants?
STAUFFACHER. Might we not meet at
Brunnen or at Treib,
Where merchant vessels with their cargoes
come?
FÜRST. We must not go so openly to
work.
Hear my opinion. On the lake's left bank,
As we sail hence to Brunnen, right against
The Mytenstein, deep-hidden in the wood
A meadow lies, by shepherds called the
Rootli,
Because the wood has been uprooted there.
[To MELCHTHAL.] 'T is where our canton
bound'ries verge on yours —
[To STAUFFACHER.] Your boat will carry
you across from Schwytz.
Thither by lonely bypaths let us wend
At midnight, and deliberate o'er our plans.
Let each bring with him there ten trusty
men,
All one at heart with us; and then we
may
Consult together for the general weal,
And, with God's guidance, fix what next to
do.
STAUFFACHER. So let it be. And now
your true right hand! —

Yours, too, young man! — and as we now three men
Among ourselves thus knit our hands together
In all sincerity and truth, e'en so
Shall we three cantons, too, together stand
In victory and defeat, in life and death.
FÜRST AND MELCHTHAL. In life and death!

[*They hold their hands clasped together for some moments in silence.*]

MELCHTHAL. Alas, my old blind father!
The day of freedom, that thou canst not see,
But thou shalt hear it, when from Alp to Alp
The beacon fires throw up their flaming signs,
And the proud castles of the tyrants fall,
Into thy cottage shall the Switzer burst,
Bear the glad tidings to thine ear, and o'er
Thy darkened way shall Freedom's radiance pour.

ACT II

SCENE I: *The mansion of the* BARON OF ATTINGHAUSEN. *A Gothic hall, decorated with escutcheons and helmets.*

[*The* BARON, *a gray-headed man, eighty-five years old, tall and of a commanding mien, clad in a furred pelisse, and leaning on a staff tipped with chamois horn,* KUONI *and six hinds standing round him with rakes and scythes.* ULRICH OF RUDENZ *enters in the costume of a knight.*]

RUDENZ. Uncle, I'm here! Your will?
ATTINGHAUSEN. First let me share,
After the ancient custom of our house,
The morning cup, with these my faithful servants!

[*He drinks from a cup, which is then passed round.*]

Time was, I stood myself in field and wood,
With mine own eyes directing all their toil,
Even as my banner led them in the fight.
Now I am only fit to play the steward:
And, if the genial sun come not to me,
I can no longer seek it on the hills.

Thus slowly, in an ever-narrowing sphere,
I move on to the narrowest and the last,
Where all life's pulses cease. I now am but
The shadow of my former self, and that
Is fading fast — 't will soon be but a name.
KUONI [*offering* RUDENZ *the cup*]. A pledge, young master!

[RUDENZ *hesitates to take the cup.*]

Nay, sir, drink it off!
One cup, one heart! You know our proverb, sir?
ATTINGHAUSEN. Go, children, and at eve, when work is done,
We'll meet and talk the country's business over. [*Exeunt Servants.*]
Belted and plumed, and all thy bravery on!
Thou art for Altdorf — for the castle, boy?
RUDENZ. Yes, uncle. Longer may I not delay —
ATTINGHAUSEN [*sitting down*]. Why in such haste? Say, are thy youthful hours
Doled in such niggard measure, that thou must
Be chary of them to thy aged uncle?
RUDENZ. I see my presence is not needed here;
I am but as a stranger in this house.
ATTINGHAUSEN [*gazes fixedly at him for a considerable time*]. Aye, pity 't is thou art! Alas, that home
To thee has grown so strange! O Uly! Uly!
I scarce do know thee now, thus decked in silks,
The peacock's feather flaunting in thy cap,
And purple mantle round thy shoulders flung;
Thou look'st upon the peasant with disdain;
And tak'st his honest greeting with a blush.
RUDENZ. All honor due to him I gladly pay,
But must deny the right he would usurp.
ATTINGHAUSEN. The sore displeasure of its monarch rests
Upon our land, and every true man's heart
Is full of sadness for the grievous wrongs
We suffer from our tyrants. Thou alone
Art all unmoved amid the general grief.
Abandoning thy friends, thou tak'st thy stand

Beside thy country's foes, and, as in scorn
Of our distress, pursuest giddy joys,
Courting the smiles of princes all the while
Thy country bleeds beneath their cruel
    scourge.
RUDENZ. The land is sore oppressed, I
    know it, uncle.
But why? Who plunged it into this dis-
    tress?
A word, one little easy word, might buy
Instant deliverance from all our ills,
And win the good-will of the Emperor.
Woe unto those who seal the people's eyes,
And make them adverse to their country's
    good —
The men who, for their own vile, selfish
    ends,
Are seeking to prevent the Forest States
From swearing fealty to Austria's House,
As all the countries round about have done!
It fits their humor well to take their seats
Amid the nobles on the Herrenbank;
They'll have the Kaiser for their lord,
    forsooth, —
That is to say, they'll have no lord at all.
ATTINGHAUSEN. Must I hear this, and
    from thy lips, rash boy?
RUDENZ. You urged me to this answer.
    Hear me out.
What, uncle, is the character you've
    stooped
To fill contentedly through life? Have you
No higher pride than in these lonely wilds
To be the Landamman or Banneret,
The petty chieftain of a shepherd race?
How! Were it not a far more glorious
    choice
To bend in homage to our royal lord,
And swell the princely splendors of his
    court,
Than sit at home, the peer of your own
    vassals,
And share the judgment-seat with vulgar
    clowns?
ATTINGHAUSEN. Ah, Uly, Uly; all too
    well I see
The tempter's voice has caught thy willing
    ear,
And poured its subtle poison in thy heart.
RUDENZ. Yes, I conceal it now. It doth
    offend
My inmost soul to hear the strangers' gibes,

That taunt us with the name of "Peasant
    Nobles!"
Think you the heart that's stirring here can
    brook,
While all the young nobility around
Are reaping honor under Hapsburg's
    banner,
That I should loiter, in inglorious ease,
Here on the heritage my fathers left,
And, in the dull routine of vulgar toil,
Lose all life's glorious spring? In other
    lands
Great deeds are done. A world of fair re-
    nown
Beyond these mountains stirs in martial
    pomp.
My helm and shield are rusting in the hall;
The martial trumpet's spirit-stirring blast,
The herald's call, inviting to the lists,
Rouse not the echoes of these vales, where
    naught
Save cowherd's horn and cattle bell is
    heard,
In one unvarying dull monotony.
ATTINGHAUSEN. Deluded boy, seduced
    by empty show!
Despise the land that gave thee birth!
    Ashamed
Of the good ancient customs of thy sires!
The day will come when thou, with burn-
    ing tears,
Wilt long for home, and for thy native hills,
And that dear melody of tuneful herds,
Which now, in proud disgust, thou dost
    despise!
A day when wistful pangs shall shake thy
    heart,
Hearing their music in a foreign land.
Oh, potent is the spell that binds to home!
No, no, the cold, false world is not for thee.
At the proud court, with thy true heart,
    thou wilt
Forever feel a stranger among strangers.
The world asks virtues of far other stamp
Than thou hast learned within these simple
    vales.
But go — go thither — barter thy free soul,
Take land in fief, be minion to a prince,
Where thou might'st be lord paramount,
    and prince
Of all thine own unburdened heritage!
O Uly, Uly, stay among thy people!

Go not to Altdorf. Oh, abandon not
The sacred cause of thy wronged native
    land!
I am the last of all my race. My name
Ends with me. Yonder hang my helm and
    shield;
They will be buried with me in the grave.
And must I think, when yielding up my
    breath,
That thou but wait'st the closing of mine
    eyes,
To stoop thy knee to this new feudal court,
And take in vassalage from Austria's hands
The noble lands, which I from God
    received,
Free and unfettered as the mountain air!
    RUDENZ. 'T is vain for us to strive
    against the King.
The world pertains to him: — shall we
    alone,
In mad, presumptuous obstinacy, strive
To break that mighty chain of lands which
    he
Hath drawn around us with his giant
    grasp?
His are the markets, his the courts — his,
    too,
The highways; nay, the very carrier's
    horse,
That traffics on the Gotthardt, pays him
    toll.
By his dominions, as within a net,
We are enclosed and girded roundabout.
— And will the Empire shield us? Say,
    can it
Protect itself 'gainst Austria's growing
    power?
To God and not to emperors must we look!
What store can on their promises be placed
When they, to meet their own necessities,
Can pawn and even alienate the towns
That flee for shelter 'neath the eagle's
    wings?
No, uncle! It is wise and wholesome
    prudence,
In times like these, when faction's all
    abroad,
To vow attachment to some mighty chief.
The imperial crown's transferred from line
    to line.
It has no memory for faithful service:
But to secure the favor of these great

Hereditary masters were to sow
Seed for a future harvest.
    ATTINGHAUSEN. Art so wise?
Wilt thou see clearer than thy noble sires,
Who battled for fair freedom's priceless gem
With life, and fortune, and heroic arm?
Sail down the lake to Lucerne, there in-
    quire
How Austria's thralldom weighs the can-
    tons down.
Soon she will come to count our sheep, our
    cattle,
To portion out the Alps, e'en to their peaks,
And in our own free woods to hinder us
From striking down the eagle or the stag;
To set her tolls on every bridge and gate,
Impoverish us, to swell her lust of sway,
And drain our dearest blood to feed her
    wars.
No, if our blood must flow, let it be shed
In our own cause! We purchase liberty
More cheaply far than bondage.
    RUDENZ. What can we,
A shepherd race, against great Albert's
    hosts?
    ATTINGHAUSEN. Learn, foolish boy, to
    know this shepherd race!
I know them, I have led them on in fight —
I saw them in the battle at Favenz.
What! Austria try, forsooth, to force on us
A yoke we are determined not to bear!
Oh, learn to feel from what a stock thou'rt
    sprung;
Cast not, for tinsel trash and idle show,
The precious jewel of thy worth away.
To be the chieftain of a freeborn race,
Bound to thee only by their unbought love,
Ready to stand — to fight — to die with
    thee,
Be that thy pride, be that thy noblest
    boast!
Knit to thy heart the ties of kindred —
    home —
Cling to the land, the dear land of thy
    sires,
Grapple to that with thy whole heart and
    soul!
Thy power is rooted deep and strongly
    here,
But in yon stranger world thou'lt stand
    alone,
A trembling reed beat down by every blast.

Oh, come! 't is long since we have seen thee,
Uly!
Tarry but this one day. Only to-day!
Go not to Altdorf. Wilt thou? Not to-day!
For this one day, bestow thee on thy
friends. [*Takes his hand.*]
RUDENZ. I gave my word. Unhand me!
I am bound.
ATTINGHAUSEN [*drops his hand and says
sternly*]. Bound, didst thou say?
Oh, yes, unhappy boy,
Thou art, indeed. But not by word or oath.
'T is by the silken mesh of love thou 'rt
bound. [RUDENZ *turns away.*]
Aye, hide thee, as thou wilt. 'T is she, I
know,
Bertha of Bruneck, draws thee to the court;
'T is she that changed thee to the Em-
peror's service.
Thou think'st to win the noble knightly
maid
By thy apostasy. Be not deceived.
She is held out before thee as a lure;
But never meant for innocence like thine.
RUDENZ. No more; I 've heard enough.
So fare you well. [*Exit.*]
ATTINGHAUSEN. Stay, Uly! Stay! —
Rash boy, he's gone! I can
Nor hold him back, nor save him from
destruction.
And so the Wolfshot has deserted us —
Others will follow his example soon.
This foreign witchery, sweeping o'er our
hills,
Tears with its potent spell our youth away.
Oh, luckless hour, when men and manners
strange
Into these calm and happy valleys came,
To warp our primitive and guileless ways!
The new is pressing on with might. The
old,
The good, the simple, all fleet fast away.
New times come on. A race is springing up,
That think not as their fathers thought
before!
What do I hear? All, all are in the grave
With whom erewhile I moved, and held
converse;
My age has long been laid beneath the sod:
Happy the man who may not live to see
What shall be done by those that follow
me!

SCENE II: *A meadow surrounded by high
rocks and wooded ground. On the rocks are
tracks, with rails and ladders, by which the
peasants are afterward seen descending. In
the background the lake is observed, and over
it a moon rainbow in the early part of the
scene. The prospect is closed by lofty mountains, with glaciers rising behind them. The
stage is dark, but the lake and glaciers glisten
in the moonlight.*

[*Enter* MELCHTHAL, BAUMGARTEN, WINK-
ELRIED, MEYER VON SARNEN, BURK-
HART AM BUHEL, ARNOLD VON SEWA,
KLAUS VON DER FLUE, *and four other
Peasants, all armed.*]

MELCHTHAL [*behind the scenes*]. The
mountain pass is open. Follow me!
I see the rock, and little cross upon it:
This is the spot; here is the Rootli.
[*They enter with torches.*]
WINKELRIED. Hark!
SEWA. The coast is clear.
MEYER. None of our comrades come?
We are the first, we Unterwaldeners.
MELCHTHAL. How far is 't i' the night?
BAUMGARTEN. The beacon watch
Upon the Selisberg has just called two.
[*A bell is heard at a distance.*]
MEYER. Hush! Hark!
BUHEL. The forest chapel's matin bell
Chimes clearly o'er the lake from Switzer-
land.
VON FLUE. The air is clear, and bears
the sound so far.
MELCHTHAL. Go, you and you, and
light some broken boughs;
Let's bid them welcome with a cheerful
blaze. [*Two Peasants exeunt.*]
SEWA. The moon shines fair to-night.
Beneath its beams
The lake reposes, bright as burnished
steel.
BUHEL. They 'll have an easy passage.
WINKELRIED [*pointing to the lake*]. Ha!
Look there!
Do you see nothing?
MEYER. Aye, indeed, I do!
A rainbow in the middle of the night.
MELCHTHAL. Formed by the bright re-
flection of the moon!

VON FLUE. A sign most strange and wonderful, indeed!
Many there be who ne'er have seen the like.
SEWA. 'T is doubled, see, — a paler one above!
BAUMGARTEN. A boat is gliding yonder right beneath it.
MELCHTHAL. That must be Werner Stauffacher! I knew
The worthy patriot would not tarry long.
    [Goes with BAUMGARTEN toward the shore.]
MEYER. The Uri men are like to be the last.
BUHEL. They're forced to take a winding circuit through
The mountains; for the Viceroy's spies are out.
    [In the mean while the two Peasants have kindled a fire in the center of the stage.]
MELCHTHAL [on the shore]. Who's there? The word?
STAUFFACHER [from below]. Friends of the country.
    [All retire up the stage, toward the party landing from the boat.]

[Enter STAUFFACHER, ITEL REDING, HANS AUF DER MAUER, JORG IM HOFE, CONRAD HUNN, ULRICH DER SCHMIDT, JOST VON WEILER, and three other Peasants, armed.]

ALL. Welcome!
    [While the rest remain behind exchanging greetings, MELCHTHAL comes forward with STAUFFACHER.]
MELCHTHAL. Oh, worthy Stauffacher, I've looked but now
On him who could not look on me again;
I've laid my hands upon his rayless eyes,
And on their vacant orbits sworn a vow
Of vengeance, only to be cooled in blood.
STAUFFACHER. Speak not of vengeance. We are here, to meet
The threatened evil, not to avenge the past.
Now, tell me what you've done, and what secured,
To aid the common cause in Unterwald.
How stand the peasantry disposed, and how

Yourself escaped the wiles of treachery?
MELCHTHAL. Through the Surenen's fearful mountain chain,
Where dreary ice-fields stretch on every side,
And sound is none, save the hoarse vulture's cry,
I reached the Alpine pasture, where the herds
From Uri and from Engelberg resort,
And turn their cattle forth to graze in common.
Still, as I went along, I slaked my thirst
With the coarse oozings of the glacier heights
That through the crevices come foaming down,
And turned to rest me in the herdsmen's cots,
Where I was host and guest, until I gained
The cheerful homes and social haunts of men.
Already through these distant vales had spread
The rumor of this last atrocity;
And wheresoe'er I went, at every door,
Kind words saluted me and gentle looks.
I found these simple spirits all in arms
Against our rulers' tyrannous encroachments.
For as their Alps through each succeeding year
Yield the same roots — their streams flow ever on
In the same channels — nay, the clouds and winds
The selfsame course unalterably pursue,
So have old customs there, from sire to son,
Been handed down, unchanging and unchanged;
Nor will they brook to swerve or turn aside
From the fixed even tenor of their life.
With grasp of their hard hands they welcomed me —
Took from the walls their rusty falchions down —
And from their eyes the soul of valor flashed
With joyful luster, as I spoke those names,
Sacred to every peasant in the mountains,
Your own and Walter Fürst's. Whate'er your voice

Should dictate as the right, they swore to
do;
And you they swore to follow e'en to
death.
— So sped I on from house to house, secure
In the guest's sacred privilege — and
when
I reached at last the valley of my home,
Where dwell my kinsmen, scattered far
and near —
And when I found my father, stripped and
blind,
Upon the stranger's straw, fed by the alms
Of charity —
STAUFFACHER. Great Heaven!
MELCHTHAL. Yet wept I not!
No — not in weak and unavailing tears
Spent I the force of my fierce burning
anguish;
Deep in my bosom, like some precious
treasure,
I locked it fast, and thought on deeds alone.
Through every winding of the hills I
crept —
No valley so remote but I explored it;
Nay, at the very glacier's ice-clad base,
I sought and found the homes of living
men;
And still, where'er my wandering footsteps
turned,
The selfsame hatred of these tyrants met
me.
For even there, at vegetation's verge,
Where the numbed earth is barren of all
fruits,
Their grasping hands had been for plunder
thrust.
Into the hearts of all this honest race,
The story of my wrongs struck deep, and
now
They, to a man, are ours; both heart and
hand.
STAUFFACHER. Great things, indeed,
you've wrought in little time.
MELCHTHAL. I did still more than this.
The fortresses,
Rossberg and Sarnen, are the country's
dread;
For from behind their adamantine walls
The foe, like eagle from his eyrie, swoops,
And, safe himself, spreads havoc o'er the
land.

With my own eyes I wished to weigh its
strength,
So went to Sarnen, and explored the castle.
STAUFFACHER. How! Venture even into
the tiger's den?
MELCHTHAL. Disguised in pilgrim's
weeds I entered it;
I saw the Viceroy feasting at his board —
Judge if I'm master of myself or no!
I saw the tyrant, and I slew him not!
STAUFFACHER. Fortune, indeed, upon
your boldness smiled.
[Meanwhile the others have arrived
and join MELCHTHAL and
STAUFFACHER.]
Yet tell me now, I pray, who are the
friends,
The worthy men, who came along with
you
Make me acquainted with them, that we
may
Speak frankly, man to man, and heart to
heart.
MEYER. In the three cantons, who, sir,
knows not you?
Meyer of Sarnen is my name; and this
Is Struth of Winkelried, my sister's son.
STAUFFACHER. No unknown name. A
Winkelried it was
Who slew the dragon in the fen at Weiler,
And lost his life in the encounter, too.
WINKELRIED. That, Master Stauffacher,
was my grandfather.
MELCHTHAL [pointing to two Peasants].
These two are men who till the
cloister lands
Of Engelberg, and live behind the forest.
You'll not think ill of them, because
they're serfs,
And sit not free upon the soil, like us.
They love the land, and bear a good repute.
STAUFFACHER [to them]. Give me your
hands. He has good cause for
thanks,
That to no man his body's service owes.
But worth is worth, no matter where 't is
found.
HUNN. That is Herr Reding, sir, our old
Landamman.
MEYER. I know him well. I am at law
with him
About a piece of ancient heritage. —

Herr Reding, we are enemies in court,
Here we are one.   [*Shakes his hand.*]
STAUFFACHER. That's well and bravely
    said.
WINKELRIED. Listen! They come. The
    horn of Uri! Hark!
    [*On the right and left armed men
    are seen descending the rocks
    with torches.*]
MAUER. Look, is not that the holy man
    of God?
A worthy priest! The terrors of the night
And the way's pains and perils scare not
    him,
A faithful shepherd caring for his flock.
BAUMGARTEN. The Sacrist follows him,
    and Walter Fürst.
But where is Tell? I do not see him there.

[WALTER FÜRST, RÖSSELMANN *the Pastor*,
    PETERMANN *the Sacrist*, KUONI *the
    Shepherd*, WERNI *the Huntsman*,
    RUODI *the Fisherman, and five other
    countrymen, thirty-three in all, advance
    and take their places round the fire.*]

FÜRST. Thus must we, on the soil our
    fathers left us,
Creep forth by stealth to meet like
    murderers,
And in the night, that should her mantle
    lend
Only to crime and black conspiracy, .
Assert our own good rights, which yet are
    clear
As is the radiance of the noonday sun.
MELCHTHAL. So be it. What is hatched
    in gloom of night
Shall free and boldly meet the morning
    light.
RÖSSELMANN. Confederates! Listen to
    the words which God
Inspires my heart withal. Here we are met,
To represent the general weal. In us
Are all the people of the land convened.
Then let us hold the Diet, as of old,
And as we're wont in peaceful times to do.
The time's necessity be our excuse,
If there be aught informal in this meeting.
Still, wheresoe'er men strike for justice,
    there
Is God, and now beneath his heaven we
    stand.

STAUFFACHER. 'T is well advised. —
    Let us, then, hold the Diet,
According to our ancient usages. —
Though it be night, there's sunshine in our
    cause.
MELCHTHAL. Few though our numbers
    be, the hearts are here
Of the whole people; here the best are met.
HUNN. The ancient books may not be
    near at hand,
Yet they are graven in our inmost hearts.
RÖSSELMANN. 'T is well. And now,
    then, let a ring be formed,
And plant the swords of power within the
    ground.
MAUER. Let the Landamman step into
    his place,
And by his side his secretaries stand.
SACRIST. There are three cantons here.
    Which hath the right
To give the head to the united Council?
Schwytz may contest that dignity with
    Uri,
We Unterwald'ners enter not the field.
MELCHTHAL. We stand aside. We are
    but suppliants here,
Invoking aid from our more potent friends.
STAUFFACHER. Let Uri have the sword.
    Her banner takes,
In battle, the precedence of our own.
FÜRST. Schwytz, then, must share the
    honor of the sword;
For she's the honored ancestor of all.
RÖSSELMANN. Let me arrange this gen-
    erous controversy.
Uri shall lead in battle — Schwytz in
    Council.
FÜRST [*gives* STAUFFACHER *his hand*].
    Then take your place.
STAUFFACHER. Not I. Some older man.
HOFE. Ulrich, the smith, is the most
    aged here.
MAUER. A worthy man, but not a free-
    man; no!
— No bondman can be judge in Switzer-
    land.
STAUFFACHER. Is not Herr Reding here,
    our old Landamman?
Where can we find a worthier man than
    he?
FÜRST. Let him be Amman and the
    Diet's chief!

You that agree with me, hold up your hands!

        [All hold up their right hands.]

REDING *[stepping into the center]*. I cannot lay my hands upon the books; But by yon everlasting stars I swear, Never to swerve from justice and the right.

      [The two swords are placed before him, and a circle formed; Schwytz in the center, Uri on his right, Unterwald on his left.]

REDING *[resting on his battle-sword]*. Why, at the hour when spirits walk the earth, Meet the three cantons of the mountains here, Upon the lake's inhospitable shore? What may the purport be of this new league We here contract beneath the starry heaven?

    STAUFFACHER *[entering the circle]*. 'T is no new league that here we now contract, But one our fathers framed, in ancient times, We purpose to renew! For know, confederates, Though mountain ridge and lake divide our bounds, And each canton by its own laws is ruled, Yet are we but one race, born of one blood, And all are children of one common home.

    WINKELRIED. Is, then, the burden of our legends true, That we came hither from a distant land? Oh, tell us what you know, that our new league May reap fresh vigor from the leagues of old.

    STAUFFACHER. Hear, then, what aged herdsmen tell. There dwelt A mighty people in the land that lies Back to the north. The scourge of famine came; And in this strait 't was publicly resolved That each tenth man, on whom the lot might fall, Should leave the country. They obeyed — and forth, With loud lamentings, men and women went,

A mighty host; and to the south moved on, Cutting their way through Germany by the sword, Until they gained these pine-clad hills of ours; Nor stopped they ever on their forward course, Till at the shaggy dell they halted, where The Müta flows through its luxuriant meads. No trace of human creature met their eye, Save one poor hut upon the desert shore, Where dwelt a lonely man, and kept the ferry. A tempest raged — the lake rose mountains high And barred their further progress. Thereupon They viewed the country — found it rich in wood, Discovered goodly springs, and felt as they Were in their own dear native land once more. Then they resolved to settle on the spot; Erected there the ancient town of Schwytz; And many a day of toil had they to clear The tangled brake and forest's spreading roots. Meanwhile their numbers grew, the soil became Unequal to sustain them, and they crossed To the black mountain, far as Weissland, where, Concealed behind eternal walls of ice, Another people speak another tongue. They built the village Stanz, beside the Kernwald; The village Altdorf, in the vale of Reuss; Yet, ever mindful of their parent stem, The men of Schwytz, from all the stranger race, That since that time have settled in the land, Each other recognize. Their hearts still know, And beat fraternally to kindred blood.

      [Extends his hand right and left.]

    MAUER. Aye, we are all one heart, one blood, one race!

    ALL *[joining hands]*. We are one people, and will act as one.

STAUFFACHER. The nations round us bear a foreign yoke,
For they have to the conqueror succumbed.
Nay, e'en within our frontiers may be found
Some that owe villein service to a lord,
A race of bonded serfs from sire to son.
But we, the genuine race of ancient Swiss,
Have kept our freedom from the first till now.
Never to princes have we bowed the knee;
Freely we sought protection of the Empire.
RÖSSELMANN. Freely we sought it — freely it was given.
'T is so set down in Emperor Frederick's charter.
STAUFFACHER. For the most free have still some feudal lord.
There must be still a chief, a judge supreme,
To whom appeal may lie, in case of strife.
And therefore was it that our sires allowed,
For what they had recovered from the waste,
This honor of the Emperor, the lord
Of all the German and Italian soil;
And, like the other free men of his realm,
Engaged to aid him with their swords in war;
The free man's duty this alone should be,
To guard the Empire that keeps guard for him.
MELCHTHAL. He's but a slave that would acknowledge more.
STAUFFACHER. They followed, when the Heribann went forth,
The imperial standard, and they fought its battles!
To Italy they marched in arms, to place
The Cæsars' crown upon the Emperor's head.
But still at home they ruled themselves in peace,
By their own laws and ancient usages.
The Emperor's only right was to adjudge
The penalty of death; he therefore named
Some mighty noble as his delegate,
That had no stake or interest in the land,
Who was called in, when doom was to be passed,
And, in the face of day, pronounced decree,
Clear and distinctly, fearing no man's hate.

What traces here, that we are bondsmen? Speak,
If there be any can gainsay my words!
HOFE. No! You have spoken but the simple truth;
We never stooped beneath a tyrant's yoke.
STAUFFACHER. Even to the Emperor we did not submit,
When he gave judgment 'gainst us for the Church;
For when the Abbey of Einsiedlen claimed
The Alp our fathers and ourselves had grazed,
And showed an ancient charter, which bestowed
The land on them as being ownerless —
For our existence there had been concealed —
What was our answer? This: "The grant is void.
No Emperor can bestow what is our own:
And if the Empire shall deny our rights,
We can, within our mountains, right ourselves!"
Thus spake our fathers! And shall we endure
The shame and infamy of this new yoke,
And from the vassal brook what never king
Dared, in his plenitude of power, attempt?
This soil we have created for ourselves,
By the hard labor of our hands; we've changed
The giant forest, that was erst the haunt
Of savage bears, into a home for man;
Extirpated the dragon's brood, that wont
To rise, distent with venom, from the swamps;
Rent the thick misty canopy that hung
Its blighting vapors on the dreary waste;
Blasted the solid rock; across the chasm
Thrown the firm bridge for the wayfaring man.
By the possession of a thousand years
The soil is ours. And shall an alien lord,
Himself a vassal, dare to venture here,
Insult us by our own hearth fires — attempt
To forge the chains of bondage for our hands,
And do us shame on our own proper soil?
Is there no help against such wrong as this?
[*Great sensation among the people.*]

Yes! There's a limit to the despot's power!
When the oppressed for justice looks in
vain,
When his sore burden may no more be
borne,
With fearless heart he makes appeal to
Heaven,
And thence brings down his everlasting
rights,
Which there abide, inalienably his,
And indestructible as are the stars.
Nature's primeval state returns again,
Where man stands hostile to his fellow
man;
And if all other means shall fail his need,
One last resource remains — his own good
sword.
Our dearest treasures call to us for aid,
Against the oppressor's violence; we stand
For country, home, for wives, for children
here!
    ALL [clasping their swords]. Here stand
        we for our homes, our wives, and
        children.
    RÖSSELMANN [stepping into the circle].
        Bethink ye well, before ye draw the
        sword.
Some peaceful compromise may yet be
made;
Speak but one word, and at your feet
you'll see
The men who now oppress you. Take the
terms
That have been often tendered you; re-
nounce
The Empire, and to Austria swear alle-
giance!
    MAUER. What says the priest? To
        Austria allegiance?
    BUHEL. Hearken not to him!
    WINKELRIED. 'T is a traitor's counsel,
        His country's foe!
    REDING. Peace, peace, confederates!
    SEWA. Homage to Austria, after wrongs
        like these!
    VON FLUE. Shall Austria extort from us
        by force
What we denied to kindness and entreaty?
    MEYER. Then should we all be slaves,
        deservedly.
    MAUER. Yes! Let him forfeit all a
        Switzer's rights,

Who talks of yielding thus to Austria's
yoke!
I stand on this, Landamman. Let this be
The foremost of our laws!
    MELCHTHAL. Even so! Whoe'er
Shall talk of bearing Austria's yoke, let
him
Of all his rights and honors be despoiled,
No man thenceforth receive him at his
hearth!
    ALL [raising their right hands]. Agreed!
        Be this the law!
    REDING [after a pause]. The law it is.
    RÖSSELMANN. Now you are free — this
        law hath made you free.
Never shall Austria obtain by force
What she has failed to gain by friendly
suit.
    WEILER. On with the order of the day!
        Proceed!
    REDING. Confederates! Have all gentler
        means been tried?
Perchance the Emperor knows not of our
wrongs,
It may not be his will we suffer thus;
Were it not well to make one last attempt,
And lay our grievances before the throne,
Ere we unsheath the sword? Force is at
best
A fearful thing e'en in a righteous cause;
God only helps, when man can help no
more.
    STAUFFACHER [to CONRAD HUNN]. Here
        you can give us information. Speak!
    HUNN. I was at Rheinfeld, at the Em-
        peror's court,
Deputed by the cantons to complain
Of the oppressions of these governors,
And of our liberties the charter claim,
Which each new King till now has ratified.
I found the envoys there of many a town,
From Swabia and the valley of the Rhine,
Who all received their parchments as they
wished,
And straight went home again with merry
heart.
But me, your envoy, they to the Council
sent,
Where I with empty cheer was soon dis-
missed:
"The Emperor at present was engaged;
Some other time he would attend to us!"

I turned away, and passing through the
hall,
With heavy heart, in a recess I saw
The Grand Duke John in tears, and by his
side
The noble lords of Wart and Tegerfeld,
Who beckoned me, and said: "Redress
yourselves.
Expect not justice from the Emperor.
Does he not plunder his own brother's
child,
And keep from him his just inheritance?"
The Duke claims his maternal property,
Urging he's now of age, and 't is full time
That he should rule his people and estates;
What is the answer made to him? The
King
Places a chaplet on his head. "Behold
The fitting ornament," he cries, "of
youth!"
MAUER. You hear. Expect not from the
Emperor
Or right or justice! Then redress your-
selves!
REDING. No other course is left us.
Now, advise
What plan most likely to insure success.
FÜRST. To shake a thralldom off that
we abhor,
To keep our ancient rights inviolate,
As we receive them from our fathers —
this,
Not lawless innovation, is our aim.
Let Cæsar still retain what is his due;
And he that is a vassal, let him pay
The service he is sworn to faithfully.
MEYER. I hold my land of Austria in
fief.
FÜRST. Continue, then, to pay your
feudal dues.
WEILER. I'm tenant of the lords of
Rapperswil.
FÜRST. Continue, then, to pay them
rent and tithe.
RÖSSELMANN. Of Zurich's abbess hum-
ble vassal I.
FÜRST. Give to the cloister what the
cloister claims.
STAUFFACHER. The Empire only is my
feudal lord.
FÜRST. What needs must be, we'll do,
but nothing more.

We'll drive these tyrants and their minions
hence,
And raze their towering strongholds to the
ground,
Yet shed, if possible, no drop of blood.
Let the Emperor see that we were driven
to cast
The sacred duties of respect away;
And when he finds we keep within our
bounds,
His wrath, belike, may yield to policy;
For truly is that nation to be feared
That, arms in hand, is temperate in its
wrath.
REDING. But prithee tell us how may
this be done?
The enemy is armed as well as we,
And, rest assured, he will not yield in peace.
STAUFFACHER. He will, whene'er he sees
us up in arms;
We shall surprise him, ere he is prepared.
MEYER. Easily said, but not so easily
done.
Two strongholds dominate the country —
they
Protect the foe, and should the King in-
vade us,
Our task would then be dangerous, indeed.
Rossberg and Sarnen both must be secured,
Before a sword is drawn in either canton.
STAUFFACHER. Should we delay, the foe
would soon be warned;
We are too numerous for secrecy.
MEYER. There is no traitor in the For-
est States.
RÖSSELMANN. But even zeal may heed-
lessly betray.
FÜRST. Delay it longer, and the keep at
Altdorf
Will be complete — the Governor secure.
MEYER. You think but of yourselves.
SACRISTAN. You are unjust!
MEYER. Unjust! said you? Dares Uri
taunt us so?
REDING. Peace, on your oath!
SACRISTAN. If Schwytz be leagued with
Uri,
Why, then, indeed, we must perforce be
dumb.
REDING. And let me tell you, in the
Diet's name,
Your hasty spirit much disturbs the peace

Stand we not all for the same common
cause?

WINKELRIED. What, if till Christmas
we delay? 'T is then
The custom for the serfs to throng the
castle,
Bringing the Governor their annual gifts.
Thus may some ten or twelve selected men
Assemble unobserved, within its walls,
Bearing about their persons pikes of steel,
Which may be quickly mounted upon
staves,
For arms are not admitted to the fort.
The rest can fill the neighboring wood,
prepared
To sally forth upon a trumpet's blast,
Soon as their comrades have secured the
gate;
And thus the castle will with ease be ours.

MELCHTHAL. The Rossberg I will un-
dertake to scale.
I have a sweetheart in the garrison,
Whom with some tender words I could
persuade
To lower me at night a hempen ladder.
Once up, my friends will not be long be-
hind.

REDING. Are all resolved in favor of
delay?
[The majority raise their hands.]

STAUFFACHER [counting them]. Twenty
to twelve is the majority.

FÜRST. If on the appointed day the
castles fall,
From mountain on to mountain we shall
speed
The fiery signal: in the capital
Of every canton quickly rouse the Land-
sturm.
Then, when these tyrants see our martial
front,
Believe me, they will never make so bold
As risk the conflict, but will gladly take
Safe conduct forth beyond our boundaries.

STAUFFACHER. Not so with Gessler. He
will make a stand.
Surrounded with his dread array of horse,
Blood will be shed before he quits the field,
And even expelled he'd still be terrible.
'T is hard, nay, dangerous, to spare his life.

BAUMGARTEN. Place me where'er a life
is to be lost;

I owe my life to Tell, and cheerfully
Will pledge it for my country. I have
cleared
My honor, and my heart is now at rest.

REDING. Counsel will come with cir-
cumstance. Be patient!
Something must still be to the moment
left.
Yet, while by night we hold our Diet here,
The morning, see, has on the mountain tops
Kindled her glowing beacon. Let us part,
Ere the broad sun surprise us.

FÜRST. Do not fear.
The night wanes slowly from these vales of
ours.
[All have involuntarily taken off
their caps, and contemplate the
breaking of day, absorbed in
silence.]

RÖSSELMANN. By this fair light which
greeteth us, before
Those other nations, that, beneath us far,
In noisome cities pent, draw painful breath,
Swear we the oath of our confederacy!
A band of brothers true we swear to be,
Never to part in danger or in death!
[They repeat his words with three
fingers raised.]
We swear we will be free, as were our sires,
And sooner die than live in slavery!
[All repeat as before.]
We swear, to put our trust in God Most
High,
And not to quail before the might of man!
[All repeat as before, and embrace
each other.]

STAUFFACHER. Now every man pursue
his several way
Back to his friends, his kindred, and his
home.
Let the herd winter up his flock, and gain
In secret friends for this great league of
ours!
What for a time must be endured, endure,
And let the reckoning of the tyrants grow,
Till the great day arrive, when they shall
pay
The general and particular debt at once.
Let every man control his own just rage,
And nurse his vengeance for the public
wrongs:
For he whom selfish interests now engage,

Defrauds the general weal of what to it
  belongs.

> [*As they are going off in profound
> silence, in three different direc-
> tions, the orchestra plays a sol-
> emn air. The empty scene re-
> mains open for some time, show-
> ing the rays of the sun rising over
> the glaciers.*]

ACT III

SCENE I: *Court before* TELL'S *house.*

[*Enter* TELL *with an axe.* HEDWIG *engaged
in her domestic duties.* WALTER *and*
WILLIAM *in the background, playing
with a little crossbow.*]

WALTER [*sings*]

With his crossbow, and his quiver,
  The huntsman speeds his way,
Over mountain, dale, and river,
  At the dawning of the day.
As the eagle, on wild pinion,
  Is the king in realms of air,
So the hunter claims dominion
  Over crag and forest lair.
Far as ever bow can carry,
  Through the trackless airy space,
All he sees he makes his quarry,
  Soaring bird and beast of chase.

WILLIAM [*runs forward*]. My string has
  snapped! Oh, father, mend it, do!
TELL. Not I; a true-born archer helps
  himself.   [*Boys retire.*]
HEDWIG. The boys begin to use the
  bow betimes.
TELL. 'T is early practice only makes
  the master.
HEDWIG. Ah! Would to Heaven they
  never learned the art!
TELL. But they shall learn it, wife, in
  all its points.
Whoe'er would carve an independent way
Through life, must learn to ward or plant
  a blow.
HEDWIG. Alas! Alas! And they will
  never rest
Contentedly at home.
TELL. No more can I!
I was not framed by nature for a shepherd.

My restless spirit ever yearns for change;
I only feel the flush and joy of life
If I can start fresh quarry every day.
HEDWIG. Heedless the while of all your
  wife's alarms,
As she sits watching through long hours at
  home.
For my soul sinks with terror at the tales
The servants tell about the risks you run.
Whene'er we part, my trembling heart
  forebodes
That you will ne'er come back to me again.
I see you on the frozen mountain steeps,
Missing, perchance, your leap from crag to
  crag.
I see the chamois, with a wild rebound,
Drag you down with him o'er the precipice.
I see the avalanche close o'er your head —
The treacherous ice give way, and you sink
  down
Entombed alive within its hideous gulf.
Ah! In a hundred varying forms does
  death
Pursue the Alpine huntsman on his course.
That way of life can surely ne'er be blessed
Where life and limb are periled every hour.
TELL. The man that bears a quick and
  steady eye,
And trusts in God, and his own lusty thews,
Passes, with scarce a scar, through every
  danger.
The mountain cannot awe the mountain
  child.

> [*Having finished his work, he
> lays aside his tools.*]

And now, methinks, the door will hold
  awhile —
Axe in the house oft saves the carpenter.
            [*Takes his cap.*]
HEDWIG. Whither away?
TELL. To Altdorf, to your father.
HEDWIG. You have some dangerous en-
  terprise in view?
Confess!
TELL. Why think you so?
HEDWIG. Some scheme's on foot
Against the Governors. There was a Diet
Held on the Rootli — that I know — and
  you
Are one of the confederacy, I'm sure.
TELL. I was not there. Yet will I not
  hold back,

Whene'er my country calls me to her aid.

HEDWIG. Wherever danger is will you be placed.

On you, as ever, will the burden fall.

TELL. Each man shall have the post that fits his powers.

HEDWIG. You took — aye, 'mid the thickest of the storm —

The man of Unterwald across the lake.

'T is marvel you escaped. Had you no thought

Of wife and children, then?

TELL. Dear wife, I had;

And therefore saved the father for his children.

HEDWIG. To brave the lake in all its wrath! 'T was not

To put your trust in God! 'T was tempting Him.

TELL. Little will he that's overcautious do.

HEDWIG. Yes, you've a kind and helping hand for all;

But be in straits, and who will lend you aid?

TELL. God grant I ne'er may stand in need of it!

[Takes up his crossbow and arrows.]

HEDWIG. Why take your crossbow with you? leave it here.

TELL. I want my right hand, when I want my bow.

[The boys return.]

WALTER. Where, father, are you going?

TELL. To grand-dad, boy —

To Altdorf. Will you go?

WALTER. Aye, that I will!

HEDWIG. The Viceroy's there just now. Go not to Altdorf!

TELL. He leaves to-day.

HEDWIG. Then let him first be gone,

Cross not his path — You know he bears us grudge.

TELL. His ill-will cannot greatly injure me.

I do what's right, and care for no man's hate.

HEDWIG. 'T is those who do what's right whom most he hates.

TELL. Because he cannot reach them. Me, I ween,

His knightship will be glad to leave in peace.

HEDWIG. Aye! — Are you sure of that?

TELL. Not long ago,

As I was hunting through the wild ravines

Of Shechenthal, untrod by mortal foot —

There, as I took my solitary way

Along a shelving ledge of rocks, where 't was

Impossible to step on either side —

For high above rose, like a giant wall,

The precipice's side, and far below

The Shechen thundered o'er its rifted bed —

[The boys press toward him, looking upon him with excited curiosity.]

There, face to face, I met the Viceroy. He

Alone with me — and I myself alone —

Mere man to man, and near us the abyss;

And when his lordship had perused my face,

And knew the man he had severely fined

On some most trivial ground, not long before,

And saw me, with my sturdy bow in hand,

Come striding toward him, his cheek grew pale,

His knees refused their office, and I thought

He would have sunk against the mountainside.

Then, touched with pity for him, I advanced

Respectfully, and said, "'T is I, my lord."

But ne'er a sound could he compel his lips

To frame in answer. Only with his hand

He beckoned me in silence to proceed.

So I passed on, and sent his train to seek him.

HEDWIG. He trembled, then, before you? Woe the while

You saw his weakness! That he'll ne'er forgive.

TELL. I shun him, therefore, and he'll not seek me.

HEDWIG. But stay away to-day. Go hunt instead!

TELL. What do you fear?

HEDWIG. I am uneasy. Stay!

TELL. Why thus distress yourself without a cause?

HEDWIG. Because there is no cause. Tell, Tell! Stay here!

TELL. Dear wife, I gave my promise I would go.

HEDWIG. Must you? — Then go. But leave the boys with me.

WALTER. No, mother, dear, I go with father, I.

HEDWIG. How, Walter! Will you leave your mother, then?

WALTER. I'll bring you pretty things from grandpapa.

[*Exit with his father.*]

WILLIAM. Mother, I'll stay with you!

HEDWIG [*embracing him*]. Yes, yes! thou art

My own dear child. Thou'rt all that's left to me.

[*She goes to the gate of the court and looks anxiously after* TELL *and her son for a considerable time.*]

SCENE II: *A retired part of the forest — brooks dashing in spray over the rocks.*

Enter BERTHA *in a hunting-dress. Immediately afterward* RUDENZ.]

BERTHA. He follows me. Now, then, to speak my mind!

RUDENZ [*entering hastily*]. At length, dear lady, we have met alone

In this wild dell; with rocks on every side,

No jealous eye can watch our interview.

Now, let my heart throw off this weary silence.

BERTHA. But are you sure they will not follow us?

RUDENZ. See, yonder goes the chase! Now, then, or never!

I must avail me of this precious chance —

Must hear my doom decided by thy lips,

Though it should part me from thy side forever.

Oh, do not arm that gentle face of thine

With looks so stern and harsh! Who — who am I,

That dare aspire so high, as unto thee?

Fame hath not stamped me yet; nor may I take

My place amid the courtly throng of knights,

That, crowned with glory's luster, woo thy smiles.

Nothing have I to offer, but a heart

That overflows with truth and love for thee.

BERTHA [*sternly and with severity*]. And dare you speak to me of love — of truth?

You, that are faithless to your nearest ties!

You, that are Austria's slave — bartered and sold

To her — an alien, and your country's tyrant!

RUDENZ. How! This reproach from thee! Whom do I seek,

On Austria's side, my own beloved, but thee?

BERTHA. Think you to find me in the traitor's ranks?

Now, as I live, I'd rather give my hand

To Gessler's self, all despot though he be,

Than to the Switzer who forgets his birth,

And stoops to be a tyrant's servile tool.

RUDENZ. O Heaven, what words are these?

BERTHA. Say! What can lie

Nearer the good man's heart than friends and kindred?

What dearer duty to a noble soul,

Than to protect weak, suffering innocence,

And vindicate the rights of the oppressed?

My very soul bleeds for your countrymen.

I suffer with them, for I needs must love them;

They are so gentle, yet so full of power;

They draw my whole heart to them. Every day

I look upon them with increased esteem.

But you, whom nature and your knightly vow

Have given them as their natural protector,

Yet who desert them and abet their foes

In forging shackles for your native land,

You — you incense and wound me to the core.

It tries me to the utmost not to hate you.

RUDENZ. Is not my country's welfare all my wish?

What seek I for her, but to purchase peace

'Neath Austria's potent scepter?

BERTHA. Bondage, rather!

You would drive Freedom from the last
stronghold
That yet remains for her upon the earth.
The people know their own true interests
better:
Their simple natures are not warped by
show.
But round your head a tangling net is
wound.

RUDENZ. Bertha, you hate me — you
despise me!

BERTHA. Nay!
And if I did, 't were better for my peace.
But to see him despised and despicable —
The man whom one might love —

RUDENZ. Oh, Bertha! You
Show me the pinnacle of heavenly bliss,
Then, in a moment, hurl me to despair!

BERTHA. No, no! The noble is not all
extinct
Within you. It but slumbers — I will
rouse it.
It must have cost you many a fiery struggle
To crush the virtues of your race within
you.
But, Heaven be praised, 't is mightier than
yourself,
And you are noble in your own despite!

RUDENZ. You trust me, then? Oh,
Bertha, with thy love
What might I not become!

BERTHA. Be only that
For which your own high nature destined
you.
Fill the position you were born to fill —
Stand by your people and your native
land —
And battle for your sacred rights!

RUDENZ. Alas!
How can I win you — how can you be
mine,
If I take arms against the Emperor?
Will not your potent kinsmen interpose,
To dictate the disposal of your hand?

BERTHA. All my estates lie in the Forest
Cantons;
And I am free when Switzerland is free.

RUDENZ. Oh, what a prospect, Bertha,
hast thou shown me!

BERTHA. Hope not to win my hand by
Austria's grace;

Fain would they lay their grasp on my
estates,
To swell the vast domains which now they
hold.
The selfsame lust of conquest, that would
rob
You of your liberty, endangers mine.
Oh, friend, I'm marked for sacrifice — to
be
The guerdon of some parasite, perchance!
They'll drag me hence to the imperial
court,
That hateful haunt of falsehood and
intrigue,
And marriage bonds I loathe await me
there.
Love, love alone, — your love, — can res-
cue me.

RUDENZ. And thou couldst be content,
love, to live here;
In my own native land to be my own?
Oh, Bertha, all the yearnings of my soul
For this great world and its tumultuous
strife,
What were they, but a yearning after thee?
In glory's path I sought for thee alone,
And all my thirst of fame was only love.
But if in this calm vale thou canst abide
With me, and bid earth's pomps and pride
adieu,
Then is the goal of my ambition won;
And the rough tide of the tempestuous
world
May dash and rave around these firm-set
hills!
No wandering wishes more have I to send
Forth to the busy scene that stirs beyond.
Then may these rocks, that girdle us, ex-
tend
Their giant walls impenetrably round,
And this sequestered, happy vale alone
Look up to heaven, and be my paradise!

BERTHA. Now, art thou all my fancy
dreamed of thee.
My trust has not been given to thee in vain.

RUDENZ. Away, ye idle phantoms of my
folly!
In mine own home I'll find my happiness.
Here, where the gladsome boy to manhood
grew,
Where every brook, and tree, and mountain peak,

Teems with remembrances of happy hours,
In mine own native land thou wilt be mine.
Ah, I have ever loved it well, I feel
How poor without it were all earthly joys.
    BERTHA. Where should we look for
        happiness on earth,
If not in this dear land of innocence?
Here, where old truth hath its familiar
    home,
Where fraud and guile are strangers, envy
    never
Shall dim the sparkling fountain of our
    bliss,
And ever bright the hours shall over us
    glide.
There do I see thee, in true manly worth,
The foremost of the free and of thy peers,
Revered with homage pure and uncon-
    strained,
Wielding a power that kings might envy
    thee.
    RUDENZ. And thee I see, thy sex's
        crowning gem,
With thy sweet woman's grace and wake-
    ful love,
Building a heaven for me within my home,
And, as the springtime scatters forth her
    flowers,
Adorning with thy charms my path of life,
And spreading joy and sunshine all around.
    BERTHA. And this it was, dear friend,
        that caused my grief,
To see thee blast this life's supremest bliss
With thine own hand. Ah! What had
    been my fate,
Had I been forced to follow some proud
    lord,
Some ruthless despot, to his gloomy keep!
Here are no keeps, here are no bastioned
    walls
To part me from a people I can bless.
    RUDENZ. Yet, how to free myself; to
        loose the coils
Which I have madly twined around my
    head?
    BERTHA. Tear them asunder with a
        man's resolve.
Whate'er ensue, firm by thy people stand!
It is thy post by birth.
        [*Hunting-horns are heard in the
            distance.*]
But hark! The chase!

Farewell — 't is needful we should part —
    away!
Fight for thy land; thou fightest for thy
    love.
One foe fills all our souls with dread; the
    blow
That makes one free, emancipates us all.
                    [*Exeunt severally.*]

    SCENE III: *A meadow near Altdorf. Trees
in the foreground. At the back of the stage
a cap upon a pole. The prospect is bounded
by the Bannberg, which is surmounted by a
snow-capped mountain.*

    [FRIESSHARDT *and* LEUTHOLD *on guard.*]

    FRIESSHARDT. We keep our watch in
        vain. Zounds! not a soul
Will pass and do obeisance to the cap.
But yest rday the place swarmed like a
    fair;
Now the old green looks like a desert,
    quite,
Since yonder scarecrow hung upon the pole.
    LEUTHOLD. Only the vilest rabble show
        themselves
And wave their tattered caps in mockery
    at us.
All honest citizens would sooner make
A weary circuit over half the town,
Than bend their backs before our master's
    cap.
    FRIESSHARDT. They were obliged to
        pass this way at noon,
As they were coming from the Council
    House.
I counted then upon a famous catch,
For no one thought of bowing to the cap.
But Rösselmann, the priest, was even with
    me:
Coming just then from some sick man, he
    takes
His stand before the pole — lifts up the
    Host —
The Sacrist, too, must tinkle with his
    bell —
When down they dropped on knee — my-
    self and all —
In reverence to the Host, but not the cap.
    LEUTHOLD. Hark ye, companion, I've
        a shrewd suspicion,
Our post's no better than the pillory.

It is a burning shame, a trooper should
Stand sentinel before an empty cap,
And every honest fellow must despise us.
To do obeisance to a cap, too! Faith,
I never heard an order so absurd!
FRIESSHARDT. Why not, an't please you,
    to an empty cap?
You've ducked, I'm sure, to many an
    empty sconce.

[Enter HILDEGARD, MECHTHILD, and ELS-
BETH with their children, and station
themselves around the pole.]

LEUTHOLD. And you are a time-serving
    sneak, that takes
Delight in bringing honest folks to harm.
For my part, he that likes may pass the
    cap —
I'll shut my eyes and take no note of him.
MECHTHILD. There hangs the Viceroy!
    Your obeisance, children!
ELSBETH. I would to God he'd go, and
    leave his cap!
The country would be none the worse for it.
FRIESSHARDT [driving them away]. Out
    of the way! Confounded pack of
    gossips!
Who sent for you? Go, send your husbands
    here,
If they have courage to defy the order.

[Enter TELL with his crossbow, leading his
son WALTER by the hand. They pass
the hat without noticing it, and advance
to the front of the stage.]

WALTER [pointing to the Bannberg].
    Father, is't true that on the moun-
    tain there
The trees, if wounded with a hatchet,
    bleed?
TELL. Who says so, boy?
WALTER. The master herdsman, father!
He tells us there's a charm upon the
    trees,
And if a man shall injure them, the hand
That struck the blow will grow from out
    the grave.
TELL. There is a charm about them —
    that's the truth.
Dost see those glaciers yonder — those
    white horns —
That seem to melt away into the sky?

WALTER. They are the peaks that
    thunder so at night,
And send the avalanches down upon us.
TELL. They are; and Altdorf long ago
    had been
Submerged beneath these avalanches'
    weight,
Did not the forest there above the town
Stand like a bulwark to arrest their fall.
WALTER [after musing a little]. And are
    there countries with no mountains,
    father?
TELL. Yes, if we travel downward from
    our heights,
And keep descending where the rivers
    go,
We reach a wide and level country, where
Our mountain torrents brawl and foam no
    more,
And fair large rivers glide serenely on.
All quarters of the heaven may there be
    scanned
Without impediment. The corn grows
    there
In broad and lovely fields, and all the
    land
Is like a garden fair to look upon.
WALTER. But, father, tell me, where-
    fore haste we not
Away to this delightful land, instead
Of toiling here, and struggling as we do?
TELL. The land is fair and bountiful as
    heaven;
But they who till it never may enjoy
The fruits of what they sow.
WALTER. Live they not free,
As you do, on the land their fathers left
    them?
TELL. The fields are all the bishop's or
    the King's.
WALTER. But they may freely hunt
    among the woods?
TELL. The game is all the monarch's —
    bird and beast.
WALTER. But they, at least, may
    surely fish the streams?
TELL. Stream, lake, and sea, all to the
    King belong.
WALTER. Who is this King, of whom
    they're so afraid?
TELL. He is the man who fosters and
    protects them.

WALTER. Have they not courage to protect themselves?

TELL. The neighbor there dare not his neighbor trust.

WALTER. I should want breathing-room in such a land.

I'd rather dwell beneath the avalanches.

TELL. 'T is better, child, to have these glacier peaks

Behind one's back, than evil-minded men!

[They are about to pass on.]

WALTER. See, father, see the cap on yonder pole!

TELL. What is the cap to us? Come, let's begone.

[As he is going, FRIESSHARDT, presenting his pike, stops him.]

FRIESSHARDT. Stand, I command you, in the Emperor's name!

TELL [seizing the pike]. What would ye? Wherefore do ye stop me thus?

FRIESSHARDT. You've broke the mandate, and with us must go.

LEUTHOLD. You have not done obeisance to the cap.

TELL. Friend, let me go.

FRIESSHARDT. Away, away to prison!

WALTER. Father to prison! Help!

[Calling to the side scene.]

This way, you men!

Good people, help! They're dragging him to prison!

[Enter RÖSSELMANN the Priest, and t e Sacristan, with three other men.]

SACRISTAN. What's here amiss?

RÖSSELMANN. Why do you seize this man?

FRIESSHARDT. He is an enemy of the King — a traitor.

TELL [seizing him with violence]. A traitor, I!

RÖSSELMANN. Friend, thou art wrong. 'T is Tell,

An honest man, and worthy citizen.

WALTER [descries FÜRST and runs up to him]. Grandfather, help; they want to seize my father!

FRIESSHARDT. Away to prison!

FÜRST [running in]. Stay, I offer bail. —

For God's sake, Tell, what is the matter here?

[Enter MELCHTHAL and STAUFFACHER.]

LEUTHOLD. He has contemned the Viceroy's sovereign power,

Refusing flatly to acknowledge it.

STAUFFACHER. Has Tell done this?

MELCHTHAL. Villain, you know 't is false!

LEUTHOLD. He has not made obeisance to the cap.

FÜRST. And shall for this to prison? — Come, my friend,

Take my security, and let him go.

FRIESSHARDT. Keep your security for yourself — you'll need it.

We only do our duty. — Hence with him!

MELCHTHAL [to the country people]. This is too bad! Shall we stand by and see

Him dragged away before our very eyes?

SACRISTAN. We are the strongest.

Friends, endure it not,

Our countrymen will back us to a man.

FRIESSHARDT. Who dares resist the Governor's commands?

OTHER THREE PEASANTS [running in]. We'll help you. What's the matter? Down with them!

[HILDEGARD, MECHTHILD, and ELSBETH return.]

TELL. Go, go, good people; I can help myself.

Think you, had I a mind to use my strength,

These pikes of theirs should daunt me?

MECHTHILD [to FRIESSHARDT]. Only try —

Try from our midst to force him, if you dare!

FÜRST AND STAUFFACHER. Peace, peace, friends!

FRIESSHARDT [loudly]. Riot! Insurrection, ho! [Hunting-horns without.]

WOMEN. The Governor!

FRIESSHARDT [raising his voice]. Rebellion! Mutiny!

STAUFFACHER. Roar till you burst, knave!

RÖSSELMANN AND MELCHTHAL. Will you hold your tongue?

FRIESSHARDT [calling still louder]. Help, help, I say, the servants of the law!

Fürst. The Viceroy here! Then we shall smart for this!

[*Enter* Gessler *on horseback, with a falcon on his wrist;* Rudolph der Harras, Bertha, *and* Rudenz, *and a numerous train of armed attendants, who form a circle of lances round the whole stage.*]

Harras. Room for the Viceroy!

Gessler. Drive the clowns apart. Why throng the people thus? Who calls for help? [*General silence.*] Who was it? I will know.

[Friesshardt *steps forward.*]

And who art thou? And why hast thou this man in custody?

[*Gives his falcon to an attendant.*]

Friesshardt. Dread sir, I am a soldier of your guard, And stationed sentinel beside the cap. This man I apprehended in the act Of passing it without obeisance due; So, as you ordered, I arrested him, Whereon to rescue him the people tried.

Gessler [*after a pause*]. And do you, Tell, so lightly hold your King, And me, who act as his viceregent here, That you refuse obeisance to the cap I hung aloft to test your loyalty? I read in this a disaffected spirit.

Tell. Pardon me, good my lord! The action sprang From inadvertence — not from disrespect. Were I discreet, I were not William Tell. Forgive me now — I'll not offend again.

Gessler [*after a pause*]. I hear, Tell, you're a master with the bow — From every rival bear the palm away.

Walter. That's very truth, sir! At a hundred yards He'll shoot an apple for you off the tree.

Gessler. Is that boy thine, Tell?

Tell. Yes, my gracious lord.

Gessler. Hast any more of them?

Tell. Two boys, my lord.

Gessler. And, of the two, which dost thou love the most?

Tell. Sir, both the boys are dear to me alike.

Gessler. Then, Tell, since at a hundred yards thou canst Bring down the apple from the tree, thou shalt Approve thy skill before me. Take thy bow — Thou hast it there at hand — make ready, then, To shoot an apple from the stripling's head! But take this counsel — look well to thine aim, See that thou hit'st the apple at the first, For, shouldst thou miss, thy head shall pay the forfeit.

[*All give signs of horror.*]

Tell. What monstrous thing, my lord, is this you ask? What, from the head of mine own child! — No, no! It cannot be, kind sir; you meant not that — God, in his grace, forbid! You could not ask A father seriously to do that thing!

Gessler. Thou art to shoot an apple from his head! I do desire — command it so.

Tell. What, I! Level my crossbow at the darling head Of mine own child? No — rather let me die!

Gessler. Or thou must shoot, or with thee dies the boy.

Tell. Shall I become the murderer of my child? You have no children, sir, — you do not know The tender throbbings of a father's heart.

Gessler. How now, Tell, on a sudden so discreet? I had been told thou wert a visionary — A wanderer from the paths of common men. Thou lovest the marvelous. So have I now Culled out for thee a task of special daring. Another man might pause and hesitate — Thou dashest at it, heart and soul, at once.

Bertha. Oh, do not jest, my lord, with these poor souls! See, how they tremble, and how pale they look, So little used are they to hear thee jest.

GESSLER. Who tells thee that I jest?
[*Grasping a branch above his head.*]
Here is the apple.
Room there, I say! And let him take his
    distance —
Just eighty paces — as the custom is —
Not an inch more or less! It was his boast,
That at a hundred he could hit his man. —
Now, archer, to your task, and look you
    miss not!
HARRAS. Heavens! This grows serious.
    — Down, boy, on your knees,
And beg the Governor to spare your life.
FÜRST [*aside to* MELCHTHAL, *who can
    scarcely restrain his indignation*].
    Command yourself! — Be calm, I
    beg of you!
BERTHA [*to the Governor*]. Let this suffice
    you, sir! It is inhuman
To trifle with a father's anguish thus.
Although this wretched man had forfeited
Both life and limb for such a slight offense,
Already has he suffered tenfold death.
Send him away uninjured to his home;
He'll know thee well in future; and this
    hour
He and his children's children will re-
    member.
GESSLER. Open a way there — quick!
    Why this delay? —
Thy life is forfeited; I might dispatch thee,
And see, I graciously repose thy fate
Upon the skill of thine own practiced
    hand. —
No cause has he to say his doom is harsh
Who's made the master of his destiny. —
Thou boastest thine unerring aim. 'T is
    well!
Now is the fitting time to show thy skill;
The mark is worthy and the prize is great.
To hit the bull's-eye in the target — that
Can many another do as well as thou; —
But he, methinks, is master of his craft,
Who can at all times on his skill rely,
Nor lets his heart disturb or eye or hand.
FÜRST. My lord, we bow to your
    authority;
But oh, let justice yield to mercy here!
Take half my property, nay, take it all,
But spare a father this unnatural doom!
WALTER. Grandfather, do not kneel to
    that bad man!

Say, where am I to stand? I do not fear;
My father strikes the bird upon the wing,
And will not miss now when 't would harm
    his boy!
STAUFFACHER. Does the child's inno-
    cence not touch your heart?
RÖSSELMANN. Bethink you, sir, there is
    a God in heaven,
To whom you must account for all your
    deeds.
GESSLER [*pointing to the boy*]. Bind him
    to yonder lime tree!
WALTER. What! Bind me?
No, I will not be bound! I will be still —
Still as a lamb — nor even draw my breath!
But if you bind me, I cannot be still.
Then I shall writhe and struggle with my
    bonds.
HARRAS. But let your eyes at least be
    bandaged, boy!
WALTER. And why my eyes? No! Do
    you think I fear
An arrow from my father's hand? Not I!
I'll wait it firmly, nor so much as wink! —
Quick, father, show them what thy bow
    can do.
He doubts thy skill — he thinks to ruin us.
Shoot, then, and hit, though but to spite
    the tyrant!
    [*He goes to the lime tree, and an
    apple is placed on his head.*]
MELCHTHAL [*to the country people*].
    What! Is this outrage to be per-
    petrated
Before our very eyes? Where is our oath?
STAUFFACHER. Resist we cannot!
    Weapons we have none,
And see the wood of lances round us! See!
MELCHTHAL. Oh, would to Heaven that
    we had struck at once!
God pardon those who counseled the delay!
GESSLER [*to* TELL]. Now, to your task!
Men bear not arms for naught.
To carry deadly tools is dangerous,
And on the archer oft his shaft recoils.
This right, these haughty peasant churls
    assume,
Trenches upon their master's privileges:
None should be armed but those who bear
    command. —
It pleases you to carry bow and bolt —
Well, be it so. I will prescribe the mark.

TELL [*bends the bow, and fixes the arrow*]. A lane there! Room!

STAUFFACHER. What, Tell? You would — no, no! You shake — your hand's unsteady — your knees tremble.

TELL [*letting the bow sink down*]. There's something swims before mine eyes!

WOMEN. Great Heaven!

TELL. Release me from this shot! Here is my heart! [*Tears open his breast.*] Summon your troopers — let them strike me down!

GESSLER. 'T is not thy life I want — I want the shot. Thy talent's universal! Nothing daunts thee! The rudder thou canst handle like the bow! No storms affright thee, when a life's at stake. Now, savior, help thyself — thou savest all!

[TELL *stands fearfully agitated by contending emotions, his hands moving convulsively, and his eyes turning alternately to the Governor and to heaven. Suddenly he takes a second arrow from his quiver, and sticks it in his belt. The Governor notes all he does.*]

WALTER [*beneath the lime tree*]. Shoot, father, shoot! Fear not!

TELL. It must be!

[*Collects himself and levels the bow.*]

RUDENZ [*who all the while has been standing in a state of violent excitement, and has with difficulty restrained himself, advances*]. My lord, you will not urge this matter further; You will not. It was surely but a test. You've gained your object. Rigor pushed too far Is sure to miss its aim, however good, As snaps the bow that's all too straitly bent.

GESSLER. Peace, till your counsel's asked for!

RUDENZ. I will speak! Aye, and I dare! I reverence my King; But acts like these must make his name abhorred.

He sanctions not this cruelty. I dare Avouch the fact. And you outstep your powers In handling thus my harmless countrymen.

GESSLER. Ha! Thou grow'st bold, methinks!

RUDENZ. I have been dumb To all the oppressions I was doomed to see. I've closed mine eyes to shut them from my view, Bade my rebellious, swelling heart be still, And pent its struggles down within my breast. But to be silent longer were to be A traitor to my King and country both.

BERTHA [*casting herself between him and the Governor*]. Oh, Heavens! You but exasperate his rage!

RUDENZ. My people I forsook — renounced my kindred — Broke all the ties of nature, that I might Attach myself to you. I madly thought That I should best advance the general weal By adding sinews to the Emperor's power. The scales have fallen from mine eyes — I see The fearful precipice on which I stand. You've led my youthful judgment far astray — Deceived my honest heart. With best intent, I had well-nigh achieved my country's ruin.

GESSLER. Audacious boy, this language to thy lord?

RUDENZ. The Emperor is my lord, not you! I'm free As you by birth, and I can cope with you In every virtue that beseems a knight. And if you stood not here in that King's name, Which I respect e'en where 't is most abused, I'd throw my gauntlet down, and you should give An answer to my gage in knightly sort. Aye, beckon to your troopers! Here I stand; But not like these [*pointing to the people*] — unarmed. I have a sword, And he that stirs one step —

STAUFFACHER [*exclaims*]. The apple's down!
[*While the attention of the crowd has been directed to the spot where* BERTHA *had cast herself between* RUDENZ *and* GESSLER, TELL *has shot.*]
RÖSSELMANN. The boy's alive!
MANY VOICES. The apple has been struck!
[WALTER FÜRST *staggers and is about to fall.* BERTHA *supports him.*]
GESSLER [*astonished*]. How? Has he shot? The madman!
BERTHA. Worthy father!
Pray you, compose yourself. The boy's alive.
WALTER [*runs in with the apple*]. Here is the apple, father! Well I knew
You would not harm your boy!
[TELL *stands with his body bent forward, as if still following the arrow. His bow drops from his hand. When he sees the boy advancing, he hastens to meet him with open arms, and embracing him, passionately sinks down with him quite exhausted. All crowd round them deeply affected.*]
BERTHA. Oh, ye kind Heavens!
FÜRST [*to father and son*]. My children, my dear children!
STAUFFACHER. God be praised!
LEUTHOLD. Almighty powers! That was a shot, indeed!
It will be talked of to the end of time.
HARRAS. This feat of Tell, the archer, will be told
Long as these mountains stand upon their base. [*Hands the apple to* GESSLER.]
GESSLER. By Heaven! The apple's cleft right through the core.
It was a master shot, I must allow.
RÖSSELMANN. The shot was good. But woe to him who drove
The man to tempt his God by such a feat!
STAUFFACHER. Cheer up, Tell, — rise!
You've nobly freed yourself,
And now may go in quiet to your home.

RÖSSELMANN. Come, to the mother let us bear her son!
[*They are about to lead him off.*]
GESSLER. A word, Tell.
TELL. Sir, your pleasure?
GESSLER. Thou didst place
A second arrow in thy belt — nay, nay!
I saw it well. Thy purpose with it? Speak!
TELL [*confused*]. It is a custom with all archers, sir.
GESSLER. No, Tell, I cannot let that answer pass.
There was some other motive, well I know.
Frankly and cheerfully confess the truth: —
Whate'er it be, I promise thee thy life.
Wherefore the second arrow?
TELL. Well, my lord,
Since you have promised not to take my life,
I will, without reserve, declare the truth.
[*He draws the arrow from his belt, and fixes his eyes sternly upon the Governor.*]
If that my hand had struck my darling child,
This second arrow I had aimed at you,
And, be assured, I should not then have missed.
GESSLER. Well, Tell, I promised thou shouldst have thy life;
I gave my knightly word, and I will keep it.
Yet, as I know the malice of thy thoughts,
I'll have thee carried hence, and safely penned,
Where neither sun nor moon shall reach thine eyes.
Thus from thy arrows I shall be secure. —
Seize on him, guards, and bind him!
[*They bind him.*]
STAUFFACHER. How, my lord —
How can you treat in such a way a man
On whom God's hand has plainly been revealed?
GESSLER. Well, let us see if it will save him twice!
Remove him to my ship; I'll follow straight,
At Küssnacht I will see him safely lodged.
RÖSSELMANN. You dare not do 't. Nor durst the Emperor's self
So violate our dearest chartered rights.
GESSLER. Where are they? Has the Emp'ror confirmed them?

He never has. And only by obedience
May you that favor hope to win from
him.
You are all rebels 'gainst the Emp'ror's
power —
And bear a desperate and rebellious spirit.
I know you all — I see you through and
through.
Him do I single from among you now,
But in his guilt you all participate.
If you are wise, be silent and obey!

    [*Exit, followed by* BERTHA, RU-
    DENZ, HARRAS, *and attendants.*
    FRIESSHARDT *and* LEUTHOLD
    remain.]

FÜRST [*in violent anguish*]. All's over
    now! He is resolved to bring
Destruction on myself and all my house.
STAUFFACHER [*to* TELL]. Oh, why did
    you provoke the tyrant's rage?
TELL. Let him be calm who feels the
    pangs I felt.
STAUFFACHER. Alas! alas! Our every
    hope is gone.
With you we all are fettered and enchained.
COUNTRY PEOPLE [*surrounding* TELL].
    Our last remaining comfort goes
    with you!
LEUTHOLD [*approaching him*]. I'm sorry
    for you, Tell, but must obey.
TELL. Farewell!
WALTER TELL [*clinging to him in great
    agony*]. O father, father, father,
    dear!
TELL [*pointing to heaven*]. Thy Father is
    on high — appeal to Him!
STAUFFACHER. Have you no message,
    Tell, to send your wife?
TELL [*clasping the boy passionately to his
    breast*]. The boy's uninjured; God
    will succor me!

    [*Tears himself suddenly away, and
    follows the soldiers of the guard.*]

ACT IV

SCENE I: *Eastern shore of the Lake of
Lucerne; rugged and singularly shaped rocks
close the prospect to the west. The lake is
agitated, violent roaring and rushing of wind,
with thunder and lightning at intervals.*

[*Enter* KUNZ OF GERSAU, *Fisherman and
    Boy.*]

KUNZ. I saw it with these eyes! Be-
    lieve me, friend,
It happened all precisely as I've said.
FISHERMAN. How! Tell a prisoner, and
    to Küssnacht borne?
The best man in the land, the bravest arm,
Had we for liberty to strike a blow!
KUNZ. The Viceroy takes him up the
    lake in person:
They were about to go on board as I
Started from Flüelen; but the gathering
    storm,
That drove me here to land so suddenly,
May well have hindered them from setting
    out.
FISHERMAN. Our Tell in chains, and in
    the Viceroy's power!
Oh, trust me, Gessler will entomb him,
    where
He never more shall see the light of day;
For, Tell once free, the tyrant well might
    dread
The just revenge of one so deeply wronged.
KUNZ. The old Landamman, too, —
    Von Attinghaus, —
They say, is lying at the point of death.
FISHERMAN. Then the last anchor of
    our hopes gives way!
He was the only man that dared to raise
His voice in favor of the people's rights.
KUNZ. The storm grows worse and
    worse. So, fare ye well!
I'll go and seek out quarters in the village.
There's not a chance of getting off to-day.
    [*Exit.*]
FISHERMAN. Tell dragged to prison, and
    the Baron dead!
Now, Tyranny, exalt thy brazen front —
Throw every shame aside! Truth's voice
    is dumb!
The eye that watched for us, in darkness
    closed,
The arm that should have struck thee
    down, in chains!
BOY. 'T is hailing hard — come, let us
    to the hut!
This is no weather to be out in, father!
FISHERMAN. Rage on, ye winds! Ye
    lightnings, flash your fires!

Burst ye, swollen clouds! Ye cataracts of
   heaven,
Descend, and drown the country! In the
   germ
Destroy the generations yet unborn!
Ye savage elements, be lords of all!
Return, ye bears; ye ancient wolves, return
To this wide, howling waste! The land is
   yours.
Who would live here, when liberty is gone?
   Boy. Hark! How the wind whistles,
   and the whirlpool roars!
I never saw a storm so fierce as this!
   Fisherman. To level at the head of his
   own child!
Never had father such command before.
And shall not Nature, rising in wild wrath,
Revolt against the deed? I should not
   marvel,
Though to the lakes these rocks should bow
   their heads,
Though yonder pinnacles, yon towers of
   ice,
That, since creation's dawn have known no
   thaw,
Should, from their lofty summits, melt
   away —
Though yonder mountains, yon primeval
   cliffs,
Should topple down, and a new deluge
   whelm
Beneath its waves all living men's abodes!
                    [Bells heard.]
   Boy. Hark! They are ringing on the
   mountain, yonder!
They surely see some vessel in distress,
And toll the bell that we may pray for it.
                [Ascends a rock.]
   Fisherman. Woe to the bark that now
   pursues its course,
Rocked in the cradle of these storm-tossed
   waves!
Nor helm nor steersman here can aught
   avail;
The storm is master. Man is like a ball,
Tossed 'twixt the winds and billows. Far
   or near,
No haven offers him its friendly shelter!
Without one ledge to grasp, the sheer
   smooth rocks
Look down inhospitably on his despair,
And only tender him their flinty breasts.

   Boy [calling from above]. Father, a ship:
   from Flüelen bearing down.
   Fisherman. Heaven pity the poor
   wretches! When the storm
Is once entangled in this strait of ours,
It rages like some savage beast of prey,
Struggling against its cage's iron bars!
Howling, it seeks an outlet — all in vain;
For the rocks hedge it round on every side,
Walling the narrow gorge as high as heaven.
               [He ascends a cliff.]
   Boy. It is the Governor of Uri's ship;
By its red poop I know it, and the flag.
   Fisherman. Judgments of Heaven! Yes,
   it is he himself,
It is the Governor! Yonder he sails,
And with him bears the burden of his
   crimes.
The avenger's arm has not been slow to
   strike!
Now over him he knows a mightier lord.
These waves yield no obedience to his voice.
These rocks bow not their heads before his
   cap.
Boy, do not pray; stay not the Judge's
   arm!
   Boy. I pray not for the Governor, I
   pray
For Tell, who's with him there on board
   the ship.
   Fisherman. Alas, ye blind, unreasoning
   elements!
Must ye, in punishing one guilty head,
Destroy the vessel and the pilot too?
   Boy. See, see, they've cleared the Bug-
   gisgrat; but now
The blast, rebounding from the Devil's
   Minster,
Has driven them back on the Great Axen-
   berg.
I cannot see them now.
   Fisherman. The Hakmesser
Is there, that's foundered many a gallant
   ship.
If they should fail to double that with skill,
Their bark will go to pieces on the rocks
That hide their jagged peaks below the
   lake.
The best of pilots, boy, they have on board.
If man could save them, Tell is just the
   man,
But he is manacled both hand and foot.

[*Enter* TELL, *with his crossbow. He enters precipitately, looks wildly round, and testifies the most violent agitation. When he reaches the center of the stage, he throws himself upon his knees, stretching out his hands, first toward the earth, and then toward heaven.*]

BOY [*observing him*]. See, father! A man on's knees; who can it be?

FISHERMAN. He clutches at the earth with both his hands,
And looks as though he were beside himself.

BOY [*advancing*]. What do I see? Come, father, come and look!

FISHERMAN [*approaches*]. Who is it? God in heaven! What! Tell! How came you hither? Speak, Tell!

BOY. Were you not
In yonder ship, a prisoner, and in chains?

FISHERMAN. Were they not carrying you to Küssnacht, Tell?

TELL [*rising*]. I am released.

FISHERMAN AND BOY. Released, oh, miracle!

BOY. Whence came you here?

TELL. From yonder vessel!

FISHERMAN. What?

BOY. Where is the Viceroy?

TELL. Drifting on the waves.

FISHERMAN. Is it possible? But you! How are you here?
How 'scaped you from your fetters and the storm?

TELL. By God's most gracious providence. Attend.

FISHERMAN AND BOY. Say on, say on!

TELL. You know what passed at Altdorf.

FISHERMAN. I do — say on!

TELL. How I was seized and bound,
And ordered by the Governor to Küssnacht.

FISHERMAN. And how at Flüelen he embarked with you.
All this we know. Say, how have you escaped?

TELL. I lay on deck, fast bound with cords, disarmed,
In utter hopelessness. I did not think
Again to see the gladsome light of day,
Nor the dear faces of my wife and boys,
And eyed disconsolate the waste of waters —

FISHERMAN. Oh, wretched man!

TELL. Then we put forth; the Viceroy, Rudolph der Harras, and their suite. My bow
And quiver lay astern beside the helm;
And just as we had reached the corner, near
The Little Axen, Heaven ordained it so
That from the Gotthardt's gorge, a hurricane
Swept down upon us with such headlong force
That every oarsman's heart within him sank,
And all on board looked for a watery grave.
Then heard I one of the attendant train,
Turning to Gessler, in this wise accost him:
"You see our danger, and your own, my lord,
And that we hover on the verge of death!
The boatmen there are powerless from fear,
Nor are they confident what course to take.
Now, here is Tell, a stout and fearless man,
And knows to steer with more than common skill:
How if we should avail ourselves of him
In this emergency?" The Viceroy then
Addressed me thus: "If thou wilt undertake
To bring us through this tempest safely, Tell,
I might consent to free thee from thy bonds."
I answered: "Yes, my lord; so help me God,
I'll see what can be done!" On this they loosed
The cords that bound me, and I took my place
Beside the helm, and steered as best I could,
Yet ever eyed my shooting gear askance,
And kept a watchful eye upon the shore,
To find some point where I might leap to land:
And when I had descried a shelving crag,
That jutted, smooth atop into the lake —

FISHERMAN. I know it. At the foot of the Great Axen;

TELL. So steep it looks, I never could have dreamed

That from a boat a man could leap to it.

TELL. I bade the men to row with all
their force
Until we came before the shelving ledge.
For there, I said, the danger will be past!
Stoutly they pulled, and soon we neared
the point;
One prayer to God for his assisting grace,
And, straining every muscle, I brought
round
The vessel's stern close to the rocky wall;
Then snatching up my weapons, with a
bound
I swung myself upon the flattened shelf,
And with my feet thrust off, with all my
might,
The puny bark into the watery hell.
There let it drift about, as Heaven ordains!
Thus am I here, delivered from the might
Of the dread storm, and man's more dread-
ful still.

FISHERMAN. Tell, Tell, the Lord has
manifestly wrought
A miracle in thy behalf! I scarce
Can credit my own eyes. But tell me, now,
Whither you purpose to betake yourself?
For you will be in peril, should perchance
The Viceroy escape this tempest with his
life.

TELL. I heard him say, as I lay bound
on board,
At Brunnen he proposed to disembark,
And, crossing Schwytz, convey me to his
castle.

FISHERMAN. Means he to go by land?

TELL. So he intends.

FISHERMAN. Oh, then conceal yourself
without delay!
Not twice will Heaven release you from
his grasp.

TELL. Which is the nearest way to Arth
and Küssnacht?

FISHERMAN. The public road leads by
the way of Steinen,
But there's a nearer road, and more retired,
That goes by Lowerz, which my boy can
show you.

TELL [gives him his hand]. May Heaven
reward your kindness! Fare ye well.
[As he is going, he comes back.]
Did not you also take the oath at Rootli?

I heard your name, methinks.

FISHERMAN. Yes, I was there,
And took the oath of the confederacy.

TELL. Then do me this one favor: speed
to Bürglen —
My wife is anxious at my absence — tell
her
That I am free, and in secure concealment.

FISHERMAN. But whither shall I tell her
you have fled?

TELL. You'll find her father with her,
and some more,
Who took the oath with you upon the
Rootli;
Bid them be resolute, and strong of
heart —
For Tell is free and master of his arm;
They shall hear further news of me ere long.

FISHERMAN. What have you, then, in
view? Come, tell me frankly!

TELL. When once 't is done, 't will be
in every mouth. [Exit.]

FISHERMAN. Show him the way, boy.
Heaven be his support!
Whate'er he has resolved, he'll execute.
[Exit.]

SCENE II: Baronial mansion of Attinghausen.

[The Baron upon a couch dying. WALTER
FÜRST, STAUFFACHER, MELCHTHAL,
and BAUMGARTEN attending round
him. WALTER TELL kneeling before
the dying man.]

FÜRST. All now is over with him. He is
gone.

STAUFFACHER. He lies not like one dead.
The feather, see,
Moves on his lips! His sleep is very calm,
And on his features plays a placid smile.
[BAUMGARTEN goes to the door and
speaks with some one.]

FÜRST. Who's there?

BAUMGARTEN [returning]. Tell's wife,
your daughter; she insists
That she must speak with you, and see her
boy. [WALTER TELL rises.]

FÜRST. I who need comfort — can I
comfort her?
Does every sorrow center on my head?

HEDWIG [*forcing her way in*]. Where is
my child? Unhand me! I must see
him.

STAUFFACHER. Be calm! Reflect, you're
in the house of death!

HEDWIG [*falling upon her boy's neck*].
My Walter! Oh, he yet is mine!

WALTER. Dear mother!

HEDWIG. And is it surely so? Art thou
unhurt?

[*Gazing at him with anxious tenderness.*]

And is it possible he aimed at thee?
How could he do it? Oh, he has no heart —
And he could wing an arrow at his child!

FÜRST. His soul was racked with anguish when he did it.

No choice was left him but to shoot or die!

HEDWIG. Oh, if he had a father's heart,
he would

Have sooner perished by a thousand
deaths!

STAUFFACHER. You should be grateful
for God's gracious care,

That ordered things so well.

HEDWIG. Can I forget
What might have been the issue? God of
Heaven,

Were I to live for centuries, I still
Should see my boy tied up — his father's
mark —

And still the shaft would quiver in my
heart!

MELCHTHAL. You know not how the
Viceroy taunted him!

HEDWIG. Oh, ruthless heart of man!
Offend his pride,

And reason in his breast forsakes her
seat;

In his blind wrath he'll stake upon a cast
A child's existence and a mother's heart!

BAUMGARTEN. Is then your husband's
fate not hard enough,

That you embitter it by such reproaches?
Have you no feeling for his sufferings?

HEDWIG [*turning to him and gazing full
upon him*]. Hast thou tears only
for thy friend's distress?

Say, where were you when he — my noble
Tell —

Was bound in chains? Where was your
friendship then?

The shameful wrong was done before your
eyes;

Patient you stood, and let your friend be
dragged,

Aye, from your very hands. Did ever Tell
Act thus to you? Did he stand whining by,
When on your heels the Viceroy's horsemen
pressed,

And full before you roared the storm-
tossed lake?

Oh, not with idle tears his pity showed;
Into the boat he sprang, forgot his home,
His wife, his children, and delivered thee!

FÜRST. It had been madness to attempt
his rescue,

Unarmed, and few in numbers as we were!

HEDWIG [*casting herself upon his bosom*].
Oh, father, and thou, too, hast lost
my Tell!

The country — all have lost him! All
lament

His loss; and, oh, how he must pine for us!
Heaven keep his soul from sinking to despair!

No friend's consoling voice can penetrate
His dreary dungeon walls. Should he fall
sick!

Ah! In the vapors of the murky vault
He must fall sick. Even as the Alpine rose
Grows pale and withers in the swampy air,
There is no life for him, but in the sun,
And in the breath of heaven's fresh-blow-
ing airs.

Imprisoned! Liberty to him is breath;
He cannot live in the rank dungeon air!

STAUFFACHER. Pray you be calm! And
hand in hand we'll all

Combine to burst his prison doors.

HEDWIG. He gone,
What have you power to do? While Tell
was free,

There still, indeed, was hope — weak innocence

Had still a friend, and the oppressed a stay.
Tell saved you all! You cannot all combined

Release him from his cruel prison bonds.

[*The* BARON *wakes.*]

BAUMGARTEN. Hush, hush! He starts!

ATTINGHAUSEN [*sitting up*]. Where is
he?

STAUFFACHER. Who?

ATTINGHAUSEN. He leaves me —
In my last moments he abandons me.
STAUFFACHER. He means his nephew.
Have they sent for him?
FÜRST. He has been summoned. —
Cheerly, sir! Take comfort!
He has found his heart at last, and is our
own.
ATTINGHAUSEN. Say, has he spoken for
his native land?
STAUFFACHER. Aye, like a hero!
ATTINGHAUSEN. Wherefore comes he
not,
That he may take my blessing ere I die?
I feel my life fast ebbing to a close.
STAUFFACHER. Nay, talk not thus, dear
sir! This last short sleep
Has much refreshed you, and your eye is
bright.
ATTINGHAUSEN. Life is but pain, and
that has left me now;
My sufferings, like my hopes, have passed
away.
[*Observing the Boy.*] What boy is that?
FÜRST. Bless him. Oh, good my lord!
He is my grandson, and is fatherless.
[HEDWIG *kneels with the Boy be-
fore the dying man.*]
ATTINGHAUSEN. And fatherless — I
leave you all, aye, all!
Oh, wretched fate, that these old eyes
should see
My country's ruin, as they close in death!
Must I attain the utmost verge of life,
To feel my hopes go with me to the grave?
STAUFFACHER [*to* FÜRST]. Shall he de-
part 'mid grief and gloom like this?
Shall not his parting moments be illumed
By hope's inspiring beams? — My noble
lord,
Raise up your drooping spirit! We are not
Forsaken quite — past all deliverance.
ATTINGHAUSEN. Who shall deliver you?
FÜRST. Ourselves. For know,
The cantons three are to each other pledged
To hunt the tyrants from the land. The
league
Has been concluded, and a sacred oath
Confirms our union. Ere another year
Begins its circling course, the blow shall
fall.
In a free land your ashes shall repose.

ATTINGHAUSEN. The league concluded!
Is it really so?
MELCHTHAL. On one day shall the
cantons rise together.
All is prepared to strike — and to this hour
The secret closely kept, though hundreds
share it;
The ground is hollow 'neath the tyrants'
feet;
Their days of rule are numbered, and ere
long
No trace will of their hateful sway be left.
ATTINGHAUSEN. Aye, but their castles,
how to master them?
MELCHTHAL. On the same day they,
too, are doomed to fall.
ATTINGHAUSEN. And are the nobles
parties to this league?
STAUFFACHER. We trust to their as-
sistance, should we need it;
As yet the peasantry alone have sworn.
ATTINGHAUSEN [*raising himself up in
great astonishment*]. And have the
peasantry dared such a deed
On their own charge, without the nobles'
aid —
Relied so much on their own proper
strength?
Nay, then, indeed, they want our help no
more;
We may go down to death cheered by the
thought
That after us the majesty of man
Will live, and be maintained by other
hands.
[*He lays his hand upon the head of
the Child who is kneeling before
him.*]
From this boy's head, whereon the apple
lay,
Your new and better liberty shall spring;
The old is crumbling down — the times
are changing —
And from the ruins blooms a fairer life.
STAUFFACHER [*to* FÜRST]. See, see, what
splendor streams around his eye!
This is not nature's last expiring flame,
It is the beam of renovated life.
ATTINGHAUSEN. From their old towers
the nobles are descending,
And swearing in the towns the civic
oath.

In Uechtland and Thurgau the work's
    begun;
The noble Berne lifts her commanding
    head,
And Freyburg is a stronghold of the free;
The stirring Zurich calls her guilds to
    arms —
And now, behold! — the ancient might of
    kings
Is shivered 'gainst her everlasting walls.
    [*He speaks what follows with a
    prophetic tone; his utterance ris-
    ing into enthusiasm.*]
I see the princes and their haughty peers,
Clad all in steel, come striding on to crush
A harmless shepherd race with mailèd
    hand.
Desp'rate the conflict: 't is for life or
    death;
And many a pass will tell to after years
Of glorious victories sealed in foemen's
    blood.
The peasant throws himself with naked
    breast,
A willing victim on their serried spears;
They yield — the flower of chivalry's cut
    down,
And Freedom waves her conquering ban-
    ner high.
    [*Grasps the hands of* WALTER
    FÜRST *and* STAUFFACHER.]
Hold fast together, then — forever fast!
Let freedom's haunts be one in heart and
    mind!
Set watches on your mountain tops, that
    league
May answer league, when comes the hour
    to strike.
Be one — be one — be one —
    [*He falls back upon the cushion.
    His lifeless hands continue to
    grasp those of* FÜRST *and* STAUF-
    FACHER, *who regard him for some
    moments in silence, and then
    retire, overcome with sorrow.
    Meanwhile the servants have
    quietly pressed into the chamber,
    testifying different degrees of
    grief. Some kneel down beside
    him and weep on his body: while
    this scene is passing, the castle
    bell tolls.*]

RUDENZ [*entering hurriedly*]. Lives he?
    Oh, say, can he still hear my voice?
FÜRST [*averting his face*]. You are our
    seignior and protector now;
Henceforth this castle bears another name.
RUDENZ [*gazing at the body with deep
    emotion*]. O God! Is my repentance.
    then, too late?
Could he not live some few brief moments
    more,
To see the change that has come o'er my
    heart?
Oh, I was deaf to his true counseling voice,
While yet he walked on earth. Now he is
    gone —
Gone, and forever — leaving me the
    debt —
The heavy debt I owe him — undis-
    charged!
Oh, tell me! Did he part in anger with me?
STAUFFACHER. When dying, he was told
    what you had done,
And blessed the valor that inspired your
    words!
RUDENZ [*kneeling down beside the dead
    body*]. Yes, sacred relics of a man
    beloved!
Thou lifeless corpse! Here, on thy death-
    cold hand,
Do I abjure all foreign ties forever!
And to my country's cause devote myself.
I am a Switzer, and will act as one,
With my whole heart and soul.
[*Rises.*] Mourn for our friend,
Our common parent, yet be not dismayed!
'T is not alone his lands that I inherit —
His heart — his spirit — have devolved on
    me;
And my young arm shall execute the task
Which in his hoary age he could not pay.
Give me your hands, ye venerable sires!
Thine, Melchthal, too! Nay, do not hesi-
    tate,
Nor from me turn distrustfully away.
Accept my plighted vow — my knightly
    oath!
FÜRST. Give him your hands, my
    friends! A heart like this,
That sees and owns its error, claims our
    trust.
MELCHTHAL. You ever held the peasan-
    try in scorn.

What surety have we, that you mean us
fair?
RUDENZ. Oh, think not of the error of
my youth!
STAUFFACHER [to MELCHTHAL]. Be one!
They were our father's latest words.
See they be not forgotten!
MELCHTHAL. Take my hand —
A peasant's hand — and with it, noble sir,
The gage and the assurance of a man!
Without us, sir, what would the nobles
be?
Our order is more ancient, too, than yours!
RUDENZ. I honor it — will shield it
with my sword!
MELCHTHAL. The arm, my lord, that
tames the stubborn earth,
And makes its bosom blossom with increase,
Can also shield its owner's breast at need.
RUDENZ. Then you shall shield my
breast, and I will yours,
Thus each be strengthened by the other's
strength.
Yet wherefore talk we, while our native
land
Is still to alien tyranny a prey?
First let us sweep the foemen from the soil,
Then reconcile our difference in peace!
[After a moment's pause.] How! You are
silent! Not a word for me!
And have I yet no title to your trust? —
Then must I force my way, despite your
will,
Into the League you secretly have formed.
You've held a Diet on the Rootli — I
Know this — know all that was transacted
there;
And though not trusted with your secret, I
Have kept it closely like a sacred pledge.
Trust me — I never was my country's foe,
Nor would I ever have against you stood!
Yet you did wrong — to put your rising
off.
Time presses! We must strike, and swiftly
too!
Already Tell is lost through your delay.
STAUFFACHER. We swore that we should
wait till Christmastide.
RUDENZ. I was not there — I did not
take the oath.
If you delay, I will not!
MELCHTHAL. What! You would —

RUDENZ. I count me now among the
country's chiefs,
And my first duty is to guard your rights.
FÜRST. Your nearest and your holiest
duty is
Within the earth to lay these dear remains.
RUDENZ. When we have set the coun-
try free, we'll place
Our fresh victorious wreaths upon his bier.
Oh, my dear friends, 't is not your cause
alone! —
I with the tyrants have a cause to fight,
That more concerns myself. My Bertha's
gone,
Has disappeared — been carried off by
stealth —
Stolen from among us by their ruffian
hands!
STAUFFACHER. So fell an outrage has
the tyrant dared
Against a lady free and nobly born?
RUDENZ. Alas! My friends, I promised
help to you,
And I must first implore it for myself!
She that I love is stolen — is forced away,
And who knows where she's by the tyrant
hid,
Or with what outrages his ruffian crew
May force her into nuptials she detests?
Forsake me not! — Oh, help me to her
rescue!
She loves you! Well, oh, well, has she
deserved
That all should rush to arms in her behalf!
STAUFFACHER. What course do you
propose?
RUDENZ. Alas! I know not.
In the dark mystery that shrouds her
fate —
In the dread agony of this suspense —
Where I can grasp at naught of certainty —
One single ray of comfort beams upon me.
From out the ruins of the tyrant's power
Alone can she be rescued from the grave.
Their strongholds must be leveled, every
one,
Ere we can penetrate her dungeon walls.
MELCHTHAL. Come, lead us on! We
follow! Why defer
Until to-morrow what to-day may do?
Tell's arm was free when we at Rootli
swore.

This foul enormity was yet undone.
And change of circumstance brings change
　　of vow;
Who such a coward as to waver still?
RUDENZ [*to* WALTER FÜRST]. Meanwhile
　　to arms, and wait in readiness
The fiery signal on the mountain-tops!
For swifter than a boat can scour the lake
Shall you have tidings of our victory;
And when you see the welcome flames
　　ascend,
Then, like the lightning, swoop upon the
　　foe,
And lay the despots and their creatures
　　low!

SCENE III: *The Pass near Küssnacht,
sloping down from behind, with rocks on
either side.*
　　*The Travelers are visible upon the heights,
before they appear on the stage. Rocks all
round the stage. Upon one of the foremost
a projecting cliff overgrown with brushwood.*

[*Enter* TELL, *with his crossbow.*]

TELL. Through this ravine he needs
　　must come. There is
No other way to Küssnacht. Here I'll do
　　it!
The ground is everything I could desire.
Yon elder bush will hide me from his view,
And from that point my shaft is sure to
　　hit.
The straitness of the gorge forbids pursuit.
Now, Gessler, balance thine account with
　　Heaven!
Thou must away from earth — thy sand
　　is run.
Quiet and harmless was the life I led,
My bow was bent on forest game alone;
No thoughts of murder rested on my soul.
But thou hast scared me from my dream
　　of peace;
The milk of human kindness thou hast
　　turned
To rankling poison in my breast; and made
Appalling deeds familiar to my soul.
He who could make his own child's head
　　his mark,
Can speed his arrow to his foeman's heart.
My boys, poor innocents, my loyal wife,
Must be protected, tyrant, from thy rage!

When last I drew my bow — with trem-
　　bling hand —
And thou, with fiendishly remorseless glee,
Forced me to level at my own boy's head,
When I, imploring pity, writhed before
　　thee,
Then in the anguish of my soul I vowed
A fearful oath, which met God's ear alone,
That when my bow next winged an arrow's
　　flight,
Its aim should be thy heart. The vow I
　　made,
Amid the hellish torments of that moment,
I hold a sacred debt, and I will pay it.
Thou art my lord, my Emperor's dele-
　　gate;
Yet would the Emperor not have stretched
　　his power
So far as thou hast done. He sent thee here
To deal forth law — stern law — for he is
　　wroth;
But not to wanton with unbridled will
In every cruelty, with fiendlike joy:
There lives a God to punish and avenge.
Come forth, thou bringer once of bitter
　　pangs,
My precious jewel now — my chiefest
　　treasure —
A mark I'll set thee, which the cry of grief
Could never penetrate — but thou shalt
　　pierce it —
And thou, my trusty bowstring, that so oft
For sport has served me faithfully and well,
Desert me not in this dread hour of need —
Only be true this once, my own good cord,
That hast so often winged the biting shaft:
For shouldst thou fly successless from my
　　hand,
I have no second to send after thee.
　　　　　　[*Travelers pass over the stage.*]
I'll sit me down upon this bench of stone,
Hewn for the wayworn traveler's brief re-
　　pose —
For here there is no home. Men hurry past
Each other, with quick step and careless
　　look,
Nor stay to question of their grief. Here
　　goes
The merchant, all anxiety — the pilgrim,
With scantly furnished scrip — the pious
　　monk,
The scowling robber, and the jovial player,

The carrier with his heavy-laden horse,
That comes to us from the far haunts of
　men;
For every road conducts to the world's end.
They all push onward — every man intent
On his own several business — mine is
　murder! [Sits down.]
Time was, my dearest children, when
　with joy
You hailed your father's safe return to
　home
From his long mountain toils; for, when he
　came,
He ever brought with him some little gift —
A lovely Alpine flower — a curious bird —
Or elf-bolt, such as on the hills are found.
But now he goes in quest of other game,
Sits in this gorge, with murder in his
　thoughts,
And for his enemy's life-blood lies in wait.
But still it is of you alone he thinks,
Dear children. 'T is to guard your inno-
　cence,
To shield you from the tyrant's fell re-
　venge,
He bends his bow to do a deed of blood!
[Rises.]
Well — I am watching for a noble
　prey —
Does not the huntsman, with unflinching
　heart,
Roam for whole days, when winter frosts
　are keen,
Leap at the risk of death from rock to
　rock —
And climb the jagged, slippery steeps, to
　which
His limbs are glued by his own streaming
　blood —
And all to hunt a wretched chamois down?
A far more precious prize is now my aim —
The heart of that dire foe who seeks my
　life!
[Sprightly music heard in the dis-
　tance, which comes gradually
　nearer.]
From my first years of boyhood I have
　used
The bow — been practiced in the archer's
　feats;
The bull's-eye many a time my shafts have
　hit,

And many a goodly prize have I brought
　home
From competitions. But this day I'll
　make
My master-shot, and win what's best to
　win
In the whole circuit of our mountain range.
[A bridal party passes over the
　stage, and goes up the pass.
　TELL gazes at it, leaning on his
　bow.]

[Enter STUSSI, the Ranger.]

STUSSI. There goes the cloister bailiff's
　bridal train
Of Mörlischachen. A rich fellow he!
And has some half-score pastures on the
　Alps.
He goes to fetch his bride from Imisee.
At Küssnacht there will be high feast to-
　night.
Come with us — ev'ry honest man is asked.
TELL. A gloomy guest fits not a wedding
　feast.
STUSSI. If you've a trouble, dash it from
　your heart!
Take what Heaven sends! The times are
　heavy now,
And we must snatch at pleasure as it flies.
Here 't is a bridal, there a burial.
TELL. And oft the one close on the
　other treads.
STUSSI. So runs the world we live in.
　Everywhere
Mischance befalls and misery enough.
In Glarus there has been a landslip, and
A whole side of the Glärnisch has fallen
　in.
TELL. How! Do the very hills begin to
　quake?
There is stability for naught on earth.
STUSSI. Of strange things, too, we hear
　from other parts.
I spoke with one but now, from Baden
　come,
Who said a knight was on his way to court,
And, as he rode along, a swarm of wasps
Surrounded him, and settling on his horse,
So fiercely stung the beast that it fell dead,
And he proceeded to the court on foot.
TELL. The weak are also furnished with
　a sting.

[*Enter* ARMGART *with several children, and places herself at the entrance of the pass.*]

STUSSI. 'T is thought to bode disaster to the land —
Some horrid deeds against the course of nature.
TELL. Why, every day brings forth such fearful deeds;
There needs no prodigy to herald them.
STUSSI. Aye, happy he who tills his field in peace,
And sits at home untroubled with his kin.
TELL. The very meekest cannot be at peace
If his ill neighbor will not let him rest.
[TELL *looks frequently with restless expectation toward the top of the pass.*]
STUSSI. So fare you well! You're waiting some one here?
TELL. I am.
STUSSI. God speed you safely to your home!
You are from Uri, are you not? His Grace
The Governor's expected thence to-day.
TRAVELER [*entering*]. Look not to see the Governor to-day.
The streams are flooded by the heavy rains,
And all the bridges have been swept away.
[TELL *rises.*]
ARMGART [*coming forward*]. Gessler not coming?
STUSSI. Want you aught with him?
ARMGART. Alas, I do!
STUSSI. Why, then, thus place yourself
Where you obstruct his passage down the pass?
ARMGART. Here he cannot escape me. He must hear me.
FRIESSHARDT [*coming hastily down the pass and calls upon the stage*]. Make way, make way! My lord, the Governor,
Is close behind me, riding down the pass.
[*Exit* TELL.]
ARMGART [*excitedly*]. The Viceroy comes.
[*She goes toward the pass with her children.*]

[GESSLER *and* RUDOLPH DER HARRAS *appear on horseback at the upper end of the pass.*]

STUSSI [*to* FRIESSHARDT]. How got ye through the stream,
When all the bridges have been carried down?
FRIESSHARDT. We've fought, friend, with the tempest on the lake;
An Alpine torrent's nothing after that.
STUSSI. How! Were you out, then, in that dreadful storm?
FRIESSHARDT. We were! I'll not forget it while I live.
STUSSI. Stay, speak —
FRIESSHARDT. I can't — must to the castle haste,
And tell them that the Governor's at hand.
[*Exit.*]
STUSSI. If honest men, now, had been in the ship,
It had gone down with every soul on board:
Some folks are proof 'gainst fire and water both.
[*Looking round.*] Where has the huntsman gone with whom I spoke? [*Exit.*]

[*Enter* GESSLER *and* RUDOLPH DER HARRAS *on horseback.*]

GESSLER. Say what you will; I am the Emperor's liege,
And how to please him my first thought must be.
He did not send me here to fawn and cringe,
And coax these boors into good humor. No!
Obedience he must have. The struggle's this:
Is King or peasant to be sovereign here?
ARMGART. Now is the moment! Now for my petition!
GESSLER. 'T was not in sport that I set up the cap
In Altdorf — or to try the people's hearts —
All this I knew before. I set it up
That they might learn to bend those stubborn necks
They carry far too proudly; and I placed
What well I knew their pride could never brook

Full in the road, which they perforce must
pass,
That, when their eye fell on it, they might
call
That lord to mind whom they too much
forget.
HARRAS. But surely, sir, the people
have some rights —
GESSLER. This is no time to settle what
they are.
Great projects are at work, and hatching
now.
The imperial house seeks to extend its
power.
Those vast designs of conquest which the
sire
Has gloriously begun, the son will end.
This petty nation is a stumbling-block —
One way or other it must be put down.
[*They are about to pass on.* ARM-
GART *throws herself down before*
GESSLER.]
ARMGART. Mercy, Lord Governor! Oh,
pardon, pardon!
GESSLER. Why do you cross me on the
public road?
Stand back, I say.
ARMGART. My husband lies in prison;
My wretched orphans cry for bread. Have
pity,
Pity, my lord, upon our sore distress!
HARRAS. Who are you? and your hus-
band, what is he?
ARMGART. A poor wild-hayman of the
Rigiberg,
Kind sir, who on the brow of the abyss
Mows the unownered grass from craggy
shelves,
To which the very cattle dare not climb.
HARRAS [*to* GESSLER]. By Heaven! a sad
and pitiable life!
I pray you set the wretched fellow free.
How great soever may be his offense,
His horrid trade is punishment enough.
[*To* ARMGART.] You shall have justice. To
the castle bring
Your suit. This is no place to deal with it.
ARMGART. No, no, I will not stir from
where I stand
Until your grace gives me my husband
back.
Six months already has he been shut up,

And waits the sentence of a judge in vain.
GESSLER. How! Would you force me,
woman? Hence! Begone!
ARMGART. Justice, my lord! Aye, jus-
tice! Thou art judge:
Viceregent of the Emperor — of Heaven.
Then do thy duty: as thou hopest for
justice
From Him who rules above, show it to us!
GESSLER. Hence! Drive this insolent
rabble from my sight!
ARMGART [*seizing his horse's reins*]. No,
no, by Heaven, I've nothing more
to lose. —
Thou stir'st not, Viceroy, from this spot,
until
Thou do'st me fullest justice! Knit thy
brows,
And roll thine eyes — I fear not. Our dis-
tress
Is so extreme, so boundless, that we care
No longer for thine anger.
GESSLER. Woman, hence!
Give way, or else my horse shall ride you
down.
ARMGART. Well, let it! — there —
[*Throws her children and herself
upon the ground before him.*]
Here on the ground I lie,
I and my children. Let the wretched
orphans
Be trodden by thy horse into the dust!
It will not be the worst that thou hast done.
HARRAS. Are you mad, woman?
ARMGART [*continuing with vehemence*].
Many a day thou hast
Trampled the Emperor's lands beneath thy
feet!
Oh, I am but a woman! Were I man,
I'd find some better thing to do than here
Lie groveling in the dust!
[*The music of the bridal party is
again heard from the top of the
pass, but more softly.*]
GESSLER. Where are my knaves?
Drag her away, lest I forget myself,
And do some deed I may repent me of.
HARRAS. My lord, the servants cannot
force their way;
The pass is blocked up by a bridal train.
GESSLER. Too mild a ruler am I to this
people;

Their tongues are all too bold — nor have
they yet
Been tamed to due submission, as they
shall be.
I must take order for the remedy;
I will subdue this stubborn mood of theirs,
This braggart spirit of freedom I will crush,
I will proclaim a new law through the land;
I will —

[*An arrow pierces him — he puts
his hand on his heart, and is
about to sink — with a feeble
voice:*]

O God, have mercy on my soul!

HARRAS. My lord! My lord! O God!
What's this? Whence came it?

ARMGART [*starts up*]. Dead, dead! He
reels, he falls! 'T is in his heart!

HARRAS [*springs from his horse*]. Horror
of horrors! Heavenly powers! Sir
Knight,
Address yourself for mercy to your God!
You are a dying man.

GESSLER. That shot was Tell's!

[*He slides from his horse into the
arms of* RUDOLPH DER HAR-
RAS, *who lays him down upon
the bench.*]

[TELL *appears above upon the rocks.*]

TELL. Thou know'st the marksman —
I, and I alone!
Now are our homesteads free, and inno-
cence
From thee is safe: thou'lt be our curse no
more!

[TELL *disappears. People rush in.*]

STUSSI. What is the matter? Tell me
what has happened?

ARMGART. The Viceroy's shot — pierced
by a crossbow bolt!

PEOPLE [*running in*]. Who has been
shot?

[*While the foremost of the marriage
party are coming on the stage,
the hindmost are still upon the
heights. The music continues.*]

HARRAS. He's bleeding fast to death.
Away, for help — pursue the murderer! —
Unhappy man, is this to be your end?
You would not listen to my warning
words.

STUSSI. By Heaven, his cheek is pale!
Life's ebbing fast.

MANY VOICES. Who did the deed?

HARRAS. What! Are the people mad,
That they make music to a murder?
Silence! —

[*Music breaks off suddenly. People
continue to flock in.*]

Speak, if you can, my lord. Have you no
charge
To trust me with?

[GESSLER *makes signs with his
hand, which he repeats with
vehemence when he finds they are
not understood.*]

Where shall I take you to?
To Küssnacht? What you say I can't make
out.
Oh, do not grow impatient! Leave all
thought
Of earthly things and make your peace with
Heaven.

[*The whole marriage party gather
round the dying man.*]

STUSSI. See there! How pale he grows!
Death's gathering now
About his heart — his eyes grow dim and
glazed.

ARMGART [*holds up a child*]. Look, children, how a tyrant dies!

HARRAS. Mad hag!
Have you no touch of feeling, that your
eyes
Gloat on a sight so horrible as this? —
Help me — take hold! What, will not one
assist
To pull the torturing arrow from his breast?

WOMEN. What! touch the man whom
God's own hand has struck!

HARRAS. All curses light on you!

[*Draws his sword.*]

STUSSI [*seizes his arm*]. Gently, Sir
Knight!
Your power is at end. 'T were best for-
bear.
Our country's foe has fallen. We will brook
No further violence. We are free men.

ALL. The country's free!

HARRAS. And is it come to this?
Fear and obedience at an end so soon?

[*To the soldiers of the guard who
are thronging in.*]

You see, my friends, the bloody piece of
work
Has here been done. 'T is now too late for
help,
And to pursue the murderer were vain.
We've other things to think of. On to
Küssnacht,
And let us save that fortress for the King!
For in a moment such as this, all ties
Of order, fealty, and faith, are rent,
And we can trust to no man's loyalty.

> [As he is going out with the soldiers,
> six Fratres Misericordiæ ap-
> pear.]

ARMGART. Here comes the brotherhood
of mercy. Room!
STUSSI. The victim's slain, and now the
ravens stoop.
BROTHERS OF MERCY [form a semicircle
round the body, and sing in solemn
tones].

Death hurries on with hasty stride,
No respite man from him may gain;
He cuts him down, when life's full tide
Is throbbing strong in every vein.
Prepared or not the call to hear,
He must before his Judge appear.

> [While they are repeating the last
> two lines, the curtain falls.]

ACT V

SCENE I: A common near Altdorf. In the
background to the right the keep of Uri, with
the scaffold still standing, as in the third
scene of the First Act. To the left the view
opens upon numerous mountains, on all of
which signal fires are burning. Day is breaking, and distant bells are heard ringing in
several directions.

[Enter RUODI, KUONI, WERNI, Master
Mason, and many other country people,
also women and children.]

RUODI. See there! The beacons on the
mountain heights!
MASON. Hark how the bells above the
forest toll!
RUODI. The enemy's routed!
MASON. And the forts are stormed!
RUODI. And we of Uri, do we still en-
dure

Upon our native soil the tyrant's keep?
Are we the last to strike for liberty?
MASON. Shall the yoke stand, that was
to curb our necks?
Up! Tear it to the ground!
ALL. Down, down with it!
RUODI. Where is the Stier of Uri?
URI. Here. What would ye?
RUODI. Up to your tower, and wind us
such a blast
As shall resound afar, from peak to peak;
Rousing the echoes of each glen and hill,
To rally swiftly all the mountain men!

> [Exit STIER OF URI.]

> [Enter WALTER FÜRST.]

FÜRST. Stay, stay, my friends! As yet
we have not learned
What has been done in Unterwald and
Schwytz.
Let's wait till we receive intelligence!
RUODI. Wait, wait for what? The ac-
cursed tyrant's dead,
And on us freedom's glorious day has
dawned!
MASON. How! Are these flaming sig-
nals not enough,
That blaze on every mountain-top around?
RUODI. Come all, fall to — come, men
and women, all!
Destroy the scaffold! Burst the arches!
Down,
Down with the walls, let not a stone re-
main!
MASON. Come, comrades, come! We
built it, and we know
How best to hurl it down.
ALL. Come! Down with it!

> [They fall upon the building on
> every side.]

FÜRST. The floodgate's burst! They're
not to be restrained.

[Enter MELCHTHAL and BAUMGARTEN.]

MELCHTHAL. What! Stands the fortress
still, when Sarnen lies
In ashes, and the Rossberg's in our hands?
FÜRST. You, Melchthal, here? D'ye
bring us liberty?
Are all the cantons from our tyrants freed?
MELCHTHAL. We've swept them from
the soil. Rejoice, my friend:

Now, at this very moment, while we speak,
There's not one tyrant left in Switzerland!
FÜRST. How did you get the forts into your power?
MELCHTHAL. Rudenz it was who by a bold assault
With manly valor mastered Sarnen's keep.
The Rossberg I had stormed the night before.
But hear, what chanced. Scarce had we driven the foe
Forth from the keep, and given it to the flames,
That now rose crackling upward to the skies,
When from the blaze rushed Diethelm, Gessler's page,
Exclaiming, "Lady Bertha will be burned!"
FÜRST. Good Heavens!
[*The beams of the scaffold are heard falling.*]
MELCHTHAL. 'T was she herself. Here had she been
By Gessler's orders secretly immured.
Up sprang Rudenz in frenzy. For even now
The beams and massive posts were crashing down,
And through the stifling smoke the piteous shrieks
Of the unhappy lady.
FÜRST. Is she saved?
MELCHTHAL. 'T was not a time to hesitate or pause!
Had he been but our baron, and no more,
We should have been most chary of our lives;
But he was our confederate, and Bertha
Honored the people. So, without a thought,
We risked the worst, and rushed into the flames.
FÜRST. But is she saved?
MELCHTHAL. She is. Rudenz and I
Bore her between us from the blazing pile,
With crashing timbers toppling all around.
And when she had revived, the danger past,
And raised her eyes to look upon the sun,
The Baron fell upon my breast; and then
A silent vow between us two was sworn —
A vow that, welded in yon furnace heat,

Will last through ev'ry shock of time and fate.
FÜRST. Where is the Landenberg?
MELCHTHAL. Across the Brünig.
'T was not my fault he bore his sight away,
He who had robbed my father of his eyes!
He fled — I followed — overtook him soon,
And dragged him to my father's feet. The sword
Already quivered o'er the caitiff's head,
When from the pity of the blind old man,
He wrung the life which, craven-like, he begged.
He swore Urphede, never to return:
He'll keep his oath, for he has felt our arm.
FÜRST. Oh, well for you, you have not stained with blood
Our spotless victory!
CHILDREN [*running across the stage with fragments of wood*]. We're free!
We're free!
FÜRST. Oh, what a joyous scene! These children will
Remember it when all their heads are gray.
[*Girls bring in the cap upon a pole. The whole stage is filled with people.*]
RUODI. Here is the cap to which we were to bow!
BAUMGARTEN. What shall we do with it? Do you decide!
FÜRST. Heavens! 'T was beneath this cap my grandson stood!
SEVERAL VOICES. Destroy the emblem of the tyrant's power!
Let it be burned!
FÜRST. No. Rather be preserved;
'T was once the instrument of despots — now
'T will of our freedom be a lasting sign.
[*Peasants, men, women, and children, some standing, others sitting upon the beams of the shattered scaffold, all picturesquely grouped, in a large semicircle.*]
MELCHTHAL. Thus, now, my friends, with light and merry hearts,
We stand upon the wreck of tyranny;
And gloriously the work has been fulfilled,
Which we at Rootli pledged ourselves to do.
FÜRST. No, not fulfilled. The work is but begun:

Courage and concord firm, we need them
both;
For, be assured, the King will make all
speed
To avenge his Viceroy's death, and rein-
state,
By force of arms, the tyrant we've expelled.
MELCHTHAL. Why, let him come, with
all his armaments!
The foe's expelled that pressed us from
within;
The foe without we are prepared to meet!
RUODI. The passes to our cantons are
but few;
These with our bodies we will block — we
will!
BAUMGARTEN. Knit are we by a league
will ne'er be rent,
And all his armies shall not make us quail.

[*Enter* RÖSSELMANN *and* STAUFFACHER.]

RÖSSELMANN [*speaking as he enters*].
These are the awful judgments of
the Lord!
PEASANT. What is the matter?
RÖSSELMANN. In what times we live!
FÜRST. Say on, what is't? — Ha, Wer-
ner, is it you?
What tidings?
PEASANT. What's the matter?
RÖSSELMANN. Hear and wonder!
STAUFFACHER. We are released from
one great cause of dread.
RÖSSELMANN. The Emperor is mur-
dered!
FÜRST. Gracious Heaven!
[*Peasants rise up and throng round*
STAUFFACHER.]
ALL. Murdered! — the Emp'ror? What!
The Emp'ror! Hear!
MELCHTHAL. Impossible! How came
you by the news?
STAUFFACHER. 'T is true! Near Bruck,
by the assassin's hand,
King Albert fell. A most trustworthy man,
John Müller, from Schaffhausen, brought
the news.
FÜRST. Who dared commit so horrible
a deed?
STAUFFACHER. The doer makes the deed
more dreadful still;
It was his nephew, his own brother's son,

Duke John of Austria, who struck the blow.
MELCHTHAL. What drove him to so dire
a parricide?
STAUFFACHER. The Emp'ror kept his
patrimony back,
Despite his urgent importunities;
'T was said, he meant to keep it for himself,
And with a miter to appease the Duke.
However this may be, the Duke gave ear
To the ill counsel of his friends in arms;
And with the noble lords, Von Eschenbach,
Von Tegerfeld, Von Wart, and Palm, re-
solved,
Since his demands for justice were despised,
With his own hands to take revenge at
least.
FÜRST. But say — the dreadful deed,
how was it done?
STAUFFACHER. The King was riding
down from Stein to Baden.
Upon his way to join the court at Rhein-
feld —
With him a train of high-born gentlemen,
And the young Princes John and Leopold;
And when they'd reached the ferry of the
Reuss,
The assassins forced their way into the
boat,
To separate the Emperor from his suite.
His Highness landed, and was riding on
Across a fresh-ploughed field — where once,
they say,
A mighty city stood in pagan times —
With Hapsburg's ancient turrets in sight,
That was the cradle of his princely race,
When Duke John plunged a dagger in his
throat,
Palm ran him through the body with his
lance,
And Eschenbach, to end him, clove his
skull;
So down he sank, all weltering in his blood,
On his own soil, by his own kinsmen slain.
Those on the opposite bank beheld the
deed,
But, parted by the stream, could only raise
An unavailing cry of loud lament.
A poor old woman, sitting by the way,
Raised him, and on her breast he bled to
death.
MELCHTHAL. Thus has he dug his own
untimely grave,

Who sought insatiably to grasp at all.
STAUFFACHER. The country round is
filled with dire alarm,
The passes are blockaded everywhere,
And sentinels on ev'ry frontier set;
E'en ancient Zurich barricades her gates,
That have stood open for these thirty
years,
Dreading the murd'rers and th' avengers
more.
For cruel Agnes comes, the Hungarian
Queen,
By all her sex's tenderness untouched,
Armed with the thunders of the ban, to
wreak
Dire vengeance for her parent's royal
blood,
On the whole race of those that murdered
him —
Their servants, children, children's children
— yea,
Upon the stones that built their castle
walls!
Deep has she sworn a vow to immolate
Whole generations on her father's tomb,
And bathe in blood as in the dew of May.
MELCHTHAL. Is 't known which way the
murderers have fled?
STAUFFACHER. No sooner had they done
the deed than they
Took flight, each following a different
route,
And parted ne'er to see each other more.
Duke John must still be wand'ring in the
mountains.
FÜRST. And thus their crime has borne
no fruit for them.
Revenge bears never fruit. Itself, it is
The dreadful food it feeds on; its delight
Is murder — its satiety despair.
STAUFFACHER. The assassins reap no
profit by their crime;
But we shall pluck with unpolluted hands
The teeming fruits of their most bloody
deed.
For we are ransomed from our heaviest
fear;
The direst foe of liberty has fallen,
And 't is reported that the crown will pass
From Hapsburg's house into another line;
The Empire is determined to assert
Its old prerogative of choice, I hear.

FÜRST AND SEVERAL OTHERS. Is any
named?
STAUFFACHER. The Count of Luxem-
bourg's
Already chosen by the general voice.
FÜRST. 'T is well we stood so stanchly
by the Empire!
Now we may hope for justice, and with
cause.
STAUFFACHER. The Emperor will need
some valiant friends.
He will 'gainst Austria's vengeance be our
shield. [The peasantry embrace.]

[Enter Sacristan with Imperial Messenger.]

SACRISTAN. Here are the worthy chiefs
of Switzerland!
RÖSSELMANN AND SEVERAL OTHERS.
Sacristan, what news?
SACRISTAN. A courier brings this letter.
ALL [to WALTER FÜRST]. Open and read
it.
FÜRST [reading]. "To the worthy men
Of Uri, Schwytz, and Unterwald, the
Queen
Elizabeth sends grace and all good wishes!"
MANY VOICES. What wants the Queen
with us? Her reign is done.
FÜRST [reading]. "In the great grief and
doleful widowhood,
In which the bloody exit of her lord
Has plunged the Queen, still in her mind
she bears
The ancient faith and love of Switzerland."
MELCHTHAL. She ne'er did that in her
prosperity.
RÖSSELMANN. Hush, let us hear!
FÜRST [reading]. "And she is well as-
sured,
Her people will in due abhorrence hold
The perpetrators of this damnèd deed.
On the three cantons, therefore, she relies,
That they in nowise lend the murderers
aid;
But rather, that they loyally assist,
To give them up to the avenger's hand,
Remembering the love and grace which
they
Of old received from Rudolph's royal
house."
[Symptoms of dissatisfaction among
the peasantry.]

MANY VOICES. The love and grace!
STAUFFACHER. Grace from the father
  we, indeed, received,
But what have we to boast of from the son?
Did he confirm the charter of our freedom,
As all preceding Emperors had done?
Did he judge righteous judgment, or afford
Shelter, or stay, to innocence oppressed?
Nay, did he e'en give audience to the men
We sent to lay our grievances before him?
Not one of all these things did the King do,
And had we not ourselves achieved our
  rights
By our own stalwart hands, the wrongs we
  bore
Had never touched him. Gratitude to him!
Within these vales he sowed no seeds of
  that;
He stood upon an eminence — he might
Have been a very father to his people,
But all his aim and pleasure was to raise
Himself and his own house: and now may
  those
Whom he has aggrandized lament for him!
    FÜRST. We will not triumph in his fall,
      nor now
Recall to mind the wrongs that we endured.
Far be 't from us! Yet, that we should
  avenge
The sovereign's death, who never did us
  good,
And hunt down those who ne'er molested
  us,
Becomes us not, nor is our duty. Love
Must be a tribute free, and unconstrained;
From all enforced duties death absolves,
And unto him we owe no further debt.
    MELCHTHAL. And if the Queen laments
      within her bower,
Accusing Heaven in sorrow's wild despair,
Here see a people, from its anguish freed,
To that same Heaven send up its thankful
  praise.
Who would reap tears, must sow the seeds
  of love.
                [Exit the Imperial Courier.]
    STAUFFACHER [to the People]. But where
      is Tell? Shall he, our freedom's
      founder,
Alone be absent from our festival?
He did the most — endured the worst of
  all.

Come — to his dwelling let us all repair,
And bid the savior of our country hail!
                            [Exeunt omnes.]

SCENE II: *Interior of* TELL'S *cottage. A
fire burning on the hearth. The open door
shows the scene outside.*

[*Enter* HEDWIG, WALTER, WILLIAM.]

    HEDWIG. My own dear boys, your
      father comes to-day;
He lives, is free, and we and all are free;
The country owes its liberty to him!
    WALTER. And I, too, mother, bore my
      part in it!
I must be named with him. My father's
  shaft
Ran my life close, but yet I never flinched.
    HEDWIG [embracing him]. Yes, yes, thou
      art restored to me again!
Twice have I seen thee given to my sad
  eyes,
Twice suffered all a mother's pangs for
  thee!
But this is past — I have you both, boys, —
  both!
And your dear father will be back to-day.

    [*A Monk appears at the door.*]

    WILLIAM. See, mother, yonder stands a
      holy friar;
He comes for alms, no doubt.
    HEDWIG. Go lead him in,
That we may give him cheer, and make
  him feel
That he has come into the house of joy.
            [*Exit and returns immediately with
              a cup.*]
    WILLIAM [to the Monk]. Come in, good
      man. Mother will give you food!
    WALTER. Come in and rest, then go re-
      freshed away!
    MONK [glancing round in terror, with un-
      quiet looks]. Where am I? In what
      country? Tell me.
    WALTER. How!
Are you bewildered, that you know not
  where?
You are at Bürglen, in the land of Uri,
Just at the entrance of the Shechenthal.
    MONK [to HEDWIG]. Are you alone?
      Your husband, is he here?

HEDWIG. I am expecting him. But what ails you, man?
There's something in your looks that omens ill!
Whoe'er you be, you are in want — take that. [*Offers him the cup.*]
MONK. Howe'er my sinking heart may yearn for food,
Naught will I taste till you have promised first —
HEDWIG. Touch not my garments; come not near me, monk!
You must stand farther back, if I'm to hear you.
MONK. Oh, by this hearth's bright, hospitable blaze,
By your dear children's heads, which I embrace — [*Grasps the Boys.*]
HEDWIG. Stand back, I say! What is your purpose, man?
Back from my boys! You are no monk — no, no,
Beneath the robe you wear peace should abide,
But peace abides not in such looks as yours.
MONK. I am the wretchedest of living men.
HEDWIG. The heart is never deaf to wretchedness;
But your look freezes up my inmost soul.
WALTER [*springs up*]. Mother, here's father!
HEDWIG. O my God!
[*Is about to follow, trembles and stops.*]
WILLIAM [*running after his brother*]. My father!
WALTER [*without*]. Here, here once more!
WILLIAM [*without*]. My father, my dear father!
TELL [*without*]. Yes, here once more! Where is your mother, boys?
WALTER. There at the door she stands, and can no further,
She trembles so with terror and with joy.
TELL. Oh, Hedwig, Hedwig, mother of my children;
God has been kind and helpful in our woes.
No tyrant's hand shall e'er divide us more.
HEDWIG [*falling on his neck*]. Oh, Tell, what anguish have I borne for thee!
[*Monk becomes attentive.*]

TELL. Forget it now, and live for alone!
I'm here again with you! This is my c
I stand again upon mine own hearthston
WILLIAM. But, father, where 's you crossbow? Not with you?
TELL. Thou shalt not ever see it more, my boy.
Within a holy shrine it has been placed,
And in the chase shall ne'er be used again.
HEDWIG. Oh, Tell! Tell!
[*Steps back, dropping his hand.*]
TELL. What alarms thee, dearest wife?
HEDWIG. How — how dost thou return to me? This hand —
Dare I take hold of it? This hand — O God! —
TELL [*with firmness and animation*]. Has shielded you and set my country free;
Freely I raise it in the face of Heaven.
[*Monk gives a sudden start — TELL looks at him.*]
Who is this friar here!
HEDWIG. Ah, I forgot him;
Speak thou with him; I shudder at his presence.
MONK [*stepping nearer*]. Are you the Tell who slew the Governor?
TELL. Yes, I am he. I hide the fact from no man.
MONK. And you are Tell! Ah! It is God's own hand,
That hath conducted me beneath your roof.
TELL [*examining him closely*]. You are no monk. Who are you?
MONK. You have slain
The Governor, who did you wrong. I, too,
Have slain a foe, who robbed me of my rights.
He was no less your enemy than mine.
I've rid the land of him!
TELL [*drawing back*]. You are — oh, horror! —
In — children, children — in, without a word.
Go, my dear wife! Go! Go! — Unhappy man,
You should be —
HEDWIG. Heav'ns, who is it?
TELL. Do not ask.

Away! Away! The children must not hear
   it —
Out of the house — away! You must not
   rest
'Neath the same roof with this unhappy
   man!
HEDWIG. Alas! What is it? Come.
                  [*Exit with the children.*]
TELL [*to the Monk*]. You are the Duke
Of Austria — I know it. You have slain
The Emperor, your uncle and liege lord!
JOHN. He robbed me of my patrimony.
TELL. How!
Slain him — your King, your uncle! And
   the earth
Still bears you! And the sun still shines on
   you!
JOHN. Tell, hear me; are you —
TELL. Reeking, with the blood
Of him that was your Emperor, your kins-
   man,
Dare you set foot within my spotless house,
Dare to an honest man to show your face,
And claim the rites of hospitality?
JOHN. I hoped to find compassion at
   your hands.
You took, like me, revenge upon your foe!
TELL. Unhappy man! Dare you con-
   found the crime
Of blood-imbrued ambition with the act
Forced on a father in mere self-defense?
Had you to shield your children's darling
   heads,
To guard your fireside's sanctuary — ward
   off
The last, the direst doom from all you
   loved?
To Heaven I raise my unpolluted hands,
To curse your act and you! I have avenged
That holy nature which you have pro-
   faned.
I have no part with you! You murdered, I
Have shielded all that was most dear to
   me.
JOHN. You cast me off to comfortless
   despair!
TELL. I shrink with horror while I talk
   with you.
Hence, on the dread career you have be-
   gun!
Cease to pollute the home of innocence!
                [JOHN *turns to depart.*]

JOHN. I cannot and I will not live this
   life!
TELL. And yet my soul bleeds for you.
   Gracious Heaven,
So young, of such a noble line, the grandson
Of Rudolph, once my lord and Emperor,
An outcast — murderer — standing at my
   door,
The poor man's door — a suppliant, in
   despair!   [*Covers his face.*]
JOHN. If you have power to weep, oh,
   let my fate
Move your compassion — it is horrible!
I am — say, rather was — a prince. I
   might
Have been most happy, had I only curbed
Th' impatience of my passionate desires:
But envy gnawed my heart — I saw the
   youth
Of mine own cousin Leopold endowed
With honor, and enriched with broad do-
   mains,
The while myself, of equal age with him,
In abject slavish nonage was kept back.
TELL. Unhappy man, your uncle knew
   you well,
When from you land and subjects he with-
   held!
You, by your mad and desperate act, have
   set
A fearful seal upon his wise resolve.
Where are the bloody partners of your
   crime?
JOHN. Where'er th' avenging furies
   may have borne them;
I have not seen them since the luckless
   deed.
TELL. Know you the Empire's ban is
   out — that you
Are interdicted to your friends, and given
An outlawed victim to your enemies?
JOHN. Therefore I shun all public
   thoroughfares,
And venture not to knock at any door —
I turn my footsteps to the wilds, and
   through
The mountains roam, a terror to myself!
From mine own self I shrink with horror
   back,
If in a brook I see my ill-starred form!
If you have pity or a human heart —
              [*Falls down before him.*]

TELL. Stand up, stand up! I say.

JOHN. Not till you give
Your hand in promise of assistance to me.

TELL. Can I assist you? Can a sinful
man?
Yet get ye up — how black soe'er your
crime —
You are a man. I, too, am one. From Tell
Shall no one part uncomforted. I will
Do all that lies within my power.

JOHN [springing up and grasping him
ardently by the hand]. Oh, Tell,
You save me from the terrors of despair!

TELL. Let go my hand! You must
away. You cannot
Remain here undiscovered, and, discovered,
You cannot count on succor. Which way,
then,
Would you be going? Where do you hope
to find
A place of rest?

JOHN. Alas! I know not where.

TELL. Hear, then, what Heaven unto
my heart suggests.
You must to Italy — to Saint Peter's
city —
There cast yourself at the Pope's feet —
confess
Your guilt to him, and ease your laden soul!

JOHN. Will he not to th' avengers yield
me up?

TELL. Whate'er he does, accept it as
from God.

JOHN. But how am I to reach that unknown land?
I have no knowledge of the way, and dare
not
Attach myself to other travelers.

TELL. I will describe the road, so mark
me well!
You must ascend, keeping along the Reuss,
Which from the mountains dashes wildly
down.

JOHN [in alarm]. What! See the Reuss?
The witness of my deed!

TELL. The road you take lies through
the river's gorge,
And many a cross proclaims where travelers
Have been by avalanches done to death.

JOHN. I have no fear for nature's terrors, so
I can appease the torments of my soul.

TELL. At every cross kneel down and
expiate
Your crime with burning penitential
tears —
And if you 'scape the perils of the pass,
And are not whelmed beneath the drifted
snows,
That from the frozen peaks come sweeping
down,
You 'll reach the bridge that 's drenched
with drizzling spray.
Then if it give not way beneath your guilt,
When you have left it safely in your rear,
Before you frowns the gloomy Gate of
Rocks,
Where never sun did shine. Proceed
through this,
And you will reach a bright and gladsome
vale.
Yet must you hurry on with hasty steps,
You must not linger in the haunts of peace.

JOHN. Oh, Rudolph, Rudolph, royal
grandsire! Thus
Thy grandson first sets foot within thy
realms!

TELL. Ascending still, you gain the
Gotthardt's heights,
Where are the tarns, the everlasting tarns,
That from the streams of heaven itself are
fed,
There to the German soil you bid farewell;
And thence, with sweet descent, another
stream
Leads you to Italy, your promised land.
[Ranz des Vaches sounded on Alp-
horns is heard without.]
But I hear voices! Hence!

HEDWIG [hurrying in]. Where art thou,
Tell?
My father comes, and in exulting bands
All the confederates approach.

JOHN [covering himself]. Woe 's me!
I dare not tarry 'mong these happy men!

TELL. Go, dearest wife, and give this
man to eat.
Spare not your bounty; for his road is long,
And one where shelter will be hard to find.
Quick — they approach!

HEDWIG. Who is he?

TELL. Do not ask!
And when he quits you, turn your eyes
away,

So that they do not see which way he goes.
[JOHN *advances hastily toward*
TELL, *but he beckons him aside,*
and exit.]

SCENE III: *The whole valley before* TELL'S
house, the heights which enclose it occupied
by peasants, grouped into tableaux. Some
are seen crossing a lofty bridge, which crosses
the Shechen.

[WALTER FÜRST *with the two Boys,* WER-
NER, *and* STAUFFACHER, *come forward.*
Others throng after them. When TELL
appears, all receive him with loud
cheers.]

ALL. Long live brave Tell, our shield,
our savior!
[*While those in front are crowding*
round TELL, *and embracing*
him, RUDENZ *and* BERTHA *ap-*
pear. The former salutes the
peasantry, the latter embraces
HEDWIG. *The music from the*
mountains continues to play.
When it has stopped, BERTHA
steps into the center of the crowd.]

BERTHA. Peasants! Confederates! Into
your league
Receive me, who was happily the first
That found deliverance in the land of
freedom.
To your brave hands I now entrust my
rights.
Will you protect me as your citizen?
PEASANTS. Aye, that we will, with life
and goods!
BERTHA. 'T is well!
And now to him [*turning to* RUDENZ] I
frankly give my hand —
A free Swiss maiden to a free Swiss man!
RUDENZ. And from this moment all my
serfs are free!
[*Music, and the curtain falls.*]

RASMUS MONTANUS

By HOLBERG

Translated by OSCAR JAMES CAMPBELL *and* FREDERIC SCHENCK

CHARACTERS

JEPPE BERG, *a well-to-do peasant*

NILLE, *his wife*

RASMUS BERG, *called* ERASMUS MONTANUS
    their elder son, a student at the University

JACOB, *the younger son*

JERONIMUS, *a wealthy freeholder*

MAGDELONE, *his wife*

LISBED, *their daughter, betrothed to* RASMUS

PEER, *the Deacon*

JESPER, *the Bailiff*

A Lieutenant

NIELS, *the Corporal*

RASMUS MONTANUS

ACT I

A village street showing JEPPE'S *house.*

[*Enter* JEPPE, *with a letter in his hand.*]

JEPPE. It is a shame that the Deacon is not in town, for there's so much Latin in my son's letter that I can't understand. Tears come to my eyes when I think that a poor peasant's son has got so much book-learning, especially as we are n't tenants of the university. I have heard from people who know about learning that he can dispute with any clergyman alive. Oh, if only my wife and I could have the joy of hearing him preach on the hill, before we die, we should n't grudge all the money we have spent on him! I can see that Peer, the Deacon, does n't much relish the idea of my son's coming. I believe that he is afraid of Rasmus Berg. It is a terrible thing about these scholarly people. They are so jealous of each other, and no one of them can endure the thought that another is as learned as he. The good man preaches fine sermons here in the village and can talk about envy so that the tears come to my eyes; but it seems to me that he is n't entirely free from that fault himself. I can't understand why it should be so. If any one said that a neighbor of mine understood farming better than I, should I take that to heart? Should I hate my neighbor for that? No, indeed, Jeppe Berg would never do such a thing. But if here is n't Peer, the Deacon!

[*Enter* PEER, *the Deacon.*]

Welcome home again, Peer.

PEER. Thank you, Jeppe Berg.

JEPPE. Oh, my dear Peer, I wish you could explain to me some Latin in my son's last letter.

PEER. That's nothing! Do you think I don't understand Latin as well as your son? I am an old *academicus*, I'd have you know, Jeppe Berg.

JEPPE. I know it. — I just wondered if you understood the new Latin, for that language must change, just as the language of Sjælland has done. In my youth the people here on the hill did n't talk the way they do now; what they now call a "lackey" used to be called a "boy"; what they now call a "*mysterious*" used to be called a "whore"; a "mademoiselle," a "housemaid"; a "musician," a "fiddler"; and a "secretary," a "clerk." So I suppose Latin may have changed, too, since you were in Copenhagen. [*Pointing to a line in the letter.*] Will you please explain that? I can read the letters, but I don't get the meaning.

PEER. Your son writes that he is now studying his *Logicam, Rhetoricam,* and *Metaphysicam.*

JEPPE. What does *Logicam* mean?

PEER. That's his pulpit.

JEPPE. I'm glad of that. I wish he could become a pastor!

PEER. But a deacon first.

JEPPE. What is the second subject?

PEER. That is *Rhetorica*, which in Danish means the Ritual. The third subject must be written wrong, or else it must be in French, because if it were Latin, I could read it easily. I am able, Jeppe Berg, to recite the whole Aurora: *ala*, that's a wing; *ancilla*, a girl; *barba*, a beard; *cœna*, a chamber-pot; *cerevisia*, ale; *campana*, a bell; *cella*, a cellar; *lagena*, a bottle; *lana*, a wolf; *ancilla*, a girl; *janua*, a door; *cerevisia*, butter; —

JEPPE. You must have the devil's own memory, Peer!

PEER. Yes, I never thought I should have to stay in a poverty-stricken deacon's living so long. I could have been something else years ago, if I had been willing to tie myself to a girl. But I prefer to help myself rather than have people say of me that I got a living through my wife.

JEPPE. But, my dear Peer, here is more

Latin that I can't understand. Look at this line.

PEER. *Die Veneris Hafnia domum profecturus sum.* That's rather high-flown, but I understand it perfectly, though any other man might cudgel his brains over it. That means in Danish: There is come *profecto* a lot of Russes to Copenhagen.

JEPPE. What are the Russians doing here again?

PEER. These are n't Muscovites, Jeppe Berg, but young students, who are called "Russes."

JEPPE. Oh, I see. I suppose there is a great celebration on the days when the boys get their salt and bread and become students.

PEER. When do you expect him home?

JEPPE. To-day or to-morrow. Wait a bit, my dear Peer; I will run and tell Nille to bring us out a drink of ale.

PEER. I'd rather have a glass of brandy — it's early in the day to drink ale.

[*Exit* JEPPE *into house.*]

To tell the truth, I am not very anxious to have Rasmus Berg come home. Not that I am afraid of his learning, for I was an old student when he was still at school, getting beatings — saving your presence — on his rump. They were different fellows who graduated in my time from what they are now. I graduated from Slagelse School with Peer Monsen, Rasmus Jespersen, Christen Klim, Mads Hansen, — whom we used to call Mads Pancake in school, — Poul Iversen, — whom we called Poul Barlycorn, — all boys with bone in their skulls and beards on their chins, able to argue on any subject that might come up. I'm only a deacon, but I'm content so long as I get my daily bread and understand my office. I have made the income a deal bigger, and get more than any of my predecessors did; so my successors won't curse me in my grave. People think that there are no fine points for a deacon to know, but I can tell you, a deacon's position is a hard one if you want to keep it on such a footing that it will support a man. Before my time people here in the village thought one funeral-song as good as another, but I have arranged things so that I can say to a peasant, "Which hymn will you have? This one costs so much and this one so much"; and when it comes to scattering earth on the body, "Will you have fine sand or just common or garden dirt?" Then there are various other touches that my predecessor, Deacon Christoffer, had no idea of; but he was uneducated. I can't understand how the fellow ever came to be a deacon; yet deacon he was, all the same. I tell you, Latin helps a man a great deal in every sort of business. I would n't give up the Latin I know for a hundred rix-dollars. It has been worth more than a hundred rix-dollars to me in my business; yes, that and a hundred more.

[*Enter* NILLE *and* JEPPE.]

NILLE [*offering the deacon a glass of brandy*]. Your health, Peer!

PEER. Thank you, mother. I never drink brandy unless I have a stomach-ache, but I have a bad stomach most of the time.

NILLE. Do you know, Peer, my son is coming home to-day or to-morrow! You'll find him a man you can talk to, for the boy's not tongue-tied, from all I hear.

PEER. Yes, I suppose he can talk a lot of Cloister-Latin.

NILLE. Cloister-Latin? That must be the best Latin, just as cloister-linen is the best linen.

PEER. Ha, ha, ha, ha!

JEPPE. What are you laughing at, Peer?

PEER. At nothing at all, Jeppe Berg. Just another drop! Your health, mother! It's true, as you say: cloister-linen is good linen, but —

NILLE. If that linen is n't made in a cloister, why is it called cloister-linen?

PEER. Yes, that's right enough, ha, ha, ha! But won't you give me a bite to eat with my brandy?

NILLE [*getting a plate from the house*]. Here's a little bread and cheese already cut, if you will eat it.

PEER. Thank you, mother. Do you know what bread is in Latin?

NILLE. No, indeed, I don't.

PEER [*eating and talking at the same time*]. It's called *panis;* genitive, *pani;* dative, *pano;* vocative, *panus;* ablative, *pano.*

JEPPE. Goodness, Peer! That language is long-winded. What is coarse bread in Latin?

PEER. That's *panis gravis;* and fine bread is *panis finis.*

JEPPE. Why, that's half Danish!

PEER. True. There are many Latin words that were originally Danish. I'll tell you why: there was once an old rector at the school in Copenhagen, called Saxo Grammatica, who improved Latin in this country, and wrote a Latin grammar, and that's why he was called Saxo Grammatica. This same Saxo greatly enriched the Latin language with Danish words, for in his day Latin was so poor that a man could n't write one sentence which people could understand.

JEPPE. But what does that word "Grammatica" mean?

PEER. The same as "Donat." When it is bound in a Turkish cover it is called "Donat," but when it's in white parchment it's called "Grammatica," and declined just like *ala.*

NILLE. I never shall see how people can keep so much in their head. My head swims just from hearing them talk about it.

JEPPE. That's why learned folk usually are n't quite right in their heads.

NILLE. What nonsense! Do you think our son Rasmus Berg is n't quite right?

JEPPE. It only seems a little queer, mother, that he should write a Latin letter to me.

PEER. Jeppe's right there, certainly. That was a little foolish. It is just as if I were to talk Greek to the bailiff, to show him that I understood the language.

JEPPE. Do you know Greek, Peer?

PEER. Why, twenty years ago I could repeat the whole Litany in Greek, standing on one foot. I still remember that the last word was "Amen."

JEPPE. Oh, Peer, it will be splendid, when my son comes back, to get you two together!

PEER. If he wants to dispute with me, he will find that I can hold my own; and if he wants to have a singing match with me, he will get the worst of it. I once had a singing contest with ten deacons and beat every one of them, for I outsang them in the *Credo,* all ten of them. Ten years ago I was offered the position of choirmaster in Our Lady's School, but I did n't want it. Why should I take it, Jeppe? Why should I leave my parish, which loves and honors me, and which I love and honor in return? I live in a place where I earn my daily bread, and where I am respected by every one. The governor himself never comes here but he sends for me at once to pass the time with him and sing for him. Last year on this occasion he gave me two marks for singing "Ut, re, mi, fa, sol." He swore that he took more pleasure in that than in the best vocal music he had heard in Copenhagen. If you give me another glass of brandy, Jeppe, I will sing the same thing for you.

JEPPE. Do, please. Pour another glass of brandy, Nille. [*Exit* NILLE.]

PEER. I don't sing for every one, but you are my good friend, Jeppe, whom I serve with pleasure. [*He sings.*] *Ut, re, mi, fa, sol, la, si, ut;* now down — *ut, si, la, sol, fa, mi, re, ut.*

[*Reënter* NILLE *with brandy. He drinks.*]

Now you shall hear how high I can go, *ut, re, mi, fa, sol, la, si, ut, re, mi, fa, sol, la, si, ut, re* —

JEPPE. Heavens! That last was fine. Our little pigs can't go any higher with a squeak.

PEER. Now I will sing rapidly: *Ut, re, mi, re* — No! that was n't right. *Ut, re, mi, do, re, mi, ut* — No, that went wrong, too. It's cursed hard, Jeppe, to sing so fast. But there comes Monsieur Jeronimus.

[*Enter* JERONIMUS, MAGDELONE, *and* LISBED.]

JERONIMUS. Good-morning, kinsman! Have you any news from your son?

JEPPE. Yes; he is coming to-day or to-morrow.

LISBED. Oh, is it possible? Then my dream has come true.

JERONIMUS. What did you dream?

LISBED. I dreamed that I slept with him last night.

MAGDELONE. There is something in dreams, I tell you. Dreams are not to be despised.

JERONIMUS. That's true enough, but if you girls did n't think so much about the menfolk in the daytime, you would n't have so many dreams about them at night. I suppose you used to dream just as much about me in the days when we were engaged, Magdelone?

MAGDELONE. I did, indeed, but upon my word I have n't dreamed about you for some years now.

JERONIMUS. That's because your love is n't as hot now as it used to be.

LISBED. But is it possible that Rasmus Berg is coming home to-morrow?

JERONIMUS. Come, daughter, you should n't show that you are so much in love.

LISBED. Oh, but is it sure that he is coming home to-morrow?

JERONIMUS. Yes, yes; you hear, don't you, that's when he is coming?

LISBED. How long is it till to-morrow, father, dear?

JERONIMUS. What confounded nonsense! These people in love act as if they were crazy.

LISBED. I tell you, I shall count every hour.

JERONIMUS. You should ask how long an hour is, so that people would think that you were completely mad. Stop this twaddle and let us elders talk together. — Listen, my dear Jeppe Berg! Do you think it is wise for these two young people to marry before he gets a position?

JEPPE. That is as you think best. I can support them well enough, but it would be better that he should get a position first.

JERONIMUS. I don't think it would be wise for them to marry until then. [LISBED weeps and wails.] Fie, shame on you! It's a disgrace for a girl to carry on so!

LISBED [sobbing]. Can't he get a position soon, then?

JEPPE. There's no doubt about it; he'll get a position soon enough, for from what I hear he is so learned he can read any book there is. He wrote me a Latin letter just lately.

NILLE. And, marry, it's one that can stand alone, as the deacon can tell you.

LISBED. Was it so well written?

PEER. Yes, well written for one so young. He may amount to something, mamselle! But there's a lot left to learn. I thought I was learned, myself, at his age, but —

JEPPE. Yes, you learned folk never praise one another —

PEER. Nonsense! Do you think I am jealous of him? Before he was born I had been up for a flogging before the school three times, and when he was in the fourth form I had been eight years a deacon.

JEPPE. One man may have a better head than another; one may learn as much in a year as others in ten.

PEER. For that matter, the Deacon dares set his head against any one's.

JERONIMUS. Yes, yes, you may both be right. Let us go home, children. Good-bye, Jeppe! I happened to be passing, and I thought I might as well talk to you on the way.

LISBED. Be sure to let me know as soon as he comes!

[Exeunt JERONIMUS, MAGDELONE, and LISBED.]

[Enter JACOB.]

JEPPE. What do you want, Jacob?

JACOB. Father! Have you heard the news? Rasmus Berg is back.

JEPPE. Heavens, is it possible! How does he look?

JACOB. Oh, he looks mighty learned. Rasmus Nielsen, who drove him, swears that he did nothing all the way but dispute with himself in Greek and Elamite; and sometimes with so much zeal that he struck Rasmus Nielsen in the back of the neck three or four times, with his clenched fist, shouting all the while, "Probe the Major! Probe the Major!" I suppose he must have had a dispute with a major before he started out. Part of the way he sat still and stared at the moon and the stars with such a rapt expression that he fell off the wagon three times and nearly broke his neck from sheer learning. Rasmus Nielsen laughed at that, and said to himself, "Rasmus Berg may be a wise man in the heavens, but he is a fool on earth."

JEPPE. Let us go and meet him. Come with us, dear Peer. It may be that he has forgotten his Danish and won't be able to talk anything but Latin. In that case you can be interpreter.

PEER [aside]. Not if I know it! [Aloud.] I have other things to attend to.

ACT II

A room in JEPPE'S *house.*

[*Enter* MONTANUS, *whose stockings are falling down around his ankles.*]

MONTANUS. I have been away from Copenhagen only a day, and I miss it already. If I didn't have my good books with me, I couldn't exist in the country. *Studia secundas res ornant, adversis solatium prœbent.* I feel as if I had lost something, after going three days without a disputation. I don't know whether there are any learned folk in the village, but if there are, I shall set them to work, for I can't live without disputation. I can't talk much to my poor parents, for they are simple folk and know hardly anything beyond their catechism; so I can't find much comfort in their conversation. The Deacon and the Schoolmaster are said to have studied, but I don't know how much that has amounted to; still, I shall see what they are good for. My parents were astonished to see me so early, for they had not expected me to travel by night from Copenhagen. [*He strikes a match, lights his pipe, and puts the bowl of his pipe through a hole he has made in his hat.*] That's what they call smoking *studentikos* — it's a pretty good invention for any one who wants to write and smoke at the same time.

[*Sits down and begins to read.*]

[*Enter* JACOB. *He kisses his own hand and extends it to his brother.*]

JACOB. Welcome home again, my Latin brother!

MONTANUS. I am glad to see you, Jacob. But as for being your brother, that was well enough in the old days, but it will hardly do any more.

JACOB. How so? Aren't you my brother?

MONTANUS. Of course I don't deny, you rogue, that I am your brother by birth, but you must realize that you are still a peasant boy, whereas I am a Bachelor of Philosophy. But listen, Jacob, — how are my sweetheart and her father?

JACOB. Very well. They were here awhile ago and asked how soon brother would be at home.

MONTANUS. Brother again! It's not from mere pride that I object, Jacob, but it simply won't do.

JACOB. Then what shall I call you, brother?

MONTANUS. You must call me "Monsieur Montanus," for that is what I am called in Copenhagen.

JACOB. If I could only keep it in my head. Was is "Monsieur Dromedarius"?

MONTANUS. Can't you hear? I say "Monsieur Montanus."

JACOB. Mossur Montanus, Mossur Montanus.

MONTANUS. That's right. "Montanus" in Latin is the same as "Berg" in Danish.

JACOB. Then can't I be called "Jacob Montanus"?

MONTANUS. When you have been to school as long as I have and passed your examinations, then you can give yourself a Latin name, too; but as long as you are a peasant boy, you must be satisfied with plain Jacob Berg. By the way, have you noticed that my sweetheart has been longing for me?

JACOB. Indeed, she has. She has been very impatient at your staying away so long, brother.

MONTANUS. There you go again, yokel!

JACOB. I meant to say: Mossur's sweetheart has been impatient because brother stayed away so long.

MONTANUS. Well, I'm here now, Jacob, and all for her sake; but I shall not stay very long, for as soon as we've had the wedding I shall take her to Copenhagen with me.

JACOB. Won't mossur take me along?

MONTANUS. What would you do there?

JACOB. I should like to look around in the world a bit.

MONTANUS. I wish you were six or seven years younger, so that I could put you into a Latin school, and then you could be a college man, too.

JACOB. No, that would n't do.

MONTANUS. Why not?

JACOB. If that happened, our parents would have to go begging.

MONTANUS. Hear how the fellow talks!

JACOB. Oh, I am full of ideas. If I had studied, I should have been the devil of a rogue.

MONTANUS. I have been told that you had a good head. But what else should you like to do in Copenhagen?

JACOB. I should like to see the Round Tower and the cloister where they make the linen.

MONTANUS. Ha, ha, ha! They're busy with other things besides linen-making in the cloister. But tell me, has my future father-in-law as much money as they say?

JACOB. He surely has. He is a rich old man, and owns nearly a third of the village.

MONTANUS. Have you heard whether he intends to give his daughter a dowry?

JACOB. Oh, I think he will give her a good one, especially if he once hears mossur preach here in the village.

MONTANUS. That will never happen. I should lower myself too much by preaching here in the country. Besides, I am interested only in disputation.

JACOB. I thought it was better to be able to preach.

MONTANUS. Do you know what disputation really means?

JACOB. Of course! I dispute every day here at home with the maids, but I don't gain anything by it.

MONTANUS. Oh, we have plenty of that kind of disputation.

JACOB. What is it, then, that mossur disputes about?

MONTANUS. I dispute about weighty and learned matters. For example, whether angels were created before men; whether the earth is round or oval; about the moon, sun, and stars, their size and distance from the earth; and other things of a like nature.

JACOB. That's not the sort of thing I dispute about, for that's not the sort of thing that concerns me. If only I can get the servants to work, they can say the world is eight-cornered, for all I care.

MONTANUS. Oh, *animal brutum!* — Listen, Jacob, do you suppose any one has let my sweetheart know that I have come home?

JACOB. I don't believe so.

MONTANUS. Then you had better run over to Master Jeronimus's and inform him of the event.

JACOB. Yes, I can do that, but shall I not tell Lisbed first?

MONTANUS. Lisbed? Who is that?

JACOB. Don't you know, brother, that your betrothed's name is Lisbed?

MONTANUS. Have you forgotten all I have just taught you, you rascal?

JACOB. You may call me "rascal" as much as you like, but I'm your brother just the same.

MONTANUS. If you don't shut up, I'll *profecto* hit you over the head with this book.

JACOB. It would n't be proper to throw the Bible at people.

MONTANUS. This is no Bible.

JACOB. Marry, I know a Bible when I see one. That book is big enough to be the Bible. I can see that it's not a Gospel Book, nor a Catechism. But whatever it is, it's a bad thing to throw books at your brother.

MONTANUS. Shut up, rascal!

JACOB. I may be a rascal, but I earn with my hands the money for my parents that you spend.

MONTANUS. If you don't shut up, I'll maim you.

[*Throws the book at him.*]

JACOB. Ow, ow, ow!

[*Enter* JEPPE *and* NILLE.]

JEPPE. What is all this noise?

JACOB. Oh, my brother Rasmus is beating me.

NILLE. What does this mean? He would n't hit you without good reason.

MONTANUS. No, mother, that is so. He comes here and bandies words with me as though he were my equal.

NILLE. What a devil's own rogue! Don't you know enough to respect such a learned man? Don't you know that he is an honor to our whole family? My dear and respected son, you must n't pay any attention to him; he is an ignorant lout.

MONTANUS. I sit here speculating about important questions, and this *importunissimus* and *audacissimus juvenis* comes and hinders me. It is no child's play to have to deal with these *transcendentalibus*. I would n't have had it happen for two marks.

JEPPE. Oh, don't be angry, my dear son! This shall never happen again. I am so much afraid that my honored son has allowed himself to get over-excited. Learned folk can't stand many shocks. I know that Peer, the Deacon, got excited once and did n't recover for three days.

MONTANUS. Peer, the Deacon! Is he learned?

JEPPE. I should say he was! As far back as I can remember, we have never had a deacon here in the village who could sing as well as he can.

MONTANUS. For all that, he may have no learning at all.

JEPPE. He preaches beautifully, too.

MONTANUS. For all that, too, he might have no learning at all.

NILLE. Oh, honored son! How can a man lack learning if he preaches well?

MONTANUS. Surely, mother! All the ignorant folk preach well, for inasmuch as they can't compose anything out of their own heads, they use borrowed sermons, and learn good men's compositions by heart, though sometimes they don't understand them themselves. A learned man, on the other hand, won't use such methods; he composes out of his own head. Believe me, it is a common mistake in this country to judge a student's learning altogether too much from his sermons. But let the fellow dispute as I do — there's the touchstone of learning. If any one says this table is a candlestick, I will justify the statement. If any one says that meat or bread is straw, I

will justify that, too; that has been done many a time. Listen, father! Will you admit that the man who drinks well is blessed?

JEPPE. I think rather that he is accursed, for a man can drink himself out of both reason and money.

MONTANUS. I will prove that he is blessed. *Quicunque bene bibit, bene dormit.* But, no, — you don't understand Latin; I must say it in Danish. Whoever drinks well, sleeps well. Is n't that so?

JEPPE. That's true enough, for when I am half-drunk I sleep like a horse.

MONTANUS. He who sleeps well does not sin. Is n't that true, too?

JEPPE. True, too; so long as a man's asleep he does n't sin.

MONTANUS. He who does not sin is blessed.

JEPPE. That is also true.

MONTANUS. *Ergo*, he who drinks well is blessed. — Little mother, I will turn you into a stone.

NILLE. Oh, nonsense! That is more than even learning can do.

MONTANUS. You shall hear whether it is or not. A stone cannot fly.

NILLE. No, indeed it can't, unless it is thrown.

MONTANUS. You cannot fly.

NILLE. That is true, too.

MONTANUS. *Ergo*, little mother is a stone. [NILLE *cries.*] Why are you crying, little mother?

NILLE. Oh! I am so much afraid that I shall turn into a stone. My legs already begin to feel cold.

MONTANUS. Don't worry, little mother. I will immediately turn you into a human being again. A stone neither thinks nor talks.

NILLE. That is so. I don't know whether it can think or not, but it surely cannot talk.

MONTANUS. Little mother can talk.

NILLE. Yes, thank God, I talk as well as a poor peasant woman can!

MONTANUS. Good! *Ergo*, little mother is no stone.

NILLE. Ah! That did me good! Now I am beginning to feel like myself again. Faith, it must take strong heads to study. I don't see how your brains can stand it. —

Jacob, after this you shall wait on your brother; you have nothing else to do. If your parents see that you annoy him, you shall get as many blows as your body can stand.

MONTANUS. Little mother, I should like very much to break him of the habit of calling me "brother." It is not decent for a peasant boy to call a learned man "brother." I should like to have him call me "monsieur."

JEPPE. Do you hear that, Jacob? When you speak to your brother after this, you are to call him mossur.

MONTANUS. I should like to have the Deacon invited here to-day, so that I can see what he is good for.

JEPPE. Yes, surely, it shall be done.

MONTANUS. In the mean time I will go to visit my sweetheart.

NILLE. But I am afraid it is going to rain. Jacob can carry your cloak for you.

MONTANUS. Jacob.

JACOB. Yes, mossur.

MONTANUS. Walk behind me and carry my cloak.

[*Exit* MONTANUS *followed by* JA-COB *bearing the cloak.*]

JEPPE. Have n't we cause to be pleased with a son like that, Nille?

NILLE. Yes, indeed, not a penny has been wasted on him.

JEPPE. We shall hear to-day what the Deacon is good for. But I am afraid that he won't come if he hears that Rasmus Berg is here, — there is no need of our letting him know that. We will write the Bailiff, too; he is glad enough to come, for he likes our ale.

NILLE. It is very dangerous, husband, to treat the Bailiff; a man like that must n't find out how our affairs stand.

JEPPE. He is welcome to know. Every man here in the village is aware that we are well-to-do folks. As long as we pay our taxes and land rent, the Bailiff can't touch a hair of our head.

NILLE. Oh, dear husband, I wonder if it is too late to let our Jacob get an education. Just think, if he could be a learned lad like his brother, what a joy it would be for his old parents!

JEPPE. No, wife, one is enough; we must have one at home who can give us a hand and do our work.

NILLE. Oh, at such work as that a man cannot do more than live from hand to mouth. Rasmus Berg, who is a scholar, can do our family more good, with his brain, in an hour than the other in a year.

JEPPE. That makes no difference, little mother; our fields must be tilled and our crops looked after. We can't possibly get along without Jacob. Look, here he is now, coming back again!

[*Enter* JACOB.]

JACOB. Ha! ha, ha, ha, ha, ha, ha! My brother may be a very learned man, but he is a great simpleton for all that.

NILLE. You wicked rascal! Do you call your brother a simpleton?

JACOB. I really don't know what I ought to call such a thing, little mother. It rained until it poured, and yet he let me walk along behind him with the cloak on my arm.

JEPPE. Could n't you have been civil enough to have said, "Mossur, it is raining. Won't you put on your cloak?"

JACOB. It seems to me, little father, it would have been very strange for me to say to the person whose parents had spent so much money upon him to teach him wisdom and cleverness, when so much rain was falling on him that he was wet to his shirt, "It is raining, sir; won't you put on your cloak?" He had no need of my warning; the rain gave him warning enough.

JEPPE. Did you walk the whole way, then, with the cloak on your arm?

JACOB. Marry, I did not; I wrapped myself up comfortably in the cloak; so my clothes are perfectly dry. I understand that sort of thing better than he, though I've not spent so much money learning wisdom. I grasped it at once, although I don't know one Latin letter from another.

JEPPE. Your brother was plunged in thought, as deeply learned folk usually are.

JACOB. Ha, ha! the devil split such learning!

JEPPE. Shut up, you rogue, or shame on your mouth! What does it matter if your brother is absent-minded about such things as that, when in so many other matters he displays his wisdom and the fruit of his studies?

JACOB. Fruit of his studies! I shall tell you what happened next on our trip. When we came to Jeronimus's gate, he went right to the side where the watch-dog stood, and he would have had his learned legs well caulked if I had not dragged him to the other side; for watch-dogs are no respecters of persons; they measure all strangers with the same stick, and bite at random whatever legs they get hold of, whether Greek or Latin. When he entered the court, Mossur Rasmus Berg absent-mindedly went into the stable and shouted, "Hey, is Jeronimus at home?" But the cows all turned their tails to him and none of them would answer a word. I am certain that if any of them could have talked, they would have said, "What a confounded lunk-head that lad must be!"

NILLE. Oh, my dear husband, can you stand hearing him use such language?

JEPPE. Jacob, you will get into trouble if you talk like that any more.

JACOB. Little father ought rather to thank me, for I set him to rights and took him out of the stable toward the house. Just think what might happen to such a lad if he should go on a long journey alone; for I'm sure that if I had not been with him, he would have been standing in the stable yet, gazing at the cows' tails, from sheer learning.

JEPPE. A plague on your impudent mouth! [JACOB runs off, JEPPE after him.]

NILLE. The confounded rogue! — I have sent word to the Bailiff and the Deacon, so that my son can have some one to dispute with when he comes back.

ACT III

Same as Act II.

[*Enter* NILLE.]

NILLE [*alone*]. My son Montanus is gone a long time. I wish he would come home before the Bailiff goes, for he wants very much to talk with him, and is eager to ask him about several things which — But there, I see him coming.

[*Enter* MONTANUS.]

Welcome home, my dear son. Our kind friend Jeronimus was no doubt very glad to see our honored son in good health after so long an absence.

MONTANUS. I have spoken neither to Jeronimus nor to his daughter, on account of that fellow with whom I got into a dispute.

NILLE. What kind of a man was he? Perhaps it was the Schoolmaster.

MONTANUS. No, it was a stranger, who is going away to-day. I know him, although I have not associated with him in Copenhagen. I am annoyed almost to death by these people who imagine they have absorbed all wisdom, and still are idiots. I'll tell you, mother, how it is: This fellow has been *ordinarius opponens* once or twice; therein lies his sole achievement. But how did he perform his *Partes? Misere et hæsitanter absque methodo.* Once when *Præses* wished to distinguish *inter rem et modum rei,* he asked, *Quid hoc est?* — Wretch, you should have known that *antequam in arenam descendis. Quid hoc est? Quæ bruta!* A fellow who ignores the *distinctiones cardinales,* and then wants to dispute *publice!*

NILLE. Oh, my respected son, you mustn't take such things as that to heart. I can see from what you say that he must be a fool.

MONTANUS. An *ignoramus.*

NILLE. Nothing could be plainer.

MONTANUS. An idiot.

NILLE. I can't see that he is anything else.

MONTANUS. *Et quidem plane hospes in philosophia.* Let the dog turn away from what he committed in the presence of so many worthy people.

NILLE. Is that what he did? By that you may know a swine.

MONTANUS. No, little mother, he did something worse than that; he openly confounded *materiam cum forma.*

NILLE. Plague take him!

MONTANUS. Does the fellow imagine that he can dispute?

NILLE. The devil he can!

MONTANUS. Not to mention the mistake he made in his *Prœmio,* when he said, *"Lectissimi et doctissimi auditores."*

NILLE. What a fool he must be!

MONTANUS. For putting *"lectissimi"* in front of *"doctissimi,"* when *"lectissimi"* is a predicate, one can give a *Deposituro.*

NILLE. But did n't you get a chance to talk with Jeronimus, my son?

MONTANUS. No; just as I was about to go into the house, I saw the fellow passing by the gate, and as we knew each other, I went out to speak to him, whereupon we immediately began to talk of learned matters, and finally to dispute, so that I had to postpone my visit.

NILLE. I am very much afraid that Monsieur Jeronimus will be offended when he hears that my son has been in his yard, but went away without talking with him.

MONTANUS. Well, I can't help that. When any one attacks philosophy, he attacks my honor. I am fond of Mademoiselle Lisbed, but my *Metaphysica* and my *Logica* have priority.

NILLE. Oh, my dear son, what did I hear? Are you engaged to two other girls in Copenhagen? That will be a bad business in the matrimonial courts.

MONTANUS. You don't understand me; I did n't mean it in that way. They are not two girls, but two sciences.

NILLE. Oh, that is another matter. But here comes the Bailiff. Don't be angry any more.

MONTANUS. I can't be angry with him, for he is a simple, ignorant man, with whom I cannot get into a dispute.

[*Enter* JEPPE *and* JESPER, *the Bailiff.*]

JESPER. *Serviteur,* monsieur. I congratulate you on your arrival.

MONTANUS. I thank you, Mr. Bailiff.

JESPER. I am glad that we have such a learned man here in the village. It must have cost you many a racking of the brain to have advanced so far. I congratulate you, too, Jeppe Berg, upon your son. Now, happiness has come to you in your old age.

JEPPE. Yes, that is true.

JESPER. But listen, my dear Monsieur Rasmus, I should like to ask you something.

MONTANUS. My name is Montanus.

JESPER [*aside to* JEPPE]. Montanus? Is that the Latin for Rasmus?

JEPPE. Yes, it must be.

JESPER. Listen, my dear Monsieur Montanus Berg. I have heard that learned folk have such extraordinary ideas. Is it true that people in Copenhagen think the earth is round? Here on the hill no one believes it; for how can that be, when the earth looks perfectly flat?

MONTANUS. That is because the earth is so large that one cannot notice its roundness.

JESPER. Yes, it is true, the earth is large; it is almost a half of the universe. But listen, monsieur, how many stars will it take to make a moon?

MONTANUS. A moon! In comparison to the stars the moon is like Pebling Pond in comparison with all Sjælland.

JESPER. Ha, ha, ha! Learned folk are never just right in the head. Will you believe it, I have heard people say that the earth moves and the sun stands still. You certainly don't believe that, too, monsieur?

MONTANUS. No man of sense doubts it any longer.

JESPER. Ha, ha, ha! If the earth should move, surely we should fall and break our necks.

MONTANUS. Can't a ship move with you, without your breaking your neck?

JESPER. Yes, but you say that the earth turns round. Now, if a ship should turn over, would n't the people fall off then into the sea?

MONTANUS. No. I will explain it to you more plainly, if you will have the patience.

JESPER. Indeed, I won't hear anything about it. I should have to be crazy to believe such a thing. Could the earth turn over, and we not fall heels over head to the devil and clear down into the abyss? Ha, ha, ha! But, my Monsieur Berg, how is it that the moon is sometimes so small and sometimes so big?

MONTANUS. If I tell you why, you won't believe me.

JESPER. Oh, please tell me.

MONTANUS. It is because, when the moon has grown large, pieces are clipped off it to make stars of.

JESPER. That certainly is curious. I really did n't know that before. If pieces were not clipped off, it would get too large and grow as broad as all Sjælland. After all, nature does regulate everything very wisely. But how is it that the moon does n't give warmth like the sun, although it is just as big?

MONTANUS. That is because the moon is not a light, but made of the same dark material as the earth, and gets its light and brilliance from the sun.

JESPER. Ha, ha, ha, ha, ha, ha! Let us talk of something else. That's stuff and nonsense; a man might go stark mad over it.

[*Enter* PEER.]

JEPPE. Welcome, Peer. Where good folk are gathered, good folk come. Here, you see, is my son, who has just come back.

PEER. Welcome, Monsieur Rasmus Berg!

MONTANUS. In Copenhagen, I am accustomed to be called " Montanus." I beg you to call me that.

PEER. Yes, surely, it's all the same to me. How are things in Copenhagen? Did many graduate this year?

MONTANUS. About as many as usual.

PEER. Was any one rejected this year?

MONTANUS. Two or three *conditionaliter*.

PEER. Who is *Imprimatur* this year?

MONTANUS. What does that mean?

PEER. I mean, who is *Imprimatur* of the verse and the books which are published?

MONTANUS. Is that supposed to be Latin?

PEER. Yes, in my day it was good Latin.

MONTANUS. If it was good Latin then, it must be so still. But it has never been Latin in the sense in which you use it.

PEER. Yes, it is, — good Latin.

MONTANUS. Is it a *nomen* or a *verbum* ?

PEER. It is a *nomen*.

JESPER. That is right, Peer, just speak up for yourself.

MONTANUS. *Cuius declinationis* is *Imprimatur*, then?

PEER. All the words that can be mentioned may be referred to eight things, which are: *nomen, pronomen, verbum, principium, conjugatio, declinatio, interjectio.*

JESPER. Yes, yes, just listen to Peer when he shakes his sleeves! That's right, keep at him!

MONTANUS. He's not answering what I ask him. What is the genitive of "*Imprimatur*"?

PEER. *Nominativus, ala; genitivus, alæ; dativus, ala; vocativus, alo; ablativus, ala.*

JESPER. Ah, ah, Monsieur Montanus, we have some folk here on the hill, too!

PEER. I should say so. In my time the fellows that graduated were of a different sort from nowadays. They were lads who got shaved twice a week, and could scan all kinds of verse.

MONTANUS. That is certainly a wonderful thing! Boys in the second class can do that to-day. Nowadays there are graduates from the schools in Copenhagen who can write Hebrew and Chaldean verse.

PEER. Then they can't know much Latin.

MONTANUS. Latin! If you went to school now, you could n't get above the bottom class.

JESPER. Don't say that, Montanus. The deacon is, I know, a thoroughly educated man; that I have heard both the district bailiff and the tax-collector say.

MONTANUS. Perhaps they understand Latin just as little as he.

JESPER. But I can hear that he answers splendidly.

MONTANUS. Yes, but he does n't answer what I ask him — *E qua schola dimissus es, mi Domine* ?

PEER. *Adjectivum et substantivum genere, numero et caseo conveniunt.*

JESPER. He's giving him his bucket full. Good for you, Peer; as sure as you live, we shall drink a half-pint of brandy together.

MONTANUS. If you knew, Mr. Bailiff, what his answers were, you would laugh until you split. I ask him from what school he graduated and he answers at random something entirely different.

PEER. *Tunc tua res agitur, paries cum proximus ardet.*

JESPER. Yes, yes, that's a good lead for you. Answer that, now.

MONTANUS. I can't answer that; it is mere mincemeat. Let us talk Danish, so the others can understand; then you will be able to hear what kind of a fellow he is.

[NILLE *cries.*]

JESPER. What are you crying for, my good woman?

NILLE. Oh, I am so sorry that my son must admit himself beaten in Latin.

JESPER. Oh, it's no wonder, my good woman. Peer is, of course, much older than he; it is no wonder. Let them talk Danish, then, as we all understand it.

PEER. Yes, certainly. I am ready for whichever one of the two he wishes. We shall propose certain questions to each other; for example, who was it that screamed so loud that he could be heard over the whole world?

MONTANUS. I know no one who screams louder than asses and country deacons.

PEER. Nonsense! Can they be heard over the whole world? It was the ass in Noah's ark; for the whole world was in the ark.

JESPER. Ha, ha, ha! That is true, to be sure. Ha, ha, ha! Peer, the Deacon, has a fine head on his shoulders.

PEER. Who was it killed a quarter of the world?

MONTANUS. Bah! I refuse to answer such stupid questions.

PEER. It was Cain, who killed his brother Abel.

MONTANUS. Prove that there were no more than four human beings at the time.

PEER. You prove that there were more.

MONTANUS. That is n't necessary; for *affirmante incumbit probatio.* Do you understand that?

PEER. Of course I do. *Omnia conando docilis solertia vincit.* Do you understand that?

MONTANUS. I am a perfect fool to stand here and dispute with a dunce. You wish to dispute, and yet know neither Latin nor Danish; much less do you know what logic is. Let's hear once, *quid est logica?*

PEER. *Post molestam senectutam, post molestam senectutam nos habebat humus.*

MONTANUS. Are you trying to make a fool of me, you rascal?

[*He grabs him by the hair. The Deacon escapes and shouts, "Dunce, dunce!" Exeunt all except the Bailiff.*]

[*Enter* JERONIMUS.]

JERONIMUS. Your servant, Mr. Bailiff. I am surprised to find you here. I have come to see my future son-in-law, Rasmus Berg.

JESPER. He will be here in a moment. It is a shame that you did n't come a half-hour sooner. You would then have heard him and the Deacon disputing together.

JERONIMUS. How did it come out?

JESPER. Shame on Peer, the Deacon! He is worse than I thought. I see well enough that he has forgot nothing either of his Latin or Hebrew.

JERONIMUS. I believe that well enough, for he probably never knew much of either.

JESPER. Don't say that, Monsieur Jeronimus! He has a devilish clever tongue. It is really a joy to hear the man talk Latin.

JERONIMUS. That is more than I should have expected. But how does my son look?

JESPER. He looks confoundedly learned. You would hardly recognize him. He has another name, too.

JERONIMUS. Another name! What does he call himself?

JESPER. He calls himself Montanus, which is said to be the same as Rasmus in Latin.

JERONIMUS. Oh, shame! that is wicked. I have known many who have changed their Christian names in that way, but they never have prospered. Some years ago I knew a person who was christened Peer, and afterwards, when he had become a man of consequence, wanted to be coined again, and called himself Peter. But that name cost him dear, for he broke his leg and died in great misery. Our Lord does n't allow such a thing, Mr. Bailiff.

JESPER. I don't care what his name is, but I don't like it that he has such peculiar opinions in religion.

JERONIMUS. What kind of opinions has he, then?

JESPER. Oh, it's terrible! My hair stands on end when I think of it. I can't remember all that I heard, but I know that among other things he said that the earth was round. What can I call such a thing, Monsieur Jeronimus? That is nothing else than overthrowing all religion and leading folk away from the faith. A heathen certainly cannot speak worse.

JERONIMUS. He must have said that only in jest.

JESPER. It is going rather too far to joke about such things as that. See, here he comes himself.

[*Enter* MONTANUS.]

MONTANUS. How do you do, my dear father-in-law. I am delighted to see you in good health.

JERONIMUS. People of my age can't enjoy remarkable health.

MONTANUS. You look mighty well, however.

JERONIMUS. Do you think so?

MONTANUS. How is Miss Lisbed?

JERONIMUS. Oh, well enough.

MONTANUS. But what is the matter? It seems to me, my dear father-in-law, that you answer me rather coldly.

JERONIMUS. I have no good reason to do otherwise.

MONTANUS. What wrong have I done?

JERONIMUS. I have been told that you have such peculiar opinions that people might really think that you had become mad or deranged, for how can a sane man be foolish enough to say that the earth is round?

MONTANUS. But, *profecto*, it is round. I must speak the truth.

JERONIMUS. The deuce it is the truth! Such a notion can't possibly come from anywhere but from the devil, who is the father of lies. I am sure there is n't a single man here in the village who would not condemn such an opinion. Just ask the Bailiff, who is an intelligent man, if he does not agree with me.

JESPER. It is really all one to me whether it is oblong or round; but I must believe my own eyes, which show me that the earth is as flat as a pancake.

MONTANUS. It is all one to me, too, what the Bailiff or the others here in the village think on the subject; for I know that the earth is round.

JERONIMUS. The deuce it is round! You must be crazy. You surely have eyes in your head as well as other men.

MONTANUS. It is known for certain, my dear father-in-law, that people live right under us with their feet turned toward ours.

JESPER. Ha, ha, ha; hi, hi, hi; ha, ha, ha!

JERONIMUS. Yes, you may well laugh, Mr. Bailiff, for he really has a screw loose in his head. Just you try to walk here on the ceiling with your head down, and see then what will happen.

MONTANUS. That is an entirely different thing, father-in-law, because —

JERONIMUS. I will never in the world be your father-in-law. I love my daughter too well to throw her away like that.

MONTANUS. I love your daughter as my own soul, but that I should give up my philosophy for her sake and drive my reason into exile, — that is more than you can demand.

JERONIMUS. Ha, ha! I see you have another lady-love in mind. You can keep your Lucy or your Sophy. I certainly shall not force my daughter on you.

MONTANUS. You mistake me. Philosophy is nothing other than a science, which has opened my eyes, in this respect as in others.

JERONIMUS. It has rather blinded both your eyes and your understanding. How can you believe such a thing is good?

MONTANUS. That is something which is beyond proof. No learned man doubts that any longer.

JESPER. I warrant you will never get Peer, the Deacon, to agree with you.

MONTANUS. Peer, the Deacon! Yes, he is a great fellow. I am a fool to stand here and talk about philosophy with you. But in order to please Monsieur Jeronimus, I will nevertheless present one or two proofs. First, we learn it from travelers, who, when they go a few thousand miles from here, have day while we have night: they see other heavens, other stars.

JERONIMUS. Are you crazy? Is there more than one heaven and one earth?

JESPER. Yes, indeed, Monsieur Jeronimus, there are twelve heavens, one above the other, until the crystal heaven is reached. So far he is right.

MONTANUS. Ah! *Quantæ tenebræ!*

JERONIMUS. In my youth I went sixteen times to the neighborhood of Kiel, but as sure as I am an honorable man, I never saw a different heaven from what we have here.

MONTANUS. You must travel sixteen times as far, *Domine Jeronime*, before you can notice such a thing, because —

JERONIMUS. Stop talking such nonsense; it is neither here nor there. Let's hear your other proof.

MONTANUS. The other proof is taken from the eclipse of the sun and moon.

JESPER. Just hear that! Now he is stark mad.

MONTANUS. What do you really suppose an eclipse to be?

JESPER. Eclipses are certain signs which are placed upon the sun and moon when some misfortune is going to happen on the earth, — a thing I can prove from my own experience: when my wife had a miscarriage three years ago, and when my daughter Gertrude died, both times there were eclipses just before.

MONTANUS. Oh, such nonsense will drive me mad.

JERONIMUS. The Bailiff is right, for an eclipse never occurs unless it is a warning of something. When the last eclipse happened, everything seemed to be well, but that did n't last long; for a fortnight afterwards we got news from Copenhagen that six candidates for degrees were rejected at one time, all persons belonging to the gentry, and two of them the sons of deacons. If a man does n't hear of misfortune at one place after such an eclipse, he hears of it at another.

MONTANUS. That is true enough, for no day passes that some misfortune does not happen somewhere in the world. But as far as these persons you mentioned are con-

cerned, they have no need to blame the eclipse, for if they had studied more, they would have passed.

JERONIMUS. What is an eclipse of the moon, then?

MONTANUS. It is nothing other than the earth's shadow, which deprives the moon of the sunlight, and since the shadow is round, we thereby see that the earth is round, too. It all happens in a natural way, for eclipses can be predicted, and therefore it is folly to say that such things are prophetic warnings of misfortune.

JERONIMUS. Oh, Mr. Bailiff, I feel ill. Unlucky was the day on which your parents allowed you to become a scholar.

JESPER. Yes, he comes mighty near to being an atheist. I must bring him and Peer, the Deacon, together again. There is a man who speaks with force. He will persuade you yet, in either Latin or Greek, that the earth, thank God, is as flat as my hand. But here comes Madame Jeronimus with her daughter.

[*Enter* MAGDELONE *and* LISBED.]

MAGDELONE. Oh, my dear son-in-law, it is a delight to me to see you back again in good health.

LISBED. Oh, my darling, let me hug you.

JERONIMUS. Slowly, slowly, my child, not so ardently.

LISBED. May I not hug my sweetheart when I have n't seen him for years?

JERONIMUS. Keep away from him, I tell you, or else you will get a beating.

LISBED [*weeping*]. I know one thing, that we have been publicly betrothed.

JERONIMUS. That is true enough, but since that time something has occurred to hinder. [LISBED *weeps*.] You must know, my child, that when he became engaged to you he was an honest man and a good Christian. But now he is a heretic and a fanatic, who ought to be introduced to the Litany rather than into our family.

LISBED. If that is all, father, dear, we can still make everything right.

JERONIMUS. Keep away from him, I tell you.

MAGDELONE. What does this mean, Mr. Bailiff?

JESPER. It's a bad business, madame. He introduces false doctrine into this village, saying that the earth is round, and other things of such a nature that I should blush to mention them.

JERONIMUS. Don't you think that the good old parents are to be pitied who have spent so much money on him?

MAGDELONE. Oh, is that all? If he loves our daughter, he will give up his opinion and say that the earth is flat, for her sake.

LISBED. Oh, my dear, for my sake say that it is flat!

MONTANUS. I cannot humor you in this, so long as I am in full possession of my reason. I cannot give the earth another shape from what it has by nature. For your sake I will say and do whatever is possible for me; but in this one thing I can never humor you, for if the brothers in my order should find out that I had given expression to such an opinion, I should be thought a fool, and despised. Besides, we learned folk never give up our opinions, but defend what we have once said to the uttermost drop of our inkhorns.

MAGDELONE. See here, husband, I don't think it matters so much that we should break off the match on that account.

JERONIMUS. And merely on that account I should try to have them divorced even if they had been actually married.

MAGDELONE. You had better believe I have something to say in this matter, too; for if she is your daughter, she is mine as well.

LISBED [weeping]. Oh, my dear, do say that it is flat.

MONTANUS. Profecto, I really cannot.

JERONIMUS. Listen, wife: you must know that I am the head of the house, and that I am her father.

MAGDELONE. You must also know that I am the mistress of the house, and that I am her mother.

JERONIMUS. I say that a father is always more than a mother.

MAGDELONE. And I say not, for there can be no doubt that I am her mother, but whether you — I had better not say any more, for I am getting excited.

LISBED [weeping]. Oh, my heart, can't you say just for my sake that it is flat?

MONTANUS. I cannot, my doll, nam contra naturam est.

JERONIMUS. What did you mean by that, my wife? Am I not her father as surely as you are her mother? — Listen, Lisbed, am I not your father?

LISBED. I think so, for my mother says so; but I know that she is my mother.

JERONIMUS. What do you think of this talk, Mr. Bailiff?

JESPER. I can't say that mamselle is wrong in this matter, for —

JERONIMUS. That is enough. Come, let us go — You may be sure, my good Rasmus Berg, that you will never get my daughter so long as you cling to your delusions.

LISBED [weeping]. Oh, my heart, do say that it is flat!

JERONIMUS. Out, out of the door!

[Exeunt JERONIMUS, MAGDELONE, and LISBED.]

ACT IV

Before JEPPE's *house.*

[Enter MONTANUS.]

MONTANUS. Here I have been worried for a good hour by my parents, who with sighing and weeping try to persuade me to give up my opinions; but they don't know Erasmus Montanus. Not if I were to be made an emperor for it would I renounce what I once have said. I love Mademoiselle Elisabet, to be sure; but that I should sacrifice philosophy for her sake, and repudiate what I have publicly maintained — that is out of the question. I hope, though, that it will all come out right, and that I shall win my sweetheart without losing my reputation. Once I get a chance to talk to Jeronimus, I can convince him of his errors so conclusively that he will agree to the match. But there are the Deacon and the Bailiff, coming from my father-and mother-in-law's.

[Enter PEER and JESPER.]

JESPER. My dear Monsieur Montanus, we have been working hard for you this day.

MONTANUS. What's that?

JESPER. We have intervened between your parents and your parents-in-law to bring about a reconciliation.

MONTANUS. Well, what have you accomplished? Did my father-in-law give way?

JESPER. The last words he said to us were, " There has never been any heresy in our family. You tell Rasmus Berg" — I merely quote his words; he never once said Montanus Berg — "You tell Rasmus Berg from me," said he, "that my wife and I are both honest, God-fearing people, who would rather wring our daughter's neck than marry her to any one who says that the earth is round, and brings false doctrine into the village."

PEER. To tell the truth, we have always had pure faith here on the hill, and Monsieur Jeronimus is n't far wrong in wishing to break off the match.

MONTANUS. My good friends, tell Monsieur Jeronimus from me that he is committing a sin in attempting to force me to repudiate what I once have said — a thing contrary to *leges scholasticas* and *consuetudines laudabiles*.

PEER. Oh, Dominus! Will you give up your pretty sweetheart for such trifles? Every one will speak ill of it.

MONTANUS. The common man, *vulgus*, will speak ill of it; but my *commilitiones*, my comrades, will praise me to the skies for my constancy.

PEER. Do you consider it a sin to say that the earth is flat or oblong?

MONTANUS. No, I do not, but I consider it shameful and dishonorable for me, a *Baccalaureus Philosophiæ*, to repudiate what I have publicly maintained, and to do anything that is improper for one of my order. My duty is to see to it that *ne quid detrimenti patiatur respublica philosophica.*

PEER. But if you can be convinced that what you believe is false, do you consider it a sin to give up your opinion?

MONTANUS. Prove to me that it is false, and that *methodice.*

PEER. That is an easy thing for me to do. Now, a great many fine people live here in the village: first, your father-in-law, who has become distinguished by the mere use of his pen; next, myself, unworthy man, who have been deacon here for fourteen full years; then this good man, the Bailiff, besides the parish Constable, and various other good men established here who have paid their taxes and land-rent in both good times and bad.

MONTANUS. That's the deuce of a *syllogismus.* What does all such nonsense lead to?

PEER. I'm coming to that directly. I say, just ask any one of these good men who live here in the village and see if any of them will agree with you that the world is round. I'm sure a man ought to believe what so many say, rather than what only one says. *Ergo,* you are wrong.

MONTANUS. You may bring all the people on the hill and let them oppose me both in this matter and others, and I shall close the mouths of all of them. Such people have no convictions; they must believe what I and other folk say.

PEER. But if you should say the moon was made of green cheese, would they believe that, too?

MONTANUS. Why not? Tell me, what do the people here think you are?

PEER. They believe that I am a good, honest man and deacon here in this place; which is true.

MONTANUS. And I say it is a lie. I say you are a cock, and I shall prove it, as surely as two and three make five.

PEER. The devil you will! Now, how can I be a cock? How can you prove that?

MONTANUS. Can you tell me anything to prevent you from being one?

PEER. In the first place I can talk; a cock cannot talk; *ergo,* I am not a cock.

MONTANUS. Talking does not prove anything. A parrot or a starling can talk, too; that does not make them human beings by any means.

PEER. I can prove it from something else besides talking. A cock has no human intelligence. I have human intelligence; *ergo,* I am not a cock.

MONTANUS. *Proba minorem.*

JESPER. Aw, talk Danish.

MONTANUS. I want him to prove that he has the intelligence of a human being.

PEER. See here, I discharge the duties of my office irreproachably, don't I?

MONTANUS. What are the main duties of your office wherein you show human intelligence?

PEER. First, I never forget to ring for service at the hour appointed.

MONTANUS. Nor does a cock forget to crow and make known the hour and tell people when to get up.

PEER. Second, I can sing as well as any deacon in Sjælland.

MONTANUS. And our cock crows as well as any cock in Sjælland.

PEER. I can mould wax candles, which no cock can do.

MONTANUS. Over against that, a cock can make a hen lay eggs, which you can't do. Don't you see that the intelligence you show in your calling fails to prove that you are better than a cock? Let us see, in a nutshell, what points you have in common with a cock: A cock has a comb on his head, you have horns on your forehead; a cock crows, you crow, too; a cock is proud of his voice and ruffles himself up, you do likewise; a cock gives warning when it is time to get up, you when it is time for service. *Ergo*, you are a cock. Have you anything else to say? [PEER *cries.*]

JESPER. Here, don't cry, Peer! Why do you heed such things?

PEER. A plague on me if it's not sheer falsehood. I can get a certificate from the whole village that I am not a rooster; that not one of my forbears has been anything but a Christian human being.

MONTANUS. Refute, then, this *syllogismus, quem tibi propono.* A cock has certain peculiarities which distinguish him from other animals: he wakes people by a noise when it's time to get up; announces the hours; plumes himself on his voice; wears protuberances on his head. You have the same peculiarities. *Ergo*, you are a cock. Refute me that argument.

[PEER *weeps again.*]

JESPER. If the Deacon can't shut you up, I can.

MONTANUS. Let us hear your argument, then!

JESPER. First, my conscience tells me that your opinion is false.

MONTANUS. One cannot pass judgment in all matters according to a bailiff's conscience.

JESPER. In the second place, I say that everything you have said is sheer falsehood.

MONTANUS. Prove it.

JESPER. In the third place, I am an honest man, whose word has always deserved to be believed.

MONTANUS. That sort of talk will convince no one.

JESPER. In the fourth place, I say that you have spoken like a knave and that the tongue ought to be cut out of your mouth.

MONTANUS. I still hear no proof.

JESPER. And, finally, in the fifth place, I will prove it to you abundantly either with swords or with bare fists.

MONTANUS. No, I do not care for either, thank you; but as long as you wish to dispute with the mouth only, you shall find that I can justify not only the things which I have said, but more, too. Come on, Mr. Bailiff, I will prove by sound logic that you are a bull.

JESPER. The devil you will.

MONTANUS. Just have the patience to hear my argument.

JESPER. Come, Peer, let's go.

MONTANUS. I prove it in this way. *Quicunque* — [JESPER *shrieks and puts his hand over* ERASMUS's *mouth.*] If you do not wish to hear my proof this time, you can meet me another time, whenever you please.

JESPER. I am too good to associate with such a fanatic.

[*Exeunt* JESPER *and* PEER.]

MONTANUS. I can dispute dispassionately with these people, however harshly they speak to me. I do not become hotheaded unless I dispute with people who imagine that they understand *methodum disputandi* and that they are just as well versed in philosophy as I. For this reason I was ten times as zealous when I argued against the student to-day; for he had some appearance of learning. But here come my parents.

[*Enter* JEPPE *and* NILLE.]

JEPPE. Oh, my dear son, don't carry on so, and don't quarrel with everybody. The Bailiff and Deacon, who at our request undertook to make peace between you and your father-in-law, have, I hear, been made sport of. What is the use of turning good folk into cocks and bulls?

MONTANUS. For this purpose I have studied, for this purpose I have racked my brains: that I may say what I choose, and justify it.

JEPPE. It seems to me that it would have been better never to have studied in that way.

MONTANUS. Keep your mouth shut, old man!

JEPPE. You're not going to beat your parents?

MONTANUS. If I did, I should justify that, too, before the whole world.

[*Exeunt* JEPPE *and* NILLE *weeping.*]

[*Enter* JACOB.]

I will not abandon my opinions, even if they all go mad at once.

JACOB. I have a letter for mossur.

[*Gives him the letter, and exit.*]

MONTANUS [*reading*].

"*My dearest friend!* I could never have imagined that you would so easily abandon her who for so many years has loved you with such faith and constancy. I can tell you for a certainty that my father is so set against the notion that the earth is round, and considers it such an important article of faith, that he will never give me to you unless you assent to the belief that he and the other good folk here in the village hold. What difference can it make to you whether the earth is oblong, round, eight-cornered, or square? I beg of you, by all the love I have borne you, that you conform to the faith in which we here on the hill have been happy for so long. If you do not humor me in this, you may be sure that I shall die of grief, and the whole world will abhor you for causing the death of one who has loved you as her own soul.

"*Elisabeth, daughter of Jeronimus,*
"*by her own hand.*"

Oh, Heavens! This letter moves me and throws me into great irresolution —

Utque securi
Saucia trabs ingens, ubi plaga novissima restat,
Quo cadat in dubio est, omnique a parte timetur,
Sic animus —

On the one hand is Philosophy, bidding me stand firm; on the other, my sweetheart reproaching me with coldness and faithlessness. But should Erasmus Montanus for any reason renounce his conviction, hitherto his one virtue? No, indeed, by no means. Yet here is necessity, which knows no law. If I do not submit in this, I shall make both myself and my sweetheart miserable. She will die of grief, and all the world will hate me and reproach me with my faithlessness. Ought I abandon her, when she has loved me constantly for so many years? Ought I be the cause of her death? No, that must not be. Still, consider what you are doing, *Erasmus Montane, Musarum et Apollonis pulle!* Here you have the chance to show that you are a true *philosophus.* The greater the danger, the larger the laurel wreath you win *inter philosophos.* Think what your *commilitiones* will say when they hear something like this: "He is no longer the Erasmus Montanus who hitherto has defended his opinions to the last drop of his blood." If common and ignorant people reproach me with unfaithfulness to my sweetheart, *philosophi,* for their part, will exalt me to the skies. The very thing which disgraces me in the eyes of the one party crowns me with honor among the other. I must therefore resist the temptation. I am resisting it. I conquer it. I have already conquered it. The earth is round. *Jacta est alea. Dixi.* [*Calls.*] Jacob!

[*Enter* JACOB.]

Jacob, the letter which you delivered to me from my sweetheart has had no influence upon me. I adhere to what I have said. The earth is round, and it shall never become flat as long as my head remains on my shoulders.

JACOB. I believe, too, that the earth is round, but if any one gave me a seed-cake to say it was oblong, I should say that it was oblong, for it would make no difference to me.

MONTANUS. That might be proper for you, but not for a *philosophus*, whose principal virtue is to justify to the uttermost what he once has said. I will dispute publicly on the subject here in the village and challenge all who have studied.

JACOB. But might I ask mossur one thing: If you win the disputation, what will be the result?

MONTANUS. The result will be that I shall have the honor of winning and shall be recognized as a learned man.

JACOB. Mossur means a talkative man. I have noticed, from the people here in the village, that wisdom and talking are not the same thing. Rasmus Hansen, who is always talking, and whom no one can stand against in the matter of words, is granted by every one to have just plain goose sense. On the other hand, the parish Constable, Niels Christensen, who says little and always gives in, is admitted to have an understanding of the duties of Chief Bailiff.

MONTANUS. Will you listen to the rascal? Faith, he's trying to argue with me.

JACOB. Mossur must n't take offense. I talk only according to my simple understanding, and ask only in order to learn. I should like to know whether, when mossur wins the dispute, Peer, the Deacon, will thereupon be turned into a cock?

MONTANUS. Nonsense! He will stay the same as he was before.

JACOB. Well, then, mossur would lose!

MONTANUS. I shall not allow myself to be drawn into dispute with a rogue of a peasant like you. If you understood Latin, I should readily oblige you. I am not accustomed to disputation in Danish.

JACOB. That is to say, mossur has become so learned that he cannot make clear his meaning in his mother tongue.

MONTANUS. Be silent, *audacissime juvenis!* Why should I exert myself to explain my opinions to coarse and common folk, who don't know what *universalia entia rationis formæ substantiales* are? It certainly is *absurdissimum* to try to prate of

colors to the blind. *Vulgus indoctum est monstrum horrendum informe, cui lumen ademptum.* Not long ago a man ten times as learned as you wished to dispute with me, but when I found that he did not know what *quidditas* was, I promptly refused him.

JACOB. What does that word *quidditas* mean? Was n't that it?

MONTANUS. I know well enough what it means.

JACOB. Perhaps mossur knows it himself, but can't explain it to others. What little I know, I know in such a way that all men can grasp it when I say it to them.

MONTANUS. Yes, you are a learned fellow, Jacob. What do you know?

JACOB. What if I could prove that I am more learned than mossur?

MONTANUS. I should like to hear you.

JACOB. He who studies the most important things, I think, has the most thorough learning.

MONTANUS. Yes, that is true enough.

JACOB. I study farming and the cultivation of the soil. For that reason I am more learned than mossur.

MONTANUS. Do you believe that rough peasants' work is the most important?

JACOB. I don't know about that. But I do know that if we farmers should take a pen or a piece of chalk in our hands to calculate how far it is to the moon, you learned men would soon suffer in the stomach. You scholars spend the time disputing whether the earth is round, square, or eight-cornered, and we study how to keep the earth in repair. Does mossur see now that our studies are more useful and important than his, and, therefore, Niels Christensen is the most learned man here in the village, because he has improved his farm so that an acre of it is rated at thirty rix-dollars more than in the time of his predecessor, who sat all day with a pipe in his mouth, smudging and rumpling Dr. Arent Hvitfeld's *Chronicle* or a book of sermons?

MONTANUS. You will be the death of me; it is the devil incarnate who is talking. I never in all my life thought such words could come from a peasant-boy's mouth. For although all you have said is false and ungodly, still it is an unusual speech for one in your walk of life. Tell me this minute from whom you have learned such nonsense.

JACOB. I have not studied, mossur, but people say I have a good head. The District Judge never comes to town but he sends for me at once. He has told my parents a hundred times that I ought to devote myself to books, and that something great might be made of me. When I have nothing to do, I go speculating. The other day I made a verse on Morten Nielsen, who drank himself to death.

MONTANUS. Let us hear the verse.

JACOB. You must know, first, that the father and the grandfather of this same Morten were both fishermen, and were drowned at sea. This was how the verse went: —

Here lies the body of Morten Nielsen;
To follow the footsteps of his forbears,
Who died in the water as fishermen,
He drowned himself in brandy.

I had to read the verse before the District Judge the other day, and he had it written down and gave me two marks for it.

MONTANUS. The poem, though *formaliter* very bad, is none the less *materialiter* excellent. The prosody, which is the most important thing, is lacking.

JACOB. What does that mean?

MONTANUS. Certain lines have not *pedes*, or feet, enough to walk on.

JACOB. Feet! I would have you know that in a few days it ran over the whole countryside.

MONTANUS. I see you have a crafty head. I could wish that you had studied and understood your *Philosophiam instrumentalem*, so you could dispute under me. Come, let us go.   [*Exeunt.*]

ACT V

Same as in Act IV.

[*Enter a Lieutenant,* JESPER, *the Bailiff.*]

LIEUTENANT. How can I manage to see the fellow, Mr. Bailiff? I should like to have a talk with him. Is he a likely looking fellow?

JESPER. Oh, he looks pretty well, and he has a mouth like a razor.

LIEUTENANT. That makes no difference, so long as he's strong and active.

JESPER. He can say anything he wants, and maintain it. He proved beyond a doubt that Peer, the Deacon, was a cock.

LIEUTENANT. Is he good and broad across the shoulders?

JESPER. A big, strong lad. Every one in the house here is afraid of him, even his parents, for he can turn them into cows, oxen, and horses, then back again into people, — that is, he can prove that they are, from books.

LIEUTENANT. Does he look as if he could stand knocking about?

JESPER. And he proved that the earth was round, too.

LIEUTENANT. That doesn't matter to me. Does he look as if he were brave, and had a stout heart?

JESPER. He would stake his life for a letter of the alphabet, not to mention anything else. He has set every one here by the ears, but that makes no difference to him — he won't budge from his opinions and his learning.

LIEUTENANT. Mr. Bailiff, from all I hear, he will make a perfect soldier.

JESPER. How can you make a soldier of him, Lieutenant? He is a student.

LIEUTENANT. That has nothing to do with it. If he can turn people into sheep, oxen, and cocks, I'll have a try at turning a student into a soldier, for once.

JESPER. I should be happy if you could. I should laugh my belly in two.

LIEUTENANT. Just keep quiet about it, Jesper! When a bailiff and a lieutenant put their heads together, such things are not impossible. But I see some one coming this way. Is that he, by any chance?

JESPER. Yes, it is. I shall run off, so that he won't suspect me.   [*Exit.*]

[*Enter* MONTANUS.]

LIEUTENANT. Welcome to the village.

MONTANUS. I humbly thank you.

LIEUTENANT. I have taken the liberty of addressing you, because there aren't many educated people hereabouts for a man to talk to.

MONTANUS. I am delighted that you have been a scholar. When did you graduate, if I may inquire?

LIEUTENANT. Oh, ten years ago.

MONTANUS. Then you are an old *academicus*. What was your specialty when you were a student?

LIEUTENANT. I read mostly the old Latin authors, and studied natural law and moral problems, as in fact I do still.

MONTANUS. That is mere trumpery, not *academicum*. Did you lay no stress on *Philosophiam instrumentalem?*

LIEUTENANT. Not especially.

MONTANUS. Then you have never done any disputation?

LIEUTENANT. No.

MONTANUS. Well, is that studying? *Philosophia instrumentalis* is the only solid *studium;* the rest are all very fine, but they are not learned. One who is well drilled in *Logica* and *Metaphysica* can get himself out of any difficulty and dispute on all subjects, even if he is unfamiliar with them. I know of nothing which I should take upon myself to defend and not get out of it very well. There was never any disputation at the university in which I did not take part. A *philosophus instrumentalis* can pass for a *polyhistor.*

LIEUTENANT. Who is the best disputer nowadays?

MONTANUS. A student called Peer Iverson. When he has refuted his opponent so that he has n't a word to say for himself, he says, "Now, if you will take my proposition, I will defend yours." In all that sort of thing his *Philosophia instrumentalis* is the greatest help. It is a shame that the lad did not become a lawyer; he could have made a mighty good living. Next to him, I am the strongest, for the last time I disputed, he whispered in my ear, "*Jam sumus ergo pares.*" Yet I will always yield him the palm.

LIEUTENANT. But I have heard it said that monsieur can prove that it is the duty of a child to beat his parents. That seems to be absurd.

MONTANUS. If I said it, I am the man to defend it.

LIEUTENANT. I dare wager a ducat that you are not clever enough for that.

MONTANUS. I will risk a ducat on it.

LIEUTENANT. Good. It is agreed. Now, let's hear you.

MONTANUS. He whom one loves most, he beats most. One ought to love nobody more than his parents, *ergo*, there is nobody whom one ought to beat more. Now, in another syllogism: what one has received he ought, according to his ability, to return. In my youth I received blows from my parents. *Ergo*, I ought to give them blows in return.

LIEUTENANT. Enough, enough, I have lost. Faith, you shall have your ducat.

MONTANUS. Oh, you were not in earnest; I will *profecto* take no money.

LIEUTENANT. Upon my word, you shall take it. I swear you shall.

MONTANUS. Then I will take it to keep you from breaking an oath.

LIEUTENANT. But may I not also try to turn you into something? *Par exemple*, I will turn you into a soldier.

MONTANUS. Oh, that is very easy, for all students are soldiers of the intellect.

LIEUTENANT. No, I shall prove that you are a soldier in body. Whoever has taken press-money is an enlisted soldier. You have done so, *ergo* —

MONTANUS. *Nego minorem.*

LIEUTENANT. *Et ego probo minorem* by the two rix-dollars you took into your hand.

MONTANUS. *Distinguendum est inter nummos.*

LIEUTENANT. No distinction! You are a soldier.

MONTANUS. *Distinguendum est inter* the two: *simpliciter* and *relative accipere.*

LIEUTENANT. No nonsense! The contract is closed, and you have taken the money.

MONTANUS. *Distinguendum est inter contractum verum et apparentem.*

LIEUTENANT. Can you deny that you have received a ducat from me?

MONTANUS. *Distinguendum est inter rem et modum rei.*

LIEUTENANT. Come, follow me straight, comrade! You must get your uniform.

MONTANUS. There are your two rix-dollars back. You have no witnesses to my taking the money.

[*Enter* JESPER *and* NIELS, *the Corporal.*]

JESPER. I can bear witness that I saw the Lieutenant put money into his hand.

NIELS. I, too.

MONTANUS. But why did I take the money? *Distinguendum est inter* —

LIEUTENANT. Oh, we won't listen to any talk. Niels, you stay here, while I fetch the uniform. [*Exit the Lieutenant.*]

MONTANUS. Oh, help!

NIELS. If you don't shut up, you dog, I'll stick a bayonet through your body. Has n't he enlisted, Mr. Bailiff?

JESPER. Yes, of course he has.

[*Enter the Lieutenant.*]

LIEUTENANT. Come, now, pull off that black coat and put on this red one. [MON-TANUS *cries while they put on his uniform.*] Oh, come, it looks bad for a soldier to cry. You are far better off than you were before. — Drill him well, now, Niels. He is a learned fellow, but he is raw yet in his exercises. [NIELS, *the Corporal, leads* MONTANUS *about, drilling him and beating him. Exeunt the Lieutenant and* JESPER.]

[*Reënter the Lieutenant.*]

Well, Niels, can he go through the drill?

NIELS. He'll learn in time, but he is a lazy dog. He has to be beaten every minute.

MONTANUS [*crying*]. Oh, gracious sir, have mercy on me. My health is weak and I cannot endure such treatment.

LIEUTENANT. It seems a little hard at first, but when your back has once been well beaten and toughened, it won't hurt so much.

MONTANUS [*crying*]. Oh, would that I had never studied! Then I never should have got into this trouble.

LIEUTENANT. Oh, this is only a beginning. When you have sat a half-score of times on the wooden horse, or stood on the stake, then you will think this sort of thing is a mere bagatelle.

[MONTANUS *weeps again.*]

[*Enter* JERONIMUS, MAGDELONE, JEPPE, *and* NILLE.]

JERONIMUS. Are you sure of it?

JEPPE. Indeed I am; the Bailiff told me a moment ago. Ah, now my anger is turned to pity.

JERONIMUS. If we could only get him back to the true faith, I should be glad to buy him off.

LISBED [*rushing in*]. Oh, poor wretch that I am!

JERONIMUS. Don't raise a hubbub, daughter, you won't gain anything by that.

LISBED. Oh, father, dear, if you were as much in love as I am, you would n't ask me to keep quiet.

JERONIMUS. Fie, fie, it is not proper for a girl to show her feelings like that. But there he is, I do believe. Look here, Rasmus Berg! What is going on?

MONTANUS. Oh, my dear Monsieur Jeronimus, I've become a soldier.

JERONIMUS. Yes, now you have something else to do besides turning men into beasts and deacons into cocks.

MONTANUS. Oh, alas! I lament my former folly, but all too late.

JERONIMUS. Listen, my friend. If you will give up your former foolishness, and not fill the land with disagreements and disputations, I shall not fail to do everything in my power to get you off.

MONTANUS. Oh, I don't deserve anything better, after threatening my old parents with blows. But if you will have pity on me and work for my release, I swear to you, that hereafter I shall live a different life, devote myself to some business, and never bother any one with disputations any more.

JERONIMUS. Stay here for a moment; I will go and talk to the Lieutenant.

[*Enter the Lieutenant.*]

Oh, my dear Lieutenant, you have always been a friend of our house. The person who has enlisted as a soldier is engaged to my only daughter, who is much in love with him. Set him free again. I shall be glad to present you with a hundred rix-dollars, if you do. I admit that at first I was delighted myself that he had been punished in such a way, for his singular behavior had exasperated me, and all the good folk here in the village, against him. But when I saw him in this plight, and at the same time heard him lament his former folly and promise amendment, my heart was ready to burst with sympathy.

LIEUTENANT. Listen, my dear Monsieur Jeronimus. What I have done has been only for his own good. I know that he is engaged to your daughter, and therefore merely for the good of your house I have reduced him to this condition and treated him with such great harshness, so that he might be brought to confess his sins. But for your sake I will give the money to the poor, inasmuch as I hear that he has experienced a change of heart. Let him come here. — Listen, my friend, your parents have spent much money on you in the hope that you would become an honor and a comfort to them in their old age. But you go off a sensible fellow and come back entirely deranged, arouse the whole village, advance strange opinions, and defend them with stubbornness. If that is to be the fruit of studies, then one ought to wish that there never had been any books. It seems to me that the principal thing a man ought to learn in school is just the opposite of what you are infected with, and that a learned man ought particularly to be distinguished from others in that he is more temperate, modest, and considerate in his speech than the uneducated. For true philosophy teaches us that we ought to restrain and quiet disagreements, and to give up our opinions as soon as we are persuaded, even by the humblest person, that they are mistaken. The first rule of philosophy is, Know thyself; and the further one advances, the lower opinion one should have of himself, the more one should realize what there remains to be learned. But you make philosophy into a kind of fencing, and consider a man a philosopher if he can warp the truth by subtle distinctions and talk himself out of any opinion; in so doing

you incur hatred and bring contempt upon learning, for people imagine that your extraordinary manners are the natural fruits of education. The best advice I can give you is to strive to forget, and to rid your head of what you have burned so much midnight oil in learning; and that you take up some calling in which you can make your way to success; or, if you are bound to pursue your studies, that you go about them in some other fashion.

MONTANUS. Oh, my good sir, I will follow your advice, and do my best to be a different man from now on.

LIEUTENANT. Good; then I will let you go as soon as you have given your word both to your own parents and to your future parents-in-law, and have begged their pardon.

MONTANUS. I humbly beg all of you, as I weep salt tears, to forgive me; and I promise to lead an entirely different life henceforward. I condemn my former ways, and I have been cured of them not so much by the fix I had got into as by this good man's wise and profound words. Next to my parents I shall always hold him in the highest esteem.

JERONIMUS. Then you don't believe any longer, my dear son-in-law, that the world is round? For that is the point that I take most to heart.

MONTANUS. My dear father-in-law, I won't argue about it any further. But I will only say this, that nowadays all learned folk are of the opinion that the earth is round.

JERONIMUS. Oh, Mr. Lieutenant, let him be made a soldier again until the earth becomes flat.

MONTANUS. My dear father-in-law, the earth is as flat as a pancake. Now are you satisfied?

JERONIMUS. Yes, now we are good friends again, — now you shall have my daughter. Come to my house, now, all together, and drink to the reconciliation. Mr. Lieutenant, won't you do us the honor of joining us? [Exeunt.]

A DOLL'S HOUSE

(EL DUKKETHEIM)

By HENRIK IBSEN

Translated by WILLIAM ARCHER

CHARACTERS

TORVALD HELMER

NORA, *his wife*

DOCTOR RANK

MRS. LINDEN

NILS KROGSTAD

THE HELMERS' *three children*

ANNA, *their nurse*

ELLEN, *a maidservant*

A Porter

The action passes in Helmer's house (a flat) in Christiania.

A DOLL'S HOUSE

ACT I

*A room, comfortably and tastefully, but not
expensively, furnished. In the back, on the
right, a door leads to the hall; on the left another door leads to* HELMER'S *study. Between
the two doors a pianoforte. In the middle of
the left wall a door, and nearer the front a
window. Near the window a round table with
armchairs and a small sofa. In the right wall,
somewhat to the back, a door, and against the
same wall, further forward, a porcelain stove;
in front of it a couple of armchairs and a
rocking-chair. Between the stove and the side-
door a small table. Engravings on the walls.
A what-not with china and bric-à-brac. A
small bookcase filled with handsomely bound
books. Carpet. A fire in the stove. It is a
winter day. A bell rings in the hall outside.
Presently the outer door of the flat is heard to
open.*

[NORA *enters, humming gayly. She is in outdoor dress, and carries several parcels,
which she lays on the right-hand table.
She leaves the door into the hall open,
and a Porter is seen outside, carrying a
Christmas tree and a basket, which he
gives to the Maidservant who has opened
the door.*]

NORA. Hide the Christmas tree carefully, Ellen; the children must on no account see it before this evening, when it's
lighted up. [*To the Porter, taking out her
purse.*] How much?

PORTER. Fifty öre.

NORA. There is a crown. No, keep the
change.

[*The Porter thanks her and goes.*
NORA *shuts the door. She continues smiling in quiet glee as
she takes off her outdoor things.
Taking from her pocket a bag of
macaroons, she eats one or two.
Then she goes on tiptoe to her
husband's door and listens.*]

Yes; he is at home.

[*She begins humming again, crossing to the table on the right.*]

HELMER [*in his room*]. Is that my lark
twittering there?

NORA [*busy opening some of her parcels*].
Yes, it is.

HELMER. Is it the squirrel frisking
around?

NORA. Yes!

HELMER. When did the squirrel get
home?

NORA. Just this minute. [*Hides the bag
of macaroons in her pocket and wipes her
mouth.*] Come here, Torvald, and see what
I've been buying.

HELMER. Don't interrupt me. [*A little
later he opens the door and looks in, pen in
hand.*] Buying, did you say? What! All
that? Has my little spendthrift been making the money fly again?

NORA. Why, Torvald, surely we can
afford to launch out a little now. It's the
first Christmas we have n't had to pinch.

HELMER. Come, come; we can't afford
to squander money.

NORA. Oh, yes, Torvald, do let us squander a little, now — just the least little bit!
You know you'll soon be earning heaps of
money.

HELMER. Yes, from New Year's Day.
But there's a whole quarter before my first
salary is due.

NORA. Never mind; we can borrow in
the mean time.

HELMER. Nora! [*He goes up to her and
takes her playfully by the ear.*] Still my little
featherbrain! Supposing I borrowed a
thousand crowns to-day, and you made
ducks and drakes of them during Christmas week, and then on New Year's Eve a
tile blew off the roof and knocked my brains
out.

NORA [*laying her hand on his mouth*].
Hush! How can you talk so horridly?

HELMER. But supposing it were to happen — what then?

NORA. If anything so dreadful happened, it would be all the same to me
whether I was in debt or not.

HELMER. But what about the creditors?

NORA. They! Who cares for them? They're only strangers.

HELMER. Nora, Nora! What a *woman* you are! But seriously, Nora, you know my principles on these points. No debts! No borrowing! Home life ceases to be free and beautiful as soon as it is founded on borrowing and debt. We two have held out bravely till now, and we are not going to give in at the last.

NORA [*going to the fireplace*]. Very well — as you please, Torvald.

HELMER [*following her*]. Come, come; my little lark must n't droop her wings like that. What? Is my squirrel in the sulks? [*Takes out his purse.*] Nora, what do you think I have here?

NORA [*turning round quickly*]. Money!

HELMER. There! [*Gives her some notes.*] Of course, I know all sorts of things are wanted at Christmas.

NORA [*counting*]. Ten, twenty, thirty, forty. Oh, thank you, thank you, Torvald! This will go a long way.

HELMER. I should hope so.

NORA. Yes, indeed; a long way! But come here, and let me show you all I've been buying. And so cheap! Look, here's a new suit for Ivar, and a little sword. Here are a horse and a trumpet for Bob. And here are a doll and a cradle for Emmy. They're only common; but they're good enough for her to pull to pieces. And dress-stuffs and kerchiefs for the servants. I ought to have got something better for old Anna.

HELMER. And what's in that other parcel?

NORA [*crying out*]. No, Torvald, you're not to see that until this evening!

HELMER. Oh! Ah! But now, tell me, you little spendthrift, have you thought of anything for yourself?

NORA. For myself! Oh, I don't want anything.

HELMER. Nonsense! Just tell me something sensible you would like to have.

NORA. No, really I don't know of anything — Well, listen, Torvald —

HELMER. Well?

NORA [*playing with his coat-buttons, without looking him in the face*]. If you really want to give me something, you might, you know — you might —

HELMER. Well? Out with it!

NORA [*quickly*]. You might give me money, Torvald. Only just what you think you can spare; then I can buy something with it later on.

HELMER. But, Nora —

NORA. Oh, please do, dear Torvald, please do! I should hang the money in lovely gilt paper on the Christmas tree. Would n't that be fun?

HELMER. What do they call the birds that are always making the money fly?

NORA. Yes, I know — spendthrifts, of course. But please do as I ask you, Torvald. Then I shall have time to think what I want most. Is n't that very sensible, now?

HELMER [*smiling*]. Certainly; that is to say, if you really kept the money I gave you, and really spent it on something for yourself. But it all goes in housekeeping, and for all manner of useless things, and then I have to pay up again.

NORA. But, Torvald —

HELMER. Can you deny it, Nora dear? [*He puts his arm round her.*] It's a sweet little lark, but it gets through a lot of money. No one would believe how much it costs a man to keep such a little bird as you.

NORA. For shame! How can you say so? Why, I save as much as ever I can.

HELMER [*laughing*]. Very true — as much as you can — but that's precisely nothing.

NORA [*hums and smiles with covert glee*]. H'm! If you only knew, Torvald, what expenses we larks and squirrels have.

HELMER. You're a strange little being! Just like your father — always on the lookout for all the money you can lay your hands on; but the moment you have it, it seems to slip through your fingers; you never know what becomes of it. Well, one must take you as you are. It's in the blood. Yes, Nora, that sort of thing is hereditary.

NORA. I wish I had inherited many of papa's qualities.

HELMER. And I don't wish you anything but just what you are — my own, sweet little song-bird. But I say — it strikes me you look so — so — what shall I call it? — so suspicious to-day —

NORA. Do I?

HELMER. You do, indeed. Look me full in the face.

NORA [looking at him]. Well?

HELMER [threatening with his finger]. Has n't the little sweet-tooth been playing pranks to-day?

NORA. No; how can you think such a thing!

HELMER. Did n't she just look in at the confectioner's?

NORA. No, Torvald; really —

HELMER. Not to sip a little jelly?

NORA. No; certainly not.

HELMER. Has n't she even nibbled a macaroon or two?

NORA. No, Torvald, indeed, indeed!

HELMER. Well, well, well; of course I'm only joking.

NORA [goes to the table on the right]. I should n't think of doing what you disapprove of.

HELMER. No, I'm sure of that; and, besides, you 've given me your word — [Going toward her.] Well, keep your little Christmas secrets to yourself, Nora darling. The Christmas tree will bring them all to light, I dare say.

NORA. Have you remembered to invite Doctor Rank?

HELMER. No. But it's not necessary; he 'll come as a matter of course. Besides, I shall ask him when he looks in to-day. I 've ordered some capital wine. Nora, you can't think how I look forward to this evening.

NORA. And I, too. How the children will enjoy themselves, Torvald!

HELMER. Ah, it's glorious to feel that one has an assured position and ample means. Is n't it delightful to think of?

NORA. Oh, it's wonderful!

HELMER. Do you remember last Christmas? For three whole weeks beforehand you shut yourself up every evening till long past midnight to make flowers for the Christmas tree, and all sorts of other marvels that were to have astonished us. I was never so bored in my life.

NORA. I did n't bore myself at all.

HELMER [smiling]. But it came to little enough in the end, Nora.

NORA. Oh, are you going to tease me about that again? How could I help the cat getting in and pulling it all to pieces?

HELMER. To be sure you could n't, my poor little Nora. You did your best to give us all pleasure, and that 's the main point. But, all the same, it 's a good thing the hard times are over.

NORA. Oh, is n't it wonderful?

HELMER. Now I need n't sit here boring myself all alone; and you need n't tire your blessed eyes and your delicate little fingers —

NORA [clapping her hands]. No, I need n't, need I, Torvald? Oh, how wonderful it is to think of? [Takes his arm.] And now I 'll tell you how I think we ought to manage, Torvald. As soon as Christmas is over — [The hall doorbell rings.] Oh, there 's a ring! [Arranging the room.] That 's somebody come to call. How tiresome!

HELMER. I 'm "not at home" to callers; remember that.

ELLEN [in the doorway]. A lady to see you, ma'am.

NORA. Show her in.

ELLEN [to HELMER]. And the doctor has just come, sir.

HELMER. Has he gone into my study?

ELLEN. Yes, sir.

[HELMER goes into his study.]

[ELLEN ushers in MRS. LINDEN, in traveling costume, and goes out, closing the door.]

MRS. LINDEN [embarrassed and hesitating]. How do you do, Nora?

NORA [doubtfully]. How do you do?

MRS. LINDEN. I see you don't recognize me.

NORA. No, I don't think — oh, yes! — I believe — [Suddenly brightening.] What, Christina! Is it really you?

MRS. LINDEN. Yes; really I!

NORA. Christina! And to think I did n't know you! But how could I — [More softly.] How changed you are, Christina!

MRS. LINDEN. Yes, no doubt. In nine or ten years —

NORA. Is it really so long since we met? Yes, so it is. Oh, the last eight years have been a happy time, I can tell you. And now you have come to town? All that long journey in mid-winter! How brave of you! MRS. LINDEN. I arrived by this morning's steamer.

NORA. To have a merry Christmas, of course. Oh, how delightful! Yes, we *will* have a merry Christmas. Do take your things off. Are n't you frozen? [*Helping her.*] There; now we 'll sit cozily by the fire. No, you take the armchair; I shall sit in this rocking-chair. [*Seizes her hands.*] Yes, now I can see the dear old face again. It was only at the first glance — But you 're a little paler, Christina, — and perhaps a little thinner.

MRS. LINDEN. And much, much older, Nora.

NORA. Yes, perhaps a little older — not much — ever so little. [*She suddenly checks herself; seriously.*] Oh, what a thoughtless wretch I am! Here I sit chattering on, and — Dear, dear Christina, can you forgive me!

MRS. LINDEN. What do you mean, Nora?

NORA [*softly*]. Poor Christina! I forgot: you are a widow.

MRS. LINDEN. Yes; my husband died three years ago.

NORA. I know, I know; I saw it in the papers. Oh, believe me, Christina, I did mean to write to you; but I kept putting it off, and something always came in the way.

MRS. LINDEN. I can quite understand that, Nora, dear.

NORA. No, Christina; it was horrid of me. Oh, you poor darling! how much you must have gone through! — And he left you nothing?

MRS. LINDEN. Nothing.

NORA. And no children?

MRS. LINDEN. None.

NORA. Nothing, nothing at all?

MRS. LINDEN. Not even a sorrow or a longing to dwell upon.

NORA [*looking at her incredulously*]. My dear Christina, how is that possible?

MRS. LINDEN [*smiling sadly and stroking her hair*]. Oh, it happens so sometimes, Nora.

NORA. So utterly alone! How dreadful that must be! I have three of the loveliest children. I can't show them to you just now; they 're out with their nurse. But now you must tell me everything.

MRS. LINDEN. No, no; I want you to tell me —

NORA. No, you must begin; I won't be egotistical to-day. To-day I 'll think only of you. Oh! but I must tell you one thing — perhaps you 've heard of our great stroke of fortune?

MRS. LINDEN. No. What is it?

NORA. Only think! my husband has been made manager of the Joint Stock Bank.

MRS. LINDEN. Your husband! Oh, how fortunate!

NORA. Yes; is n't it? A lawyer's position is so uncertain, you see, especially when he won't touch any business that 's the least bit — shady, as of course Torvald never would; and there I quite agree with him. Oh! You can imagine how glad we are. He is to enter on his new position at the New Year, and then he 'll have a large salary, and percentages. In future we shall be able to live quite differently — just as we please, in fact. Oh, Christina, I feel so light-hearted and happy! It 's delightful to have lots of money, and no need to worry about things, is n't it?

MRS. LINDEN. Yes; at any rate, it must be delightful to have what you need.

NORA. No, not only what you need, but heaps of money — *heaps!*

MRS. LINDEN [*smiling*]. Nora, Nora, have n't you learned reason yet? In our schooldays you were a shocking little spendthrift.

NORA [*quietly smiling*]. Yes; that 's what Torvald says I am still. [*Holding up her forefinger.*] But "Nora, Nora," is not so silly as you all think. Oh! I have n't had the chance to be much of a spendthrift. We have both had to work.

MRS. LINDEN. You, too?

NORA. Yes, light fancy work: crochet, and embroidery, and things of that sort; [*carelessly*] and other work too. You know, of course, that Torvald left the Government service when we were married. He had little chance of promotion, and of course he required to make more money. But in the first year after our marriage he overworked himself terribly. He had to under take all sorts of extra work, you know, and to slave early and late. He could n't stand it, and fell dangerously ill. Then the doctors declared he must go to the South.

MRS. LINDEN. You spent a whole year in Italy, did n't you?

NORA. Yes, we did. It was n't easy to manage, I can tell you. It was just after Ivar's birth. But of course we had to go. Oh, it was a wonderful, delicious journey! And it saved Torvald's life. But it cost a frightful lot of money, Christina.

MRS. LINDEN. So I should think.

NORA. Twelve hundred dollars! Four thousand eight hundred crowns! Is n't that a lot of money?

MRS. LINDEN. How lucky you had the money to spend.

NORA. We got it from father, you must know.

MRS. LINDEN. Ah, I see. He died just about that time, did n't he?

NORA. Yes, Christina, just then. And only think! I could n't go and nurse him! I was expecting little Ivar's birth daily; and then I had my poor sick Torvald to attend to. Dear, kind old father! I never saw him again, Christina. Oh! That's the hardest thing I have had to bear since my marriage.

MRS. LINDEN. I know how fond you were of him. But then you went to Italy?

NORA. Yes; you see, we had the money, and the doctors said we must lose no time. We started a month later.

MRS. LINDEN. And your husband came back completely cured.

NORA. Sound as a bell.

MRS. LINDEN. But — the doctor?

NORA. What do you mean?

MRS. LINDEN. I thought as I came in your servant announced the doctor —

NORA. Oh, yes; Doctor Rank. But he does n't come professionally. He is our best friend, and never lets a day pass without looking in. No, Torvald has n't had an hour's illness since that time. And the children are so healthy and well, and so am I. [*Jumps up and claps her hands.*] Oh, Christina, Christina, what a wonderful thing it is to live and to be happy! — Oh but it's really too horrid of me! Here am I talking about nothing but my own con-

cerns. [*Seats herself upon a footstool close to* CHRISTINA, *and lays her arms on her friend's lap.*] Oh, don't be angry with me! Now, tell me, is it really true that you did n't love your husband? What made you marry him, then?

MRS. LINDEN. My mother was still alive, you see, bedridden and helpless; and then I had my two younger brothers to think of. I did n't think it would be right for me to refuse him.

NORA. Perhaps it would n't have been. I suppose he was rich then?

MRS. LINDEN. Very well off, I believe. But his business was uncertain. It fell to pieces at his death, and there was nothing left.

NORA. And then —?

MRS. LINDEN. Then I had to fight my way by keeping a shop, a little school, anything I could turn my hand to. The last three years have been one long struggle for me. But now it is over, Nora. My poor mother no longer needs me; she is at rest. And the boys are in business, and can look after themselves.

NORA. How free your life must feel!

MRS. LINDEN. No, Nora; only inexpressibly empty. No one to live for! [*Stands up restlessly.*] That's why I could not bear to stay any longer in that out-of-the-way corner. Here it must be easier to find something to take one up — to occupy one's thoughts. If I could only get some settled employment — some office work.

NORA. But, Christina, that's such drudgery, and you look worn out already. It would be ever so much better for you to go to some watering-place and rest.

MRS. LINDEN [*going to the window*]. I have no father to give me the money, Nora.

NORA [*rising*]. Oh, don't be vexed with me.

MRS. LINDEN [*going to her*]. My dear Nora, don't you be vexed with me. The worst of a position like mine is that it makes one so bitter. You have no one to work for, yet you have to be always on the strain. You must live; and so you become selfish. When I heard of the happy change in your fortunes — can you believe it? — I was glad for my own sake more than for yours.

NORA. How do you mean? Ah, I see! You think Torvald can perhaps do something for you.

MRS. LINDEN. Yes; I thought so.

NORA. And so he shall, Christina. Just you leave it all to me. I shall lead up to it beautifully! — I shall think of some delightful plan to put him in a good humor! Oh, I should so love to help you.

MRS. LINDEN. How good of you, Nora, to stand by me so warmly! Doubly good in you, who know so little of the troubles and burdens of life.

NORA. I? I know so little of — ?

MRS. LINDEN [smiling]. Oh, well — a little fancy-work, and so forth. — You're a child, Nora.

NORA [tosses her head and paces the room]. Oh, come, you must n't be so patronizing!

MRS. LINDEN. No?

NORA. You're like the rest. You all think I'm fit for nothing really serious —

MRS. LINDEN. Well, well —

NORA. You think I've had no troubles in this weary world.

MRS. LINDEN. My dear Nora, you've just told me all your troubles.

NORA. Pooh — those trifles! [Softly.] I have n't told you the great thing.

MRS. LINDEN. The great thing? What do you mean?

NORA. I know you look down upon me, Christina; but you have no right to. You are proud of having worked so hard and so long for your mother.

MRS. LINDEN. I am sure I don't look down upon any one; but it's true I am both proud and glad when I remember that I was able to keep my mother's last days free from care.

NORA. And you're proud to think of what you have done for your brothers, too.

MRS. LINDEN. Have I not the right to be?

NORA. Yes, indeed. But now let me tell you, Christina, — I, too, have something to be proud and glad of.

MRS. LINDEN. I don't doubt it. But what do you mean?

NORA. Hush! Not so loud. Only think, if Torvald were to hear! He must n't — not for worlds! No one must know about it, Christina, — no one but you.

MRS. LINDEN. Why, what can it be?

NORA. Come over here. [Draws her down beside her on the sofa.] Yes, Christina, — I, too, have something to be proud and glad of. I saved Torvald's life.

MRS. LINDEN. Saved his life? How?

NORA. I told you about our going to Italy. Torvald would have died but for that.

MRS. LINDEN. Well — and your father gave me the money.

NORA [smiling]. Yes, so Torvald and every one believes; but —

MRS. LINDEN. But —?

NORA. Papa did n't give us one penny. It was I that found the money.

MRS. LINDEN. You? All that money?

NORA. Twelve hundred dollars. Four thousand eight hundred crowns. What do you say to that?

MRS. LINDEN. My dear Nora, how did you manage it? Did you win it in the lottery?

NORA [contemptuously]. In the lottery? Pooh! Any one could have done that!

MRS. LINDEN. Then, wherever did you get it from?

NORA [hums and smiles mysteriously]. H'm; tra-la-la-la.

MRS. LINDEN. Of course you could n't borrow it.

NORA. No? Why not?

MRS. LINDEN. Why, a wife can't borrow without her husband's consent.

NORA [tossing her head]. Oh! When the wife has some idea of business, and knows how to set about things —

MRS. LINDEN. But, Nora, I don't understand —

NORA. Well, you need n't. I never said I borrowed the money. There are many ways I may have got it. [Throws herself back on the sofa.] I may have got it from some admirer. When one is so — attractive as I am —

MRS. LINDEN. You're too silly, Nora.

NORA. Now, I'm sure you're dying of curiosity, Christina, —

MRS. LINDEN. Listen to me, Nora, dear: have n't you been a little rash?

NORA [sitting upright again]. Is it rash to save one's husband's life?

MRS. LINDEN. I think it was rash of you, without his knowledge —

NORA. But it would have been fatal for him to know! Can't you understand that? He was n't even to suspect how ill he was. The doctors came to me privately and told me his life was in danger — that nothing could save him but a winter in the South. Do you think I did n't try diplomacy first? I told him how I longed to have a trip abroad, like other young wives; I wept and prayed; I said he ought to think of my condition, and not to thwart me; and then I hinted that he could borrow the money. But then, Christina, he got almost angry. He said I was frivolous, and that it was his duty as a husband not to yield to my whims and fancies — so he called them. Very well, thought I, but saved you must be; and then I found the way to do it.

MRS. LINDEN. And did your husband never learn from your father that the money was not from him?

NORA. No; never. Papa died at that very time. I meant to have told him all about it, and begged him to say nothing. But he was so ill — unhappily, it was n't necessary.

MRS. LINDEN. And you have never confessed to your husband?

NORA. Good Heavens! What can you be thinking of? *Tell him*, when he has such a loathing of debt! And, besides, — how painful and humiliating it would be for Torvald, with his manly self-respect, to know that he owed anything to me! It would utterly upset the relation between us; our beautiful, happy home would never again be what it is.

MRS. LINDEN. Will you never tell him?

NORA [*thoughtfully, half-smiling*]. Yes, some time, perhaps, — many, many years hence, when I 'm — not so pretty. You must n't laugh at me! Of course, I mean when Torvald is not so much in love with me as he is now; when it does n't amuse him any longer to see me dancing about, and dressing up and acting. Then it might be well to have something in reserve. [*Breaking off.*] Nonsense! Nonsense! That time will never come. Now, what do you say to my grand secret, Christina? Am I

fit for nothing now? You may believe it has cost me a lot of anxiety. It has been no joke to meet my engagements punctually. You must know, Christina, that in business there are things called installments, and quarterly interest, that are terribly hard to provide for. So I 've had to pinch a little here and there, wherever I could. I could n't save much out of the housekeeping, for, of course, Torvald had to live well. And I could n't let the children go about badly dressed; all I got for them, I spent on them, the blessed darlings!

MRS. LINDEN. Poor Nora! So it had to come out of your own pocket-money.

NORA. Yes, of course. After all, the whole thing was my doing. When Torvald gave me money for clothes, and so on, I never spent more than half of it; I always bought the simplest and cheapest things. It's a mercy that everything suits me so well — Torvald never had any suspicions. But it was often very hard, Christina, dear. For it's nice to be beautifully dressed — now, is n't it?

MRS. LINDEN. Indeed it is.

NORA. Well, and besides that, I made money in other ways. Last winter I was so lucky — I got a heap of copying to do. I shut myself up every evening and wrote far into the night. Oh, sometimes I was so tired, so tired. And yet it was splendid to work in that way and earn money. I almost felt as if I was a man.

MRS. LINDEN. Then how much have you been able to pay off?

NORA. Well, I can't precisely say. It's difficult to keep that sort of business clear. I only know that I 've paid everything I could scrape together. Sometimes I really did n't know where to turn. [*Smiles.*] Then I used to sit here and pretend that a rich old gentleman was in love with me —

MRS. LINDEN. What! What gentleman?

NORA. Oh, nobody! — that he was dead now, and that when his will was opened, there stood in large letters: "Pay over at once everything of which I die possessed to that charming person, Mrs. Nora Helmer."

MRS. LINDEN. But, my dear Nora, — what gentleman do you mean?

Nora. Oh, dear, can't you understand? There was n't any old gentleman: it was only what I used to dream and dream when I was at my wits' end for money. But it does n't matter now — the tiresome old creature may stay where he is for me. I care nothing for him or his will; for now my troubles are over. [*Springing up.*] Oh, Christina, how glorious it is to think of! Free from all anxiety! Free, quite free. To be able to play and romp about with the children; to have things tasteful and pretty in the house, exactly as Torvald likes it! And then the spring will soon be here, with the great blue sky. Perhaps then we shall have a little holiday. Perhaps I shall see the sea again. Oh, what a wonderful thing it is to live and to be happy!   [*The hall doorbell rings.*]

Mrs. Linden [*rising*]. There's a ring. Perhaps I had better go.

Nora. No; do stay. No one will come here. It's sure to be some one for Torvald.

Ellen [*in the doorway*]. If you please, ma'am, there's a gentleman to speak to Mr. Helmer.

Nora. Who is the gentleman?

Krogstad [*in the doorway*]. It is I, Mrs. Helmer.

[Mrs. Linden *starts and turns away to the window.*]

Nora [*goes a step toward him, anxiously, speaking low*]. You? What is it? What do you want with my husband?

Krogstad. Bank business — in a way. I hold a small post in the Joint Stock Bank, and your husband is to be our new chief, I hear.

Nora. Then it is — ?

Krogstad. Only tiresome business, Mrs. Helmer; nothing more.

Nora. Then will you please go to his study.

[Krogstad *goes. She bows indifferently while she closes the door into the hall. Then she goes to the stove and looks to the fire.*]

Mrs. Linden. Nora — who was that man?

Nora. A Mr. Krogstad — a lawyer.

Mrs. Linden. Then it was really he?

Nora. Do you know him?

Mrs. Linden. I used to know him — many years ago. He was in a lawyer's office in our town.

Nora. Yes, so he was.

Mrs. Linden. How he has changed!

Nora. I believe his marriage was unhappy.

Mrs. Linden. And he is a widower now?

Nora. With a lot of children. There! Now it will burn up.

[*She closes the stove, and pushes the rocking-chair a little aside.*]

Mrs. Linden. His business is not of the most creditable, they say?

Nora. Is n't it? I dare say not. I don't know. But don't let us think of business — it's so tiresome.

[Doctor Rank *comes out of* Helmer's *room.*]

Rank [*still in the doorway*]. No, no; I'm in your way. I shall go and have a chat with your wife. [*Shuts the door and sees* Mrs. Linden.] Oh, I beg your pardon. I'm in the way here too.

Nora. No, not in the least. [*Introduces them.*] Doctor Rank — Mrs. Linden.

Rank. Oh, indeed; I've often heard Mrs. Linden's name; I think I passed you on the stairs as I came up.

Mrs. Linden. Yes; I go so very slowly. Stairs try me so much.

Rank. Ah — you are not very strong?

Mrs. Linden. Only overworked.

Rank. Nothing more? Then no doubt you've come to town to find rest in a round of dissipation?

Mrs. Linden. I have come to look for employment.

Rank. Is that an approved remedy for overwork?

Mrs. Linden. One must live, Doctor Rank.

Rank. Yes, that seems to be the general opinion.

Nora. Come, Doctor Rank, — you want to live yourself.

Rank. To be sure I do. However wretched I may be, I want to drag on as long as possible. All my patients, too, have the same mania. And it's the same with people whose complaint is moral. At this very moment Helmer is talking to just such a moral incurable —

MRS. LINDEN [*softly*]. Ah!

NORA. Whom do you mean?

RANK. Oh, a fellow named Krogstad, a man you know nothing about, — corrupt to the very core of his character. But even he began by announcing, as a matter of vast importance, that he must live.

NORA. Indeed? And what did he want with Torvald?

RANK. I have n't an idea; I only gathered that it was some bank business.

NORA. I did n't know that Krog — that this Mr. Krogstad had anything to do with the Bank?

RANK. Yes. He has got some sort of place there. [*To* MRS. LINDEN.] I don't know whether, in your part of the country, you have people who go grubbing and sniffing around in search of moral rottenness — and then, when they have found a "case," don't rest till they have got their man into some good position, where they can keep a watch upon him. Men with a clean bill of health they leave out in the cold.

MRS. LINDEN. Well, I suppose the — delicate characters require most care.

RANK [*shrugs his shoulders*]. There we have it! It's that notion that makes society a hospital.

[NORA, *deep in her own thoughts, breaks into half-stifled laughter and claps her hands.*]

Why do you laugh at that? Have you any idea what "society" is?

NORA. What do I care for your tiresome society? I was laughing at something else — something excessively amusing. Tell me, Doctor Rank, are all the employees at the Bank dependent on Torvald now?

RANK. Is that what strikes you as excessively amusing?

NORA [*smiles and hums*]. Never mind, never mind! [*Walks about the room.*] Yes, it is funny to think that we — that Torvald has such power over so many people. [*Takes the bag from her pocket.*] Doctor Rank, will you have a macaroon?

RANK. What! — macaroons! I thought they were contraband here.

NORA. Yes; but Christina brought me these.

MRS. LINDEN. What! I — ?

NORA. Oh, well! Don't be frightened. You could n't possibly know that Torvald had forbidden them. The fact is, he's afraid of me spoiling my teeth. But, oh, bother, just for once! — That's for you, Doctor Rank! [*Puts a macaroon into his mouth.*] And you too, Christina. And I'll have one while we're about it — only a tiny one, or at most two. [*Walks about again.*] Oh, dear, I am happy! There's only one thing in the world I really want.

RANK. Well; what's that?

NORA. There's something I should so like to say — in Torvald's hearing.

RANK. Then why don't you say it?

NORA. Because I dare n't, it's so ugly.

MRS. LINDEN. Ugly!

RANK. In that case you'd better not. But to us you might — What is it you would so like to say in Helmer's hearing?

NORA. I should so love to say, "Damn it all!"

RANK. Are you out of your mind?

MRS. LINDEN. Good gracious, Nora — !

RANK. Say it — there he is!

NORA [*hides the macaroons*]. Hush — sh —

[HELMER *comes out of his room, hat in hand, with his overcoat on his arm.*]

[*Going to him*]. Well, Torvald, dear, have you got rid of him?

HELMER. Yes; he has just gone.

NORA. Let me introduce you — this is Christina, who has come to town —

HELMER. Christina? Pardon me, I don't know —

NORA. Mrs. Linden, Torvald, dear, — Christina Linden.

HELMER [*to* MRS. LINDEN]. Indeed! A school-friend of my wife's, no doubt?

MRS. LINDEN. Yes; we knew each other as girls.

NORA. And only think! She has taken this long journey on purpose to speak to you.

HELMER. To speak to me!

MRS. LINDEN. Well, not quite —

NORA. You see, Christina is tremendously clever at office work, and she's so anxious to work under a first-rate man of business in order to learn still more —

HELMER [to MRS. LINDEN]. Very sensible, indeed.

NORA. And when she heard you were appointed manager — it was telegraphed, you know — she started off at once, and — Torvald, dear, for my sake, you must do something for Christina. Now, can't you?

HELMER. It's not impossible. I presume Mrs. Linden is a widow?

MRS. LINDEN. Yes.

HELMER. And you have already had some experience of business?

MRS. LINDEN. A good deal.

HELMER. Well, then, it's very likely I may be able to find a place for you.

NORA [clapping her hands]. There now! There now!

HELMER. You have come at a fortunate moment, Mrs. Linden.

MRS. LINDEN. Oh, how can I thank you — ?

HELMER [smiling]. There is no occasion. [Puts on his overcoat.] But for the present you must excuse me —

RANK. Wait; I am going with you.
[Fetches his fur coat from the hall and warms it at the fire.]

NORA. Don't be long, Torvald, dear.

HELMER. Only an hour; not more.

NORA. Are you going, too, Christina?

MRS. LINDEN [putting on her walking things]. Yes; I must set about looking for lodgings.

HELMER. Then perhaps we can go together?

NORA [helping her]. What a pity we haven't a spare room for you; but it's impossible —

MRS. LINDEN. I shouldn't think of troubling you. Good-bye, dear Nora, and thank you for all your kindness.

NORA. Good-bye for the present. Of course, you'll come back this evening. And you, too, Doctor Rank. What! If you're well enough? Of course you'll be well enough. Only wrap up warmly. [They go out, talking, into the hall. Outside on the stairs are heard children's voices.] There they are! There they are! [She runs to the outer door and opens it. The Nurse, ANNA, enters the hall with the children.] Come in! Come in! [Stoops down and kisses the children.] Oh, my sweet darlings! Do you see them, Christina? Are n't they lovely?

RANK. Don't let us stand here chattering in the draught.

HELMER. Come, Mrs. Linden; only mothers can stand such a temperature.
[DOCTOR RANK, HELMER, and MRS. LINDEN go down the stairs.]

[ANNA enters the room with the children; NORA also, shutting the door.]

NORA. How fresh and bright you look! And what red cheeks you've got! Like apples and roses. [The children chatter to her during what follows.] Have you had great fun? That's splendid! Oh, really! You've been giving Emmy and Bob a ride on your sledge! — both at once, only think! Why, you're quite a man, Ivar. Oh, give her to me a little, Anna. My sweet little dolly! [Takes the smallest from the nurse and dances with her.] Yes, yes; mother will dance with Bob, too. What! Did you have a game of snowballs? Oh, I wish I'd been there. No; leave them, Anna; I'll take their things off. Oh, yes, let me do it; it's such fun. Go to the nursery; you look frozen. You'll find some hot coffee on the stove.
[The Nurse goes into the room on the left. NORA takes off the children's things and throws them down anywhere, while the children talk all together.]
Really! A big dog ran after you? But he did n't bite you? No; dogs don't bite dear little dolly children. Don't peep into those parcels, Ivar. What is it? Would n't you like to know? Take care — it'll bite! What? Shall we have a game? What shall we play at? Hide-and-seek? Yes, let's play hide-and-seek. Bob shall hide first. Am I to? Yes, let me hide first.
[She and the children play, with laughter and shouting, in the room and the adjacent one to the right. At last NORA hides under the table; the children come rushing in, look for her, but cannot find her, hear her half-choked

*laughter, rush to the table, lift up
the cover and see her. Loud
shouts. She creeps out, as though
to frighten them. Fresh shouts.*]

[*Meanwhile there has been a knock at the
door leading into the hall. No one has
heard it. Now the door is half opened
and* KROGSTAD *appears. He waits a
little; the game is renewed.*]

KROGSTAD. I beg your pardon, Mrs.
Helmer —

NORA [*with a suppressed cry, turns round
and half jumps up*]. Ah! What do you
want?

KROGSTAD. Excuse me; the outer door
was ajar — somebody must have forgotten
to shut it —

NORA [*standing up*]. My husband is not
at home, Mr. Krogstad.

KROGSTAD. I know it.

NORA. Then what do you want here?

KROGSTAD. To say a few words to you.

NORA. To me? [*To the children, softly.*]
Go in to Anna. What? No, the strange
man won't hurt mamma. When he's gone
we'll go on playing. [*She leads the children
into the left-hand room, and shuts the door
behind them. Uneasy, in suspense.*] It is to
me you wish to speak?

KROGSTAD. Yes, to you.

NORA. To-day! But it's not the first
yet —

KROGSTAD. No, to-day is Christmas Eve.
It will depend upon yourself whether you
have a merry Christmas.

NORA. What do you want? I'm not
ready to-day —

KROGSTAD. Never mind that just now.
I have come about another matter. You
have a minute to spare?

NORA. Oh, yes, I suppose so; although —

KROGSTAD. Good. I was sitting in the
restaurant opposite, and I saw your husband go down the street —

NORA. Well?

KROGSTAD. With a lady.

NORA. What then?

KROGSTAD. May I ask if the lady was a
Mrs. Linden?

NORA. Yes.

KROGSTAD. Who has just come to town?

NORA. Yes. To-day.

KROGSTAD. I believe she is an intimate
friend of yours.

NORA. Certainly. But I don't understand —

KROGSTAD. I used to know *her* too.

NORA. I know you did.

KROGSTAD. Ah! You know all about it.
I thought as much. Now, frankly, is Mrs.
Linden to have a place in the Bank?

NORA. How dare you catechize me in
this way, Mr. Krogstad — you, a subordinate of my husband's? But since you ask,
you shall know. Yes, Mrs. Linden is to be
employed. And it is I who recommended
her, Mr. Krogstad. Now you know.

KROGSTAD. Then my guess was right.

NORA [*walking up and down*]. You see
one has a wee bit of influence, after all.
It does n't follow because one's only a
woman — When people are in a subordinate position, Mr. Krogstad, they ought
really to be careful how they offend anybody who — h'm —

KROGSTAD. Who has influence?

NORA. Exactly.

KROGSTAD [*taking another tone*]. Mrs.
Helmer, will you have the kindness to employ your influence on my behalf?

NORA. What? How do you mean?

KROGSTAD. Will you be so good as to
see that I retain my subordinate position
in the Bank?

NORA. What do you mean? Who wants
to take it from you?

KROGSTAD. Oh, you need n't pretend
ignorance. I can very well understand that
it cannot be pleasant for your friend to
meet me; and I can also understand now
for whose sake I am to be hounded out.

NORA. But I assure you —

KROGSTAD. Come, come, now, once for
all: there is time yet, and I advise you to
use your influence to prevent it.

NORA. But, Mr. Krogstad, I have no
influence — absolutely none.

KROGSTAD. None? I thought you said a
moment ago —

NORA. Of course, not in that sense. I!
How can you imagine that I should have
any such influence over my husband?

KROGSTAD. Oh, I know your husband

from our college days. I don't think he is any more inflexible than other husbands.

NORA. If you talk disrespectfully of my husband, I must request you to leave the house.

KROGSTAD. You are bold, madam.

NORA. I am afraid of you no longer. When New Year's Day is over, I shall soon be out of the whole business.

KROGSTAD [controlling himself]. Listen to me, Mrs. Helmer. If need be, I shall fight as though for my life to keep my little place in the Bank.

NORA. Yes, so it seems.

KROGSTAD. It's not only for the salary: that is what I care least about. It's something else — Well, I had better make a clean breast of it. Of course, you know, like every one else, that some years ago I — got into trouble.

NORA. I think I've heard something of the sort.

KROGSTAD. The matter never came into court; but from that moment all paths were barred to me. Then I took up the business you know about. I had to turn my hand to something; and I don't think I've been one of the worst. But now I must get clear of it all. My sons are growing up; for their sake I must try to recover my character as well as I can. This place in the Bank was the first step; and now your husband wants to kick me off the ladder, back into the mire.

NORA. But I assure you, Mr. Krogstad, I have n't the least power to help you.

KROGSTAD. That is because you have not the will; but I can compel you.

NORA. You won't tell my husband that I owe you money?

KROGSTAD. H'm; suppose I were to?

NORA. It would be shameful of you. [With tears in her voice.] The secret that is my joy and my pride — that he should learn it in such an ugly, coarse way — and from you. It would involve me in all sorts of unpleasantness —

KROGSTAD. Only unpleasantness?

NORA [hotly]. But just do it. It's you that will come off worst, for then my husband will see what a bad man you are, and then you certainly won't keep your place.

KROGSTAD. I asked whether it was only domestic unpleasantness you feared?

NORA. If my husband gets to know about it, he will, of course, pay you off at once, and then we shall have nothing more to do with you.

KROGSTAD [coming a pace nearer]. Listen, Mrs. Helmer: either your memory is defective, or you don't know much about business. I must make the position a little clearer to you.

NORA. How so?

KROGSTAD. When your husband was ill, you came to me to borrow twelve hundred dollars.

NORA. I knew of nobody else.

KROGSTAD. I promised to find you the money —

NORA. And you did find it.

KROGSTAD. I promised to find you the money, on certain conditions. You were so much taken up at the time about your husband's illness, and so eager to have the wherewithal for your journey, that you probably did not give much thought to the details. Allow me to remind you of them. I promised to find you the amount in exchange for a note of hand, which I drew up.

NORA. Yes, and I signed it.

KROGSTAD. Quite right. But then I added a few lines, making your father security for the debt. Your father was to sign this.

NORA. Was to —? He did sign it!

KROGSTAD. I had left the date blank. That is to say, your father was himself to date his signature. Do you recollect that?

NORA. Yes, I believe —

KROGSTAD. Then I gave you the paper to send to your father, by post. Is not that so?

NORA. Yes.

KROGSTAD. And of course you did so at once; for within five or six days you brought me back the document with your father's signature; and I handed you the money.

NORA. Well? Have I not made my payments punctually?

KROGSTAD. Fairly — yes. But to return to the point: You were in great trouble at the time, Mrs. Helmer.

NORA. I was, indeed!

KROGSTAD. Your father was very ill, I believe?

NORA. He was on his death-bed.

KROGSTAD. And died soon after?

NORA. Yes.

KROGSTAD. Tell me, Mrs. Helmer; do you happen to recollect the day of his death? The day of the month, I mean?

NORA. Father died on the 29th of September.

KROGSTAD. Quite correct. I have made inquiries. And here comes in the remarkable point — [*produces a paper*] which I cannot explain.

NORA. What remarkable point? I don't know —

KROGSTAD. The remarkable point, madam, that your father signed this paper three days after his death!

NORA. What! I don't understand —

KROGSTAD. Your father died on the 29th of September. But look here: he has dated his signature October 2d! Is not that remarkable, Mrs. Helmer? [NORA *is silent.*] Can you explain it? [NORA *continues silent.*] It is noteworthy, too, that the words "October 2d" and the year are not in your father's handwriting, but in one which I believe I know. Well, this may be explained; your father may have forgotten to date his signature, and somebody may have added the date at random, before the fact of your father's death was known. There is nothing wrong in that. Everything depends on the signature. Of course, it is genuine, Mrs. Helmer? It was really your father himself who wrote his name here?

NORA [*after a short silence, throws her head back and looks defiantly at him*]. No, it was not. *I* wrote father's name.

KROGSTAD. Ah! — Are you aware, madam, that that is a dangerous admission?

NORA. How so? You will soon get your money.

KROGSTAD. May I ask you one more question? Why did you not send the paper to your father?

NORA. It was impossible. Father was ill. If I had asked him for his signature, I should have had to tell him why I wanted the money; but he was so ill I really could not tell him that my husband's life was in danger. It was impossible.

KROGSTAD. Then it would have been better to have given up your tour.

NORA. No, I could n't do that; my husband's life depended on that journey. I could n't give it up.

KROGSTAD. And did it never occur to you that you were deceiving me?

NORA. That was nothing to me. I did n't care in the least about you. I could n't endure you for all the cruel difficulties you made, although you knew how ill my husband was.

KROGSTAD. Mrs. Helmer, you evidently do not realize what you have been guilty of. But I can assure you it was nothing more and nothing worse that made me an outcast from society.

NORA. You! You want me to believe that you did a brave thing to save your wife's life?

KROGSTAD. The law takes no account of motives.

NORA. Then it must be a very bad law.

KROGSTAD. Bad or not, if I produce this document in court, you will be condemned according to law.

NORA. I don't believe that. Do you mean to tell me that a daughter has no right to spare her dying father trouble and anxiety? — that a wife has no right to save her husband's life? I don't know much about the law, but I'm sure you'll find, somewhere or another, that that is allowed. And you don't know that — you, a lawyer! You must be a bad one, Mr. Krogstad.

KROGSTAD. Possibly. But business — such business as ours — I do understand. You believe that? Very well; now, do as you please. But this I may tell you, that if I am flung into the gutter a second time, you shall keep me company.

[*Bows and goes out through hall.*]

NORA [*stands a while thinking, then tosses her head*]. Oh, nonsense! He wants to frighten me. I'm not so foolish as that. [*Begins folding the children's clothes. Pauses.*] But — ? No, it's impossible! Why, I did it for love!

CHILDREN [*at the door, left*]. Mamma, the strange man has gone now.

NORA. Yes, yes, I know. But don't tell any one about the strange man. Do you hear? Not even papa!

CHILDREN. No, mamma; and now will you play with us again?

NORA. No, no; now not.

CHILDREN. Oh, do, mamma; you know you promised.

NORA. Yes, but I can't just now. Run to the nursery; I have so much to do. Run along, run along, and be good, my darlings! [*She pushes them gently into the inner room, and closes the door behind them. Sits on the sofa, embroiders a few stitches, but soon pauses.*] No! [*Throws down the work, rises, goes to the hall door and calls out.*] Ellen, bring in the Christmas tree! [*Goes to table, left, and opens the drawer; again pauses.*] No, it's quite impossible!

ELLEN [*with Christmas tree*]. Where shall I stand it, ma'am?

NORA. There, in the middle of the room.

ELLEN. Shall I bring in anything else?

NORA. No, thank you, I have all I want.

[ELLEN, *having put down the tree, goes out.*]

NORA [*busy dressing the tree*]. There must be a candle here — and flowers there. — That horrible man! Nonsense, nonsense! there's nothing to be afraid of. The Christmas tree shall be beautiful. I'll do everything to please you, Torvald; I'll sing and dance, and —

[*Enter* HELMER *by the hall door, with a bundle of documents.*]

NORA. Oh! You're back already?

HELMER. Yes. Has anybody been here?

NORA. Here? No.

HELMER. That's odd. I saw Krogstad come out of the house.

NORA. Did you? Oh, yes, by the bye, he was here for a minute.

HELMER. Nora, I can see by your manner that he has been begging you to put in a good word for him.

NORA. Yes.

HELMER. And you were to do it as if of your own accord? You were to say nothing to me of his having been here. Did n't he suggest that, too?

NORA. Yes, Torvald; but —

HELMER. Nora, Nora! And you could condescend to that! To speak to such a man, to make him a promise! And then to tell me an untruth about it!

NORA. An untruth!

HELMER. Did n't you say that nobody had been here? [*Threatens with his finger.*] My little bird must never do that again! A song-bird must sing clear and true; no false notes. [*Puts his arm round her.*] That's so, is n't it? Yes, I was sure of it. [*Lets her go.*] And now we'll say no more about it. [*Sits down before the fire.*] Oh, how cozy and quiet it is here! [*Glances into his documents.*]

NORA [*busy with the tree, after a short silence*]. Torvald!

HELMER. Yes.

NORA. I'm looking forward so much to the Stenborgs' fancy ball the day after to-morrow.

HELMER. And I'm on tenterhooks to see what surprise you have in store for me.

NORA. Oh, it's too tiresome!

HELMER. What is?

NORA. I can't think of anything good. Everything seems so foolish and meaningless.

HELMER. Has little Nora made that discovery?

NORA [*behind his chair, with her arms on the back*]. Are you very busy, Torvald?

HELMER. Well —

NORA. What papers are those?

HELMER. Bank business.

NORA. Already!

HELMER. I have got the retiring manager to let me make some necessary changes in the staff and the organization. I can do this during Christmas week. I want to have everything straight by the New Year.

NORA. Then that's why that poor Krogstad —

HELMER. H'm.

NORA [*still leaning over the chair-back and slowly stroking his hair*]. If you had n't been so very busy, I should have asked you a great, great favor, Torvald.

HELMER. What can it be? Out with it.

NORA. Nobody has such perfect taste as you; and I should so love to look well at the fancy ball. Torvald, dear, couldn't you take me in hand, and settle what I'm to be, and arrange my costume for me?

HELMER. Aha! So my willful little woman is at a loss, and making signals of distress.

NORA. Yes, please, Torvald. I can't get on without your help.

HELMER. Well, well, I'll think it over, and we'll soon hit upon something.

NORA. Oh, how good that is of you! [Goes to the tree again; pause.] How well the red flowers show. — Tell me, was it anything so very dreadful this Krogstad got into trouble about?

HELMER. Forgery, that's all. Don't you know what that means?

NORA. May n't he have been driven to it by need?

HELMER. Yes; or, like so many others, he may have done it in pure heedlessness. I am not so hard-hearted as to condemn a man absolutely for a single fault.

NORA. No, surely not, Torvald!

HELMER. Many a man can retrieve his character, if he owns his crime and takes the punishment.

NORA. Punishment — ?

HELMER. But Krogstad did n't do that. He evaded the law by means of tricks and subterfuges; and that is what has morally ruined him.

NORA. Do you think that — ?

HELMER. Just think how a man with a thing of that sort on his conscience must be always lying and canting and shamming. Think of the mask he must wear even toward those who stand nearest him — toward his own wife and children. The effect on the children — that's the most terrible part of it, Nora.

NORA. Why?

HELMER. Because in such an atmosphere of lies home life is poisoned and contaminated in every fiber. Every breath the children draw contains some germ of evil.

NORA [closer behind him]. Are you sure of that?

HELMER. As a lawyer, my dear, I have seen it often enough. Nearly all cases of early corruption may be traced to lying mothers.

NORA. Why — mothers?

HELMER. It generally comes from the mother's side; but of course the father's influence may act in the same way. Every lawyer knows it too well. And here has this Krogstad been poisoning his own children for years past by a life of lies and hypocrisy — that is why I call him morally ruined. [Holds out both hands to her.] So my sweet little Nora must promise not to plead his cause. Shake hands upon it. Come, come, what's this? Give me your hand. That's right. Then it's a bargain. I assure you it would have been impossible for me to work with him. It gives me a positive sense of physical discomfort to come in contact with such people.

[NORA draws her hand away, and moves to the other side of the Christmas tree.]

NORA. How warm it is here. And I have so much to do.

HELMER [rises and gathers up his papers]. Yes, and I must try to get some of these papers looked through before dinner. And I shall think over your costume too. Perhaps I may even find something to hang in gilt paper on the Christmas tree. [Lays his hand on her head.] My precious little songbird!

[He goes into his room and shuts the door.]

NORA [softly, after a pause]. It can't be. It's impossible. It must be impossible!

ANNA [at the door, left]. The little ones are begging so prettily to come to mamma.

NORA. No, no, no; don't let them come to me! Keep them with you, Anna.

ANNA. Very well, ma'am.

[Shuts the door.]

NORA [pale with terror]. Corrupt my children! — Poison my home! [Short pause She throws back her head.] It's not true! It can never, never be true!

ACT II

The same room. In the corner, beside the piano, stands the Christmas tree, stripped, and with the candles burnt out. NORA's *outdoor things lie on the sofa.*

[NORA, *alone, is walking about restlessly. At last she stops by the sofa, and takes up her cloak.*]

NORA [*dropping the cloak*]. There's somebody coming! [*Goes to the hall door and listens.*] Nobody; of course nobody will come to-day, Christmas Day; nor to-morrow either. But perhaps — [*Opens the door and looks out.*] — No, nothing in the letter box; quite empty. [*Comes forward.*] Stuff and nonsense! Of course he won't really do anything. Such a thing could n't happen. It's impossible! Why, I have three little children.

[ANNA *enters from the left, with a large cardboard box.*]

ANNA. I've found the box with the fancy dress at last.

NORA. Thanks; put it down on the table.

ANNA [*doing so*]. But I'm afraid it's very much out of order.

NORA. Oh, I wish I could tear it into a hundred thousand pieces!

ANNA. Oh, no. It can easily be put to rights — just a little patience.

NORA. I shall go and get Mrs. Linden to help me.

ANNA. Going out again? In such weather as this! You'll catch cold, ma'am, and be ill.

NORA. Worse things might happen. — What are the children doing?

ANNA. They're playing with their Christmas presents, poor little dears; but—

NORA. Do they often ask for me?

ANNA. You see they've been so used to having their mamma with them.

NORA. Yes; but, Anna, I can't have them so much with me in future.

ANNA. Well, little children get used to anything.

NORA. Do you think they do? Do you believe they would forget their mother if she went quite away?

ANNA. Gracious me! Quite away?

NORA. Tell me, Anna, — I've so often wondered about it, — how could you bring yourself to give your child up to strangers?

ANNA. I had to when I came to nurse my little Miss Nora.

NORA. But how could you make up your mind to it?

ANNA. When I had the chance of such a good place? A poor girl who's been in trouble must take what comes. That wicked man did nothing for me.

NORA. But your daughter must have forgotten you.

ANNA. Oh, no, ma'am, that she has n't. She wrote to me both when she was confirmed and when she was married.

NORA [*embracing her*]. Dear old Anna — you were a good mother to me when I was little.

ANNA. My poor little Nora had no mother but me.

NORA. And if my little ones had nobody else, I'm sure you would — Nonsense, nonsense! [*Opens the box.*] Go in to the children. Now I must — You'll see how lovely I shall be to-morrow.

ANNA. I'm sure there will be no one at the ball so lovely as my Miss Nora.

[*She goes into the room on the left.*]

NORA [*takes the costume out of the box, but soon throws it down again*]. Oh, if I dared go out. If only nobody would come. If only nothing would happen here in the mean time. Rubbish; nobody is coming. Only not to think. What a delicious muff! Beautiful gloves, beautiful gloves! To forget — to forget! One, two, three, four, five, six — [*With a scream.*] Ah, there they come.

[*Goes toward the door, then stands irresolute.*]

[MRS. LINDEN *enters from the hall, where she has taken off her things.*]

NORA. Oh, it's you, Christina. There's nobody else there? I'm so glad you have come.

MRS. LINDEN. I hear you called at my lodgings.

NORA. Yes, I was just passing. There's something you *must* help me with. Let us sit here on the sofa — so. To-morrow evening there's to be a fancy ball at Consul Stenborg's overhead, and Torvald wants me to appear as a Neapolitan fisher-girl, and dance the *tarantella;* I learned it at Capri.

MRS. LINDEN. I see — quite a performance.

NORA. Yes, Torvald wishes it. Look, this is the costume; Torvald had it made for me in Italy. But now it's all so torn, I don't know —

MRS. LINDEN. Oh, we shall soon set that to rights. It's only the trimming that has come loose here and there. Have you a needle and thread? Ah, here's the very thing.

NORA. Oh, how kind of you.

MRS. LINDEN [*sewing*]. So you're to be in costume to-morrow, Nora? I'll tell you what — I shall come in for a moment to see you in all your glory. But I've quite forgotten to thank you for the pleasant evening yesterday.

NORA [*rises and walks across the room*]. Oh, yesterday, it did n't seem so pleasant as usual. — You should have come to town a little sooner, Christina. — Torvald has certainly the art of making home bright and beautiful.

MRS. LINDEN. You, too, I should think, or you would n't be your father's daughter. But tell me — is Doctor Rank always so depressed as he was last evening?

NORA. No, yesterday it was particularly noticeable. You see, he suffers from a dreadful illness. He has spinal consumption, poor fellow. They say his father was a horrible man, who kept mistresses and all sorts of things — so the son has been sickly from his childhood, you understand.

MRS. LINDEN [*lets her sewing fall into her lap*]. Why, my darling Nora, how do you come to know such things?

NORA [*moving about the room*]. Oh, when one has three children, one sometimes has visits from women who are half — half doctors — and they talk of one thing and another.

MRS. LINDEN [*goes on sewing; a short pause*]. Does Doctor Rank come here every day?

NORA. Every day of his life. He has been Torvald's most intimate friend from boyhood, and he's a good friend of mine, too. Doctor Rank is quite one of the family.

MRS. LINDEN. But tell me — is he quite sincere? I mean, is n't he rather given to flattering people?

NORA. No, quite the contrary. Why should you think so?

MRS. LINDEN. When you introduced us yesterday he said he had often heard my name; but I noticed afterwards that your husband had no notion who I was. How could Doctor Rank — ?

NORA. He was quite right, Christina. You see, Torvald loves me so indescribably, he wants to have me all to himself, as he says. When we were first married, he was almost jealous if I even mentioned any of my old friends at home; so naturally I gave up doing it. But I often talk of the old times to Doctor Rank, for he likes to hear about them.

MRS. LINDEN. Listen to me, Nora! You are still a child in many ways. I am older than you, and have had more experience. I'll tell you something? You ought to get clear of all this with Doctor Rank.

NORA. Get clear of what?

MRS. LINDEN. The whole affair, I should say. You were talking yesterday of a rich admirer who was to find you money —

NORA. Yes, one who never existed, worse luck. What then?

MRS. LINDEN. Has Doctor Rank money?

NORA. Yes, he has.

MRS. LINDEN. And nobody to provide for?

NORA. Nobody. But — ?

MRS. LINDEN. And he comes here every day?

NORA. Yes, I told you so.

MRS. LINDEN. I should have thought he would have had better taste.

NORA. I don't understand you a bit.

MRS. LINDEN. Don't pretend, Nora. Do you suppose I can't guess who lent you the twelve hundred dollars?

NORA. Are you out of your senses? How can you think such a thing? A friend who comes here every day! Why, the position would be unbearable!

MRS. LINDEN. Then it really is not he?
NORA. No, I assure you. It never for a moment occurred to me — Besides, at that time he had nothing to lend; he came into his property afterwards.
MRS. LINDEN. Well, I believe that was lucky for you, Nora, dear.
NORA. No, really, it would never have struck me to ask Doctor Rank — And yet, I'm certain that if I did —
MRS. LINDEN. But of course you never would.
NORA. Of course not. It's inconceivable that it should ever be necessary. But I'm quite sure that if I spoke to Doctor Rank —
MRS. LINDEN. Behind your husband's back?
NORA. I must get clear of the other thing; that's behind his back too. I *must* get clear of that.
MRS. LINDEN. Yes, yes, I told you so yesterday; but —
NORA [*walking up and down*]. A man can manage these things much better than a woman.
MRS. LINDEN. One's own husband, yes.
NORA. Nonsense. [*Stands still.*] When everything is paid, one gets back the paper.
MRS. LINDEN. Of course.
NORA. And can tear it into a hundred thousand pieces, and burn it up, the nasty, filthy thing!
MRS. LINDEN [*looks at her fixedly, lays down her work, and rises slowly*]. Nora, you are hiding something from me.
NORA. Can you see it in my face?
MRS. LINDEN. Something has happened since yesterday morning. Nora, what is it?
NORA [*going toward her*]. Christina —!
[*Listens.*] Hush! There's Torvald coming home. Do you mind going into the nursery for the present? Torvald can't bear to see dressmaking going on. Get Anna to help you.
MRS. LINDEN [*gathers some of the things together*]. Very well; but I shan't go away until you have told me all about it.
[*She goes out to the left.*]

[HELMER *enters from the hall.*]

NORA [*runs to meet him*]. Oh, how I've been longing for you to come, Torvald, dear!

HELMER. Was that the dressmaker —?
NORA. No, Christina. She's helping me with my costume. You'll see how nice I shall look.
HELMER. Yes, wasn't that a happy thought of mine?
NORA. Splendid! But isn't it good of me, too, to have given in to you about the *tarantella*?
HELMER [*takes her under the chin*]. Good of you! To give in to your own husband? Well, well, you little madcap, I know you don't mean it. But I won't disturb you. I dare say you want to be "trying on."
NORA. And you are going to work, I suppose?
HELMER. Yes. [*Shows her a bundle of papers.*] Look here. I've just come from the Bank —   [*Goes toward his room.*]
NORA. Torvald.
HELMER [*stopping*]. Yes?
NORA. If your little squirrel were to beg you for something so prettily —
HELMER. Well?
NORA. Would you do it?
HELMER. I must know first what it is.
NORA. The squirrel would skip about and play all sorts of tricks if you would only be nice and kind.
HELMER. Come, then, out with it.
NORA. Your lark would twitter from morning till night —
HELMER. Oh, that she does in any case.
NORA. I'll be an elf and dance in the moonlight for you, Torvald.
HELMER. Nora — you can't mean what you were hinting at this morning?
NORA [*coming nearer*]. Yes, Torvald, I beg and implore you!
HELMER. Have you really the courage to begin that again?
NORA. Yes, yes; for my sake, you *must* let Krogstad keep his place in the Bank.
HELMER. My dear Nora, it's his place I intend for Mrs. Linden.
NORA. Yes, that's so good of you. But instead of Krogstad, you could dismiss some other clerk.
HELMER. Why, this is incredible obstinacy! Because you have thoughtlessly promised to put in a word for him, I am to —!

NORA. It's not that, Torvald. It's for your own sake. This man writes for the most scurrilous newspapers; you said so yourself. He can do you no end of harm. I'm so terribly afraid of him —

HELMER. Ah, I understand; it's old recollections that are frightening you.

NORA. What do you mean?

HELMER. Of course, you're thinking of your father.

NORA. Yes — yes, of course. Only think of the shameful slanders wicked people used to write about father. I believe they would have got him dismissed if you had n't been sent to look into the thing, and been kind to him, and helped him.

HELMER. My little Nora, between your father and me there is all the difference in the world. Your father was not altogether unimpeachable. I am; and I hope to remain so.

NORA. Oh, no one knows what wicked men may hit upon. We could live so quietly and happily now, in our cozy, peaceful home, you and I and the children, Torvald! That's why I beg and implore you —

HELMER. And it is just by pleading his cause that you make it impossible for me to keep him. It's already known at the Bank that I intend to dismiss Krogstad. If it were now reported that the new manager let himself be turned round his wife's little finger —

NORA. What then?

HELMER. Oh, nothing, so long as a willful woman can have her way — ! I am to make myself a laughing-stock to the whole staff, and set people saying that I am open to all sorts of outside influence? Take my word for it, I should soon feel the consequences. And besides — there is one thing that makes Krogstad impossible for me to work with —

NORA. What thing?

HELMER. I could perhaps have overlooked his moral failings at a pinch —

NORA. Yes, could n't you, Torvald?

HELMER. And I hear he is good at his work. But the fact is, he was a college chum of mine —there was one of those rash friendships between us that one so often repents of later. I may as well confess it at once — he calls me by my Christian name; and he is tactless enough to do it even when others are present. He delights in putting on airs of familiarity — Torvald here, Torvald there! I assure you it's most painful to me. He would make my position at the Bank perfectly unendurable.

NORA. Torvald, surely you're not serious?

HELMER. No? Why not?

NORA. That's such a petty reason.

HELMER. What! Petty! Do you consider me petty!

NORA. No, on the contrary, Torvald, dear; and that's just why —

HELMER. Never mind; you call my motives petty; then I must be petty too. Petty! Very well! — Now we'll put an end to this, once for all. [Goes to the door into the hall and calls.] Ellen!

NORA. What do you want?

HELMER [searching among his papers]. To settle the thing.

[ELLEN enters.]

Here; take this letter; give it to a messenger. See that he takes it at once. The address is on it. Here's the money.

ELLEN. Very well, sir.

[Goes with the letter.]

HELMER [putting his papers together]. There, Madam Obstinacy.

NORA [breathless]. Torvald — what was in the letter?

HELMER. Krogstad's dismissal.

NORA. Call it back again, Torvald! There's still time. Oh, Torvald, call it back again! For my sake, for your own, for the children's sake! Do you hear, Torvald? Do it! You don't know what that letter may bring upon us all.

HELMER. Too late.

NORA. Yes, too late.

HELMER. My dear Nora, I forgive your anxiety, though it's anything but flattering to me. Why should you suppose that I would be afraid of a wretched scribbler's spite? But I forgive you all the same, for it's a proof of your great love for me. [Takes her in his arms.] That's as it should be, my own dear Nora. Let what will happen — when it comes to the pinch, I shall have strength and courage enough. You shall see: my shoulders are broad enough to bear the whole burden.

NORA [terror-struck]. What do you mean by that?

HELMER. The whole burden, I say —

NORA [with decision]. That you shall never, never do!

HELMER. Very well; then we'll share it, Nora, as man and wife. That is how it should be. [Petting her.] Are you satisfied now? Come, come, come, don't look like a scared dove. It's all nothing — foolish fancies. — Now you ought to play the tarantella through and practice with the tambourine. I shall sit in my inner room and shut both doors, so that I shall hear nothing. You can make as much noise as you please. [Turns round in doorway.] And when Rank comes, just tell him where I'm to be found. [He nods to her, and goes with his papers into his room, closing the door.]

NORA [bewildered with terror, stands as though rooted to the ground, and whispers]. He would do it. Yes, he would do it. He would do it, in spite of all the world. — No, never that, never, never! Anything rather than that! Oh, for some way of escape! What shall I do —! [Hall bell rings.] Doctor Rank —! Anything, anything, rather than —!

[NORA draws her hands over her face, pulls herself together, goes to the door and opens it. RANK stands outside hanging up his fur coat. During what follows it begins to grow dark.]

NORA. Good-afternoon, Doctor Rank. I knew you by your ring. But you must n't go to Torvald now. I believe he's busy.

RANK. And you? [Enters and closes the door.]

NORA. Oh, you know very well, I have always time for you.

RANK. Thank you. I shall avail myself of your kindness as long as I can.

NORA. What do you mean? As long as you can?

RANK. Yes. Does that frighten you?

NORA. I think it's an odd expression. Do you expect anything to happen?

RANK. Something I have long been prepared for; but I did n't think it would come so soon.

NORA [catching at his arm.] What have you discovered? Doctor Rank, you must tell me!

RANK [sitting down by the stove]. I am running down hill. There's no help for it.

NORA [drawing a long breath of relief]. It's you —?

RANK. Who else should it be? — Why lie to one's self? I am the most wretched of all my patients, Mrs. Helmer. In these last days I have been auditing my life-account — bankrupt! Perhaps before a month is over, I shall lie rotting in the churchyard.

NORA. Oh! What an ugly way to talk.

RANK. The thing itself is so confoundedly ugly, you see. But the worst of it is, so many other ugly things have to be gone through first. There is only one last investigation to be made, and when that is over I shall know pretty certainly when the break-up will begin. There's one thing I want to say to you: Helmer's delicate nature shrinks so from all that is horrible: I will not have him in my sick-room —

NORA. But, Doctor Rank —

RANK. I won't have him, I say — not on any account. I shall lock my door against him. — As soon as I am quite certain of the worst, I shall send you my visiting-card with a black cross on it; and then you will know that the final horror has begun.

NORA. Why, you're perfectly unreasonable to-day; and I did so want you to be in a really good humor.

RANK. With death staring me in the face? — And to suffer thus for another's sin! Where's the justice of it? And in one way or another you can trace in every family some such inexorable retribution —

NORA [stopping her ears]. Nonsense, nonsense! Now, cheer up!

RANK. Well, after all, the whole thing's only worth laughing at. My poor innocent spine must do penance for my father's wild oats.

NORA [at table, left]. I suppose he was too fond of asparagus and Strasbourg pâté, was n't he?

RANK. Yes; and truffles.

NORA. Yes, truffles, to be sure. And oysters, I believe?

RANK. Yes, oysters; oysters, of course.

NORA. And then all the port and champagne! It's sad that all these good things should attack the spine.

RANK. Especially when the luckless spine attacked never had any good of them.

NORA. Ah, yes, that's the worst of it.

RANK [looks at her searchingly]. H'm —

NORA [a moment later]. Why did you smile?

RANK. No; it was you that laughed.

NORA. No; it was you that smiled, Doctor Rank.

RANK [standing up]. I see you're deeper than I thought.

NORA. I'm in such a crazy mood to-day.

RANK. So it seems.

NORA [with her hands on his shoulders]. Dear, dear Doctor Rank, death shall not take you away from Torvald and me.

RANK. Oh, you'll easily get over the loss. The absent are soon forgotten.

NORA [looks at him anxiously]. Do you think so?

RANK. People make fresh ties, and then —

NORA. Who make fresh ties?

RANK. You and Helmer will, when I am gone. You yourself are taking time by the forelock, it seems to me. What was that Mrs. Linden doing here yesterday?

NORA. Oh! — you're surely not jealous of poor Christina?

RANK. Yes, I am. She will be my successor in this house. When I am out of the way, this woman will, perhaps —

NORA. Hush! Not so loud! She's in there.

RANK. To-day as well? You see!

NORA. Only to put my costume in order — dear me, how unreasonable you are! [Sits on sofa.] Now, do be good, Doctor Rank! To-morrow you shall see how beautifully I shall dance; and then you may fancy that I'm doing it all to please you — and of course Torvald as well. [Takes various things out of box.] Doctor Rank, sit down here, and I'll show you something.

RANK [sitting]. What is it?

NORA. Look here. Look!

RANK. Silk stockings.

NORA. Flesh-colored. Are n't they lovely? It's so dark here now; but to-morrow — No, no, no; you must only look at the feet. Oh, well, I suppose you may look at the rest too.

RANK. H'm —

NORA. What are you looking so critical about? Do you think they won't fit me?

RANK. I can't possibly give any competent opinion on that point.

NORA [looking at him a moment]. For shame! [Hits him lightly on the ear with the stockings.] Take that.
[Rolls them up again.]

RANK. And what other wonders am I to see?

NORA. You shan't see anything more; for you don't behave nicely.
[She hums a little and searches among the things.]

RANK [after a short silence]. When I sit here gossiping with you, I can't imagine — I simply cannot conceive — what would have become of me if I had never entered this house.

NORA [smiling]. Yes, I think you do feel at home with us.

RANK [more softly — looking straight before him]. And now to have to leave it all —

NORA. Nonsense. You shan't leave us.

RANK [in the same tone]. And not to be able to leave behind the slightest token of gratitude; scarcely even a passing regret — nothing but an empty place, that can be filled by the first comer.

NORA. And if I were to ask you for — ? No —

RANK. For what?

NORA. For a great proof of your friendship.

RANK. Yes — yes?

NORA. I mean — for a very, very great service —

RANK. Would you really, for once, make me so happy?

NORA. Oh, you don't know what it is.

RANK. Then tell me.

NORA. No, I really can't, Doctor Rank. It's far, far too much — not only a service, but help and advice, besides —

RANK. So much the better. I can't think what you can mean. But go on. Don't you trust me?

NORA. As I trust no one else. I know you are my best and truest friend. So I will tell you. Well, then, Doctor Rank, there is something you must help me to prevent. You know how deeply, how wonderfully Torvald loves me; he would n't hesitate a moment to give his very life for my sake.

RANK [bending toward her]. Nora — do you think he is the only one who — ?

NORA [with a slight start]. Who — ?

RANK. Who would gladly give his life for you?

NORA [sadly]. Oh!

RANK. I have sworn that you shall know it before I — go. I shall never find a better opportunity. — Yes, Nora, now I have told you; and now you know that you can trust me as you can no one else.

NORA [standing up; simply and calmly]. Let me pass, please.

RANK [makes way for her, but remains sitting]. Nora —

NORA [in the doorway]. Ellen, bring the lamp. [Crosses to the stove.] Oh, dear, Doctor Rank, that was too bad of you.

RANK [rising]. That I have loved you as deeply as — any one else? Was that too bad of me?

NORA. No, but that you should have told me so. It was so unnecessary —

RANK. What do you mean? Did you know — ?

[ELLEN enters with the lamp; sets it on the table and goes out again.]

Nora — Mrs. Helmer — I ask you, did you know?

NORA. Oh, how can I tell what I knew or did n't know? I really can't say — How could you be so clumsy, Doctor Rank? It was all so nice!

RANK. Well, at any rate, you know now that I am at your service, body and soul. And now, go on.

NORA [looking at him]. Go on — now?

RANK. I beg you to tell me what you want.

NORA. I can tell you nothing now.

RANK. Yes, yes! You must n't punish me in that way. Let me do for you whatever a man can.

NORA. You can do nothing for me now. — Besides, I really want no help. You shall see it was only my fancy. Yes, it must be so. Of course! [Sits in the rocking-chair, looks at him and smiles.] You are a nice person, Doctor Rank! Are n't you ashamed of yourself, now that the lamp is on the table?

RANK. No; not exactly. But perhaps I ought to go — forever.

NORA. No, indeed you must n't. Of course, you must come and go as you've always done. You know very well that Torvald can't do without you.

RANK. Yes, but you?

NORA. Oh, you know I always like to have you here.

RANK. That is just what led me astray. You are a riddle to me. It has often seemed to me as if you liked being with me almost as much as being with Helmer.

NORA. Yes; don't you see? There are people one loves, and others one likes to talk to.

RANK. Yes — there's something in that.

NORA. When I was a girl, of course, I loved papa best. But it always delighted me to steal into the servants' room. In the first place they never lectured me, and in the second it was such fun to hear them talk.

RANK. Ah, I see; then it's their place I have taken.

NORA [jumps up and hurries toward him]. Oh, my dear Doctor Rank, I don't mean that. But you understand, with Torvald it's the same as with papa —

[ELLEN enters from the hall.]

ELLEN. Please, ma'am —
    [Whispers to NORA, and gives her a card.]

NORA [glancing at card]. Ah!
    [Puts it in her pocket.]

RANK. Anything wrong?

NORA. No, no, not in the least. It's only — it's my new costume —

RANK. Your costume! Why, it's there.

NORA. Oh, that one, yes. But this is another that — I have ordered it — Torvald must n't know —

RANK. Aha! So that's the great secret.

NORA. Yes, of course. Please go to him; he's in the inner room. Do keep him while I —

RANK. Don't be alarmed; he shan't escape. [*Goes into* HELMER'S *room.*]

NORA [*to* ELLEN]. Is he waiting in the kitchen?

ELLEN. Yes, he came up the back stair—

NORA. Did n't you tell him I was engaged?

ELLEN. Yes, but it was no use.

NORA. He won't go away?

ELLEN. No, ma'am, not until he has spoken to you.

NORA. Then let him come in; but quietly. And, Ellen — say nothing about it; it's a surprise for my husband.

ELLEN. Oh, yes, ma'am, I understand. [*She goes out.*]

NORA. It is coming! The dreadful thing is coming, after all. No, no, no, it can never be; it shall not!

[*She goes to* HELMER'S *door and slips the bolt.*]

[ELLEN *opens the hall door for* KROGSTAD, *and shuts it after him. He wears a traveling-coat, high boots, and a fur cap.*]

NORA [*goes toward him*]. Speak softly; my husband is at home.

KROGSTAD. All right. That's nothing to me.

NORA. What do you want?

KROGSTAD. A little information.

NORA. Be quick, then. What is it?

KROGSTAD. You know I have got my dismissal.

NORA. I could n't prevent it, Mr. Krogstad. I fought for you to the last, but it was of no use.

KROGSTAD. Does your husband care for you so little? He knows what I can bring upon you, and yet he dares —

NORA. How could you think I should tell him?

KROGSTAD. Well, as a matter of fact, I did n't think it. It was n't like my friend Torvald Helmer to show so much courage—

NORA. Mr. Krogstad, be good enough to speak respectfully of my husband.

KROGSTAD. Certainly, with all due respect. But since you are so anxious to keep the matter secret, I suppose you are a little clearer than yesterday as to what you have done.

NORA. Clearer than you could ever make me.

KROGSTAD. Yes, such a bad lawyer as I —

NORA. What is it you want?

KROGSTAD. Only to see how you are getting on, Mrs. Helmer. I've been thinking about you all day. Even a mere money-lender, a gutter-journalist, a — in short, a creature like me — has a little bit of what people call feeling.

NORA. Then show it; think of my little children.

KROGSTAD. Did you and your husband think of mine? But enough of that. I only wanted to tell you that you need n't take this matter too seriously. I shall not lodge any information, for the present.

NORA. No, surely not. I knew you would n't.

KROGSTAD. The whole thing can be settled quite amicably. Nobody need know. It can remain among us three.

NORA. My husband must never know.

KROGSTAD. How can you prevent it? Can you pay off the balance?

NORA. No, not at once.

KROGSTAD. Or have you any means of raising the money in the next few days?

NORA. None — that I will make use of.

KROGSTAD. And if you had, it would not help you now. If you offered me ever so much money down, you should not get back your I O U.

NORA. Tell me what you want to do with it.

KROGSTAD. I only want to keep it — to have it in my possession. No outsider shall hear anything of it. So, if you have any desperate scheme in your head —

NORA. What if I have?

KROGSTAD. If you should think of leaving your husband and children —

NORA. What if I do?

KROGSTAD. Or if you should think of — something worse —

NORA. How do you know that?

KROGSTAD. Put all that out of your head.

NORA. How did you know what I had in my mind?

KROGSTAD. Most of us think of *that* at first. I thought of it, too; but I had n't the courage —

NORA [*tonelessly*]. Nor I.

KROGSTAD [*relieved*]. No, one has n't. You have n't the courage either, have you?

NORA. I have n't, I have n't.

KROGSTAD. Besides, it would be very foolish. — Just one domestic storm, and it 's all over. I have a letter in my pocket for your husband —

NORA. Telling him everything?

KROGSTAD. Sparing you as much as possible.

NORA [*quickly*]. He must never read that letter. Tear it up. I will manage to get the money somehow —

KROGSTAD. Pardon me, Mrs. Helmer, but I believe I told you —

NORA. Oh, I'm not talking about the money I owe you. Tell me how much you demand from my husband — I will get it.

KROGSTAD. I demand no money from your husband.

NORA. What *do* you demand, then?

KROGSTAD. I will tell you. I want to regain my footing in the world. I want to rise; and your husband shall help me to do it. For the last eighteen months my record has been spotless; I have been in bitter need all the time; but I was content to fight my way up, step by step. Now, I've been thrust down again, and I will not be satisfied with merely being reinstated as a matter of grace. I want to rise, I tell you. I must get into the Bank again, in a higher position than before. Your husband shall create a place on purpose for me —

NORA. He will never do that!

KROGSTAD. He will do it; I know him — he won't dare to show fight! And when he and I are together there, you shall soon see! Before a year is out I shall be the manager's right hand. It won't be Torvald Helmer, but Nils Krogstad, that manages the Joint Stock Bank.

NORA. That shall never be.

KROGSTAD. Perhaps you will — ?

NORA. *Now* I have the courage for it.

KROGSTAD. Oh, you don't frighten me! A sensitive, petted creature like you —

NORA. You shall see, you shall see!

KROGSTAD. Under the ice, perhaps? Down into the cold, black water? And next spring to come up again, ugly, hairless, unrecognizable —

NORA. You can't terrify me.

KROGSTAD. Nor you me. People don't do that sort of thing, Mrs. Helmer. And, after all, what would be the use of it? I have your husband in my pocket, all the same.

NORA. Afterwards? When I am no longer — ?

KROGSTAD. You forget, your reputation remains in my hands! [NORA *stands speechless and looks at him.*] Well, now you are prepared. Do nothing foolish. As soon as Helmer has received my letter, I shall expect to hear from him. And remember that it is your husband himself who has forced me back again into such paths. That I will never forgive him. Good-bye, Mrs. Helmer.

[*Goes out through the hall.* NORA *hurries to the door, opens it a little, and listens.*]

NORA. He's going. He's not putting the letter into the box. No, no, it would be impossible! [*Opens the door further and further.*] What's that. He's standing still; not going downstairs. Has he changed his mind? Is he —? [*A letter falls into the box.* KROGSTAD'S *footsteps are heard gradually receding down the stair.* NORA *utters a suppressed shriek, and rushes forward towards the sofatable; pause.*] In the letter-box! [*Slips shrinkingly up to the hall door.*] There it lies. — Torvald, Torvald — now we are lost!

[MRS. LINDEN *enters from the left with the costume.*]

MRS. LINDEN. There, I think it's all right now. Shall we just try it on?

NORA [*hoarsely and softly*]. Christina, come here.

MRS. LINDEN [*throws down the dress on the sofa*]. What's the matter? You look quite distracted.

NORA. Come here. Do you see that letter? *There*, see, — through the glass of the letter-box.

MRS. LINDEN. Yes, yes, I see it.

NORA. That latter is from Krogstad —

MRS. LINDEN. Nora — it was Krogstad who lent you the money?

NORA. Yes; and now Torvald will know everything.

MRS. LINDEN. Believe me, Nora, it's the best thing for both of you.

NORA. You don't know all yet. I have forged a name —

MRS. LINDEN. Good Heavens!

NORA. Now, listen to me, Christina; you shall bear me witness —

MRS. LINDON. How " witness " ? What am I to —

NORA. If I should go out of my mind — it might easily happen —

MRS. LINDEN. Nora!

NORA. Or if anything else should happen to me — so that I could n't be here — !

MRS. LINDEN. Nora, Nora, you're quite beside yourself!

NORA. In case any one wanted to take it all upon himself — the whole blame — you understand —

MRS. LINDEN. Yes, yes; but how can you think — ?

NORA. You shall bear witness that it's not true, Christina. I'm not out of my mind at all; I know quite well what I'm saying; and I tell you nobody else knew anything about it; I did the whole thing, I myself. Remember that.

MRS. LINDEN. I shall remember. But I don't understand what you mean —

NORA. Oh, how should you? It's the miracle coming to pass.

MRS. LINDEN. The miracle?

NORA. Yes, the miracle. But it's so terrible, Christina; it must n't happen for all the world.

MRS. LINDEN. I shall go straight to Krogstad and talk to him.

NORA. Don't; he'll do you some harm.

MRS. LINDEN. Once he would have done anything for me.

NORA. He?

MRS. LINDEN. Where does he live?

NORA. Oh, how can I tell ? — Yes — [*Feels in her pocket.*] Here's his card. But the letter, the letter — !

HELMER [*knocking outside*]. Nora!

NORA [*shrieks in terror*]. Oh, what is it? What do you want?

HELMER. Well, well, don't be frightened. We're not coming in; you've bolted the door. Are you trying on your dress?

NORA. Yes, yes, I'm trying it on. It suits me so well, Torvald.

MRS. LINDEN [*who has read the card*]. Why, he lives close by here.

NORA. Yes, but it's no use now. We are lost. The letter is there in the box.

MRS. LINDEN. And your husband has the key?

NORA. Always.

MRS. LINDEN. Krogstad must demand his letter back, unread. He must find some pretext —

NORA. But this is the very time when Torvald generally —

MRS. LINDEN. Prevent him. Keep him occupied. I shall come back as quickly as I can. [*She goes out hastily by the hall door.*]

NORA [*opens* HELMER'S *door and peeps in*]. Torvald!

HELMER. Well, may one come into one's own room again at last? Come, Rank, we'll have a look — [*In the doorway.*] But how's this?

NORA. What, Torvald, dear?

HELMER. Rank led me to expect a grand transformation.

RANK [*in the doorway*]. So I understood. I suppose I was mistaken.

NORA. No, no one shall see me in my glory till to-morrow evening.

HELMER. Why, Nora, dear, you look so tired. Have you been practicing too hard?

NORA. No, I have n't practiced at all yet.

HELMER. But you'll have to —

NORA. Oh, yes, I must, I must! But, Torvald, I can't get on at all without your help. I've forgotten everything.

HELMER. Oh, we shall soon freshen it up again.

NORA. Yes, do help me, Torvald. You must promise me — Oh, I'm so nervous about it. Before so many people — This evening you must give yourself up entirely to me. You must n't do a stroke of work; you must n't even touch a pen. Do promise, Torvald, dear!

HELMER. I promise. All this evening I shall be your slave. Little helpless thing —! But, by the bye, I must just —

[Going to hall door.]

NORA. What do you want there?

HELMER. Only to see if there are any letters.

NORA. No, no, don't do that, Torvald.

HELMER. Why not?

NORA. Torvald, I beg you not to. There are none there.

HELMER. Let me just see.

[Is going. NORA, at the piano, plays the first bars of the tarantella.]

[At the door, stops]. Aha!

NORA. I can't dance to-morrow if I don't rehearse with you first.

HELMER [going to her]. Are you really so nervous, dear Nora?

NORA. Yes, dreadfully! Let me rehearse at once. We have time before dinner. Oh, do sit down and play for me, Torvald, dear; direct me and put me right, as you used to do.

HELMER. With all the pleasure in life, since you wish it.

[Sits at piano. NORA snatches the tambourine out of the box, and hurriedly drapes herself in a long parti-colored shawl; then, with a bound, stands in the middle of the floor.]

NORA. Now, play for me! Now I'll dance!

[HELMER plays and NORA dances. RANK stands at the piano behind HELMER and looks on.]

HELMER [playing]. Slower! Slower!

NORA. Can't do it slower!

HELMER. Not so violently, Nora.

NORA. I must! I must!

HELMER [stops]. No, no, Nora, — that will never do.

NORA [laughs and swings her tambourine]. Did n't I tell you so!

RANK. Let me play for her.

HELMER [rising]. Yes, do, — then I can direct her better.

[RANK sits down to the piano and plays; NORA dances more and more wildly. HELMER stands by the stove and addresses frequent corrections to her; she seems not to hear. Her hair breaks loose, and falls over her shoulders. She does not notice it, but goes on dancing.]

[MRS. LINDEN enters and stands spellbound in the doorway.]

MRS. LINDEN. Ah —!

NORA [dancing]. We're having such fun here, Christina!

HELMER. Why, Nora, dear, you're dancing as if it were a matter of life and death.

NORA. So it is.

HELMER. Rank, stop! This is the merest madness. Stop, I say!

[RANK stops playing, and NORA comes to a sudden standstill.]

[Going toward her]. I could n't have believed it. You've positively forgotten all I taught you.

NORA [throws the tambourine away]. You see for yourself.

HELMER. You really do want teaching.

NORA. Yes, you see how much I need it. You must practice with me up to the last moment. Will you promise me, Torvald?

HELMER. Certainly, certainly.

NORA. Neither to-day nor to-morrow must you think of anything but me. You must n't open a single letter — must n't look at the letter-box.

HELMER. Ah, you're still afraid of that man —

NORA. Oh, yes, yes, I am.

HELMER. Nora, I can see it in your face — there's a letter from him in the box.

NORA. I don't know, I believe so. But you're not to read anything now; nothing ugly must come between us until all is over.

RANK [softly, to HELMER]. You must n't contradict her.

HELMER [putting his arm around her]. The child shall have her own way. But to-morrow night, when the dance is over —

NORA. Then you shall be free.

[ELLEN *appears in the doorway, right.*]

ELLEN. Dinner is on the table, ma'am.

NORA. We'll have some champagne, Ellen.

ELLEN. Yes, ma'am. [*Goes out.*]

HELMER. Dear me! Quite a banquet.

NORA. Yes, and we'll keep it up till morning. [*Calling out.*] And macaroons, Ellen, — plenty, — just this once.

HELMER [*seizing her hand*]. Come, come, don't let us have this wild excitement! Be my own little lark again.

NORA. Oh, yes, I will. But now go into the dining-room; and you, too, Doctor Rank. Christina, you must help me to do up my hair.

RANK [*softly, as they go*]. There's nothing in the wind? Nothing — I mean — ?

HELMER. Oh, no, nothing of the kind. It's merely this babyish anxiety I was telling you about. [*They go out to the right.*]

NORA. Well?

MRS. LINDEN. He's gone out of town.

NORA. I saw it in your face.

MRS. LINDEN. He comes back to-morrow evening. I left a note for him.

NORA. You should n't have done that. Things must take their course. After all, there's something glorious in waiting for the miracle.

MRS. LINDEN. What is it you're waiting for?

NORA. Oh, you can't understand. Go to them in the dining-room; I shall come in a moment.

[MRS. LINDEN *goes into the dining-room.* NORA *stands for a moment as though collecting her thoughts; then looks at her watch.*]

Five. Seven hours till midnight. Then twenty-four hours till the next midnight. Then the *tarantella* will be over. Twenty-four and seven? Thirty-one hours to live.

[HELMER *appears at the door, right.*]

HELMER. What has become of my little lark?

NORA [*runs to him with open arms*]. Here she is!

ACT III

The same room. The table, with the chairs around it, in the middle. A lighted lamp on the table. The door to the hall stands open. Dance music is heard from the floor above.

[MRS. LINDEN *sits by the table and absently turns the pages of a book. She tries to read, but seems unable to fix her attention; she frequently listens and looks anxiously toward the hall door.*]

MRS. LINDEN [*looks at her watch*]. Not here yet; and the time is nearly up. If only he has n't — [*Listens again.*] Ah, there he is. [*She goes into the hall and cautiously opens the outer door; soft footsteps are heard on the stairs; she whispers.*] Come in; there is no one here.

KROGSTAD [*in the doorway*]. I found a note from you at my house. What does it mean?

MRS. LINDEN. I *must* speak to you.

KROGSTAD. Indeed? And in this house?

MRS. LINDEN. I could not see you at my rooms. They have no separate entrance. Come in; we are quite alone. The servants are asleep, and the Helmers are at the ball upstairs.

KROGSTAD [*coming into the room*]. Ah! So the Helmers are dancing this evening? Really?

MRS. LINDEN. Yes. Why not?

KROGSTAD. Quite right. Why not?

MRS. LINDEN. And now, let us talk a little.

KROGSTAD. Have we two anything to say to each other?

MRS. LINDEN. A great deal.

KROGSTAD. I should not have thought so.

MRS. LINDEN. Because you have never really understood me.

KROGSTAD. What was there to understand? The most natural thing in the world — a heartless woman throws a man over when a better match offers.

MRS. LINDEN. Do you really think me so heartless? Do you think I broke with you lightly?

KROGSTAD. Did you not?

MRS. LINDEN. Do you really think so?

KROGSTAD. If not, why did you write me that letter?

MRS. LINDEN. Was it not best? Since I had to break with you, was it not right that I should try to put an end to all that you felt for me?

KROGSTAD [*clenching his hands together*]. So that was it? And all this — for the sake of money!

MRS. LINDEN. You ought not to forget that I had a helpless mother and two little brothers. We could not wait for you, Nils, as your prospects then stood.

KROGSTAD. Perhaps not; but you had no right to cast me off for the sake of others, whoever the others might be.

MRS. LINDEN. I don't know. I have often asked myself whether I had the right.

KROGSTAD [*more softly*]. When I had lost you, I seemed to have no firm ground left under my feet. Look at me now. I am a shipwrecked man clinging to a spar.

MRS. LINDEN. Rescue may be at hand.

KROGSTAD. It *was* at hand; but then you came and stood in the way.

MRS. LINDEN. Without my knowledge, Nils. I did not know till to-day that it was you I was to replace in the Bank.

KROGSTAD. Well, I take your word for it. But now that you do know, do you mean to give way?

MRS. LINDEN. No; for that would not help you in the least.

KROGSTAD. Oh, help, help — ! I should do it whether or no.

MRS. LINDEN. I have learned prudence. Life and bitter necessity have schooled me.

KROGSTAD. And life has taught me not to trust fine speeches.

MRS. LINDEN. Then life has taught you a very sensible thing. But deeds you *will* trust?

KROGSTAD. What do you mean?

MRS. LINDEN. You said you were a shipwrecked man, clinging to a spar.

KROGSTAD. I have good reason to say so.

MRS. LINDEN. I, too, am shipwrecked, and clinging to a spar. I have no one to mourn for, no one to care for.

KROGSTAD. You made your own choice.

MRS. LINDEN. No choice was left me.

KROGSTAD. Well, what then?

MRS. LINDEN. Nils, how if we two shipwrecked people could join hands?

KROGSTAD. What!

MRS. LINDEN. Two on a raft have a better chance than if each clings to a separate spar.

KROGSTAD. Christina!

MRS. LINDEN. What do you think brought me to town?

KROGSTAD. Had you any thought of me?

MRS. LINDEN. I must have work or I can't bear to live. All my life, as long as I can remember, I have worked; work has been my one great joy. Now I stand quite alone in the world, aimless and forlorn. There is no happiness in working for one's self. Nils, give me somebody and something to work for.

KROGSTAD. I cannot believe in all this. It is simply a woman's romantic craving for self-sacrifice.

MRS. LINDEN. Have you ever found me romantic?

KROGSTAD. Would you really — ? Tell me: do you know all my past?

MRS. LINDEN. Yes.

KROGSTAD. And do you know what people say of me?

MRS. LINDEN. Did you not say just now that with me you could have been another man?

KROGSTAD. I am sure of it.

MRS. LINDEN. Is it too late?

KROGSTAD. Christina, do you know what you are doing? Yes, you do; I see it in your face. Have you the courage, then — ?

MRS. LINDEN. I need some one to be a mother to, and your children need a mother. You need me, and I — I need you. Nils, I believe in your better self. With you I fear nothing.

KROGSTAD [*seizing her hands*]. Thank you — thank you, Christina. Now I shall make others see me as you do. — Ah, I forgot —

MRS. LINDEN [*listening*]. Hush! The *tarantella!* Go! Go!

KROGSTAD. Why? What is it?

MRS. LINDEN. Don't you hear the dancing overhead? As soon as that is over they will be here.

KROGSTAD. Oh, yes, I shall go. Nothing will come of this, after all. Of course, you don't know the step I have taken against the Helmers.

Mrs. Linden. Yes, Nils, I do know.

Krogstad. And yet you have the courage to — ?

Mrs. Linden. I know to what lengths despair can drive a man.

Krogstad. Oh, if I could only undo it!

Mrs. Linden. You could. Your letter is still in the box.

Krogstad. Are you sure?

Mrs. Linden. Yes; but —

Krogstad [looking to her searchingly]. Is that what it all means? You want to save your friend at any price. Say it out — is that your idea?

Mrs. Linden. Nils, a woman who has once sold herself for the sake of others, does not do so again.

Krogstad. I shall demand my letter back again.

Mrs. Linden. No, no.

Krogstad. Yes, of course. I shall wait till Helmer comes; I shall tell him to give it back to me — that it's only about my dismissal — that I don't want it read —

Mrs. Linden. No, Nils, you must not recall the letter.

Krogstad. But tell me, was n't that just why you got me to come here?

Mrs. Linden. Yes, in my first alarm. But a day has passed since then, and in that day I have seen incredible things in this house. Helmer must know everything; there must be an end to this unhappy secret. These two must come to a full understanding. They must have done with all these shifts and subterfuges.

Krogstad. Very well, if you like to risk it. But one thing I can do, and at once —

Mrs. Linden [listening]. Make haste! Go, go! The dance is over; we're not safe another moment.

Krogstad. I shall wait for you in the street.

Mrs. Linden. Yes, do; you must see me home.

Krogstad. I never was so happy in all my life!

[Krogstad goes out by the outer door. The door between the room and the hall remains open.]

Mrs. Linden [arranging the room and getting her outdoor things together]. What a change! What a change! To have some one to work for, to live for; a home to make happy! Well, it shall not be my fault if I fail. — I wish they would come. — [Listens.] Ah, there they are! I must get my things on. [Takes bonnet and cloak.]

[Helmer's and Nora's voices are heard outside, a key is turned in the lock, and Helmer drags Nora almost by force into the hall. She wears the Italian costume with a large black shawl over it. He is in evening dress and wears a black domino, open.]

Nora [struggling with him in the doorway]. No, no, no! I won't go in! I want to go upstairs again; I don't want to leave so early! Helmer. But, my dearest girl — !

Nora. Oh, please, please, Torvald, I beseech you — only one hour more!

Helmer. Not one minute more, Nora, dear; you know what we agreed. Come, come in; you're catching cold here.

[He leads her gently into the room in spite of her resistance.]

Mrs. Linden. Good-evening.

Nora. Christina!

Helmer. What, Mrs. Linden! You here so late?

Mrs. Linden. Yes, I ought to apologize. I did so want to see Nora in her costume.

Nora. Have you been sitting here waiting for me?

Mrs. Linden. Yes; unfortunately, I came too late. You had gone upstairs already; and I felt I could n't go away without seeing you.

Helmer [taking Nora's shawl off]. Well, then, just look at her! I assure you she's worth it. Is n't she lovely, Mrs. Linden?

Mrs. Linden. Yes, I must say —

Helmer. Is n't she exquisite? Every one said so. But she's dreadfully obstinate, dear little creature. What's to be done with her? Just think, I had almost to force her away.

Nora. Oh, Torvald, you'll be sorry some day that you did n't let me stay, if only for one half-hour more.

Helmer. There! You hear her, Mrs. Linden? She dances her tarantella with wild applause, and well she deserved it, I must say, — though there was, perhaps, a little too much nature in her rendering of the idea, — more than was, strictly speaking, artistic. But never mind — the point is, she made a great success, a tremendous success. Was I to let her remain after that — to weaken the impression? Not if I know it. I took my sweet little Capri girl — my capricious little Capri girl, I might say — under my arm; a rapid turn round the room, a curtsy to all sides, and — as they say in novels — the lovely apparition vanished! An exit should always be effective, Mrs. Linden; but I can't get Nora to see it. By Jove! it's warm here. [*Throws his domino on a chair and opens the door to his room.*] What! No light there? Oh, of course. Excuse me —

[*Goes in and lights candles.*]

NORA [*whispers breathlessly*]. Well?

MRS. LINDEN [*softly*]. I've spoken to him.

NORA. And — ?

MRS. LINDEN. Nora — you must tell your husband everything —

NORA [*tonelessly*]. I knew it!

MRS. LINDEN. You have nothing to fear from Krogstad; but you must speak out.

NORA. I shall not speak!

⌐ MRS. LINDEN. Then the letter will.

NORA. Thank you, Christina. Now I know what I have to do. Hush — !

HELMER [*coming back*]. Well, Mrs. Linden, have you admired her?

MRS. LINDEN. Yes; and now I must say good-night.

HELMER. What, already? Does this knitting belong to you?

MRS. LINDEN [*takes it*]. Yes, thanks; I was nearly forgetting it.

HELMER. Then you do knit?

MRS. LINDEN. Yes.

HELMER. Do you know, you ought to embroider instead?

MRS. LINDEN. Indeed! Why?

HELMER. Because it's so much prettier. Look, now! You hold the embroidery in the left hand, so, and then work the needle with the right hand, in a long, graceful curve — don't you?

MRS. LINDEN. Yes, I suppose so.

HELMER. But knitting is always ugly.

Just look — your arms close to your sides, and the needles going up and down — there's something Chinese about it. — They really gave us splendid champagne to-night.

MRS. LINDEN. Well, good-night, Nora, and don't be obstinate any more.

HELMER. Well said, Mrs. Linden!

MRS. LINDEN. Good-night, Mr. Helmer.

HELMER [*accompanying her to the door*]. Good-night, good-night; I hope you'll get safely home. I should be glad to — but you have such a short way to go. Good-night, good-night. [*She goes;* HELMER *shuts the door after her and comes forward again.*] At last we've got rid of her: she's a terrible bore.

NORA. Aren't you very tired, Torvald?

HELMER. No, not in the least.

NORA. Nor sleepy?

HELMER. Not a bit. I feel particularly lively. But you? You do look tired and sleepy.

NORA. Yes, very tired. I shall soon sleep now.

HELMER. There, you see. I was right, after all, not to let you stay longer.

NORA. Oh, everything you do is right.

HELMER [*kissing her forehead*]. Now my lark is speaking like a reasonable being. Did you notice how jolly Rank was this evening?

NORA. Indeed? Was he? I had no chance of speaking to him.

HELMER. Nor I, much; but I haven't seen him in such good spirits for a long time. [*Looks at* NORA *a little, then comes nearer her.*] It's splendid to be back in our own home, to be quite alone together! — Oh, you enchanting creature!

NORA. Don't look at me in that way, Torvald.

HELMER. I am not to look at my dearest treasure? — at all the loveliness that is mine, mine only, wholly and entirely mine?

NORA [*going to the other side of the table*]. You mustn't say these things to me this evening.

HELMER [*following*]. I see you have the *tarantella* still in your blood — and that makes you all the more enticing. Listen! the other people are going now. [*More softly.*] Nora — soon the whole house will be still.

NORA. Yes, I hope so.

HELMER. Yes, don't you, Nora, darling? When we are among strangers, do you know why I speak so little to you, and keep so far away, and only steal a glance at you now and then — do you know why I do it? Because I am fancying that we love each other in secret, that I am secretly betrothed to you, and that no one dreams that there is anything between us.

NORA. Yes, yes, yes. I know all your thoughts are with me.

HELMER. And then, when the time comes to go, and I put the shawl about your smooth, soft shoulders, and this glorious neck of yours, I imagine you are my bride, that our marriage is just over, that I am bringing you for the first time to my home — that I am alone with you for the first time — quite alone with you, in your trembling loveliness! All this evening I have been longing for you, and you only. When I watched you swaying and whirling in the *tarantella* — my blood boiled — I could endure it no longer; and that's why I made you come home with me so early —

NORA. Go, now, Torvald! Go away from me. I won't have all this.

HELMER. What do you mean? Ah, I see you're teasing me, little Nora! Won't — won't! Am I not your husband —?

[*A knock at the outer door.*]

NORA [*starts*]. Did you hear — ?

HELMER [*going toward the hall*]. Who's there?

RANK [*outside*]. It is I; may I come in for a moment?

HELMER [*in a low tone, annoyed*]. Oh! What can he want just now? [*Aloud.*] Wait a moment. [*Opens door.*] Come, it's nice of you to look in.

RANK. I thought I heard your voice, and that put it into my head. [*Looks round.*] Ah, this dear old place! How cozy you two are here!

HELMER. You seemed to find it pleasant enough upstairs, too.

RANK. Exceedingly. Why not? Why should n't one take one's share of everything in this world? All one can, at least,

and as long as one can. The wine was splendid —

HELMER. Especially the champagne.

RANK. Did you notice it? It's incredible the quantity I contrived to get down.

NORA. Torvald drank plenty of champagne, too.

RANK. Did he?

NORA. Yes, and it always puts him in such spirits.

RANK. Well, why should n't one have a jolly evening after a well-spent day?

HELMER. Well-spent! Well, I have n't much to boast of in that respect.

RANK [*slapping him on the shoulder*]. But I *have*, don't you see?

NORA. I suppose you have been engaged in a scientific investigation, Doctor Rank?

RANK. Quite right.

HELMER. Bless me! Little Nora talking about scientific investigations!

NORA. Am I to congratulate you on the result?

RANK. By all means.

NORA. It was good, then?

RANK. The best possible, both for doctor and patient — certainty.

NORA [*quickly and searchingly*]. Certainty?

RANK. Absolute certainty. Was n't I right to enjoy myself after that?

NORA. Yes, quite right, Doctor Rank.

HELMER. And so say I, provided you don't have to pay for it to-morrow.

RANK. Well, in this life nothing is to be had for nothing.

NORA. Doctor Rank — I'm sure you are very fond of masquerades?

RANK. Yes, when there are plenty of amusing disguises —

NORA. Tell me, what shall we two be at our next masquerade?

HELMER. Little featherbrain! Thinking of your next already!

RANK. We two? I'll tell you. You must go as a good fairy.

HELMER. Ah, but what costume would indicate *that*?

RANK. She has simply to wear her everyday dress.

HELMER. Capital! But don't you know what you will be yourself?

RANK. Yes, my dear friend, I am perfectly clear upon that point.

HELMER. Well?

RANK. At the next masquerade I shall be invisible.

HELMER. What a comical idea!

RANK. There's a big black hat — have n't you heard of the invisible hat? It comes down all over you, and then no one can see you.

HELMER [with a suppressed smile]. No, you're right there.

RANK. But I'm quite forgetting what I came for. Helmer, give me a cigar — one of the dark Havanas.

HELMER. With the greatest pleasure. [Hands cigar-case.]

RANK [takes one and cuts the end off]. Thank you.

NORA [striking a wax match]. Let me give you a light.

RANK. A thousand thanks. [She holds the match. He lights his cigar at it.] And now, good-bye!

HELMER. Good-bye, good-bye, my dear fellow.

NORA. Sleep well, Doctor Rank.

RANK. Thanks for the wish.

NORA. Wish me the same.

RANK. You? Very well, since you ask me — sleep well. And thanks for the light. [He nods to them both and goes out.]

HELMER [in an undertone]. He's been drinking a good deal.

NORA [absently]. I dare say. [HELMER takes his bunch of keys from his pocket and goes into the hall.] Torvald, what are you doing there?

HELMER. I must empty the letter-box; it's quite full; there will be no room for the newspapers to-morrow morning.

NORA. Are you going to work to-night?

HELMER. You know very well I am not. — Why, how is this? Some one has been at the lock.

NORA. The lock — ?

HELMER. I'm sure of it. What does it mean? I can't think that the servants — ? Here's a broken hairpin. Nora, it's one of yours.

NORA [quickly]. It must have been the children —

HELMER. Then you must break them of such tricks. — There! At last I've got it open. [Takes contents out and calls into the kitchen.] Ellen! — Ellen, just put the hall door lamp out.

[He returns with letters in his hand, and shuts the inner door.]

Just see how they've accumulated. [Turning them over.] Why, what's this?

NORA [at the window]. The letter! Oh, no, no, Torvald!

HELMER. Two visiting-cards — from Rank.

NORA. From Doctor Rank?

HELMER [looking at them]. Doctor Rank. They were on the top. He must just have put them in.

NORA. Is there anything on them?

HELMER. There's a black cross over the name. Look at it. What an unpleasant idea! It looks just as if he were announcing his own death.

NORA. So he is.

HELMER. What! Do you know anything? Has he told you anything?

NORA. Yes. These cards mean that he has taken his last leave of us. He is going to shut himself up and die.

HELMER. Poor fellow! Of course, I knew we could n't hope to keep him long. But so soon — ! And to go and creep into his lair like a wounded animal —

NORA. When we must go, it is best to go silently. Don't you think so, Torvald?

HELMER [walking up and down]. He had so grown into our lives, I can't realize that he is gone. And he and his sufferings and his loneliness formed a sort of cloudy background to the sunshine of our happiness. — Well, perhaps it's best as it is — at any rate, for him. [Stands still.] And perhaps for us, too, Nora. Now we two are thrown entirely upon each other. [Takes her in his arms.] My darling wife! I feel as if I could never hold you close enough. Do you know, Nora, I often wish some danger might threaten you, that I might risk body and soul, and everything, everything, for your dear sake.

NORA [tears herself from him and says firmly]. Now you shall read your letters, Torvald.

HELMER. No, no; not to-night. I want to be with you, my sweet wife.

NORA. With the thought of your dying friend — ?

HELMER. You are right. This has shaken us both. Unloveliness has come between us — thoughts of death and decay. We must seek to cast them off. Till then — we will remain apart.

NORA [her arms round his neck]. Torvald! Good-night! good-night!

HELMER [kissing her forehead]. Good-night, my little song-bird. Sleep well, Nora. Now I shall go and read my letters.

[He goes with the letters in his hand into his room and shuts the door.]

NORA [with wild eyes, gropes about her, seizes HELMER's domino, throws it round her, and whispers quickly, hoarsely, and brokenly]. Never to see him again. Never, never, never. [Throws her shawl over her head.] Never to see the children again. Never, never. — Oh, that black, icy water! Oh that bottomless — ! If it were only over! Now he has it; he's reading it. Oh, no, no, no, not yet. Torvald, good-bye — ! Good-bye, my little ones — !

[She is rushing out by the hall; at the same moment HELMER flings his door open, and stands there with an open letter in his hand.]

HELMER. Nora!

NORA [shrieks]. Ah — !

HELMER. What is this? Do you know what is in this letter?

NORA. Yes, I know. Let me go! Let me pass!

HELMER [holds her back]. Where do you want to go?

NORA [tries to break away from him]. You shall not save me, Torvald!

HELMER [falling back]. True! Is what he writes true? No, no, it is impossible that this can be true.

NORA. It is true. I have loved you beyond all else in the world.

HELMER. Pshaw — no silly evasions!

NORA [a step nearer him]. Torvald — !

HELMER. Wretched woman — what have you done!

NORA. Let me go — you shall not save me! You shall not take my guilt upon yourself!

HELMER. I don't want any melodramatic airs. [Locks the outer door.] Here you shall stay and give an account of yourself. Do you understand what you have done? Answer! Do you understand it?

NORA [looks at him fixedly, and says with a stiffening expression]. Yes; now I begin fully to understand it.

HELMER [walking up and down]. Oh, what an awful awakening! During all these eight years — she who was my pride and my joy — a hypocrite, a liar — worse, worse — a criminal. Oh, the unfathomable hideousness of it all! Ugh! Ugh!

[NORA says nothing, and continues to look fixedly at him.]

I ought to have known how it would be. I ought to have foreseen it. All your father's want of principle — be silent! — all your father's want of principle you have inherited — no religion, no morality, no sense of duty. How I am punished for screening him! I did it for your sake; and you reward me like this.

NORA. Yes — like this.

HELMER. You have destroyed my whole happiness. You have ruined my future. Oh, it's frightful to think of! I am in the power of a scoundrel; he can do whatever he pleases with me, demand whatever he chooses; he can domineer over me as much as he likes, and I must submit. And all this disaster and ruin is brought upon me by an unprincipled woman!

NORA. When I am out of the world, you will be free.

HELMER. Oh, no fine phrases. Your father, too, was always ready with them. What good would it do me, if you were "out of the world," as you say? No good whatever! He can publish the story all the same; I might even be suspected of collusion. People will think I was at the bottom of it all and egged you on. And for all this I have you to thank — you whom I have done nothing but pet and spoil during our whole married life. Do you understand now what you have done to me?

NORA [with cold calmness]. Yes.

HELMER. The thing is so incredible, I can't grasp it. But we must come to an understanding. Take that shawl off. Take it off, I say! I must try to pacify him in one way or another — the matter must be hushed up, cost what it may. — As for you and me, we must make no outward change in our way of life — no *outward* change, you understand. Of course, you will continue to live here. But the children cannot be left in your care. I dare not trust them to you. — Oh, to have to say this to one I have loved so tenderly — whom I still — ! But that must be a thing of the past. Henceforward there can be no question of happiness, but merely of saving the ruins, the shreds, the show — [*A ring;* HELMER *starts.*] What's that? So late! Can it be the worst? Can he — ? Hide yourself, Nora; say you are ill.

[NORA *stands motionless.* HELMER *goes to the door and opens it.*]

ELLEN [*half dressed, in the hall*]. Here is a letter for you, ma'am.

HELMER. Give it to me. [*Seizes the letter and shuts the door.*] Yes, from him. You shall not have it. I shall read it.

NORA. Read it!

HELMER [*by the lamp*]. I have hardly the courage to. We may both be lost, both you and I. Ah! I *must* know. [*Hastily tears the letter open; reads a few lines, looks at an enclosure; with a cry of joy.*] Nora!

[NORA *looks inquiringly at him.*]

Nora! — Oh! I must read it again. — Yes, yes, it is so. I am saved! Nora, I am saved!

NORA. And I?

HELMER. You, too, of course; we are both saved, both of us. Look here — he sends you back your promissory note. He writes that he regrets and apologizes that a happy turn in his life — Oh, what matter what he writes. We are saved, Nora! No one can harm you. Oh, Nora, Nora; but first to get rid of this hateful thing. I'll just see — [*Glances at the I O U.*] No, I will not look at it; the whole thing shall be nothing but a dream to me. [*Tears the I O U and both letters in pieces. Throws them into the fire and watches them burn.*] There! it's gone! — He said that ever since Christmas Eve — Oh, Nora, they must have been three terrible days for you!

NORA. I have fought a hard fight for the last three days.

HELMER. And in your agony you saw no other outlet but — No; we won't think of that horror. We will only rejoice and repeat — it's over, all over! Don't you hear, Nora? You don't seem able to grasp it. Yes, it's over. What is this set look on your face? Oh, my poor Nora, I understand; you cannot believe that I have forgiven you. But I have, Nora; I swear it. I have forgiven everything. I know that what you did was all for love of me.

NORA. That is true.

HELMER. You loved me as a wife should love her husband. It was only the means that, in your inexperience, you misjudged. But do you think I love you the less because you cannot do without guidance? No, no. Only lean on me; I will counsel you, and guide you. I should be no true man if this very womanly helplessness did not make you doubly dear in my eyes. You must n't dwell upon the hard things I said in my first moment of terror, when the world seemed to be tumbling about my ears. I have forgiven you, Nora, — I swear I have forgiven you.

NORA. I thank you for your forgiveness.

[*Goes out, to the right.*]

HELMER. No, stay — ! [*Looking through the doorway.*] What are you going to do?

NORA [*inside*]. To take off my masquerade dress.

HELMER [*in the doorway*]. Yes, do, dear. Try to calm down, and recover your balance, my scared little song-bird. You may rest secure. I have broad wings to shield you. [*Walking up and down near the door.*] Oh, how lovely — how cozy our home is, Nora! Here you are safe; here I can shelter you like a hunted dove whom I have saved from the claws of the hawk. I shall soon bring your poor beating heart to rest; believe me, Nora, very soon. To-morrow all this will seem quite different — everything will be as before. I shall not need to tell you again that I forgive you; you will feel for yourself that it is true. How could you think I could find it in my heart to drive you away, or even so much as to reproach you? Oh, you don't know a true man's heart, Nora. There is something indescribably sweet and soothing to a man in having forgiven his wife — honestly forgiven her, from the bottom of his heart. She becomes his property in a double sense. She is as though born again; she has become, so to speak, at once his wife and his child. That is what you shall henceforth be to me, my bewildered, helpless darling. Don't be troubled about anything, Nora; only open your heart to me, and I will be both will and conscience to you.

[NORA *enters in everyday dress.*]

Why, what's this? Not gone to bed? You have changed your dress?

NORA. Yes, Torvald; now I have changed my dress.

HELMER. But why now, so late —?

NORA. I shall not sleep to-night.

HELMER. But, Nora, dear —

NORA [*looking at her watch*]. It's not so late yet. Sit down, Torvald; you and I have much to say to each other.

[*She sits at one side of the table.*]

HELMER. Nora — what does this mean? Your cold, set face —

NORA. Sit down. It will take some time. I have much to talk over with you.

[HELMER *sits at the other side of the table.*]

HELMER. You alarm me, Nora. I don't understand you.

NORA. No, that is just it. You don't understand me; and I have never understood you — till to-night. No, don't interrupt. Only listen to what I say. — We must come to a final settlement, Torvald.

HELMER. How do you mean?

NORA [*after a short silence*]. Does not one thing strike you as we sit here?

HELMER. What should strike me?

NORA. We have been married eight years. Does it not strike you that this is the first time we two, you and I, man and wife, have talked together seriously?

HELMER. Seriously! What do you call seriously?

NORA. During eight whole years, and more — ever since the day we first met — we have never exchanged one serious word about serious things.

HELMER. Was I always to trouble you with the cares you could not help me to bear?

NORA. I am not talking of cares. I say that we have never yet set ourselves seriously to get to the bottom of anything.

HELMER. Why, my dearest Nora, what have you to do with serious things?

NORA. There we have it! You have never understood me. — I have had great injustice done me, Torvald; first by father, and then by you.

HELMER. What! By your father and me? — By us, who have loved you more than all the world?

NORA [*shaking her head*]. You have never loved me. You only thought it amusing to be in love with me.

HELMER. Why, Nora, what a thing to say!

NORA. Yes, it is so, Torvald. While I was at home with father, he used to tell me all his opinions, and I held the same opinions. If I had others, I said nothing about them, because he would n't have liked it. He used to call me his doll-child, and played with me as I played with my dolls. Then I came to live in your house —

HELMER. What an expression to use about our marriage!

NORA [*undisturbed*]. I mean I passed from father's hands into yours. You arranged everything according to your taste; and I got the same tastes as you; or I pretended to — I don't know which — both ways, perhaps; sometimes one and sometimes the other. When I look back on it now, I seem to have been living here like a beggar, from hand to mouth. I lived by performing tricks for you, Torvald. But you would have it so. You and father have done me a great wrong. It is your fault that my life has come to nothing.

HELMER. Why, Nora, how unreasonable and ungrateful you are! Have you not been happy here?

NORA. No, never. I thought I was; but I never was.

HELMER. Not — not happy!

NORA. No; only merry. And you have always been so kind to me. But our house has been nothing but a play-room. Here I have been your doll-wife, just as at home I used to be papa's doll-child. And the children, in their turn, have been my dolls. I thought it fun when you played with me, just as the children did when I played with them. That has been our marriage, Torvald.

HELMER. There is some truth in what you say, exaggerated and overstrained though it be. But henceforth it shall be different. Play-time is over; now comes the time for education.

NORA. Whose education? Mine, or the children's?

HELMER. Both, my dear Nora.

NORA. Oh, Torvald, you are not the man to teach me to be a fit wife for you.

HELMER. And you can say that?

NORA. And I — how have I prepared myself to educate the children?

HELMER. Nora!

NORA. Did you not say yourself, a few minutes ago, you dared not trust them to me?

HELMER. In the excitement of the moment! Why should you dwell upon that?

NORA. No — you were perfectly right. That problem is beyond me. There is another to be solved first — I must try to educate myself. You are not the man to help me in that. I must set about it alone. And that is why I am leaving you.

HELMER [jumping up]. What — do you mean to say —?

NORA. I must stand quite alone if I am ever to know myself and my surroundings; so I cannot stay with you.

HELMER. Nora! Nora!

NORA. I am going at once. I dare say Christina will take me in for to-night —

HELMER. You are mad! I shall not allow it! I forbid it!

NORA. It is of no use your forbidding me anything now. I shall take with me what belongs to me. From you I will accept nothing, either now or afterwards.

HELMER. What madness this is!

NORA. To-morrow I shall go home — I mean to what was my home. It will be easier for me to find some opening there.

HELMER. Oh, in your blind inexperience —

NORA. I must try to gain experience, Torvald.

HELMER. To forsake your home, your husband, and your children! And you don't consider what the world will say.

NORA. I can pay no heed to that. I only know that I must do it.

HELMER. This is monstrous ! Can you forsake your holiest duties in this way?

NORA. What do you consider my holiest duties?

HELMER. Do I need to tell you that? Your duties to your husband and your children.

NORA. I have other duties equally sacred.

HELMER. Impossible! What duties do you mean?

NORA. My duties toward myself.

HELMER. Before all else you are a wife and a mother.

NORA. That I no longer believe. I believe that before all else I am a human being, just as much as you are — or at least that I should try to become one. I know that most people agree with you, Torvald, and that they say so in books. But henceforth I can't be satisfied with what most people say, and what is in books. I must think things out for myself, and try to get clear about them.

HELMER. Are you not clear about your place in your own home? Have you not an infallible guide in questions like these? Have you not religion?

NORA. Oh, Torvald, I don't really know what religion is.

HELMER. What do you mean?

NORA. I know nothing but what Pastor Hansen told me when I was confirmed. He explained that religion was this and that. When I get away from all this and stand alone, I will look into that matter too. I will see whether what he taught me is right, or, at any rate, whether it is right for me.

HELMER. Oh, this is unheard of! And from so young a woman! But if religion cannot keep you right, let me appeal to your conscience — for I suppose you have some moral feeling? Or, answer me: perhaps you have none?

NORA. Well, Torvald, it's not easy to say. I really don't know — I am all at sea about these things. I only know that I think quite differently from you about them. I hear, too, that the laws are different from what I thought; but I can't believe that they can be right. It appears that a woman has no right to spare her dying father, or to save her husband's life! I don't believe that.

HELMER. You talk like a child. You don't understand the society in which you live.

NORA. No, I do not. But now I shall try to learn. I must make up my mind which is right — society or I.

HELMER. Nora, you are ill; you are feverish; I almost think you are out of your senses.

NORA. I have never felt so much clearness and certainty as to-night.

HELMER. You are clear and certain enough to forsake husband and children?

NORA. Yes, I am.

HELMER. Then there is only one explanation possible.

NORA. What is that?

HELMER. You no longer love me.

NORA. No; that is just it.

HELMER. Nora! — Can you say so!

NORA. Oh, I'm so sorry, Torvald; for you've always been so kind to me. But I can't help it. I do not love you any longer.

HELMER [mastering himself with difficulty]. Are you clear and certain on this point too?

NORA. Yes, quite. That is why I will not stay here any longer.

HELMER. And can you also make clear to me how I have forfeited your love?

NORA. Yes, I can. It was this evening, when the miracle did not happen; for then I saw you were not the man I had imagined.

HELMER. Explain yourself more clearly; I don't understand.

NORA. I have waited so patiently all these eight years; for, of course, I saw clearly enough that miracles don't happen every day. When this crushing blow threatened me, I said to myself so confidently, "Now comes the miracle!" When Krogstad's letter lay in the box, it never for a moment occurred to me that you would think of submitting to that man's conditions. I was convinced that you would say to him, "Make it known to all the world"; and that then —

HELMER. Well? When I had given my own wife's name up to disgrace and shame — ?

NORA. Then I firmly believed that you would come forward, take everything upon yourself, and say, "I am the guilty one."

HELMER. Nora — !

NORA. You mean I would never have accepted such a sacrifice? No, certainly not. But what would my assertions have been worth in opposition to yours? — *That* was the miracle that I hoped for and dreaded. And it was to hinder *that* that I wanted to die.

HELMER. I would gladly work for you day and night, Nora, — bear sorrow and want for your sake. But no man sacrifices his honor, even for one he loves.

NORA. Millions of women have done so.

HELMER. Oh, you think and talk like a silly child.

NORA. Very likely. But you neither think nor talk like the man I can share my life with. When your terror was over — not for what threatened me, but for yourself — when there was nothing more to fear — then it seemed to you as though nothing had happened. I was your lark again, your doll, just as before — whom you would take twice as much care of in future, because she was so weak and fragile. [Stands up.] Torvald — in that moment it burst upon me that I had been living here these eight years with a strange man, and had borne him three children. — Oh, I can't bear to think of it! I could tear myself to pieces!

HELMER [sadly]. I see it, I see it; an abyss has opened between us. — But, Nora, can it never be filled up?

NORA. As I now am, I am no wife for you.

HELMER. I have strength to become another man.

NORA. Perhaps — when your doll is taken away from you.

HELMER. To part — to part from you ! No, Nora, no; I can't grasp the thought.

NORA [going into room on the right]. The more reason for the thing to happen.

[She comes back with outdoor things and a small traveling-bag, which she places on a chair.]

HELMER. Nora, Nora, not now! Wait till to-morrow.

NORA [putting on cloak]. I can't spend the night in a strange man's house.

HELMER. But can we not live here, as brother and sister — ?

NORA [fastening her hat]. You know very well that would n't last long. [Puts on the shawl.] Good-bye, Torvald. No, I won't go to the children. I know they are in better hands than mine. As I now am, I can be nothing to them.

HELMER. But some time, Nora — some time — ?

NORA. How can I tell? I have no idea what will become of me.

HELMER. But you are my wife, now and always!

NORA. Listen, Torvald, — when a wife leaves her husband's house, as I am doing, I have heard that in the eyes of the law he is free from all duties toward her. At any rate, I release you from all duties. You must not feel yourself bound, any more than I shall. There must be perfect freedom on both sides. There, I give you back your ring. Give me mine.

HELMER. That, too?

NORA. That, too.

HELMER. Here it is.

NORA. Very well. Now it is all over. I lay the keys here. The servants know about everything in the house — better than I do. To-morrow, when I have started, Christina will come to pack up the things I brought with me from home. I will have them sent after me.

HELMER. All over! All over! Nora, will you never think of me again?

NORA. Oh, I shall often think of you, and the children, and this house.

HELMER. May I write to you, Nora?

NORA. No — never. You must not.

HELMER. But I must send you —

NORA. Nothing, nothing.

HELMER. I must help you if you need it.

NORA. No, I say. I take nothing from strangers.

HELMER. Nora — can I never be more than a stranger to you?

NORA [taking her traveling-bag]. Oh, Torvald, then the miracle of miracles would have to happen —

HELMER. What is the miracle of miracles?

NORA. Both of us would have to change so that — Oh, Torvald, I no longer believe in miracles.

HELMER. But I will believe. Tell me! We must so change that — ?

NORA. That communion between us shall be a marriage. Good-bye.

[She goes out by the hall door.]

HELMER [sinking into a chair by the door with his face in his hands.] Nora! Nora! [He looks round and rises.] Empty. She is gone. [A hope springs up in him.] Ah! The miracle of miracles — ?

[From below is heard the reverberation of a heavy door closing.]

APPENDIX

APPENDIX

I. NOTES ON THE AUTHORS

ÆSCHYLUS

ÆSCHYLUS, the earliest of the great Greek tragic poets, was born in Athens B.C. 525. Tradition asserts that he fought at Marathon and at Salamis. He brought out his first tragedy when he was about twenty-five; and we have the titles of seventy-nine of his plays, of which only seven survive. He was the father of Greek tragedy, which had been almost wholly lyrical before him, with only a single actor. Æschylus made use of a second performer, causing the pair of them to assume as many characters as he might need. In the later plays he followed the example of Sophocles and utilized three actors. He wrote on an average two plays every year; and he diminished the portion of pure lyric while intensifying the action, the clash of will, which is the essential element of drama. To him we owe the trilogy, the linking of three plays together, presenting successive parts of the same long story. He took the first prize at least thirteen times; and his constant success was due to the lofty elevation of his choral odes, to his masterly presentation of character at the moment of crisis, and to his intensifying of the dramatic interest of his plots, which, simple as they may seem to us, were more effective than any that the Athenians had earlier been familiar with. He died in B.C. 456, and was buried at Gela in Sicily. Upon his tombstone were placed two lines which may have been written by the poet himself: "Beneath this stone lies Æschylus, son of Euphorion, the Athenian, who perished in the wheat-bearing land of Gela; of his prowess the grove of Marathon can speak, and the long-haired Persian, who knows it well."

SOPHOCLES

Sophocles, the second of the great Athenian tragic poets was born at Colonus about B.C. 495. He was therefore about thirty years younger than Æschylus. His life covers the most splendid period of the Athenian Empire. It is believed that he was the leader of the chorus of boys at the celebration of the victory of Salamis; and it is recorded also that he served as a general with Pericles in the Samian War. He was intimate with Pericles, Phidias, Herodotus, Thucydides, and Socrates. He lived to be nearly ninety, dying only in B.C. 406. He is said to have written seventy tragedies besides nearly a score of satyric after-pieces. Of these only seven tragedies and a large portion of one satyr-play are extant. His tragedies called for the service of three actors, whereas Æschylus in his earlier plays had utilized only two performers. Æschylus had elaborated the dramatic action while still preserving the predominance of the lyric element out of which tragedy had been evolved; and Sophocles still further strengthened the plot and made his choral odes subordinate to the dramatic struggle and yet helpful to its effect. He also developed the spectacular possibilities of tragic performance; and he was highly skillful in the training of his actors and in the drilling of his chorus in their circlings about the altar. He is a master of the art of construction, and the best of his plots are as skillfully articulated as those in the pieces of the most adroit of the modern playwrights. He combines as did no other Greek the utmost technical accomplishment with largeness of vision, with loftiness of poetic outlook, and with imaginative energy.

EURIPIDES

The third of the great Attic tragedians was born probably in B.C. 484, perhaps eleven years after Sophocles and forty-one after Æschylus. He is credited with the authorship of at least ninety tragedies, of which eighteen survive; and there is also extant one of his half-dozen or more satyric dramas. All through his career as a dramatist he was overshadowed by the fame of his two mighty predecessors in playmaking. He sought to broaden the scope of Attic tragedy, to relax its austerity, to widen its circle of subjects, to get closer to everyday humanity. As a result of his departure from the traditional path in which Æschylus and Sophocles had been content to walk, he seemed to his contemporaries as a daring and disrespectful innovator deliberately lowering the tone of tragedy and often descending to overt melodrama. To the Greeks of a later generation his appeal was more immediate than to his contemporaries; and to many more recent critics, he has appeared as the least Attic of the great Greek dramatists and therefore as the most modern of them all. After his death and when the taste of the Greeks had been transformed, he became more popular than Sophocles or Æschylus; and it is due to this belated appreciation that we have now more of his plays than those of his two rivals taken together. Euripides departed intentionally from the noble form constantly exemplified in Sophocles, and for this he was violently attacked by Aristophanes, yet modern criticism recognizes that the older tragedy was no longer possible in the changing order at Athens; and it has tended toward a more sympathetic appreciation of Euripides for what he actually accomplished, and to refrain from depreciation for his failure to abjure his own personality. He died B.C. 406.

ARISTOPHANES

Aristophanes is the only one of the writers of Greek comedy of whom we now have a group of complete plays. He was born about B.C. 446; and if so he was nearly forty years younger than Euripides. His earliest play is the *Acharnians*, produced when he was apparently only twenty-one. Eleven of his comedies are extant; and more than thirty others are known by name and sometimes by a few fragments. Except the latest, — *Plutus*, produced in 388, about which date he died, — all the existing pieces belong to what is known as Old Comedy, a type of play peculiar to Athens and to be likened only to our latter-day theatrical review, in that it combined parody, burlesque, comic situation, and comic character. This nondescript form exactly suited the fertility and the variety of the genius of Aristophanes, who was supremely endowed for these different departments of literature. He was a soaring lyrist with a fecundity and an ethereal elevation which can be paralleled only in Shelley; he was a scourging and scorching satirist with a vehemence akin to that of Juvenal; and he was a bold and robust humorist with an earthy streak as broad as that of Rabelais. In politics he was a bitter reactionary; and when the liberties of the Athenians were restricted the license of the stage-satirists was curbed. In *Plutus*, probably his last play, he deals with a theme of permanent and universal interest, — the power of money, — eschewing altogether his customary incursions into contemporary and local politics. *Plutus* is an example of the so-called Middle Comedy which prepared the way for the New Comedy of Menander, a type approximating more obviously to the modern idea of that comedy of contemporary manners which reaches its culmination in Molière.

PLAUTUS

We do not know the date or the place of the birth of Titus Maccius Plautus — possibly in B.C. 254 and in Umbria. After failing in business, as a result of which he sank into extreme poverty, he commenced playwright when he was about thirty. More than a hundred plays have been credited to him, probably without warrant. Twenty of these have been preserved. Before his death, in B.C. 184, he had witnessed the splendid expansion of Rome, from its position as the foremost city of Italy to its empire over all the shores of the Mediterranean; and his life covers also the period when the subtler Greek intellect made its abiding impression on the solider Latin character. The coarse Roman farces, which might have been lifted into literature, — as Molière elevated the improvized comedy-of-masks of the Italians, — had its evolution inhibited by the importation of the fully developed comedy of the Athenians. All the plays of Plautus are adaptations of Attic comedies, chiefly Menander's; and yet the Latin playwright managed to give to his pieces an intensely Roman flavor, a recognizable Latin local color in spite of their Greek plots and their Greek characters. Even though the scene of the story might be Athens or some other Greek city, Plautus abounded in allusions to Roman conditions; and he often suggested the aroma of tenement-house life in the Italian metropolis. His humor is bold and broad; and his style is racy. He knew the unlettered spectators of Rome, so different from the cultivated audiences of Athens; and he was fertile in devices for evoking the hearty laughter of these illiterate playgoers.

TERENCE

Publius Terentius Afer was a native of Carthage and he was born between B.C. 190 and 185, a few years before Plautus died. He was brought to Rome as a slave to a member of the noble family of Terentius. His master early recognized his intellect, in consequence of which he had Terence educated and set him free. Terence seems to have established himself as a dramatist some years before he was thirty; and he was early admitted into the society of the cultivated Romans newly taken captive by the charm of Greek literature. We do not possess a complete list of his comedies, of which only six have come down to us. Apparently most of them were adaptations from Menander, far closer to the original than the few paraphrases of Plautus. They are also far less comic than the farces of his Latin predecessor — or even than their Greek originals, if we may credit the saying of Julius Cæsar that Terence was " only a half Menander." He died about B.C. 158. Plautus is primarily a playwright, desirous above all else of stimulating the interest of the rude mob of Roman playgoers in the theater itself, and as careless of the subsequent approval of the reader in the library as was Shakespeare. Terence, on the other hand, although he reveals his disappointment at the comparative non-success of his plays on the stage, is essentially a man of letters, wishful more especially of the approval of his fellow men of letters. Where Plautus complicates his plot and descends to horseplay to amuse the rough Roman audiences, Terence refines his style and seeks to be as Greek as possible, more or less contemptuous of the spectators whose suffrage he was seeking. In other words, Plautus is akin to Labiche, and even to Molière, whereas Terence is rather to be likened to Congreve.

LOPE DE VEGA

Lope Felix de Vega Carpio was born in Madrid in 1562. He studied at Alcala; he went on the expedition to the Azores; and he served in the Armada. He became the most popular as he was the most prolific of men of letters. He put forth a constant succession of epistles and elegies, sonnets and romances, pastorals and epics; and one of these last, *La Dragontea*, had Sir Francis Drake for the hero-villain. In 1608 or 1609 Lope, then the undisputed master of the Spanish stage, delivered a metrical address on the "New Art of Writing Plays in those Times," in which he admitted the validity of the classicist code of dramatic doctrine and defended himself for his disregard of these rules by pleading the necessity of pleasing the unlearned spectators. He had found the drama more or less formless and more or less unliterary. He re-formed it, reducing the customary number of acts from four to three, choosing themes of higher import, constructing plots with more dexterous workmanship, and indulging to the full the Spanish tendency toward ornate grandiloquence. Some of his pieces were improvized with breathless speed — on one occasion five in a single fortnight; others were more deliberately planned and elaborated. He is said to have composed nearly eighteen hundred plays, of which more than four hundred have been preserved. He had a career as rich in adventure (military, political, and amorous) as that of any of his heroes. Late in life he became a familiar of the Inquisition; and the Pope made him a doctor of theology. He died in August, 1635, mourned by all Spain.

CALDERON

Pedro Calderon de la Barca was born in Madrid in January, 1600; he was thus nearly forty years the junior of his great rival, Lope de Vega. He was educated at the Jesuit College of his native city; and he studied law at Salamanca. He accepted the formulas of the Spanish drama as these had been developed by Lope de Vega; and he proved himself almost equally fecund. He was not as vigorously creative as Lope was; and not a few of his plays are only rehandlings of pieces by his predecessors, generally with an intensifying of their dramatic power. His *Alcalde of Zalamea*, for example, is a far firmer and more vital drama than the hasty play by Lope on which it was founded. In fact, in many cases Calderon did very much what Shakespeare had done in making his tragic masterpieces, *Hamlet* and *King Lear*, out of melodramas already popular on the stage. Yet even Calderon's masterpieces tend to be melodramatic — that is to say, he is often willing to sacrifice veracity of character to the immediate effectiveness of situation. And he is often content to utilize the stock characters employed by Lope and Tirso de Molina. He is an adroit playwright even if he is rarely a subtle psychologist; and he is a genuine poet, although he overindulges in the flowery flamboyance which is a common characteristic of Spanish literature. Toward the end of his career he returned to his early intention of joining the priesthood. He was appointed prebend of Toledo in 1635; and in 1663 he became honorary chaplain to Philip IV. Despite his immense popularity he seems to have passed the final years of his life in poverty. He died in May, 1681.

CORNEILLE

Pierre Corneille was born at Rouen in June, 1606. Educated by the Jesuits, he was admitted to the bar. His first piece was presented in 1629. He went up to Paris and was one of the five authors who wrote plays under the direction of Richelieu. After composing several comedies and dramas in accord with the practice of his predecessors, he was advised to learn Spanish. It was from Spanish playwrights that he derived the plots of his first important tragedy, the *Cid*, acted in 1637, and of his first important comedy, the *Liar*, acted in 1644. From Roman history he took the themes of *Horatius*, produced in 1640; *Cinna*, produced in the same year, and *Polyeucte*, produced in 1643. When he commenced playwright he had not heard of the so-called "rules of the drama" elaborated by the Italian theorists; but after the *Cid* he accepted these as binding, although he constantly chafed against their restrictions. It was Corneille who established the formula of French tragedy as Lope de Vega had established the formula of the Spanish cloak-and-sword drama. He prided himself justly on his adroitness in composing the mechanism of a plot; and he was a born playwright, with an instinctive insistence upon the stark assertion of the human will. Toward the end of his career his powers weakened and his plays became less spontaneous and more obviously mechanical in the conduct of their stories. In the last years of his life he sank into honorable poverty; and he had the pain of seeing popular preference go to the plays of his younger rival, Racine. He died in September, 1684.

MOLIÈRE

Jean Baptiste Poquelin was born in Paris in January, 1622. His father was a prosperous tradesman and he was sent to the best school in Paris, the Jesuit Collège de Clermont. He studied law; but when he was twenty-one he turned actor, taking the name of Molière. After vain struggles in Paris the company which he had joined began its strolling in the provinces; and it did not return to Paris until 1658. Molière had become the foremost of French comic actors; he was the chief of the company; and he was already known as a playwright. He brought out in Paris under the patronage of Louis XIV the two or three plays already presented in the provinces, brisk comic pieces which attained an immediate popularity. In the next fifteen years he wrote nearly thirty other plays, steadily revealing a firmer technic, a richer humor, and a deeper understanding of humanity. He took an unexpected step forward in 1664 when *Tartuffe* was first performed. He followed this in 1665 with the *Festin de Pierre*, in which Don Juan was the chief character. In 1666 he produced the *Misanthrope*, generally accepted by French critics as his masterpiece and as the model of modern comedy. In 1672 he brought out the *Femmes Savantes* (the "Learned Ladies"); and it is in these four plays that his loftiest power is most amply displayed. But while he climbed to these heights he recurred again and again to the humbler type of comic piece, the aim of which was to arouse irresistible laughter; and he also wrote pieces to order to please the king. His last play was the *Imaginary Invalid*, first seen in February, 1673; and at the fourth performance of this he had a seizure, breaking a blood-vessel. He died on February 17, 1673. He had made many enemies by his attacks on pretense and hypocrisy in medicine, in religion, and in society; and his wife had to throw herself at the king's feet to obtain permission for a Christian burial.

RACINE

Jean Racine was born at La Ferté-Milon in December, 1639, being just a third of a century younger than Corneille. He was educated at the Jansenist school at Port-Royal; and he became an accomplished Greek scholar. Intended for the Church, he was lured into literature; and he quarreled ungratefully with his Jansenist teachers. His first play was brought out in 1664 by Molière's company, and so was his second the next year. But Racine again showed his ingratitude by surreptitiously taking this piece to a rival company. *Andromache* produced in 1667, was the first of his tragedies to be triumphantly successful; and in the next ten years it was followed by six others of which the last was *Phædra*, acted in 1677. Disheartened by attacks upon him, Racine suddenly renounced the drama, although he yielded in 1689 and in 1691 to the appeal of Mme. de Maintenon and composed, for the pupils of her school at Saint-Cyr, two plays on religious themes, *Esther* and *Athaliah*. He had been appointed historiographer to Louis XIV in 1677. In the later years of his life he was reconciled to the Jansenists and he bitterly repented his earlier errors. He died in April, 1699. He had begun by imitating Corneille, but he had soon discovered that his genius was not, like Corneille's, fitted for sturdy historic contentions. He developed a unique gift for the subtle and searching analysis of passion at the moment of climax. His plots are seemingly simple, but they are articulated with meticulous skill. The English critics who have dismissed his plays as empty and cold have merely disclosed their incapacity to peer beneath the surface and to perceive the fiery lava that flows through the veins of the characters immeshed in a plot in which the action is internal rather than external.

BEAUMARCHAIS

Pierre Augustin Caron was born in Paris in 1732. He was a watchmaker and a musician. When he married in 1756 he took the name of Beaumarchais from a small fief belonging to his wife. In 1764 he made a trip to Spain to vindicate a sister who had been engaged to a man named Clavijo; and his brilliant account of his successful adventure served Goethe as the basis of *Clavigo*. Beaumarchais's first play, a drama called *Eugénie* (brought out in 1767), met with only moderate success; and his second, the *Two Friends* (produced in 1770), failed. They were serious and sentimental pieces; and they did not display his special qualities — invention, ingenuity, briskness, brilliance. Involved in a long litigation he issued a series of witty memoirs which made him one of the most popular personalities in Paris. In 1775 he brought out the *Barber of Seville* which was instantly triumphant. And almost immediately he undertook a vast enterprise for supplying the revolted American colonies with arms, ammunition, and supplies; and he published a complete edition of Voltaire. Then he wrote a sequel to the *Barber*, the *Marriage of Figaro*, which was so daring in its satire that its production was not permitted until 1784, when the crush at the first performance was such that three persons were stifled to death. Thereafter he wrote the libretto for Salieri's *Tarare*, and also a heavy play, the *Guilty Mother*, which had only a slight success. He survived the French Revolution, dying in 1799.

VICTOR HUGO

Victor Hugo was born at Besançon in 1802. When scarcely more than a boy he began to publish both in verse and in prose, displaying a precocious eloquence. His first story, *Hans of Iceland*, appeared in 1823; and he was soon acclaimed as the chief of the insurgent Romanticists. His unactable drama, *Cromwell*, was published in 1827 with a preface which set forth the doctrines of the new school. *Marion de Lorme*, intended for acting, was prohibited in 1828; and not until 1830, with the production of *Hernani*, did he win the success on the stage which was necessary for the triumph of the new doctrines of dramatic art. After three plays in verse Hugo wrote three dramas in prose, returning to verse in *Ruy Blas*, which was brought out in 1838 and which still holds the stage by the side of the earlier *Hernani*. Because of the chilly greeting given to the *Burgraves*, in 1843, Hugo declined again to submit to the fiery ordeal of the footlights; but he continued to pour forth poetry and fiction; and he aspired also after eminence in public life. After Louis Napoleon made himself Emperor in 1852, Hugo went into exile, returning to France at the downfall of the Empire in 1870. Thirty years after *Notre Dame de Paris* had been published (in 1831), he followed it with another mighty prose-fiction, *Les Misérables* (issued in 1862). Unfailingly fecund in oratory, in history, in poetry, and in fiction, Hugo survived to be more than fourscore, dying at last in May, 1885. His body lay in state under the Arch of Triumph; and his funeral was a superb manifestation of national appreciation.

ÉMILE AUGIER *and* JULES SANDEAU

Augier was born at Valence in 1820, a grandson of Pigault-Lebrun. He was well educated and studied for the bar. His first play, the *Hemlock Draft*, acted in 1844, was a pale and unpromising attempt at Greek comedy. He revealed a firmer grasp on life and a keener understanding of the stage in the *Adventuress*, produced in 1848. In 1854 he brought forth the *Son-in-law of M. Poirier*, written in collaboration with Jules Sandeau (who had been born in 1811, and who died in 1883). Augier had other collaborators, Alfred de Musset, Labiche, and Édouard Foussier; but he was always the senior partner in the joint undertaking, and all the plays which he wrote in partnership are stamped with his trademark. After the younger Dumas had set the example of social satire on the stage, Augier was stimulated to a series of keen analyses of French society as he saw it in the final years of the Second Empire and in the early years of the Third Republic. His last play was the *Fourchambault*, produced successfully in 1878; and he did not die until 1889. Certain characteristics mark all his plays — a frank sincerity, and an engaging honesty, a hearty manliness, an abiding regard for the home and the family, and a total absence of false sentimentality. As a playwright he was fertile and dextrous, with the power of projecting character sharply and powerfully. He utilized the framework of the "well-made play" to carry a social message; and he may be considered as the most important factor in the development of the social drama between Scribe and Ibsen.

ALEXANDRE DUMAS Fils

Alexandre Dumas was born in Paris in July, 1824, a natural son of the author of *Monte Cristo* and the *Three Guardsmen* by whom he was acknowledged and legitimated. His schooldays left painful memories, which he utilized in his *Affaire Clémenceau*. As a young man he shared his father's alternations from penury to extravagance. Determined to be independent, he turned author, issuing a volume of verse and half a dozen novels, of which only one had any vitality. This was the *Lady of the Camellias*, published in 1848; it was dramatized by its author and ultimately performed in 1852. It has held the stage not only in France, but all over the world, for more than threescore years. His next play was also a dramatization of a novel of his own, *Diane de Lys*. Then in 1855 he brought out a wholly original play, the *Outer Edge of Society;* and thereafter his position was secure as the wittiest and most adroit of dramatists, as a writer of comedy in its higher aspect, second only to Augier. In later years he began to charge his plays with a more or less paraded moral purpose. When this overt didacticism overweighted the dramatic effectiveness, the play failed, as was the case with the *Ideas of Madame Aubray;* but in most instances his mastery of the craft of playmaking served him in good stead. In *Denise* he rehandled the theme of *Madame Aubray;* he modified the plot only a little, but he strengthened the emotional appeal, so that the later play was immediately successful. He prefixed suggestive prefaces to his several plays when he issued them in a complete edition. His last piece *Francillon*, a comedy brisk in its action, brilliant in its dialogue, and biting in its social satire, was produced in 1887. He died in November, 1895.

GOLDONI

Carlo Goldoni was born in Venice in February, 1707. His boyhood was spent in Perugia and Rimini. He studied law for a few months; he joined a company of strolling players; he wrote satires and even tragedies. At last, after having come under the influence of Molière, whom he revered always as the master of modern comedy, he turned to the comic drama. He became the salaried playwright of a Venetian theater; and there was one year in which he provided it with sixteen plays, most of them in the local dialect of Venice. In 1761 he went to Paris, writing pieces for the Italian company and teaching Italian. One of his best comedies, the *Benevolent Bear*, was composed in French. He received a pension from the king of France; and he amused his old age by writing a lively autobiography. When the Revolution broke out his pension was taken away, and he sank into abject penury. He died at Versailles in February, 1793, having attained to more than fourscore years. Goldoni is justly regarded as the father of modern comedy in Italy. He profited greatly by his constant admiration for Molière; and the influence of the great French dramatist is evident even in his lighter Venetian sketches. And it is in these unpretending pieces, in which he sets on the stage the swarming life of his native city, that he is seen at his best. He is ingenious in intrigue, fresh in invention, easy in the portrayal of character, and lively in the action of the stories he has devised.

LESSING

Ephraim Gotthold Lessing was born in Kamenz, in Saxony, in January, 1729. His father was a pastor and Lessing was intended for the ministry. He went to the University of Leipzig to study theology, but he felt stronger attractions toward medicine and literature. His first play was acted before he was twenty; and his second, *Miss Sara Sampson*, was successfully brought out at Frankfort in 1755. He supported himself by criticism, by editing and by hackwork of various kinds, seizing every opportunity to broaden his knowledge and to deepen his scholarship. In 1766 he published his *Laocoön*, the most stimulating of all eighteenth-century contributions to æsthetic doctrine; and the year after he issued his best comedy, *Minna von Barnhelm*. Almost immediately he went to Hamburg to serve as adviser and critic to a short-lived theatrical enterprise; and to this we owe his illuminating articles on dramatic art, in which he combated the influence of the French classicists. His discussion of the fundamental principles of dramaturgy are more fragmentary than his analysis of æsthetic principles; but they are almost as significant, and they formed the solid basis of the Romanticist revolt under Goethe and Schiller. He continued to wander and to study and to write. He published *Emilia Galotto* in 1772 and *Nathan der Weise* in 1779. He had married in 1776 a widow to whom he had long been attached; and she died two years thereafter to his abiding grief. The later years of his life were occupied largely with theological controversy, in which he revealed himself as independent and as acute as he had shown himself in æsthetic and dramatic discussion, desirous always of piercing to the center and of getting at the kernel of truth. His health failed, partly in consequence of overwork; and he died in February, 1781.

GOETHE

Johann Wolfgang Goethe was born in Frankfort-on-the-Main in August, 1749. He studied law at Leipzig and later at Strassburg; but he took little interest in legal history, devoting his mind to literature. In 1772 he published his first play, *Goetz von Berlichingen*. Two years later he issued his first novel, the *Sorrows of Werther*, following it almost immediately by another play, *Clavigo*. In 1775, on the invitation of Karl August, he moved to Weimar, where he was to make his home for the rest of his life. He was already, at twenty-six, the most famous of German authors. He had the large fecundity of genius, and he was constantly attracted by the stage, having played with a puppet-show in his boyhood and becoming in early manhood the manager of the ducal theater at Weimar. He wrote many plays, *Tasso, Iphigenie, Egmont;* and his most important poem, *Faust*, originally issued in 1790, is cast in dramatic form. But although he was the greatest poet of his country and of his century, he was not a born playwright. His comments on acting, on stage management, on dramatic construction are often very acute; but he lacked a large share of the native gift of playmaking. Technically *Clavigo* is probably the play of his which is most skillfully put together. Even after his friendship with Schiller, who was more richly endowed with the dramaturgic instinct, he was still groping for a satisfactory dramatic formula. In his later years he gave himself whole-heartedly to scientific studies. He outlived all his contemporaries, surviving until March, 1832.

SCHILLER

Johann Christoph Friedrich Schiller was born at Marbach in November, 1759. He studied at a military school, and when this was transferred to Stuttgart, he was allowed to devote himself to medicine. He became an army surgeon in 1781; and the next year he published and saw acted his first play, the *Robbers*, a drama of ardent revolt, composed while he was still a student. In 1783 he was attached to the theater at Mannheim, where he brought out *Fiesco* and *Intrigue and Love*. His first play in verse, *Don Carlos*, was published in 1787; it conformed to the French classicist type; and it is evidence that Schiller, like Goethe, then and later suffered from the chaotic conditions of the contemporary German theater, and especially from the absence of native traditional formulas wherein German dramatists could express themselves spontaneously. In 1793 Schiller wrote a *History of the Thirty Years' War;* and the next year he began the memorable friendship with Goethe, which ultimately led him to settle in Weimar and to assist Goethe in the management of the ducal theater. Under the stimulus of Goethe's companionship Schiller wrote a series of superb ballads, of which the best and the best known is the *Song of the Bell*. He returned to his early love of the drama, publishing his trilogy of *Wallenstein* in 1799, his *Mary Stuart* in 1800, his *Maid of Orleans* in 1801, and his *Bride of Messina* in 1803 — the last being an attempt to emulate the stern severity of the Attic tragedians. His last drama, *William Tell*, was issued in 1804. His health broke in these final years at Weimar; and he died there in May, 1805.

HOLBERG

Ludwig Holberg was born at Bergen, in Norway, in December, 1684. He studied for a little while at the University of Copenhagen; but his real education was rather the result of his incessant travels in England, France, and Italy. His earlier writings were historical; and they were in Danish. This was a departure from the practice of Scandinavian men of letters who were wont to write only in Latin; and it is perhaps not too much to say that Holberg's writings were as influential in the founding of Danish literature as Dante's were in Italian, Chaucer's in English, and Luther's in German. Holberg not only founded Scandinavian literature; he was also its foremost and most fecund contributor, pouring forth prose and verse in abundance. In 1718 he became a professor at the University of Copenhagen; and there he dwelt for the rest of his life. In 1722 the attempt was made to organize a company of Danish actors to perform in their native tongue; and Holberg was appointed manager of the new theater erected in Copenhagen. As there were no plays in Danish, Holberg turned playwright and disclosed a striking talent for the drama; and during the five years that the theater was able to keep its doors open, Holberg composed twenty-eight pieces, most of them comedies. As Goldoni was to do later, Holberg wisely patterned himself upon the incomparable master of modern comedy, and as Goldoni is the Italian Molière, so Holberg is the Danish Molière, — with a large share of Molière's simplicity of plot, swiftness of action, naturalness of dialogues and insight into character. When the theater reopened a few years later, Holberg composed for it five more comedies. He continued to write books in almost every department of literature until the day of his death, which took place in January, 1754.

HENRIK IBSEN

Henrik Ibsen was born at Skien, in Norway, in March, 1828. He served for seven years as apprentice to a druggist. When he was twenty-two he entered the university at Christiania; and he began to write verse. He managed to get a play on the stage; and he contributed to the newspapers. Then in 1851 he became connected with the theater at Bergen, where he remained five years as play-reader, stage manager and resident playwright, — thus acquiring the intimate knowledge of the theater which is all-important for a dramatist. At Bergen, and afterward at a Christiania theater of which he became manager, he brought out several poetic dramas, more or less in imitation of the Danish playwrights, Oehlenschläger and Hertz. His first modern play, *Love's Comedy*, written in rhymed verse, was published in 1862. Two years later, after vain struggles, he left Norway to settle in Rome, where he wrote *Brand* and *Peer Gynt*. In 1868 he removed to Dresden, moving on later to Munich. His books began to sell and he was in receipt of a "poet's pension" from his native land. The wars between Denmark and Prussia, Prussia and Austria, and Prussia and France forced him to revise his conceptions of the social organization. Abandoning the historical and poetic drama and relinquishing verse, he wrote a dozen social dramas in prose, beginning with the *Pillars of Society* (1877) and the *Doll's House* (1879), including *Ghosts* (1881), *Hedda Gabler* (1890), the *Master Builder* (1892), and ending with *When we Dead Awaken* (1900). In 1901 he returned to Norway; and it was in his native land that he died in May, 1906.

II. NOTES ON THE PLAYS

AGAMEMNON

Agamemnon is the first play of a trilogy, of three pieces dealing with successive stages of a tragic story. This is the only Greek trilogy which survives complete. It was not brought out until B.C. 458, possibly after the poet's death. The story of the whole trilogy has a striking similarity to that of *Hamlet*, as it presents the murder of a king by the paramour of the queen, and the subsequent vengeance taken by the son of the murdered man. In the *Agamemnon*, we see the king return from Troy, to be welcomed treacherously by his false wife and to be slain by her and her accomplice. In the second play of the series, the *Choëphori*, we are made spectators of the vengeance of Orestes, the son of Agamemnon and Clytemnestra, with the slaying of the assassins; and in the third piece, the *Eumenides*, we see the atonement made by Orestes for his matricide. Of all the extant tragedies of Æschylus, the *Agamemnon* is probably the most effective when acted before a modern audience. Simple as the plot is, it abounds in moments of tense suspense; and the thick horror of the unseen murder of the king can be paralleled only by the similar moment in *Macbeth*.

In reading the tragedies of Æschylus, Sophocles, and Euripides an attempt should be made to visualize a performance at Athens with thousands of citizens seated in tiers on the sides of the hill on which the Acropolis still stands. In the center of the semicircular orchestra stood the altar; and in this leveled space the actors and the chorus stood and moved, spoke and chanted, their figures relieved against the long, narrow building which took the place of a stage. On the roof of this building stood the solitary Watchman, waiting and looking for the distant beacon-fire which announced the fall of Troy. A central door in this building served as the entrance to the palace of the king.

Although the Attic dramatist could people his play with as many characters as he chose, he was allowed only three actors; and he had so to construct his plot that no more than three persons should appear at once. The protagonist or most important actor would impersonate the most important character, although he might also undertake one or more of the minor parts. The other characters were divided between the deuteragonist and the tritagonist. In *Agamemnon*, there can be but little doubt that the protagonist impersonated only Clytemnestra, leaving the deuteragonist the briefer parts of the Herald, Cassandra, and Ægisthus, and to the tritagonist the Watchman and Agamemnon.

ŒDIPUS THE KING

This play has been recognized by the most competent critics from Aristotle to Jebb as the mighty masterpiece of Greek tragedy, the supreme effort of the consummate technician who was also an inspired poet, capable of seeing life steadily and seeing it whole. Its plot is intricate; and yet there is no moment when the spectator does not follow its clear unrolling with understanding and with breathless interest. Its movement is as straightforward as it is massive; and the doom which finally overtakes the hero is felt to be inevitable. The characters are projected simply yet powerfully; they reveal themselves instantly; and they are artfully contrasted. There are frequent moments of acute suspense, but the weight of the impending catastrophe is never weakened by any shock of mere surprise. The choral odes are ingeniously utilized to heighten the force of the action itself and to interpret the message of the story to the spectators. And the poetry which is omnipresent is always direct, elevated, and imaginative. Even to-day, twenty-five centuries after it was originally composed, the tragedy meets the ultimate test of a play, — that it is even more appealing on the stage than in the study. In a French translation it is kept in the repertory of the Théâtre Français; and in *Œdipus* Mounet-Sully found his most powerful part. At the original performance in Athens the protagonist impersonated Œdipus only, the deuteragonist probably assuming the parts of Iocasta, the Priest, the Herdsman, and the Second Messenger, while to the tritagonist was entrusted Creon, Teiresias, and the First Messenger.

MEDEA

In this play we can discover all the chief characteristics of Euripides as a playwright. The story is moving and picturesque; the situations are violent to the verge of melodrama; the characters are strong of purpose and intense in passion; and the spectacular possibilities of the theme are skillfully utilized. The choral odes have a less integral and intimate relation to the action, such as we perceive in the plays of Sophocles; and they seem sometimes to be introduced only in deference to the tradition of Attic drama. They are beautiful lyrics, which, like our modern interact music, serve to fill the intervals between the episodes. While the loftier tragedies of Sophocles have an obvious likeness to the massive music-dramas of Wagner, the more realistic plays of Euripides resemble rather the operas which Meyerbeer and Halévy composed to librettos by Scribe, also a most ingenious deviser of effective plots. Like the *Agamemnon* and the *Œdipus*, *Medea* has proved itself to be impressive when adequately represented in the modern theater. Indeed, Medea herself is akin to a host of modern heroines in that she is "a woman with a past." Probably the protagonist played only Medea, the deuteragonist "doubling" the Nurse and Jason, and the tritagonist being charged with four parts, the Teacher, Creon, Ægeus, and the Messenger. The central door of the stage building that shut in the orchestra served as the entrance to the abode of Medea; and it was on the roof of this building that Medea stood before she was swung through the air in a dragon-chariot, — which was perhaps a decorated basket raised and lowered by a crane.

THE FROGS

In the *Knights* Aristophanes attacked Cleon and in the *Clouds* he assailed Socrates. In the *Frogs* the shining mark of his satire is Euripides, whom he selects, perhaps partly, because the author of *Medea* was then the most popular and the most quoted of dramatic poets and therefore the best known to the Attic spectators, and partly because of a conservative dislike for the novelties of realism, of sentimentalism, and of sensationalism which he found in the plays of Euripides and which seemed to him degrading to the austere nobility of Greek tragedy as exemplified in the works of Æschylus and of Sophocles. The adventures of Bacchus and of his attendant, Xanthias, on their way to Hades are rich in fun; they combine the humor of character and situation with the wit of dialogue; and the final trial-at-law is a masterly example of parody, proving the existence of a high degree of literary cultivation and æsthetic understanding in the Attic audience. The criticism of the methods of Euripides may be a little unfair, but it is unfailingly acute. In spite of the delicacy of the literary criticism, the general tone of the original performance was probably not very different from that of a rollicking undergraduate burlesque with its topical songs, its local hits, and its atmosphere of boyish high-spirits.

THE CAPTIVES

The prologue of the *Captives* was probably prefixed twenty or thirty years after the death of Plautus and after the Roman audiences had so degenerated in attention and in intelligence that it was held to be necessary to explain the plot in advance to lazy-minded spectators, many of whom might be only doubtfully familiar with Latin. The *Captives* has been chosen to represent Plautus in this volume because it is by far the cleanest of his plays, the author himself in the final lines drawing attention to the inoffensiveness of the story. Lessing was emphatic in his praise of the piece, and probably Plautus owed this merit to the Greek dramatist from whom he took over the play. The comedy is less comic than the other plays of Plautus; in fact the humor is centered in the traditional character of the Parasite, always hungry and always in search of a gratuitous meal. The other plays are rather robust and ingenious farces, only rarely attaining the higher level of comedy. The *Captives* is akin to our modern " domestic dramas," with a finer sentiment rising at times to genuine feeling. The playhouse in which it was originally performed seems to have had a wide and shallow stage with an elaborate architectural back wall, pierced with three doors, — which might serve as the entrances to the residences of three different characters, if need be.

PHORMIO

Phormio is an exception among Terence's comedies in that it is an adaptation not from Menander, but from another Athenian comic dramatist of the same school, Apollodorus. It is an exception also in that its plot is more truly comic than the plots of most of the other plays, with an ingenuity of situation which makes its performance amusing even on the modern stage. Its two chief characters are a parasite, a variant of the traditional type, and an intriguing slave, one of the stable figures of Greek comedy, which was transmitted through the Latin comic drama to the Italian comedy-of-masks and from that to the French stage. Geta is the remote ancestor of Molière's Mascarille and Beaumarchais's Figaro; and *Phormio*, which Terence took over from Apollodorus, supplied a part of the plot of Molière's *Fourberies de Scapin*. It may be noted also that Terence's earliest play, *Andria*, was utilized by Molière's pupil, Baron, in his *Adrienne*, and afterward by Steele in his *Conscious Lovers*. In the plays of Terence, as in those of Plautus (and probably also in the comedies of Menander), the scene is laid in the open street, where all the characters may meet and where they do not hesitate to discuss their most private affairs. Here the dramatists are observing the customs of the country; and even to-day in southern Italy the lower classes seem to use their homes only for sleeping purposes, carrying on the business of life in the streets, where they converse, cook, and court.

THE STAR OF SEVILLE

No play of Lope's is more characteristic of his method than the *Star of Seville*. It is a typical example of the comedy-of-cloak-and-sword, with its high-strung hero, its high-strung heroine, its traditional comic servant, allowed to comment at will on the story as it unrolls itself. There is a swift succession of situations, always effective, in spite of the occasional artificiality by which they are brought about — situations effective because they have been artfully prepared for, skillfully led up to, and powerfully handled when at last they are presented. The dialogue is sometimes stiff with rhetorical embroidery; but in general it is easy with the freedom almost of improvisation. Throughout the play we cannot fail to perceive the facility and the felicity of the born playwright, joying in his task, carrying on his story with a light hand and yet holding with a firm grasp. Lope adjusts his plays to the conditions of the theater in Madrid, — a stage bare of scenery, a courtyard in which the ruder sort of spectators stood, and a stand of seats at the back of the courtyard for the richer element of the audience. As there was no scenery, there could be no other indication of a change of place than that afforded by the dialogue of the characters who entered after the stage had been left empty; — this leaving of the stage empty seeming to serve as a conventional notice to the spectators that the next scene would be laid in a different place.

LIFE IS A DREAM

This play was published in 1636 or 1637, when Calderon was not yet forty; and it represents his work when he was in the full maturity of his power both as playwright and as poet. The story is interesting and the structure is skillful, although it reveals that the Spanish drama had not even then departed very widely from the primitive methods of the mediæval theater. The theme is a mediæval anecdote; and the implied moral is also a little mediæval. The characters are effectively projected and boldly contrasted. Clarin, the *gracioso*, is the equivalent of the Elizabethan comic character, who is more or less characterless, serving only as a mouthpiece for miscellaneous and irrelevant witticisms, frequently bald puns. The dialogue is often a tissue of grandiloquent figures of speech, in which the lyrist recklessly revels in flowers and birds and stars. The more heroic characters are sometimes ultra-heroic in their high-flown exuberance of rhetoric. Sometimes again they voice sentiments of universal appeal in language that is at once lofty and direct.

THE CID

Although Corneille borrowed the plot of the *Cid* from a Spanish play by Guillen de Castro, he revealed his own individuality and his own originality in the changes he imposed upon the Spanish story. In his hands the three acts of the Spanish piece became five; the story was simplified and strengthened; and it was made to possess a unity of purpose foreign to the looser methods of the Spanish stage. Moreover, the characters are reduced in number and raised in energy, in self-will and in recognition of duty. They have an accent of veracity and a faculty of self-analysis which may be sought in vain in the Spanish drama. In Corneille's play they all know what they ought to do in obedience to moral obligation, and they are highly resolved to do it, at whatever conflict with their own passions and at whatever cost to their own desires. The serried arguments which we find in the vibrating dialogue of Corneille's play have little or no counterpart in the speeches of the persons in Guillen de Castro's piece. The influence of the Spanish original, and perhaps also of the French mediæval drama, is seen in the affluence of the lyrical stanzas. And a careful reading will reveal the fact that Corneille frankly lays his scene on the stage of the semi-mediæval French theater, — a bare stage, with hangings at the back and sides and with doors and other properties which serve to localize the residences of different characters. The stage is a neutral ground, nowhere in particular, where all the characters can meet at will without asking where they are.

TARTUFFE

In the spring of 1664 Louis XIV gave a series of sumptuous entertainments at Versailles in the course of which Molière presented the first three acts of *Tartuffe*. The king immediately prohibited its further performance as likely to be offensive to the devout. Molière thereupon gave readings of it at the houses of important personages; and in 1667, believing that the interdict on the play had been raised, he ventured to produce it at his own theater in the Palais Royal, having made various modifications and calling it then the *Imposter*. It was again forbidden; and not until 1669 was its performance permitted, the definite version taking again the original title. *Tartuffe* is the model of modern comedy; it is the first comedy which deals deeply ,and sincerely with society in its more serious aspects; and it has served as the pattern for every social drama which has since been written, not only in French, but in all the other modern languages. Its abiding influence can be seen in the *School for Scandal* of Sheridan and the *Marriage of Figaro* of Beaumarchais, in the *Outer Edge of Society* of the younger Dumas, and in the *Son-in-law of M. Poirier* of Augier and Sandeau, in the *Pillars of Society* of Ibsen and the *Second Mrs. Tanqueray* of Pinero. The plot is knotted with the utmost adroitness; and especially noteworthy is the skill by which Tartuffe's hypocrisy is made evident to the spectators in spite of the fact that he is not permitted to have a single aside in which to reveal his true self.

PHÆDRA

When Racine began to write for the stage he was fortunate in finding ready to his hand the tragic formula developed by Corneille; and the younger poet accepted this pattern, but shifted the interest from the action to the chief character, or rather to delineation of the single overmastering passion by which that character was driven to destruction. Racine's plots are far simpler than Corneille's, simpler even than those of Euripides which he borrowed. In *Phædra* the story is taken up so close to its culmination that one might almost say that very little happens in the play itself, and that we are shown only the inevitable and irresistible results of what has already taken place. The action is internal; and it is concentrated so as to set forth only the final moments of that struggle between desire and duty, in the fire of which the heroine is finally consumed. Beneath the stately courtesies of characters whose language and whose manners are contemporary with Louis XIV, there is an almost brutal realism of emotional expression perhaps all the more burning because of the moderation of the terms in which it is expressed. In *Phædra*, as in most of Racine's other plays, the "star-part" demands all our attention and the other characters are "feeders," who exist only to set off the sufferings of the heroine. Aricia is introduced only to give Phædra cause for jealousy; Theseus is reported dead only so that she may avow her love; and the return of Theseus is only to compel her to send Hippolytus to his death.

THE BARBER OF SEVILLE

When it was produced originally the *Barber* was welcomed and denounced as a bold novelty, partly because it was in prose and partly because it departed widely from the type of a comedy then prevalent on the French stage. Yet it was only a return to the manner of Regnard and even of Molière in his lighter plays. Its story was one which had been utilized more than once by both Regnard and Molière. What was indisputably new was the individuality of Beaumarchais himself, his wit, his satire, his irony, his incessant and effervescent liveliness. The play reveals all his characteristics as a comic dramatist; it has perfect clarity of plot, swiftness of exposition, ingenuity of intrigue, briskness of action, and a consummate understanding of theatrical effect. These qualities are all displayed perhaps even more amply in the *Marriage of Figaro;* and it is partly from a study of Beaumarchais that Scribe acquired his methods of dramatic construction out of which he developed the formula of the "well-made play," in which the closely knit sequence of situations was made all-sufficient unto itself and in which the characters were only profile figures.

HERNANI

The first performances of *Hernani* were a series of pitched battles between the partisans of the outworn classicist formulas and the youthful advocates of the Romanticist doctrines. The play was full of juvenile ardor; it had an impetuous energy unknown on the French stage since the *Cid* of Corneille; and its arbitrary and melodramatic plot was draped with the golden brocade of the poet's superb lyricism. That the plot is arbitrary is obvious enough now; and it is evident that Hugo had modeled it upon the popular melodramas of the unliterary theaters, relying upon the splendor of his verse to supply literary merit. The story itself is straggling and the successive situations are monotonous; the characters are stage types, lending themselves to fervent acting; and not a few other defects have been dwelt upon by cold critics. Yet in the theater itself the piece still discloses its old-time power to rivet the attention of the average spectator and to hold his interest unflagging to the highly wrought and exquisitely phrased death of the hero and heroine. It is true that the interest dies down a little in the fourth act and that the monologue of the king seems interminably tedious.

THE SON–IN–LAW OF M. POIRIER

The source of this masterly comedy is a novelette by Jules Sandeau; and it is probable that Sandeau was more or less responsible for the caressing portrait of the heroine. But if we may judge from the plays which Sandeau wrote alone and from the plays which Augier wrote alone, the vigor and the veracity of this play due to their collaboration must be credited to Augier. It is the masterpiece of French comedy in the nineteenth century; and it is unmatched in the dramatic literature of any other language. It is the chief modern exemplar of high comedy, of which Molière first made the pattern in *Tartuffe* and the *Learned Ladies*. The story is interesting; the plot is simple, moving, and adroitly articulated; the characters are few, veracious, and sharply contrasted; and the struggle which sustains the action is clearly presented in the opening scenes and steadily maintained to the end. It proves that Augier had inherited the large tradition of the comedy of Molière, than which there can be no higher commendation.

THE OUTER EDGE OF SOCIETY

It is not easy to find an approximate translation for *demi-monde*, as Dumas used it originally. *Monde* means "Society" in the narrow sense of fashionable circles; and perhaps the nearest approach to an exact rendering of the French compound word would be "Near-Society." It is into a highly specialized circle in the Paris of the middle of the nineteenth century that Dumas takes us and that he makes us understand. In no other of his comedies did he more fully utilize his mastery of stagecraft. His exposition is immediate and clear; his characters reveal themselves at once by word and by act; his situations are logically knit together and they steadily increase in effectiveness; and his dialogue is almost too incessantly glittering. It is true that after many years we may now feel that the method is a little old-fashioned, that the plotting is a little arbitrary, and that the Olivier de Jalin, whom the author extols as a true gentleman, is little better than a cad. Yet the comedy justifies itself even now, although it is seen to be inferior to its chief rival, the *Son-in-law of M. Poirier*, because the segment of society that it presents so sharply is far more limited.

THE MISTRESS OF THE INN

Goldoni's gift of playmaking is amply revealed in this unpretending little comedy. Simple as it is in story, its successive episodes are effectively put together; and its lively situations follow one another with effortless ease and with unfailing vivacity. It is above all an actable piece, with its four men all cajoled and managed and maneuvered by the single woman who dominated the lively comedy from beginning to end, radiant with humor and with good humor. She fills it with the fragrant charm of her exuberant femininity. These five characters are sharply drawn and boldly contrasted. They are all easy to act and they all reward the actor's endeavor. Yet, amusing as the play is in the reading, no mere reader can conceive of its brilliancy when the incomparable Duse impersonated the fascinating Mandolina.

MINNA von BARNHELM

Although Lessing, in his desire to disestablish the sovereignty of French drama in Germany, was inclined to underestimate Molière, his *Minna von Barnhelm* reveals the result of his careful study of the founder of modern comedy. In fact, the German had to go to the Frenchman for a model, as there was no other for him to profit by. *Minna* is less comic than Molière's lighter plays and it is less weighty than Molière's major masterpieces. But Lessing's comedy is like the best of Molière's in that it is interesting in story, clear in action, effective in acting, and healthy in sentiment. It is one of the earliest plays in any language in which there is only one set to the act and in which there are different sets in different acts. Yet it respects the so-called "unity of place," since all the sets represent rooms in the same inn. It is a comedy of manners rather than a comedy of intrigue; and it presents us with a gallery of figures veraciously studied from contemporary German life. It may be noted also that Lessing is as frank as Shakespeare in causing his heroines, both mistress and maid, Minna and Fanciska, to display their readiness to make advances to their male wooers.

GOETZ von BERLICHINGEN

Goetz was not written with an eye to immediate performance. It was the result of Goethe's discovery of Shakespeare; and its model is the disjointed Elizabethan chronicle-play, of which *Henry V* is an example. But in writing his series of English "histories" Shakespeare was utilizing a form made popular in the playhouse of his predecessors, whereas Goethe in borrowing its loose framework was using a form unknown in his time and entirely foreign to the traditions of the contemporary German theater. Moreover, Shakespeare, even in the loose-jointed chronicle-play, is always a "theater-poet," — to employ Goethe's own term, — thinking out his succession of scenes in accord with the existing conditions of his own theater, whereas Goethe paid far too little attention to the exigencies or to the possibilities of the actual playhouse. Goethe confessed to Eckermann that a play "which is not originally by the intent and skill of the poet, written for the boards, will not succeed; but no matter what is done, it will remain unmanageable. What trouble have I taken with *Goetz* — but it will not go right as an acting play." And therefore, although Goetz himself, strong-willed and self-reliant, is a most promising hero for a stage-play of compelling power, the merits of Geothe's piece are rather literary than dramatic. Even if it is not a well-knit piece, with its single action sweeping steadily forward to an inevitable culmination, it is a stirring evocation of life in the Middle Ages, a picturesque panorama of an epoch unduly neglected. It is the herald of the Romanticist revival of the drama; and its influence upon the *Waverley Novels* is indisputable.

WILLIAM TELL

As a poet Schiller is less liberally endowed than Goethe; but as a maker of plays he is more richly gifted. He has in a larger degree than Goethe the intuitive feeling for effective situations and the instinctive faculty for combining them so as to stir the emotions of an audience. Yet he is never a strenuous seeker for technical victory, to be won only by unrelenting conscientiousness of attention to the details of construction, exposition, and climax. His dramas impress us by their mass and by their fire, wherein they reveal the innate dramatic power of the born playwright. In *William Tell* he handles a historical theme with liberal freedom, not tied down to the mere facts as they happen to be recorded, but striving rather to express the larger truth of the theme. While he is careful in the characterization of his hero, he is even more concerned with the characterization of the Swiss patriots as representatives of a forward movement for human freedom.

RASMUS MONTANUS

Holberg was the first man to compose a play in Danish for Danish actors; and his comic dramas have the primitive simplicity which might be expected under these circumstances. This play has the straightforward directness of certain of Molière's lighter pieces, such as the *Physician in Spite of Himself*. There is no complexity of plot-making; the characters are drawn in the primary colors; and the story moves forward with the swift simplicity of a fable. It discloses Holberg's intimate understanding of the rustic Danes who take part in the action and a knowledge equally intimate of the dwellers in the semi-rural capital of Denmark before whom it was to be performed. Holberg follows Molière in letting his characters reveal themselves freely in explanatory soliloquies, addressed obviously to the spectators. But it is interesting to note that Holberg in this play, written in 1731, anticipated Lessing in changing his scenes only between the acts, using always the same set throughout the act.

A DOLL'S HOUSE

Prior to the production of the *Doll's House*, Ibsen had composed several dramatic poems and poetic dramas; and he had also brought out two or three plays in prose dealing with contemporary society. Yet in no one of these had he amply revealed his individuality or given promise of his later mastery over the modern drama. And the *Doll's House* itself, up to the middle of the third act, is not much more than an ingeniously invented story, departing in its content only a little from the formula worked out in France by Augier and Dumas. The effective incident of the shawl-dance might have been devised by Sardou. But when husband and wife settle down to talk over their relation to one another, the tone of the play changes and a deeper note is struck for the first time, — the note that was to be heard again and again in the series of searching social dramas which followed at two-year intervals during the remainder of Ibsen's life. In the prose-plays preceding the *Doll's House*, Ibsen is only one of a group of accomplished playwrights; whereas in the succession of social dramas following the *Doll's House*, he takes his position as the foremost and most powerful dramatist of the later nineteenth century.

III. A READING LIST IN EUROPEAN DRAMATISTS

No attempt has been made to provide an exhaustive bibliography. Books are cited for availability and general usefulness.

THE ART OF THE DRAMA.

Recent discussions of the principles of the dramatist's art are Brander Matthews, *A Study of the Drama* (1910); William Archer, *Playmaking; a Manual of Craftsmanship* (1913); and Clayton Hamilton, *The Theory of the Theater* (1910), and *Studies in Stagecraft* (1913). Much that is significant can be gleaned in Lessing's *Hamburg Dramaturgy* (English translation in Bohn's Library). Important also are three Publications of the Dramatic Museum of Columbia University, *The Law of the Drama*, by Brunetière, with an introduction by Henry Arthur Jones; *The Autobiography of a Play*, by Bronson Howard, with an introduction by Augustus Thomas; and *Robert Louis Stevenson as a Dramatist*, by Sir Arthur Wing Pinero, with an introduction by Clayton Hamilton. There is a translation of Freytag's *Technic of the Drama*, but the theories it sets forth are now discredited.

HISTORIES OF THE DRAMA.

In Bohn's Library there is a translation of Schlegel's *Lectures on Dramatic Literature*. In Sir Walter Scott's miscellaneous works will be found an interesting account of *The Drama*. The only recent book which attempts to cover the entire history of the art is Brander Matthews, *The Development of the Drama* (1903).

THE GREEK DRAMA.

An account of the Greek theater and of its methods will be found in Barnett, *Greek Drama* (1900); in Haigh, *The Attic Theater* (3d edition, 1908), and in the first volume of Mantzius, *History of Theatrical Art* (1904). Very useful also is Butcher, *Aristotle's Theory of Poetry and Fine Art* (2d edition, 1898). Haigh, *The Tragic Drama of the Greeks* (1899), may be heartily recommended. There is unfortunately no translation of Patin, *Les Tragiques Grecs*. The Athenian dramatists are admirably dealt with in Jebb, *Primer of Greek Literature* (1877), and in Gilbert Murray, *Ancient Greek Literature* (1897). See also the *Lectures on Greek Literature*, Columbia University Press (1911), for discussions of Greek tragedy by J. R. Wheeler and of Greek comedy by Edward Capps.

ÆSCHYLUS.

There are translations of all the tragedies by Swanwick, Morshead, Campbell.
Among the translations of separate plays may be mentioned *Agamemnon*, by Browning, and *Prometheus*, by Mrs. Browning.

SOPHOCLES.

There are translations of all the tragedies by Franklin, Potter, Plumptre, and Lewis Campbell.
Among the translations of separate plays may be mentioned *Œdipus the King*, by Gilbert Murray.
In the series of *Classical Writers* there is a study of Sophocles by Lewis Campbell.

EURIPIDES.

There are translations of all or of most of the tragedies by A. S. Way, E. P. Coleridge, and Gilbert Murray.
There is a version of *Alcestis* included in Browning's *Balaustion*.
In the series of *Classical Writers* there is a study of Euripides by J. P. Mahaffy. See also Gilbert Murray's *Euripides and his Age* (1913).

ARISTOPHANES.

There are translations more or less complete by Hickie, Mitchell, Hookham Frere, and B. B. Rogers. Gilbert Murray has translated the *Frogs*.

THE LATIN DRAMA.

There is unhappily no book about the Roman theater as satisfactory as Haigh's *Attic Theater*. Perhaps the account most easily available is that in the first volume of Mantzius, *History of Theatrical Art*. The most useful history of Latin literature is Mackail's (1895).

PLAUTUS.
There are translations by Bonnell Thorton and by Sugden. A volume in *Ancient Classics for English Readers*, by W. L. Collins deals with Plautus and Terence.

TERENCE.
There is a translation by George Colman the elder.

THE SPANISH DRAMA.
George Ticknor's *History of Spanish Literature* (last edition, 1863) is still the most authoritative account; but it can be supplemented by Fitzmaurice-Kelly's more recent volume. See, also, George Henry Lewes, *The Spanish Drama* (1846), and H. A. Rennert, *The Spanish Stage in the Time of Lope de Vega* (1912).

LOPE DE VEGA.
A translation of the *Gardener's Dog*, by W. H. H. Chambers, will be found in Bates, *The Drama* (1903) ; and a translation of *Castelvines and Montreses*, by F. W. Cosens, was privately printed in 1869. W. T. Brewster's rendering of *Lope's New Art of Writing Plays in these Times* was issued in 1914 as the first of the Publications of the Dramatic Museum of Columbia University. The amplest and the latest biography is H. A. Rennert's *Life of Lope de Vega* (1904).

CALDERON.
There are translations of a dozen of Calderon's plays by Dennis Florence Mac-Carthy. Edward FitzGerald made free versions of six of Calderon's dramas. See, also, Trench's study (1880), and E. J. Hasell's brief critical biography in *Foreign Classics for English Readers* (1879).

THE FRENCH DRAMA.
It is to be regretted that there is no English translation of Brunetière's suggestive and stimulating *Epochs of the French Drama;* nor is there any history in English of the development of the French drama as thorough as that by Lentilhac now in course of completion. But attention should be called to the brief account of the beginnings of the French theater in the fourth volume of Mantzius, *History of Theatrical Art* (1905). For Hugo, Augier, Dumas *fils*, and their contemporaries, see Brander Matthews, *French Dramatists of the 19th Century* (3d edition, enlarged, 1901).

CORNEILLE.
Apparently the *Cid* is the only one of Corneille's plays which has been translated into English. Consult Dorothy Canfield, *Corneille and Racine in England*, for a record of stage-adaptations.

MOLIÈRE.
There are complete prose translations of Molière's plays by Van Laun, Waller, and C. H. Wall (in Bohn's Library) ; and Curtis Hidden Page has admirably rendered several of the most important comedies into English verse. The most recent biographies are by H. C. Chatfield-Taylor (1906) and by Brander Matthews (1910). See also the fourth volume of Mantzius, *History of Theatrical Art* (1905).

RACINE.
There is a complete translation by R. B. Boswell in Bohn's Library. An excellent critical consideration of Racine by Professor F. M. Warren will be found in Warner's *Library of the World's Best Literature*.

BEAUMARCHAIS.
Although most of the plays of Beaumarchais have been acted in English adaptations, there is no complete translation. Lomenie's *Beaumarchais and his Times* is not recent, and it may be supplemented by Austin Dobson's biographical sketch prefixed to his Clarendon Press Edition of the *Barber of Seville*.

VICTOR HUGO.
There are translations of several of Hugo's plays by Mrs. Newton Crosland and F. L. Slous in Bohn's Library. A brief biographical sketch by Swinburne will be found in the *Encyclopædia Britannica* (11th edition). There is a semi-autobiography entitled *Victor Hugo Narrated by a Witness of his Life*. An acute analysis of the plays will be found in Archer's *About the Theater* (1886).

AUGIER *and* SANDEAU.

Neither the plays written by Augier and Sandeau nor the plays written by either of them separately have been completely rendered into English. The only available translation is Barrett H. Clark's *Four Plays by Émile Augier* (1915), with a preface by Brieux.

DUMAS *fils*.

Very few of the plays of Dumas have been translated for readers, although most of them at one time or another have been seen on the English-speaking stage in mangled perversions. Two essays will be found in Henry James, *Notes on Novelists* (1914).

THE ITALIAN DRAMA.

The account of Italian dramatic literature given in most of the histories is likely to be misleading in that it discusses various closet-dramas as if they had contributed to the development of a genuine drama. The peculiarities of the improvised comedy-of-masks are described in John Addington Symonds's introduction to his translation of Gozzi's *Memoirs* and in Chatfield-Taylor's *Life of Goldoni*.

GOLDONI.

There are many English translations of different plays by Goldoni; four of them edited by Helen Zimmern were published in 1892 in a volume of a series called *Masterpieces of Foreign Authors*. The most illuminating life is that by H. C. Chatfield-Taylor (1913). To his abridged edition of Goldoni's autobiography W. D. Howells prefixed a biographical criticism.

THE GERMAN DRAMA.

The most recent and the most acute history of German literature is that by Calvin Thomas (1909).

LESSING.

Lessing's comedies and tragedies, translated by Ernest Bell, fill two volumes in Bohn's Library. There is a brief biography by Helen Zimmern and a larger life by James Sime. Attention must also be called to the stimulating essay by James Russell Lowell.

GOETHE.

In his biography of Goethe, George Henry Lewes pays especial attention to the dramatic works. Translations of Goethe's plays fill one volume of Bohn's Library. See also the paper on Goethe in H. H. Boyesen, *Essays on German Literature* (1892).

SCHILLER.

The latest and most satisfactory biography of Schiller is that by Calvin Thomas (1901). Translations of his plays are to be found in two volumes of the Bohn Library.

THE SCANDINAVIAN DRAMA.

There does not exist in English anywhere an adequate account of the origin and evolution of the drama in Denmark, Norway, and Sweden.

HOLBERG.

A translation by Oscar James Campbell and Frederic Schenck of three of Holberg's plays was published in New York in 1914, by the American-Scandinavian Foundation. To be noted also are O. J. Campbell's the *Comedies of Holberg* (1914) and the article by W. M. Payne in Warner's *Library of the World's Best Literature*.

IBSEN.

Nearly all of Ibsen's plays have been rendered into English by different hands; the most nearly completed edition is that edited by William Archer (1900–01). The latest biography is that by Edmund Gosse (1907). H. H. Boyesen issued in 1892 a *Commentary on Ibsen*. Very suggestive are the extracts from the author's manuscripts entitled *From Ibsen's Workshop* translated by A. G. Chater (1911).